# Abbreviations/Abbreviazioni

*adj* adjective
*admin* administration
*adv* adverb
*aero* aeronautics
*agg* aggettivo
*agric* agriculture, agricoltura
*anat* anatomy, anatomia
*arch* architecture, architettura
*art* article, articolo
*astrol* astrology, astrologia
*astron* astronomy, astronomia
*auto* automobilismo
*aux* auxiliary
*avv* avverbio
*biol* biology, biologia
*bot* botany, botanica
*chem* chemistry
*chim* chimica
*coll* colloquial
*comm* commerce, commercio
*cong* congiunzione
*conj* conjunction
*derog* derogatory
*dir* diritto
*econ* economics, economia
*elec* electricity
*elett* elettricità
*f* feminine, femminile
*fam* familiar, familiare
*ferr* ferrovia
*fig* figurato
*filos* filosofia
*fis* fisica
*foto* fotografia
*gastr* gastronomia
*geog* geography, geografia
*geol* geology, geologia

*geom* geometry, geometria
*gramm* grammar, grammatica
*impol* impolite
*inter* interiezione
*interj* interjection
*invar* invariable, invariabile
*m* masculine, maschile
*mar* marina
*mat* matematica
*math* mathematics
*mec* mechanical, meccanica
*med* medicine, medicina
*mil* military, militare
*n* noun
*naut* nautical
*phone* telephone
*phot* photography
*phys* physics
*pl* plural, plurale
*pol* politics, politica
*prep* preposition, preposizione
*pron* pronoun, pronome
*psic* psicologia, psichiatria
*psych* psychology, psychiatry
*rail* railways
*rel* religion, religione
*s* sostantivo
*sing* singular, singolare
*spreg* spregiativo
*tec* tecnologia
*tech* technical
*TV* television, televisione
*v* verb, verbo
*V* vide (see, vedi)
*volg* volgare
*zool* zoology, zoologia

# *Italian pronunciation*

As wide variations exist between pronunciations in different parts of Italy, we have favoured the standard accepted in the north as this is rapidly gaining general acceptance.

a sano ['sano]

ɛ bene ['bɛne]

e festa ['festa]

i tinto ['tinto]

ɔ brodo ['brɔdo]

o mondo ['mondo]

u fune ['fune]

b bene ['bɛne]

d dito ['dito]

f fine ['fine]

g gallo ['gallo]

j lezione [le'tsjone]

k capo ['kapo]

l legge ['leddʒe]

m mago ['mago]

n nitido ['nitido]

p pulce ['pultʃe]

r rete ['rete]

s sabbia ['sabbja]

t tanto ['tanto]

v via ['via]

w quando ['kwando]

z viso ['vizo]

dz zucchero ['dzukkero]

ts anzi ['antsi]

ʃ sciame ['ʃame]

tʃ cibo ['tʃibo]

dʒ gentile [dʒen'tile]

ʎ figlio ['fiʎo]

ɲ ragno ['raɲo]

ŋ smoking ['zmɔkiŋ]

The symbol ' indicates that the following syllable should be stressed.

# PENGUIN POCKET ITALIAN DICTIONARY
## ENGLISH–ITALIANO
## ITALIAN–INGLESE

Daniele O. Arati

Jonathan J. Griffith

PENGUIN BOOKS

PENGUIN BOOKS

Published by the Penguin Group
Penguin Books Ltd, 80 Strand, London WC2R 0RL, England
Penguin Group (USA) Inc., 375 Hudson Street, New York, New York 10014, USA
Penguin Group (Canada), 90 Eglinton Avenue East, Suite 700, Toronto, Ontario, Canada M4P 2Y3
(a division of Pearson Penguin Canada Inc.)
Penguin Ireland, 25 St Stephen's Green, Dublin 2, Ireland
(a division of Penguin Books Ltd)
Penguin Group (Australia), 250 Camberwell Road, Camberwell, Victoria 3124, Australia
(a division of Pearson Australia Group Pty Ltd)
Penguin Books India Pvt Ltd, 11 Community Centre,
Panchsheel Park, New Delhi – 110 017, India
Penguin Group (NZ), cnr Airborne and Rosedale Roads, Albany,
Auckland 1310, New Zealand (a division of Pearson New Zealand Ltd)
Penguin Books (South Africa) (Pty) Ltd, 24 Sturdee Avenue,
Rosebank 2196, Johannesburg, South Africa

Penguin Books Ltd, Registered Offices: 80 Strand, London WC2R 0RL, England

www.penguin.com

First published 2006
1

Copyright © Market House Books Ltd, 2006
All rights reserved

The moral right of the authors has been asserted

Set in Stone Sans and ITC Stone Serif
Printed in England by Clays Ltd, St Ives plc

ISBN-13: 978-0-141-02719-7
ISBN-10: 0-141-02719-3

PENGUIN REFERENCE
Penguin Pocket Italian Dictionary

Daniele Ottorino Arati was born in Berne and studied literature, linguistics and journalism in Italy and Switzerland. He lives with his family in the United Kingdom and works as a specialist interpreter and a correspondent for the Italian media.

Jonathan James Griffith was born in London and now lives with his family in Surrey. He is a director of a company that provides a range of linguistic services, notably specialized translations and lexicographical compilations.

## Pronuncia inglese

a hat [hat]
e bell [bel]
i big [big]
o dot [dot]
ʌ bun [bʌn]
u book [buk]
ə alone [ə'loun]
a: card [ka:d]
ə: word [wə:d]
i: team [ti:m]
o: torn [to:n]
u: spoon [spu:n]
ai die [dai]
ei ray [rei]
oi toy [toi]
au how [hau]
ou road [roud]
eə lair [leə]
iə fear [fiə]
uə poor [puə]
b back [bak]
d dull [dʌl]
f find [faind]
g gaze [geiz]
h hop [hop]

j yell [jel]
k cat [kat]
l life [laif]
m mouse [maus]
n night [nait]
p pick [pik]
r rose [rouz]
s sit [sit]
t toe [tou]
v vest [vest]
w week [wi:k]
z zoo [zu:]
θ think [θiŋk]
ð those [ðouz]
ʃ shoe [ʃu:]
ʒ treasure ['treʒə]
tʃ chalk [tʃo:k]
dʒ jump [dʒʌmp]
ŋ sing [siŋ]

Il simbolo ' precede la sillaba che ha l'accento tonico principale.
Il simbolo , precede la sillaba che ha l'accento tonico secondario.

# Guide to the dictionary

Irregular plural forms are shown at the headword and in the text. The follow-ing categories of Italian plural forms are considered regular:

| | |
|---|---|
| alber**o** | alber**i** |
| vial**e** | vial**i** |
| chies**a** | chies**e** |
| ami**ca** | ami**che** |
| lun**ga** | lun**ghe** |
| città | città |
| tesi | tesi |

In addition, masculine Italian words ending in **-a** are considered regular if they form their plural in **-i**. Masculine words ending in **-co** and **-go** form their plurals in **-chi** and **-ghi** unless the word is of more than two syllables and the **-co** or **-go** preceded by a vowel, in which case the plural is formed in **-ci** and **-gi**. Exceptions to this rule are considered irregular.

Irregular verbs listed in the verb tables are marked with an asterisk in the headword list. Compounds are not listed in the verb tables.

Adverbs are shown only if their formation is irregular. English adverbs are considered regular if they are formed by adding *-ly* or *-ally* to the adjective. Italian adverbs are considered regular if they are formed by adding *-mente* to the feminine form of the adjective.

# Guida all'uso del vocabulario

I plurali irregolari dei sostantivi sono indicati sia sotto la voce di partenza sia nel testo stesso. Le seguenti categorie vengono considerate di formazione regolare in inglese:

|          |           |
|----------|-----------|
| cat      | cats      |
| glass    | glasses   |
| fly      | flies     |
| half     | halves    |
| wife     | wives     |

I verbi irregolari nell'apposita tavola sono contraddistinti con un asterisco nella lista delle voci di partenza. Non sono compresi nella tavola i verbi composti.

Gli avverbi sono indicati con voci proprie solo quando si tratta di formazioni irregolari. Vengono considerati regolari in inglese gli avverbi formati con l'aggiunta di -ly o di -ally all'aggettivo. Vengono considerati regolari in italiano gli avverbi formati mediante l'aggiunta di -mente al femminile dell'aggettivo.

# Italian irregular verbs

| Infinitive | Present | Past Absolute | Future | Past Participle |
|---|---|---|---|---|
| **addurre** | adduco | addussi | addurrò | addotto |
| **affiggere** | affiggo | affissi | affiggerò | affisso |
| **affliggere** | affliggo | afflissi | affliggerò | afflitto |
| **alludere** | alludo | allusi | alluderò | alluso |
| **andare** | vado | andai | andrò | andato |
| **annettere** | annetto | annettei | annetterò | annesso |
| **apparire** | appaio | apparvi | apparirò | apparso |
| **appendere** | appendo | appesi | appenderò | appeso |
| **aprire** | apro | aprii | aprirò | aperto |
| **ardere** | ardo | arsi | arderò | arso |
| **assistere** | assisto | assistetti | assisterò | assistito |
| **assolvere** | assolvo | assolsi | assolverò | assolto |
| **assumere** | assumo | assunsi | assumerò | assunto |
| **avere** | ho | ebbi | avrò | avuto |
| **bere** | bevo | bevvi | berrò | bevuto |
| **cadere** | cado | caddi | cadrò | caduto |
| **cogliere** | colgo | colsi | coglierò | colto |
| **comprimere** | comprimo | compressi | comprimerò | compresso |
| **concedere** | concedo | concedetti | concederò | concesso |
| **conoscere** | conosco | conobbi | conoscerò | conosciuto |
| **correre** | corro | corsi | correrò | corso |
| **crescere** | cresco | crebbi | crescerò | cresciuto |
| **cuocere** | cuocio | cossi | cuocerò | cotto |
| **dare** | do | diedi | darò | dato |
| **dire** | dico | dissi | dirò | detto |
| **dirigere** | dirigo | diressi | dirigerò | diretto |
| **discutere** | discuto | discussi | discuterò | discusso |
| **dissuadere** | dissuado | dissuasi | dissuaderò | dissuaso |
| **distinguere** | distinguo | distinsi | distinguerò | distinto |
| **dolere** | dolgo | dolsi | dorrò | doluto |
| **dovere** | debbo | dovetti | dovrò | dovuto |
| **emergere** | emergo | emersi | emergerò | emerso |
| **erigere** | erigo | eressi | erigerò | eretto |
| **esigere** | esigo | esigetti | esigerò | esatto |
| **espellere** | espello | espulsi | espellerò | espulso |
| **esplodere** | esplodo | esplosi | esploderò | esploso |
| **essere** | sono | fui | sarò | stato |
| **estinguere** | estinguo | estinsi | estinguerò | estinto |
| **evadere** | evado | evasi | evaderò | evaso |
| **fare** | faccio | feci | farò | fatto |
| **flettere** | fletto | flettei | fletterò | flesso |
| **fondere** | fondo | fusi | fonderò | fuso |
| **friggere** | friggo | frissi | friggerò | fritto |
| **giacere** | giaccio | giacqui | giacerò | giaciuto |
| **godere** | godo | godetti | godrò | goduto |
| **incutere** | incuto | incussi | incuterò | incusso |
| **infliggere** | infliggo | inflissi | infliggerò | inflitto |
| **invadere** | invado | invasi | invaderò | invaso |
| **leggere** | leggo | lessi | leggerò | letto |

| Infinitive | Present | Past Absolute | Future | Past Participle |
|---|---|---|---|---|
| **mettere** | metto | misi | metterò | messo |
| **mordere** | mordo | morsi | morderò | morso |
| **morire** | muoio | morii | morirò | morto |
| **muovere** | muovo | mossi | muoverò | mosso |
| **nascere** | nasco | nacqui | nascerò | nato |
| **nascondere** | nascondo | nascosi | nasconderò | nascosto |
| **nuocere** | nuoccio | nocqui | nuocerò | nociuto |
| **offrire** | offro | offersi | offrirò | offerto |
| **parere** | paio | parvi | parrò | parso |
| **perdere** | perdo | perdetti | perderò | perso |
| **persuadere** | persuado | persuasi | persuaderò | persuaso |
| **piacere** | piaccio | piacque | piacerò | piaciuto |
| **porgere** | porgo | porsi | porgerò | porto |
| **porre** | pongo | posi | porrò | posto |
| **potere** | posso | potei | potrò | potuto |
| **proteggere** | proteggo | protessi | proteggerò | protetto |
| **redigere** | redigo | redassi | redigerò | redatto |
| **redimere** | redimo | redensi | redimerò | redento |
| **reggere** | reggo | ressi | reggerò | retto |
| **rifulgere** | rifulgo | rifulsi | rifulgerò | rifulso |
| **rimanere** | rimango | rimasi | rimarrò | rimasto |
| **rispondere** | rispondo | risposi | risponderò | risposto |
| **rodere** | rodo | rosi | roderò | roso |
| **rompere** | rompo | ruppi | romperò | rotto |
| **sapere** | so | seppi | saprò | saputo |
| **scegliere** | scelgo | scelsi | sceglierò | scelto |
| **scindere** | scindo | scissi | scinderò | scisso |
| **sciogliere** | sciolgo | sciolsi | scioglierò | sciolto |
| **scoprire** | scopro | scoprii | scoprirò | scoperto |
| **scorgere** | scorgo | scorsi | scorgerò | scorto |
| **scrivere** | scrivo | scrissi | scriverò | scritto |
| **scuotere** | scuoto | scossi | scuoterò | scosso |
| **sedere** | siedo | sedetti | sederò | seduto |
| **solere** | soglio | solei | solerò | solito |
| **sommergere** | sommergo | sommersi | sommergerò | sommerso |
| **sorgere** | sorgo | sorsi | sorgerò | sorto |
| **spandere** | spando | spansi | spanderò | spanto |
| **spargere** | spargo | sparsi | spargerò | sparso |
| **spegnere** | spengo | spensi | spegnerò | spento |
| **stare** | sto | stetti | starò | stato |
| **stringere** | stringo | strinsi | stringerò | stretto |
| **struggere** | struggo | strussi | struggerò | strutto |
| **svellere** | svello | svelsi | svellerò | svelto |
| **tacere** | taccio | tacqui | tacerò | taciuto |
| **tenere** | tengo | tenni | terrò | tenuto |
| **togliere** | tolgo | tolsi | toglierò | tolto |
| **torcere** | torco | torsi | torcerò | torto |
| **trarre** | traggo | trassi | trarrò | tratto |
| **udire** | odo | udii | udirò | udito |
| **ungere** | ungo | unsi | ungerò | unto |
| **uscire** | esco | uscii | uscirò | uscito |
| **valere** | valgo | valsi | varrò | valso |

| Infinitive | Present | Past Absolute | Future | Past Participle |
|---|---|---|---|---|
| **vedere** | vedo | vidi | vedrò | visto |
| **venire** | vengo | venni | verrò | venuto |
| **vincere** | vinco | vinsi | vincerò | vinto |
| **vivere** | vivo | vissi | vivrò | vissuto |
| **volere** | voglio | volli | vorrò | voluto |
| **volgere** | volgo | volsi | volgerò | volto |

For verbs ending in:

-**cedere** see **concedere**
-**durre** see **addurre**
-**endere** see **appendere**
-**figgere** see **affiggere**
-**idere** or -**udere** see **alludere**
-**nettere** see **annettere**

-**ngere** (except **stringere**) see **ungere**
-**parire** see **apparire**
-**primere** see **comprimere**
-**sistere** see **assistere**

# Verbi inglesi irregolari

| Infinitive | Passato | Participio Passato |
|------------|---------|--------------------|
| **abide** | abode | abode |
| **arise** | arose | arisen |
| **awake** | awoke | awoken |
| **be** | was | been |
| **bear** | bore | borne *or* born |
| **beat** | beat | beaten |
| **become** | became | become |
| **begin** | began | begun |
| **behold** | beheld | beheld |
| **bend** | bent | bent |
| **bet** | bet | bet |
| **beware** | | |
| **bid** | bid | bidden *or* bid |
| **bind** | bound | bound |
| **bite** | bit | bitten |
| **bleed** | bled | bled |
| **blow** | blew | blown |
| **break** | broke | broken |
| **breed** | bred | bred |
| **bring** | brought | brought |
| **build** | built | built |
| **burn** | burnt *or* burned | burnt *or* burned |
| **burst** | burst | burst |
| **buy** | bought | bought |
| **can** | could | |
| **cast** | cast | cast |
| **catch** | caught | caught |
| **choose** | chose | chosen |
| **cling** | clung | clung |
| **come** | came | come |
| **cost** | cost | cost |
| **creep** | crept | crept |
| **cut** | cut | cut |
| **deal** | dealt | dealt |
| **dig** | dug | dug |
| **do** | did | done |
| **draw** | drew | drawn |
| **dream** | dreamed *or* dreamt | dreamed *or* dreamt |
| **drink** | drank | drunk |
| **drive** | drove | driven |
| **dwell** | dwelt | dwelt |
| **eat** | ate | eaten |
| **fall** | fell | fallen |

| Infinitive | Passato | Participio Passato |
|---|---|---|
| **feed** | fed | fed |
| **feel** | felt | felt |
| **fight** | fought | fought |
| **find** | found | found |
| **flee** | fled | fled |
| **fling** | flung | flung |
| **fly** | flew | flown |
| **forbid** | forbade | forbidden |
| **forget** | forgot | forgotten |
| **forgive** | forgave | forgiven |
| **forsake** | forsook | forsaken |
| **freeze** | froze | frozen |
| **get** | got | got |
| **give** | gave | given |
| **go** | went | gone |
| **grind** | ground | ground |
| **grow** | grew | grown |
| **hang** | hung *or* hanged | hung *or* hanged |
| **have** | had | had |
| **hear** | heard | heard |
| **hide** | hid | hidden |
| **hit** | hit | hit |
| **hold** | held | held |
| **hurt** | hurt | hurt |
| **keep** | kept | kept |
| **kneel** | knelt | knelt |
| **knit** | knitted *or* knit | knitted *or* knit |
| **know** | knew | known |
| **lay** | laid | laid |
| **lead** | led | led |
| **lean** | leant *or* leaned | leant *or* leaned |
| **leap** | leapt *or* leaped | leapt *or* leaped |
| **learn** | learnt *or* learned | learnt *or* learned |
| **leave** | left | left |
| **lend** | lent | lent |
| **let** | let | let |
| **lie** | lay | lain |
| **light** | lit *or* lighted | lit *or* lighted |
| **lose** | lost | lost |
| **make** | made | made |
| **may** | might | |
| **mean** | meant | meant |
| **meet** | met | met |
| **mow** | mowed | mown |
| **must** | | |
| **ought** | | |

| Infinitive | Passato | Participio Passato |
|---|---|---|
| **pay** | paid | paid |
| **put** | put | put |
| **quit** | quitted *or* quit | quitted *or* quit |
| **read** | read | read |
| **rid** | rid | rid |
| **ride** | rode | ridden |
| **ring** | rang | rung |
| **rise** | rose | risen |
| **run** | ran | run |
| **saw** | sawed | sawn *or* sawed |
| **say** | said | said |
| **see** | saw | seen |
| **seek** | sought | sought |
| **sell** | sold | sold |
| **send** | sent | sent |
| **set** | set | set |
| **sew** | sewed | sewn *or* sewed |
| **shake** | shook | shaken |
| **shear** | sheared | sheared *or* shorn |
| **shed** | shed | shed |
| **shine** | shone | shone |
| **shoe** | shod | shod |
| **shoot** | shot | shot |
| **show** | showed | shown |
| **shrink** | shrank | shrunk |
| **shut** | shut | shut |
| **sing** | sang | sung |
| **sink** | sank | sunk |
| **sit** | sat | sat |
| **sleep** | slept | slept |
| **slide** | slid | slid |
| **sling** | slung | slung |
| **slink** | slunk | slunk |
| **slit** | slit | slit |
| **smell** | smelt *or* smelled | smelt *or* smelled |
| **sow** | sowed | sown *or* sowed |
| **speak** | spoke | spoken |
| **speed** | sped *or* speeded | sped *or* speeded |
| **spell** | spelt *or* spelled | spelt *or* spelled |
| **spend** | spent | spent |
| **spill** | spilt *or* spilled | spilt *or* spilled |
| **spin** | spun | spun |
| **spit** | spat | spat |
| **split** | split | split |
| **spread** | spread | spread |
| **spring** | sprang | sprung |

| Infinitive | Passato | Participio Passato |
|---|---|---|
| **stand** | stood | stood |
| **steal** | stole | stolen |
| **stick** | stuck | stuck |
| **sting** | stung | stung |
| **stink** | stank *or* stunk | stunk |
| **stride** | strode | stridden |
| **strike** | struck | struck |
| **string** | strung | strung |
| **strive** | strove | striven |
| **swear** | swore | sworn |
| **sweep** | swept | swept |
| **swell** | swelled | swollen *or* swelled |
| **swim** | swam | swum |
| **swing** | swung | swung |
| **take** | took | taken |
| **teach** | taught | taught |
| **tear** | tore | torn |
| **tell** | told | told |
| **think** | thought | thought |
| **throw** | threw | thrown |
| **thrust** | thrust | thrust |
| **tread** | trod | trodden |
| **wake** | woke | woken |
| **wear** | wore | worn |
| **weave** | wove | woven |
| **weep** | wept | wept |
| **win** | won | won |
| **wind** | wound | wound |
| **wring** | wrung | wrung |
| **write** | wrote | written |

# English – Italiano

## A

**a, an** [ə, ən] *art* un, uno *m*; una *f*.

**aback** [ə'bak] *adv* **be taken aback** essere colto di sorpresa.

**abandon** [ə'bandən] *v* abbandonare. *n* abbandono *m*.

**abashed** [ə'baʃt] *adj* confuso.

**abate** [ə'beit] *v* diminuire. **abatement** *n* diminuzione *f*.

**abattoir** ['abətwa:] *n* macello *m*.

**abbey** ['abi] *n* abbazia *f*. **abbess** *n* badessa *f*. **abbot** *n* abate *m*.

**abbreviate** [ə'bri:vieit] *v* abbreviare. **abbreviation** *n* abbreviazione *f*.

**abdicate** ['abdikeit] *v* abdicare. **abdication** *n* abdicazione *f*.

**abdomen** ['abdəmən] *n* addome *m*. **abdominal** *adj* addominale.

**abduct** [əb'dʌkt] *v* rapire. **abduction** *n* rapimento *m*.

**aberration** [abə'reiʃən] *n* aberrazione *f*. **aberrant** *adj* aberrante.

**abet** [ə'bet] *v* favoreggiare. **aid and abet** farsi complice di.

**abeyance** [ə'beiəns] *n* sospensione *f*. **in abeyance** in sospeso.

**abhor** [əb'ho:] *v* aborrire. **abhorrence** *n* aborrimento *m*. **abhorrent** *adj* aborrevole, odioso.

*****abide** [ə'baid] *v* (*wait*) aspettare; (*tolerate*) soffrire. **abide by** sostenere, restar fedele a.

**ability** [ə'biləti] *n* abilità *f*. **to the best of one's ability** come meglio potrà.

**abject** [,abdʒekt] *adj* abietto.

**ablaze** [ə'bleiz] *adj* in fiamme, risplendente.

**able** ['eibl] *adj* capace; (*talented*) abile. **able-bodied** *adj* robusto. **be able** potere, essere in grado di.

**abnormal** [ab'no:ml] *adj* anormale. **abnormality** *n* anormalità *f*.

**aboard** [ə'bo:d] *adv, prep* a bordo (di). **all aboard!** tutti a bordo! **go aboard** imbarcarsi.

**abode** [ə'boud] *V* **abide**. *n* dimora *f*.

**abolish** [ə'boliʃ] *v* abolire. **abolition** *n* abolizione *f*.

**abominable** [ə'bominəbl] *adj* abominevole. **abominate** *v* detestare. **abomination** *n* abominazione *f*.

**aborigine** [abə'ridʒini] *n* indigeno *m*.

**abortion** [ə'bo:ʃən] *n* aborto *m*. **abort** *v* abortire.

**abound** [ə'baund] *v* abbondare.

**about** [ə'baut] *adv* (*around*) intorno; (*nearly*) verso, presso; circa; (*concerning*) su. *prep* di, su; intorno a. **be about to** stare per.

**above** [ə'bʌv] *adv* in alto, di sopra. *prep* sopra, al di sopra di; (*number*) più di; (*rank*) superiore a. **above all** sopratutto. **above-mentioned** *adj* suddetto. **from above** dall'alto.

**abrasion** [ə'breiʒən] *n* abrasione *f*. **abrasive** *adj* abrasivo.

**abreast** [ə'brest] *adv* **keep abreast of** or

**with** tenersi al corrente di. **two abreast** due per due.

**abridge** [ə'brɪdʒ] v abbreviare. **abridgement** n abbreviazione f.

**abroad** [ə'brɔːd] adv all'estero.

**abrupt** [ə'brʌpt] adj brusco.

**abscess** ['abses] n ascesso m.

**abscond** [əb'skɒnd] v rendersi latitante.

**abseil** ['abseil] v calarsi a corda doppia; calarsi con la corda.

**absent** ['absənt] adj assente. **absent-minded** adj distratto. v **absent oneself** assentarsi. **absence** n assenza f. **absentee** n assente m. **absenteeism** n assenteismo m.

**absolute** ['absəluːt] adj assoluto. **absolutely** adv assolutamente, perfettamente. **absolutism** n assolutismo m.

**absolve** [əb'zɒlv] v assolvere. **absolution** n assoluzione f.

**absorb** [əb'zɔːb] v assorbire. **be absorbed in** essere concentrato in. **absorbent** adj assorbente. **absorbing** adj (coll) molto interessante. **absorption** n assorbimento m.

**abstain** [əb'stein] v astenersi. **abstention** n astensione f.

**abstemious** [əb'stiːmiəs] adj astemio.

**abstinence** ['abstinəns] n astinenza f.

**abstract** ['abstrakt; v ab'strakt] adj astratto. v astrarre. **abstractedly** adv distrattamente. **abstraction** n astrazione f.

**absurd** [əb'səːd] adj assurdo, ridicolo. **absurdity** n assurdità f.

**abundance** [ə'bʌndəns] n abbondanza f. **abundant** adj abbondante.

**abuse** [ə'bjuːs; v ə'bjuːz] n abuso m; insulto m. v abusare di, maltrattare; insultare, oltraggiare. **abusive** adj offensivo; abusivo.

**abyss** [ə'bis] n abisso m. **abysmal** adj abissale; profondo.

**academy** [ə'kadəmi] n accademia f. **academic** n, adj accademico, -a.

**accede** [ak'siːd] v accedere.

**accelerate** [ak'seləreit] v accelerare. **acceleration** n accelerazione f. **accelerator** n acceleratore m.

**accent** ['aksənt] n accento m. v accentuare; (gramm) accentare.

**accept** [ək'sept] v accettare, accogliere. **acceptable** adj (agreeable) gradevole; accettabile. **acceptance** n accettazione f.

**access** ['akses] n accesso m. **accessible**

adj accessibile.

**accessory** [ək'sesəri] n accessorio m; (law) complice m, f. adj accessorio.

**accident** ['aksidənt] n accidente m, infortunio m. **by accident** per caso. **accidental** adj fortuito.

**acclaim** [ə'kleim] v acclamare. n also **acclamation** acclamazione f.

**acclimatize** [ə'klaimətaiz] v acclimatare.

**accolade** [ə'kəleid] n abbraccio m.

**accommodate** [ə'kɒmədeit] v accomodare; (lodge) ospitare; (provide) provvedere (di). **accommodating** adj cortese, conciliante. **accommodation** n (housing) alloggio m; (hotel) posto m.

**accompany** [ə'kʌmpəni] v accompagnare. **accompaniment** n accompagnamento m. **accompanist** n accompagnatore, -trice m, f.

**accomplice** [ə'kʌmplis] n complice m, f.

**accomplish** [ə'kʌmpliʃ] v compiere, realizzare. **accomplished** adj (talented) compito. **accomplishment** n effettuazione f; talento m.

**accord** [ə'kɔːd] v concedere, accordare. n accordo m. **of one's own accord** spontaneamente. **in accordance with** in conformità con. **accordingly** adv pertanto, quindi, di conseguenza. **according to** secondo.

**accordion** [ə'kɔːdiən] n fisarmonica f.

**accost** [ə'kɒst] v rivolgersi a.

**account** [ə'kaunt] n (report) relazione f, versione f; (status) importanza f; (bank) conto m. **by all accounts** a quanto si dice. **on no account** a nessuna condizione. **on one's own account** per propria iniziativa. v **account for** spiegare la ragione di, giustificare. **accountant** n contabile m, f, ragioniere m.

**accrue** [ə'kruː] v accrescere.

**accumulate** [ə'kjuːmjuleit] v accumulare. **accumulation** n ammasso m, accumulamento m.

**accurate** ['akjurət] adj accurato, preciso. **accuracy** n accuratezza f, precisione f.

**accuse** [ə'kjuːz] v accusare, incolpare. **the accused** n l'imputato, -a m, f. **accusation** n accusa f.

**accustom** [ə'kʌstəm] v abituare.

**ace** [eis] n asso m. **within an ace of** a un dito di.

**ache** [eik] *n* dolore *m*. *v* far male, dolere.

**achieve** [ə'tʃiːv] *v* concludere, ottenere, compiere. **achievement** *n* compimento *m*, successo *m*.

**acid** ['asid] *nm, adj* acido.

**acid rain** *n* pioggia acida *m*.

**acknowledge** [ək'nolidʒ] *v* riconoscere, ammettere. **acknowledge receipt of** accusare ricevuta di. **acknowledgement** *n* riconoscimento *m*; ricevuta *f*.

**acne** ['akni] *n* acne *f*.

**acorn** ['eikoːn] *n* ghianda *f*.

**acoustic** [ə'kuːstik] *adj* acustico. **acoustics** *pl n* acustica *f sing*.

**acquaint** [ə'kweint] *v* avvertire, mettere al corrente. **acquaintance** *n* (*knowledge*) conoscenza *f*; (*person*) conoscente *m, f*. **become acquainted with** (*person*) fare la conoscenza di; (*thing*) informarsi su.

**acquiesce** [akwi'es] *v* acconsentire tacitamente. **acquiescence** *n* acquiescenza *f*. **acquiescent** *adj* acquiescente.

**acquire** [ə'kwaiə] *v* acquisire, acquistare.

**acquisition** [akwi'ziʃən] *n* acquisto *m*; acquisizione *f*. **acquisitive** *adj* avido di guadagno.

**acquit** [ə'kwit] *v* esonerare. **acquit oneself** comportarsi. **acquittal** *n* (*law*) assoluzione *f*.

**acrid** ['akrid] *adj* acre, pungente.

**acrimony** ['akriməni] *n* acrimonia *f*. **acrimonious** *adj* acrimonioso, astioso.

**acrobat** ['akrəbat] *n* acrobata *m, f*. **acrobatic** *adj* acrobatico. **acrobatics** *pl n* acrobazie *f pl*.

**acronym** ['akrənim] *n* acronimo *m*.

**across** [ə'kros] *adv* per traverso; (*crossword*) orizzontali. *prep* al di là di, attraverso.

**acrylic** [ə'krilik] *adj* acrilico.

**act** [akt] *v* agire; (*theatre*) recitare; (*behave*) comportarsi. **act as** fungere da. **act for** agire per conto di. *n* (*deed*) azione *f*; (*theatre*) atto *m*; (*law*) decreto *m*. **actor** *n* attore *m*. **actress** *n* attrice *f*.

**action** ['akʃən] *n* azione *f*; (*law*) processo *m*; (*mil*) combattimento *m*. **out of action** fuori uso.

**active** ['aktiv] *adj* attivo, energico. **activate** *v* attivare. **activist** *n* attivista *m, f*. **activity** *n* attività *f*.

**actual** ['aktʃuəl] *adj* effettivo, reale. **actually** *adv* effettivamente.

**actuate** ['aktjueit] *v* mettere in atto *or* moto.

**acupuncture** ['akjupʌŋktʃə] *n* acupuntura *f*.

**acute** [ə'kjuːt] *adj* acuto, perspicace.

**adamant** ['adəmənt] *adj* inflessibile.

**Adam's apple** [adəm'zapl] *n* pomo d'Adamo *m*.

**adapt** [ə'dapt] *v* adattare, modificare. **adaptability** *n* adattabilità *f*. **adaptable** *adj* adattabile. **adaptation** *n* adattamento *m*. **adapter** *n* (*theatre*) riduttore *m*; (*elec*) raccordo *m*.

**add** [ad] *v* aggiungere. **add to** aumentare. **add up** fare la somma di, sommare. **addition** *n* addizione *f*. **additional** *adj* supplementare.

**addendum** [ə'dendəm] *n* aggiunta *f*.

**adder** ['adə] *n* vipera *f*.

**addict** ['adikt; *v* ə'dikt] *n* (*drug*) drogato, -a *m, f*, tossicomane *m, f*. **be addicted to** essere abituato *or* dedito a. **addiction** *n* dedizione *f*; tossicomania *f*. **addictive** *adj* che dà assuefazione.

**additive** ['aditiv] *n* aggiunta *f*.

**address** [ə'dres] *v* (*letter*) indirizzare; (*meeting, etc.*) rivolgere la parola a, fare un discorso a. **address oneself to** mettersi a. *n* (*speech*) discorso *m*; (*letter*) indirizzo *m*, recapito *m*. **addressee** *n* destinatario *m*.

**adenoids** ['adənoidz] *pl n* adenoidi *f pl*.

**adept** [ə'dept] *nm, adj* esperto.

**adequate** ['adikwət] *adj* sufficiente, adeguato.

**adhere** [əd'hiə] *v* aderire, attaccarsi. **adhesion** *n* adesione *f*. **adhesive** *nm, adj* adesivo.

**adherent** [əd'hiərənt] *n* partigiano *m*, seguace *m*.

**adjacent** [ə'dʒeisənt] *adj* adiacente, contiguo.

**adjective** ['adʒiktiv] *n* aggettivo *m*.

**adjoin** [ə'dʒoin] *v* confinare (con). **adjoining** *adj* adiacente.

**adjourn** [ə'dʒəːn] *v* aggiornare, rinviare. **adjournment** *n* rinvio *m*.

**adjudicate** [ə'dʒuːdikeit] *v* aggiudicare. **adjudicator** *n* arbitro *m*.

**adjust** [ə'dʒʌst] *v* regolare, mettere a punto. **adjustment** *n* adattamento *m*, rettifica *f*.

**ad-lib** ['ad'lib] *v* improvvisare.

**administer** [əd'ministə] v amministrare; (med) somministrare. **administration** n amministrazione f. **administrative** adj amministrativo. **administrator** n amministratore, -trice m, f.

**admiral** ['admərəl] n ammiraglio m.

**admire** [əd'maiə] v ammirare. **admirable** adj ammirevole. **admiration** n ammirazione f. **admiringly** adv con meraviglia.

**admit** [əd'mit] v ammettere; concedere; confessare. **admissible** adj ammissibile. **admission** n ammissione f. **admittance** n ingresso m, entrata f.

**adolescence** [adə'lesns] n adolescenza f. **adolescent** n(m+f), adj adolescente.

**adopt** [ə'dopt] v adottare. **adopted** adj (child) adottivo. **adoption** n adozione f.

**adore** [ə'do:] v adorare. **adoration** n adorazione f.

**adorn** [ə'do:n] v abbellire, guarnire. **adornment** n ornamento m.

**adrenaline** [ə'drenəlin] n adrenalina f.

**adrift** [ə'drift] adv alla deriva.

**adroit** [ə'droit] adj abile, destro.

**adulation** [adju'leifən] n adulazione f.

**adult** ['adʌlt] n, adj adulto, -a.

**adulterate** [ə'dʌltəreit] v adulterare; (wine) sofisticare.

**adultery** [ə'dʌltəri] n adulterio m. **adulterer** n adultero, -a m, f.

**advance** [əd'va:ns] v avanzare, progredire, anticipare. n avanzamento m; (mil) marcia in avanti f; (cash) anticipo m. **book in advance** prenotare.

**advantage** [əd'va:ntidʒ] n vantaggio m, beneficio m. **take advantage of** approfittare di. **advantageous** adj vantaggioso.

**advent** ['advənt] n avvento m.

**adventure** [əd'ventʃə] n avventura f, impresa rischiosa f. **adventurer** n avventuriero m. **adventurous** adj avventuroso.

**adverb** ['advə:b] n avverbio m.

**adversary** ['advəsəri] n avversario, -a m, f.

**adverse** ['advə:s] adj avverso. **adversity** n avversità f.

**advertise** ['advətaiz] v annunziare, fare pubblicità a. **advertisement** n annunzio m, inserzione f. **advertising** n pubblicità f.

**advise** [əd'vaiz] v consigliare, raccomandare. **ill-advised** adj imprudente, inopportuno. **well-advised** adj saggio. **advice** n consiglio m, suggerimento m. **advisable**

adj opportuno, consigliabile. **adviser** n consulente m, f. **advisory** adj consultivo.

**advocate** ['advəkeit] v sostenere.

**aerial** ['eəriəl] adj aereo. n antenna f.

**aerobics** [eə'roubiks] n aerobica f.

**aerodynamics** [eərədai'namiks] n aerodinamica f.

**aeronautics** [eərə'no:tiks] n aeronautica f.

**aeroplane** ['eərəplein] n aereo m.

**aerosol** ['eərəsol] n aerosol m.

**aesthetic** [i:s'θetik] adj estetico. **aesthetics** n estetica f.

**affair** [ə'feə] n affare m. **have an affair** avere una relazione intima.

**affect**[1] [ə'fekt] v (influence) colpire, toccare.

**affect**[2] [ə'fekt] v (pretend) fingere, simulare.

**affection** [ə'fekʃən] n affetto m, affezione f. **affectionate** adj affezionato.

**affiliate** [ə'filieit] v affiliare. **affiliation** n affiliazione f.

**affinity** [ə'finəti] n affinità f.

**affirm** [ə'fə:m] v affermare, confermare. **affirmation** n affermazione f, conferma f. **affirmative** adj affermativo.

**affix** [ə'fiks] v affiggere.

**afflict** [ə'flikt] v affliggere, angosciare. **affliction** n afflizione f, dolore m.

**affluent** ['afluənt] adj ricco, opulento. **affluence** n affluenza f, ricchezza f.

**afford** [ə'fo:d] v avere i mezzi per; (produce) dare, offrire; (allow oneself to) permettersi di.

**affront** [ə'frʌnt] n affronto m, offesa f. v insultare, offendere.

**afloat** [ə'flout] adv a galla.

**afoot** [ə'fut] adv a piedi; (fig) in atto.

**aforesaid** [ə'fo:sed] adj suddetto, soprannominato.

**afraid** [ə'freid] adj impaurito, pauroso, spaventato. **be afraid of** temere, aver paura di.

**afresh** [ə'freʃ] adv da capo, nuovamente.

**Africa** ['afrikə] n Africa f. **African** n, adj africano, -a.

**aft** [a:ft] adv a poppa.

**after** ['a:ftə] prep dopo, in seguito a. adv dopo, poi. conj dopo che. **after all** dopo tutto, insomma. **afterwards** adv dopo, poi.

**afternoon** [a:ftə'nu:n] n pomeriggio m, dopo pranzo m. **good afternoon!** buona sera!

**aftershave** ['a:ftəʃeiv] n dopobarba m invar.

**again** [ə'gen] adv di nuovo, ancora. **again and again** ripetutamente. **never again** mai più.

**against** [ə'genst] prep contro, in opposizione a.

**age** [eidʒ] n età f; era f. **of age** maggiorenne. **old age** vecchiaia f. **under age** minorenne. v invecchiare. **aged** adj vecchio; (seasoned) invecchiato.

**agency** ['eidʒənsi] n agenzia f, rappresentanza f.

**agenda** [ə'dʒendə] n ordine del giorno m.

**agent** ['eidʒənt] n agente m, f; rappresentante m, f.

**aggravate** ['agrəveit] v aggravare; (coll) irritare. **aggravation** n aggravamento m; (coll) irritazione f.

**aggregate** ['agrigət] nm, adj aggregato.

**aggression** [ə'greʃən] n aggressione f. **aggressive** adj aggressivo. **aggressor** n aggressore m.

**aghast** [ə'ga:st] adj stupefatto, atterrito.

**agile** ['adʒail] adj agile. **agility** n agilità f.

**agitate** ['adʒiteit] v agitare, turbare. **agitation** n agitazione f. **agitator** n agitatore, -trice m, f.

**agnostic** [ag'nostik] n, adj agnostico, -a. **agnosticism** n agnosticismo m.

**ago** [ə'gou] adv fa.

**agog** [ə'gog] adj bramoso.

**agony** ['agəni] n agonia f, angoscia f. **be in agony** soffrire dolori atroci.

**agree** [ə'gri:] v essere or andare d'accordo, convenire, accordarsi. **agreeable** adj piacevole, simpatico. **agreement** n accordo m, patto m, contratto m.

**agriculture** ['agrikʌltʃə] n agricoltura f. **agricultural** adj agricolo.

**aground** [ə'graund] adv arenato. **run aground** incagliarsi.

**ahead** [ə'hed] adv (in) avanti.

**aid** [eid] v aiutare, sovvenire, soccorrere. n aiuto m, sussidio m. **first aid** pronto soccorso m. **in aid of** a favore di.

**Aids** n (med) aids m.

**aim** [eim] v puntare, prendere di mira; aspirare. n mira f; (purpose) scopo m, proposito m.

**air** [eə] n aria f; (bearing) aspetto m, contegno m. v ventilare.

**airbed** ['eəbed] n materassino pneumatico m.

**airborne** ['eəbo:n] adj aerotrasportato.

**air-conditioned** adj ad aria condizionata.

**aircraft** ['eəkra:ft] n aereo m. **aircraft-carrier** n portaerei f invar.

**airfield** ['eəfi:ld] n campo d'aviazione m.

**air force** n aviazione f.

**air-hostess** n assistente di volo f, hostess f invar.

**air lift** n ponte aereo m.

**airline** ['eəlain] n linea aerea f.

**airmail** ['eəmeil] n posta aerea f.

**airport** ['eəpo:t] n aeroporto m.

**air-raid** n incursione aerea f. **air-raid shelter** rifugio contraereo m.

**airtight** ['eətait] adj ermetico, impenetrabile all'aria.

**air traffic controller** n controllore di voli m.

**airy** ['eəri] adj arioso, ben ventilato.

**aisle** [ail] n navata f.

**ajar** [ə'dʒa:] adj socchiuso.

**akin** [ə'kin] adj simile, parente.

**alabaster** ['aləba:stə] n alabastro m.

**alarm** [ə'la:m] n allarme m. **alarm clock** sveglia f. v allarmare.

**alas** [ə'las] interj purtroppo!

**Albania** [al'beinjə] n Albania f. **Albanian** n(m+f), adj albanese.

**albatross** ['albatros] n albatro m.

**albino** [al'bi:nou] n, adj albino, -a.

**album** ['albəm] n album m.

**alchemy** ['alkəmi] n alchimia f. **alchemist** n alchimista m, f.

**alcohol** ['alkəhol] n alcool m.

**alcoholic** [alkə'holik] adj alcoolico. n alcoolizzato, -a m, f. **alcoholism** n alcoolismo m.

**alcove** ['alkouv] n nicchia f.

**alderman** ['o:ldəmən] n assessore municipale m.

**ale** [eil] n birra f.

**alert** [ə'lə:t] adj vigilante. v avvertire. **be on the alert** stare all'erta.

**algebra** ['aldʒibrə] n algebra f.

**alias** ['eiliəs] adv altrimenti detto.

**alibi** ['alibai] n alibi m invar.

**alien** ['eiliən] n, adj straniero, -a, forestiero, -a. **alienate** v alienare. **alienation** n alienazione f.

**alight**[1] [ə'lait] v scendere, smontare.

**alight**[2] [ə'lait] adj acceso, illuminato.

**align** [ə'lain] v allineare.

**alike** [ə'laik] adj simile, somigliante. adv ugualmente. **be alike** assomigliarsi.

**alimentary canal** [ali'mentəri] adj alimentare.

**alimony** ['aliməni] n alimenti m pl.

**alive** [ə'laiv] adj vivo, vivente. **alive to** sensibile a.

**alkaline** ['alkəlain] adj alcalino.

**all** [o:l] adj tutto. adv completamente. n tutti m pl, tutte f pl. **all right!** va bene! **All Saints' Day** Ognissanti m. **All Souls' Day** giorno dei morti m. **all the same** con tutto ciò. **not at all** niente affatto.

**allay** [ə'lei] v calmare.

**allege** [ə'ledʒ] v allegare, asserire. **alleged** adj sedicente.

**allegiance** [ə'li:dʒəns] n obbedienza f, fedeltà f.

**allegory** ['aligəri] n allegoria f.

**allergy** ['alədʒi] n allergia f. **allergic** adj allergico.

**alleviate** [ə'li:vieit] v alleviare, attenuare.

**alley** ['ali] n vicolo m.

**alliance** [ə'laiəns] n alleanza f, patto m.

**alligator** ['aligeitə] n alligatore m.

**alliteration** [əlitə'reifən] n allitterazione f.

**allocate** ['aləkeit] v assegnare, collocare. **allocation** n assegnamento m.

**allot** [ə'lot] v assegnare. **allotment** n (land) lotto m, pezzo di terreno m; (portion) parte assegnata f.

**allow** [ə'lau] v permettere, concedere. **allow for** tener conto di. **allow me!** permetta! **allowance** n (grant) assegno m; (reduction) sconto m.

**alloy** ['aloi; v ə'loi] n lega f. v legare, amalgamare.

**allude** [ə'lu:d] v riferirsi (a), alludere (a). **allusion** n allusione f, riferimento m.

**allure** [ə'ljuə] n fascino m. v affascinare. **alluring** adj seducente.

**ally** ['alai; v ə'lai] n alleato, -a m, f. v alleare.

**almanac** ['o:lmənak] n almanacco m.

**almighty** [o:l'maiti] adj onnipotente. **the Almighty** n il Padreterno m.

**almond** ['a:mənd] n (nut) mandorla f; (tree) mandorlo m.

**almost** ['o:lmoust] adv quasi.

**alms** [a:mz] pl n elemosina f sing. **give alms** fare l'elemosina. **almshouse** n ospizio dei poveri m.

**aloft** [ə'loft] adv in alto.

**alone** [ə'loun] adj solo. adv solo, da solo. (only) solamente. **leave alone** lasciar stare.

**along** [ə'loŋ] prep lungo. **along with** insieme a. **come along!** su! avanti! **alongside** prep accanto a.

**aloof** [ə'lu:f] adj riservato, freddo. adv a distanza.

**aloud** [ə'laud] adv ad alta voce.

**alphabet** ['alfəbit] n alfabeto m.

**Alps** [alps] pl n the Alps le Alpi f pl. **alpine** adj alpino.

**already** [o:l'redi] adv già

**also** ['o:lsou] adv anche, pure, inoltre.

**altar** ['o:ltə] n altare m. **altarpiece** n pala d'altare f. **high altar** altare maggiore m.

**alter** ['o:ltə] v alterare, cambiare, alterarsi. **alteration** n cambiamento m, mutamento m.

**alternate** ['o:ltəneit; adj o:l'tə:nət] v alternare, alternarsi, succedersi. adj alterno. **alternation** n alternazione f, successione reciproca f.

**alternative** [o:l'tə:nətiv] adj alternativo. n alternativa f.

**although** [o:l'ðou] conj sebbene, benché.

**altitude** ['altitju:d] n altezza f, altitudine f; (aircraft) quota f.

**altogether** [o:ltə'geðə] adv complessivamente, nell'insieme.

**altruistic** [altru'istik] adj altruistico. **altruism** n altruismo m. **altruist** n altruista m, f.

**aluminium** [alju'miniəm] n alluminio m.

**always** ['o:lweiz] adv sempre.

**am** [am] V **be**.

**amalgamate** [ə'malgəmeit] v amalgamare. **amalgam** n amalgama m.

**amass** [ə'mas] v accumulare.

**amateur** ['amətə] n dilettante m, f. **amateurish** adj da dilettante.

**amaze** [ə'meiz] v stupire, meravigliare. **amazement** n stupore m, meraviglia f. **amazing** adj straordinario, stupendo.

**ambassador** [am'basədə] n ambasciatore, -trice m, f.

**amber** ['ambə] n ambra f.

**ambidextrous** [ambi'dekstrəs] adj

ambidestro.

**ambiguous** [am'bigjuəs] *adj* ambiguo.

**ambition** [am'bifən] *n* ambizione *f*. **ambitious** *adj* ambizioso.

**ambivalent** [am'bivələnt] *adj* ambivalente.

**amble** ['ambl] *v* camminare lentamente.

**ambulance** ['ambjuləns] *n* ambulanza *f*.

**ambush** ['ambuʃ] *n* imboscata *f*, agguato *m*. *v* tendere un agguato.

**ameliorate** [ə'mi:liəreit] *v* migliorare.

**amenable** [ə'mi:nəbl] *adj* trattabile, suscettibile.

**amend** [ə'mend] *v* emendare, correggere. **amendment** *n* emendamento *m*, correzione *f*. **make amends** fare ammenda.

**amenity** [ə'mi:nəti] *n* amenità *f*. **amenities** *pl n* comodità *f*.

**America** [ə'merikə] *n* America *f*. **American** *n, adj* americano, -a.

**amethyst** ['aməθist] *n* ametista *f*.

**amiable** ['eimiəbl] *adj* gentile, amabile.

**amicable** ['amikəbl] *adj* amichevole.

**amid** [ə'mid] *prep* fra, tra, in mezzo a.

**amiss** [ə'mis] *adv* **take amiss** aversene a male.

**ammonia** [ə'mouniə] *n* ammoniaca *f*.

**ammunition** [amju'nifən] *n* munizioni *f pl*.

**amnesia** [am'ni:ziə] *n* amnesia *f*.

**amnesty** ['amnəsti] *n* amnistia *f*.

**amoeba** [ə'mi:bə] *n* ameba *f*.

**among** [ə'mʌŋ] *prep* fra, tra, in mezzo a.

**amoral** [ei'morəl] *adj* amorale.

**amorous** ['amərəs] *adj* amoroso.

**amorphous** [ə'mo:fəs] *adj* amorfo.

**amount** [ə'maunt] *n* quantità *f*, importo *m*, somma *f*. *v* ammontare, equivalere.

**ampere** ['ampeə] *n* ampere *m invar*.

**amphetamine** [am'fetəmi:n] *n* amfetamina *f*, anfetamina *f*.

**amphibian** [am'fibiən] *nm, adj* anfibio.

**amphitheatre** ['amfiθiətə] *n* anfiteatro *m*.

**ample** ['ampl] *adj* ampio, abbondante.

**amplify** ['amplifai] *v* amplificare, ampliare. **amplification** *n* amplificazione *f*. **amplifier** *n* amplificatore *m*.

**amputate** ['ampjuteit] *v* amputare. **amputation** *n* amputazione *f*.

**amuse** [ə'mju:z] *v* divertire, dilettare. **amusement** *n* divertimento *m*, svago *m*. **amusing** *adj* divertente, buffo.

**amusement arcade** *n* sala giochi *f*.

**anachronism** [ə'nakrənizəm] *n* anacronismo *m*.

**anaemia** [ə'ni:miə] *n* anemia *f*. **anaemic** *adj* anemico.

**anaesthetic** [anəs'θetik] *nm, adj* anestetico. **anaesthesia** *n* anestesia *f*. **anaesthetist** *n* anestesista *m, f*. **anaesthetize** *v* anestetizzare.

**anagram** ['anəgram] *n* anagramma *m*.

**anal** ['einl] *adj* anale.

**analogy** [ə'nalədʒi] *n* analogia *f*. **analogous** *adj* analogo (*m pl* -ghi).

**analysis** [ən'aləsis] *n, pl* -ses analisi *f*. **analyse** *v* analizzare, **analyst** *n* analista *m, f*. **analytical** *adj* analitico.

**anarchy** ['anəki] *n* anarchia *f*. **anarchic** *adj* anarchico. **anarchist** *n* anarchico, -a *m, f*.

**anathema** [ə'naθəmə] *n* anatema *m*.

**anatomy** [ə'natəmi] *n* anatomia *f*. **anatomical** *adj* anatomico. **anatomist** *n* anatomista *m, f*.

**ancestor** ['ansestə] *n* antenato *m*. **ancestral** *adj* avito. **ancestry** *n* stirpe *f*, lignaggio *m*.

**anchor** ['aŋkə] *n* ancora *f*. *v* ancorare.

**anchovy** ['antʃəvi] *n* acciuga *f*.

**ancient** ['einʃənt] *adj* antico (*m pl* -chi), anziano.

**ancillary** [an'siləri] *adj* ausiliario, sussidiario.

**and** [and] *conj* e, ed.

**anecdote** ['anikdout] *n* aneddoto *m*.

**anemone** [ə'neməni] *n* anemone *f*.

**anew** [ə'nju:] *adv* da capo, di nuovo.

**angel** ['eindʒəl] *n* angelo *m*. **angelic** *adj* angelico.

**anger** ['aŋgə] *n* rabbia *f*, stizza *f*, ira *f*. *v* far arrabbiare.

**angina** [an'dʒainə] *n* (*med*) angina *f*.

**angle** ['aŋgl] *n* (*corner*) angolo *m*; (*viewpoint*) punto di vista *m*.

**angling** ['aŋliŋ] *n* pesca all'amo *f*. **angler** *n* pescatore *m*.

**angry** ['aŋgri] *adj* arrabbiato, stizzito.

**anguish** ['aŋgwiʃ] *n* angoscia *f*, tormento *m*. *v* angosciare, tormentare.

**angular** ['aŋgjulə] *adj* angolare.

**animal** ['animəl] *n* animale *m*, bestia *f*. *adj* animale.

**animate** ['animət; *v* 'animeit] *adj* animato,

vivente. *v* animare. **animated** *adj* vivace.
**animation** *n* animazione f.
**animosity** [ani'mosəti] *n* animosità f.
**aniseed** ['anisi:d] *n* anice m.
**ankle** ['aŋkl] *n* caviglia f.
**annals** ['anlz] *pl n* annali m pl.
**annex** [ə'neks; n 'aneks] *v* annettere. *n*
annesso m; (hotel) dipendenza f. **annexa-
tion** *n* annessione f.
**annihilate** [ə'naiəleit] *v* annientare. **anni-
hilation** *n* annientamento m.
**anniversary** [ˌani'vəːsəri] *nm, adj* anniversario.
**annotate** ['anəteit] *v* annotare.
**announce** [ə'nauns] *v* annunciare, rendere
noto. **announcement** *n* annuncio m.
**announcer** *n* annunciatore, -trice m, f.
**annoy** [ə'noi] *v* dar noia a, disturbare, seccare. **annoyance** *n* fastidio m, noia f.
**annoying** *adj* seccante, fastidioso.
**annual** ['anjuəl] *adj* annuale, annuo. *n*
(book) annuario m; (plant) pianta annuale f.
**annually** *adv* annualmente.
**annuity** [ə'njuːəti] *n* annualità f. **life annuity** *n* vitalizio m.
**annul** [ə'nʌl] *v* annullare. **annulment** *n*
annullamento m.
**Annunciation** [əˌnʌnsi'eiʃn] *n* (rel)
Annunziazione f.
**anode** ['anoud] *n* anodo m.
**anomaly** [ə'noməli] *n* anomalia f. **anomalous** *adj* anomalo, irregolare.
**anonymous** [ə'noniməs] *adj* anonimo.
**anorak** ['anərak] *n* giacca a vento f.
**anorexia** [anə'reksiə] (nervosa) *n* anoressia
(nervosa) f.
**another** [ə'nʌðə] *adj, pron* un altro. **one
another** l'un l'altro.
**answer** ['aːnsə] *v* rispondere (a). **answer
for** rispondere di. *n* risposta f.
**answering machine** *n* segreteria telefonica, segreteria automatica f.
**ant** [ant] *n* formica f. **ant-hill** *n* formicaio
m.
**antagonize** [an'tagənaiz] *v* provocare l'ostilità (di). **antagonism** *n* antagonismo m.
**antagonist** *n* antagonista m, f.
**antecedent** [ˌanti'siːdənt] *adj* antecedente.
**antecedents** *pl n* precedenti m pl; (for-
bears) antenati m pl.
**antelope** ['antəloup] *n* antilope f.

**antenatal** [anti'neitl] *adj* prenatale.
**antenna** [an'tenə] *n* antenna f.
**anthem** ['anθəm] *n* inno m.
**anthology** [an'θolədʒi] *n* antologia f.
**anthropology** [anθrə'polədʒi] *n*
antropologia f. **anthropologist** *n* antropologo, -a m, f.
**anti-aircraft** [anti'eəkra:ft] *adj* contraereo.
**antibiotic** [antibai'otik] *nm, adj* antibiotico.
**antibody** ['antiˌbodi] *n* anticorpo m.
**anticipate** [an'tisipeit] *v* anticipare, prevenire. **in anticipation** in anticipo.
**anticlimax** [anti'klaimaks] *n* conclusione
banale f.
**anticlockwise** [anti'klokwaiz] *adj, adv* in
senso antiorario.
**antics** ['antiks] *pl n* buffoneria f sing.
**anticyclone** [anti'saikloun] *n* anticiclone m.
**antidepressant** [ˌantidi'presənt] *adj* antidepressivo.
**antidote** ['antidout] *n* antidoto m.
**antifreeze** ['antifriːz] *n* antigelo m.
**antipathy** [an'tipəθi] *n* antipatia f.
**antique** [an'tiːk] *adj* antico (m pl -chi). *n*
oggetto antico m. **antique dealer** *n* antiquario m. **antiquity** *n* antichità f.
**anti-Semitic** [antisə'mitik] *n* antisemita m,
f. **anti-Semitism** *n* antisemitismo m.
**antiseptic** [anti'septik] *nm, adj* antisettico.
**antisocial** [anti'souʃəl] *adj* antisociale.
**anti-tank** [anti'taŋk] *adj* anticarro.
**antithesis** [an'tiθəsis] *n, pl -ses* antitesi f.
**antler** ['antlə] *n* corno m.
**antonym** ['antənim] *n* antonimo m.
**anus** ['einəs] *n* ano m.
**anvil** ['anvil] *n* incudine f.
**anxious** ['aŋkʃəs] *adj* ansioso, preoccupato.
**anxiety** *n* ansia f, ansietà f.
**any** ['eni] *adj* del, della, etc.; qualche *invar*;
alcuno. *pron* alcuno, nessuno, ne. **anybody** *or* **anyone** *pron* qualcuno, alcuno;
chiunque. **anyhow** *or* **anyway** *adv* in ogni
caso, tuttavia; ad ogni modo. **anything**
*pron* qualcosa, qualche cosa; (everything)
qualunque cosa. **anywhere** *adv* in
qualunque luogo, in alcun luogo; (everywhere) dovunque.
**apart** [ə'paːt] *adv* a parte, in disparte.
**come apart** disfarsi. **tell apart** distinguere
l'uno dall'altro.

**apartment** [ə'pɑːtmənt] *n* appartamento *m*, alloggio *m*.

**apathy** ['apəθi] *n* apatia *f*. **apathetic** *adj* apatico.

**ape** [eip] *n* scimmia *f*. *v* scimmiottare, imitare.

**aperitif** [əperi'tiːf] *n* aperitivo *m*.

**aperture** ['apətjuə] *n* apertura *f*.

**apex** ['eipeks] *n* vertice *m*, apice *m*.

**aphid** ['eifid] *n* afide *m*.

**aphrodisiac** [afrə'diziak] *n* afrodisiaco *m*.

**apiece** [ə'piːs] *adv* a testa, per ciascuno, per uno.

**apology** [ə'polədʒi] *n* scusa *f*, giustificazione *f*. **apologetic** *adj* apologetico. **apologize** *v* chiedere scusa, scusarsi.

**apoplexy** ['apəpleksi] *n* apoplessia *f*. **apoplectic** *adj* apoplettico. **apoplectic fit** colpo apoplettico *m*.

**apostle** [ə'posl] *n* apostolo *m*.

**apostrophe** [ə'postrəfi] *n* (*punctuation*) apostrofo *m*; (*speech*) apostrofe *f*.

**appal** [ə'poːl] *v* inorridire, sgomentare. **appalling** *adj* terribile, spaventoso.

**apparatus** [apə'reitəs] *n* apparecchio *m*, apparato *m*.

**apparent** [ə'parənt] *adj* apparente, evidente, manifesto.

**apparition** [apə'riʃən] *n* visione *f*, fantasma *m*.

**appeal** [ə'piːl] *n* appello *m*. *v* appellarsi, fare appello; (*law*) ricorrere in appello. **appealing** *adj* attraente, commovente.

**appear** [ə'piə] *v* apparire, sembrare, parere. **appearance** *n* apparenza *f*, aspetto *m*. **put in an appearance** fare atto di presenza.

**appease** [ə'piːz] *v* calmare, pacificare. **appeasement** *n* pacificazione *f*.

**appendix** [ə'pendiks] *n* appendice *f*. **appendicitis** *n* appendicite *f*.

**appetite** ['apitait] *n* appetito *m*. **appetizing** *adj* gustoso, succulento.

**applaud** [ə'ploːd] *v* applaudire. **applause** *n* applauso *m*.

**apple** ['apl] *n* (*fruit*) mela *f*; (*tree*) melo *m*.

**apply** [ə'plai] *v* rivolgersi, fare domanda; (*refer*) riferirsi; (*use*) applicare. **apply oneself to** dedicarsi a. **appliance** *n* apparecchio *m*, strumento *m*. **applicable** *adj* applicabile, idoneo. **applicant** *n* candidato *m*. **application** *n* domanda *f*, richiesta *f*. **application form** modulo di richiesta *m*.

**appoint** [ə'point] *v* nominare; (*arrange*) fissare. **appointment** *n* (*engagement*) appuntamento *m*; (*post*) nomina *f*.

**apportion** [ə'poːʃən] *v* distribuire.

**appraisal** [ə'preizl] *n* valutazione *f*. **appraise** *v* stimare, valutare.

**appreciate** [ə'priːʃieit] *v* (*esteem*) apprezzare, stimare; (*be aware of*) rendersi conto di; (*increase in value*) aumentare di valore. **appreciable** *adj* apprezzabile, sensibile. **appreciation** *n* apprezzamento *m*, stima *f*.

**apprehend** [apri'hend] *v* cogliere, arrestare. **apprehension** *n* arresto *m*; (*worry*) timore *m*. **apprehensive** *adj* timoroso, preoccupato.

**apprentice** [ə'prentis] *n* apprendista *m*, *f*. **apprenticeship** *n* tirocinio *m*, apprendistato *m*.

**approach** [ə'proutʃ] *v* avvicinare; (*come near*) avvicinarsi (a). *n* avvicinamento *m*, accesso *m*.

**appropriate** [ə'proupriət; *v* ə'prouprieit] *adj* adatto, opportuno. *v* impadronirsi di.

**approve** [ə'piuːv] *v* approvare, dare il benestare. **approval** *n* approvazione *f*, benestare *m*. **on approval** in visione, in esame. **approved** *adj* approvato, convalidato, riconosciuto.

**approximate** [ə'proksimeit; *adj* ə'proksimət] *v* approssimare. *adj* approssimativo. **approximately** *adv* approssimativamente, all'incirca, su per giù.

**apricot** ['eiprikot] *n* (*fruit*) albicocca *f*; (*tree*) albicocco *m*.

**April** ['eiprəl] *n* aprile *m*.

**apron** ['eiprən] *n* grembiule *m*, grembiale *m*.

**apt** [apt] *adj* atto, adatto.

**aptitude** ['aptitjuːd] *n* abilità *f*, attitudine *f*.

**aqualung** ['akwəlʌŋ] *n* autorespiratore *m*.

**aquarium** [ə'kweəriəm] *n* acquario *m*.

**Aquarius** [ə'kweəriəs] *n* Acquario *m*.

**aquatic** [ə'kwatik] *adj* acquatico.

**aqueduct** ['akwidʌkt] *n* acquedotto *m*.

**Arab** ['arəb] *n*, *adj* arabo, -a. **Arabia** *n* Arabia *f*. **Arabic** *n* (*language*) arabo *m*.

**arable** ['arəbl] *adj* arabile.

**arbitrary** ['aːbitrəri] *adj* arbitrario.

**arbitrate** ['aːbitreit] *v* arbitrare. **arbitration** *n* arbitraggio *m*.

**arc** [aːk] *n* arco *m*. **arc lamp** lampada ad arco *f*.

**arcade** [a:'keid] *n* portico *m*, galleria *f*.

**arch**[1] [a:tʃ] *n* arco *m*, volta *f*. *v* curvare, arcuare.

**arch**[2] [a:tʃ] *adj* (*chief*) arci-.

**archaeology** [a:ki'olədʒi] *n* archeologia *f*. **archaeologist** *n* archeologo, -a *m, f*.

**archaic** [a:'keiik] *adj* arcaico.

**archbishop** [a:tʃ'biʃəp] *n* arcivescovo *m*.

**archduke** [a:tʃ'dju:k] *n* arciduca *m*.

**archery** ['a:tʃəri] *n* tiro all'arco *m*. **archer** *n* arciere *m*.

**archetype** ['a:kitaip] *n* archetipo *m*.

**archipelago** [a:ki'peləgou] *n* arcipelago (*pl* -ghi) *m*.

**architect** ['a:kitekt] *n* architetto, -a *m, f*. **architecture** *n* architettura *f*.

**archives** ['a:kaivz] *pl n* archivio *m sing*.

**arctic** ['a:ktik] *adj* artico.

**ardent** ['a:dənt] *adj* ardente, appassionato.

**ardour** ['a:də] *n* ardore *m*, fervore *m*.

**arduous** ['a:djuəs] *adj* arduo, difficile.

**are** [a:] *V* **be**.

**area** ['eəriə] *n* area *f*, superficie *f*, zona *f*.

**arena** [ə'ri:nə] *n* arena *f*.

**argue** ['a:gju:] *v* argomentare, discutere, disputare. **arguable** *adj* discutibile. **argument** *n* argomento *m*, discussione *f*. **argumentative** *adj* polemico.

**arid** ['arid] *adj* arido.

**Aries** ['eəri:z] *n* Ariete *m*.

**\*arise** [ə'raiz] *v* alzarsi, sorgere.

**arisen** [ə'rizn] *V* **arise**.

**aristocracy** [ari'stokrəsi] *n* aristocrazia *f*. **aristocrat** *n* aristocratico, -a *m, f*. **aristocratic** *adj* aristocratico.

**arithmetic** [ə'riθmətik] *n* aritmetica *f*.

**ark** [a:k] *n* arca *f*. **Noah's Ark** arca di Noè *f*.

**arm**[1] [a:m] *n* (*limb*) braccio *m* (*pl* -a *f*). **armchair** *n* poltrona *f*. **arm in arm** a braccetto. **armpit** *n* ascella *f*. **within arm's reach** a portata di mano.

**arm**[2] [a:m] *n* (*weapon*) arma (*pl* -i) *f*. **bear arms** essere sotto le armi. **be up in arms against** essere in rivolta contro. **coat of arms** stemma *m*. *v* armare.

**armistice** ['a:mistis] *n* armistizio *m*.

**armour** ['a:mə] *n* armatura *f*, corazza *f*. **armourer** *n* armiere *m*. **armour-plated** *adj* corazzato. **armoury** *n* arsenale *m*.

**army** ['a:mi] *n* esercito *m*, armata *f*.

**aroma** [ə'roumə] *n* aroma *m*.

**arose** [ə'rouz] *V* **arise**.

**around** [ə'raund] *prep* attorno a, intorno a. *adv* intorno. **all around** tutto intorno.

**arouse** [ə'rauz] *v* destare, eccitare.

**arrange** [ə'reindʒ] *v* accomodare, ordinare; (*music*) adattare; (*meeting, etc.*) organizzare; (*put in order*) sistemare. **arrangement** *n* combinazione *f*; accomodamento *m*; adattamento *m*. **come to an arrangement** mettersi d'accordo.

**array** [ə'rei] *n* schieramento *m*; mostra imponente *f*. *v* ornare, schierare.

**arrears** [ə'riəz] *pl n* arretrati *m pl*. **be in arrears** avere degli arretrati.

**arrest** [ə'rest] *n* arresto *m*. **under arrest** in stato d'arresto. *v* arrestare, sospendere.

**arrive** [ə'raiv] *v* arrivare, giungere. **arrival** *n* arrivo *m*; (*person*) arrivato, -a *m, f*.

**arrogant** ['arəgənt] *adj* arrogante. **arrogance** *n* arroganza *f*.

**arrow** ['arou] *n* freccia *f*.

**arse** [a:s] *n* (*vulgar*) culo *m*.

**arsenal** ['a:sənl] *n* arsenale *m*.

**arsenic** ['a:snik] *n* arsenico *m*.

**arson** ['a:sn] *n* incendio doloso *m*.

**art** [a:t] *n* arte *f*. **art gallery** galleria d'arte *f*, pinacoteca *f*. **artful** *adj* astuto.

**artefact** ['a:tifakt] *n* artefatto *m*.

**artery** ['a:təri] *n* arteria *f*.

**arthritis** [a:'θraitis] *n* artrite *f*.

**artichoke** ['a:titʃouk] *n* carciofo *m*.

**article** ['a:tikl] *n* articolo *m*; oggetto *m*.

**articulate** [a:'tikjuleit; *adj* a:'tikjulət] *v* articolare. *adj* articolato, distinto.

**artifice** ['a:tifis] *n* artifizio *m*, astuzia *f*.

**artificial** [a:ti'fiʃəl] *adj* artificiale, finto. **artificiality** *n* artificiosità *f*.

**artillery** [a:'tiləri] *n* artiglieria *f*.

**artisan** [a:ti'zan] *n* artigiano, -a *m, f*.

**artist** ['a:tist] *n* artista *m, f*. **artistic** *adj* artistico.

**as** [az] *adv* come, quanto. *conj* come; (*while*) mentre; (*because*) poiché, siccome. **as ... as** così ... come, tanto ... quanto. *prep* da. **as far as** (*distance*) sino a. **as for** or **to** per quanto riguarda. **as if** come se. **as long as** finché, purché. **as much** altrettanto. **as soon as** (non) appena. **as well** anche. **as well as** (*in addition to*) oltre a.

**asbestos** [az'bestos] *n* asbesto *m*,

amianto m.

**ascend** [ə'send] v salire, ascendere. **ascendancy** n ascendente m. **ascension** n ascensione f. **ascent** n ascesa f, salita f.

**ascertain** [asə'tein] v accertarsi di, verificare.

**ascetic** [ə'setik] adj ascetico. n asceta m, f.

**ash**¹ [aʃ] n (cinder) cenere f. **ashen** adj cinereo. **ashtray** n portacenere m.

**ash**² [aʃ] n (tree) frassino m.

**ashamed** [ə'ʃeimd] adj vergognoso. **be ashamed of** vergognarsi di.

**ashore** [ə'ʃo:] adv a terra, sulla riva.

**Ash Wednesday** n mercoledì delle Ceneri m.

**Asia** ['eiʃə] n Asia f. **Asian** n, adj asiatico, -a.

**aside** [ə'said] adv da parte, a parte, in disparte. n (theatre) parole dette a parte f pl.

**ask** [a:sk] v domandare, chiedere. **ask about** informarsi di or su. **ask after** chiedere notizie di.

**askew** [ə'skju:] adv di traverso.

**asleep** [ə'sli:p] adj addormentato. **fall asleep** addormentarsi.

**asparagus** [ə'sparəgəs] n asparago m.

**aspect** ['aspekt] n aspetto m, apparenza f.

**asphalt** ['asfalt] n asfalto m.

**asphyxiate** [əs'fiksieit] v asfissiareo.

**aspire** [ə'spaiə] v ambire. **aspiration** n ambizione f.

**aspirin** ['aspərin] n aspirina f.

**ass** [as] n asino m, somaro m.

**assail** [ə'seil] v assalire, aggredire. **assailant** n aggressore m.

**assassinate** [ə'sasineit] v assassinare. **assassin** n assassino, -a m, f. **assassination** n assassinio m.

**assault** [ə'so:lt] n assalto m, attacco m. v assalire, attaccare.

**assemble** [ə'sembl] v riunire, riunirsi; (put together) montare. **assembly** n assemblea f, riunione f. **assembly line** catena di montaggio f.

**assent** [ə'sent] v assentire, approvare. n assenso m, consenso m.

**assert** [ə'sə:t] v asserire, sostenere. **assert oneself** farsi valere, imporsi. **assertion** n asserzione f, rivendicazione f. **assertive** adj sicuro di sé, consapevole.

**assess** [ə'ses] v valutare, stimare. **assessment** n valutazione f, imposizione di tassa

f. **assessor** n assessore m, agente del fisco m.

**asset** ['aset] n bene m. **assets** pl n attività f pl.

**assiduous** [ə'sidjuəs] adj assiduo.

**assign** [ə'sain] v assegnare; (law) delegare. **assignee** n mandatario m. **assignment** n assegnazione f, attribuzione f.

**assimilate** [ə'simileit] v assimilare. **assimilation** n assimilazione f.

**assist** [ə'sist] v assistere, aiutare. **assistance** n assistenza f, soccorso m. **assistant** n assistente m, f, aiutante m, f; (shop) commesso, -a m, f.

**associate** [ə'sousieit; n ə'sousiət] v associare, associarsi. **associate with** frequentare. n socio, -a m, f, collega m, f. **association** n associazione f, società f; (club) circolo m.

**assorted** [ə'so:tid] adj assortito. **assortment** n assortimento m.

**assume** [ə'sju:m] v assumere; presumere. **assumption** n assunzione f, supposizione f. **assuming that** supposto che.

**assure** [ə'ʃuə] v assicurare. **assurance** n assicurazione f, certezza f, promessa f.

**asterisk** ['astərisk] n asterisco m.

**asthma** ['asmə] n asma m.

**astonish** [ə'stoniʃ] v stupire, meravigliare. **astonishing** adj sbalorditivo, sorprendente. **astonishment** n sorpresa f, stupore m.

**astound** [ə'staund] v stupefare, stupire. **astounding** adj stupefacente, sbalorditivo.

**astray** [ə'strei] adv fuori strada. **go astray** smarrirsi. **lead astray** sviare, traviare.

**astride** [ə'straid] adv a cavalcioni.

**astringent** [ə'strindʒənt] adj astringente.

**astrology** [ə'strolədʒi] n astrologia f. **astrologer** n astrologo, -a m, f.

**astronaut** ['astrəno:t] n astronauta m, f.

**astronomy** [ə'stronəmi] n astronomia f. **astronomer** n astronomo, -a m, f. **astronomic(al)** adj astronomico.

**astute** [ə'stjut] adj astuto, furbo.

**asunder** [ə'sʌndə] adv a pezzi.

**asylum** [ə'sailəm] n ricovero m, rifugio m; (for the insane) manicomio m.

**at** [at] prep a, in, da.

**ate** [et] V eat.

**atheism** ['eiθiizəm] n ateismo m. **atheist** n ateo, -a m, f.

**Athens** ['aθinz] n Atene f. **Athenian** n(m+f), adj ateniese.

**athlete** ['aθli:t] n atleta m, f. **athletic** adj atletico. **athletics** n atletica f.

**Atlantic** [ət'lantik] nm, adj atlantico.

**atlas** ['atləs] n atlante m.

**atmosphere** ['atməsfiə] n atmosfera f; ambiente m. **atmospheric** adj atmosferico. **atmospherics** pl n disturbi atmosferici m pl.

**atom** ['atəm] n atomo m. **atomic** adj atomico.

**atone** [ə'toun] v espiare, fare ammenda. **atonement** n espiazione f.

**atrocious** [ə'troufəs] adj atroce, terribile. **atrocity** n atrocità f.

**attach** [ə'tatʃ] v attaccare, attribuire. **become attached to** affezionarsi a. **attachment** n (friendship) affezione f; (law) sequestro m; (tech) accessorio m.

**attaché** [ə'taʃei] n addetto m. **attaché case** n valigetta rigida f, borsa per documenti f.

**attack** [ə'tak] v attaccare, assalire. n attacco m; offensiva f; (med) accesso. **attacker** n aggressore m.

**attain** [ə'tein] v ottenere, raggiungere. **attainment** n raggiungimento m, conseguimento m. **attainments** pl n coltura f sing.

**attempt** [ə'tempt] v tentare, provare. n tentativo m, prova f; (crime) attentato m.

**attend** [ə'tend] v (wait on) servire, accompagnare; (listen) prestar attenzione; (be present at) assistere. **attendance** n presenza f; servizio m. **attendant** n inserviente m, f; sorvegliante m, f, assistente m, f.

**attention** [ə'tenʃən] n attenzione f, cura f. **pay attention** far attenzione, stare attento. **attentive** adj attento, sollecito, premuroso.

**attic** ['atik] n attico m, soffitta f.

**attire** [ə'taiə] n abbigliamento m. v vestire.

**attitude** ['atitju:d] n atteggiamento m, posa f.

**attorney** [ə'tə:ni] n procuratore m. **power of attorney** procura f.

**attract** [ə'trakt] v attrarre, attirare; affascinare. **attraction** n attrazione f; fascino m. **attractive** adj attraente; affascinante.

**attribute** ['atribju:t; v ə'tribju:t] n attributo m, qualità f. v attribuire, ascrivere. **attribution** n attribuzione f.

**attrition** [ə'triʃən] n attrito m.

**atypical** [ei'tipikl] adj atipico.

**aubergine** ['oubəʒi:n] n melanzana f.

**auburn** ['o:bən] adj invar color rame.

**auction** ['o:kʃən] n asta f. v vendere all'asta. **auctioneer** n venditore all'asta m, banditore m.

**audacious** [o:'deiʃəs] adj audace, intrepido. **audacity** n temerità f.

**audible** ['o:dəbl] adj udibile. **audibility** n udibilità f.

**audience** ['o:djəns] n pubblico m; (assembly of spectators) uditorio m; (formal interview) udienza f.

**audiovisual** [o:diou'viʒuəl] adj audiovisivo.

**audit** ['o:dit] n controllo m, verifica dei conti f, revisione f. v rivedere, verificare i conti. **auditor** n revisore di conti m; sindaco m.

**audition** [o:'diʃən] n audizione f. v ascoltare in audizione.

**auditorium** [o:di'to:riəm] n sala per concerti f, auditorio m.

**augment** [o:g'ment] v aumentare, crescere.

**August** ['o:gəst] n agosto m.

**aunt** [a:nt] n zia f.

**au pair** [ou 'peə] n ragazza alla pari f.

**aura** ['o:rə] n aura f.

**auspicious** [o:'spiʃəs] adj propizio, di buon augurio.

**austere** [o:'stiə] adj austero. **austerity** n austerità f.

**Australia** [o'streiljə] n Australia f. **Australian** n, adj australiano, -a.

**Austria** ['ostriə] n Austria f. **Austrian** n, adj austriaco, -a.

**authentic** [o:'θentik] adj autentico. **authenticate** v convalidare. **authenticity** n autenticità f.

**author** ['o:θə] n autore, -trice m, f.

**authority** [o:'θorəti] n autorità f; (influence) ascendente m; (accepted source) fonte autorevole f. **on good authority** da fonte autorevole. **authoritative** adj autorevole. **authoritarian** adj autoritario.

**authorize** ['o:θəraiz] v autorizzare. **authorization** n autorizzazione f.

**autism** ['o:tizəm] n autismo m. **autistic** adj autistico.

**autobiography** [o:toubai'ogrəfi] n autobiografia f. **autobiographical** adj autobiografico.

**autocratic** [o:tou'kratik] *adj* autocratico.

**autograph** ['o:təgra:f] *n* autografo *m*. *v* autografare.

**automatic** [o:tə'matik] *adj* automatico. **automation** *n* automazione *f*.

**automobile** ['o:təməbi:l] *n* automobile *f*; (*fam*) macchina *f*.

**autonomous** [o:'tonəməs] *adj* autonomo.

**autopsy** ['o:topsi] *n* autopsia *f*.

**autumn** ['o:təm] *n* autunno *m*. **autumnal** *adj* autunnale.

**auxiliary** [o:g'ziljəri] *n*, *adj* ausiliario, -a.

**avail** [ə'veil] *v* servire, giovare a. **avail oneself of** servirsi di. *n* vantaggio *m*. **be of no avail** non servire a nulla.

**available** [ə'veiləbl] *adj* disponibile, libero; (*to hand*) sotto mano. **availability** *n* disponibilità *f*.

**avalanche** ['avəla:nʃ] *n* valanga *f*.

**avarice** ['avəris] *n* avarizia *f*. **avaricious** *adj* avaro.

**avenge** [ə'vendʒ] *v* vendicare, vendicarsi. **avenger** *n* vendicatore, -trice *m*, *f*.

**avenue** ['avinju:] *n* viale *m*.

**average** ['avəridʒ] *n* media *f*. **on average** in media. *adj* medio. *v* fare la media.

**aversion** [ə'və:ʃən] *n* avversione *f*, antipatia *f*. **not be averse to** non aver nulla in contrario a.

**avert** [ə'və:t] *n* (*turn away*) distogliere; (*ward off*) allontanare; (*prevent*) prevenire.

**aviary** ['eiviəri] *n* uccelliera *f*.

**aviation** [eivi'eiʃən] *n* aviazione *f*.

**avid** ['avid] *adj* avido.

**avocado** [avə'ka:dou] *n* pera avocado *f*.

**avoid** [ə'void] *v* evitare, schivare. **avoidance** *n* fuga *f*; l'evitare *m*.

**await** [ə'weit] *v* aspettare, attendere.

**\*awake** [ə'weik] *adj* sveglio. *v* svegliare, svegliarsi. **awaken** *v* risvegliare, risvegliarsi. **awakening** *n* risveglio *m*.

**award** [ə'wo:d] *n* premio *m*; (*honour*) onorificenza *f*. *v* aggiudicare, premiare, conferire.

**aware** [ə'weə] *adj* consapevole, conscio. **be aware of** sapere, rendersi conto di. **awareness** *n* consapevolezza *f*, sensibilità *f*.

**away** [ə'wei] *adv* lontano, via; (*absent*) fuori.

**awe** [o:] *n* timore reverenziale *m*. **awestruck** *adj* in preda a timore. **awe-inspir-**

**ing** *adj* che incute rispetto.

**awful** ['o:ful] *adj* terribile, spaventoso. **awfully** *adv* terribilmente; (*coll*) molto.

**awkward** ['o:kwəd] *adj* goffo, sgraziato.

**awl** [o:l] *n* lesina *f*.

**awning** ['o:niŋ] *n* tenda *f*.

**awoke** [ə'wouk] *V* **awake**.

**awoken** [ə'woukn] *V* **awake**.

**axe** [aks] *n* ascia *f*, scure *f*.

**axiom** ['aksiəm] *n* assioma *m*.

**axis** ['aksis] *n* asse *m*.

**axle** ['aksl] *n* asse *m*; perno *m*.

# B

**babble** ['babl] *v* balbettare, ciarlare. *n* balbettio *m*.

**baby** ['beibi] *n* bimbo, -a *m*, *f*, bebè *m*. **babysitter** *n* babysitter *m*, *f invar*. **babyish** *adj* bambinesco.

**bachelor** ['batʃələ] *n* scapolo *m*. **Bachelor of Arts/Science** *n* laureato, -a in lettere/scienze *m*, *f*.

**back** [bak] *n* (*anat*) dorso *m*, schiena *f*; (*chair*) schienale *m*; (*reverse*) rovescio *m*. **back to front** a rovescio. *adv* dietro, indietro, di ritorno. *v* appoggiare, sostenere; (*bet on*) scommettere su, puntare su. **back out** ritirarsi.

**\*backbite** ['bakbait] *v* calunniare, sparlare di.

**backbone** ['bakboun] *n* spina dorsale *f*.

**backdate** [bak'deit] *v* retrodatare.

**backfire** [bak'faiə] *v* far ritorno di flamma; (*coll*) andare all'aria.

**background** ['bakgraund] *n* sfondo *m*; (*milieu*) ambiente *m*.

**backhand** ['bakhand] *n* rovescio *m*.

**backlash** ['baklaʃ] *n* contraccolpo *m*.

**backlog** ['baklog] *n* arretrati *m pl*.

**back pay** *n* arretrati di paga *m pl*.

**backside** ['baksaid] *n* sedere *m*.

**\*backslide** ['bakslaid] *v* ricadere nell'errore.

**backstage** ['baksteidʒ] *adv* dietro le quinte.

**backstroke** ['bakstrouk] *n* nuoto sul dorso *m*.

**back-up** n (computer) back-up; ((support)) riserva m+f.

**backward** ['bakwəd] adj tardivo, arretrato.

**backwards** ['bakwədz] adv indietro, all'indietro.

**backwater** ['bakwo:tə] n (pool) acqua stagnante f; (place) posto dove non succede mai nulla m.

**bacon** ['beikən] n pancetta f.

**bacteria** [bak'tiəriə] pl n batteri m pl.

**bad** [bad] adj cattivo, malvagio, dannoso, brutto; (serious) grave. **bad language** parolacce f pl. **feel bad** sentirsi male. **go bad** andare a male. **badly** adv male, malamente; (seriously) gravemente.

**badge** [badʒ] n distintivo m, emblema m.

**badger** ['badʒə] n tasso m. v molestare.

**baffle** ['bafl] v sconcertare, confondere. **baffling** adj sconcertante.

**bag** [bag] n sacco m, borsa f, borsetta f. v insaccare; (coll) impadronirsi di, prendere.

**bail¹** [beil] n (law) cauzione f, garanzia f. **grant bail** concedere libertà provvisoria (su cauzione). **stand bail for** rendersi garante per. v dar garanzia per, prestar cauzione a. **bail out** ottenere libertà provvisoria (su cauzione) per.

**bail²** or **bale** [beil] v **bail out** (flooded boat) aggottare; (from aircraft) lanciarsi.

**bailiff** ['beilif] n (law) funzionario incaricato a fare sequestri m; (of estate) fattore m.

**bait** [beit] n (fishing) esca f; (lure) lusinga f. v adescare; (annoy) tormentare.

**bake** [beik] v cuocere al forno. **baker** n fornaio panettiere m. **bakery** n panificio m. **baking powder** lievito minerale m, bicarbonato m. **baking tin** teglia f.

**balance** ['baləns] n equilibrio m, armonia f; (scales) bilancia f; (comm) bilancio m. **balance of payments** bilancia dei pagamenti f. v bilanciare, equilibrare; (comm) fare il bilancio.

**balcony** ['balkəni] n balcone m; (theatre) balconata f.

**bald** [bo:ld] adj calvo; (naked) nudo, disadorno. **baldness** n calvizie f invar.

**bale¹** [beil] n balla f. v imballare.

**bale²** V **bail².**

**baleful** ['beilful] adj maligno, distruttivo.

**ball¹** [bo:l] n palla f; (inflatable) pallone m; (sphere) sfera f. **ball-bearings** pl n cuscinetti a sfere m pl. **ball-point pen** penna a sfera f.

**ball²** [bo:l] n (dance) ballo m. **ballroom** n sala da ballo f.

**ballad** ['baləd] n ballata f; (music) canzone popolare f.

**ballast** ['baləst] n zavorra f. v zavorrare.

**ballet** ['balei] n balletto m. **ballet dancer** ballerino, -a m, f.

**ballistic** [bə'listik] adj balistico. **ballistic missile** proiettile balistico m.

**balloon** [bə'lu:n] n pallone m, aerostato m; (toy) palloncino m. **balloonist** n aeronauta m.

**ballot** ['balət] n votazione f, scrutinio m; (paper) scheda f. v ballottare, votare segretamente. **ballot-box** n urna elettorale f.

**bamboo** [bam'bu:] n bambù m.

**ban** [ban] n proibizione f, bando m, interdizione f. v proibire, interdire.

**banal** [bə'na:l] adj banale.

**banana** [bə'na:nə] n (fruit) banana f; (tree) banano m.

**band¹** [band] n (troop) banda f, schiera f; (music) banda f, orchestrina f. **bandstand** n palco per banda m. v **band together** legare insieme.

**band²** [band] n (strip) striscia f, fascia f.

**bandage** ['bandidʒ] n benda f, fascia f. v bendare, fasciare.

**bandit** ['bandit] n bandito m.

**bandy** ['bandi] adj storto, curvo. **bandy-legged** adj a gambe storte. v **bandy words** scambiare parole.

**bang** [baŋ] n colpo m, botta f. v sbattere.

**bangle** ['baŋgl] n braccialetto m.

**banish** ['baniʃ] v bandire, esiliare. **banishment** n bando m, esilio m.

**banister** ['banistə] n ringhiera f.

**banjo** ['bandʒou] n banjo m invar.

**bank¹** [baŋk] n (edge) sponda f; (river) riva f. v arginare.

**bank²** [baŋk] n banca f, banco m. **bank account** conto in banca m. **bank holiday** festa legale f. **bank manager** direttore di banca m. v depositare in banca. **bank on** contare su.

**bankrupt** ['baŋkrʌpt] adj fallito. v far fallire. **bankruptcy** n fallimento m.

**banner** ['banə] n stendardo m, insegna f.

**banquet** ['baŋkwit] n banchetto m.

**banter** ['bantə] v canzonare, prendere in

giro. *n* presa in giro *f*.

**baptize** [bap'taiz] *v* battezzare. **baptism** *n* battesimo *m*. **baptismal** *adj* battesimale. **Baptist** *n* battista *m*.

**bar** [ba:] *n* (*metal*) sbarra *f*, stanga *f*; (*line*) striscia *f*; (*chocolate*) tavoletta *f*; (*law*) ordine degli avvocati *m*; barriera *f*; (*drinks*) bar *m invar*; (*music*) battuta *f*. **barmaid** *n* cameriera al banco *f*, barista *f*. **barman** *n* barista *m*. *v* proibire, impedire, escludere. *prep* eccetto, tranne.

**barbarian** [ba:'beəriən] *n*, *adj* barbaro, -a.

**barbecue** ['ba:bikju:] *n* arrosto all'aperto *m*. *v* arrostire all'aperto.

**barb** [ba:b] *n* spina *f*. **barbed** *adj* pungente. **barbed wire** filo spinato *m*.

**barber** ['ba:bə] *n* barbiere *m*, parrucchiere *m*.

**barbiturate** [ba:'bitjurət] *n* barbiturato *m*.

**bar code** *n* codice a barre *m*.

**bare** [beə] *adj* (*without covering*) scoperto; (*simple*) semplice; (*naked, unadorned*) nudo; (*just sufficient*) appena sufficiente. *v* denudare, rivelare. **barefoot** *adj*, *adv* scalzo, a piedi scalzi. **barely** *adv* appena.

**bargain** ['ba:gin] *n* (*transaction*) affare *m*; (*offer*) occasione *f*. **into the bargain** per giunta, in più. *v* contrattare, mercanteggiare.

**barge** [ba:dʒ] *n* barcone *m*, chiatta *f*. *v* **barge in** intervenire a sproposito, irrompere. **barge into** imbattersi per caso.

**baritone** ['baritoun] *n* baritono *m*.

**bark**¹ [ba:k] *n* (*dog*) latrato *m*. *v* abbaiare, latrare.

**bark**² [ba:k] *n* (*tree*) scorza *f*, corteccia *f*.

**barley** ['ba:li] *n* orzo *m*. **barley sugar** zucchero d'orzo *m*. **barley water** tisana d'orzo *f*.

**barn** [ba:n] *n* granaio *m*.

**barometer** ['bə'romitə] *n* barometro *m*.

**baron** ['barən] *n* barone *m*. **baroness** *n* baronessa *f*. **baronet** *n* baronetto *m*.

**baroque** [bə'rok] *nm*, *adj* barocco.

**barracks** ['baraks] *pl n* caserma *f sing*.

**barrage** ['bara:ʒ] *n* sbarramento *m*.

**barrel** ['barəl] *n* (*cask*) barile *m*, botte *f*; (*gun, etc.*) canna *f*. **barrel organ** organetto *m*.

**barren** ['barən] *adj* sterile, infecondo.

**barricade** [bari'keid] *n* barricata *f*. *v* barricare.

**barrier** ['bariə] *n* barriera *f*.

**barrister** ['baristə] *n* avvocato *m*.

**barrow** ['barou] *n* carretta *f*; (*archaeol*) tumulo *m*.

**barter** ['ba:tə] *v* barattare. *n* baratto *m*.

**base**¹ [beis] *v* fondare, basare. *n* base *f*, fondamento *m*. **baseless** *adj* infondato.

**base**² [beis] *adj* vile, basso. **baseness** *n* bassezza *f*.

**basement** ['beismənt] *n* sottosuolo *m*.

**bash** [baʃ] *n* colpo violento *m*. *v* colpire violentemente.

**bashful** ['baʃful] *adj* timido, vergognoso.

**basic** ['beisik] *adj* fondamentale; (*chem*) basico.

**basil** ['bazl] *n* basilico *m*.

**basin** ['beisin] *n* bacino *m*, catino *m*; (*wash-basin*) lavabo *m*.

**basis** ['beisis] *n*, *pl* -ses base *f*, fondamento *m*.

**bask** [bask] *v* crogiolarsi.

**basket** ['ba:skit] *n* cesto *m*, paniere *m*. **basketball** *n* pallacanestro *f*.

**Basle** [ba:l] *n* Basilea *f*.

**bas-relief** ['basri,li:f] *n* bassorilievo *m*.

**bass**¹ [beis] *n* basso *m*.

**bass**² [bas] *n* (*sea*) branzino *m*, spigola *f*; (*freshwater*) pesce persico *m*.

**bassoon** [bə'su:n] *n* fagotto *m*.

**bastard** ['ba:stəd] *n*, *adj* bastardo, -a.

**baste** [beist] *v* (*cookery*) arrosolare; (*sewing*) imbastire; (*beat*) bastonare.

**bastion** ['bastjən] *n* bastione *m*.

**bat**¹ [bat] *n* (*cricket, baseball*) mazza *f*; (*table tennis*) racchetta *f*. *v* battere.

**bat**² [bat] *n* (*zool*) pipistrello *m*. **blind as a bat** cieco come una talpa.

**batch** [batʃ] *n* lotto *m*, partita *f*; (*bread*) infornata *f*.

**bath** [ba:θ] *n* bagno *m*. *v* fare un bagno; lavare. **bathchair** *n* carrozzella per invalidi *f*. **bathmat** *n* stuoia da bagno *f*. **bathrobe** *n* accappatoio *m*. **bathroom** *n* stanza da bagno *f*.

**bathe** [beið] *v* bagnare, fare un *or* il bagno. **bather** *n* bagnante *m*, *f*. **bathing cap** cuffia da bagno *f*. **bathing costume** costume da bagno *m*. **bathing trunks** calzoncini da bagno *m pl*.

**baton** ['batn] *n* (*mil*) bastone *m*; (*music*) bacchetta *f*.

**battalion** [bə'taljən] *n* battaglione *m*.

**batter**[1] ['batə] *v* percuotere, colpire con violenza. **battering ram** (*mil*) ariete *m*.

**batter**[2] ['batə] *n* (*cookery*) pastella *f*.

**battery** ['batəri] *n* batteria *f*, pila *f*.

**battery farming** *n* allevamento di animali in batteria *m*.

**battle** ['batl] *n* battaglia *f*, combattimento *m*. **battlefield** *n* campo di battaglia *m*. **battleship** *n* nave da battaglia *f*. *v* combattere, lottare.

**bawdy** ['bo:di] *adj* licenzioso.

**bawl** [bo:l] *v* urlare, gridare.

**bay**[1] [bei] *n* (*geog*) baia *f*, golfo *m*, insenatura *f*.

**bay**[2] [bei] *v* (*cry*) abbaiare. *n* latrato *m*. **at bay** a bada.

**bay**[3] [bei] *n* (*tree*) lauro *m*.

**bayonet** ['beiənit] *n* baionetta *f*.

**bay window** *n* finestra sporgente *f*.

**\*be** [bi:] *v* essere, esistere; (*remain*) stare.

**beach** [bi:tʃ] *n* spiaggia *f*, lido *m*.

**beacon** ['bi:kən] *n* faro *m*; (*fire*) falò *m*.

**bead** [bi:d] *n* grano *m*; (*liquid*) goccia *f*.

**beagle** ['bi:gl] *n* cane da caccia *m*.

**beak** [bi:k] *n* becco *m*, rostro *m*.

**beaker** ['bi:kə] *n* coppa *f*.

**beam** [bi:m] *n* (*wood*) trave *f*; (*light*) raggio *m*; (*radio*) segnale *m*; (*smile*) sorriso *m*. *v* irradiare; (*smile*) sorridere.

**bean** [bi:n] *n* fava *f*, fagiolo *m*; (*coffee*) chicco *m*. **French bean** fagiolino *m*. **full of beans** energico.

**\*bear**[1] [beə] *v* (*carry*) portare; (*support weight*) reggere; (*tolerate*) soffrire, sopportare; (*give birth to*) dare alla luce. **bear oneself** comportarsi. **bear with** aver pazienza con. **bearable** *adj* sopportabile. **bearer** *n* portatore, -trice *m, f*.

**bear**[2] [beə] *n* orso, -a *m, f*.

**beard** [biəd] *n* barba *f*. *v* sfidare. **bearded** *adj* barbuto. **beardless** *adj* imberbe.

**bearing** ['beəriŋ] *n* condotta *f*, contegno *m*; (*aircraft*) rilevamento *m*; (*mech*) cuscinetto *m*. **bearings** *pl n* orientamento *m sing*, senso di direzione *m sing*. **lose one's bearings** disorientarsi.

**beast** [bi:st] *n* bestia *f*, animale *m*. **beastly** *adj* bestiale; (*coll*) veramente cattivo.

**\*beat** [bi:t] *v* battere; (*hit*) bastonare; (*heart*) palpitare; (*defeat*) sconfiggere; (*eggs, etc.*) sbattere. *n* battito *m*, palpito *m*; (*music*) battuta *f*; (*police*) ronda *f*. **beating** *n* bastonata *f*, sconfitta *f*.

**beaten** ['bi:tn] *V* beat.

**beauty** ['bju:ti] *n* bellezza *f*. **beautiful** *adj* bello. **beautify** *v* abbellire.

**beaver** ['bi:və] *n* castoro *m*.

**became** [bi'keim] *V* become.

**because** [bi'koz] *conj* perché, poiché. **because of** a causa di.

**beckon** ['bekən] *v* chiamare con un cenno.

**\*become** [bi'kʌm] *v* diventare, divenire. **becoming** *adj* che sta bene; (*suitable*) conveniente.

**bed** [bed] *n* letto *m*; (*sea*) fondo *m*; (*coal*) giacimento *m*; (*flowers*) aiuola *f*. **bedbug** *n* cimice *f*. **bedroom** *n* camera da letto *f*. **bedside** *n* capezzale *m*. **bedsitter** *n* camera studio *f*. **bedspread** *n* copriletto *m*. **double bed** letto matrimoniale *m*. **go to bed** andare a letto. **twin beds** letti gemelli *m pl*. **bedding** *n* (*sheets*) lenzuola *f pl*; (*covers*) coperte *f pl*. **bed and breakfast** *n* pensione (*stabilimento*), camera e prima colazione (*servizio offerto*) *f*.

**bedevil** [bi'devl] *v* vessare.

**bedlam** ['bedləm] *n* confusione *f*.

**bedraggled** [bi'dragld] *adj* fradicio, inzaccherato.

**bee** [bi:] *n* ape *f*. **beehive** *n* alveare *m*. **beekeeper** *n* apicoltore *m*.

**beech** [bi:tʃ] *n* faggio *m*.

**beef** [bi:f] *n* manzo *m*. **beefsteak** *n* bistecca *f*. **beefburger** *n* hamburger (*di manzo*) *m*.

**been** [bi:n] *V* be.

**beer** [biə] *n* birra *f*.

**beetle** ['bi:tl] *n* scarabeo *m*. **black beetle** scarafaggio *m*.

**beetroot** ['bi:tru:t] *n* barbabietola *f*.

**before** [bi'fo:] *adv* prima, già; *prep* prima di, davanti a. *conj* prima che. **beforehand** *adv* in anticipo.

**befriend** [bi'frend] *v* sostenere, mostrarsi amico a.

**beg** [beg] *v* implorare, pregare; (*for alms*) chiedere l'elemosina. **beggar** *n* mendicante *m, f*.

**began** [bi'gan] *V* begin.

**\*begin** [bi'gin] *v* cominciare, iniziare. **to begin with** anzitutto. **beginner** *n* principiante *m, f*. **beginning** *n* principio *m*, inizio *m*.

**begrudge** [bi'grʌdʒ] v invidiare.

**begun** [bi'gʌn] V **begin**.

**behalf** [bi'haːf] n **on behalf of** a nome di.

**behave** [bi'heiv] v comportarsi. **behaviour** n condotta f, comportamento m.

**behead** [bi'hed] v decapitare.

**beheld** [bi'held] V **behold**.

**behind** [bi'haind] adv dietro, indietro; (late) in ritardo. prep dietro a or di, dopo. **behindhand** adv in arretrato, in ritardo. n (coll) sedere m.

**\*behold** [bi'hould] v vedere. **beholder** n osservatore, -trice m, f.

**beige** [beiʒ] adj beige invar.

**being** ['biːiŋ] n essere m, creatura f. **for the time being** per il momento.

**Belarus** ['belərʌs] n Bielorussia f.

**belated** [bi'leitid] adj tardivo.

**belch** [beltʃ] v ruttare. n rutto m.

**belfry** ['belfri] n campanile m.

**Belgium** ['beldʒəm] n Belgio m. **Belgian** n(m+f), adj belga (m pl -gi).

**believe** [bi'liːv] v credere, pensare, aver fede in. **make believe** v far finta. **belief** n, pl -s fede f, credenza f, opinione f. **believable** adj credibile. **believer** n credente m, f, fedele m, f.

**bell** [bel] n campana f; (door) campanello m. **bellringer** n campanaro m. **bell-tower** n campanile m.

**belligerent** [bi'lidʒərənt] adj belligerente.

**bellow** ['belou] v urlare, muggire.

**bellows** ['belouz] pl n soffietto m sing, mantice m sing.

**belly** ['beli] n pancia f, ventre m.

**belong** [bi'loŋ] v appartenere, spettare, far parte (di). **belongings** pl n roba f sing, effetti personali m pl.

**beloved** [bi'lʌvid] n, adj amato, -a.

**below** [bi'lou] adv sotto, di sotto, giù. prep sotto, al di sotto di, inferiore a.

**belt** [belt] n cintura f; (mech) cinghia f; (zone) fascia f. v (coll: hit) picchiare; (coll: rush) precipitarsi.

**bench** [bentʃ] n (workshop) banco m; (long seat) panchina f, panca f; (law) magistratura f.

**\*bend** [bend] v piegare, curvare. n curva f, svolta f.

**beneath** [bi'niːθ] adv giù, abbasso. prep sotto, al di sotto di.

**benefactor** ['benəfaktə] n benefattore, -trice m, f. **benefaction** n beneficenza f.

**benefit** ['benəfit] n beneficio m, vantaggio m, utilità f. v giovare a, far bene a, approfittare. **beneficial** adj vantaggioso, utile. **beneficiary** n, adj beneficiario, -a.

**benevolent** [bi'nevələnt] adj benevolo, caritatevole. **benevolence** n benevolenza f.

**benign** [bi'nain] adj benevolo; (med) benigno.

**bent** [bent] V **bend**. adj curvato; (determined) risoluto; (dishonest) corrotto. n tendenza f.

**bequeath** [bi'kwiːð] v lasciare per testamento. **bequest** n lascito m.

**bereaved** [bi'riːvd] **be bereaved** essere in lutto. **bereavement** n lutto m.

**beret** ['berei] n beretto m.

**berry** ['beri] n bacca f, chicco m.

**berserk** [bə'səːk] adv **go berserk** montare su tutte le furie.

**berth** [bəːθ] n (sleeping) cuccetta f; (naut) posto d'ormeggio m. **give a wide berth to** evitare. v ancorare.

**beside** [bi'said] prep accanto a, presso, vicino a. **be beside oneself** essere fuori di sé. **besides** adv d'altronde, inoltre, per di più.

**besiege** [bi'siːdʒ] v assediare.

**best** [best] adj il migliore. adv meglio. **as best one can** come meglio si può, il meglio possibile. **come off best** avere la meglio. **do one's best** fare del proprio meglio. **the best** il meglio. **to the best of my knowledge** per quanto ne sappia.

**bestial** ['bestjəl] adj bestiale.

**bestow** [bi'stou] v conferire, dare.

**bet** [bet] n scommessa f. v scommettere.

**betray** [bi'trei] v tradire, svelare. **betrayal** n tradimento m.

**better** ['betə] adj meglio, migliore. adv meglio, in modo migliore. v migliorare. **all the better** tanto meglio. **be** or **feel better** star meglio. **get the better of** aver la meglio su.

**between** [bi'twiːn] adv in mezzo. prep tra, fra, in mezzo a.

**beverage** ['bevəridʒ] n bevanda f, bibita f.

**\*beware** [bi'weə] v guardarsi da, stare attento a. **beware of the dog!** attenti al cane!

**bewilder** [bi'wildə] v sconcertare, confondere. **bewildered** adj sconcertato, perplesso. **bewildering** adj sconcertante. **bewilderment** n disorientamento m.

**beyond** [bi'jɒnd] adv oltre, più in là. prep oltre, al di là di.

**bias** ['baiəs] n inclinazione f, pregiudizio m, preconcetto m. **on the bias** (tailoring) per sbieco. **biased** adj prevenuto.

**bib** [bib] n bavaglino m.

**Bible** ['baibl] n bibbia f. **biblical** adj biblico.

**bibliography** [bibli'ɒgrəfi] n bibliografia f. **bibliographer** n bibliografo, -a m, f. **bibliographical** adj bibliografico.

**biceps** ['baiseps] n bicipite m.

**bicker** ['bikə] v litigare, bisticciare. **bickering** n bisticciarsi m invar.

**bicycle** ['baisikl] n bicicletta f.

*bid [bid] n offerta f; (cards) dichiarazione f. v (order) comandare; (auction) offrire; (cards) dichiarare. **bidder** n offerente m, f; dichiarante, -trice m, f. **bidding** n ordine m; dichiarazione f.

**bide** [baid] v bide one's time aspettare il momento propizio.

**bidet** ['bi:dei] n bidè m.

**biennial** [bai'eniəl] adj biennale.

**bifocals** [bai'foukəlz] pl n lenti bifocali f pl.

**big** [big] adj grande, grosso, importante.

**bigamy** ['bigəmi] n bigamia f. **bigamist** n bigamo m. **bigamous** adj bigamo.

**bigot** ['bigət] n bigotto m, fanatico, -a m, f. **bigoted** adj bigotto, fanatico. **bigotry** n bigotteria f, fanatismo m.

**bikini** [bi'ki:ni] n bikini m invar.

**bilateral** [bai'latərəl] adj bilaterale.

**bilingual** [bai'liŋgwəl] adj bilingue.

**bilious** ['biljəs] adj (med) biliare; (irritable) collerico; (sickly) nauseante. **bile** n bile f. **biliousness** n travaso di bile m.

**bill¹** [bil] n (hotel, restaurant) conto m; (shop, invoice) fattura f; (pol) progetto di legge m, atto m; (poster) affisso m; (theatre) cartellone m. **bill of fare** menù m. v fatturare; (poster) affiggere; (theatre) mettere in programma.

**bill²** [bil] n (beak) becco m, rostro m.

**billiards** ['biljədz] n biliardo m.

**billion** ['biljən] n ($10^{12}$) bilione m, mille miliardi m pl; ($10^9$) miliardo m.

**billow** ['bilou] n onda f; (smoke) ondata f. v (sail) gonfiarsi; (smoke) emanare.

**bin** [bin] n recipiente m; (dustbin) pattumiera f.

**binary** ['bainəri] adj binario.

*bind [baind] v legare, attaccare; (book) rilegare; (force) costringere. n (slang) scocciatura f.

**binding** ['baindiŋ] n legatura f, legame m; (book) rilegatura f. adj impegnativo, obbligatorio.

**binoculars** [bi'nɒkjuləz] pl n binocolo m sing.

**biodegradable** [ˌbaioudi'greidəbl] adj biodegradabile.

**biography** [bai'ɒgrəfi] n biografia f. **biographer** n biografo, -a m, f. **biographical** adj biografico.

**biology** [bai'ɒlədʒi] n biologia f. **biological** adj biologico. **biologist** n biologo, -a m, f.

**birch** [bə:tʃ] n betulla f.

**bird** [bə:d] n uccello m. **bird's-eye view** veduta a volo d'uccello f.

**Biro®** ['baiərou] n biro f.

**birth** [bə:θ] n nascita f; origine f; discendenza f. **birth certificate** atto di nascita m. **birth control** controllo delle nascite m. **birthday** n compleanno m. **birthmark** n voglia f. **birthplace** n luogo di nascita m. **birth rate** natalità f, indice demografico m. **give birth to** mettere al mondo, dare alla luce.

**biscuit** ['biskit] n biscotto m.

**bishop** ['biʃəp] n (church) vescovo m; (chess) alfiere m.

**bison** ['baisən] n bisonte m.

**bit¹** [bit] V bite. n (horse) morso m; (drill) punta f, morsa f.

**bit²** [bit] n (morsel) boccone m; (small piece) pezzo m, pezzetto m. **bit by bit** poco a poco. **do one's bit** fare la propria parte. **wait a bit!** aspetta un po'!

**bitch** [bitʃ] n cagna f; (slang) antipatica f. **bitchy** adj malvagio.

*bite [bait] n morso m; (insect) puntura f; (fish) l'abboccare m; (food) boccone m. v mordere, addentare. **biting** adj pungente, mordente.

**bitten** ['bitn] V bite.

**bitter** ['bitə] adj amaro, aspro, accanito. **bitter-sweet** adj agrodolce. **to the bitter end** ad oltranza. **bitterness** n amarezza f, rancore m.

**bizarre** [bi'za:] adj bizzarro, strano.

**black** [´blak] *adj* nero. **things look black** le cose si mettono male. *n* (*colour*) nero *m*; (*person*) negro, -a *m*, *f*. **blacken** *v* annerire.

**blackberry** [´blakbəri] *n* (*fruit*) mora *f*; (*bush*) rovo *m*.

**blackbird** [´blakbə:d] *n* merlo *m*.

**blackboard** [´blakbo:d] *n* lavagna *f*.

**blackcurrant** [ˌblak´kʌrənt] *n* ribes nero *m invar*.

**blackhead** [´blakhed] *n* comedone *m*.

**blackleg** [´blakleg] *n* crumiro *m*.

**blackmail** [´blakmeil] *n* ricatto *m*. *v* ricattare. **blackmailer** *n* ricattatore, -trice *m*, *f*.

**black market** *n* borsa nera *f*.

**blackout** [´blakaut] *n* oscuramento *m*; (*med*) svenimento *m*.

**blacksmith** [´blaksmiθ] *n* fabbro *m*.

**blackshirt** [´blakʃə:t] *n* camicia nera *f*.

**bladder** [´bladə] *n* vescica *f*.

**blade** [bleid] *n* lama *f*; (*oar, propeller*) pala *f*; (*grass*) filo d'erba *m*.

**blame** [bleim] *n* biasimo *m*, responsabilità *f*. *v* biasimare, incolpare, rimproverare. **blameless** *adj* innocente.

**blanch** [bla:ntʃ] *v* (*cookery*) sbollentare; (*go pale*) impallidire.

**bland** [bland] *adj* blando.

**blank** [blaŋk] *adj* vuoto, in bianco; (*puzzled*) perplesso. *n* spazio vuoto *m*; (*cartridge*) cartuccia a salve *f*. **point blank** a bruciapelo.

**blanket** [´blaŋkit] *n* coperta *f*. *v* ricoprire.

**blare** [bleə] *v* squillare, sonare con tutta forza. *n* (*trumpet*) squillo *m*; (*loud noise*) chiasso *m*.

**blaspheme** [blas´fi:m] *v* bestemmiare. **blasphemous** *adj* blasfemo, empio. **blasphemy** *n* bestemmia *f*.

**blast** [bla:st] *n* (*wind*) raffica *f*; esplosione *f*. *v* far esplodere, far saltare. **blast-furnace** *n* altoforno (*pl* altiforni) *m*.

**blatant** [´bleitənt] *adj* vistoso, evidente.

**blaze** [bleiz] *n* (*flame*) fiamma *f*; (*sudden outburst of fire*) vampata *f*. *v* ardere, divampare. **blazer** *n* giacca sportiva *f*.

**bleach** [bli:tʃ] *v* scolorire, candeggiare. *n* candeggina *f*.

**bleak** [bli:k] *adj* (*desolate*) triste; (*dreary*) squallido; (*depressing*) deprimente.

**bleat** [bli:t] *v* belare.

**bled** [bled] *V* **bleed**.

**\*bleed** [bli:d] *v* sanguinare, perder sangue. **bleeding** *n* emorragia *f*, perdita di sangue *f*.

**blemish** [´blemiʃ] *n* difetto *m*, imperfezione *f*. *v* sfigurare, macchiare.

**blend** [blend] *v* mescolare, combinare. *n* miscela intima *f*.

**bless** [bles] *v* benedire. **be blessed with** godere di, essere dotato di. **bless you!** salute! **blessing** *n* benedizione *f*.

**blew** [blu:] *V* **blow**[2].

**blight** [blait] *v* ((*fig*)) rovinare, appassire.

**blind** [blaind] *adj* cieco. **blind drunk** ubriaco fradicio. **blind spot** punto cieco *m*. **turn a blind eye to** chiudere gli occhi davanti a. **blindness** *n* cecità *f*. *v* accecare, ingannare. *n* (*window*) tendina *f*, persiana *f*; (*pretence*) finzione *f*.

**blindfold** [´blaindfould] *n* benda (agli occhi) *f*. *v* bendare gli occhi.

**blink** [bliŋk] *v* battere le palpebre; (*wink*) ammiccare.

**bliss** [blis] *n* beatitudine *f*. **blissful** *adj* beato.

**blister** [´blistə] *n* bolla *f*, vescica *f*. *v* far venire vesciche; coprirsi di vesciche.

**blizzard** [´blizəd] *n* tormenta *f*, bufera *f*.

**blob** [blob] *n* macchia *f*.

**bloc** [blok] *n* blocco *m*.

**block** [blok] *v* bloccare, sbarrare. *n* blocco *m*, ceppo *m*; (*large building*) palazzo *m*; (*obstacle*) ostacolo *m*. **block letter** stampatello *m*; (*capital*) maiuscola *f*.

**blockade** [blo´keid] *n* blocco *m*, assedio *m*. *v* bloccare.

**blockade** [blo´keid] *n* blocco; ostruzione *m+f*.

**bloke** [blouk] *n* (*coll*) tipo *m*.

**blond** [blond] *adj* biondo. **blonde** *n* bionda *f*.

**blood** [blʌd] *n* sangue *m*; (*descent*) stirpe *f*. **blood clot** coagulo di sangue *m*. **blood-curdling** *adj* raccapricciante. **blood group** gruppo sanguigno *m*. **bloodhound** *n* segugio *m*. **blood poisoning** setticemia *f*. **blood pressure** pressione sanguigna *f*. **bloodshed** *n* carneficina *f*. **bloodshot** *adj* arrossato. **bloodthirsty** *adj* assetato di sangue. **bloody** *adj* macchiato di sangue; (*slang*) maledetto.

**bloom** [blu:m] *v* fiorire. *n* fiore *m*,

fioritura f.

**blossom** ['blosəm] n fiore; fioritura m+f.

**blot** [blot] n macchia f, sgorbio m. v macchiare. **blot out** cancellare. **blotting paper** carta assorbente f.

**blouse** [blauz] n blusa f, camicetta f.

**blow¹** [blou] n colpo m; (fist) pugno m; (stick) bastonata f. **come to blows** venire alle mani.

**\*blow²** [blou] v soffiare; (trumpet, etc.) suonare. **blow away** spazzar via. **blow one's nose** soffiarsi il naso. **blow out** spegnere. **blow up** (explode) far saltare; (inflate) gonfiare. **blow-dry** v asciugare (con l'asciugacapelli).

**blown** [bloun] V **blow²**.

**blubber** ['blʌbə] n (whale) grasso di balene m. v (weep) piangere singhiozzando.

**blue** [bluː] nm, adj azzurro; (pale) celeste; (dark) blu. **bluebell** n giacinto selvatico m. **blueprint** n progetto m.

**bluff** [blʌf] v ingannare; (cards) bluffare. n vanteria infondata f; (poker) bluff m invar.

**blunder** ['blʌndə] n errore m, papera f. v commettere un errore.

**blunt** [blʌnt] adj (not sharp) ottuso, spuntato; (frank) brusco. v smussare, ottundere.

**blur** [bləː] v rendere confuso, oscurare. n offuscamento m, macchia f.

**blush** [blʌʃ] v arrossire. n rossore m.

**boar** [boː] n cinghiale m.

**board** [boːd] v (ship, etc.) abbordare, imbarcarsi. n (wood) asse m, tavola f; (food) vitto m; (examiners) commissione f. **board of directors** consiglio d'amministrazione m. **full board** pensione completa f. **half board** mezza pensione f. **on board** a bordo. **boarding house** pensione f. **boarding school** collegio m.

**boast** [boust] n vanto m. v vantare. **boastful** adj millantatore, vanaglorioso.

**boat** [bout] n barca f, battello m. **boat race** gara di canottaggio f. **boating** n canottaggio m.

**bob** [bob] v **bob up** (come to surface) venire a galla. **bob up and down** muoversi in su e in giù.

**bobbin** ['bobin] n bobina f.

**bodice** ['bodis] n busto m, liseuse f.

**body** ['bodi] n corpo m; entità f; gruppo m; (corpse) cadavere m; (organization) ente m. **bodyguard** n guardia del corpo f.

**bog** [bog] n palude f, pantano m.

**bogus** ['bougəs] adj falso.

**bohemian** [bə'hiːmiən] adj da artista.

**boil¹** [boil] v bollire, far bollire, lessare. **boiler** n caldaia f. **boiler suit** tuta f. **boiling point** punto d'ebollizione f.

**boil²** [boil] n (swelling) foruncolo m.

**boisterous** ['boistərəs] adj chiassoso, impetuoso.

**bold** [bould] adj audace, ardito, sfacciato. n (typeface) grassetto m. **boldness** n audacia f, coraggio m.

**bollard** ['bolaːd] n bitta (d'ormeggio); colonnetta usata per bloccare l'accesso al traffico f.

**bolster** ['boulstə] n capezzale m, cuscino m. v **bolster up** sostenere.

**bolt** [boult] n (for nut) bullone m; (door) catenaccio m; (arrow) freccia f. v (bar) sprangare; (run away) scappare. **a bolt from the blue** un fulmine a ciel sereno. **bolt upright** diritto come un fuso.

**bomb** [bom] n bomba f. v bombardare. **bombing** n bombardamento m.

**bond** [bond] n (tie) legame m, vincolo m; (agreement) impegno m; (comm) titolo m; (law) cauzione f. **bonded warehouse** magazzino doganale m. **bondage** n schiavitù f.

**bone** [boun] n osso m (pl -a f). v disossare. **bony** adj ossuto.

**bonfire** ['bonfaiə] n falò m.

**bonnet** ['bonit] n (hat) cappellino m; (car) cofano m.

**bonus** ['bounəs] n gratifica f, premio m.

**booby trap** ['buːbi] n mina nascosta f, trappola esplosiva f; (pitfall) trabocchetto m.

**book** [buk] n libro m. v (reserve) prenotare.

**bookcase** ['bukkeis] n scaffale m.

**booking** ['bukin] n prenotazione f.

**bookkeeping** ['bukkiːpiŋ] n contabilità f. **bookkeeper** n contabile m, f.

**booklet** ['buklit] n opuscolo m.

**bookmaker** ['bukmeikə] n bookmaker m invar, allibratore m.

**bookmark** ['bukmaːk] n segnalibro m.

**bookseller** ['bukselə] n libraio m.

**bookshop** ['bukʃop] n libreria f.

**bookstall** ['bukstoːl] n edicola f.

**boom** [buːm] v (noise) rimbombare, tuonare; (econ) essere in gran voga. n rimbombo *m*, tuono *m*; (*econ*) boom *m invar*.

**boorish** ['buərif] *adj* grossolano.

**boost** [bu:st] *n* pressione *f*, spinta *f*. *v* aumentare, spingere.

**boot** [bu:t] *n* (*shoe*) stivale *m*; (*car*) portabagagli *m*.

**booth** [bu:ð] *n* baracca *f*, cabina *f*.

**boot up** (*computer*) avviare.

**booze** [bu:z] (*coll*) *n* bevanda alcoolica *f*. *v* ubriacarsi, sbronzarsi.

**border** ['bo:də] *n* orlo *m*, limite *m*, frontiera *f*. *v* (*embroidery*) orlare; (*geog*) confinare (con). **borderline case** caso limite *m*.

**bore**¹ [bo:] *n* (*hole*) buco *m*, foro *m*; (*gun*) calibro *m*. *v* forare, trapanare; (*mech*) alesare.

**bore**² [bo:] *v* (*weary*) seccare, annoiare. *n* (*person*) seccatore, -trice *m*, *f*; (*matter*) seccatura *f*; noia *f*.

**bore**³ [bo:] *V* **bear**¹.

**born** [bo:n] *adj* nato. **be born** nascere.

**borne** [bo:n] *V* **bear**¹.

**borough** ['bʌrə] *n* comune *m*, borgo *m*.

**borrow** ['borou] *v* prendere a prestito, farsi prestare.

**Bosnia** Bosnia *f*. **Bosnian** *n*(*m*+*f*), *adj* bosniaco.

**bosom** ['buzəm] *n* petto *m*, seno *m*.

**boss** [bos] *n* capo *m*, direttore *m*. *v* comandare. **bossy** *adj* prepotente.

**botany** ['botəni] *n* botanica *f*. **botanical** *adj* botanico. **botanist** *n* botanico, -a *m*, *f*.

**both** [bouθ] *adj*, *pron* ambedue, entrambi, tutti e due.

**bother** ['boðə] *n* seccatura *f*, noia *f*. *v* seccare, preoccuparsi.

**bottle** ['botl] *n* bottiglia *f*. *v* imbottigliare. **bottleneck** *n* ingorgo *m*. **bottle-opener** *n* apribottiglie *m invar*.

**bottom** ['botəm] *n* fondo *m*. *adj* ultimo, inferiore. **bottomless** *adj* senza fondo.

**bough** [bau] *n* ramo *m*.

**bought** [bo:t] *V* **buy**.

**boulder** ['bouldə] *n* macigno *m*, masso roccioso *m*.

**bounce** [bauns] *v* (far) rimbalzare. *n* balzo *m*, rimbalzo *m*.

**bound**¹ [baund] *v* saltare, rimbalzare. *n* salto *m*, balzo *m*. **by leaps and bounds** a passi da gigante.

**bound**² [baund] *n* confine *m*, restrizione *f*.

*v* porre limiti a, confinare. **boundary** *n* limite *m*, frontiera *f*. **boundless** *adj* illimitato.

**bound**³ [baund] *adj* **bound for** diretto per, con destinazione per.

**bound**⁴ [baund] *V* **bind**.

**bouquet** [bu:kei] *n* mazzo *m*.

**bourgeois** ['buəʒwa:] *n*(*m*+*f*), *adj* borghese.

**bout** [baut] *n* periodo d'attività *m*; (*illness*) attacco *m*; (*match*) ripresa *f*.

**bow**¹ [bau] *n* (*greeting*) saluto *m*; (*bend*) inchino *m*. *v* inchinarsi, salutare, chinare.

**bow**² [bou] *n* (*archery*) arco *m*; (*violin, etc.*) archetto *m*; (*ribbon*) fiocco *m*. **bow-legged** *adj* dalle gambe storte. **bow-tie** *n* cravatta a farfalla *f*.

**bow**³ [bau] *n* (*naut*) prua *f*, prora *f*.

**bowels** ['bauəlz] *pl n* viscere *f pl*.

**bowl**¹ [boul] *n* (*basin*) scodella *f*, bacino *m*.

**bowl**² [boul] *n* (*ball*) boccia *f*. *v* far rotolare, servire la palla. **bowls** *n* gioco delle bocce *m*. **bowler** *n* (*hat*) bombetta *f*.

**box**¹ [boks] *n* scatola *f*, cassetta *f*; (*theatre*) palco *m*. **box number** casella postale *f*. **box office** botteghino *m*.

**box**² [boks] *v* fare a pugni, fare del pugilato, fare la boxe. **boxing** *n* pugilato *m*, boxe *f*.

**Boxing Day** *n* giorno di San Stefano *m*.

**boy** [boi] *n* ragazzo *m*. **boyhood** *n* fanciullezza *f*. **boyish** *adj* da ragazzo.

**boycott** ['boikot] *n* boicottaggio *m*. *v* boicottare.

**bra** [bra:] *n* reggipetto *m*, reggiseno *m*.

**brace** [breis] *v* fortificare, rinvigorire. *n* sostegno *m*; (*tool*) trapano *m*; (*pair*) coppia *f*. **braces** *pl n* bretelle *f pl*.

**bracelet** ['breislit] *n* braccialetto *m*.

**bracken** ['brakən] *n* felce *f*.

**bracket** ['brakit] *n* mensola *f*, braccio *m*; (*printing*) parentesi *f invar*. **put in brackets** mettere fra parentesi. **bracket together** accoppiare.

**brag** [brag] *v* vantarsi. **braggart** *n* fanfarone *m*.

**braid** [breid] *n* (*hair*) treccia *f*.

**brain** [brein] *n* cervello *m*. **brainwashing** *n* lavaggio del cervello *m*. **brainwave** *n* idea geniale *f*. **brainy** *adj* intelligente.

**braise** [breiz] *v* brasare, cuocere a stufato.

**brake** [breik] *n* freno *m*. *v* frenare, serrare

il freno.

**bramble** ['brambl] n (bush) rovo m; (fruit) mora f.

**bran** [bran] n crusca f.

**branch** [bra:ntʃ] n ramo m; (office) succursale f. **branch off** biforcarsi. **branch out** estendersi.

**brand** [brand] n (trademark) marchio m; (grade, make) marca f; (marking) marchio m, stigma m; (burning wood) tizzone m. **brand-new** adj nuovo di zecca, nuovo fiammante. v marchiare, stigmatizzare.

**brandish** ['brandiʃ] v brandire.

**brandy** ['brandi] n cognac m, acquavite f.

**brass** [bra:s] n ottone m. **brassy** adj d'ottone; (impudent) sfacciato.

**brassiere** ['brasiə] V **bra**.

**brave** [breiv] adj prode, coraggioso, ardito. v sfidare, affrontare. **bravery** n audacia f, coraggio m.

**brawl** [bro:l] n rissa f, zuffa f. v rissare, azzuffarsi.

**brawn** [bro:n] n (strength) forza muscolare f; (meat) testina f.

**brazen** ['breizn] adj sfacciato, impudente; (brass) di ottone.

**breach** [bri:tʃ] n violazione f, rottura f; (mil) breccia f. v far una breccia in, rompere.

**bread** [bred] n pane m. **breadcrumbs** pl n briciole di pane f pl.

**breadth** [bredθ] n larghezza f, ampiezza f, (cloth) altezza f.

**\*break** [breik] n rottura f, frattura f; interruzione f, pausa f; (chance) opportunità f. v rompere, spezzare, infrangere; (record) battere. **at breakneck speed** a rompicollo. **break away** fuggire, distaccarsi. **break off** mandare a monte. **break out** (war) scoppiare. **breakthrough** n scoperta f, innovazione f. **breakable** adj fragile. **breakage** n rottura f. **break-in** n (burglary) scasso m.

**breakdown** ['breikdaun] n crollo m; (car) panna f; (nerves) esaurimento nervoso m. v **break down** demolire; analizzare; (car) avere una panna; (nerves) avere un esaurimento nervoso.

**breakfast** ['brekfəst] n prima colazione f.

**breast** [brest] n petto m, seno m. **breast-bone** n sterno m. **breast-stroke** n nuoto a rana m.

**breath** [breθ] n respiro m, fiato m, soffio m.

**breathless** adj ansimante. **breathtaking** adj sorprendente.

**breathalyser** ['breθəlaizə] n analizzatore del fiato m.

**breathe** [bri:ð] v respirare, prender fiato; (sigh) sospirare. **breathing** n respirazione f.

**bred** [bred] V **breed**.

**\*breed** [bri:d] v generare, allevare. n razza f, stirpe f. **breeding** n (animals) allevamento m; (manners) educazione f.

**breeze** [bri:z] n brezza f. **breezily** adj con disinvoltura.

**brew** [bru:] v (beer) far fermentare; (tea) preparare; (storm) essere nell'aria. n miscela f. **brewer** n birraio m. **brewery** n birreria f.

**bribe** [braib] v corrompere, allettare. n dono a scopo di corruzione m; (coll) bustarella f. **bribery** n corruzione f.

**brick** [brik] n mattone m. **bricklayer** n muratore m. **drop a brick** fare una gaffe.

**bride** [braid] n sposa f, sposina f. **bridal** adj nuziale. **bridegroom** n sposo m. **bridesmaid** n damigella d'onore della sposa f.

**bridge¹** [bridʒ] n ponte m. v congiungere. **bridge a gap** colmare una lacuna.

**bridge²** [bridʒ] n (cards) bridge m.

**bridle** ['braidl] n briglia f, freno m. v risentirsi. **bridle-path** n sentiero percorribile a cavallo m.

**brief** [bri:f] adj breve. n riassunto m; istruzioni f pl; lettera f. v riassumere per sommi capi; (law) affidare una causa. **brief-case** n borsa f.

**brigade** [bri'geid] n brigata f.

**bright** [brait] adj lucido, risplendente; (lively) vivace; (clever) intelligente. **brighten** v rendere più brillante, illuminare. **brightness** n luminosità f, splendore m.

**brilliant** ['briljənt] adj brillante.

**brim** [brim] n orlo m, bordo m; (hat) falda f. **brimful** adj colmo.

**brine** [brain] n acqua salata f.

**\*bring** [briŋ] v portare, condurre. **bring about** causare. **bring back** riportare; restituire. **bring up** educare; vomitare.

**brink** [briŋk] n orlo m.

**brisk** [brisk] adj vivace, arzillo.

**bristle** ['brisl] n (human) pelo duro m; (animal) setola f. v rizzarsi.

**Britain** ['britn] n Gran Bretagna f. **British** adj britannico. **Briton** n britannico, -a m, f.

**brittle** ['britl] adj fragile.

**broach** [brəutʃ] v (*subject*) intavolare un discorso su.

**broad** [brɔ:d] adj (*wide*) largo, ampio; (*overall*) generale. **broad bean** fava f. **broad-minded** adj di larghe vedute. **broaden** v allargare.

***broadcast** ['brɔ:dka:st] v trasmettere alla radio. adj radiodiffuso. n trasmissione radio f.

**broccoli** ['brɒkəli] n broccolo m.

**brochure** ['brəuʃuə] n opuscolo m.

**broke** [brəuk] V **break**. adj (*coll*) al verde, rovinato.

**broken** ['brəukn] V **break**.

**broker** ['brəukə] n agente m, commissionario m, sensale m.

**bronchitis** [brɒŋ'kaitis] n bronchite f.

**bronze** [brɒnz] n bronzo m. v abbronzare.

**brooch** [brəutʃ] n spilla f.

**brood** [bru:d] n covata f, figliolanza f. v covare; (*think*) meditare.

**brook** [bruk] n ruscello m. v ammettere.

**broom** [bru:m] n (*brush*) scopa f; (*plant*) ginestra f.

**broth** [brɒθ] n brodo m.

**brothel** ['brɒθl] n bordello m.

**brother** ['brʌðə] n fratello m. **brother-in-law** n cognato m. **brotherhood** n fratellanza f, fraternità f. **brotherly** adj fraterno.

**brought** [brɔ:t] V **bring**.

**brow** [brau] n fronte f; (*hill*) cima f. **browbeat** v intimidire.

**brown** [braun] nm, adj bruno, marrone, castano. v abbrunire, abbronzare; (*cooking*) rosolare.

**browse** [brauz] v brucare, scartabellare; (*Internet*) navigare. **browser** n browser, navigatore m.

**bruise** [bru:z] v ammaccare, intaccare. n livido m, contusione f. **bruised** adj (*person*) contuso; (*fruit*) ammaccato.

**brunette** [bru:'net] nf, adj bruna, brunetta.

**brush** [brʌʃ] n spazzola f; spazzolino m; (*paint*) pennello m; (*encounter*) scontro m. v spazzolare. **brush against** sfiorare. **brush aside** ignorare. **brush up** (*revise*) ripassare.

**brusque** [brusk] adj brusco.

**Brussels** ['brʌsəlz] n Brusselle f. **Brussels sprouts** cavoli di Brusselle m pl.

**brute** [bru:t] nm, adj bruto. **brutal** adj brutale.

**bubble** ['bʌbl] n bolla f. v formar bolle, gorgogliare.

**buck¹** [bʌk] n maschio m; (*deer*) daino m. **buck-tooth** n dente sporgente m. **pass the buck** scaricare la responsabilità. **v buck up** (*rear up*) impennarsi; (*coll: cheer up*) rallegrarsi.

**buck²** n (*dollar*) quattrino, dollaro m.

**bucket** ['bʌkit] n secchio m, secchia f.

**buckle** ['bʌkl] n fibbia f, fermaglio m. v affibbiare.

**bud** [bʌd] n bocciolo m, gemma f. v germogliare, sbocciare. **nip in the bud** troncare sul nascere.

**Buddhism** ['budizəm] n buddismo m. **Buddhist** n(m+f), adj buddista.

**budge** [bʌdʒ] v scostarsi.

**budget** ['bʌdʒit] n bilancio preventivo m. v fare un bilancio preventivo.

**buffalo** ['bʌfələu] n bufalo, -a m, f.

**buffer** ['bʌfə] n (*trains*) respingente m. **buffer state** stato cuscinetto m.

**buffet¹** ['bʌfit] v (*hit*) schiaffeggiare. n schiaffo m.

**buffet²** ['bufei] n (*cafeteria*) buffet m, caffè ristorante m; (*sideboard*) credenza f. **cold buffet** cibi freddi m pl.

**bug** [bʌg] n cimice f; (*coll*) piccolo insetto m.

**bugger** ['bʌgə] n (*impol*) sodomita m; (*fellow*) tizio m; (*derog*) brutto ceffo m. v inculare. **bugger off** v svignarsela. **bugger off!** va a quel paese! va al diavolo! **buggery** n sodomia f, pederastia f.

**buggy** ['bʌgi] n passeggino m.

**bugle** ['bju:gl] n tromba f.

***build** [bild] v costruire, fabbricare. n corporatura f. **building** n edificio m, costruzione f. **building society** n società immobiliare f, credito edilizio m.

**built** [bilt] V **build**.

**bulb** [bʌlb] n (*plant*) bulbo m; (*light*) lampadina f.

**Bulgaria** [bʌl'geəriə] n Bulgaria f. **Bulgarian** n, adj bulgaro, -a.

**bulge** [bʌldʒ] n protuberanza f, gonfiore m. v gonfiarsi, sporgere.

**bulimia** [bu:'limiə] n bulimia f.

**bulk** [bʌlk] n massa f, volume m. **the bulk** la maggior parte f. **bulky** adj massiccio, voluminoso.

**bull** [bul] n toro m; (*papal*) bolla f. **bull-dog**

*n* mastino *m*. **bulldozer** *n* livellatrice *f*.
**bullfight** *n* corrida *f*. **bull's eye** centro (del bersaglio) *m*.

**bullet** ['bulit] *n* pallottola *f*. **bullet-proof** *adj* blindato, corazzato.

**bulletin** ['bulətin] *n* bollettino *m*.

**bullion** ['buliən] *n* lingotto (di metallo prezioso) *m*.

**bully** ['buli] *n* prepotente *m*. *v* tiranneggiare, maltrattare.

**bum** [bʌm] (*coll*) *n* sedere *m*. *adj* scadente. *v* **bum around** vagabondare.

**bump** [bʌmp] *v* urtare. *n* protuberanza *f*, bernoccolo *m*. **bump into** (*collide*) andare a sbattere contro; (*meet*) incontrare per caso. **bumpy** *adj* irregolare.

**bumper** ['bʌmpə] *n* (*mot*) paraurti *m*. *adj* abbondante.

**bun** [bʌn] *n* (*cake*) focaccia, ciambella dolce *f*; (*hair*) crocchia *f*.

**bunch** [bʌntʃ] *n* fascio *m*, mazzo *m*, gruppo *m*; (*grapes*) grappolo d'uva *m*. *v* riunire, raggruppare.

**bundle** ['bʌndl] *n* fagotto *m*, involto *m*. *v* mettere insieme alla rinfusa, fare un involto di, affastellare.

**bungalow** ['bʌngəlou] *n* bungalow *m*, villino ad un piano *m*.

**bungle** ['bʌngl] *v* sciupare, lavorar male. *n* lavoro malfatto *m*. **bungler** *n* confusionario *m*, guastamestieri *m*.

**bunion** ['bʌnjən] *n* protuberanza callosa *f*.

**bunk** [bʌnk] *n* cuccetta *f*. **bunk beds** *n* letti a castello *m pl*.

**bunker** ['bʌnkə] *n* (*coal*) carbonaia *f*; (*mil*) ricovero militare seminterrato *m*; (*golf*) ostacolo *m*.

**buoy** [boi] *n* gavitello *m*, boa *f*. **buoyancy** *n* galleggiabilità *f*. **buoyant** *adj* galleggiante.

**burden** ['bə:dn] *n* peso *m*, onere *m*. *v* caricare, tassare.

**bureau** ['bjuərou] *n* (*desk*) scrittoio *m*; (*office*) ufficio *m*.

**bureaucracy** [bju'rokrəsi] *n* burocrazia *f*. **bureaucrat** *n* burocrate *m, f*. **bureaucratic** *adj* burocratico.

**burglar** ['bə:glə] *n* scassinatore *m*, ladro *m*. **burgle** *v* scassinare, svaligiare.

**\*burn** [bə:n] *v* bruciare, scottare, risplendere. **burn down** incendiare. *n* ustione *f*, scottatura *f*. **burner** *n* bruciatore *m*, becco

a gas *m*.

**burnt** [bə:nt] *V* **burn**.

**burrow** ['bʌrou] *n* tana *f*, covo *m*. *v* farsi una tana, scavare.

**\*burst** [bə:st] *n* scoppio *m*, raffica *f*. *v* scoppiare, esplodere.

**bury** ['beri] *v* seppellire, sotterrare. **burial** *n* sepoltura *f*.

**bus** [bʌs] *n* autobus *m invar*. **bus station** capolinea (*pl* capilinea) *m*. **bus stop** fermata dell'autobus *f*.

**bush** [buʃ] *n* (*shrub*) cespuglio *m*; (*woodland*) macchia *f*. **bushy** *adj* folto.

**business** ['biznis] *n* affare *m*, mestiere *m*. **business-like** *adj* metodico. **businessman** *n* uomo d'affari *m*.

**bust**[1] [bʌst] *n* (*anat*) busto *m*, petto *m*.

**bust**[2] [bʌst] *adj* (*coll: bankrupt*) rovinato. *v* rovinare.

**bustle** ['bʌsl] *n* trambusto *m*, agitazione *f*. *v* agitarsi, affaccendarsi.

**busy** ['bizi] *adj* occupato, attivo, indaffarato. **busybody** *n* ficcanaso *m*. *v* **busy oneself with** occuparsi di.

**but** [bʌt] *conj* ma. *adv* (*only*) solo, soltanto. *prep* (*except*) eccetto, tranne.

**butane** ['bju:tein] *n* butano *m*.

**butcher** [butʃə] *n* macellaio *m*. **butcher's shop** macelleria *f*. *v* macellare, massacrare. **butchery** *n* strage *f*, massacro *m*.

**butler** ['bʌtlə] *n* maggiordomo *m*.

**butt**[1] [bʌt] *n* (*gun*) calcio *m*, impugnatura *f*; (*cigarette*) mozzicone *m*.

**butt**[2] [bʌt] *n* (*laughing-stock*) bersaglio *m*, zimbello *m*.

**butt**[3] [bʌt] *n* (*hit*) cornata *f*, cozzo *m*. *v* cozzare, urtare con la testa. **butt in** interrompere, intromettersi.

**butter** ['bʌtə] *n* burro *m*. *v* imburrare.

**buttercup** ['bʌtəkʌp] *n* ranuncolo *m*.

**butterfly** ['bʌtəflai] *n* farfalla *f*.

**buttocks** ['bʌtəks] *pl n* natiche *f pl*.

**button** ['bʌtn] *n* bottone *m*, bottone *m* occhiello *m*, asola *f*. *v* attaccare un bottone. **button up** abbottonare.

**buttress** ['bʌtris] *n* sostegno *m*, sperone *m*. *v* sostenere.

**\*buy** [bai] *v* acquistare, comprare. *n* acquisto *m*. **buyer** *n* compratore *m*.

**buzz** [bʌz] *n* ronzio *m*; (*phone*) telefonata *f*. *v* ronzare; telefonare.

**by** [bai] *adv* vicino. *prep* da, con, a, di, per, entro. **by and large** generalmente parlando. **by the way** a proposito. **by-law** *n* legge locale *f.* **bypass** *n* circonvallazione *f*; deviazione stradale *f.* **by-product** *n* prodotto secondario *m.* **bystander** *n* astante *m, f.* **byword** *n* detto *m.*

**byte** [bait] *n* byte *m.*

# c

**cab** [kab] *n* tassì *m.*

**cabaret** ['kabərei] *n* caffè concerto *m,* cabaret *m invar.*

**cabbage** ['kabidʒ] *n* cavolo *m.*

**cabin** ['kabin] *n* cabina *f,* capanna *f.*

**cabinet** ['kabinit] *n* (*furniture*) armadietto *m*; (*pol*) gabinetto *m*; (*cocktails*) bar *m invar.* **cabinet-maker** *n* ebanista *m.*

**cable** ['keibl] *n* cavo *m*; telegramma *m.* *v* telegrafare. **cable-car** *n* funivia *f.* **cable television** *n* televisione via cavo *f.*

**cache** [kaʃ] *n* (*comp*) cache *m.*

**cackle** ['kakl] *v* (*hens*) schiamazzare; (*people*) chiacchierare. *n* schiamazzo *m,* chiacchiera *f.*

**cactus** ['kaktəs] *n* cactus *m.*

**caddie** ['kadi] *n* (*golf*) caddie *m.*

**cadence** ['keidəns] *n* cadenza *f.*

**cadet** [kə'det] *n* cadetto *m.*

**Caesarean** [si'zeəriən] *n* taglio cesareo *m.*

**café** ['kafei] *n* caffè *m.*

**cafeteria** [kafə'tiəriə] *n* bar-ristorante *m.*

**caffeine** ['kafi:n] *n* caffeina *f.*

**cage** [keidʒ] *n* gabbia *f.* *v* ingabbiare. **cagey** *adj* cauto.

**cake** [keik] *n* (*sweet*) torta *f,* focaccia *f,* dolce *m*; (*soap*) saponetta *f,* pezzo di sapone *m.* *v* incrostarsi.

**calamine** ['kaləmain] *n* calamina *f.*

**calamity** [kə'laməti] *n* calamità *f,* disgrazia *f.*

**calcium** ['kalsiəm] *n* calcio *m.*

**calculate** ['kalkjuleit] *v* calcolare. **calculation** *n* calcolo *m.* **calculator** *n* calcolatore *m,* macchina calcolatrice *f.*

**calendar** ['kaləndə] *n* calendario *m.*

**calf**[1] [ka:f] *n* (*animal*) vitello, -a *m, f.*

**calf**[2] [ka:f] *n* (*leg*) polpaccio *m.*

**calibre** ['kalibə] *n* calibro *m,* qualità *f.*

**call** [ko:l] *n* chiamata *f,* appello *m,* grido *m,* visita *f.* **call-box** *n* cabina telefonica *f.* **call-girl** *n* ragazza squillo *f.* *v* chiamare. **call off** annullare. **call on** visitare. **call up** telefonare; (*mil*) richiamare sotto le armi. **calling** *n* vocazione *f.*

**callous** ['kaləs] *adj* insensibile. *n* insensibilità *f.*

**calm** [ka:m] *adj* calmo. *v* calmare. **calm down** calmarsi. *n* calma *f.*

**calorie** ['kaləri] *n* caloria *f.*

**camcorder** ['kamko:də] *n* videocamera *f.*

**came** [keim] *V* **come.**

**camel** ['kaməl] *n* cammello *m.*

**camera** ['kamərə] *n* macchina fotografica *f.* **(film/television) cameraman** *n* operatore (cinematografico/televisivo) *m.*

**camouflage** ['kaməfla:ʒ] *n* mimetizzazione *f,* mascheramento *m.* *v* mimetizzare, mascherare.

**camp** [kamp] *n* campo *m,* accampamento *m.* **camp-bed** *n* branda *f.* **campsite** *n* campeggio *m.* *v* accamparsi, campeggiare.

**campaign** [kam'pein] *n* campagna *f.* *v* fare una campagna.

**campus** ['kampəs] *n* campo universitario *m.*

**camshaft** ['kamʃa:ft] *n* albero a camme *or* eccentrici *m.*

**\*can**[1] [kan] *v* (*be able*) potere, essere in grado di; (*know how*) sapere.

**can**[2] [kan] *n* scatola *f,* recipiente *m.* **can-opener** *n* apriscatole *m invar.* *v* mettere in scatola.

**Canada** ['kanədə] *n* Canadà *m.* **Canadian** *n(m+f ), adj* canadese.

**canal** [kə'nal] *n* canale *m.*

**canary** [kə'neəri] *n* canarino *f.*

**cancel** ['kansəl] *v* annullare, disdire. **cancellation** *n* annullamento *m.*

**cancer** ['kansə] *n* cancro *m.* **Cancer** *n* Cancro *m.*

**candid** ['kandid] *adj* candido, sincero.

**candidate** ['kandidət] *n* candidato, -a *m, f.*

**candle** ['kandl] *n* candela *f*; (*church*) cero *m.* **candlelight** *n* lume di candela *m.* **candlestick** *n* candeliere *m.*

**candour** ['kandə] *n* franchezza *f.*

candy ['kandi] n (US) caramella f. candied adj candito.

cane [kein] n canna f, bastone m; (school) verga f. v bastonare.

canine ['keinain] adj canino.

canister ['kanistə] n latta f.

cannabis ['kanəbis] n hascisc m.

cannibal ['kanibəl] n cannibale m. cannibalism n cannibalismo m.

cannon ['kanən] n cannone m. cannonball n palla di cannone f.

canoe [kə'nu:] n canoa f.

canon ['kanən] n canone m, criterio m; (church dignitary) canonico m. canonical adj canonico. canonize v canonizzare.

canopy ['kanəpi] n baldacchino m.

canteen [kan'ti:n] n (dining place) mensa f; (cutlery) posateria f.

canter ['kantə] n piccolo galoppo m. v andare al piccolo galoppo.

canvas ['kanvəs] n tela f; (sails) velatura f.

canvass ['kanvəs] v (orders, votes) sollecitare. canvasser n sollecitatore, -trice m, f.

canyon ['kanjən] n burrone m.

cap [kap] n (hat) berretto m; (bathing) cuffia f; (mech) coperchio m, cappello m. v coprire; sorpassare.

capable ['keipəbl] adj capace. capability n capacità f.

capacity [kə'pasəti] n capacità f, abilità f. in the capacity of nella qualità di.

cape¹ [keip] n (cloak) mantellina f.

cape² [keip] n (geog) capo m, promontorio m.

caper¹ ['keipə] n (bot) cappero m.

caper² ['keipə] n capriola f.

capillary [kə'piləri] adj capillare. n vaso capillare m.

capital ['kapitl] n capitale f; (arch) capitello m; (letter) maiuscola f. adj capitale. capitalism n capitalismo m. capitalist n(m+f), adj capitalista. capitalize v capitalizzare.

Capitol ['kapitl] n Campidoglio m.

capitulate [kə'pitjuleit] v capitolare. capitulation n resa f.

capricious [kə'prifəs] adj capriccioso.

Capricorn ['kaprikɔ:n] n Capricorno m.

capsicum ['kapsikəm] n peperone m.

capsize [kap'saiz] v capovolgere, capovolgersi.

capsule ['kapsju:l] n capsula f.

captain ['kaptin] n (chief) capo m; (army, team) capitano m; (navy) capitano di vascello m; comandante m. v comandare.

caption ['kapfən] n didascalia f.

captive ['kaptiv] n, adj prigioniero, -a; schiavo, -a. captivate v cattivare. captivity n cattività f, prigionia f.

capture ['kaptfə] v catturare. n cattura f. captor n catturatore m.

car [ka:] n macchina f, automobile f. car park parcheggio m. go by car andare in macchina.

carafe [kə'raf] n caraffa f.

carat ['karət] n carato m.

caravan ['karəvan] n (vehicle) roulotte (pl -s) f; (travelling group) carovana f.

caraway ['karəwei] n cumino m.

carbohydrate [ka:bə'haidreit] n carboidrato m.

carbon ['ka:bən] n carbonio m. carbon paper carta carbone f.

carbon monoxide n monossido di carbonio m.

carbuncle ['ka:bʌŋkl] n carbonchio m, pustola f.

carburettor ['ka:bjuretə] n carburatore m.

carcass ['ka:kəs] n carcassa f.

card [ka:d] n carta f; (greetings, etc.) cartolina f; (playing) carta da gioco f; (visiting) biglietto da visita m; (index) scheda f.

cardboard ['ka:dbo:d] n cartone m, cartoncino m.

cardiac ['ka:diak] adj cardiaco. cardiac arrest arresto cardiaco m.

cardigan ['ka:digən] n golf m, giacca f.

cardinal ['ka:dənl] nm, adj cardinale.

care [keə] v curare; preoccuparsi; interessarsi. n cura f, premura f; ansietà f; responsabilità f. carefree adj spensierato. care of presso. caretaker n custode m, f. careworn adj preoccupato. careful adj attento; (thorough) curato. careless adj disattento, trascurato. carelessness n trascuratezza f.

career [kə'riə] n carriera f.

caress [kə'res] n carezza f. v accarezzare.

cargo ['ka:gou] n carico (pl -chi) m.

Caribbean [kari'bi:ən] adj caraibico.

caricature ['karikətjuə] n caricatura f. v mettere in caricatura. caricaturist n caricaturista *m, f.*

**carnage** ['kɑ:nidʒ] *n* strage *f.*

**carnal** ['kɑ:nl] *adj* carnale, sensuale.

**carnation** [kɑ:'neiʃən] *n* garofano *m.*

**carnival** ['kɑ:nivəl] *n* carnevale *m.*

**carnivorous** [kɑ:'nivərəs] *adj* carnivoro. **carnivore** *n* carnivoro *m.*

**carol** ['kærəl] *n* cantico *m.* **Christmas carol** cantico di Natale *m.*

**carpenter** ['kɑ:pəntə] *n* falegname *m.* **carpentry** *n* falegnameria *f*, ebanisteria *f.*

**carpet** ['kɑ:pit] *n* tappeto *m*, moquette *f.*

**carriage** ['kæridʒ] *n (vehicle)* carrozza *f*, vettura *f; (bearing)* portamento *m; (railway)* vagone *m.*

**carrier** ['kæriə] *n* portatore, -trice *m, f; (comm)* trasportatore *m; (med)* vettore *m.* **carrier bag** sacchetto per acquisti *m.* **carrier pigeon** piccione viaggiatore *m.*

**carrot** ['kærət] *n* carota *f.*

**carry** ['kæri] *v* portare, trasportare. **carrycot** *n* culla portabile *f.* **carry on** proseguire, gestire. **carry out** eseguire, realizzare. **carry over** riportare.

**cart** [kɑ:t] *n* carro *m*, carretta *f.* **cartload** *n* carrettata *f.* **turn cartwheels** fare la ruota. *v* **cart off** portar via.

**cartilage** ['kɑ:təlidʒ] *n* cartilagine *f.*

**cartography** [kɑ:'tɒgrəfi] *n* cartografia *f.* **cartographer** *n* cartografo, -a *m, f.*

**carton** ['kɑ:tən] *n* scatola di cartone *f; (cigarettes)* stecca *f.*

**cartoon** [kɑ:'tu:n] *n (drawing)* cartone *m; (film)* cartone animato *m*, caricatura *f.* **cartoonist** *n* disegnatore, -trice *m, f;* caricaturista *m, f.*

**cartridge** ['kɑ:tridʒ] *n* cartuccia *f.*

**carve** [kɑ:v] *v (meat)* tagliare, trinciare; *(art)* scolpire, intagliare. **carving** *n* intaglio *m.* **carving knife** trinciante *m.*

**cascade** [kæs'keid] *n* cascata *f.* *v* scrosciare.

**case¹** [keis] *n (matter)* caso *m*, fatto *m*, questione *f;* cosa *f; (law)* causa *f*, processo *m.* **in any case** ad ogni modo. **in case** qualora. **in most cases** in genere. **in that case** allora.

**case²** [keis] *n (box)* scatola *f; (luggage)* valigia *f; (glasses, pens)* astuccio *m.*

**cash** [kæʃ] *v* incassare, riscuotere. *n* denaro *m;* contanti *m pl.* **cash desk** cassa *f.* **cash dispenser** sportello automatico *m.* **cash payment** pagamento in contanti *m.* **petty**

**cash** spese varie *f pl.*

**cashier¹** [kæ'ʃiə] *n* cassiere, -a *m, f.*

**cashier²** [kæ'ʃiə] *v* destituire.

**cashmere** [kæʃ'miə] *n* cachemire *m invar.*

**casing** ['keisiŋ] *n* copertura *f*, rivestimento *m.*

**casino** [kə'si:nou] *n* casinò *m.*

**casket** ['kɑ:skit] *n* cofanetto *m; (coffin)* cassa da morto *f.*

**casserole** ['kæsəroul] *n* casseruola *f.* *v* cucinare in umido.

**cassette** [kə'set] *n* cassetta *f.*

**cassock** ['kæsək] *n* tonaca *f.*

***cast** [kɑ:st] *n (throw)* lancio *m*, getto *m; (mould)* forma *f*, calco *m; (metal)* fusione *f; (theatre)* complesso *m*, insieme degli attori *m; (plaster)* ingessatura *f.* *v* lanciare, gettare; *(metal)* fondere; *(theatre)* dare la parte. **cast away** gettar via. **cast iron** ghisa *f.* **cast-off** *adj* abbandonato.

**caste** [kɑ:st] *n* casta *f.*

**castle** ['kɑ:sl] *n* castello *m.*

**castor** ['kɑ:stə] *n (furniture)* rotella al piede di mobili *f; (condiments)* ampolliera *f.* **castor oil** olio di ricino *m.* **castor sugar** zucchero semolato *m.*

**castrate** [kə'streit] *v* castrare. **castration** *n* castratura *f.*

**casual** ['kæʒuəl] *adj* casuale, fortuito, disinvolto.

**casualty** ['kæʒuəlti] *n* vittima *f; (accident)* incidente *m; (hospital)* pronto soccorso *m.*

**cat** [kæt] *n* gatto, -a *m, f.* **cat's eye** catarifrangente *m.* **catty** *adj* malevolo.

**catalogue** ['kætəlɒg] *n* catalogo (*pl* -ghi) *m*, elenco *m.* *v* elencare.

**catalyst** ['kætəlist] *n* catalizzatore *m.* **catalysis** *n*, *pl* **-ses** catalisi *f.*

**catalytic converter** *n* catalizzatore *m.*

**catamaran** [kætəmə'ræn] *n* catamarano *m.*

**catapult** ['kætəpʌlt] *n* catapulta *f*, fionda *f.* *v* scagliare.

**cataract** ['kætərækt] *n* cateratta *f.*

**catarrh** [kə'tɑ:] *n* catarro *m.*

**catastrophe** [kə'tæstrəfi] *n* catastrofe *f.* **catastrophic** *adj* catastrofico.

***catch** [kætʃ] *n* preda *f*, cattura *f; (door)* spranga *f; (fish)* retata *f.* *v* prendere, acchiappare; *(fish)* pescare. **catch-phrase** *n* frase fatta *f.* **catch up with** raggiungere. **catchword** *n* slogan *m.* **catching** *adj (med)* contagioso, infettivo.

**category** ['katəgəri] n categoria f. **categorical** adj categorico.

**cater** ['keitə] v provvedere cibo. **cater for** provvedere a. **caterer** n approvvigionatore, -trice m, f. **catering** n approvvigionamento m.

**caterpillar** ['katəpilə] n bruco m.

**cathedral** [kə'θi:drəl] n cattedrale f.

**catheter** ['kaθətə] n catetere m.

**cathode** ['kaθoud] n catodo m.

**catholic** ['kaθəlik] n, adj cattolico, -a. **catholicism** n cattolicesimo m.

**catkin** ['katkin] n gattino m.

**cattle** ['katl] n bestiame m.

**caught** [ko:t] V **catch**.

**cauliflower** ['koliflauə] n cavolfiore m.

**cause** [ko:z] n causa f, ragione f, motivo m. v causare, provocare, suscitare.

**causeway** ['ko:zwei] n strada rialzata f; (main highway) strada maestra f.

**caustic** ['ko:stik] adj caustico.

**caution** ['ko:ʃən] n cautela f, circospezione f; (law) diffida f, ammonimento m. v ammonire, mettere in guardia. **cautious** adj cauto, prudente.

**cavalry** ['kavəlri] n cavalleria f.

**cave** [keiv] n caverna f, grotta f.

**caviar** ['kavia:] n caviale m.

**cavity** ['kavəti] n cavità f, buco m.

**CCTV** n televisione a circuito chiuso f.

**cease** [si:s] v cessare, smettere. **cease-fire** n tregua f, cessate il fuoco m invar. **ceaseless** adj continuo, incessante.

**cedar** ['si:də] n cedro m.

**ceiling** ['si:liŋ] n soffitto m.

**celebrate** ['seləbreit] v celebrare, festeggiare, far festa. **celebration** n festa f, commemorazione f. **celebrity** n celebrità f.

**celery** ['seləri] n sedano m.

**celestial** [sə'lestiəl] adj celestiale, celeste.

**celibate** ['selibət] n, adj celibe m. **celibacy** n celibato m.

**cell** [sel] n (room) cella f; (biol) cellula f; (elec) pila f.

**cellar** ['selə] n cantina f, sottosuolo m.

**cello** ['tʃelou] n violoncello m. **cellist** n violoncellista m, f.

**cellular** ['seljulə] adj cellulare.

**cement** [sə'ment] n cemento m. v cementare, consolidare.

**cemetery** ['semətri] n cimitero m, camposanto m.

**censor** ['sensə] n censore m. v censurare. **censorious** adj ipercritico. **censorship** n censura f.

**censure** ['senʃə] n censura f.

**census** ['sensəs] n censimento m.

**cent** [sent] n centesimo m, soldo m.

**centenary** [sen'ti:nəri] n, adj centenario.

**centigrade** ['sentigreid] adj centigrado.

**centimetre** ['sentimi:tə] n centimetro m.

**centipede** ['sentipi:d] n millepiedi m invar.

**centre** ['sentə] n centro m. v centrare, accentrare. **central** adj centrale. **central heating** riscaldamento centrale m. **centralization** n centralizzazione f. **centralize** v centralizzare.

**centrifugal** [sen'trifjugəl] adj centrifugo (m pl -ghi). **centrifuge** n centrifuga f.

**century** ['sentʃuri] n secolo m.

**ceramic** [sə'ramik] adj ceramico. **ceramics** n ceramica f.

**cereal** ['siəriəl] nm, adj cereale.

**cerebral** ['serəbrəl] adj cerebrale.

**ceremony** ['serəməni] n cerimonia f, funzione f. **stand on ceremony** far complimenti. **ceremonial** adj solenne, rituale. **ceremonious** adj formalista, cerimonioso.

**certain** ['sə:tn] adj certo, sicuro. **certainly** adv certo, certamente, senza dubbio. **certainty** n certezza f, sicurezza f.

**certificate** [sə'tifikət] n certificato m, atto m, diploma m. **certify** v certificare, attestare, vidimare; (declare insane) classificare come pazzo.

**cervix** ['sə:viks] n cervice f.

**cesspool** ['sespu:l] n cloaca f.

**chafe** [tʃeif] v irritarsi.

**chaffinch** ['tʃafintʃ] n fringuello m.

**chain** [tʃein] n catena f. **chain-smoke** v fumare ininterrottamente. **chain store** magazzino a catena m. v incatenare.

**chair** [tʃeə] n sedia f, seggio m; (university) cattedra f. **chairlift** n seggiovia f. **chairman** n presidente m. v presiedere.

**chalk** [tʃo:k] n gesso m. **chalky** adj gessoso; pallido.

**challenge** ['tʃalindʒ] n sfida f, provocazione f. v sfidare, opporsi a, provocare. **challenging** adj stimolante, provocatorio.

**chamber** ['tʃeimbə] n camera f. **chamber-**

**maid** n cameriera f. **chamber music** musica da camera f.

**chameleon** [kəˈmiːliən] n camaleonte m.

**chamois** [ˈʃamwaː] n camoscio m; (leather) pelle di camoscio f.

**champagne** [ʃamˈpein] n champagne m.

**champion** [ˈtʃampiən] n campione, -essa m, f. **championship** n campionato m. v difendere, sostenere.

**chance** [tʃaːns] n caso m, fortuna f, opportunità f, rischio m. **by chance** per caso. v (risk) arrischiare; (happen) capitare. adj fortuito.

**chancellor** [ˈtʃaːnsələ] n cancelliere m; (university) rettore titolare m.

**chandelier** [ʃandəˈliə] n lampadario m.

**change** [tʃeindʒ] n cambio m, mutamento m; (money) resto m, spiccioli m pl. v cambiare, mutare, cambiarsi. **changeable** adj variabile, mutevole. **changeability** n variabilità f. **changeless** adj immutevole, costante.

**channel** [ˈtʃanl] n canale m. **English Channel** Manica f. **Channel tunnel** tunnel sotto la Manica m. v incanalare.

**chant** [tʃaːnt] n canto m, salmodia f. v cantare, salmodiare.

**chaos** [ˈkeios] n caos m.

**chap**[1] [tʃap] v screpolare, screpolarsi. n fessura f.

**chap**[2] [tʃap] n (fellow) tipo m, tizio m.

**chapel** [ˈtʃapəl] n cappella f.

**chaperon** [ˈʃapəroun] n chaperon m. v accompagnare.

**chaplain** [ˈtʃaplin] n cappellano m.

**chapter** [ˈtʃaptə] n capitolo m.

**char**[1] [tʃaː] v carbonizzare, bruciare.

**char**[2] [tʃaː] v fare i lavori di casa. **charwoman** n donna di servizio f, donna a mezzo servizio f.

**character** [ˈkarəktə] n carattere m, indole f, qualità f; (acting) personaggio m. **characterization** n caratterizzazione f. **characterize** v caratterizzare.

**characteristic** [karəktəˈristik] adj caratteristico. n caratteristica f.

**charcoal** [ˈtʃaːkoul] n carbone di legna m.

**charge** [tʃaːdʒ] n spesa f, costo m; cura f, custodia f; (law) accusa f; (mil) carica f. **free of charge** gratis, gratuito. **charge card** carta di credito f. **in charge** addetto, incaricato. **take charge of** incaricarsi di. v

addebitare; caricare. **chargeable** adj addebitabile.

**charisma** [kəˈrizmə] n carisma m. **charismatic** adj carismatico.

**charity** [ˈtʃarəti] n carità f, elemosina f. **charitable** adj caritatevole.

**charm** [tʃaːm] n fascino m, incantesimo m; (trinket) portafortuna m invar. v affascinare, incantare. **charming** adj incantevole, affascinante.

**chart** [tʃaːt] n mappa f, diagramma m, grafico m, quadro m. v tracciare un diagramma or grafico di.

**charter** [ˈtʃaːtə] n carta f, documento m; (flight) volo charter m. v (document) istituire; (hire) noleggiare. **chartered accountant** ragioniere diplomato m.

**chase** [tʃeis] n caccia f, inseguimento m. v cacciare, inseguire; (jewellery) incastonare; (metal) cesellare.

**chasm** [ˈkazəm] n abisso m.

**chassis** [ˈʃasi] n telaio m.

**chaste** [tʃeist] adj casto, austero. **chastity** n castità f, purezza f.

**chastise** [tʃasˈtaiz] v castigare, punire. **chastisement** n castigo (pl -ghi) m, punizione f.

**chat** [tʃat] n chiacchiera f, chiacchierata f. v chiacchierare.

**chatter** [ˈtʃatə] v chiacchierare; (teeth) battere. n chiacchiera f.

**chauffeur** [ˈʃoufə] n autista m, f.

**chauvinism** [ˈʃouvinizəm] n sciovinismo m. **chauvinist** n(m+f), adj sciovinista.

**cheap** [tʃiːp] adj economico, a buon mercato, poco caro; (derog) spregevole. **cheapen** v abbassare il prezzo di, screditare.

**cheat** [tʃiːt] n imbroglione, -a m, f, truffatore, -trice m, f; (cards) baro, -a m, f. v imbrogliare, truffare; barare. **cheating** n imbroglio m, truffa f.

**check** [tʃek] n controllo m, pausa f, ostacolo m; (chess) scacco m. v controllare, verificare, fermare; (chess) dare scacco. **check in** registrare all'arrivo. **check up** on informarsi su.

**cheek** [tʃiːk] n guancia f; (insolence) faccia tosta f. **cheeky** adj sfacciato, sfrontato.

**cheer** [tʃiə] n (shout) applauso m; (mood) allegria f, buonumore m. **cheerio!** interj ciao! arrivederci! v applaudire. **cheer up** rallegrare, rallegrarsi. **cheerful** adj allegro, di buonumore. **cheerless** adj triste.

**cheese** [tʃiːz] n formaggio m. **cheesecloth**

*n* garza *f.* **cheese-paring** *adj* tirchio.

**chef** [ʃef] *n* capocuoco (*pl* -chi) *m.*

**chemical** ['kemikl] *n* prodotto chimico *m.* *adj* chimico.

**chemistry** ['kemistri] *n* chimica *f.* **chemist** *n* chimico, -a *m, f,* farmacista *m, f.* **chemist's shop** farmacia *f.*

**cheque** *or US* **check** [tʃek] *n* assegno *m.* **cheque-book** *n* libretto d'assegni *m.*

**cherish** ['tʃeriʃ] *v* tener caro, nutrire, amare.

**cherry** ['tʃeri] *n* (*fruit*) ciliegia *f.;* (*tree*) ciliegio *m.*

**chess** [tʃes] *n* scacchi *m pl.* **chessboard** *n* scacchiera *f.*

**chest** [tʃest] *n* cassa *f.;* (*anat*) petto *m,* torace *m.* **chest of drawers** cassettone *m.*

**chestnut** ['tʃesnʌt] *n* (*fruit*) castagna *f.;* (*tree*) castagno *m.* *adj* castano.

**chew** [tʃu:] *v* masticare. **chew over** meditare. **chewing-gum** *n* chewing gum *m invar,* gomma da masticare *f.*

**chicken** ['tʃikin] *n* pollo *m;* (*chick*) pulcino *m.* **chicken-coop** *n* pollaio *m.* **chicken-pox** *n* varicella *f.*

**chicory** ['tʃikəri] *n* cicoria *f,* indivia *f.*

**chick-pea** ['tʃik‚pi:] *n* cece *m.*

**chide** [tʃaid] *v* sgridare.

**chief** [tʃi:f] *nm, pl* -s, *adj* capo, principale.

**chilblain** ['tʃilblein] *n* gelone *m.*

**child** [tʃaild] *n, pl* **children** bambino, -a *m, f;* ragazzo, -a *m, f;* (*offspring*) figlio, -a *m, f.* **childbirth** *n* parto *m.* **childhood** *n* infanzia *f.* **childish** *adj* puerile, infantile. **childlike** *adj* da bambino, semplice, innocente. **child-minder** *n* (*coll*) baby sitter; vigilatore d'infanzia (*titolo. ufficiale*); precettore (*raro*) *m+f.*

**chill** [tʃil] *v* raffreddare, agghiacciare. *adj* freddo, gelido. *n* freddo *m,* brivido *m;* (*illness*) raffreddore *m.* **catch a chill** buscarsi un raffreddore. **take the chill off** intiepidire. **chilly** *adj* freddo, fresco, freddoloso.

**chilli** ['tʃili] *n* peperone *m,* pepe rosso *m.*

**chime** [tʃaim] *v* suonare, scampanare. *n* scampanio *m,* rintocco *m.*

**chimney** ['tʃimni] *n* camino *m,* caminetto *m.* **chimney-pot** *n* ciminiera *f,* fumaiolo *m.* **chimney-sweep** *n* spazzacamino *m.*

**chimpanzee** [tʃimpən'zi:] *n* scimpanzè *m.*

**chin** [tʃin] *n* mento *m.* **chin-strap** *n* sottogola *m invar.*

**china** ['tʃainə] *n* porcellana *f,* ceramica *f.* **china clay** caolino *m.*

**China** ['tʃainə] *n* Cina *f.* **Chinese** *n*(*m+f*), *adj* cinese.

**chink**[1] [tʃiŋk] *n* (*fissure*) fessura *f,* crepa *f.*

**chink**[2] [tʃiŋk] *n* (*sound*) tintinnio *m.* *v* tintinnare.

**chip** [tʃip] *n* scheggia *f,* frammento *m,* truciolo *m;* (*gambling*) cip (*pl* -s) *m,* gettone *m.* **chips** *pl n* (*cookery*) patatine fritte *f pl.* *v* scheggiare. **chip in** intervenire; (*contribute money*) contribuire.

**chiropodist** [ki'ropədist] *n* pedicure *m, f invar.*

**chirp** [tʃə:p] *v* cinguettare, pigolare. *n* cinguettio *m,* pigolio *m.* **chirpy** *adj* allegro.

**chisel** ['tʃizl] *n* cesello *m,* bulino *m.* *v* cesellare.

**chivalry** ['ʃivəlri] *n* galanteria *f.* **chivalrous** *adj* galante.

**chive** [tʃaiv] *n* erba cipollina *f.*

**chlorine** ['klɔ:ri:n] *n* cloro *m.*

**chlorophyll** ['klɔrəfil] *n* clorofilla *f.*

**chocolate** ['tʃɔkəlat] *n* cioccolato *m,* cioccolatino *m;* (*drink*) cioccolata *f.* *adj* cioccolato *invar.*

**choice** [tʃois] *n* scelta *f,* assortimento *m.* *adj* scelto, di prima qualità.

**choir** ['kwaiə] *n* coro *m.*

**choke** [tʃouk] *v* soffocare, strozzare. *n* (*motor*) valvola dell'aria *f,* diffusore *m.*

**cholera** ['kɔlərə] *n* colera *m.*

**cholesterol** [kə'lestərol] *n* colesterolo *m.*

**\*choose** [tʃu:z] *v* scegliere, eleggere, preferire.

**chop**[1] [tʃop] *n* (*meat*) braciola *f;* (*blow*) colpo *m.* *v* (*split*) spaccare; (*mince*) tagliuzzare, tritare. **chop down** abbattere. **chopper** *n* accetta *f.* **chopping-block** *n* tagliere *m.* **choppy sea** maretta *f.*

**chop**[2] [tʃop] *v* **chop and change** fare e disfare. **chop logic** cavillare.

**chops** [tʃops] *pl n* mascelle *f pl.* **lick one's chops** leccarsi i baffi.

**chord** [kɔ:d] *n* corda *f,* accordo *m.*

**chore** [tʃɔ:] *n* (*task*) lavoro *m,* compito *m.* **household chores** lavori domestici *m pl.*

**choreography** [kɔri'ogrəfi] *n* coreografia *f.* **choreographer** *n* coreografo; -a *m, f.*

**chorus** ['kɔ:rəs] *n* coro *m.* **choral** *adj* corale. **chorister** *n* corista *m, f.*

**chose** [tʃouz] V **choose**.

**chosen** ['tʃouzn] V **choose**.

**Christ** [kraist] n Cristo m.

**christen** ['krisn] v battezzare; (name) chiamare. **christening** n battesimo m.

**Christian** ['kristʃən] n, adj cristiano, -a. **Christian Democrat** democriziano, -a m, f. **Christian name** nome di battesimo m. **Christendom** n cristianesimo m. **Christianity** n cristianità f.

**Christmas** ['krisməs] n Natale m. adj di Natale; natalizio.

**chromatic** [krə'matik] adj cromatico.

**chromium** ['kroumiəm] n cromo m. **chromium-plate** v cromare. **chromium-plating** n cromatura f.

**chromosome** ['krouməsoum] n cromosoma m.

**chronic** ['kronik] adj cronico.

**chronicle** ['kronikl] n cronaca f. v narrare, fare la cronaca di.

**chronological** [kronə'lodʒikəl] adj cronologico.

**chrysalis** ['krisəlis] n crisalide f.

**chrysanthemum** [kri'sanθəməm] n crisantemo m.

**chubby** ['tʃʌbi] adj paffuto, grassoccio.

**chuck** [tʃʌk] v gettare, buttare. **chuck out** buttar fuori.

**chuckle** ['tʃʌkl] v ridacchiare, ridere di soppiatto.

**chunk** [tʃʌŋk] n grosso pezzo m; (food) fetta f.

**church** [tʃə:tʃ] n chiesa f. **church-goer** n praticante m, f. **churchyard** n cimitero m, camposanto m.

**churlish** ['tʃə:liʃ] adj burbero.

**churn** [tʃə:n] n zangola f. v agitare, sbattere.

**chute** [ʃu:t] n (slide) scivolo m; (waterfall) cascata f.

**cider** ['saidə] n sidro m.

**cigar** [si'ga:] n sigaro m.

**cigarette** [sigə'ret] n sigaretta f. **cigarette-end** n mozzicone m. **cigarette-lighter** n accendino m.

**cinder** ['sində] n tizzone m, cenere f. **burnt to a cinder** carbonizzato.

**cine camera** ['sini] n macchina da presa f.

**cinema** ['sinəmə] n cinema m.

**cinnamon** ['sinəmən] n cannella f.

**circle** ['sə:kl] n cerchio m, circolo m;

(theatre) galleria f; (environment) cerchia f, ambiente m. v girare attorno a, accerchiare; (aeroplane) volteggiare. **circular** adj circolare. n volantino m. **circulate** v circolare, mettere in circolazione, girare. **circulation** n (movement) circolazione f; (distribution) tiratura f.

**circuit** ['sə:kit] n circuito m, giro m.

**circumcise** ['sə:kəmsaiz] v circoncidere. **circumcision** n circoncisione f.

**circumference** [sə'kʌmfərəns] n circonferenza f.

**circumscribe** ['sə:kəmskraib] v circoscrivere.

**circumstance** ['sə:kəmstans] n circostanza f, condizione f. **circumstantial** adj particolareggiato. **circumstantial evidence** prove indiziarie indirette f pl.

**circus** ['sə:kəs] n circo m; (convergence of streets) largo m.

**cistern** ['sistən] n cisterna f, serbatoio m.

**cite** [sait] v citare. **citation** n citazione f; (mil) encomio m.

**citizen** ['sitizn] n cittadino, -a m, f. **citizenship** n cittadinanza f.

**citrus fruits** ['sitrəs] pl n agrumi m pl.

**city** ['siti] n città f; (business centre) centro degli affari m. **city hall** municipio m.

**civic** ['sivik] adj civico, municipale.

**civil** ['sivl] adj civile; (polite) cortese, educato. **civil engineer** ingegnere civile m. **civil engineering** ingegneria civile f. **civil servant** funzionario, -a statale m, f. **Civil Service** amministrazione dello Stato f. **civil war** guerra civile f.

**civilian** [sə'viljən] n(m+f), adj civile, borghese. **in civilian clothes** in borghese.

**civilization** [sivilai'zeiʃən] n civiltà f, civilizzazione f. **civilize** v civilizzare, incivilire. **civilized** adj civilizzato.

**clad** [klad] adj vestito.

**claim** [kleim] n (right) diritto m; (title) titolo m; (complaint) reclamo m; (insurance) rivendicazione f; asserzione f. v chiedere, esigere; rivendicare; asserire.

**clairvoyant** [kleə'voiənt] n chiaroveggente m, f.

**clam** [klam] n vongola f.

**clamber** ['klambə] v arrampicarsi.

**clammy** ['klami] adj viscido.

**clamour** ['klamə] n clamore m, schiamazzo m. v strepitare, vociferare. **clamorous** adj clamoroso, strepitoso.

**clamp** [klamp] *n* morsa f, morsetto *m*. *v* tener fermo, stringere. **clamp down on** far smettere.

**clan** [klan] *n* tribù f, famiglia f. **clannish** *adj* imbevuto di spirito di parte.

**clandestine** [klan'destin] *adj* clandestino.

**clang** [klaŋ] *n* suono metallico *m*, strepito *m*. *v* strepitare.

**clap** [klap] *n* (*blow, noise*) colpo *m*, scoppio *m*; applauso *m*, battimano *m*. *v* applaudire. **clap hands** battere le mani. **clap into prison** sbattere in prigione. **clapper** *n* (*bell*) battaglio *m*. **claptrap** *n* sproloquio *m*.

**claret** ['klarət] *n* chiaretto *m*.

**clarify** ['klarəfai] *v* chiarire, raffinare.

**clarinet** [klarə'net] *n* clarinetto *m*. **clarinettist** *n* clarinettista *m, f*.

**clash** [klaʃ] *n* (*noise*) strepito *m*; (*collision*) urto *m*; (*conflict*) scontro *m*, contrasto *m*; (*colours, sounds*) stonatura f. *v* urtare, urtarsi; scontrarsi; stonare.

**clasp** [kla:sp] *n* (*device*) fermaglio *m*; (*grasp*) stretta f; (*embrace*) abbraccio *m*. **clasp-knife** *n* coltello a serramanico *m*. *v* agganciare, stringere, abbracciare.

**class** [kla:s] *n* classe f, categoria f, qualità f. **class-mate** *n* compagno, -a di classe *m, f*. **classroom** *n* aula f. *v also* **classify** classificare. **classy** *adj* di classe.

**classic** ['klasik] *nm, adj* classico.

**clatter** ['klatə] *n* fracasso *m*. *v* far fracasso.

**clause** [klɔ:z] *n* clausola f, proposizione f, articolo *m*.

**claustrophobia** [klɔ:strə'foubiə] *n* claustrofobia f. **claustrophobic** *adj* claustrofobico.

**claw** [klɔ:] *n* artiglio *m*; (*tool*) raffio *m*. *v* (*seize*) aggraffare; (*scratch*) graffiare.

**clay** [klei] *n* argilla f, creta f.

**clean** [kli:n] *adj* pulito, nitido. **clean-shaven** *adj* sbarbato. **make a clean breast** confessare tutto. *v* pulire; (*remove stains*) smacchiare. **cleanliness** *n* pulizia f, nettezza f.

**cleanse** [klenz] *v* pulire, depurare.

**clear** [kliə] *adj* chiaro, limpido; ovvio; libero. **keep clear of** tenersi lontano da. *v* chiarire, chiarificare; (*empty*) vuotare; (*overcome*) superare; (*law*) assolvere; (*comm*) sdoganare. **clear away** portar via; (*table*) sparecchiare. **clear off** andarsene. **clear up** chiarire, mettere in chiaro; (*weather*)

rasserenarsi; (*tidy*) rassettare. **clearance** *n* (*customs*) sdoganamento *m*; (*sale*) liquidazione f; (*distance*) gioco *m*. **clearing** *n* (*land*) radura f; (*bank*) clearing *m*; (*emptying*) sgombro *m*.

**clef** [klef] *n* chiave f.

**clench** [klentʃ] *v* stringere. **with clenched fists** a pugni stretti.

**clergy** ['klə:dʒi] *n* clero *m*. **clergyman** *n* ecclesiastico *m*, pastore *m*, prete *m*.

**clerical** ['klerikəl] *adj* (*church*) clericale; (*office*) d'ufficio, impiegatizio. **clerical error** *n* errore materiale *m*, errore di trascrizione *m*.

**clerk** [kla:k] *n* impiegato, -a *m, f*; commesso, -a *m, f*.

**clever** ['klevə] *adj* abile, ingegnoso, bravo. **cleverness** *n* abilità f, ingegnosità f, intelligenza f.

**cliché** [kli:ʃei] *n* espressione stereotipata f, frase fatta f.

**click** [klik] *n* scatto *m*, schiocco *m*. *v* scattare, schioccare.

**client** ['klaiənt] *n* cliente *m, f*.

**cliff** [klif] *n* scoglio *m*.

**climate** ['klaimət] *n* clima *m*.

**climax** ['klaimaks] *n* apice *m*, apogeo *m*.

**climb** [klaim] *v* scalare, salire, arrampicarsi. *n* scalata f, salita f. **climb down** scendere; (*withdraw*) tirarsi indietro. **climb over** scavalcare.

**\*cling** [kliŋ] *v* aggrapparsi, aderire.

**clinic** ['klinik] *n* clinica f, ambulatorio *m*. **clinical** *adj* clinico.

**clip¹** [klip] *n* (*cut*) taglio *m*; (*slap*) scappellotto *m*. *v* tagliare, tosare. **clip the wings of** tarpare le ali a.

**clip²** [klip] *n* (*fastener*) fermaglio *m*, graffa f.

**clipper** ['klipə] *n* (*boat*) clipper *m*, goletta f.

**clitoris** ['klitəris] *n* clitoride f.

**cloak** [klouk] *n* (*garment*) mantello *m*, cappa f; (*mask*) maschera f; (*pretext*) pretesto *m*, scusa f. *v* (*conceal*) celare. **cloak and dagger** cappa e spada. **cloakroom** *n* guardaroba *m*.

**clock** [klok] *n* orologio *m*. **clockmaker** *n* orologiaio *m*. **clockwork** *n* meccanismo d'orologeria *m*. **clockwise** *adv* in senso orario.

**clog** [klog] *n* (*shoe*) zoccolo *m*. *v* intasare.

**cloister** ['kloistə] *n* chiostro *m*. *v* rinchiudere in convento.

**clone** n clone m, v clonare.

**close¹** [klouz] v chiudere, concludere. **close down** (shop) chiudere bottega. **close ranks** serrare le file. n (end) fine f.

**close²** [klous] n (place) recinto m. adj vicino, stretto; intimo. **close by** vicino.

**closet** ['klozit] n gabinetto m, studio m. v rinchiudere.

**clot** [klot] n grumo m, coagulo m; (coll) scemo, -a m, f. v raggrumare, coagulare, coagularsi, rapprendersi. **clotted cream** panna rappresa f.

**cloth** [kloθ] n panno m, stoffa f, tessuto m; (for dishes) strofinaccio m.

**clothe** [klouð] v vestire, abbigliare; (dress) vestirsi. **clothes** pl n vestiti m pl, abiti m pl, indumenti m pl. **clothes line** corda per il bucato f. **clothes peg** molletta f. **clothing** n vestiario m, abbigliamento m.

**cloud** [klaud] n nuvola f. **cloudburst** n acquazzone m. v annuvolare; (obscure) offuscare. **cloud over** annuvolarsi; **cloudy** adj nuvoloso; (liquid) torbido.

**clove¹** [klouv] n (plant) garofano m; (spice) chiodo di garofano m.

**clove²** [klouv] n (part of bulb) spicchio m.

**clover** ['klouvə] n trifoglio m.

**clown** [klaun] n pagliaccio m, buffone, -a m, f. v fare il pagliaccio. **clownery** n pagliacciata f. **clownish** adj pagliaccesco.

**club** [klʌb] n (stick) mazza f, randello m; (golf) bastone da golf m; (social) circolo m, club m; (cards) fiore m. v picchiare, bastonare. **club together** associarsi, riunirsi.

**clue** [klu:] n indizio m, chiave f.

**clump** [klʌmp] n gruppo m, cespo m.

**clumsy** ['klʌmzi] adj maldestro, goffo. **clumsiness** n goffaggine f, malaccortezza f.

**clung** [klʌn] V **cling**.

**cluster** ['klʌstə] n gruppo m; (bunch) grappolo m.

**clutch** [klʌtʃ] n presa f; (mot) frizione f. **fall into the clutches of** cadere nelle grinfie di. v afferrare, aggrapparsi a.

**clutter** ['klʌtə] n ingombro m, confusione f. v ingombrare.

**coach** [koutʃ] n carrozza f; (bus) corriera f, torpedone m; (tutor) ripetitore, -trice m, f; (sport) allenatore, -trice m, f. **coachbuilder** n carrozziere m. **coachwork** n carrozzeria f. v (teach) dare lezioni private; (sport) allenare.

**coagulate** [kou'agjuleit] v coagulare, coagularsi, accagliarsi. **coagulant** n coagulante m.

**coal** [koul] n carbone m. **coal-tar** n catrame m. **coalmine** n miniera di carbone f.

**coalition** [kouə'liʃən] n coalizione f.

**coarse** [ko:s] adj (rude) grossolano, rozzo; (rough) ruvido. **coarseness** n volgarità f, ruvidezza f.

**coast** [koust] n costa f, litorale m. v (cycling) scendere a ruota libera; (motoring) andare in folle. **coastal** adj costiero.

**coat** [kout] n soprabito m, cappotto m; (jacket) giacca f; (animal) pelame m, pelliccia f; (paint) mano f. **coat-hanger** n attaccapanni m. **coat-of-arms** n stemma m. **coating** n rivestimento m. v coprire, rivestire.

**coax** [kouks] v blandire, lusingare.

**cobbler** ['koblə] n ciabattino m, calzolaio m.

**cobra** ['koubrə] n cobra m.

**cobweb** ['kobweb] n ragnatela f.

**cocaine** [kə'kein] n cocaina f.

**cock¹** [kok] n (male bird) uccello maschio m; (chicken) gallo m; (tap) rubinetto m; (gun) cane m; (vulgar) cazzo m. **cocky** adj impertinente, pieno di sè.

**cock²** [kok] v (gun) armare; (ears) drizzare. **cock a snook** fare marameo.

**cockle** ['kokl] n cardio m. **cockle-shell** n conchiglia f.

**cockpit** ['kokpit] n (plane) carlinga f, cabina di guida f; (naval) cassero m.

**cockroach** ['kokroutʃ] n scarafaggio m.

**cocktail** ['kokteil] n cocktail m.

**cocoa** ['koukou] n cacao m.

**coconut** ['koukənʌt] n noce di cocco f.

**cocoon** [kə'ku:n] n bozzolo m.

**cod** [kod] n merluzzo m. **cod-liver oil** olio di fegato di merluzzo m.

**code** [koud] n cifrario m, codice m.

**codeine** ['koudi:n] n codeina f.

**coeducation** [kouedju'keiʃən] n scuola mista f.

**coerce** [kou'ə:s] v costringere, forzare.

**coexist** [kouig'zist] v coesistere. **coexistence** n coesistenza f.

**coffee** ['kofi] n caffè m. **coffee bean** chicco di caffè m. **coffee pot** caffettiera f.

**coffin** ['kofin] n cassa da morto f, bara f,

feretro m.

**cog** [kog] n dente m.

**cohabit** [kou'hæbit] v coabitare.

**coherent** [kou'hiərənt] adj coerente. **cohesion** n coesione f.

**coil** [koil] n rotolo m, bobina f. v avvolgere, attorcigliare, ravvolgere.

**coin** [koin] n moneta f.

**coincide** [kouin'said] v coincidere. **coincidence** n coincidenza f.

**colander** ['koləndə] n colabrodo m, colino m.

**cold** [kould] adj freddo, gelido; (unfriendly) riservato. **be cold** (person) aver freddo; (weather) far freddo. n freddo m; (illness) raffreddore m. **catch a cold** prendere un raffreddore, raffreddarsi. **have a cold** essere raffreddato.

**colic** ['kolik] n colica f.

**collaborate** [kə'læbəreit] v collaborare. **collaboration** n collaborazione f. **collaborator** n collaboratore, -trice m, f.

**collapse** [kə'læps] v crollare, afflosciarsi. n crollo m, collasso m, rovina f.

**collar** ['kolə] n colletto m, bavero m; (animal) collare m; (mech) manicotto m. v afferrare per il collo; (take possession) appropriarsi di.

**colleague** ['koli:g] n collega (m pl -ghi) m, f.

**collect** [kə'lekt] v raccogliere, riunire; (take delivery) prendere in consegna, ricuperare; (make collection of) far collezione di; (meet) radunarsi. **collect call** n (US) chiamata rovesciata f. **collected** adj calmo, padrone di sè. **collection** n collezione f, raccolta f; (charity) colletta f. **collective** adj collettivo. **collector** n collezionista m, f.

**college** ['kolidʒ] n collegio m, istituto m, università f.

**collide** [kə'laid] v scontrarsi, investire. **collision** n urto m, scontro m, investimento m.

**colloid** ['koloid] n colloide m.

**colloquial** [kə'loukwiəl] adj familiare. **colloquialism** n espressione familiare f.

**colon** ['koulon] n (biol) colon m invar; (gramm) due punti.

**colonel** ['kə:nl] n colonnello m.

**colonnade** [kolə'neid] n colonnata f, portico m.

**colony** ['koləni] n colonia f. **colonial** n, adj coloniale. **colonize** v colonizzare.

**colossal** [kə'losəl] adj colossale, enorme.

**colour** ['kʌlə] n colore m, tinta f. **colour bar** discriminazione razziale f. **colour-blind** adj daltonico. v colorare, tingere, colorire. **coloured** adj colorato, colorito, a colori; (person) di colore. **colourful** adj pittoresco, a tinte vivaci. **colouring** n colorito m.

**colt** [koult] n puledro m.

**column** ['koləm] n colonna f; (newspaper) rubrica f, cronaca f. **columnist** n cronista m, f, giornalista m, f.

**coma** ['koumə] n coma m invar.

**comb** [koum] n pettine m; (horse) striglia f; (birds) cresta f. v pettinare, strigliare. **comb one's hair** pettinarsi.

**combat** ['kombat] n combattimento m, lotta f. v combattere, lottare. **combatant** n combattente m, f.

**combine** [kəm'bain; n 'kombain] v combinare, unire, abbinare, combinarsi. n associazione f, consorzio m.
**combine-harvester** n mietitrebbiatrice f. **combination** n combinazione f.

**combustion** [kəm'bʌstʃən] n combustione f. **internal combustion engine** motore a combustione interna m.

*****come** [kʌm] v venire, arrivare, giungere. **come about** accadere. **come across** incontrare per caso, trovare per caso. **come in** entrare. **come into force** entrare in vigore. **come off** (succeed) riuscire. **come to blows** venire alle mani. **come to light** venire alla luce. **come up** salire; (to the surface) venire a galla.

**comedy** ['komədi] n commedia f. **comedian** n commediante m, f, comico, -a m, f.

**comet** ['komit] n cometa f.

**comfort** ['kʌmfət] n agio m, conforto m, consolazione f, agiatezza f. v consolare, confortare.

**comic** ['komik] n comico, -a m, f; (periodical) giornaletto a fumetti m. adj comico. **comic opera** opera buffa f. **comic strip** fumetto m. **comical** adj comico.

**comma** ['komə] n virgola f. **in inverted commas** fra virgolette.

**command** [kə'ma:nd] n comando m, ordine m. v comandare; (mil) ordinare, avere il comando di. **commander** n comandante m, capo m. **commanding position** posizione dominante f. **com-**

**mandment** n comandamento m, precetto m.

**commandeer** [komən'diə] v requisire.

**commando** [kə'ma:ndou] n truppe d'assalto f pl, commando m invar.

**commemorate** [kə'meməreit] v commemorare. **commemoration** n commemorazione f.

**commence** [kə'mens] v cominciare, iniziare. **commencement** n inizio m, principio m.

**commend** [kə'mend] v raccomandare, lodare. **commendable** adj lodevole, encomiabile. **commendation** n lode f, encomio m.

**comment** ['koment] n commento m, osservazione f, rilievo m. v commentare, fare delle osservazioni. **commentary** n commentario m, cronaca f. **commentator** n commentatore, -trice m, f; cronista m, f; radiocronista m, f.

**commerce** ['komə:s] n commercio m, scambi m pl. **commercial** adj commerciale.

**commiserate** [kə'mizəreit] v commiserare, compiangere.

**commission** [kə'miʃən] n commissione f, delegazione f; (authority) incarico m; (comm) provvigione f; (mil) brevetto da ufficiale m. v incaricare, dare una carica; nominare ufficiale; (ship) armare. **commissionaire** n portiere m. **commissioned officer** ufficiale m. **non-commissioned officer** sottufficiale m. **commissioner** n commissario m.

**commit** [kə'mit] v commettere; affidare, rimettere. **commit oneself** impegnarsi. **commit to memory** imparare a memoria. **commitment** n impegno m. **committed** adj impegnato.

**committee** [kə'miti] n comitato m, commissione f.

**commodity** [kə'modəti] n merce f, derrata f.

**common** ['komən] adj comune, ordinario, volgare. n parco demaniale m. **commonplace** adj ordinario, banale. **common sense** buonsenso m.

**commotion** [kə'mouʃən] n agitazione f, confusione f.

**commune¹** [kə'mju:n] v intrattenersi, discutere.

**commune²** ['komju:n] n comune m, comunità f. **communal** adj comunale, in comune.

**communicate** [kə'mju:nikeit] v comunicare, informare, trasmettere. **communicate with** essere in comunicazione con. **communication** n comunicazione f, informazione f, rapporto m.

**communion** [kə'mju:njən] n comunione f.

**communism** ['komjunizəm] n comunismo m. **communist** n(m+f), adj comunista.

**community** [kə'mju:nəti] n comunità f.

**commute** [kə'mju:t] v commutare; (travel) fare il pendolare. **commuter** n pendolare m, f.

**compact¹** [kəm'pakt, n 'kompakt] adj compatto, serrato. n (powder) portacipria m invar.

**compact²** ['kompakt] n (agreement) patto m, accordo m.

**companion** [kəm'panjən] n compagno, -a m, f. **companionship** n compagnia f, cameratismo m, amicizia f.

**company** ['kʌmpəni] n compagnia f, comitiva f; (comm) ditta f, società f; (ship) equipaggio m. **in the company of** accompagnato da. **part company with** separarsi da.

**compare** [kəm'peə] v paragonare, confrontare, essere paragonabile a. **comparable** adj paragonabile, comparabile. **comparative** adj comparativo, relativo. **compared with** rispetto a, di fronte a. **comparison** n confronto m, paragone m.

**compartment** [kəm'pa:tmənt] n compartimento m, casella f; (railway) scompartimento m.

**compass** ['kʌmpəs] n bussola f. **compasses** pl n compasso m sing. v cingere, circondare.

**compassion** [kəm'paʃən] n compassione f, pietà f, misericordia f. **compassionate** adj misericordioso, pieno di compassione.

**compatible** [kəm'patəbl] adj compatibile. **compatibility** n compatibilità f.

**compel** [kəm'pel] v costringere, obbligare, forzare. **compel respect** farsi rispettare. **compelling** adj irresistibile.

**compensate** ['kompənseit] v compensare, ricompensare, indennizzare. **compensation** n compenso m, ricompensa f; (comm) compensazione f.

**compete** [kəm'pi:t] v concorrere, fare concorrenza a, gareggiare. **competition** n (contest) gara f; (rivalry) concorrenza f; (exam) concorso m. **competitive** adj competitivo.

**competitor** n concorrente m, f; rivale m, f.

**competent** ['kɒmpətənt] adj competente, capace. **competence** n competenza f, capacità f.

**compile** [kəm'pail] v compilare. **compilation** n compilazione f.

**complacent** [kəm'pleisnt] adj soddisfatto di sè.

**complain** [kəm'plein] v lamentarsi, lagnarsi. **complaint** n (discontent) lamentela f; (merchandise) reclamo m; (illness) malattia f.

**complement** ['kɒmpləmənt] n complemento m. v completare, fare da complemento a. **complementary** adj complementare.

**complete** [kəm'pli:t] adj completo, intero. v completare, finire. **completion** n fine f, compimento m.

**complex** ['kɒmpleks] nm, adj complesso.

**complexion** [kəm'plekʃən] n (skin) colorito m; (nature) aspetto m.

**complicate** ['kɒmplikeit] v complicare. **complicated** adj complicato, complesso. **complication** n difficoltà f.

**complicity** [kəm'plisəti] n complicità f.

**compliment** ['kɒmpləmənt] n complimento m. v congratularsi con. **complimentary** adj (flattering) lusinghiero; (free) di favore.

**comply** [kəm'plai] v ubbidire, acconsentire. **in compliance with** conforme a.

**component** [kəm'pounənt] nm, adj componente.

**compose** [kəm'pouz] v comporre. **composed** adj calmo. **composer** n compositore, -trice m, f. **composite** adj composto, misto. **composition** n composizione f.

**compost** ['kɒmpɒst] n concime m.

**composure** [kəm'pouʒə] n compostezza f, calma f.

**compound**[1] [kəm'paund; n 'kɒmpaund] v (compose) comporre; (mix) mescolare; (settle) regolare. n composto m, miscela f. adj composto.

**compound**[2] ['kɒmpaund] n (enclosure) campo m, accampamento m.

**comprehend** [kɒmpri'hend] v comprendere, capire. **comprehensible** adj comprensibile. **comprehension** n comprensione f. **comprehensive** adj comprensivo, esauriente.

**compress** [kəm'pres; n 'kɒmpres] v comprimere. n compressa f. **compression** n compressione f.

**comprise** [kəm'praiz] v includere.

**compromise** ['kɒmprəmaiz] n compromesso m. v giungere a un compromesso; (endanger) compromettere. **compromising** adj compromettente, imbarazzante.

**compulsion** [kəm'pʌlʃən] n costrizione f, obbligo m. **compulsive** adj coercitivo. **compulsory** adj obbligatorio.

**compunction** [kəm'pʌŋkʃən] n rimorso m.

**computer** [kəm'pju:tə] n computer (pl -s) m, elaboratore elettronico m.

**comrade** ['kɒmrid] n compagno, -a m, f; camerata m, f. **comradeship** n cameratismo m.

**concave** [kɒn'keiv] adj concavo.

**conceal** [kən'si:l] v celare, nascondere.

**concede** [kən'si:d] v concedere, ammettere, riconoscere.

**conceit** [kən'si:t] n vanità f, presunzione f. **conceited** adj vanitoso, presuntuoso.

**conceive** [kən'si:v] v concepire; immaginare. **conceivable** adj concepibile, immaginabile.

**concentrate** ['kɒnsəntreit] v concentrare. n concentrato m. **concentration** n concentrazione f. **concentration camp** campo di concentramento m.

**concentric** [kən'sentrik] adj concentrico.

**concept** ['kɒnsept] n concetto m, nozione f.

**conception** [kən'sepʃən] n concezione f, idea f.

**concern** [kən'sə:n] n (care) sollecitudine f, preoccupazione f; (business) affare m, faccenda f; interesse m; (firm) azienda f, ditta f. v riguardare, toccare. **concerned** adj in questione; (anxious) preoccupato. **concerning** prep riguardo a, in merito a, inerente a.

**concert** ['kɒnsət] n concerto m. **concerted** adj predisposto, stabilito d'accordo con altri.

**concertina** [kɒnsə'ti:nə] n fisarmonica f.

**concerto** [kən'tʃə:tou] n concerto m.

**concession** [kən'seʃən] n concessione f.

**conciliate** [kən'silieit] v conciliare. **conciliation** n conciliazione f. **conciliatory** adj conciliatorio.

**concise** [kən'sais] adj conciso, breve.

**conclude** [kən'klu:d] v concludere, dedurre. **conclusion** n conclusione f, fine f. **in conclusion** adv in fine, insomma. **conclusive**

*adj* conclusivo.

**concoct** [kən'kɒkt] *v* (*contrive*) inventare. **concoction** *n* intruglio *m*, pasticcio *m*.

**concrete** ['kɒŋkri:t] *adj* concreto. *n* calcestruzzo *m*, cemento *m*. **concrete mixer** betoniera *f*. **reinforced concrete** cemento armato *m*. *v* cementare, rivestire di calcestruzzo.

**concussion** [kən'kʌʃən] *n* commozione cerebrale *f*.

**condemn** [kən'dem] *v* condannare. **condemnation** *n* condanna *f*.

**condense** [kən'dens] *v* condensare. **condensation** *n* condensazione *f*.

**condescend** [kɒndi'send] *v* degnarsi. **condescending** *adj* condiscendente. **condescension** *n* condiscendenza *f*.

**condition** [kən'diʃən] *n* condizione *f*. *v* condizionare. **conditional** *adj* condizionale.

**conditioner** *n* balsamo (per capelli) *m*.

**condolence** [kən'dəuləns] *n* condoglianza *f*. **express condolences** fare le condoglianze.

**condom** ['kɒndɒm] *n* preservativo *m*.

**condone** [kən'dəun] *v* perdonare.

**conducive** [kən'dju:siv] *adj* contribuire.

**conduct** [kən'dʌkt; *n* 'kɒndʌkt] *v* condurre; (*music*) dirigere. **conduct oneself** comportarsi. *n* condotta *f*, comportamento *m*.

**conductor** [kən'dʌktə] *n* (*transport*) bigliettaio, -a *m*, *f*; (*music*) direttore d'orchestra *m*; (*physics*) conduttore *m*.

**cone** [kəun] *n* cono *m*; (*fir*) pigna *f*.

**confectioner** [kən'fekʃənə] *n* pasticciere, -a *m*, *f*. **confectioner's shop** *n* pasticceria *f*.

**confederate** [kən'fedərət] *adj* confederato, alleato. *v* confederarsi, allearsi.

**confer** [kən'fə:] *v* conferire, consultarsi. **conference** *n* conferenza *f*. **conferment** *n* conferimento *m*.

**confess** [kən'fes] *v* confessare, ammettere; (*rel*) confessarsi. **confession** *n* confessione *f*, professione *f*. **confessor** *n* confessore *m*.

**confetti** [kən'feti] *n* coriandoli *m pl*.

**confide** [kən'faid] *v* confidare. **confidant, -e** *n* confidente *m*, *f*. **confidence** *n* fiducia *f*; sicurezza di sè *f*. **have confidence in** aver fiducia in. **in confidence** in confidenza. **confident** *adj* fiducioso, sicuro. **confidential** *adj* riservato.

**confine** [kən'fain] *n* confine *m*. *v* relegare; (*to barracks*) consegnare. **be confined**

(*childbirth*) partorire. **confinement** *n* imprigionamento *m*, segregazione *f*; (*childbirth*) parto *m*.

**confirm** [kən'fə:m] *v* confermare; (*statement*) ribadire; (*rel*) cresimare; (*law*) omologare. **confirmation** *n* conferma *f*; (*law*) ratifica *f*; (*rel*) confermazione *f*; cresima *f*. **confirmed** *adj* confermato; (*belief*) convinto, impenitente.

**confiscate** ['kɒnfiskeit] *v* confiscare.

**conflict** ['kɒnflikt; *v* kən'flikt] *n* conflitto *m*, lotta *f*, contrasto *m*. *v* **conflict with** essere in disaccordo *or* contrasto con. **conflicting** *adj* (*evidence*) contradditorio; (*interests*) contrastante.

**conform** [kən'fɔ:m] *v* conformare, adattarsi. **conformist** *n* conformista *m*, *f*. **conformity** *n* conformità *f*. **in conformity with** conforme a, conformemente a.

**confound** [kən'faund] *v* sconcertare, sconvolgere.

**confront** [kən'frʌnt] *v* affrontare; (*law*) mettere a confronto. **confrontation** *n* confronto *m*.

**confuse** [kən'fju:z] *v* confondere, sconcertare, disorientare, scambiare. **confusing** *adj* sconcertante, che rende perplesso. **confusion** *n* confusione *f*, disordine *m*.

**congeal** [kən'dʒi:l] *v* (*freeze*) congelare, congelarsi; coagulare, coagularsi.

**congenial** [kən'dʒi:niəl] *adj* congeniale.

**congenital** [kən'dʒenitl] *adj* congenito, innato.

**congested** [kən'dʒestid] *adj* congestionato. **congestion** *n* congestione *f*.

**conglomeration** [kən,glɒmə'reiʃən] *n* conglomerazione *f*.

**congratulate** [kən'gratjuleit] *v* congratularsi con, felicitare, felicitarsi con. **congratulation** *n* felicitazione *f*. **congratulations!** *interj* auguri!

**congregate** ['kɒngrigeit] *v* congregare, riunirsi. **congregation** *n* (*rel*) comunità *f*, adunanza dei fedeli *f*.

**congress** ['kɒngres] *n* congresso *m*.

**conical** ['kɒnikəl] *adj* conico.

**conifer** ['kɒnifə] *n* conifera *f*.

**conjecture** [kən'dʒektʃə] *v* supporre. *n* supposizione *f*.

**conjugal** ['kɒndʒugəl] *adj* coniugale.

**conjugate** ['kɒndʒugeit] *v* coniugare. **conjugation** *n* coniugazione *f*.

**conjunction** [kən'dʒʌŋkʃən] *n* congiunzione *f*.

**conjunctivitis** [kən,dʒʌŋkti'vaitis] *n* congiuntivite *f*.

**conjure** ['kʌndʒə; (*invoke*) kən'dʒuə] *v* fare giochi di prestigio; (*invoke*) scongiurare. **conjure up** evocare. **conjurer** *n* prestigiatore, -trice *m*, *f*. **conjuring trick** gioco di prestigio *m*.

**connect** [kə'nekt] *v* connettere, congiungere; associare; (*trains*) far coincidenza. **connection** *n* connessione *f*, rapporto *m*; coincidenza *f*. **in connection with** in merito a.

**connoisseur** [konə'sə:] *n* intenditore, -trice *m*, *f*.

**connotation** [konə'teiʃən] *n* significato implicito *m*.

**conquer** ['koŋkə] *v* conquistare, vincere. **conqueror** *n* conquistatore, -trice *m*, *f*; vincitore, -trice *m*, *f*. **conquest** *n* conquista *f*, vittoria *f*.

**conscience** ['konʃəns] *n* coscienza *f*.

**conscientious** [konʃi'enʃəs] *adj* conscienzioso, diligente. **conscientious objector** obiettore di coscienza *m*.

**conscious** ['konʃəs] *adj* conscio, cosciente; (*deliberate*) intenzionale. **consciousness** *n* coscienza *f*.

**conscript** ['konskript] *v* chiamare alle armi, arruolare. *n* soldato di leva *m*. **conscription** *n* leva *f*.

**consecrate** ['konsikreit] *v* consacrare. **consecration** *n* consacrazione *f*.

**consecutive** [kən'sekjutiv] *adj* consecutivo.

**consensus** [kən'sensəs] *n* consenso *m*, assenso *m*.

**consent** [kən'sent] *v* consentire, acconsentire. *n* consenso *m*, benestare *m*, accordo *m*.

**consequence** ['konsikwəns] *n* conseguenza *f*, effetto *m*, importanza *f*. **consequently** *adv* di conseguenza, quindi, perciò.

**conserve** [kən'sə:v] *v* conservare, preservare. *n* conserva *f*. **conservation** *n* preservazione *f*. **conservative** *adj* conservativo, cauto; (*pol*) conservatore. **conservatoire** *n* (*music*) conservatorio *m*. **conservatory** *n* serra *f*.

**consider** [kən'sidə] *v* considerare, giudicare, ritenere, pensare. **considerable** *adj* notevole. **considerate** *adj* sollecito, riguardoso. **consideration** *n* considerazione *f*, riflessione *f*; (*feeling, regard*) riguardo *m*, sollecitudine *f*, delicatezza *f*.

**consign** [kən'sain] *v* consegnare, affidare. **consignee** *n* destinatario, -a *m*, *f*. **consignor** *or* **n** mittente *m*, *f*. **consignment** *n* spedizione *f*, invio *m*; (*goods*) partita di merce *f*.

**consist** [kən'sist] *v* consistere (in), essere composto. **consistency** *n* consistenza *f*. **consistent** *adj* regolare, costante, coerente.

**console**[1] [kən'soul] *v* confortare. **consolation** *n* consolazione *f*, conforto *m*.

**console**[2] ['konsoul] *n* (*arch*) mensola *f*; (*furniture*) mobile *m*; (*tech*) quadro di comando *m*.

**consolidate** [kən'solideit] *v* consolidare. **consolidation** *n* consolidazione *f*.

**consommé** [kən'somei] *n* brodo *m*.

**consonant** ['konsənənt] *n* consonante *f*.

**consortium** [kən'so:tiəm] *n* consorzio *m*.

**conspicuous** [kən'spikjuəs] *adj* cospicuo, evidente.

**conspire** [kən'spaiə] *v* complottare. **conspiracy** *n* complotto *m*, congiura *f*.

**constable** ['kʌnstəbl] *n* vigile *m*, poliziotto *m*.

**constant** ['konstənt] *adj* costante, invariabile. *n* costante *f*.

**constellation** [konstə'leiʃən] *n* costellazione *f*.

**constipation** [konsti'peiʃən] *n* stitichezza *f*. **constipated** *adj* stitico.

**constitute** ['konstitju:t] *v* costituire, creare. **constituent** *nf*, *adj* costituente. **constituency** *n* collegio elettorale *m*. **constitution** *n* costituzione *f*; statuto *m*; (*health*) salute *f*.

**constraint** [kən'streint] *n* (*restriction*) costrizione *f*; (*embarrassment*) imbarazzo *m*.

**constrict** [kən'strikt] *v* stringere, restringere, comprimere. **constriction** *n* restringimento *m*; (*tight feeling*) oppressione *f*.

**construct** [kən'strʌkt] *v* costruire. **construction** *n* costruzione *f*; (*building*) edificio *m*; (*meaning*) senso *m*. **constructive** *adj* costruttivo, positivo.

**consul** ['konsəl] *n* console *m*. **consulate** *n* consolato *m*.

**consult** [kən'sʌlt] *v* consultare; (*consider*) tener conto di. **consultant** *n* consulente *m*, *f*, esperto, -a *m*, *f*. **consultation** *n* consultazione *f*; (*med*) consulta *f*. **consulting room** (*med*) studio *m*.

**consume** [kən'sju:m] *v* consumare. **con-**

**sumer** *n* consumatore, -trice *m, f.* **consumer goods** generi di consumo *m pl.*

**contact** ['kɒntakt] *n* contatto *m; (acquaintance)* conoscenza *f.* *v* mettere in contatto con, mettersi in contatto. **contact lens** *n* lente a contatto *f.*

**contagious** [kən'teidʒəs] *adj* contagioso.

**contain** [kən'tein] *v* contenere, includere. **container** *n* recipiente *m.*

**contaminate** [kən'tamineit] *v* contaminare, inquinare. **contamination** *n* contaminazione *f*, inquinamento *m.*

**contemplate** ['kɒntəmpleit] *v* contemplare, meditare; *(intend to)* proporsi, aver intenzione di. **contemplation** *n* contemplazione *f.*

**contemporary** [kən'tempərəri] *n, adj* contemporaneo, -a; coetaneo, -a.

**contempt** [kən'tempt] *n* disprezzo *m.* **contempt of court** oltraggio alla corte *m.* **contemptible** *adj* spregevole. **contemptuous** *adj* sprezzante, altezzoso.

**contend** [kən'tend] *v* contendere, sostenere, affermare. **bone of contention** pomo della discordia *m.*

**content**[1] ['kɒntent] *n* contenuto *m.*

**content**[2] [kən'tent] *adj* contento, soddisfatto. *v* accontentare.

**contest** [kɒntest; *v* kən'test] *n* gara *f*, lotta *f.* *v* contestare, impugnare.

**context** ['kɒntekst] *n* contesto *m.*

**continent** ['kɒntinənt] *nm, adj* continente. **continental** *adj* continentale.

**contingency** [kən'tindʒənsi] *n* contingenza *f.*

**continue** [kən'tinju:] *v* continuare, proseguire. **continual** *or* **continuous** *adj* continuo, ininterrotto. **continuation** *n* seguito *m.* **continuity** *n* continuità *f; (film)* sceneggiatura *f.*

**contort** [kən'to:t] *v* contorcere. **contortion** *n* contorcimento *m.* **contortionist** *n* contorsionista *m.*

**contour** ['kɒntuə] *n* contorno *m.* **contour map/line** curva/curva ipsometrica *f.*

**contraband** ['kɒntrəband] *n* contrabbando *m.*

**contraception** [kɒntrə'sepʃən] *n* pratiche antifecondative *f pl.* **contraceptive** *nm, adj* anticoncezionale, anticoncettivo, antifecondativo.

**contract** ['kɒntrakt; *v* kən'trakt] *n* patto *m*, accordo *m*, contratto *m.* *v (draw together)* contrarre, restringere; *(acquire, take on)* contrarre; *(enter into)* contrattare. **contraction** *n* contrazione *f.*

**contradict** [kɒntrə'dikt] *v* contraddire, smentire. **contradiction** *n* contraddizione *f*, smentita *f.*

**contralto** [kən'traltou] *n* contralto *m.*

**contraption** [kən'trapʃən] *n* congegno *m*, aggeggio *m.*

**contrary** ['kɒntrəri] *nm, adj* contrario, opposto. **contrary to** contrariamente a. **on the contrary** al contrario, anzi.

**contrast** ['kɒntra:st; *v* kən'tra:st] *n* contrasto *m*, antitesi *f invar.* *v* contrastare, confrontare, mettere in contrasto.

**contravene** [kɒntrə'vi:n] *v* contravvenire a.

**contribute** [kən'tribjut] *v* contribuire. **contributor** *n* contributore, -trice *m, f; (writer)* collaboratore, -trice *m, f.* **contribution** *n* contributo *m; (writing)* articolo *m.*

**contrive** [kən'traiv] *v* riuscire a, escogitare.

**control** [kən'troul] *v* controllare, dominare. *n* controllo *m*, autorità *f.* **controls** *pl n* comandi *m pl.* **remote control** controllo a distanza *m*, telecontrollo *m.*

**controversy** [kən'trɒvəsi] *n* controversia *f.* **controversial** *adj* controverso.

**convalesce** [kɒnvə'les] *v* rimettersi in salute. **convalescence** *n* convalescenza *f.* **convalescent home** convalescenziario *m.*

**convector** [kən'vektə] *nm, adj* convettore.

**convenience** [kən'vi:njəns] *n* comodo *m*, comodità *f*, convenienza *f.* **at the earliest convenience** alla prima occasione. **public convenience** gabinetto pubblico *m.* **convenient** *adj* conveniente, comodo.

**convent** ['kɒnvənt] *n* convento *m.*

**convention** [kən'venʃən] *n* convenzione *f; (meeting)* adunata *f; (agreement)* accordo *m.* **convene** *v* convocare, adunare. **conventional** *adj* convenzionale.

**converge** [kən'və:dʒ] *v* convergere.

**converse** [kən'və:s; *n, adj* kɒnvə:s] *v* conversare. *nm, adj* contrario, opposto. **conversation** *n* conversazione *f.*

**convert** [kən'və:t; *n* 'kɒnvə:t] *v* convertire, trasformare. *n* convertito, -a *m, f.* **convertible** *n (car)* auto decapottabile *f.*

**convex** ['kɒnveks] *adj* convesso.

**convey** [kən'vei] *v* trasportare; *(impart)* esprimere. **conveyance** *n* mezzo di trasporto m; (*law*) atto di cessione m. **con-veyor belt** nastro trasportatore m.

**convict** [kən'vikt; n 'konvikt] v condannare. n carcerato, -a m, f; prigioniero, -a m, f.

**conviction** [kən'vikʃən] n (*sentence*) condanna f; persuasione f, convinzione f.

**convince** [kən'vins] v convincere, persuadere.

**convivial** [kən'viviəl] adj allegro.

**convoy** ['konvoi] n convoglio m, scorta f. v convogliare, scortare.

**convulsion** [kən'vʌlʃən] n convulsione f. v **be convulsed (with laughter)** contorcersi (dalle risa).

**cook** [kuk] n cuoco, -a m, f. v cuocere, cucinare, far la cucina. **cook the books** falsificare i registri. **cooker** n fornello m. **cookery** or **cooking** n cucina f, arte culinaria f.

**cool** [ku:l] adj fresco, calmo. v rinfrescare, raffreddare. **cooler** n refrigerante m; (*slang*) gattabuia f.

**coop** [ku:p] n stia f. v **coop up** stipare, pigiarsi.

**cooperate** [kou'opəreit] v cooperare. **cooperation** n cooperazione f, collaborazione f. **cooperative** adj cooperativo. **cooperator** n collaboratore, -trice m, f.

**coordinate** [kou'o:dineit] v coordinare. n coordinata f. adj coordinato. **coordination** n coordinazione f.

**cop** [kop] n (*slang*) poliziotto m. v pescare. **cop it** prenderle.

**cope¹** [koup] v riuscire. **cope with** far fronte a.

**cope²** [koup] n cappa f.

**Copenhagen** [koupən'heigən] n Copenhagen f.

**copious** ['koupiəs] adj abbondante.

**copper¹** ['kopə] n rame m. adj color rame.

**copper²** ['kopə] n (*slang*) poliziotto m.

**copulate** ['kopju:leit] v accoppiarsi. **copulation** n accoppiamento m, copulazione f.

**copy** ['kopi] v copiare; ricopiare, riprodurre; imitare. n copia f, trascrizione f, imitazione f; (*book*) esemplare m. **copyright** n diritti d'autore m pl.

**coral** ['korəl] n corallo m.

**cord** [ko:d] n corda f; (*string*) spago m; (*elec*) filo m, cavo m.

**cordial** ['ko:diəl] adj cordiale, caloroso.

**cordon** ['ko:dn] n cordone m. **cordon off** fare cordone intorno a, isolare.

**corduroy** ['ko:dəroi] n fustagno m.

**core** [ko:] n centro m; (*fruit*) torsolo m; (*mech*) anima f.

**cork** [ko:k] n (*bark*) sughero m; (*stopper*) tappo m, turacciolo m. **corkscrew** n cavatappi m invar. v turare. **corked** adj (*wine*) che sa di turacciolo.

**corn¹** [ko:n] n (*grain*) grano m; (*wheat*) frumento m; (*maize*) mais m invar, granturco m. **cornflour** n farina finissima di granturco f. **corny** adj banale.

**corn²** [ko:n] n (*toe*) callo m.

**corner** ['ko:nə] n angolo m; (*football*) corner m invar, calcio d'angolo m. v (*prevent escape*) mettere alle strette; (*stock*) accaparrare; (*drive*) fare una curva.

**cornet** ['ko:nit] n (*music*) cornetta f; (*ice-cream*) cono m.

**coronary** ['korənəri] adj coronario. **coronary thrombosis** trombosi coronaria f.

**coronation** [korə'neiʃən] n incoronazione f.

**corporal¹** ['ko:pərəl] adj (*bodily*) corporale; (*material*) corporeo.

**corporal²** ['ko:pərəl] n caporale, -a m, f.

**corporation** [ko:pə'reiʃən] n corporazione f, ente m. **corporate** adj corporativo.

**corps** [ko:] n corpo m.

**corpse** [ko:ps] n cadavere m.

**correct** [kə'rekt] v correggere. adj corretto, giusto, esatto. **correction** n correzione f, rettifica f.

**correlate** ['korəleit] v mettere in correlazione. **correlated** adj correlativo. **correlation** n correlazione f.

**correspond** [korə'spond] v corrispondere, equivalere; (*letters*) essere in corrispondenza, scambiare lettere. **correspondence** n corrispondenza f, scambio di lettere m. **correspondent** n corrispondente m, f. **corresponding** adj corrispondente.

**corridor** ['korido:] n corridoio m.

**corrode** [kə'roud] v corrodere, corrodersi. **corrosion** n corrosione f. **corrosive** adj corrosivo.

**corrupt** [kə'rʌpt] v corrompere. adj corrotto. **corruption** n corruzione f.

**corset** ['ko:sit] n busto m; (*orthopaedic*) corsetto m.

**Corsica** ['ko:sikə] n Corsica f. **Corsican** n, adj corso, -a.

**cosh** [koʃ] *n* randello *m*.

**cosmetic** [koz'metik] *nm, adj* cosmetico. **cosmetics** *pl n* prodotti di bellezza *m pl*.

**cosmic** ['kozmik] *adj* cosmico. **cosmonaut** *n* cosmonauta *m, f*.

**cosmopolitan** [kozmə'politən] *nm, adj* cosmopolitano.

*****cost** [kost] *n* costo *m*, prezzo *m*. *v* costare. **costly** *adj* costoso, caro.

**costume** ['kostju:m] *n* costume *m*, abito *m*; (*suit*) tailleur *m*.

**cosy** ['kouzi] *adj* comodo, intimo, accogliente.

**cot** [kot] *n* lettino *m*, culla *f*.

**cottage** ['kotidʒ] *n* villino *m*, casetta *f*.

**cotton** ['kotn] *n* cotone *m*. **cotton-wool** *n* bambagia *f*, ovatta *f*; (*med*) cotone idrofilo *m*.

**couch** [kautʃ] *n* divano *m*, canapè *m*.

**cough** [kof] *n* tosse *f*. **cough mixture** sciroppo per la tosse *m*. *v* tossire.

**could** [kud] *V* **can**[1]

**council** ['kaunsəl] *n* consiglio *m*; (*rel*) concilio *m*. **councillor** *n* consigliere *m*, membro del consiglio *m*.

**council house** *n* casa popolare *f*.

**counsel** ['kaunsəl] *n* (*advice*) consiglio *m*; (*lawyer*) avvocato *m*. *v* raccomandare, consigliare. **counsellor** *n* consigliere, -a *m, f*; (*consultant*) consulente *m, f*.

**count**[1] [kaunt] *v* contare, includere. **count on** contare su, fare affidamento su. *n* conto *m*, calcolo *m*; (*law*) capo d'accusa *m*.

**count**[2] [kaunt] *n* conte *m*. **countess** *n* contessa *f*.

**countenance** ['kauntinəns] *n* espressione *f*. *v* tollerare.

**counter**[1] ['kauntə] *n* (*token*) gettone *m*; (*table top*) banco *m*; (*device*) calcolatore *m*.

**counter**[2] ['kauntə] *v* opporsi a, controbattere. *adj* contrario, opposto.

**counteract** [kauntə'rakt] *v* neutralizzare, invalidare, mandare a vuoto.

**counter-attack** *n* contrattacco *m*. *v* contrattaccare.

**counterfeit** ['kauntəfit] *adj* falsificato, falso. *v* falsificare.

**counterfoil** ['kauntəfoil] *n* matrice *f*, figlia *f*.

**counterpart** ['kauntəpa:t] *n* contropartita *f*, complemento *m*.

**country** ['kʌntri] *n* (*countryside*) campagna *f*; (*state*) paese *m*; (*homeland*) patria *f*.

**county** ['kaunti] *n* provincia *f*, regione *f*.

**coup** [ku:] *n* **coup de grace** colpo di grazia *m*. **coup d'état** colpo di stato *m*.

**couple** ['kʌpl] *n* coppia *f*, paio *m* (*pl* -a *f*). *v* accoppiare, abbinare.

**coupon** ['ku:pon] *n* tagliando *m*, scontrino *m*.

**courage** ['kʌridʒ] *n* coraggio *m*. **courageous** *adj* coraggioso.

**courgette** [kuə'ʒet] *n* zucchina *f*, zucchino *m*.

**courier** ['kuriə] *n* accompagnatore, -trice *m, f*; messaggero, -a *m, f*.

**course** [ko:s] *n* corso *m*, percorso *m*, linea *f*; (*food*) piatto *m*; (*aircraft*) rotta *f*. **in due course** a tempo debito. **in the course of** durante, nel corso di. **of course** naturalmente, beninteso.

**court** [ko:t] *n* corte *f*; (*law*) tribunale *m*; (*tennis*) campo *m*. **court-martial** *n* corte marziale *f*. **courtyard** *n* cortile *m*. *v* corteggiare, far la corte a.

**courteous** ['kə:tiəs] *adj* cortese, gentile. **courtesy** *n* cortesia *f*, gentilezza *f*.

**cousin** ['kʌzn] *n* cugino, -a *m, f*.

**cove** [kouv] *n* insenatura *f*.

**cover** ['kʌvə] *n* coperta *f*, copertura *f*; (*shelter*) riparo *m*; (*book*) copertina *f*. *v* coprire, ricoprire; (*travel*) percorrere; (*journalism*) riferire. **covering** *n* copertura *f*. **covering letter** lettera d'accompagnamento *f*.

**cow** [kau] *n* vacca *f*, mucca *f*. *v* intimidire.

**coward** ['kauəd] *n* vigliacco, -a *m, f*; vile *m, f*. **cowardly** *adj* vigliacco, vile. **cowardice** *n* vigliaccheria *f*.

**cower** ['kauə] *v* accovacciarsi, rannicchiarsi.

**cowl** [kaul] *n* (*chimney*) comignolo *m*; (*hood*) cappa *f*; (*car*) cofano *m*.

**coy** [koi] *adj* ritroso, timido.

**crab** [krab] *n* granchio *m*.

**crack** [krak] *n* (*opening*) screpolatura *f*, fessura *f*; (*whip*) schiocco *m*; (*rifle*) scoppio *m*; (*noise*) schianto *m*. **have a crack at** provare a fare. *v* spaccare, schioccare, screpolare.

**cracker** ['krakə] *n* (*biscuit*) cracker (*pl* -s) *m*, gallettina *f*; (*firework*) mortaretto *m*.

**crackle** ['krakl] *v* crepitare, scricchiolare. *n* crepitio *m*, scricchiolio *m*.

**cradle** ['kreidl] *n* culla *f*. *v* cullare.

**craft** [kra:ft] *n* mestiere *m*, professione *f*; (*cunning*) astuzia *f*; (*boat*) imbarcazione *f*. **crafty** *adj* astuto.

**cram** [kram] *v* ficcare, cacciare.

**cramp** [kramp] *n* (*med*) crampo *m*. *v* paralizzare, bloccare.

**cranberry** ['kranbəri] *n* mirtillo rosso *m*.

**crane** [krein] *n* gru *f invar*. *v* **crane one's neck** allungare il collo.

**crank** [kraŋk] *n* (*mech*) gomito *m*, manovella *f*; eccentrico, -a *m*, *f*. *v* **crank up** avviare.

**crap** [krap] *n* (*vulgar*) merda *f*; (*impol: nonsense*) scemenze *f pl*, stupidaggini *f pl*. *v* (*vulgar*) cacare.

**crash** [kraʃ] *n* (*collision*) scontro *m*; (*noise*) fracasso *m*; (*collapse*) crollo *m*; (*aircraft*) caduta *f*. **crash-helmet** *n* casco paraurti *m*. **crash-landing** *n* atterraggio di fortuna *m*. *v* (*clash*) scontrarsi; fracassare; crollare; precipitare.

**crate** [kreit] *n* cassa *f*. *v* imballare.

**crater** ['kreitə] *n* cratere *m*.

**crave** [kreiv] *v* ambire, bramare. **craving** *n* smania *f*, brama *f*.

**crawl** [kro:l] *v* trascinarsi, strisciare. *n* (*swimming*) crawl *m invar*.

**crayfish** ['kreifiʃ] *n* gambero (di fiume) *m*.

**crayon** ['kreiən] *n* pastello *m*, matita colorata *f*.

**craze** [kreiz] *n* mania *f*, pazzia *f*. **crazy** *adj* pazzo, matto. **drive crazy** far impazzire.

**creak** [kri:k] *v* cigolare, scricchiolare. *n* cigolio *m*, scricchiolio *m*.

**cream** [kri:m] *n* panna *f*, crema *f*. *v* scremare. **creamy** *adj* cremoso; (*soft*) morbido.

**crease** [kri:s] *n* piega *f*, grinza *f*. *v* sgualcirsi, raggrinzarsi. **creased** *adj* raggrinzato; (*clothes*) sgualcito.

**create** [kri'eit] *v* creare, provocare. **creation** *n* creazione *f*. **creative** *adj* creativo, originale. **creativity** *n* potenza creativa *f*, originalità *f*. **creator** *n* creatore, -trice *m*, *f*. **creature** *n* creatura *f*.

**créche** *n* asilo infantile, (asilo) nido *m*.

**credentials** [kri'denʃəlz] *pl n* credenziali *f pl*.

**credible** ['kredəbl] *adj* credibile. **credibility** *n* credibilità *f*.

**credit** ['kredit] *n* credito *m*; (*trustworthyness*) fiducia *f*; considerazione *f*; (*bank*) attivo *m*. **credit balance** saldo attivo *m*. **credit card**

carta di credito *f*. *v* (*comm*) accreditare; (*have faith in*) credere, prestar fede a; (*ascribe*) attribuire. **creditable** *adj* degno di lode, che fa onore. **creditor** *n* creditore, -trice *m*, *f*.

**credulous** ['kredjuləs] *adj* credulo, ingenuo.

**creed** [kri:d] *n* credo *m*, professione di fede *f*.

***creep** [kri:p] *v* strisciare, insinuarsi; (*plants*) arrampicarsi. **creeper** *n* (*plant*) pianta rampicante *f*. **creepy** *adj* che dà i brividi.

**cremate** [kri'meit] *v* cremare. **cremation** *n* cremazione *f*. **crematorium** *n* crematorio *m*.

**crept** [krept] *V* creep.

**crescent** ['kresnt] *n* mezzaluna *f*.

**cress** [kres] *n* crescione *m*. **mustard and cress** crescione inglese *m*, agretto *m*. **watercress** *n* crescione d'acqua *m*.

**crest** [krest] *n* cresta *f*, ciuffo *m*; (*heraldry, helmet*) cimiero *m*. **crestfallen** *adj* mortificato.

**crevice** ['krevis] *n* crepa *f*, fessura *f*.

**crew** [kru:] *n* equipaggio *m*, squadra *f*.

**crib** [krib] *n* (*rel*) presepio *m*; (*bed*) lettino *m*; (*manger*) mangiatoia *f*; (*coll*) bigino *m*. *v* plagiare.

**cricket¹** ['krikit] *n* (*insect*) grillo *m*.

**cricket²** ['krikit] *n* (*sport*) cricket *m*.

**crime** [kraim] *n* delitto *m*, reato *m*. **criminal** *n*(*m+f*), *adj* criminale.

**crimson** ['krimzn] *adj* cremisi.

**cringe** [krindʒ] *v* comportarsi in modo servile.

**crinkle** ['kriŋkl] *n* grinza *f*. *v* raggrinzare.

**cripple** ['kripl] *n* storpio, -a *m*, *f*; invalido, -a *m*, *f*. *v* storpiare, mutilare, paralizzare.

**crisis** ['kraisis] *n*, *pl* **-ses** crisi *f invar*.

**crisp** [krisp] *adj* (*lively*) nitido; (*bracing*) invigorante; (*firm, fresh*) fresco; (*brittle*) croccante; (*crinkled*) crespo. **crisps** *pl n* patatine fritte croccanti *f pl*.

**criterion** [krai'tiəriən] *n*, *pl* **-ria** criterio *m*.

**criticize** ['kritisaiz] *v* criticare, esprimere un giudizio su. **critic** *n* critico *m*. **critical** *adj* critico. **criticism** *n* critica *f*; (*philosophy*) criticismo *m*. **critique** *n* saggio critico *m*.

**croak** [krouk] *v* gracchiare, gracidare; (*grumble*) brontolare. *n* gracchiare *m*, gracchio *m*, gracidio *m*.

**Croatia** [krou'eiʃə] n Croazia f. **Croatian** n(m+f), adj croato.

**crochet** ['krouʃei] v lavorare all'uncinetto.

**crockery** ['krokəri] n vasellame m, stoviglie f pl.

**crocodile** ['krokə,dail] n coccodrillo m.

**crocus** ['kroukəs] n croco m.

**crook** [kruk] n (hook) uncino m; (bishop's) pastorale m; (shepherd's) bastone da pastore m; (criminal) truffatore, -trice m, f. v piegare, curvare.

**crooked** ['krukid] adj (bent) piegato, storto; disonesto.

**crop** [krop] n (produce) raccolto m; (riding) frusta f; (gullet) gozzo m. v (clip hair) tagliar corto; (trees) mozzare; (cut grain, etc.) mietere. **come a cropper** far fiasco.

**croquet** ['kroukei] n croquet m invar.

**cross** [kros] n croce f. adj arrabbiato. **be cross** arrabbiarsi. v incrociare; (street, etc.) attraversare; (threshold) varcare; (cheque) sbarrare; (annoy) ostacolare. **cross oneself** segnarsi. **cross one's mind** venire in mente a uno. **cross out** cancellare. **cross-examine** v sottoporre a interrogatorio. **cross-examination** n interrogatorio m. **cross-eyed** adj strabico. **cross-fire** n fuoco incrociato m **cross-legged** adj a gambe accavallate. **cross-reference** n richiamo m. **crossroads** n crocevia m, incrocio m. **crossword** n cruciverba m invar, parole incrociate f pl. **crossing** n traversata f.

**crotchet** ['krotʃit] n (music) semiminima f; (hook) uncinetto m. **crotchety** adj irritabile.

**crouch** [krautʃ] v ranicchiarsi.

**crow¹** [krou] n (bird) corvo m, cornacchia f. **as the crow flies** in linea diretta. **crow's nest** coffa f. **crow's foot** ruga f, zampa di gallina f.

**crow²** [krou] v cantare, esultare; (boast) vantarsi, trionfare.

**crowd** [kraud] n folla f, massa f, compagnia f. v affollare, ammassare. **crowded** adj affollato, stipato, pieno zeppo.

**crown** [kraun] n corona f; (hat) cocuzzolo m; (head) calotta f; (road) colmo m. **crown-prince** n principe ereditario m. v incoronare; (reward) ricompensare; (tooth) mettere una corona a. **to crown it all** come se non bastasse.

**crucial** ['kru:ʃəl] adj decisivo, critico.

**crucify** ['kru:si,fai] v crocifiggere, mettere in croce; tormentare, mortificare. **crucifix** n crocifisso m. **crucifixion** n crocifissione f.

**crude** [kru:d] adj (rough, vulgar) grossolano, rozzo, volgare; (unrefined) grezzo.

**cruel** ['kru:əl] adj crudele. **be cruel to** maltrattare. **cruelty** n crudeltà f.

**cruise** [kru:z] n crociera f. **go on a cruise** fare una crociera.

**crumb** [krʌm] n briciola f.

**crumble** ['krʌmbl] v sgretolare; (collapse) crollare. **crumbly** adj friabile.

**crumple** ['krʌmpl] v sgualcire, sgualcirsi; (collapse) sfasciarsi, accasciarsi.

**crunch** [krʌntʃ] v sgretolare, sgranocchiare. n scricchiolio m; (critical point) momento di crisi m.

**crusade** [kru:'seid] n crociata f. **crusader** n crociato m.

**crush** [krʌʃ] v schiacciare, frantumare; (destroy) annientare. n calca f, ressa f. **have a crush on** prendersi una cotta per. **crusher** n frantoio m.

**crust** [krʌst] n crosta f, corteccia f. **crusty** adj crostoso; (surly) burbero.

**crutch** [krʌtʃ] n gruccia f, stampella f.

**crux** [krʌks] n **the crux of the matter** il nodo della questione m.

**cry** [krai] n urlo m, strillo m, lamento m. v urlare, gridare; (weep) piangere.

**crypt** [kript] n cripta f. **cryptic** adj ambiguo, misterioso.

**crystal** ['kristl] n cristallo m. **crystallization** n cristallizzazione f. **crystallize** v cristallizzare.

**cub** [kʌb] n cucciolo m.

**cube** [kju:b] n cubo m. v elevare al cubo. **cubic** adj cubico.

**cubicle** ['kju:bikl] n stanzino m; (changing-room) spogliatoio m.

**cuckold** ['kʌkould] n cornuto m. v fare le corna a.

**cuckoo** ['kuku:] n cuculo m, cucù m.

**cucumber** [kju'kʌmbə] n cetriolo m.

**cuddle** ['kʌdl] v coccolare, abbracciare teneramente. n abbraccio tenero m.

**cue¹** [kju:] n (theatre) battuta d'entrata f; (hint) spunto m.

**cue²** [kju:] n (billiards) stecca f.

**cuff¹** [kʌf] n (shirt) polsino m. **cuff-links** pl n gemelli m pl.

**cuff²** [kʌf] n (hit) schiaffo m, sberla f.

*v* schiaffeggiare.

**culinary** ['kʌlinəri] *adj* culinario, gastronomico.

**culminate** ['kʌlmi‚neit] *v* concludersi. **culmination** *n* culmine *m*.

**culprit** ['kʌlprit] *n* colpevole *m, f*.

**cult** [kʌlt] *n* culto *m*.

**cultivate** ['kʌlti‚veit] *v* coltivare. **cultivation** *n* coltivazione *f*, coltura *f*.

**culture** ['kʌltʃə] *n* cultura *f*; (*land, plants*) coltura *f*. **cultural** *adj* culturale. **cultured** *adj* colto.

**cumbersome** ['kʌmbəsəm] *adj* ingombrante.

**cunning** ['kʌniŋ] *adj* scaltro, astuto. *n* astuzia *f*, scaltrezza *f*.

**cup** [kʌp] *n* tazza *f*; (*sport*) coppa *f*.

**cupboard** ['kʌbəd] *n* armadio *m*, credenza *f*. **cupboard love** amore interessato *m*.

**curate** ['kjuərət] *n* curato *m*, parroco *m*.

**curator** [kjuə'reitə] *n* direttore, -trice di museo *m, f*; curatore, -trice *m, f*.

**curb** [kə:b] *v* frenare.

**curdle** ['kə:dl] *v* cagliare, cagliarsi; (*blood*) gelare.

**cure** [kjuə] *n* cura *f*, rimedio *m*. *v* sanare, guarire; (*food*) conservare; (*salt*) salare; (*smoke*) affumicare.

**curfew** ['kə:fju:] *n* coprifuoco *m*.

**curious** ['kjuəriəs] *adj* (*odd*) strano, curioso, insolito; (*inquisitive*) curioso.

**curl** [kə:l] *n* ricciolo *m*. *v* arricciare, arrotolare; (*lip*) torcere. **curl up** rannicchiarsi; (*animal*) accucciarsi. **curler** *n* bigodino *m*.

**currant** ['kʌrənt] *n* ribes *m invar*; (*dried*) uva passa *f*, uvetta *f*.

**currency** ['kʌrənsi] *n* decorrenza *f*; (*money*) valuta *f*, moneta legale *f*.

**current** ['kʌrənt] *n* corrente *f*. *adj* corrente, comune.

**curriculum** [kə'rikjuləm] *n* curriculum *m*.

**curry** ['kʌri] *n* curry *m invar*. *v* **curry favour** ingraziarsi.

**curse** [kə:s] *n* (*oath*) bestemmia *f*; (*evil*) maledizione *f*. *v* bestemmiare, maledire. **be cursed with** essere afflitto da.

**cursor** ['kə:sə] *n* cursore *m*.

**curt** [kə:t] *adj* brusco.

**curtail** [kə:'teil] *v* limitare, ridurre.

**curtain** ['kə:tn] *n* cortina *f*; (*cloth*) tenda *f*, tendina *f*; (*theatre*) sipario *m*.

**curtsy** ['kə:tsi] *n* inchino *m*. *v* inchinarsi.

**curve** [kə:v] *n* curva *f*, svolta *f*. *v* curvare, svoltare.

**cushion** ['kuʃən] *n* cuscino *m*; (*billiards*) sponda *f*. *v* smorzare, assorbire.

**custody** ['kʌstədi] *n* custodia *f*, guardia *f*. **take into custody** arrestare. **custodian** *n* guardiano *m*, custode *m, f*.

**custom** ['kʌstəm] *n* costume *m*, usanza *f*, abitudine *f*. **customs** *n* dogana *f*. **customs officer** doganiere, -a *m, f*. **customary** *adj* abituale, solito. **customer** *n* cliente *m, f*.

**\*cut** [kʌt] *n* taglio *m*, incisione *f*; (*wound*) ferita *f*. *v* tagliare, incidere; (*wound*) ferire; (*cards*) alzare le carte. **cut down** ridurre; (*fell*) abbattere. **cut off** tagliar via; (*suspend*) sospendere. **cut out** ritagliare; omettere; (*elec*) interrompere. **cut it out!** piantala! **cut price** prezzo ridotto *m*. **cut-throat** *adj* spietato.

**cute** [kju:t] *adj* grazioso, ingegnoso.

**cutlery** ['kʌtləri] *n* posate *f pl*, posateria *f*; (*knives*) coltelleria *f*.

**cutlet** ['kʌtlit] *n* costoletta *f*, cotoletta *f*.

**cutting** ['kʌtiŋ] *adj* tagliente. *n* (*newspaper*) ritaglio *m*; (*plant*) margotta *f*; (*railway*) trincea *f*.

**cyberspace** ['saibəspeis] *n* cyber-spazio *m*.

**cycle** ['saikl] *n* ciclo *m*, periodo *m*; (*bicycle*) bicicletta *f*. *v* andare in bicicletta. **cyclic** *adj* ciclico. **cycling** *n* ciclismo *m*. **cyclist** *n* ciclista *m, f*.

**cyclone** ['saikloun] *n* ciclone *m*.

**cylinder** ['silində] *n* cilindro *m*; (*revolver*) tamburo *m*; (*printing*) rullo *m*; (*gas*) bombola *f*.

**cymbal** ['simbəl] *n* cembalo *m*.

**cynic** ['sinik] *n* cinico, -a *m, f*. **cynical** *adj* cinico. **cynicism** *n* cinismo *m*.

**cypress** ['saiprəs] *n* cipresso *m*.

**Cyprus** ['saiprəs] *n* Cipro *m*. **Cypriot** *n* (*m+f*), *adj* cipriota.

**cyst** [sist] *n* cisti *f*.

**Czech Republic** *n* Repubblica Ceca *f*. **Czech** *n*, *adj* ceco, -a.

# D

**dab** [dab] v toccare leggermente; applicare. n (*small quantity*) tocco m; (*light blow*) colpetto m.

**dabble** ['dabl] v (*dip, paddle*) guazzare. **dabble in** dilettarsi a; fare da dilettante.

**dad** [dad] n babbo m, papà m.

**daffodil** ['dafədil] n narciso m.

**daft** [da:ft] adj scemo, sciocco.

**dagger** ['dagə] n pugnale m, stiletto m. **be at daggers drawn** essere ai ferri corti.

**daily** ['deili] adj giornaliero, quotidiano. n giornale m; (*maid*) domestica a giornata f. adv ogni giorno, quotidianamente.

**dainty** ['deinti] adj delicato, squisito.

**dairy** ['deəri] n latteria f. **dairy produce** latticini m pl.

**daisy** ['deizi] n margherita f.

**dam** [dam] n diga f, argine m. v sbarrare, arginare.

**damage** ['damidʒ] n danno m, guasto m; (*law*) indennizzo m. v danneggiare, guastare, nuocere. **damaging** adj dannoso.

**damn** [dam] v dannare, maledire. interj maledizione! n (*negligible amount*) bel niente m.

**damp** [damp] adj umido, madido. n umido m. v also **dampen** (*moisten*) inumidire; (*dull*) smorzare, deprimere. **damper** n (*furnace*) valvola di tiraggio f; (*elec*) smorzatore m; (*music*) sordina f.

**damson** ['damzən] n (*fruit*) susina selvatica f; (*tree*) susino selvatico m.

**dance** [da:ns] n danza f, ballo m. v danzare, ballare. **dancer** n danzatore, -trice m, f; ballerino, -a m, f.

**dandelion** ['dandi,laiən] n dente di leone m.

**dandruff** ['dandrəf] n forfora f.

**danger** ['deindʒə] n pericolo m. **dangerous** adj pericoloso.

**dangle** ['dangl] v (far) ciondolare or dondolare.

**Danish** ['deiniʃ] nm, adj danese. **Dane** n danese m, f.

**dare** [deə] v (*be bold*) osare; (*challenge*) sfidare. **I dare say** suppongo; probabilmente; (*not deny*) non nego.

**daring** ['deəriŋ] adj audace. n audacia f.

**dark** [da:k] n also **darkness** buio m, oscurità f. adj buio, oscuro, cupo. **darken** v scurire, offuscare, rabbuiarsi.

**darling** ['da:liŋ] n tesoro m, gioia f, favorito, -a m, f. adj carissimo, amatissimo.

**darn** [da:n] v rammendare. n rammendo m, rammendatura f.

**dart** [da:t] n dardo m, freccia f. v (*move swiftly*) balzare, slanciarsi, precipitarsi; (*throw*) lanciare.

**dash** [daʃ] v buttare, urtare; (*spoil*) frustrare; (*rush*) scappare. n spruzzo m; (*rush*) slancio m; (*drink*) goccio m; (*pinch*) pizzico m; (*printing*) lineetta f. **dashboard** n cruscotto m.

**data** ['deitə] pl n dati m pl, elementi m pl. **database** n banca dati f. **data processing** elaborazione di dati f.

**date¹** [deit] n (*calendar*) data f; (*appointment*) appuntamento m. v datare, fare appuntamento con. **date from** risalire a. **out of date** fuori moda, antiquato. **up to date** aggiornato.

**date²** [deit] n (*fruit*) dattero m.

**daughter** ['do:tə] n figlia f, figliola f. **daughter-in-law** n nuora f.

**daunt** [do:nt] v intimidire.

**dawdle** ['do:dl] v sprecar tempo, bighellonare. **dawdler** n fannullone, -a m, f; bighellone, -a m, f.

**dawn** [do:n] n alba f, aurora f; (*beginning*) inizio m. v albeggiare; (*appear*) apparire, manifestarsi.

**day** [dei] n giorno m, giornata f. **by day** di giorno. **daybreak** n alba f, spuntar del giorno m. **daylight** n luce del giorno f. **every other day** un giorno sì e uno no. **the day before yesterday** ieri l'altro. **the day after tomorrow** dopodomani.

**daydream** ['deidri:m] v sognare ad occhi aperti, fantasticare. n sogno ad occhi aperti m, fantasticheria f.

**daze** [deiz] v stordire, sbalordire. n stupore m.

**dazzle** ['dazl] v abbagliare.

**dead** [ded] adj morto, defunto; (*coll: absolute*) assoluto, completo. **dead drunk** ubriaco fradicio. **deadline** n scadenza f. **deadlock** n punto morto m; incaglio m. **dead slow** a passo d'uomo. **deaden** v attutire. **deadly** adj mortale.

**deaf** [def] adj sordo. **turn a deaf ear** fare orecchi da mercante. **deaf-mute** n sordomuto, -a m, f. **deafen** v rendere sordo, intontire. **deafness** n sordità f.

*****deal** [di:l] v (cards) dare le carte. **deal in** commerciare in. **deal with** occuparsi di; (things) trattare di; (people) avere rapporti con. n (business) affare m; (agreement) accordo m; (amount) quantità f. **dealer** n commerciante m, f; (retail) dettagliante m, f; (wholesale) grossista m, f.

**dealt** [delt] V **deal**.

**dean** [di:n] n (university) preside di facoltà m, f; (rel) decano m.

**dear** [diə] adj caro. **oh dear!** ahimè! Dio mio!

**death** [deθ] n morte f. **death certificate** certificato di morte m. **death duties** tassa di successione f sing. **death warrant** sentenza di morte f. **deathly** adj, adv mortale; cadaverico.

**debase** [di'beis] v degradare, svalutare.

**debate** [di'beit] v dibattere, discutere. n dibattito m, discussione f.

**debit** ['debit] n debito m; (accounts) dare m. v addebitare.

**debris** ['deibri:] n detrito m, macerie f pl.

**debt** [det] n debito m; (obligation) obbligo m. **debt collector** n esattore, -trice m, f. **debtor** n debitore, -trice m, f.

**decade** ['dekeid] n decennio m.

**decadent** ['dekədənt] adj decadente.

**decaffeinated** [di'kafineitid] adj decaffeinato.

**decant** [di'kant] v travasare. **decanter** n caraffa f.

**decay** [di'kei] v deperire, putrefare, putrefarsi, andare in rovina; (teeth) cariare. n sfacelo m, rovina f, deperimento m.

**deceased** [di'si:st] n, adj defunto, -a. **decease** n decesso m.

**deceit** [di'si:t] n inganno m, truffa f. **deceitful** adj falso, perfido.

**deceive** [di'si:v] v ingannare, imbrogliare, illudersi.

**December** [di'sembə] n dicembre m.

**decent** ['di:sənt] adj (proper) decente; (fitting) decoroso; (fair) discreto; (respectable) bravo. **decency** n decenza f, decoro m.

**deceptive** [di'septiv] adj ingannevole, illusorio. **deception** n inganno m, imbroglio m.

**decibel** ['desi,bel] n decibel m invar.

**decentralization** [di:,sentrəlai'zeiʃn] n decentramento m.

**decide** [di'said] v decidere, decidersi. **decided** adj deciso, risoluto.

**deciduous** [di'sidjuəs] adj deciduo.

**decimal** ['desiməl] nm, adj decimale.

**decipher** [di'saifə] v decifrare.

**decision** [di'siʒən] n decisione f. **decisive** adj decisivo.

**deck** [dek] n (naut) ponte m, coperta f; (cards) mazzo m. v ornare. **deck-chair** n sedia a sdraio f.

**declare** [di'kleə] v dichiarare, proclamare. **declaration** n dichiarazione f, proclama m.

**decline** [di'klain] v (refuse) rifiutare; (gramm) declinare; (deteriorate) deperire. n (gradual loss) declino m, deterioramento m; decadenza f.

**decode** [di:'koud] v decodificare.

**decompose** [,di:kəm'pouz] v decomporre. **decomposition** n decomposizione f, putrefazione f.

**decorate** ['dekə,reit] v decorare, ornare; (house) verniciare. **decoration** n decorazione f, ornamento m. **decorator** n (interior) arredatore, -trice m, f; (building) decoratore, -trice m, f, pittore, -trice m, f. **decorous** adj decoroso. **decorum** n decoro m.

**decoy** ['di:koi] n richiamo m, uccello da richiamo m, esca f; (person) adescatore, -trice m, f.

**decrease** [di'kri:s] v diminuire. n diminuzione f, ribasso m.

**decree** [di'kri:] n decreto m, ordinanza f. v decretare.

**decrepit** [di'krepit] adj decrepito.

**dedicate** ['dedi,keit] v dedicare. **dedication** n dedicazione f; (book) dedica f.

**deduce** [di'dju:s] v dedurre, inferire. **deduction** n (inference) deduzione f.

**deduct** [di'dʌkt] v dedurre, sottrarre. **deduction** n (subtraction) sottrazione f.

**deed** [di:d] n fatto m, azione f; (law) atto notarile m, strumento m; (undertaking) impresa f. **good deed** buona azione f.

**deep** [di:p] adj profondo, alto; (colour) scuro, cupo. **deep-rooted** or **deep-seated** adj radicato. **deepen** v approfondire.

**deep-freeze** v surgelare. n congelatore m, freezer m invar.

**deer** [diə] n (roe) capriolo m; (fallow) daino m.

**deface** [di'feis] v sfregiare, mutilare.

**defamatory** [di'fæmətəri] adj diffamatorio. **defamation** n diffamazione f, calunnia f.

**default** [di'fɔːlt] v rendersi contumace. n **by default** in contumacia. **in default of** in difetto di.

**defeat** [di'fiːt] n sconfitta f, disfatta f. v sconfiggere. **defeatism** n disfattismo m. **defeatist** n disfattista m, f.

**defect¹** ['diːfekt] n difetto m, mancanza f. **defective** adj difettoso, imperfetto; (gramm) difettivo.

**defect²** [di'fekt] v disertare. **defection** n diserzione f, defezione f.

**defend** [di'fend] v difendere, proteggere. **defence** n difesa f. **defenceless** adj indifeso, senza difesa. **defendant** n imputato, -a m, f. **defender** n difensore m.

**defensive** [di'fensiv] adj difensivo. n difensiva f. **be on the defensive** stare sulla difesa.

**defer¹** [di'fəː] v (put off) rimandare, rinviare.

**defer²** [di'fəː] v (yield to) sottoporsi. **deferential** adj rispettoso, deferente.

**deficient** [di'fiʃənt] adj deficiente, incompleto, insufficiente. **deficiency** n deficienza f, mancanza f, carenza f.

**deficit** ['defisit] n deficit m invar, disavanzo m.

**define** [di'fain] v definire, precisare. **definition** n definizione f.

**definite** ['definit] adj definito, determinato, preciso.

**deflate** [di'fleit] v sgonfiare; (comm) deflazionare. **deflation** n sgonfiamento m, deflazione f.

**deflect** [di'flekt] v deflettere, deviare. **deflection** n deviazione f.

**deflect** [di'flekt] v .

**deform** [di'fɔːm] v deformare. **deformity** or **deformation** n deformazione f.

**defraud** [di'frɔːd] v frodare, defraudare.

**defray** [di'frei] v **defray expenses** rimborsare le spese.

**defrost** [diː'frost] v scongelare.

**deft** [deft] adj destro, lesto. **deftness** n destrezza f, agilità f.

**defunct** [di'fʌŋkt] adj defunto.

**defuse** [diː'fjuːz] v disinnescare.

**defy** [di'fai] v sfidare, provocare. **defiance** n (resistance) sfida f; dispetto m. **in defi-**

**ance of** a dispetto di. **defiant** adj ribelle, ricalcitrante.

**degenerate** [di'dʒenərit; v di'dʒenəreit] adj degenerato, perverso. v degenerare. **degeneracy** or **degeneration** n degenerazione f.

**degrade** [di'greid] v degradare. **degrading** adj degradante.

**degree** [di'griː] n grado m; (diploma) titolo di studio m, laurea f.

**dehydrate** [diː'haidreit] v disidratare. **dehydration** n disidratazione f.

**de-icer** [diː'aisə] n dispositivo antighiaccio m.

**deign** [dein] v degnarsi.

**deity** ['diːəti] n divinità f, deità f.

**dejected** [di'dʒektid] adj avvilito, abbattuto.

**delay** [di'lei] n ritardo m, indugio m. v ritardare, differire.

**delegate** ['deligit; v 'deligeit] n delegato, -a m, f. v delegare, autorizzare. **delegation** n delegazione f.

**delete** [di'liːt] v espungere. **deletion** n cancellatura f, espunzione f.

**deliberate** [di'libərət; v di'libəreit] adj (intentional) voluto; (unhurried) misurato; (carefully considered) ponderato. v deliberare, riflettere. **deliberation** n riflessione f, deliberazione f.

**delicate** ['delikət] adj delicato, fine; (sensitive) sensibile. **delicacy** n delicatezza f; sensibilità f; (food) leccornia f.

**delicatessen** [ˌdelikə'tesn] n ghiottonerie pl.

**delicious** [di'liʃəs] adj delizioso; (food) squisito.

**delight** [di'lait] n delizia f, diletto m. v dilettare. **delight in** rallegrarsi di. **delighted** adj ben lieto. **delightful** adj delizioso, incantevole, simpaticissimo.

**delinquency** [di'liŋkwənsi] n delinquenza f. **delinquent** n (m+f), adj delinquente.

**delirious** [di'liriəs] adj (feverish) delirante; (wildly excited) ebbro.

**deliver** [di'livə] v (hand over) recapitare, consegnare; (set free) liberare; (save) salvare; (speech) pronunciare. **deliverance** n liberazione f. **delivery** n consegna f; (birth) parto m; (diction) dizione f.

**delta** ['deltə] n delta m.

**delude** [di'luːd] v deludere, deludersi. **delusion** n delusione f.

**deluge** ['delju:dʒ] *n* diluvio *m*. *v* diluviare.

**delve** [delv] *v* (*dig*) scavare; (*research*) far ricerche.

**demand** [di'ma:nd] *v* esigere, pretendere. *n* pretesa *f*, richiesta *f*. **in demand** ricercato. **on demand** su richiesta. **demanding** *adj* esigente.

**demented** [di'mentid] *adj* demente, impazzito.

**democracy** [di'mokrəsi] *n* democrazia *f*. **democrat** *n* democratico, -a *m*, *f*. **democratic** *adj* democratico.

**demolish** [di'moliʃ] *v* demolire, abbattere. **demolition** *n* demolizione *f*.

**demon** ['di:mən] *n* demonio *m*, diavolo *m*.

**demonstrate** ['demən,streit] *v* dimostrare. **demonstrable** *adj* dimostrabile. **demonstration** *n* dimostrazione *f*; (*proof*) prova *f*; (*meeting*) manifestazione *f*. **demonstrative** *adj* dimostrativo; (*feeling*) espansivo.

**demoralize** [di'morə,laiz] *v* demoralizzare, scoraggiare.

**demure** [di'mjuə] *adj* modesto, schivo.

**den** [den] *n* tana *f*.

**denial** [di'naiəl] *n* (*contradiction*) smentita *f*; (*negation*) diniego *m*; (*refusal*) rifiuto *m*.

**denim** [di'nim] *n* tela pesante *f*.

**Denmark** ['denma:k] *n* Danimarca *f*.

**denomination** [di,nomi'neiʃən] *n* denominazione *f*; (*belief*) setta *f*, religione *f*; (*money*) taglio *m*. **denominator** *n* denominatore *m*.

**denote** [di'nout] *v* denotare, indicare.

**denounce** [di'nauns] *v* denunciare; (*openly accuse*) inveire contro.

**dense** [dens] *adj* denso, fitto. **density** *n* densità *f*.

**dent** [dent] *n* tacca *f*, ammaccatura *f*. *v* intaccare, ammaccare.

**dental** ['dentl] *adj* dentale; (*of dentistry*) dentistico.

**dentist** ['dentist] *n* dentista *m*, *f*. **dentistry** *n* odontoiatria *f*.

**denture** ['dentʃə] *n* dentiera *f*.

**denude** [di'nju:d] *v* denudare, privare.

**denunciation** [dinʌnsi'eiʃən] *n* denuncia *f*.

**deny** [di'nai] *v* negare, smentire. **deny oneself** privarsi di, fare a meno di.

**deodorant** [di:'oudərənt] *nm*, *adj* deodorante.

**depart** [di'pa:t] *v* (*leave*) partire; (*diverge*)

deviare. **departure** *n* partenza *f*, deviazione *f*.

**department** [di'pa:tmənt] *n* reparto *m*. **department store** grande magazzino *m*.

**depend** [di'pend] *v* dipendere, fare assegnamento. **depend on** dipendere da, fare assegnamento su. **dependable** *adj* fidato. **dependence** *n* dipendenza *f*. **dependent** *n(m+f)*, *adj* dipendente.

**depict** [di'pikt] *v* rappresentare, descrivere.

**deplete** [di'plit] *v* esaurire, vuotare.

**deplore** [di'plo:] *v* biasimare, disapprovare. **deplorable** *adj* riprensibile, biasimevole.

**deport** [di'po:t] *v* deportare, espellere. **deportation** *n* deportazione *f*, espulsione *f*.

**depose** [di'pouz] *v* (*dismiss*) deporre; (*witness*) testimoniare. **deposition** *n* deposizione *f*, testimonianza *f*.

**deposit** [di'pozit] *v* depositare, posare. *n* deposito *m*; (*security*) cauzione *f*, pegno *m*. **deposit account** conto vincolato *m*.

**depot** ['depou] *n* deposito *m*, magazzino *m*, parco *m*.

**deprave** [di'preiv] *v* corrompere, depravare.

**depreciate** [di'pri:ʃi,eit] *v* deprezzare; (*money*) svalutare; (*belittle*) screditare, denigrare. **depreciation** *n* deprezzamento *m*, svalutazione *f*; discredito *m*, denigrazione *f*.

**depress** [di'pres] *v* deprimere. **depressed** *adj* depresso, abbattuto; (*market*) basso. **depressing** *adj* deprimente, triste. **depression** *n* depressione *f*; (*comm*) crisi *f invar*.

**deprive** [di'praiv] *v* privare. **deprivation** *n* privazione *f*.

**depth** [depθ] *n* profondità *f*, altezza *f*. **be out of one's depth** non essere all'altezza.

**deputy** ['depjuti] *n* delegato *m*, deputato *m*. **deputation** *n* deputazione *f*.

**derail** [di'reil] *v* uscire dalle rotaie, deragliare. **derailment** *n* deragliamento *m*.

**derelict** ['derilikt] *adj* derelitto, abbandonato.

**deride** [di'raid] *v* deridere, schernire. **derision** *n* derisione *f*, scherno *m*. **derisive** *or* **derisory** *adj* irrisorio, derisivo.

**derive** [di'raiv] *v* derivare, provenire. **derivation** *n* derivazione *f*, provenienza *f*, origine *f*.

**derogatory** [di'rogətəri] *adj* sprezzante, diffamante.

**descend** [di'send] *v* scendere; (*come from*) derivare, discendere. **descent** *n* discesa *f*;

(*ancestry*) discendenza *f*, lignaggio *m*.
**descendant** *n* discendente *m*, *f*.
**describe** [di'skraib] *v* descrivere. **description** *n* descrizione *f*.
**desert**[1] ['dezət] *n* deserto *m*.
**desert**[2] [di'zə:t] *v* disertare, abbandonare. **deserter** *n* disertore *m*. **desertion** *n* diserzione *f*, abbandono *m*.
**desert**[3] [di'zə:t] *n* **get one's just deserts** ricevere quel che si merita.
**deserve** [di'zə:v] *v* meritare, essere degno di.
**design** [di'zain] *v* disegnare; (*plan*) progettare; (*intend*) destinare. *n* disegno *m*, progetto *m*; (*intention*) proposito *m*. **have designs on** avere delle mire su. **designer** *n* stilista *m*, *f*; disegnatore (grafico) *m*, progettista *m*, *f*, modellista *m*, *f*.
**designate** ['dezig,neit] *v* designare. *adj* designato.
**designer** ; progettista.
**desire** [di'zaiə] *v* desiderare, bramare. *n* (*wish*) desiderio *m*; (*craving*) brama *f*; passione *f*. **desirable** *adj* desiderabile.
**desk** [desk] *n* scrivania *f*; (*school*) banco *m*; (*cash*) cassa *f*.
**desolate** ['desələt] *adj* desolato; (*barren*) deserto; (*lonely*) solitario; (*sad*) afflitto, rattristato.
**despair** [di'speə] *n* disperazione *f*. *v* disperare.
**desperate** ['despərət] *adj* disperato; (*hopeless*) senza speranza. **desperation** *n* disperazione *f*.
**despise** [di'spaiz] *v* disprezzare.
**despite** [di'spait] *prep* malgrado.
**despondent** [di'spondənt] *adj* accasciato, depresso.
**despot** ['despot] *n* despota *m*, *f*.
**dessert** [di'zə:t] *n* dessert *m invar*.
**destine** ['destin] *v* destinare. **destination** *n* destinazione *f*, recapito *m*. **destiny** *n* destino *m*, sorte *f*.
**destitute** ['destitju:t] *adj* indigente.
**destroy** [di'stroi] *v* distruggere. **destruction** *n* distruzione *f*.
**detach** [di'tat∫] *v* staccare, distaccare. **detached** *adj* staccato; (*house*) isolato; (*aloof*) distaccato; (*objective*) obiettivo. **detachment** *n* distacco *m*; (*army*) distaccamento *m*; indifferenza *f*; obiettività *f*.
**detail** ['di:teil] *n* particolare *m*, dettaglio *m*.

*v* dettagliare, descrivere minutamente.
**detain** [di'tein] *v* detenere; (*delay*) tratenere. **detainee** *n* detenuto, -a *m*, *f*; carcerato, -a *m*, *f*.
**detect** [di'tekt] *v* scoprire, individuare. **detection** *n* scoperta *f*. **detective** *n* detective *m invar*, investigatore, -trice *m*, *f*. **detective novel** romanzo poliziesco *m*, romanzo giallo *m*.
**détente** [dei'tã:nt] *n* distensione *f*.
**detention** [di'ten∫ən] *n* detenzione *f*.
**deter** [di'tə:] *v* dissuadere, scoraggiare. **deterrent** *n* deterrente *m*.
**detergent** [di'tə:dʒənt] *nm, adj* detergente, detersivo.
**deteriorate** [di'tiəriə,reit] *v* deteriorare, peggiorare. **deterioration** *n* deterioramento *m*, peggioramento *m*.
**determine** [di'tə:min] *v* determinare, stabilire; decidere. **determination** *n* determinazione *f*, risolutezza *f*. **determined** *adj* determinato, risoluto.
**detest** [di'test] *v* detestare, odiare. **detestable** *adj* detestabile, odioso.
**detonate** ['detə,neit] *v* detonare, esplodere. **detonation** *n* detonazione *f*, esplosione *f*. **detonator** *n* detonatore *m*.
**detour** ['di:tuə] *n* deviazione *f*.
**detract** [di'trakt] *v* detrarre.
**detriment** ['detrimənt] *n* **to the detriment of** a scapito di.
**deuce** [dju:s] *n* (*cards*) due *m*; (*tennis*) quaranta pari.
**devalue** [di:'valju:] *v* svalutare. **devaluation** *n* svalutazione *f*.
**devastate** ['devə,steit] *v* devastare, rovinare. **devastating** *adj* devastatore; (*highly effective*) schiacciante.
**develop** [di'veləp] *v* sviluppare; elaborare; (*land*) usare come terreno da costruzione. **develop into** diventare. **developer** *n* (*phot*) sviluppatore *m*; (*land*) persona che apporta migliorie *f*. **development** *n* sviluppo *m*; evoluzione *f*; (*land*) valorizzazione di terreno *f*.
**deviate** ['di:vi,eit] *v* deviare. **deviation** *n* deviazione *f*.
**device** [di'vais] *n* (*contrivance*) congegno *m*; (*crafty scheme*) schema *m*, espediente *m*; (*heraldry*) motto *m*, divisa *f*.
**devil** ['devl] *n* diavolo *m*, demonio *m*. **devilish** *adj* diabolico, infernale.

**devious** ['di:viəs] *adj* indiretto, tortuoso.

**devise** [di'vaiz] *v* escogitare, progettare.

**devoid** [di'void] *adj* privo.

**devolution** [ˌdi:və'lu:ʃən] *n* devoluzione *f*.

**devote** [di'vout] *v* dedicare, consacrare. **devoted** *adj* devoto, affezionato. **devotion** *n* devozione *f*; (*prayer*) preghiere *f pl*.

**devour** [di'vuə] *v* divorare.

**devout** [di'vaut] *adj* devoto, pio, fervente.

**dew** [dju:] *n* rugiada *f*.

**dextrous** ['dekstrəs] *adj* destro, abile. **dexterity** *n* destrezza *f*.

**diabetes** [ˌdiəə'bi:ti:z] *n* diabete *m*. **diabetic** *n*, *adj* diabetico.

**diagnose** [ˌdiəəg'nouz] *v* fare la diagnosi. **diagnosis** *n*, *pl* **-ses** diagnosi *f*. **diagnostic** *adj* diagnostico.

**diagonal** [dai'agənəl] *nf*, *adj* diagonale.

**diagram** ['daiəˌgram] *n* diagramma *m*.

**dial** ['daiəl] *n* (*watch*) quadrante *m*; (*telephone*) disco combinatore *m*. *v* (*number*) comporre.

**dialect** ['daiəlekt] *n* dialetto *m*.

**dialogue** ['daiəlog] *n* dialogo (*pl* -ghi) *m*.

**diameter** [dai'amitə] *n* diametro *m*.

**diamond** ['daiəmənd] *n* diamante *m*. **diamonds** *pl n* (*cards*) quadri *m pl*.

**diaper** ['daiəpə] *n* (*US*) pannolino (per neonati) *m*.

**diaphragm** ['daiəˌfram] *n* diaframma *m*.

**diarrhoea** [ˌdaiə'riə] *n* diarrea *f*.

**diary** ['daiəri] *n* diario *m*, agenda *f*.

**dice** [dais] *n* dado *m*.

**dictate** [dik'teit] *v* dettare, imporre. *n* (*order*) comando *m*; (*rule*) regola *f*. **dictation** *n* dettato *m*. **dictator** *n* dittatore *m*. **dictatorial** *adj* dittatoriale. **dictatorship** *n* dittatura *f*.

**dictionary** ['dikʃənəri] *n* dizionario *m*, vocabolario *m*.

**did** [did] *V* **do**.

**die** [dai] *v* morire. **die away** scomparire. **die down** spegnersi lentamente.

**diehard** ['daihaːd] *n(m+f)*, *adj* tradizionalista, intransigente.

**diesel** ['di:zəl] *n* **diesel engine** motore diesel *m*. **diesel oil** gasolio *m*, nafta *f*.

**diet** ['daiət] *n* dieta *f*; (*food*) alimentazione *f*, vitto *m*. **be on a diet** stare a dieta, stare *or* essere a regime. **dietary** *adj* dietetico.

**differ** ['difə] *v* essere diverso, differire; (*dis-*

*agree*) dissentire. **difference** *n* differenza *f*.

**different** *adj* differente, diverso.

**difficult** ['difikəlt] *adj* difficile; (*troublesome*, *tricky*) difficoltoso. **difficulty** *n* difficoltà *f*.

**diffident** ['difidənt] *adj* timido.

**\*dig** [dig] *v* scavare; (*agric*) vangare. *n* (*archaeol*) scavi *m pl*.

**digest** [dai'dʒest; *n* 'daidʒest] *v* digerire, assimilare. *n* sommario *m*, selezione *f*. **digestible** *adj* digeribile. **digestion** *n* digestione *f*.

**digit** ['didʒit] *n* (*figure*) numero semplice *m*, cifra *f*; (*finger*, *toe*) dito *m*.

**digital** *adj* digitale.

**dignified** ['digniˌfaid] *adj* dignitoso, nobile.

**dignity** ['dignəti] *n* dignità *f*.

**digress** [dai'gres] *v* digredire, deviare. **digression** *n* digressione *f*.

**digs** [digz] *pl n* alloggio *m sing*.

**dilapidated** [di'lapiˌdeitid] *adj* decrepito.

**dilate** [dai'leit] *v* dilatare.

**dilemma** [di'lemə] *n* dilemma *m*.

**diligent** ['dilidʒənt] *adj* diligente, assiduo.

**dilute** [dai'lu:t] *v* diluire, allungare. *adj* diluito.

**dim** [dim] *v* attenuare, affievolire. *adj* fioco, tenue; (*stupid*) poco intelligente.

**dimension** [di'menʃən] *n* dimensione *f*.

**diminish** [di'miniʃ] *v* diminuire, ridurre.

**diminutive** [di'minjutiv] *adj* diminutivo, minuscolo.

**dimple** ['dimpl] *n* fossetta *f*.

**din** [din] *n* fracasso *m*, baccano *m*.

**dine** [dain] *v* pranzare. **dining car** vagone ristorante *m*. **dining room** sala da pranzo *f*.

**dinghy** ['diŋgi] *n* barca *f*.

**dingy** ['dindʒi] *adj* squallido.

**dinner** ['dinə] *n* pranzo *m*, cena *f*.

**dinosaur** ['dainəˌsoː] *n* dinosauro *m*.

**diocese** ['daiəsis] *n* diocesi *f invar*.

**dip** [dip] *v* abbassare, tuffare, immergere. *n* immersione *f*; (*swim*) nuotata *f*; (*incli-*) nazione *f*.

**diphthong** ['difθoŋ] *n* dittongo *m*.

**diploma** [di'ploumə] *n* diploma *m*.

**diplomacy** [di'plouməsi] *n* diplomazia *f*. **diplomat** *n* diplomatico *m*. **diplomatic** *adj* diplomatico.

**dipstick** ['dipstik] *n* asta di livello *f*.

**dire** [daiə] *adj* **dire need** bisogno urgente *m*. **dire straits** miseria squallida *f sing*.

**direct** [di'rekt] *adj* diretto, immediato; sincero. *v* dirigere, amministrare. **direction** *n* direzione *f*; (*management*) amministrazione; (*address*) indirizzo *m*; (*stage*) didascalia *f*. **director** *n* (*comm*) amministratore, -trice *m, f*; (*theatre*) regista *m, f*. **directory** *n* annuario *m*, guida *f*; (*phone*) elenco telefonico *m*.

**dirt** [də:t] *n* sporcizia *f*. **dirty** *adj* sporco, sudicio. **dirty word** parolaccia *f*.

**disability** [disə'biləti] *n* incapacità *f*, inabilità *f*. **disabled** *nm, adj* invalido, mutilato.

**disadvantage** [,disəd'va:ntidʒ] *n* svantaggio *m*.

**disagree** [,disə'gri:] *v* non andar d'accordo, non essere d'accordo. **disagree with** (*food*) far male a. **disagreeable** *adj* sgradevole, antipatico. **disagreement** *n* disaccordo *m*, dissenso *m*.

**disappear** [disə'piə] *v* sparire, scomparire. **disappearance** *n* scomparsa *f*.

**disappoint** [,disə'point] *v* deludere. **disappointed** *adj* deluso, scontento. **disappointment** *n* delusione *f*.

**disapprove** [,disə'pru:v] *v* disapprovare, riprovare. **disapproval** *n* disapprovazione *f*.

**disarm** [dis'a:m] *v* disarmare. **disarmament** *n* disarmo *m*.

**disaster** [di'za:stə] *n* disastro *m*, disgrazia *f*; calamità *f*. **disastrous** *adj* disastroso.

**disband** [dis'band] *v* sbandare, sciogliere, congedare.

**disc** *or US* **disk** [disk] *n* disco *m*.

**discard** [dis'ka:d] *v* scartare.

**discern** [di'sə:n] *v* discernere, scorgere. **discerning** *adj* avveduto, accorto. **discernment** *n* discernimento *m*, giudizio *m*.

**discharge** [dis'tʃa:dʒ] *v* scaricare; (*dismiss*) licenziare; (*law*) assolvere; (*radiation*) emettere; (*med*) suppurare; (*a duty*) adempiere; (*a debt*) saldare. *n* scarico *m*; licenziamento *m*; assoluzione *f*; emissione *f*; suppurazione *f*; (*elec*) scarica *f*.

**disciple** [di'saipl] *n* discepolo, -a *m, f*.

**discipline** ['disiplin] *n* disciplina *f*. *v* disciplinare. **disciplinary** *adj* disciplinare.

**disclaim** [dis'kleim] *v* ripudiare, sconfessare, smentire. **disclaimer** *n* ripudio *m*, smentita *f*; denunzia di un contratto *f*.

**disclose** [dis'klouz] *v* svelare, rivelare. **disclosure** *n* rivelazione *f*.

**disco** ['diskou] *n* discoteca *f*.

**discolour** [dis'kʌlə] *v* scolorire, sbiadire.

**discomfort** [dis'kʌmfət] *n* disagio *m*. *v* mettere a disagio.

**disconcert** [diskən'sə:t] *v* sconcertare. **disconcerting** *adj* sconcertante.

**disconnect** [diskə'nekt] *v* sconnettere; (*mech*) disinnestare.

**disconsolate** [dis'konsələt] *adj* sconsolato, desolato.

**discontinue** [diskən'tinju:] *v* sospendere, interrompere, terminare.

**discord** ['disko:d] *n* discordia *f*, dissenso *m*; (*music*) dissonanza *f*, disarmonia *f*. **discordant** *adj* discorde; (*noise*) discordante; dissonante.

**discotheque** ['diskətek] *n* discoteca *f*.

**discount** ['diskaunt] *v* (*disregard*) non badare a. *n* sconto *m*, ribasso *m*.

**discourage** [dis'kʌridʒ] *v* scoraggiare. **discouragement** *m* scoraggiamento *m*. **discouraging** *adj* scoraggiante.

**discover** [dis'kʌvə] *v* scoprire. **discovery** *n* scoperta *f*.

**discredit** [dis'kredit] *v* screditare, mettere in dubbio.

**discreet** [di'skri:t] *adj* discreto, riservato. **discretion** *n* discrezione *f*; prudenza *f*; (*judgment*) giudizio *m*. **discretionary** *adj* discrezionale.

**discrepancy** [di'skrepənsi] *n* divario *m*, disaccordo *m*.

**discrete** [di'skri:t] *adj* separato, distinto, discreto.

**discriminate** [di'skrimi,neit] *v* discriminare, differenziare. **discriminating** *adj* penetrante, giudizioso. **discrimination** *n* discriminazione *f*, distinzione *f*.

**discus** ['diskəs] *n* disco *m*.

**discuss** [di'skʌs] *v* discutere, dibattere. **discussion** *n* discussione *f*, dibattimento *m*.

**disease** [di'zi:z] *n* malattia *f*. **diseased** *adj* malato, ammalato.

**disembark** [disim'ba:k] *v* sbarcare.

**disengage** [disin'geidʒ] *v* disimpegnare, liberare; (*mech*) disinnestare. **disengaged** *adj* libero.

**disfigure** [dis'figə] *v* sfigurare, deturpare.

**disgrace** [dis'greis] *n* disonore *m*, vergogna *f*, scandalo *m*, ignominia *f*. *v* disonorare, screditare. **disgraceful** *adj* vergognoso.

**disgruntled** [dis'grʌntld] *adj* di cattivo umore, scontento.

**disguise** [dis'gaiz] *v* camuffare, mascherare. *n* maschera *f*, travestimento *m*.

**disgust** [dis'gʌst] *n* disgusto *m*, ribrezzo *m*, schifo *m*. *v* disgustare, far schifo, nauseare. **disgusting** *adj* disgustoso, schifoso.

**dish** [diʃ] *n* piatto *m*. **dishcloth** *n* strofinaccio per i piatti *m*. **dishwasher** *n* lavapiatti *m*, *f*.

**dishearten** [dis'ha:tn] *v* scoraggiare.

**dishevelled** [di'ʃevəld] *adj* scapigliato, arruffato.

**dishonest** [dis'onist] *adj* disonesto. **dishonesty** *n* disonestà *f*.

**dishonour** [dis'onə] *v* disonorare. *n* disonore *m*, infamia *f*. **dishonourable** *adj* disonorevole.

**disillusion** [disi'lu:ʒən] *v* disilludere, disingannare. *n* disillusione *f*, disinganno *m*.

**disinfect** [disin'fekt] *v* disinfettare. **disinfectant** *nm*, *adj* disinfettante.

**disinherit** [disin'herit] *v* diseredare.

**disintegrate** [dis'inti,greit] *v* disintegrare, disgregare, disfare, disfarsi. **disintegration** *n* disfacimento *m*, sfacelo *m*, disintegrazione *f*.

**disinterested** [dis'intristid] *adj* disinteressato.

**disjointed** [dis'dʒointid] *adj* sconnesso, incoerente.

**disk** *n* disco *m*.

**disk drive** drive del disco *m*.

**dislike** [dis'laik] *v* detestare, sentire antipatia per. *n* antipatia *f*, avversione *f*.

**dislocate** ['dislə,keit] *v* dislocare; (*joint*) lussare. **dislocation** *n* dislocazione *f*; lussazione *f*.

**dislodge** [dis'lodʒ] *v* sloggiare, scacciare.

**disloyal** [dis'loiəl] *adj* sleale, infedele. **disloyalty** *n* slealtà *f*, infedeltà *f*.

**dismal** ['dizməl] *adj* triste, lugubre, malinconico.

**dismantle** [dis'mantl] *v* smantellare.

**dismay** [dis'mei] *v* costernare, sgomentare. *n* costernazione *f*, sgomento *m*.

**dismiss** [dis'mis] *v* (*send away*) respingere; (*discard*) scartare; (*discharge*) licenziare. **dismissal** *n* licenziamento *m*.

**dismount** [dis'maunt] *v* smontare.

**disobey** [disə'bei] *v* disubbidire, disobbedire. **disobedience** *n* disubbidienza *f*. **disobedient** *adj* disubbidiente.

**disorder** [dis'o:də] *n* disordine *m*, confusione *f*; (*med*) disturbo *m*. **disorderly** *adj* disordinato.

**disorganized** [dis'o:gənaizd] *adj* disorganizzato. **disorganization** *n* disorganizzazione *f*.

**disown** [dis'oun] *v* ripudiare, rinnegare.

**disparage** [di'sparidʒ] *v* denigrare, screditare.

**disparity** [dis'pariti] *n* disparità *f*.

**dispassionate** [dis'paʃənit] *adj* spassionato, obiettivo.

**dispatch** [di'spatʃ] *v* spedire, inviare; (*settle*) sbrigare; (*kill*) spacciare. *n* spedizione *f*; (*mil*) dispaccio *m*; (*speed*) prontezza *f*, sollecitudine *f*.

**dispel** [di'spel] *v* dissipare, scacciare.

**dispense** [di'spens] *v* dispensare, distribuire; (*justice*) amministrare. **dispense with** fare a meno di. **dispensary** *n* dispensario *m*, farmacia *f*.

**disperse** [di'spə:s] *v* disperdere, sparpagliare, dileguarsi. **dispersion** *n* dispersione *f*, diffusione *f*.

**displace** [dis'pleis] *v* spostare; (*take place of* ) soppiantare. **displaced person** profugo (*pl* -ghi) *m*, -a *f*. **displacement** *n* spostamento *m*.

**display** [di'splei] *v* mostrare, esibire, ostentare, manifestare. *n* mostra *f*, manifestazione *f*, esposizione *f*.

**displease** [dis'pli:z] *v* spiacere, dispiacere, scontentare. **displeasure** *n* dispiacere *m*, ira *f*.

**dispose** [di'spouz] *v* disporre, sistemare. **dispose of** sbarazzarsi di, eliminare. **disposal** *n* (*control*) disposizione *f*; (*act of disposing*) sistemazione *f*. **disposed** *adj* disposto, intenzionato. **disposition** *n* disposizione *f*, tendenza *f*; (*character*) indole *f*.

**disprove** [dis'pru:v] *v* confutare.

**dispute** [di'spju:t] *n* disputa *f*, vertenza *f*; (*quarrel*) lite *f*. *v* contestare.

**disqualify** [dis'kwoli,fai] *v* (*sport*) squalificare; (*render unfit*) incapacitare; (*law*) interdire. **disqualification** *n* squalifica *f*, incapacità *f*, interdizione *f*.

**disregard** [disrə'ga:d] *v* non far caso a, ignorare. *n* noncuranza *f*, inosservanza *f*.

**disreputable** [dis'repjutəbl] *adj* malfamato, vergognoso.

**disrespect** [disrə'spekt] *n* mancanza di rispetto *f*, irreverenza *f*. **disrespectful** *adj* poco rispettoso, che non mostra rispetto.

**disrupt** [dis'rʌpt] *v* scompigliare, mettere in confusione. **disruption** *n* scompiglio *m*.

**dissatisfy** [di'satisfai] *v* scontentare. **dissatisfaction** *n* insoddisfazione *f*.

**dissect** [di'sekt] *v* sezionare; (*corpse*) dissecare; (*analyse*) analizzare. **dissection** *n* sezionamento *m*; dissezione *f*; analisi *f*.

**dissent** [di'sent] *n* dissenso *m*. *v* dissentire.

**dissident** ['disidənt] *n*(*m*+*f*), *adj* dissidente.

**dissimilar** [di'similə] *adj* dissimile.

**dissipated** ['disipeitid] *adj* dissoluto.

**dissociate** [di'sousieit] *v* dissociare, sdoppiare. **dissociation** *n* dissociazione *f*, sdoppiamento *m*.

**dissolve** [di'zolv] *v* sciogliere, sciogliersi, dissolvere. **dissolute** *adj* dissoluto, licenzioso.

**dissuade** [di'sweid] *v* dissuadere, distogliere. **dissuasion** *n* dissuasione *f*, distoglimento *m*.

**distance** ['distəns] *n* distanza *f*, lontananza *f*; (*reserve*) riserbo *m*. **distant** *adj* distante, lontano, remoto; riservato.

**distaste** [dis'teist] *n* avversione *f*. **distasteful** *adj* sgradevole.

**distemper** [di'stempə] *n* (*paint*) intonaco *m*; (*canine*) cimurro *m*. *v* intonacare.

**distended** [di'stendid] *adj* dilatato.

**distil** [di'stil] *v* distillare. **distillation** *n* distillazione *f*. **distillery** *n* distilleria *f*.

**distinct** [di'stiŋkt] *adj* differente, diverso; distinto; (*clear*) chiaro. **distinction** *n* distinzione *f*; differenza *f*. **distinctive** *adj* caratteristico, distintivo.

**distinguish** [di'stiŋgwiʃ] *v* distinguere, differenziare, individuare. **distinguish oneself** farsi notare. **distinguishable** *adj* distinguibile. **distinguished** *adj* distinto, insigne.

**distort** [di'sto:t] *v* deformare, alterare. **distortion** *n* deformazione *f*, alterazione *f*.

**distract** [di'strakt] *v* distrarre; (*disturb*) turbare. **distraction** *n* distrazione *f*.

**distraught** [di'stro:t] *adj* turbato.

**distress** [di'stres] *n* (*anxiety*) angoscia *f*; (*poverty*) miseria *f*; (*ship*) pericolo *m*; (*worry*) preoccupazione *f*. *v* angosciare, affliggere,

preoccupare. **distressed** *adj* dolente, angosciato. **distressing** *adj* penoso, doloroso.

**distribute** [di'stribjut] *v* distribuire. **distribution** *n* distribuzione *f*. **distributor** *n* distributore *m*.

**district** ['distrikt] *n* distretto *m*, quartiere *m*, zona *f*.

**distrust** [dis'trʌst] *v* diffidare di, sospettare, non aver fiducia in. *n* sospetto *m*, sfiducia *f*, diffidenza *f*.

**disturb** [di'stə:b] *v* disturbare, incomodare. **disturbance** *n* disturbo *m*; (*breach of peace*) sommossa *f*.

**ditch** [ditʃ] *n* fossa *f*, fossato *m*. *v* (*abandon*) piantare.

**ditto** ['ditou] *adv* idem.

**divan** [di'van] *n* divano *m*.

**dive** [daiv] *v* tuffarsi, fare un tuffo, sommergersi. *n* (*plunge*) tuffo *m*; (*coll*) taverna *f*, bettola *f*. **diver** *n* palombaro *m*. **diving board** trampolino *m*. **diving suit** scafandro *m*.

**diverge** [dai'və:dʒ] *v* divergere.

**diversify** [dai'və:sifai] *v* diversificare, differenziare.

**divert** [dai'və:t] *v* deviare; distrarre; (*amuse*) divertire. **diversion** *n* (*distraction*) diversivo *m*, distrazione *f*; (*mil*) diversione *f*; deviazione *f*.

**divide** [di'vaid] *v* dividere, separare. **divided** *adj* diviso. **dividers** *pl n* compasso *m sing*. **division** *n* divisione *f*.

**dividend** ['dividend] *n* dividendo *m*.

**divine** [di'vain] *adj* divino, sacro. *n* teologo *m*, sacerdote *m*. *v* scoprire, indovinare; (*prophesy*) pronosticare. **diviner** *n* (*soothsayer*) indovino, -a *m*, *f*; (*user of divining rod*) rabdomante *m*. **divinity** *n* divinità *f*.

**divorce** [di'vo:s] *n* divorzio *m*. *v* divorziare, divorziarsi.

**divulge** [dai'vʌldʒ] *v* divulgare, diffondere.

**dizzy** ['dizi] *adj* vertiginoso. **feel dizzy** avere il capogiro; sentirsi girare la testa. **dizziness** *n* capogiro *m*, vertigine *f*.

**\*do** [du:] *v* fare; (*suffice*) bastare; (*achieve*) compiere; (*carry out*) eseguire. **do away with** abolire; (*kill*) uccidere. **do-it-yourself** *adj* da fare da soli. **do out of** deprivare di. **do up** (*clothes, etc.*) abbottonare. **do without** fare a meno di. **how do you do?** come sta? come stai? **make do** arrangiarsi.

**docile** ['dousail] *adj* docile, mansueto.

**dock¹** [dok] *n* (*wharf*) banchina *f*; (*water-way*) bacino *m*; (*port area*) zona portuale *f*. *v* attraccare. **docker** *n* portuale *m*. **dockyard** *n* cantiere navale *m*.

**dock²** [dok] *v* mozzare, troncare.

**dock³** [dok] *n* (*law*) banco degli imputati *m*.

**docket** ['dokit] *n* bolletta *f*.

**doctor** ['doktə] *n* dottore, -essa *m*, *f*; (*med*) medico, -chessa *m*, *f*. **doctorate** *n* dottorato *m*.

**doctrine** ['doktrin] *n* dottrina *f*. **doctrinal** *adj* dottrinale.

**document** ['dokjumənt] *n* documento *m*. *v* documentare. **documentary** *n* documentario *m*. **documentation** *n* documentazione *f*.

**dodge** [dodʒ] *v* schivare, scansare. *n* sotterfugio *m*, stratagemma *f*.

**doe** [dou] *n* selvaggina femmina *f*; (*deer*) daina *f*; (*rabbit*) femmina del coniglio *f*; (*hare*) lepre femmina *f*.

**dog** [dog] *n* cane *m*. **dog-eared** *adj* (*page*) accartocciato, con le orecchie. **dogrose** *n* rosa canina *f*. **dog-tired** *adj* stanco morto. **dogtooth** *n* dente canino *m*. *v* pedinare. **be dogged by** essere perseguitato da. **dogged** *adj* ostinato, accanito.

**doge** [doudʒ] *n* doge *m*.

**dogma** ['dogmə] *n* dogma *m*. **dogmatic** *adj* dogmatico.

**dole** [doul] *n* sussidio di disoccupazione *m*. *v* **dole out** distribuire.

**doll** [dol] *n* bambola *f*, pupa *f*. *v* **doll up** agghindarsi, abbellirsi.

**dollar** ['dolə] *n* dollaro *m*.

**dolphin** ['dolfin] *n* delfino *m*.

**domain** [də'mein] *n* (*land*) proprietà *f*; (*law*) demanio *m*; (*control, sphere of activity*) dominio *m*.

**dome** [doum] *n* cupola *f*.

**domestic** [də'mestik] *adj* domestico; (*not foreign*) nazionale. *n* domestico, -a *m*, *f*. **domesticate** *v* addomesticare. **domesticity** *n* domesticità *f*.

**domicile** ['domisail] *n* domicilio *m*.

**dominate** ['domi,neit] *v* dominare. **dominant** *adj* dominante.

**domineer** [domi'niə] *v* signoreggiare. **domineering** *adj* imperioso; (*overbearing*) prepotente.

**dominion** [də'minjən] *n* dominio *m*; autorità *f*.

**domino** ['dominou] *n* domino *m*.

**don¹** [don] *v* vestire, indossare.

**don²** [don] *n* (*Spanish title*) don *m invar*; (*scholar*) docente universitario, -a *m*, *f*.

**donate** [də'neit] *v* donare. **donation** *n* dono *m*, donazione *f*. **donor** *n* donatore, -trice *m*, *f*.

**done** [dʌn] *V* do.

**donkey** ['doŋki] *n* asino, -a *m*, *f*; somaro, -a *m*, *f*.

**doodle** ['du:dl] *n* scarabocchio, ghirigoro *m*.

**doom** [du:m] *n* destino *m*, sorte *f*; (*ruin*) rovina *f*. *v* destinare, condannare. **doomed** *adj* condannato. **doomsday** *n* giorno del giudizio *m*.

**door** [do:] *n* porta *f*, uscio *m*. **doorbell** *n* campanello *m*. **door-handle** *n* maniglia *f*. **door-keeper** *n* portiere, -a *m*, *f*, portinaio, -a *m*, *f*. **door-knocker** *n* battiporta *m*, batacchio *m*. **doormat** *n* zerbino *m*, stoino *m*. **doorstep** *n* soglia *f*. **doorway** *n* entrata *f*, portone *m*.

**dope** [doup] *n* (*slang: drug*) stupefacente *m*, droga *f*; (*slang: information*) notizie *f pl*. *v* drogare. **dopey** *adj* inebetito.

**dormant** ['do:mənt] *adj* addormentato, latente.

**dormitory** ['do:mitəri] *n* dormitorio *m*.

**dormouse** ['do:,maus] *n* ghiro *m*.

**dose** [dous] *n* dose *f*. *v* dosare.

**dot** [dot] *n* punto *m*. *v* punteggiare. **on the dot** in orario. **dotty** *adj* (*coll*) picchiatello.

**dote** [dout] *v* **dote on** essere infatuato di.

**double** ['dʌbl] *v* raddoppiare. **double up** piegare *or* piegarsi in due; contorcersi. *adj* doppio. *n* doppio *m*; (*person*) sosia *m invar*. **at the double** a passo di corsa. **double-barrelled** *adj* a doppia canna. **double bass** contrabbasso *m*. **double bed** letto matrimoniale *m*. **double-breasted** *adj* a doppio petto. **double-cross** *v* fare il doppio gioco, tradire.

**doubt** [daut] *n* dubbio *m*, incertezza *f*. *v* dubitare, mettere in dubbio. **doubtful** *adj* dubbio, incerto, problematico. **doubtless** *adv* senza dubbio.

**dough** [dou] *n* pasta *f*; (*slang*) quattrini *m pl*. **doughnut** *n* ciambella *f*, krapfen *m invar*.

**dove** [dʌv] n colomba f. **dovecot** n colombaia f. **dovetail** v (carpentry) incastrare a coda di rondine; (fit exactly) combaciare, far combaciare.

**dowdy** ['daudi] adj sciatto, trasandato.

**down**[1] [daun] adv giù, di sotto, per terra. adj depresso, abbattuto. **down and out** ridotto in miseria. v **down tools** abbandonare il lavoro.

**down**[2] [daun] n (plumage) piumino m, lanugine f; (soft hair) peluria f.

**down-and-out** [daunən'aut] n (coll) indigente, barbone m.

**downcast** ['daun,ka:st] adj abbattuto, depresso.

**downfall** ['daun,fo:l] n rovina f, caduta f.

**downhearted** [,daun'ha:tid] adj depresso, scoraggiato.

**downhill** [,daun'hil] adv in discesa.

**download** [daun'loud] v scaricare.

**downpour** ['daun,po:] n acquazzone m.

**downright** ['daun,rait] adv categoricamente, nettamente.

**Down's Syndrome** n sindrome di Down f.

**downstairs** [,daun'steəz] adv da basso, al piano inferiore. **go downstairs** scendere le scale.

**downstream** [,daun'stri:m] adv a valle, seguendo la corrente.

**downtrodden** [daun,trodn] adj oppresso.

**downward** ['daunwəd] adj discendente.

**downwards** ['daunwədz] adv in giù, verso il basso.

**dowry** ['dauəri] n dote f.

**doze** [douz] v sonnecchiare, fare un pisolino. **doze off** assopirsi. **dozy** adj sonnolento.

**dozen** ['dʌzn] n dozzina f.

**drab** [drab] adj squallido, scialbo.

**draft** [dra:ft] n (sketch) abbozzo m; (preliminary copy) brutta copia f; (conscription) leva f; (written order) tratta f, cambiale f; (bank) assegno circolare m. v abbozzare, delineare; (conscript) chiamare sotto le armi, arruolare.

**drag** [drag] v trascinare; (search) dragare; (extract) strappare. n trazione f. **in drag** vestito da donna.

**dragon** ['dragən] n drago m; (woman) megera f. **dragon-fly** n libellula f.

**drain** [drein] n fogna f, tubo di scarico m. v (draw off) scolare, prosciugare; (med) drenare; (exhaust) esaurire; (drink up) bere fino all'ultimo. **drainage** n scarico m, fognatura f, drenaggio m. **draining board** scolatoio m. **drainpipe** n grondaia f.

**drama** ['dra:mə] n dramma m. **dramatic** adj drammatico, impressionante. **dramatist** n drammaturgo, -a m, f. **dramatize** v drammatizzare.

**drank** [draŋk] V **drink**.

**drape** [dreip] v drapeggiare.

**draper** ['dreipə] n negoziante di tessuti m, f. **drapery** n tessuti m pl; tendaggio m.

**drastic** ['drastik] adj drastico.

**draught** or US **draft** [dra:ft] n (air current) corrente d'aria f; (drink) sorso m; (pull) tiro m; (fishing) retata f. **draughts** n gioco della dama m. **draughtsman** n disegnatore, -trice m, f, progettista m, f; (of documents) compilatore, -trice m, f. **it's draughty** c'è una corrente d'aria.

**\*draw** [dro:] v (pull) tirare; (attract) attirare, attrarre; (picture) disegnare; (sport) pareggiare; (extract) estrarre. **draw back** ritirarsi. **drawback** n inconveniente m. **drawbridge** n ponte levatoio m. **draw near** avvicinarsi. **draw on** (funds) attingere (a). n (sport) pareggio m. **drawing** n disegno m. **drawing-board** n tavola da disegno f. **drawing-pin** n puntina da disegno f. **drawing-room** n salotto m.

**drawer** ['dro:ə] n cassetto m. **chest of drawers** cassettone m. **drawers** pl n (underclothes) mutandine f pl.

**drawl** [dro:l] v strascicare le parole.

**drawn** [dro:n] V **draw**.

**dread** [dred] v aver paura di. n timore m, paura f, fobia f. **dreadful** adj spaventoso.

**\*dream** [dri:m] n sogno m; visione f. v sognare; immaginare. **dreamer** n sognatore, -trice m, f; visionario, -a m, f. **dreamy** adj (vague) vago.

**dreamt** [dremt] V **dream**.

**dreary** ['driəri] adj triste; (boring) noioso. **dreariness** n tristezza f.

**dredge** [dredʒ] v dragare.

**dregs** [dregz] pl n feccia f sing; (coffee) fondo m sing.

**drench** [drentʃ] v inzuppare, bagnare.

**dress** [dres] v (clothe) vestire; (salad, etc.) condire; (wounds) bendare. n abito m, vestito m. **dress circle** prima galleria f. **dress-maker** n sarta f. **dressmaking** n confezione di abiti da donna f. **dress rehearsal** prova generale f. **dressing** n condimento m; benda f. **dressing down** rimprovero m. **dressing-gown** n vestaglia f. **dressing-room** n camerino m. **dressing-table** n toilette (pl -s) f.

**dresser**[1] ['dresə] n (furniture) credenza f.

**dresser**[2] ['dresə] n (theatre) vestiarista m, f; (med) assistente medico, -a m, f.

**drew** [dru:] V **draw**.

**dribble** ['dribl] v sbavare; (trickle) gocciolare; (ball) palleggiare. n bava f; gocciolamento m; palleggio m.

**drier** ['draiə] n (clothes) asciugatrice f; (hair) asciugacapelli m.

**drift** [drift] v andare alla deriva; (wander aimlessly) lasciarsi andare. **drift apart** perdersi di vista. n tendenza f, direzione f; (movement) deriva f; (current) corrente f.

**drill**[1] [dril] n trivella f, sonda f, trapano m. v trapanare, sondare.

**drill**[2] [dril] n esercitazioni f pl, addestramento m. v esercitare, fare esercitazioni, addestrare.

*****drink** [drink] v bere. n bibita f, bevanda f. **drinkable** adj bevibile, potabile. **drinking fountain** fontanella f. **drinking water** acqua potabile f.

**drip** [drip] v gocciolare. n gocciolio m, gocciolatura f; (slang) persona insulsa f.

**dripping** n stillicidio m; (fat) grasso colato m.

*****drive** [draiv] v condurre; (car) guidare; (push) spingere. **drive away** scacciare. n (road) viale m; (trip) corsa f, giro m; energia f, iniziativa f; (golf) colpo forte m. **driver** n guidatore, -trice m, f. **driving-licence** n patente di guida f. **driving-test** n esame di guida m.

**drivel** ['drivl] n (nonsense) sciocchezze f pl. v dir sciocchezze.

**driven** ['drivn] V **drive**.

**drizzle** ['drizl] v piovigginare. n pioggerella f.

**drone** [droun] n (bee) fuco m, pecchione m; (idler) fannullone m; (hum) ronzio m. v (hum) ronzare. **droning** adj ronzante, monotono.

**droop** [dru:p] v afflosciarsi, accasciarsi. n accasciamento m. **drooping** adj piegato in giù, floscio.

**drop** [drop] n goccia f; (fall) caduta f. v (fall) cadere; (let fall) far cadere; (lower) calare; diminuire, abbassarsi. **dropper** n contagocce m. **droppings** pl n sterco m sing.

**dropout** ['dropaut] n emarginato, -a m, f. v **drop out** ritirarsi, rinunciare.

**drought** [draut] n siccità f.

**drove** [drouv] V **drive**.

**drown** [draun] v annegare, affogare.

**drowsy** ['drauzi] adj sonnolento, assopito.

**drudge** [drʌdʒ] v sfacchinare, sgobbare. n sgobbone, -a m, f. **drudgery** n sfacchinata f.

**drug** [drʌg] n medicinale m, droga f, stupefacente m. **drug-addict** n drogato, -a m, f, tossicomane m, f. v narcotizzare, drogare.

**drum** [drʌm] n tamburo m, timpano m; (cylinder) cilindro m, rullo m. **drumstick** n bacchetta da tamburo f; (chicken) coscia di pollo f. v suonare il tamburo; (beat) tamburellare. **drummer** n tamburo m.

**drunk** [drʌŋk] V **drink**. adj ubriaco (m pl -chi), sbronzo. **get drunk** ubriacarsi. **drunkard** n ubriacone, -a m, f; sbronzo, -a m, f. **drunkenness** n ubriachezza f.

**dry** [drai] adj asciutto, secco; (uninteresting) monotono; (caustic) mordace. v asciugare, seccare. **dry-clean** v lavare a secco. **dry-cleaning** n lavaggio a secco m. **dry rot** carie del legno f.

**dual** ['djuəl] adj doppio, duplice. **dual carriageway** strada a doppia carreggiata f.

**dubbed** ['dʌbd] adj (film) doppiato; (name) qualificato.

**dubious** ['djubiəs] adj dubbio, equivoco, incerto. **dubiousness** n incertezza f.

**duchess** ['dʌtʃis] n duchessa f.

**duck**[1] [dʌk] n (zool) anitra f. **duckling** n anatroccolo m.

**duck**[2] [dʌk] v (plunge) tuffare, immergere; (dodge) schivare; (lower the head) chinarsi di colpo.

**dud** [dʌd] adj inutile. n (explosive) proiettile che non esplode m.

**due** [dju:] adj (owing) da pagarsi; (rightful, proper) debito; (attributable) dovuto; (expected) atteso, in arrivo. adv direttamente. **due to** a causa di. **dues** pl n dazio m sing, diritti m pl.

**duel** ['djuəl] n duello m, lotta f.

**duet** [dju'et] n duetto m.

**duffel bag** ['dʌfəl] n sacca da viaggio f.

**duffel coat** ['dʌfəl] n montgomery m invar.

**dug** [dʌg] V **dig**.

**duke** [dju:k] n duca m.

**dull** [dʌl] adj (unintelligent) ottuso; (boring) noioso; (slow) lento; monotono; (not sharp) non tagliente; (weather) grigio. v attutire, attenuare, intorpidire. **dullness** n lentezza f; noia f.

**duly** ['dju:li] adv debitamente.

**dumb** [dʌm] adj muto, reticente; (slang: foolish) scemo. **dumbfound** v sbalordire, stupire.

**dummy** ['dʌmi] adj falso, finto. n (man of straw) uomo di paglia m; (cards) morto m; (baby's) biberon m invar, poppatoio m; (model) manichino m.

**dump** [dʌmp] n (tip) luogo di scarico m; (coll) posto triste m. v (get rid of ) scartare, disfarsi di; (unload) scaricare.

**dunce** [dʌns] n ignorante m, f.

**dune** [dju:n] n duna f.

**dung** [dʌŋ] n letame m, sterco m.

**dungarees** [ˌdʌŋgəˈriːz] pl n (overalls) tuta f sing.

**dungeon** ['dʌndʒən] n segreta f, cella sotterranea f.

**duplicate** ['dju:plikət; v 'dju:plikeit] adj duplice, doppio. n duplicato m, duplice copia f, doppione m. v duplicare.

**durable** ['djuərəbl] adj durevole, duraturo.

**duration** [dju'reiʃən] n durata f.

**during** ['djuriŋ] prep durante, nel corso di.

**dusk** [dʌsk] n crepuscolo m.

**dust** [dʌst] n polvere f. v (clean) spolverare; (sprinkle) cospargere. **dustbin** n pattumiera f. **dustman** n spazzino m. **dustpan** n paletta per la spazzatura f. **duster** n spolverino m, strofinaccio m. **dusty** adj polveroso.

**Dutch** [dʌtʃ] adj olandese. **Dutch person** olandese m, f. **go Dutch** fare or pagare alla romana.

**duty** ['dju:ti] n dovere m; (customs) dogana f.

**duvet** ['du:vei] n piumino m.

**dwarf** [dwo:f] n nano m. v (make appear small) far sembrar piccolo; (render insignificant) sminuire.

*****dwell** [dwel] v (reside) dimorare. **dwell on** soffermarsi su. **dwelling** n dimora f, abitazione f.

**dwelt** [dwelt] V **dwell**.

**dwindle** ['dwindl] v diminuire; (decline) deperire.

**dye** [dai] n colorante m, tintura f. v colorare, tingere. **dyed in the wool** inveterato, radicato. **dyer** n tintore m.

**dyke** [daik] n diga f, argine m.

**dynamic** [dai'namik] adj dinamico. **dynamics** n dinamica f.

**dynamite** ['dainəˌmait] n dinamite f.

**dynamo** ['dainəˌmou] n dinamo f invar.

**dynasty** ['dinəsti] n dinastia f.

**dysentery** ['disəntri] n dissenteria f.

**dyslexia** [dis'leksiə] n dislessia f.

**dyspepsia** [dis'pepsiə] n dispepsia f.

# E

**each** [i:tʃ] adj ogni, ciascuno. pron ognuno. adv (apiece) l'uno, l'una. **each other** l'un l'altro.

**eager** ['i:gə] adj avido, premuroso; impaziente. **eagerness** n impazienza f; zelo m; brama f.

**eagle** ['i:gl] n aquila f.

**ear**[1] [iə] n orecchio m. **be up to one's ears in ...** aver ... fin sopra i capelli. **earache** n mal d'orecchi m. **eardrum** n timpano m. **earmark** v contrassegnare; (set aside) mettere da parte; (money) stanziare. **ear-plug** n tappo per orecchi m. **ear-ring** n orecchino m. **ear-splitting** adj assordante. **within earshot** a portata d'orecchio.

**ear**[2] [iə] n spiga f.

**earl** [ə:l] n conte m.

**early** ['ə:li] adv presto, di buon'ora. adj primo; (morning) mattiniero, mattutino; (before time) prematuro; (ancient) antico (m pl -chi).

**earn** [ə:n] v guadagnare, meritare. **earnings** pl n guadagni m pl, stipendio m.

**earnest** ['ə:nist] adj serio, coscienzioso. **be in earnest** fare sul serio. **earnestness** n serietà f.

**earth** [ə:θ] n terra f; (world) mondo m; (soil) terreno m. **earthquake** n terremoto m. v (elec) mettere a terra. **earthenware** n terraglia f. **earthly** adj terrestre. **earthy** adj (*coarse*) grossolano; robusto.

**earwig** ['iəwig] *n* forbicina *f*.

**ease** [i:z] *n* agio *m*, comodo *m*. **at ease** tranquillo. **ill at ease** a disagio. *v* agevolare, alleggerire.

**easel** ['i:zl] *n* cavalletto *m*.

**east** [i:st] *adj* orientale, dell'est. *n* oriente *m*, est *m*. **Middle/Near/Far East** medio/prossimo/estremo oriente *m*. **eastward** *adv*, *adj* verso est, ad est, verso oriente.

**Easter** ['i:stə] *n* Pasqua *f*.

**easy** ['i:zi] *adj* facile, semplice; (*informal*) disinvolto; (*compliant*) accomodante. **easy chair** poltrona *f*. **easy-going** *adj* (*placid*) bonaccione, paciente; indolente; tollerante.

**\*eat** [i:t] *v* mangiare. **eatable** *adj* mangiabile, mangereccio.

**eaten** ['i:tn] *V* **eat**.

**eavesdrop** ['i:vzdrop] *v* origliare.

**ebb** [eb] *n* riflusso *m*; declino *m*. *v* rifluire; declinare.

**eccentric** [ik'sentrik] *nm*, *adj* eccentrico. **eccentricity** *n* eccentricità *f*.

**ecclesiastical** [ikli:zi:'astikl] *adj* ecclesiastico.

**echo** ['ekou] *v* echeggiare, far eco a. *n* eco *f*, *m* (*pl* -i *m*).

**eclair** [ei'kleə] *n* bignè *m invar*.

**eclipse** [i'klips] *n* eclissi *f*. *v* eclissare.

**ecology** [i'kolədʒi] *n* ecologia *f*.

**e-commerce** ['i:,komə:s] *n* commercio elettronico, e-commercio *m*.

**economy** [i'konəmi] *n* economia *f*. **economical** *or* **economic** *adj* economico, a buon prezzo; (*thrifty*) frugale. **economics** *n* economia *f*, scienze economiche *f pl*. **economist** *n* economista *m*, *f*. **economize** *v* economizzare, fare economia.

**ecstasy** ['ekstəsi] *n* estasi *f*. **ecstatic** *adj* estatico.

**eczema** ['eksimə] *n* eczema *m*.

**edge** [edʒ] *n* orlo *m*, margine *m*; (*blade*) filo *m*; (*road*) ciglio *m*; (*river*) sponda *f*. **be on edge** avere i nervi. *v* orlare.

**edible** ['edəbl] *adj* mangereccio, mangiabile.

**Edinburgh** ['edinbərə] *n* Edimburgo *f*.

**edit** ['edit] *v* curare, redigere, dirigere. **editor** *n* redattore, -trice *m*, *f*; (*newspaper*) direttore, -trice *m*, *f*. **editorial** *n* articolo di fondo *m*. **edition** *n* edizione *f*.

**educate** ['edju,keit] *v* educare, istruire. **educated** *adj* colto, istruito. **education** *n* educazione *f*, istruzione *f*; (*teaching*) insegnamento *m*, pedagogia *f*.

**eel** [i:l] *n* anguilla *f*.

**eerie** ['iəri] *adj* (*strange*) misterioso; (*causing fear*) pauroso.

**effect** [i'fekt] *n* effetto *m*; conseguenza *f*, risultato *m*; impressione *f*. **take effect** entrare in vigore. **with effect from** a partire da. *v* effettuare, realizzare. **effective** *adj* efficace, efficiente.

**effeminate** [i'feminət] *adj* effeminato.

**effervescent** [efə'vesənt] *adj* effervescente.

**efficient** [i'fiʃənt] *adj* efficiente, capace. **efficiency** *n* efficienza *f*, capacità *f*; (*machine*) rendimento *m*.

**effigy** ['efidʒi] *n* effigie *f*.

**effort** ['efət] *n* sforzo *m*, fatica *f*. **make an effort** sforzarsi, fare di tutto. **effortless** *adj* senza sforzo.

**egg** [eg] *n* uovo *m* (*pl* -a *f*). **egg-cup** *n* portauovo *m*. **egg-shaped** *adj* ovale. **egg-shell** *n* guscio d'uovo *m*. **egg-whisk** *n* frullino *m*. **v egg on** aizzare.

**ego** ['i:gou] *n* ego *m*. **egocentric** *adj* egocentrico. **egoism** *n* egoismo *m*. **egoist** *n* egoista *m*, *f*. **egoistic(al)** *adj* egoista, egoistico. **egotism** *n* egotismo *m*. **egotist** *n* egotista *m*, *f*. **egotistic(al)** *adj* egotista, -a.

**Egypt** ['i:dʒipt] *n* Egitto *m*. **Egyptian** *n*, *adj* egiziano, -a; (*ancient*) egizio, -a.

**eiderdown** ['aidədaun] *n* piumino *m*.

**eight** [eit] *nm*, *adj* otto. **eighth** *nm*, *adj* ottavo.

**eighteen** [ei'ti:n] *nm*, *adj* diciotto. **eighteenth** *nm*, *adj* diciottesimo.

**eighty** ['eiti] *nm*, *adj* ottanta. **eightieth** *nm*, *adj* ottantesimo.

**either** ['aiðə] *pron*, *adj* l'uno o l'altro; (*each*) ciascuno dei due, tutti e due. *adv* nemmeno, neppure, neanche. *conj* **either ... or ...** o ... o ..., sia ... che ..., sia ... sia ....

**ejaculate** [i'dʒakjuleit] *v* eiaculare; esclamare. **ejaculation** *n* eiaculazione *f*, esclamazione *f*.

**eject** [i'dʒekt] *v* espellere, gettar fuori. **ejector seat** sedile eiettabile *m*.

**eke** [i:k] *v* **eke out** supplire. **eke out a living** sbarcare il lunario.

**elaborate** [i'læbəreit; *adj* i'læbərət] *v* elaborare, sviluppare. *adj* elaborato, minuzioso.

**elapse** [i'læps] *v* passare, decorrere.

**elastic** [i'læstik] *nm, adj* elastico.

**elated** [i'leitid] *adj* giubilante, euforico.

**elbow** ['elbou] *n* gomito *m*. **elbow-room** *n* libertà di movimento *f*. *v* (*jostle*) dar gomitate.

**elder**[1] ['eldə] *adj* più vecchio, maggiore. *n* anziano, -a *m, f*. **elderly** *adj* di una certa età, anziano.

**elder**[2] ['eldə] *n* sambuco (*pl* -chi) *m*. **elderberry** *n* bacca di sambuco *f*.

**eldest** ['eldist] *adj* più vecchio, maggiore, primogenito.

**elect** [i'lekt] *v* eleggere, scegliere. *adj* eletto, scelto. **election** *n* elezione *f*. **electioneering** *n* campagna elettorale *f*. **electorate** *n* elettorato *m*. **elector** *n* elettore, -trice *m, f*.

**electricity** [elek'trisəti] *n* elettricità *f*. **electric** *adj* elettrico. **electric appliances** elettrodomestici *m pl*. **electrician** *n* elettricista *m*. **electrify** *v* elettrificare. **electrocution** *n* elettroesecuzione *f*. **electrode** *n* elettrodo *m*. **electrolysis** *n* elettrolisi *f*. **electron** *n* elettrone *m*. **electronic** *adj* elettronico. **electronics** *n* elettronica *f*.

**elegant** ['eligənt] *adj* elegante, fine. **elegance** *n* eleganza *f*, finezza *f*.

**elegy** ['elidʒi] *n* elegia *f*. **elegiac** *adj* elegiaco.

**element** ['eləmənt] *n* elemento *m*, fattore *m*. **elemental** *adj* fondamentale. **elementary** *adj* elementare.

**elephant** ['elifənt] *n* elefante *m*. **elephantine** *adj* elefantesco.

**elevate** ['eliveit] *v* elevare, innalzare; (*exalt*) esaltare. **elevated** *adj* elevato, eminente. **elevation** *n* (*altitude*) altezza *f*; (*drawing*) proiezione ortogonale *f*; (*grandeur*) elevatezza *f*. **elevator** *n* (*lift*) ascensore *m*.

**eleven** [i'levn] *nm, adj* undici. **eleventh** *nm, adj* undicesimo.

**elf** [elf] *n* elfo *m*, folletto *m*.

**eligible** ['elidʒəbl] *adj* eleggibile; desiderabile.

**eliminate** [i'limineit] *v* eliminare, scartare. **elimination** *n* eliminazione *f*.

**elite** [ei'li:t] *n* élite (*pl* -s) *f*, fior fiore *m invar*.

**ellipse** [i'lips] *n* ellisse *f*.

**elm** [elm] *n* olmo *m*.

**elocution** [elə'kju:ʃən] *n* elocuzione *f*.

**elope** [i'loup] *v* fuggire. **elopement** *n* fuga *f*.

**eloquent** ['eləkwənt] *adj* eloquente, retorico. **eloquence** *n* eloquenza *f*, retorica *f*.

**else** [els] *adv, pron* altro, altrimenti. **elsewhere** *adv* altrove.

**elucidate** [i'lu:sideit] *v* chiarire, spiegare.

**elude** [i'lu:d] *v* eludere, evitare. **elusive** *adj* evasivo, elusivo.

**emaciated** [i'meisieitid] *adj* scarno, emaciato.

**e-mail** ['i:meil] *n* e-mail *m*, posta electronica *f*. *v* spedire un e-mail.

**emanate** ['eməneit] *v* emanare, emettere, scaturire. **emanation** *n* emanazione *f*, emissione *f*.

**emancipate** [i'mansipeit] *v* emancipare. **emancipation** *n* emancipazione *f*.

**embalm** [im'ba:m] *v* imbalsamare.

**embankment** [im'baŋkmənt] *n* argine *m*, lungofiume *m*.

**embargo** [im'ba:gou] *n* embargo *m*, sanzioni *f pl*, proibizione *f*.

**embark** [im'ba:k] *v* imbarcare. **embark on** intraprendere.

**embarrass** [im'barəs] *v* mettere in imbarazzo. **embarrassment** *n* imbarazzo *m*.

**embassy** ['embəsi] *n* ambasciata *f*.

**embellish** [im'beliʃ] *v* abbellire, ornare. **embellishment** *n* abbellimento *m*.

**ember** ['embə] *n* tizzone *m*. **embers** *pl n* brace *f pl*.

**embezzle** [im'bezl] *v* appropriarsi indebitamente. **embezzlement** *n* appropriazione indebita *f*, malversazione *f*. **embezzler** *n* malversatore, -trice *m, f*.

**embitter** [im'bitə] *v* rendere amaro, amareggiare.

**emblem** ['embləm] *n* emblema *m*, simbolo *m*.

**embody** [im'bodi] *v* incorporare; (*comprise*) comprendere; incarnare; concretare.

**emboss** [im'bos] *v* sbalzare, fare in rilievo, scolpire in rilievo.

**embrace** [im'breis] *v* abbracciare. *n* abbraccio *m*.

**embroider** [im'broidə] *v* ricamare; (*embellish*) abbellire. **embroidery** *n* ricamo *m*.

**embryo** ['embriou] *n* embrione *m*. **embry-**

**onic** *adj* embrionale.

**emerald** ['emərəld] *n* smeraldo *m*.

**emerge** [i'mɜːdʒ] *v* emergere.

**emergency** [i'mɜːdʒənsi] *n* emergenza *f*, caso imprevisto *m*. **emergency exit** uscita di sicurezza *f*. **in case of emergency** in caso di urgenza.

**emigrate** ['emigreit] *v* emigrare. **emigration** *n* emigrazione *f*.

**eminent** ['eminənt] *adj* eminente, distinto.

**emit** [i'mit] *v* emettere, emanare. **emission** *n* emissione *f*.

**emotion** [i'məuʃən] *n* emozione *f*, sentimento *m*, commozione *f*. **emotional** *adj* emotivo; impressionabile. **emotive** *adj* emozionale.

**empathy** ['empəθi] *n* empatia *f*, immedesimazione *f*.

**emphasis** ['emfəsis] *n*, *pl* -ses enfasi *f*, veemenza *f*, rilievo *m*. **emphasize** *v* dare rilievo a, mettere in evidenza. **emphatic** *adj* enfatico, risoluto, intenso.

**empire** ['empaiə] *n* impero *m*. **emperor** *n* imperatore *m*. **empress** *n* imperatrice *f*.

**empirical** [im'pirikəl] *adj* empirico.

**employ** [im'ploi] *v* impiegare; (*use*) adoperare, usare. **employee** *n* impiegato, -a *m*, *f*. **employer** *n* padrone, -a *m*, *f*; datore, -trice di lavoro *m*, *f*. **employment** *n* impiego (*pl* -ghi) *m*, lavoro *m*. **employment agency** ufficio di collocamento *m*.

**empower** [im'pauə] *v* autorizzare.

**empty** ['empti] *adj* vuoto. *v* vuotare, scaricare. **empty-handed** *adj* a mani vuote.

**emulate** ['emjuːleit] *v* emulare. **emulation** *n* emulazione *f*.

**emulsion** [i'mʌlʃən] *n* emulsione *f*.

**enable** [i'neibl] *v* mettere in grado di, permettere; (*law*) abilitare.

**enact** [i'nakt] *v* (*ordain*) ordinare; (*decree*) decretare; (*put into operation*) promulgare; (*theatre*) recitare.

**enamel** [i'naməl] *n* smalto *m*. *v* smaltare.

**enamoured** [i'naməd] *adj* innamorato.

**enchant** [in'tʃaːnt] *v* incantare, affascinare, ammaliare. **enchanting** *adj* incantevole. **enchantment** *n* incanto *m*, incantesimo *m*, fascino *m*.

**encircle** [in'sɜːkl] *v* cingere, accerchiare. **encirclement** *n* accerchiamento *m*.

**enclose** [in'klouz] *v* rinchiudere; (*letter*) allegare. **enclosure** *n* recinto *m*; (*letter*) allegato

*m*; (*rel*) clausura *f*.

**encore** ['oŋkoː] *nm*, *interj* bis.

**encounter** [in'kauntə] *v* incontrare, affrontare. *n* incontro *m*; (*battle*) lotta *f*.

**encourage** [in'kʌridʒ] *v* incoraggiare, favorire, stimolare. **encouragement** *n* incitamento *m*, stimolo *m*.

**encroach** [in'krəutʃ] *v* **encroach on** abusare di; (*intrude on*) invadere.

**encumber** [in'kʌmbə] *v* ingombrare, impacciare; (*burden*) sopraffare. **encumbrance** *n* (*hindrance*) impaccio *m*; (*burden*) carico (*pl* -chi) *m*.

**encyclopedia** [insaiklə'piːdiə] *n* enciclopedia *f*.

**end** [end] *n* fine *f*, termine *m*; (*purpose*) scopo *m*; (*result*) conclusione *f*. **in the end** infine. **make ends meet** sbarcare il lunario. *v* finire, concludere, terminare. **endless** *adj* interminabile, senza fine.

**endanger** [in'deindʒə] *v* mettere in pericolo, compromettere.

**endear** [in'diə] *v* rendere caro. **endearing** *adj* simpatico, amabile, avvincente, irresistibile.

**endeavour** [in'devə] *v* cercare, tentare. *n* sforzo *m*, tentativo *m*.

**endemic** [en'demik] *n* endemico.

**endive** ['endiv] *n* indivia *f*, cicoria *f*.

**endorse** [in'doːs] *v* approvare; (*sign*) vistare; (*cheque*) girare; (*record infringement*) annotare le infrazioni commesse. **endorsement** *n* visto *m*, girata *f*, annotazione delle infrazioni commesse *f*.

**endow** [in'dau] *v* dotare, fornire. **endowment** *n* dotazione *f*, donazione *f*.

**endure** [in'djuə] *v* tollerare, sopportare; (*last*) durare; resistere. **endurance** *n* resistenza *f*.

**enema** ['enəmə] *n* clistere *m*, enteroclisma *m*.

**enemy** ['enəmi] *n* nemico, -a *m*, *f*; avversario, -a *m*, *f*.

**energy** ['enədʒi] *n* energia *f*. **energetic** *adj* energico.

**enfold** [in'fould] *v* avvolgere.

**enforce** [in'foːs] *v* imporre, far valere, far rispettare. **enforced** *adj* obbligatorio, imposto. **enforcement** *n* imposizione *f*, applicazione *f*.

**engage** [in'geidʒ] *v* (*employ*) assumere, impiegare; (*occupy*) impegnare, occupare;

(*mil*) attaccare; (*interlock*) ingranare, innestare; (*reserve*) prenotare. **engaged** *adj* (*busy*) occupato; (*betrothed*) fidanzato. **get engaged** fidanzarsi. **engagement** *n* fidanzamento *m*; (*employment*) impiego (*pl* -ghi) *m*; (*obligation*) impegno *m*; (*appointment*) appuntamento *m*.

**engine** ['endʒin] *n* motore *m*, macchina *f*; (*rail*) locomotiva *f*.

**engineer** [endʒi'niə] *n* ingegnere, -a *m*, *f*; meccanico, -a *m*, *f*; tecnico, -a *m*, *f*; (*mil*) geniere *m*. *v* (*construct*) costruire; (*contrive*) macchinare, tramare. **engineering** *n* costruzione *f*; (*study, science*) ingegneria *f*.

**England** ['iŋɡlənd] *n* Inghilterra *f*. **English** *n*(*m+f*), *adj* inglese.

**engrave** [in'greiv] *v* incidere, intagliare; (*printing*) imprimere. **engraver** *n* incisore *m*. **engraving** *n* incisione *f*.

**engrossed** [in'groust] *adj* preso (da), immerso.

**engulf** [in'ɡʌlf] *v* ingolfare.

**enhance** [in'haːns] *v* intensificare, aumentare, migliorare.

**enigma** [i'niɡmə] *n* enigma *m*. **enigmatic** *adj* enigmatico, misterioso.

**enjoy** [in'dʒoi] *v* godere, apprezzare. **enjoy oneself** divertirsi. **enjoyable** *adj* divertente, piacevole. **enjoyment** *n* piacere *m*, godimento *m*, gioia *f*, divertimento *m*.

**enlarge** [in'laːdʒ] *v* ingrandire. **enlarge on** dilungarsi su. **enlargement** *n* ingrandimento *m*; (*med*) ipertrofia *f*.

**enlighten** [in'laitn] *v* illuminare, chiarire. **enlightenment** *n* schiarimento *m*, delucidazione *f*; (*history*) illuminismo *m*.

**enlist** [in'list] *v* arruolare; (*obtain*) ottenere. **enlistment** *n* arruolamento *m*.

**enliven** [in'laivn] *v* animare, ravvivare.

**enmity** ['enmiti] *n* ostilità *f*.

**enormous** [i'noːməs] *adj* enorme, immenso.

**enough** [i'nʌf] *adv* abbastanza, sufficientemente. *adj* sufficiente, abbastanza, bastante. **be enough** bastare. *interj* basta!

**enquire** [in'kwaiə] *V* **inquire**.

**enrage** [in'reidʒ] *v* far arrabbiare. **enraged** *adj* arrabbiato, furioso.

**enrich** [in'ritʃ] *v* arricchire, abbellire.

**enrol** [in'roul] *v* (*mil*) arruolare; (*college, etc.*) iscrivere. **enrolment** *n* arruolamento *m*; iscrizione *f*.

**enslave** [in'sleiv] *v* far schiavo, assoggettare. **enslavement** *n* schiavitù *f*.

**ensue** [in'sjuː] *v* seguire, risultare.

**ensure** [in'ʃuə] *v* assicurare, garantire.

**entail** [in'teil] *v* comportare, implicare.

**entangle** [in'taŋɡl] *v* impigliare, aggrovigliare; (*involve*) coinvolgere. **entanglement** *n* impiccio *m*, imbroglio *m*.

**enter** ['entə] *v* entrare (in); penetrare; (*join*) iscriversi a; (*record*) notare.

**enterprise** ['entəpraiz] *n* impresa *f*, iniziativa *f*. **enterprising** *adj* intraprendente, pieno d'iniziativa.

**entertain** [entə'tein] *v* (*amuse*) divertire; (*receive guests*) ricevere ospitare; (*consider*) concepire, prendere in considerazione. **entertainer** (*actor*) attore, -trice *m*, *f*; (*singer*) cantante *m*, *f*. **entertaining** *adj* divertente, piacevole. **entertainment** *n* divertimento *m*, spettacolo *m*.

**enthral** [in'θroːl] *v* affascinare.

**enthusiasm** [in'θuːziˌazəm] *n* entusiasmo *m*. **enthusiast** *n* entusiasta *m*, *f*; (*fam*) tifoso, -a *m*, *f*. **enthusiastic** *adj* entusiastico, appassionato.

**entice** [in'tais] *v* sedurre, allettare. **enticement** *n* seduzione *f*, allettamento *m*.

**entire** [in'taiə] *adj* intero, completo, assoluto. **in its entirety** nel suo insieme.

**entitle** [in'taitl] *v* dar diritto a, qualificare, autorizzare; (*name*) intitolare. **entitlement** *n* diritto *m*, titolo *m*.

**entity** ['entəti] *n* entità *f*.

**entrails** ['entreilz] *pl n* viscere *f pl*.

**entrance**[1] ['entrəns] *n* entrata *f*, ingresso *m*, ammissione *f*.

**entrance**[2] [in'traːns] *v* incantare, estasiare.

**entrant** ['entrənt] *n* candidato, -a *m*, *f*; concorrente *m*, *f*.

**entreat** [in'triːt] *v* supplicare, implorare. **entreaty** *n* supplica *f*, preghiera *f*.

**entrée** ['ontrei] *n* (*main course*) piatto principale *m*, secondo piatto *m*; (*first course*) primo piatto *m*.

**entrench** [in'trentʃ] *v* trincerare, rafforzare. **entrenched** *adj* (*set*) radicato.

**entrepreneur** [ˌontrəprə'nəː] *n* imprenditore, -trice *m*, *f*.

**entrust** [in'trʌst] *v* affidare.

**entry** ['entri] *n* entrata *f*; (*book-keeping*) partita *f*; annotazione *f*.

**entwine** [in'twain] *v* intrecciare.

**enumerate** [i'nju:mǝreit] v annoverare, elencare.

**enunciate** [i'nʌnsi‚eit] v enunciare; articolare.

**envelop** [in'veləp] v avvolgere.

**envelope** ['envǝ‚loup] n busta f.

**environment** [in'vaiǝrǝnmǝnt] n ambiente m. **environmental** adj ambientale.

**envisage** [in'vizidʒ] v contemplare, immaginare.

**envoy** ['envoi] n inviato, -a m, f.

**envy** ['envi] n invidia f. v invidiare. **envious** adj invidioso.

**enzyme** ['enzaim] n enzima m.

**ephemeral** [i'femǝrǝl] adj effimero, passeggero.

**epic** ['epik] adj epico. n epopea f.

**epicure** ['epikjuǝ] n epicureo m; (gourmet) buongustaio, -a m, f.

**epidemic** [epi'demik] n epidemia f. adj epidemico.

**epilepsy** ['epilepsi] n epilessia f. **epileptic** nm, adj epilettico.

**epilogue** ['epilog] n epilogo (pl -ghi) m.

**Epiphany** [i'pifǝni] n Epifania f.

**episcopal** [i'piskǝpǝl] adj vescovile.

**episode** ['episoud] n episodio m, incidente m.

**epitaph** ['epi‚ta:f] n epitaffio m.

**epitome** [i'pitǝmi] n epitome f, compendio m.

**epoch** ['i:pok] n epoca f.

**equable** ['ekwǝbl] adj equanime, sereno, uniforme.

**equal** ['i:kwǝl] adj eguale, uguale, pari. v uguagliare; (in calculations) fare. **equality** n uguaglianza f, parità f. **equalize** v ragguagliare; (sport) pareggiare.

**equanimity** [ekwǝ'nimǝti] n equanimità f, serenità f.

**equate** [i'kweit] v uguagliare, paragonare. **equation** n equazione f.

**equator** [i'kweitǝ] n equatore m.

**equestrian** [i'kwestriǝn] adj equestre.

**equilateral** [i:kwi'latǝrǝl] adj equilatero.

**equilibrium** [i:kwi'libriǝm] n equilibrio m. **equilibrate** v equilibrare, bilanciare.

**equinox** ['ekwinoks] n equinozio m.

**equip** [i'kwip] v (array) allestire; (furnish) attrezzare, fornire (di), dotare (di). **equipment** n equipaggiamento m, attrezzatura f.

**equity** ['ekwǝti] n giustizia f; imparzialità f; (property) valore netto m; (securities) azioni ordinarie f pl.

**equivalent** [i'kwivǝlǝnt] nm, adj equivalente.

**era** ['iǝrǝ] n era f, epoca f.

**eradicate** [i'radi‚keit] v sradicare, estirpare.

**erase** [i'reiz] v cancellare.

**erect** [i'rekt] v erigere, costruire. adj eretto, dritto. **erection** n erezione f.

**ermine** ['ǝ:min] n ermellino m.

**erode** [i'roud] v erodere. **erosion** n erosione f.

**erotic** [i'rotik] adj erotico.

**err** [ǝ:] v errare; (make mistakes) sbagliare; (sin) peccare.

**errand** ['erǝnd] n commissione f. **errandboy** n fattorino m.

**erratic** [i'ratik] adj erratico.

**error** ['erǝ] n errore m, sbaglio m, torto m. **erroneous** adj erroneo.

**erudite** ['erudait] adj erudito, dotto. **erudition** n erudizione f.

**erupt** [i'rupt] v (volcano) eruttare; (burst out) erompere. **eruption** n eruzione f.

**escalate** ['eskǝ‚leit] v intensificare. **escalation** n intensificazione f. **escalator** n scala mobile f.

**escalope** ['eskǝ‚lop] n scaloppina f.

**escape** [is'keip] v fuggire, sfuggire; (avoid) evitare. n fuga f, evasione f. **escapism** n escapismo m, evasione dalla realtà f.

**escort** ['esko:t; v i'sko:t] n scorta f. v scortare.

**esoteric** [esǝ'terik] adj esoterico.

**especial** [i'speʃǝl] adj notevole, particolare. **especially** adv specie, specialmente.

**espionage** ['espiǝ‚na:ʒ] n spionaggio m.

**esplanade** [‚esplǝ'neid] n spianata f; lungomare m.

**essay** ['esei] n saggio m, tema m.

**essence** ['esns] n essenza f; (gist) nocciolo m.

**essential** [i'senʃǝl] adj essenziale, indispensabile.

**establish** [i'stabliʃ] v stabilire, fondare; (ascertain) constatare; (set up) istituire, instaurare; (fix) determinare. **established** adj (set) radicato; (beyond question) indubbio. **establishment** n costituzione f, fondazione f; (*house*) casa f; (*organization*) personale effettivo m.

**estate** [i'steit] n (*property*) tenuta f; (*possessions*) beni m pl, patrimonio m. **estate agent** agente immobiliare m. **estate car** giardinetta f. **housing estate** quartiere residenziale m.

**esteem** [i'sti:m] n stima f, considerazione f. v stimare, apprezzare.

**estimate** ['esti,meit; n 'estimət] v (*value*) valutare; (*judge*) stimare; (*assess cost*) preventivare. n preventivo m; valutazione f. **estimation** n valutazione f; considerazione f.

**Estonia** [e'stouniə] n Estonia f. **Estonian** n(m+f), adj estone f.

**estrange** [i'streindʒ] v alienare. **estrangement** n alienazione f; allontanamento m.

**estuary** ['estjuəri] n estuario m.

**eternal** [i'tə:nl] adj eterno. **eternity** n eternità f.

**ether** ['i:θə] n etere m.

**ethereal** [i'θiəriəl] adj etereo, evanescente.

**ethical** ['eθikl] adj etico, morale. **ethics** pl n etica f sing, morale f sing.

**ethnic** ['eθnik] adj etnico. **ethnology** n etnologia f.

**etiquette** ['eti,ket] n etichetta f, comportamento m, cerimoniale m.

**etymology** [,eti'molədʒi] n etimologia f. **etymological** adj etimologico.

**EU** n UE f.

**Eucharist** ['ju:kərist] n eucaristia f.

**eunuch** ['ju:nək] n eunuco (pl -chi) m.

**euphemism** ['ju:fə,mizəm] n eufemismo m. **euphemistic** adj eufemistico.

**euphoria** [ju'fo:riə] n euforia f. **euphoric** adj euforico.

**Europe** ['juərəp] n Europa f. **European** n, adj europeo, -a. **Europian Union** n Unione Europea f.

**euthanasia** [ju:θə'neiziə] n eutanasia f.

**evacuate** [i'vakju,eit] v evacuare, sfollare. **evacuation** n evacuazione f, sfollamento m.

**evade** [i'veid] v evadere, evitare, eludere. **evasion** n evasione f. **evasive** adj evasivo, elusivo.

**evaluate** [i'valju,eit] v valutare. **evaluation** n valutazione f.

**evangelical** [,i:van'dʒelikəl] adj evangelico. **evangelist** n evangelista m.

**evaporate** [i'vapə,reit] v evaporare, far evaporare. **evaporation** n evaporazione f.

**eve** [i:v] n vigilia f.

**even** ['i:vən] adj (*flat*) piano, piatto; (*regular*) uniforme, regolare; (*not odd*) pari. adv (*still*) ancora; (*indeed*) perfino. **even if** benchè, sebbene, quantunque. v livellare, uguagliare.

**evening** ['i:vniŋ] n sera f, serata f. **evening class** classe or scuola serale f. **evening dress** abito da sera m.

**evensong** ['i:vən,soŋ] n vespro m.

**event** [i'vent] n avvenimento m, evento m; (*outcome*) eventualità f; (*sport*) gara f. **eventful** adj ricco di vicende, memorabile. **eventual** adj finale, contingente. **eventually** adv alla fine, ultimamente.

**ever** ['evə] adv sempre, mai. **ever since** da quando, da allora. **evergreen** nm, adj sempreverde. **everlasting** adj eterno, perpetuo, perenne. **hardly ever** quasi mai.

**every** ['evri] adj ogni, ognuno, ciascuno. **everybody** or **everyone** pron ognuno, tutti pl. **everyday** adj quotidiano, normale. **every now and then** di tanto in tanto. **every other day** un giorno sì un giorno no. **everything** pron tutto, ogni cosa. **everywhere** adv dovunque, dappertutto.

**evict** [i'vikt] v sfrattare. **eviction** n sfratto m.

**evidence** ['evidəns] n prova f, evidenza f; (*law*) testimonianza f, deposizione f. **give evidence** (*law*) deporre, testimoniare. **evident** adj evidente, manifesto, ovvio.

**evil** ['i:vl] adj cattivo, malvagio. n male m, peccato m. **evil-doer** malfattore, -trice m, f. **evil eye** malocchio m. **evil-looking** adj losco. **evil-minded** adj malintenzionato.

**evoke** [i'vouk] v evocare.

**evolve** [i'volv] v evolvere, sviluppare. **evolution** n evoluzione f.

**ewe** [ju:] n pecora (femmina) f.

**exacerbate** [ig'zasə,beit] v esacerbare, inasprire, irritare.

**exact** [ig'zakt] adj esatto, preciso. v esigere, richiedere. **exacting** adj esigente, impegnativo. **exactitude** n esattezza f, precisione f.

**exaggerate** [ig'zadʒə,reit] v esagerare. **exaggeration** n esagerazione f.

**exalt** [ig'zolt] v esaltare; (*praise*) vantare, lodare. **exaltation** n esaltazione f.

**examine** [ig'zamin] v esaminare; verificare;

(*med*) visitare; (*law*) interrogare. **examination** *n* esame *m*; verifica *f*; visita medica *f*; (*law*) interrogatorio *m*. **examiner** *n* ispettore, -trice *m, f.*

**example** [ig'za:mpl] *n* esempio *m*; (*specimen*) esemplare *m*. **for example** per esempio.

**exasperate** [ig'za:spə,reit] *v* esasperare; esacerbare; irritare. **exasperating** *adj* esasperante. **exasperation** *n* esasperazione *f.*

**excavate** ['ekskə,veit] *v* scavare. **excavation** *n* scavo *m.*

**exceed** [ik'si:d] *v* eccedere, superare. **exceedingly** *adv* estremamente.

**excel** [ik'sel] *v* eccellere.

**excellent** ['eksələnt] *adj* eccellente, ottimo. **excellence** *n* eccellenza *f*, superiorità *f.* **Excellency** *n* Eccellenza *f.*

**except** [ik'sept] *prep* eccetto, salvo, tranne, all'infuori di. *v* escludere, eccettuare.

**excerpt** ['eksə:pt] *n* estratto *m*, brano *m.*

**excess** [ik'ses] *n* eccesso *m*, sovrabbondanza *f.* **excess baggage** eccedenza di bagaglio *f.* **excess weight** soprappeso *m.* **excessive** *adj* eccessivo, smoderato.

**exchange** [iks'tʃeindʒ] *n* cambio *m*, scambio *m*; (*phone*) centralino *m.* **rate of exchange** cambio *m. v* cambiare, scambiare.

**exchequer** [iks'tʃekə] *n* tesoro *m*, erario *m.*

**excise** ['eksaiz] *n* imposta di consumo *f. v* recidere, tagliar via.

**excite** [ik'sait] *v* eccitare, stimolare, provocare. **excitable** *adj* eccitabile, impressionabile. **excitement** *n* eccitamento *m*, agitazione *f*, emozione *f.*

**exclaim** [ik'skleim] *v* esclamare. **exclamation** *n* esclamazione *f.* **exclamation mark** punto esclamativo *m.*

**exclude** [ik'sklu:d] *v* escludere. **excluding** *prep* escluso, eccetto. **exclusion** *n* esclusione *f.* **exclusive** *adj* esclusivo. **exclusivity** *n* esclusiva *f.*

**excommunicate** [ekskə'mju:ni,keit] *v* scomunicare. **excommunication** *n* scomunica *f.*

**excrement** ['ekskrəmənt] *n* sterco *m*, feci *f pl.* **excrete** *v* defecare. **excretion** *n* escrezione *f.*

**excruciating** [ik'skru:ʃieitiŋ] *adj* atroce.

**excursion** [ik'skə:ʃən] *n* escursione *f*, gita *f.*

**excuse** [ik'skjus; *v* ik'skju:z] *n* scusa *f*, pretesto *m.* **make excuses** scusarsi. *v* scusare, perdonare; giustificare. **excuse from** esentare da. **excuse me!** scusi!

**execute** ['eksi,kju:t] *v* eseguire, mettere in esecuzione, effettuare; (*kill*) giustiziare. **execution** *n* esecuzione *f*; (*death*) esecuzione capitale *f.* **executioner** *n* boia *m invar.*

**executive** [ig'zekjutiv] *adj* esecutivo. *n* (*body*) esecutivo *m*; (*person*) funzionario, -a *m, f.* **executor** *n* esecutore, -trice *m, f.* testamentario, -a *m, f.*

**exemplify** [ig'zempli,fai] *v* esemplificare, illustrare.

**exempt** [ig'zempt] *v* esentare, esonerare. *adj* esente. **exemption** *n* esenzione *f*, dispensa *f.*

**exercise** ['eksə,saiz] *n* esercizio *m*, uso *m*; (*task*) compito *m*; (*mil*) manovra *f. v* esercitare, usare. **exercise-book** *n* quaderno *m.*

**exert** [ig'zə:t] *v* esercitare. **exert oneself** sforzarsi. **exertion** *n* sforzo *m.*

**exhale** [eks'heil] *v* emanare; (*breathe out*) esalare.

**exhaust** [ig'zo:st] *v* stancare, esaurire, estenuare. *n* scarico (*pl* -chi) *m*, scappamento *m.* **exhausted** *adj* sfinito, esausto. **exhausting** *adj* faticoso, estenuante. **exhaustion** *n* esaurimento *m.*

**exhibit** [ig'zibit] *v* esibire, esporre. *n* oggetto per mostra *m*; (*law*) oggetto di appoggio *m.* **exhibition** *n* mostra *f*, esposizione *f.* **exhibitionism** *n* esibizionismo *m.* **exhibitionist** *n* esibizionista *m, f.* **exhibitor** *n* esibitore, -trice *m, f.*

**exhilarating** [ig'ziləreitiŋ] *adj* esilarante, rallegrante.

**exigency** [ig'zidʒənsi] *n* esigenza *f*, necessità *f.*

**exile** ['eksail] *n* (*expulsion*) esilio *m*; (*person*) esule *m, f*, esiliato, -a *m, f. v* esiliare, mettere al bando.

**exist** [ig'zist] *v* esistere, vivere. **existence** *n* esistenza *f*, vita *f.* **existentialism** *n* esistenzialismo *m.* **existing** *adj* esistente, attuale.

**exit** ['egzit] *n* uscita *f. v* uscire.

**exodus** ['eksədəs] *n* esodo *m.*

**exonerate** [ig'zonə,reit] *v* esonerare, assolvere.

**exorbitant** [ig'zo:bitənt] *adj* esorbitante, esagerato.

**exorcize** ['ekso:saiz] v esorcizzare. **exorcism** n esorcismo m. **exorcist** n esorcista m, f.

**exotic** [ig'zotik] adj esotico; (strange) strano.

**expand** [ik'spand] v espandere, estendere. **expansion** n espansione f.

**expanse** [ik'spans] n spazio m, distesa f.

**expatriate** [eks'peitrieit; n, adj eks'peitriət] v espatriare, emigrare. n, adj espatriato, -a.

**expect** [ik'spekt] v (await) aspettare; anticipare; (believe) credere. **expectant** adj in attesa. **expectation** n aspettativa f, attesa f, prospettiva f.

**expedient** [ik'spi:diənt] n espediente m, accorgimento m. adj opportuno, conveniente.

**expedition** [,ekspi'diʃən] n spedizione f. **expeditious** adj sbrigativo.

**expel** [ik'spel] v espellere, scacciare.

**expenditure** [ik'spenditʃə] n spesa f, consumo m.

**expense** [ik'spens] n spesa f. **expense account** conto spese m. **expensive** adj caro, costoso.

**experience** [ik'spiəriəns] v provare, subire. n esperienza f; incidente m, avventura f.

**experiment** [ik'sperimənt] n esperimento m, prova f. v sperimentare, provare, fare esperimenti. **experimental** adj sperimentale.

**expert** ['ekspə:t] adj esperto, perito, competente. n esperto, -a m, f, perito, -a m, f; conoscitore, -trice m, f.

**expertise** [,ekspə:'ti:z] n perizia f, maestria f.

**expire** [ik'spaiə] v scadere, terminare; (die) morire. **expiry** n termine m, scadenza f.

**explain** [ik'splein] v spiegare, chiarire. **explanation** n spiegazione f, chiarimento m. **explanatory** adj esplicativo.

**expletive** [ek'spli:tiv] n (profanity) bestemmia f.

**explicit** [ik'splisit] adj esplicito, chiaro.

**explode** [ik'sploud] v esplodere, far saltare, scoppiare; (discredit) screditare. **explosion** n esplosione f.

**exploit¹** ['eksploit] n impresa f. **exploits pl** n gesta f pl.

**exploit²** [ik'sploit] v sfruttare, valorizzare. **exploitation** n sfruttamento m, valorizzazione f.

**explore** [ik'splo:] v esplorare; studiare. **exploration** n esplorazione f; studio m. **exploratory** adj esploratorio.

**exponent** [ik'spounənt] n esponente m, f; (representative) interprete m, f, rappresentante m, f. **exponential** adj esponenziale.

**export** ['ekspo:t; v ik'spo:t] n esportazione f. v esportare.

**expose** [ik'spouz] v esporre, mostrare; (reveal) svelare; (unmask) smascherare. **exposition** n spiegazione f; mostra f.

**exposure** n esposizione f; smascheramento m; rivelazione f; (phot) posa f.

**express** [ik'spres] adj espresso, esplicito. **express train** direttissimo m, rapido m. v esprimere. **expression** n espressione f; manifestazione f; (phrase) modo di dire m. **expressionless** adj impassibile. **expressive** adj espressivo.

**expulsion** [ik'spʌlʃən] n espulsione f.

**expurgate** ['ekspəgeit] v espurgare.

**exquisite** ['ekswizit] adj squisito; (intense) vivo, acuto.

**extend** [ik'stend] v estendere, prolungare. **extension** n estensione f; (time) proroga f; (phone) telefono interno m. **extensive** adj esteso, vasto.

**extent** [ik'stent] n estensione f; limite m.

**extenuating** [ik'stenjueitiŋ] adj attenuante.

**exterior** [ik'stiəriə] nm, adj esterno.

**exterminate** [ik'stə:mi,neit] v sterminare, annientare. **extermination** n sterminio m, annientamento m.

**external** [ik'stə:nl] adj esterno.

**extinct** [ik'stiŋkt] adj estinto.

**extinguish** [ik'stiŋgwiʃ] v estinguere, spegnere. **fire extinguisher** n estintore m.

**extol** [ik'stoul] v esaltare, lodare.

**extort** [ik'sto:t] v estorcere, strappare. **extortion** n estorsione f. **extortionate** adj esorbitante, esagerato.

**extra** ['ekstrə] adj extra invar, straordinario, supplementare, in più. n (theatre) comparsa f; (additional charge) spesa extra f. adv in più.

**extract** [ik'strakt] v estrarre; (tooth) cavare. **extraction** n estrazione f; ceppo m.

**extradite** ['ekstrə,dait] v estradare. **extraditable** adj passibile di estradizione. **extradition** n estradizione f.

**extramural** [,ekstrə'mjuərəl] adj fuori le mura; (university) al di fuori dell'università.

**extramural course** corso libero *m*.

**extraneous** [ik'streiniəs] *adj* estraneo.

**extraordinary** [ik'stro:dənəri] *adj* straordinario, eccezionale, fenomenale.

**extravagant** [ik'stravəgənt] *adj* stravagante; (*wasteful*) prodigo, spendereccio; (*exaggerated*) esagerato. **extravagance** *n* stravaganza *f*, prodigalità *f*.

**extreme** [ik'stri:m] *adj* estremo, ultimo. *n* estremo *m*. **extremist** *n* estremista *m*, *f*. **extremity** *n* estremità *f*.

**extricate** ['ekstri,keit] *v* **extricate oneself** districarsi, tirarsi d'impaccio, liberarsi.

**extrovert** ['ekstrəvə:t] *nm, adj* estroverso.

**exuberant** [ig'zju:bərənt] *adj* esuberante. **exuberance** *n* esuberanza *f*.

**exude** [ig'zju:d] *v* emanare.

**exult** [ig'zʌlt] *v* esultare. **exultant** *adj* esultante, trionfante. **exultation** *n* esultazione *f*, trionfo *m*.

**eye** [ai] *n* occhio *m*; (*needle*) cruna *f*. **see eye to eye (with)** vederla allo stesso modo (di). *v* adocchiare, osservare.

**eyeball** ['aibo:l] *n* bulbo oculare *m*.

**eyebrow** ['aibrau] *n* sopracciglio *m*.

**eyelash** ['ailaʃ] *n* ciglio *m* (*pl* -a *f*).

**eyelet** ['ailit] *n* occhiello *m*.

**eyelid** ['ailid] *n* palpebra *f*.

**eye-opener** *n* fatto rivelatore *m*.

**eye shadow** *n* bistro *m*, ombretto *m*.

**eyesight** ['aisait] *n* vista *f*, visione *f*.

**eyesore** ['aiso:] *n* pugno in un occhio *m*.

**eyewitness** ['ai,witnis] *n* testimonio oculare *m*.

# F

**fable** ['feibl] *n* favola *f*.

**fabric** ['fabrik] *n* (*cloth*) tessuto *m*, stoffa *f*; (*structure*) struttura *f*.

**fabricate** ['fabrikeit] *v* (*make up*) inventare; (*fake*) falsificare; (*construct*) fabbricare. **fabrication** *n* costruzione *f*, invenzione *f*.

**fabulous** ['fabjuləs] *adj* favoloso.

**façade** [fə'sa:d] *n* facciata *f*.

**face** [feis] *n* faccia *f*, volto *m*, viso *m*; (*clock*) quadrante *m*; (*type*) carattere *m*. *v* (*look towards*) fronteggiare; (*confront*) affrontare; (*cover*) rivestire. **face-cloth** *n* pezzuola per lavarsi *f*. **face-lift** *n* plastica facciale *f*; (*restyling*) restauro *m*. **face-pack** *n* maschera di bellezza *f*. **face value** valore nominale *m*. **lose face** perdere prestigio.

**facet** ['fasit] *n* (*small plane*) faccetta *f*; (*aspect*) aspetto *m*.

**facetious** [fə'si:ʃəs] *adj* arguto, spiritoso.

**facial** ['feiʃəl] *adj* facciale.

**facile** ['fasail] *adj* (*glib*) superficiale, pronto; (*easy*) facile.

**facilitate** [fə'sili,teit] *v* facilitare, agevolare.

**facility** [fə'siləti] *n* facilità *f*; (*help*) facilitazione *f*, agevolazione *f*; opportunità *f*. **facilities** *pl n* servizi *m pl*.

**facing** ['feisiŋ] *n* (*covering*) rivestimento *m*; (*dress*) risvolto *m*.

**facsimile** [fak'siməli] *n* facsimile *m invar*.

**fact** [fakt] *n* fatto *m*, verità *f*. **as a matter of fact** in effetti. **fact-finding** *adj* di inchiesta. **in fact** infatti. **factual** *adj* effettivo.

**faction** ['fakʃən] *n* fazione *f*, dissenso *m*. **factious** *adj* fazioso, partigiano.

**factor** ['faktə] *n* fattore *m*; agente *m*, *f*.

**factory** ['faktəri] *n* fabbrica *f*, stabilimento *m*.

**faculty** ['fakəlti] *n* facoltà *f*.

**fad** [fad] *n* capriccio *m*; (*fashion*) moda *f*.

**fade** [feid] *v* (*colour*) sbiadire; (*lose freshness*) appassire; (*disappear*) svanire. **fade away** affievolirsi.

**fag** [fag] *v* sfacchinare. *n* (*hard work*) sgobbata *f*; (*slang*) sigaretta *f*. **fag-end** *n* cicca *f*. **fagged out** stanco morto.

**fail** [feil] *v* fallire; (*fall short*) mancare; (*not pass*) bocciare, essere respinto. **without fail** senza fallo. **failure** *n* insuccesso *m*, mancanza *f*.

**failing** ['feiliŋ] *n* debole *m*, difetto *m*. *adj* debole. *prep* salvo.

**faint** [feint] *v* svenire. *adj* fiacco, tenue, appena percettibile. **feel faint** sentirsi venir meno. **not have the faintest idea** non avere la più pallida idea.

**fair**[1] [feə] *adj* (*colouring*) biondo, chiaro; (*unbiased*) giusto, imparziale; (*moderately good*) discreto. **fair copy** bella copia *f*. **fair play** comportamento leale *m*. *adv* secondo le regole. **fairly** *adv* (*moderately*) abbastanza; (*properly*) giustamente. **in all fairness**

in tutta franchezza.

**fair²** [feə] n fiera f, mercato m.

**fairy** ['feəri] n fata f. **fairy-tale** n fiaba f.

**faith** [feiθ] n (belief) fede f; (confidence) fiducia f. **faith-healer** n guaritore, -trice per suggestione m, f. **faithful** adj fedele. **faithless** adj che non ha fede, sleale.

**fake** [feik] v contraffare, fingere. n (object) contraffazione; (person) impostore, -a m, f.

**falcon** ['fo:lkən] n falco m, falcone m.

**\*fall** [fo:l] v cadere, cascare; (collapse) crollare; (lower) abbassarsi. **fall asleep** addormentarsi. **fall back on** riccorrere a. **fall behind** rimanere indietro; (fig) essere in arretrato. **fall ill** ammalarsi. **fall-out** n pioggia radioattiva f. **fall through** fallire. n caduta f; crollo m, rovina f; abbassamento m; (US: autumn) autunno m.

**fallacy** ['faləsi] n falsità f. **fallacious** adj fallace, falso.

**fallen** ['fo:ltə] V **fall**.

**fallible** ['faləbl] adj fallibile. **fallibility** n fallibilità f.

**fallow** ['falou] adj a maggese.

**false** [fo:ls] adj falso, artificiale, finto. **false alarm** falso allarme m. **false pretences** (law) millantato credito m. **false teeth** denti artificiali m pl. **falsehood** n menzogna f. **falseness** n perfidia f. **falsify** v falsificare.

**falsetto** [fo:l'setou] n falsetto m.

**falter** ['fo:ltə] v (waver) vacillare, titubare; (speak hesitatingly) balbettare. **faltering** adj titubante.

**fame** [feim] n fama f, rinomanza f. **famed** adj rinomato.

**familiar** [fə'miljə] adj familiare; intimo; (impudent) sfacciato; (well-known) noto. **be on familiar terms with** aver dimestichezza con. **familiarity** n familiarità f; intimità f; (impertinence) sfacciataggine f.

**family** ['faməli] n famiglia f. **family tree** albero genealogico m.

**famine** ['famin] n carestia f.

**famished** ['famiʃt] adj affamato.

**famous** ['feiməs] adj famoso, celebre.

**fan¹** [fan] n ventaglio m; (mechanical) ventilatore m. **fan-belt** n cinghia per ventilatore f. v (flames) soffiare su; (excite) aizzare. **fan oneself** farsi vento.

**fan²** [fan] n (admirer) tifoso, -a m, f.

**fanatic** [fə'natik] n, adj fanatico, -a; (sport)

tifoso, -a. **fanaticism** n fanatismo m; tifo m.

**fancy** ['fansi] adj elaborato, raffinato, di fantasia. **fancy-dress** n costume m. **fancy-dress ball** ballo in maschera m. n immaginazione f, fantasia f, capriccio m. v desiderare, immaginare. **fanciful** adj fantasioso, capriccioso.

**fanfare** ['fanfeə] n fanfara f.

**fang** [fan] n zanna f.

**fantastic** [fan'tastik] adj fantastico, strano.

**fantasy** ['fantəsi] n fantasia f, capriccio m.

**far** [fa:] adv, adj lontano, distante; (much) molto. **as far as** (place) fino a. **as far as I know** a quanto sappia. **far-fetched** adj improbabile, forzato. **far-reaching** adj di gran portata. **far-sighted** adj (prudent) previdente. **so far** (up to this point) fin qui.

**farce** [fa:s] n farsa f.

**fare** [feə] n tariffa f, prezzo del biglietto m; (person) viaggiatore, -trice m, f; (food) vitto m. v vivere, trovarsi.

**farewell** [feə'wel] n addio m, congedo m. interj addio!

**farm** [fa:m] n fattoria f, podere m. **farmhouse** n casa colonica f. v coltivare, fare l'agricoltore. **farm out** dare in appalto. **farmer** n agricoltore m, contadino, -a m, f. **farming** n agricoltura f, coltivazione f.

**fart** [fa:t] (vulgar) n scoreggia f. v fare scoregge.

**farther** ['fa:ðə] adj, adv più lontano; ulteriore. **farthest** adj il più lontano.

**fascinate** ['fasineit] v affascinare, incantare. **fascinating** adj affascinante, avvincente. **fascination** n fascino m, attrattiva f.

**fascism** ['faʃizəm] n fascismo m. **fascist** n(m+f), adj fascista.

**fashion** ['faʃən] n (manner) modo m, maniera f; (dress) moda f; (style) stile m; (vogue) voga f. **after a fashion** in un certo modo. **in fashion** alla moda. **out of fashion** fuori moda. v foggiare, modellare. **fashionable** adj elegante, di moda.

**fast¹** [fa:st] adj rapido, veloce; (firmly held) fisso, saldo; (colour) solido. adv presto, rapidamente. **the clock is … fast** l'orologio va avanti di …

**fast²** [fa:st] n digiuno m. v digiunare.

**fasten** ['fa:sn] v legare, fissare, agganciare, attaccare. **fastener** or **fastening** n chiusura f, fermaglio m.

**fastidious** [fa'stidiəs] *adj* meticoloso, schifiltoso.

**fat** [fat] *adj, nm* grasso. **fatten** *v* ingrassare. **fatty** *adj* grasso, untuoso.

**fatal** ['feitl] *adj* fatale, ineluttabile. **fatalism** *n* fatalismo. **fatalist** *n* fatalista *m, f.* **fatality** *n* fatalità *f.*

**fate** [feit] *n* fato *m,* destino *m.* **fated** *adj* destinato. **fateful** *adj* decisivo.

**father** ['fa:ðə] *n* padre *m;* (*coll*) babbo *m.* *v* procreare, originare. **fatherhood** *n* paternità *f.* **father-in-law** *n* suocero *m.* **fatherland** *n* patria *f.* **fatherly** *adj* paterno.

**fathom** ['faðəm] *v* (*understand*) indovinare, penetrare; (*depth*) sondare. *n* braccio *m.*

**fatigue** [fə'ti:g] *n* stanchezza *f,* esaurimento *m.* *v* stancare.

**fatuous** ['fatjuəs] *adj* fatuo, frivolo, vuoto.

**fault** [fo:lt] *n* (*flaw*) difetto *m,* imperfezione *f;* errore *m;* (*cause for blame*) colpa *f;* (*geol*) faglia *f;* (*tennis*) fallo *m.* **be at fault** essere colpevole. **find fault with** criticare, biasimare. **faultless** *adj* senza colpa. **faulty** *adj* difettoso.

**favour** ['feivə] *n* favore *m,* piacere *m.* *v* favorire, favoreggiare, preferire. **favourable** *adj* favorevole, vantaggioso.

**favourite** ['feivrit] *adj* preferito. *n* favorito, -a *m, f.*

**fawn¹** [fo:n] *n* (*zool*) daino *m,* cerbiatto *m.* *adj* (*colour*) fulvo.

**fawn²** [fo:n] *v* **fawn on** adulare.

**fax** [faks] *n, v* fax, faxare *m.*

**fear** [fiə] *v* temere, aver paura di. *n* timore *m,* paura *f.* **fearful** *adj* terribile, spaventoso. **fearless** *adj* intrepido.

**feasible** ['fi:zəbl] *adj* fattibile, realizzabile. **feasibility** *n* praticabilità *f.*

**feast** [fi:st] *n* festa *f,* banchetto *m.*

**feat** [fi:t] *n* impresa *f,* azione *f.*

**feather** ['feðə] *n* penna *f,* piuma *f.* **feather-bed** *n* letto di piume *m.* **feathered** *adj* pennuto.

**feature** ['fi:tʃə] *n* caratteristica *f,* tratto distintivo *m;* (*newspaper*) elzeviro *m;* (*geog*) configurazione *f.* **features** *pl n* (*anat*) lineamenti *m pl.* *v* dar rilievo a; (*theatre*) presentare. **featureless** *adj* scialbo.

**February** ['februəri] *n* febbraio *m.*

**fed** [fed] *V* **feed.**

**federal** ['fedərəl] *adj* federale. **federation** *n* federazione *f.*

**fee** [fi:] *n* onorario *m,* parcella *f;* (*school*) retta *f;* (*entrance fee*) tassa d'iscrizione *f.*

**feeble** ['fi:bl] *adj* debole, fiacco. **feeble-minded** *adj* cretino, debole di mente. **feebleness** *n* debolezza *f.*

**\*feed** [fi:d] *v* nutrire; (*supply*) alimentare; (*eat*) mangiare, nutrirsi. *n* mangime *m,* nutrimento *m;* (*baby*) poppata *f.* **feedback** *n* retroreazione *f,* feedback *m invar;* (*response*) reazione. **fed up** (*coll*) stufo.

**\*feel** [fi:l] *v* (*touch*) tastare, toccare; (*emotion*) sentire. **feel like** sentirsi disposto a. **feeler** *n* tentacolo *m;* (*proposal*) sondaggio *m.* **feeling** *n* (*physical*) senso *m,* sensazione *f;* (*emotion*) sensibilità *f,* suscettibilità *f;* (*affection*) affetto *m.*

**feet** [fi:t] *V* **foot.**

**feign** [fein] *v* fingere, simulare, far finta.

**feline** ['fi:lain] *adj* felino.

**fell¹** [fel] *V* **fall.**

**fell²** [fel] *v* (*cut down*) abbattere; (*strike down*) atterrare.

**fellow** ['felou] *n* individuo *m,* tipo *m;* (*companion*) compagno *m,* collega *m, f;* (*member*) membro *m,* socio *m.* **fellow-countryman** *n* compatriota *m, f.* **fellowship** *n* (*companionship*) cameratismo *m;* (*rel*) comunità *f;* (*allowance*) borsa di studio *f.*

**felony** ['feləni] *n* crimine *m.* **felon** *n* delinquente *m, f.*

**felt¹** [felt] *V* **feel.**

**felt²** [felt] *n* feltro *m.*

**female** ['fi:meil] *n* femmina *f.* *adj also* **feminine** femminile.

**feminism** ['feminizəm] *n* femminismo *m.* **feminist** *n* femminista *m, f.*

**fence** [fens] *n* (*barrier*) steccato *m,* palizzata *f;* (*receiver of stolen goods*) ricettatore, -trice *m, f.* *v* (*sport*) tirar di scherma. **fence in** recintare. **fencing** *n* recinto *m;* (*sport*) scherma *f.*

**fend** [fend] *v* **fend for oneself** provvedere a se stesso, arrangiarsi. **fend off** parare, schivare.

**fender** ['fendə] *n* paracenere *m invar;* (*US*) paraurti *m.*

**fennel** ['fenl] *n* finocchio *m.*

**ferment** [*n* 'fə:ment; *v* fə'ment] *n* fermento *m.* *v* fermentare. **fermentation** *n* fermentazione *f.*

**fern** [fə:n] *n* felce *f.*

**ferocious** [fə'rouʃəs] *adj* feroce. **ferocity** *n*

ferocia f.

**ferret** ['ferit] n furetto m. v **ferret out** scovare.

**ferry** ['feri] n traghetto m. v traghettare.

**fertile** ['fə:tail] adj fertile, fecondo. **fertility** n fertilità f, fecondità f. **fertilize** v (enrich) fertilizzare; fecondare. **fertilizer** n fertilizzante m, concime m.

**fervent** ['fə:vənt] adj fervente, fervido. **fervour** n fervore m, ardore m.

**fester** ['festə] v suppurare; (rankle) bruciare.

**festival** ['festəvəl] n festival m invar, festa f. **festivity** n festività f. **festive** adj festivo.

**festoon** [fə'stu:n] v decorare con festoni. n festone m.

**fetch** [fetʃ] v andare a prendere; (call) chiamare; (a price) realizzare. **fetching** adj attraente.

**fête** [feit] n festa f. v festeggiare.

**fetid** ['fi:tid] adj fetido, puzzolente.

**fetish** ['fetiʃ] n feticcio m, idolo m.

**fetter** ['fetə] n catena f. v incatenare.

**feud** [fju:d] n lite f. v essere in lotta.

**feudal** ['fju:dl] adj feudale. **feudalism** n feudalesimo m.

**fever** ['fi:və] n febbre f. **feverish** adj febbricitante; (restless) febbrile.

**few** [fju:] pron, adj pochi, -e. **a few** alcuni, -e. **quite a few** parecchi, parecchie. **fewer** adj meno invar. **fewest** adj meno invar.

**fiancé** [fi'onsei] n fidanzato m. **fiancée** n fidanzata f.

**fiasco** [fi'askou] n fiasco m.

**fib** [fib] (coll) n frottola f. v raccontar frottole.

**fibre** ['faibə] n fibra f. **fibreglass** n fibra di vetro f. **fibrous** adj fibroso.

**fickle** ['fikl] adj volubile. **fickleness** n volubilità f.

**fiction** ['fikʃən] n (invention) finzione f; (novels, etc.) novellistica f, narrativa f. **fictional** or **fictitious** adj fittizio, immaginario.

**fiddle** ['fidl] n violino m; (coll: fraud) imbroglio m, truffa f. v suonare il violino; (coll: cheat) truffare, imbrogliare. **fit as a fiddle** sano come un pesce.

**fidelity** [fi'deləti] n fedeltà f.

**fidget** ['fidʒit] v muoversi irrequietamente, dimenarsi. **fidgety** adj irrequieto, nervoso.

**field** [fi:ld] n campo m; (of knowledge, etc.) settore m. **field glasses** binocolo m sing. **field marshal** maresciallo m.

**fiend** [fi:nd] n demonio m. **fiendish** adj infernale, diabolico.

**fierce** [fiəs] adj feroce, intenso.

**fiery** ['faiəri] adj focoso, ardente.

**fifteen** [fif'ti:n] nm, adj quindici. **fifteenth** nm, adj quindicesimo.

**fifth** [fifθ] nm, adj quinto.

**fifty** ['fifti] nm, adj cinquanta. **fiftieth** nm, adj cinquantesimo.

**fig** [fig] n fico m.

**\*fight** [fait] v lottare, combattere. n lotta f, combattimento m; (scuffle) zuffa f.

**figment** ['figmənt] n **figment of the imagination** finzione f.

**figure** ['figə] n (numeral) cifra f; (shape) forma f; (pictorial) figura f; (character) personaggio m; (bodily form) linea f. **figurehead** n (naut) polena f; (derog) uomo di paglia m. **figure of speech** modo di dire m. v (appear) apparire. **figure out** calcolare.

**filament** ['filəmənt] n filamento m.

**file¹** [fail] n (dossier) pratica f; archivio m; (for papers) cartella f; (card with details) scheda f; (row) fila f. v archiviare, mettere in ordine, registrare. **filing** n schedare m. **filing cabinet** schedario m. **single file** fila indiana f.

**file²** [fail] n (tool) lima f. v limare, levigare.

**filial** ['filiəl] adj filiale.

**fill** [fil] v riempire; (tooth) otturare. **fill in** completare, inserire. **fill up** (mot) fare il pieno. **filling** n (cookery) ripieno m; (tooth) otturazione f. **filling station** stazione di rifornimento f.

**fillet** ['filit] n (meat) filetto m. v disossare.

**film** [film] n pellicola f; (phot, cinema) film m invar. **film star** divo, -a del cinema m, f. v girare un film.

**filter** ['filtə] n filtro m. **filter-tip** n filtro m. v filtrare.

**filth** [filθ] n sudiciume m, sporcizia f; oscenità f. **filthy** adj sudicio, sporco; lurido, osceno.

**fin** [fin] n pinna f.

**final** ['fainl] adj finale, ultimo. n finale f. **finalist** n finalista m, f. **finally** adv infine.

**finance** [fai'nans] n finanza f. v finanziare. **financial** adj finanziario. **financier** n finanziere m, finanziatore m.

**finch** [fintʃ] n fringuello m.

**\*find** [faind] v scoprire, trovare. **find out** scoprire.

**fine¹** [fain] adj (high quality) pregiato, raffinato; (minute) fine; (accomplished) bravo; (beautiful) bello. adv bene.

**fine²** [fain] n (penalty) multa f. v multare.

**finesse** [fi'nes] n finezza f.

**finger** ['fiŋgə] n dito m (pl dita f). **cross one's fingers** toccar ferro. **finger bowl** lavadita m invar. **finger-mark** n ditata f. **fingernail** n unghia f. **fingerprint** n impronta digitale f. **fingertip** n punta delle dita f. v (touch) palpare.

**finish** ['finiʃ] v finire, concludere. n fine f, conclusione f; (surface) finitura f; (textile) appretto m.

**finite** ['fainait] adj limitato, circoscritto; (math) finito.

**Finland** ['finlənd] n Finlandia f. **Finn** n finlandese m, f. **Finnish** nm, adj finlandese.

**fir** [fə:] n abete m.

**fire** ['faiə] n fuoco m; (conflagration) incendio m; (heater) stufa f. **catch fire** prender fuoco. **hang fire** indugiare. **set fire to** appiccare il fuoco a, incendiare. v (shoot) sparare; (dismiss) licenziare, silurare; (inflame) eccitare, infiammare; (inspire) ispirare.

**fire alarm** n allarme d'incendio m.

**firearm** ['faiə,a:m] n arma da fuoco f.

**fire brigade** n corpo dei vigili del fuoco m.

**fire door** n esercitazione antincendio f.

**fire drill** n pompa antincendio f.

**fire engine** n uscita di sicurezza f.

**fire escape** n uscita di sicurezza f.

**fire extinguisher** n estintore m.

**firefly** ['faiəflai] n lucciola f.

**fire-guard** n parafuoco m, paracenere m invar.

**fireman** ['faiəmən] n pompiere m, vigile del fuoco m.

**fireplace** ['faiə,pleis] n focolare m, camino m, caminetto m.

**fireproof** ['faiə,pru:f] adj incombustibile, resistente al fuoco.

**fireside** ['faiə,said] n focolare m.

**fire station** n caserma dei pompieri f.

**firewood** ['faiə,wud] n legna da ardere f.

**fireworks** ['faiə,wə:ks] pl n fuochi d'artificio m pl.

**firing squad** n plotone d'esecuzione m.

**firm¹** [fə:m] adj fermo; (steady) saldo; (steadfast) risoluto; solido; stabile. **stand firm** tener duro. **firmness** n fermezza f; saldezza f; risolutezza f.

**firm²** [fə:m] n (comm) ditta f, azienda f.

**first** [fə:st] adj primo. adv prima; in primo luogo; anzitutto. **first aid** pronto soccorso m. **first-class** adj ottimo, di prima qualità, eccellente; (rail, etc.) di prima classe. **first floor** primo piano m. **first-hand** adj, adv di prima mano. **first name** nome di battesimo m.

**fiscal** ['fiskəl] adj fiscale.

**fish** [fiʃ] n pesce m. v pescare. **fishy** adj (coll) losco.

**fishbone** ['fiʃ,boun] n lisca f.

**fisherman** ['fiʃəmən] n pescatore m.

**fish fingers** pl n bastoncini di pesce m pl.

**fishing** ['fiʃiŋ] n pesca f. **fishing boat** peschereccio m. **fishing rod** canna da pesca f.

**fishmonger** ['fiʃ,mʌŋgə] n pescivendolo, -a m, f.

**fishpond** ['fiʃ,pond] n vivaio m.

**fission** ['fiʃən] n fissione f.

**fissure** ['fiʃə] n fessura f.

**fist** [fist] n pugno m.

**fit¹** [fit] adj (suitable) adatto; competente; (healthy) sano. **keep fit** mantenersi sano, mantenersi in forma. n misura f. v (clothes, etc.) star bene; (suit) adeguare, convenire. **fit in** incastrare. **fitting** adj conveniente, adatto. **fittings** pl n suppellettili m pl, arredi m pl. **fitted carpet** n moquette f.

**fit²** [fit] n accesso m, attacco m. **fitful** adj intermittente.

**five** [faiv] nm, adj cinque.

**fix** [fiks] v fissare, stabilire. **fix up** sistemare, mettere a posto. n (coll) difficoltà f, guaio m. **fixation** n fissazione f. **fixed** adj fisso, stabile. **fixture** n (accessory) attrezzatura f; (sport) avvenimento sportivo m.

**fizz** [fiz] v frizzare. n spumante m. **fizzy** adj effervescente, frizzante.

**fizzle** ['fizl] v **fizzle out** far cilecca.

**flabbergast** ['flabəga:st] v sbalordire.

**flabby** ['flabi] adj floscio, flaccido.

**flag¹** [flag] n (banner) bandiera f. **flag-pole** n asta di bandiera f. **flagship** n nave ammiraglia f. v **flag down** intimare di fermarsi.

**flag²** [flag] v (tire) indebolirsi, accasciarsi.

**flag³** [flag] n (stone) lastra (di pietra) f.

**flagon** ['flagən] n bottiglione m.

**flagrant** ['fleigrənt] adj flagrante.

**flagstone** ['flagstoun] n lastra di pietra f.

**flair** [fleə] n intuito m, inclinazione f.

**flake** [fleik] v sfaldare, sfaldarsi. n falda f, scaglia f. **flaky** adj a scaglie. **flaky pastry** sfoglia f.

**flamboyant** [flam'boiənt] adj sgargiante.

**flame** [fleim] n fiamma f. v fiammeggiare, risplendere. **burst into flames** divampare. **flaming** adj fiammeggiante, violento.

**flamingo** [flə'miŋgou] n fiammingo m.

**flan** [flan] n sformato m, torta f.

**flank** [flaŋk] v fiancheggiare. n fianco m, lato m.

**flannel** ['flanl] n (fabric) flanella f; (facecloth) pezzuola per lavarsi f. v (slang) abbindolare con le chiacchiere.

**flap** [flap] v agitare; (wings) battere; (coll) agitarsi. n lembo m; (wings) colpo m; panico m.

**flare** [fleə] n fiammata f, bagliore m; (rocket) razzo m. v brillare; (clothes) svasare. **flare up** divampare; (anger, etc.) arrabbiarsi.

**flash** [flaʃ] n baleno m, lampo m. v balenare. **flashback** n scena retrospettiva f, flashback m invar. **flash bulb** lampadina flash f. **flashlight** n fotolampo m, flash m invar.

**flask** [fla:sk] n flacone m, borraccia f.

**flat¹** [flat] adj piatto, piano; (tyre) a terra; (net) netto; (stale) svanito, insipido. n (music) bemolle m. **flat-footed** adj con i piedi piatti. **flat out** a briglia sciolta. **flatten** v appiattire, livellare.

**flat²** [flat] n appartamento m.

**flatter** ['flatə] v adulare, lusingare. **flatterer** n adulatore, -trice m, f. **flattering** adj lusinghiero. **flattery** n lusinghe f pl, adulazione f.

**flatulence** ['flatjuləns] n flatulenza f. **flatulent** adj flatulento.

**flaunt** [flo:nt] v ostentare, pavoneggiarsi.

**flautist** ['flo:tist] n flautista m, f.

**flavour** ['fleivə] n sapore m, gusto m. v condire. **flavouring** n condimento m.

**flaw** [flo:] n tacca f, difetto m. **flawed** adj difettoso. **flawless** adj perfetto.

**flax** [flaks] n lino m. **flaxen** adj di lino; (colour) biondissimo.

**flea** [fli:] n pulce f.

**fleck** [flek] n chiazza f, macchia f. v chiazzare, macchiare.

**fled** [fled] V **flee**.

**\*flee** [fli:] v fuggire, scappare.

**fleece** [fli:s] n vello m. (jacket) n felpa f. v (coll) pelare, derubare.

**fleet** [fli:t] n flotta f; (of cars) parco m.

**fleeting** ['fli:tiŋ] adj fugace, transitorio.

**Flemish** ['flemiʃ] nm, adj fiammingo.

**flesh** [fleʃ] n carne f; (fruit) polpa f.

**flew** [flu:] V **fly¹**.

**flex** [fleks] v flettere. n filo or cavo elettrico m. **flexible** adj flessibile. **flexibility** n flessibilità f.

**flick** [flik] n colpetto m. v dare un colpetto a.

**flicker** ['flikə] v tremolare. n tremolio m.

**flight¹** [flait] n (flying) volo m; (steps) rampa f. **flighty** adj frivolo.

**flight²** [flait] n (fleeing) fuga f.

**flimsy** ['flimzi] adj tenue, fragile; (inadequate) insufficiente.

**flinch** [flintʃ] v (wince) sussultare; (shrink from) sottrarsi a. **without flinching** senza batter ciglio.

**\*fling** [fliŋ] v lanciare, scagliare, buttare. n **have one's fling** godersela.

**flint** [flint] n selce f; (lighter) pietrina f.

**flip** [flip] n colpetto m. v dare un colpetto a. **flip a coin** fare testa e croce. **flip through** sfogliare, dare una scorsa a.

**flippant** ['flipənt] adj poco serio, frivolo. **flippancy** n mancanza di serietà f.

**flirt** [flə:t] v flirtare. n dongiovanni m; civetta f.

**flit** [flit] v svolazzare; (disappear) squaliarsela.

**float** [flout] v galleggiare, stare a galla. n galleggiante m; (angling) sughero m; (procession) carro m.

**flock¹** [flok] n (animals) branco m; (birds) stormo m; (sheep) gregge m; (crowd) folla f. v accorrere in massa, affluire. **flock together** radunarsi.

**flock²** [flok] n fiocco m; (mattress filling) borra f.

**flog** [flog] v bastonare, frustare; (sell) spacciare.

**flood** [flʌd] v inondare, allagare. n inondazione f, alluvione f, diluvio m; (outpouring) torrente m, ondata f. **floodlight** n riflettore m. **floodlit** adj illuminato a giorno.

**floor** [flo:] n pavimento m; (storey) piano m. **floorboard** n tavola di pavimento f. **take the floor** (speak) prendere la parola; (dance) ballare. v pavimentare; (knock down) atterrare.

**flop** [flop] n tonfo m; (coll) fiasco m. v cader di schianto; (coll) fallire.

**Florence** ['florəns] n Firenze f. **Florentine** n, adj fiorentino, -a.

**florist** ['florist] n fioraio, -a m, f; fiorista m, f.

**flotsam** ['flotsəm] n relitti m pl. **flotsam and jetsam** (people) relitti umani m pl.

**flounce**[1] [flauns] v dimenare.

**flounce**[2] [flauns] n balza f.

**flounder** ['flaundə] v dibattersi, dimenarsi; (speech) impappinarsi. n passera di mare f.

**flour** ['flauə] n farina f. **floury** adj farinoso.

**flourish** ['flʌriʃ] v (prosper) fiorire; (brandish) brandire. n (fanfare) squillo di tromba m; (writting) ghirigoro m; (speech) fiorettatura f; (gesture) largo gesto m.

**flout** [flaut] v sprezzare, schernire.

**flow** [flou] n corrente f, flusso m. v scorrere, circolare.

**flower** ['flauə] n fiore m. **flower-bed** n aiuola f. **flower-pot** n vaso da fiori m. v fiorire, essere in fiore. **flowering** adj in fiore. **flowery** adj fiorito.

**flown** [floun] V **fly**[1].

**flu** [flu:] n influenza f.

**fluctuate** ['flʌktju,eit] v fluttuare. **fluctuation** n fluttuazione f.

**flue** [flu:] n gola del camino f.

**fluent** ['fluənt] adj corrente, scorrevole. **speak fluently** parlare correntemente.

**fluff** [flʌf] n lanugine f, peluria f.

**fluid** ['fluid] nm, adj fluido, liquido.

**fluke** [flu:k] n (lucky chance) colpo fortunato m.

**flung** [flʌŋ] V **fling**.

**fluorescent** [fluə'resnt] adj fluorescente.

**fluoride** ['fluəraid] n fluoruro m. **fluoridation** n fluorizzazione f.

**flush**[1] [flʌʃ] n (colouring) rossore m; (rush of liquid) flusso m; (blushing) vampa f; (poker) flush m invar. v (wash out) pulire con un getto d'acqua; (lavatory) vuotare; (redden) arrossire, avvampare.

**flush**[2] [flʌʃ] adj (level) a livello, rasente; (slang: rich) ben fornito.

**fluster** ['flʌstə] v turbare, confondere.

**flute** [flu:t] n flauto m.

**flutter** ['flʌtə] v battere; agitare, confondere; (fly) svolazzare. n battito m, agitazione f; (bet) scommessa f.

**flux** [flʌks] n flusso m.

***fly**[1] [flai] v volare; (flutter) svolazzare; (flag) sventolare; (flee) fuggire, scappare. **fly away** or **off** volar via. **flyleaf** n risguardo m. **flyover** n cavalcavia m invar. **flysheet** n volantino m. **flywheel** n volano m. **flying squad** squadra mobile f.

**fly**[2] [flai] n (insect) mosca f.

**flying saucer** n disco volante m.

**foal** [foul] n puledro m.

**foam** [foum] n schiuma f. **foam rubber** gommapiuma m. v spumeggiare.

**focus** ['foukəs] n fuoco m, centro m. v concentrare; (bring into focus) mettere a fuoco. **focal** adj focale.

**fodder** ['fodə] n mangime m, foraggio m.

**foe** [fou] n nemico, -a m, f; avversario, -a m, f.

**foetus** ['fi:təs] n feto m.

**fog** [fog] n nebbia f. **fog-bound** adj fermo per la nebbia. **fog-horn** n sirena da nebbia f. **foggy** adj nebbioso.

**foible** ['foibl] n debole m.

**foil**[1] [foil] v frustrare, sventare.

**foil**[2] [foil] n lamina (di metallo) f; (tinfoil) stagnolo m; (contrast) contrappeso m.

**foist** [foist] v rifilare, affibbiare.

**fold**[1] [fould] v piegare; (envelop) avvolgere. **fold one's arms** incrociare le braccia. **fold (up)** (collapse) chiudere, cessare l'esercizio. n piega f, ripiegatura f. **folder** n cartella f. **folding** adj pieghevole.

**fold**[2] [fould] n (enclosure) ovile m.

**foliage** ['fouliidʒ] n fogliame m.

**folk** [fouk] n gente f, popolo m. **folk dance** danza rustica f. **folklore** n folclore m. **folk song** canto popolare m.

**follicle** ['folikl] n follicolo m.

**follow** ['folou] v seguire, succedere; (understand) capire; (result) risultare, conseguire. **follower** n seguace m, f. **following** adj seguente, successivo.

**folly** ['foli] *n* follia *f*.

**fond** [fond] *adj* affettuoso, affezionato.
**become fond of** affezionarsi a. **be fond of** voler bene a; (*person*) amare.

**fondle** ['fondl] *v* accarezzare, coccolare.

**font**¹ [font] *n* fonte battesimale *f*.

**font**² *n* (*typface*) serie di caratteri *f*.

**food** [fu:d] *n* cibo *m*, vitto *m*; (*foodstuffs*) generi alimentari *m pl*. **food processor** *n* tritatutto (per alimenti) *m*, *f*.

**fool** [fu:l] *n* sciocco, -a *m*, *f*; cretino, -a *m*, *f*; (*jester*) buffone, -a *m*, *f*, pagliaccio *m*. **fool-hardy** *adj* temerario. **foolproof** *adj* sicurissimo. *v* (*deceive*) ingannare. **foolish** *adj* sciocco, insensato. **foolishness** *n* sciocchezza *f*.

**foolscap** ['fu:lskap] *n* carta protocollo *f*.

**foot** [fut] *n*, *pl* **feet** piede *m*; (*birds, animals*) zampa *f*. **v foot the bill** saldare il conto. **on foot** a piedi. **put one's foot down** farsi valere. **put one's foot in it** fare una gaffe.

**football** ['fut,bo:l] *n* football *m invar*, pallone *m*. **footballer** *n* calciatore *m*.

**foot-bridge** ['fut,bridʒ] *n* passerella *f*.

**foothold** ['fut,hould] *n* punto d'appoggio *m*.

**footing** ['futin] *n* (*foundation*) base *f*; (*mutual standing*) relazioni *f pl*.

**footlights** ['fut,laits] *pl n* luci della ribalta *f pl*.

**footnote** ['fut,nout] *n* postilla *f*, nota in calce *f*.

**footpath** ['fut,pa:θ] *n* sentiero *m*.

**footprint** ['fut,print] *n* orma *f*.

**footstep** ['fut,step] *n* passo *m*.

**footwear** ['fut,weə] *n* calzatura *f*.

**for** [fo:] *prep* per, a favore di, a, di, da. *conj* poiché.

**forage** ['foridʒ] *v* foraggiare. *n* foraggio *m*.

**forbade** [fo:'bad] *V* **forbid**.

*****forbear** [fo:'beə] *v* astenersi da, pazientare.

*****forbid** [fo:'bid] *v* proibire, vietare. **forbidding** *adj* austero, formidabile.

**forbidden** [fo:'bidn] *V* **forbid**.

**force** [fo:s] *n* forza *f*. **in force** in vigore. *v* forzare; (*compel*) costringere. **forceful** *adj* energico.

**forceps** ['fo:seps] *pl n* forcipe *m sing*.

**ford** [fo:d] *n* guado *m*. *v* guadare.

**fore** [fo:] *adj* anteriore. **come to the fore**

venire alla ribalta.

**forearm** ['fo:ra:m] *n* avambraccio *m*.

**forebear** ['fo:beə] *n* antenato, -a *m*, *f*.

**foreboding** [fo:'boudin] *n* presagio *m*.

*****forecast** ['fo:ka:st] *n* previsione *f*, pronostico *m*. *v* prevedere.

**forecourt** ['fo:ko:t] *n* cortile *m*.

**forefather** ['fo:fa:ðə] *n* antenato *m*, avo *m*.

**forefinger** ['fo:fingə] *n* indice *m*.

**forefront** ['fo:frʌnt] *n* prima linea *f*.

**foreground** ['fo:graund] *n* primo piano *m*.

**forehand** ['fo:hand] *nm*, *adj* (*tennis*) diritto *m*.

**forehead** ['forid] *n* fronte *f*.

**foreign** ['forən] *adj* straniero, forestiero; (*trade, etc.*) estero; (*not belonging*) estraneo. **foreigner** *n* straniero, -a *m*, *f*; forestiero, -a *m*, *f*.

**foreleg** ['fo:leg] *n* zampa anteriore *f*.

**foreman** ['fo:mən] *n* caposquadra (*pl* capisquadra) *m*, capo operaio *m*; (*jury*) presidente *m*.

**foremost** ['fo:moust] *adj* principale, primo. *adv* in primo luogo. **first and foremost** anzitutto.

**forename** ['fo:neim] *n* nome di battesimo *m*.

**forensic** [fə'rensik] *adj* forense. **forensic medicine** medicina legale *f*.

**forerunner** ['fo:rʌnə] *n* precursore *m*.

*****foresee** [fo:'si:] *v* prevedere. **foreseeable** *adj* prevedibile.

**foreshadow** [fo:'ʃadou] *v* adombrare.

**foreshorten** [fo:'ʃo:tn] *v* scorciare. **foreshortened** *adj* di scorcio.

**foresight** ['fo:sait] *n* (*prevision*) preveggenza *f*; (*care for future*) previdenza *f*.

**foreskin** ['fo:skin] *n* prepuzio *m*.

**forest** ['forist] *n* foresta *f*. **forester** *n* guardia forestale *f*. **forestry** *n* selvicoltura *f*.

**forestall** [fo:'sto:l] *v* anticipare, prevenire.

**foretaste** ['fo:teist] *n* pregustazione *f*.

*****foretell** [fo:'tel] *v* predire, pronosticare.

**forethought** ['fo:θo:t] *n* premeditazione *f*, previdenza *f*.

**forever** [fə'revə] *adv* per sempre.

**foreword** ['fo:wə:d] *n* prefazione *f*.

**forfeit** ['fo:fit] *n* (*pawn*) pegno *m*; (*fine*) multa *f*. *v* (*give up*) dover abbandonare; pagare il fio.

**forgave** [fə'geiv] *V* **forgive**.

**forge¹** [fo:dʒ] v (counterfeit) falsificare, contraffare; (metal) forgiare. n fucina f. **forger** n falsario, -a m, f. **forgery** n contraffazione f, falso m.

**forge²** [fo:dʒ] v avanzare. **forge ahead** farsi strada; (take lead) distanziarsi, staccarsi.

**\*forget** [fə'get] v dimenticare, scordare, non ricordarsi di. **forget-me-not** n nontiscordardimé m. **forget oneself** lasciarsi andare. **forgetful** adj smemorato.

**\*forgive** [fə'giv] v perdonare, rimettere. **forgiveness** n perdono m, indulgenza f. **forgiving** adj clemente, indulgente.

**forgiven** [fə'givn] V **forgive.**

**\*forgo** [fo:'gou] v rinunciare a.

**forgot** [fə'got] V **forget.**

**forgotten** [fə'gotn] V **forget.**

**fork** [fo:k] n (cutlery) forchetta f; (agriculture) forca f, forcone m; (road) bivio m; (branching) biforcazione f. v forcare; biforcarsi. **fork out** (slang: pay) metter mano alla borsa.

**forlorn** [fə'lo:n] adj disperato, desolato.

**form** [fo:m] n forma f; (document) modulo m; (bench) banco m; (school) classe f. v formare. **formation** n formazione f. **formative** adj formativo.

**formal** [fo:məl] adj formale, esplicito. **formality** n formalità f, cerimonia f.

**format** [fo:mat] n formato m.

**former** [fo:mə] adj precedente, anteriore. **the former** il primo. **formerly** adv in passato, già, in altri tempi.

**formidable** [fo:'midəbl] adj formidabile, spaventoso, terribile.

**formula** [fo:mjulə] n, pl -ae formula f.

**formulate** [fo:mju,leit] v formulare. **formulation** n formulazione f.

**\*forsake** [fə'seik] v abbandonare.

**forsaken** [fə'seikn] V **forsake.**

**forsook** [fə'suk] V **forsake.**

**fort** [fo:t] n fortezza f, forte m.

**forth** [fo:θ] adv avanti; (out of concealment) fuori. **and so forth** e così via. **forthcoming** adj imminente, prossimo. **forthright** adj franco, schietto. **forthwith** adv immediatamente.

**fortify** [fo:ti,fai] v fortificare, rafforzare, dar forza a; (wine) alcolizzare. **fortification** n fortificazione f.

**fortitude** [fo:ti,tju:d] n forza d'animo f; (virtue) fortezza f.

**fortnight** [fo:tnait] n quindicina f, due settimane f pl. **fortnightly** nm, adj quindicinale, bimensile.

**fortress** [fo:tris] n fortezza f.

**fortuitous** [fo:'tju:itəs] adj fortuito.

**fortune** [fo:tʃən] n fortuna f; (riches) ricchezza f; futuro m. **fortune-teller** n chiromante m, f. **fortune-telling** n chiromanzia f. **fortunate** adj fortunato.

**forty** [fo:ti] nm, adj quaranta. **fortieth** nm, adj quarantesimo.

**forum** [fo:rəm] n foro m; (court) tribuna f.

**forward** [fo:wəd] adj avanzato; presuntuoso. adv also **forwards** avanti, in avanti. **look forward to** anticipare con piacere. **put forward** proporre. v spedire, inoltrare; (mail) rispedire.

**fossil** [fosl] n fossile m. **fossilized** adj fossilizzato.

**foster** [fostə] v (child) allevare; incoraggiare; nutrire, alimentare. **foster child** bambino in affidamento m. **foster father** padre affidatario m. **foster mother** madre affidataria f. **foster parents** genitori affidatari m pl. **foster home** casa d'accoglimento f.

**fought** [fo:t] V **fight.**

**foul** [faul] adj lurido, schifoso; (weather) pessimo. **foul play** (crime) delitto m; (sport) gioco falloso m.

**found¹** [faund] V **find.**

**found²** [faund] v fondare, istituire, basare. **foundation** n fondazione f; istituto m; (base) fondamento m, base f. **founder** n fondatore, -trice m, f.

**founder** [faundə] v (sink) colare a picco.

**foundry** [faundri] n fonderia f.

**fountain** [fauntin] n fontana f. **fountain pen** penna stilografica f.

**four** [fo:] nm, adj quattro. **foursome** n quattro m. **on all fours** (a) carponi. **fourth** nm, adj quarto.

**fourteen** [fo:'ti:n] nm, adj quattordici. **fourteenth** nm, adj quattordicesimo.

**fowl** [faul] n pollame m; (chicken) pollo m.

**fox** [foks] n volpe f; (sly person) furbacchione m, furbo, -a m, f. **foxglove** n digitale f. **fox-hound** n bracco m. v (coll) ingannare. **foxed** adj perplesso.

**foyer** [foiei] n ridotto m.

**fraction** [frakʃən] n frazione f.

**fracture** ['fraktʃə] n frattura f, rottura f. v rompere, fratturare.

**fragile** ['fradʒail] adj fragile; (delicate) gracile.

**fragment** ['fragmənt] n frammento m.

**fragrant** ['freigrənt] adj fragrante, profumato. **fragrance** n profumo m.

**frail** [freil] adj fragile, gracile.

**frame** [freim] n struttura f; (skeleton) ossatura f; (picture) cornice f; (machine) telaio m. **frame of mind** disposizione d'animo f, umore m. **framework** n (mech) intelaiatura f; (outline) abbozzo m. v incorniciare, costruire; (compose) redigere; (fabricate evidence) calunniare.

**France** [fra:ns] n Francia f.

**franchise** ['frantʃaiz] n (privilege) franchigia f; (comm) concessione f.

**frank** [fraŋk] adj sincero, schietto. **frankness** n sincerità f, schiettezza f.

**frantic** ['frantik] adj frenetico.

**fraternal** [frə'tə:nl] adj fraterno. **fraternity** n fratellanza f; (friendship) fraternità f. **fraternize** v fraternizzare.

**fraud** [fro:d] n (deceit) frode f, inganno m; (deceiver) impostore, -a m, f; truffatore, -trice m, f. **fraudulent** adj fraudolento, doloso.

**fraught** [fro:t] adj (tense) nervoso. **fraught with** pieno or denso di.

**fray**[1] [frei] v (unravel) logorare, consumare. **frayed** adj (clothes, etc.) logoro dall'uso, liso. **frayed nerves** nervi scoperti m pl.

**fray**[2] [frei] n (brawl) mischia f.

**freak** [fri:k] n fenomeno m; figura grottesca f, mostro m.

**freckle** ['frekl] n lentiggine f. **freckled** adj lentigginoso.

**free** [fri:] adj libero; (without payment) gratis, gratuito; (unconstrained) disinvolto, sciolto; (lavish) generoso. **free from** esente da. **freehold** n prprietà fondiaria assoluta f. **freelance** adj indipendente. **Freemason** n massone m. **free speech** libertà di parola f. **free trade** libero scambio m. **free will** libero arbitrio m. v liberare. **freedom** n libertà f.

**free-range** adj di allevamento all'aperto.

**freesia** ['fri:ziə] n fresia f.

*****freeze** [fri:z] v gelare, congelare; (block) bloccare. n gelo m. **freezer** n congelatore m, freezer m invar. **freezing** adj gelido.

below **freezing** sotto zero. **freezing point** punto di congelamento m.

**freight** [freit] n (cargo) carico m; (charge) nolo m; (conveyance) trasporto m. **freight train** treno merci m. v trasportare. **freighter** n nave da carico f.

**French** [frentʃ] nm, adj francese. **French bean** n fagiolino verde m, cornetto m. **French horn** corno (a pistoni) m. **Frenchman/woman** n francese m, f. **French window** portafinestra f. **French fries** n patatine fritte f pl.

**frenzy** ['frenzi] n frenesia f. **frenzied** adj frenetico.

**frequent** ['fri:kwənt; v fri'kwent] adj frequente. v frequentare. **frequency** n frequenza f.

**fresco** ['freskou] n affresco m.

**fresh** [freʃ] adj fresco; (water) dolce; (brisk) vigoroso; (cheeky) insolente. **fresh from** appena venuto da. **freshman** n matricola f. **freshen** v rinfrescare, rinnovare. **freshness** n freschezza f, vigore m.

**fret**[1] [fret] v inquietarsi. **fretful** adj irritabile.

**fret**[2] [fret] n (pattern) fregio m. v ornare con fregi, traforare. **fretwork** n lavoro di traforo m.

**friar** ['fraiə] n frate m. **friary** n convento di frati m.

**friction** ['frikʃən] n attrito m; (conflict) dissenso m.

**Friday** ['fraidei] n venerdì m.

**fridge** [fridʒ] n (coll) frigorifero m.

**fried** [fraid] adj fritto.

**friend** [frend] n amico, -a m, f. **make friends** fare amicizia. **friendless** adj senza amici. **friendliness** n amichevolezza f, cordialità f. **friendly** adj amichevole, cordiale, gentile. **be friendly with** essere amico di. **friendship** n amicizia f.

**frieze** [fri:z] n fregio m.

**frigate** ['frigit] n fregata f.

**fright** [frait] n spavento m. **frighten** v spaventare, allarmare. **be frightened** aver paura. **frightening** adj spaventevole, terribile. **frightful** adj terribile.

**frigid** ['fridʒid] adj freddo; (woman) frigido. **frigidity** n freddezza f; frigidità f.

**frill** [fril] n fronzolo m. **frilly** adj carico di fronzoli.

**fringe** [frindʒ] n (border) orlo m; limite m;

(*ornamental border, hair*) frangia *f*; periferia *f*. *v* ornare di frange.

**frisk** [frisk] *v* saltellare; (*search*) perquisire. **frisky** *adj* vivace.

**fritter**[1] ['fritə] *v* **fritter away** sprecare.

**fritter**[2] ['fritə] *n* (*cookery*) frittella *f*.

**frivolity** [fri'voliti] *n* frivolezza *f*. **frivolous** *adj* superficiale, frivolo.

**frizz** [friz] *v* arricciare. *n* ricciolo *m*. **frizzy** *adj* ricciuto.

**fro** [frou] *adv* **to and fro** avanti e indietro.

**frock** [frok] *n* vestito *m*.

**frog** [frog] *n* rana *f*. **frogman** *n* uomo rana *m*.

**frolic** ['frolik] *v* trastullarsi, scherzare. *n* scherzo *m*.

**from** [from] *prep* da, per, da parte di.

**front** [frʌnt] *n* parte anteriore *f*; (*mil, pol*) fronte *m*; (*arch*) facciata *f*; (*seaside*) lungomare *m*. *adj* primo, anteriore. **front door** portone *m*. **in front of** davanti a.

**frontier** ['frʌntiə] *n* frontiera *f*, confine *m*.

**frost** [frost] *n* gelo *m*. **frost-bite** *n* gelone *m*. *v* brinare; (*cookery*) glassare. **frosted glass** vetro smerigliato *m*. **frosty** *adj* (*weather*) gelido; (*manner*) freddo.

**froth** [froθ] *n* schiuma *f*. *v* spumare, schiumare.

**frown** [fraun] *v* aggrottare le ciglia, corrugare la fronte. **frown at** guardare in cagnesco. *n* cipiglio *m*, viso arcigno *m*.

**froze** [frouz] V **freeze**.

**frozen** ['frouzn] V **freeze**. *adj* gelato, congelato; bloccato.

**frugal** ['fru:gəl] *adj* frugale, sobrio.

**fruit** [fru:t] *n* frutto *m*; (*collectively*) frutta *f*; (*result*) risultato *m*. **fruit salad** macedonia di frutta *f*. *v* (*bear fruit*) fruttare. **fruiterer** *n* fruttivendolo, -a *m*, *f*. **fruitful** *adj* fecondo; (*profitable*) redditizio. **fruition** *n* realizzazione *f*. **fruitless** *adj* infruttuoso; inutile. **fruity** *adj* saporito; di frutta; (*wine*) dal gusto d'uva.

**frustrate** [frʌ'streit] *v* frustrare. **frustration** *n* frustrazione *f*.

**fry** [frai] *v* friggere. **frying pan** padella *f*.

**fuchsia** ['fju:ʃə] *n* fucsia *f*.

**fuck** [fʌk] *v* (*vulgar*) fottere, chiavare.

**fuel** ['fjuəl] *n* combustibile *m*; (*mot*) carburante *m*. **fuel oil** gasolio *m*, nafta *f*. *v* alimentare.

**fugitive** ['fju:dʒitiv] *adj* (*runaway*) fuggitivo, fuggiasco; (*fleeting*) effimero, fugace. *n* fuggiasco, -a *m*, *f*; profugo, -a *m*, *f*.

**fugue** [fju:g] *n* fuga *f*.

**fulcrum** ['fulkrəm] *n* fulcro *m*.

**fulfil** [ful'fil] *v* adempiere, compiere, soddisfare. **fulfilment** *n* adempimento *m*, realizzazione *f*.

**full** [ful] *adj* pieno; completo; intero. **full-length** *adj* di lunghezza normale; (*portrait*) in piedi. **full moon** luna piena *f*. **full-sized** *adj* di grandezza naturale. **full stop** punto *m*. **full-time** *adj, adv* a tempo intero, a orario completo. **fully** *adv* completamente.

**fumble** ['fʌmbl] *v* brancolare.

**fume** [fju:m] *v* emettere fumo; (*coll: rage*) arrabbiarsi, imperversare. *n* fumo *m*, esalazione *f*.

**fumigate** ['fju:migeit] *v* suffumicare.

**fun** [fʌn] *n* spasso *m*, divertimento *m*, scherzo *m*. **funfair** *n* luna park *m invar*. **in fun** per ridere. **make fun of** prendere in giro.

**function** ['fʌŋkʃən] *n* funzione *f*; (*purpose*) scopo *m*; (*duty*) mansione *f*; (*ceremony*) cerimonia *f*. *v* funzionare. **functional** *adj* funzionale.

**fund** [fʌnd] *n* fondo *m*, riserva *f*, capitale *m*. **funds** *pl n* soldi *m pl*.

**fundamental** [fʌndə'mentl] *adj* fondamentale, basilare.

**funeral** ['fju:nərəl] *n* funerale *m*. *adj* funebre. **funereal** *adj* funereo.

**fungus** ['fʌŋgəs] *n*, *pl* -gi fungo *m*. **fungicide** *n* anticrittogamico *m*.

**funnel** ['fʌnl] *n* imbuto *m*; (*ship*) ciminiera *f*.

**funny** ['fʌni] *adj* divertente, comico; (*odd*) strano. **funny story** barzelletta *f*. **the funny thing is** il bello è.

**fur** [fə:] *n* (*skin*) pelo *m*; pelliccia *f*. *v* incrostarsi. **furrier** *n* pellicciaio *m*. **furry** *adj* peloso.

**furious** ['fjuəriəs] *adj* furibondo, arrabbiatissimo.

**furnace** ['fə:nis] *n* fornace *f*.

**furnish** ['fə:niʃ] *v* (*supply*) fornire, dotare; (*house, etc.*) arredare, ammobiliare.

**furniture** ['fə:nitʃə] *n* mobilio *m*, mobili *m pl*; (*fittings*) attrezzatura *f*.

**furrow** ['fʌrou] *n* solco *m*; (*brow*) ruga *f*, grinza *f*.

**further** ['fə:ðə] *adj* ulteriore, più lontano. *adv* più lontano, oltre. **furthermore** *adv* inoltre. **further on** più avanti. **further up** più in su. *v* favorire, promuovere.

**furthest** ['fə:ðist] *adj* in più lontano, estremo.

**furtive** ['fə:tiv] *adj* furtivo, di soppiatto.

**fury** ['fjuəri] *n* furia *f.* **fuse¹** [fju:z] *n (elec)* valvola *f,* fusibile *m.* **blow a fuse** saltare la corrente. *v (melt)* fondere; *(blend)* amalgamare, unire. **fusion** *n* fusione *f.*

**fuse²** [fju:z] *n (bomb)* detonatore *m.*

**fuselage** ['fju:zə,la:ʒ] *n* fusoliera *f.*

**fuss** [fʌs] *v* lamentarsi, agitarsi. **fuss over** affaccendarsi attorno a. *n* scalpore *m,* trambusto *m.* **make a fuss** fare un gran chiasso. **fussy** *adj* pignolo, meticoloso.

**futile** ['fju:tail] *adj* vano, inutile. **futility** *n* inutilità *f.*

**future** ['fju:tʃə] *n* futuro *m,* avvenire *m. adj* futuro.

**fuzz** [fʌz] *n* lanugine *f,* peluria *f.* **fuzzy** *adj* peloso; *(unclear)* sfocato.

# G

**gabble** ['gabl] *v* borbottare. *n* borbottio *m.*

**gaberdine** [gabə'di:n] *n* gabardina *f.*

**gable** ['geibl] *n* pigna *f,* frontone *m.*

**gadget** ['gadʒit] *n* congegno *m,* dispositivo *m.*

**gag¹** [gag] *n* bavaglio *m. v* imbavagliare.

**gag²** [gag] *n (joke)* battuta *f.*

**gaiety** ['geiəti] *n* allegria *f.*

**gaily** ['geili] *adv* allegramente.

**gain** [gein] *n* guadagno *m,* profitto *m. v* guadagnare; *(obtain)* ottenere.

**gait** [geit] *n* andatura *f,* passo *m.*

**gala** ['ga:lə] *n* festa *f.*

**galaxy** ['galəksi] *n* galassia *f.*

**gale** [geil] *n* bufera *f,* burrasca *f.*

**gallant** ['galənt] *adj (courageous)* prode; *(courtly)* galante. *n* cavaliere *m.* **gallantry** *n* valore *m,* coraggio *m;* galanteria *f.*

**gall-bladder** ['go:l,bladə] *n* cistifellea *f,* vescica biliare *f.*

**galleon** ['galiən] *n* galeone *m.*

**gallery** ['galəri] *n* galleria *f; (theatre)* loggione *m.*

**galley** ['gali] *n (naut)* galea *f; (kitchen)* cambusa *f.*

**gallop** ['galəp] *n* galoppo *m;* galoppata *f. v* galoppare, andare al galoppo.

**gallows** ['galouz] *n* patibolo *m.*

**gallstone** ['go:lstoun] *n* calcolo biliare *m.*

**galore** [gə'lo:] *adv* in quantità.

**galvanize** ['galvənaiz] *v* galvanizzare. **galvanometer** *n* galvanometro *m.*

**gambit** ['gambit] *n* gambetto *m.*

**gamble** ['gambl] *v (risk)* rischiare, arrischiare; *(game)* giocare *n* impresa rischiosa *f,* speculazione *f.* **gambler** *n* giocatore, -trice *m, f.* **gambling** *n* gioco d'azzardo *m.*

**game** [geim] *n* gioco *m; (match)* partita *f; (hunting)* selvaggina *f.* **gamekeeper** *n* guardacaccia *m. adj (plucky)* che ha del fegato.

**gammon** ['gamən] *n* prosciutto *m.*

**gander** ['gandə] *n* papero *m.*

**gang** [gaŋ] *n* squadra *f,* gruppo *m; (youths, thieves, etc.)* banda *f. v* **gang up** allearsi. **gangster** *n* gangster *m invar,* bandito *m.*

**gangling** ['ganglin] *adj* allampanato.

**gangrene** ['gangri:n] *n* cancrena *f.*

**gangway** ['ganwei] *n* passaggio *m,* corsia *f; (naut)* barcarizzo *m.*

**gaol** *V* **jail.**

**gap** [gap] *n (breach)* breccia *f; (opening)* apertura *f; (hole)* buco *m; (vacant space)* vuoto *m;* intervallo *m; (divergence)* distacco *m.*

**gape** [geip] *v* stare a bocca aperta; *(open wide)* spalancare.

**garage** ['gara:dʒ] *n* garage *m invar; (repairs)* autorimessa *f.*

**garbage** ['ga:bidʒ] *(US) n* rifiuti *m pl.* **garbage can** bidone della spazzatura *m.*

**garble** ['ga:bl] *v* mutilare.

**garden** ['ga:dn] *n* giardino *m. v* fare del giardinaggio. **gardener** *n* giardiniere, -a *m, f.* **gardening** *n* giardinaggio *m.*

**gargle** ['ga:gl] *v* gargarizzare. *n* gargarismo *m.*

**garish** ['geəriʃ] *adj* vistoso.

**garland** ['ga:lənd] *n* ghirlanda *f. v* inghirlandare.

**garlic** ['ga:lik] *n* aglio *m.*

**garment** ['gaːmənt] *n* indumento *m*, capo di vestiario *m*.

**garnish** ['gaːniʃ] *v* guarnire, adornare. *n* ornamento *m*, guarnizione *f*.

**garret** ['garət] *n* soffitta *f*.

**garrison** ['garisn] *n* guarnigione *f*, presidio *m*. *v* presidiare.

**garrulous** ['garələs] *adj* loquace.

**garter** ['gaːtə] *n* giarrettiera *f*.

**gas** [gas] *n* gas *m invar*; (*US: petrol*) benzina *f*. **gas cooker** fornello a gas *m*. **gas fire** stufa a gas *f*. **gas mask** maschera antigas *f*. *v* asfissiare.

**gash** [gaʃ] *n* sfregio *m*, squarcio *m*. *v* sfregiare, squarciare.

**gasket** ['gaskit] *n* guarnizione *f*.

**gasoline** ['gasəliːn] *n* (*US*) benzina *f*.

**gasp** [gaːsp] *v* boccheggiare, ansimare. *n* rantolo *m*.

**gastric** ['gastrik] *adj* gastrico.

**gastronomy** [ga'stronəmi] *n* gastronomia *f*. **gastronomic** *adj* gastronomico.

**gate** [geit] *n* cancello *m*, porta *f*. **gatecrash** *v* fare il portoghese, entrare senza invito or pagare. **gatepost** *n* montante del cancello *m*. **gateway** *n* entrata *f*, portone *m*.

**gateau** ['gatou] *n* pasticcino *m*, gateau *m*.

**gather** ['gaðə] *v* cogliere; (*bring together*) raccogliere; (*infer*) dedurre; (*assemble*) radunarsi. **gathering** *n* riunione *f*, adunata *f*.

**gaudy** ['goːdi] *adj* vistoso.

**gauge** [geidʒ] *n* (*measure*) misura *f*; (*instrument*) calibro *m*; (*rail*) scartamento *m*. *v* misurare, calibrare.

**gaunt** [goːnt] *adj* emaciato, desolato.

**gauze** [goːz] *n* garza *f*.

**gave** [geiv] *V* **give**.

**gay** [gei] *adj* vivace, allegro; (*slang*) omosessuale.

**gaze** [geiz] *v* mirare, guardare fissamente. **gaze at** fissare. *n* sguardo fisso *m*.

**gazelle** [gə'zel] *n* gazzella *f*.

**gazette** [gə'zet] *n* gazzetta ufficiale *f*.

**gazetteer** [gazə'tiə] *n* dizionario geografico *m*.

**gear** [giə] *n* (*mot*) marcia *f*, velocità *f*; (*equipment, tools*) arnesi *m pl*, attrezzatura *f*; (*belongings*) roba *f*. **change gear** cambiare velocità. **gearbox** *n* scatola del cambio *f*. **gear lever** leva del cambio *f*. *v* preparare,

adattare.

**gelatine** ['dʒelə,tiːn] *n* gelatina *f*.

**gelignite** ['dʒelig,nait] *n* gelatina esplosiva *f*.

**gem** [dʒem] *n* gemma *f*.

**Gemini** ['dʒemini] *n* Gemelli *m pl*.

**gender** ['dʒendə] *n* genere *m*, sesso *m*.

**gene** [dʒiːn] *n* gene *m*.

**genealogy** [,dʒiːni'alədʒi] *n* genealogia *f*. **genealogical** *adj* genealogico.

**general** ['dʒenərəl] *nm, adj* generale. **general practitioner** medico generico *m*. **generalization** *n* generalizzazione *f*. **generalize** *v* generalizzare.

**generate** ['dʒenəreit] *v* generare, produrre. **generation** *n* generazione *f*. **generator** *n* generatore *m*.

**generic** [dʒi'nerik] *adj* generico.

**generous** ['dʒenərəs] *adj* generoso. **generosity** *n* generosità *f*.

**genetic** [dʒi'netik] *adj* genetico. **geneticist** *n* genetista *m, f*. **genetics** *n* genetica *f*. **genetically modified** *adj* geneticamente modificato.

**Geneva** [dʒi'niːvə] *n* Ginevra *f*.

**genial** ['dʒiːniəl] *adj* gioviale, simpatico.

**genital** ['dʒenitl] *adj* genitale. **genitals** *pl n* organi genitali *m pl*.

**genius** ['dʒiːnjəs] *n* genio *m*.

**Genoa** ['dʒenouə] *n* Genova *f*. **Genoese** *n(m+f)*, *adj* genovese.

**genteel** [dʒen'tiːl] *adj* signorile. **gentility** *n* signorilità *f*.

**gentle** ['dʒentl] *adj* tenero; (*mild*) mite; (*not steep*) dolce. **gentleman** *n* signore *m*; (*of good breeding, etc.*) gentiluomo *m*. **gentlemanly** *adj* signorile. **gentleness** *n* dolcezza *f*. **gently** *adv* dolcemente; adagio, piano.

**gentry** ['dʒentri] *n* piccola nobiltà *f*.

**gents** [dʒents] *n* (*sign*) uomini, signori.

**genuine** ['dʒenjuin] *adj* genuino, autentico; sincero. **genuinely** *adv* (*really*) veramente.

**genus** ['dʒiːnəs] *n* genere *m*.

**geography** [dʒi'ogrəfi] *n* geografia *f*. **geographer** *n* geografo, -a *m, f*. **geographical** *adj* geografico.

**geology** [dʒi'olədʒi] *n* geologia *f*. **geological** *adj* geologico. **geologist** *n* geologo, -a *m, f*.

**geometry** [dʒi'omətri] *n* geometria *f*. **geometric** *adj* geometrico.

**geranium** [dʒəˈreiniəm] n geranio m.

**geriatric** [dʒeriˈatrik] adj geriatrico. **geriatrics** n geriatria f.

**germ** [dʒəːm] n germe m.

**Germany** [ˈdʒəːməni] n Germania f. **German** n, adj tedesco, -a. **German measles** rosolia f, rubeola f.

**germinate** [ˈdʒəːmineit] v germinare. **germination** n germinazione f.

**gerund** [ˈdʒerənd] n gerundio m.

**gesticulate** [dʒeˈstikjuˌleit] v gesticolare. **gesticulation** n gesticolazione f.

**gesture** [ˈdʒestʃə] n gesto m. v gesticolare, fare gesti.

**\*get** [get] v (obtain) ottenere, procurare; (fetch) andare a prendere; (receive) ricevere; (understand) capire; (become) diventare; (reach) arrivare. **get across** attraversare; (make understand) far capire. **get along with** andare d'accordo con. **get at** (reach) raggiungere; (hint) alludere. **getaway** n fuga f. **get off** scendere. **get out** uscire. **get up** alzarsi.

**geyser** [ˈgiːzə] n (geog) geyser m; (waterheater) scaldabagno m.

**ghastly** [ˈgaːstli] adj orrendo; (pale) spettrale.

**gherkin** [ˈgəːkin] n cetriolino m.

**ghetto** [ˈgetou] n ghetto m.

**ghost** [goust] n fantasma m, spettro m. **ghostly** adj spettrale.

**giant** [ˈdʒaiənt] n gigante, -essa m, f. adj gigantesco, gigante.

**gibberish** [ˈdʒibəriʃ] n discorso incomprensibile m.

**gibe** [dʒaib] n beffa f; scherno m. v **gibe at** beffarsi di, beffare.

**giblets** [ˈdʒiblits] pl n rigaglie f pl, frattaglie f pl.

**giddy** [ˈgidi] adj (flighty) incostante, volubile; (dizzy) preso da vertigini; (height) vertiginoso. **feel giddy** avere il capogiro. **giddiness** n capogiro m, vertigini f pl.

**gift** [gift] n dono m, regalo m. **gifted** adj dotato.

**gigantic** [dʒaiˈgantik] adj gigantesco.

**giggle** [ˈgigl] v ridere scioccamente. n risatina sciocca f. **have the giggles** avere la ridarella.

**gill** [gil] n (fish) branchia f; (mushroom) lamella f.

**gilt** [gilt] n doratura f. adj dorato.

**gimmick** [ˈgimik] n (coll: device) congegno m; stratagemma m.

**gin** [dʒin] n gin m invar.

**ginger** [ˈdʒindʒə] n zenzero m. adj fulvo.

**gingerly** [ˈdʒindʒəli] adj cauto.

**gipsy** [ˈdʒipsi] n zingaro, -a m, f.

**giraffe** [dʒiˈraːf] n giraffa f.

**girder** [ˈgəːdə] n trave maestra f, putrella f.

**girdle** [ˈgəːdl] n busto m, cintura f. v cingere.

**girl** [gəːl] n ragazza f. **girlfriend** n amica f. **girlish** adj da ragazza.

**giro** [ˈdʒairou] n giroconto m, postagiro m.

**girth** [gəːθ] n circonferenza f.

**gist** [dʒist] n nocciolo m.

**\*give** [giv] v dare; (present) regalare; (relinquish) cedere. **give away** regalare; (betray) tradire; (secret) rivelare. **give back** restituire. **give in** cedere. **give oneself up** costituirsi. **give out** distribuire. **give rise to** risultare in. **give up** abbandonare; (cease) smettere. n elasticità f.

**given** [ˈgivn] V give.

**glacier** [ˈglasiə] n ghiacciaio m.

**glad** [glad] adj lieto, contento. **gladden** v rallegrare. **gladly** adv con piacere.

**glamour** [glamə] n fascino m. **glamorous** adj affascinante.

**glance** [glaːns] n sguardo m. **at a glance** a prima vista. v dare un'occhiata.

**gland** [gland] n ghiandola f. **glandular** adj ghiandolare.

**glare** [gleə] n (light) bagliore m; (fierce look) sguardo torvo m. v **glare at** guardare con cipiglio, guardare con occhio torvo.

**glass** [glaːs] n vetro m; (container) bicchiere m. **glasses** pl n occhiali m pl. **glassy** adj vitreo.

**glaze** [gleiz] n smalto m, patina f. v smaltare, verniciare; (fit with glass) fornire di vetri.

**gleam** [gliːm] v luccicare. n barlume m, luccichio m.

**glean** [gliːn] v racimolare.

**glee** [gliː] n gioia f. **gleeful** adj pieno di gioia.

**glib** [glib] adj facondo.

**glide** [glaid] v scivolare, scorrere; (aero) planare. **glider** n aliante m. **gliding** n volo a vela m.

**glimmer** [ˈglimə] v luccicare; (of dawn)

albeggiare. *n* barlume *m*, luccichio *m*.

**glimpse** [glimps] *n* occhiata *f*, visione *f*. *v* intravedere.

**glint** [glint] *n* luccichio *m*. *v* luccicare, scintillare.

**glisten** ['glisn] *v* luccicare, brillare.

**glitter** ['glitə] *v* brillare, scintillare. *n* lucentezza *f*.

**gloat** [glout] *v* gongolare (malignamente).

**global warming** *n* riscaldamento globale *m*.

**globe** [gloub] *n* globo *m*. **global** *adj* globale.

**gloom** [glu:m] *n* (*darkness*) oscurità *f*; (*depression*) malinconia *f*, tristezza *f*. **gloomy** *adj* malinconico, triste.

**glory** ['glo:ri] *n* gloria *f*, splendore *m*. **glorify** *v* glorificare. **glorious** *adj* illustre, splendido.

**gloss**[1] [glos] *n* (*lustre*) lucentezza *f*; (*appearance*) apparenza *f*. **glossy** *adj* lucido.

**gloss**[2] [glos] *n* (*explanation*) chiosa *f*. *v* chiosare, commentare.

**glossary** ['glosəri] *n* lessico *m*.

**glove** [glʌv] *n* guanto *m*.

**glow** [glou] *v* risplendere; ardere. *n* rossore *m*; (*colour*) luminosità *f*. **glowing** *adj* acceso, ardente.

**glucose** ['glu:kous] *n* glucosio *m*.

**glue** [glu:] *n* colla *f*. *v* incollare.

**glum** [glʌm] *adj* tetro, cupo.

**glut** [glʌt] *n* sovrabbondanza *f*. *v* saturare.

**glutton** ['glʌtən] *n* ghiottone, -a *m*, *f*; goloso, -a *m*, *f*. **gluttonous** *adj* ghiotto, goloso. **gluttony** *n* golosità *f*.

**gnarled** [na:ld] *adj* nodoso.

**gnash** [naʃ] *v* **gnash one's teeth** digrignare i denti.

**gnat** [nat] *n* zanzara *f*.

**gnaw** [no:] *v* rodere, rosicchiare. **gnawing** *adj* rosicante.

**gnome** [noum] *n* gnomo *m*.

**\*go** [gou] *v* andare; (*become*) diventare. **go away** andarsene. **go back** ritornare. **go-between** *n* intermediario *m*. **go by** passare; (*be guided by*) regolarsi su. **go down** scendere; (*sink*) affondare. **go in** entrare. **go off** esplodere; (*spoil*) guastarsi; (*leave*) andarsene. **go on** continuare. **go out** uscire. **go up** salire. **go without** fare a meno di. *n* energia *f*; (*try*) colpo *m*. **on the go** molto attivo.

**goad** [goud] *n* pungolo *m*. *v* incitare.

**goal** [goul] *n* (*aim*) meta *f*; (*sport*) porta *f*, rete *f*. **goalkeeper** *n* portiere *m*. **goal-post** *n* palo della porta *m*.

**goat** [gout] *n* capra *f*.

**gobble** ['gobl] *v* inghiottire.

**goblin** ['goblin] *n* folletto *m*.

**god** [god] *n* dio (*pl* dei) *m*. **goddaughter** *n* figlioccia *f*. **godfather** *n* padrino *m*. **godmother** *n* madrina *f*. **godson** *n* figlioccio *m*. **goddess** *n* dea *f*.

**goggles** ['goglz] *pl n* occhiali di protezione *m pl*.

**gold** [gould] *n* oro *m*. **goldfinch** *n* cardellino *m*. **goldfish** *n* pesce dorato *or* rosso *m*. **gold mine** miniera d'oro *f*. **goldsmith** *n* orefice *m*. **golden** *adj* d'oro; (*colour*) aureo. **golden rule** regola d'oro *f*.

**golf** [golf] *n* golf *m*. **golf course** campo di golf *m*. **golfer** *n* giocatore, -trice di golf *m*, *f*.

**gondola** ['gondələ] *n* gondola *f*.

**gone** [gon] *V* go.

**gong** [gon] *n* gong *m invar*.

**gonorrhoea** [gonə'riə] *n* gonorrea *f*.

**good** [gud] *adj* buono; valido; (*well-behaved, clever*) bravo. **good afternoon** buon giorno; (*later*) buona sera. **goodbye** *interj* addio; arrivederci; (*coll*) ciao. **good-for-nothing** *n* benvenuto a nulla *m*. **good-looking** *adj* bello. **good morning** buon giorno. **goodnight** *interj* buona notte. **goodwill** *n* benevolenza *f*; (*comm*) avviamento *m*, *n* bene *m*, vantaggio *m*. **be no good** non servire. **for good** per sempre. **goodness** *n* bontà *f*, gentilezza *f*, virtù *f*.

**Good Friday** *n* Venerdì Santo *m*.

**goods** [gudz] *pl n* merce *f pl*, beni *m pl*. **goods train** treno merci *m*.

**goose** [gu:s] *n*, *pl* **geese** oca *f*.

**gooseberry** ['guzbəri] *n* uva spina *f*.

**gore** [go:] *v* trafiggere.

**gorge** [go:dʒ] *n* (*geol*) gola *f*. *v* rimpinzarsi (di).

**gorgeous** ['go:dʒəs] *adj* splendido.

**gorilla** [gə'rilə] *n* gorilla *m invar*.

**gorse** [go:s] *n* ginestrone *m*.

**gory** [go:ri] *adj* cruento.

**gosling** ['gozlin] *n* papero, -a *m*, *f*.

**gospel** ['gospəl] *n* vangelo *m*; (*coll: truth*) verità implicita *f*.

**gossip** ['gosip] *n* ciarla *f*, pettegolezzo *m*; (*person*) ciarlone, -a *m, f*, chiacchierone, -a *m, f*. *v* ciarlare, chiacchierare.

**got** [got] *V* get.

**Gothic** ['goθik] *adj* gotico.

**gourd** [guəd] *n* zucca *f*.

**gourmet** ['guəmei] *n* buongustaio, -a *m, f*.

**gout** [gaut] *n* gotta *f*.

**govern** ['gʌvən] *v* governare *f*; (*gramm*) reggere. **governess** *n* governante *f*. **government** *n* governo *m*. **governor** *n* governatore *m*; (*coll: boss*) capo *m*.

**gown** [gaun] *n* (*dress*) veste *f*; (*robe*) toga *f*.

**grab** [grab] *v* arraffare. *n* strappo *m*.

**grace** [greis] *n* grazia *f*, eleganza *f*. *v* adornare. **graceful** *adj* grazioso. **gracious** *adj* benigno.

**grade** [greid] *n* grado *m*; (*level*) livello *m*; classe *f. v* classificare.

**gradient** ['greidiənt] *n* gradiente *m*; (*slope*) pendio *m*.

**gradual** ['gradjuəl] *adj* graduale. **gradually** *adv* poco a poco.

**graduate** ['gradjuət; *v* 'gradjueit] *n* laureato, -a *m, f. v* laurearsi.

**graft¹** [gra:ft] *n* (*bot*) innesto *m*; (*med*) trapianto *m*; (*hard work*) sgobbata *f. v* innestare; trapiantare; sgobbare.

**graft²** [gra:ft] *n* (*bribery*) corruzione *f. v* corrompere.

**grain** [grein] *n* (*seed*) chicco *m*, granello *m*; (*wheat*) grano *m*; (*wood*) venatura *f*; (*leather*) grana *f*. **against the grain** contro pelo.

**gram** [gram] *n* grammo *m*.

**grammar** ['gramə] *n* grammatica *f*. **grammatical** *adj* grammaticale.

**gramophone** ['graməfoun] *n* grammofono *m*.

**granary** ['granəri] *n* granaio *m*.

**grand** [grand] *adj* (*imposing*) grandioso; (*first rate*) splendido. **grandchild** *n* nipote *m, f*; nipotino, -a *m, f*. **grandfather** *n* nonno *m*. **grandmother** *n* nonna *f*. **grand piano** pianoforte a coda *m*. **grandstand** *n* tribuna coperta *f*. **grandeur** *n* grandiosità *f*.

**granite** ['granit] *n* granito *m*.

**grant** [gra:nt] *v* (*confer*) concedere, accordare; (*give*) dare; (*admit*) ammettere. **take for granted** ritenere per certo. *n* (*student*) borsa di studio *f*; concessione *f*.

**granule** ['granju:l] *n* granello *m*.

**grape** [greip] *n* acino *m*, chicco d'uva *m*. **grapes** *pl n* uva *f sing*. **grapevine** *n* vite *f*; (*coll*) canali confidenziali *m pl*.

**grapefruit** ['greipfru:t] *n* pompelmo *m*.

**graph** [graf] *n* (*math*) grafico *m*; diagramma *m*. **graphic** *adj* grafico. **graph paper** carta millimetrata *f*.

**grapple** ['grapl] *v* **grapple with** venire alle prese con.

**grasp** [gra:sp] *v* afferrare; (*understand*) capire. *n* stretta *f*. **grasping** *adj* avaro.

**grass** [gra:s] *n* erba *f*; (*lawn*) prato *m*. **grasshopper** *n* cavalletta *f*. **grassy** *adj* erboso.

**grate¹** [greit] *n* graticola *f*. **grating** *n* inferriata *f*.

**grate²** [greit] *v* grattugiare; (*sound harshly*) stridere; (*irritate*) dare sui nervi.

**grateful** ['greitful] *adj* riconoscente, grato.

**gratify** ['grati,fai] *v* appagare.

**gratitude** ['gratitju:d] *n* gratitudine *f*.

**gratuitous** [grə'tjuitəs] *adj* (*free*) gratuito; (*without cause*) ingiustificato.

**gratuity** [grə'tjuəti] *n* (*tip*) mancia *f*; (*unsolicited gift*) gratifica *f*.

**grave¹** [greiv] *n* tomba *f*, sepolcro *m*. **gravedigger** *n* becchino *m*. **gravestone** *n* lapide funeraria *f*. **graveyard** *n* cimitero *m*.

**grave²** [greiv] *adj* grave.

**gravel** ['gravəl] *n* ghiaia *f*.

**gravity** ['gravəti] *n* gravità *f*. **gravitate** *v* gravitare.

**gravy** ['greivi] *n* sugo di carne *m*; salsa *f*.

**graze¹** [greiz] *v* (*touch*) sfiorare; (*scrape*) scalfire. *n* scalfittura *f*, lesione superficiale *f*.

**graze²** [greiz] *v* (*animal*) pascolare.

**grease** [gri:s] *n* grasso *m*, unto *m*. **greaseproof paper** carta oleata *f. v* ungere, ingrassare. **greasy** *adj* grasso, unto; (*slippery*) scivoloso.

**great** [greit] *adj* grande; (*very good*) magnifico; (*very large*) grandissimo. **Great Britain** Gran Bretagna *f*. **greatly** *adv* molto. **greatness** *n* grandezza *f*.

**Greece** [gri:s] *n* Grecia *f*. **Greek** *n, adj* greco (*pl* -ci), -a.

**greed** [gri:d] *n* ingordigia *f*. **greedy** *adj* ingordo.

**green** [gri:n] *adj* verde. *n* verde *m*; (*land*) prato *m*; (*golf*) green *m*. **greenfly** *n* afide *m*. **greengage** *n* prugna verde *f*. **greengrocer** *n* erbivendolo, -a *m, f*, fruttivendolo, -a *m, f.* **greenhouse** *n* serra *f.* **green light** luce verde *f.* **greens** *pl n* verdura *f sing.*

**greenhouse effect** *n* effetto serra *m.*

**Greenland** ['gri:nlənd] *n* Groenlandia *f.* **Greenlander** *n* groenlandese *m, f.*

**greet** [gri:t] *v* salutare. **greeting** *n* saluto *m.*

**gregarious** [gri'geəriəs] *adj* gregario, socievole.

**grenade** [grə'neid] *n* granata *f.*

**grew** [gru:] *V* **grow**.

**grey** [grei] *adj* grigio.

**grid** [grid] *n* (network) rete *f;* (map) reticolo *m;* (grating) grata *f.*

**grief** [gri:f] *n* dolore *m,* afflizione *f.* **come to grief** far fiasco *or* cilecca.

**grieve** [gri:v] *v* (upset) affliggere, addolorare; (sorrow) affliggersi. **grievance** *n* (injustice) ingiustizia *f;* (complaint) lamentela *f.* **grievous** *adj* doloroso, atroce.

**grill** [gril] *n* (cookery) graticola *f,* gratella *f;* (grilled meat) carne ai ferri *f. v* (cookery) cucinare ai ferri; (question severely) sottoporre a un interrogatorio severo.

**grille** [gril] *n* inferriata *f,* grata *f.*

**grim** [grim] *adj* (unrelenting) inesorabile; (fierce) feroce; (forbidding) arcigno. **grimly** *adv* con severità.

**grimace** [gri'meis] *n* smorfia *f. v* fare smorfie.

**grime** [graim] *n* sudiciume *m.* **grimy** *adj* sudicio.

**grin** [grin] *v* fare un largo sorriso. *n* largo sorriso *m.*

***grind** [graind] *v* (pulverize) macinare; (sharpen) affilare; (teeth) digrignare. *n.* (coll: hard work) sgobbata *f.*

**grip** [grip] *v* stringere; (hold interest) avvincere; (take firm hold) far presa. *n* presa *f,* stretta *f;* (control) padronanza *f.* **come to grips with** venire alle prese con.

**gripe** [graip] *n* colica *f. v* (coll) lagnarsi.

**grisly** ['grizli] *adj* orribile, macabro.

**gristle** ['grisl] *n* cartilagine *f.* **gristly** *adj* cartilaginoso.

**grit** [grit] *n* (sand) sabbia *f;* (mech) graniglia *f;* (coll: courage) fegato *m. v* (teeth) digrignare. **gritty** *adj* sabbioso.

**groan** [groun] *n* gemito *m,* lamento *m. v* gemere, lamentarsi.

**grocer** ['grousə] *n* droghiere, -a *m, f.* **grocer's** *n* (shop) drogheria *f.* **groceries** *pl n*

generi coloniali *m pl.*

**groin** [groin] *n* inguine *m.*

**groom** [gru:m] *n* stalliere *m;* (bridegroom) sposo *m. v* preparare; (horse) strigliare.

**groove** [gru:v] *n* solco *m. v* scanalare.

**grope** [group] *v* brancolare. **grope for** cercare a tentoni, brancolare in cerca di.

**gross** [grous] *adj* grossolano, volgare; (not net) lordo. *v* (income) avere un introito lordo di. *n* grossa *f.*

**grotesque** [grə'tesk] *adj* fantastico; (incongruous) grottesco.

**grotto** ['grotou] *n* grotta *f.*

**ground¹** [graund] *V* **grind**.

**ground²** [graund] *n* (soil) terreno *m;* (earth, floor) terra *f;* (sport) campo *m;* (reason) motivo *m;* (bottom) fondo *m.* **ground floor** pianterreno *m.* **grounds** *pl n* (sediment) deposito *m sing;* (dregs) fondi *m pl. v* (base) fondare; (teach) insegnare i primi elementi; (aircraft) impedire di volare. **grounding** *n* base *f.* **groundless** *adj* infondato.

**group** [gru:p] *n* gruppo *m. v* raggruppare, disporre.

**grouse¹** [graus] *n* (bird) urogallo *m.*

**grouse²** [graus] *(coll) v* brontolare, lamentarsi. *n* lagnanza *f.*

**grove** [grouv] *n* boschetto *m.*

**grovel** ['grovl] *v* umiliarsi; (cringe) strisciare.

***grow** [grou] *v* (become larger) crescere; (thrive) prosperare; (become) diventare. **grown-up** *n, adj* adulto, -a. **grow on** piacere sempre più. **grow up** crescere, sorgere. **grower** *n* coltivatore, -trice *m, f.* **growth** *n* crescita *f,* progresso *m;* (med) escrescenza *f,* tumore *m.*

**growl** [graul] *v* ringhiare; (rumble) brontolare. *n* ringhio *m;* brontolio *m.*

**grown** [groun] *V* **grow**.

**grub** [grʌb] *n* (insect) larva *f,* bruco *m;* (coll) roba da mangiare *f. v* ripulire; (uproot) sradicare.

**grubby** ['grʌbi] *adj* (dirty) sudicio; (contemptible) abietto.

**grudge** [grʌdʒ] *n* rancore *m.* **bear a grudge against** nutrire rancore verso. *v* (give reluctantly) dare malvolentieri; (resent) invidiare. **grudgingly** *adv* malvolentieri.

**gruelling** ['gruəliŋ] *adj* faticoso.

**gruesome** ['gru:səm] *adj* raccapricciante.

**gruff** [grʌf] *adj* (surly) burbero; (hoarse) rauco; (harsh) aspro.

**grumble** ['grʌmbl] *v* (complain) lagnarsi;

(*growl*) brontolare. *n* lagnanza *f*, brontolio *m*.

**grumpy** ['grʌmpi] *adj* scontroso.

**grunt** [grʌnt] *v* grugnire. *n* grugnito *m*.

**guarantee** [garən'tiː] *v* garantire, rispondere di. *n* garanzia *f*.

**guard** [gaːd] *v* (*keep safe*) custodire; (*watch over*) sorvegliare; (*keep watch*) stare in guardia. **guard against** badare a. *n* guardia *m*, *f*; (*appliance*) protezione *f*; (*railway*) capotreno *m*. **guarded** *adj* cauto.
**guardian** *n* custode *m*; (*legal*) tutore *m*.

**guerrilla** [gə'rilə] *n* guerrigliero *m*. **guerrilla warfare** guerriglia *f*.

**guess** [ges] *n* congettura *f*, supposizione *f*. **at a rough guess** a occhio e croce. *v* indovinare.

**guest** [gest] *n* ospite *m*, *f*; (*of hotel*) cliente *m*, *f*. **guest-house** *n* pensione *f*.

**guide** [gaid] *n* guida *f*; (*of tourists*) cicerone *m*. **guidebook** *n* guida *f*. *v* guidare; (*advise*) consigliare; (*direct*) dirigere. **be guided by** seguire il consiglio di. **guidance** *n* (*leadership*) guida *f*; (*instruction*) norma *f*.

**guild** [gild] *n* corporazione *f*.

**guile** [gail] *n* astuzia *f*. **guileless** *adj* ingenuo.

**guillotine** ['gilətiːn] *n* ghigliottina *f*.

**guilt** [gilt] *n* colpa *f*. **guiltless** *adj* innocente. **guilty** *adj* colpevole. **have a guilty conscience** avere la coscienza sporca *or* cattiva.

**guinea-pig** ['ginipig] *n* cavia *f*.

**guitar** [gi'taː] *n* chitarra *f*. **guitarist** *n* chitarrista *m*, *f*.

**gulf** [gʌlf] *n* (*geog*) golfo *m*; (*wide separation*) abisso *m*.

**gull** [gʌl] *n* gabbiano *m*.

**gullet** ['gʌlit] *n* (*throat*) gola *f*; (*oesophagus*) esofago *m*.

**gullible** ['gʌləbl] *adj* credulo. **gullibility** *n* credulità *f*.

**gully** ['gʌli] *n* (*canyon*) burrone *m*; (*ditch*) cunetta *f*.

**gulp** [gʌlp] *n* (*food*) boccone *m*; (*drink*) sorso *m*. *v* (*food*) ingoiare; (*drink*) tracannare; (*choke*) soffocare.

**gum¹** [gʌm] *n* (*secretion*) gomma *f*; (*glue*) colla *f*. *v* ingommare; incollare.

**gum²** [gʌm] *n* (*mouth*) gengiva *f*.

**gun** [gʌn] *n* fucile *m*; cannone *m*. **gunfire** *n* sparatoria *f*. **gunman** *n* bandito armato

*m*. **gunner** *n* artigliere *m*. **gunpowder** *n* polvere da sparo *f*. **gunshot** *n* colpo di fucile *m*.

**gurgle** ['gəːgl] *v* gorgogliare. *n* gorgoglio *m*.

**gush** [gʌʃ] *n* sgorgo *m*; (*language*) torrente *m*. *v* (*liquid*) scaturire; (*speech*) parlare con effusione.

**gust** [gʌst] *n* raffica *f*.

**gusto** ['gʌstou] *n* fervore *m*.

**gut** [gʌt] *n* budello *m* (*pl* -a *f*). **guts** *pl n* (*coll*) fegato *m sing*. *v* sbudellare.

**gutter** ['gʌtə] *n* (*house*) grondaia *f*; (*street*) cunetta *f*; (*conduit*) condotto *m*. **guttersnipe** *n* scugnizzo *m*.

**guy¹** [gai] *n* tipo *m*, individuo *m*.

**guy²** [gai] *n* (*rope*) tirante *m*.

**gymnasium** [dʒim'neiziəm] *n* palestra *f*. **gymnast** *n* ginnasta *m*, *f*. **gymnastics** *n* ginnastica *f*.

**gynaecology** [gainə'kolədʒi] *n* ginecologia *f*. **gynaecological** *adj* ginecologico. **gynaecologist** *n* ginecologo, -a *m*, *f*.

**gypsum** ['dʒipsəm] *n* gesso *m*.

**gyrate** [dʒai'reit] *v* girare, roteare.

**gyroscope** ['dʒairə,skoup] *n* giroscopio *m*.

# H

**haberdasher** ['habədaʃə] *n* merciaio, -a *m*, *f*. **haberdashery** *n* merceria *f*.

**habit** ['habit] *n* abitudine *f*; (*dress*) tonaca *f*. **habitual** *adj* abituale. **habitually** *adv* di solito.

**habitable** ['habitəbl] *adj* abitabile.

**habitat** ['habitat] *n* ambiente *m*.

**hack¹** [hak] *v* tagliare, troncare. **hacksaw** *n* seghetto *m*.

**hack²** [hak] *n* (*horse*) ronzino *m*; (*writer*) scribacchino *m*.

**hackneyed** ['haknid] *adj* trito, comune.

**had** [had] *V* **have**.

**haddock** ['hadək] *n* eglefino *m*.

**haemorrhage** ['heməridʒ] *n* emorragia *f*.

**haemorrhoids** ['heməroidz] *pl n* emorroidi *f pl*.

**hag** [hag] *n* vecchiaccia *f*, strega *f*.

**haggard** ['hagəd] *adj* smunto, scarno.

**haggle** ['hagl] v mercanteggiare.

**Hague** [heig] n l'Aia f.

**hail¹** [heil] n grandine f. **hailstone** n chicco di grandine m. v grandinare.

**hail²** [heil] v salutare; (call) chiamare. **hail from** essere oriundo di. interj salve! n saluto m.

**hair** [heə] n capelli m pl; (single strand) capello m; (of animals) pelo m. **split hairs** cercare il pelo nell'uovo. **hairy** adj capelluto; peloso.

**hairbrush** ['heəbrʌʃ] n spazzola per capelli f.

**haircut** ['heəkʌt] n taglio dei capelli m. **have a haircut** farsi tagliare i capelli.

**hairdresser** ['heə,dresə] n parrucchiere, -a m, f.

**hair-dryer** ['heə,draiə] n asciugacapelli m invar.

**hairpin** ['heəpin] n forcina f.

**hair-raising** ['heə,reiziŋ] adj raccapricciante.

**hake** [heik] n nasello m.

**half** [ha:f] adj mezzo. n mezzo m, metà f; (sport: period) tempo m. **in half** in due. **half-and-half** adj, adv metà e metà.

**half-back** ['ha:fbak] n mediano m.

**half-baked** [,ha:f'beikt] adj (coll) inesperto, immaturo.

**half-breed** ['ha:fbri:d] nm, adj ibrido.

**half-brother** ['ha:fbrʌðə] n fratellastro m.

**half-hearted** [,ha:f'ha:tid] adj esitante, poco entusiasta.

**half-hour** [,ha:f'auə] n mezz'ora f.

**half-mast** [,ha:f'ma:st] n **at half-mast** a mezz'asta.

**half-moon** [,ha:f'mu:n] n mezzaluna f.

**half-sister** ['ha:fsistə] n sorellastra f.

**half-time** [,ha:f'taim] n intervallo m.

**half-tone** ['ha:ftoun] n mezzatinta f, fotoriproduzione f.

**halfway** [,ha:f'wei] adj, adv a metà strada. **meet halfway** giungere a un compromesso.

**half-witted** [,ha:f'witid] adj scemo, deficiente.

**halibut** ['halibət] n halibut m invar, ippoglosso m.

**hall** [ho:l] n (entrance) entrata f; (room) sala f, salone m; (building) villa f, casa signorile f.

**hallmark** ['ho:lma:k] n marchio d'autenticità m; elemento caratteristico m. v marcare.

**hallowed** ['haloud] adj venerato.

**hallucination** [hə,lu:si'neiʃən] n allucinazione f.

**halo** ['heilou] n aureola f; (astron) alone m.

**halt** [ho:lt] n fermata f; (temporary) sosta f. v sostare, fermare, fermarsi. interj alt!

**halter** ['ho:ltə] n capestro m; cavezza f.

**halve** [ha:v] v dimezzare, ridurre della or alla metà.

**ham** [ham] n prosciutto m.

**hamburger** ['hambə:gə] n hamburger m invar.

**hammer** ['hamə] n martello m. v martellare.

**hammock** ['hamək] n amaca f.

**hamper¹** ['hampə] v intralciare, ostacolare.

**hamper²** ['hampə] n paniere m.

**hamster** ['hamstə] n criceto m.

**hand** [hand] n mano (pl -i) f; (clock) lancetta f; (worker) operaio, -a m, f. **at hand** a portata di mano. **by hand** a mano. **hands down** completamente, con facilità. **hands off!** via le mani! **hands up!** alto le mani! **in hand** (under control) sotto controllo; (available) a disposizione; (being dealt with) in corso. **on hand** presente; (available) disponibile. **on the other hand** d'altra parte. v (give) dare, porgere. **hand down** trasmettere, tramandare. **hand in** or **over** consegnare. **hand out** distribuire. **handful** n manata f; piccolo gruppo m.

**handbag** ['handbag] n borsetta f.

**handbill** ['handbil] n volantino m.

**handbook** ['handbuk] n manuale m.

**handbrake** ['handbreik] n freno a mano m.

**handcuff** ['handkʌf] n manetta f. v ammanettare.

**handicap** ['handikap] n svantaggio m, impedimento m; (sport) handicap m invar. v impedire.

**handicraft** ['handikra:ft] n artigianato m; (trade) mestiere m.

**handiwork** ['handiwə:k] n (personal work) opera f.

**handkerchief** ['haŋkətʃif] n fazzoletto m.

**handle** ['handl] n manico m; (door) maniglia f; (crank) manovella f. v (manipulate) maneggiare; (deal with) trattare. **handlebar** n manubrio m.

**handmade** [‚hand'meid] *adj* fatto a mano.

**hand-out** ['handaut] *n* comunicato *m*, campione pubblicitario *m*.

**hand-pick** [hand'pik] *v* scegliere a mano.

**handrail** ['handreil] *n* ringhiera *f*.

**handshake** ['handʃeik] *n* stretta di mano *f*.

**handsome** ['hansəm] *adj* bello; generoso, considerevole.

**handstand** ['hand‚stand] *n* posata verticale sulle mani *f*.

**hand-towel** ['hand‚tauəl] *n* asciugamano *m*.

**handwriting** ['hand‚raitiŋ] *n* calligrafia *f*.

**handy** ['handi] *adj* (*accessible*) a portata di mano; (*deft*) destro, abile; (*convenient*) comodo.

**\*hang** [haŋ] *v* pendere, appendere, sospendere; (*execute*) impiccare. **hang around** bazzicare. **hanger** *n* (*clothes*) attaccapanni *m invar*. **hanger-on** *n* scroccone *m*. **hangman** *n* boia *m invar*. **hang on** persistere, indugiare; (*phone*) restare in linea. **hangover** *n* postumi di una sbornia *m pl*.

**hangar** ['haŋə] *n* hangar *m invar*; aviorimessa *f*.

**hanker** ['haŋkə] *v* **hanker after** bramare. **hankering** *n* forte desiderio *m*, brama *f*.

**haphazard** [‚hap'hazəd] *adj* casuale.

**happen** ['hapən] *v* (*take place*) accadere, succedere. **as it happens** per caso. **happening** *n* avvenimento *m*.

**happy** ['hapi] *adj* felice, contento, lieto; (*in greetings*) buono. **happy-go-lucky** *adj* spensierato. **happiness** *n* felicità *f*, contentezza *f*.

**harass** ['harəs] *v* molestare, tormentare, irritare. **harassment** *n* tormento *m*, molestia *f*.

**harbour** ['ha:bə] *n* porto *m*. *v* (*shelter*) dare asilo a.

**hard** [ha:d] *adj* duro; difficile; severo. *adv* molto; (*solidly*) sodo. **hard and fast** immutabile. **hard-boiled** *adj* (*egg*) sodo; (*person*) duro. **hard core** nucleo *m*. **hard-headed** *adj* accorto, pratico. **hard-hearted** *adj* insensibile. **hard shoulder** corsia d'emergenza *f*. **hard up** al corto di quattrini. **hardware** *n* ferramenta *f pl*; (*computer*) meccanismo *m*. **hard-wearing** *adj* duraturo, durevole. **hard work** lavoro faticoso *m*. **try hard** provare assiduamente. **work hard** lavorar sodo. **hardness** *n*

durezza *f*. **hardship** *n* privazione *f*.

**hardly** ['ha:dli] *adv* (*not quite*) non esattamente; (*barely, almost not*) quasi, appena; (*with difficulty*) a stento.

**hardy** ['ha:di] *adj* robusto, resistente; (*courageous*) coraggioso.

**hare** [heə] lepre *f*. **hare-brained** *adj* scervellato.

**harm** [ha:m] *n* male *m*, danno *m*. *v* nuocere a, far male a. **harmful** *adj* nocivo, dannoso. **harmless** *adj* innocuo, inoffensivo.

**harmony** ['ha:məni] *n* armonia *f*, accordo *m*. **harmonic** *adj* armonico, armonioso. **harmonize** *v* armonizzare.

**harness** ['ha:nis] *n* briglia *f*. *v* imbrigliare.

**harp** [ha:p] *n* arpa *f*. **harpist** *n* arpista *m, f*.

**harpoon** [ha:'pu:n] *n* rampone *m*. *v* ramponare.

**harpsichord** ['ha:psi‚ko:d] *n* clavicembalo *m*.

**harrowing** ['harouiŋ] *adj* straziante.

**harsh** [ha:ʃ] *adj* aspro, duro. **harshness** *n* asprezza *f*, durezza *f*.

**harvest** ['ha:vist] *n* raccolto *m*. *v* raccogliere, mietere.

**has** [haz] *V* **have**.

**hash** [haʃ] *n* carne tritata *f*; (*coll: mess*) confusione *f*, pasticcio *m*. **make a hash of** sciupare, mandare a rotoli.

**hashish** ['haʃi:ʃ] *n* (h)ascisc *m invar*.

**haste** [heist] *n* fretta *f*. **hasten** *v* precipitare, affrettarsi. **hasty** *adj* frettoloso.

**hat** [hat] *n* cappello *m*.

**hatch**[1] [hatʃ] *v* (*bring forth*) covare; (*contrive*) tramare.

**hatch**[2] [hatʃ] *n* (*naut*) boccaporto *m*; (*opening*) portello *m*, sportello *m*.

**hatchet** ['hatʃit] *n* accetta *f*.

**hate** [heit] *v* odiare. *n also* **hatred** odio *m*. **hateful** *adj* odioso.

**haughty** ['ho:ti] *adj* altezzoso, arrogante.

**haul** [ho:l] *n* tiro *m*; (*fish*) retata *f*; (*coll: booty*) bottino *m*. *v* tirare.

**haunch** [ho:ntʃ] *n* anca *f*.

**haunt** [ho:nt] *v* perseguitare, ossessionare. *n* ritrovo *m*. **haunting** *adj* ossessionante.

**\*have** [hav] *v* avere. **have to** avere da, dovere. **have it in for** avercela con. **have on** (*wear*) portare; (*have planned*) aver intenzione di fare, aver da fare; (*coll: tease*) prendere in giro.

**haven** ['heivn] n (*harbour*) porto m; (*shelter*) rifugio m.

**haversack** ['havəsak] n bisaccia f.

**havoc** ['havək] n **play havoc with** rovinare, far strage di.

**hawk¹** [ho:k] n falco m, falcone m.

**hawk²** [ho:k] v spacciare; fare il venditore ambulante.

**hawthorn** ['ho:θo:n] n biancospino m.

**hay** [hei] n fieno m. **go haywire** perdere le staffe. **hay fever** raffreddore del fieno m.

**haystack** n fienile m.

**hazard** ['hazəd] n (*danger*) pericolo m; (*risk*) rischio m. v azzardare. **hazardous** adj pericoloso, rischioso.

**haze** [heiz] n foschia f. **hazy** adj nebuloso, indistinto.

**hazel** ['heizl] n (*tree*) nocciolo m. **hazelnut** n nocciola f. adj color nocciola invar.

**he** [hi:] pron egli, lui. **he who** colui che.

**head** [hed] n testa f; (*leader*) capo m. v (*lead*) essere a capo di; (*direct*) dirigere.

**headache** ['hedeik] n mal di testa m; (*coll*) preoccupazione f.

**headdress** ['heddres] n copricapo m.

**heading** n (*title*) intestazione f; (*topic*) voce f.

**headlamp** ['hedlamp] n also **headlight** (*mot*) faro m, fanale m.

**headland** ['hedlənd] n promontorio m.

**headline** ['hedlain] n titolo m. **headlines** pl n (*news*) sommario m sing.

**headlong** ['hedloŋ] adv a capofitto.

**headmaster** [,hed'ma:stə] n preside m.

**head office** n sede centrale m.

**headphones** ['hedfounz] pl n cuffia f sing.

**headquarters** [,hed'kwo:təz] n (*mil*) quartiere generale m; (*office*) sede f, direzione f.

**headrest** ['hedrest] n appoggiatesta m invar.

**headscarf** ['hedska:f] n foulard m invar.

**headstrong** ['hedstroŋ] adj testardo, cocciuto.

**headway** ['hedwei] n progresso m. **make headway** fare strada.

**heady** ['hedi] adj impetuoso; (*intoxicating*) che dà alla testa.

**heal** [hi:l] v guarire, sanare.

**health** [helθ] n salute f. **healthy** adj (*person*) sano; (*climate, etc.*) salubre.

**heap** [hi:p] n mucchio m. v ammucchiare.

**\*hear** [hiə] v udire, sentire; (*be informed of*) venire a sapere. **hear about** aver notizie di. **hear from** aver notizie da. **hearing** n udito m; (*audience*) udienza f. **hearsay** n voce f.

**heard** [hə:d] V hear.

**hearse** [hə:s] n carro funebre m.

**heart** [ha:t] n cuore m; (*feeling*) animo m; (*essential part*) parte centrale f, centro m. **by heart** a memoria. **hearts** pl n (*cards*) cuori m pl. **take to heart** prendersi a cuore.

**heart attack** n attacco cardiaco m.

**heartbeat** ['ha:tbi:t] n battito del cuore m.

**heart-breaking** ['ha:tbreikiŋ] adj straziante. **heart-broken** adj accorato, affranto.

**heartburn** ['ha:tbə:n] n bruciore di stomaco m.

**heartening** ['ha:tniŋ] adj incoraggiante.

**heartfelt** ['ha:tfelt] adj sincero.

**hearth** [ha:θ] n focolare m.

**heartless** ['ha:tləs] adj spietato, insensibile.

**hearty** ['ha:ti] adj (*warm-hearted*) caloroso; sincero; vigoroso.

**heat** [hi:t] n calore m, caldo m; (*sport*) batteria f; (*oestrum*) estro m. **heat wave** calura f. v scaldare, riscaldare. **heated** adj animato. **heater** n riscaldatore m; stufa elettrica f. **heating** n riscaldamento m.

**heath** [hi:θ] n brughiera f.

**heathen** ['hi:ðn] n, adj pagano, -a.

**heather** ['heðə] n erica f.

**heave** [hi:v] v sollevare; (*retch*) avere i conati di vomito. **heave a sigh** tirare un sospiro. n sollevamento m.

**heaven** ['hevn] n cielo m, paradiso m. **for heaven's sake!** per l'amor del cielo! **good heavens!** santo cielo! **heavenly** adj divino, delizioso.

**heavy** ['hevi] adj pesante, forte. **heavyweight** n peso massimo m.

**Hebrew** ['hi:bru:] n (*language*) ebraico m; (*person*) ebreo, -a m, f. adj ebraico; ebreo.

**heckle** ['hekl] v interrompere con domande imbarazzanti.

**hectare** ['hekta:] n ettaro m.

**hectic** ['hektik] adj febbrile.

**hedge** [hedʒ] n siepe f; (*bet*) copertura f. v (*bet*) coprire dai rischi. **as a hedge against** per mettersi al riparo contro.

**hedgehog** ['hedʒhog] *n* riccio *m.*

**heed** [hi:d] *v* badare a, dar retta a. **heedless** *adj* noncurante.

**heel** [hi:l] *n* (*anat*) calcagno *m*; (*shoe*) tacco *m.* **Achilles' heel** tallone d'Achille *m.*

**hefty** ['hefti] *adj* robusto.

**heifer** ['hefə] *n* giovenca *f.*

**height** [hait] *n* altezza *f*; (*hill*) collina *f*; (*highest degree*) colmo *m*; (*highest point*) culmine *m.* **heighten** *v* intensificare.

**heir** [eə] *n* erede *m, f.*

**held** [held] *V* **hold**[1].

**helicopter** ['helikoptə] *n* elicottero *m.*

**hell** [hel] *n* inferno *m.* **hellish** *adj* infernale.

**hello** [hə'lou] *interj* (*on meeting*) ciao! (*phone*) pronto!

**helm** [helm] *n* timone *m.*

**helmet** ['helmit] *n* elmo *m*, elmetto *m*; (*motorcyclist, airman*) casco *m.*

**help** [help] *n* aiuto *m*, assistenza *f*; (*remedy*) rimedio *m. v* aiutare, assistere. **helpful** *adj* utile, vantaggioso. **helping** *n* porzione *f.* **helpless** *adj* impotente, indifeso.

**hem** [hem] *n* orlo *m. v* orlare. **hem in** rinchiudere, accerchiare.

**hemisphere** ['hemi,sfiə] *n* emisfera *f.*

**hemp** [hemp] *n* canapa *f.*

**hen** [hen] *n* gallina *f.*

**hence** [hens] *adv* quindi.

**henna** ['henə] *n* tintura di henna *f.*

**her** [hə:] *pron* (*direct object*) la; (*indirect object*) le; (*after prep*) lei. *adj* (il) suo, (la) sua; (*pl*) (i) suoi, (le) sue.

**herald** ['herəld] *n* araldo *m*, messaggero *m.*

**heraldry** ['herəldri] *n* araldica *f.*

**herbs** [hə:bz] *pl n* erbe aromatiche *f pl.*

**herd** [hə:d] *n* gregge *m*, mandria *f*; (*people*) massa *f.* **herd together** raggruppare, radunare.

**here** [hiə] *adv* qui, qua; (*emphasizing*) ecco. **here I am!** eccomi qua!

**hereabouts** ['hiərə,bauts] *adv* qui vicino.

**hereafter** [,hiər'a:ftə] *adv* d'ora innanzi, in futuro. *n* **the hereafter** l'al di là *m.*

**hereby** [,hiə'bai] *adv* così, con questo.

**hereditary** [hi'reditri] *adj* ereditario.

**heredity** [hi'redəti] *n* eredità *f.*

**heresy** ['herəsi] *n* eresia *f.* **heretic** *n* eretico, -a *m, f.* **heretical** *adj* eretico.

**herewith** [,hiə'wið] *adv* con questo; (*correspondence*) con la presente.

**heritage** ['heritidʒ] *n* patrimonio *m.*

**hermit** ['hə:mit] *n* eremita *m.*

**hernia** ['hə:niə] *n* ernia *f.*

**hero** ['hiərou] *n* eroe *m*; (*principal character*) protagonista *m.* **heroic** *adj* eroico. **heroine** *n* eroina *f*; protagonista *f.*

**heroin** ['herouin] *n* eroina *f.*

**heron** ['herən] *n* airone *m.*

**herring** ['heriŋ] *n* aringa *f.* **herring-bone** *adj* a lisca di pesce.

**hers** [hə:z] *pron* il suo, la sua; (*pl*) i suoi, le sue.

**herself** [hə:'self] *pron* lei stessa; (*after prep*) sè (stessa); (*reflexive*) si; (*emphatic*) proprio lei.

**hesitate** ['heziteit] *v* esitare. **hesitant** *adj* esitante. **hesitation** *n* esitazione *f.* **without hesitation** decisamente.

**heterogeneous** [hetərə'dʒi:niəs] *adj* eterogeneo.

**heterosexual** [hetərə'sekʃuəl] *adj* eterosessuale.

**hexagon** ['heksəgən] *n* esagono *m.* **hexagonal** *adj* esagonale.

**heyday** ['heidei] *n* (*prime*) fiore *m*; più bel periodo *m*; (*splendour*) fulgore *m.*

**hiatus** [hai'eitəs] *n* interruzione *f*; (*med*) iato *m.*

**hibernate** ['haibəneit] *v* svernare; (*of animals*) ibernare.

**hiccup** ['hikʌp] *n* singhiozzo *m. v* singhiozzare. **have hiccups** avere il singhiozzo.

**hid** [hid] *V* **hide**[1].

**hidden** ['hidn] *V* **hide**[1].

***hide***[1] [haid] *v* nascondere, nascondersi. **hide-out** *n* nascondiglio *m.*

**hide**[2] [haid] *n* (*raw*) pelle *f*; (*dressed*) cuoio *m.* **hidebound** *adj* gretto, di mentalità ristretta.

**hideous** ['hidiəs] *adj* oriendo, ripugnante.

**hiding**[1] ['haidiŋ] *n* **be in hiding** essere *or* tenersi nascosto. **go into hiding** nascondersi, darsi alla macchia.

**hiding**[2] ['haidiŋ] *n* (*beating*) batosta *f.*

**hierarchy** ['haiəra:ki] *n* gerarchia *f.*

**high** [hai] *adj* alto, elevato; (*of meat*) andato a male. **it's high time** è ora. **leave high and dry** piantare in asso. *adv* in alto. *n* culmine *f*; (*weather*) anticiclone *m.*

**highness** n altezza f.
**highbrow** ['haibrau] n(m+f), adj intellettuale.
**high chair** n seggiolina f.
**high-fidelity** adj ad alta fedeltà.
**high frequency** adj ad alta frequenza.
**high jump** n salto in alto m.
**highlight** ['hailait] v mettere in rilievo. n clou m invar, culmine m.
**high-pitched** [,hai'pitʃd] adj acuto.
**high point** n culmine m.
**high-powered** adj potente, dinamico.
**high pressure** n alta pressione f. **high-pressure** adj ad alta pressione; (coll) aggressivo.
**high-rise** adj a molti piani.
**high-spirited** [,hai'spiritid] adj vivace. **high spirits** pl n buonumore m sing.
**high street** n corso m.
**highway** ['haiwei] n strada maestra f. **highway code** codice della strada m.
**hijack** ['haidʒak] v (goods) rubare in transito; (aero) dirottare. **hijacker** n dirottatore m, pirata dell'aria m. **hijacking** n dirottamento m.
**hike** [haik] n gita a piedi f. v fare una gita or escursione a piedi.
**hilarious** [hi'leəriəs] adj divertente, allegro.
**hill** [hil] n colle m, collina f; (slope) salita f.
**him** [him] pron (direct object) lo; (indirect object) gli; (after prep) lui.
**himself** [him'self] pron lui stesso; (after prep) sè (stesso); (reflexive) si; (emphatic) proprio lui.
**hinder** ['hində] v (make difficult) intralciare; (make impossible) impedire.
**Hindu** [hin'du:] n(m+f), adj indù invar. **Hinduism** n induismo m.
**hinge** [hindʒ] n cardine m, perno m. v (depend) dipendere (da).
**hint** [hint] n cenno m, allusione f; (clue) suggerimento m; (slight amount) traccia f. v far capire, accennare, alludere.
**hip** [hip] n fianco m, anca f.
**hippopotamus** [hipə'potəməs] n ippopotamo m.
**hire** [haiə] v prendere a nolo, noleggiare. **hire out** dare a nolo, noleggiare. n nolo m, noleggio m. **hire purchase** vendita a rate f. **hire car** n auto a noleggio m.
**his** [hiz] adj (il) suo, (la) sua; (pl) (i) suoi,

(le) sue. pron il suo, la sua; (pl) i suoi, le sue.
**hiss** [his] v sibilare. n sibilo m. **hissing** adj sibilante.
**history** ['histəri] n storia f; (past) passato m. **historian** n storico m. **historic** adj storico; memorabile.
**\*hit** [hit] n colpo m, botta f; successo m. v colpire, battere. **hit on** scoprire. **hit-or-miss** adv alla buona.
**hitch** [hitʃ] v attaccare. **hitch-hike** v fare l'autostop. **hitch up** tirar su. n (obstacle) intoppo m; (knot) nodo m.
**hitherto** [,hiðə'tu:] adv finora.
**hive** [haiv] n alveare m.
**hoard** [ho:d] n scorta f, mucchio m. v ammucchiare.
**hoarding** ['ho:diŋ] n (billboard) tabellone m.
**hoarse** [ho:s] adj rauco. **hoarseness** n raucedine f.
**hoax** [houks] n beffa f.
**hobble** ['hobl] v zoppicare.
**hobby** ['hobi] n passatempo m, hobby m invar.
**hock¹** [hok] n (joint) garretto m.
**hock²** [hok] n (wine) vino bianco del Reno m.
**hockey** ['hoki] n hockey m invar.
**hoe** [hou] n zappa f. v zappare.
**hog** [hog] n maiale m, porco m. v (coll) monopolizzare.
**hoist** [hoist] n montacarichi m invar. v sollevare.
**\*hold¹** [hould] n presa f, stretta f; (dominating influence) ascendente m. **get hold of** (grasp) afferrare; (obtain) ottenere. v tenere; contenere; esser valido. **hold back** trattenere. **hold out** resistere. **hold up** (delay) ostacolare; (stop by force) fermare per derubare; (exhibit) esibire. **hold-up** n intoppo m; (robbery) rapina a mano armata f. **holder** n supporto m; detentore m. **holding** n (land) tenuta f; (shares) pacchetto (di azioni) m.
**hold²** [hould] n (naut) stiva f.
**hole** [houl] n buco m; (in the ground) buca f; (burrow) tana f; (predicament) guaio m.
**holiday** ['holədi] n (day) giorno festivo m, festa f; (period) vacanza f. **go on holiday** andare in vacanza or villeggiatura. **holiday-maker** n villeggiante m, f.
**Holland** ['holənd] n Olanda f.

**hollow** ['holou] *adj* cavo; concavo; (*not solid*) vuoto; (*of sound*) cupo; falso. *n* buca *f*, cavità *f*; (*anat*) cavo *m*.

**holly** ['holi] *n* agrifoglio *m*.

**holster** ['houlstə] *n* fondina *f*.

**holy** ['houli] *adj* santo, sacro.

**homage** ['homidʒ] *n* omaggio *m*. **pay homage to** rendere omaggio a.

**home** [houm] *n* (*house*) casa *f*, domicilio *m*; (*land*) patria *f*; (*institution*) ricovero *m*, rifugio *m*; (*habitat*) ambiente naturale *m*. **at home** a casa. **feel at home** sentirsi a proprio agio. **leave home** lasciare la casa paterna. *adj* domestico, casalingo. *adv* a casa; in patria; (*all the way*) a fondo. **strike home** colpire nel vivo.

**homecoming** ['houm,kʌmiŋ] *n* ritorno in casa *or* patria *m*.

**home-grown** [houm'groun] *adj* nostrano.

**homeless** ['houmləs] *adj* senza tetto.

**homely** ['houmli] *adj* semplice, senza pretese; (*unattractive*) brutto.

**home-made** [,houm'meid] *adj* fatto in casa.

**homeopathic** [,homiə'paθik] *adj* omeopatico.

**homesick** ['houmsik] *adj* nostalgico.

**homework** ['houmwə:k] *n* compiti di casa *m pl*.

**homicide** ['homisaid] *n* (*crime*) omicidio *m*; (*murderer*) omicida *m, f*. **homicidal** *adj* micidiale.

**homogeneous** [homə'dʒi:niəs] *adj* omogeneo.

**homosexual** [homə'sekʃuəl] *n*(*m+f*), *adj* omosessuale.

**honest** ['onist] *adj* onesto. **honestly!** *interj* davvero! **honesty** *n* onestà *f*.

**honey** ['hʌni] *n* miele *m*. **honeycomb** *n* favo *m*. **honeymoon** *n* luna di miele *f*.

**honeysuckle** ['hʌnisʌkl] *n* caprifoglio *m*.

**honour** ['onə] *n* onore *m*; (*respect*) stima *f*. *v* onorare; (*comm*) far onore a. **honours** *pl n* (*titles*) onorificenza *f sing*. **honorary** *adj* onorario. **honourable** *adj* onorevole, stimato, probo.

**hood** [hud] *n* cappuccio *m*; (*mot*) cappotta *f*.

**hoof** [hu:f] *n* zoccolo *m*.

**hook** [huk] *n* gancio *m*; (*fishing*) amo *m*. *v* agganciare.

**hooligan** ['hu:ligən] *n* teppista *m*.

**hoop** [hu:p] *n* cerchio *m*.

**hoot** [hu:t] *v* (*car*) suonare il clacson; (*shriek*) stridere; (*hiss*) fischiare. **hooter** *n* sirena *f*; (*car*) clacson *m invar*.

**hop¹** [hop] *v* salterellare. *n* salterello *m*.

**hop²** [hop] *n* (*bot*) luppolo *m*.

**hope** [houp] *n* speranza *f*. *v* sperare. **hopeful** *adj* pieno di speranza, fiducioso; (*promising*) promettente. **hopeless** *adj* senza speranza, disperato; (*not resolvable*) irrimediabile.

**horde** [ho:d] *n* banda *f*.

**horizon** [hə'raizn] *n* orizzonte *m*. **horizontal** *adj* orizzontale.

**hormone** ['ho:moun] *n* ormone *m*.

**horn** [ho:n] *n* corno (*pl* -a) *m*; (*mot*) clacson *m invar*.

**hornet** ['ho:nit] *n* calabrone *m*.

**horoscope** ['horəskoup] *n* oroscopo *m*.

**horrible** ['horibl] *adj* also **horrid** orribile, orrendo.

**horrify** ['horifai] *v* inorridire, raccapricciare. **horrifying** *adj* raccapricciante.

**horror** ['horə] *n* orrore *m*, spavento *m*.

**hors d'oeuvre** [o:'də:vr] *n* antipasto *m*.

**horse** [ho:s] *n* cavallo *m*.

**horseback** ['ho:sbak] *n* **on horseback** a cavallo.

**horse-chestnut** *n* ippocastano *m*.

**horse-fly** *n* tafano *m*.

**horseman** ['ho:smən] *n* cavaliere *m*.

**horsepower** ['ho:s,pauə] *n* cavallo vapore *m*.

**horse-race** *n* corsa ippica *f*.

**horseradish** ['ho:s,radiʃ] *n* cren *m invar*; (*plant*) barbaforte *m*.

**horseshoe** ['ho:ʃʃu:] *n* ferro di cavallo *m*.

**horsewoman** ['ho:s,wumən] *n* cavallerizza *f*.

**horticulture** ['ho:tikʌltʃə] *n* orticultura *f*.

**hose** [houz] *n* (*stocking*) calza *f*, calzino *m*; (*pipe*) tubo flessibile *m*, manichetta *f*. *v* **hose (down)** dare una lavata a, annaffiare.

**hosiery** ['houziəri] *n* calzetteria *f*.

**hospitable** [ho'spitəbl] *adj* ospitale.

**hospital** ['hospitl] *n* ospedale *m*. **hospitalize** far ricoverare in ospedale.

**hospitality** [,hospi'taliti] *n* ospitalità *f*.

**host¹** [houst] *n* oste *m*, ospite *m*. **hostess** *n* ospite *f*, ostessa *f*.

**host²** [houst] *n* moltitudine *f*, gran numero *m*.

**host³** [houst] *n* (*rel*) ostia *f*.

**hostage** ['hostidʒ] *n* ostaggio *m*.

**hostel** ['hostəl] *n* ostello *m*, alloggio *m*.

**hostile** ['hostail] *adj* ostile. **hostility** *n* antagonismo *m*. **hostilities** *pl n* ostilità *f pl*.

**hot** [hot] *adj* caldo; ardente, impetuoso; (*pungent, peppery*) forte, piccante. **be hot** aver caldo. **hot-blooded** *adj* dal sangue caldo. **hot-headed** *adj* impetuoso. **hothouse** *n* serra *f*. **hotplate** *n* scaldavivande *m invar*; (*hob*) fornello *m*. **hot-tempered** *adj* irascibile.

**hotel** [hou'tel] *n* albergo *m*. **hotel-keeper** *n* albergatore, -trice *m, f*.

**hound** [haund] *n* bracco *m*.

**hour** ['auə] *n* ora *f*. **hours** *pl n* (*time spent*) orario *m sing*. **kilometres/miles per hour** chilometri/miglia all'ora.

**hourly** ['auəli] *adj* orario. *adv* (*every hour*) ogni ora; (*hour by hour*) d'ora in ora, continuamente.

**house** [haus; *v* hauz] *n* casa *f*; (*theatre attendance*) sala *f*; (*audience*) pubblico *m*; (*dynasty*) dinastia *f*, famiglia *f*; (*comm*) ditta *f*. *v* (*shelter*) alloggiare; (*put in safe place*) mettere al sicuro.

**houseboat** ['hausbout] *n* casa galleggiante *f*, houseboat *f invar*.

**housebound** ['hausbaund] *adj* costretto a stare a casa.

**housebreaking** ['haus,breikiŋ] *n* scasso *m*.

**household** ['haushould] *n* famiglia *f*, casa *f*. *adj* casalingo, domestico.

**housekeeper** ['haus,ki:pə] *n* massaia *f*, governante *f*. **housekeeping** *n* economia domestica *f*.

**housemaid** ['hausmeid] *n* domestica *f*, cameriera *f*.

**house-to-house** *adj* di porta in porta.

**housewife** ['hauswaif] *n* massaia *f*, casalinga *f*.

**housework** ['hauswə:k] *n* lavori di casa *m pl*.

**housing** ['hauziŋ] *n* alloggio *m*. **housing estate** quartiere residenziale *m*.

**hovel** ['hovəl] *n* tugurio *m*.

**hover** ['hovə] *v* librarsi. **hovercraft** *n* hovercraft *m invar*.

**how** [hau] *adv* come, in che modo; (*to what extent*) quanto. **how are you?** come sta? **how do you do** (*after introduction*) piacere;

buon giorno. **how much** quanto. **how many** quanti. **how often** quante volte. *conj* che.

**however** [hau'evə] *adv* comunque, tuttavia. *conj* nonostante, tuttavia.

**howl** [haul] *v* ululare, lamentarsi. *n* ululato *m*, lamento *m*.

**hub** [hʌb] *n* parte centrale *f*; (*of wheel*) mozzo *m*. **hub cap** coppa *f*.

**hubbub** ['hʌbʌb] *n* baccano *m*.

**huddle** ['hʌdl] *v* **huddle together** affollarsi, accalcarsi.

**hue** [hju:] *n* colore *m*, tinta *f*.

**huff** [hʌf] *n* stizza *f*, risentimento *m*. **in a huff** offeso.

**hug** [hʌg] *v* abbracciare. *n* abbraccio *m*.

**huge** [hju:dʒ] *adj* enorme, immenso.

**hulk** [hʌlk] *n* carcassa *f*. **hulking** *adj* goffo.

**hull** [hʌl] *n* (*shell*) guscio *m*; (*husk*) buccia *f*; (*of nuts*) mallo *m*; (*pod*) baccello *m*; (*naut*) scafo *m*.

**hum** [hʌm] *v* ronzare; cantare a bocca chiusa, canterellare. *n* ronzio *m*.

**human** ['hju:mən] *adj* umano. **human being** essere umano *m*.

**humane** [hju:'mein] *adj* umanitario, umano, compassionevole.

**humanism** ['hju:mənizəm] *n* umanesimo *m*. **humanist** *n* umanista *m, f*.

**humanitarian** [hju:,mæni'teəriən] *adj* filantropico. *n* filantropo, -a *m, f*.

**humanity** [hju:'mænəti] *n* umanità *f*; compassione *f*.

**humble** ['hʌmbl] *adj* umile, modesto. *v* umiliare.

**humdrum** ['hʌmdrʌm] *adj* monotono, noioso.

**humid** ['hju:mid] *adj* umido. **humidity** *n* umidità *f*.

**humiliate** [hju:'milieit] *v* umiliare.

**humility** [hju:'miləti] *n* umiltà *f*.

**humour** ['hju:mə] *n* (*mood*) umore *m*; stato d'animo *m*, disposizione *f*; (*comic quality*) comicità *f*. *v* compiacere, accontentare.

**humorist** *n* umorista *m, f*. **humorous** *adj* divertente, spiritoso.

**hump** [hʌmp] *n* gobba *f*; (*hill*) cresta *f*.

**hunch** [hʌntʃ] *n* gobba *f*. **have a hunch** (*coll*) avere un sospetto. **hunchback** *n* gobbo *m*. **hunchbacked** *adj* gobbo.

**hundred** ['hʌndrəd] *nm, adj* cento. **hun-**

**dredth** *nm, adj* centesimo.

**hung** [hʌŋ] V **hang**.

**Hungary** ['hʌŋgəri] *n* Ungheria *f*.
**Hungarian** *n(m+f)*, *adj* ungherese.

**hunger** ['hʌŋgə] *n* fame *f*, appetito *m*. **hungry** *adj* affamato. **be hungry** aver fame.

**hunt** [hʌnt] *n* caccia *f*; (*pursuit*) inseguimento *m*; (*search*) ricerca affannosa *f*. *v* andare a caccia di; inseguire; cercare affannosamente. **hunter** *n* cacciatore *m*.

**hurdle** ['həːdl] *n* ostacolo *m*. *v* fare la corsa a ostacoli.

**hurl** [həːl] *v* scagliare, scaraventare.

**hurrah** [hu'raː] *interj* evviva!

**hurricane** ['hʌrikən] *n* uragano *m*. **hurricane lamp** lanterna controvento *f*.

**hurry** ['hʌri] *n* fretta *f*. **be in a hurry** aver fretta. *v* affrettare. **hurry up** sbrigarsi.

*****hurt** [həːt] *v* far male a, nuocere a; (*wound*) ferire; (*feel painful*) dolere. *n* dolore *m*, male *m*; ferita *f*; offesa *f*. **feel hurt** rimanere offeso.

**husband** ['hʌzbənd] *n* marito *m*.

**hush** [hʌʃ] *n* silenzio *m*. *interj* zitto! *v* far tacere. **hush-hush** *adj* (*coll*) segretissimo. **hush up** nascondere, dissimulare; (*suppress*) soffocare.

**husk** [hʌsk] *n* guscio *m*, baccello *m*.

**husky** ['hʌski] *adj* (*of voice*) rauco, fioco; (*burly*) grande e grosso.

**hustle** ['hʌsl] *n* spintone *m*. *v* spingere, sbrigarsi.

**hut** [hʌt] *n* capanna *f*, baracca *f*.

**hutch** [hʌtʃ] *n* conigliera *f*.

**hyacinth** ['haiəsinθ] *n* giacinto *m*.

**hybrid** ['haibrid] *nm, adj* ibrido.

**hydrant** ['haidrənt] *n* idrante *m*.

**hydraulic** [hai'droːlik] *adj* idraulico.

**hydrocarbon** [,haidrou'kaːbən] *n* idrocarburo *m*.

**hydro-electric** [,haidroui'lektrik] *adj* idroelettrico.

**hydrofoil** ['haidroufoil] *n* aliscafo *m*.

**hydrogen** ['haidrədʒən] *n* idrogeno *m*.

**hyena** [hai'iːnə] *n* iena *f*.

**hygiene** ['haidʒiːn] *n* igiene *f*. **hygienic** *adj* igienico.

**hymn** [him] *n* inno *m*, canto sacro *m*.

**hyperactive** [haipər'aktiv] *adj* iperattivo.

**hypermarket** ['haipə,maːkit] *n* ipermercato *m*.

**hyphen** ['haifən] *n* lineetta *f*.

**hypnosis** [hip'nousis] *n* ipnosi *f*. **hypnotic** *adj* ipnotico. **hypnotism** *n* ipnotismo *m*, ipnosi *f*. **hypnotist** *n* ipnotizzatore, -trice *m, f*.

**hypochondria** [haipə'kondriə] *n* ipocondria *f*. **hypochondriac** *n, adj* ipocondriaco, -a.

**hypocrisy** [hi'pokrəsi] *n* ipocrisia *f*. **hypocrite** *n* ipocrita *m, f*. **hypocritical** *adj* ipocrita.

**hypodermic** [haipə'dəːmik] *adj* ipodermico.

**hypotenuse** [hai'potənjuːz] *n* ipotenusa *f*.

**hypothesis** [hai'poθəsis] *n, pl* -**ses** ipotesi *f*. **hypothetical** *adj* ipotetico.

**hysterectomy** [histə'rektəmi] *n* isterectomia *f*.

**hysteria** [his'tiəriə] *n* isterismo *m*. **hysterical** *adj* isterico. **hysterics** *pl n* crisi isterica *f* sing.

# I

**I** [ai] *pron* io.

**ice** [ais] *n* ghiaccio *m*. **iceberg** *n* iceberg *m invar*. **ice-cold** *adj* freddo come il ghiaccio, glaciale, gelido. **ice cream** gelato *m*. **ice lolly** ghiacciolo *m*. **ice rink** pista di pattinaggio *f*. *v* (*cookery*) glassare; (*cover with ice*) ghiacciare. **icing** *n* glassa *f*. **icy** *adj* glaciale, gelido.

**Iceland** ['aislənd] *n* Islanda *f*. **Icelander** *n* islandese *m, f*. **Icelandic** *adj* islandese.

**icicle** ['aisikl] *n* ghiacciolo *m*.

**icon** ['aikon] *n* icona *f*. **iconoclast** *n* iconoclasta *m, f*.

**idea** [ai'diə] *n* idea *f*, concetto *m*, impressione *f*.

**ideal** [ai'diəl] *nm, adj* ideale. **idealist** *n* idealista *m, f*. **idealistic** *adj* idealistico. **idealize** *v* idealizzare.

**identical** [ai'dentikəl] *adj* identico.

**identify** [ai'dentifai] *v* identificare. **identification** *n* identificazione *f*.

**identity** [ai'dentiti] *n* identità *f*. **identity card** carta d'identità *f*. **identity parade** confronto all'americana *m*. **mistaken**

**identity** errore di persona *m*.

**ideology** [aidi'olədʒi] *n* ideologia *f*. **ideological** *adj* ideologico.

**idiom** ['idiəm] *n* (*expression*) frase idiomatica *f*; (*language*) idioma *m*.

**idiosyncrasy** [,idiə'siŋkrəsi] *n* idiosincrasia *f*.

**idiot** ['idiət] *n* idiota *m*, *f*; cretino, -a *m*, *f*. **idiotic** *adj* idiota, cretino, imbecille.

**idle** ['aidl] *adj* (*lazy*) pigro; (*doing nothing*) disoccupato; (*machine*) fermo; (*worthless*) vano. *v* stare senza far nulla; (*machine*) girare a folle. **idler** *n* fannullone, -a *m*, *f*.

**idol** ['aidl] *n* idolo *m*. **idolatry** *n* idolatria *f*. **idolize** *v* idoleggiare.

**idyllic** [i'dilik] *adj* idillico.

**if** [if] *conj* se. **as if** come se. **if not** se no. **if you please** per piacere.

**ignite** [ig'nait] *v* accendere, dar fuoco a; (*catch fire*) prender fuoco.

**ignition** [ig'niʃən] *n* accensione *f*. **ignition key** interruttore dell'accensione *m*.

**ignorant** ['ignərant] *adj* ignorante. **be ignorant of** ignorare. **ignorance** *n* ignoranza *f*.

**ignore** [ig'no:] *v* (*disregard*) non badare a, trascurare; (*refrain from seeing/recognizing/hearing*) fingere di non vedere/riconoscere/sentire.

**ill** [il] *adj* (*sick*) malato; (*bad*) cattivo. *nm*, *adv* male. **ill-advised** *adj* malavveduto. **ill-bred** or **ill-mannered** *adj* maleducato. **ill-treat** *v* maltrattare. **illness** *n* malattia *f*. **ill feeling** cattivo sangue *m*.

**illegal** [i'li:gəl] *adj* illegale.

**illegible** [i'ledʒəbl] *adj* illeggibile.

**illegitimate** [,ili'dʒitimit] *adj* illegittimo.

**illicit** [i'lisit] *adj* illecito.

**illiterate** [i'litərit] *n*(*m+f*), *adj* analfabeta.

**illogical** [i'lodʒikəl] *adj* illogico.

**illuminate** [i'lu:mi,neit] *v* illuminare, rischiarare. **illuminating** *adj* illuminante. **illumination** *n* illuminazione *f*.

**illusion** [i'lu:ʒən] *n* illusione *f*.

**illustrate** ['ilə,streit] *v* illustrare. **illustration** *n* illustrazione *f*.

**illustrious** [i'lʌstriəs] *adj* illustre, celebre.

**image** ['imidʒ] *n* immagine *f*, ritratto *m*. **imagery** *n* immagini *f pl*.

**imagine** [i'mædʒin] *v* farsi un'idea di, immaginarsi; (*suppose*) supporre; (*believe*) credere. **imaginary** *adj* immaginario.

**imagination** *n* immaginazione *f*, fantasia *f*.

**imbalance** [im'baləns] *n* squilibrio *m*.

**imbecile** ['imbə,si:l] *n*(*m+f*), *adj* imbecille.

**imitate** ['imi,teit] *v* imitare, contraffare. **imitation** *n* imitazione *f*, copia *f*, contraffattura *f*.

**immaculate** [i'makjulit] *adj* immacolato.

**immaterial** [,imə'tiəriəl] *adj* (*unimportant*) di nessuna importanza.

**immature** [,imə'tjuə] *adj* immaturo. **immaturity** *n* immaturità *f*.

**immediate** [i'mi:diət] *adj* immediato. **immediately** *adv* immediatamente, subito.

**immense** [i'mens] *adj* immenso.

**immerse** [i'mə:s] *v* immergere. **immersion** *n* immersione *f*. **immersion heater** riscaldatore a immersione *m*.

**immigrate** ['imi,greit] *v* immigrare. **immigrant** *n*(*m+f*) immigrante. **immigration** *n* immigrazione *f*.

**imminent** ['iminənt] *adj* imminente.

**immobile** [i'moubail] *adj* immobile, fermo. **immobilize** *v* immobilizzare.

**immoral** [i'morəl] *adj* immorale. **immorality** *n* immoralità *f*.

**immortal** [i'mo:tl] *adj* immortale. **immortality** *n* immortalità *f*. **immortalize** *v* immortalare.

**immovable** [i'mu:vəbl] *adj* inamovibile, fisso.

**immune** [i'mju:n] *adj* immune. **immunity** *n* immunità *f*. **immunization** *n* immunizzazione *f*. **immunize** *v* immunizzare.

**imp** [imp] *n* folletto *m*.

**impact** ['impakt] *n* urto *m*, scontro *m*; (*effect*) impressione *f*.

**impair** [im'peə] *v* danneggiare, menomare.

**impale** [im'peil] *v* impalare.

**impart** [im'pa:t] *v* impartire.

**impartial** [im'pa:ʃəl] *adj* imparziale. **impartiality** *n* imparzialità *f*.

**impasse** [am'pa:s] *n* impasse *m*, intoppo *m*.

**impatient** [im'peiʃənt] *adj* impaziente. **get impatient** impazientirsi. **impatience** *n* impazienza *f*.

**impeach** [im'pi:tʃ] *v* accusare; (*call in question*) mettere in dubbio, imputare.

**impeccable** [im'pekəbl] *adj* impeccabile.

**impede** [im'pi:d] *v* ostacolare, impedire.

**impediment** [im'pedimənt] *n* impedimento *m*, ostacolo *m*. **speech impediment** difetto *or* impedimento di lingua *m*.

**impel** [im'pel] *v* spingere, impellere.

**impending** [im'pendiŋ] *adj* imminente.

**imperative** [im'perətiv] *nm, adj* imperativo.

**imperfect** [im'pə:fikt] *nm, adj* imperfetto.

**imperial** [im'piəriəl] *adj* imperiale. **imperialism** *n* imperialismo *m*.

**imperil** [im'perəl] *v* mettere in pericolo, compromettere.

**impersonal** [im'pə:sənl] *adj* impersonale, comune.

**impersonate** [im'pə:sə,neit] *v* impersonare; (*theatre*) interpretare.

**impertinent** [im'pə:tinənt] *adj* impertinente. **impertinence** *n* impertinenza *f*.

**impervious** [im'pə:viəs] *adj* impervio; impermeabile; (*fig*) sordo.

**impetuous** [im'petjuəs] *adj* impetuoso.

**impetus** ['impətəs] *n* impeto *m*, slancio *m*.

**impinge** [im'pindʒ] *v* **impinge on** colpire.

**implement** ['implimənt; *v* 'impliment] *n* attrezzo *m*, utensile *m*. *v* adempiere. **implementation** *n* adempimento *m*.

**implicate** ['implikeit] *v* implicare, coinvolgere. **implication** *n* implicazione *f*.

**implicit** [im'plisit] *adj* implicito.

**implore** [im'plo:] *v* supplicare.

**imply** [im'plai] *v* (*mean*) significare; (*suggest*) far pensare a.

**impolite** [impə'lait] *adj* scortese, sgarbato.

**import** [im'po:t] *v* importare. *n* (*comm*) importazione *f*; importanza *f*. **importer** *n* importatore *m*.

**importance** [im'po:təns] *n* importanza *f*. **important** *adj* importante.

**impose** [im'pouz] *v* imporre. **impose on** abusare di. **imposing** *adj* imponente. **imposition** *n* imposizione *f*.

**impossible** [im'posəbl] *adj* impossibile. **impossibility** *n* impossibilità *f*.

**impostor** [im'postə] *n* impostore *m*.

**impotent** ['impətənt] *adj* impotente. **impotence** *n* impotenza *f*.

**impound** [im'paund] *v* confiscare.

**impoverish** [im'povəriʃ] *v* impoverire.

**impractical** [im'praktikəl] *adj* (*person*) privo di senso pratico; (*thing*) inservibile, non pratico.

**impregnate** ['impreg,neit] *v* impregnare. **impregnation** *n* impregnazione *f*.

**impress** [im'pres] *v* colpire, fare impressione su; (*urge*) raccomandare; (*print*) imprimere, stampare. **impression** *n* impressione *f*; (*print*) stampa *f*, ristampa *f*. **impressive** *adj* impressionante.

**imprint** ['imprint] *n* impronta *f*.

**imprison** [im'prizn] *v* carcerare. **imprisonment** *n* carcerazione *f*.

**improbable** [im'probəbl] *adj* improbabile. **improbability** *n* improbabilità *f*.

**impromptu** [im'promptju:] *adj* improvvisato. *adv* all'improvviso.

**improper** [im'propə] *adj* (*inappropriate*) improprio; (*unseemly*) indecente, indecoroso.

**improve** [im'pru:v] *v* migliorare; (*increase value*) valorizzare; (*get better*) star meglio. **improve on** perfezionare. **improvement** *n* miglioramento *m*; (*making more valuable*) miglioria *f*.

**improvise** ['imprə,vaiz] *v* improvvisare. **improvisation** *n* improvvisazione *f*.

**impudent** ['impjudənt] *adj* sfacciato. **impudence** *n* sfacciataggine *f*.

**impulse** ['impʌls] *n* impulso *m*, stimolo *m*. **impulsive** *adj* impulsivo.

**impure** [im'pjuə] *adj* impuro. **impurity** *n* impurità *f*.

**in** [in] *prep* in; (*within*) tra, entro. *adv* dentro, a casa, in sede.

**inability** [,inə'biləti] *n* incapacità *f*.

**inaccessible** [,inak'sesəbl] *adj* inaccessibile.

**inaccurate** [in'akjurit] *adj* inesatto. **inaccuracy** *n* inesattezza *f*.

**inactive** [in'aktiv] *adj* inattivo, passivo.

**inadequate** [in'adikwit] *adj* inadeguato, insufficiente, inetto. **inadequacy** *n* inadeguatezza *f*.

**inadmissible** [inəd'misəbl] *adj* inammissibile.

**inadvertent** [,inəd'və:tənt] *adj* involontario.

**inane** [in'ein] *adj* insensato, futile.

**inanimate** [in'animit] *adj* (*not animate*) inanimato; (*lifeless*) esanime.

**inarticulate** [,ina:'tikjulit] *adj* (*person*) che non sa esprimersi; inarticolato.

**inasmuch** [,inəz'mʌtʃ] *conj* dacchè, poichè.

**inaudible** [in'o:dəbl] *adj* inaudibile.

**inaugurate** [iˈnɔːgjuˌreit] v inaugurare. **inaugural** adj inaugurale. **inauguration** n inaugurazione f.

**inauspicious** [inɔːˈspiʃəs] adj infausto.

**inbred** [ˌinˈbred] adj (inborn) innato; (resulting from inbreeding) endogamo. **inbreeding** n endogamia f.

**incalculable** [inˈkalkjuləbl] adj incalcolabile, imprevedibile.

**incapable** [inˈkeipəbl] adj incapace, inetto.

**incendiary** [inˈsendiəri] adj incendiario.

**incense¹** [ˈinsens] n incenso m.

**incense²** [inˈsens] v irritare, provocare.

**incentive** [inˈsentiv] n incentivo m.

**incessant** [inˈsesənt] adj continuo.

**incest** [ˈinsest] n incesto m. **incestuous** adj incestuoso.

**inch** [intʃ] n pollice m. **inch by inch** gradatamente. v **inch forward** avanzare poco alla volta.

**incident** [ˈinsidənt] n caso m, episodio m; (event with serious consequences) incidente f. **incidental** adj incidentale. **incidentally** adv tra parentesi, a proposito.

**incinerator** [inˈsinəˌreitə] n inceneritore m. **incinerate** v incenerire.

**incisive** [inˈsaisiv] adj acuto.

**incite** [inˈsait] v incitare, spronare. **incitement** n incitamento m.

**incline** [inˈklain] v inclinare, chinare. **be inclined to** essere propenso or disposto a. n piano inclinato m, pendio m. **inclination** n inclinazione f; propensione f.

**include** [inˈkluːd] v includere. **inclusion** n inclusione f. **inclusive** adj compreso.

**incoherent** [ˌinkəˈhiərənt] adj incoerente.

**income** [ˈinkʌm] n entrata f, reddito m. **income tax** imposta sull'entrata f. **incoming** adj in arrivo.

**incompatible** [inkəmˈpatəbl] adj incompatibile. **incompatibility** n incompatibilità f.

**incompetent** [inˈkompitənt] adj incompetente. **incompetence** n incompetenza f.

**incomplete** [ˌinkəmˈpliːt] adj incompleto.

**incomprehensible** [inˌkompriˈhensəbl] adj incomprensibile.

**inconceivable** [inkənˈsiːvəbl] adj inconcepibile.

**inconclusive** [inkənˈkluːsiv] adj inconcludente.

**incongruous** [inˈkoŋgruəs] adj incongruo.

**inconsiderate** [ˌinkənˈsidərit] adj sconsiderato; (person) che manca di riguardo.

**inconsistent** [ˌinkənˈsistənt] adj inconsistente. **inconsistency** n inconsistenza f.

**incontinence** [inˈkontinəns] n incontinenza f. **incontinent** adj incontinente.

**inconvenience** [inkənˈviːnjəns] n sconvenienza f. v sconvenire, disturbare. **inconvenient** adj sconveniente, scomodo.

**incorporate** [inˈkoːpəˌreit] v incorporare.

**incorrect** [inkəˈrekt] adj scorretto.

**increase** [inˈkriːs] v aumentare, ingrandirsi, crescere. n aumento m. **increasingly** adv sempre più.

**incredible** [inˈkredəbl] adj incredibile.

**incredulous** [inˈkredjuləs] adj incredulo.

**increment** [ˈiŋkrəmənt] n incremento m, aumento m.

**incriminate** [inˈkrimineit] v incolpare.

**incubate** [ˈiŋkjuˌbeit] v incubare. **incubation** n incubazione f. **incubator** n incubatrice f.

**incumbent** [inˈkʌmbənt] adj **be incumbent on** spettare a.

**incur** [inˈkəː] v incorrere in.

**incurable** [inˈkjuərəbl] adj incurabile.

**indebted** [inˈdetid] adj (owing money) indebitato; (under obligation) riconoscente.

**indecent** [inˈdiːsnt] adj indecente. **indecency** n indecenza f; (law) oltraggio al pudore m.

**indeed** [inˈdiːd] adv infatti, effettivamente, proprio. interj davvero!

**indefatigable** [indiˈfatigəbl] adj indefesso.

**indefinite** [inˈdefinit] adj indefinito, vago, illimitato.

**indelible** [inˈdeləbl] adj indelebile; (memory) indimenticabile.

**indemnity** [inˈdemnəti] n indennità f; (sum paid) indennizzo m. **indemnify** v indennizzare.

**indent** [inˈdent] v (notch) dentellare; (make recess) incavare. **indentation** n incavo m, dentellatura f, rientranza f; (printing) capoverso m.

**independent** [ˌindiˈpendənt] adj indipendente. **independence** n indipendenza f.

**index** [ˈindeks] n indice m. **index card** scheda f. **index finger** indice m.

**India** [ˈindjə] n India f. **India rubber**

gomma f. **Indian** n, adj indiano, -a.
**Indian ink** inchiostro di china m.
**indicate** ['indikeit] v indicare.
**indict** [in'dait] v accusare. **indictment** n
accusa f; (law) atto d'accusa m.
**indifferent** [in'difrənt] adj indifferente.
**indifference** n indifferenza f.
**indigenous** [in'didʒinəs] adj indigeno.
**indigestion** [,indi'dʒestʃən] n indigestione
f.
**indignant** [in'dignənt] adj sdegnato. **feel
indignant** indignarsi, sdegnarsi (contro).
**indignity** [in'dignəti] n indegnità f.
**indirect** [,indi'rekt] adj indiretto.
**indiscreet** [,indi'skri:t] adj indiscreto.
**indiscretion** n indiscrezione f.
**indiscriminate** [,indi'skriminit] adj indiscriminato.
**indispensable** [,indi'spensəbl] adj indispensabile.
**indisposed** [,indi'spouzd] adj indisposto.
**individual** [,indi'vidjuəl] n individuo m. adj
individuale, particolare.
**indoctrinate** [in'doktri,neit] v indottrinare.
**indoctrination** n indottrinamento m.
**indolent** ['indələnt] adj indolente. **indo-
lence** n indolenza f.
**indoor** ['indo:] adj di or da casa. **indoors**
adv in casa, all'interno, dentro.
**induce** [in'dju:s] v indurre.
**indulge** [in'dʌldʒ] v (gratify) appagare, soddisfare; essere indulgente verso. **indulge in**
abbandonarsi a, dedicarsi a. **indulgence** n
indulgenza f. **indulgent** adj indulgente.
**industry** ['indəstri] n industria f; diligenza
f, zelo m. **industrial** adj industriale. **industrialize** v industrializzare. **industrious** adj
diligente, operoso.
**inebriated** [i'ni:brieitid] adj ubriaco.
**inedible** [in'edibl] adj immangiabile.
**inefficient** [,ini'fiʃnt] adj inefficiente. **inef-
ficiency** n inefficienza f.
**inept** [i'nept] adj inetto, incapace.
**inequality** [,ini'kwoləti] n ineguaglianza f.
**inert** [i'nə:t] adj inerte. **inertia** n inerzia f.
**inevitable** [in'evitəbl] adj inevitabile.
**inexcusable** [,inik'skju:zəbl] adj imperdonabile, ingiustificabile.
**inexhaustible** [,inig'zo:stəbl] adj inesauri-
bile.
**inexpensive** [,inik'spensiv] adj a buon mer-

cato, poco caro.
**inexperienced** [,inik'spiəriənst] adj inesperto.
**inexplicable** [inik'splikəbl] adj inspiegabile.
**infallible** [in'faləbl] adj infallibile. **infallibility** n infallibilità f.
**infamous** ['infəməs] adj infame. **infamy** n
infamia f.
**infancy** ['infənsi] n infanzia f.
**infant** ['infənt] n infante m, bambino, -a m,
f. **infantile** adj infantile, puerile. **infant
prodigy** bambino prodigio m.
**infantry** ['infəntri] n fanteria f.
**infatuated** [in'fatjueitid] adj infatuato. **be
infatuated** prendere una cotta.
**infect** [in'fekt] v infettare. **infection** n
infezione f. **infectious** adj infettivo.
**infer** [in'fə:] v dedurre, desumere. **infer-
able** adj deducibile. **inference** n inferenza
f, deduzione f.
**inferior** [in'fiəriə] n(m+f), adj inferiore.
**inferiority** n inferiorità f.
**infernal** [in'fə:nl] adj infernale.
**infest** [in'fest] v infestare.
**infidelity** [,infi'deliti] n infedeltà f.
**infiltrate** [in'fil,treit] v infiltrare. **infiltra-
tion** n infiltrazione f.
**infinite** ['infinit] nm, adj infinito. **infinity**
n infinità f, infinito m.
**infinitive** [in'finitiv] nm, adj infinito.
**infirm** [in'fə:m] adj infermo. **infirmity** n
infermità f.
**inflame** [in'fleim] v infiammare. **inflammable** adj infiammabile. **inflammation** n
infiammazione f.
**inflate** [in'fleit] v gonfiare. **inflation** n
inflazione f. **inflatable** adj gonfiabile.
**inflection** [in'flekʃən] n inflessione f.
**inflexible** [in'fleksəbl] adj inflessibile.
**inflict** [in'flikt] v infliggere.
**influence** ['influəns] n influenza f, ascendente m. v influire su, influenzare. **influen-
tial** adj autorevole, importante.
**influenza** [,influ'enzə] n influenza f.
**influx** ['inflʌks] n afflusso m, affluenza f.
**inform** [in'fo:m] v informare, far sapere a.
**inform against** or **on** (denounce) denunziare. **informant** n informatore, -trice m, f.
**informer** n spia f, delatore, -trice m, f.
**informal** [in'fo:ml] adj alla buona, senza
cerimonia, non ufficiale. **informality** n

mancanza di formalità f.

**information** [ˌinfəˈmeiʃən] n informazioni f pl, notizie f pl. **for your information** a titolo d'informazione. **information technology** tecnologia dell'informazione f, m.

**infra-red** [ˌinfrəˈred] adj infrarosso.

**infrequent** [inˈfriːkwənt] adj raro.

**infringe** [inˈfrindʒ] v violare, trasgredire. **infringement** n violazione f.

**infuriate** [inˈfjuəriˌeit] v fare arrabbiare. **be infuriated** essere furibondo or arrabbiatissimo.

**ingenious** [inˈdʒiːnjəs] adj ingegnoso. **ingenuity** n ingegnosità f.

**ingot** [ˈiŋgət] n lingotto m.

**ingredient** [inˈgriːdjənt] n ingrediente m.

**inhabit** [inˈhabit] v abitare, vivere, dimorare. **inhabitant** n abitante m, f.

**inhale** [inˈheil] v inalare. **inhaler** n inalatore m.

**inherent** [inˈhiərənt] adj inerente.

**inherit** [inˈherit] v ereditare. **inheritance** n eredità f.

**inhibit** [inˈhibit] v inibire. **inhibition** n inibizione f.

**inhuman** [inˈhjuːmən] adj inumano. **inhumanity** n inumanità f.

**iniquity** [iˈnikwəti] n iniquità f. **iniquitous** adj iniquo.

**initial** [iˈniʃl] nf, adj iniziale. v siglare.

**initiate** [iˈniʃiˌeit] v iniziare, istituire. **initiation** n iniziazione f, inizio m.

**initiative** [iˈniʃiətiv] n iniziativa f.

**inject** [inˈdʒekt] v iniettare; (introduce) immettere. **injection** n iniezione f.

**injure** [ˈindʒə] v (damage) danneggiare; (hurt) far male a; (wound) ferire; (law) ledere. **injurious** adj dannoso, nocivo. **injury** n male m; danno m; torto m; ferita f.

**injustice** [inˈdʒʌstis] n ingiustizia f.

**ink** [iŋk] n inchiostro m. **ink-well** n calamaio m.

**inkling** [ˈiŋkliŋ] n sospetto m, sentore m.

**inland** [ˈinlənd] adv inˈland] adj interno. adv all' or nell'interno.

**in-laws** [ˈinˌlɔːs] pl n (coll) parenti acquisiti m pl.

***inlay** [ˈinlei] v intarsiare. n intarsio m.

**inlet** [ˈinlet] n (geog) insenatura f.

**inmate** [ˈinmeit] n (of hospital, etc.) ricoverato, -a m, f; (of prison) carcerato, -a m, f.

**inn** [in] n locanda f, osteria f, albergo m.

**innkeeper** n locandiere, -a m, f; oste, -essa m, f; albergatore, -trice m, f.

**innate** [iˈneit] adj innato.

**inner** [ˈinə] adj interno, interiore; (thoughts, etc.) intimo. **inner city** centro città m. **inner tube** camera d'aria f.

**innocent** [ˈinəsnt] n(m+f), adj innocente. **innocence** n innocenza f.

**innocuous** [iˈnokjuəs] adj innocuo.

**innovation** [ˌinəˈveiʃən] n innovazione f, novità f. **innovate** v innovare. **innovator** n innovatore, -trice m, f.

**innuendo** [ˌinjuˈendou] n insinuazione f.

**innumerable** [iˈnjuːmərəbl] adj innumerevole.

**inoculate** [iˈnokjuˌleit] v inoculare. **inoculation** n inoculazione f.

**inorganic** [ˌinoːˈganik] adj inorganico.

**input** [ˈinput] n (elec) alimentazione f; (computer) input m invar.

**inquest** [ˈinkwest] n inchiesta f, istruttoria f.

**inquire** [inˈkwaiə] v chiedere, domandare. **inquiry** n domanda f, informazione f, inchiesta f.

**inquisition** [ˌinkwiˈziʃən] n inquisizione f, inchiesta f.

**inquisitive** [inˈkwizətiv] adj curioso.

**insane** [inˈsein] adj pazzo, matto. **insanity** n pazzia f, follia f.

**insatiable** [inˈseiʃəbl] adj insaziabile.

**inscribe** [inˈskraib] v (enrol) inscrivere; (engrave) incidere. **inscription** n iscrizione f, dedica f.

**insect** [ˈinsekt] n insetto m. **insecticide** n insetticida m.

**insecure** [ˌinsiˈkjuə] adj malsicuro, instabile. **insecurity** n incertezza f, instabilità f.

**inseminate** [inˈsemineit] v inseminare. **insemination** n inseminazione f.

**insensible** [inˈsensəbl] adj insensibile; (unconscious) privo di sensi.

**insensitive** [inˈsensətiv] adj insensibile, indifferente.

**inseparable** [inˈsepərəbl] adj inseparabile.

**insert** [inˈsəːt; n ˈinsəːt] v inserire. n also **insertion** inserzione f.

**inshore** [ˌinˈʃoː] adj costiero. adv verso la riva.

**inside** [ˌinˈsaid] adv dentro, internamente.

*prep* dentro, all'interno. *adj* interno, interiore; (*confidential*) riservato. *n* interno *m*; (*soccer*) mezzala *f*. **inside out** a rovescio.

**insidious** [in'sidiəs] *adj* insidioso, perfido.

**insight** ['insait] *n* discernimento *m*, intuito *m*.

**insignificant** [,insig'nifikənt] *adj* insignificante.

**insincere** [,insin'siə] *adj* insincero.

**insinuate** [in'sinjueit] *v* insinuare, dare ad intendere. **insinuation** *n* insinuazione *f*.

**insipid** [in'sipid] *adj* insipido.

**insist** [in'sist] *v* insistere. **insistence** *n* insistenza *f*. **insistent** *adj* insistente.

**insolent** ['insələnt] *adj* impertinente. **insolence** *n* impertinenza *f*.

**insoluble** [in'soljubl] *adj* insolubile; (*not solvable*) insolvibile.

**insomnia** [in'somniə] *n* insonnia *f*. **insomniac** *n* insonne *m*, *f*.

**inspect** [in'spekt] *v* ispezionare, verificare; (*troops*) passare in rivista. **inspection** *n* ispezione *f*, verifica *f*; rivista *f*. **inspector** *n* ispettore, -trice *m*, *f*; (*bus, train*) controllore, -a *m*, *f*; (*police*) commissario *m*.

**inspire** [in'spaiə] *v* ispirare, infondere. **inspiration** *n* ispirazione *f*.

**instability** [,instə'biləti] *n* instabilità *f*.

**install** [in'stoːl] *v* installare. **installation** *n* installazione *f*.

**instalment** [in'stoːlmənt] *n* (*comm*) rata *f*; (*serial*) puntata *f*.

**instance** ['instəns] *n* esempio *m*. **for instance** per esempio.

**instant** ['instənt] *adj* immediato; urgente; (*comm*) corrente; (*of food*) istantaneo. *n* istante *m*, momento *m*. **instantaneous** *adj* istantaneo.

**instead** [in'sted] *adv* invece.

**instep** ['instep] *n* (*anat*) collo del piede *m*; (*shoe*) collo della scarpa *m*.

**instigate** ['instigeit] *v* istigare. **instigation** *n* istigazione *f*.

**instil** [in'stil] *v* instillare, infondere.

**instinct** ['instiŋkt] *n* istinto *m*. **instinctive** *adj* istintivo.

**institute** ['institjuːt] *n* istituto *m*. *v* istituire, iniziare. **institution** *n* istituzione *f*.

**instruct** [in'strʌkt] *v* (*teach*) istruire; (*direct*) dare istruzioni *or* disposizioni a. **instruction** *n* istruzione *f*, disposizioni *f pl*. **instructive** *adj* istruttivo. **instructor** *n*

istruttore, -trice *m*, *f*, insegnante *m*, *f*.

**instrument** ['instrəmənt] *n* strumento *m*; (*tool*) arnese *m*; (*law*) titolo *m*, atto *m*. **instrumental** *adj* strumentale. **be instrumental in** essere utile a.

**insubordinate** [,insə'boːdənət] *adj* insubordinato. **insubordination** *n* insubordinazione *f*.

**insufficient** [,insə'fiʃənt] *adj* insufficiente.

**insular** ['insjulə] *adj* insulare; (*outlook*) gretto.

**insulate** ['insjuleit] *v* isolare. **insulating tape** nastro isolante *m*. **insulation** *n* isolamento *m*.

**insulin** ['insjulin] *n* insulina *f*.

**insult** [in'sʌlt; *n* 'insʌlt] *v* insultare, offendere. *n* insulto *m*, offesa *f*.

**insure** [in'ʃuə] *v* assicurare. **insurance** *n* assicurazione *f*.

**intact** [in'takt] *adj* intatto.

**intake** ['inteik] *n* (*consumption*) consumo *m*; (*employment*) assunzione *f*; (*people newly taken on*) reclute *f pl*.

**intangible** [in'tandʒəbl] *adj* intangibile.

**integral** ['intigrəl] *adj* integrale.

**integrate** ['intigreit] *v* integrare. **integration** *n* integrazione *f*.

**integrity** [in'tegrəti] *n* integrità *f*.

**intellect** ['intilekt] *n* intelletto *m*. **intellectual** *n*(*m*+*f*), *adj* intellettuale.

**intelligent** [in'telidʒənt] *adj* intelligente. **intelligence** *n* intelligenza *f*; informazioni *f pl*. **intelligentsia** *n* intellighenzia *f*.

**intelligible** [in'telidʒəbl] *adj* intelligibile.

**intend** [in'tend] *v* intendere, aver l'intenzione di. **intended** *adj* premeditato, voluto.

**intense** [in'tens] *adj* intenso, profondo.

**intent**[1] [in'tent] *n* intento *m*, proposito *m*, intenzione *f*. **to all intents and purposes** a tutti gli effetti.

**intent**[2] [in'tent] *adj* intento, assorto. **intent on** deciso a.

**intention** [in'tenʃən] *n* intenzione *f*, proposito *m*. **intentional** *adj* intenzionale.

**inter** [in'təː] *v* seppellire. **interment** *n* sepoltura *f*.

**interact** [,intər'akt] *v* esercitare un'azione reciproca, interagire. **interaction** *n* azione reciproca *f*. **interactive** *adj* interattivo.

**intercede** [,intə'siːd] *v* intercedere.

**intercept** [ˌɪntə'sept] v intercettare. **interception** n intercettazione f.

**interchange** [ˌɪntə'tʃaɪndʒ] v scambiare. **interchangeable** adj intercambiabile, scambievole.

**intercom** ['ɪntəkɒm] n citofono m.

**intercourse** ['ɪntəkɔːs] n rapporti m pl.

**interest** ['ɪntrɪst] v interessare. **be interested in** interessarsi di. n interesse m. **interesting** adj interessante.

**interest rate** n tasso d'interessi m.

**interfere** [ˌɪntə'fɪə] v interferire, immischiarsi. **interference** n interferenza f.

**interim** ['ɪntərɪm] n interim m. adj provvisorio, temporaneo.

**interior** [ɪn'tɪərɪə] nm, adj interno. **interior decorator** arredatore, -trice m, f.

**interjection** [ˌɪntə'dʒekʃən] n interiezione f.

**interlude** ['ɪntəluːd] n interludio m.

**intermediary** [ˌɪntə'miːdɪərɪ] n intermediario m.

**intermediate** [ˌɪntə'miːdɪət] adj intermedio.

**interminable** [ɪn'tə:mɪnəbl] adj senza fine.

**intermission** [ˌɪntə'mɪʃən] n interruzione f.

**intermittent** [ˌɪntə'mɪtənt] adj intermittente.

**intern** [ɪn'tə:n] v internare. **internment** n internamento m.

**internal** [ɪn'tə:nl] adj interno, interiore.

**international** [ˌɪntə'naʃənl] adj internazionale.

**interpose** [ˌɪntə'pəuz] v frapporre.

**interpret** [ɪn'tə:prɪt] v interpretare. **interpretation** n interpretazione f. **interpreter** n interprete m, f.

**interrogate** [ɪn'terəgeɪt] v interrogare. **interrogation** n interrogazione f. **interrogative** adj, nm interrogativo.

**interrupt** [ˌɪntə'rʌpt] v interrompere. **interruption** n interruzione f.

**intersect** [ˌɪntə'sekt] v intersecare. **intersection** n intersezione f.

**intersperse** [ˌɪntə'spə:s] v cospargere.

**interval** ['ɪntəvəl] n intervallo m.

**intervene** [ˌɪntə'viːn] v intervenire. **intervention** n intervento m.

**interview** ['ɪntəvjuː] n intervista f, colloquio m. v intervistare.

**intestine** [ɪn'testɪn] n intestino m. **intestinal** adj intestinale.

**intimate¹** ['ɪntɪmət] adj intimo, familiare. **intimacy** n intimità f.

**intimate²** ['ɪntɪmeɪt] v intimare, suggerire. **intimation** n intimazione f.

**intimidate** [ɪn'tɪmɪdeɪt] v intimidire, intimorire. **intimidation** n intimidazione f.

**into** ['ɪntu] prep in, dentro.

**intolerable** [ɪn'tɒlərəbl] adj insopportabile, intollerabile.

**intolerant** [ɪn'tɒlərənt] adj intollerante. **intolerance** n intolleranza f.

**intonation** [ˌɪntə'neɪʃən] n intonazione f.

**intoxicate** [ɪn'tɒksɪkeɪt] v intossicare; (with drink) ubriacare; (excite) esaltare. **intoxicated** adj ubriaco, eccitato.

**intransigent** [ɪn'transɪdʒənt] adj intransigente.

**intransitive** [ɪn'transɪtɪv] adj intransitivo.

**intravenous** [ˌɪntrə'viːnəs] adj endovenoso.

**intrepid** [ɪn'trepɪd] adj intrepido.

**intricate** ['ɪntrɪkət] adj complicato, complesso. **intricacy** n complicazione f.

**intrigue** ['ɪntriːg; v ɪn'triːg] n intrigo (pl -ghi) m. v (plot) intrigare; (excite curiosity) incuriosire. **intriguing** adj interessante, affascinante.

**intrinsic** [ɪn'trɪnsɪk] adj intrinseco.

**introduce** [ˌɪntrə'djuːs] v introdurre; (people) presentare. **introduction** n introduzione f, presentazione f. **introductory** adj introduttorio, introduttivo.

**introspective** [ˌɪntrə'spektɪv] adj introspettivo. **introspection** n introspezione f.

**introvert** ['ɪntrəvə:t] adj, n introverso, -a.

**intrude** [ɪn'truːd] v intrudere. **intrusion** n intrusione f.

**intuition** [ˌɪntju:'ɪʃən] n intuito m; (psychol, etc.) intuizione f. **intuitive** adj intuitivo.

**inundate** ['ɪnʌndeɪt] v inondare, allagare. **inundation** n allagamento m.

**invade** [ɪn'veɪd] v invadere. **invader** n invasore m. **invasion** n invasione f.

**invalid¹** ['ɪnvəlɪd] n, adj invalido, -a; malato, -a.

**invalid²** [ɪn'valɪd] adj (not valid) invalido, senza validità, nullo. **invalidate** v invalidare, annullare.

**invaluable** [ɪn'valjuəbl] adj inestimabile, incalcolabile.

**invariable** [ɪn'veərɪəbl] adj invariabile, costante.

**invective** [in'vektiv] *n* invettiva *f.*

**invent** [in'vent] *v* inventare. **invention** *n* invenzione *f.*

**inventory** ['invəntri] *n* inventario *m.*

**invert** [in'və:t] *v* invertire; (*inside out*) rovesciare; (*upside down*) capovolgere. **inverted commas** virgolette *f pl.* **inversion** *n* inversione *f,* rovesciamento *m.*

**invertebrate** [in'və:tibrət] *nm, adj* invertebrato.

**invest** [in'vest] *v* investire. **investment** *n* investimento *m.*

**investigate** [in'vestigeit] *v* investigare, svolgere indagini. **investigation** *n* indagine *f.*

**invigorating** [in'vigəreitiŋ] *adj* che invigorisce, fortificante.

**invincible** [in'vinsəbl] *adj* invincibile.

**invisible** [in'vizəbl] *adj* invisibile. **invisibility** *n* invisibilità *f.*

**invite** [in'vait] *v* invitare; provocare; (*lay oneself open to*) esporsi a. **invitation** *n* invito *m.* **inviting** *adj* attraente, seducente.

**invoice** ['invois] *n* fattura *f. v* fatturare.

**invoke** [in'vouk] *v* invocare. **invocation** *n* invocazione *f.*

**involuntary** [in'volǝntəri] *adj* involontario.

**involve** [in'volv] *v* (*imply*) implicare; (*implicate*) coinvolgere; (*entail*) comportare. **involvement** *n* implicazione *f.*

**inward** ['inwəd] *adj* interno, intimo. **inwardly** *adv* interiormente. **inwards** *adv* verso il centro.

**iodine** ['aiədi:n] *n* iodio *m.*

**ion** ['aiən] *n* ione *m.*

**irate** [ai'reit] *adj* arrabbiato.

**Ireland** ['aiələnd] *n* Irlanda *f.* **Irish** *n(m+f),* *adj* irlandese.

**iris** ['aiəris] *n* (*anat*) iride *f;* (*bot*) giaggiolo *m.*

**irk** [ə:k] *v* infastidire, dar noia a. **irksome** *adj* seccante, noioso.

**iron** ['aiən] *n* ferro *m;* (*for pressing*) ferro da stiro *m.* **iron curtain** cortina di ferro *f.* **ironmonger's** *n* ferramenta *f. v* stirare. **ironing board** tavola da stiro *f.*

**irony** ['aiərəni] *n* ironia *f.* **ironic** *adj* ironico.

**irrational** [i'raʃənl] *adj* irrazionale.

**irregular** [i'regjulə] *adj* irregolare. **irregularity** *n* irregolarità *f.*

**irrelevant** [i'reləvənt] *adj* non pertinente.

**irreparable** [i'repərəbl] *adj* irreparabile.

**irresistible** [,iri'zistəbl] *adj* irresistibile.

**irrespective** [,iri'spektiv] *adj* **irrespective of** senza riguardo a, senza tener conto di.

**irresponsible** [,iri'sponsəbl] *adj* irresponsabile. **irresponsibility** *n* irresponsabilità *f.*

**irrevocable** [i'revəkəbl] *adj* irrevocabile.

**irrigate** ['irigeit] *v* irrigare. **irrigation** *n* irrigazione *f.*

**irritate** ['iriteit] *v* irritare. **irritating** *adj* irritante. **irritation** *n* irritazione *f.*

**Islam** ['izla:m] *n* Islam *m.* **Islamic** *adj* islamico.

**island** ['ailənd] *n* isola *f.*

**isolate** ['aisəleit] *v* isolare. **isolation** *n* isolamento *m.*

**issue** ['iʃu:] *n* questione *f,* problema *m;* (*outcome*) conclusione *f;* edizione *f;* (*shares, etc.*) emissione *f. v* pubblicare; emettere; uscire.

**isthmus** ['isməs] *n* istmo *m.*

**it** [it] *pron* (*subject*) esso, -a; (*direct object*) lo, la; (*indirect object*) gli, le.

**italic** [i'talik] *adj* (*handwriting*) italico; (*printing*) corsivo. **in italics** in (carattere) corsivo.

**Italy** ['itəli] *n* Italia *f.* **Italian** *n, adj* italiano, -a; (*language*) italiano *m.*

**itch** [itʃ] *n* (*sensation*) prurito *m;* (*desire*) gran voglia *f. v* sentire prurito.

**item** ['aitəm] *n* voce *f,* capo *m,* pezzo *m.*

**itinerary** [ai'tinərəri] *n* itinerario *m.*

**its** [its] *adj* (il) suo, (la) sua; (*pl*) (i) suoi, (le) sue.

**itself** [it'self] *pron* (*reflexive*) si; (*after prep*) sè; (*emphatic*) se esso, -a, se stesso, -a.

**ivory** ['aivəri] *n* avorio *m.*

**ivy** ['aivi] *n* edera *f.*

# J

**jab** [dʒab] *n* puntura *f. v* pungere, punzecchiare.

**jack** [dʒak] *n* (*car*) cricco *m;* (*cards*) fante *m;* (*bowls*) boccino *m.* **v jack up** alzare.

**jackdaw** ['dʒakdɔ:] *n* taccola *f.*

**jacket** ['dʒakit] n giacca f; (of book) copertina f; (boiler, etc.) rivestimento m. **jacket potato** patata in camicia f.

**jack-knife** ['dʒaknaif] n coltello a serramanico m.

**jackpot** ['dʒakpot] n posta intera f, monte premi m. **hit the jackpot** avere un colpo di fortuna.

**jade** [dʒeid] n giada f.

**jaded** ['dʒeidid] adj stracco, spossato.

**jagged** ['dʒagid] adj scabro, intaccato, dentellato.

**jaguar** ['dʒagjuə] n giaguaro m.

**jail** or **gaol** [dʒeil] n prigione f, carcere m. v incarcerare, mettere in prigione.

**jam¹** [dʒam] v (block) bloccare; (cause to stop functioning) intralciare; (squeeze) pigiare; (radio) disturbare; (traffic) intasare. **jam on the brakes** bloccare i freni. n (traffic) intasamento m. **get into a jam** mettersi nei pasticci.

**jam²** [dʒam] n marmellata f, conserva di frutta f.

**janitor** ['dʒanitə] n portinaio, -a m, f.

**January** ['dʒanjuəri] n gennaio m.

**Japan** [dʒə'pan] n Giappone m. **Japanese** n(m+f), adj giapponese.

**jar¹** [dʒaː] n (vessel) brocca f; (usually with lid) barattolo m.

**jar²** [dʒaː] v vibrare; produrre un suono aspro. **jarring** adj discorde.

**jargon** ['dʒaːgən] n gergo m.

**jasmine** ['dʒazmin] n gelsomino m.

**jaundice** ['dʒɔːndis] n itterizia f. **jaundiced** adj distorto, invelenito.

**jaunt** [dʒɔːnt] n gita f.

**jaunty** ['dʒɔːnti] adj vivace, disinvolto.

**javelin** ['dʒavəlin] n giavellotto m.

**jaw** [dʒɔː] n (upper) mascella f; (lower) mandibola f.

**jay** [dʒei] n ghiandaia f.

**jazz** [dʒaz] n jazz m invar.

**jealous** ['dʒeləs] adj geloso. **become jealous** ingelosirsi. **make jealous** ingelosire. **jealousy** n gelosia f.

**jeans** [dʒiːns] pl n jeans m pl.

**jeep** [dʒiːp] n jeep f invar.

**jeer** [dʒiə] v schernire, canzonare. n derisione f, scherno m.

**jelly** ['dʒeli] n gelatina f, budino di gelatina m.

**jeopardize** ['dʒepədaiz] v mettere a repentaglio, arrischiare. **jeopardy** n repentaglio m.

**jerk** [dʒaːk] n (shock) scossa f; (pull) strappo m; (sudden start) scatto m. v scuotere; dare uno strappoa; scattare.

**jersey** ['dʒaːzi] n (fabric) jersey m invar; (garment) maglione m.

**jest** [dʒest] n scherzo m, burla f. v scherzare. **jester** n buffone m.

**Jesuit** ['dʒezjuit] adj, nm gesuita. **Jesuitical** adj gesuitico.

**Jesus** ['dʒiːzəs] n Gesù m. **Jesus Christ** Gesù Cristo.

**jet** [dʒet] n getto m, zampillo m; (spout) becco m; (aero) aviogetto m, aeroplano a reazione m. **jet-black** adj (nero) ebano invar. **jet engine** motore a reazione m.

**jettison** ['dʒetisn] v buttar via, disfarsi di.

**jetty** ['dʒeti] n molo m, banchina f.

**Jew** [dʒuː] n ebreo, -a m, f. **Jewish** adj (person) ebreo; (thing) ebraico.

**jewel** ['dʒuːəl] n gioiello m; (watch) rubino m; (treasure) tesoro m. **jeweller** n gioielliere m. **jewellery** n gioielleria f.

**jib¹** [dʒib] n (sail) fiocco m; (crane) braccio m.

**jib²** [dʒib] v **jib at** essere restio or ritroso a.

**jig¹** [dʒig] n (machine tool) maschera di montaggio f. v lavorare con maschere.

**jig²** n (dance) giga f. v ballare la giga. **jig up and down** salterellare su e giù.

**jiggle** ['dʒigl] v dondolare, muoversi in qua e in là.

**jigsaw** ['dʒigsɔː] n sega da traforo f. **jigsaw puzzle** puzzle m.

**jilt** [dʒilt] v piantare in asso.

**jingle** ['dʒingl] n (sound) tintinnio m; (song) ritornello m, cantilena f. v tintinnare.

**jinx** [dʒiŋks] n malocchio m.

**job** [dʒob] n impiego (pl -ghi) m, lavoro m; (coll) affare m, mestiere m.

**jockey** ['dʒoki] n fantino m. v maneggiare.

**jocular** ['dʒokjulə] adj faceto.

**jodhpurs** ['dʒodpəz] pl n calzoni da equitazione m pl.

**jog** [dʒog] v (sport) fare il footing; (horse) andare al piccolo trotto. **jog the memory** richiamare alla memoria. n (push) spinta f; (nudge) colpetto m; (elbowing) gomitata f; (trot) piccolo trotto m.

**join** [dʒoin] *n* giuntura *f*. *v* unire, congiungere, unirsi a; (*become member*) iscriversi a, entrare. **join in** entrare a far parte di.

**joiner** ['dʒoinə] *n* falegname *m*.

**joint** [dʒoint] *n* (*join*) giuntura *f*; articolazione *f*; (*plant*) nodo *m*; (*meat*) taglio (di carne) *m*; (*coll: bar, etc.*) bettola *f*. *adj* comune, collettivo.

**joist** [dʒoist] *n* trave *f*, travicello *m*.

**joke** [dʒouk] *n* scherzo *m*, barzelletta *f*. **no joke** un affare serio *m*. *v* scherzare. **joker** *n* burlone *m*; (*cards*) jolly *m invar*, matta *f*.

**jolly** ['dʒoli] *adj* divertente, ameno, gaio. *adv* molto.

**jolt** [dʒoult] *v* scuotere, far sobbalzare. *n* scossa *f*, sobbalzo *m*.

**jostle** ['dʒosl] *n* (*push*) spinta *f*; (*elbowing*) gomitata *f*. *v* fare a gomitate, spingersi avanti.

**journal** ['dʒə:nl] *n* periodico *m*; (*daily record*) diario *m*, giornale *m*; (*day-book*) brogliaccio *m*. **journalism** *n* giornalismo *m*. **journalist** *n* giornalista *m, f*.

**journey** ['dʒə:ni] *n* viaggio *m*. *v* viaggiare. **go on a journey** andare *or* mettersi in viaggio.

**jovial** ['dʒouviəl] *adj* gioviale, lieto.

**jowl** [dʒaul] *n* (*jaw*) mascella *f*; (*flesh*) gota *f*.

**joy** [dʒoi] *n* gioia *f*, allegrezza *f*, allegria *f*. **joyful** *or* **joyous** *adj* gioioso.

**jubilant** ['dʒu:bilənt] *adj* giubilante.

**jubilee** ['dʒu:bili:] *n* giubileo *m*.

**Judaism** ['dʒu:dei,izəm] *n* giudaismo *m*.

**judge** [dʒʌdʒ] *n* giudice *m*; (*of competition*) arbitro *m*, giudice *m*; (*expert*) intenditore, -trice *m, f*. *v* giudicare, considerare. **judgment** *n* giudizio *m*; (*law*) sentenza *f*; (*opinion*) parere *m*. **Last Judgment** giudizio universale *m*.

**judicial** [dʒu:'diʃəl] *adj* giudiziario; legale.

**judiciary** [dʒu:'diʃəri] *n* magistratura *f*.

**judicious** [dʒu:'diʃəs] *adj* giudizioso, prudente.

**judo** ['dʒu:dou] *n* judo *m invar*, giudò *f*.

**jug** [dʒʌg] *n* brocca *f*, caraffa *f*.

**juggernaut** ['dʒʌgəno:t] *n* (*lorry*) grosso autotreno *m*.

**juggle** ['dʒʌgl] *v* giocolare, prestigiare; (*trick*) truffare. **juggle with** svisare, travisare. **juggler** *n* giocoliere, -a *m, f*; prestigiatore, -trice *m, f*.

**jugular** ['dʒʌgjulə] *adj* giugulare.

**juice** [dʒu:s] *n* succo *m*, sugo *m*. **juicy** *adj* sugoso, succolento.

**jukebox** ['dʒu:kboks] *n* jukebox *m invar*.

**July** [dʒu'lai] *n* luglio *m*.

**jumble** ['dʒʌmbl] *n* miscuglio *m*, confusione *f*. **jumble sale** bazar di beneficenza *m invar*.

**jump** [dʒʌmp] *n* salto *m*; (*sudden rise*) balzo *m*; (*nervous*) sussulto *m*. **long/high jump** salto in lungo/alto *m*. *v* saltare, fare un salto; sussultare; (*of prices*) rincarare. **jump at** accettare con entusiasmo. **jump off** lanciarsi da. **jump over** scavalcare.

**jumper** ['dʒʌmpə] *n* (*pullover*) maglione *m*, pullover *m invar*; (*jacket*) casacca *f*; (*person*) saltatore, -trice *m, f*.

**junction** ['dʒʌŋkʃən] *n* congiunzione *f*; (*rail*) nodo ferroviario *m*.

**juncture** ['dʒʌŋkʃə] *n* frangente *m*, momento (critico) *m*.

**June** [dʒu:n] *n* giugno *m*.

**jungle** ['dʒʌŋgl] *n* giungla *f*.

**junior** ['dʒu:njə] *adj* minore, più giovane.

**juniper** ['dʒu:nipə] *n* ginepro *m*.

**junk¹** [dʒʌŋk] *n* (*rubbish*) roba vecchia *f*, robaccia *f*, rifiuti *m pl*. **junk mail** corrispondenza non sollecitata *f*.

**junk²** [dʒʌŋk] *n* (*boat*) giunca *f*.

**junta** ['dʒʌntə] *n* giunta *f*.

**jurisdiction** [dʒuəris'dikʃən] *n* giurisdizione *f*.

**jury** ['dʒuəri] *n* giuria *f*. **juror** *n* giurato, -a *m, f*.

**just** [dʒʌst] *adj* giusto, preciso. *adv* giusto, per l'appunto, proprio; (*barely*) appena; (*not more than*) soltanto.

**justice** ['dʒʌstis] *n* giustizia *f*; (*judge*) giudice *m*, magistrato *m*. **do justice to** (*show appreciation*) far onore a; (*concede what is due*) apprezzare, stimare.

**justify** ['dʒʌstifai] *v* giustificare, scusare. **justifiable** *adj* giustificabile, scusabile, legittimo. **justification** *n* giustificazione *f*, scusa *f*.

**jut** [dʒʌt] *v* sporgere, protendere (in fuori).

**jute** [dʒu:t] *n* giuta *f*.

**juvenile** ['dʒu:vənail] *adj* giovanile, per ragazzi, minorenne.

**juxtapose** [,dʒʌkstə'pouz] *v* giustapporre. **juxtaposition** *n* giustapposizione *f*.

# K

**kaleidoscope** [kə'laidəskoup] *n* caleidoscopio *m*.

**kangaroo** [kaŋgə'ru:] *n* canguro *m*.

**karate** [kə'ra:ti] *n* karatè *m invar*.

**keel** [ki:l] *n* chiglia *f*. *v* **keel over** capovolgersi.

**keen** [ki:n] *adj* (*cutting*) tagliente; (*sharp*) aguzzo; (*perceptive*) vivo, perspicace; (*biting*) mordace; (*eager*) appassionato, entusiasta. **keenness** *n* passione *f*, entusiasmo *m*, intensità *f*; (*eagerness*) ardore *m*.

**\*keep** [ki:p] *v* tenere; mantenere; conservare; (*hold in custody*) custodire; (*manage*) gestire; (*observe*) osservare, rispettare. **keep at** persistere, continuare a fare. **keep back** (*stay behind*) stare indietro; (*withhold*) trattenere. **keep down** reprimere. **keep good time** (*watch*) funzionare bene. **keep in with** mantenersi in buoni rapporti con. **keep on** continuare. **keep out** non lasciar entrare; restar fuori. **keep to** aderire a. *n* **earn one's keep** mantenersi. **for keeps** per sempre.

**keeper** ['ki:pə] *n* guardiano, -a *m, f*; custode *m, f*.

**keeping** ['ki:piŋ] *n* custodia *f*. **in keeping with** conforme *or* consono a.

**keepsake** ['ki:pseik] *n* ricordo *m*.

**keg** [keg] *n* barilotto *m*.

**kennel** ['kenl] *n* canile *m*.

**kept** [kept] *V* **keep**.

**kerb** [kə:b] *n* banchina *f*.

**kernel** ['kə:nl] *n* nocciolo *m*, nucleo *m*.

**kerosene** ['kerəsi:n] *n* cherosene *m*.

**kettle** ['ketl] *n* bollitore *m*, pentola *f*.

**kettledrum** ['ketldrʌm] *n* timpano *m*.

**key** [ki:] *n* chiave *f*; (*part of keyboard*) tasto *m*. **keyboard** *n* tastiera *f*. **keyhole** *n* buco della chiave *m*. **keynote** *n* nota determinante *f*.

**khaki** ['ka:ki] *adj* cachi.

**kick** [kik] *v* dare un calcio a, dare una pedata a; protestare. **kick off** iniziare. **kick out** buttar fuori. **kick up** scatenare, provocare. *n* calcio *m*, pedata *f*; (*force*) forza *f*.

**kid¹** [kid] *n* (*child*) bimbo, -a *m, f*; (*goat*) capretto *m*. **handle with kid gloves** trattare coi guanti.

**kid²** [kid] *v* (*coll*) prendere in giro.

**kidnap** ['kidnap] *v* rapire. **kidnapper** *n* rapitore, -trice *m, f*.

**kidney** ['kidni] *n* (*organ*) rene *m*; (*food*) rognone *f*. **kidney bean** fagiolo *m*.

**kill** [kil] *v* uccidere, ammazzare. **killer** *n* assassino, -a *m, f*.

**kiln** [kiln] *n* forno *m*.

**kilo** ['ki:lou] *n* chilo *m*. **kilogram** *n* chilogrammo *m*.

**kilometre** ['kiləmi:tə] *n* chilometro *m*.

**kilt** [kilt] *n* gonnellino scozzese *m*.

**kin** [kin] *n* parenti *m pl*; (*kinship*) parentela *f*. **kinsman** *n* parente *m*. **next of kin** parente prossimo *m*.

**kind¹** [kaind] *adj* gentile, cortese, buono; (*well-meant*) cordiale. **kind-hearted** *adj* benevolo. **kindly** *adv* gentilmente; (*please*) per cortesia, per favore. **kindness** *n* gentilezza *f*, cortesia *f*.

**kind²** [kaind] *n* genere *m*, specie *f*, razza *f*.

**kindergarten** ['kindəga:tn] *n* giardino d'infanzia *m*, asilo (infantile) *m*.

**kindle** ['kindl] *v* accendere; (*excite*) eccitare.

**kindred** ['kindrid] *n* parentela *f*. *adj* affine, simile. **kindred spirit** anima gemella *f*.

**kinetic** [kin'etik] *adj* chinetico.

**king** [kiŋ] *n* re *m invar*. **kingdom** *n* regno *m*.

**kingfisher** ['kiŋfiʃə] *n* martin pescatore *m*.

**kink** [kiŋk] *n* attorcigliamento *m*, piega *f*; (*whim*) ghiribizzo *m*. **kinky** *adj* (*odd*) strambo; (*coll*) pervertito.

**kiosk** ['ki:osk] *n* chiosco *m*; (*newsagent*) edicola *f*.

**kipper** ['kipə] *n* aringa affumicata *f*.

**kiss** [kis] *n* bacio *m*. *v* baciare.

**kit** [kit] *n* (*tools*) attrezzi *m pl*, utensili *m pl*; (*outfit*) corredo *m*. *v* attrezzare. **kit out** equipaggiare.

**kitchen** ['kitʃin] *n* cucina *f*.

**kite** [kait] *n* aquilone *m*; (*bird*) nibbio *m*.

**kitten** ['kitn] *n* micio *m*, gattino *m*.

**kitty** ['kiti] *n* (*joint pool*) fondo comune *m*; (*cards*) posta *f*.

**kleptomania** [kleptə'meiniə] *n* cleptomania *f*. **kleptomaniac** *n* cleptomane *m, f*.

**knack** [nak] *n* desterità *f*, bernoccolo *m*.

**knapsack** ['napsak] *n* zaino *m*.

**knave** [neiv] *n* furfante *m*; (*cards*) fante *m*.

**knead** [ni:d] *v* impastare.

**knee** [ni:] *n* ginocchio *m* (*pl* -a *f*). **kneecap** *n* rotula *f*, patella *f*. **knee-deep** *adj* che arriva fino al ginocchio; (*submerged*) sommerso.

**\*kneel** [ni:l] *v* inginocchiarsi, mettersi in ginocchio.

**knelt** [nelt] *V* **kneel**.

**knew** [nju:] *V* **know**.

**knickers** ['nikəz] *pl n* mutandine *f pl*.

**knife** [naif] *n* coltello *m*. *v* accoltellare.

**knight** [nait] *n* cavaliere *m*.

**\*knit** [nit] *v* lavorare a maglia, fare la calza; (*join together*) unire. **knit one's brows** aggrottare le ciglia. **knitting needle** ferro da calza *m*. **knitwear** *n* maglieria *f*.

**knob** [nob] *n* pomo *m*, manopola *f*; (*protuberance*) bitorzolo *m*. **knobbly** *adj* bitorzoluto, nodoso.

**knock** [nok] *v* (*at door*) bussare; (*hit*) colpire, battere; (*of motor engine*) battere in testa. **knock about** (*mistreat*) malmenare; (*wander aimlessly*) fare vita randagia. **knock down** (*strike*) abbattere; demolire; (*lower*) abbassare. **knock-kneed** *adj* dalle gambe a X. **knock off** (*stop work*) tralasciare, smettere; (*deduct*) dedurre; (*coll: steal*) far man bassa, portar via; (*complete hurriedly*) buttar giù. **knock out** (*stun*) far perdere i sensi a; (*put out of action*) mettere fuori combattimento. **knock together** (*make hurriedly*) acciabattare. **knock up** (*wake*) svegliare; (*tennis*) fare del palleggio. *n* colpo *m*; bussata *f*; (*blow*) batosta *f*. **knocker** *n* battiporta *m invar*, picchiotto *m*.

**knot** [not] *n* nodo *m*. *v* annodare. **knotted** *adj* nodoso, annodato, pieno di nodi. **knotty** *adj* pieno di nodi; difficile, complesso.

**\*know** [nou] *v* (*facts*) sapere; (*be acquainted with*) conoscere; (*understand*) capire; (*recognize*) riconoscere. **as far as is known** per quanto si sappia. **know about** essere informato su, essere al corrente di. **know how to** sapere. *n* **in the know** (*coll*) al corrente. **knowing** *adj* accorto, intelligente. **known** *adj* noto, conosciuto. **make known** far sapere *or* conoscere, divulgare, render noto.

**knowledge** ['nolidʒ] *n* cognizione *f*, conoscenze *f pl*.

**known** [noun] *V* **know**.

**knuckle** ['nʌkl] *n* nocca *f*. **knuckle down** applicarsi. **knuckle under** sottomettersi, piegarsi.

**kosher** ['kouʃə] *adj* kasher, cascer.

**L**

**lab** [lab] *n* laboratorio *m*.

**label** ['leibl] *n* etichetta *f*; (*strip of paper*) cartellino *m*; definizione *f*. *v* etichettare, qualificare.

**laboratory** [lə'borətəri] *n* laboratorio *m*.

**labour** ['leibə] *n* (*toil*) lavoro *m*; (*hard work, task*) fatica *f*; (*effort*) sforzo *m*; (*workforce*) manodopera *f*; (*childbirth*) doglie del parto *f pl*, travaglio del parto *m*. **Labour Party** partito laburista *m*. **labour-saving** *adj* che risparmia fatica. *v* faticare, lavorare. **labour under** essere vittima di. **laborious** *adj* laborioso, faticoso.

**laburnum** [lə'bə:nəm] *n* laburno *m*.

**labyrinth** ['labərinθ] *n* labirinto *m*.

**lace** [leis] *n* pizzo *m*, merletto *m*, brina *f*; (*string, cord*) laccio *m*; (*braid*) gallone *m*. *v* (*fasten*) allacciare; (*trim with lace*) ornare di pizzi; (*add to drink*) correggere. **lacemaker** *n* trinaia *f*.

**lacerate** ['lasəreit] *v* lacerare.

**lack** [lak] *n* mancanza *f*, insufficienza *f*. *v* mancare (di).

**lackadaisical** [ˌlakə'deizikəl] *adj* svogliato, infingardo.

**lacquer** ['lakə] *n* lacca *f*. *v* laccare.

**lad** [lad] *n* ragazzo *m*, giovanotto *m*.

**ladder** ['ladə] *n* scala *f*; (*stocking*) smagliatura *f*. *v* smagliarsi. **ladder-proof** *adj* indemagliabile.

**laden** ['leidn] *adj* carico (*m pl* -chi).

**ladle** ['leidl] *n* (*dish-shaped*) mestolo *m*; (*cup-shaped*) ramaiuolo *m*, cucchiaione *m*. *v* scodellare.

**lady** ['leidi] *n* signora *f*. **lady of the house** padrona di casa *f*.

**ladybird** ['leidibə:d] *n* coccinella *f*.

**lag¹** [lag] *v* avanzare lentamente. **lag behind** rimanere indietro. *n* ritardo *m*, intervallo *m*.

**lag²** [lag] *v* (*cover*) rivestire di materiale isolante, isolare. **lagging** *n* rivestimento isolante *m*.

**lager** ['la:gə] *n* birra (chiara) *f*.

**lagoon** [lə'gu:n] *n* laguna *f*.

**laid** [leid] *V* **lay¹**.

**laid-back** *adj* calmo, rilassato; pacifico; indifferente.

**lain** [lein] V **lie**¹.

**lair** [leə] n tana f.

**laity** ['leiəti] n **the laity** i laici m pl.

**lake** [leik] n lago m.

**lamb** [lam] n agnello m.

**lame** [leim] adj zoppo, storpio; (poor) debole, insufficiente. **lame duck** fallito m.

**lament** [lə'ment] n lamento m. v lamentare, compiangere. **lamented** adj compianto.

**laminate** ['lamineit] v laminare.

**lamp** [lamp] n lampada f, lume m; (of car, ship) fanale m. **lamp-holder** n portalampada m. **lamp-post** n lampione m. **lampshade** n paralume m.

**lance** [la:ns] n lancia f. v incidere col bisturi. **lancet** n bisturi m invar.

**land** [land] n terra f; (country) paese m; (agricultural area) campagna f; (site, soil) terreno m. v (put on shore) sbarcare, approdare; (from the air) atterrare; (obtain) ottenere. **landing** n sbarco m; atterraggio m; (of stairs) pianerottolo m.

**landlady** ['landleidi] n padrona di casa f, proprietaria f.

**landlord** ['landlo:d] n padrone di casa m, proprietario m; (of inn) oste m.

**landmark** ['landma:k] n punto di riferimento m.

**landscape** ['landskeip] n paesaggio m.

**landslide** ['landslaid] n frana f.

**lane** [lein] n (between houses) vicolo m; (track) sentiero m; (part of road, sports track) corsia f.

**language** ['langwidʒ] n (of a nation) lingua f; (means of expression) linguaggio m.

**languish** ['langwiʃ] v languire.

**lanky** ['lanki] adj alto e magro.

**lantern** ['lantən] n lanterna f.

**lap**¹ [lap] n (anat) grembo m; (loose fold) falda f, piega f; (circuit) giro m; (part of journey) tappa f.

**lap**² [lap] v lambire. **lap up** lappare; (coll) ascoltare or accettare con avidità.

**lapel** [lə'pel] n risvolto m.

**Lapland** ['lapland] n Lapponia f. **Lapp** n (m+f), adj lappone.

**lapse** [laps] n svista f, errore m; (time) corso m, periodo m; (law) scadenza f; decadenza f. v (become void) scadere; (decline) decadere; (time) trascorrere. **lapsed** adj (law) decadu-

to; (rel) apostata.

**larceny** ['la:səni] n furto m.

**larch** [la:tʃ] n larice m.

**lard** [la:d] n strutto m.

**larder** ['la:də] n dispensa f.

**large** [la:dʒ] adj grande, ampio. **at large** in libertà (in general) in complesso.

**lark**¹ [la:k] n (bird) allodola f.

**lark**² [la:k] (coll) n burla f. v **lark about** divertirsi.

**larva** ['la:və] n, pl **larvae** larva f.

**larynx** ['larinks] n laringe f. **laryngitis** n laringite f.

**laser** ['leizə] n laser m invar. **laser printer** stampante laser f.

**lash** [laʃ] n sferzata f; (eye) ciglio m (pl -a f). v (whip) sferzare; (tie) legare. **lash out** menar colpi; (coll: money) non badare a spese. **lash out at** inveire contro.

**lass** [las] n fanciulla f, giovane f.

**lassitude** ['lasitju:d] n stanchezza f.

**lasso** [la'su:] n lasso m, laccio m. v catturare al lasso or laccio.

**last**¹ [la:st] adj finale, ultimo; (past) scorso, passato. **last but one** penultimo. **last night** ieri sera. adv (after all others) per ultimo; (most recently) l'ultima volta; finalmente. **at last** alla fine, finalmente.

**last**² [la:st] v durare. **lasting** adj durevole.

**latch** [latʃ] n saliscendi m invar, chiavistello m. v chiudere con saliscendi. **latch on to** afferrare.

**late** [leit] adj tardo; recente; (former) precedente; (dead) defunto, fu. adv (not on time) in ritardo; (not early) tardi. **lately** adv recentemente. **lateness** n ritardo m. **later** adv più tardi, dopo. **see you later!** a più tardi! **latest** adj ultimo; recentissimo. **at the latest** al più tardi.

**latent** ['leitənt] adj latente.

**lateral** ['latərəl] adj laterale.

**lathe** [leið] n tornio m.

**lather** ['la:ðə] n schiuma f. v (of soap) far schiuma.

**Latin** ['latin] nm, adj latino.

**latitude** ['latitju:d] n latitudine f.

**latrine** [lə'tri:n] n latrina f.

**latter** ['latə] adj secondo, ultimo. **the latter** il secondo, questo.

**lattice** ['latis] n traliccio m, grata f.

**Latvia** ['latviə] n Lettonia f. **Latvian**

*n* (m+f), *adj* lettone.

**laugh** [la:f] *v* ridere. **laugh at** ridere per *or* di. *n* risata *f*; (*coll*) spasso *m*. **have a laugh** fare una risata. **laughable** *adj* ridicolo, risibile. **laughing stock** zimbello *m*. **laughter** *n* riso *m* (*pl* -a *f*), risata *f*.

**launch¹** [lo:ntʃ] *v* varare; (*give a start*) lanciare; (*attack*) sferrare.

**launch²** [lo:ntʃ] *n* (*naut*) lancia *f*.

**launder** ['lo:ndə] *v* fare il bucato, lavare e stirare. **launderette** *n* lavanderia automatica *f*, lavanderia a gettoni *f*. **laundry** *n* (*place*) lavanderia *f*; (*clothes, etc.*) bucato *m*.

**laurel** ['lorəl] *n* alloro *m*, lauro *m*.

**lava** ['la:və] *n* lava *f*.

**lavatory** ['lavətəri] *n* gabinetto *m*, ritirata *f*.

**lavender** ['lavində] *n* lavanda *f*.

**lavish** ['laviʃ] *adj* prodigo, generoso. *v* dispensare *or* spendere largamente.

**law** [lo:] *n* legge *f*; (*profession*) diritto *m*; (*rule*) norma *f*, regola *f*. **law-abiding** *adj* ligio alla legge. **lawsuit** *n* causa *f*, processo *m*. **lawful** *adj* legittimo, lecito. **lawyer** *n* avvocato, -essa *m*, *f*.

**lawn** [lo:n] *n* prato rasato *m*. **lawn-mower** *n* falciatrice *or* tosatrice per prati *f*.

**lax** [laks] *adj* rilassato; negligente.

**laxative** ['laksətiv] *nm*, *adj* lassativo.

**\*lay¹** [lei] *v* posare, mettere; (*eggs*) deporre; (*table*) apparecchiare. **lay-by** *n* area *or* piazzola di sosta *or* parcheggio *f*. **lay down** posare per terra; stabilire. **lay off** (*workers*) sospendere. **lay on** disporre, installare. **layout** *n* disposizione *f*; (*sketch*) tracciato *m*, pianta *f*. **lay out** (*spread*) stendere; (*coll: spend*) sborsare. **be laid up** essere costretto di rimanere a letto.

**lay²** [lei] *adj* laico; non professionale. **layman** *n* laico, -a *m*, *f*; profano, -a *m*, *f*.

**lay³** [lei] *V* **lie¹**.

**layer** ['leiə] *n* strato *m*.

**lazy** ['leizi] *adj* pigro, indolente. **laziness** *n* pigrizia *f*.

**\*lead¹** [li:d] *v* condurre; influenzare; (*bring*) portare; (*be at head of*) essere in testa di, essere al comando di; (*act as guide*) guidare; (*make go*) indurre. *n* direzione *f*, comando *m*; (*for dog*) guinzaglio *m*; (*theatre*) primo attore, prima attrice *m*, *f*. **be in the lead** (*sport*) essere in testa. **take the lead** (*sport*) passare in testa. **leader** *n* capo *m*, dirigente *m*, *f*; (*newspaper*) articolo di fondo *m*. **leadership** *n* direzione *f*, comando *m*. **leading** *adj* principale, primo.

**lead²** [led] *n* piombo *m*. **leaden** *adj* di piombo.

**leaf** [li:f] *n* (*plant*) foglia *f*; (*paper*) foglio *m*; (*table*) asse *f*. *v* **leaf through** sfogliare. **leaflet** *n* volantino *m*, manifestino *m*.

**league** [li:g] *n* lega *f*; classe *f*.

**leak** [li:k] *n* (*escape*) fuga *f*; (*crack*) fessura *f*; (*boat*) falla *f*; (*news*) trapelamento *m*. *v* perdere; (*boat*) far acqua; trapelare.

**\*lean¹** [li:n] *v* appoggiare, inclinare, pendere. **lean against** appoggiarsi a. **lean out** sporgersi. **lean towards** tendere verso. **leaning** *n* inclinazione *f*, propensione *f*.

**lean²** [li:n] *adj* magro, scarno; (*poor*) povero.

**leant** [lent] *V* **lean¹**.

**\*leap** [li:p] *n* salto *m*, balzo *m*. **by leaps and bounds** a passi da gigante. *v* saltare, balzare. **leap-frog** *n* cavallina *f*. **leap year** anno bisestile *m*.

**leapt** [lept] *V* **leap**.

**\*learn** [lə:n] *v* imparare, studiare; (*become informed*) sentire, apprendere. **learned** *adj* dotto, erudito, colto. **learner** *n* (*beginner*) principiante *m*, *f*; allievo, -a *m*, *f*; apprendista *m*, *f*. **learning** *n* cultura *f*, erudizione *f*.

**learnt** [lə:nt] *V* **learn**.

**lease** [li:s] *n* affitto *m*, contratto d'affitto *m*. *v* affittare.

**leash** [li:ʃ] *n* guinzaglio *m*.

**least** [li:st] *adj* minimo, -a. **at least** almeno. **not in the least** per nulla, affatto.

**leather** ['leðə] *n* cuoio *m*, pelle *f*. **leather goods** pelletteria *f sing*.

**\*leave¹** [li:v] *v* lasciare; abbandonare; (*go out from*) uscire da; (*depart*) partire. **leave alone** lasciar stare, lasciare in pace. **leave home** andar via. **leave out** omettere. **be left** rimanere. **be left over** avanzare.

**leave²** [li:v] *n* permesso *m*; (*holiday*) licenza *f*, congedo *m*.

**lecherous** ['letʃərəs] *adj* lussurioso, lascivo. **lecher** *n* libertino *m*. **lechery** *n* lascivia *f*.

**lectern** ['lektən] *n* leggio *m*.

**lecture** ['lektʃə] *n* lezione *f*, conferenza *f*; (*reprimand*) ramanzina *f*, sgridata *f*. *v* tenere una conferenza; dare un corso di lezioni;

(*rebuke*) predicare, fare una paternale a. **lecturer** *n* conferenziere, -a *m, f*; (*university*) docente *m, f*.

**led** [led] *V* **lead¹**.

**ledge** [ledʒ] *n* (*window*) davanzale *m*; (*projecting part*) sporgenza *f*.

**ledger** ['ledʒə] *n* (libro) mastro *m*.

**lee** [li:] *n* (*shelter*) riparo *m*; (*naut*) sottovento *m*. **leeward** *adj, adv* sottovento.

**leech** [li:tʃ] *n* sanguisuga *f*.

**leek** [li:k] *n* porro *m*.

**leer** [liə] *v* guardare di sbieco. *n* sguardo sbieco *m*.

**leeway** ['li:wei] *n* (*naut*) deriva *f*. **make up leeway** recuperare lo svantaggio.

**left¹** [left] *V* **leave¹**.

**left²** [left] *adj* sinistro. *n* sinistra *f*. **the Left** (*pol*) la Sinistra. *adv* a sinistra, verso sinistra, sulla sinistra. **left-hand** *adj* sinistro. **left-handed** *adj* mancino.

**leg** [leg] *n* gamba *f*; (*furniture*) piede *m*; (*lap*) tappa *f*; (*poultry*) coscia *f*; (*meat*) cosciotto *m*.

**legacy** ['legəsi] *n* lascito *m*, eredità *f*.

**legal** ['li:gəl] *adj* lecito, legittimo, legale. **legality** *n* legalità *f*. **legalize** *v* legalizzare, legittimare.

**legend** ['ledʒənd] *n* leggenda *f*. **legendary** *adj* leggendario.

**Leghorn** [,leg'ho:n] *n* Livorno *m*.

**legible** ['ledʒəbl] *adj* leggibile. **legibility** *n* leggibilità *f*.

**legion** ['li:dʒən] *n* legione *f*.

**legislate** ['ledʒisleit] *v* promulgare leggi. **legislation** *n* legislazione *f*.

**legitimate** [lə'dʒitimət] *adj* legittimo, lecito. *v* legittimare. **legitimacy** *n* legittimità *f*.

**leisure** ['leʒə] *n* agio *m*, tempo libero *m*. **leisurely** *adj* fatto con comodo. *adv* comodamente.

**lemon** ['lemən] *n* limone *m*. *adj* color limone *invar*. **lemonade** *n* limonata *f*. **lemon juice** succo di limone *m*.

***lend** [lend] *v* prestare, dare in prestito.

**length** [leŋθ] *n* lunghezza *f*; (*time*) durata *f*; (*cloth*) taglio *m*. **at length** per disteso. **lengthen** *v* allungare. **lengthy** *adj* lungo.

**lenient** ['li:niənt] *adj* benigno, indulgente. **leniency** *n* indulgenza *f*.

**lens** [lenz] *n* lente *f*; (*camera*) obiettivo *m*.

**lent** [lent] *V* **lend**.

**Lent** [lent] *n* quaresima *f*.

**lentil** ['lentil] *n* lenticchia *f*.

**Leo** ['li:ou] *n* Leone *m*.

**leopard** ['lepəd] *n* leopardo *m*.

**leotard** ['li:əta:d] *n* calzamaglia (*pl* calzemaglie) *f*.

**leper** ['lepə] *n* lebbroso, -a *m, f*. **leprosy** *n* lebbra *f*.

**lesbian** ['lezbiən] *n* lesbica *f*.

**less** [les] *adj* minore, meno. *nm, adv, prep* meno. **lessen** *v* diminuire. **lesser** *adj* minore, inferiore.

**lesson** ['lesn] *n* lezione *f*.

**lest** [lest] *conj* per paura che.

***let** [let] *v* lasciare, permettere; (*rent*) affittare. **let down** (*lower*) calare; (*hair*) sciogliere; (*disappoint*) deludere; (*dress*) allungare. **let go** lasciar andare. **let in** fare entrare. **let know** far sapere. **let out** far uscire, liberare; (*dress*) allargare; (*secret*) lasciar sfuggire; (*emit*) fare.

**lethal** ['li:θəl] *adj* letale.

**lethargy** ['leθədʒi] *n* letargia *f*. **lethargic** *adj* letargico.

**letter** ['letə] *n* lettera *f*; (*character*) carattere *m*. **letter-box** *n* buca delle lettere *f*. **lettering** *n* iscrizione *f*.

**lettuce** ['letis] *n* lattuga *f*.

**leukaemia** [lu:'ki:miə] *n* leucemia *f*.

**level** ['levl] *n* livello *m*, piano *m*; (*height, position*) altezza *f*. *v* livellare, spianare. *adj* piano, uniforme; (*equal*) pari. **be level with** essere a livello di. **level crossing** passaggio a livello *m*. **level-headed** *adj* equilibrato.

**lever** ['li:və] *n* leva *f*. **leverage** *n* leva *f*, stimolo *m*.

**levy** ['levi] *n* imposta *f*, contributo *m*. *v* imporre, esigere.

**lewd** [lu:d] *adj* lascivo, osceno.

**liable** ['laiəbl] *adj* responsabile. **liable to** soggetto a, passibile di. **liability** *n* obbligo *m*, responsabilità *f*; (*comm*) passività *f*, deficit *m invar*.

**liaise** *v* fare da intermediario.

**liaison** [li:'eizon] *n* legame *m*; (*sexual*) relazione amorosa *f*.

**liar** ['laiə] *n* bugiardo, -a *m, f*.

**libel** ['laibəl] *n* diffamazione *f*, calunnia *f*. *v* diffamare, calunniare. **libellous** *adj*

diffamatorio, calunnioso.
**liberal** ['lɪbərəl] *adj* liberale, generoso. *n* liberale *m, f.* **liberalism** *n* liberalismo *m*.
**liberate** ['lɪbəreɪt] *v* liberare, mettere in libertà. **liberation** *n* liberazione *f*.
**liberty** ['lɪbətɪ] *n* libertà *f*.
**Libra** ['liːbrə] *n* Libra *f*.
**library** ['laɪbrərɪ] *n* biblioteca *f*. **librarian** *n* bibliotecario, -a *m, f*.
**libretto** [lɪ'bretəʊ] *n* libretto *m*.
**lice** [laɪs] *V* **louse**.
**licence** ['laɪsəns] *n* licenza *f*, permesso *m*; (*driving*) patente (di guida) *f*; (*arms*) porto d'armi *m*. **license** *v* autorizzare. **licensee** *n* gestore autorizzato *m*, concessionario *m*.
**lichen** ['laɪkən] *n* lichene *m*.
**lick** [lɪk] *v* leccare. *n* leccata *f*.
**lid** [lɪd] *n* coperchio *m*.
**\*lie¹** [laɪ] *v* giacere, stare sdraiato. **lie down** coricarsi, sdraiarsi. **lie in** (*stay in bed*) restare a letto; (*consist of*) consistere di. **lie with** spettare a.
**lie²** [laɪ] *n* (*untruth*) bugia *f*, menzogna *f*. *v* mentire, dire una bugia.
**lieu** [luː] *n* **in lieu of** invece di.
**lieutenant** [ləf'tenənt] *n* tenente *m*.
**life** [laɪf] *n* vita *f*. **lifeless** *adj* esanime.
**lifebelt** ['laɪfbelt] *n* salvagente *m*.
**lifeboat** ['laɪfbəʊt] *n* scialuppa di salvataggio *f*.
**lifebuoy** ['laɪfbɔɪ] *n* salvagente *m*.
**life insurance** *n* assicurazione sulla vita *f*.
**life-jacket** *n* cintura di salvataggio *f*.
**lifelike** ['laɪflaɪk] *adj* realistico, vivido.
**lifeline** ['laɪflaɪn] *n* linea di communicazione vitale *f*.
**lifelong** ['laɪflɒŋ] *adj* di tutta la vita.
**lifestyle** ['laɪfstaɪl] *n* stile di vita *m*.
**lifetime** ['laɪftaɪm] *n* vita *f*, durata della vita *f*.
**lift** [lɪft] *n* ascensore *m*; (*coll: ride*) autostop *m*. *v* sollevare, alzare.
**\*light¹** [laɪt] *n* luce *f*, lume *m*; illuminazione *f*. **switch on/off the light** accendere/spegnere la luce. *adj* chiaro. **light bulb** ampolla *f*. **lighthouse** *n* faro *m*.
**light-year** *n* anno luce *m*. *v* accendere.
**lighten** *v* rischiarare, illuminare. **lighter** *n* (*for cigarette*) accendino *m*. **lighting** *n* illuminazione *f*.
**light²** [laɪt] *adj* leggero. **light-headed** *adj*

frivolo; (*giddy*) preso da vertigini. **light-hearted** *adj* gaio. **lighten** *v* alleggerire, alleviare. **lightness** *n* leggerezza *f*.
**\*light³** [laɪt] *v* **light upon** imbattersi in.
**lightning** ['laɪtnɪŋ] *n* fulmine *m*, lampo *m*. **lightning conductor** *n* parafulmine *m*.
**like¹** [laɪk] *adj* simile, uguale. *prep* come. **be** or **look like** rassomigliare a. **liken** *v* paragonare. **likeness** *n* somiglianza *f*; (*portrait*) ritratto *m*. **likewise** *adv* parimenti, altrettanto.
**like²** [laɪk] *v* gradire; (*want*) volere. **I like ...** mi piace ... **likeable** *adj* simpatico. **liking** *n* simpatia *f*, gusto *m*. **have a liking for** trovar simpatico *or* gradevole.
**likely** ['laɪklɪ] *adj* probabile, verosimile. *adv* probabilmente. **likelihood** *n* probabilità *f*.
**lilac** ['laɪlək] *nm, adj* lilla *invar*.
**lily** ['lɪlɪ] *n* giglio *m*. **lily-of-the-valley** *n* mughetto *m*.
**limb** [lɪm] *n* arto *m*, membro *m* (*pl* -a *f*).
**limbo** ['lɪmbəʊ] *n* limbo *m*.
**lime¹** [laɪm] *n* calce *f*. **limestone** *n* calcare *m*.
**lime²** [laɪm] *n* (*fruit*) limetta *f*; (*linden*) tiglio *m*.
**limelight** ['laɪm,laɪt] *n* luci della ribalta *f pl*. **be in the limelight** essere alla ribalta.
**limit** ['lɪmɪt] *n* limite *m*, ambito *m*. *v* limitare. **limitation** *n* limitazione *f*. **limitless** *adj* illimitato.
**limousine** ['lɪmə,ziːn] *n* berlina *f*, limousine *f invar*.
**limp¹** [lɪmp] *v* zoppicare. *n* zoppicamento *m*.
**limp²** [lɪmp] *adj* floscio; (*weak*) debole.
**limpet** ['lɪmpɪt] *n* patella *f*.
**line** [laɪn] *n* linea *f*; (*row*) fila *f*; (*string*) corda *f*; (*wrinkle*) ruga *f*; (*of letters*) riga *f*. *v* rigare; (*clothes*) foderare; (*border*) fiancheggiare. **line up** allineare. **linear** *adj* lineare.
**linen** ['lɪnɪn] *n* lino *m*; (*sheets, etc.*) biancheria *f. adj* di lino.
**liner** ['laɪnə] *n* (*naut*) transatlantico *m*; (*aero*) aereo di linea *m*.
**linger** ['lɪŋgə] *v* indugiare, soffermarsi. **lingering** *adj* protratto.
**lingerie** ['lãʒərɪ] *n* biancheria per signora *f*.
**linguist** ['lɪŋgwɪst] *n* linguista *m, f*; poliglotta *m, f*. **linguistic** *adj* linguistico. **linguistics** *n* linguistica *f*.
**lining** ['laɪnɪŋ] *n* (*clothes*) fodera *f*; rivesti-

mento interno *m*.

**link** [liŋk] *n* (*of chain*) anello *m*; (*bond*) legame *m*; (*mech*) collegamento *m*. *v* collegare, congiungere.

**linoleum** [li'nouliəm] *n* linoleum *m invar*.

**linseed** ['lin,si:d] *n* semi di lino *m pl*. **linseed oil** olio di semi di lino *m*.

**lint** [lint] *n* filaccia (di lino) *f*.

**lion** ['laiən] *n* leone *m*. **lioness** *n* leonessa *f*.

**lip** [lip] *n* labbro *m* (*pl* -a *f*). **lip-read** *v* capire dal movimento delle labbra. **lipstick** *n* rossetto *m*.

**liqueur** [li'kjuə] *n* liquore *m*.

**liquid** ['likwid] *nm*, *adj* liquido. **liquidate** *v* liquidare; eliminare. **liquidation** *n* liquidazione *f*.

**liquor** ['likə] *n* bevanda alcoolica *f*.

**liquorice** ['likəris] *n* liquirizia *f*.

**lisp** [lisp] *v* essere *or* parlar bleso. *n* blesità *f*.

**list¹** [list] *n* lista *f*, elenco *m*. *v* elencare, registrare.

**list²** [list] *v* (*naut*) sbandare. *n* sbandamento *m*.

**listen** ['lisn] *v* ascoltare; (*heed*) badare. **listener** *n* ascoltatore, -trice *m*, *f*.

**listless** ['listlis] *adj* languido, svogliato.

**lit** [lit] *V* **light**.

**litany** ['litəni] *n* litania *f*.

**literal** ['litərəl] *adj* letterale. **literally** *adv* alla lettera, letteralmente.

**literary** ['litərəri] *adj* (*writing*) letterario; (*people*) letterato.

**literate** ['litərət] *adj* che sa leggere e scrivere. **literacy** *n* il saper leggere e scrivere *m*.

**literature** ['litrətʃə] *n* letteratura *f*.

**Lithuania** [liθju'einiə] *n* Lituania *f*. **Lithuanian** *adj* lituano, -a.

**litigation** [liti'geiʃən] *n* lite *f*, causa *f*. **litigate** *v* essere in causa.

**litre** ['li:tə] *n* litro *m*.

**litter** ['litə] *n* rifiuti *m pl*, immondizia *f*; (*zool*) figliata *f*; (*bed, etc.*) lettiga *f*. *v* sparpagliare, lasciare in disordine.

**little** ['litl] *adj* piccolo, piccino; (*not much*) un po' di, poco; (*short*) breve. *nm*, *adv* poco. **little by little** a poco a poco.

**liturgy** ['litədʒi] *n* liturgia *f*.

**live¹** [liv] *v* vivere; (*reside*) abitare, stare. **live by** *or* **on** vivere di. **live down** far dimenticare. **live up to** mettere in pratica, giustificare.

**live²** [laiv] *adj* vivo; (*broadcast*) dal vivo, in ripresa diretta; (*coal, etc.*) ardente; (*wire*) sotto tensione.

**livelihood** ['laivlihud] *n* vita *f*.

**lively** ['laivli] *adj* vivace, animato. **liveliness** *n* vivacità *f*.

**liven** ['laivn] *v* **liven up** animare.

**liver** ['livə] *n* fegato *m*.

**livestock** ['laivstok] *n* bestiame *m*.

**livid** ['livid] *adj* livido.

**living** ['liviŋ] *adj* vivente, vivo. *n* vita *f*. **living room** stanza di soggiorno *f*.

**lizard** ['lizəd] *n* lucertola *f*.

**load** [loud] *n* carico (*pl* -chi) *m*; (*weight*) peso *m*; (*quantity carried*) portata *f*; (*elec*) carica *f*. *v* caricare. **loaded** *adj* caricato, carico; (*question*) insidioso; (*slang*) ricco.

**loaf¹** [louf] *n* pane *m*.

**loaf²** [louf] *v* oziare, girellare, stare con le mani in mano. **loafer** *n* bighellone, -a *m*, *f*; fannullone, -a *m*, *f*.

**loan** [loun] *n* prestito *m*. *v* prestare, dare in prestito.

**loathe** [louð] *v* aborrire, detestare. **loathing** *n* disgusto *m*. **loathsome** *adj* disgustoso.

**lob** [lob] (*sport*) *n* pallonetto *m*. *v* fare un pallonetto.

**lobby** ['lobi] *n* atrio *m*, anticamera *f*; (*theatre*) ridotto *m*. *v* influenzare con manovre di anticamera.

**lobe** [loub] *n* (*anat*) lobo *m*.

**lobster** ['lobstə] *n* aragosta *f*.

**local** ['loukəl] *adj* locale, del luogo. **locality** *n* località *f*. **localize** *v* circoscrivere, delimitare.

**locate** [lə'keit] *v* individuare; determinare la posizione di; situare. **location** *n* posizione *f*, sito *m*; (*cinema*) set *m invar*.

**lock¹** [lok] *n* serratura *f*; (*canal*) conca *f*. **locksmith** *n* magnano *m*. **lock, stock, and barrel** barca e barattini. **under lock and key** sotto chiave. *v* serrare, chiudere a chiave; (*mech*) bloccare. **lock away** mettere al sicuro. **lock in** rinchiudere. **lock out** chiudere fuori; (*workers*) fare una serrata. **lock up** chiudere a chiave, mettere sotto chiave.

**lock²** [lok] *n* (*of hair*) ciocca *f*, ricciolo *m*.

**locker** ['lokə] *n* armadietto *m*.

**locket** ['lokit] *n* medaglione *m*.

**locomotive** [ˌloukə'moutiv] n locomotiva f.

**locust** ['loukəst] n cavalletta f.

**lodge** [lodʒ] n capanna f; (porter's) portineria f. v alloggiare; (put in place, deposit) deporre, collocare; (report) presentare. **lodge a complaint** sporgere querela. **lodger** n pensionante m, f. **lodging** n alloggio m.

**loft** [loft] n solaio m, soffitta f. **lofty** adj alto; (style) nobile.

**log** [log] n ceppo m, tronco m. **logbook** n registro m; (naut) giornale di bordo m; (mot) libretto di circolazione m. v registrare.

**logarithm** ['logəriðəm] n logaritmo m.

**loggerheads** ['logəhedz] n **be at loggerheads** prendersi per i capelli, essere ai ferri corti.

**logic** ['lodʒik] n logica f. **logical** adj logico.

**log on** v connettersi.

**log off** v disconnettersi.

**loin** [loin] n (cookery) lombata f. **gird up one's loins** apprestarsi.

**loiter** ['loitə] v bighellonare, passare oziando.

**lollipop** ['loli,pop] n lecca lecca m invar.

**London** ['lʌndən] n Londra f.

**lonely** ['lounli] adj solitario, solo. **loneliness** n solitudine f.

**long¹** [loŋ] adj lungo. adv a lungo. **as long as** finquanto. **long-distance** adj a lunga distanza; (phone) interurbano. **long-playing record** disco microsolco m. **long-range** adj (distance) a lunga portata; (time) a lunga scadenza. **long-sighted** adj presbite; (having foresight) previdente. **long-standing** adj di vecchia data. **long-wave** adj (radio) a onde lunghe. **long-winded** adj prolisso.

**long²** [loŋ] v bramare, aver gran desiderio (di). **longing** n brama f, desiderio ardente m.

**longevity** [lon'dʒevəti] n longevità f.

**longitude** ['londʒitjuːd] n longitudine f.

**long wave** n onda lunga f.

**loo** [luː] n (coll) gabinetto m.

**look** [luk] n sguardo m, occhiata f; (appearance) aspetto m; espressione f. v guardare; (appear, seem) sembrare, parere. **look after** (care for) occuparsi di, badare a. **look at** guardare, considerare. **look down on** guardare con disprezzo. **look for** cercare. **look forward to** aspettare con impazienza. **look out** guardar fuori, affacciarsi; (be on guard) stare attento. **look over** ripassare, riesaminare.

**loom¹** [luːm] v apparire (indistintamente), intravedere; (be imminent) incombere.

**loom²** [luːm] n telaio m.

**loop** [luːp] n cappio m, laccio m, anello m. v fare un cappio o laccio, allacciare.

**loophole** ['luːphoul] n scappatoia f.

**loose** [luːs] adj sciolto, libero; (tooth) caduco. **come** or **get loose** allentarsi. **let loose** liberare. **loose-fitting** adj ampio. **loose-leaf** adj a fogli staccati. **loosely** adv scioltamente; in senso lato. **loosen** v sciogliere, allentare.

**loot** [luːt] n bottino m. v far man bassa, saccheggiare. **looting** n saccheggio m.

**lop** [lop] v potare. **lop off** mozzare.

**lopsided** [ˌlop'saidid] adj sbilenco, asimmetrico.

**lord** [loːd] n signore m; (English title) lord m invar. **lordship** n signoria f.

**lorry** ['lori] n autocarro m, camion m invar. **lorry-driver** n camionista m.

***lose** [luːz] v perdere, smarrire; (clock) ritardare. **lose interest** non interessarsi più. **lose one's temper** arrabbiarsi.

**loss** [los] n perdita f, danno m. **be at a loss** non sapere cosa fare, essere disorientato.

**lost** [lost] V **lose**. adj perso, smarrito. **lost cause** causa persa f. **lost property** oggetti smarriti m pl.

**lot** [lot] n (destiny) sorte f; (of land) lotto m; (method of decision) sorteggio m; (comm) partita f; (coll: large amount) grande quantità f. **a lot of** molto. **lots of** tanti. **the whole lot** tutto quanto. **what a lot of** quanto.

**lotion** ['louʃən] n lozione f.

**lottery** ['lotəri] n lotteria f.

**lotus** ['loutəs] n loto m.

**loud** [laud] adj forte, alto; (gaudy) vistoso. adv forte. **loud-mouthed** adj sguaiato. **loudspeaker** n altoparlante m. **loudness** n forza f, altezza di voce f.

**lounge** [laundʒ] n salotto m; sala di ritrovo f. v oziare, dondolarsi.

**louse** [laus] n, pl **lice** pidocchio m. **lousy** adj pidocchioso; (slang: bad) schifoso.

**love** [lʌv] n amore m; (tennis) zero m. **fall in love (with)** innamorarsi (di). **love affair** relazione amorosa f. **make love (to)** fare all'amore (con). **with love** (in letter)

affettuosamente. *v* amare, voler bene a.
**lovable** *adj* amabile, simpatico. **lovely** *adj*
bello, grazioso, incantevole. **lover** *n*
amante *m, f*; (*enthusiast*) appassionato, -a
*m, f.* **loving** *adj* affettuoso.

**low** [lou] *adj* basso; (*coll*) depresso; volgare.
*adv* basso, in basso. **lowbrow** *adj* incolto,
popolare. **low-lying** *adj* situato in pianura.
**low-necked** *adj* scollato. **lowly** *adj* umile,
dimesso.

**lower** ['louə] *adj* più basso, inferiore. *v*
abbassare, ridurre; (*flag*) ammainare;
degradare.

**loyal** ['loiəl] *adj* fedele, devoto, leale. **loyalty** *n* fedeltà *f*, devozione *f*, lealtà *f*.

**lozenge** ['lozindʒ] *n* pastiglia *f*, pasticca *f*.

**lubricate** ['lu:brikeit] *v* lubrificare. **lubricant** *nm, adj* lubrificante. **lubrication** *n*
lubrificazione *f*.

**lucid** ['lu:sid] *adj* (*easily understood*) chiaro;
(*clear*) limpido; (*bright*) lucido.

**luck** [lʌk] *n* fortuna *f*; (*chance*) sorte *f.* **bad
luck** sfortuna *f.* **be in/out of luck** essere
fortunato/sfortunato. **good luck** buona
fortuna *f.* **lucky** *adj* fortunato.

**lucrative** ['lu:krativ] *adj* lucroso, redditizio.

**ludicrous** ['lu:dikrəs] *adj* ridicolo, irrisorio.

**lug** [lʌg] *v* tirare, trascinare.

**luggage** ['lʌgidʒ] *n* bagaglio *m.* **hand luggage** bagaglio a mano *m.* **left luggage**
deposito bagagli *m.* **luggage rack** *n* (*rail*)
rete portabagagli *f.*

**lukewarm** ['lu:kwo:m] *adj* tiepido.

**lull** [lʌl] *n* momento di calma *m*; (*truce*)
tregua *f. v* (*put to sleep*) far addormentare;
calmare.

**lumbago** [lʌm'beigou] *n* lombaggine *f.*

**lumber**[1] ['lʌmbə] *n* legname *m*; (*useless
articles*) cianfrusaglie *f pl. v* (*encumber*)
ingombrare, accatastare. **lumberjack** *n*
boscaiolo *m.*

**lumber**[2] ['lʌmbə] *v* (*move clumsily*) muoversi pesantemente *or* goffamente.

**luminous** ['lu:minəs] *adj* luminoso.

**lump** [lʌmp] *n* massa *f*; (*swelling*) gonfiore
*m.* **lump sum** somma globale *f.* **lump
together** mettere insieme. **lumpy** *adj* gru-
moso.

**lunacy** ['lu:nəsi] *n* pazzia *f.*

**lunar** ['lu:nə] *adj* lunare.

**lunatic** ['lunətik] *n, adj* pazzo, -a, matto, -a.
**lunatic asylum** manicomio *m.*

**lunch** [lʌntʃ] *n* colazione *f*, pranzo *m. v* far
colazione, pranzare.

**lung** [lʌŋ] *n* polmone *m.*

**lunge** [lʌndʒ] *v* scagliarsi. *n* rapido movimento in avanti *m.*

**lurch**[1] [lə:tʃ] *v* barcollare, sbandare. *n* bar-
collamento *m*, sbandamento *m.*

**lurch**[2] [lə:tʃ] *n* **leave in the lurch** piantare
in asso.

**lure** [luə] *n* (*bait*) esca *f*; (*fascination*) fascino *m. v* adescare, attirare, affascinare.

**lurid** ['luərid] *adj* raccapricciante.

**lurk** [lə:k] *v* (*be in hiding*) nascondersi; (*lie
in wait*) stare in agguato.

**luscious** ['lʌʃəs] *adj* succulento.

**lush** [lʌʃ] *adj* lussureggiante.

**lust** [lʌst] *n* brama *f*; (*sexual*) libidine *f*;
concupiscenza *f. v* **lust after** aver brama *or*
sete di.

**lustre** ['lʌstə] *n* splendore *m.*

**lute** [lu:t] *n* liuto *m.*

**Luxembourg** ['lʌksəm,bə:g] *n*
Lussemburgo *m.*

**luxury** ['lʌkʃəri] *n* lusso *m.* **luxuriant** *adj*
lussureggiante, rigoglioso. **luxurious** *adj*
lussuoso, di lusso.

**lynch** [lintʃ] *v* linciare.

**lynx** [links] *n* lince *f.*

**lyre** [laiə] *n* lira *f.*

**lyrical** ['lirikəl] *adj* lirico.

**lyrics** ['liriks] *pl n* parole (di una canzone) *f
pl.*

# M

**mac** [mak] *n* (*coll*) impermeabile *m.*

**macabre** [mə'ka:br] *adj* macabro.

**macaroni** [makə'rouni] *n* maccheroni *m pl.*

**mac**[1] [meis] *n* (*club*) mazza *f.*

**mace**[2] [meis] *n* (*spice*) macis *f invar.*

**machine** [mə'ʃi:n] *n* macchina *f.* **machine-
gun** *n* mitragliatrice *f.* **machine tool**
macchina utensile *f. v* lavorare a macchina.
**machinery** *n* macchinario *m*; meccanismo
*m*; (*system*) organizzazione *f.* **machinist** *n*
macchinista *m, f.*

**mackerel** ['makrəl] *n* sgombro *m.*

**mackintosh** ['makin,toʃ] n impermeabile m.

**mad** [mad] adj matto, pazzo; furioso. **drive mad** far impazzire. **go mad** impazzire. **madden** v far impazzire. **madness** n pazzia f.

**madam** ['madəm] n signora f.

**made** [meid] V **make**.

**magazine** [,magə'zi:n] n (publication) rivista f, periodico m; (phot) magazzino m; (rifle) caricatore m.

**maggot** ['magət] n larva f.

**magic** ['madʒik] adj magico. n magia f, incanto m. **magician** n mago m, stregone m; (conjurer) illusionista m.

**magistrate** ['madʒistreit] n magistrato m, pretore m. **magistrature** n magistratura f, pretura f.

**magnanimous** [mag'nanimǝs] adj magnanimo. **magnanimity** n magnanimità f.

**magnate** ['magneit] n magnate m.

**magnet** ['magnǝt] n magnete m, calamita f. **magnetic** adj magnetico. **magnetism** n magnetismo m. **magnetize** v magnetizzare.

**magnificent** [mag'nifisnt] adj magnifico, splendido. **magnificence** n magnificenza f.

**magnify** ['magnifai] v magnificare, ingrandire. **magnifying glass** lente d'ingrandimento f. **magnification** n ingrandimento m.

**magnitude** ['magnitju:d] n grandezza f.

**magnolia** [mag'nouliǝ] n magnolia f.

**magpie** ['magpai] n gazza f.

**mahogany** [mǝ'hogǝni] n mogano m.

**maid** [meid] n domestica f, donna di servizio f. **old maid** vecchia zitella f.

**maiden** ['meidǝn] n fanciulla f. adj primo; (journey) inaugurale. **maiden lady** signorina f. **maiden name** nome da ragazza m.

**mail**[1] [meil] n posta f. **mail order** vendita per catalogo f. v imbucare, mandare per posta.

**mail**[2] [meil] n (armour) maglia di ferro f. **mailed fist** pugno di ferro m.

**maim** [meim] v mutilare, storpiare.

**main** [mein] adj principale, essenziale. **mainland** n terra ferma f. **mainspring** (of watch) molla principale f; (impelling cause) movente principale f. **mainstay** n (chief support) sostegno m, braccio destro m. **mainstream** n tendenza dominante f. **in the main** nel complesso, in genere. **mainly** adv soprattutto; in genere.

**maintain** [mein'tein] v mantenere; (support) sostenere; (assert) affermare. **maintenance** n mantenimento m; (machinery, etc.) manutenzione f; (alimony) alimenti m pl.

**maisonette** [meizǝ'net] n casetta f.

**maize** [meiz] n mais m invar, granturco m invar.

**majesty** ['madʒǝsti] n maestà f. **majestic** adj maestoso.

**major** ['meidʒǝ] nm, adj maggiore. **majority** n maggioranza f; (age) maggiore età f.

***make** [meik] v fare; produrre. **make believe** dare da intendere, far finta di. **make-believe** n finzione f, illusione f. **make do** arrangiarsi. **make out** preparare; decifrare; (understand) capire. **make up** costituire, costruire; inventare; compensare; (cosmetics) truccare. **make-up** n trucco m, truccatura f; composizione f; costituzione f. **maker** n creatore, -trice m, f; fabbricante m, f.

**makeover** n rifacimento, ristrutturazione f.

**makeshift** ['meikʃift] adj di fortuna, improvvisato. n espediente m.

**maladjusted** [malǝ'dʒʌstid] adj disadattato.

**malaise** [ma'leiz] n malessere m.

**malaria** [mǝ'leǝriǝ] n malaria f.

**male** [meil] n maschio m. adj maschio, maschile.

**malevolent** [mǝ'levǝlǝnt] adj malevolo. **malevolence** n malevolenza f.

**malfunction** [mal'fʌŋkʃǝn] n funzionamento difettoso m.

**malice** ['malis] n malizia f, malignità f. **with malice aforethought** con premeditazione maliziosa. **malicious** adj malizioso, maligno.

**malignant** [mǝ'lignǝnt] adj maligno. **malignancy** n malignità f.

**malinger** [mǝ'liŋgǝ] v darsi malato, scansar fatiche. **malingerer** n scansafatiche m, f invar.

**mall** [mo:l] n viale m.

**mallet** ['malit] n maglio m, martello (di legno) m. **malleable** adj malleabile.

**malnutrition** [malnju'triʃǝn] n malnutrizione f.

**malt** [mo:lt] *n* malto *m*.

**Malta** ['mo:ltə] *n* Malta *f*. **Maltese** *n(m+f)*, *adj* maltese.

**maltreat** [mal'tri:t] *v* maltrattare. **maltreatment** *n* maltrattamento *m*.

**mammal** ['maməl] *n* mammifero *m*.

**mammoth** ['maməθ] *n* mammut *m*. *adj* enorme, mastodontico.

**man** [man] *n*, *pl* **men** uomo (*pl* uomini) *m*. *v* equipaggiare, presidiare. **manly** *adj* virile.

**manage** ['manidʒ] *v* dirigere, amministrare; (*cope*) farcela. **manage to** riuscire a, fare in modo da. **manage without** fare a meno di. **manageable** *adj* (*people*) trattabile, docile; (*things*) maneggevole. **management** *n* amministrazione *f*, direzione *f*. **manager** *n* direttore *m*. **manageress** *n* direttrice *f*. **managing director** consigliere delegato *m*.

**mandarin** ['mandərin] *n* mandarino *m*.

**mandate** ['mandeit] *n* mandato *m*. **mandatory** *adj* mandatorio.

**mandolin** ['mandəlin] *n* mandolino *m*.

**mane** [mein] *n* criniera *f*.

**mange** [meindʒ] *n* rogna *f*. **mangy** *adj* rognoso.

**mangle**[1] ['mangl] *v* (*disfigure*) deformare, mutilare.

**mangle**[2] ['mangl] *n* (*wringer*) mangano *m*. *v* manganare.

**manhandle** [man'handl] *v* manovrare a mano; (*treat harshly*) malmenare.

**manhole** ['manhoul] *n* botola *f*. **manhole cover** tombino *m*.

**mania** ['meiniə] *n* mania *f*. **maniac** *n* maniaco, -a *m, f*. **maniacal** *adj* maniaco.

**manicure** ['manikjuə] *n* manicure *f invar*.

**manifest** ['manifest] *adj* evidente, palese. *v* manifestare, dimostrare. *n* (*comm*) manifesto (di bordo) *m*, nota di carico *f*.

**manifesto** [mani'festou] *n* manifesto *m*, proclama *m*.

**manifold** ['manifould] *adj* molteplice, vario. *n* (*tech*) collettore *m*.

**manipulate** [mə'nipjuleit] *v* maneggiare. **manipulation** *n* maneggio *m*. **manipulative** *adj* manipolatore.

**mankind** [man'kaind] *n* umanità *f*, genere umano *m*.

**man-made** [man'meid] *adj* artificiale, sintetico.

**manner** ['manə] *n* modo *m*, maniera *f*; stile *m*; sorta *f*, specie *f*. **manners** *pl n* maniere *f pl*, educazione *f sing*. **mannerism** *n* affettazione *f*, manierismo *m*.

**manoeuvre** [mə'nu:və] *n* manovra *f*. *v* manovrare, maneggiare.

**manor** ['manə] *n* castello *m*, maniero *m*.

**manpower** ['man,pauə] *n* manodopera *f*; forze di lavoro *f pl*; capacità lavorativa *f*.

**mansion** ['manʃən] *n* palazzo *m*, casa signorile *f*.

**mantelpiece** ['mantlpi:s] *n* mensola (del caminetto) *f*.

**manual** ['manjuəl] *nm, adj* manuale. **manually** *adv* a mano.

**manufacture** [manju'faktʃə] *n* manifattura *f*, fabbricazione *f*, confezione *f*. *v* fabbricare. **manufacturer** *n* fabbricante *m*.

**manure** [mə'njuə] *n* concime *f*, fertilizzante *m*.

**manuscript** ['manjuskript] *nm, adj* manoscritto.

**many** ['meni] *adj, pron* molti, -e. **as many** altrettanti, -e. **how many** quanti, -e. **so many** tanti, -e. **too many** troppi, -e.

**map** [map] *n* mappa *f*, carta geografica *f*; (*of town*) pianta *f*. **off the map** remoto. *v* **map out** tracciare.

**maple** ['meipl] *n* acero *m*.

**mar** [ma:] *v* guastare, rovinare.

**marathon** ['marəθən] *n* maratona *f*.

**marble** ['ma:bl] *n* marmo *m*; (*glass ball*) bilia *f*. *adj* di marmo, marmoreo.

**march** [ma:tʃ] *n* marcia *f*. *v* marciare. **march-past** *n* sfilata *f*.

**March** [ma:tʃ] *n* marzo *m*.

**marchioness** [,ma:ʃə'nes] *n* marchesa *f*.

**mare** [meə] *n* cavalla *f*.

**margarine** [,ma:dʒə'ri:n] *n* margarina *f*.

**margin** ['ma:dʒin] *n* margine *m*. **marginal** *adj* marginale.

**marguerite** [,ma:gə'ri:t] *n* margherita *f*.

**marigold** ['marigould] *n* calendola *f*.

**marijuana** [mari'wa:nə] *n* marijuana *f invar*, canapa indiana *f*.

**marina** [mə'ri:nə] *n* porticciuolo *m*.

**marinade** [,mari'neid] *n* marinata *f*. *v* marinare.

**marine** [mə'ri:n] *adj* marino, marittimo. *n* (*fleet*) marina *f*; (*soldier*) soldato di marina *m*.

**marital** ['maritl] *adj* coniugale. **marital**

**status** stato civile *m*.

**maritime** ['maritaim] *adj* marittimo.

**marjoram** ['ma:dʒərəm] *n* maggiorana *f*.

**mark¹** [ma:k] *n* segno *m*; (*brand*) marchio *m*; (*rating*) voto *m*; (*trace*) traccia *f*. **marksman** *n* tiratore scelto *m*. *v* segnare; notare; osservare; (*correct, grade*) dare i voti a. **mark off** delimitare. **mark out** tracciare. **marking** *n* marchio *m*. **markings** *pl n* segni caratteristici *m pl*.

**mark²** [ma:k] *n* (*money*) marco *m*.

**market** ['ma:kit] *n* mercato *m*. **market garden** orto *m*. **market research** ricerca di mercato *f*. *v* mettere in vendita. **marketing** *n* marketing *m invar*.

**marmalade** ['ma:məleid] *n* marmellata *f*.

**maroon¹** [mə'ru:n] *nm, adj* (*colour*) marrone rossastro.

**maroon²** [mə'ru:n] *v* abbandonare.

**marquee** [ma:'ki:] *n* grande tenda *f*; padiglione *m*.

**marquess** ['ma:kwis] *n* marchese *m*.

**marriage** ['maridʒ] *n* matrimonio *m*. **marriage licence** dispensa di matrimonio *f*.

**marrow** ['marou] *n* zucca *f*.

**marry** ['mari] *v* sposare. **married** *adj* sposato. **get married** sposarsi.

**Mars** [ma:z] *n* Marte *m*. **Martian** *n, adj* marziano, -a.

**marsh** [ma:ʃ] *n* palude *f*. **marshy** *adj* paludoso.

**marshal** ['ma:ʃəl] *v* disporre; (*mil*) schierare. *n* maresciallo *m*.

**martial** ['ma:ʃəl] *adj* marziale.

**martin** ['ma:tin] *n* balestruccio *m*.

**martyr** ['ma:tə] *n* martire *m, f*. *v* martirizzare. **martyrdom** *n* martirio *m*.

**marvel** ['ma:vəl] *n* meraviglia *f*. *v* meravigliarsi. **marvel at** stupirsi di, ammirare.

**marvellous** ['ma:vələs] *adj* meraviglioso.

**marzipan** [ma:zi'pan] *n* marzapane *m*.

**mascara** [ma'ska:rə] *n* mascara *m invar*.

**mascot** ['maskət] *n* portafortuna *m invar*, mascotte *f*.

**masculine** ['maskjulin] *adj* maschile, virile. **masculinity** *n* mascolinità *f*, virilità *f*.

**mash** [maʃ] *v* ridurre in polpa, schiacciare; (*cookery*) fare un purè di. *n* (*cookery*) passata *f*, purè *m*.

**mask** [ma:sk] *n* maschera *f*. *v* mascherare; (*hide*) nascondere.

**masochist** ['masəkist] *n* masochista *m, f*. *adj* masochistico. **masochism** *n* masochismo *m*.

**mason** ['meisn] *n* muratore *m*; (*freemason*) massone *m*. **masonic** *adj* massonico. **masonry** *n* muratura *f*.

**masquerade** [maskə'reid] *n* mascherata *f*. *v* **masquerade as** mascherarsi da, farsi passare per.

**mass¹** [mas] *n* massa *f*, (*bulk*) mole *f*; (*great number*) gran numero *m*; (*large amount*) grande quantità *f*. **masses** *pl n* (*coll*) mucchio *m sing*. **mass meeting** adunata popolare *f*. **mass-produced** *adj* prodotto in serie. **mass-production** *n* produzione in serie *or* massa *f*.

**mass²** [mas] *n* (*rel*) messa *f*.

**massacre** ['masəkə] *n* massacro *m*, strage *f*. *v* massacrare, far strage di.

**massage** ['masa:ʒ] *n* massaggio *m*. *v* massaggiare. **masseur** *n* massaggiatore *m*. **masseuse** *n* massaggiatrice *f*.

**massive** ['masiv] *adj* massiccio, solido.

**mast** [ma:st] *n* albero *m*.

**mastectomy** [ma'stektəmi] *n* mastectomia *f*.

**master** ['ma:stə] *n* padrone *m*, signore *m*; (*of ship*) capitano *m*; (*school*) professore *m*. **masterpiece** *n* capolavoro *m*. *v* dominare, impadronirsi di; (*learn*) conoscere a perfezione. **masterly** *adj* magistrale.

**masturbate** ['mastəbeit] *v* masturbarsi. **masturbation** *n* masturbazione *f*.

**mat** [mat] *n* (*covering*) tappeto *m*; (*for floor*) stuoia *f*; (*at door*) zerbino *m*; (*on table*) sottopiatto *m*.

**match¹** [matʃ] *n* (*light*) fiammifero *m*. **matchbox** *n* scatola da fiammiferi *f*.

**match²** [matʃ] *v* (*clothes, colours, etc.*) andare bene insieme; corrispondere; (*oppose*) opporre; (*equal*) uguagliare. *n* (*equal*) uguale *m, f*, pari *m, f*; (*contest, partner*) partita *f*. **matchmaker** *n* sensale di matrimoni *m*. **meet one's match** trovare un degno avversario.

**mate** [meit] *n* compagno, -a *m, f*; (*help*) aiuto *m*, assistente *m, f*; (*naut*) secondo *m*.

**material** [mə'tiəriəl] *n* (*substance*) sostanza *f*, materia *f*; materiale *m*; (*fabric*) stoffa *f*. *adj* materiale, essenziale. **materialize** *v* realizzarsi, prender corpo.

**maternal** [mə'tə:nl] *adj* materno. **maternity** *n* maternità *f*.

**mathematics** [maθə'matiks] *n* matematica f. **mathematical** *adj* matematico. **mathematician** *n* matematico, -a *m, f*.

**matinee** ['matinei] *n* rappresentazione diurna f.

**matins** ['matinz] *n* mattutino *m*.

**matriarch** ['meitria:k] *n* matrona f. **matriarchal** *adj* matriarcale.

**matrimony** ['matriməni] *n* matrimonio *m*. **matrimonial** *adj* matrimoniale.

**matrix** ['meitriks] *n* matrice f.

**matron** ['meitrən] *n* (*hospital*) capoinfermiera f; (*institution*) direttrice f.

**matt** [mat] *adj* matto, opaco.

**matter** ['matə] *v* importare. *n* materia f; (*thing, affair*) cosa f, affare *m*; (*of book, etc.*) argomento *m*, questione f. **as a matter of fact** in realtà, fatto sta che. **matter-of-fact** *adj* pratico. **what's the matter?** cosa c'è?

**mattress** ['matris] *n* materasso *m*.

**mature** [mə'tjuə] *v* maturare; (*become due*) scadere. **maturity** *n* maturità f.

**maudlin** ['mo:dlin] *adj* lamentevole, querulo.

**maul** [mo:l] *v* dilaniare.

**mausoleum** [mo:sə'liəm] *n* mausoleo *m*.

**mauve** [mouv] *adj* (*color*) malva *invar*.

**maxim** ['maksim] *n* massima f.

**maximum** ['maksiməm] *nm, adj* massimo.

**\*may** [mei] *v* potere. **maybe** può darsi, forse.

**May** [mei] *n* maggio *m*.

**mayonnaise** [ˌmeiə'neiz] *n* maionese f.

**mayor** [meə] *n* sindaco *m*.

**maze** [meiz] *n* labirinto *m*.

**me** [mi:] *pron* mi; (*after prep*) me. **it's me** sono io.

**meadow** ['medou] *n* prato *m*.

**meagre** ['mi:gə] *adj* scarso.

**meal**[1] [mi:l] *n* (*food*) pasto *m*.

**meal**[2] [mi:l] *n* (*grain*) farina f.

**\*mean**[1] [mi:n] *v* significare, voler dire; intendere; destinare.

**mean**[2] [mi:n] *adj* gretto; (*miserly*) avaro; (*shabby*) meschino; (*low*) basso. **meanness** *n* grettezza f; avarizia f.

**mean**[3] [mi:n] *n* (*average*) media f. *adj* medio.

**meander** [mi'andə] *v* divagare.

**meaning** ['mi:nin] *n* significato *m*, senso *m*. *adj* significativo.

**means** [mi:nz] *n* mezzi *m pl*. **by means of** per mezzo di. **by no means** niente affatto. **by some means or other** in qualche modo.

**meant** [ment] *V* **mean**[1].

**meanwhile** ['mi:nwail] *adv* also **in the meantime** nel frattempo, intanto.

**measles** ['mi:zlz] *n* morbillo *m*. **German measles** *n* rosolio f, rubeola f. **measly** *adj* (*wretched*) miserabile.

**measure** ['meʒə] *n* misura f; (*action*) provvedimento *m*. **made to measure** fatto su misura. *v* misurare; (*estimate*) valutare. **measurement** *n* misura f. **measurements** *pl n* dimensioni f *pl*.

**meat** [mi:t] *n* carne f. **meaty** *adj* sostanzioso.

**mechanic** [mi'kanik] *n* meccanico *m*. **mechanical** *adj* meccanico. **mechanism** *n* meccanismo *m*. **mechanized** *adj* meccanizzato.

**medal** ['medl] *n* medaglia f.

**meddle** ['medl] *v* immischiarsi, intromettersi. **meddler** *n* ficcanaso *m invar*.

**media** ['mi:diə] *pl n* mezzi di comunicazione *m pl*.

**median** ['mi:diən] *adj* mediano. *n* mediana f.

**mediate** ['mi:dieit] *v* fare da mediatore *or* intermediario. **mediation** *n* mediazione f. **mediator** *n* mediatore, -trice *m, f*.

**medical** ['medikəl] *adj* medico. *n* (*examination*) esame medico *m*. **medication** *n* medicazione f. **medicinal** *adj* medicinale.

**medicine** *n* (*science*) medicina f; (*substance*) medicinale *m*, farmaco *m*.

**medieval** [medi'i:vəl] *adj* medievale.

**mediocre** [mi:di'oukə] *adj* mediocre. **mediocrity** *n* mediocrità f.

**meditate** ['mediteit] *v* meditare. **meditation** *n* meditazione f.

**Mediterranean** [ˌmeditə'reiniən] *n* Mediterraneo *m*. *adj* mediterraneo.

**medium** ['mi:diəm] *n* (*spiritualist*) medium *m, f invar*; (*biology*) brodo (di coltura) *m*; (*agency*) mezzo *m*. **happy medium** giusto mezzo *m*. *adj* medio.

**medley** ['medli] *n* miscuglio *m*, pasticcio *m*.

**meek** [mi:k] *adj* mansueto, mite. **meekness** *n* mansuetudine f.

**\*meet** [mi:t] *v* incontrare; (*by arrangement*) trovare; (*gather*) riunirsi. **meeting** *n* incontro *m*; riunione *f*.

**megaphone** ['megəfoun] *n* megafono *m*.

**melancholy** ['melənkəli] *n* malinconia *f*. *adj also* **melancholic** malinconico.

**mellow** ['melou] *adj* maturo; (*wine*) amabile; (*soft*) morbido. *v* maturare; (*person*) intenerirsi.

**melodrama** ['melədramə] *n* melodramma *m*. **melodramatic** *adj* melodrammatico.

**melody** ['melədi] *n* melodia *f*. **melodious** *adj* melodioso.

**melon** ['melən] *n* melone *m*.

**melt** [melt] *v* fondere, sciogliere; (*feeling*) intenerire. **melt down** fondere. **melting point** punto di fusione *m*. **melting pot** crogiuolo *m*.

**member** ['membə] *n* membro *m*; (*of society, club, etc.*) socio, -a *m, f*; (*of parliament*) deputato, -a *m, f*. **membership** *n* (*number*) numero dei soci *m*; (*condition*) l'essere socio *m*.

**membrane** ['membrein] *n* membrana *f*.

**memento** [mə'mentou] *n* ricordo *m*.

**memo** ['memou] *n* appunto *m*.

**memoirs** ['memwa:z] *pl n* memorie *f pl*.

**memorandum** [memə'randəm] *n* appunto *m*, promemoria *m invar*; (*document*) memorandum *m invar*.

**memorial** [mi'mo:riəl] *n* monumento *m*. *adj* commemorativo.

**memory** ['meməri] *n* (*faculty*) memoria *f*; (*recollection*) ricordo *m*. **memorable** *adj* memorabile. **memorize** *v* imparare a memoria.

**men** [men] *V* **man**.

**menace** ['menis] *n* minaccia *f*. *v* minacciare. **menacing** *adj* minaccioso.

**menagerie** [mi'nadʒəri] *n* serraglio *m*.

**mend** [mend] *v* riparare, aggiustare; (*get better*) migliorare. **mend one's ways** ravvedersi. *n* be on the mend stare rimettendosi. **mending** *n* rammendo *m*.

**menial** ['mi:niəl] *adj* servile, umile.

**meningitis** [menin'dʒaitis] *n* meningite *f*.

**menopause** ['menəpo:z] *n* menopausa *f*.

**menstrual** ['menstruəl] *adj* mestruale. **menstruate** *v* mestruare. **menstruation** *n* mestruazione *f*.

**mental** ['mentl] *adj* mentale; (*home, hospital*) psichiatrico. **mentality** *n* mentalità *f*.

**menthol** ['menθəl] *n* mentolo *m*.

**mention** ['menʃən] *v* accennare a, parlare di, citare. **don't mention it!** prego! *n* menzione *f*, cenno *m*; citazione *f*.

**menu** ['menju:] *n* menu *m invar*, lista dei cibi *f*.

**mercantile** ['mə:kən,tail] *adj* mercantile.

**mercenary** ['mə:sinəri] *nm, adj* mercenario.

**merchandise** ['mə:tʃəndaiz] *n* merce *f*.

**merchant** ['mə:tʃənt] *n* commerciante *m, f*. **merchant navy** marina mercantile *f*.

**mercury** ['mə:kjuri] *n* mercurio *m*.

**mercy** ['mə:si] *n* pietà *f*, carità *f*. **at the mercy of** alla mercè di. **merciful** *adj* pietoso, caritatevole.

**mere** [miə] *adj* puro, mero.

**merge** [mə:dʒ] *v* fondere, amalgamare. **merger** *n* fusione *f*.

**meridian** [mə'ridiən] *n* meridiano *m*.

**meringue** [mə'raŋ] *n* meringa *f*.

**merit** ['merit] *n* merito *m*, valore *m*. *v* meritare.

**mermaid** ['mə:meid] *n* sirena *f*.

**merry** ['meri] *adj* allegro; (*coll*) brillo. **merry-go-round** *n* carosello *m*. **merry-making** *n* festa *f*.

**mesh** [meʃ] *n* maglia *f*; (*net*) rete *f*. **in mesh** ingranato.

**mesmerize** ['mezməraiz] *v* ipnotizzare; affascinare.

**mess** [mes] *n* confusione *f*, pasticcio *m*; (*eating place*) mensa *f*. **be in a mess** (*of things*) essere in disordine; (*of people*) trovarsi nei guai. **make a mess of** rovinare. *v* **mess about** perdersi in cose inutili; (*inconvenience*) disturbare. **mess up** rovinare. **messy** *adj* confuso, disordinato; (*dirty*) sporco.

**message** ['mesidʒ] *n* messaggio *m*. **messenger** *n* messaggero *m*; (*errand boy*) fattorino *m*.

**met** [met] *V* **meet**.

**metabolism** [mi'tabəlizm] *n* metabolismo *m*. **metabolic** *adj* metabolico.

**metal** ['metl] *n* metallo *m*. **metallic** *adj* metallico. **metallurgy** *n* metallurgia *f*.

**metamorphosis** [metə'mo:fəsis] *n* metamorfosi *f invar*.

**metaphor** ['metəfə] *n* metafora *f*. **metaphoric(al)** *adj* metaforico.

**metaphysics** [metə'fiziks] *n* metafisica *f*. **metaphysical** *adj* metafisico.

**meteor** ['mi:tiə] *n* meteora *f.* **meteoric** *adj* meteorico; rapidissimo.

**meteorology** [,mi:tiə'rolədʒi] *n* meteorologia *f.* **meteorological** *adj* meteorologico. **meteorologist** *n* meteorologo, -a *m, f.*

**meter** ['mi:tə] *n* contatore *m; (parking)* parchimetro *m.* *v* misurare.

**methane** ['mi:θein] *n* metano *m.*

**method** ['meθəd] *n* metodo *m*, modo *m.* **methodical** *adj* metodico, sistematico.

**methylated spirits** ['meθileitid] *n* alcool denaturato *m.*

**meticulous** [mi'tikjuləs] *adj* meticoloso.

**metre** ['mi:tə] *n* metro *m.* **metric** *adj* metrico.

**metronome** ['metrənoum] *n* metronomo *m.*

**metropolis** [mə'tropəlis] *n* metropoli *f.* **metropolitan** *adj* metropolitano.

**mettle** ['metl] *n* **put someone on his mettle** mettere qualcuno alla prova.

**mews** [mju:z] *n* vicolo *m.*

**Mexico** ['meksikou] *n* Messico *m.* **Mexican** *n, adj* messicano, -a.

**miaow** [mi'au] *v* miagolare.

**mice** [mais] *V* **mouse.**

**microbe** ['maikroub] *n* microbo *m.*

**microfilm** ['maikrə,film] *n* microfilm *m invar.*

**microphone** ['maikrəfoun] *n* microfono *m.*

**microscope** ['maikrəskoup] *n* microscopio *m.* **microscopic** *adj* microscopico. **microscopy** *n* microscopia *f.*

**microwave oven** *n* fornello a micro-onde *m.*

**mid** [mid] *adj* **in mid** ... a metà ..., in mezzo a ..., in pieno .... **midday** *n* mezzogiorno *m.* **midnight** *n* mezzanotte *f.* **mid-ocean** *n* alto mare *m.* **midsummer** *n* mezza estate *f.* **midway** *adv* a metà strada.

**middle** ['midl] *n* mezzo *m*, centro *m.* *adj* medio. **middle-aged** *adj* di mezza età. **Middle Ages** Medio Evo *m sing.* **middle-class** *adj* borghese. **middle man** *n* intermediario *m.*

**midge** [midʒ] *n* zanzara *f.*

**midget** ['midʒit] *n* nano *m.*

**midst** [midst] *n* mezzo *m*, centro *m.* **in the midst of** nel mezzo di, in mezzo a, fra.

**midwife** ['midwaif] *n* levatrice *f.* **midwifery** *n* ostetricia *f.*

**might¹** [mait] *V* **may.**

**might²** [mait] *n (power)* forza *f*, potenza *f.*

**mighty** ['maiti] *adj* forte, potente. *adv (coll)* estremamente.

**migraine** ['mi:grein] *n* emicrania *f.*

**migrate** [mai'greit] *v* migrare. **migrant** *n, adj* migratore, -trice. **migration** *n* migrazione *f.* **migratory** *adj* migratorio.

**Milan** [mi'lan] *n* Milano *f.* **Milanese** *n(m+f), adj* milanese.

**mild** [maild] *adj* mite. **mildness** *n* mitezza *f.*

**mildew** ['mildju:] *n* muffa *f.* **mildewy** *adj* ammuffito.

**mile** [mail] *n* miglio *m (pl* -a *f).* **mileage** *n* distanza percorsa in miglia *f*, chilometraggio *m.* **mileometer** *n* contachilometri *m invar.*

**militant** ['militənt] *n(m+f), adj* militante, attivista.

**military** ['militəri] *adj* militare. **militarism** *n* militarismo *m.* **militate** *v* militare. **militia** *n* milizia *f.*

**milk** [milk] *n* latte *m.* **milkman** *n* lattaio *m.* *v* mungere; *(exploit)* sfruttare.

**Milky Way** *n* Via Lattea *f.*

**mill** [mil] *n (flour)* mulino *m; (textiles)* stabilimento *m; (tech)* fresa *f; (coffee)* macinino *m.* **millstone** *n* macina *f; (burden)* macigno *m.* *v* macinare; *(metal)* laminare; *(crowd)* circolare. **milling** *n (corn)* macinatura *f; (metal)* laminatura *f; (tech)* fresatura *f; (coins)* zigrinatura *f.*

**millennium** [mi'leniəm] *n* millennio *m.*

**millet** ['milit] *n* miglio *m.*

**milligram** ['mili,gram] *n* milligrammo *m.*

**millilitre** ['mili,li:tə] *n* millilitro *m.*

**millimetre** ['mili,mi:tə] *n* millimetro *m.*

**milliner** ['milinə] *n* modista *f.*

**million** ['miljən] *n* milione *m.* **millionaire** *n* milionario, -a *m, f.* **millionth** *nm, adj* milionesimo.

**mime** [maim] *n (art)* mimica *f; (artist)* mimo, -a *m, f.* *v* mimare.

**mimic** ['mimik] *v* contraffare; *(ape)* scimmiottare. *n* imitatore, -trice *m, f;* contraffattore, -trice *m, f.* **mimicry** *n* mimica *f; (zool)* mimetismo *m.*

**mimosa** [mi'mouzə] *n* mimosa *f.*

**minaret** [minə'ret] *n* minareto *m.*

**mince** [mins] *v* tritare, tagliuzzare. **not**

**mince one's words** parlare apertamente. *n* (*meat*) carne tritata *f*. **make mincemeat of** (*coll*) demolire. **mincer** *n* tritatutto *m invar*.

**mind** [maind] *n* mente *f*, intelletto *m*, spirito *m*; (*reason*) ragione *f*; (*opinion*) parere *m*. **bear in mind** tenere a mente. **make up one's mind** decidersi. **peace of mind** serenità *f*. **piece of one's mind** (*reprimand*) rimprovero *m*. **speak one's mind** parlar chiaro. **state of mind** stato d'animo *m*. *v* badare a, occuparsi di; (*watch out*) far attenzione. **do you mind if ... ?** ti dispiace se ... ? **never mind!** non importa! **mindful** *adj* attento. **mindless** *adj* (*heedless*) sbadato; (*senseless*) insensato.

**minder** *n* guardia del corpo; sorvegliante *f*; *m*.

**mine¹** [main] *pron* il mio, la mia; (*pl*) i miei, le mie.

**mine²** [main] *n* miniera *f*; (*explosive*) mina *f*. *v* (*dig*) scavare; (*extract*) estrarre; (*mil*) minare. **mine-detector** *n* rilevatore di mine *m*. **minefield** *n* campo minato *m*. **minesweeper** *n* dragamine *m invar*. **miner** *n* minatore *m*.

**mineral** ['minərəl] *nm, adj* minerale. **mineral water** *n* acqua minerale *f*.

**mingle** ['miŋgl] *v* mescolare, mischiarsi.

**miniature** ['minitʃə] *n* miniatura *f*. *adj* in miniatura.

**minim** ['minim] *n* (*music*) minima *f*.

**minimum** ['miniməm] *n* minimo *m*. **minimal** *adj* minimo. **minimize** *v* minimizzare.

**mining** ['mainiŋ] *n* estrazione *f*, scavo *m*; (*mil*) posa di mine *f*. *adj* minerario.

**minister** ['ministə] *n* (*pol*) ministro, -a *m, f*; (*rel*) sacerdote *m*; (*diplomat*) incaricato, -a *m, f*. *v* **minister to** soccorrere. **minister to the needs of** provvedere ai bisogni di. **ministerial** *adj* ministeriale. **ministry** *n* ministero *m*; (*clergy*) clero *m*.

**mink** [miŋk] *n* visone *m*.

**minor** ['mainə] *adj* minore, più piccolo, meno importante. *n* minorenne *m, f*. **minority** *n* minoranza *f*; (*age*) minorità *f*, età minore *f*.

**minstrel** ['minstrəl] *n* menestrello *m*, cantante *m*.

**mint¹** [mint] *n* (*bot*) menta *f*.

**mint²** [mint] *n* zecca *f*. **be in mint condition** essere nuovo di zecca. **have a mint of money** avere un mucchio di soldi. *v* coniare.

**minuet** [minju'et] *n* minuetto *m*.

**minus** ['mainəs] *prep* meno.

**minute¹** ['minit] *n* minuto *m*; momento *m*. **minutes** *pl n* (*of meeting*) verbale *m sing*. *v* (*record*) prendere nota; (*enter in minutes*) mettere agli atti.

**minute²** [mai'nju:t] *adj* minuto; (*detailed*) minuzioso.

**minx** [miŋks] *n* (*coll*) civetta *f*.

**miracle** ['mirəkl] *n* miracolo *m*. **miraculous** *adj* miracoloso.

**mirage** ['mira:ʒ] *n* miraggio *m*.

**mirror** ['mirə] *n* specchio *m*. *v* riflettere, rispecchiare.

**mirth** [mə:θ] *n* ilarità *f*, allegria *f*.

**misadventure** [misəd'ventʃə] *n* infortunio *m*, disavventura *f*.

**misanthropist** [miz'anθrəpist] *n* misantropo, -a *m, f*. **misanthropic** *adj* misantropico. **misanthropy** *n* misantropia *f*.

**misapprehension** [misapri'henʃən] *n* equivoco *m*, malinteso *m*. **misapprehend** *v* fraintendere.

**misbehave** [misbi'heiv] *v* comportarsi male. **misbehaviour** *n* cattiva condotta *f*.

**miscalculate** [mis'kalkjuleit] *v* calcolar male. **miscalculation** *n* calcolo errato *m*.

**miscarriage** [mis'karidʒ] *n* (*med*) aborto *m*. **miscarry** *v* abortire.

**miscellaneous** [misə'leiniəs] *adj* miscellaneo.

**mischance** [mis'tʃa:ns] *n* sventura *f*.

**mischief** ['mistʃif] *n* (*harm*) danno *m*; (*of child, etc.*) fastidi *m pl*; (*teasing*) malizia *f*. **be up to mischief** combinare un brutto tiro. **make mischief** creare discordia. **mischief-maker** *n* attaccabrighe *m invar*. **mischievous** *adj* malizioso; (*of child*) birichino.

**misconception** [miskən'sepʃən] *n* malinteso *m*.

**misconduct** [mis'kondʌkt] *n* cattiva condotta *f*.

**misdeed** [mis'di:d] *n* misfatto *m*, delitto *m*.

**misdemeanour** [misdi'mi:nə] *n* (*misbehaviour*) cattiva condotta *f*; (*crime*) delitto *m*.

**miser** ['maizə] *n* avaro, -a *m, f*. **miserly** *adj* avaro.

**miserable** ['mizərəbl] *adj* (*unhappy*) infelice, triste; (*pitiful*) pietoso; (*painful*) penoso; depresso.

**misery** ['mizəri] *n* miseria *f*; sofferenze *f pl*.

**misfire** [mis'faiə] v fare cilecca or fiasco.

**misfit** ['misfit] n (person) spostato, -a m, f.

**misfortune** [mis'fo:tʃən] n sfortuna f, disgrazia f.

**misgiving** [mis'giviŋ] n dubbio m.

**misguided** [mis'gaidid] adj fuori posto, sviato.

**mishap** ['mishap] n disgrazia f, contrattempo m.

**misjudge** [mis'dʒʌdʒ] v farsi un'idea sbagliata di, giudicare male.

***mislay** [mis'lei] v smarrire.

***mislead** [mis'li:d] v ingannare. **misleading** adj ingannevole.

**misnomer** [mis'noumə] n termine improprio m.

**misplace** [mis'pleis] v mettere fuori posto.

**misprint** ['misprint] n errore tipografico m.

**miss¹** [mis] n colpo mancato m. v mancare (a); (not catch) perdere; (skip) saltare; (not find) non trovare; (regret absence of) sentire la mancanza di. **miss out** omettere. **be missing** mancare.

**miss²** [mis] n signorina f.

**missile** ['misail] n missile m.

**mission** ['miʃən] n missione f. **missionary** n, adj missionario, -a.

**mist** [mist] n caligine f, foschia f. v offuscare. **misty** adj caliginoso, fosco.

***mistake** [mi'steik] n errore m, sbaglio m. **by mistake** per errore. **make a mistake** sbagliare, fare un errore. v (confuse) confondere, scambiare. **mistaken** adj sbagliato, falso.

**mistletoe** ['misltou] n vischio m.

**mistress** ['mistris] n padrona f; (school) insegnante f; (lover) amante f.

**mistrust** [mis'trʌst] v diffidare di, non aver fiducia in. n diffidenza f, sfiducia f. **mistrustful** adj diffidente.

***misunderstand** [misʌndə'stand] v fraintendere, capir male. **misunderstanding** n malinteso m, equivoco m. **misunderstood** adj incompreso.

**misuse** [mis'ju:s; v mis'ju:z] n abuso m; uso incorretto m. v abusare; (ill-treat) maltrattare; (use badly) adoperare male.

**mitigate** ['mitigeit] v mitigare; (law) attenuare. **mitigation** n (law) attenuante f.

**mitre** ['maitə] n (rel) mitra f; (carpentry) ugnatura f. v ugnare.

**mitten** ['mitn] n mezzo quanto m, muffola f.

**mix** [miks] v mescolare, mischiare; combinare. **mix up** confondere. **mix-up** n confusione f. **mixed** adj misto. **mixer** n (tech) agitatore m. **be a good mixer** essere socievole. **mixture** n miscela f; miscuglio m.

**moan** [moun] n (complaint) lamento m; (groan) gemito m. v lamentarsi; gemere.

**moat** [mout] n fosso m, fossato m.

**mob** [mob] n folla f, marmaglia f, plebaglia f. v molestare, assalire.

**mobile** ['moubail] adj mobile. **mobility** n mobilità f. **mobilization** n mobilitazione f. **mobilize** v mobilitare. **mobile phone** n (telefono) cellulare m.

**moccasin** ['mokasin] n mocassino m.

**mock** [mok] v deridere, canzonare. adj finto, falso. **mockery** n presa in giro f, derisione f. **mocking** adj beffardo. **mockingbird** n mimo m.

**mode** [moud] n modo m, maniera f.

**model** ['modl] n modello m; (art) modello, -a m, f; (fashion) indossatore, -trice m, f. adj modello, esemplare. v modellare, fare l'indossatore.

**moderate** ['modərət; v 'modəreit] adj misurato, moderato; (price) modico. v moderare. **moderation** n misura f, moderazione f. **in moderation** moderatamente.

**modern** ['modən] adj moderno. **modernization** n rimodernamento m. **modernize** v rimodernare.

**modest** ['modist] adj modesto. **modesty** n modestia f.

**modify** ['modifai] v modificare. **modification** n modifica f.

**modulate** ['modjuleit] v modulare. **modulation** n modulazione f.

**module** ['modju:l] n modulo m.

**mohair** ['mouheə] n mohair m invar.

**moist** [moist] adj umido. **moisten** v inumidire; (surface) umettare. **moisture** n umidità f. **moisturize** v umidificare.

**molar** ['moulə] nm, adj molare.

**molasses** [mə'lasiz] n melassa f.

**mold** (US) V **mould**.

**Moldova** [mol'douvə] n Moldavia f.

**mole¹** [moul] n (on skin) neo m.

**mole²** [moul] n (zool) talpa f.

**molecule** ['molikju:l] n molecola f. **molecu-**

**lar** *adj* molecolare.
**molest** ['mə'lest] *v* molestare.
**mollify** ['mɔlifai] *v* placare.
**mollusc** ['mɔləsk] *n* mollusco *m*.
**mollycoddle** ['mɔlikodl] *v* coccolare.
**molt** *(US) V* **moult**.
**molten** ['moultən] *adj* fuso.
**moment** ['moumənt] *n* momento *m*, istante *m*. **at the moment** attualmente. **momentary** *adj* momentaneo. **momentous** *adj* grave, importante. **momentum** *n* impeto *m*, slancio *m*.
**Monaco** ['mɔnəˌkou] *n* Monaco *f*.
**monarch** ['mɔnək] *n* monarca *m, f*. **monarchist** *n, adj* monarchico, -a. **monarchy** *n* monarchia *f*.
**monastery** ['mɔnəstəri] *n* monastero *m*. **monastic** *adj* monastico.
**Monday** ['mʌndi] *n* lunedì *m*.
**money** ['mʌni] *n* denaro *m*, soldi *m pl*. **money-box** *n* salvadanaio *m*. **moneylender** *n* usuraio *m*. **money order** vaglia (postale) *m invar*. **monetary** *adj* monetario.
**Mongolia** [mɔŋ'goulia] *n* Mongolia *f*. **Mongolian** *n, adj* mongolo, -a.
**mongrel** ['mʌŋgrəl] *nm, adj* bastardo.
**monitor** ['mɔnitə] *n (radio)* ascoltatore *m*; *(tech)* monitor *m invar*. *v (radio)* ascoltare; controllare. **monitoring service** servizio d'ascolto *m*.
**monk** [mʌŋk] *n* monaco *m*, frate *m*.
**monkey** ['mʌŋki] *n* scimmia *f*.
**monogamy** [mə'nɔgəmi] *n* monogamia *f*. **monogamous** *adj* monogamo.
**monogram** ['mɔnəgram] *n* monogramma *m*.
**monograph** ['mɔnəgraːf] *n* monografia *f*.
**monolithic** [ˌmɔnə'li θik] *adj* monolitico.
**monologue** ['mɔnəlog] *n* monologo *(pl -ghi) m*.
**monopolize** [mə'nɔpəlaiz] *v* monopolizzare. **monopoly** *n* monopolio *m*.
**monosyllable** ['mɔnəsiləbl] *n* monosillabo *m*. **monosyllabic** *adj* monosillabico, monosillabo.
**monotony** [mə'nɔtəni] *n* monotonia *f*. **monotone** *n* tono uniforme *m*. **monotonous** *adj* monotono.
**monsoon** [mɔn'suːn] *n* monsone *m*.

**monster** ['mɔnstə] *n* mostro *m*. **monstrosity** *n* mostruosità *f*. **monstrous** *adj* mostruoso.
**month** [mʌnθ] *n* mese *m*.
**monthly** ['mʌnθli] *n (periodical)* rivista mensile *f*. *adj* mensile. *adv* al mese, mensilmente.
**monument** ['mɔnjumənt] *n* monumento *m*. **monumental** *adj* monumentale.
**mood**[1] [muːd] *n* umore *m*, stato d'animo *m*. **feel in the mood to** sentirsi disposto a, aver voglia di. **moodiness** *n* malumore *m*; volubilità *f*. **moody** *adj* capriccioso; *(sulky)* di malumore.
**mood**[2] [muːd] *n (gramm)* modo *m*.
**moon** [muːn] *n* luna *f*. **moonlight** *n* chiaro di luna *m*.
**moor**[1] [muə] *n* brughiera *f*. **moorhen** *n* gallinella d'acqua *f*.
**moor**[2] [muə] *v* ormeggiare, ancorare. **mooring** *n* ormeggio *m*, ancoraggio *m*.
**moose** [muːs] *n* alce *m*.
**moot** [muːt] *adj* discutibile.
**mop** [mɔp] *n* scopa di cotone per lavaggio *f*; *(of hair)* zazzera *f*. *v* **mop one's brow** asciugarsi la fronte. **mop up** asciugare; rastrellare.
**mope** [moup] *v* fare il broncio, immusonirsi.
**moped** ['mouped] *n* ciclomotore *m*.
**moral** ['mɔrəl] *nf, adj* morale. **morals** *pl n* morale *f sing*. **morale** *n* morale *m*. **moralist** *n* moralista *m, f*. **morality** *n* moralità *f*, buon costume *m*.
**morbid** ['mɔːbid] *adj* morboso, patologico.
**more** [mɔː] *adv* più, di più; *(again)* ancora. *nm, adj* più. **more and more** sempre più. **more than** più di *or* che.
**moreover** [mɔː'rouvə] *adv* inoltre, per di più.
**morgue** [mɔːg] *n* obitorio *m*.
**morning** ['mɔːniŋ] *n* mattina *m*, mattinata *f*. **this morning** stamane. **tomorrow morning** domattina. *adj* del mattino, mattutino.
**moron** ['mɔːron] *n* deficiente *m, f*. **moronic** *adj* deficiente, scemo.
**morose** [mə'rous] *adj* scontroso.
**morphine** ['mɔːfiːn] *n* morfina *f*.
**Morse code** [mɔːs] *n* alfabeto Morse *m*.
**morsel** ['mɔːsəl] *n* boccone *m*.

**mortal** ['mɔːtl] n(m+f), adj mortale. **mortality** n mortalità f.

**mortar** ['mɔːtə] n (vessel, arms) mortaio m; (building) malta f.

**mortgage** ['mɔːgidʒ] n ipoteca f. v ipotecare, impegnare.

**mortify** ['mɔːtifai] v mortificare. **mortification** n mortificazione f.

**mortuary** ['mɔːtʃuəri] n camera ardente or mortuaria f.

**mosaic** [mə'zeiik] n mosaico m.

**Moscow** ['mɔskou] n Mosca f.

**mosque** [mɔsk] n moschea f.

**mosquito** [mə'skiːtou] n zanzara f.

**moss** [mɔs] n muschio m, musco m. **mossy** adj muscoso.

**most** [moust] adj (majority) la maggior parte di, il più di; (greatest) il più grande, il maggiore. n il più m; (greatest part) la maggior parte f; (majority) la maggioranza f, i più m pl. adv il più; n; (very) molto, assai.

**motel** [mou'tel] n motel m invar, autostello m.

**moth** [mɔθ] n lepidottero m. **clothes moth** tarma f. **mothball** n pallina antitarmica f.

**mother** ['mʌðə] n madre f; (coll) mamma f. v aver cura di come una madre. **mother-in-law** n suocera f. **mother-of-pearl** n madreperla f. **mother tongue** madrelingua f. **motherly** adj materno.

**motion** ['mouʃən] n moto m, movimento m; (proposal) mozione f; (law) istanza f. **go through the motions** far finta. **set in motion** avviare, mettere in moto. v accennare a, far cenno a. **motionless** adj immobile.

**motivate** ['moutiveit] v motivare, spingere. **motivation** n spinta f, stimolo m.

**motive** ['moutiv] n motivo m, ragione f.

**motor** ['moutə] nm, adj motore. **motorboat** n motoscafo m. **motor car** automobile f, macchina f. **motorcycle** n motocicletta f. **motorcyclist** n motociclista m, f. **motorway** n autostrada f. v andare in macchina. **motoring** n automobilismo m. **motorist** n automobilista m, f. **motorize** v motorizzare.

**mottled** ['mɔtld] adj chiazzato.

**motto** ['motou] n motto m, massima f.

**mould¹** or US **mold** [mould] n stampo m, forma f. v formare, foggiare, modellare.

**mould²** or US **mold** [mould] n muffa f. **mouldy** adj ammuffito. **go mouldy** ammuffire.

**moult** or US **molt** [moult] v mutare, fare la muta.

**mound** [maund] n tumulo m; (heap) mucchio m.

**mount¹** [maunt] v montare. n (setting) montatura f.

**mount²** [maunt] n monte m.

**mountain** ['mauntən] n montagna f. **mountaineer** n alpinista m, f. **mountaineering** n alpinismo m. **mountainous** adj montuoso, alpestre.

**mourn** [mɔːn] v rimpiangere, essere in lutto per. **mourning** n lutto m, cordoglio m. **mournful** adj triste; lugubre.

**mouse** [maus] n, pl **mice** topo m. (comp) mouse m. **mouse-trap** n trappola (per topi) f. **mousy** adj (colour) grigio topo; timido. **mouse mat** tappetino per il mouse m.

**mousse** [muːs] n mousse f, spuma f.

**moustache** [mə'staːʃ] n baffi m pl.

**mouth** [mauθ] n bocca f; (of river) foce f. **mouth organ** armonica f. **mouthpiece** n (spokesman) portavoce m invar; (of pipe) bocchino m. v declamare. **mouthful** n boccone m.

**move** [muːv] v muovere, spostare; (house) traslocare; (arouse feelings) commuovere; (propose) proporre. **move away** or **off** allontanare; (depart) partire. **move back** indietreggiare; (return) tornare. **move forward** avanzare. **move in** occupare. **move out** uscire; (get closer) avvicinarsi. n mossa f, passo m; (house) trasloco m. **movable** adj movibile. **movement** n movimento m; (sign) cenno m; (tech) meccanismo m. **moving** adj commovente; (in motion) in moto.

**movie** ['muːvi] n (US) film m invar.

***mow** [mou] v falciare.

**mown** [moun] V **mow**.

**Mr** ['mistə] n signor m.

**Mrs** ['misiz] n signora f.

**much** [mʌtʃ] pron, adj molto. adv molto, assai. **as much as** (tanto) quanto. **how much** quanto. **so much** tanto. **too much** troppo.

**muck** [mʌk] n letame m; (coll: filth) porcheria f. v **muck about** (coll) bighellonare. **muck up** (coll) rovinare.

**mucus** ['mju:kəs] *n* muco *m*. **mucous membrane** mucosa *f*.

**mud** [mʌd] *n* fango *m*. **mudguard** *n* parafango *m*. **mudslinger** *n* maldicente *m, f*. **muddy** *adj* fangoso, inzaccherato.

**muddle** ['mʌdl] *n* confusione *f*, pasticcio *m*. *v* **muddle through** arrabattarsi. **muddle up** confondere. **muddler** *n* confusionario, -a *m, f*.

**muff** [mʌf] *n* manicotto *m*. *v* mancare, sbagliare.

**muffle** ['mʌfl] *v* smorzare, attutire.

**mug** [mʌg] *n* (*cup*) tazza *f*; (*coll: face*) muso *m*, ceffo *m*; (*slang: fool*) gonzo *m*. *v* assalire. **mugger** *n* rapinatore *m*, ladro *m*.

**mulberry** ['mʌlbəri] *n* (*fruit*) mora di gelso *f*; (*tree*) gelso *m*.

**mule¹** [mju:l] *n* (*zool*) mulo *m*. **mulish** *adj* (*stubborn*) duro.

**mule²** [mju:l] *n* (*slipper*) ciabatta *f*, pianella *f*.

**mullet** ['mʌlit] *n* (*grey*) muggine *m*; (*red*) triglia *f*.

**multicoloured** [,mʌlti'kʌləd] *adj* multicolore.

**multimillionaire** [,mʌltimiljə'neə] *n* multimilionario, -a *m, f*.

**multiple** ['mʌltipl] *adj* multiplo, molteplice. *n* multiplo *m*.

**multiply** ['mʌltiplai] *v* moltiplicare. **multiplication** *n* moltiplicazione *f*. **multiplicity** *n* varietà *f*.

**multiracial** [,mʌlti'reiʃəl] *adj* multirazziale.

**multitude** ['mʌltitju:d] *n* moltitudine *f*, massa *f*.

**mum** [mʌm] *adj* **keep mum** star zitto.

**mumble** ['mʌmbl] *v* borbottare.

**mummy¹** ['mʌmi] *n* (*corpse*) mummia *f*. **mummify** *v* mummificare.

**mummy²** ['mʌmi] *n* (*coll: mother*) mamma *f*, mammina *f*.

**mumps** [mʌmps] *n* orecchioni *m pl*.

**munch** [mʌntʃ] *v* sgranocchiare.

**mundane** [mʌn'dein] *adj* mondano.

**municipal** [mju'nisipəl] *adj* municipale. **municipality** *n* comune *m*.

**mural** ['mjuərəl] *n* pittura murale *f*.

**murder** ['mə:də] *n* assassinio *m*. *v* assassinare, ammazzare; (*coll*) massacrare. **murderer** *n* assassino *m*. **murderess** *n* assassina *f*. **murderous** *adj* micidiale.

**murmur** ['mə:mə] *n* mormorio *m*. *v* mormorare.

**muscle** ['mʌsl] *n* muscolo *m*.

**muse¹** [mju:z] *n* musa *f*.

**muse²** [mju:z] *v* meditare, riflettere.

**museum** [mju'ziəm] *n* museo *m*.

**mushroom** ['mʌʃrum] *n* fungo *m*. *v* (*gather*) raccogliere funghi; (*spread*) dilagare, svilupparsi rapidamente.

**music** ['mju:zik] *n* musica *f*. **musician** *n* musicista *m, f*.

**musical** ['mju:zikl] *adj* musicale; (*gifted*) dotato per la musica. *n* musical *m invar*.

**musk** [mʌsk] *n* (*zool*) muschio *m*.

**musket** ['mʌskit] *n* moschetto *m*.

**Muslim** ['mʌzlim] *n, adj* musulmano, -a.

**muslin** ['mʌzlin] *n* mussola *f*.

**mussel** ['mʌsl] *n* mitilo *m*, cozza *f*.

***must¹** [mʌst] *v* dovere. *n* (*coll*) cosa essenziale *f*.

**must²** [mʌst] *n* (*wine*) mosto *m*.

**mustard** ['mʌstəd] *n* senape *f*, mostarda *f*.

**muster** ['mʌstə] *v* radunare. **muster up courage** farsi coraggio. *n* **pass muster** essere accettabile.

**mute** [mju:t] *adj* muto, taciturno. *n* muto, -a *m, f*; (*music*) sordina *f*.

**mutilate** ['mju:tileit] *v* mutilare, mozzare. **mutilation** *n* mutilazione *f*.

**mutiny** ['mju:tini] *n* ammutinamento *m*, ribellione *f*. *v* ammutinarsi, ribellarsi. **mutinous** *adj* ammutinato, ribelle.

**mutter** ['mʌtə] *v* brontolare, borbottare.

**mutton** ['mʌtn] *n* carne ovina *f*, castrato *m*. **dead as mutton** morto stecchito.

**mutual** ['mju:tʃuəl] *adj* mutuo, reciproco; comune.

**muzzle** ['mʌzl] *n* (*gun*) imboccatura *f*; (*animal*) muso *m*; (*device*) museruola *f*. *v* mettere la museruola a; (*silence*) far tacere.

**my** [mai] *adj* (il) mio, (la) mia; (*pl*) (i) miei, (le) mie.

**myself** [mai'self] *pron* io stesso; (*after prep*) me stesso; (*reflexive*) mi.

**myopia** [mai'oupiə] *n* miopia *f*. **myopic** *adj* miope.

**mystery** ['mistəri] *n* mistero *m*, segreto *m*. **mysterious** *adj* misterioso, strano.

**mystic** ['mistik] *n* mistico, -a *m, f*. **mystical** *adj* mistico, misterioso. **mysticism** *n* misticismo *m*, mistica *f*.

**mystify** ['mistifai] v mistificare, disorientare.

**mystique** [mi'sti:k] n mistica f.

**myth** [miθ] n mito m. **mythical** adj mitico. **mythological** adj mitologico. **mythology** n mitologia f.

# N

**nag**[1] [nag] v rimbrottare, brontolare. **nagging** adj bisbetico, irritante, fastidioso.

**nag**[2] [nag] n ronzino m.

**nail** [neil] n (anat) unghia f; (metal) chiodo m. **nail-brush** n spazzolino per le unghie m. **nail-file** n lima per le unghie f. **nail polish** smalto per le unghie m. **nail-scissors** pl n forbici per le unghie f pl.

**naive** [nai'i:v] adj ingenuo. **naivety** n ingenuità f.

**naked** ['neikid] adj nudo, scoperto. **strip naked** spogliare. **nakedness** n nudità f.

**name** [neim] v chiamare. n nome m. **go by the name of** chiamarsi. **my name is ...** mi chiamo .... **namesake** n omonimo m. **nameless** adj anonimo. **namely** adv cioè.

**nanny** ['nani] n bambinaia f.

**nap**[1] [nap] n (doze) pisolino m. v fare or schiacciare un pisolino.

**nap**[2] [nap] n (cloth) pelo m.

**nape** [neip] n nuca f.

**napkin** ['napkin] n tovagliolo m.

**nappy** ['napi] n pannolino m.

**narcotic** [naːˈkotik] nm, adj narcotico.

**narrate** [nəˈreit] v narrare, raccontare. **narration** n racconto m. **narrative** n narrativa f. **narrator** n narratore, -trice m, f.

**narrow** ['narou] adj stretto; limitato; (person, mind, etc.) ristretto. **narrow-gauge** adj (railway) a scartamento ridotto. **narrow-minded** adj gretto, di mente ristretta. v restringere, limitare. **narrowly** adv per un pelo, a stento.

**nasal** ['neizəl] adj nasale.

**nasturtium** [nəˈstəːʃəm] n nasturzio m.

**nasty** ['naːsti] adj (filthy) disgustoso; (offensive) ripugnante; (unpleasant) cattivo, sgradevole. **nastiness** n cattiveria f.

**nation** ['neiʃən] n nazione f. **national** adj nazionale. **national insurance** assicurazione sociale f. **nationalism** n nazionalismo m. **nationalist** n(m+f), adj nazionalista. **nationality** n nazionalità f. **nationalization** n nazionalizzazione f. **nationalize** v nazionalizzare.

**native** ['neitiv] n, adj (original inhabitant) indigeno, -a; (of town, etc.) nativo, -a, oriundo, -a.

**nativity** [nəˈtivəti] n natività f.

**natural** ['natʃərəl] adj naturale; normale; istintivo. **naturalization** n naturalizzazione f. **naturalize** v naturalizzare.

**nature** ['neitʃə] n natura f; (condition) indole f; disposizione f.

**naught** [noːt] n nulla m. **come to naught** ridurre a zero.

**naughty** ['noːti] adj cattivo; (mischievous) birichino; indecente, spinto.

**nausea** ['noːziə] n nausea f; fastidio m. **nauseous** adj nauseabondo, disgustoso.

**nautical** ['noːtikəl] adj nautico.

**naval** ['neivəl] adj navale, marittimo.

**nave**[1] [neiv] n (of church) navata f.

**nave**[2] [neiv] n (hub) mozzo m.

**navel** ['neivəl] n ombelico m.

**navigate** ['navigeit] v navigare, pilotare. **navigable** adj navigabile. **navigation** n navigazione f. **navigator** n navigatore m; (officer) ufficiale di rotta m.

**navy** ['neivi] n marina militare f. **navy blue** adj blu marino.

**near** [niə] adj vicino. prep vicino a, accanto a. adv vicino. v avvicinare. **near at hand** a portata di mano. **near-sighted** adj miope. **nearby** adj, adv, prep vicino (a). **nearly** adv quasi.

**neat** [niːt] adj (orderly) ordinato, accurato; elegante; (undiluted) liscio. **neatness** n ordine m; eleganza f.

**nebulous** ['nebjuləs] adj vago, nebuloso.

**necessary** ['nesisəri] adj necessario, indispensabile. **necessity** n necessità f, bisogno m.

**neck** [nek] n (anat) collo m; (of dress) scollatura f. **have a stiff neck** avere il torcicollo. **neck and neck** testa a testa. **necklace** n collana f. **necktie** n cravatta f.

**nectar** ['nektə] n nettare m. **nectarine** n pesca noce f.

**nectarine** ['nektəri:n] n (pesca) nettarina f.

**née** [nei] adj nata.

**need** [ni:d] *n* bisogno *m*, necessità *f*; *(poverty)* miseria *f*. **if need be** caso mai, se c'è bisogno. *v* aver bisogno di; *(require)* richiedere. **needed** *adj* necessario. **needless** *adj* inutile, superfluo. **needy** *adj* indigente, bisognoso.

**needle** ['ni:dl] *n* ago *m*; *(knitting)* ferro *m*; *(gramophone)* puntina *f*. **needlework** *n* *(sewing)* cucitura *f*; *(embroidery)* ricamo *m*. *v* *(coll)* punzecchiare.

**negative** ['negətiv] *adj* negativo. *n* negativa *f*. **answer in the negative** rispondere di no.

**neglect** [ni'glekt] *n* negligenza *f*, trascuratezza *f*. *v* trascurare. **neglect to** mancare di. **neglectful** *adj* negligente. **negligible** *adj* trascurabile.

**negligée** ['negliʒei] *n* negligé *m invar*, vestaglia *f*.

**negotiate** [ni'gouʃieit] *v* trattare, negoziare; *(obstacle, etc.)* superare. **negotiable** *adj* negoziabile. **negotiation** *n* trattativa *f*, negoziato *m*.

**Negro** ['ni:grou] *nm*, *adj* negro. **Negress** *n* negra *f*.

**neigh** [nei] *v* nitrire. *n* nitrito *m*.

**neighbour** ['neibə] *n* vicino, -a *m*, *f*. **next-door neighbour** vicino di casa *m*. **neighbourhood** *n* vicinanza *f*, paraggi *m pl*. **neighbouring** *adj* adiacente, vicino. **neighbourly** *adj* socievole, da buon vicino.

**neither** ['naiðə] *adj* nè l'uno nè l'altro. *adv* **neither ... nor ...** nè ... nè ... *pron* nessuno, nè l'uno nè l'altro.

**neon** ['ni:on] *n* neon *m*.

**nephew** ['nefju:] *n* nipote *m*.

**nepotism** ['nepətizəm] *n* nepotismo *m*.

**nerve** [nə:v] *n* nervo *m*; coraggio *m*; *(coll: cheek)* sfacciataggine *f*, faccia tosta *f*. **get on the nerves of** dare sui nervi a. **nerve-racking** *adj* snervante. **nervous** *adj* nervoso; apprensivo. **get nervous** inquietarsi. **nervous breakdown** esaurimento nervoso *m*.

**nest** [nest] *n* nido *m*. **nest egg** gruzzolo *m*. *v* annidarsi.

**nestle** ['nesl] *v* annidarsi, accoccolarsi.

**net¹** [net] *n* rete *f*. **network** *n* rete *f*. *v* *(enclose)* cintare con reti; *(catch)* prendere con reti; *(ball)* mandare in rete. **netting** *n* reticolato *m*.

**net²** [net] *adj* netto.

**Netherlands** ['neðələndz] *pl n* Paesi Bassi *m pl*.

**nettle** ['netl] *n* ortica *f*. **nettle-rash** *n* orticaria *f*. *v* irritare.

**neurosis** [nju'rousis] *n* nevrosi *f*. **neurotic** *n*, *adj* nevrotico, -a.

**neuter** ['nju:tə] *adj* neutro. *v* castrare.

**neutral** ['nju:trəl] *adj* neutrale; *(tech)* neutro. *n* neutrale *m*, *f*. **neutrality** *n* neutralità *f*. **neutralize** *v* neutralizzare. **neutron** *n* neutrone *m*.

**never** ['nevə] *adv* (non ...) mai. **never-ending** *adj* interminabile.

**nevertheless** [nevəðə'les] *adv*, *conj* ciononostante, tuttavia.

**new** [nju:] *adj* nuovo. **new-born** *adj* neonato. **newcomer** *n* nuovo venuto, nuova venuta *m*, *f*.

**news** [nju:z] *n* novità *f pl*, notizie *f pl*, informazioni *f pl*. **news agency** agenzia d'informazioni *f*. **newsagent** *n* giornalaio *m*. **news bulletin** notiziario *m*; *(radio)* giornale radio *m*. **news item** notizia *f*. **newspaper** *n* giornale *m*. **newsprint** *n* carta da giornale *f*. **newsreel** *n* cinegiornale *m*.

**newt** [nju:t] *n* tritone *m*.

**New Year** *n* Anno nuovo *m*. **Happy New Year!** Buon Anno! **New Year's Day** il Capodanno *m*. **New Zealand** *n* Nuova Zelanda *f*. **New Zealander** neozelandese *m*, *f*.

**next** [nekst] *adj* prossimo; *(nearest)* più vicino; *(following)* successivo, seguente. *adv* *(after)* dopo, poi; *(later)* in seguito. **next-of-kin** *n* parente prossimo *m*, *f*.

**nib** [nib] *n* pennino *m*.

**nibble** ['nibl] *n* *(morsel)* bocconcino *m*. *v* rosicchiare.

**nice** [nais] *adj* bello; piacevole, simpatico; *(subtle)* sottile; delicato; *(refined)* elegante, fine. **nicely** *adv* proprio bene. **nicety** *n* esattezza *f*. **niceties** *pl n* finezze *f pl*, sfumature *f pl*.

**niche** [nitʃ] *n* nicchia *f*.

**nick** [nik] *v* intaccare; *(slang: steal)* arraffare; *(slang: catch)* acchiappare. *n* tacca *f*. **in the nick of time** all'ultimo momento.

**nickel** ['nikl] *n* nichel *m*; *(US: coin)* nichelino *m*.

**nickname** ['nikneim] *n* nomignolo *m*, soprannome *m*. *v* soprannominare.

**nicotine** ['nikəti:n] *n* nicotina *f*.

**niece** [niːs] n nipote f.

**niggling** ['niglin] adj insignificante.

**night** [nait] n notte f; (evening) sera f. **have a good/bad night** dormir bene/male. **night-club** n night m invar. **nightdress** n camicia da notte f. **nightfall** n tramonto m. **nightmare** n incubo m. **nightmarish** adj opprimente, spaventoso. **stay the night** pernottare.

**nightingale** ['naitiŋ,geil] n usignolo m.

**nightly** ['naitli] adj notturno; (every night) di tutte le sere. adv ogni notte or sera.

**nil** [nil] n nulla m, niente m, zero m.

**nimble** ['nimbl] adj agile, svelto. **nimbleness** n agilità f.

**nine** [nain] nm, adj nove. **ninepins** n birilli m pl. **ninth** nm, adj nono.

**nineteen** [nain'tiːn] nm, adj diciannove. **nineteenth** nm, adj diciannovesimo.

**ninety** ['nainti] nm, adj novanta. **ninetieth** nm, adj novantesimo.

**nip¹** [nip] v pizzicare; (bite) morsicare. **nip in** intromettersi, entrare lestamente. **nip in the bud** stroncare sul nascere. **nip out** fare un salto. n (frost) gelo m; (bite) morso m. **nippy** adj (speedy) svelto; (cold) frizzante.

**nip²** [nip] n (drop) bicchierino m, sorso m.

**nipple** ['nipl] n capezzolo m; (tech) rubinetto m.

**nit** [nit] n lendine m; (coll) stupido, -a m, f.

**nitrogen** ['naitrədʒən] n azoto m.

**no** [nou] adj nessuno, neppure uno; (forbidden) vietato. adv no; (with comparative) non. n no m invar.

**noble** ['noubl] n(m+f), adj nobile. **nobility** n nobiltà f.

**nobody** ['noubodi] pron nessuno. n zero m, sconosciuto, -a m, f.

**nocturnal** [nok'təːnəl] adj notturno.

**nod** [nod] n cenno col capo m. v fare un cenno col capo; (doze) sonnecchiare; (assent) annuire; (greet) salutare. **nodding acquaintance** conoscenza superficiale f.

**noise** [noiz] n rumore m; (loud) baccano m. **background noise** rumori di fondo m pl. **big noise** (coll) pezzo grosso m. **noiseless** adj silenzioso. **noisy** adj rumoroso, chiassoso.

**nomad** ['noumad] n(m+f), adj nomade.

**nominal** ['nominl] adj nominale; simbolico.

**nominate** ['nomineit] v nominare; (propose) proporre. **nomination** n nomina f.

**nominative** ['nominətiv] nm, adj nominativo.

**nonchalant** ['nonʃələnt] adj indifferente, noncurante. **nonchalance** n indifferenza f, noncuranza f.

**nonconformist** [nonkən'foːmist] n(m+f), adj dissidente, anti-conformista.

**nondescript** ['nondiskript] adj inclassificabile, qualunque.

**none** [nʌn] pron nessuno, nulla, niente. adv affatto, punto. **none other than** nientedimeno che.

**nonentity** [non'entəti] n nullità f, zero m.

**nonetheless** [,nʌnðə'les] adv ciononostante, tuttavia.

**nonsense** ['nonsəns] n nonsenso m, assurdo m; (coll) sciocchezze f pl. **nonsensical** adj assurdo, sciocco. **talk nonsense** dire sciocchezze.

**non-stick** [non'stik] adj antiaderente.

**non-stop** [non'stop] adj continuo, ininterrotto.

**noodles** ['nuːdlz] pl n tagliatelle f pl, taglierini m pl.

**nook** [nuk] n cantuccio m, angolo m.

**noon** [nuːn] n mezzogiorno m.

**no-one** ['nouwʌn] pron nessuno.

**noose** [nuːs] n nodo scorsoio m, laccio m.

**nor** [noː] conj nè, neppure, nemmeno.

**norm** [noːm] n norma f, modello m. **normal** adj normale, regolare. **normally** adv di solito.

**north** [noːθ] n nord m, settentrione m. adj also **northern** del nord, settentrionale. **northerly** adj di nordo; da nordo; a nordo. **north-east** n nordest m. **north-eastern** del nordest. **north-west** n nordovest m. **north-western** del nordovest.

**Northern Ireland** n Irlanda del Nord f.

**Norway** ['noːwei] n Norvegia f. **Norwegian** n(m+f), adj norvegese.

**nose** [nouz] n naso m; (of animal, aeroplane, etc.) muso m. v fiutare. **nose around** esplorare. **nosy** adj (coll) curioso.

**nostalgia** [no'staldʒə] n nostalgia f, rimpianto m. **nostalgic** adj nostalgico.

**nostril** ['nostrəl] n narice f.

**not** [not] adv non. **not at all** niente affatto. **not even** neppure, neanche.

**notable** ['noutəbl] *adj* notevole, degno di nota.

**notary** ['noutəri] *n* notaio *m*.

**notch** [notʃ] *n* tacca *f*, intaglio *m*. *v* intaccare.

**note** [nout] *n* nota *f*, appunto *m*, commento *m*; (*money*) biglietto *m*. **note-book** *n* taccuino *m*. **notepaper** *n* carta da lettere *or* scrivere. **noteworthy** *adj* degno di nota, notevole. **take note of** prendere atto di. **take notes** prendere appunti. **notation** *n* notazione *f*. *v* notare; osservare. **noted** *adj* noto, rinomato.

**nothing** ['nʌθiŋ] *n* niente *m*, zero *m*. *adv* per nulla, niente (affatto). **next to nothing** quasi nulla. **nothing but** null'altro che. **nothing less than** semplicemente.

**notice** ['noutis] *n* avviso *m*, annuncio *m*; (*advance warning*) preavviso *m*; (*criticism*) recensione *f*. **give notice** (*dismiss*) licenziare. **notice-board** *n* tabellone *m*. **take notice of** fare attenzione a. *v* notare, rilevare. **noticeable** *adj* apparente, percettibile.

**notify** ['noutifai] *v* notificare, avvertire. **notification** *n* notifica *f*.

**notion** ['noufən] *n* nozione *f*, idea *f*.

**notorious** [nou'to:riəs] *adj* notorio, famigerato. **notoriety** *n* notorietà *f*.

**notwithstanding** [notwið'standiŋ] *prep* nonostante, malgrado. *adv* ciononostante, con tutto ciò.

**nougat** ['nu:ga:] *n* torrone *m*.

**nought** [no:t] *n* zero *m*.

**noun** [naun] *n* nome *m*, sostantivo *m*.

**nourish** ['nʌriʃ] *v* nutrire, alimentare. **nourishing** *adj* nutriente. nutritivo. **nourishment** *n* cibo *m*, alimento *m*.

**novel¹** ['novəl] *n* romanzo *m*. **novelist** *n* romanziere, -a *m*, *f*.

**novel²** ['novəl] *adj* nuovo, originale; (*unusual*) insolito. **novelty** *n* novità *f*.

**November** [nə'vembə] *n* novembre *m*.

**novice** ['novis] *n* novizio, -a *m*, *f*.

**now** [nau] *adv* ora, adesso. **from now on** d'ora in poi. **just now** or ora. **nowadays** *adv* oggigiorno, al giorno d'oggi. **now and again** ogni tanto, di quando in quando. **until now** finora.

**nowhere** ['nouweə] *adv* in nessun luogo.

**noxious** ['nokʃəs] *adj* nocivo, malefico.

**nozzle** ['nozl] *n* (*spout*) becco *m*; (*tech*) ugello *m*.

**nuance** ['nju:ãs] *n* sfumatura *f*.

**nuclear** ['nju:kliə] *adj* nucleare.

**nucleus** ['nju:kliəs] *n* nucleo *m*.

**nude** ['nju:d] *n*, *adj* nudo, -a. **nudism** *n* nudismo *m*. **nudist** *n* nudista *m*, *f*. **nudity** *n* nudità *f*.

**nudge** [nʌdʒ] *n* colpetto *m*. *v* dare un colpetto a.

**nugget** ['nʌgit] *n* pepita *f*.

**nuisance** ['nju:sns] *n* fastidio *m*, seccatura *f*; (*law*) infrazione *f*. **make a nuisance of oneself** seccare tutti.

**null** [nʌl] *adj* nullo. **null and void** senza validità legale.

**numb** [nʌm] *adj* intorpidito; (*stunned*) intontito. *v* intorpidire, paralizzare. **numbness** *n* torpore *m*.

**number** ['nʌmbə] *n* numero *m*; (*numeral*) cifra *f*; quantità *f*. **number plate** targa *f*. *v* numerare, contare. **numberless** *adj* innumerevole.

**numeral** ['nju:mərəl] *n* cifra *f*.

**numerical** [nju:'merikl] *adj* numerico.

**numerous** ['nju:mərəs] *adj* numeroso.

**nun** [nʌn] *n* monaca *f*, suora *f*. **become a nun** prendere il velo. **nunnery** *n* convento *m*.

**nurse** [nə:s] *v* curare, fare l'infermiere; (*suckle*) allattare; (*hope, grievance, etc.*) nutrire, covare. *n* infermiere, -a *m*, *f*; (*children's*) balia *f*, bambinaia *f*. **nursing** *n* professione d'infermiera *f*. **nursing home** casa di cura *f*, clinica *f*.

**nursery** ['nə:səri] *n* (*children's*) camera dei bambini *f*; (*plants, etc.*) vivaio *m*, serra *f*. **day nursery** asilo infantile *m*. **nursery rhyme** filastrocca *f*. **nursery school** giardino d'infanzia *m*.

**nurture** ['nə:tʃə] *v* (*feed*) nutrire; (*rear*) allevare. *n* nutrimento *m*; allevamento *m*.

**nut** [nʌt] *n* noce *f*; (*tech*) dado *m*; (*coll: head*) zucca *f*. **be nuts** (*coll*) essere matto. **in a nutshell** in poche parole. **nutcrackers** *pl n* schiaccianoci *m invar*. **nutmeg** *n* noce moscata *f*. **nut-tree** *n* noce *m*.

**nutrient** ['nju:triənt] *adj* nutriente. *n* nutrimento *m*.

**nutrition** [nju:'triʃən] *n* alimentazione *f*. **nutritious** *adj* nutriente.

**nuzzle** ['nʌzl] *v* accucciolarsi, rannicchiarsi.

**nylon** ['nailon] *n* nailon *m*.

**nymph** [nimf] *n* ninfa f. **nymphomaniac** *n* ninfomane f.

# O

**oak** [ouk] *n* quercia f.

**oar** [o:] *n* remo m.

**oasis** [ou'eisis] *n*, *pl* -**ses** oasi f invar.

**oath** [ouθ] *n* (*promise*) giuramento m; (*profanity*) bestemmia f.

**oats** [outs] *pl n* avena f *sing*. **oatmeal** *n* farina d'avena f.

**obedient** [ə'bi:diənt] *adj* ubbidiente, obbediente. **obedience** *n* ubbidienza f, obbedienza f

**obese** [ə'bi:s] *adj* obeso. **obesity** *n* obesità f.

**obey** [ə'bei] *v* ubbidire, obbedire.

**obituary** [ə'bitjuəri] *n* necrologia f.

**object** ['obʒikt; *v* əb'ʒekt] *n* oggetto m; (*aim*) scopo m. *v* obiettare, protestare. **objection** *n* obiezione f, protesta f. **have no objection to** aver nulla in contrario a. **objectionable** *adj* offensivo, sgradevole, riprensibile. **objective** *nm*, *adj* obiettivo.

**oblige** [ə'blaidʒ] *v* costringere, obbligare; fare un favore a. **be obliged to** (*have to*) dovere; (*be grateful to*) essere riconoscente a. **obligation** *n* (*law*) obbligazione f; (*binding promise*) obbligo (*pl* -ghi) m; (*duty*) dovere m. **obligatory** *adj* obbligatorio. **obliging** *adj* cortese, accomodante.

**oblique** [ə'bli:k] *adj* obliquo; indiretto.

**obliterate** [ə'blitəreit] *v* obliterare, cancellare; (*destroy*) distruggere. **obliteration** *n* distruzione f.

**oblivion** [ə'bliviən] *n* oblio m. **oblivious** *adj* dimentico (*m pl* -chi).

**oblong** ['oblon] *adj* bislungo.

**obnoxious** [əb'nokʃəs] *adj* odioso, offensivo.

**oboe** ['oubou] *n* oboe m. **oboist** *n* oboista m, f.

**obscene** [əb'si:n] *adj* osceno. **obscenity** *n* oscenità f.

**obscure** [əb'skjuə] *adj* (*not clear*) ambiguo, oscuro; (*inconspicuous*) vago. *v* offuscare, velare. **obscurity** *n* oscurità f.

**observe** [əb'zə:v] *v* (*see*) osservare; notare, rilevare; (*rel*) praticare. **observance** *n* osservanza f. **observant** *adj* osservante. **observation** *n* osservazione f, attenzione f. **keep under observation** tenere in osservazione. **observatory** *n* osservatorio m. **observer** *n* osservatore, -trice m, f.

**obsess** [əb'ses] *v* ossessionare. **obsession** *n* ossessione f. **obsessive** *adj* ossessivo.

**obsolescent** [obsə'lesnt] *adj* che sta cadendo in disuso.

**obsolete** ['obsəli:t] *adj* caduto in disuso; antiquato.

**obstacle** ['obstəkl] *n* ostacolo m.

**obstetrics** [ob'stetriks] *n* ostetricia f. **obstetrician** *n* ostetrico, -a m.

**obstinate** ['obstinət] *adj* ostinato. **obstinacy** *n* ostinatezza f.

**obstreperous** [əb'strepərəs] *adj* ribelle.

**obstruct** [əb'strʌkt] *v* impacciare, ostacolare. **obstruction** *n* impaccio m, ostacolo m.

**obtain** [əb'tein] *v* ottenere, procurare. **obtainable** *adj* ottenibile, raggiungibile.

**obtrusive** [əb'tru:siv] *adj* importuno; invadente. **obtrusion** *n* invadenza f.

**obtuse** [əb'tju:s] *adj* ottuso.

**obverse** ['obvə:s] *n* faccia f, diritto m; (*counterpart*) inverso m.

**obvious** ['obviəs] *adj* ovvio, evidente. **obviously** *adv* ovviamente.

**occasion** [ə'keiʒən] *v* causare. *n* (*time*) occasione f, volta f; (*cause*) motivo m, ragione f. **rise to the occasion** mostrarsi all'altezza. **occasional** *adj* saltuario, sporadico. **occasionally** *adv* ogni tanto.

**occult** ['okʌlt] *adj* occulto. *n* forze occulte f pl.

**occupy** ['okjupai] *v* occupare. **occupant** or **occupier** *n* occupante m, f. **occupation** *n* occupazione f; (*trade*) mestiere m, professione f. **occupational** *adj* del lavoro, professionale.

**occur** [ə'kə:] *v* succedere, capitare; (*come to mind*) venire in mente. **occurrence** *n* avvenimento m, caso m.

**ocean** ['ouʃən] *n* oceano m.

**ochre** ['oukə] *n* ocra f. *adj* (*color*) ocra.

**o'clock** [ə'klok] *adv* **one o'clock** l'una. **two/three/etc. o'clock** le due/tre/etc.

**octagon** ['oktəgən] *n* ottagono m. **octagonal** *adj* ottagonale.

**octane** ['oktein] *n* ottano m.

**octave** ['oktiv] n ottava f.

**October** [ok'toubə] n ottobre m.

**octopus** ['oktəpəs] n polpo m.

**oculist** ['okjulist] n oculista m, f.

**odd** [od] adj (not even) dispari; (not paired) scompagnato; (strange) strano, bizzarro; casuale; (approximately) circa. **oddity** n stranezza f; (person) eccentrico, -a m, f. **odd-ments** pl n rimasugli m pl, scampoli m pl.

**odds** [odz] pl n probabilità f pl, differenza f sing; (betting) posta f sing. **be at odds with** essere in disaccordo con. **lay odds** scommettere. **odds and ends** cosette varie f pl, rimasugli m pl.

**ode** [oud] n ode f.

**odious** ['oudiəs] adj odioso.

**odour** ['oudə] n odore m. **odourless** adj inodoro.

**oesophagus** [i:'sofəgəs] n esofago m.

**of** [ov] prep di.

**off** [of] adv via, distante. prep lontano da, fuori (di). adj (holiday) libero; (food) marcio, non buono. **be off** (cancelled) non aver luogo.

**offal** ['ofəl] n frattaglie f pl.

**offend** [ə'fend] v offendere. **offence** n offesa f; (law) infrazione alla legge f. **take offence** offendersi. **offender** n colpevole m, f; trasgreditore, -trice m, f.

**offensive** [ə'fensiv] adj offensivo; (disagreeable) sgradevole; insolente. n offensiva f.

**offer** ['ofə] v offrire, presentare, dare. n offerta f, proposta f. **on offer** in offerta.

**offhand** [of'hand] adj noncurante. adv all'improvviso.

**office** ['ofis] n (place) ufficio m; (post, function) carica f. **head office** n sede (centrale) f. **officer** n funzionario, -a m, f; (mil, etc.) ufficiale m.

**official** [ə'fiʃəl] adj ufficiale. n funzionario, -a m, f.

**officious** [ə'fiʃəs] adj inframmettente, invadente.

**offing** ['ofin] n **in the offing** in vista.

**off-line** [of'lain] adj fuori linea, scollegato.

**off-load** [of'loud] v scaricare.

**off-peak** [of'pi:k] adj non di punta.

**off-putting** ['of,putin] adj sconcertante, che lascia perplesso.

**off-road vehicle** ['ofroud] n fuoristrada m.

**off-season** [of'si:zn] adj fuori stagione.

**offset** [of'set; n 'ofset] v compensare, controbilanciare. n (print) offset m invar.

**offshoot** ['ofʃu:t] n ramo m.

**offshore** ['ofʃo:] adv al largo. adj di terra.

**offside** [of'said] adv, adj fuori gioco.

**offspring** ['ofsprin] n prole f; frutto m.

**offstage** ['ofsteidʒ] adv, adj fuori scena.

**often** ['ofn] adv spesso, sovente, molte volte. **how often** quante volte. **too often** troppe volte.

**ogre** ['ougə] n orco m.

**oil** [oil] n olio m; petrolio m; gasolio m. **oil-field** n giacimento petrolifero m. **oilfired** adj a gasolio or nafta. **oil-painting** n pittura a olio f. **oilskin** n tela impermeabile f. **oil-well** n pozzo petrolifero m. v ungere, lubrificare. **oily** adj oleoso, untuoso.

**ointment** ['ointmənt] n unguento m.

**old** [ould] adj vecchio, antico (m pl -chi); (not new) usato. **old age** vecchiaia f. **old-fashioned** adj fuori moda. **old man** vecchio m. **old people** vecchi m pl. **old woman** vecchia f. **oldish** adj vecchiotto.

**olive** ['oliv] n oliva f. **olive green** adj verde oliva. **olive grove** oliveto m. **olive oil** olio d'oliva m. **olive-tree** n olivo m.

**Olympic** [ə'limpik] adj olimpico. **Olympic Games** olimpiadi f pl.

**omelette** ['omlit] n frittata f.

**omen** ['oumən] n presagio m, segno m.

**ominous** ['ominəs] adj sinistro, minaccioso.

**omit** [ou'mit] v omettere, tralasciare. **omission** n omissione f.

**omnipotent** [om'nipətənt] adj onnipotente. **omnipotence** n onnipotenza f.

**on** [on] prep su, sopra; a. adv su. adj (gas, elec, etc.) acceso; (tap) aperto.

**once** [wʌns] adv una volta. **all at once** ad un tratto. **at once** subito.

**one** [wʌn] n, adj uno, -a. pron uno; (impersonal) si. **oneself** pron sè (stesso); (reflexive) si. **one by one** a uno a uno. **one-off** adj unico, straordinario. **one-sided** adj unilaterale; parziale; ineguale. **one-way street** senso unico m. **the one** quello, -a. **which one?** quale?

**ongoing** adv in corso.

**onion** ['ʌnjən] n cipolla f.

**on-line** [on'lain] adj in linea, collegato.

**onlooker** ['onlukə] n spettatore, -trice m, f.

**only** ['ounli] *adj* solo, unico. *conj* ma. *adv* solo, soltanto. **only just** appena.

**onset** ['onset] *n* inizio *m*.

**onshore** ['onʃo:] *adv* a terra.

**onslaught** ['onslo:t] *n* attacco *m*, assalto *m*.

**onus** ['ounəs] *n* onere *m*, obbligo (*pl* -ghi) *m*.

**onward** ['onwəd] *adj* che progredisce *or* avanza. **onwards** *adv* (in) avanti.

**onyx** ['oniks] *n* onice *m*.

**ooze** [u:z] *v* colare, trasudare.

**opal** ['oupəl] *n* opale *m*.

**opaque** [ə'paik] *adj* opaco (*m pl* -chi). **opacity** *n* opacità *f*.

**open** ['oupən] *v* aprire; iniziare; inaugurare. **open wide** spalancare. *nm, adj* aperto. **lay oneself open to** esporsi a. **open-handed** *adj* generoso. **open-hearted** *adj* sincero. **open-minded** *adj* spregiudicato, libero da preconcetti. **open-mouthed** *adj, adv* a bocca aperta.

**opening** ['oupənin] *adj* introduttivo, inaugurale. *n* apertura *f*; inaugurazione *f*.

**opera** ['opərə] *n* opera *f*. **opera glasses** binocoli da teatro *m pl*. **opera house** teatro dell'opera *m*. **opera singer** cantante lirico, -a *m, f*. **operetta** *n* operetta *f*.

**operate** ['opəreit] *v* operare. **operation** *n* operazione *f*; (*activity*) attività *f*; (*surgical*) intervento (chirurgico) *m*. **come into operation** entrare in vigore. **operative** *adj* operativo; attivo; (*surgical*) operatorio. **operator** *n* operatore, -trice *m, f*; (*phone*) telefonista *m, f*.

**ophthalmic** [of'θalmik] *adj* oftalmico.

**opinion** [ə'pinjən] *n* opinione *f*, parere *m*, giudizio *m*. **in the opinion of** secondo. **opinionated** *adj* dogmatico, intransigente.

**opium** ['oupiəm] *n* oppio *m*.

**opponent** [ə'pounənt] *n* avversario, -a *m, f*.

**opportune** [opə'tju:n] *adj* opportuno, giusto.

**opportunity** [opə'tju:nəti] *n* occasione *f*.

**oppose** [ə'pouz] *v* opporre, combattere; contrastare. **opposed** *adj* opposto, contrario. **opposition** *n* opposizione *f*.

**opposite** ['opəzit] *nm, adj* opposto, contrario. *prep* di fronte a, dirimpetto a.

**oppress** [ə'pres] *v* opprimere. **oppression** *n* oppressione *f*. **oppressive** *adj* oppressivo, opprimente. **oppressor** *n* oppressore *m*.

**opt** [opt] *v* optare. **opt out** decidere di non partecipare.

**optical** ['optikl] *adj* ottico. **optician** *n* ottico *m*. **optics** *n* ottica *f*.

**optimism** ['optimizəm] *n* ottimismo *m*. **optimist** *n* ottimista *m, f*. **optimistic** *adj* ottimistico.

**optimum** ['optiməm] *n* optimum *m*, meglio *m*. *adj* migliore.

**option** ['opʃən] *n* opzione *f*, scelta *f*. **optional** *adj* facoltativo.

**opulent** ['opjulənt] *adj* opulento. **opulence** *n* opulenza *f*.

**or** [o:] *conj* o, oppure. **either ... or ...** o ... o .... **or else** altrimenti.

**oracle** ['orəkl] *n* oracolo *m*.

**oral** ['o:rəl] *adj* orale.

**orange** ['orindʒ] *n* (*fruit*) arancia *f*; (*tree, colour*) arancio *m*. *adj* (*colour*) arancio, arancione. **orange juice** succo d'arancio *m*; (*drink*) spremuta d'arancio *f*. **orange squash** aranciata *f*.

**orator** ['orətə] *n* oratore, -trice *m, f*. **oration** *n* orazione *f*.

**orbit** ['o:bit] *n* orbita *f*.

**orchard** ['o:tʃəd] *n* frutteto *m*.

**orchestra** ['o:kəstrə] *n* orchestra *f*. **orchestral** *adj* orchestrale. **orchestrate** *v* orchestrare. **orchestration** *n* orchestrazione *f*.

**orchid** ['o:kid] *n* orchidea *f*.

**ordain** [o:'dein] *v* ordinare.

**ordeal** [o:'di:l] *n* dura prova *f*, travaglio *m*.

**order** ['o:də] *n* ordine *m*; comando *m*; classe *f*, grado *m*; (*commission*) ordinazione *f*. **in order that** affinché, perché. **in order to** per, allo scopo di. **out of order** guasto. *v* ordinare. **order about** mandar qua e là.

**orderly** ['o:dəli] *adj* ordinato, regolare. *n* attendente *m*, inserviente *m*.

**ordinal** ['o:dinl] *adj* ordinale.

**ordinary** ['o:dənəri] *nm, adj* ordinario, solito, comune.

**ore** [o:] *n* minerale *m*.

**oregano** [ori'ga:nou] *n* origano *m*.

**organ** ['o:gən] *n* organo *m*. **organ-pipe** *n* canna d'organo *f*. **organic** *adj* organico. **organist** *n* organista *m, f*.

**organism** ['o:gənizəm] *n* organismo *m*.

**organize** ['o:gənaiz] *v* organizzare. **organization** *n* organizzazione *f*. **organizer** *n* organizzatore, -trice *m, f*.

**orgasm** ['o:gazəm] *n* orgasmo *m*.

**orgy** ['ɔ:dʒi] *n* orgia *f*.

**orient** ['ɔ:riənt] *n* oriente *m*. *v* orientare. **oriental** *adj* orientale.

**orientate** ['ɔ:riənteit] *v* orientare. **orientation** *n* orientamento *m*.

**origin** ['ɔridʒin] *n* origine *f*. **originate** *v* originare. **originate from** derivare *or* provenire da. **originator** *n* creatore, -trice *m, f*; originatore, -trice *m, f*.

**original** [ə'ridʒinl] *adj* originale; (*authentic, primitive*) originario. *n* originale *m*. **originality** *n* originalità *f*. **originally** *adv* in origine.

**ornament** ['ɔ:nəmənt] *n* ornamento *m*; (*music*) abbellimento *m*; (*object, fitting*) suppellittile *f*. *v* abbellire. **ornamentation** *n* abbellimento *m*.

**ornate** [ɔ:'neit] *adj* ornato.

**ornithology** [ɔ:ni'θɔlədʒi] *n* ornitologia *f*. **ornithologist** *n* ornitologo, -a *m, f*.

**orphan** ['ɔ:fən] *n* orfano, -a *m, f*. *v* rendere orfano. **be orphaned** rimanere orfano. **orphanage** *n* orfanotrofio *m*.

**orthodox** ['ɔ:θədɔks] *adj* ortodosso. **orthodoxy** *n* ortodossia *f*.

**orthopaedic** [ɔ:θə'pi:dik] *adj* ortopedico. **orthopaedics** *n* ortopedia *f*. **orthopaedist** *n* ortopedico, -a *m, f*.

**oscillate** ['ɔsileit] *v* (far) oscillare; (*fluctuate*) vacillare. **oscillation** *n* oscillazione *f*.

**ostensible** [o'stensəbl] *adj* ostensibile.

**ostentatious** [osten'teiʃəs] *adj* ostentato, ostentoso.

**osteopath** ['ɔstiəpaθ] *n* osteologo, -a *m, f*.

**ostracize** ['ɔstrəsaiz] *v* osteggiare, mettere al bando.

**ostrich** ['ɔstritʃ] *n* struzzo *m*.

**other** ['ʌðə] *adj* altro, diverso. **on the other hand** d'altra parte. **other people** gli altri. *pron* altro. **each other** l'un l'altro.

**otherwise** ['ʌðəwaiz] *adv* altrimenti.

**otter** ['ɔtə] *n* lontra *f*.

**\*ought** [ɔ:t] *v* dovere.

**our** [auə] *adj* (il) nostro, (la) nostra; (*pl*) (i) nostri, (le) nostre.

**ours** [auəz] *pron* il nostro, la nostra; (*pl*) i nostri, le nostre.

**ourselves** [auə'selvz] *pron* noi (stessi); (*reflexive*) ci.

**oust** [aust] *v* espellere, soppiantare.

**out** [aut] *adj* (*not alight*) spetto. *adv* via, fuori; (*to the end*) alla fine. **feel out of it** sentirsi a disagio. **out of** (*without*) senza. **out of action** fuori servizio, guasto. **out of date** antiquato; (*ticket, etc.*) scaduto. **out of doors** all'aperto. **out of place** inopportuno. **out of pocket** in perdita. **out of print** esaurito, fuori stampa. **out of tune** stonato. **out of work** disoccupato.

**outboard** ['autbo:d] *adj* fuoribordo.

**outbreak** ['autbreik] *n* scoppio *m*; (*riot*) sommossa; eruzione *f*; epidemia *f*.

**outbuilding** ['autbildiŋ] *n* edificio annesso *m*, dipendenza *f*.

**outburst** ['autbə:st] *n* scoppio *m*; (*invective*) tirata *f*.

**outcast** ['autka:st] *n, adj* proscritto, -a, reietto, -a.

**outcome** ['autkʌm] *n* esito *m*, risultato *m*.

**outcry** ['autkrai] *n* grido *m*, scalpore *m*.

**outdated** [aut'deitid] *adj* fuori moda; antiquato.

**\*outdo** [aut'du:] *v* sorpassare.

**outdoor** ['autdo:] *adj* all'aperto.

**outer** ['autə] *adj* esterno, esteriore.

**outfit** ['autfit] *n* corredo *m*, equipaggiamento *m*; (*coll*) compagnia *f*.

**outgoing** ['autgouiŋ] *adj* uscente, in partenza; (*person*) estroverso, espansivo. **outgoings** *pl n* spese *f pl*.

**\*outgrow** [aut'grou] *v* (*grow taller than*) sorpassare in altezza; (*clothes*) diventare troppo grande per.

**outhouse** ['authaus] *n* fabbricato annesso *m*.

**outing** ['autiŋ] *n* gita *f*, scampagnata *f*.

**outlandish** [aut'landiʃ] *adj* esotico.

**outlast** [aut'la:st] *v* durare più a lungo di, sopravvivere a.

**outlaw** ['autlo:] *n* fuorilegge *m, f invar*. *v* mettere al bando, proscrivere.

**outlay** ['autlei] *n* spesa *f*, dispendio *m*.

**outlet** ['autlit] *n* sfogo *m*, sbocco *m*.

**outline** ['autlain] *v* delineare; (*draft*) abbozzare. *n* contorno *m*; (*general sketch*) abbozzo *m*. **outlines** *pl n* elementi *m pl*.

**outlive** [aut'liv] *v* sopravvivere a.

**outlook** ['autluk] *n* (*view*) veduta *f*; (*future prospect*) prospettiva *f*; (*mental view*) modo di vedere *m*, vedute *f pl*.

**outlying** ['autlaiiŋ] *adj* periferico, lontano.

**outnumber** [aut'nʌmbə] *v* superare

in numero.

**outpatient** ['autpeiʃənt] n paziente esterno or ambulatoriale m, f.

**outpost** ['autpoust] n avamposto m.

**output** ['autput] n produzione f; (yield) rendimento m.

**outrage** ['autreidʒ] n oltraggio m. v oltraggiare.

**outrageous** [aut'reidʒəs] adj (disgraceful) vergognoso; offensivo; (excessive) esagerato.

**outright** ['autrait; adv aut'rait] adj completo, categorico. adv (at once) subito; (entirely) completamente; (openly) apertamente.

**outset** ['autset] n at the outset al principio.

**outside** [aut'said; adj 'autsaid] adj esterno, esteriore; (extraneous) estraneo. adv fuori, all'aperto. prep fuori di; (except) all'infuori di. n esterno m. at the outside (coll) tutt'al più. **outsider** n estraneo m; (sport) outsider m invar.

**outsize** ['autsaiz] adj di taglia forte, fuori misura.

**outskirts** ['autskə:tz] pl n dintorni m pl, periferia f sing.

**outspoken** [aut'spoukən] adj franco, esplicito, schietto.

**outstanding** [aut'standiŋ] adj (striking) eminente, notevole; (unpaid) in sospeso, arretrato.

**outstrip** [aut'strip] v distanziare.

**outward** ['autwəd] adj esterno, esteriore, superficiale; (journey) d'andata. **outwardly** adv in apparenza.

**outweigh** [aut'wei] v superare in importanza.

**outwit** [aut'wit] v superare in astuzia.

**oval** ['ouvəl] nm, adj ovale.

**ovary** ['ouvəri] n ovaia f.

**ovation** [ou'veiʃən] n ovazione f.

**oven** ['ʌvn] n forno m.

**over** ['ouvə] adv oltre, al di sopra; (in excess) in più; (finished) finito. prep su, sopra; (across) al di là di; (more than) più di. **over here** qui, da questa parte. **over there** là, laggiù.

**overall** ['ouvəro:l] adj globale, completo. n (workman's) tuta f; (scientist's) camice m; (woman's) grembiulone m. adv in complesso.

**overbalance** [ouvə'baləns] v sbilanciare, perdere l'equilibrio.

**overbearing** [ouvə'beəriŋ] adj prepotente, altezzoso.

**overboard** ['ouvəbo:d] adv in mare or acqua.

**overcast** [ouvə'ka:st] adj coperto, nuvoloso.

**overcharge** [ouvə'tʃa:dʒ] v far pagare troppo.

**overcoat** ['ouvəkout] n cappotto m, soprabito m.

**\*overcome** [ouvə'kʌm] v superare. adj sopraffatto, commosso.

**overcrowded** [ouvə'kraudid] adj sovraffollato. **overcrowding** n sovraffollamento m.

**\*overdo** [ouvə'du:] v esagerare; (overcook) stracuocere.

**overdose** ['ouvədous] n dose eccessiva f.

**overdraft** ['ouvədra:ft] n scoperto (di conto) m.

**\*overdraw** [ouvə'dro:] v andare allo scoperto.

**overdrive** ['ouvədraiv] n marcia sovramoltiplicata f.

**overdue** [ouvə'dju:] adj in ritardo, tardivo; (bill) scaduto.

**overestimate** [ouvə'estimeit] v sopravvalutare.

**overexpose** [ouvəik'spouz] v sovraesporre. **overexposure** n sovraesposizione f.

**overflow** [ouvə'flou; n 'ouvəflou] v (flood) inondare; (river) straripare; (vessel) traboccare. n (outlet) troppopieno m. **overflow pipe** scarico del troppopieno m.

**overgrown** [ouvə'groun] adj ricoperto di vegetazione.

**\*overhang** [ouvə'haŋ; n 'ouvəhaŋ] v sporgere sopra; (impend) incombere su, minacciare. n aggetto m; (mountaineering) strapiombo m.

**overhaul** [ouvə'ho:l] v (investigate) esaminare; (repair) ripassare, riparare. n esame minuzioso m.

**overhead** [ouvə'hed] adv in alto, di sopra. adj di sopra, aereo. **overheads** pl n spese generali f pl.

**\*overhear** [ouvə'hiə] v udire per caso; (eavesdrop) origliare.

**overheat** [ouvə'hi:t] v surriscaldare.

**overjoyed** [ouvə'dʒoid] adj felicissimo, colmo di gioia.

**overland** [ouvə'land] adj, adv per terra.

**overlap** [ouvə'lap] v sovrapporre, accavallare; coincidere *or* corrispondere in parte con.

**overlay** [ouvə'lei; *v* ouvə'lei] *n* copertura *f.* *v* ricoprire; incrostare.

**overleaf** [ouvə'li:f] *adv see* overleaf vedi retro.

**overload** [ouvə'loud; *n* 'ouvəloud] *v* sovraccaricare. *n* sovraccarico *m.*

**overlook** [ouvə'luk] *v* (*miss*) lasciarsi sfuggire, non rilevare; condonare; (*ignore*) non tener conto di, trascurare; (*house, etc.*) dare su.

**overnight** [ouvə'nait] *adv* di notte; (*suddenly*) d'un tratto. **stay overnight** pernottare.

**overpower** [ouvə'pauə] *v* sopraffare, dominare. **overpowering** *adj* irresistibile.

**overrate** [ouvə'reit] *v* sopravvalutare.

**overreach** [ouvə'ri:tʃ] *v* **overreach oneself** sopravvalutare le proprie forze.

**overriding** [ouvə'raidiŋ] *adj* di primaria importanza.

**overrule** [ouvə'ru:l] *v* (*decision*) annullare; (*plea*) respingere.

**overrun** [ouvə'rʌn] *v* invadere, infestare.

**overseas** [ouvə'si:z] *adv* oltremare. *adj* d'oltremare, straniero.

**overseer** [ouvə'siə] *n* ispettore, -trice *m, f,* sorvegliante *m, f.*

**overshadow** [ouvə'ʃadou] *v* oscurare; (*render insignificant*) eclissare.

**overshoot** [ouvə'ʃu:t] *v* (*miss*) fallire; (*go beyond*) oltrepassare. **overshoot the mark** passare il segno. **overshoot the runway** atterrare lungo.

**oversight** ['ouvəsait] *n* svista *f,* inavvertenza *f.*

**oversleep** [ouvə'sli:p] *v* dormire troppo a lungo, dormire oltre all'ora stabilita.

**overspill** ['ouvəspil] *n* sovrappiù *m.*

**overt** [ou'və:t] *adj* manifesto, palese.

**overtake** [ouvə'teik] *v* sorpassare.

**overthrow** [ouvə'θrou; *n* 'ouvəθrou] *v* rovesciare, sconfiggere. *n* rovesciamento *m.*

**overtime** ['ouvətaim] *n* ore straordinarie *f pl.*

**overtone** ['ouvətoun] *n* (*implication*) sfumatura *f.*

**overture** ['ouvətjuə] *n* (*music*) ouverture *f,* preludio *m;* (*proposal*) proposta *f;* (*political*) apertura *f.*

**overturn** [ouvə'tə:n] *v* rovesciare, capovolgere.

**overweight** [ouvə'weit] *adj* **be overweight** pesare troppo.

**overwhelm** [ouvə'welm] *v* (*defeat*) sopraffare; (*crush*) schiacciare; (*with kindness, etc.*) colmare. **overwhelmingly** *adv* in modo schiacciante.

**overwork** [ouvə'wə:k] *v* (far) lavorar troppo. *n* eccesso di lavoro *m.*

**overwrought** [ouvə'ro:t] *adj* teso, turbato, agitato.

**ovulate** ['ovjuleit] *v* ovulare. **ovulation** *n* ovulazione *f.*

**owe** [ou] *v* dovere. **owing** *adj* dovuto. **owing to** dovuto a, grazie a.

**owl** [aul] *n* gufo *m,* civetta *f.*

**own** [oun] *adj* proprio. **get one's own back** rendere pan per focaccia. **on one's own** da solo. *v* possedere; (*recognize*) riconoscere; confessare. **owner** *n* proprietario, -a *m, f.* **ownership** *n* proprietà *f,* possesso *m.*

**ox** [oks] *n, pl* oxen bue (*pl* buoi) *m.* **oxtail** *n* coda di bue *f.*

**oxygen** ['oksidʒən] *n* ossigeno *m.*

**oyster** ['oistə] *n* ostrica *f.*

**ozone** ['ouzoun] *n* ozono *m.* **ozone layer** strato d'ozono *m.*

# P

**pace** [peis] *n* passo *m;* (*speed*) velocità *f.* **keep pace with** (*walking*) camminare di pari passo con; (*keep up to date*) tenersi al corrente di. *v* **pace off** misurare a passi. **pace up and down** andare su e giù.

**pacemaker** *n* (*med*) segnapasso cardiaco *m.*

**Pacific** [pə'sifik] *nm, adj* pacifico.

**pacifism** ['pasifizəm] *n* pacifismo *m.* **pacifist** *n* pacifista *m, f.*

**pacify** ['pasifai] *v* pacificare.

**pack** [pak] *n* (*parcel, package*) pacco *m;* (*of goods*) imballo *m;* (*rucksack*) zaino *m;* (*cards*) mazzo *m;* (*thieves*) banda *f;* (*hounds*) muta *f.* **pack of lies** tessuto di bugie *m.* *v* imballare; (*suitcases*) fare (le valige); (*cram*) pigiare. **packed** adj (full) pieno zeppo. **packing** n confezione f, imballaggio m; (tech) guarnizione f. **do one's packing** fare le valige, fare i bagagli.

**package** ['pakidʒ] n pacco m. adj (deal, etc.) comprensivo.

**packet** ['pakit] n pacchetto m.

**pact** [pakt] n patto m.

**pad¹** [pad] n (cushion) cuscinetto m, tampone m; (notepaper) taccuino m; (paw) zampa f. v imbottire. **pad out** (speech, essay, etc.) infarcire. **padding** n imbottitura f; infarcimento m.

**pad²** [pad] v camminare a passo felpato.

**paddle¹** ['padl] n (of boat) pagaia f; (tech) spatola f; (zool) pinna f. **paddle-boat** n piroscafo a ruote m. v remare piano.

**paddle²** ['padl] v sguazzare (nell'acqua). **paddling pool** piscina per bambini f.

**paddock** ['padək] n recinto m; (racing) paddock m invar.

**paddy-field** ['padifi:ld] n risaia f.

**padlock** ['padlok] n lucchetto m. v chiudere col lucchetto.

**paediatric** [pi:di'atrik] adj pediatrico. **paediatrician** n pediatra m, f. **paediatrics** n pediatria f.

**pagan** ['peigən] n, adj pagano, -a.

**page¹** [peidʒ] n (book) pagina f.

**page²** [peidʒ] n also **page-boy** paggio m; (hotel) piccolo m. v (coll) chiamare.

**pageant** ['padʒənt] n corteo storico m. **pageantry** n fasto m.

**paid** [peid] V pay.

**pain** [pein] n dolore m, sofferenza f. **be at pains to** sforzarsi di. **on pain of** sotto pena di. **painkiller** n analgesico m. **painstaking** adj laborioso, **v** addolorare, far male a. **painful** adj doloroso. **painless** adj indolore.

**paint** [peint] v dipingere, pitturare; (decorate) verniciare. n colore m, vernice f. **paint-box** n scatola di colori f. **paint-brush** n pennello m. **painter** n pittore, -trice m, f; decoratore m. **painting** n guadro m, pittura f.

**pair** [peə] n paio m (pl -a f), coppia f. v accoppiare.

**Pakistan** [paki'sta:n] n Pachistan m. **Pakistani** n, adj pachistano, -a.

**pal** [pal] n (coll) compagno, -a m, f.

**palace** ['paləs] n palazzo m. **palatial**

adj sontuoso.

**palate** ['palit] n palato m. **palatable** adj saporito.

**pale¹** [peil] adj pallido. v impallidire. **paleness** n pallore m.

**pale²** [peil] n (stake) palo m. **beyond the pale** adj (coll) impossibile.

**palette** ['palit] n tavolozza f. **palette knife** spatola f.

**pall¹** [po:l] v smettere or cessare di interessare; (weary) stancare.

**pall²** [po:l] n drappo funebre m.

**palm¹** [pa:m] n (of hand) palmo m. v **palm off** affibbiare. **palmist** n chiromante m, f. **palmistry** n chiromanzia f.

**palm²** [pa:m] n (tree) palma f. **Palm Sunday** Domenica delle Palme f.

**palpitation** [,palpi'teiʃən] n palpitazione f.

**pamper** ['pampə] v viziare.

**pamphlet** ['pamflit] n opuscolo m; (polemical) libello m.

**pan** [pan] n pentola f, casseruola f, padella f. **pancake** n fritella f. **Pancake Tuesday** martedì grasso m.

**pancreas** ['paŋkriəs] n pancreas m invar. **pancreatic** adj pancreatico.

**panda** ['pandə] n panda m invar.

**pander** ['pandə] v **pander to** favorire, andare incontro a.

**pane** [pein] n vetro m.

**panel** ['panl] n pannello m; (jury) lista f; (instruments) cruscotto m. **panelling** n rivestimento a pannelli m.

**pang** [paŋ] n dolore acuto m, spasimo m.

**panic** ['panik] n panico m, allarme m. **panic-stricken** adj colto dal panico. v essere in preda al panico. **panicky** adj apprensivo.

**panorama** [,panə'ra:mə] n panorama m.

**pansy** ['panzi] n (flower) viola del pensiero f; (coll: homosexual) finocchio m.

**pant** [pant] v anelare, sbuffare.

**panther** ['panθə] n pantera f.

**pantomime** ['pantəmaim] n pantomina f; (Christmas) spettacolo di Natale m.

**pantry** ['pantri] n dispensa f.

**pants** [pants] pl n mutande f pl.

**papal** ['peipl] adj papale. **papacy** n papato m.

**paper** ['peipə] n carta f; documento m; (treatise) discorso m; (news) giornale m.

**paperback** *n* edizione economica *f*. **paper-clip** *n* fermaglio *m*, agrafe *f*. **paper-mill** *n* cartiera *f*. **paperweight** *n* fermacarte *m* invar. **paperwork** *n* lavoro d'ufficio *m*; documenti *m pl*. *v* tappezzare.

**paprika** ['paprikə] *n* paprica *f*.

**par** [pa:] *n* **above/below par** sopra/sotto la pari. **feel below par** sentirsi (un po') giù. **on a par with** alla pari con.

**parable** ['parəbl] *n* parabola *f*.

**parabola** [pə'rabələ] *n* parabola *f*.

**parachute** ['parəʃu:t] *n* paracadute *m* invar. *v* scendere col paracadute. **parachutist** *n* paracadutista *m*, *f*.

**parade** [pə'reid] *n* (display) sfoggio *m*; (mil) sfilata *f*; (sea-front) lungomare *m*. *v* ostentare, sfoggiare; sfilare.

**paradise** ['parədais] *n* paradiso *m*.

**paradox** ['parədoks] *n* paradosso *m*. **paradoxical** *adj* paradossale.

**paraffin** ['parəfin] *n* paraffina liquida *f*; (oil) cherosene *m*, petrolio da illuminazione *m*.

**paragon** ['parəgən] *n* modello (di perfezione) *m*.

**paragraph** ['parəgra:f] *n* paragrafo *m*; (news item) trafiletto *m*.

**parallel** ['parəlel] *adj* parallelo. **parallel line** parallela *f*. *n* parallelo *m*; (comparison) paragone *m*.

**paralyse** ['parəlaiz] *v* paralizzare. **paralysis** *n*, *pl* -ses paralisi *f*. **paralytic** *n*, *adj* paralitico, -a.

**paramedic** [parə'medik] *n* paramedico *m*.

**parameter** [pə'ramitə] *n* parametro *m*.

**paramilitary** [,parə'militəri] *adj* paramilitare.

**paramount** ['parəmaunt] *adj* sommo, supremo.

**paranoia** [,parə'noiə] *n* paranoia *f*. **paranoiac** or **paranoid** *n*, *adj* paranoico, -a.

**parapet** ['parəpit] *n* parapetto *m*.

**paraphernalia** [,parəfə'neiliə] *n* oggetti vari *m pl*, cianfrusaglie *f pl*.

**paraphrase** ['parəfreiz] *n* parafrasi *f*. *v* parafrasare.

**paraplegic** [,parə'pli:dʒik] *n*, *adj* paraplegico, -a. **paraplegia** *n* paraplegia *f*.

**parasite** ['parəsait] *n* parassita *m*, *f*. **parasitic** *adj* parassita, parassitico.

**parasol** ['parəsol] *n* parasole *m*.

**paratrooper** ['parə,tru:pə] *n* (soldato) para-

cadutista *m*.

**parcel** ['pa:səl] *n* pacco *m*, pacchetto *m*. **by parcel post** a mezzo pacco postale. **part and parcel of** parte integrale di. *v* **parcel up** impacchettare.

**parched** [pa:tʃt] *adj* riarso. **be parched with thirst** morire dalla sete.

**parchment** ['pa:tʃmənt] *n* pergamena *f*, cartapecora *f*. **parchment paper** carta pergamenata *f*.

**pardon** ['pa:dn] *n* perdono *m*; (law) grazia *f*; (for minor fault) scusa *f*. **I beg your pardon** mi scusi. *v* scusare; perdonare; graziare. *interj* prego? **pardonable** *adj* perdonabile.

**pare** [peə] *v* sbucciare, pelare. **pare down** ridurre.

**parent** ['peərənt] *n* padre, madre *m*, *f*. **parents** *pl n* genitori *m pl*. **parental** *adj* dei genitori. **parenthood** *n* l'essere genitori *m*.

**parenthesis** [pə'renθəsis] *n*, *pl* -ses parentesi *f*.

**pariah** [pə'raiə] *n* paria *m* invar.

**Paris** ['paris] *n* Parigi *f*. **Parisian** *n*, *adj* parigino, -a.

**parish** ['pariʃ] *n* parrocchia *f*; (civil) comune *m*. **parish priest** parroco (pl -chi) *m*.

**parishioner** *n* parrocchiano, -a *m*, *f*.

**parity** ['pariti] *n* parità *f*.

**park** [pa:k] *n* parco *m*. *v* parcheggiare, posteggiare. **parking** *n* posteggio *m*, parcheggio *m*. **parking meter** parchimetro *m*. **park-and-ride** *n* parcheggio periferico *m*.

**parliament** ['pa:ləmənt] *n* parlamento *m*. **member of parliament** deputato *m*. **parliamentary** *adj* parlamentare.

**parlour** ['pa:lə] *n* salotto *m*. **parlour game** gioco di società *m*.

**Parmesan** [,pa:mi'zan] *n* (cheese) (formaggio) parmigiano *m*, grana *m* invar.

**parochial** [pə'roukiəl] *adj* provinciale.

**parody** ['parədi] *n* parodia *f*. *v* parodiare.

**parole** [pə'roul] *v* rilasciare sulla parola. *n* rilascio sulla parola *m*.

**paroxysm** ['parəksizəm] *n* parossismo *m*, accesso *m*.

**parrot** ['parət] *n* pappagallo *m*.

**parsley** ['pa:sli] *n* prezzemolo *m*.

**parsnip** ['pa:snip] *n* pastinaca *f*.

**parson** ['pa:sn] *n* prete *m*, parroco *m*. **parsonage** *n* casa parrocchiale *f*, presbiterio *m*.

**part** [pɑːt] *n* parte *f*; (*theatre*) ruolo *m*; (*district*) quartiere *f*. **part-time** *adv*, *adj* a mezzo tempo. **spare part** pezzo di ricambio *m*. **take part** prender parte. *v* separare, spartire; (*hair*) dividere. **part with** rinunciare a. **parting** *n* separazione *f*, addio *m*; (*hair*) divisa dei capelli *f*, riga *f*.

**\*partake** [pɑːteik] *v* **partake of** consumare.

**partial** [ˈpɑːʃəl] *adj* parziale. **be partial to** avere un debole per. **partiality** *n* preferenza *f*. **partially** *adv* in parte.

**participate** [pɑːˈtisipeit] *v* partecipare. **participant** *n* partecipante *m*, *f*. **participation** *n* partecipazione *f*.

**participle** [ˈpɑːtisipl] *n* participio *m*.

**particle** [ˈpɑːtikl] *n* particella *f*.

**particular** [pəˈtikjulə] *adj* particolare, speciale; (*exacting*) esigente. *n* particolare *m*, dettaglio *m*. **particularly** *adv* in particolare, specie.

**partisan** [pɑːtiˈzan] *n*, *adj* partigiano, -a.

**partition** [pɑːˈtiʃən] *n* spartizione *f*; (*of room*) tramezzo *m*. *v* spartire; tramezzare.

**partly** [ˈpɑːtli] *adv* in parte.

**partner** [ˈpɑːtnə] *n* (*comm*) socio *m*; compagno, -a *m*, *f*, partner (*pl* -s) *m*, *f* v far da compagno a, associarsi a. **partnership** *n* società *f*, associazione *f*.

**partridge** [ˈpɑːtridʒ] *n* pernice *f*.

**party** [ˈpɑːti] *n* (*group*) compagnia *f*, gruppo *m*; (*entertainment*) festa *f*, trattenimento *m*; (*pol*) partito *m*; (*law*) parte *f*. **third party** terzi *m pl*.

**pass** [pɑːs] *n* (*mountain*) passo *m*, valico (*pl* -chi) *m*; (*permit*) permesso *m*; (*mil*) libera uscita *f*; (*school*) promozione *f*; (*sport*) allungo *m*. *v* passare; superare; promuovere; allungare. **pass by** (*disregard*) non curarsi di; (*in front of*) passare davanti a. **pass off** far passare (per). **pass on** trasmettere; (*die*) morire. **pass out** (*faint*) svenire.

**passage** [ˈpasidʒ] *n* passaggio *m*; (*in book*) brano *m*.

**passenger** [ˈpasindʒə] *n* viaggiatore, -trice *m*, *f*. **passenger train** treno viaggiatori *m*.

**passer-by** [ˌpasəˈbai] *n* passante *m*, *f*.

**passing** [ˈpasiŋ] *adj* passeggero, transitorio; casuale. **in passing** di passaggio *or* sfuggita; (*by the way*) tra parentesi.

**passion** [ˈpaʃən] *n* passione *f*, entusiasmo *m*. **passionate** *adj* appassionato, ardente.

**passive** [ˈpasiv] *nm*, *adj* passivo. **passivity** *n* passività *f*.

**Passover** [ˈpɑːsouvə] *n* Pasqua degli ebrei *f*.

**passport** [ˈpɑːspɔːt] *n* passaporto *m*.

**password** [ˈpɑːswəːd] *n* parola d'ordine *f*.

**past** [pɑːst] *prep* al di là di, oltre; (*after*) dopo. **five past six** le sei e cinque. *adj* passato, scorso; (*former*) ex. *adv* davanti, oltre. *n* passato *m*.

**pasta** [ˈpɑstə] *n* pasta *f*, pastasciutta *f*.

**paste** [peist] *n* pasta *f*; (*adhesive*) colla *f*. *v* incollare.

**pastel** [ˈpɑstəl] *n* pastello *m*.

**pasteurize** [ˈpɑstʃəraiz] *v* pastorizzare. **pasteurization** *n* pastorizzazione *f*.

**pastime** [ˈpɑːstaim] *n* passatempo *m*.

**pastoral** [ˈpɑːstərəl] *adj* pastorale.

**pastry** [ˈpeistri] *n* pasta *f*. **pastry-cook** *n* pasticciere, -a *m*, *f*.

**pasture** [ˈpɑːstʃə] *n* pascolo *m*, pastura *f*. *v* pascolare.

**pasty¹** [ˈpeisti] *adj* pallido; (*consistency*) pastoso.

**pasty²** [ˈpasti] *n* (*pie*) pasticcio *m*.

**pat¹** [pat] *adj* pronto, apposito. *adv* (*aptly*) a proposito; (*exactly*) precisamente.

**pat²** [pat] *n* (*light blow*) colpetto *m*; (*of butter*) pezzetto *m*. *v* dare un colpetto a.

**patch** [patʃ] *n* (*material*) pezza *f*, toppa *f*; (*land*) pezzo *m*. **go through a bad patch** attraversare un momento brutto. *v* rattoppare. **patch up** rattoppare, accomodare; (*quarrel*) comporre. **patchy** *adj* rattoppato; (*not uniform*) irregolare.

**pâté** [ˈpatei] *n* pasticcio *m*, pâté *m invar*.

**patent** [ˈpeitənt] *adj* manifesto, ovvio. **patent leather** pelle verniciata *f*. **patent medicine** specialità medicinale *f*. *n* brevetto *m*. *v* brevettare.

**paternal** [pəˈtəːnl] *adj* paterno. **paternity** *n* paternità *f*.

**path** [pɑːθ] *n* sentiero *m*; (*course, way*) via *f*, strada *f*.

**pathetic** [pəˈθetik] *adj* patetico, commovente.

**pathology** [pəˈθolədʒi] *n* anatomia patologica *f*. **pathological** *adj* patologico. **pathologist** *n* anatomo patologo, anatoma patologa *m*, *f*.

**patient** [ˈpeiʃənt] *adj* paziente. *n* paziente *m*, *f*, malato, -a *m*, *f*. **be patient** pazientare, aver pazienza. **patience** *n* pazienza *f*.

**patio** ['patiou] n patio m invar.

**patriarchal** ['peitriəkəl] adj patriarcale. **patriarch** n patriarca m.

**patriot** ['patriət] n patriota m, f. **patriotic** adj patriottico. **patriotism** n patriottismo m.

**patrol** [pə'troul] n pattuglia f. v andare in pattuglia, ispezionare.

**patron** ['peitrən] n patrono m, protettore m; (customer) cliente abituale m, f, avventore, -a m, f. **patronage** n protezione f, auspici m pl. **patronize** v favorire, proteggere; frequentare. **patronizing** adj condiscendente.

**patter**[1] ['patə] n (sound) picchiettare. n picchiettio m.

**patter**[2] ['patə] n (speech) cicalata f, ciancia f. v cicalare, cianciare.

**pattern** ['patən] n modello m, tipo m; disegno m. v modellare.

**paunch** [po:ntʃ] n pancia f. **paunchy** adj panciuto.

**pauper** ['po:pə] n povero, -a m, f; mendicante m, f. **pauperize** v impoverire.

**pause** [po:z] n pausa f; esitazione f. v fare una pausa; esitare.

**pave** [peiv] v pavimentare. **pave the way** preparare il terreno. **pavement** n marciapiede m. **paving stone** lastra da selciato f.

**pavilion** [pə'viljən] n padiglione m.

**paw** [po:] n zampa f. v (ground) scalpitare; (handle) palpeggiare.

**pawn**[1] [po:n] n (deposit) pegno m. **pawnbroker** n prestatore su pegno m. **pawnshop** n monte di pietà m. v pignorare, dare in pegno.

**pawn**[2] [po:n] n (chess) pedina f.

*****pay** [pei] n paga f, stipendio m. **in the pay of** al servizio di. **pay-roll** n organico m. v pagare; (settle) saldare; (profit) rendere; (attention, etc.) fare. **pay back** rimborsare, restituire. **pay in** versare. **pay off** liquidare. **payable** adj pagabile. **payee** n beneficiario, -a m, f. **payment** n pagamento m, versamento m.

**pea** [pi:] n pisello m.

**peace** [pi:s] n pace f; tranquillità f. **breach of the peace** violazione dell'ordine pubblico f. **peace-loving** adj pacifico. **peace offering** dono propiziatorio m. **peacetime** n tempo di pace m. **peaceful** adj pacifico.

**peach** [pi:tʃ] n (fruit) pesca f; (tree) pesco m.

**peacock** ['pi:kok] n pavone m. **peacock blue** nm, adj. blu pavone. **peahen** n pavona f.

**peak** [pi:k] n cima f, vetta f; (highest point) massimo m; (on cap) visiera f. **peak hours** ore di punta f pl. **peak load** carico massimo m. v raggiungere il massimo.

**peal** [pi:l] n (bells) scampanio m; (thunder, laughter) scoppio m, scroscio m. v scampanare; (thunder) rimbombare.

**peanut** ['pi:nʌt] n arachide f.

**pear** [peə] n (fruit) pera f; (tree) pero m.

**pearl** [pə:l] n perla f. **pearly** adj (like pearl) perlaceo; (adorned with pearls) perlato.

**peasant** ['peznt] n contadino, -a m, f.

**peat** [pi:t] n torba f.

**pebble** ['pebl] n ciottolo m. **pebbly** adj ciottoloso.

**peck** [pek] v beccare; (food) mangiucchiare; (kiss) dare un bacetto a, baciucchiare. n beccata f; baciucchio m.

**peckish** ['pekiʃ] adj feel peckish sentirsi vuoto or affamato.

**peculiar** [pi'kju:liə] adj strano, particolare. **peculiarity** n particolarità f, stranezza f.

**pedal** ['pedl] n pedale m. v pedalare.

**pedantic** [pi'dantik] adj pedante. **pedant** n pedante m, f. **pedantry** n pedanteria f.

**peddle** ['pedl] v spacciare.

**pedestal** ['pedistl] n piedistallo m.

**pedestrian** [pi'destriən] adj pedonale; (commonplace) pedestre. n pedone m. **pedestrian precinct** zona pedonale f.

**pedigree** ['pedigri:] n genealogia f; (of animals) pedigree m invar. di razza.

**pedlar** ['pedlə] n (salesman) venditore ambulante m.

**peel** [pi:l] n buccia f. v sbucciare; (paint, skin) staccarsi. **peeler** n sbucciatore m. **peelings** pl n bucce f pl.

**peep** [pi:p] n occhiata (furtiva) f, sguardo furtivo m. v dare un'occhiatina, spiare. **peep-hole** n spiraglio m. **peep out** mostrarsi appena.

**peer**[1] [piə] v peer at scrutare, guardare da presso.

**peer**[2] [piə] n pari m. **peerage** n nobiltà f.

**peevish** ['pi:viʃ] adj permaloso, scontroso.

**peg** [peg] n piolo m; (violin, etc.) bischero m; (washing) molletta f. **off the peg** adj pronto. v (*prices*) stabilire. **peg out** (*coll: die*) crepare.

**pejorative** [pəˈdʒɔrətiv] *adj* peggiorativo.

**Peking** [piːˈkiŋ] *n* Pechino *f*. **Pekingese** *n* (*dog*) (*cane*) pechinese *m*.

**pelican** [ˈpelikən] *n* pellicano *m*.

**pellet** [ˈpelit] *n* pallottola *f*, pallina *f*; (*pill*) pillola *f*.

**pelmet** [ˈpelmit] *n* mantovana *f*.

**pelt**[1] [pelt] *v* scagliare; (*rain*) piovere dirottamente, diluviare. *n* **at full pelt a** piena velocità.

**pelt**[2] [pelt] *n* pelliccia *f*.

**pelvis** [ˈpelvis] *n* pelvi *f*, bacino *m*. **pelvic** *adj* pelvico.

**pen**[1] [pen] *n* (*for writing*) penna *f*. *v* scrivere.

**pen**[2] [pen] *n* recinto *m*; (*for sheep*) ovile *m*; (*for pigs*) porcile *m*. *v* **pen in** rinchiudere.

**penal** [ˈpiːnl] *adj* penale. **penalize** *v* punire. **penalty** *n* pena *f*; (*fine*) multa *f*. **penalty kick** (*sport*) calcio di rigore *m*.

**penance** [ˈpenəns] *n* penitenza *f*.

**pencil** [ˈpensl] *n* matita *f*. **pencil-sharpener** *n* temperamatite *m invar*.

**pendant** [ˈpendənt] *n* ciondolo *m*.

**pending** [ˈpendiŋ] *adj* in sospeso. *prep* in attesa di.

**pendulum** [ˈpendjuləm] *n* pendolo *m*. **pendulum clock** orologio a pendolo *m*.

**penetrate** [ˈpenitreit] *v* penetrate. **penetration** *n* penetrazione *f*.

**pen-friend** *n* amico, -a per corrispondenza *m, f*.

**penguin** [ˈpeŋgwin] *n* pinguino *m*.

**penicillin** [peniˈsilin] *n* penicillina *f*.

**peninsula** [pəˈninsjulə] *n* penisola *f*. **peninsular** *adj* peninsulare.

**penis** [ˈpiːnis] *n* pene *m*.

**penitent** [ˈpenitənt] *n*(*m+f*), *adj* penitente. **penitence** *n* penitenza *f*, pentimento *m*. **penitentiary** *n* (*prison*) penitenziario *m*; (*church dignitary*) penitenziere *m*.

**penknife** [ˈpennaif] *n* temperino *m*.

**pen-name** *n* pseudonimo *m*.

**pennant** [ˈpenənt] *n* pennello *m*.

**penniless** [ˈpeniləs] *adj* al verde, senza un soldo.

**pension** [ˈpenʃən] *n* pensione *f*. *v* **pension off** mettere a riposo, mettere in pensione. **pensioner** *n* pensionato, -a *m, f*.

**pensive** [ˈpensiv] *adj* pensoso, pensieroso, preoccupato.

**pentagon** [ˈpentəgən] *n* pentagono *m*. **pentagonal** *adj* pentagonale.

**penthouse** [ˈpenthaus] *n* attico *m*.

**pent-up** [ˌpentˈʌp] *adj* represso.

**penultimate** [piˈnʌltimit] *adj* penultimo.

**people** [ˈpiːpl] *n* popolo *m*, nazione *f*. *pl n* gente *f sing*; (*coll: family*) i suoi *m pl*. *v* popolare. **people carrier** monovolume *m*.

**pepper** [ˈpepə] *n* pepe *m*. **peppercorn** *n* grano di pepe *m*. **pepper-mill** *n* macinapepe *m invar*. **peppermint** *n* (*herb*) menta piperita *f*; (*sweet*) mentina *f*. **pepper-pot** *n* pepaiola *f*. *v* (*season*) pepare; (*dot*) cospargere; (*hit*) tempestare.

**per** [pəː] *prep* a. **as per** secondo. **per cent** percento. **percentage** *n* percentuale *f*.

**perceive** [pəˈsiːv] *v* rilevare, scorgere, accorgersi di.

**perceptible** [pəˈseptibl] *adj* percettibile; visibile. **perceptibility** *n* percettibilità *f*; visibilità *f*.

**perception** [pəˈsepʃən] *n* percezione *f*. **perceptive** *adj* percettivo, sensibile.

**perch**[1] [pəːtʃ] *n* posatoio *m*. *v* posarsi.

**perch**[2] [pəːtʃ] *n* (*fish*) pesce persico *m*.

**percolate** [ˈpəːkəleit] *v* filtrare. **percolator** *n* percolatore *m*.

**percussion** [pəˈkʌʃən] *n* percussione *f*.

**perennial** [pəˈreniəl] *adj* perenne; perpetuo. *v* pianta perenne *f*.

**perfect** [ˈpəːfikt; *v* pəˈfekt] *adj* perfetto, ideale; (*real*) vero. *v* perfezionare. **perfection** *n* perfezione *f*.

**perforate** [ˈpəːfəreit] *v* perforare. **perforation** *n* perforazione *f*.

**perform** [pəˈfoːm] *v* eseguire, compire; (*music, theatre*) recitare. **performance** *n* esecuzione *f*; recita *f*; (*show*) spettacolo *m*. **performer** *n* artista *m, f*.

**perfume** [ˈpəːfjuːm] *n* profumo *m*. *v* profumare. **perfumery** *n* profumeria *f*.

**perfunctory** [pəˈfʌŋktəri] *adj* fatto alla buona, meccanico, indifferente.

**perhaps** [pəˈhaps] *adv* forse, magari.

**peril** [ˈperil] *n* rischio *m*. **perilous** *adj* rischioso, pericoloso.

**perimeter** [pəˈrimitə] *n* perimetro *m*.

**period** [ˈpiəriəd] *n* periodo *m*; (*full stop*) punto fermo *m*; (*med*) mestruazione *f*. *adj* antico (*m pl* -chi), storico. **periodic** *adj* periodico. **periodical** *nm, adj* periodico.

**peripheral** [pə'rifərəl] *adj* periferico.
**periphery** *n* periferia *f*.

**periscope** ['periskoup] *n* periscopio *m*.

**perish** ['periʃ] *v* perire; (*food, etc.*) guastarsi, deperire. **perishable** *adj* deperibile.

**perjure** ['pə:dʒə] *v* spergiurare. **perjurer** *n* spergiuro, -a *m*, *f*. **perjury** *n* spergiuro *m*, giuramento falso *m*.

**perk**[1] [pə:k] *v* **perk up** rianimarsi, ravvivarsi. **perky** *adj* vispo.

**perk**[2] *n* (*fringe benefit*) vantaggio addizionale *m*.

**perm** [pə:m] *n* permanente *f*. **have a perm** farsi fare la permanente.

**permanent** ['pə:mənənt] *adj* permanente.

**permeate** ['pə:mieit] *v* permeare.

**permit** ['pə:mit; *v* pə'mit] *n* permesso *m*, licenza *f*. *v* permettere. **permissible** *adj* permissibile. **permission** *n* permesso *m*. **permissive** *adj* permissivo.

**permutation** [pə:mju'teiʃən] *n* permutazione *f*.

**pernicious** [pə'niʃəs] *adj* pernicioso.

**pernickety** [pə'nikəti] *adj* pignolo.

**perpendicular** [,pə:pen'dikjulə] *nf, adj* perpendicolare.

**perpetrate** ['pə:pitreit] *v* commettere. **perpetration** *n* perpetrazione *f*. **perpetrator** *n* perpetratore, -trice *m*, *f*.

**perpetual** [pə'petʃuəl] *adj* perpetuo.

**perpetuate** [pə'petʃueit] *v* perpetuare. **perpetuation** *n* perpetuazione *f*. **in perpetuity** in perpetuo.

**perplex** [pə'pleks] *v* confondere, rendere perplesso. **perplexed** *adj* perplesso, confuso. **perplexing** *adj* imbarazzante. **perplexity** *n* perplessità *f*, imbarazzo *m*.

**persecute** ['pə:sikju:t] *v* perseguitare. **persecution** *n* persecuzione *f*.

**persevere** [,pə:si'viə] *v* perseverare. **perseverance** *n* perseveranza *f*, assiduità *f*. **persevering** *adj* perseverante, assiduo.

**persist** [pə'sist] *v* persistere, ostinarsi, perseverare. **persistence** *n* perseveranza *f*, persistenza *f*, ostinazione *f*. **persistent** *adj* ostinato, persistente.

**person** ['pə:sn] *n* persona *f*, individuo *m*. **personage** *n* personaggio *m*. **personal** *adj* personale; (*disparaging*) offensivo, di carattere personale. **personality** *n* personalità *f*; carattere *m*; celebrità *f*.

**personal assistant** *n* segretaria

personale *f*.

**personify** [pə'sonifai] *v* personificare. **personification** *n* personificazione *f*.

**personnel** [pə:sə'nel] *n* personale *m*, impiegati *m pl*.

**perspective** [pə'spektiv] *n* prospettiva *f*.

**perspire** [pə'spaiə] *v* sudare. **perspiration** *n* sudore *m*.

**persuade** [pə'sweid] *v* persuadere. **persuasion** *n* persuasione *f*. **persuasive** *adj* persuasivo.

**pert** [pə:t] *adj* (*lively*) vispo; impudente, insolente.

**pertain** [pə'tein] *v* **pertain to** riguardare, appartenere a. **pertinent** *adj* pertinente, a proposito. **pertinence** *n* pertinenza *f*.

**perturb** [pə'tə:b] *v* turbare, sconcertare.

**peruse** [pə'ru:z] *v* leggere attentamente.

**pervade** [pə'veid] *v* pervadere. **pervasive** *adj* penetrante.

**perverse** [pə'və:s] *adj* perverso. **perversity** *n* perversità *f*.

**pervert** ['pə:və:t; *v* pə'və:t] *n* pervertito, -a *m*, *f*. *v* pervertire. **perversion** *n* perversione *f*, pervertimento *m*.

**pessimism** ['pesimizəm] *n* pessimismo *m*. **pessimist** *n* pessimista *m*, *f*. **pessimistic** *adj* pessimista, pessimistico.

**pest** [pest] *n* animale *or* parassita nocivo *m*; (*coll: nuisance*) seccatore *m*. **pest control** disinfestazione *f*. **pesticide** *n* pesticida *m*.

**pester** ['pestə] *v* seccare.

**pet** [pet] *n* animale favorito *m*; (*favourite*) cocco, -a *m*, *f*. *adj* prediletto. **pet aversion** avversione spiccata *f*. **pet name** nomignolo *m*. *v* coccolare. **petting** *n* (*slang*) carezze amorose *f pl*.

**petal** ['petl] *n* petalo *m*.

**petition** [pə'tiʃən] *n* petizione *f*, supplica *f*. *v* presentare una petizione *or* supplica.

**petrify** ['petrifai] *v* pietrificare, paralizzare. **petrified** *adj* allibito, pietrificato.

**petrol** ['petrəl] *n* benzina *f*. **petrol-tank** *n* serbatoio *m*.

**petroleum** [pə'trouliəm] *n* petrolio *m*.

**petticoat** ['petikout] *n* sottana *f*.

**petty** ['peti] *adj* insignificante; (*mean*) meschino. **petty cash** piccola cassa *f*, fondo per le piccole spese *m*. **petty officer** capo *m*. **pettiness** *n* piccolezza *f*, meschinità *f*.

**petulant** ['petjulənt] *adj* scontroso, irritabile. **petulance** *n* scontrosità *f*, irritabilità *f*.

**pew** [pju:] *n* banco (di chiesa) *m*.

**pewter** ['pju:tə] *n* peltro *m*.

**phantom** ['fæntəm] *n* fantasma *m*.

**pharmacy** ['fɑ:məsi] *n* farmacia *f*. **pharmaceutical** *adj* farmaceutico. **pharmacist** *n* farmacista *m*, *f*.

**pharynx** ['færiŋks] *n* faringe *f*.

**phase** [feiz] *n* fase *f*.

**pheasant** ['feznt] *n* fagiano *m*.

**phenomenon** [fə'nomənən] *n*, *pl* **-ena** fenomeno *m*. **phenomenal** *adj* fenomenale.

**phial** ['faiəl] *n* fiala *f*.

**philanthropy** [fi'lænθrəpi] *n* filantropia *f*. **philanthropic** *adj* filantropico. **philanthropist** *n* filantropo, -a *m*, *f*.

**philately** [fi'lætəli] *n* filatelia *f*. **philatelist** *n* filatelico, -a *m*, *f*.

**philosophy** [fi'losəfi] *n* filosofia *f*. **philosopher** *n* filosofo, -a *m*, *f*. **philosophical** *adj* filosofico.

**phlegm** [flem] *n* (*mucus*) muco *m*; (*sluggishness*) flemma *f*.

**phlegmatic** [fleg'mætik] *adj* flemmatico.

**phobia** ['foubiə] *n* fobia *f*.

**phone** [foun] *n* (*coll*) telefono *m*. *v* telefonare (a). **phone book** elenco telefonico *m*. **phone-in** *n* chiamare una trasmissione.

**phonetic** [fə'netik] *adj* fonetico. **phonetics** *n* fonetica *f*.

**phoney** ['founi] (*coll*) *adj* falso, fasullo. *n* ipocrita *m*, *f*; impostore *m*.

**phosphate** ['fosfeit] *n* fosfato *m*.

**phosphorescence** [fosfə'resəns] *n* fosforescenza *f*. **phosphorescent** *adj* fosforescente.

**phosphorus** ['fosfərəs] *n* fosforo *m*.

**photo** ['foutou] *n* (*coll*) foto *f*.

**photocopy** ['foutou,kopi] *n* fotocopia *f*. *v* fotocopiare.

**photogenic** [,foutou'dʒenik] *adj* fotogenico.

**photograph** ['foutəgrɑ:f] *n* fotografia *f*. *v* fotografare. **photographer** *n* fotografo *m*. **photographic** *adj* fotografico. **photography** *n* fotografia *f*.

**phrase** [freiz] *n* frase *f*, modo di dire *m*. *v* esprimere, formulare.

**physical** ['fizikəl] *adj* fisico.

**physician** [fi'ziʃən] *n* medico *m*.

**physics** ['fiziks] *n* fisica *f*. **physicist** *n* fisico, -a *m*, *f*.

**physiology** [,fizi'olədʒi] *n* fisiologia *f*. **physiological** *adj* fisiologico. **physiologist** *n* fisiologo, -a *m*, *f*.

**physiotherapy** [,fiziou'θerəpi] *n* fisioterapia *f*. **physiotherapist** *n* fisioterapista *m*, *f*.

**physique** [fi'zi:k] *n* fisico *m*.

**piano** [pi'ænou] *n* pianoforte *m*. **pianist** *n* pianista *m*, *f*.

**pick¹** [pik] *v* (*choose*) scegliere; (*pluck*) cogliere. **pick out** scegliere. **pickpocket** *n* borsaiolo *m*. **pick up** raccogliere; (*recover*) star meglio; (*passenger*) far salire; (*learn*) imparare. **pick-up** *n* pick-up. *m*. *n* (*choice*) scelta *f*; (*best*) fior fiore *m*.

**pick²** [pik] *n* piccone *m*.

**picket** ['pikit] *n* picchetto *m*. *v* picchettare.

**pickle** ['pikl] *v* marinare; (*in vinegar*) mettere sott'aceto. *n* (*coll*: *predicament*) pasticcio *m*. **pickles** *pl n* sottaceti *m pl*. **pickled** *adj* sottaceto.

**picnic** ['piknik] *n* picnic *m invar*, colazione all'aperto *f*.

**pictorial** [pik'to:riəl] *adj* illustrato.

**picture** ['piktʃə] *v* immaginare, figurare. *n* (*painting*) quadro *m*; foto *f*; (*image*) immagine *f*; film *m*. **be in the picture** essere informato. **pictures** *n* (*coll*) cinema *m*. **put in the picture** mettere al corrente.

**picturesque** [piktʃə'resk] *adj* pittoresco.

**pidgin** ['pidʒən] *n* linguaggio bastardo *or* maccheronico *m*.

**pie** [pai] *n* pasticcio *m*; (*sweet*) crostata *f*.

**piece** [pi:s] *n* pezzo *m*. **piecemeal** *adv* gradualmente, un po' alla volta. **piecework** *n* lavoro a cottimo *m*. *v* rappezzare. **piece together** aggiustare, mettere assieme.

**Piedmont** ['pi:dmənt] *n* Piemonte *m*.

**pier** [piə] *n* molo *m*, banchina *f*.

**pierce** [piəs] *v* forare, penetrare. **piercing** *adj* acuto, penetrante; (*wind*) pungente.

**piety** ['paiəti] *n* devozione religiosa *f*.

**pig** [pig] *n* maiale *m*, porco (*pl* -ci) *m*. **pig-headed** *adj* ostinato, testardo. **pig-headedness** *n* testardaggine *f*. **pig-iron** *n* ghisa *f*. **piglet** *n* porcellino *m*. **pigskin** *adj* cinghiale. **pigsty** *n* porcile *m*. **pigtail** *n* codino *m*.

**pigeon** ['pidʒən] *n* piccione *m*. **carrier**

**pigeon** piccione viaggiatore *m*. **clay pigeon** piattello *m*.

**pigeon-hole** *n* casella *f*. *v* incasellare.

**pigment** ['pigmənt] *n* pigmento *m*.

**pike** [paik] *n* (*fish*) luccio *m*.

**pilchard** ['piltʃəd] *n* sardina *f*, sarda *f*.

**pile**[1] [pail] *n* (*heap*) mucchio *m*; (*building*) fabbricato *m*. *v* accumulare. **pile on** (*coll*) esagerare. **pile up** accatastare.

**pile**[2] [pail] *n* (*post*) palo *m*. **pile-driver** *n* battipalo *m*.

**pile**[3] [pail] *n* (*of carpet, etc.*) pelo *m*.

**piles** [pailz] *pl n* (*med*) emorroidi *f pl*.

**pilfer** ['pilfə] *v* rubacchiare. **pilferer** *n* ladruncolo *m*.

**pilgrim** ['pilgrim] *n* pellegrino *m*. **pilgrimage** *n* pellegrinaggio *m*.

**pill** [pil] *n* pillola *f*. **pillbox** *n* scatoletta per pillole *f*; (*mil*) casamatta *f*.

**pillage** ['pilidʒ] *n* saccheggio *m*. *v* saccheggiare.

**pillar** ['pilə] *n* pilastro *m*, colonna *f*. **pillarbox** *n* buca delle lettere *f*.

**pillion** ['piljən] *n* sella posteriore *f*, sedile posteriore *m*. **ride pillion** viaggiare sul sedile posteriore.

**pillow** ['pilou] *n* guanciale *m*. **pillowslip** *n* federa *f*.

**pilot** ['pailət] *n* pilota *m, f*. *v* pilotare.

**pimento** [pi'mentou] *n* (*allspice*) pimento *m*; (*capsicum*) peperone *m*.

**pimp** [pimp] *n* ruffiano *m*.

**pimple** ['pimpl] *n* pustoletta *f*, foruncolo *m*.

**pin** [pin] *n* spillo *m*; (*brooch*) spilla *f*. **pincushion** *n* portaspilli *m invar*. **pinpoint** *v* determinare con precisione. **pinprick** *n* (*annoyance*) seccatura *f*. *v* puntare. **pin down** inchiodare. **pin-up** *n* (*girl*) ragazza da copertina *f*, pin-up *f invar*.

**pinafore** ['pinəfo:] *n* grembiulino *m*.

**pincers** ['pinsəz] *pl n* pinza *f sing*, tenaglia *f sing*.

**pinch** [pintʃ] *v* pizzicare; (*hurt*) far male a; (*coll: steal*) rubare; (*coll: catch*) acchiappare. *n* (*nip*) pizzicotto *m*; (*small quantity*) pizzico (*pl* -chi) *m*. **at a pinch** caso mai.

**pine**[1] [pain] *n* (*tree*) pino *m*. **pine-cone** *n* pigna *f*.

**pine**[2] [pain] *v* languire. **pine for** desiderare ardentemente.

**pineapple** ['painapl] *n* ananas *m*.

**pinion**[1] ['pinjən] *n* (*tech*) pignone *m*.

**pinion**[2] ['pinjən] *v* (*shackle*) legare.

**pink** [piŋk] *adj* rosa *invar*. *n* (*colour*) rosa *m invar*; (*flower*) garofano *m*. **in the pink of condition** in ottima forma.

**pinnacle** ['pinəkl] *n* cima *f*, colmo *m*; (*arch*) pinnacolo *m*.

**pioneer** [,paiə'niə] *n* pioniere, -a *m, f*. *v* aprire la strada a.

**pious** ['paiəs] *adj* pio, devoto.

**pip**[1] [pip] *n* (*seed*) seme *m*, granello *m*.

**pip**[2] [pip] *n* (*phone*) segnale acustico *m*.

**pipe** [paip] *n* tubo *m*, condotto *m*; (*for smoking*) pipa *f*. **pipe-cleaner** *n* nettapipe *m invar*. **pipedream** *n* illusione *f*. **pipeline** *n* oleodotto *m*; linea di communicazione *f*. *v* **pipe down!** sta zitto! **pipe up** farsi sentire. **piping** *n* (*sewing*) cordonetto *m*. **piping hot** caldo bollente.

**piquant** ['pi:kənt] *adj* piccante, mordace.

**pique** [pi:k] *n* dispetto *m*. *v* **feel piqued** risentirsi.

**pirate** ['paiərət] *n* pirata *m*. **pirate radio** radiopirata *m*. *v* (*radio*) servirsi abusivamente di; (*book*) plagiare. **piracy** *n* pirateria *f*.

**pirouette** [piru'et] *n* piroetta *f*. *v* piroettare.

**Pisces** ['paisi:z] *n* Pesci *m pl*.

**piss** [pis] (*vulgar*) *n* piscia *f*. *v* pisciare. **pissed** *adj* sbronzo.

**pistachio** [pi'sta:ʃiou] *n* pistacchio *m*.

**pistol** ['pistl] *n* pistola *f*.

**piston** ['pistən] *n* pistone *m*.

**pit** [pit] *n* fossa *f*; (*theatre*) platea *f*; (*scar*) buttero *m*. *v* **pit against** opporre.

**pitch**[1] [pitʃ] *n* lancio *m*; (*degree*) grado *m*; (*music*) tono *m*, registro *m*; (*sport*) campo *m*, terreno *m*. *v* lanciare; (*tent*) piantare; (*fix*) fissare; (*ship*) beccheggiare. **pitchfork** *n* forcone *m*.

**pitch**[2] [pitʃ] *n* pece *f*. **pitch-dark** *adj* buio pesto.

**pitfall** ['pitfo:l] *n* trappola *f*, tranello *m*.

**pith** [piθ] *n* midollo *m*. **pithy** *adj* succinto.

**pittance** ['pitəns] *n* somma irrisoria *f*.

**pituitary** [pi'tju:itəri] *n* ipofisi *f*, glandola pituitaria *f*.

**pity** ['piti] *n* pietà *f*, compassione *f*; (*shame*) peccato *m*. **what a pity!** che peccato! *v* avere pietà di, compatire. **pitiful** *adj* (*wretched*) pietoso; (*contemptible*) miserabile.

**pitiless** *adj* spietato.

**pivot** ['pivət] *n* perno *m*, fulcro *m*. *v* imperniare.

**placard** ['plaka:d] *n* cartellone *m*.

**placate** [plə'keit] *v* placare, conciliare.

**place** [pleis] *n* luogo *m*, posto *m*. **out of place** inopportuno. **put in one's place** umiliare. **take place** aver luogo, accadere. *v* mettere, posare, porre; (*order*) piazzare.

**placenta** [plə'sentə] *n* placenta *f*.

**placid** ['plasid] *adj* placido.

**plagiarize** ['pleidʒəraiz] *v* plagiare. **plagiarism** *n* plagio *m*. **plagiarist** *n* plagiario, -a *m*, *f*.

**plague** [pleig] *n* (*disease*) peste *f*; (*calamity*) piaga *f*. *v* tormentare, affliggere.

**plaice** [pleis] *n* passera di mare *f*.

**plaid** [plad] *n* plaid *m invar*.

**plain** [plein] *adj* chiaro; (*simple*) semplice; (*frank*) schietto; (*not patterned*) a tinta unita; (*unattractive*) brutto. **in plain clothes** in borghese. **plain cooking** cucina semplice *or* casalinga *f*. *n* pianura *f*.

**plaintiff** ['pleintif] *n* querelante *m*, *f*; attore, -trice *m*, *f*.

**plaintive** ['pleintiv] *adj* querulo, lamentoso.

**plait** [plat] *n* (*braid*) treccia *f*; (*pleat*) piega *f*. *v* intrecciare; piegare.

**plan** [plan] *n* piano *m*, progetto *m*; intenzione *f*; (*drawing*) disegno *m*; (*map*) pianta *f*. *v* progettare; intendere; (*econ*) pianificare.

**plane**[1] [plein] *n* (*flat surface*) piano *m*, livello *m*; (*coll*) aereo *m*. *adj* piano.

**plane**[2] [plein] *n* (*tool*) pialla *f*. *v* piallare.

**plane**[3] [plein] *n* (*tree*) platano *m*.

**planet** ['planit] *n* pianeta *m*. **planetarium** *n* planetario *m*. **planetary** *adj* planetario.

**plank** [plaŋk] *n* asse *f*, tavola *f*.

**plankton** ['plaŋktən] *n* plancton *m invar*.

**plant** [pla:nt] *n* (*bot*) pianta *f*; (*manufacturing*) impianto *m*, stabilimento *m*. *v* piantare. **plantation** *n* piantagione *f*.

**plaque** [pla:k] *n* placca *f*.

**plasma** ['plazmə] *n* plasma *m*.

**plaster** ['pla:stə] *n* (*med*) intonaco *m*; (*med*) impiastro *m*; (*for wound*) cerotto *m*. **plaster of Paris** gesso *m*. *v* intonacare; impiastrare; ingessare.

**plastic** ['plastik] *adj* plastico. *n* plastica *f*.

**plate** [pleit] *n* (*dish*) piatto *m*; (*of metal*) lamiera *f*, lastra *f*; (*denture*) dentiera *f*; (*metallic ware*) argenteria *f*; (*in book*) tavola *f*, illustrazione *f*. **plate-glass** *n* cristallo *m*. *v* galvanizzare; (*silver*) argentare.

**plateau** ['platou] *n* altipiano *m*.

**platform** ['platfo:m] *n* piattaforma *f*; (*rail*) binario *m*.

**platinum** ['platinəm] *n* platino *m*.

**platonic** [plə'tonik] *adj* platonico.

**platoon** [plə'tu:n] *n* plotone *m*.

**plausible** ['plo:zəbl] *adj* ammissibile, credibile.

**play** [plei] *v* giocare; (*musical instrument*) suonare; (*act*) recitare. **play down** minimizzare. **play fair** comportarsi lealmente. **play truant** marinare la scuola. *n* gioco *m*, divertimento *m*; (*theatre*) spettacolo *m*. **playboy** *n* playboy *m*, buontempone *m*. **playground** *n* cortile di scuola *m*. **playmate** *n* compagno, -a di gioco *m*, *f*. **playpen** *n* recinto per bambini *m*, box *m invar*. **play-school** *n* asilo *m*. **playwright** *n* commediografo, -a *m*, *f*; drammaturgo, -a *m*, *f*. **player** *n* giocatore, -trice *m*, *f*; (*music*) suonatore, -trice *m*, *f*; (*theatre*) attore, -trice *m*, *f*. **playful** *adj* scherzoso, giocoso. **playing card** carta da gioco *f*. **playing field** campo sportivo *m*.

**plea** [pli:] *n* difesa *f*, supplica *f*; (*excuse*) scusa *f*.

**plead** [pli:d] *v* implorare; perorare. **plead guilty/innocent** dichiararsi colpevole/innocente. **plead with** intercedere presso. **pleading** *n* perorazione *f*.

**please** [pli:z] *v* piacere (a), contentare, soddisfare. **please oneself** fare il proprio comodo. *adv* per favore, per cortesia. **pleased** *adj* contento, lieto, soddisfatto. **pleasing** *adj* piacevole, gradevole. **pleasure** *n* piacere *m*, favore *m*.

**pleat** [pli:t] *n* piega *f*. *v* pieghettare.

**pledge** [pledʒ] *n* promessa solenne *f*; (*undertaking*) impegno *m*. *v* impegnare, garantire; promettere solennemente.

**plenty** ['plenti] *n* abbondanza *f*. **in plenty** in abbondanza. **plenty of** abbastanza. **plentiful** *adj* abbondante.

**pleurisy** ['pluərisi] *n* pleurite *f*.

**pliable** ['plaiəbl] *adj* flessibile. **pliability** *n* flessibilità *f*.

**pliers** ['plaiəz] *pl n* pinza *f sing*, tenaglia *f sing*.

**plight** [plait] *n* stato *m*.

**plimsoll** ['plimsəl] *n* scarpa da tennis *f.*

**plod** [plod] *v* **plod along** tirare avanti. **plodder** *n* sgobbone, -a *m, f.*

**plonk** [ploŋk] *n* (*coll*) vino comune *m.*

**plot**[1] [plot] *n* (*story*) trama *f*, intreccio *m*; (*secret plan*) congiura *f*, complotto *m. v* tramare, complottare; (*trace*) tracciare. **plotter** *n* cospiratore, -trice *m, f.*

**plot**[2] [plot] *n* (*land*) lotto *or* pezzo di terreno *m.*

**plough** [plau] *n* aratro *m. v* arare; (*coll: fail exam*) trombare. **plough back** riinvestire. **plough through** (*book, etc.*) leggere con fatica.

**pluck** [plʌk] *v* cogliere; (*feathers*) spennare; (*tug at*) strappare. **pluck up courage** farsi coraggio. *n* (*courage*) fegato *m.* **be plucky** aver fegato.

**plug** [plʌg] *n* tappo *m*; (*elec*) spina *f*; (*mot*) candela *f. v* tappare.

**plum** [plʌm] *n* (*fruit*) prugna *f*, susina *f*; (*tree*) prugno *m*, susino *m. adj* (*colour*) prugna.

**plumage** ['plu:midʒ] *n* piumaggio *m.*

**plumb** [plʌm] *adj* verticale. *adv* a piombo; (*absolutely*) proprio. *n* piombo *m*, scandaglio *m. v* sondare; (*naut*) scandagliare. **plumber** *n* idraulico *m.*

**plume** [plu:m] *n* penna *f*, piuma *f*; (*on helmet*) pennacchio *m.*

**plummet** ['plʌmit] *v* piombare.

**plump**[1] [plʌmp] *adj* (*fat*) grassoccio, paffuto.

**plump**[2] [plʌmp] *v* **plump for** scegliere.

**plunder** ['plʌndə] *n* bottino *m. v* spogliare, depredare.

**plunge** [plʌndʒ] *n* tuffo *m. v* tuffare; immergere; (*rush*) lanciarsi. **plunger** *n* (*tech*) stantuffo *m.*

**pluperfect** [plu:'pəfikt] *n* trapassato remoto *m.*

**plural** ['pluərəl] *nm, adj* plurale. **in the plural** al plurale.

**plus** [plʌs] *adj* addizionale. *prep* più.

**plush** [plʌʃ] *n* felpa *f. adj* lussuoso.

**plutocrat** ['plu:təkrat] *n* plutocrate *m, f.*

**ply**[1] [plai] *v* (*travel*) viaggiare regolarmente; (*trade*) esercitare.

**ply**[2] [plai] *n* (*layer*) strato *m*; (*wool*) filo *m.* **plywood** *n* legno compensato *m.*

**pneumatic** [nju'matik] *adj* pneumatico.

**pneumonia** [nju'mouniə] *n* polmonite *f.*

**poach**[1] [poutʃ] *v* (*game*) cacciare di frodo; (*fish*) pescare di frodo; (*encroach on*) usurpare. **poacher** *n* bracconiere *m.*

**poach**[2] [poutʃ] *v* (*cookery*) lessare. **poached egg** uovo affogato *m*, uovo in camicia *m.*

**pocket** ['pokit] *n* tasca *f*, taschino *m*; (*billiards*) buca *f.* **be out of pocket** rimetterci. *v* intascare. *adj* tascabile. **pocket-book** *n* taccuino *m.* **pocket-knife** *n* temperino *m.* **pocket-money** *n* soldi per le piccole spese *m pl.*

**pod** [pod] *n* baccello *m.*

**podgy** ['podʒi] *adj* grassotto, paffuto.

**poem** ['pouim] *n* poesia *f.*

**poet** ['pouit] *n* poeta *m.* **poetess** *n* poetessa *f.* **poetic** *adj* poetico. **poetry** *n* poesia *f.*

**poignant** ['poinjənt] *adj* intenso, vivo, commovente.

**point** [point] *n* punto *m*; (*sharp end*) punta *f*; (*elec*) presa *f.* **be on the point of** stare per. **make a point of** insistere su. **point-blank** *adv* a bruciapelo; (*coll*) di punto in bianco. *v* indicare, additare; (*aim*) puntare; (*brickwork*) affilettare. **pointed** *adj* acuto. **pointer** *n* (*hint*) indicazione *f*; (*dog*) pointer *m.* **pointing** *n* affilettatura *f.* **pointless** *adj* inutile.

**poise** [poiz] *n* equilibrio *m*, compostezza *f*, portamento *m. v* equilibrare, essere in equilibrio.

**poison** ['poizən] *n* veleno *m. v* avvelenare. **poisonous** *adj* velenoso.

**poke** [pouk] *n* spinta *f*, gomitata *f. v* (*stick into*) ficcare; (*thrust*) cacciare; (*fire*) attizzare. **poke about** frugare. **poke fun at** beffarsi di. **poker** *n* attizzatoio *m.* **poky** *adj* meschino, piccolo.

**poker** ['poukə] *n* (*cards*) poker *m.* **poker-faced** *adj* impassibile.

**Poland** ['poulənd] *n* Polonia *f.* **Pole** *n* polacco, -a *m, f.* **Polish** *nm, adj* polacco.

**polar** ['poulə] *adj* polare. **polar bear** orso bianco *m.* **polarize** *v* polarizzare. **polarity** *n* polarità *f.*

**pole**[1] [poul] *n* (*post*) palo *m*, asta *f.* **pole-vault** *n* salto all'asta *m.*

**pole**[2] [poul] *n* (*geog*) polo *m.*

**police** [pə'li:s] *n* polizia *f.* **policeman** *n* carabiniere *m*, poliziotto *m*, vigile *m.* **police station** questura *f. v* mantenere l'ordine, sorvegliare, vigilare.

**policy¹** ['polǝsi] *n* politica *f*, linea di condotta *f*.

**policy²** ['polǝsi] *n* (*insurance*) polizza *f*.

**polio** ['pouliou] *n* poliomielite *f*.

**polish** ['poliʃ] *n* (*for shoes, etc.*) lucido *m*; (*for nails*) smalto *m*; raffinatezza *f*. *v* lucidare, lustrare. **polish off** (*dispose of quickly*) sbrigare; liquidare. **polish up** ripassare.

**polite** [pǝ'lait] *adj* cortese, garbato. **politeness** *n* cortesia *f*, garbo *m*.

**politically correct** *adv* politicamente corretto.

**politics** ['politiks] *n* politica *f*. **politic** *adj* espediente. **political** *adj* politico. **politician** *n* uomo politico *m*.

**polka** ['polkǝ] *n* polca *f*.

**poll** [poul] *n* elezione *f*; (*casting of votes*) votazione *f*; (*votes cast*) voti *m pl*. **opinion poll** sondaggio d'opinioni *m*. *v* ottenere voti. **polling booth** cabina elettorale *f*.

**pollen** ['polǝn] *n* polline *m*. **pollinate** *v* impollinare. **pollination** *n* impollinazione *f*.

**pollute** [pǝ'lu:t] *v* inquinare. **pollution** *n* inquinamento *m*.

**polo** ['poulou] *n* polo *m*. **polo-neck** *n* collo ciclista *m*. **polo-neck sweater** ciclista *f*.

**polygamy** [pǝ'ligǝmi] *n* poligamia *f*. **polygamist** *n* poligamo *m*. **polygamous** *adj* poligamo.

**polygon** ['poligǝn] *n* poligono *m*. **polygonal** *adj* poligonale.

**polytechnic** [ˌpoli'teknik] *n* politecnico *m*.

**polythene** ['poliθi:n] *n* politene *m*.

**pomegranate** ['pomigranit] *n* melagrana *f*.

**pomp** [pomp] *n* pompa *f*, sfarzo *m*. **pompous** *adj* pomposo, ampolloso.

**pond** [pond] *n* stagno *m*.

**ponder** ['pondǝ] *v* ponderare; valutare. **ponderous** *adj* ponderoso, pesante.

**pontiff** ['pontif] *n* pontefice *m*, papa *m*. **pontifical** *adj* pontificio. **pontificate** *v* pontificare.

**pontoon** [pon'tu:n] *n* pontone *m*; (*cards*) ventuno *m*.

**pony** ['pouni] *n* pony *m*.

**poodle** ['pu:dl] *n* cane barbone *m*.

**poof** [pu:f] *n* (*derog*) finocchio *m*.

**pool¹** [pu:l] *n* (*pond*) stagno *m*; (*puddle*) pozzanghera *f*; (*swimming*) piscina *f*.

**pool²** [pu:l] *v* mettere in comune. *n* fondo comune *m*; (*football*) totocalcio *m*.

**poor** [puǝ] *adj* povero; mediocre; (*meagre*) magro; (*not good*) cattivo.

**poorly** ['puǝli] *adj* malaticcio. *adv* male. **feel poorly** non sentirsi troppo bene.

**pop¹** [pop] *v* schioccare, saltare. **pop in** fare una breve visita. **pop out** saltar fuori. **pop up** apparire. *n* schiocco *m*; (*drink*) bibita gassata *f*.

**pop²** [pop] *adj* popolare. **pop-art** *n* pop-art *f*. **pop music** musica pop *f*.

**pope** [poup] *n* papa *m*.

**poplar** ['poplǝ] *n* pioppo *m*.

**poppy** ['popi] *n* papavero *m*.

**popular** ['popjulǝ] *adj* popolare; (*favourite*) ben visto. **popularity** *n* popolarità *f*. **popularize** *v* divulgare.

**population** [ˌpopju'leiʃǝn] *n* popolazione *f*. **populate** *v* popolare.

**porcelain** ['po:slin] *n* porcellana *f*.

**porch** [po:tʃ] *n* portico *m*.

**porcupine** ['po:kjupain] *n* porcospino *m*.

**pore¹** [po:] *n* (*opening*) poro *m*.

**pore²** [po:] *v* **pore over** meditare su, essere assorto in.

**pork** [po:k] *n* carne suina *f*, carne di maiale *f*.

**pornography** [po:'nogrǝfi] *n* pornografia *f*. **pornographic** *adj* pornografico.

**porous** ['po:rǝs] *adj* poroso.

**porpoise** ['po:pǝs] *n* focena *f*.

**porridge** ['poridʒ] *n* pappa di fiocchi d'avena *f*.

**port¹** [po:t] *n* (*harbour*) porto *m*.

**port²** [po:t] *n* (*naut: left*) sinistra *f*, babordo *m*.

**port³** [po:t] *n* (*wine*) porto *m invar*.

**portable** ['po:tǝbl] *adj* portatile.

**portent** ['po:tent] *n* (*omen*) presagio *m*; (*marvel*) portento *m*. **portentous** *adj* prodigioso, portentoso; grave.

**porter** ['po:tǝ] *n* (*janitor*) portinaio, -a *m, f*; (*carrier*) facchino *m*.

**portfolio** [po:t'fouliou] *n* (*pol*) portafoglio *m*; (*case*) cartella *f*.

**porthole** ['po:thoul] *n* oblò *m*.

**portion** ['po:ʃǝn] *n* porzione *f*. *v* ripartire.

**portrait** ['po:trǝt] *n* ritratto *m*. **portrait-painter** *n* ritrattista *m, f*.

**portray** [po:'trei] *v* rappresentare.

**Portugal** ['po:tjugl] *n* Portogallo *m*.

**Portuguese** n(m+f), adj portoghese.
**pose** [pouz] n posa f; (posture) atteggiamento m. v posare, atteggiarsi (a); (propound) porre.
**posh** [poʃ] adj elegante.
**position** [pə'ziʃən] n posizione f, situazione f; (employment) posto m. v collocare, piazzare.
**positive** ['pozətiv] adj positivo; (certain) sicuro. n (phot) positiva f; (gramm) positivo m.
**possess** [pə'zes] v possedere, avere. **possessed** adj ossesso, frenetico. **possession** n possesso m. **possessions** pl n (goods) beni personali m pl. **possessive** nm, adj possessivo. **possessor** n possessore m, posseditrice f.
**possible** ['posəbl] adj possibile. **possibility** n possibilità f. **possibly** adv (perhaps) forse, può darsi; (if possible) possibilmente.
**post¹** [poust] n (pole) palo m. v affiggere.
**post²** [poust] n (job) posto m. v collocare.
**post³** [poust] n (mail) posta f. **post-box** n buca da lettere f. **postcard** n cartolina f. **postman** n postino m. **postmark** n timbro postale m. **postmarked** adj timbrato. **post office** posta f, ufficio postale m. **post office box** casella postale f. v imbucare; (book-keeping) registrare. **keep posted** tenere al corrente. **postage** n tariffa postale f. **postage stamp** francobollo m. **postal** adj postale. **postal order** vaglia postale m invar.
**poste restante** [poust'restät] adv fermo posta.
**poster** ['poustə] n cartellone m, manifesto m, avviso pubblicitario m.
**posterior** [po'stiəriə] adj posteriore.
**posterity** [po'sterəti] n posterità f.
**postgraduate** [poust'gradjuit] adj di perfezionamento or specializzazione. n laureato, -a che continua gli studi universitari m, f.
**posthumous** ['postjuməs] adj postumo.
**post-mortem** [poust'mo:təm] n autopsia f.
**postpone** [pous'poun] v posporre, rinviare. **postponement** n rinvio m.
**postscript** ['pousskript] n poscritto m.
**postulate** ['postjuleit; n 'postjulət] v postulare. n postulato m.
**posture** ['postʃə] n posizione f; (attitude) atteggiamento m. v assumere una posa.

**pot** [pot] n vaso m; (pan) pentola f; (container) recipiente m. v (plant) piantare in vaso; (billiards) mandare in buca. **pot-belly** n pancione m. **pot-bellied** adj panciuto. **take pot luck** mangiare alla buona.
**potassium** [pə'tasjəm] n potassio m. **potash** n potassa f.
**potato** [pə'teitou] n patata f.
**potent** ['poutənt] adj potente, forte. **potency** n potenza f.
**potential** [pə'tenʃəl] adj, nm potenziale.
**pot-hole** ['pothoul] n (cave) spelonca f; (in road) buca f. **pot-holer** n speleologo, -a m, f. **pot-holing** n speleologia f.
**potion** ['pouʃən] n pozione f.
**potter¹** ['potə] v **potter about** lavoricchiare.
**potter²** ['potə] n ceramista m, f, vasaio, -a m, f.
**pottery** ['potəri] n (ware) ceramica f; (workshop) laboratorio di ceramiche m.
**potty¹** ['poti] adj (coll) matto.
**potty²** ['poti] n (coll) vaso da notte m, pitale m.
**pouch** [pautʃ] n borsa f, tasca f, sacchetto m.
**poultice** ['poultis] n cataplasma m.
**poultry** ['poultri] n pollame m. **poulterer** n pollivendolo, -a m, f.
**pounce** [pauns] n sbalzo m. v balzare. **pounce on** piombare su, saltare addosso a.
**pound¹** [paund] v (hit) pestare, battere. n colpo m.
**pound²** [paund] n (weight) libbra f; (sterling) lira sterlina f.
**pound³** [paund] n (enclosure) recinto m.
**pour** [po:] v versare, riversarsi; (rain) scrosciare.
**pout** [paut] v fare il broncio. n broncio m.
**poverty** ['povəti] n povertà f, miseria f. **poverty-stricken** adj bisognoso, indigente.
**powder** ['paudə] n polvere f; (cosmetic) cipria f. **powder compact** portacipria m invar. **powder puff** piumino per la cipria m. v polverizzare, incipriare. **powdery** adj polveroso.
**power** ['pauə] n potere m; (pol, phys, etc.) potenza f; (tech) energia f, forza f. **powers** pl n facoltà f pl. **power point** presa elettrica f. **power station** centrale elettrica f. **powerful** adj potente. **powerless** adj

impotente, incapace.

**practicable** ['præktikəbl] *adj* fattibile.

**practical** ['præktikəl] *adj* pratico. **for practical purposes** in pratica. **practical joke** beffa *f*. **practically** *adv* in effetto, quasi.

**practice** ['præktis] *n* pratica *f*; esercizio *m*; clientela *f*; (*sport*) allenamento *m*. **normal practice** regola *f*. **out of practice** fuori esercizio.

**practise** ['præktis] *v* praticare, esercitare; (*music*) esercitarsi; (*sport*) allenarsi. **practised** *adj* esperto, pratico. **practising** *adj* (*rel*) praticante.

**practitioner** [præk'tiʃənə] *n* **general practitioner** medico generico *m*.

**pragmatic** [præg'mætik] *adj* prammatico; (*officious*) inframmettente; dogmatico. **pragmatism** *n* pragmatismo *m*; dogmatismo *m*.

**Prague** [pra:g] *n* Praga *f*.

**prairie** ['preəri] *n* prateria *f*.

**praise** [preiz] *n* lode *f*, elogio *m*. *v* lodare, elogiare. **praiseworthy** *adj* lodevole.

**pram** [præm] *n* carrozzella *f*.

**prance** [pra:ns] *v* pavoneggiarsi; (*child*) saltellare; (*horse*) impennarsi.

**prank** [præŋk] *n* burla *f*, tiro *m*. **play a prank on** fare un tiro a.

**prattle** ['prætl] *v* cianciare, ciarlare.

**prawn** [prɔ:n] *n* gambero *m*, palemone *m*.

**pray** [prei] *v* pregare. **prayer** *n* preghiera *f*. **prayer-book** *n* libro di preghiere *m*; (*missal*) messale *m*.

**preach** [pri:tʃ] *v* predicare. **preach a sermon** fare una predica. **preacher** *n* predicatore *m*.

**preamble** [pri:'æmbl] *n* preambolo *m*.

**prearrange** [pri:ə'reindʒ] *v* predisporre.

**precarious** [pri'keəriəs] *adj* precario, incerto.

**precaution** [pri'kɔ:ʃən] *n* precauzione *f*.

**precede** [pri'si:d] *v* precedere. **precedence** *n* precedenza *f*. **precedent** *n* precedente *m*.

**precinct** ['pri:siŋkt] *n* (*area*) zona *f*; ambito *m*.

**precious** ['preʃəs] *adj* prezioso.

**precipice** ['presipis] *n* precipizio *m*.

**precipitate** [pri'sipiteit; *adj* pri'sipitət] *v* precipitare; (*hurry up*) affrettare. *n* precipitato *m*. *adj* precipitoso.

**précis** ['preisi] *n* sunto *m*.

**precise** [pri'sais] *adj* preciso, esatto; (*strict*) puntiglioso. **precision** *n* precisione *f*, esattezza *f*.

**preclude** [pri'klu:d] *v* precludere.

**precocious** [pri'kouʃəs] *adj* precoce. **precociousness** *n* precocità *f*.

**preconceive** [,pri:kən'si:v] *v* avere preconcetti su. **preconception** *n* preconcetto *m*.

**precursor** [,pri:'kə:sə] *n* precursore *m*.

**predatory** ['predətəri] *adj* predatore, rapace.

**predecessor** ['pri:disesə] *n* predecessore *m*.

**predestine** [pri'destin] *v* predestinare. **predestination** *n* predestinazione *f*.

**predicament** [pri'dikəmənt] *n* situazione imbarazzante *f*, pasticcio *m*.

**predicate** ['predikət] *n* predicato *m*.

**predict** [pri'dikt] *v* predire, pronosticare. **predictable** *adj* prevedibile. **prediction** *n* predizione *f*.

**predispose** [,pri:di'spouz] *v* predisporre. **predisposition** *n* predisposizione *f*.

**predominate** [pri'domineit] *v* predominare, prevalere. **predominance** *n* predominio *m*, ascendente *m*.

**pre-eminent** [pri:'eminənt] *adj* preminente, per eccellenza. **pre-eminence** *n* preminenza *f*.

**preen** [pri:n] *v* **preen oneself** (*bird*) lisciarsi le penne; (*person*) agghindarsi.

**prefabricate** [pri:'fæbrikeit] *v* prefabbricare. **prefab** *n* (*coll*) casa prefabbricata *f*.

**preface** ['prefis] *n* prefazione *f*. *v* premettere.

**prefect** ['pri:fekt] *n* prefetto *m*; (*school*) capoclasse *m*.

**prefer** [pri'fə:] *v* preferire. **preferable** *adj* preferibile. **preference** *n* preferenza *f*. **preference shares** azioni privilegiate *f pl*. **preferential** *adj* preferenziale, di favore.

**prefix** ['pri:fiks] *n* prefisso *m*. *v* prefiggere.

**pregnant** ['pregnənt] *adj* incinta; (*animal*) gravida. **pregnancy** *n* gravidanza *f*.

**prehistoric** [,pri:hi'storik] *adj* preistorico. **prehistory** *n* preistoria *f*.

**prejudice** ['predʒədis] *n* pregiudizio *m*, prevenzione *f*. **have a prejudice against** esser prevenuto contro. *v* pregiudicare, compromettere. **prejudiced** *adj* prevenuto.

**preliminary** [pri'liminəri] *nm, adj* preliminare.

**prelude** ['prelju:d] *n* preludio *m*.

**premarital** [priːˈmaritl] *adj* prematrimoniale.

**premature** [premɘˈtʃuɘ] *adj* prematuro.

**premeditate** [priːˈmediteit] *v* premeditare. **premeditation** *n* premeditazione *f*.

**premier** [ˈpremiɘ] *adj* primo, primario. *n* primo ministro *m*.

**premiere** [ˈpremiɘ] *n* prima (rappresentazione) *f*.

**premise** [ˈpremis] *n* premessa *f*. **premises** *n* locali *m pl*. **off the premises** fuori. **on the premises** sul posto.

**premium** [ˈpriːmiɘm] *n* premio *m*; (*finance*) aggio *m*. **at a premium** (*econ*) sopra la pari.

**premonition** [ˌpremɘˈniʃɘn] *n* premonizione *f*.

**preoccupied** [priːˈokjupaid] *adj* preoccupato. **preoccupation** *n* preoccupazione *f*.

**prepare** [priːˈpeɘ] *v* preparare. **preparation** *n* preparazione *f*. **preparatory** *adj* preparatorio.

**preposition** [ˌprepɘˈziʃɘn] *n* preposizione *f*.

**preposterous** [priːˈpostɘrɘs] *adj* assurdo.

**prerequisite** [priːˈrekwizit] *n* prerequisito *m*, requisito (principale) *m*.

**prerogative** [priːˈrogɘtiv] *n* prerogativa *f*.

**prescribe** [priːˈskraib] *v* prescrivere. **prescription** *n* prescrizione *f*; (*med*) ricetta medica *f*.

**presence** [ˈprezns] *n* presenza *f*; (*appearance*) aspetto *m*.

**present¹** [ˈpreznt] *adj* presente, attuale. *n* (*time*) presente *m*. **at present** attualmente. **for the present** per ora. **presently** *adv* quanto prima.

**present²** [priˈzent; *n* ˈpreznt] *v* presentare, offrire. *n* (*gift*) regalo *m*. **presentable** *adj* presentabile. **presentation** *n* presentazione *f*.

**preserve** [priˈzɘːv] *v* conservare, preservare; (*appearances*) salvare. *n* (*food*) conserva *f*; (*reserve*) riserva *f*. **preservation** *n* preservazione *f*. **preservative** *nm*, *adj* preservativo.

**preside** [priˈzaid] *v* **preside over** presiedere a.

**president** [ˈprezidɘnt] *n* presidente *m*. **presidency** *n* presidenza *f*. **presidential** *adj* presidenziale.

**press** [pres] *v* premere; (*squeeze*) comprimere, schiacciare; far pressione su; insis-

tere su; (*iron*) stirare. **press-button** *n* pulsante *m*. **press-stud** *n* bottone automatico *m*. *n* (*newspapers*) stampa *f*; (*printing*) macchina da stampa *f*; (*publishing house*) casa editrice *f*; (*tech*) torchio *m*. **press cutting** ritaglio (di giornale) *m*. **pressing** *adj* urgente.

**pressure** [ˈpreʃɘ] *n* pressione *m*. **pressure-cooker** *n* pentola a pressione *f*. **pressure group** gruppo di pressione *m*. **pressurize** *v* pressurizzare; (*force*) far pressione su.

**prestige** [preˈstiːʒ] *n* prestigio *m*.

**presume** [priˈzjuːm] *v* presumere, supporre. **presumption** *n* presunzione *f*, supposizione *f*; arroganza *f*. **presumptuous** *adj* presuntuoso. **presumptive** *adj* presunto. *adv* presumibilmente.

**pretend** [priˈtend] *v* pretendere; (*feign*) fingere, far finta. **pretence** *n* pretesa *f*; (*pretext*) pretesto *m*. **pretension** *n* pretensione *f*. **pretentious** *adj* pretenzioso, pieno di pretese.

**pretext** [ˈpriːtekst] *n* pretesto *m*.

**pretty** [ˈpriti] *adj* carino, simpatico. *adv* (*quite*) piuttosto, abbastanza; (*moderately*) quasi.

**prevail** [priˈveil] *v* prevalere. **prevail upon** persuadere, indurre. **prevalent** *adj* prevalente.

**prevent** [priˈvent] *v* impedire. **prevention** *n* prevenzione *f*; (*med*) profilassi *f*.

**preview** [ˈpriːvjuː] *n* anteprima *f*.

**previous** [ˈpriːviɘs] *adj* precedente, anteriore. **previously** *adv* prima.

**prey** [prei] *n* preda *f*. **be/fall a prey to** essere/cadere in preda a. *v* **prey on** predare; (*fear, etc.*) rodere.

**price** [prais] *n* prezzo *m*. **price-list** *n* listino dei prezzi *m*. *v* valutare, fare il prezzo di. **priceless** *adj* impagabile; (*very amusing*) divertentissimo.

**prick** [prik] *v* pungere, punzecchiare. **prick up one's ears** drizzare le orecchie. *n* puntura *f*.

**prickle** [ˈprikl] *n* spina *f*. **prickly** *adj* spinoso; (*sensitive*) difficile. **prickly pear** fico d'India *m*.

**pride** [praid] *n* orgoglio *m*, amor proprio *m*; (*best part*) fiore *m*. *v* **pride oneself on** essere orgoglioso di.

**priest** [priːst] *n* prete *m*, sacerdote *m*. **priesthood** *n* sacerdozio *m*.

**prig** [prig] *n* borioso, -a *m*, *f*. **priggish**

*adj* borioso.

**prim** [prim] *adj* affettato, compassato; (*formal*) cerimonioso.

**primary** ['praiməri] *adj* primario, fondamentale, primo. **primary school** scuola elementare *f*.

**primate** ['praimət] *n* primate *m*. **primacy** *n* primato *m*.

**prime** [praim] *adj* primo; di prima qualità. *n* fiore *m*, primavera *f*. *v* (*arms*) innescare; (*paint*) mesticare; (*information*) mettere al corrente; (*pump*) adescare. **primer** *n* (*book*) testo elementare *m*; (*paint*) mestica *f*.

**primitive** ['primitiv] *adj* primitivo.

**primrose** ['primrouz] *n* primula *f*.

**primus stove** ['praiməs] *n* fornello a petrolio *m*.

**prince** [prins] *n* principe *m*. **princess** *n* principessa *f*.

**principal** ['prinsəpəl] *adj* principale, primo. *n* (*of business*) principale *m*, *f*; (*of school*) direttore, -trice *m*, *f*; (*comm*) capitale *m*.

**principle** ['prinsəpəl] *n* principio *m*.

**print** [print] *v* stampare, imprimere; (*handwriting*) scrivere a stampatello. *n* stampa *f*; impressione *f*; (*phot*) copia *f*. **out of print** esaurito. **printer** *n* tipografo *m*. (*computer*) stampante *f*. **printing** *n* tipografia *f*; (*edition*) tiratura *f*.

**prior**[1] ['praiə] *adj* precedente, anteriore. **prior to** prima di. **priority** *n* precedenza *f*.

**prior**[2] ['praiə] *n* priore *m*. **prioress** *n* priora *f*. **priory** *n* convento *m*, monastero *m*.

**prise** [praiz] *v* far leva su. **prise open** forzare.

**prism** ['prizm] *n* prisma *m*.

**prison** ['prizn] *n* prigione *f*. **prisoner** *n* prigioniero, -a *m*, *f*. **take prisoner** far prigioniero.

**private** ['praivət] *adj* privato, personale. *n* soldato semplice *m*. **privacy** *n* intimità *f*.

**privet** ['privət] *n* ligustro *m*.

**privilege** ['privəlidʒ] *n* privilegio *m*.

**privy** ['privi] *adj* privato. **be privy to** essere a conoscenza di.

**prize** [praiz] *n* (*reward*) premio *m*. **prize-fighter** *n* pugile *m*. **prize-giving** *n* distribuzione dei premi *f*. **prizewinner** *n* vincitore, -trice *m*, *f*. *v* apprezzare, valutare.

**probable** ['probəbl] *adj* probabile. **probability** *n* probabilità *f*.

**probation** [prə'beiʃən] *n* (*law*) libertà condizionata *f*; (*for job, etc.*) periodo di prova *m*. **probationary** *adj* di prova.

**probe** [proub] *v* esplorare, sondare. *n* (*investigation*) sondaggio *m*, inchiesta *f*; (*instrument*) sonda *f*.

**problem** ['probləm] *n* problema *m*. **problematic** *adj* problematico.

**proceed** [prə'si:d] *v* procedere, proseguire. **proceeds** *pl n* ricavo *m sing*, incasso *m sing*. **procedure** *n* procedura *f*; (*proceeding*) procedimento *m*.

**process** ['prouses] *n* processo *m*, andamento *m*; (*procedure*) procedimento *m*. *v* trattare, trasformare. **processed cheese** formaggio fuso *m*.

**procession** [prə'seʃən] *n* processione *f*, sfilata *f*.

**proclaim** [prə'kleim] *v* proclamare. **proclamation** *n* proclama *m*.

**procrastinate** [prə'krastineit] *v* procrastinare, rimandare.

**procreate** ['proukrieit] *v* procreare. **procreation** *n* procreazione *f*.

**procure** [prə'kjuə] *v* procurare. **procurement** *n* approvvigionamento *m*.

**prod** [prod] *v* (*incite*) sollecitare; (*push*) spingere.

**prodigy** ['prodidʒi] *n* prodigio *m*.

**produce** [prə'dju:s; *n* 'prodju:s] *v* produrre; (*pull out*) tirar fuori; (*theatre*) mettere in scena. *n* prodotti *or* generi agricoli *m pl*. **producer** *n* produttore, -trice *m*, *f*; (*theatre, etc.*) regista *m*, *f*. **product** *n* prodotto *m*, frutto *m*. **production** *n* produzione *f*; messa in scena *f*. **productive** *adj* produttivo; fertile. **productivity** *n* produttività *f*.

**profane** [prə'fein] *adj* profano. **profanity** *n* profanità *f*; (*language*) bestemmia *f*.

**profess** [prə'fes] *v* professare, manifestare; (*practise*) esercitare; (*imply*) pretendere di. **professed** *adj* (*avowed*) dichiarato. **profession** *n* professione *f*; dichiarazione *f*.

**professional** [prə'feʃənl] *n* professionista *m*, *f*. *adj* professionale. **professionalism** *n* professionismo *m*.

**professor** [prə'fesə] *n* professore, -essa *m*, *f*.

**proficient** [prə'fiʃənt] *adj* competente, provetto. **proficiency** *n* perizia *f*, competenza *f*.

**profile** ['proufail] *n* profilo *m*.

**profit** ['profit] *n* profitto *m*, guadagno *m*. *v* (*be of benefit to*) giovare a, essere utile a.

**profit from** approfittare di, trarre profitto da. **profitable** adj vantaggioso; lucroso.

**profound** [prə'faund] adj profondo.

**profuse** [prə'fju:s] adj abbondante, prodigo. **apologize profusely** profondersi in scuse. **profusion** n abbondanza f.

**prognosis** [prog'nousis] n prognosi f.

**programme** ['prougram] n programma m. v programmare. **programmer** n programmatore m, f. **programming** n programmazione.

**progress** ['prougres] v progredire, avanzare. n progresso m, andamento m. **progression** n progressione f. **progressive** adj progressivo.

**prohibit** [prə'hibit] v proibire, vietare. **prohibition** n proibizione f, divieto m; (of alcohol) proibizionismo m.

**project** ['prodʒekt; v prə'dʒekt] n progetto m, disegno m. v (plan) progettare; (math, screen) proiettare; (protrude) sporgere. **projectile** n proiettile m. **projection** n proiezione f; sporgenza f. **projector** n proiettore m.

**proletariat** [proulə'teəriət] n proletariato m. **proletarian** n, adj proletario, -a.

**proliferate** [prə'lifəreit] v proliferare.

**prolific** [prə'lifik] adj prolifico.

**prologue** ['proulog] n prologo (pl -ghi) m.

**prolong** [prə'loŋ] v prolungare.

**promenade** [promə'na:d] v fare una passeggiata. n passeggiata f; (sea-front) lungomare m.

**prominent** ['prominənt] adj prominente; eminente, importante. **prominence** n prominenza; eminenza f. **give prominence to** dar risalto a.

**promiscuous** [prə'miskjuəs] adj indiscriminato. **promiscuity** n promiscuità f.

**promise** ['promis] v promettere, assicurare. n promessa f, assicurazione f. **promising** adj che promette bene.

**promontory** ['proməntəri] n promontorio m.

**promote** [prə'mout] v promuovere; (comm) lanciare. **promotion** n promozione f; lancio m.

**prompt** [prompt] adj pronto, sollecito. v ispirare, suggerire.

**prone** [proun] adv bocconi. **be prone to** essere disposto or propenso a.

**prong** [proŋ] n rebbio m. v infilzare.

**pronoun** ['prounaun] n pronome m.

**pronounce** [prə'nauns] v pronunciare; dichiarare. **pronounced** adj pronunciato, spiccato. **pronouncement** n dichiarazione f. **pronunciation** n pronuncia f.

**proof** [pru:f] n prova f; (printing) bozza f. adj impenetrabile, resistente (a). v impermeabilizzare.

**prop**[1] [prop] n appoggio m, sostegno m; (building) puntello m. v **prop up** sorreggere, appoggiare; puntellare.

**prop**[2] [prop] n (coll) oggetto teatrale m.

**propaganda** [propə'gandə] n propaganda f.

**propagate** ['propageit] v propagare. **propagation** n propagazione f.

**propel** [prə'pel] v spingere avanti, azionare. **propellant** n propellente m. **propeller** n elica f.

**proper** ['propə] adj proprio; (right) particolare; (good) buono. **properly** adv come si deve; correttamente; (well) bene.

**property** ['propəti] n proprietà f; possesso m, beni m pl.

**prophecy** ['profəsi] n profezia f. **prophesy** v fare il profeta, predire.

**prophet** ['profit] n profeta m. **prophetess** n profetessa f. **prophetic** adj profetico.

**propitious** [prə'pifəs] adj propizio, favorevole.

**proportion** [prə'po:fən] n proporzione f. **out of proportion** sproporzionato, smisurato. **proportional** adj proporzionale.

**propose** [prə'pouz] v proporre, intendere; fare una proposta di matrimonio. **proposal** n proposta f; offerta di matrimonio f. **proposition** n proposta f; (gramm) proposizione f.

**proprietor** [prə'praiətə] n proprietario m, padrone m. **proprietress** n proprietaria f, padrona f.

**propriety** [prə'praiəti] n decoro m, decenza f.

**propulsion** [prə'pʌlʃən] n propulsione f.

**prose** [prouz] n prosa f. **prosaic** adj prosaico, banale.

**prosecute** ['prosikju:t] v citare in giudizio, processare. **prosecution** n processo m. **prosecutor** n procuratore m, pubblico ministero m.

**prospect** ['prospekt; v prə'spekt] n prospettiva *f*, aspettativa *f*; (*view*) prospetto *m*. *v* esplorare. **prospective** *adj* futuro.

**prospectus** [prə'spektəs] *n* prospetto *m*.

**prosper** ['prɒspə] *v* prosperare. **prosperity** *n* prosperità *f*. **prosperous** *adj* prospero, benestante.

**prostitute** ['prɒstitjuːt] *v* prostituire. *n* prostituta *f*, puttana *f*. **prostitution** *n* prostituzione *f*.

**prostrate** [prɒ'streit; *adj* 'prɒstreit] *v* prostrare, prosternare. *adj* abbattuto.

**protagonist** [prou'tægənist] *n* protagonista *m*, *f*.

**protect** [prə'tekt] *v* proteggere. **protection** *n* protezione *f*. **protective** *adj* protettivo. **protector** *n* protettore, -trice *m*, *f*. **protectorate** *n* protettorato *m*.

**protégé** ['prɒtəʒei] *n* protetto, -a *m*, *f*.

**protein** ['proutiːn] *n* proteina *f*.

**protest** [prə'test; *n* 'proutest] *v* protestare. *n* protesta *f*; (*comm*) protesto *m*; (*pol*) contestazione. **under protest** protestando.

**Protestant** ['prɒtistənt] *n*(*m*+*f*), *adj* protestante. **Protestantism** *n* protestantesimo *m*.

**protocol** ['proutəkɒl] *n* protocollo *m*.

**proton** ['prouton] *n* protone *m*.

**protoplasm** ['proutəplazəm] *n* protoplasma *m*.

**prototype** ['proutətaip] *n* prototipo *m*.

**protract** [prə'trakt] *v* protrarre, prolungare.

**protractor** [prə'traktə] *n* goniometro *m*.

**protrude** [prə'truːd] *v* sporgere.

**proud** [praud] *adj* orgoglioso, fiero.

**prove** [pruːv] *v* dimostrare, confermare.

**proverb** ['prɒvəːb] *n* proverbio *m*.

**provide** [prə'vaid] *v* provvedere, fornire. **provide against** premunirsi contro. **provided that** purché. **providence** *n* provvidenza *f*.

**province** ['prɒvins] *n* provincia *f*. **provincial** *adj* provinciale.

**provision** [prə'viʒən] *n* provvedimento *m*. **provisions** *pl n* viveri *m pl*, provviste *f pl*. **provisional** *adj* provvisorio.

**proviso** [prə'vaizou] *n* stipulazione *f*, condizione *f*.

**provoke** [prə'vouk] *v* provocare, irritare. **provocation** *n* provocazione *f*. **provocative** *adj* provocativo.

**prow** [prau] *n* prua *f*, prora *f*.

**prowess** ['prauis] *n* (*ability*) bravura *f*; (*bravery*) prodezza *f*, valore *m*.

**prowl** [praul] *v* girare furtivamente, vagare.

**proximity** [prɒk'siməti] *n* prossimità *f*.

**proxy** ['prɒksi] *n* (*agency, authorization*) procura *f*; (*person*) procuratore, -trice *m*, *f*.

**prude** [pruːd] *n* persona che affetta pudore, puritano, -a *m*, *f*. **prudish** *adj* che affetta pudore, puritano.

**prudent** ['pruːdənt] *adj* prudente, cauto. **prudence** *n* prudenza *f*, avvedutezza *f*.

**prune¹** [pruːn] *v* sfrondare; (*tree*) potare.

**prune²** [pruːn] *n* prugna secca *f*.

**pry** [prai] *v* curiosare, ficcare il naso (in).

**psalm** [saːm] *n* salmo *m*.

**pseudonym** ['sjuːdənim] *n* pseudonimo *m*.

**psychedelic** [,saikə'delik] *adj* psichedelico.

**psychiatry** [sai'kaiətri] *n* psichiatria *f*. **psychiatric** *adj* psichiatrico. **psychiatrist** *n* psichiatra *m*, *f*.

**psychic** ['saikik] *adj* psichico.

**psychoanalysis** [saikouə'naləsis] *n* psicanalisi *f*. **psychoanalyse** *v* psicanalizzare. **psychoanalyst** *n* psicanalista *m*, *f*. **psychoanalytic** *adj* psicanalitico.

**psychology** [sai'kɒlədʒi] *n* psicologia *f*. **psychological** *adj* psicologico. **psychologist** *n* psicologo, -a *m*, *f*.

**psychopath** ['saikəpaθ] *n* psicopatico, -a *m*, *f*.

**psychosis** [sai'kousis] *n* psicosi *f*. **psychotic** *n*, *adj* psicotico, -a.

**psychosomatic** [,saikəsə'matik] *adj* psicosomatico.

**psychotherapy** [,saikə'θerəpi] *n* psicoterapia *f*. **psychotherapist** *n* psicoterapista *m*, *f*.

**pub** [pʌb] *n* bar *m invar*.

**puberty** ['pjuːbəti] *n* pubertà *f*.

**pubic** ['pjuːbik] *adj* pubico.

**public** ['pʌblik] *nm*, *adj* pubblico. **public holiday** festa civile *f*. **public library** biblioteca comunale *f*. **public school** collegio privato *m*. **public-spirited** *adj* dotato di senso civico. **publican** proprietario del bar *m*, oste *m*.

**publication** [,pʌbli'keiʃən] *n* pubblicazione *f*.

**publicity** [pʌb'lisəti] *n* pubblicità *f*. **publicist** *n* pubblicista *m*, *f*.

**publicize** ['pʌblisaiz] *v* divulgare; (*advertise*) fare la pubblicità a.

**publish** ['pʌblɪʃ] v pubblicare. **publisher** n (*person*) editore m; (*firm*) casa editrice f.

**pucker** ['pʌkə] v corrugare, raggrinzare.

**pudding** ['pudɪŋ] n budino m, dolce m.

**puddle** ['pʌdl] n pozzanghera f.

**puerile** ['pjuəraɪl] adj puerile.

**puff** [pʌf] n (*of wind*) soffio m; (*of smoke*) buffata f; (*of breath*) alito m; (*powder*) piumino m; (*pipe, cigarette*) boccata f. **puff pastry** pasta sfoglia f. v sbuffare.

**pull** [pul] n tirata f, strappo m; (*influence*) ascendente m. v tirare; (*haul*) trascinare. **pull back** tirare indietro, trattenere. **pull down** tirar giù; demolire. **pull in** (*train*) entrare in stazione. **pull oneself together** riprendere animo. **pull up** tirar su; (*plant, etc.*) strappare; (*stop*) fermarsi.

**pulley** ['puli] n puleggia f.

**pullover** ['pul,ouvə] n pullover m invar.

**pulp** [pʌlp] n polpa f. v ridurre in polpa.

**pulpit** ['pulpit] n pulpito m.

**pulsate** [pʌl'seit] v palpitare, pulsare. **pulsation** n pulsazione f.

**pulse**[1] [pʌls] n (*beat*) polso m; (*elec*) impulso m; vitalità f. v pulsare.

**pulse**[2] [pʌls] n (*vegetables*) legumi m pl.

**pulverize** ['pʌlvəraiz] v polverizzare.

**pump** [pʌmp] n pompa f. **petrol pump** distributore di benzina m. v pompare; (*bullets*) scaricare.

**pumpkin** ['pʌmpkin] n zucca f.

**pun** [pʌn] n gioco di parole m. v fare giochi di parole.

**punch**[1] [pʌntʃ] v (*hit*) picchiare, dare un pugno o cazzotto a. n pugno m; (*coll*) cazzotto m; (*energy*) forza f. **punch-drunk** adj stordito.

**punch**[2] [pʌntʃ] n (*drink*) ponce m.

**punch**[3] [pʌntʃ] n (*tool*) punzone m. v (*tickets*) forare; (*tech*) punzonare; (*stamp*) timbrare.

**punctual** ['pʌŋktjuəl] adj puntuale. **punctuality** n puntualità f.

**punctuate** ['pʌŋktjueit] v interrompere ripetutamente; (*sentence*) mettere la punteggiatura. **punctuation** n punteggiatura f.

**puncture** ['pʌŋktʃə] n puntura f; (*tyre*) foratura f. **have a puncture** avere una gomma a terra. v forare, bucare.

**pungent** ['pʌndʒənt] adj pungente, aspro; caustico.

**punish** ['pʌniʃ] v punire, castigare. **punishment** n punizione f, castigo (pl -ghi) m. **punitive** adj punitivo.

**punk** [pʌŋk] adj (*coll*) marcio, malmesso.

**punt**[1] [pʌnt] n (*boat*) barchino m.

**punt**[2] [pʌnt] v (*bet*) puntare. **punter** n giocatore d'azzardo m, scommettitore m.

**puny** ['pjuːni] adj sparuto, debole.

**pupil**[1] ['pjuːpl] n (*school*) allievo, -a m, f, alunno, -a m, f.

**pupil**[2] ['pjuːpl] n (*anat*) pupilla f.

**puppet** ['pʌpit] n burattino m.

**puppy** ['pʌpi] n cagnolino m.

**purchase** ['pəːtʃəs] v acquistare, comprare. n acquisto m; (*tech*) presa f. **purchaser** n compratore, -trice m, f.

**pure** ['pjuə] adj puro. **purify** v purificare, depurare. **purity** n purezza f.

**purée** ['pjuərei] n purè m.

**purgatory** ['pəːgətəri] n purgatorio m.

**purge** [pəːdʒ] v (*purify*) purgare; (*pol*) epurare. n purga f, epurazione f.

**puritan** ['pjuəritən] n, adj puritano, -a. **puritanism** n puritanesimo m.

**purl** [pəːl] v (*knitting*) lavorare a punto rovescio; (*edge*) smerlare. n punto rovescio m; punto smerlo m.

**purple** ['pəːpl] n porpora f. adj purpureo; (*of face*) paonazzo.

**purpose** ['pəːpəs] n scopo m, proposito m. **on purpose** apposta.

**purr** [pəː] n fusa f pl. v far le fusa.

**purse** [pəːs] n borsa f; (*for money*) borsellino m. v contrarre.

**purser** ['pəːsə] n commissario di bordo m.

**pursue** [pə'sjuː] v (*seek to attain*) perseguire; (*follow closely*) perseguitare; (*continue*) seguire, proseguire. **pursuit** n (*quest*) ricerca f; (*chase*) inseguimento m; (*activity*) impiego (pl -ghi) m.

**pus** [pʌs] n pus m, materia f.

**push** [puʃ] n spinta f; (*effort*) sforzo m, energia f; iniziativa f. **push-chair** n carozzina f. v spingere; (*urge*) spronare; (*product*) lanciare. **push away** allontanare. **push back** respingere. **push-over** n vittima facile f. **pushing** adj energico, aggressivo.

**\*put** [put] v mettere, porre; (*question*) rivolgere; (*idea*) esprimere. **put about** (*rumour*) diffondere. **put across** (*explain*) spiegare. **put aside** or **by** mettere da parte, risparmiare. **put down** (*suppress*) sopprimere; (*land*) atterrare; (*ascribe*) attribuire. **put forward** proporre, nominare. **put off** rinviare; (*get rid of*) sbarazzarsi di; (*cause to dislike*) ripugnare. **put out** (*extinguish*) spegnere; (*inconvenience*) disturbare. **put up** offrire alloggio a; (*stay*) prendere alloggio; (*raise*) alzare; (*notice, etc.*) affiggere. **put up with** sopportare.

**putrid** ['pju:trid] *adj* putrido.

**putt** [pʌt] *v* colpire leggermente, fare il putting. *n* colpo leggero *m*, putting *m invar*.

**putty** ['pʌti] *n* stucco *m*. *v* stuccare.

**puzzle** ['pʌzl] *n* indovinello *m*; enigma *m*. *v* confondere, rendere perplesso. **puzzled** *adj* perplesso.

**pygmy** ['pigmi] *n*, *adj* pigmeo, -a.

**pyjamas** [pə'dʒaːməz] *pl n* pigiama *m sing*.

**pylon** ['pailən] *n* pilone *m*.

**pyramid** ['pirəmid] *n* piramide *f*.

**python** ['paiθən] *n* pitone *m*.

# Q

**quack¹** [kwak] *v* (*duck*) schiamazzare.

**quack²** [kwak] *n* (*med*) ciarlatano *m*, medicastro *m*.

**quadrangle** ['kwodraŋgl] *n* (*math*) quadrangolo *m*; (*arch*) corte quadrangolare *f*.

**quadrant** ['kwodrənt] *n* quadrante *m*.

**quadrilateral** [kwodrə'latərəl] *nm*, *adj* quadrilatero.

**quadruped** ['kwodruped] *n* quadrupede *m*.

**quadruple** [kwod'ruːpl] *adj* quadruplo.

**quagmire** ['kwagmaiə] *n* pantano *m*.

**quail¹** [kweil] *n* (*bird*) quaglia *f*.

**quail²** [kweil] *v* aver paura, sgomentarsi.

**quaint** [kweint] *adj* interessante *or* pittoresco in un modo insolito.

**quake** [kweik] *v* tremare; (*person*) fremere. *n* (*coll: earthquake*) terremoto *m*.

**Quaker** ['kweikə] *n* quacchero, -a *m*, *f*.

**qualify** ['kwolifai] *v* qualificare; (*define*) precisare. **qualification** *n* qualifica *f*; (*limitation*) riserva *f*. **qualified** *adj* qualificato, idoneo; (*limited*) condizionato.

**quality** ['kwoləti] *n* qualità *f*.

**qualm** [kwaːm] *n* scrupolo *m*, apprensione *f*.

**quandary** ['kwondəri] *n* situazione difficile *f*, imbarazzo *m*.

**quantify** ['kwontifai] *v* quantificare.

**quantity** ['kwontəti] *n* quantità *f*.

**quantum** ['kwontəm] *n* quanto *m*.

**quarantine** ['kworəntiːn] *n* quarantena *f*. *v* mettere in quarantena.

**quarrel** ['kworəl] *n* lite *f*, bisticcio *m*. **pick a quarrel** attaccar briga. **quarrelsome** *adj* litigioso.

**quarry¹** ['kwori] *n* (*prey*) preda *f*.

**quarry²** ['kwori] *n* (*mining*) cava *f*. *v* scavare.

**quarter** ['kwoːtə] *n* quarto *m*; (*three months*) trimestre *m*; (*district, mercy*) quartiere *m*. **at close quarters** da vicino. **quarters** *pl n* (*mil*) accantonamento *m sing*. *v* dividere in quattro; (*mil*) acquartierare. **quarterly** *nm*, *adj* trimestrale.

**quartet** [kwoː'tet] *n* quartetto *m*.

**quartz** [kwoːts] *n* quarzo *m*.

**quash** [kwoʃ] *v* sopprimere; (*law*) annullare, cassare.

**quaver** ['kweivə] *n* (*music*) croma *f*; (*shaky voice*) tremolio *m*. *v* tremolare.

**quay** [kiː] *n* banchina *f*.

**queasy** ['kwiːzi] *adj* che sente nausea.

**queen** [kwiːn] *n* regina *f*.

**queer** [kwiə] *adj* strambo, bizzarro. **feel queer** sentirsi male. *n* (*coll: homosexual*) finocchio *m*.

**quell** [kwel] *v* reprimere, sopprimere.

**quench** [kwentʃ] *v* spegnere. **quench one's thirst** dissetarsi.

**query** ['kwiəri] *n* domanda *f*, quesito *m*. *v* chiedersi; (*raise doubt*) mettere in dubbio.

**quest** [kwest] *n* ricerca *f*.

**question** ['kwestʃən] *n* questione *f*, domanda *f*; (*gramm*) interrogazione *f*; problema *m*. **question mark** punto interrogativo *m*. *v* interrogare; (*query*) mettere in dubbio.

**queue** [kjuː] *n* coda *f*. *v* fare la coda, mettersi in coda.

**quibble** ['kwibl] *n* cavillo *m*. *v* cavillare.

**quick** [kwik] *adj* rapido, veloce; (*lively*) vivace. **quicksand** *n* sabbia mobile *f*. **quicksilver** *n* argento vivo *m*. **quick-tempered** *adj* impulsivo. **quick-witted** *adj* sveglio. *adv* presto. *n* **cut to the quick** toccare sul vivo. **quicken** *v* affrettare, accelerare.

**quid** [kwid] n (coll) sterlina f.

**quiet** ['kwaiət] adj tranquillo, quieto. **keep quiet** tacere, star zitto. n quiete f, tranquillità f, silenzio m. **on the quiet** di nascosto. **quieten** v calmare, acquietare.

**quill** [kwil] n penna f.

**quilt** [kwilt] v trapuntare. n trapunta f; (duvet) piumino m.

**quince** [kwins] n cotogna f.

**quinine** [kwi'ni:n] n chinino m.

**quinsy** ['kwinzi] n angina f.

**quintet** [kwin'tet] n quintetto m.

**quirk** [kwə:k] n ticchio m, vezzo m.

***quit** [kwit] v lasciare, abbandonare; (depart) partire.

**quite** [kwait] adv perfettamente, bene, affatto, proprio; (somewhat) abbastanza.

**quits** [kwits] adj pari. **call it quits** far pari e patta. **double or quits** lascia o raddoppia.

**quiver¹** ['kwivə] v fremere; (voice) tremolare. n fremito m; tremolio m.

**quiver²** ['kwivə] n (arrows) faretra f.

**quiz** [kwiz] n quiz m invar. v interrogare. **quizzical** adj (odd) curioso; (ridiculing) beffardo.

**quota** ['kwoutə] n quota f, rata f; (trade) contingente m.

**quote** [kwout] v citare; (price) quotare. **quotation** n citazione f. **quotation marks** virgolette f pl.

**quotient** ['kwouʃnt] n quoziente m.

# R

**rabbi** ['rabai] n rabbino m.

**rabbit** ['rabit] m coniglio m.

**rabble** ['rabl] n plebaglia f.

**rabies** ['reibi:z] n rabbia f. **rabid** adj (med) idrofobo; furioso; fanatico.

**race¹** [reis] n (sport) corsa f, gara f. **racecourse** n ippodromo m. **racehorse** n cavallo da corsa m. **racetrack** n autodromo m, pista f. v correre; (compete) gareggiare con. **racing** adj da corsa. **racy** adj vivace, piccante.

**race²** [reis] n razza f. **racial** adj razziale. **racialism** or **racism** n razzismo m. **racial-**

**ist** or **racist** n(m+f), adj razzista.

**rack¹** [rak] n rastrelliera f; (for plates) scolapiatti m invar, (tech) cremagliera f; (for luggage) rete f. v **rack one's brains** scervellarsi, lambiccarsi il cervello.

**rack²** [rak] n **go to rack and ruin** andare in malora.

**racket¹** ['rakit] n (bat) racchetta f.

**racket²** ['rakit] n (noise) baccano m, chiasso m; (dishonest scheme) truffa f.

**radar** ['reida:] n radar m.

**radial** ['reidiəl] adj radiale.

**radiant** ['reidiənt] adj raggiante; splendido; (joyful) esultante; (phys, tech) radiante. **radiance** n splendore m.

**radiate** ['reidieit] v irradiare, raggiare. **radiation** n irradiazione f; (phys) radiazione f. **radiator** n (car) radiatore m; (central heating) termosifone m.

**radical** ['radikəl] n(m+f), adj radicale.

**radio** ['reidiou] nf invar, adj radio. **radioactive** [reidiou'aktiv] adj radioattivo. **radioactivity** n radioattività f.

**radiography** [reidi'ogrəfi] n radiografia f.

**radiology** [reidi'olədʒi] n radiologia f. **radiologist** n radiologo, -a m, f.

**radish** ['radiʃ] n ravanello m.

**radium** ['reidiəm] n radio m.

**radius** ['reidiəs] n raggio m.

**raffia** ['rafiə] n rafia f.

**raffle** ['rafl] n riffa f.

**raft** [ra:ft] n zattera f.

**rafter** ['ra:ftə] n trave f.

**rag¹** [rag] n (cloth) straccio m, cencio m; (derog: newspaper) giornalaccio m. **ragged** adj lacero, cencioso.

**rag²** [rag] (coll) v prendere in giro. n baldoria f.

**rage** [reidʒ] n rabbia f, collera f; (enthusiasm) passione f, moda f. **be in a rage** essere furioso or arrabbiato. **fly into a rage** infuriarsi. v montare su tutte le furie, infuriarsi; (storm, etc.) imperversare. **rage against** inveire contro. **raging** adj furioso, violento.

**raid** [reid] n incursione f, razzia f. v fare un'incursione in, razziare, invadere. **raider** n razziatore m.

**rail¹** [reil] n (bar) sbarra f; (barrier) ringhiera f; (handrail) corrimano m invar; (for train) rotaia f, binario m. **by rail** col treno. **go off the rails** perdere le staffe. **railway** n ferrovia f. **railway line** linea ferroviaria f.

**railings** ['reilinz] *pl n* cancellata *f sing*, inferriata *f sing.*

**rain** [rein] *n* pioggia f. **rainbow** *n* arcobaleno *m.* **raincoat** *n* impermeabile *m.* **raindrop** *n* goccia di pioggia f. **rainforest** *n* foresta pluviale f. *v* piovere. **rain cats and dogs** piovere a catinelle. **rainy** *adj* piovoso.

**raise** [reiz] *v* (*lift up*) alzare; (*rear*) allevare; (*bring up*) sollevare; (*increase*) aumentare; (*cause*) suscitare.

**raisin** ['reizən] *n* uva secca f.

**rake** [reik] *n* (*tool*) rastrello *m.* *v* rastrellare. **rake up the past** rivangare il passato.

**rally** ['rali] *n* (*meeting*) raduno *m;* (*mot*) rally *m invar;* (*recovery*) ricupero di forze *m*, ripresa f; (*tennis, etc.*) scambio di colpi *m.* *v* radunare; riprendersi.

**ram** [ram] *n* montone *m.* *v* ficcare; (*of ships*) speronare.

**ramble** ['rambl] *n* gita f, giro *m.* *v* vagare, girovagare; (*speech*) divagare; (*mind*) delirare. **rambling** *adj* (*unconnected*) sconnesso, sconclusionato. **rambling rose** rosa rampicante f.

**ramp** [ramp] *n* rampa f.

**rampage** [ram'peidʒ] *n* **go on the rampage** andare su tutte le furie.

**rampant** ['rampənt] *adj* (*unchecked*) sfrenato; (*heraldry*) rampante.

**rampart** ['rampa:t] *n* bastione *m.*

**ramshackle** ['ramʃakl] *adj* cadente.

**ran** [ran] *V* **run**.

**ranch** [ra:ntʃ] *n* fattoria (per l'allevamento di bestiame) f, ranch *m invar.*

**rancid** ['ransid] *adj* rancido.

**rancour** ['raŋkə] *n* amarezza f, rancore *m.*

**random** ['randəm] *adj* casuale, fortuito. *n* **at random** a casaccio.

**randy** ['randi] *adj* lascivo.

**rang** [ran] *V* **ring²**.

**range** [reindʒ] *n* (*assortment*) gamma f; (*mountains*) catena f; (*scope*) portata f; (*for shooting*) campo di tiro *m;* (*of voice*) estensione f; (*stove*) fornello *m.* **out of range** fuori tiro. **range-finder** *n* telemetro *m.* **within range** a portata; (*of gun*) a tiro. *v* (*arrange*) disporre; (*set in order*) schierare; (*between limits*) estendersi, variare.

**rank¹** [raŋk] *n* (*class*) grado *m;* (*row*) fila f. **ranks** *pl n* truppe *f pl.* *v* (*arrange*) schierare;

classificare; considerare.

**rank²** [raŋk] *adj* (*excessive*) rigoglioso; (*utter*) assoluto; (*smell*) puzzolente.

**rankle** ['raŋkl] *v* bruciare; (*cause bitterness*) amareggiare.

**ransack** ['ransak] *v* mettere sossopra, rovistare.

**ransom** ['ransəm] *n* riscatto *m.* *v* riscattare.

**rap** [rap] *v* picchiare, colpire. **rap over the knuckles** rimproverare. *n* colpetto *m.* **take the rap** accollarsi il biasimo.

**rape** [reip] *n* stupro *m*, violenza carnale f; (*abduction*) rapimento *m.* *v* violentare, stuprare; rapire.

**rapid** ['rapid] *adj* rapido, veloce. **rapidity** *n* rapidità f.

**rapier** ['reipiə] *n* spada f, stocco *m.*

**rapture** ['raptʃə] *n* estasi f. **rapturous** *adj* estatico.

**rare¹** ['reə] *adj* (*scarce*) raro. **rarity** *n* rarità f.

**rare²** ['reə] *adj* (*meat*) al sangue.

**rascal** ['ra:skəl] *n* briccone *m*, mascalzone *m.*

**rash¹** [raʃ] *adj* avventato, sconsiderato. **rashness** *n* avventatezza f, imprudenza f.

**rash²** [raʃ] *n* (*med*) eruzione f.

**rasher** ['raʃə] *n* fetta (di prosciutto) f.

**raspberry** ['ra:zbəri] *n* lampone *m.* **blow a raspberry** (*coll*) fare una pernacchia.

**rat** [rat] *n* ratto *m;* (*coll: traitor*) traditore *m.* **smell a rat** (*coll*) avere dei sospetti.

**rate** [reit] *n* (*charge*) tasso *m;* (*speed*) velocità f, passo *m;* (*degree*) grado *m.* **at any rate** comunque. **at this rate** a questo passo. **ratepayer** *n* contribuente *m*, f. **rates** *pl n* imposta *f sing.* *v* stimare, valutare, considerare.

**rather** ['ra:ðə] *adv* piuttosto, anzi. *interj* certo! altro che! **I would rather ...** preferirei ....

**ratify** ['ratifai] *v* ratificare. **ratification** *n* ratifica f.

**ratio** ['reiʃiou] *n* rapporto *m*, proporzione f.

**ration** ['raʃən] *n* razione f. **rations** *pl n* viveri *m pl.* *v* razionare.

**rational** ['raʃənl] *adj* razionale.

**rattle** ['ratl] *v* sbatacchiare; (*disconcert*) sconcertare. *n* sbatacchio *m;* (*toy, instrument*) raganella f; (*in throat*) rantolo *m.*

**raucous** ['rɔ:kəs] *adj* rauco.

**ravage** ['rævidʒ] v devastare. n devastazione f.

**rave** [reiv] v delirare. **rave about** andar pazzo di.

**raven** ['reivən] n corvo m.

**ravenous** ['rævənəs] adj vorace. **be ravenous** avere una fame da lupo.

**ravine** [rə'viːn] n burrone m.

**ravish** ['ræviʃ] v (delight) incantare; (rape) violentare. **ravishing** adj incantevole.

**raw** [rɔː] adj (not cooked) crudo; (not refined) greggio; (untrained) inesperto. **raw material** materia prima f. **touch on the raw** toccare sul vivo.

**ray¹** [rei] n raggio m.

**ray²** [rei] n (fish) razza f.

**rayon** ['reiɔn] n raion m.

**razor** ['reizə] n rasoio m. **razor blade** lametta f.

**reach** [riːtʃ] n portata f; (continuous stretch) tratto m. **out of reach** fuori mano. **within reach** a portata di mano. v (get to) raggiungere; (hand) porgere.

**react** [ri'ækt] v reagire. **reaction** n reazione f. **reactionary** n, adj reazionario, -a. **reactor** n reattore m.

*****read** [riːd] v leggere; studiare. **well-read** adj istruito. **readable** adj leggibile. **reader** n lettore, -trice m, f. **readership** n lettori m pl. **reading** n lettura f; interpretazione f.

**readjust** [riːə'dʒʌst] v raggiustare.

**ready** ['redi] adj pronto, preparato; (willing) disposto. **get ready** preparare, prepararsi. **ready-made** adj confezionato. **ready money** contanti m pl.

**real** [riəl] adj reale, effettivo, genuino. **real estate** beni immobili m pl. **realism** n realismo m. **realist** n realista m, f. **realistic** adj realistico. **reality** n realtà f.

**realize** ['riəlaiz] v realizzare. **realization** n realizzazione f.

**really** ['riəli] adv effettivamente; (before adj) proprio. **interj** davvero.

**realm** [relm] n dominio m; (special field) campo m.

**reap** [riːp] v mietere; (profit, etc.) raccogliere.

**reappear** [riːə'piə] v riapparire. **reappearance** n ricomparsa f.

**rear¹** [riə] n (back) dietro m, parte posteriore f; (mil) retroguardia f. **at the rear of** dietro a. **rear-view mirror** retrovisore m.

stay **in the rear** restare per ultimo. adj posteriore.

**rear²** [riə] v (raise) allevare; (horse, etc.) impennarsi; (elevate) innalzare.

**rearm** [riː'ɑːm] v riarmare. **rearmament** n riarmo m.

**rearrange** [riːə'reindʒ] v riordinare. **rearrangement** n riordinamento m.

**reason** ['riːzn] n ragione f, causa f; (judgment) ragionevolezza f. **it stands to reason** è evidente. v ragionare. **reasonable** adj ragionevole, giusto. **reasoning** n modo di ragionare m.

**reassure** [riːə'ʃuə] v rassicurare. **reassurance** n rassicurazione f.

**rebate** ['riːbeit] n sconto m.

**rebel** ['rebl] v ribellarsi. n ribelle m, f. **rebellion** n ribellione f. **rebellious** adj ribelle.

**rebound** [ri'baund; n 'riːbaund] v rimbalzare. n rimbalzo m.

**rebuff** [ri'bʌf] v respingere, rifiutare. n scacco m, rifiuto m.

*****rebuild** [riː'bild] v ricostruire. **rebuilding** n ricostruzione f.

**rebuke** [ri'bjuːk] n rimprovero m. v rimproverare.

**recall** [ri'kɔːl] v richiamare; (remember) rievocare, ricordare. n richiamo m, memoria f. **past recall** irrevocabile.

**recap** ['riːkap] (coll) v ricapitolare. n ricapitolazione f.

**recede** [ri'siːd] v recedere, inclinarsi all'indietro.

**receipt** [rə'siːt] v quietanzare. n ricevuta f. **receipts** pl n incasso m sing, entrate f pl.

**receive** [rə'siːv] v ricevere; (sustain) sostenere, riportare; (stolen goods) ricettare. **receiver** n ricettatore, -trice m, f; (bankruptcy) curatore fallimentare m; (phone) ricevitore m.

**recent** ['riːsnt] adv recente. **recently** adv di recente, poco fa.

**receptacle** [rə'septəkl] n recipiente m; (bot) ricettacolo m.

**reception** [rə'sepʃən] n ricevimento m; (radio) ricezione f. **receptionist** n segretaria f, receptionist f invar. **receptive** adj ricettivo.

**recess** [ri'ses] n nicchia f; pausa f; (holiday) vacanza f. **recesses** pl n (of mind, etc.) recessi m pl.

**recession** [rə'seʃən] n recessione f.

**recharge** [riːˈtʃɑːdʒ] v ricaricare.

**recipe** [ˈresəpi] n ricetta f.

**recipient** [rəˈsipiənt] n destinatario, -a m, f. adj ricevente.

**reciprocate** [rəˈsiprəkeit] v contraccambiare, reciprocare; (tech) alternarsi. **reciprocal** adj reciproco. **reciprocity** n reciprocità f.

**recite** [rəˈsait] v recitare. **recital** n (narrative) racconto m; (entertainment) recital m invar. **recitation** n recitazione f.

**reckless** [ˈrekləs] adj imprudente, avventato. **recklessness** n avventatezza f.

**reckon** [ˈrekən] v contare; (consider) giudicare. **reckon on** contare su. **reckon with** prendere in considerazione. **reckoning** n (bill) resa dei conti f.

**reclaim** [riˈkleim] v redimere; (land) bonificare; (material) ricuperare. **reclamation** n bonifica f.

**recline** [rəˈklain] v appoggiarsi.

**recluse** [rəˈkluːs] n eremita m.

**recognize** [ˈrekəgnaiz] v riconoscere. **recognition** n riconoscimento m. **recognizable** adj riconoscibile.

**recoil** [rəˈkoil] v rinculare. **recoil from** rifuggire da. n rinculo m.

**recollect** [rekəˈlekt] v rammentarsi di. **recollection** n memoria f, ricordo m.

**recommence** [riːkəˈmens] v ricominciare.

**recommend** [rekəˈmend] v raccomandare, consigliare. **recommendation** n raccomandazione f.

**recompense** [ˈrekəmpens] v compensare, risarcire. n indennizzo m, risarcimento m.

**reconcile** [ˈrekənsail] v mettere d'accordo, riconciliare. **reconcile oneself to** rassegnarsi a. **reconciliation** n rappacificazione f.

**reconnoitre** [rekəˈnoitə] v fare un sopralluogo; (mil) fare una ricognizione. **reconnaissance** n esplorazione f, sopralluogo (pl -ghi) m; (mil) ricognizione f.

**reconstruct** [riːkənˈstrʌkt] v ricostruire. **reconstruction** n ricostruzione f.

**record** [rəˈkoːd; n ˈrekoːd] v registrare; notare; (as document) mettere a verbale. n nota f, registro m; (court report) verbale m; (sport) record m invar; disco m; (dossier) stato di servizio m. **keep a record of** prendere nota di. **off the record** ufficiosamente. **record-player** n giradischi m invar.

**recorder** n (music) flautino m. **recording** n registrazione f.

**recount** [riˈkaunt] v riferire, raccontare.

**recoup** [riˈkuːp] v rifarsi di, compensare.

**recourse** [rəˈkoːs] n **have recourse to** ricorrere a. **without recourse** senza rivalsa.

**recover** [rəˈkʌvə] v (get back) riprendere, ricuperare; (regain health) rimettersi. **recovery** n ricupero m; (health) guarigione f.

**recreation** [rekriˈeiʃən] n ricreazione f, passatempo m, svago m.

**recrimination** [rəkrimiˈneiʃən] n recriminazione f.

**recruit** [rəˈkruːt] n recluta f. v arruolare. **recruitment** n reclutamento m.

**rectangle** [ˈrektaŋgl] n rettangolo m. **rectangular** adj rettangolare.

**rectify** [ˈrektifai] v rettificare; (elec) raddrizzare.

**rectum** [ˈrektəm] n retto m.

**recuperate** [rəˈkjuːpəreit] v ricuperare; (get well again) rimettersi. **recuperation** n ricupero m.

**recur** [riˈkəː] v ricorrere, ritornare. **recurrence** n ricorrenza f; (of illness) ricaduta f. **recurrent** adj ricorrente.

**recycle** [riːˈsaikl] v riciclare. **recycling** n riciclaggio m.

**red** [red] adj rosso. **go red** (person) arrossire; (thing) diventar rosso. **redcurrant** n ribes m invar. **red-handed** adj in flagrante. **red herring** diversivo m. **red-hot** adj rovente. **Red Indian** n pellerossa (pl pellirosse) m, f. n **in the red** scoperto. **reddish** adj rossastro.

**Red Cross** n Croce Rossa f.

**redeem** [rəˈdiːm] v redimere, estinguere, svincolare. **redeeming feature** particolare che salva m. **redeemable** adj redimibile. **redemption** n redenzione f; salvezza f; liberazione f.

**redress** [rəˈdres] n riparazione f, soddisfazione f. v soddisfare, correggere.

**reduce** [rəˈdjuːs] v ridurre. **reduced** adj ridotto. **reduction** n riduzione f.

**redundant** [rəˈdʌndənt] adj superfluo. **make redundant** (employee) mettere in cassa d'integrazione.

**reed** [riːd] n canna f; (of musical instrument) linguetta f.

**reef** [riːf] n scogliera f.

**reek** [ri:k] v puzzare. n puzzo m.

**reel**[1] [ri:l] n rocchetto m; (fishing) mulinello m; (film) rotolo m. v arrotolare. **reel off** rifilare.

**reel**[2] [ri:l] v (sway) barcollare; (of head) girare.

**refectory** [rə'fektəri] n refettorio m.

**refer** [rə'fə:] v (report, ascribe) riferire; (consult) ricorrere, rivolgersi; (send back) rimandare. **referring to** con riferimento a. **reference** n riferimento m; (testimonial) referenza f, attestato m.

**referee** [refə'ri:] n arbitro m. v arbitrare.

**referendum** [refə'rendəm] n referendum m.

**refill** ['ri:fil] n refill m invar, pezzo di ricambio m.

**refine** [rə'fain] v raffinare. **refined** adj raffinato, squisito. **refinement** n (tech) raffinazione f; (manners) raffinatezza f. **refinery** n raffineria f.

**reflation** [rə'fleiʃn] n reflazione f.

**reflect** [rə'flekt] v riflettere; (manifest) rispecchiare. **reflection** n riflessione f. **on reflection** a pensarci su. **reflector** n riflettore m; (of vehicle) catarifrangente m.

**reflex** ['ri:fleks] nm, adj riflesso. **reflexive** adj riflessivo.

**reform** [rə'fo:m] n riforma f. v riformare, correggere. **reformation** n riforma f. **reformatory** n riformatorio m. **reformer** n riformatore, -trice m, f.

**refract** [rə'frakt] v rifrangere. **refraction** n rifrazione f.

**refractory** [rə'fraktəri] adj refrattario; (stubborn) ostinato.

**refrain**[1] [rə'frein] v astenersi, trattenersi.

**refrain**[2] [rə'frein] n ritornello m, ripresa f.

**refresh** [rə'freʃ] v rinfrescare, ristorare. **refresher course** corso di aggiornamento m. **refreshments** pl n rinfreschi m pl.

**refrigerator** [rə'fridʒəreitə] n frigorifero m.

**refuel** [ri:'fju:əl] v rifornirsi di carburante.

**refuge** ['refju:dʒ] n rifugio m. **take refuge** rifugiarsi. **refugee** n profugo, -a m, f.

**refund** [ri'fʌnd; n 'ri:fʌnd] v rimborsare. n rimborso m.

**refuse**[1] [rə'fju:z] v rifiutare, dire di no; (deny) negare, respingere; (prohibit) vietare. **refusal** n rifiuto m; (option) diritto di opzione m.

**refuse**[2] ['refju:s] n rifiuti m pl, immondizia f.

**refute** [ri'fju:t] v confutare.

**regain** [ri'gein] v riacquistare, riprendere. **regain consciousness** riprendere i sensi, rianimarsi.

**regal** ['ri:gəl] adj regale.

**regard** [rə'ga:d] v (consider) stimare; (concern) riguardare. n riguardo m; rispetto m; considerazione f; deferenza f. **with regard to** riguardo a, per quanto riguarda. **regardless of** senza badare or riguardo a.

**regatta** [rə'gatə] n regata f.

**regent** ['ri:dʒənt] n reggente m. **regency** n reggenza f.

**regime** [rei'ʒi:m] n regime m.

**regiment** ['redʒimənt] n reggimento m. v irreggimentare. **regimental** adj reggimentale. **regimentation** n irreggimentazione f.

**region** ['ri:dʒən] n regione f, zona f. **regional** adj regionale.

**register** ['redʒistə] n registro m; (voting) lista elettorale f; (professional) albo m. v registrare; (show) indicare; (enter formally) iscriversi. **registered letter** (lettera) raccomandata f. **registered office** sede legale f. **registrar** n segretario m; ufficiale di stato civile m. **registration** n registrazione f; iscrizione f. **registry office** ufficio di stato civile m.

**regress** [ri'gres] v regredire. **regression** n regressione f. **regressive** adj regressivo.

**regret** [rə'gret] n dispiacere m, rammarico m. **regrets** pl n (sorrow) rimorsi m pl; (excuses) scuse f pl. v rimpiangere, rammicarsi di. **regretful** adj spiacente. **regrettable** adj spiacevole.

**regular** ['regjulə] adj regolare. **regularity** n regolarità f.

**regulate** ['regjuleit] v regolare. **regulation** n regolamento m; (rule) regola f.

**rehabilitate** [ri:hə'biliteit] v riabilitare. **rehabilitation** n riabilitazione f.

**rehearse** [rə'hə:s] v (theatre) provare; (enumerate) ripetere, recitare. **rehearsal** n prova f. **dress rehearsal** prova generale f.

**reign** [rein] n regno m. v regnare; prevalere.

**reimburse** [ri:im'bə:s] v rimborsare. **reimbursement** n rimborso m.

**rein** [rein] n redine f, briglia f. **give free rein to** dare libero sfogo a. v **rein in** frenare.

**reincarnation** [ˌriːinkaːˈneiʃən] *n* reincarnazione *f*.

**reindeer** [ˈreindiə] *n* renna *f*.

**reinforce** [ˌriːinˈfoːs] *v* rinforzare. **reinforced concrete** cemento armato *m*. **reinforcement** *n* rinforzo *m*.

**reinstate** [ˌriːinˈsteit] *v* reintegrare. **reinstatement** *n* reintegrazione *f*.

**reinvest** [riːinˈvest] *v* rinvestire.

**reissue** [riːˈiʃuː] *n* nuova emissione *f*, ristampa *f*. *v* emettere di nuovo, ristampare.

**reject** [rəˈdʒekt; *n* ˈriːdʒekt] *v* rifiutare, respingere; (*discard*) scartare. *n* scarto *m*. **rejection** *n* rifiuto *m*.

**rejoice** [rəˈdʒois] *v* rallegrarsi, gioire. **rejoicing** *n* allegrezza *f*, allegria *f*.

**rejoin** [rəˈdʒoin] *v* (*join again*) ricongiungere; (*come back to*) tornare a; (*answer*) rispondere; (*law*) replicare. **rejoinder** *n* risposta *f*, replica *f*.

**rejuvenate** [rəˈdʒuːvəneit] *v* ringiovanire. **rejuvenation** *n* ringiovanimento *m*.

**relapse** [rəˈlaps] *v* ricadere; (*med*) riammalarsi. *n* ricaduta *f*.

**relate** [rəˈleit] *v* (*tell*) narrare, (*refer*) riferire, riguardare; (*be connected*) aver rapporto. **related** *adj* associato, congiunto; (*family*) parente.

**relation** [rəˈleiʃn] *n* (*family*) parente *m, f*; (*connection*) rapporto *m*; (*narration*) racconto *m*. **relationship** *n* parentela *f*, rapporto *m*.

**relative** [ˈrelətiv] *adj* relativo. **relative to** (*concerning*) riguardante. *n* parente *m, f*. **relativity** *n* relatività *f*.

**relax** [rəˈlaks] *v* rilassare, allentare; (*rest*) riposarsi. **relaxation** *n* distensione *f*, riposo *m*; (*entertainment*) svago *m*.

**relay** [ˈriːlei *o* riˈlei] *n* (*shift*) turno *m*; (*elec*) relè *m invar*, soccorritore *m*; (*radio*) trasmissione *f*. **relay race** (corsa a) staffetta *f*. *v* trasmettere.

**release** [rəˈliːs] *v* liberare, rimettere in libertà; (*launch*) lanciare; (*let go*) mollare; (*publication*) mettere in circolazione. *n* liberazione *f*; lancio *m*; (*press*) comunicato stampa *m*.

**relent** [rəˈlent] *v* placarsi, cedere. **relentless** *adj* inesorabile, spietato.

**relevant** [ˈreləvənt] *adj* pertinente, a proposito. **relevance** *n* pertinenza *f*.

**reliable** [riˈlaiəbl] *adj* fidato; sicuro; (*infor-*

*mation*) attendibile. **reliability** *n* sicurezza *f*; (*person*) fidatezza *f*; attendibilità *f*.

**relic** [ˈrelik] *n* reliquia *f*.

**relief** [rəˈliːf] *n* (*alleviation*) sollievo *m*; (*help*) soccorso *m*; (*prominence*) rilievo *m*. **relief map** *n* plastico *m*, levata topografica *f*.

**relieve** [rəˈliːv] *v* alleviare; (*help*) soccorrere. **feel relieved** sentirsi sollevato.

**religion** [rəˈlidʒən] *n* religione *f*. **religious** *adj* religioso, devoto.

**relinquish** [rəˈliŋkwiʃ] *v* abbandonare, rinunziare a.

**relish** [ˈreliʃ] *v* apprezzare, godere. *n* piacere *m*, godimento *m*.

**relocate** [ˌriːlouˈkeit] *v* trasferire, trasferirsi.

**reluctant** [rəˈlʌktənt] *adj* restio, riluttante. **reluctance** *n* riluttanza *f*. **reluctantly** *adv* di malavoglia, a malincuore.

**rely** [rəˈlai] *v* contare, fare assegnamento, fidarsi (di).

**remain** [rəˈmein] *v* rimanere, restare. **remainder** *n* resto *m*, avanzo *m*. **remains** *pl n* resti *m pl*; (*mortal*) spoglie *f pl*.

**remand** [rəˈmaːnd] *v* rinviare. *n* rinvio *m*.

**remark** [rəˈmaːk] *n* nota *f*, osservazione *f*, commento *m*. *v* notare, osservare. **remarkable** *adj* notevole.

**remarry** [riːˈmari] *v* risposarsi.

**remedy** [ˈremədi] *n* rimedio *m*. *v* rimediare, correggere; (*heal*) curare. **remedial** *adj* (*school*) correttivo; (*law*) riparatore.

**remember** [riˈmembə] *v* ricordare, ricordarsi (di), rammentare. **remembrance** *n* memoria *f*, ricordo *m*.

**remind** [rəˈmaind] *v* ricordare, rammentare, richiamare alla mente. **reminder** *n* promemoria *m invar*, ricordo *m*.

**reminiscence** [reməˈnisens] *n* reminiscenza *f*. **reminiscent of** che rammenta.

**remiss** [rəˈmis] *adj* negligente, disattento.

**remit** [rəˈmit] *v* (*transmit*) rimettere; (*abate*) mitigare; (*send back*) rinviare; perdonare. **remittance** *n* rimessa *f*.

**remnant** [ˈremnənt] *n* scampolo *m*, resto *m*.

**remorse** [rəˈmoːs] *n* rimorso *m*. **remorseful** *adj* preso *or* tormentato dal rimorso. **remorseless** *adj* spietato.

**remote** [rəˈmout] *adj* remoto, lontano; (*faint*) pallido. **remote control** telecomando *m*.

**remove** [rəˈmuːv] *v* (*take off*) togliere; (*do*

*away with*) eliminare; (*withdraw*) ritirare; (*move house*) traslocare. **removal** n (*house*) trasloco m; (*med*) ablazione f; (*act of removing*) rimozione f.

**remunerate** [rə'mju:nəreit] v ricompensare. **remuneration** n ricompensa f, rimunerazione f. **remunerative** adj rimunerativo.

**renaissance** [rə'neisəns] n rinascimento m.

**rename** [ri:'neim] v rinominare.

**render** ['rendə] v rendere; rappresentare; (*give back*) restituire; (*cookery*) struggere; (*building*) incalcinare.

**rendezvous** ['rondivu:] n appuntamento m, convegno m.

**renegade** ['renigeid] n, adj rinnegato, -a.

**renew** [rə'nju:] v rinnovare. **renewal** n rinnovamento m. **renewable** adj rinnovabile.

**renounce** [ri'nauns] v rinunciare a, ripudiare. **renouncement** or **renunciation** n rinunzia f.

**renovate** ['renəveit] v rinnovare, ripristinare; (*buildings*) restaurare. **renovation** n ripristinamento m; restauro m.

**renown** [rə'naun] n fama f. **renowned** adj rinomato, famoso, celebre.

**rent¹** [rent] v affittare; (*take, occupy*) prendere in affitto; (*let out*) dare in affitto. n affitto m.

**rent²** [rent] n (*tear*) strappo m, rottura f.

**reopen** [ri:'oupən] v riaprire. **reopening** n riapertura f.

**reorganize** [ri:'o:gənaiz] v riorganizzare. **reorganization** n riorganizzazione f.

**rep¹** [rep] n (*coll*) teatro stabile, compagnia stabile f.

**rep²** [rep] n (*coll*) rappresentante m, f.

**repair** [ri'peə] v riparare, aggiustare. n riparazione f. **beyond repair** irreparabile. **in good/bad repair** in buono/cattivo stato. **repairer** n riparatore, -trice m, f.

**repartee** [repa:'ti:] n battuta di spirito f.

**repatriate** [ri:'patrieit] v rimpatriare. **repatriation** n rimpatrio m.

*****repay** [ri'pei] v ripagare; (*refund*) rimborsare. **repayment** n rimborso m; ricompensa f.

**repeal** [rə'pi:l] v revocare, annullare. n revoca f, annullamento m.

**repeat** [rə'pi:t] v ripetere; (*food*) tornare a gola. n ripetizione f; (*music*) ripresa f.

**repel** [rə'pel] v respingere. **repellent** adj repellente.

**repent** [rə'pent] v pentirsi. **repentance** n penitenza f; (*regret*) pentimento m.

**repercussion** [ri:pə'kʌʃən] n ripercussione f.

**repertoire** ['repətwa:] n repertorio m.

**repertory** ['repətəri] n teatro stabile m. **repertory company** compagnia stabile f.

**repetition** [repə'tiʃn] n ripetizione f. **repetitive** adj che si ripete.

**replace** [rə'pleis] v rimpiazzare; (*put back*) rimettere a posto; sostituire. **replaceable** adj sostituibile. **replacement** n sostituzione f.

**replay** ['ri:plei; v ri:'plei] n rivincita f. v fare la rivincita.

**replenish** [rə'pleniʃ] v rifornire. **replenishment** n rifornimento m.

**replica** ['replikə] n facsimile m invar, copia f.

**reply** [rə'plai] n risposta f. v rispondere.

**report** [rə'po:t] n rapporto m, relazione f; (*school*) pagella f; (*rumour*) voce f; (*noise*) scoppio m. v (*relate*) riferire, fare un rapporto; denunciare; presentarsi. **reporter** n cronista m, f; reporter m invar.

**repose** [rə'pouz] n riposo m. v riposarsi.

**reprehensible** [repri'hensəbl] adj biasimevole, riprensibile.

**represent** [reprə'zent] v rappresentare; (*depict*) raffigurare. **representation** n rappresentazione f.

**representative** [reprə'zentətiv] adj rappresentativo, caratteristico. m rappresentante m, f; (*pol*) deputato, -a m, f.

**repress** [rə'pres] v reprimere. **repressed** adj represso. **repression** n repressione f. **repressive** adj repressivo.

**reprieve** [rə'pri:v] v graziare. n grazia f.

**reprimand** ['reprima:nd] v rimproverare, sgridare. n rimprovero m, predica f.

**reprint** [ri:'print; n ri:'print] v ristampare. n ristampa f.

**reprisal** [rə'praizəl] n rappresaglia f.

**reproach** [rə'proutʃ] v rimproverare, biasimare. n rimprovero m, biasimo m.

**reproduce** [ri:prə'dju:s] v riprodurre. **reproduction** n riproduzione f. **reproductive** adj riproduttivo.

**reprove** [rə'pru:v] v rimproverare, sgridare. **reproof** n rimprovero m.

**reptile** ['reptail] *n* rettile *m*.

**republic** [rə'pʌblik] *n* repubblica *f*. **republican** *n*, *adj* repubblicano, -a.

**repudiate** [rə'pju:dieit] *v* ripudiare; (*disown*) disconoscere; (*reject*) respingere. **repudiation** *n* ripudio *m*.

**repugnant** [rə'pʌgnənt] *adj* ripugnante. **repugnance** *n* ripugnanza *f*.

**repulsion** [rə'pʌlʃn] *n* ripulsione *f*, ripugnanza *f*. **repulsive** *adj* ributtante, schifoso.

**repute** [rə'pju:t] *v* reputare, stimare. *n also* **reputation** reputazione *f*, fama *f*. **reputable** *adj* rispettabile, stimabile, onorevole. **reputedly** *adv* presumibilmente.

**request** [ri'kwest] *n* richiesta *f*, domanda *f*. *v* richiedere, domandare, sollecitare.

**requiem** ['rekwiəm] *n* requiem *m invar*.

**require** [rə'kwaiə] *v* richiedere; (*demand*) esigere, pretendere; rendere necessario. **requirement** *n* esigenza *f*, bisogno *m*.

**requisite** ['rekwizit] *adj* necessario, indispensabile. *n* requisito *m*.

**requisition** [,rekwi'ziʃən] *v* requisire. *n* (*mil*) requisizione *f*, ordine *m*.

**re-route** [ri:'ru:t] *v* deviare.

**resale** [ri:'seil] *n* rivendita *f*.

**rescue** ['reskju:] *n* salvataggio *m*, soccorso *m*. *v* liberare; soccorrere. **rescuer** *n* liberatore, -trice *m*, *f*; soccorritore, -trice *m*, *f*.

**research** [ri'sə:tʃ] *n* ricerca *f*, indagine *f*. *v* fare *or* compiere ricerche, indagare. **researcher** *n* ricercatore, -trice *m*, *f*.

**resemble** [rə'zembl] *v* somigliare, rassomigliare. **resemblance** *n* somiglianza *f*, rassomiglianza *f*.

**resent** [ri'zent] *v* risentirsi di, offendersi *or* sdegnarsi per. **resentful** *adj* offeso, sdegnoso. **resentment** *n* risentimento *m*, sdegno *m*, rancore *m*.

**reserve** [rə'zə:v] *v* riservare. *n* riserva *f*; (*manner*) riserbo *m*; (*circumspection*) riservatezza *f*. **reservation** *n* riserva *f*; (*booking*) prenotazione *f*.

**reservoir** ['rezəvwa:] *n* cisterna *f*, serbatoio *m*; (*artificial lake*) lago artificiale *m*, bacino di riserva *m*.

**reside** [rə'zaid] *v* dimorare, risiedere. **residence** *n* residenza *f*, dimora *f*. **residence permit** permesso di soggiorno *m*. **resident** *n*(*m+f*), *adj* residente. **residential** *adj* residenziale.

**residue** ['rezidju:] *n* residuo *m*. **residual** *adj* residuo, rimanente.

**resign** [rə'zain] *v* dimettersi, rassegnare le dimissioni; (*surrender*) rinunciare a. **resign oneself to** rassegnarsi a. **resignation** *n* dimissioni *f pl*, rassegnazione *f*. **resigned** *adj* rassegnato.

**resilient** [rə'ziliənt] *adj* flessibile. **be resilient** (*person*) aver capacità di ricupero. **resilience** *n* flessibilità *f*, resilienza *f*; capacità di ricupero *f*.

**resin** ['rezin] *n* resina *f*. **resinous** *adj* resinoso.

**resist** [rə'zist] *v* resistere (a). **resistance** *n* resistenza *f*. **resistant** *adj* resistente.

**\*resit** [ri:'sit] *v* ripetere.

**resolute** ['rezəlu:t] *adj* deciso, risoluto. **resolution** *n* risoluzione *f*; (*determination*) risolutezza *f*; decisione *f*.

**resolve** [rə'zolv] *v* risolvere; decidere; (*clear up*) chiarire. *n* decisione *f*.

**resonant** ['rezənənt] *adj* risonante. **resonance** *n* risonanza *f*.

**resort** [rə'zo:t] *v* **resort to** ricorrere a. *n* (*recourse*) ricorso *m*; (*expedient*) risorsa *f*; (*holiday, etc.*) luogo di soggiorno *m*, stazione di villeggiatura *f*.

**resound** [rə'zaund] *v* risonare, echeggiare.

**resource** [rə'zo:s] *n* risorsa *f*. **resourceful** *adj* pieno di risorse, ingegnoso.

**respect** [rə'spekt] *v* rispettare, aver riguardo per. *n* rispetto *m*; (*esteem*) stima *f*, riguardo *m*; (*detail*) aspetto *m*. **pay one's respects** rendere omaggio a. **with due respect** coi debiti riguardi. **with respect to** riguardo a, quanto a. **respectable** *adj* rispettabile; onesto; considerevole. **respectful** *adj* rispettoso. **respectively** *adv* rispettivamente.

**respiration** [respə'reiʃn] *n* respirazione *f*. **respirator** *n* (*med*) respiratore *m*; (*gas mask*) maschera antigas *f*. **respiratory** *adj* respiratorio.

**respite** ['respait] *n* tregua *f*, proroga *f*.

**respond** [rə'spond] *v* rispondere; reagire. **respondent** *n* (*law*) imputato, -a *m*, *f*. **response** *n* risposta *f*; reazione *f*; (*church*) responsorio *m*. **responsive** *adj* sensibile.

**responsible** [rə'sponsəbl] *adj* responsabile. **responsibility** *n* responsabilità *f*.

**rest**[1] [rest] *v* riposarsi; (*place*) posare; (*stay*) stare, fermarsi. *n* riposo; (*support*) appoggio *m*. **restful** *adj* riposante, tranquillo. **restive** *adj* restio. **restless** *adj* inquieto, irrequieto.

**rest²** [rest] *n* resto *m*.

**restaurant** ['restront] *n* ristorante *m*, trattoria *f*. **restaurant car** vagone ristorante *m*.

**restore** [rə'stɔ:] *v* ristabilire; (*building, etc.*) restaurare. **restoration** *n* ristabilimento *m*; restauro *m*; (*history*) restaurazione *f*.

**restrain** [rə'strein] *v* trattenere, reprimere, frenare. **restraint** *n* freno *m*, ritegno *m*; limitazione *f*.

**restrict** [rə'strikt] *v* restringere, limitare. **restriction** *n* restrizione *f*, limitazione *f*. **restrictive** *adj* restrittivo.

**result** [rə'zʌlt] *n* risultato *m*, esito *m*. *v* risultare, derivare. **resultant** *adj* risultante.

**resume** [rə'zju:m] *v* riprendere; riassumere. **resumption** *n* ripresa *f*.

**résumé** ['reizumei] *n* riassunto *m*.

**resurgence** [ri'sə:dʒəns] *n* risurrezione *f*, rinascita *f*.

**resurrect** [rezə'rekt] *v* risuscitare. **resurrection** *n* risurrezione *f*.

**resuscitate** [rə'sʌsəteit] *v* risuscitare.

**retail** ['ri:teil] *n* vendita al dettaglio *or* minuto *f*. *v* (*sell*) vendere al dettaglio *or* minuto; (*tell*) raccontare, dettagliare. *adv*, *adj* al dettaglio *or* minuto. **retailer** *n* dettagliante *m*.

**retain** [rə'tein] *v* ritenere, mantenere. **retainer** (*law*) caparra *f*.

**retaliate** [rə'talieit] *v* contraccambiare, rendere la pariglia. **retaliation** *n* contraccambio *m*, rappresaglia *f*.

**retard** [rə'tɑ:d] *v* ritardare, ostacolare. **retarded** *adj* tardivo.

**retch** [retʃ] *v* aver conati di vomito.

**reticent** ['retisənt] *adj* reticente, riservato, taciturno. **reticence** *n* reticenza *f*, riservatezza *f*, taciturnità *f*.

**retina** ['retinə] *n* retina *f*.

**retinue** ['retinju:] *n* seguito *m*.

**retire** [rə'taiə] *v* ritirarsi; (*go to bed*) andare a letto; (*give up work*) andare in pensione. **retired** *adj* in pensione, a riposo; (*withdrawn*) ritirato, appartato. **retirement** *n* ritirata *f*; riposo *m*.

**retort¹** [rə'tɔ:t] *v* ribattere, rimbeccare. *n* (*reply*) ritorsione *f*, rimbecco *m*.

**retort²** [rə'tɔ:t] *n* (*chem*) storta *f*.

**retrace** [ri'treis] *v* (*follow up*) rintracciare; (*go back over*) ripercorrere; risalire alle origini di.

**retract** [rə'trakt] *v* (*withdraw*) ritirare, far

rientrare; (*disown*) disdire.

**retreat** [rə'tri:t] *n* ritiro *m*; rifugio *m*, asilo *m*; (*mil*) ritirata *f*. *v* ritirarsi, indietreggiare.

**retrieve** [rə'tri:v] *v* ricuperare; riparare; rimediare. **retrieval** *n* ricupero *m*. **retriever** *n* (*dog*) cane da riporto *m*.

**retrograde** ['retrəgreid] *adj* retrogrado.

**retrospect** ['retrəspekt] *n* **in retrospect** guardando indietro. **retrospective** *adj* retrospettivo.

**return** [rə'tə:n] *v* tornare, ritornare; (*put back*) rimettere; (*reciprocate*) contraccambiare; (*give back*) restituire; (*send back*) rinviare. *n* ritorno *m*; restituzione *f*; rinvio *m*; (*profit*) utile *m*; (*report*) relazione *f*, rapporto *m*; (*statement*) rendiconto *m*. **by return of post** a giro di posta. **in return for** in cambio di. **return match** rivincita *f*. **return ticket** biglietto di andata e ritorno *m*.

**reunite** [ri:ju'nait] *v* riunire. **reunion** *n* riunione *f*.

**rev** [rev] *v* (*mot*) imballare. *n* giro *m*. **rev counter** contagiri *m invar*.

**reveal** [rə'vi:l] *v* rivelare, manifestare. **revelation** *n* rivelazione *f*.

**revel** ['revl] *v* (*take pleasure*) trovar diletto; (*make merry*) far baldoria. *n also* **revelry** baldoria *f*.

**revenge** [rə'vendʒ] *n* vendetta *f*. *v* vendicare.

**revenue** ['revinju:] *n* (*income*) rendita *f*; (*yield*) reddito *m*; (*of state*) erario *m*; (*department*) fisco *m*.

**reverberate** [rə'və:bəreit] *v* (*sound*) risonare, riecheggiare; (*heat, light*) riverberare. **reverberation** *n* riverberazione *f*.

**reverence** ['revərəns] *n* riverenza *f*, venerazione *f*. **reverend** *nm*, *adj* reverendo. **reverent** *adj* riverente. **reverential** *adj* reverenziale.

**reverse** [rə'və:s] *v* rovesciare; (*inside out*) rivoltare; (*mot*) far marcia indietro. **reverse the charges** addebitare al destinatario. *adj* contrario, rovescio, inverso. *n* contrario *m*, rovescio *m*, inverso *m*; (*mot*) retromarcia *f*. **reversal** *n* rovesciamento *m*; (*law*) revoca *f*. **reversible** *adj* reversibile; (*law*) revocabile; (*fabric*) a due diritti.

**revert** [rə'və:t] *v* ritornare.

**review** [rə'vju:] *n* (*survey*) rassegna *f*, esame *m*; critica *f*, recensione *f*; (*mil, periodical*) rivista *f*. *v* riesaminare; fare la critica di; passare in rivista. **reviewer** *n* critico *m*.

**revise** [rə'vaiz] v rivedere, correggere. **revision** n revisione f.

**revive** [rə'vaiv] v rianimare, risvegliare; (*restore to use*) ripristinare. **revival** n risveglio m; ripristino m; (*theatre*) ripresa f.

**revoke** [rə'vouk] v revocare.

**revolt** [rə'voult] v ribellarsi; (*feel disgust*) provare orrore; (*cause disgust*) disgustare. **revolting** adj rivoltante, disgustoso; (*rebellious*) ribelle.

**revolution** [revə'lu:ʃən] n rivoluzione f; (*turn*) giro m. **revolutionary** n, adj rivoluzionario, -a.

**revolve** [rə'volv] v (*turn*) girare; (*depend*) basarsi (su), dipendere (da). **revolver** n rivoltella f. **revolving** adj (*door*) girevole; (*credit*) rotativo.

**revue** [rə'vju:] n rivista f.

**revulsion** [rə'vʌlʃən] n ripugnanza f, disgusto m; (*med*) revulsione f.

**reward** [rə'wo:d] n ricompensa f, compenso m. v ricompensare, rimunerare. **rewarding** adj rimunerativo.

**rhetoric** ['retərik] n retorica f. **rhetorical** adj retorico.

**rheumatism** ['ru:mətizəm] n reumatismo m. **rheumatic** adj reumatico.

**Rhine** [rain] n Reno m.

**rhinoceros** [rai'nosərəs] n rinoceronte m.

**rhododendron** [roudə'dendrən] n rododendro m.

**rhombus** ['rombəs] n rombo m.

**rhubarb** ['ru:ba:b] n rabarbaro m.

**rhyme** [raim] n rima f. v rimare, far rima.

**rhythm** ['riðəm] n ritmo m. **rhythmic** adj ritmico.

**rib** [rib] n costola f. **ribbed** adj a coste, scanalato.

**ribbon** ['ribən] n nastro m. **torn to ribbons** ridotto a brandelli.

**rice** [rais] n riso m.

**rich** [ritʃ] adj ricco; (*full*) pieno, abbondante; (*food*) pesante; (*colour*) intenso. **riches** pl n ricchezza f sing. **richness** n ricchezza f.

**rickety** ['rikəti] adj traballante, instabile; (*med*) rachitico.

**\*rid** [rid] v liberare, sbarazzare. **get rid of** sbarazzarsi di. **good riddance!** che liberazione!

**ridden** ['ridn] V **ride**.

**riddle¹** ['ridl] n indovinello m, enigma m. **speak in riddles** parlare per enigmi.

**riddle²** ['ridl] v crivellare.

**\*ride** [raid] n (*on horseback*) passeggiata a cavallo f; (*on bicycle*) passeggiata in bicicletta f; (*in vehicle*) corsa f, giro m. **take for a ride** (*make fun of*) prendere in giro; (*deceive*) imbrogliare. v cavalcare, andare a cavallo. **rider** n (*horse*) cavallerizzo, -a m, f; ciclista m, f; motociclista m, f; (*additional clause*) clausola aggiunta f, codicillo m. **riding school** maneggio m.

**ridge** [ridʒ] n (*geog*) cresta f; (*raised strip*) costa f; (*roof*) colmo m; (*meteorology*) espansione di alta pressione f. v corrugare, incresparsi.

**ridicule** ['ridikju:l] v mettere in ridicolo, canzonare. n ridicolo m. **be an object of ridicule** esser posto in ridicolo. **ridiculous** adj ridicolo, assurdo.

**rife** [raif] adj diffuso, corrente.

**rifle¹** ['raifl] n fucile m. **rifle-range** n poligono di tiro m.

**rifle²** [raifl] v svaligiare. **rifle through** rovistare or frugare in.

**rift** [rift] n crepa f, spacco m; (*in relations*) disaccordo m, screzio m; (*geol*) falda f.

**rig** [rig] n (*naut*) attrezzatura f; (*industry*) impianto m; (*fraudulent dealing*) broglio m, manipolazione f. v attrezzare; (*equip*) montare; manipolare, manovrare.

**right** [rait] adj corretto, giusto; (*geom*) retto; (*not left*) destro. **be right** aver ragione. **right-angled** adj ad angolo retto. **right-hand man** braccio destro m. **right wing** (*pol*) destra f. **right-winger** n persona di destra. f. n bene m, giusto m; (*law*) diritto m; (*not left*) destra f. **right of way** (*vehicles*) precedenza f; (*law*) servitù di passaggio f; (*path*) passaggio pubblico m. adv bene; (*exactly*) proprio; direttamente; completamente; (*direction*) a destra. **right away** subito. v (*restore to position*) raddrizzare; (*correct*) aggiustare, accomodare, metere a posto; (*redress*) riparare. **rightful** adj legittimo. **rightly** adv giustamente.

**righteous** ['raitʃəs] adj retto, giusto. **righteousness** n rettitudine f.

**rigid** ['ridʒid] adj rigido, inflessibile, rigoroso. **rigidity** n rigidezza f; (*stiffness*) rigidità f.

**rigmarole** ['rigməroul] n (*long procedure*) trafila f; (*nonsense*) filastrocca f.

**rigour** ['rigə] n rigore m. **rigorous** adj rigoroso, rigido.

**rim** [rim] n orlo m, bordo m; (of wheel) cerchio m; (of spectacles) montatura f.

**rind** [raind] n (fruit) buccia f, scorza f; (cheese) crosta f.

**ring¹** [riŋ] n anello m; (enclosure) recinto m, pista f; (boxing) quadrato m, ring m invar. v cingere, circondare. **ringlet** n (curl) ricciolo m.

**\*ring²** [riŋ] n (sound) suono m, squillo m; (inherent quality) tono m; (coll) telefonata f, colpo di telefono m. v suonare; (echo) risonare, echeggiare; telefonare (a).

**rink** [riŋk] n pista di pattinaggio f.

**rinse** [rins] v sciacquare, risciacquare. n risciacquatura f; (hair) cachet m.

**riot** ['raiət] n rivolta f, sommossa f; (uproar) baccano m, fracasso m; (profusion) orgia f. **riot squad** squadra mobile or volante f. v insorgere, far baccano. **riotous** adj tumultuoso; (noisy) chiassoso, clamoroso; dissoluto.

**rip** [rip] n strappo m, squarcio m. v strappare, squarciare. **let rip** (give vent to) dare libero sfogo a.

**ripe** [raip] adj maturo. **ripen** v (far) maturare. **ripeness** n maturità f. **ripening** n maturazione f.

**ripple** ['ripl] n increspamento m, crespa f; (sound) mormorio m. v increspare, mormorare.

**\*rise** [raiz] v sorgere; (get up) alzarsi, levarsi; (increase) aumentare, salire; (swell) gonfiarsi; (rebel) insorgere. n salita f; aumento m. **give rise to** causare.

**risen** ['rizn] V **rise**.

**risk** [risk] v rischiare, arrischiare, correre il rischio di. n rischio m. **at the risk of** a rischio di. **risky** adj rischioso.

**rissole** ['risoul] n polpetta f, crocchetta f.

**rite** [rait] n rito m.

**ritual** ['ritjuəl] nm, adj rituale.

**rival** ['raivəl] n(m+f), adj rivale. v rivaleggiare, competere. **rivalry** n rivalità f.

**river** ['rivə] n fiume m.

**rivet** ['rivit] n rivetto m. v rivettare. **riveting** adj affascinante.

**road** [roud] n strada f, via f. **road-block** n posto di blocco m. **road sign** cartello stradale m. **road-works** pl n lavori stradali m pl. **roadworthy** adj atto a prendere la strada.

**roam** [roum] v vagare, errare.

**roar** [ro:] v (wild beast) ruggire, urlare; (sea) muggire. **roar with laughter** scoppiare dalle risa. n ruggito m, urlo m; muggito m; (thunder) rombo m; (laughter) scroscio m.

**roast** [roust] v arrostire; (coffee) tostare. n arrosto m.

**rob** [rob] v derubare, rapinare; (plunder) svaligiare. **robber** n ladro m, rapinatore m. **robbery** n rapina f. **armed robbery** rapina a mano armata f.

**robe** [roub] n abito lungo m, toga f.

**robin** ['robin] n pettirosso m.

**robot** ['roubot] n automa m.

**robust** [rə'bʌst] adj robusto.

**rock¹** [rok] n (stone) roccia f, scoglio m; (support) rocca f. **on the rocks** (coll: without money) al verde; (coll: with ice) con ghiaccio. **rock-bottom** adj bassissimo. **rock-crystal** n cristallo di rocca m. **rock-salt** n salgemma m. **rocky** adj roccioso.

**rock²** [rok] v dondolare, oscillare; (baby) cullare. **off one's rocker** (coll) matto. **rocking-chair** n sedia a dondolo f. **rocking-horse** n cavallo a dondolo m.

**rocket** ['rokit] n razzo m; (reprimand) cicchetto m. v (increase sharply) andare alle stelle.

**rod** [rod] n bastone m, stecca f; (fishing) canna (da pesca) f; (piston) biella f.

**rode** [roud] V **ride**.

**rodent** ['roudənt] nm, adj roditore.

**roe¹** [rou] n (deer) capriolo m.

**roe²** [rou] n (hard) uova di pesce f pl; (soft) latte di pesce m.

**rogue** [roug] n (dishonest person) mariolo m; (rascal) briccone m, furfante m. **roguery** n bricconeria f. **roguish** adj bricconesco; (mischievous) furbo.

**role** [roul] n ruolo m, funzione f.

**roll** [roul] v rullare; (wave) ondeggiare; (rotate) roteare; (ship) rollare. **be rolling in money** guazzare nel denaro. **roll out** (pastry) spianare. **roll up** arrotolare. n rotolo m; (bread) panino m. **roll-call** n appello m. **roller** n cilindro m, rullo m. **roller-skate** n schettino m, pattino a rotelle m. **rolling-pin** n matterello m.

**romance** [rou'mans] n romanzo (cavalleresco) m; (medieval tale) romanza f; (love affair) idillio m, avventura amorosa f.

**romantic** *adj* romantico; *(fanciful)* romanzesco.

**Romania** [ru:'meinjə] *n* Romania *f*. **Romanian** *n*, *adj* romeno, -a.

**Rome** [roum] *n* Roma *f*. **Roman** *n*, *adj* romano, -a. **Roman Catholic** *adj* cattolico (romano).

**romp** [romp] *v* giocare rumorosamente, ruzzare. **romp home** *(win easily)* vincere facilmente. **romp through** *(exam)* superare con facilità. *n* trambusto *m*; *(coll)* cagnara *f*.

**roof** [ru:f] *n*, *pl* -s tetto *m*. **hit the roof** *(coll)* andare su tutte le furie. **roof of the mouth** palato *m*.

**rook** [ruk] *n* *(bird)* corvo *m*; *(chess)* torre *f*; *(swindler)* truffatore, -trice *m*, *f*. *v* barare, truffare.

**room** [ru:m] *n* stanza *f*, sala *f*, camera *f*; *(space)* posto *m*, spazio *m*; opportunità *f*. **room temperature** temperatura ambiente *f*. **roomy** *adj* spazioso, vasto.

**roost** [ru:st] *n* *(building)* pollaio *m*; *(pole)* posatoio *m*. **rule the roost** fare il gallo del pollaio. *v* appollaiarsi.

**root**[1] [ru:t] *n* radice *f*; *(cause)* fondo *m*. **root and branch** radicalmente. **root cause** causa prima *f*. **take root** mettere radice. *v* piantare, abbarbicare; *(become fixed)* mettere radici, radicare.

**root**[2] [ru:t] *v* grufolare; *(search)* frugacchiare. **root for** *(slang)* sostenere. **root out** scovare.

**rope** [roup] *n* corda *f*, fune *f*. **know the ropes** esser pratico, saperla lunga. **learn the ropes** familiarizzarsi.

**rosary** ['rouzəri] *n* rosario *m*.

**rose**[1] [rouz] *V* **rise**.

**rose**[2] [rouz] *n* rosa *f*. **rose-bush** *n* rosa *f*, rosaio *m*. **rosy** *adj* roseo.

**rosé** ['rouzei] *n* rosato *m*.

**rosemary** ['rouzməri] *n* rosmarino *m*.

**rosette** [rou'zet] *n* coccarda *f*, rosetta *f*.

**roster** ['rostə] *n* turno di servizio *m*; *(mil)* ruolino *m*.

**rostrum** ['rostrəm] *n* tribuna *f*, piattaforma *f*.

**rot** [rot] *v* putrefare, marcire; *(teeth, wood)* cariare. *n* putrefazione *f*; *(rotten matter)* marciume *m*; *(coll: nonsense)* sciocchezze *f pl*; declino *m*. **rotten** *adj* marcio; *(coll: annoying)* seccante.

**rota** ['routə] *n* turno (di servizio) *m*, lista *f*.

**rotate** [rou'teit] *v* rotare; *(crops)* avvicendare. **rotary** *adj* *(motion)* rotatorio; *(tech)* rotativo. **rotation** *n* rotazione *f*; avvicendamento *m*.

**rouge** [ru:ʒ] *n* belletto *m*, rossetto *m*.

**rough** [rʌf] *adj* *(coarse)* ruvido; *(person)* rozzo; *(ground)* malagevole, irregolare; *(sea, weather)* agitato, tempestoso; approssimativo; *(unrefined)* greggio. **rough-and-ready** *adj* improvvisato. **rough-and-tumble** *n* zuffa *f*, mischia *f*. *v* **rough it** vivere primitivamente. **rough out** abbozzare. **roughen** *v* irruvidire. **roughness** *n* ruvidezza *f*.

**roulette** [ru:'let] *n* roulette *f*.

**round** [raund] *adj* tondo, rotondo; circolare; sferico. *prep* tutto intorno a. *n* tondo *m*, cerchio *m*; *(tour)* giro *m*; *(game)* partita *f*; *(boxing)* ripresa *f*; *(ammunition)* scarica *f*; *(applause)* salva *f*. *adv* in giro. **all year round** tutto l'anno. **show round** fare da guida a. *v* **round off** completare. **round up** *(number)* arrotondare.

**roundabout** ['raundəbaut] *n* anello stradale *m*. *adj* indiretto, obliquo.

**rouse** [rauz] *v* destare. **rousing** *adj* stimolante.

**route** [ru:t] *n* strada *f*, rotta *f*. **en route** per strada.

**routine** [ru:'ti:n] *n* uso *m*, abitudine *f*.

**rove** [rouv] *v* errare, vagabondare.

**row**[1] [rou] *n* fila *f*.

**row**[2] [rou] *v* remare. *n* remata *f*. **rowing boat** barca a remi *f*.

**row**[3] [rau] *n* *(quarrel)* rissa *f*, lite *f*; *(noise)* chiasso *m*, baccano *m*. *v* litigarsi.

**rowdy** ['raudi] *adj* chiassoso, turbolento. *n* attaccabrighe *m*, *f invar*.

**royal** ['roiəl] *adj* reale, regio, regale. **royalist** *n* (*m*+*f*), *adj* realista. **royalties** *pl n* diritti d'autore *m pl*. **royalty** *n* *(people)* reali *m pl*; *(status)* regalità *f*, dignità di re *f*.

**rub** [rʌb] *v* fregare, strofinare. **rub down** *(clean)* pulire fregando; *(dry)* asciugare fregando. **rub out** cancellare. **rub shoulders** venire in contatto.

**rubber** ['rʌbə] *n* gomma *f*, caucciù *m*.

**rubbish** ['rʌbiʃ] *n* *(waste)* immondizia *f*; *(derog)* robaccia *f*; *(nonsense)* sciocchezze *f pl*. **rubbish bin** pattumiera *f*.

**rubble** ['rʌbl] *n* frantumi *m pl*, macerie *f pl*.

**ruby** ['ru:bi] n rubino m. adj (color) rubino or vermiglio.

**rucksack** ['rʌksak] n sacco da montagna m, zaino m.

**rudder** ['rʌdə] n timone m.

**rude** [ru:d] adj (discourteous) scortese; (unmannerly) rozzo, grossolano; (sturdy) robusto. **rudeness** n scortesia f; grossolanità f; robustezza f.

**rudiment** ['ru:dimənt] n rudimento m.

**rueful** ['ru:fəl] adj triste, lamentevole.

**ruff** [rʌf] n gorgiera f.

**ruffian** ['rʌfiən] n ruffiano m, farabutto m.

**ruffle** ['rʌfl] v arruffare, increspare.

**rug** [rʌg] n tappeto m; (travelling) coperta da viaggio f; (bedside) scendiletto m.

**rugby** ['rʌgbi] n rugby m invar, palla ovale f.

**rugged** ['rʌgid] adj irregolare; rude.

**ruin** ['ru:in] n rovina f. v rovinare. **ruinous** adj rovinoso.

**rule** [ru:l] n regola f, norma f; (ruler) regolo m. **as a rule** di regola or solito. v regolare, dirigere; decidere; (mark with lines) rigare. **rule out** escludere. **ruler** n sovrano m, governatore m; (school) regolo m. **ruling** n direttiva f, decisione f.

**rum** [rʌm] n rum m.

**rumble** ['rʌmbl] v rimbombare, brontolare; (stomach) gorgogliare; (coll: detect) scoprire. n brontolio m, gorgoglio m.

**rummage** ['rʌmidʒ] v frugare, rovistare.

**rummy** ['rʌmi] n ramino m.

**rumour** ['ru:mə] n diceria f, voce f. v far correre voce.

**rump** [rʌmp] n groppa f, culatta f. **rump steak** bistecca f.

*__**run**__ [rʌn] n corsa f; (outing) gita f; serie f invar, durata f. **in the long run** a lungo andare. **on the run** in fuga. v correre; (flow) scorrere; funzionare; (colour) spandere; (stockings) smagliare; (manage) dirigere. **run away** or **off** fuggire. **run-away** n, adj fuggiasco, -a. **run down** (slow) rallentarsi; (car, etc.) investire; (disparage) parlar male di; (find) trovare. **run in** rodare. **run into** (encounter) incontrare per caso, imbattersi; (collide with) urtare; (amount to) raggiungere. **run out** (supplies, etc.) esaurirsi. **run over** (car, etc.) investire; (overflow) traboccare; (rehearse) ripassare. **runway** n pista di decollo or atterraggio f.

**runner** n corridore m; (messenger) fattorino m; (carpet) passatoia f; (plant) pollone m. **runner bean** fagiolo (rampicante) m. **runner-up** n secondo arrivato, seconda arrivata m, f.

**rung**[1] [rʌŋ] n piolo m.

**rung**[2] [rʌŋ] V **ring**[2].

**running** ['rʌniŋ] n corsa f; funzionamento m; (competition) gara f. **be in the running** aver possibilità di vincere. **make the running** fare l'andatura. adj funzionante; regolare; consecutivo.

**rupture** ['rʌptʃə] n rottura f; (med) ernia f. v rompere.

**rural** ['ruərəl] adj campestre, rurale.

**rush**[1] [rʌʃ] v precipitarsi, avventarsi; (convey with haste) precipitare, spostare in fretta. n corsa precipitosa f; (intense activity) trambusto m; (haste) fretta e furia f; (sudden coming) accesso m. **rush hour** ora di punta f.

**rush**[2] [rʌʃ] n (plant) giunco m.

**rusk** [rʌsk] n biscotto (non dolce) m.

**Russia** ['rʌʃə] n Russia f. **Russian** n, adj russo, -a.

**rust** [rʌst] n ruggine f. **rustproof** adj inossidabile. v arrugginirsi. **rusty** adj arrugginito, rugginoso; (out of practice) fuori d'esercizio.

**rustic** ['rʌstik] adj rustico.

**rustle** ['rʌsl] n fruscio m. v frusciare, stormire.

**rut** [rʌt] n solco m, carreggiata f; (fixed habit) abitudine fissa f.

**ruthless** ['ru:θlis] adj spietato, implacabile.

**rye** [rai] n segala f.

# S

**sabbatical** [sə'batikəl] adj sabbatico.

**sable** ['seibl] n zibellino m. adj di zibellino.

**sabotage** ['sabətɑ:ʒ] n sabotaggio m. v sabotare. **saboteur** n sabotatore, -trice m, f.

**sabre** ['seibə] n sciabola f. **sabre-rattling** n minaccia di guerra f, bravata f.

**saccharin** ['sakərin] n saccarina f.

**sachet** ['saʃei] n sacchetto profumato m.

**sack** [sak] n sacco m; (coll; dismissal) licenziamento m. **get the sack** (coll) essere mandato a spasso. *v* (*coll*) mandare a spasso.

**sacrament** ['sakrəmənt] *n* sacramento *m*. **sacramental** *adj* sacramentale.

**sacred** ['seikrid] *adj* sacro, sacrosanto.

**sacrifice** ['sakrifais] *n* sacrificio *m*; (*comm*) perdita *f*. *v* sacrificare; (*comm*) vendere sottocosto.

**sacrilege** ['sakrəlidʒ] *n* sacrilegio *m*. **sacrilegious** *adj* sacrilego (*m pl* -ghi).

**sad** [sad] *adj* triste. **sadden** *v* rattristare. **sadness** *n* tristezza *f*.

**saddle** ['sadl] *n* sella *f*. *v* sellare.

**sadism** ['seidizəm] *n* sadismo *m*. **sadist** *n* sadico, -a *m*, *f*. **sadistic** *adj* sadico.

**safe** [seif] *adj* sicuro; (*unharmed*) salvo; innocuo. **safe and sound** sano e salvo. **safe-conduct** *n* salvacondotto *m*. **safeguard** *v* salvaguardare; proteggere. **safe keeping** custodia *f*. *n* cassaforte *f*. **safety** *n* sicurezza *f*, salvezza *f*. **safety-belt** *n* cintura di sicurezza *f*. **safety-catch** *n* sicura *f*. **safety-pin** *n* spillo di sicurezza *m*.

**saffron** ['safrən] *n* zafferano *m*.

**sag** [sag] *v* incurvarsi, piegarsi.

**saga** ['sa:gə] *n* saga *f*.

**sage¹** [seidʒ] *n*, *adj* saggio, -a. **sagacious** *adj* sagace, avveduto.

**sage²** [seidʒ] *n* (*herb*) salvia *f*.

**Sagittarius** [sadʒi'teəriəs] *n* Sagittario *m*.

**sago** ['seigou] *n* sagù *m*.

**said** [sed] *V* say.

**sail** [seil] *v* navigare; (*leave*) salpare. *n* vela *f*. **sailcloth** *n* tela olona *f*. **sailing** *n* vela *f*, sport della vela *m*. **sailing boat** barca a vela *f*. **sailor** *n* marinaio *m*.

**saint** [seint] *n* santo, -a *m*, *f*. *adj* santo. **saintly** *adj* santo, pio.

**sake** [seik] *n* beneficio *m*, interesse *m*, bene *m*. **for God's sake** per l'amor di Dio. **for the sake of** (*in order to*) tanto per. **for your own sake** per il tuo bene.

**salad** ['saləd] *n* insalata *f*.

**salami** [sə'la:mi] *n* salame *m*.

**salary** ['saləri] *n* stipendio *m*.

**sale** [seil] *n* vendita *f*; (*clearance*) liquidazione *f*, saldo *m*. **for** *or* **on sale** in vendita. **salesgirl** *n* commessa *f*. **salesman** *n* commesso *m*. **travelling salesman** commesso viaggiatore *m*.

**saline** ['seilain] *adj* salino. **salinity** *n* salinità *f*.

**saliva** [sə'laivə] *n* saliva *f*. **salivary** *adj* salivare. **salivate** *v* salivare.

**sallow** ['salou] *adj* giallastro, olivastro.

**salmon** ['samən] *n* salmone *m*.

**salon** ['salon] *n* salone *m*.

**saloon** [sə'lu:n] *n* salone *m*; (*ship*) ritrovo per passeggeri *m*. **saloon car** berlina *f*.

**salt** [so:lt] *n* sale *m*. **salt-cellar** *n* saliera *f*. *adj also* **salty** salato, piccante. *v* salare.

**salubrious** [sə'lu:briəs] *adj* salubre.

**salute** [sə'lu:t] *n* saluto *m*. *v* salutare.

**salvage** ['salvidʒ] *n* salvataggio *m*, ricupero *m*. *v* salvare, ricuperare.

**salvation** [sal'veiʃən] *n* salvezza *f*; (*theology*) salvazione *f*.

**same** [seim] *adj* stesso, medesimo; (*unchanged*) immutato. *pron* lo stesso, il medesimo. **all the same** (*nevertheless*) malgrado tutto. **at the same time** nello stesso tempo; (*notwithstanding*) con tutto ciò, ciononostante. **the same to you!** altrettanto! **sameness** *n* somiglianza *f*, uniformità *f*, monotonia *f*.

**sample** ['sa:mpl] *n* campione *m*; (*specimen*) saggio *m*. *v* campionare; (*test*) assaggiare. **sampling** *n* campionatura *f*.

**sanatorium** [sanə'to:riəm] *n* sanatorio *m*.

**sanctify** ['saŋktifai] *v* santificare, consacrare.

**sanctimonious** [saŋkti'mouniəs] *adj* santocchio, santerello.

**sanction** ['saŋkʃən] *n* sanzione *f*. *v* sanzionare, sancire.

**sanctity** ['saŋktəti] *n* santità *f*.

**sanctuary** ['saŋktʃuəri] *n* santuario *m*; (*refuge*) asilo *m*, rifugio *m*.

**sand** [sand] *n* sabbia *f*. *v* (*sprinkle*) insabbiare; (*smooth*) smerigliare. **sand-blast** *v* pulire con un getto di sabbia. **sandpaper** *n* carta vetrata *f*. **sandy** *adj* (*consistency*) sabbioso; (*colour*) biondo rossiccio.

**sandal** ['sandl] *n* sandalo *m*.

**sandwich** ['sanwidʒ] *n* sandwich *m invar*, panino imbottito *m*. *v* inserire.

**sane** [sein] *adj* equilibrato, sano di mente. **sanity** *n* sanità di mente *f*, equilibrio *m*.

**sang** [saŋ] *V* sing.

**sanitary** ['sanitəri] *adj* igienico, sanitario. **sanitary towel** *n* pannolino igienico *m*.

**sank** [saŋk] *V* sink.

**sap¹** [sap] *n* (*plant*) linfa *f*.

**sap²** [sap] *v* (*undermine*) minare, indebolire.

**sapphire** ['safaiə] *n* zaffiro *m*. *adj* zaffirino.

**sarcasm** ['sa:kazəm] *n* sarcasmo *m*. **sarcastic** *adj* sarcastico.

**sardine** [sa:'di:n] *n* sardina *f*.

**Sardinia** [sa:'dinjə] *n* Sardegna *f*. **Sardinian** *n*, *adj* sardo, -a.

**sardonic** [sa:'donik] *adj* sardonico.

**sash¹** [saʃ] *n* (*scarf*) sciarpa *f*.

**sash²** [saʃ] *n* (*frame*) telaio *m*. **sash-cord** *n* corda del contrappeso *f*. **sash-window** *n* finestra alla ghigliottina *f*.

**sat** [sat] *V* **sit**.

**satchel** ['satʃəl] *n* cartella *f*.

**satellite** ['satəlait] *nm*, *adj* satellite. **satellite town** città satellite *f*. **satellite dish** parabola (satellitare) *f*.

**satin** ['satin] *nm*, *adj* raso.

**satire** ['sataiə] *n* satira *f*. **satirical** *adj* satirico. **satirist** *n* satirista *m*, *f*.

**satisfy** ['satisfai] *v* soddisfare. **satisfaction** *n* soddisfazione *f*. **satisfactory** *adj* soddisfacente.

**saturate** ['satʃəreit] *v* saturare. **saturated** *adj* saturo. **saturation** *n* saturazione *f*.

**Saturday** ['satədi] *n* sabato *m*.

**sauce** [so:s] *n* salsa *f*; (*coll*) impertinenza *f*. **saucy** *adj* impertinente, sfacciato. **sauciness** *n* impertinenza *f*, sfacciataggine *f*.

**saucepan** ['so:spən] *n* casseruola *f*, pentola *f*.

**saucer** ['so:sə] *n* piattino *m*, sottocoppa *f*.

**sauerkraut** ['sauəkraut] *n* sarcrauti *m pl*.

**sauna** [so:nə] *n* sauna *f*.

**saunter** [so:ntə] *v* girovagare, andare a passeggio, girare. *n* giro *m*.

**sausage** ['sosidʒ] *n* salsiccia *f*, salame *m*.

**savage** ['savidʒ] *adj* selvaggio; feroce, crudele. *v* assalire, ferire. **savagery** *n* selvatichezza *f*; ferocia, crudeltà *f*.

**save¹** [seiv] *v* salvare; (*keep*) conservare; (*put aside*) risparmiare. **saver** *n* risparmiatore, -trice *m*, *f*. **saving** *n* economia *f*. **savings** *pl n* risparmi *m pl*.

**save²** [seiv] *prep* (*except*) salvo, eccetto.

**saviour** ['seivjə] *n* liberatore, -trice *m*, *f*; (*rel*) redentore *m*.

**savoury** ['seivəri] *adj* (*appetizing*) saporito, gustoso; (*piquant*) piccante. *n* piatto appetitoso *m*.

**\*saw¹** [so:] *n* sega *f*. **sawdust** *n* segatura *f*.

**sawmill** *n* segheria *f*. *v* segare.

**saw²** [so:] *V* **see¹**.

**sawn** [so:n] *V* **saw¹**.

**saxophone** ['saksəfoun] *n* sassofono *m*.

**\*say** [sei] *v* dire; (*declare*) dichiarare, affermare. **I say!** senti! guarda un po'! (*let's*) **say** (*as an estimate*) mettiamo, facciamo. **have no say** non aver voce. **have one's say** dire la sua. **saying** *n* massima *f*, motto *m*, proverbio *m*.

**scab** [skab] *n* crosta *f*; (*biol*) scabbia *f*, rogna *f*; (*derog: non-striker*) crumiro, -a *m*, *f*. **scabby** *adj* rognoso, scabbioso.

**scaffold** ['skafəld] *n* (*execution*) patibolo *m*. **scaffolding** *n* impalcatura *f*, ponteggio *m*; (*theatre*) palco *m*.

**scald** [sko:ld] *n* scottatura *f*. *v* scottare.

**scale¹** [skeil] *n* (*thin plate*) lamina *f*; (*of fish, etc.*) scaglia *f*, squama *f*; tartaro *m*; incrostazione *f*. *v* squamare; incrostare. **scaly** *adj* squamoso.

**scale²** [skeil] *n* (*music, math, etc.*) scala *f*. **to scale** in proporzione. *v* (*climb*) scalare; (*climb over*) scavalcare. **scale down** ridurre proporzionalemente.

**scales** [skeilz] *pl n* bilancia *f sing*. **tip the scales** dare il crollo alla bilancia.

**scallop** ['skaləp] *n* (*zool*) pettine *m*; (*shell*) conchiglia *f*; (*edging*) dentellatura *f*.

**scalp** [skalp] *n* scalpo *m*. *v* scalpare.

**scalpel** ['skalpəl] *n* scalpello *m*.

**scampi** ['skampi] *pl n* scampi *m pl*.

**scan** [skan] *v* scrutare; (*radar, etc.*) analizzare, sondare; (*poetry*) scandire; (*glance at*) dare una scorsa a. **scanner** *n* analizzatore *m*, dispositivo di esplorazione *m*.

**scandal** ['skandl] *n* scandalo *m*; (*gossip*) maldicenza *f*, diceria *f*. **scandalmonger** *n* maldicente *m*, *f*. **scandalize** *v* scandalizzare. **scandalous** *adj* scandaloso.

**scanty** ['skanti] *adj* *also* **scant** scarso, insufficiente. **scantily dressed** vestito succintamente.

**scapegoat** ['skeipgout] *n* capro espiatorio *m*.

**scar** [ska:] *n* cicatrice *f*, sfregio *m*. *v* (*mark*) sfregiare; (*heal*) cicatrizzare. **scarred** *adj* sfregiato.

**scarce** [skeəs] *adj* scarso, raro. **scarcely** *adv* appena. **scarcity** *n* scarsezza *f*.

**scare** [skeə] *n* paura *f*, panico *m*. *v* impaurire, spaventare. **be scared** avere paura. **be**

**scared stiff** avere una paura matta. **scare-crow** n spauracchio m. **scaremonger** n allarmista m, f.

**scarf** [ska:f] n sciarpa f; (square) foulard m invar.

**scarlet** ['ska:lit] adj scarlatto. **scarlet fever** scarlattina f. **scarlet runner** fagiolo di Spagna m.

**scathing** ['skeiðiŋ] adj sprezzante, sdegnoso.

**scatter** ['skatə] v spargere, disperdere, diffondere. **scatterbrained** adj scervellato, distratto.

**scavenge** ['skavindʒ] v (streets) spazzare; (zool) nutrirsi di cadaveri. **scavenger** n (street cleaner) spazzino m; (zool) animale necrofago m.

**scene** [si:n] n scena f, spettacolo m. **scenario** n scenario m.

**scenery** ['si:nəri] n (landscape) paesaggio m, veduta f; (theatre) scenario m.

**scent** [sent] n profumo m, odore m; (track) pista f. **throw off the scent** far perdere la traccia. v (detect) fiutare; (perfume) profumare.

**sceptic** ['skeptik] n scettico, -a m, f. **sceptical** adj scettico. **scepticism** n scetticismo m.

**sceptre** ['septə] n scettro m.

**schedule** ['fedju:l] n programma m; (time-table) orario m; lista f, specchietto m. **according to schedule** secondo il previsto or programma. v programmare; (list) elencare. **scheduled flight** volo di linea m.

**scheme** [ski:m] n schema m, progetto m, piano m; intrigo (pl -ghi) m, trama f. v progettare; tramare. **schematic** adj schematico.

**schizophrenia** [skitsə'fri:niə] n schizofrenia f. **schizophrenic** n, adj schizofrenico, -a.

**scholar** ['skolə] n persona erudita f, studioso, -a m, f; studente, -essa m, f. **scholarly** adj erudito, dotto. **scholarship** n erudizione f; studio m; (award) borsa di studio f.

**scholastic** [skə'lastik] adj scolastico.

**school¹** [sku:l] n scuola f. **schoolboy** n scolaro m. **schoolfellow** n compagno, -a di scuola m, f. **schoolgirl** n scolara f. **schoolmaster** n maestro m; insegnante m. **schoolmistress** n maestra f, insegnante f. v istruire, ammaestrare.

**school²** [sku:l] n (of fish) banco m, frotta f.

**schooner** ['sku:nə] n goletta f.

**sciatica** [sai'atikə] n sciatica f. **sciatic** adj sciatico.

**science** ['saiəns] n scienza f. **science fiction** fantascienza f. **scientific** adj scientifico. **scientist** n scienziato, -a m, f.

**scissors** ['sizəz] pl n forbici f pl.

**scoff¹** [skof] v (mock) beffare, schernire. n beffa f.

**scoff²** [skof] v (coll: eat) pappare.

**scold** [skould] v sgridare, rimproverare. **scolding** n sgridata f, lavata di capo f.

**scone** [skon] n focaccia f.

**scoop** [sku:p] n (kitchen) mestolo m; (dredge) benna f; (coll) colpo m. v scavare. **scoop out** scodellare. **scoop up** raccogliere, tirar su.

**scooter** ['sku:tə] n motoretta f, scooter m invar; (child's) monopattino m.

**scope** [skoup] n (extent) portata f; opportunità f; possibilità f; (space for activity) campo libero m.

**scorch** [sko:tʃ] n scottatura f. v abbruciacchiare. **scorcher** n (coll) giornata caldissima f.

**score** [sko:] n (sport) punteggio m; (account) conto m; (debt) debito m; (ground) causa f; (music) partitura f. **scoreboard** n tabellone m. v (sport) segnare; (points) notare; marcare; (notches) intaccare; orchestrare. **score off** aver la meglio su.

**scorn** [sko:n] n disprezzo m, sdegno m. v sdegnare, sprezzare. **scornful** adj sdegnoso, sprezzante.

**Scorpio** ['sko:piou] n Scorpione m.

**scorpion** ['sko:piən] n scorpione m.

**scotch** [skotʃ] v sopprimere.

**Scotland** ['skotlənd] n Scozia f. **Scot** n scozzese m, f. **Scotch** n (whisky) scotch m invar, whisky scozzese m. **Scottish** or **Scots** adj scozzese.

**scoundrel** ['skaundrəl] n furfante m, mascalzone m.

**scour¹** [skauə] v (clean) pulire sfregando; (rub) fregare, forbire.

**scour²** [skauə] v (search) perlustrare.

**scout** [skaut] v esplorare, perlustrare. n (mil) vedetta f; (boy) giovane esploratore m; osservatore m.

**scowl** [skaul] n cipiglio m, guardataccia f. v accigliarsi.

**scramble** ['skrambl] v (move hastily) sgambettare; (climb) arrampicarsi; (struggle) azzuffarsi, battagliare; (*radio, etc.*) disturbare. **scrambled eggs** uova strapazzate *f pl. n* confusione *f*, parapiglia *f*; (*struggle*) lotta *f*.

**scrap** [skrap] *n* (*small piece*) pezzetto *m*, frammento *m*; (*metal*) rottame *m*. **scrapbook** *n* album *m invar.* **scraps** *pl n* (*leftovers*) avanzi *m pl*, rimasugli *m pl*. **scrap yard** rottamaio *m*. *v* scartare, mettere fuori servizio. **scrappy** *adj* frammentario.

**scrape** [skreip] *v* raschiare, grattare. **scrape through** cavarsela; (*exam*) passare per il buco della serratura. **scrape together** racimolare, raccogliere. *n* (*embarrassing situation*) impaccio *m*.

**scratch** [skratʃ] *v* graffiare, grattare; cancellare; (*withdraw*) ritirarsi. *n* graffiatura *f*. **from scratch** da zero. **up to scratch** all'altezza della situazione. **scratch card** scheda gratta e vinci *f*.

**scrawl** [skro:l] *n* scarabocchio *m*. *v* scarabocchiare.

**scream** [skri:m] *v* strillare. *n* strillo *m*; (*coll: funny person*) spasso *m*.

**screech** [skri:tʃ] *v* stridere, cigolare. *n* strido *m* (*pl* -a *f*).

**screen** [skri:n] *n* paravento *m*; (*shelter*) riparo *m*; (*film, etc.*) schermo *m*. **screen-saver** salvaschermo *m*. *v* (*hide*) nascondere; (*protect*) proteggere; (*check*) vagliare; (*cinema*) proiettare. **screening** *n* (*med*) controllo (diagnostico) *m*.

**screw** [skru:] *n* vite *f*. **screwdriver** *n* cacciavite *m invar. v* avvitare. **screw up one's courage** farsi coraggio.

**scribble** ['skribl] *n* sgorbio *m*. *v* scribacchiare. **scribbler** *n* scribacchino, -a *m, f*.

**script** [skript] *n* (*handwriting*) scrittura *f*; manuscritto *m*; (*theatre*) copione *m*.

**Scripture** ['skriptʃə] *n* Sacra Scrittura *f*, Bibbia *f*.

**scroll** [skroul] *n* (*roll*) rotolo *m*; (*ornament*) voluta *f*.

**scrounge** [skraundʒ] (*coll*) *v* scroccare. **scrounger** *n* scroccone, -a *m, f*.

**scrub¹** [skrʌb] *v* lavare or pulire fregando forte. **scrubbing brush** spazzola dura *f*, spazzolone per lavare *m*.

**scrub²** [skrʌb] *n* (*bush*) macchia *f*.

**scruffy** ['skrʌfi] *adj* trasandato.

**scruple** ['skru:pl] *n* scrupolo *m*. **scrupulous** *adj* scrupoloso.

**scrutiny** ['skru:təni] *n* esame accurato *m*. **scrutinize** *v* esaminare accuratamente.

**scuffle** ['skʌfl] *n* tafferuglio *m*. *v* azzuffarsi.

**scullery** ['skʌləri] *n* retrocucina *f*.

**sculpt** [skʌlpt] *v* scolpire. **sculptor** *n* scultore *m*. **sculptress** *n* scultrice *f*. **sculptural** *adj* scultorio. **sculpture** *n* scultura *f*.

**scum** [skʌm] *n* (*on liquids*) schiuma *f*; (*on metals*) scoria *f*; (*worthless people*) feccia *f*.

**scurf** [skə:f] *n* forfora *f*. **scurfy** *adj* forforoso.

**scurrilous** ['skʌriləs] *adj* scurrile.

**scurvy** ['skə:vi] *n* scorbuto *m*.

**scuttle¹** ['skʌtl] *n* (*for coal*) secchio da carbone *m*.

**scuttle²** ['skʌtl] *v* (*run*) scorrazzare.

**scuttle³** ['skʌtl] *v* (*sink*) affondare.

**scythe** [saið] *n* falce *f*. *v* falciare.

**sea** [si:] *n* mare *m*. **at sea** in mare; perplesso. **by sea** per mare. **put out to sea** prendere il largo.

**sea bed** *n* fondo del mare *m*.

**seafaring** ['si:ˌfeəriŋ] *adj* navigatore, -trice; marinaro. **seafarer** *n* navigatore *m*.

**seafood** ['si:fu:d] *n* frutti di mare *m pl*.

**sea front** *n* marina *f*.

**seagoing** ['si:ˌgouiŋ] *adj* d'alto mare.

**sea-gull** *n* gabbiano *m*.

**sea-horse** *n* cavalluccio marino *m*.

**seal¹** [si:l] *n* (*stamp*) sigillo *m*; chiusura *f*. *v* sigillare; (*close*) chiudere. **sealing wax** ceralacca *f*.

**seal²** [si:l] *n* (*animal*) foca *f*. **sealskin** *n* pelle di foca *f*.

**sea-level** *n* livello del mare *m*.

**sea-lion** *n* leone marino *m*.

**seam** [si:m] *n* cucitura *f*, giuntura *f*; (*geol*) vena *f*. *v* cucire.

**seaman** ['si:mən] *n* marinaio *m*.

**search** [sə:tʃ] *v* frugare, rovistare. *n* (*act*) ricerca *f*; esame minuto *m*; (*for something hidden*) perquisizione *f*. **search engine** motore di ricerca *m*. **searchlight** *n* proiettore *m*. **search party** *n* squadra di ricerca *f*. **search warrant** *n* mandato di perquisizione *m*. **searching** *adj* (*careful*) minuzioso; (*observing*) indagatore, -trice *n*.

**seashore** ['si:ʃo:] *n* spiaggia *f*, costa *f*.

**seasick** ['si:sik] *adj* **be seasick** avere il mal di mare. **seasickness** *n* mal di mare *m*.

**seaside** ['si:said] *n* **at** *or* **to the seaside**

al mare.

**season** ['siːzn] *n* stagione *f*. **season ticket** abbonamento *m*. *v* (*wood*) stagionare; (*spice*) condire. **seasonable** *adj* (*timely*) opportuno. **seasoning** *n* condimento *m*.

**seat** [siːt] *n* sedile *m*; (*chair*) sedia *f*; (*place*) posto *m*; (*coll: behind*) sedere *m*; (*location*) sede *f*. **take a seat** accomodarsi. *v* (*cause to sit*) far sedere; (*provide with seat*) provvedere di posti (a sedere).

**seaweed** ['siːwiːd] *n* alga *f*.

**seaworthy** ['siːwəði] *adj* atto a tenere il mare.

**secluded** [si'kluːdid] *adj* isolato, appartato. **seclusion** *n* isolamento *m*.

**second** ['sekənd] *n* secondo *m*; (*day*) due *m*; (*gear*) seconda *f*. *adj* secondo. **on second thoughts** ripensandoci bene. **secondhand** *adj* di seconda mano. **second-rate** *adj* mediocre. **second sight** chiaroveggenza *f*.

**secondary** ['sekəndəri] *adj* secondario.

**secret** ['siːkrit] *nm, adj* segreto. **top secret** *adj* riservatissimo. **secrecy** *n* segretezza *f*. **secretive** *adj* riservato, reticente.

**secretary** ['sekrətəri] *n* segretario, -a *m, f*. **secretarial** *adj* segretariale. **secretariat** *n* segreteria *f*, segretariato *m*.

**secrete** [si'kriːt] *v* (*biol*) secernere; (*conceal*) celare. **secretion** *n* secrezione *f*.

**sect** [sekt] *n* setta *f*. **sectarian** *adj* settario.

**section** ['sekʃən] *n* sezione *f*, parte *f*.

**sector** ['sektə] *n* settore *m*.

**secular** ['sekjulə] *adj* secolare; profano; laico.

**secure** [si'kjuə] *adj* sicuro; solido. *v* mettere al sicuro, assicurare; garantire; procurarsi. **security** *n* sicurezza *f*, garanzia *f*. **securities** *pl n* titoli *m pl*, obbligazioni *f pl*.

**sedate** [si'deit] *adj* pacato, posato. *v* calmare, tranquillizzare. **sedative** *n* sedativo *m*; calmante *m*.

**sediment** ['sedimənt] *n* sedimento *m*. **sedimentation** *n* sedimentazione *f*.

**seduce** [si'djuːs] *v* sedurre. **seducer** *n* seduttore, -trice *m, f*. **seduction** *n* seduzione *f*. **seductive** *adj* seducente.

**\*see¹** [siː] *v* vedere. **see about** *or* **to** occuparsi di. **see home** accompagnare a casa. **see through** penetrare.

**see²** [siː] *n* (*bishop's*) diocesi *f*. **Holy See** Santa Sede *f*.

**seed** [siːd] *n* seme *m*; (*collective*) semenza *f*. **go to seed** (*bot*) sementire; (*decay*) scadere, declinare. *v* seminare. **seedling** *n* germoglio *m*, semenzale *m*. **seedy** *adj* (*shabby*) malconcio; indisposto.

**\*seek** [siːk] *v* cercare.

**seem** [siːm] *v* sembrare, parere. **seeming** *adj* apparente.

**seen** [siːn] *V* **see¹**.

**seep** [siːp] *v* infiltrare.

**seesaw** ['siːsoː] *n* altalena (a bilico) *f*. *adj* oscillante. *v* altalenare.

**seethe** [siːð] *v* bollire; (*be agitated*) fremere. **seethe with rage** fremere di rabbia.

**segment** ['segmənt] *n* segmento *m*, sezione *f*.

**segregate** ['segrigeit] *v* segregare. **segregation** *n* segregazione *f*.

**seize** [siːz] *v* (*grasp*) afferrare; (*by force*) impadronirsi di; confiscare. **seize up** grippare, ingranarsi. **seizure** *n* confisca *f*; conquista *f*; (*med*) attacco *m*.

**seldom** ['seldəm] *adv* raramente, di rado.

**select** [sə'lekt] *adj* scelto, distinto. *v* scegliere. **selection** *n* selezione *f*, scelta *f*. **selective** *adj* selettivo. **selectivity** *n* selettività *f*.

**self** [self] *n* io *m*, persona *f*.

**self-assured** *adj* sicuro di sè. **self-assurance** sicurezza di sè *f*.

**self-catering** *adj* (*apartment*) con uso di cucina.

**self-centred** *adj* egocentrico, egoista.

**self-confident** *adj* sicuro di sè. **self-confidence** *n* fiducia in sè.

**self-conscious** *adj* impacciato. **self-consciousness** *n* impaccio *m*.

**self-contained** *adj* (*not shared*) indipendente; (*uncommunicative*) riservato; (*self-sufficient*) autosufficiente.

**self-critical** *adj* autocritico. **self-criticism** *n* autocritica *f*.

**self-defence** *n* autodifesa *f*; (*law*) legittima difesa *f*.

**self-discipline** *n* autodisciplina *f*.

**self-employed** *adj* **be self-employed** lavorare in proprio.

**self-evident** *adj* manifesto, palese.

**self-explanatory** *adj* ovvio.

**self-expression** *n* espressione della propria personalità *f*.

**self-government** n autonomia f.

**self-interest** n interesse personale m.

**selfish** ['selfiʃ] adj egoista, egoistico. **selfishness** n egoismo m.

**selfless** ['selflis] adj altruista, altruistico. **selflessness** n altruismo m.

**self-pity** n autocommiserazione f.

**self-portrait** n autoritratto m.

**self-possessed** adj composto, padrone di sè.

**self-preservation** n conservazione f.

**self-propelled** adj che si muove per forza propria.

**self-respect** n amor proprio m. **self-respecting** adj dignitoso.

**self-restraint** n autocontrollo m.

**self-righteous** adj compiaciuto di sè stesso. **self-righteousness** n autocompiacimento m.

**self-sacrifice** n abnegazione f.

**selfsame** ['selfseim] adj identico, proprio lo stesso.

**self-satisfied** adj contento di sè. **self-satisfaction** n autocompiacimento m.

**self-service** n self-service m invar.

**self-styled** adj sedicente.

**self-sufficient** adj autosufficiente. **self-sufficiency** n autosufficienza f.

**self-willed** adj ostinato; (wilful) caparbio.

***sell** [sel] v vendere. **seller** n venditore, -trice m, f.

**sellotape®** ['seləteip] n scotch® m invar, nastro autoadesivo m.

**semantic** [sə'mantik] adj semantico. **semantics** n semantica f.

**semaphore** ['seməfo:] n semaforo m.

**semen** ['si:mən] n sperma m.

**semibreve** ['semibri:v] n semibreve f.

**semicircle** ['semisə:kl] n semicerchio m. **semicircular** adj semicircolare.

**semicolon** [,semi'koulən] n punto e virgola m.

**semifinal** [semi'fainl] n semifinale f. **semifinalist** n semifinalista m, f.

**seminar** ['semina:] n seminario m.

**seminary** ['seminəri] n seminario m.

**semi-precious** adj semiprezioso.

**semiquaver** ['semikweivə] n semicroma f.

**semitone** ['semitoun] n semitono m.

**semolina** [,semə'li:nə] n semolino m.

**senate** ['senit] n senato m. **senator** n senatore m.

***send** [send] v mandare; (dispatch) spedire; trasmettere. **send for** (person) mandare a chiamare; (thing) mandare a prendere. **send in** sottoporre. **send on** (readdress) inoltrare. **sender** n mittente m, f.

**senile** ['si:nail] adj senile. **senility** n (old age) senilità f; (mental infirmity) senilismo m.

**senior** ['si:njə] adj più anziano, maggiore. n anziano, -a m, f; superiore, -a m, f. **seniority** n anzianità f. **senior citizen** n anziano.

**sensation** [sen'seiʃən] n sensazione f. **cause a sensation** far sensazione or colpo. **sensational** adj sensazionale, che fa colpo.

**sense** [sens] n senso m. **take leave of one's senses** perder la ragione. **talk sense** parlare sensatamente. v intuire, capire.

**sensible** ['sensəbl] adj sensato, ragionevole; (appreciable) sensibile. **sensibility** n sensibilità f.

**sensitive** ['sensitiv] adj sensibile; delicato; (physiology) sensitivo. **sensitivity** n sensibilità f; suscettibilità f; delicatezza f.

**sensual** ['sensjuəl] adj sensuale. **sensuality** n sensualità f.

**sensuous** ['sensjuəs] adj gradevole ai sensi, voluttuoso.

**sent** [sent] V **send**.

**sentence** ['sentəns] n (gramm) frase f; (law) condanna f, pena f. **pass sentence** pronunciare (una) sentenza. v condannare.

**sentiment** ['sentimənt] n sentimento m. **sentimental** adj sentimentale. **sentimentality** n sentimentalità f.

**sentry** ['sentri] n sentinella f. **stand sentry** fare la guardia.

**separate** ['sepərət; v 'sepəreit] adj separato; distinto; indipendente. v separare. **separation** n separazione f.

**September** [sep'tembə] n settembre m.

**septic** ['septik] adj settico. **septicaemia** n setticemia f.

**sequel** ['si:kwəl] n seguito m; conseguenza f.

**sequence** ['si:kwəns] n **successione** f; (math, cards) sequenza f. **in sequence** in ordine successivo.

**sequin** ['si:kwin] n lustrino m.

**Serbia** ['sə:biə] n Serbia f. **Serb** adj serbo.

**serenade** [serə'neid] n serenata f. v fare una serenata a.

**serene** [sə'ri:n] *adj* sereno. **serenity** *n* serenità *f*.

**sergeant** ['sa:dʒənt] *n* (*mil*) sergente *m*; (*police*) brigadiere *m*.

**serial** ['siəriəl] *n* (*novel*) romanzo a puntate *m*; (*play*) commedia a puntate *f*. *adj* (*in instalments*) a puntate; (*tech*) di *or* in serie. **serialize** *v* pubblicare *or* trasmettere a puntate.

**series** ['siəri:z] *n* serie *f*.

**serious** ['siəriəs] *adj* serio, grave. **are you serious?** dice sul serio? **seriousness** *n* serietà *f*.

**sermon** ['sə:mən] *n* predica *f*.

**serpent** ['sə:pənt] *n* serpente *m*. **serpentine** *adj* serpentino; (*winding*) serpeggiante.

**serum** ['siərəm] *n* siero *m*.

**servant** ['sə:vənt] *n* domestico, -a *m*, *f*; servo, -a *m*, *f*.

**serve** [sə:v] *v* servire. **it serves you right!** ti sta bene! te lo sei meritato!

**service** ['sə:vis] *n* servizio *m*; (*disposal*) disposizione *f*; (*rel*) ufficio divino *m*. **of service** d'aiuto, utile. **service area/station** area/stazione di servizio *f*. *v* provvedere alla manutenzione di, controllare. **serviceable** *adj* pratico, funzionale.

**serviette** [ˌsə:vi'et] *n* tovagliolo *m*.

**servile** ['sə:vail] *adj* servile. **servility** *n* servilità *f*.

**session** ['sefən] *n* seduta *f*, sessione *f*.

*****set** [set] *adj* fisso; (*ready*) pronto; prescritto; deciso; preparato; (*prearranged*) stabilito. *n* serie *f*, assortimento *m*; (*theatre, etc.*) set *m invar*, scenario *m*; (*tennis*) set *m invar*, partita *f*. *v* (*place*) mettere, posare; (*fix*) fissare; (*solidify*) indurirsi, rapprendersi; (*sun*) tramontare; (*jewel*) incastonare; (*hair*) mettere in piega; (*bones*) mettere a posto. **set about** (*begin to*) accingersi a; (*attempt*) cercare di; (*coll*) attaccare. **set aside** *or* **by** mettere da parte. **set back** (*hinder*) impedire; (*delay*) ritardare. **setback** *n* regresso *m*, contrattempo *m*. **set free** liberare. **set off** far esplodere; (*depart*) mettersi in viaggio; (*intensify*) mettere in risalto; compensare. **set out** partire. **set up** (*erect*) erigere; (*establish*) stabilire, metter su; (*prepare*) allestire.

**setting** *n* (*environment*) ambiente *m*; (*jewel*) montatura *f*; (*theatre*) scenario *m*, messa in scena *f*; (*music*) messa in musica *f*; (*sun*) tramonto *m*.

**settee** [se'ti:] *n* canapè *m*, sofà *m*.

**settle** ['setl] *v* fissare, determinare; (*pay*) regolare, saldare; (*compose*) sistemare; decidere. **settle down** stabilizzarsi; (*live*) stabilirsi. **settlement** *n* decisione *f*; saldo *m*; colonia *f*. **settler** *n* colonizzatore, -trice *m*, *f*.

**seven** ['sevn] *nm, adj* sette. **seventh** *nm, adj* settimo.

**seventeen** [sevn'ti:n] *nm, adj* diciassette. **seventeenth** *adj* diciassettesimo.

**seventy** ['sevnti] *nm, adj* settanta. **seventieth** *adj* settantesimo.

**sever** ['sevə] *v* staccare.

**several** ['sevrəl] *pron* parecchi, diversi. *adj* parecchi, diversi; separato; (*own*) proprio.

**severe** [sə'viə] *adj* severo; grave; (*weather*) rigido; (*pain, etc.*) violento, vivo. **severity** *n* severità *f*, rigore *m*; violenza *f*.

*****sew** [sou] *v* cucire. **sewing** *n* cucito *m*. **sewing machine** macchina da cucire *f*.

**sewage** ['sjuidʒ] *n* acque di scolo *or* scarico *f pl*.

**sewer** ['sjuə] *n* fogna *f*. **sewerage** *n* fognatura *f*.

**sewn** [soun] *V* **sew**.

**sex** [seks] *n* sesso *m*. **sexual** *adj* sessuale. **sexuality** *n* sessualità *f*. **sexist** *adj* sessista.

**sextet** [seks'tet] *n* sestetto *m*.

**shabby** ['ʃabi] *adj* (*of poor appearance*) malconcio, trasandato; (*badly worn*) logoro, frusto; (*contemptible*) meschino.

**shack** [ʃak] *n* baracca *f*.

**shade** [ʃeid] *n* ombra *f*; (*colour*) tinta *f*; (*lamp*) paralume *m*. *v* ombreggiare; (*protect*) proteggere (dalla luce); (*drawing*) sfumare. **shading** *n* sfumatura *f*.

**shadow** ['ʃadou] *n* ombra *f*. *v* ombreggiare; (*follow*) pedinare. **shady** *adj* ombreggiato; (*dubious*) disonesto, losco.

**shaft** [ʃa:ft] *n* (*pole*) asta *f*; (*passageway*) condotto *m*; (*handle*) manico *m*; (*light*) fascio *m*; (*sarcasm*) frecciata *f*.

**shaggy** ['ʃagi] *adj* peloso, irsuto.

*****shake** [ʃeik] *n* scossa *f*. **no great shakes** di poco conto. *v* scuotere; agitare; (*tremble*) tremare; (*disturb*) fremere. **shake hands** stringere la mano. **shake off** liberarsi da. **shake-up** *n* riorganizzazione *f*. **shaky** *adj* tremolante; (*insecure*) malsicuro; precario.

**shaken** ['ʃeikn] *V* **shake**.

**shall** [ʃal] *aux translated by future tense*.

**shallot** [ʃə'lot] *n* scalogno *m*.

**shallow** ['ʃaləu] *adj* poco profondo, basso, superficiale. **shallows** *pl n* bassofondo (*pl* bassifondi) *m sing*.

**sham** [ʃam] *adj* finto, falso. *n* finzione *f*, inganno *m*. *v* fingere, simulare.

**shambles** ['ʃamblz] *n* macello *m*.

**shame** [ʃeim] *v* svergognare. *n* vergogna *f*. **bring shame on** recar onta a, disonorare. **shamefaced** *adj* timido, vergognoso. **what a shame!** che peccato! **shameful** *adj* vergognoso. **shameless** *adj* svergognato, spudorato; (*brazen*) sfacciato. **shamelessness** *n* spudoratezza *f*, sfacciataggine *f*.

**shampoo** [ʃam'puː] *n* shampoo *m invar*. *v* **shampoo one's hair** lavarsi i capelli.

**shamrock** ['ʃamrok] *n* trifoglio d'Irlanda *m*.

**shanty**[1] ['ʃanti] *n* (*hut*) capanna *f*. **shanty town** baraccopoli *f*, bidonville (*pl* -s) *f*.

**shanty**[2] ['ʃanti] *n* (*song*) canzone marinaresca *f*.

**shape** [ʃeip] *n* forma *f*; condizione *f*. **take shape** concretizzarsi, prender forma. *v* formare, dar forma a; modellare; adattare. **shapeless** *adj* informe, confuso. **shapely** *adj* ben fatto, bello.

**share** [ʃeə] *n* porzione *f*, parte *f*; (*comm*) azione *f*. **shareholder** *n* azionista *m, f. v* dividere; (*jointly*) condividere. **share in** prender parte a. **share out** distribuire.

**shark** [ʃaːk] *n* pescecane (*pl* pescicani) *m*.

**sharp** [ʃaːp] *adj* (*cutting*) tagliente; (*not blunt*) aguzzo; brusco; (*distinct*) netto; (*flavour*) aspro, piccante; acuto; (*alert*) sveglio; (*biting*) mordace; (*shrewd*) scaltro. *adv* bruscamente; (*punctually*) in punto. *n* (*music*) diesis *m*. **sharpen** v affilare; (*pencil*) far la punta a; rendere più acuto.

**shatter** ['ʃatə] *v* (*break into fragments*) frantumare; (*destroy*) rovinare. **shattering** *adj* (*coll*) schiacciante.

**shave** [ʃeiv] *n* rasatura *f*. **have a close shave** cavarsela per un pelo. *v* farsi la barba; (*cut closely*) radere, rasare. **shaving brush/soap** pennello/sapone da barba *m*. **shaving cream** crema da barba *f*.

**shawl** [ʃoːl] *n* scialle *m*.

**she** [ʃiː] *pron* ella, lei. **she who** colei che.

**sheaf** [ʃiːf] *n* fascio *m*; (*cereals*) covone *m*.

**\*shear** [ʃiə] *v* tosare; (*tech*) spezzarsi; (*deprive*) privare. **shears** *pl n* cesoie *f pl*.

**sheath** [ʃiːθ] *n* guaina *f*. **sheathe** *v* rivestire; (*sword*) ringuainare.

**\*shed**[1] [ʃed] *v* (*let fall*) versare; (*lose*) perdere. **shed light on** far luce su.

**shed**[2] [ʃed] *n* capannone *m*; (*outhouse*) capanna *f*, rimessa *f*.

**sheen** [ʃiːn] *n* lucentezza *f*.

**sheep** [ʃiːp] *n* pecora *f*. **sheep-dog** *n* (*cane da*) pastore *m*. **sheepish** *adj* timido.

**sheer**[1] [ʃiə] *adj* (*mere*) mero; assoluto; (*steep*) a piombo; trasparente.

**sheer**[2] [ʃiə] *v* cambiar rotta.

**sheet** [ʃiːt] *n* (*bedding*) lenzuolo *m* (*pl* -a *f*); (*paper*) foglio *m*; (*iron, etc.*) lamiera *f*; (*glass*) lastra *f*. **sheet lightning** lampeggio *m*.

**shelf** [ʃelf] *n* (*support*) mensola *f*, ripiano *m*; (*ledge*) sporgenza *f*; (*rock*) scogliera *f*. **set of shelves** scaffale *m*.

**shell** [ʃel] *n* (*of egg, etc.*) guscio *m*; (*of fish*) conchiglia *f*; (*mil*) proiettile *m*; (*hollow casing*) involucro *m*. **shellfish** *n* crostaceo *m*, mollusco *m*; (*pl*: *as food*) frutti di mare *m pl*. **shell-shock** *n* psicosi traumatica da guerra *f*. *v* (*mil*) bombardare; (*eggs, etc.*) sgusciare; (*peas*) sgranare.

**shelter** ['ʃeltə] *n* riparo *m*, rifugio *m*; protezione *f*. **take shelter** ripararsi, rifugiarsi. *v* proteggere, dare asilo a.

**shelve** [ʃelv] *v* (*put aside*) mettere da parte; (*postpone*) rimandare, archiviare.

**shepherd** ['ʃepəd] *n* pastore *m*. **shepherdess** *n* pastora *f*.

**sheriff** ['ʃerif] *n* sceriffo *m*.

**sherry** ['ʃeri] *n* sherry *m invar*.

**shield** [ʃiːld] *n* schermo *m*; (*armour*) scudo *m*. *v* proteggere.

**shift** [ʃift] *v* spostare, trasferire; (*free oneself from*) liberarsi da. **shift for oneself** fare da sè. *n* turno *m*; (*change*) cambiamento *m*; (*artifice*) espediente *m*. **shifting** *adj* instabile, mutevole; (*sands*) mobile. **shifty** *adj* malizioso.

**shimmer** ['ʃimə] *v* luccicare. *n* luccichio *m*.

**shin** [ʃin] *n* stinco *m*.

**\*shine** [ʃain] *n* splendore *m*. *v* brillare, risplendere; (*polish*) lustrare.

**shingle** ['ʃiŋgl] *n* (*roof*) lastra di copertura *f*; (*stone*) ciottolo *m*; (*extent of pebbles*) ghiaia *f*.

**shingles** ['ʃiŋglz] *n* erpete *m*; (*coll*) fuoco di Sant'Antonio *m*.

**ship** [ʃip] *n* nave *f*. **shipowner** *n* armatore *m*. **shipshape** *adv* in ordine perfetto. **shipwreck** *n* naufragio *m*. **be shipwrecked**

naufragare. **shipyard** n cantiere navale m.
v spedire. **shipper** n spedizioniere m.

**shirk** [ʃəːk] v evitare, scansare. **shirker** n
scansafatiche m, f invar.

**shirt** [ʃəːt] n camicia f.

**shit** [ʃit] (vulgar) n merda f. v cacare.

**shiver** [ʃivə] v tremare, rabbrividire. n brivido m, tremito m. **have the shivers** (cold)
avere i brividi; (fear) avere la tremarella.

**shoal** [ʃoul] n frotta f; (fish) banco m.

**shock**[1] [ʃok] n colpo m; (encounter) scontro
m; (elec) scossa f; (med) shock m invar;
impressione f. **shock absorber** ammortiz-
zatore m. v colpire; disgustare; impressionare; dare una scossa a. **shocking** adj
terribile; ripugnante, disgustoso.

**shock**[2] [ʃok] n (hair) chioma f.

**shod** [ʃod] V shoe.

**shoddy** [ʃodi] adj scadente.

*****shoe** [ʃuː] n scarpa f. **shoe-lace** n laccio
delle scarpe m. **shoemaker** n calzolaio m. v
(horse) ferrare.

**shone** [ʃon] V shine.

**shook** [ʃuk] V shake.

*****shoot** [ʃuːt] v tirare, sparare; (hit) ferire;
(kill) uccidere; (film) girare; (bot) germogliare. n (plant) rampollo m, germoglio
m; (spedizione di) caccia f. **shooting** n tiro
m, caccia f; (firing) sparatoria f. **shooting
pain** dolore lancinante m. **shooting star**
stella filante f.

**shop** [ʃop] n negozio m, bottega f; (in factory, etc.) officina f. **shopkeeper** n
negoziante m, f. **shoplifter** n taccheggiatore, -trice m, f. **shoplifting** n taccheggio
m. **shop-soiled** adj sciupato. **shop-win-
dow** n vetrina f. **shut up shop** chiudere
bottega. **talk shop** parlare d'affari. v fare
gli acquisti, fare la spesa. **shopper** n
acquirente m, f. **shopping** n acquisti m pl.
**go shopping** fare la spesa. **shopping bag**
borsa per la spesa f.

**shore**[1] [ʃoː] n sponda f, riva f. **on shore** a
terra.

**shore**[2] [ʃoː] v **shore up** puntellare.

**shorn** [ʃoːn] V shear.

**short** [ʃoːt] adj (not long) corto; breve; (not
tall) basso; brusco. adv bruscamente; (suddenly) di botto. **in short** in breve. **nothing
short of** addirittura. **run short** scarseggiare. **to cut a long story short** a farla breve.
n (film) short m invar, cortometraggio m.
**shortage** n mancanza f, carenza f. **shorten**

v accorciare, abbreviare. **shortly** adv
presto.

**shortbread** [ʃoːtbred] n biscotto di pasta
frolla m.

**short-circuit** n corto circuito m. v mettere
in corto circuito.

**shortcoming** [ʃoːtkʌmiŋ] n difetto m.

**short cut** n scorciatoia f.

**shortfall** [ʃoːtfoːl] n disavanzo; diminuzione
m; f.

**shorthand** [ʃoːthand] n stenografia f.
**shorthand typist** n stenodattilografo, -a
m, f.

**short list** n rosa dei candidati f. v mettere
nella rosa dei candidati.

**short-lived** adj di poca durata.

**shorts** [ʃoːts] pl n shorts m pl; calzoncini
corti m pl.

**short-sighted** adj miope; (lacking foresight) imprevidente. **short-sightedness** n
miopia f; imprevidenza f.

**short story** n novella f.

**short-tempered** adj irascibile.

**short-term** adj a breve scadenza.

**short-wave** adj a onde corte.

**shot**[1] [ʃot] V shoot.

**shot**[2] [ʃot] n sparo m, colpo m; (pellet) pallottola f; (pellets) pallini di piombo m pl;
(person) tiratore m; (phot) istantanea f;
(film) ripresa f. **off like a shot** via come un
bolide. **shotgun** n fucile da caccia m.

**should**[1] [ʃud] aux translated by conditional
tense.

**should**[2] [ʃud] aux translated by conditional
tense of dovere.

**shoulder** [ʃouldə] n spalla f; (road) banchina f. **give the cold shoulder** trattare con
freddezza. **shoulder-blade** n scapola f.
**shoulder-strap** n spallina f. v caricarsi
sulle spalle; (assume as burden) addossarsi.

**shout** [ʃaut] v gridare, urlare. n grido m (pl
-a f), urlo m (pl -a f). **shout at** sgridare,
alzar la voce con. **shout down** far tacere a
forza di grida.

**shove** [ʃʌv] n spinta f. v spingere.

**shovel** [ʃʌvl] v spalare. n pala f. **shovelful**
n palata f.

*****show** [ʃou] n (display) mostra f, espo-
sizione f; (theatre) spettacolo m; apparenza
f; ostentazione f. **give the show away** rivelare tutto. **run the show** essere in controllo. **show business** mondo dello

spettacolo m. **show-case** n vetrina f. **show-down** n (final reckoning) resa dei conti f.
**showman** n (theatre) impresario m; showman m invar. **show-room** n sala d'esposizione f. v mostrare, manifestare, indicare, dimostrare. **show off** ostentare, darsi delle arie. **show up** (reveal) svelare; (display) far risaltare; (appear) presentarsi.

**shower** ['ʃauə] n (bath) doccia f; (rain) acquazzone m; (blows) grandine f. **have a shower** fare la doccia. v **shower with** tempestare di, inondare di.

**shown** [ʃoun] V show.

**shrank** [ʃrank] V shrink.

**shred** [ʃred] n (piece torn off ) brandello m; (bit, scrap) briciolo m. v fare a brandelli or pezzetti.

**shrew** [ʃru:] n (woman) bisbetica f; (zool) toporagno m.

**shrewd** [ʃru:d] adj accorto, scaltro. **shrewdness** n accortezza f, scaltrezza f.

**shriek** [ʃri:k] v strillare. n strillo m.

**shrill** [ʃril] adj stridulo, acuto.

**shrimp** [ʃrimp] n gamberetto m.

**shrine** [ʃrain] n santuario m, reliquario m, tempio m.

*shrink** [ʃriŋk] v (become tight) restringersi; (withdraw) ritirarsi; (become less) ridursi. **shrink from** rifuggire da. **shrinkage** n restringimento m.

**shrivel** ['ʃrivl] v raggrinzirsi.

**shroud** [ʃraud] n lenzuolo funebre m; (mist) velo m. v avvolgere.

**Shrove Tuesday** [ʃrouv] n martedì grasso m.

**shrub** [ʃrʌb] n arbusto m.

**shrug** [ʃrʌg] v scrollare (le spalle). **shrug off** (minimize) prendere alla leggera; (shake off ) scrollarsi di dosso. n scrollata (di spalle) f.

**shrunk** [ʃrʌŋk] V shrink.

**shudder** ['ʃʌdə] n brivido m, tremito m. v rabbrividire.

**shuffle** ['ʃʌfl] v mettere in disordine; rimaneggiare; (cards) mescolare; (feet) strascicare.

**shun** [ʃʌn] v scansare, sfuggire (a).

**shunt** [ʃʌnt] v (rail) smistare; (get rid of ) mettere da parte; (elec) shuntare. n (rail) scambio m; (elec) shunt m invar.

*shut** [ʃʌt] adj chiuso. v chiudere. **shut down** (work) sospendere l'attività. **shut off**

bloccare, sottrarre a. **shut out** non lasciar entrare. **shut up** star zitto.

**shutter** ['ʃʌtə] n (window) persiana f; (phot) otturatore m.

**shuttle** ['ʃʌtl] n spola f, navetta f. **shuttle-cock** n volano m. **shuttle service** servizio di spola m, servizio pendolare m.

**shy** [ʃai] adj timido, schivo. v (horse) scartare. **shy from** rifuggire da; (shun) schivare. **shyness** n timidezza f, diffidenza f.

**sick** [sik] adj malato; (fed up) stanco, stufo. **be sick** essere malato, star male; vomitare. **feel sick** sentirsi male, avere la nausea. **make sick** (infuriate) mandare in bestia; disgustare; far vomitare. **sick-bay** n infermeria f. n vomito m. **sicken** v ammalarsi. **sickening** adj nauseabondo, disgustante. **sickness** n malattia f.

**sickle** ['sikl] n falce f.

**side** [said] n lato m, fianco m; (lake, etc.) riva f; (in battle, quarrel, etc.) parte f. **on the other side** d'altra parte. **sideboard** n credenza f. **side-issue** n questione secondaria f. **sidelight** n (mot) luce di posizione f. **sidelong** adj di traverso, furtivo. **sidestep** v schivare. **side-street** n via laterale f. **sidetrack** v distrarre. **sideways** adv lateralmente; obliquamente. v **side with** essere dalla parte di. **siding** n binario di raccordo m.

**sidle** ['saidl] v andare a sghembo. **sidle up to** accostarsi furtivamente a.

**siege** [si:dʒ] n assedio m. **lay siege** assediare. **raise the siege** togliere l'assedio.

**sieve** [siv] n setaccio m. v setacciare.

**sift** [sift] v setacciare; (examine) vagliare.

**sigh** [sai] v sospirare. n sospiro m.

**sight** [sait] n vista f; (coll) spettacolo m; (tech) mirino m. **catch sight of** intravedere. **know by sight** conoscere di vista. **lose sight of** perdere di vista. **sights** pl n luoghi d'interesse m pl. **sightseeing** n turismo m.

**sign** [sain] n segno m, cenno m; (inscription) insegna f, segnale m; (trace) traccia f. **sign-post** n indicatore m. v firmare, ratificare. **sign off** ritirarsi. **sign on** (employ) assumere; (commit oneself ) impegnarsi.

**signal** ['signəl] n segnale m. v segnalare.

**signature** ['signətʃə] n firma f. **signatory** n firmatario, -a m, f.

**signify** ['signifai] v significare; (mean) voler

dire; (be of consequence) importare. **significance** n importanza f; (meaning) significato m. **significant** adj significativo, espressivo.

**silence** ['saıləns] n silenzio m. v ridurre al silenzio, far tacere; (put to rest) porre fine a. **silencer** n silenziatore m.

**silent** ['saılənt] adj silenzioso; tacito; muto. **keep silent** tacere, rimaner zitto.

**silhouette** [silu'et] n silhouette (pl -s) f.

**silk** [silk] n seta f. **silkworm** n baco da seta m. **silken** adj di seta. **silky** adj di seta; (lustrous) lucido; (smooth) morbido.

**sill** [sil] n (window) davanzale m.

**silly** ['sili] adj sciocco. **silliness** n sciocchezza f.

**silt** [silt] n limo m. v **silt up** insabbiarsi.

**silver** ['silvə] n argento m; (cutlery, etc.) argenteria f. adj d'argento, argenteo. v argentare.

**similar** ['similə] adj simile. **similarity** n somiglianza f.

**simile** ['siməli] n (figure of speech) similitudine f; (example) paragone m.

**simmer** ['simə] v sobbollire.

**simple** ['simpl] adj semplice. **simpleton** n sempliciotto, -a m, f. **simplicity** n semplicità f. **simplification** n semplificazione f. **simplify** v semplificare.

**simulate** ['simjuleit] v simulare, fingere. **simulation** n simulazione f, finzione f.

**simultaneous** [,siməl'teinjəs] adj simultaneo.

**sin** [sin] n peccato m. v peccare. **sinful** adj peccaminoso. **sinner** n peccatore, -trice m, f.

**since** [sins] adv (from then) da allora; (subsequently) poi; (ago) fa. **prep** da. **conj** (period) da quando; dacchè; (because) poichè.

**sincere** [sin'siə] adj sincero. **sincerity** n sincerità f.

**sinew** ['sinju:] n tendine m; (force) nerbo m.

*sing [siŋ] v cantare. **singer** n cantante m, f. **singing** n canto m.

**singe** [sindʒ] v strinare; (scorch) bruciacchiare.

**single** ['singl] adj (one only) singolo, solo; (unmarried) celibe. **single-breasted** adj a un petto. **single file** fila indiana f. **single-handed** adj (unaided) solo, senza aiuto. **single-minded** adj deciso, fermo, tenace. **single mindedness** n fermezza f, tenacia f. **single parent** genitore singolo m. **single**

**ticket** biglietto di andata solo m. n singolo m. v **single out** scegliere.

**singular** ['siŋgjulə] nm, adj singolare.

**sinister** ['sinistə] adj (ominous) di cattivo augurio.

*sink [siŋk] n lavandino m. v (submerge, go under) affondare; (go down) calare, abbassarsi.

**sinuous** ['sinjuəs] adj tortuoso.

**sinus** ['sainəs] n seno m; (nasal) seno paranasale m. **sinusitis** n sinusite f.

**sip** [sip] n sorso m. v sorseggiare, bere a piccoli sorsi.

**siphon** ['saifən] n sifone m. v travasare con un sifone.

**sir** [sə:] n signore m.

**siren** ['saiərən] n sirena f.

**sirloin** ['sə:loin] n lombata f.

**sister** ['sistə] n sorella f; (nursing) infermiera capo sala f; (rel) suora f. **sister-in-law** n cognata f.

*sit [sit] v sedere; posare; (garment) cadere; (exam) dare; (be convened) essere in seduta. **sit down** sedersi, mettersi a sedere. **sit on the fence** non prendere partito. **sit tight** non lasciarsi smuovere. **sitting** n seduta f. **sitting room** salotto m.

**site** [sait] n posizione f; (building) cantiere edile m. v situare.

**situation** [sitju'eiʃən] n situazione f; (post) posizione f. **situated** adj situato.

**six** [siks] nm, adj sei. **sixth** nm, adj sesto.

**sixteen** [siks'ti:n] nm, adj sedici. **sixteenth** nm, adj sedicesimo.

**sixty** ['siksti] nm, adj sessanta. **sixtieth** nm, adj sessantesimo.

**size¹** [saiz] n dimensione f, grandezza f; (garments) misura f, taglia f. v **size up** valutare. **sizeable** adj notevole.

**size²** [saiz] n (glue) bozzima f. v imbozzimare.

**sizzle** ['sizl] v sfriggere. n sfrigolio m.

**skate¹** [skeit] n pattino. v pattinare. **skater** n pattinatore, -trice m, f. **skating** m pattinaggio m.

**skate²** [skeit] n (fish) razza f.

**skeleton** ['skelitn] n scheletro m.

**sketch** [sketʃ] n abbozzo m; (theatre) bozzetto m. v abbozzare; delineare. **sketchbook** n albo di o per schizzi m. **sketchy** adj impreciso, superficiale.

**skewer** ['skjuə] n spiedo m.

**ski** [ski:] n sci m. **ski-lift** n sciovia f. v sciare.
**skier** n sciatore, -trice m, f. **skiing** n sci m.
**ski slope** pista da sci f.

**skid** [skid] v slittare; (car) sbandare; (plane) derapare. n slittamento m; sbandamento m.

**skill** [skil] n abilità f, destrezza f. **skilful** adj abile, esperto. **skilled** adj abile, esperto; (worker) specializzato.

**skim** [skim] v (milk) scremare; (glide over) rasentare. **skim over** sfiorare; (reading) sfogliare.

**skimp** [skimp] v (food, expense, etc.) lesinare, risparmiare; (person) tenere a stecchetto; (scrimp) fare economia. **skimpy** adj (scanty) scarso; (mean) tirchio.

**skin** [skin] n pelle f; (fruit) buccia f, scorza f; (film) pellicola f; (colouring) carnagione f. **by the skin of one's teeth** per il rotto della cuffia. **skin-deep** adj superficiale. **skin-diving** n pesca subacquea f. **skinflint** n spilorcio m. **skin-graft** n innesto epidermico m. v sbucciare; (animals) scorticare. **skinny** adj magro, ossuto.

**skip** [skip] v saltare; (leap) balzellare. n balzo m.

**skipper** ['skipə] n capitano m.

**skirmish** ['skə:miʃ] n scaramuccia f. v scontrarsi.

**skirt** [skə:t] n gonna f, sottana f. v costeggiare; (edge) orlare. **skirting board** zoccolo m.

**skittle** ['skitl] n birillo m.

**skull** [skʌl] n cranio m, teschio m. **skull-cap** n calotta f, papalina f.

**skunk** [skʌŋk] n moffetta f; (coll) farabutto m.

**sky** [skai] n cielo m. **blow sky-high** far saltare per aria. **sky-blue** adj celeste. **sky-lark** n allodola f. **skylight** n lucernario m. **skyline** n profilo m, orizzonte m. **sky-scraper** n grattacielo m.

**slab** [slab] n piastra f; (thick piece) fetta f.

**slack** [slak] adj (loose) lento; (inactive) fiacco; (negligent) indolente. n (rope) imbando m; (comm) attività ridotta f. v (neglect duty) trascurare. **slacken** v rallentare.

**slacks** [slaks] pl n calzoni sportivi m pl.

**slag** [slag] n scoria f.

**slalom** ['sla:ləm] n slalom m.

**slam** [slam] v sbattere. n (bridge) slam m invar.

**slander** ['sla:ndə] n diffamazione f. v diffamare. **slanderer** n diffamatore, -trice m, f. **slanderous** adj diffamatorio.

**slang** [slaŋ] n gergo m. v vituperare. **slanging match** battibecco m.

**slant** [sla:nt] v inclinare, inclinarsi; (news) presentare in modo tendenzioso. n (slope) inclinazione f; (point of view) punto di vista m; (bias) tendenza f.

**slap** [slap] n schiaffo m; (rebuke) rabbuffo m. **slap in the face** insulto m, umiliazione f. **slap on the back** felicitazione f. v schiaffeggiare. **slap-bang** adv (right) in pieno; (suddenly) di colpo. **slapdash** adj fatto a casaccio, abborracciato. **slap-happy** adj incosciente.

**slash** [slaʃ] v tagliare, squarciare. n taglio m.

**slat** [slat] n stecca f, assicella f.

**slate** [sleit] n lavagna f; (geol) ardesia f. **have a clean slate** aver la fedina pulita. **wipe the slate clean** ricominciare dimenticando il passato.

**slaughter** ['slɔ:tə] n macello m; (massacre) strage f. v macellare, far strage di. **slaughterhouse** n macello m.

**slave** [sleiv] n schiavo, -a m, f. **slave-driver** n negriero, -a m, f. **slave labour** lavori forzati m pl. v sgobbare.

**sledge** [sledʒ] n slitta f.

**sledgehammer** ['sledʒ,hamə] n mazza f. **sledgehammer blow** mazzata f.

**sleek** [sli:k] adj (glossy) lucido; (smooth) liscio; (soft) morbido; (unctuous) mellifluo.

*sleep [sli:p] n sonno m. **go to sleep** addormentarsi, prendere sonno. **have a good sleep** fare una bella dormita. v dormire; (accommodate) alloggiare. **sleep on** dormirci su. **sleeper** n dormiente m, f; (timber beam) traversina f; (on train) vagone letto m. **be a heavy/light sleeper** avere il sonno pesante/leggero. **sleeping bag** sacco a pelo m. **sleeping partner** (econ) socio accomandante m. **sleeping pill** sonnifero m. **sleepless** adj insonne. **sleepy** adj sonnolento.

**sleet** [sli:t] n nevischio m.

**sleeve** [sli:v] n manica f; (tech) manicotto m; (record) copertina f. **up one's sleeve** di riserva.

**sleigh** [slei] n slitta f. v andare in slitta.

**slender** ['slendə] adj snello; (small) esiguo, scarso.

**slept** [slept] V sleep.

**slice** [slais] n fetta f; parte f, porzione f;

(*spatula*) paletta *f*. *v* affettare, tagliare a fette; (*sport*) tagliare.

**slick** [slik] *adj* (*sleek*) lucido; (*coll: smooth*) untuoso; (*coll: shrewd*) spigliato, scaltro.

**slid** [slid] *V* **slide**.

***slide** [slaid] *n* (*inclined plane*) scivolo *m*; (*microscope*) vetrino *m*; (*phot*) diapositiva *f*; (*hair*) fibbia *f*; (*act of sliding*) scivolata *f*. **slide-rule** *n* regolo calcolatore *m*. *v* scivolare. **let slide** lasciar correre. **sliding scale** scala mobile *f*.

**slight** [slait] *adj* leggero, (*frail*) esile. *n* affronto *m*, dispetto *m*, mancanza di rispetto *f*. *v* mancare di rispetto, ignorare.

**slim** [slim] *adj* magro, snello; (*poor*) povero; (*scant*) minimo. *v* dimagrare. **slimming** *adj* dimagrante.

**slime** [slaim] *n* melma *f*; (*secretion*) bava *f*. **slimy** *adj* melmoso; bavoso; (*servile*) untuoso.

***sling** [slin] *n* (*weapon*) fionda *f*; (*bandage*) benda *f*, fascia *f*; (*rifle*) cinghia *f*; (*hoist*) braca *f*. **have one's arm in a sling** portare un braccio al collo. *v* (*throw*) lanciare, gettare; (*suspend*) sospendere.

***slink** [slink] *v* sgattaiolare.

**slip** [slip] *n* errore *m*, svista *f*; (*garment*) sottana *f*; (*skid*) scivolata *f*; (*plant*) rampollo *m*; (*of paper*) pezzetto *m*. **slip of the tongue** lapsus linguae *m* invar. *v* scivolare. **let slip** lasciar scappare. **slip away** andarsene. **slip-knot** *n* nodo scorsoio *m*. **slip-road** *n* raccordo *m*. **slip up** fare uno sbaglio, prendere una papera.

**slipper** ['slipə] *n* pantofola *f*, ciabatta *f*.

**slippery** ['slipəri] *adj* scivoloso.

***slit** [slit] *n* taglio *m*, fessura *f*. *v* tagliare, squarciare.

**slither** ['sliðə] *v* scivolare.

**slobber** ['slobə] *v* sbavare.

**sloe** [slou] *n* (*fruit*) prugnola *f*; (*tree*) prugnolo *m*.

**slog** [slog] *v* (*walk*) avanzare a fatica; (*toil*) faticare. *n* camminata dura *f*; faticata *f*.

**slogan** ['slougən] *n* motto *m*, slogan *m* invar.

**slop** [slop] *v* versare; (*spill over*) traboccare. **slops** *pl n* (*food*) pappa *f sing*; (*dirty water*) lavatura *f sing*.

**slope** [sloup] *n* pendio *m*. *v* inclinarsi, pendere. **sloping** *adj* inclinato, obliquo.

**sloppy** ['slopi] *adj* (*wet*) bagnato; (*careless*) abborracciato; (*untidy*) scatto; sentimentale.

**slot** [slot] *n* fessura *f*, apertura *f*. **slot-machine** *n* (*vending*) apparecchio a gettoni *m*; (*gambling*) slot-machine *m* invar. *v* **slot into** incanalare.

**slouch** [slautʃ] *v* (*walk*) camminare dinoccolato; (*droop*) languire. *n* andatura dinoccolata *f*.

**Slovakia** [slou'vakiə] *n* Slovacchia *f*. **Slovakian** *adj* slovacco.

**Slovenia** [slou'vi:niə] *n* Slovenia *f*. sloveno *adj*.

**slovenly** ['slʌvnli] *adj* sciatto, trascurato.

**slow** [slou] *adj* lento; (*late*) tardo; (*clock*) indietro *invar*. *adv* piano, adagio. *v* **slow down** rallentare.

**slug** [slʌg] *n* lumaca *f*.

**sluggish** ['slʌgiʃ] *adj* lento, inerte.

**sluice** [slu:s] *n* chiusa *f*. *v* (*flush*) lavare abbondantemente.

**slum** [slʌm] *n* quartiere povero *or* basso *m*; (*tumbledown house*) tugurio *m*, catapecchia *f*.

**slumber** ['slʌmbə] *v* sonnecchiare. *n* (*heavy*) dormita *f*; (*light*) dormiveglia *m* invar.

**slump** [slʌmp] *n* crollo *m*, caduta *f*. *v* cadere, crollare.

**slung** [slʌŋ] *V* **sling**.

**slunk** [slʌŋk] *V* **slink**.

**slur** [slə:] *v* (*speech*) biascicare; (*disparage*) denigrare; (*music*) legare. **slur over** passar sopra a. *n* affronto *m*; (*blot*) macchia *f*.

**slush** [slʌʃ] *n* melma *f*. **slushy** *adj* melmoso.

**slut** [slʌt] *n* (*immoral*) sgualdrina *f*; (*slovenly*) sciattona *f*.

**sly** [slai] *adj* astuto, scaltro. **on the sly** in sordina.

**smack**[1] [smak] *n* (*hit*) schiaffo *m*; (*sound*) schiocco *m*; (*kiss*) bacione *m*. **smack in the eye** (*snub*) rabbuffo *m*; (*disappointment*) delusione *f*. *v* schiaffeggiare, schioccare. **smack one's lips** leccarsi i baffi.

**smack**[2] [smak] *n* sapore *m*. *v* **smack of** (*taste*) sapere di; (*suggest*) ricordare.

**small** [smo:l] *adj* piccolo; (*low*) basso; (*humble*) umile; insignificante. **small change** spiccioli *m pl*. **small fry** persone di poco conto *f pl*. **small-minded** *adj* gretto. **smallpox** *n* vaiolo *m*. **small talk** chiacchera *f*, cicaleccio *m*.

**smart** [sma:t] *adj* (*sharp*) acuto; intelligente; (*shrewd*) sveglio; elegante; brillante.

*v* bruciare, sentire un vivo dolore. **smarten**
*v* abbellire, ravvivarsi.

**smash** [smaʃ] *n* (*collision*) scontro *m*; (*ruin*)
rovina *f*, disastro *m*; (*tennis*) smash *m invar.*
**smash-and-grab raid** (*coll*) spaccata *f. v*
(*shatter*) fracassare; (*destroy*) annientare.
**smashing** *adj* (*coll*) magnifico.

**smear** [smiə] *v* (*grease*) ungere; (*daub*) spalmare; (*soil*) macchiare; (*defame*) calunniare.
*n* macchia *f*; (*slur*) calunnia *f.* **smear campaign** *n* campagna diffamatoria *f.* **smear
test** *n* (*med*) citodiagnosi *f.*

**\*smell** [smel] *n* odore *m*, profumo *m*; (*faculty*) odorato *m. v* sentire l'odore di; (*perceive*)
fiutare; (*stink*) puzzare. **smell a rat** fiutare
un imbroglio. **smell of** aver odore di.

**smelt** [smelt] *V* **smell**.

**smile** [smail] *n* sorriso *m. v* sorridere.

**smirk** [smə:k] *n* sorriso compiaciuto *m. v*
sorridere con aria compiaciuta.

**smock** [smok] *n* camiciotto *m*; (*artists'*)
blusa *f.* **smocking** *n* nido d'ape *m*, punto
smock *m.*

**smog** [smog] *n* smog *m invar.*

**smoke** [smouk] *n* fumo *m.* **smoke-screen** *n*
cortina di fumo *f.* **smoke-stack** *n* fumaiolo
*m. v* fumare; (*cure*) affumicare. **smokeless**
*adj* senza fumo. **smoker** *n* (*person*) fumatore, -trice *m, f*; (*compartment*) scompartimento per fumatori *m.* **smoky** *adj* fumoso,
che sa di fumo.

**smooth** [smu:ð] *adj* (*not rough*) liscio;
(*unruffled*) calmo; (*not harsh*) gradevole. *v*
lisciare, spianare, facilitare.

**smother** ['smʌðə] *v* soffocare, sopprimere.

**smoulder** ['smouldə] *v* covare (sotto la
cenere).

**smudge** [smʌdʒ] *n* sgorbio *m. v* sgorbiare.

**smug** [smʌg] *adj* soddisfatto di sé.

**smuggle** ['smʌgl] *v* **smuggle in/out** far
entrare/uscire di contrabbando. **smuggler**
*n* contrabbandiere, -a *m, f.* **smuggling** *n*
contrabbando *m.*

**snack** [snak] *n* (*light meal*) spuntino *m.*

**snag** [snag] *n* (*impediment*) intoppo *m. v*
(*stocking*) smagliare.

**snail** [sneil] *n* chiocciola *f*, lumaca *f.*

**snake** [sneik] *n* serpente *m.*

**snap** [snap] *v* (*noise*) schioccare; (*break suddenly*) spezzarsi; (*phot*) scattare. **snap out
of it** riprendersi. **snap up** non lasciarsi
sfuggire. *n* schiocco *m*; rottura improvvisa

*f*; (*sudden bite*) morsicata *f*; (*phot*) istantanea *f*; (*short spell*) ondata *f.* **snapdragon** *n*
bocca di leone *f.* *adj* istantaneo. **snappy**
*adj* irritabile; (*lively*) vivace.

**snare** [sneə] *n* laccio *m*, lacciolo *m. v* prendere al laccio; accalappiare.

**snarl¹** [sna:l] *v* (*growl*) ringhiare. *n* ringhio
*m.*

**snarl²** [sna:l] *n* (*tangle*) groviglio *m. v*
aggrovigliare.

**snatch** [snatʃ] *v* ghermire, aggguantare. *n*
strappo *m*; (*scrap*) frammento *m.*

**sneak** [sni:k] *v* muoversi furtivamente;
(*coll: steal*) squagliarsela; (*slang: tell tales*)
spifferare. *n* (*coll*) spifferone, -a *m, f*; (*despicable person*) vigliacco, -a *m, f.* **sneakers** *pl
n* scarpe da tennis *or* ginnastica *f pl.*

**sneer** [sniə] *n* (*derisory*) ghigno *m*; (*contemptuous*) sogghigno *m. v* ghignare; sogghignare. **sneer at** canzonare, burlarsi di.

**sneeze** [sni:z] *n* starnuto *m. v* starnutire.
**sneeze at** (*coll*) sprezzare.

**sniff** [snif] *v* annusare, fiutare; aspirare col
naso. *n* annusata *f*, fiuto *m.*

**snigger** ['snigə] *v* ridere sotto i baffi, ridacchiare. *n* ghigno *m.*

**snip** [snip] *v* tagliuzzare; (*cut off*) spuntare.
*n* (*piece*) ritaglio *m*; (*bargain*) occasione *f.*

**snipe** [snaip] *n* (*bird*) beccaccino *m. v*
sparare di sorpresa. **sniper** *n* tiratore scelto
che spara di soppiatto *m.*

**snivel** ['snivl] *v* moccicare; (*whine*) frignare.
**sniveller** *n* moccioso, -a *m, f*; frignone, -a
*m, f.*

**snob** [snob] *n* snob *m*, *f invar.*

**snoop** [snu:p] *v* curiosare.

**snooty** ['snu:ti] *adj* (*coll*) sdegnoso, altezzoso.

**snooze** [snu:z] *v* sonnecchiare. *n* pisolino
*m.*

**snore** [sno:] *v* russare, ronfare.

**snorkel** ['sno:kəl] *n* respiratore a tubo *m.*

**snort** [sno:t] *n* sbuffata *f. v* sbuffare.

**snout** [snaut] *n* muso *m*; (*pig*) grugno *m*;
(*nozzle*) becco *m.*

**snow** [snou] *n* neve *f.* **snowball** *n* palla di
neve *f.* **snowbound** *adj* bloccato dalla
neve. **snow-drift** *n* cumulo *or* banco di
neve *m.* **snowdrop** *n* bucaneve *m invar.*
**snowfall** *n* nevicata *f.* **snowflake** *n* fiocco
di neve *m.* **snowman** *n* pupazzo di neve *m.*
**snow-plough** *n* spazzaneve *m invar.* **snow-**

**storm** n tormenta f. v nevicare. **snowy** adj nevoso; (colour) niveo, candido.

**snub** [snʌb] n rabbuffo m, affronto m. v trattare con disprezzo. **snub-nosed** adj camuso.

**snuff¹** [snʌf] v fiutare, aspirare. n tabacco da fiuto m. **snuffbox** n tabacchiera f.

**snuff²** [snʌf] v **snuff it** (coll: die) crepare. **snuff out** spegnere.

**snug** [snʌg] adj (comfortable) comodo; (cosy) intimo; (close-fitting) aderente.

**snuggle** [snʌgl] v rannicchiarsi; (cuddle) coccolare.

**so** [sou] adv così, tanto; (to that extent) talmente. conj perciò, quindi. **and so on** eccetera. **if so** in tal caso. **in so far as** per quanto. **so-called** adj cosiddetto. **so far** finora. **so long as** finché. **so much** tanto. **so-so** adv discretamente, così così. **so to speak** per così dire.

**soak** [souk] v inzuppare, imbevere. **be soaked through** essere bagnato fradicio. **soak in** penetrare. **soak up** assorbire.

**soap** [soup] n sapone m. **soap-dish** n portasapone m invar. **soap flakes/powder** sapone in scaglie/polvere m. **soap-suds** n saponata f sing. v insaponare. **soapy** adj (covered with soap) insaponato; (like soap) saponoso.

**soar** [so:] v librarsi; (rise) salire.

**sob** [sob] n singhiozzo m. v singhiozzare.

**sober** [souba] adj sobrio, calmo. v **sober down** calmarsi. **sober up** smaltire una sbornia. **sobriety** n moderatezza f, serietà f.

**soccer** [soka] n calcio m, football m invar.

**sociable** [souʃabl] adj socievole. **sociability** n socievolezza f.

**social** [souʃal] adj (of a community) sociale; (disposition) socievole; (of polite society) mondano. **social security** previdenza sociale f. **social worker** assistente sociale m. **socialism** n socialismo m. **socialist** n(m+f), adj socialista.

**society** [sa'saiati] n società f, compagnia f.

**sociology** [sousi'oladʒi] n sociologia f. **sociological** adj sociologico. **sociologist** n sociologo, -a.

**sock¹** [sok] n (short) calzino m; (long) calza f.

**sock²** [sok] n (slang) colpo m. v picchiare; (punch) prendere a pugni.

**socket** [sokit] n cavità f; (eye) orbita f,

occhiaia f; (elec) presa f.

**soda** [souda] n (water) seltz m invar; (sodium carbonate) soda f; soda caustica f.

**sodden** [sodn] adj fradicio.

**sofa** [soufa] n sofà m invar.

**soft** [soft] adj (not hard) molle; (not rough) morbido, soffice; (pleasant) mite, dolce; (soothing) tenero; (water) dolce. adv piano. **soften** v ammorbidire, intenerirsi. **softly** adv pian piano, adagio, dolcemente.

**soggy** [sogi] adj fradicio, inzuppato.

**soil¹** [soil] n suolo m, terra f.

**soil²** [soil] v sporcare, insudiciare.

**solar** [soula] adj solare.

**sold** [sould] V **sell**.

**solder** [solda] n saldatura f. v saldare. **soldering iron** saldatore m.

**soldier** [souldʒa] n soldato m. v **soldier on** tirare avanti.

**sole¹** [soul] adj solo, unico.

**sole²** [soul] n (foot) pianta f; (shoe, tech) suola f.

**sole³** [soul] n (fish) sogliola f.

**solemn** [solam] adj solenne, serio.

**solicitor** [sa'lisita] n avvocato, -essa m, f.

**solicitous** [sa'lisitas] adj premuroso.

**solid** [solid] adj solido, sodo, compatto; (sound) serio. n (corpo) solido m. **solidarity** n solidarietà f. **solidity** n solidità f; serietà f.

**solitary** [solitari] adj solitario, solo, isolato. **solitary confinement** n reclusione or segregazione cellulare f.

**solitude** [solitju:d] n solitudine f, isolamento m.

**solo** [soulou] n assolo m, adj solitario. **soloist** n solista m, f.

**solstice** [solstis] n solstizio m.

**soluble** [soljubl] adj solubile.

**solution** [sa'lu:ʃan] n soluzione f.

**solve** [solv] v risolvere. **solvent** nm, adj solvente. **solvency** n solvenza f.

**sombre** [somba] adj tetro, fosco.

**some** [sʌm] adj del, della; (pl) dei, delle; qualche; (certain) alcuni. pron alcuni, -e; (before verb) ne. **somebody** or **someone** pron qualcuno. **somebody else** qualcun altro. **some day** un bel giorno. **somehow** adv in qualche modo, in un modo o in un altro. **some ... some ...** gli uni ... gli altri ... . **something** pron qualcosa. **something**

**else** qualcos'altro. **sometime** *adv* un giorno o l'altro, presto o tardi. **sometimes** *adv* qualche volta; (*now and then*) di tanto in tanto. **somewhat** *adv* piuttosto. **somewhere** *adv* in qualche parte. **somewhere else** altrove.

**somersault** ['sʌməsɔːlt] *n* capriola *f*, salto mortale *m*. *v* fare una capriola, fare un salto mortale.

**son** [sʌn] *n* figlio *m*. **son-in-law** *n* genero *m*.

**sonata** [sə'naːtə] *n* sonata *f*.

**song** [son] *n* canzone *f*; (*act of singing*) canto *m*. **for a song** per una sciocchezza.

**sonic** ['sonik] *adj* sonico. **sonic bang** or **boom** boato sonico *m*.

**sonnet** ['sonit] *n* sonetto *m*.

**soon** [suːn] *adv* presto, tra poco. **as soon as** appena. **how soon?** fra quanto tempo? **soon after** subito dopo. **too soon** in anticipo. **very soon** tra breve, quanto prima. **no sooner said than done** detto fatto. **sooner or later** presto o tardi, prima o poi.

**soot** [sut] *n* fuliggine *f*. **sooty** *adj* fuligginoso.

**soothe** [suːð] *v* calmare, mitigare.

**sophisticated** [sə'fistikeitid] *adj* raffinato, sofisticato.

**sopping** ['sopin] *adj* fradicio.

**soprano** [sə'praːnou] *n* soprano *m, f*.

**sordid** ['soːdid] *adj* sordido.

**sore** [soː] *adj* doloroso. **sore throat** mal di gola *m*. *n* piaga *f*, ulcera *f*.

**sorrow** ['sorou] *n* dolore *m*, dispiacere *m*; (*cause of regret*) rincrescimento *m*. **sorrowful** *adj* triste, addolorato; (*distressing*) penoso.

**sorry** ['sori] *adj* dolente, spiacente, triste; (*wretched*) meschino, miserabile. **feel sorry for** compatire. **I'm sorry** mi dispiace *or* rincresce. **interj** pardon! scusi! scusate!

**sort** [soːt] *n* sorta *f*, specie *f invar*. **a good sort** una brava persona *f*. **out of sorts** giù di giri. *v* classificare, raggruppare. **sort out** smistare; (*choose*) scegliere.

**soufflé** ['suːflei] *n* soufflé *m invar*.

**sought** [soːt] *V* **seek**.

**soul** [soul] *n* anima *f*, spirito *m*.

**sound¹** [saund] *n* suono *m*; (*noise*) rumore *m*. **sound effect** effetto sonoro *m*. **soundproof** *adj* fonoassorbente, impenetrabile al

suono. **sound-track** *n* colonna sonora *f*. *v* suonare; (*seem*) sembrare.

**sound²** [saund] *adj* (*not damaged*) sano; valido, legittimo; (*sleep, etc.*) profondo.

**sound³** [saund] *n* (*med*) sonda *f*. *v* sondare; (*naut*) scandagliare.

**soup** [suːp] *n* minestra *f*; (*broth*) brodo *m*; (*with bread*) zuppa *f*. **be in the soup** trovarsi nei pasticci. **soup-ladle** *n* cucchiaione *m*. **soup-plate** *n* fondina *f*.

**sour** [sauə] *adj* acido; (*tart, harsh*) acerbo, agro.

**source** [soːs] *n* sorgente *f*, origine *f*.

**south** [sauθ] *n* sud *m*; (*of country*) meridione *m*. *adj* also **southern, southerly** del sud; meridionale. *adv* (*direction*) verso sud; (*location*) al sud; (*origin*) dal sud. **southeast** *n* sudest *m*. **South Pole** polo sud *m*. **south-west** *n* sudovest *m*. **southernmost** *adj* il più a sud.

**South Africa** *n* Sud Africa *m*.

**South America** *n* Sud America *m*, America del Sud *f*.

**souvenir** [suːvə'niə] *n* ricordo *m*.

**sovereign** ['sovrin] *n, adj* sovrano, -a. **sovereignty** *n* sovranità *f*.

**\*sow¹** [sou] *v* seminare; disseminare.

**sow²** [sau] *n* scrofa *f*.

**sown** [soun] *V* **sow¹**.

**soya** ['soiə] *n* soia *f*.

**spa** [spaː] *n* terme *f pl*, stazione termale *f*.

**space** [speis] *n* spazio *m*. *v* scaglionare; (*printing*) spaziare. **spaceman** *n* astronauta *m*. **spaceship** *n* astronave *f*. **spacious** *adj* ampio, spazioso.

**spade** [speid] *n* badile *m*, vanga *f*. **call a spade a spade** dire pane al pane. **spades** [speidz] *pl n* (*cards*) picche *f pl*.

**Spain** [spein] *n* Spagna *f*. **Spaniard** *n* spagnolo, -a *m, f*. **Spanish** *nm, adj* spagnolo.

**span** [span] *n* (*hand*) spanna *f*; (*bridge*) arco *m*; (*extent*) portata *f*; (*time*) durata *f*. *v* stendersi attraverso.

**spaniel** ['spanjəl] *n* spaniel *m invar*.

**spank** [spaŋk] *v* sculacciare.

**spanner** ['spanə] *n* chiave *f*; (*adjustable*) chiave inglese *f*.

**spare** [speə] *adj* di riserva *or* scorta; (*surplus*) in più, disponibile; frugale; (*lean*) magro. **spare part** pezzo di ricambio *m*. **spare room** camera in più *f*. **spare time** tempo disponibile *m*. **spare wheel** ruota di scorta f. v (not harm) risparmiare; (do without) fare a meno di. **spare no expense** non badare a spese. **sparing** adj parco, sobrio, limitato.

**spark** [spɑːk] n scintilla f; (gleam) barlume m. v emettere scintille, scintillare; (elec) accendere. **sparking-plug** n candela (d'accensione) f.

**sparkle** ['spɑːkl] n scintilla f, splendore m. v scintillare, brillare, risplendere. **sparkling** adj brillante; (wine) spumante.

**sparrow** ['sparou] n passero m.

**sparse** [spɑːs] adj rado, scarso. **sparsely** adv poco.

**spasm** ['spazəm] n accesso m; (muscular) spasmo m. **spasmodic** adj spasmodico.

**spastic** ['spastik] n, adj spastico, -a.

**spat** [spat] V **spit**[1].

**spate** [speit] n piena f.

**spatial** ['speiʃl] adj spaziale.

**spatula** ['spatjulə] n spatola f.

**spawn** [spɔːn] n (zool) uova f pl; (brood) progenie f. v deporre uova; (give rise to) generare, produrre (in abbondanza); (derog) figliare.

**\*speak** [spiːk] v parlare. **so to speak** per così dire. **speaking of** a proposito di. **speak out** parlare apertamente. **speak up** (loudly) parlare ad alta voce, parlare più forte. **speak up for** parlare a favore di. **strictly speaking** per essere precisi. **speaker** n oratore m; (pol) presidente m; (hi-fi) cassa acustica.

**spear** [spiə] n lancia f. v trafiggere.

**special** ['speʃəl] adj speciale, particolare; straordinario. **specialist** n specialista m, f. **speciality** n specialità f. **specialization** n specializzazione f. **specialize** v specializzare.

**species** ['spiːʃiːz] n specie f invar, genere m.

**specify** ['spesifai] v specificare, precisare. **specific** adj specifico, preciso. **specification** n specificazione f; (detailed description) specifica f.

**specimen** ['spesimin] n esemplare m, modello m; (for test) campione m.

**speck** [spek] n (spot) macchia f; (particle) granello m. **speckle** n macchia f, chiazza f. **speckled** adj chiazzato.

**spectacle** ['spektəkl] n spettacolo m. **spectacles** pl n occhiali m pl. **spectacled** adj occhialuto.

**spectator** [spek'teitə] n spettatore, -trice m, f.

**spectrum** ['spektrəm] n spettro m.

**speculate** ['spekjuleit] v speculare, meditare. **speculation** n speculazione f. **speculative** adj speculativo. **speculator** n speculatore, -trice m, f.

**sped** [sped] V **speed**.

**speech** [spiːtʃ] n (faculty) parola f; discorso m. **speechless** adj muto, senza parole.

**\*speed** [spiːd] n velocità f. **at full speed** a tutta corsa, a velocità massima. **speed-boat** n fuoribordo m. **speed limit** limite di velocità m. **speedometer** n tachimetro m. v andare in fretta. **speed up** accelerare. **speedy** adj veloce; (ready) pronto.

**spell**[1] [spel] v (read) compitare, sillabare; (write) scrivere; significare. **spelling** n ortografia f.

**spell**[2] [spel] n (magic) incanto m, incantesimo m; fascino m. **cast a spell** incantare. **spellbind** v affascinare.

**spell**[3] [spel] n periodo m; (work) turno m; (bout) attacco m.

**spelt** [spelt] V **spell**[1].

**\*spend** [spend] v spendere; (employ) impiegare, dedicare; (time) trascorrere, passare; (consume) esaurire. **spendthrift** n, adj prodigo, -a.

**spent** [spent] V **spend**.

**sperm** [spəːm] n sperma m.

**spew** [spjuː] n vomito m. v vomitare.

**sphere** [sfiə] n sfera f. **spherical** adj sferico.

**spice** [spais] n (cookery) spezie f invar; (flavour) gusto m, sapore m. v condire (con spezie); dar gusto or interesse a. **spicy** adj piccante, aromatico; salace.

**spider** ['spaidə] n ragno m. **spider's web** ragnatela f.

**spike** [spaik] n punta f, chiodo m. v inchiodare; (frustrate) rendere inservibile.

**\*spill** [spil] v spandere, versare. **spill over** traboccare.

**spilt** [spilt] V **spill**.

**\*spin** [spin] v (thread) filare; (rotate) (far) girare. **spin-drier** n centrifuga f, idroestrattore m. **spin-dry** v asciugare con la centrifuga. **spin out** prolungare. **spin a yarn** raccontare una frottola. n rotazione f; (phys) spin m invar; (short trip) giro m.

**spinach** ['spinidʒ] n spinaci m pl.

**spindle** ['spindl] n fuso m. **spindly** adj

esile, affusolato.

**spine** [spain] n (anat) spina dorsale f; (book) dorso m. **spinal** adj spinale, vertebrale. **spine-chilling** adj agghiacciante. **spineless** adj smidollato, debole.

**spinster** ['spinstə] n nubile f; (coll) zitella f.

**spiral** ['spaiərəl] n spirale f. adj a spirale. **spiral staircase** scala a chiocciola f.

**spire** ['spaiə] n guglia f.

**spirit** ['spirit] n spirito m; (drink) superalcolico m. **be in high spirits** avere il morale alto; essere allegro. **spirit-level** n livella a bolla d'aria f. **that's the spirit!** così va bene! **spirited** adj vivace, vigoroso. **spiritless** adj (without vigour) fiacco; (not lively) abbattuto. **spiritual** adj spirituale. **spiritualism** n spiritismo m; (philos) spiritualismo m. **spiritualist** n spiritista m, f.

***spit*** [spit] v sputare; (rain) piovigginare; (cat) soffiare. **the spitting image of ...** ... nato e sputato. n also **spittle** sputo m, saliva f.

**spit²** [spit] n (skewer) spiedo m; (land) lingua di terra f. v (skewer) infilzare.

**spite** [spait] n dispetto m. **in spite of** nonostante, malgrado. v far dispetto a; (annoy) indispettire. **spiteful** adj dispettoso, maligno.

**splash** [splaʃ] v (spatter) spruzzare; (mark with colour) macchiare, chiazzare. n spruzzata f; (sound) tonfo m; (liquid splashed) spruzzo m; (patch) macchia f; (showy display) sfoggio m.

**spleen** [spli:n] n (med) milza f; (peevishness) malumore m. **vent one's spleen on** sfogarsi su.

**splendid** ['splendid] adj splendido, stupendo. **splendour** n splendore m.

**splice** [splais] v (rope) impiombare; (tape) giuntare. n impiombatura f; giuntura f.

**splint** [splint] n stecca f.

**splinter** ['splintə] n scheggia f. v frantumarsi.

***split*** [split] v (cleave) spaccare; dividere, separare. **split hairs** cavillare. **split on** (coll) denunciare. **split up** dividersi, suddividere. n fenditura f; (into fractions) scissione f; separazione f. **split second** attimo m.

**splutter** ['splʌtə] v (spit) sputacchiare; (talk confusedly) farfugliare; (splash) spruzzare; (engine) scoppiettare.

***spoil*** [spoil] v rovinare, sciupare; (indulge) viziare. **be spoiling for** aver una gran voglia di. **spoil-sport** n guastafeste m, f invar. **spoils** pl n spoglie f pl.

**spoilt** [spoilt] V **spoil**.

**spoke¹** [spouk] V **speak**.

**spoke²** [spouk] n raggio m; (rung) piolo m. **put a spoke in someone's wheel** mettere un bastone fra le ruote a qualcuno.

**spoken** ['spoukn] V **speak**.

**spokesman** ['spouksmən] n portavoce m, f invar.

**sponge** [spʌndʒ] n spugna f. **sponge-cake** n pan di Spagna m. **throw in the sponge** gettare la spugna. v lavare con la spugna; (coll: cadge) scroccare. **sponger** n scroccone, -a m, f. **spongy** adj spugnoso.

**sponsor** ['sponsə] n garante m, f; (TV, etc.) finanziatore, -trice m, f. v essere garante di; rendersi responsabile di; finanziare; (lend support) patrocinare. **sponsorship** n garanzia f; finanziamento m.

**spontaneous** [spon'teinjəs] adj spontaneo. **spontaneity** n spontaneità f.

**spool** [spu:l] n rocchetto m.

**spoon** [spu:n] n cucchiaio m. **spoonfeed** v scodellare la pappa a. **spoonful** n cucchiaiata f.

**sporadic** [spə'radik] adj isolato.

**sport** [spo:t] n sport m invar; (jesting) scherzo m. **be a sport!** sii bravo! **sportsman** n sportivo m. **sportsmanship** n abilità sportiva f; spirito sportivo m. **sportswoman** n sportiva f. v (display) sfoggiare. **sporting** adj sportivo. **sporting chance** possibilità di successo f.

**spot** [spot] n (mark) macchia f, puntino m; (pimple) piccolo foruncolo m; (place) posto m, località f. **on the spot** sul posto. **spot check** controllo saltuario m. **spotlight** n riflettore m. v macchiare, punteggiare; (see) riconoscere, scoprire, osservare. **spotless** adj immacolato. **spotter** n osservatore, -trice m, f.

**spouse** [spaus] n sposo, -a m, f, coniuge m, f.

**spout** [spaut] n becco m, beccuccio m; (chute) scivolo m; (jet) getto m. **up the spout** (lost) perduto; (in a bad way) ridotto male. v (discharge) scaricare, gettare; (gush out) scaturire; (coll: talk) declamare.

**sprain** [sprein] v (strain) storcere; (wrench) slogare. n storta f; slogatura f.

**sprang** [spraŋ] V **spring**.

**sprawl** [spro:l] v stendersi lungo disteso;

(*spread out*) estendersi. **send sprawling** mandare a gambe all'aria.

**spray¹** [sprei] *n* (*jet*) spruzzo *m*; (*appliance*) spray *m invar*, atomizzatore *m*; (*hail*) raffica *f. v* spruzzare, atomizzare; (*scatter*) spargere.

**spray²** [sprei] *n* (*branch*) frasca *f*.

**\*spread** [spred] *v* (*lay out*) stendere; (*distribute*) spargere; (*disseminate*) diffondere; (*apply layer*) spalmare. *n* estensione *f*, diffusione *f*; (*cover*) coperta *f*; (*coll: feast*) banchetto *m*.

**spreadsheet** *n* foglio (di calcolo) elettronico *m*.

**spree** [spri:] *n* baldoria *f*.

**sprig** [sprig] *n* ramoscello *m*.

**sprightly** ['spraitli] *adj* vivace.

**\*spring** [spriŋ] *v* (*rise suddenly*) saltare, balzare; (*move rapidly*) scattare. **spring a leak** aprire una falla. **spring from** derivare or provenire da. **spring up** (*arise*) nascere; (*originate*) sorgere; (*jump up*) balzare; (*come forth*) spuntare. *n* (*beginning*) origine *f*; (*source of water*) sorgente *f*; (*season*) primavera *f*; (*coil*) molla *f. adj* primaverile, giovane. **spring-board** *n* trampolino *m*. **spring onion** cipollina *f*.

**sprinkle** ['spriŋkl] *v* spargere, cospargere; (*liquid*) spruzzare. **sprinkler** *n* (*watering can*) annaffiatoio *m*; (*fire*) nebulizzatore (antincendio) *m*. **sprinkling** *n* (*of knowledge*) infarinatura *f*.

**sprint** [sprint] *n* (*sport*) sprint *m invar*; volata *f. v* correre di volata, scattare. **sprinter** *n* sprinter *m*, *f invar*, velocista *m*, *f*.

**sprout** [spraut] *v* germogliare. *n* germoglio *m*. **Brussels sprouts** cavolini di Bruxelles *m pl*.

**spruce** [spru:s] *n* abete *m*.

**sprung** [sprʌŋ] *V* spring.

**spun** [spʌn] *V* spin.

**spur** [spə:] *n* sprone *m*. **on the spur of the moment** lì per lì. *v* spur on incitare.

**spurious** ['spjuəriəs] *adj* falso, spurio.

**spurn** [spə:n] *v* sdegnare; rifiutare.

**spurt** [spə:t] *n* (*gush*) getto improvviso *m*, zampillo *m*; (*burst*) scatto *m*; (*effort*) sforzo *m. v* zampillare.

**spy** [spai] *n* spia *f. v* spiare, fare la spia. **spying** *n* spionaggio *m*.

**squabble** ['skwobl] *v* litigare, bisticciarsi. *n* alterco *m*, bisticcio *m*, lite *f*.

**squad** [skwod] *n* squadra *f*.

**squadron** ['skwodrən] *n* squadriglia *f*.

**squalid** ['skwolid] *adj* squallido.

**squall** [skwo:l] *n* raffica *f*.

**squander** ['skwondə] *v* sprecare, sperperare. **squanderer** *n* sprecone, -a *m*, *f*.

**square** [skweə] *n* quadrato *m*; (*street*) piazza *f*; (*instrument*) squadra *f. adj* quadro; (*math*) quadrato; (*corner*) ad angolo retto; perpendicolare; (*settled*) saldato; (*straightforward*) diretto, netto. **square meal** pasto sostanzioso *m. v* (*math*) quadrare; (*accounts*) saldare; (*regulate*) mettere a punto; (*coll: bribe*) corrompere. **square up to** affrontare.

**squash** [skwoʃ] *v* schiacciare, spremere; (*suppress*) sopprimere; ridurre al silenzio, umiliare. *n* (*drink*) spremuta *f*; (*sport*) squash *m invar*; (*crowd*) ressa *f*.

**squat** [skwot] *v* rannicchiarsi, accovacciarsi; (*occupy illegally*) occupare abusivamente. *adj* tarchiato, tozzo.

**squawk** [skwo:k] *v* schiamazzare. *n* schiamazzo *m*.

**squeak** [skwi:k] *v* stridere, cigolare. *n* strido *m*, cigolio *m*. **have a narrow squeak** scamparla bella.

**squeal** [skwi:l] *v* strillare; (*coll: complain*) protestare. *n* strillo *m*.

**squeamish** ['skwi:miʃ] *adj* schizzinoso, schifiltoso.

**squeeze** [skwi:z] *v* (*press*) spremere; (*force*) pigiare; (*embrace*) stringere; (*press together*) comprimere. *n* stretta *f*; (*crowd*) calca *f*; (*comm*) restrizioni *f pl*.

**squid** [skwid] *n* calamaro *m*, seppia *f*.

**squiggle** ['skwigl] *n* sgorbio *m. v* sgorbiare.

**squint** [skwint] *v* (*be cross-eyed*) essere guercio or strabico; (*glance sideways*) guardare di traverso. *n* sguardo torto *m*, strabismo *m*. **squint-eyed** *adj* guercio, strabico.

**squire** ['skwaiə] *n* gentiluomo *m*, proprietario di terre *m*.

**squirm** [skwə:m] *v* (*wriggle*) dimenarsi, contorcersi; (*feel embarrassed*) essere sulle spine.

**squirrel** ['skwirəl] *n* scoiattolo *m*.

**squirt** [skwə:t] *v* schizzare. *n* (*jet*) schizzo *m*; (*syringe*) schizzetto *m*; (*derog*) ometto *m*, tizio *m*.

**stab** [stab] *v* pugnalare, accoltellare. **stab in the back** pugnalare alle spalle. *n* pugnalata *f*, coltellata *f*; (*try*) tentativo *m*. **have a stab at** tentare di.

**stabilize** ['steibilaiz] *v* stabilizzare. **stabi-**

**lization** n stabilizzazione f. **stabilizer** n stabilizzatore m.

**stable**¹ ['steibl] n stalla f; (racing) scuderia f.

**stable**² ['steibl] adj stabile; (firm) saldo; permanente. **stability** n stabilità f, fermezza f.

**staccato** [stə'ka:tou] adj staccato.

**stack** [stak] n (heap) catasta f, mucchio m; (chimney) fumaiolo m. v accatastare, ammucchiare.

**stadium** ['steidiəm] n stadio m.

**staff** [sta:f] n (stick) bastone m; (flag-pole) asta f; (personnel) personale m; (mil) stato maggiore m. v fornire di personale, impiegare.

**stag** [stag] n cervo m. **stag-beetle** n cervo volante m.

**stage** [steidʒ] n (phase) fase f; (lap) tappa f; periodo m, momento m; teatro m; (platform) palcoscenico m. **at this stage** a questo punto. **go on the stage** fare l'attore. **stage-coach** n diligenza f. **stage-craft** n scenotecnica f. **stage fright** timor panico m. **stage-manager** n direttore di scena m. v rappresentare, mettere in scena. **staging** n messa in scena f.

**stagger** ['stagə] v barcollare; (shock) colpire, impressionare; (arrange) scaglionare. **staggering** adj sconcertante.

**stagnant** ['stagnənt] adj stagnante, inattivo. **stagnate** v ristagnare. **stagnation** n ristagno m.

**staid** [steid] adj posato, serio.

**stain** [stein] n macchia f; tinta f, colore m. **stain remover** smacchiatore m. v macchiare; colorire. **stainless steel** acciaio inossidabile m.

**stair** [steə] n (step) scalino m, gradino m. **staircase** n scala f. **stairs** pl n scale f pl.

**stake**¹ [steik] n (post) palo m; (execution) rogo m. v (support) palare. **stake out** cintare. **stake out a claim** reclamare.

**stake**² [steik] n (bet) posta f, scommessa f. **at stake** in gioco. v mettere in gioco, scommettere. **stake one's life** scommettere l'osso del collo.

**stale** [steil] adj vecchio, stantio; (bread) raffermo.

**stalemate** ['steilmeit] n stallo m; (dead-lock) punto morto m. **reach stalemate** giungere a una posizione di stallo.

**stalk**¹ [sto:k] n stelo m, gambo m.

**stalk**² [sto:k] v (follow) inseguire furtivamente; (stride haughtily) camminare impettito.

**stall**¹ [sto:l] n banco m, chiosco m; (newspapers) edicola f; (theatre) poltrona diplatea f. **stalls** pl n (theatre) platea f sing. v (engine) imballare; (aeroplane) picchiare; (stop) fermarsi.

**stall**² [sto:l] v (delay) tirar per le lunghe; (act evasively) cercar pretesti.

**stallion** ['staljən] n stallone m.

**stamina** ['staminə] n vigore m, capacità di resistenza f.

**stammer** ['stamə] v balbettare. n balbuzie f. **stammerer** n balbuziente m, f.

**stamp** [stamp] v marcare, imprimere; (envelope) affrancare; (print on) timbrare; (documents) bollare; (with foot) pestare. **stamp out** domare, annientare. n (impression) impronta f; marchio m; (document) bollo m; (postage) francobollo m; (implement) stampiglia f; (rubber) timbro m. **stamp-collector** n filatelico, -a m, f.

**stampede** [stam'pi:d] n fuga precipitosa f. v fuggire in disordine.

*****stand** [stand] n posizione f; (platform) tribuna f; (exhibition) stand m invar; (music, etc.) leggio m. v stare, essere; (be upright) stare in piedi; (remain) restare; (tolerate) sopportare, tollerare. **stand by** (wait) rimanere in attesa; (help) aiutare; (remain faithful) restar fedele a. **stand-by** n riserva f, scorta f. **stand for** significare; (support) sostenere. **stand-in** n controfigura f. **stand-offish** adj riservato. **stand out** (project) spiccare; (be conspicuous) risaltare. **standstill** n arresto m, fermata f. **come to a standstill** fermarsi. **stand up** alzarsi. **stand up for** prender la parte di. **stand up to** resistere a.

**standard** ['standəd] n standard m invar, modello m, campione m; (level) livello m; (flag) stendardo m, bandiera f. adj standard invar, normale. **standard lamp** torciera f, piantana f.

**standing** ['standiŋ] n posizione f, reputazione f; (period) durata f. adj fermo, fisso; permanente; abituale; (upright) in piedi. **leave standing** abbandonare sul posto.

**stank** [staŋk] V **stink**.

**stanza** ['stanzə] n strofa f.

**staple**¹ [steipl] n graffa f; (stationery) punto metallico m. v graffare; cucire (con punti metallici). **stapler** n cucitrice f.

**staple²** [steipl] n prodotto principale m; (textile) fiocco m. adj principale, base invar.

**star** [sta:] n stella f; (actor) divo, -a m, f. **starfish** n stella di mare f. adj principale. v (cinema, etc.) primeggiare. **starry** adj stellato. **starry-eyed** adj (coll) ingenuo.

**starboard** ['sta:bəd] n dritta f.

**starch** [sta:tʃ] n amido m, fecola f. v inamidare. **starchy** adj (food) ricco d'amido; (manner) rigido.

**stare** [steə] v fissare; (gaze fixedly) sgranare gli occhi. **stare in the face** (be obvious) saltare agli occhi, essere ovvio. n sguardo fisso m.

**stark** [sta:k] adj rigido; (bleak) brullo. **stark mad** matto da legare. **stark naked** completamente nudo, nudo nato.

**starling** ['sta:liŋ] n storno m, stornello m.

**start** [sta:t] n (beginning) inizio m; (point of departure) partenza f; (sudden movement) soprassalto m; (lead) vantaggio m. **by fits and starts** a sbalzi. v iniziare, cominciare; partire; (jump) sussultare; (set in motion) mettere in moto. **to start with** per cominciare. **starter** n starter m invar, motorino d'avviamento m.

**startle** ['sta:tl] v (far) trasalire, sbigottire. **startling** adj sorprendente.

**starve** [sta:v] v affamare; (to death) (far) morire di fame; (be very hungry) soffrire la fame. **starve of** (far) soffrire per mancanza di. **starvation** n fame f.

**state** [steit] n stato m; pompa f; (coll) ansietà f. **statesman** n uomo di stato m. adj statale; solenne. v dichiarare, affermare; specificare; indicare. **stateless** adj apolide. **stately** adj solenne, maestoso. **statement** n affermazione f, dichiarazione f; (bank, etc.) estratto conto m.

**static** ['statik] adj fisso, statico. **statics** n statica f.

**station** ['steiʃən] n stazione f; (headquarters) sede f; (rank) condizione sociale f. **stationmaster** n (pl capostazione) m. **station-wagon** n (US) giardinetta f. v appostare, collocare.

**stationary** ['steiʃənəri] adj fermo; costante, fisso.

**stationer** ['steiʃənə] n cartolaio, -a m, f. **stationer's** n cartoleria f. **stationery** n oggetti di cancelleria m pl.

**statistics** [stə'tistiks] n statistica f. **statisti-cal** adj statistico. **statistician** n statistico, -a m, f.

**statue** ['statju:] n statua f.

**stature** ['statʃə] n statura f.

**status** ['steitəs] n posizione sociale f, rango m, prestigio m.

**statute** ['statju:t] n decreto m, legge f.

**staunch** [sto:ntʃ] adj fedele, leale. v stagnare.

**stay** [stei] n soggiorno m; arresto m; (law) sospensione f. v (remain) restare, rimanere; (on holiday, etc.) soggiornare; (at hotel) alloggiare (in); (stop) sostare; sospendere. **stay in** non uscire, restare a casa. **stay on** trattenersi. **stay out** rimaner fuori, non rientrare.

**steadfast** ['stedfa:st] adj risoluto, saldo.

**steady** ['stedi] adj fermo, stabile; (responsible) serio; regolare; costante. v reggersi, tener fermo; calmare.

**steak** [steik] n (meat) bistecca f; (fish) trancia f.

***steal** [sti:l] v rubare. **steal away** andarsene di nascosto. **steal a march on** prevenire.

**stealthy** ['stelθi] adj clandestino. **stealthily** adv di nascosto or soppiatto.

**steam** [sti:m] n vapore m; (coll: energy) carica f. **let off steam** (coll) sfogarsi. v emettere vapore; (cook) cucinare a vapore. **steam up** appannarsi. **steamer** n (boat) piroscafo m; (cookery) pentola a vapore f. **steamy** adj pieno di vapore.

**steam-roller** n rullo compressore m; (coll) forza irresistibile f. v sopraffare.

**steel** [sti:l] n acciaio m. v indurire. **steely** adj d'acciaio, inflessibile.

**steep¹** [sti:p] adj (sheer) ripido; (coll: unreasonable) eccessivo.

**steep²** [sti:p] v (soak) inzuppare; (tech) macerare.

**steeple** ['sti:pl] n (spire) guglia f; (tower) campanile m.

**steer¹** [stiə] n (ox) manzo m.

**steer²** [stiə] v guidare, dirigere. **steer clear of** evitare. **steering-wheel** n volante m.

**stem¹** [stem] n (stalk) gambo m; (of pipe) cannello m; (branch) ramo m; (of word) radice f. v **stem from** derivare da.

**stem²** [stem] v contenere, arginare.

**stench** [stentʃ] n puzzo m.

**stencil** ['stensl] n (device) stampino m;

*(duplicating machine)* ciclostile *m*. *v* stampinare; ciclostilare.

**step** [step] *n* passo *m*; *(stair)* gradino *m*; *(measure)* provvedimento *m*. **out of step** non conforme. **step by step** un poco alla volta, per gradi. **step-ladder** *n* scala a libretto *f*, scaleo *m*. **watch one's step** stare attenti. *v* fare un passo; *(walk)* camminare. **step down** scendere; *(retire)* ritirarsi. **step in** entrare; intervenire. **step up** salire; aumentare; accelerare.

**stepbrother** ['stepbrʌðə] *n* fratellastro *m*.

**stepdaughter** ['stepdɔːtə] *n* figliastra *f*.

**stepfather** ['stepfɑːðə] *n* patrigno *m*.

**stepmother** ['stepmʌðə] *n* matrigna *f*.

**stepsister** ['stepsistə] *n* sorellastra *f*.

**stepson** ['stepsʌn] *n* figliastro *m*.

**stereo** ['steriou] *adj* stereo. **stereophonic** *adj* stereofonico.

**stereotype** ['steriətaip] *n* cliché *m*; *(tech)* stereotipia *f*. **stereotyped** *adj* *(trite)* stereotipato; *(tech)* stereotipo.

**sterile** ['sterail] *adj* sterile. **sterility** *n* sterilità *f*. **sterilization** *n* sterilizzazione *f*. **sterilize** *v* sterilizzare.

**sterling** ['stəːliŋ] *n* sterlina *f*. *adj* genuino.

**stern¹** [stəːn] *adj* *(harsh)* severo; *(strict)* rigoroso.

**stern²** [stəːn] *n* *(ship)* poppa *f*.

**stethoscope** ['steθəskoup] *n* stetoscopio *m*.

**stew** [stjuː] *n* spezzatino *m*, stufato *m*. **be in a stew** essere preoccupato *or* turbato. *v* cuocere (a fuoco lento).

**steward** ['stjuəd] *n* amministratore, -trice *m, f*; *(ship)* cameriere di bordo *m*, steward *m invar*. **stewardess** *n* stewardess *f invar*, assistente di volo *f*. **stewardship** *n* gestione *f*; *(office)* carica di amministratore *f*.

**stick¹** [stik] *n* *(wood)* bastone *m*; *(celery, etc.)* gambo *m*; *(small rod)* bastoncino *m*. **be in a cleft stick** non sapere che pesci pigliare.

**\*stick²** [stik] *v* attaccare, appiccicare; *(stab)* ficcare; *(remain)* rimanere. **stick it out** tener duro. **stick out** *(be conspicuous)* saltare agli occhi; *(put out)* tirar fuori. **stick to** *(not digress)* attenersi a, non divagare da; *(remain loyal)* restar fedele a. **stick up for** difendere, battersi per. **sticky** *adj* attaccaticcio; adesivo; *(weather)* pesante; *(coll: difficult)* complesso.

**sticker** *n* autocollante *m*.

**stickler** ['stiklə] *n* pignolo, -a *m, f*. **stickler for ...** persona ligia a ....

**stiff** [stif] *adj* rigido; *(hard to move, difficult)* duro; *(formal)* freddo. *adv* *(coll)* a morte. **stiffen** *v* irrigidire. **stiffness** *n* rigidezza *f*; durezza *f*.

**stifle** ['staifl] *v* soffocare.

**stigma** ['stigmə] *n* segno *m*, marchio *m*; *(disgrace)* stigma *m*.

**stile** [stail] *n* scaletta *f*.

**still¹** [stil] *adj* *(quiet)* tranquillo; *(motionless)* immobile. *adv* ancora, tuttora. **still-born** *adj* nato morto. **in silenzio** *m*; *(phot)* posa *f*. *v* calmare. **stillness** *n* silenzio *m*, tranquillità *f*.

**still²** [stil] *n* distilleria *f*; *(retort)* storta *f*.

**stilt** [stilt] *n* trampolo *m*; *(building)* palafitta *f*. **stilted** *adj* artificiale; *(pompous)* ampolloso.

**stimulus** ['stimjuləs] *n pl* -li stimolo *m*. **stimulant** *nm, adj* stimolante. **stimulate** *v* stimolare. **stimulation** *n* stimolo *m*.

**\*sting** [stiŋ] *v* *(wound)* pungere; *(incite)* spronare; *(coll: cheat)* truffare. *n* puntura *f*; *(pang)* morso *m*; *(incitement)* sprone *m*.

**stingy** ['stindʒi] *adj* tirchio, spilorcio. **stinginess** *n* tirchieria *f*, spilorceria *f*.

**\*stink** [stiŋk] *n* puzzo *m*. *v* puzzare. **stinking** *adj* puzzolente, fetente.

**stint** [stint] *n* dovere *m*, periodo di lavoro *m*. *v* risparmiare, fare economia.

**stipulate** ['stipjuleit] *v* pattuire, convenire. **stipulation** *n* patto *m*, condizione *f*, convenzione *f*.

**stir** [stəː] *v* mescolare, agitare; *(budge)* muoversi. **stir up** eccitare, incitare. *n* *(excitement)* scalpore *m*; confusione *f*. **stirring** *adj* *(touching)* commovente; eccitante.

**stirrup** ['stirəp] *n* staffa *f*.

**stitch** [stitʃ] *n* *(sewing)* punto *m*; *(knitting)* maglia *f*. *v* cucire; *(sew on)* attaccare; *(med)* suturare.

**stoat** [stout] *n* ermellino *m*.

**stock** [stok] *n* *(goods)* provvista *f*, stock *m invar*, riserva *f*; *(standing)* credito *m*; famiglia *f*; *(cookery)* brodo *m*. **stockbroker** *n* agente di cambio *m*. **stock exchange** borsa valori *f*. **stockholder** *n* azionista *m, f*. **stockpile** *v* fare scorta di. **stocks and shares** titoli *m pl*. **stocktaking** *n* inventario *m*. *v* *(supply)* fornire, rifornire; tenere in magazzino.

**stocking** ['stokiŋ] n calza f.

**stocky** ['stoki] adj tarchiato, tozzo.

**stodge** [stodʒ] (coll) n (food) cibo pesante m; (dull matter) mattone m. **stodgy** adj pesante; (tedious) noioso.

**stoical** ['stouikl] adj stoico. **stoic** n stoico, -a m, f.

**stoke** [stouk] v alimentare. **stoke up** rimpinzarsi. **stoker** n fuochista m.

**stole**[1] [stoul] V **steal**.

**stole**[2] [stoul] n stola f.

**stolen** ['stoulən] V **steal**.

**stomach** ['stʌmək] n stomaco m. **stomache** n mal di stomaco m. v (tolerate) sopportare.

**stone** [stoun] n pietra f; (pebble) sasso m; (fruit) nocciolo m; (med) calcolo m. **a stone's throw from** a due passi da. **stone-deaf** adj sordo come una campana. **stonemason** n muratore m. **stoneware** n gres m invar. v prendere a sassate; (fruit) snocciolare.

**stood** [stud] V **stand**.

**stool** [stu:l] n sgabello m. **stool-pigeon** n spia f.

**stoop** [stu:p] v curvare, chinarsi; (condescend) abbassarsi. n **walk with a stoop** camminar curvo.

**stop** [stop] n (halt) sosta f, fermata f; (punctuation) punto m; (organ) registro m. v finire, smettere; (halt) fermare; (prevent) impedire; (withhold) trattenere; (block) turare. **stop-press** n ultimissime f pl. **stopwatch** n cronometro a scatto m. **stoppage** n fermata f, arresto m; sospensione f; (med) blocco m. **stopper** n (bung) tappo m.

**store** [sto:] n (supply) provvista f, riserva f; (shop) bottega f; (warehouse) magazzino m. **storekeeper** n magazziniere m. v fare provviste di; conservare; accumulare; mettere in magazzino. **storage** n immagazzinamento m; (comm) magazzinaggio m.

**storey** ['sto:ri] n piano m.

**stork** [sto:k] n cicogna f.

**storm** [sto:m] n tempesta f; (thunder) temporale m. v (rage) infuriarsi; (rush) precipitarsi; (mil) prendere d'assalto. **stormy** adj burrascoso.

**story** ['sto:ri] n storia f, racconto m; (news) fatto di cronaca m.

**stout** [staut] adj (fat) grasso; intrepido; robusto.

**stove** [stouv] n stufa f; (cooker) cucina f.

**stow** [stou] v stivare; (fill) riempire (di). **stow away** mettere da parte; (on boat, etc.) imbarcarsi clandestinamente. **stowaway** n passeggero clandestino m. **stowage** n stivaggio m.

**straddle** ['stradl] v stare a cavalcioni, cavalcare.

**straggle** ['stragl] v disperdersi; (lag behind) rimanere indietro. **straggler** n ritardatario, -a m, f.

**straight** [streit] adj diritto; (open) franco, aperto. adv diritto, in linea retta; (directly) direttamente. **straight away** subito. **straightforward** adj franco, aperto; onesto; semplice. **straighten** v raddrizzare; (order) assettare.

**strain**[1] [strein] v filtrare, passare; (force) sforzare; (sprain) storcere. n sforzo m, tensione f; (med) storta f; (tune) melodia f. **strained** adj forzato; filtrato. **strainer** n filtro m, colino m.

**strain**[2] [strein] n (race) stirpe f, famiglia f.

**strait** [streit] n (geog) stretto m. **straits** pl n difficoltà f pl. adj **strait-laced** adj rigoroso, puritano.

**strand**[1] [strand] n (hair) ciocca f; (rope) fune f.

**strand**[2] [strand] n (shore) spiaggia f, sponda f. v arenare, incagliarsi.

**strange** [streindʒ] adj strano, misterioso; (unaccountable) inspiegabile. **stranger** n sconosciuto, -a m, f; estraneo, -a m, f; (foreigner) straniero, -a m, f.

**strangle** ['straŋgl] v strangolare. **strangulation** n strangolamento m.

**strap** [strap] n cinghia f; (on garment) spallina f; (watch) cinturino m. v **strap up** assicurare con cinghia; (med) fissare con cerotto. **strapping** adj robusto.

**strategy** ['stratədʒi] n strategia f. **strategic** adj strategico.

**stratum** ['stra:təm] n, pl **-ta** strato m.

**straw** [stro:] n paglia f; (drinking) cannuccia f.

**strawberry** ['stro:bəri] n fragola f.

**stray** [strei] v (lose one's way) smarrirsi; (roam) vagare. **stray from** deviare or allontanarsi da. adj (animal) randagio; (lost) smarrito; (occasional) isolato.

**streak** [stri:k] n (mark) riga f, striscia f; (vein) vena f; (lightning) lampo m. v striare;

venare; (*rush*) filare.

**stream** [striːm] *n* corso d'acqua *m*; (*brook*) ruscello *m*; corrente *f*. **streamline** *v* sveltire. **streamlined** *adj* aerodinamico, svelto. *v* grondare, riversarsi. **streaming cold** forte raffreddore *m*.

**street** [striːt] *n* strada *f*, via *f*. **street-cleaner** *n* spazzino *m*. **street-light** *n* lampione *m*. **the man in the street** l'uomo qualunque *m*.

**strength** [strenθ] *n* forza *f*; intensità *f*; validità *f*; (*mil*) effettivo *m*. **strengthen** *v* rinforzare; (*give weight to*) convalidare.

**strenuous** ['strenjuəs] *adj* energico, fervente; (*activity*) arduo, duro.

**stress** [stres] *n* tensione *f*; pressione *f*, spinta *f*; (*emphasis*) rilievo *m*; accento *m*; (*med*) stress *m invar*. *v* mettere in rilievo, sottolineare; accentare; sottoporre a tensione.

**stretch** [stretʃ] *v* (*pull*) tirare; (*extend*) stendere; (*reach*) estendersi. **stretch one's legs** sgranchirsi le gambe. **stretch out** allungare, sdraiarsi. *n* (*expanse*) tratto *m*; (*time*) periodo *m*. **stretcher** *n* barella *f*, lettiga *f*.

**stricken** ['strikən] *adj* colpito.

**strict** [strikt] *adj* severo, rigoroso; esatto; (*absolute*) stretto.

**\*stride** [straid] *v* camminare a grandi passi. *n* passo *m*. **take in one's stride** (*do easily*) superare con facilità; (*adjust to*) prendersela con calma.

**strife** [straif] *n* lotta *f*, conflitto *m*.

**\*strike** [straik] *v* colpire; (*deal a blow*) battere; (*match*) accendere; (*oil*) scoprire; (*not work*) scioperare. **strike home** colpire nel segno. **strike off** radiare. **strike up** (*enter upon*) stringere. *n* sciopero *m*; (*discovery*) scoperta *f*. **striking** *adj* sorprendente, impressionante.

**\*string** [strin] *n* spago *m*, corda *f*; (*series*) fila *f*. **pull strings** manovrare, raccomandare. **strings** *pl n* (*music*) strumenti a corda *m pl*. *v* (*music*) incordare; (*racket*) mettere le corde a; (*beads*) infilare.

**stringent** ['strindʒənt] *adj* rigoroso, severo.

**strip¹** [strip] *v* spogliare, denudare; (*car, etc.*) smontare; (*paint*) togliere. **strip of** privare di. **strip-tease** *n* spogliarello *m*.

**strip²** [strip] *n* striscia *f*, nastro *m*; (*comic*) fumetto *m*.

**stripe** [straip] *n* riga *f*, striscia *f*; (*mil*) gallone *m*. **striped** *adj* a righe or strisce.

**\*strive** [straiv] *v* (*try hard*) sforzarsi, adoper-

arsi; (*struggle*) lottare.

**striven** ['strivn] *V* **strive**.

**strode** [stroud] *V* **stride**.

**stroke¹** [strouk] *n* colpo *m*; (*mark*) sbarra *f*; (*swimming*) bracciata *f*; (*med*) colpo apoplettico *m*; (*clock*) tocco *m*; (*tech*) corsa *f*. **stroke of genius** lampo di genio *m*. **stroke of lightning** fulmine *m*.

**stroke²** [strouk] *v* accarezzare, lisciare.

**stroll** [stroul] *n* passeggiatina *f*. **go for a stroll** andare a far quattro passi. *v* girovagare.

**strong** [stron] *adj* forte, robusto, resistente. **stronghold** *n* roccaforte *f*. **strong language** parole grosse *f pl*. **strong-minded** *adj* risoluto. **strong point** forte *m*.

**strove** [strouv] *V* **strive**.

**struck** [strʌk] *V* **strike**.

**structure** ['strʌktʃə] *n* struttura *f*. **structural** *adj* strutturale.

**struggle** ['strʌgl] *n* (*fight*) lotta *f*; (*effort*) sforzo *m*. *v* lottare; sforzarsi.

**strum** [strʌm] *v* strimpellare.

**strung** [strʌn] *V* **string**.

**strut¹** [strʌt] *v* (*prance*) camminare impettito.

**strut²** [strʌt] *n* (*support*) puntone *m*.

**stub** [stʌb] *n* (*cigarette, pencil, etc.*) mozzicone *m*; (*cheque*) matrice *f*; (*tree*) ceppo *m*. *v* urtare. **stub out** spegnere.

**stubble** ['stʌbl] *n* stoppia *f*; (*beard*) barba ispida *f*. **stubbly** *adj* pieno di stoppie; ispido.

**stubborn** ['stʌbən] *adj* ostinato, testardo. **stubbornness** *n* ostinatezza *f*, testardaggine *f*.

**stuck** [stʌk] *V* **stick²**.

**stud¹** [stʌd] *n* (*ornament*) borchia *f*; (*nail*) ribattino *m*; (*button*) bottoncino *m*. *v* guarnire di borchie; (*jewel*) tempestare.

**stud²** [stʌd] *n* scuderia *f*. **stud-horse** *n* stallone *m*.

**student** ['stjuːdənt] *n* (*pupil*) studente, -essa *m*, *f*; (*scholar*) studioso, -a *m*, *f*.

**studio** ['stjuːdiou] *n* studio *m*.

**study** ['stʌdi] *n* studio *m*. *v* studiare; esaminare attentamente. **studied** *adj* studiato, premeditato. **studious** *adj* studioso, attento, premuroso.

**stuff** [stʌf] *n* roba *f*; (*substance*) sostanza *f*; (*fabric*) tessuto *m*. **know one's stuff** sapere il fatto proprio. *v* (*cookery*) farcire; (*animal*) imbalsamare; (*fill*) imbottire. **stuffing** *n* imbottitura *f*; (*cookery*) ripieno *m*. **stuffy** *adj* soffocante; (*tedious*) noioso; (*blocked up*) intasato; (*prim*) rigido, conservatore.

**stumble** [stʌmbl] *v* inciampare, fare un passo falso; (*speech*) impaperarsi. **stumbling block** ostacolo *m*.

**stump** [stʌmp] *n* (*tree*) ceppo *m*; (*limb*) moncone *m*.

**stun** [stʌn] *v* stordire; (*astound*) sbalordire. **stunning** *adj* sbalorditivo, stupefacente.

**stung** [stʌŋ] *V* **sting**.

**stunk** [stʌŋk] *V* **stink**.

**stunt¹** [stʌnt] *v* arrestare la crescita di.

**stunt²** [stʌnt] *n* bravata *f*; acrobazia *f*; trovata pubblicitaria *f*.

**stupid** [ˈstjuːpid] *adj* stupido, sciocco. **stupidity** *n* stupidità *f*.

**stupor** [ˈstjuːpə] *n* stupore *m*, torpore *m*.

**sturdy** [ˈstəːdi] *adj* vigoroso, robusto. **sturdiness** *n* vigoria *f*.

**sturgeon** [ˈstəːdʒən] *n* storione *m*.

**stutter** [ˈstʌtə] *n* balbuzie *f*. *v* balbettare. **stutterer** *n* balbuziente *m, f*.

**sty** [stai] *n* porcile *m*.

**stye** [stai] *n* orzaiolo *m*.

**style** [stail] *n* stile *m*. **stylish** *adj* elegante. **stylist** *n* stilista *m, f*.

**stylus** [ˈstailəs] *n* puntina *f*.

**suave** [swaːv] *adj* cortese, affabile.

**subconscious** [sʌbˈkɒnʃəs] *nm, adj* subcosciente.

**subcontract** [sʌbkənˈtrakt] *n* subappalto *m*. *v* dare in subappalto.

**subdivision** [ˌsʌbdiˈviʒən] *n* suddivisione *f*. **subdivide** *v* suddividere.

**subdue** [səbˈdjuː] *v* (*conquer*) soggiogare; (*repress*) reprimere; (*reduce intensity*) attenuare. **subdued** *adj* inibito; intimidito; attenuato.

**subject** [ˈsʌbdʒikt; *v* səbˈdʒekt] *n* soggetto *m*, argomento *m*; (*study*) materia *f*; (*pol*) suddito, -a *m, f*. *adj* **subject to** soggetto a. *v* (*bring under control*) sottomettere; (*expose*) esporre, sottoporre. **subjective** *adj* soggettivo. **subjectivity** *n* soggettività *f*.

**subjunctive** [səbˈdʒʌŋktiv] *nm, adj* congiuntivo.

**\*sublet** [ˌsʌbˈlet] *v* subaffittare.

**sublimate** [ˈsʌblimeit] *v* sublimare. *n* sublimato *m*. **sublimation** *n* sublimazione *f*.

**sublime** [səˈblaim] *adj* sublime.

**submarine** [ˈsʌbməriːn] *n* sottomarino *m*.

**submerge** [səbˈməːdʒ] *v* sommergere. **submersion** *n* sommersione *f*.

**submit** [səbˈmit] *v* (*yield*) sottomettersi, rassegnarsi; deferire; (*present*) sottoporre. **submission** *n* sottomissione *f*, rassegnazione *f*; (*theory*) tesi *f*.

**subnormal** [sʌbˈnɔːməl] *adj* subnormale.

**subordinate** [səˈbɔːdinət] *adj* subordinato, inferiore. *n* subalterno *m*. *v* subordinare. **subordination** *n* subordinazione *f*.

**subscribe** [səbˈskraib] *v* sottoscrivere, aderire; (*newspapers, etc.*) abbonarsi. **subscriber** *n* abbonato, -a *m, f*. **subscription** *n* abbonamento *m*; (*dues*) quota *f*; (*fund raised*) sottoscrizione *f*.

**subsequent** [ˈsʌbsikwənt] *adj* successivo, susseguente.

**subservient** [səbˈsəːviənt] *adj* subordinato; (*servile*) umile.

**subside** [səbˈsaid] *v* decrescere, diminuire; (*give way*) cedere, avvallare; (*abate*) quietarsi. **subsidence** *n* avvallamento *m*.

**subsidiary** [səbˈsidiəri] *adj* sussidiario, (*comm*) consociato.

**subsidize** [ˈsʌbsidaiz] *v* sovvenzionare. **subsidy** *n* sovvenzione *f*.

**subsist** [səbˈsist] *v* sostentarsi. **subsistence** *n* sostentamento *m*. **subsistence money** acconto paga *m*, trasferta *f*.

**substance** [ˈsʌbstəns] *n* sostanza *f*, materia *f*; (*wealth*) beni *m pl*. **substantial** *adj* sostanziale; (*meal*) sostanzioso; (*considerable*) notevole.

**substitute** [ˈsʌbstitjuːt] *n* (*person*) sostituto, -a *m, f*; (*thing*) surrogato *m*. *v* sostituire, rimpiazzare. **substitution** *n* sostituzione *f*.

**subterfuge** [ˈsʌbtəfjuːdʒ] *n* sotterfugio *m*.

**subterranean** [sʌbtəˈreiniən] *adj* sotterraneo.

**subtitle** [ˈsʌbtaitl] *n* sottotitolo *m*.

**subtle** [ˈsʌtl] *adj* sottile, delicato; astuto, ingegnoso. **subtlety** *n* sottigliezza *f*, finezza *f*; astuzia *f*.

**subtract** [səbˈtrakt] *v* dedurre, sottrarre. **subtraction** *n* sottrazione *f*.

**suburb** [ˈsʌbəːb] *n* sobborgo *m*. **suburban** *adj* suburbano.

**subvert** [səbˈvəːt] *v* sovvertire. **subversion** *n* sovversione *f*. **subversive** *n, adj* sovversivo, -a.

**subway** ['sʌbwei] *n* sottopassaggio *m*; (*US*) metropolitana *f*.

**succeed** [sək'siːd] *v* riuscire; (*be successful*) aver successo; (*follow*) succedere. **success** *n* successo *m*, buona riuscita *f*. **successful** *adj* (*person*) che ha successo; vittorioso; prospero, arrivato; (*thing*) riuscito. **succession** *n* successione *f*. **successive** *adj* successivo. **successor** *n* successore *m*.

**succinct** [sək'siŋkt] *adj* succinto.

**succulent** ['sʌkjulənt] *adj* succulento.

**succumb** [sə'kʌm] *v* soccombere.

**such** [sʌtʃ] *adj* tale; (*like*) del genere, simile. *adv* così. **such and such** tale dei tali. **such as** come. **such as it is** così com'è.

**suck** [sʌk] *v* succhiare; (*breast*) poppare. **suck up** assorbire; (*slang*) fare il leccapiedi.

**sucker** ['sʌkə] *n* (*plant*) pollone *m*; (*device*) ventosa *f*; (*slang: fool*) gonzo *m*.

**suckle** ['sʌkl] *v* allattare.

**suction** ['sʌkʃən] *n* aspirazione *f*. **suction pump** pompa aspirante *f*.

**sudden** ['sʌdən] *adj* improvviso, subitaneo. **all of a sudden** ad un tratto, all'improvviso.

**suds** [sʌdz] *pl n* saponata *f sing*.

**sue** [suː] *v* (*law*) citare, chiamare in giudizio, querelare. **sue for peace** chiedere *or* sollecitare la pace.

**suede** [sweid] *nm*, *adj* scamosciato.

**suet** ['suːit] *n* grasso di rognone *m*.

**suffer** ['sʌfə] *v* soffrire, patire; tollerare; (*undergo*) subire. **on sufferance** per tacita tolleranza. **suffering** *n* sofferenza *f*, dolore *m*.

**sufficient** [sə'fiʃənt] *adj* sufficiente. **sufficiency** *n* sufficienza *f*.

**suffix** ['sʌfiks] *n* suffisso *m*.

**suffocate** ['sʌfəkeit] *v* soffocare. **suffocation** *n* soffocazione *f*.

**sugar** ['ʃugə] *n* zucchero *m*. **sugar-beet** *n* barbabietola (da zucchero) *f*. **sugar-cane** *n* canna da zucchero *f*. **sugary** *adj* zuccherino, mellifluo.

**suggest** [sə'dʒest] *v* suggerire; proporre. **suggestible** *adj* suggestionabile. **suggestion** *n* suggerimento *m*; proposta *f*; (*psych*) suggestione *f*.

**suicide** ['suːisaid] *n* (*deed*) suicidio *m*; (*person*) suicida *m*, *f*. **commit suicide** suicidarsi. **suicidal** *adj* suicida.

**suit** [suːt] *n* (*garment*) abito *m*; (*law*) causa *f*; (*cards*) seme *m*, colore *m*; (*request*) preghiera *f*. **follow suit** seguire l'esempio; (*cards*) rispondere a colore. **suitcase** *n* valigia *f*. *v* accontentare, convenire a, soddisfare. **suit yourself!** fa come ti pare! **suitable** *adj* adatto; conveniente, opportuno. **suitability** *n* convenienza *f*.

**suite** [swiːt] *n* (*music*) suite *f invar*; (*retinue*) seguito *m*; (*furniture*) mobilia *f invar*; (*rooms*) fuga di stanze *f*.

**sulk** [sʌlk] *v* tenere il broncio. **sulky** *adj* imbronciato.

**sullen** ['sʌlən] *adj* accigliato, imbronciato.

**sulphur** ['sʌlfə] *n* zolfo *m*.

**sultan** ['sʌltən] *n* sultano *m*.

**sultana** [sʌl'taːnə] *n* uva sultanina *f*.

**sultry** ['sʌltri] *adj* afoso; (*person*) eccitante.

**sum** [sʌm] *n* somma *f*, addizione *f*; (*amount*) importo *m*, totale *m*. **do sums** far calcoli. *v* **sum up** riassumere. **summing-up** *n* riassunto *m*, riepilogo *m* (*pl* -ghi *m*).

**summarize** ['sʌməraiz] *v* riassumere. **summary** *nm*, *adj* sommario.

**summer** ['sʌmə] *n* estate *f*. *adj* d'estate, estivo.

**summit** ['sʌmit] *n* cima *f*, vertice *m*.

**summon** ['sʌmən] *v* convocare; (*law*) citare, chiamare in giudizio. **summon up courage** farsi coraggio.

**summons** ['sʌmənz] *v* citare in giudizio. *n* citazione *f*. **answer a summons** presentarsi in giudizio.

**sumptuous** ['sʌmptʃuəs] *adj* sontuoso.

**sun** [sʌn] *n* sole *m*. *v* **sun oneself** prendere il sole. **sunny** *adj* soleggiato; (*cheerful*) allegro.

**sunbathe** ['sʌnbeið] *v* fare i bagni di sole. **sunbathing** *n* bagni di sole *m pl*.

**sunburn** ['sʌnbəːn] *n* (*pain*) scottatura solare *f*, eritema solare *m*; (*tan*) abbronzatura *f*. **sunburnt** *adj* scottato dal sole; abbronzato.

**Sunday** ['sʌndi] *n* domenica *f*.

**sundial** ['sʌndaiəl] *n* meridiana *f*.

**sundry** ['sʌndri] *adj* diversi, parecchi. **all and sundry** tutti quanti.

**sunflower** ['sʌnflauə] *n* girasole *m*.

**sung** [sʌŋ] *V* **sing**.

**sun-glasses** ['sʌnglaːsiz] *pl n* occhiali da sole *m pl*.

**sunk** [sʌŋk] *V* **sink**.

**sunlight** ['sʌnlait] *n* luce del sole *f*.

**sunrise** ['sʌnraiz] n alba f.

**sunroof** ['sʌnru:f] n (car) tettuccio apribile m.

**sunset** ['sʌnset] n tramonto m.

**sunshine** ['sʌnʃain] n sole m; (good weather) bel tempo m. **sunshine roof** tetto scorrevole m.

**sunstroke** ['sʌnstrouk] n colpo di sole m, insolazione f.

**sun-tan** ['sʌntan] n abbronzatura f.

**super** ['su:pə] adj (coll) magnifico.

**superannuation** [ˌsu:pərənjuˈeiʃən] n (retirement) collocamento a riposo m; (pension) vitalizio m.

**superb** [su:'pə:b] adj superbo, magnifico.

**supercilious** [ˌsu:pə'siliəs] adj altero, borioso.

**superficial** [ˌsu:pə'fiʃəl] adj superficiale.

**superfluous** [su'pə:fluəs] adj superfluo.

**superhuman** [su:pə'hju:mən] adj sovrumano.

**superimpose** [ˌsu:pərim'pouz] v sovraporre.

**superintendent** [ˌsu:pərin'tendənt] n soprintendente m; (police) commissario m.

**superior** [su:'piəriə] adj superiore. n superiore, -a m, f. **superiority** n superiorità f.

**superlative** [su:'pə:lətiv] nm, adj superlativo.

**supermarket** ['su:pə,ma:kit] n supermercato m.

**supernatural** [ˌsu:pə'natʃərəl] nm, adj soprannaturale.

**supersede** [ˌsu:pə'si:d] v rimpiazzare, sostituire.

**supersonic** [ˌsu:pə'sonik] adj supersonico.

**superstition** [su:pə'stiʃən] n superstizione f. **superstitious** adj superstizioso.

**supervise** ['su:pəvaiz] v sorvegliare, soprintendere. **supervision** n sorveglianza f, soprintendenza f. **supervisor** n soprintendente m, f, sorvegliante m, f, ispettore, -trice m, f.

**supper** ['sʌpə] n cena f. **have supper** cenare.

**supple** ['sʌpl] adj flessibile; agile. **suppleness** n flessibilità f; agilità f.

**supplement** ['sʌpləmənt] n supplemento m, aggiunta f. v completare, integrare. **supplementary** adj supplementare.

**supply** [sə'plai] n provvista f, rifornimento m; (econ) offerta f. v provvedere, fornire.

**supplier** n fornitore m.

**support** [sə'po:t] n appoggio m, sostegno m. **means of support** mezzi di sostentamento m pl. v reggere, sostenere; (keep) mantenere; (tolerate) sopportare.

**suppose** [sə'pouz] v supporre; (think) ritenere, pensare. **supposed** adj presunto. **be supposed to** dovere. **supposedly** adv per supposizione. **supposing** conj supponiamo che. **supposition** n supposizione f.

**suppository** [sə'pozitri] n supposta f.

**suppress** [sə'pres] v sopprimere; (check) soffocare; (hide) nascondere.

**supreme** [su'pri:m] adj supremo, massimo. **supremacy** n supremazia f.

**surcharge** ['sə:tʃa:dʒ] n soprattassa f.

**sure** [ʃuə] adj certo, sicuro. **make sure** assicurarsi.

**surety** ['ʃuərəti] n certezza f; garanzia f. **stand surety for** farsi garante per.

**surf** [sə:f] n frangente m, risacca f. **surfing** n surfing m invar, sport dell'acquaplano m. v (internet) navigare.

**surface** ['sə:fis] n superficie f, faccia f. adj superficiale, esterno. v venire a galla, affiorare.

**surfeit** ['sə:fit] n eccesso m.

**surge** [sə:dʒ] n ondata f, riflusso m. v fluttuare, rifluire.

**surgeon** ['sə:dʒən] n chirurgo m. **surgery** n (subject) chirurgia f; (consulting room) gabinetto medico m, infermeria f. **surgical** adj chirurgico.

**surly** ['sə:li] adj scontroso.

**surmount** [sə'maunt] v superare.

**surname** ['sə:neim] n cognome m.

**surpass** [sə'pa:s] v sorpassare, superare.

**surplus** ['sə:pləs] n eccesso m, avanzo m, residuato m.

**surprise** [sə'praiz] n sorpresa f; (astonishment) stupore m, meraviglia f. **take by surprise** (amaze) stupire; (come upon unawares) cogliere all'improvviso. adj (unexpected) inaspettato. v sorprendere; cogliere all'improvviso; stupire.

**surrealism** [sə'riəlizəm] n surrealismo m. **surrealist** n(m+f), adj surrealista.

**surrender** [sə'rendə] v cedere; (mil) arrendersi. n resa f.

**surreptitious** [ˌsʌrəp'tiʃəs] adj furtivo, clandestino.

**surround** [sə'raund] v circondare; (encircle)

accerchiare. *n* bordura *f*. **surrounding** *adj* circostante. **surroundings** *pl n* dintorni *m pl*; (*environment*) ambiente *m sing*.

**surveillance** [sə'veiləns] *n* sorveglianza *f*.

**survey** ['sə:vei; *v* sə'vei] *n* quadro generale *m*; (*official examination*) perizia *f*; rapporto *m*; valutazione *f*; (*of land*) agrimensura *f*; (*geog*) rilievo topografico *m*; (*poll*) sondaggio *m*. *v* contemplare; esaminare, fare una perizia di; prendere i rilievi di. **surveyor** *n* ispettore, -trice *m, f*; (*land*) agrimensore *m*; (*house*) geometra *m, f*; (*geog*) topografo, -a *m, f*.

**survive** [sə'vaiv] *v* sopravvivere. **survival** *n* sopravvivenza *f*. **survivor** *n* superstite *m, f*.

**susceptible** [sə'septəbl] *adj* suscettibile; predisposto. **susceptibility** *n* suscettibilità *f*; predisposizione *f*.

**suspect** [sə'spekt; *n, adj* 'sʌspekt] *v* sospettare; (*surmise*) dubitare. *n* persona sospetta *f*. *adj* sospetto.

**suspend** [sə'spend] *v* sospendere. **suspense** *n* incertezza *f*, apprensione *f*. **in suspense** in sospeso. **suspension** *n* sospensione *f*. **suspension bridge** ponte sospeso *m*.

**suspicion** [sə'spiʃən] *n* sospetto *m*, dubbio *m*. **suspicious** *adj* (*distrustful*) sospettoso, diffidente; (*questionable*) sospetto.

**sustain** [sə'stein] *v* sostenere; (*injury, etc.*) subire.

**swab** [swob] *n* tampone *m*; (*sample*) prelievo *m*.

**swagger** ['swagə] *v* (*strut*) pavoneggiarsi; (*boast*) boriarsi, grandeggiare. *n* boria *f*, andatura spavalda *f*.

**swallow**[1] ['swolou] *v* inghiottire, ingoiare; (*coll: believe*) bere; (*suppress*) reprimere. *n* gorgata *f*.

**swallow**[2] ['swolou] *n* (*bird*) rondine *f*.

**swam** [swam] *V* **swim**.

**swamp** [swomp] *n* palude *f*. *v* (*flood*) inondare, allagare; (*overwhelm*) travolgere.

**swan** [swon] *n* cigno *m*.

**swank** [swaŋk] (*coll*) *v* darsi delle arie. *n* boria *f*.

**swap** *or* **swop** [swop] *n* scambio *m*. *v* scambiare.

**swarm** [swo:m] *n* (*bees*) sciame *m*; (*crowd*) folla *f*. *v* sciamare; (*throng*) accalcarsi; (*teem*) brulicare.

**swarthy** ['swo:ði] *adj* di carnagione scura.

**swat** [swot] *v* schiacciare.

**sway** [swei] *v* oscillare, vacillare; inclinare; influenzare. *n* oscillazione *f*. **hold sway over** esercitare potere su.

**\*swear** [sweə] *v* (*declare solemnly*) giurare; (*curse*) bestemmiare. **swear by** giurare su. **swear in** far prestare giuramento, insediare. **swear-word** *n*. bestemmia *f*.

**sweat** [swet] *v* sudare. *n* sudore *m*. **sweat-shirt** *n* argentina *f*. **sweater** *n* maglione *m*.

**swede** [swi:d] *n* ravizzone *m*.

**Sweden** ['swi:dn] *n* Svezia *f*. **Swede** *n* svedese *m, f*. **Swedish** *nm, adj* svedese.

**\*sweep** [swi:p] *v* spazzare; (*view*) percorrere. **sweep aside** scartare. **sweep the board** far piazza pulita. **sweep** *n* spazzata *f*; curva *f*; (*chimney*) spazzacamino *m*. **sweeping** *adj* radicale, di lunga portata. **sweeping statement** asserzione gratuita *f*.

**sweet** [swi:t] *adj* dolce; fresco; (*smell*) profumato; (*sound*) armonioso; (*temper*) amabile, carino. *n* caramella *f*; (*dessert*) dolce *m*. **sweet-and-sour** *adj* agrodolce. **sweetbread** *n* animella *f*. **sweetheart** *n* amoroso, -a *m, f*. **sweet pea** pisello odoroso *m*. **sweeten** *v* addolcire; alleviare.

**\*swell** [swel] *v* aumentare, gonfiarsi. *n* (*sea*) ondata *f*. **swelling** *n* gonfiore *m*, tumore *m*, tumefazione *f*.

**swelter** ['sweltə] *v* soffocare *or* morire dal caldo. **sweltering** *adj* soffocante.

**swept** [swept] *V* **sweep**.

**swerve** [swə:v] *v* (*change direction abruptly*) scartare, deviare, scostarsi. *n* scarto *m*; deviazione *f*.

**swift** [swift] *adj* lesto; (*prompt*) pronto. *n* rondone *m*.

**swig** [swig] *v* tracannare. *n* sorso *m*.

**swill** [swil] *v* (*swig*) tracannare; (*rinse*) risciacquare. *n* (*rubbish*) rifiuti *m pl*; (*slops*) intruglio *m*; (*for pigs*) broda (per maiali) *f*.

**\*swim** [swim] *v* nuotare. *n* nuotata *f*. **go for a swim** andare a nuotare. **in the swim** attivo. **swimmer** *n* nuotatore, -trice *m, f*. **swimming** *n* nuoto *m*. **swimming costume** costume da bagno *m*. **swimming pool** *or* **baths** piscina *f*. **swimming trunks** calzoncini da bagno *m pl*.

**swindle** ['swindl] *v* truffare, imbrogliare. *n* truffa *f*. **swindler** *n* truffatore, -trice *m, f*, imbroglione, -a *m, f*.

**swine** [swain] *n* maiale *m*, porco (*pl* -ci) *m*.

**\*swing** [swiŋ] *v* dondolare, oscillare; (*club, etc.*) vibrare; influenzare. **swing open**

spalancarsi. **swing round** voltarsi di scatto. *n* oscillazione *f*, ritmo *m*; (*in playground*) altalena *f*. **in full swing** in piena attività. **swing-door** *n* porta a due battenti *f*.

**swipe** [swaip] (*coll*) *n* botta *f*. *v* dare una botta (a); (*steal*) fregare.

**swirl** [swə:l] *v* turbinare. *n* turbine *m*.

**swish** [swiʃ] *v* (*sound*) sibilare; (*move*) brandire; (*rustle*) frusciare. *n* (*whip*) sferza *f*; (*sound*) sibilo *m*.

**Swiss** [swis] *n*, *adj* svizzero, -a.

**switch** [switʃ] *n* (*elec*) interruttore *m*; (*whip*) sferza *f*; (*change*) svolta *f*, cambiamento *m*. **switchback** *n* montagne russe *f pl*. **switchboard** *n* tavolo di controllo *m*; (*phone*) centralino *m*. *v* spostare, scambiare. **switch off** spegnere. **switch on** accendere. **switch over** commutare.

**Switzerland** ['switsələnd] *n* Svizzera *f*.

**swivel** ['swivl] *n* perno *m*. **swivel chair** sedia girevole *f*. *v* girare, rotare.

**swollen** ['swoulən] *V* **swell**. *adj* gonfio.

**swoop** [swu:p] *n* piombare, avventarsi. *n* calata improvvisa *f*. **at one fell swoop** d'un sol colpo.

**swop** *V* **swap**.

**sword** [so:d] *n* spada *f*. **cross swords** (*fight*) battersi; (*argue*) venire alle mani. **swordfish** *n* pesce spada *m*.

**swore** [swo:] *V* **swear**.

**sworn** [swo:n] *V* **swear**.

**swot** [swot] (*coll*) *v* sgobbare. *n* secchione, -a *m*, *f*.

**swum** [swʌm] *V* **swim**.

**swung** [swʌŋ] *V* **swing**.

**sycamore** ['sikəmo:] *n* sicomoro *m*.

**syllable** ['siləbl] *n* sillaba *f*.

**syllabus** ['siləbəs] *n* programma *m*, prospetto *m*.

**symbol** ['simbl] *n* simbolo *m*. **symbolic** *adj* simbolico. **symbolism** *n* simbolismo *m*. **symbolize** *v* simboleggiare.

**symmetry** ['simitri] *n* simmetria *f*. **symmetrical** *adj* simmetrico.

**sympathy** ['simpəθi] *n* simpatia *f*, comprensione *f*; compassione *f*. **sympathetic** *adj* simpatico, simpatizzante; compassionevole. **sympathetic to** favorevole a, ben disposto verso. **sympathize** *v* simpatizzare; essere d'accordo; compatire. **sympathizer** *n* simpatizzante *m*, *f*.

**symphony** ['simfəni] *n* sinfonia *f*. **sympho-** ny orchestra orchestra sinfonica *f*. **symphonic** *adj* sinfonico.

**symposium** [sim'pouziəm] *n* simposio *m*.

**symptom** ['simptəm] *n* sintomo *m*. **symptomatic** *adj* sintomatico.

**synagogue** ['sinəgog] *n* sinagoga *f*.

**synchromesh** ['siŋkroumeʃ] *n* sincronizzatore *m*.

**synchronize** ['siŋkrənaiz] *v* sincronizzare.

**syndicate** ['sindikit] *n* sindacato *f*.

**syndrome** ['sindroum] *n* sindrome *f*.

**synod** ['sinəd] *n* sinodo *m*.

**synonym** ['sinənim] *n* sinonimo *m*. **synonymous** *adj* sinonimo.

**synopsis** [si'nopsis] *n*, *pl* **-ses** sinossi *f*; (*film, etc.*) sinopsi *f*. **synoptic** *adj* sinottico.

**syntax** ['sintaks] *n* sintassi *f*. **syntactic** *adj* sintattico.

**synthesis** ['sinθisis] *n*, *pl* **-ses** sintesi *f*. **synthesize** *v* sintetizzare. **synthetic** *adj* sintetico.

**syphilis** ['sifilis] *n* sifilide *f*.

**syringe** [si'rindʒ] *n* siringa *f*. *v* siringare; (*inject*) iniettare.

**syrup** ['sirəp] *n* sciroppo *m*; (*golden*) melassa *f*. **syrupy** *adj* sciropposo.

**system** ['sistəm] *n* sistema *m*. **systematic** *adj* sistematico.

# T

**tab** [tab] *n* cartellino *m*, etichetta *f*. **keep tabs on** tener d'occhio.

**tabby** ['tabi] *n* (gatto) soriano *or* tigrato *m*.

**table** ['teibl] *n* tavola *f*; (*with modifier*) tavolo *m*; (*multiplication*) tavola pitagorica *f*; (*synopsis*) tabella *f*. **lay/clear the table** apparecchiare/sparecchiare la tavola. **table-cloth** *n* tovaglia *f*. **table-mat** *n* sottopiatto *m*. **table-napkin** *n* tovagliolo *m*. **table-spoon** *n* cucchiaio da tavola *m*; (*spoonful*) cucchiaiata *f*. **table tennis** tennis da tavolo *m*. **turn the tables** rovesciare le posizioni. *v* intavolare.

**table d'hôte** [ta:blə'dout] *adj* a prezzo fisso.

**tablet** ['tablit] *n* tavoletta *f*; (*med*) pastiglia *f*.

**taboo** [ta'bu:] *nm, adj* tabù.

**tabulate** ['tabjuleit] *v* presentare in forma sinottica.

**tacit** ['tasit] *adj* tacito.

**tack** [tak] *n* (*pin*) puntina *f*; (*naut*) bordata *f*; (*stitch*) punto lungo *m*. **get down to brass tacks** venire ai fatti. *v* (*sewing*) imbastire; (*sailing*) bordeggiare. **tack on** aggiungere. **tacking** *n* imbastitura *f*. **tacky** *adj* appiccicaticcio, appiccicoso.

**tackle** ['takl] *n* attrezzatura *f*; (*fishing*) arnesi da pesca *m pl*; (*hoisting*) paranco *m*; (*football*) carica *f*; (*rugby*) placcaggio *m*. *v* venire alle prese con, affrontare; caricare; placcare.

**tact** [takt] *n* tatto *m*, riguardo *m*. **tactful** *adj* riguardoso, diplomatico. **tactless** *adj* mancante di riguardo, senza tatto.

**tactics** ['taktiks] *pl n* tattica *f sing*. **tactical** *adj* tattico. **tactician** *n* tattico, -a *m, f*.

**tadpole** ['tadpoul] *n* girino *m*.

**taffeta** ['tafitə] *n* taffettà *m*.

**tag** [tag] *n* (*stub*) talloncino *m*; (*label*) etichetta *f*, cartellino *m*; (*refrain*) ritornello *m*; (*saying*) locuzione *f*. *v* **tag along** seguire. **tag on** aggiungere.

**tail** [teil] *n* coda *f*. **tail-board** *n* ribalta *f*. **tail-end** *n* finalino *m*. **tail-light** *n* fanalino *m*. **tails** *pl n* (*dress*) frac *m invar*; (*coin*) croce *f sing*.

**tailor** ['teilə] *n* sarto, -a *m, f*. **tailoring** *n* mestiere del sarto *m*.

**taint** [teint] *n* tara *f*, traccia di marcio *f*. *v* (*spoil*) guastare, contaminare. **tainted** *adj* tarato.

**\*take** [teik] *v* prendere; (*carry, convey*) portare; (*require*) volerci; (*bath, walk, etc.*) fare. **take after** assomigliare a. **take back** riportare. **take care** badare, far attenzione. **take care of** curarsi di. **take down** tirar giù; (*dictation*) prender nota di. **take in** (*visitors*) dare alloggio a; (*reduce*) stringere; (*understand*) comprendere; (*deceive*) ingannare. **take off** (*remove*) togliere; (*aero*) decollare; (*mimic*) parodiare. **take-off** *n* decollo *m*; caricatura *f*. **take on** assumere; (*fight*) affrontare. **take out** tirar fuori; accompagnare. **take over** (*assume control*) rilevare. **take-over** *n* rilievo *m*. **take place** accadere, aver luogo a; (*addict*) darsi a. **take to** affezionarsi a; (*addict*) darsi a.

**taken** ['teikn] *V* **take**.

**talcum powder** ['talkəm] *n* talco in polvere *m*; borotalco *m*.

**tale** [teil] *n* storia *f*, racconto *m*; (*gossip*) diceria *f*.

**talent** ['talənt] *n* talento *m*; (*gift*) dote *f*; (*aptitude*) attitudine *f*. **talented** *adj* dotato.

**talk** [to:k] *n* discorso *m*, conversazione *f*; (*lecture*) conferenza *f*; (*chat*) chiacchierata *f*. *v* parlare; conversare; chiacchierare. **talk about** parlare di. **talk nonsense** dire sciocchezze. **talk over** discutere. **talk round** persuadere. **talk sense** dire cose sensate. **talkative** *adj* loquace.

**tall** [to:l] *adj* alto. **tallboy** *n* canterano *m*. **tall order** impresa difficile *f*. **tall story** storia inverosimile *f*, frottola *f*.

**tally** ['tali] *n* (*score*) punteggio *m*; (*account*) conto *m*; (*label*) etichetta *f*, scontrino *m*. *v* corrispondere; coincidere (con).

**talon** ['talən] *n* artiglio *m*.

**tambourine** [tambə'ri:n] *n* tamburello *m*.

**tame** [teim] *adj* docile, domestico. *v* addomesticare, domare.

**tamper** ['tampə] *v* **tamper with** alterare, falsificare; (*meddle*) ingerirsi in; (*bribe*) subornare.

**tampon** ['tampon] *n* tampone *m*.

**tan** [tan] *n* (*leather*) conciare; (*sun*) abbronzare. *v* (*colour*) castano *m*; abbronzatura *f*. *adj* castano.

**tandem** ['tandəm] *n* tandem *m invar*. **in tandem** in tandem.

**tangent** ['tandʒənt] *n* tangente *f*. **fly off at a tangent** pigliare un dirizzone.

**tangerine** [tandʒə'ri:n] *n* mandarino *m*.

**tangible** ['tandʒəbl] *adj* tangibile.

**tangle** ['taŋgl] *n* groviglio *m*, confusione *f*. *v* ingarbugliare, imbrogliare. **tangle with** (*fight*) lottare con *or* contro.

**tank** [taŋk] *n* serbatoio *m*; (*pool*) vasca *f*; (*mil*) carro armato *m*. **tanker** *n* (*ship*) nave cisterna *f*; (*lorry*) autocisterna *f*.

**tankard** ['taŋkəd] *n* boccale *m*.

**tantalize** ['tantəlaiz] *v* tormentare.

**tantamount** ['tantəmaunt] *adj* **be tantamount to** equivalere a, essere come.

**tantrum** ['tantrəm] *n* accesso d'ira *m*, bizza *f*. **have tantrums** fare le bizze.

**tap¹** [tap] *v* (*strike*) picchiare, dare un colpetto a; (*knock*) bussare. *n* colpetto *m*.

**tap²** [tap] *n* rubinetto *m*; (*on cask*) spina *f*, cannella *f*. **on tap** (*beer*) alla spina; (*ready*) a disposizione, pronto. *v* (*draw off*) spillare; (*phone*) intercettare; utilizzare.

**tape** [teip] *n* nastro *m*. **red tape** burocrazia *f*. **tape-measure** *n* metro *m*. **tape-recorder** *n* registratore a nastro *m*. *v* (*tie*) allacciare; (*record*) registrare.

**taper** ['teipə] *v* affusolare, assottigliarsi. **taper off** finire a punta. *n* cerino *m*, candela sottile *f*. **tapering** *adj* affusolato, a punta.

**tapestry** ['tapəstri] *n* arazzo *m*, tappezzeria *f*.

**tapioca** [tapi'oukə] *n* tapioca *f*.

**tar** [ta:] *n* catrame *m*. *v* incatramare.

**tarantula** [tə'rantjulə] *n* tarantola *f*.

**target** ['ta:git] *n* bersaglio *m*, obiettivo *m*.

**tariff** ['tarif] *n* tariffa *f*.

**tarmac** ['ta:mak] *n* macadam al catrame; (*runway*) pista *f*.

**tarnish** ['ta:niʃ] *v* annerire, offuscare; (*stain*) macchiare. *n* annerimento *m*; macchia *f*.

**tarpaulin** [ta:'po:lin] *n* copertone *m*.

**tarragon** ['tarəgən] *n* dragoncello *m*.

**tart**[1] [ta:t] *adj* aspro, agro. **tartness** *n* asprezza *f*.

**tart**[2] [ta:t] *n* torta *f*, crostata *f*; (*slang*) puttana *f*.

**tartan** ['ta:tən] *n* tartan *m invar*, tessuto scozzese *m*.

**tartar** ['ta:tə] *n* tartaro *m*. **cream of tartar** cremor di tartaro *m*.

**task** [ta:sk] *n* compito *m*, dovere *m*. **take to task** rimproverare.

**tassel** ['tasəl] *n* nappa *f*, nappina *f*.

**taste** [teist] *n* gusto *m*, sapore *m*; (*liking*) amore *m*, apprezzamento *m*; (*small sample*) assaggio *m*. *v* assaggiare, gustare. **taste of** sapere di. **tasteful** *adj* squisito, di buon gusto. **tasteless** *adj* insipido; di cattivo gusto. **tasty** *adj* saporito, appetitoso.

**tattered** ['tatəd] *adj* stracciato, a brandelli.

**tattoo**[1] [tə'tu:] *n* tatuaggio *m*. *v* tatuare.

**tattoo**[2] [tə'tu:] *n* (*mil*) ritirata *f*.

**taught** [to:t] *V* **teach**.

**taunt** [to:nt] *v* rinfacciare, schernire. *n* derisione *f*, scherno *m*.

**Taurus** ['to:rəs] *n* Toro *m*.

**taut** [to:t] *adj* teso.

**tavern** ['tavən] *n* osteria *f*, trattoria *f*, taverna *f*.

**tawdry** ['to:dri] *adj* vistoso, volgare.

**tax** [taks] *n* tassa *f*, imposta *f*. **tax collector** esattore fiscale *m*. **tax disc** tagliando auto-

mobilistico *m*. **tax evasion** evasione fiscale *f*. **taxpayer** *n* contribuente *m*, *f*. *v* tassare, imporre una tassa su; (*make demands*) mettere alla prova. **taxation** *n* tassazione *f*, tasse *f pl*.

**taxi** ['taksi] *n* tassì *m*. **taxi-driver** *n* tassista *m*, *f*. **taxi rank** posteggio (per tassi) *m*. *v* (*aero*) rullare.

**tea** [ti:] *n* tè *m*. **teacup** *n* tazza da tè *f*. **teapot** *n* teiera *f*. **teaspoon** *n* cucchiaino *m*. **tea-towel** *n* canovaccio *m*.

**\*teach** [ti:tʃ] *v* insegnare. **teacher** *n* insegnante *m*, *f*; (*primary school*) maestro, -a *m*, *f*; (*secondary school, university*) professore, -essa *m*, *f*. **teaching** *n* insegnamento *m*. **teachings** *pl n* dottrina *f sing*, precetti *m pl*.

**teak** [ti:k] *n* tek *m*.

**team** [ti:m] *n* squadra *f*; (*animals*) tiro *m*. **teamwork** *n* affiatamento *m*. **v team up with** mettersi insieme a, collaborare con.

**\*tear**[1] [teə] *n* strappo *m*. *v* strappare. **be torn between** dibattersi tra. **tear off** strappar via; (*run*) scappar via. **tear up** stracciare. **tearing** *adj* impetuoso, terribile.

**tear**[2] [tiə] *n* lacrima *f*. **burst into tears** scoppiare in lacrime. **in tears** sciolto in lacrime. **tear-gas** *n* gas lacrimogeno *m*. **tearful** *adj* lacrimoso.

**tease** [ti:z] *v* stuzzicare, canzonare; irritare.

**teat** [ti:t] *n* (*nipple*) capezzolo *m*; (*rubber*) tettarella *f*.

**technical** ['teknikəl] *adj* tecnico. **technicality** *n* tecnicismo *m*. **technician** *n* tecnico, -a *m*, *f*. **technique** *n* tecnica *f*. **technological** *adj* tecnologico. **technologist** *n* tecnologo, -a *m*, *f*. **technology** *n* tecnologia *f*.

**teddy bear** ['tedi,beə] *n* orsacchiotto *m*.

**tedious** ['ti:diəs] *adj* noioso. **tedium** *n* noia *f*.

**tee** [ti:] *n* tee *m invar*. *v* **tee off** cominciare (dal tee). **tee up** preparare, collocare sul tee.

**teem** [ti:m] *v* (*rain*) grondare. **teem with** formicolare *or* brulicare di.

**teenage** ['ti:neidʒ] *adj* adolescente. **teenager** *n* adolescente *m*, *f*.

**teeth** [ti:θ] *V* **tooth**.

**teethe** [ti:ð] *v* mettere i denti. **teething** *n* dentizione *f*. **teething-ring** *n* dentaruolo *m*. **teething troubles** difficoltà iniziali *f pl*.

**teetotal** [ti:'toutl] *adj* astemio. **teetotaller** *n* astemio, -a *m*, *f*.

**telecommunications** [ˌtelikəmjuːni-ˈkeiʃənz] *pl n* telecomunicazioni *f pl*.

**telegram** [ˈteligram] *n* telegramma *m*.

**telegraph** [ˈteligrɑːf] *n* telegrafo *m*. *v* telegrafare. **telegraphic** *adj* telegrafico.

**telepathy** [təˈlepəθi] *n* telepatia *f*. **telepathic** *adj* telepatico.

**telephone** [ˈtelifoun] *n* telefono *m*. *v* telefonare. **telephone box** cabina telefonica *f*. **telephone call** telefonata *f*, colpo di telefono *m*. **telephone exchange** centralino *m*. **telephone operator** telefonista *m, f*.

**teleprinter** [ˈteliprintə] *n* telescrivente *m*.

**telesales** [ˈteliseilz] *npl* televendita *f*.

**telescope** [ˈteliskoup] *n* telescopio *m*. *v* incastrare, far scorrere l'uno nell'altro; (*shorten*) condensare. **telescopic** *adj* telescopico.

**television** [ˈteliviʒən] *n* televisione *f*. **television screen** video *m*. **television set** televisore *m*. **televise** *v* teletrasmettere, trasmettere per televisione.

**telex** [ˈteleks] *n* telex *m*. *v* trasmettere per telex.

***tell** [tel] *v* dire, raccontare; distinguere. **tell off** (*scold*) sgridare. **telling-off** *n* ramanzina *f*, sgridata *f*. **telling** *adj* efficace, indicativo.

**temper** [ˈtempə] *n* (*mood*) umore *m*, disposizione *f*; (*metal*) tempra *f*. **keep one's temper** contenersi, rimaner calmo. **lose one's temper** arrabbiarsi, andare in collera. *v* moderare, temperare; (*metal*) temprare.

**temperament** [ˈtempərəmənt] *n* temperamento *m*, indole *f*. **temperamental** *adj* capriccioso.

**temperate** [ˈtempərət] *adj* temperato.

**temperature** [ˈtemprətʃə] *n* temperatura *f*. **have a temperature** (*med*) avere la febbre.

**tempestuous** [temˈpestjuəs] *adj* tempestoso, burrascoso.

**temple¹** [ˈtempl] *n* (*rel*) tempio *m*.

**temple²** [ˈtempl] *n* (*anat*) tempia *f*.

**tempo** [ˈtempou] *n* tempo *m*; ritmo *m*, andamento *m*.

**temporary** [ˈtempərəri] *adj* temporaneo.

**tempt** [tempt] *v* tentare. **temptation** *n* tentazione *f*. **tempter** *n* tentatore *m*. **tempting** *adj* allettante, seducente; (*food*) appetitoso. **temptress** *n* tentatrice *f*.

**ten** [ten] *nm, adj* dieci. **tenth** *nm, adj* decimo.

**tenable** [ˈtenəbl] *adj* sostenibile, tenibile.

**tenacious** [təˈneiʃəs] *adj* tenace, ostinato; (*persistent*) accanito. **tenacity** *n* tenacia *f*, ostinazione *f*; accanimento *m*.

**tenant** [ˈtenənt] *n* inquilino, -a *m, f*. **tenancy** *n* affitto *m*.

**tend¹** [tend] *v* (*be inclined*) tendere. **tendency** *n* tendenza *f*, inclinazione *f*. **tendentious** *adj* tendenzioso.

**tend²** [tend] *v* (*care for*) curare, assistere, soccorrere.

**tender¹** [ˈtendə] *adj* tenero, delicato; (*affectionate*) affettuoso; (*sensitive*) sensibile. **tenderness** *n* tenerezza *f*; affettuosità *f*.

**tender²** [ˈtendə] *n* offerta *f*; (*comm*) preventivo *m*, appalto *m*. *v* offrire; appaltare, preventivare. **tender one's resignation** dare *or* rassegnare le dimissioni.

**tendon** [ˈtendən] *n* tendine *m*.

**tendril** [ˈtendril] *n* viticcio *m*.

**tenement** [ˈtenəmənt] *n* casamento *m*, casa popolare *f*.

**tennis** [ˈtenis] *n* tennis *m*. **tennisball/racket** *n* palla/racchetta da tennis *f*. **tennis-court** *n* campo da tennis *m*. **tennis player** giocatore, -trice di tennis *m, f*.

**tenor** [ˈtenə] *n* tenore *m*.

**tense¹** [tens] *adj* teso, rigido. **tension** *n* tensione *f*; (*mech*) trazione *f*.

**tense²** [tens] *n* tempo *m*.

**tent** [tent] *n* tenda *f*.

**tentacle** [ˈtentəkl] *n* tentacolo *m*.

**tentative** [ˈtentətiv] *adj* di prova, sperimentale; (*hesitant*) titubante.

**tenterhooks** [ˈtentəhuks] *pl n* **on tenterhooks** sulle spine.

**tenuous** [ˈtenjuəs] *adj* tenue.

**tenure** [ˈtenjə] *n* tenuta *f*, possesso *m*, esercizio *m*.

**tepid** [ˈtepid] *adj* tiepido.

**term** [təːm] *n* termine *m*; durata *f*; (*school*) trimestre *m*. **come to terms with** venire a patti con. **terms** *pl n* tariffa *f sing*; condizioni *f pl*; (*footing*) relazioni *f pl*.

**terminal** [ˈtəːminəl] *n* (*elec*) terminale *m*; (*aero*) terminal *m invar*. *adj* finale, estremo.

**terminate** [ˈtəːmineit] *v* terminare, porre termine a. **termination** *n* (*act*) terminazione *f*; (*end*) termine *m*, conclusione *f*.

**terminology** [ˌtəːmiˈnolədʒi] *n* terminologia *f*.

**terminus** ['tə:minəs] *n* stazione di testa *f*, capolinea (*pl* capilinea) *m*.

**terrace** ['terəs] *n* terrazzo *m*; (*row of houses*) fila di case *f*.

**terrain** [tə'rein] *n* terreno *m*.

**terrestrial** [tə'restriəl] *adj* terrestre.

**terrible** ['terəbl] *adj* terribile, spaventoso.

**terrier** ['teriə] *n* terrier *m invar*.

**terrific** [tə'rifik] *adj* (*coll*) tremendo, fantastico.

**terrify** ['terifai] *v* atterrire. **be terrified** avere una paura matta. **terrifying** *adj* spaventoso.

**territory** ['teritəri] *n* territorio *m*. **territorial** *adj* territoriale.

**terror** ['terə] *n* terrore *m*. **terror-stricken** *adj* terrorizzato, atterrito. **terrorism** *n* terrorismo *m*. **terrorist** *n* terrorista *m*, *f*. **terrorize** *v* terrorizzare.

**test** [test] *n* prova *f*; esame *m*; analisi *f*; (*psych*) test *m invar*; (*industry*) collaudo *m*. **test-tube** *n* provetta *f*. *v* provare; esaminare; analizzare; collaudare.

**testament** ['testəmənt] *n* testamento *m*.

**testicle** ['testikl] *n* testicolo *m*.

**testify** ['testifai] *v* testimoniare, attestare.

**testimonial** [testi'mouniəl] *n* benservito *m*, attestato di buona condotta *m*.

**testimony** ['testiməni] *n* testimonianza *f*, deposizione *f*; (*proof*) prova *f*.

**tetanus** ['tetənəs] *n* tetano *m*.

**tether** ['teðə] *n* impastoiare. *n* pastoia *f*. **be at the end of one's tether** non poterne più, essere agli sgoccioli.

**text** [tekst] *n* testo *m*. **textbook** *n* libro di testo *m*. **textual** *adj* testuale. *v* mandare un (messaggio) sms.

**textile** ['tekstail] *nm*, *adj* tessile.

**texture** ['tekstijuə] *n* struttura *f*; (*surface*) grana *f*.

**Thames** [temz] *n* Tamigi *m*.

**than** [ðən] *conj* di, che.

**thank** [θaŋk] *v* ringraziare. **thank you** grazie. **thanks** *pl n* grazie *f pl*. **thanks to** grazie a. **thankful** *adj* riconoscente, grato.

**that** [ðat] *adj*, *pron* quel(lo), quella. **that is** cioè. **that's all!** ecco tutto! *adv* talmente. *conj* che.

**thatch** [θatʃ] *n* (copertura di) paglia *f*. *v* coprire di paglia.

**thaw** [θɔ:] *n* disgelo *m*. *v* disgelare.

**the** [ðə] *art* il *or* lo, la; (*pl*) i *or* gli, le.

**theatre** ['θiətə] *n* teatro *m*; (*hospital*) sala operatoria *f*. **theatrical** *adj* teatrale.

**theft** [θeft] *n* furto *m*.

**their** [ðeə] *adj* (il) loro, (la) loro; (*pl*) (i) loro, (le) loro.

**theirs** [ðeəz] *pron* il loro, la loro; (*pl*) i loro, le loro.

**them** [ðem] *pron* (*before verb*) li, le; (*after verb or prep*) loro. **both of them** tutti e due. **none of them** nessuno di loro.

**theme** [θi:m] *n* tema *m*. **theme park** parco di divertimenti (tematico) *m*. **theme song** sigla (musicale) *f*. **thematic** *adj* tematico.

**themselves** [ðəm'selvz] *pron* loro stessi, -e; (*reflexive*) si; (*after prep*) sè stessi, -e.

**then** [ðen] *adv* (*at that time*) allora; (*next in time*) poi, dopo. **by then** a quel punto. **now and then** di tanto in tanto. *conj* dunque, allora. *adj* di allora.

**theology** [θi'olədʒi] *n* teologia *f*. **theologian** *n* teologo *m*. **theological** *adj* teologico.

**theorem** ['θiərəm] *n* teorema *m*.

**theory** ['θiəri] *n* teoria *f*. **theoretical** *adj* teorico.

**therapy** ['θerəpi] *n* terapia *f*. **therapeutic** *adj* terapeutico. **therapist** *n* terapista *m*, *f*.

**there** [ðeə] *adv* lì, là; (*to that place*) ci, vi. **thereabouts** *adv* da quelle parti, all'incirca. **thereafter** *adv* quindi, in seguito. **there are** ci sono. **thereby** *adv* così, in tal modo. **therefore** *adv* dunque, perciò, quindi. **there is** c'è; (*calling attention*) ecco. **there it is!** eccolo! **thereupon** *adv* quindi, subito dopo.

**thermal** ['θə:məl] *adj* termico; (*waters*) termale.

**thermodynamics** [θə:moudai'namiks] *n* termodinamica *f*.

**thermometer** [θə'momitə] *n* termometro *m*.

**thermonuclear** [θə:mou'njukliə] *adj* termonucleare.

**thermos** ® ['θə:məs] *n* thermos ® *m invar*.

**thermostat** ['θə:məstat] *n* termostato *m*.

**thesaurus** [θə'sɔ:rəs] *n* repertorio lessicale *m*.

**these** [ði:z] *pron*, *adj* questi, -e.

**thesis** ['θi:sis] *n*, *pl* **-ses** tesi *f*.

**they** [ðei] *pron* essi, -e, loro.

**thick** [θik] adj spesso; (hair) folto; (fog) fitto; stupido. **thick as thieves** amici per la pelle. **thickset** adj (heavily built) tarchiato; (dense) folto, fitto. **thick-skinned** adj insensibile. **through thick and thin** nella buona e nella cattiva sorte. **thicken** v addensare, ispessire, infittire. **thickness** n spessore m; (layer) strato m.

**thief** [θi:f] n ladro, -a m, f. **thieve** v rubare. **thieving** n ruberia f, il rubare m.

**thigh** [θai] n coscia f.

**thimble** ['θimbl] n ditale m.

**thin** [θin] adj sottile, fine; (lean) magro; (not dense) rado, sparso; (weak) debole. v diradare; (lose weight) dimagrire; (dilute) allungare. **thinner** n diluente m.

**thing** [θiŋ] n cosa f, oggetto m. **for one thing ... for another ...** anzitutto ... e poi .... **things** pl n (implements, possessions etc.) roba f sing, cose f pl.

*****think** [θiŋk] v pensare; (believe) credere, ritenere; (imagine) figurarsi. **thinker** n pensatore, -trice m, f.

**thinking** ['θiŋkiŋ] adj pensante, ragionevole. n pensiero m, il ragionare m. **to my way of thinking** a mio avviso.

**third** [θə:d] nm, adj terzo. **third party** terzi m pl.

**thirst** [θə:st] n sete f. v aver sete. **thirst for** or **after** bramare. **thirsty** adj assetato. **be thirsty** aver sete.

**thirteen** [θə:'ti:n] nm, adj tredici. **thirteenth** nm, adj tredicesimo.

**thirty** [θə:ti] nm, adj trenta. **thirtieth** nm, adj trentesimo.

**this** [ðis] pron, adj questo, -a.

**thistle** ['θisl] n cardo m.

**thong** n (underwear) perizoma m.

**thorn** [θɔ:n] n spina f; (shrub) spino m. **thorny** adj spinoso.

**thorough** ['θʌrə] adj accurato; profondo; radicale; diligente. **thoroughly** adv a fondo.

**thoroughbred** ['θʌrəbred] n purosangue m. adj di razzo, di puro sangue.

**thoroughfare** ['θʌrəfeə] n via f, passaggio m.

**those** [ðouz] pron, adj quei or quegli, quelle.

**though** [ðou] conj (in spite of ) sebbene, benchè; (yet, still) tuttavia, pure. **as though** come se. **even though** anche se. **it looks as though** sembra che.

**thought** [θɔ:t] V think. n pensiero m; idea f. **on second thoughts** ripensandoci (su). **thoughtful** adj (reflective) pensoso; (thought out) profondo; (considerate) premuroso, sollecito; (careful) attento, prudente. **thoughtless** adj (careless) imprudente; (heedless) sbadato; (unthinking) avventato; (inconsiderate) irrispettoso.

**thousand** ['θauzənd] adj mille. n mille m invar, migliaio (pl -a) m. **thousandth** nm, adj millesimo.

**thrash** [θraʃ] v battere, bastonare. **thrash out** discutere a fondo. **thrashing** n (defeat) batosta f; (beating) botte f pl.

**thread** [θred] n filo m; (screw) filetto m, passo m. v infilare; filettare. **threadbare** adj logoro.

**threat** [θret] n minaccia f. **threaten** v minacciare. **threatening** adj minaccioso; (letter) minatorio.

**three** [θri:] nm, adj tre. **three-cornered** adj triangolare, a tre punte. **three-dimensional** adj tridimensionale. **three-ply** adj (wood) a tre strati; (wool) a tre capi. **three-quarter** adj a tre quarti. **three-speed** adj a tre marce.

**thresh** [θreʃ] v (corn, etc.) trebbiare; battere. **threshing** n trebbiatura f.

**threshold** ['θreʃould] n soglia f.

**threw** [θru:] V throw.

**thrift** [θrift] n frugalità f, economia f. **thrifty** adj frugale, parsimonioso. **be thrifty** fare economia.

**thrill** [θril] n brivido m, fremito m; (excitement) emozione f. v far rabbrividire; emozionare; entusiasmare. **be thrilled with** (book, film) essere entusiasta di. **thriller** n (book, film) giallo m. **thrilling** adj emozionante, eccitante.

**thrive** [θraiv] v fiorire, riuscire. **thrive on** approfittare di. **thriving** adj prospero, fiorente.

**throat** [θrout] n gola f. **have a sore throat** aver mal di gola. **throaty** adj gutturale.

**throb** [θrob] v battere, palpitare. n battito m, palpito m. **throbbing** adj palpitante, pulsante.

**throes** [θrouz] pl n **in the throes of** alle prese con.

**thrombosis** [θrom'bousis] n trombosi f.

**throne** [θroun] n trono m.

**throng** [θroŋ] n folla f, calca f. v affollarsi, stiparsi.

**throttle** ['θrɒtl] v strozzare; (*suppress*) soffocare; (*mot*) regolare. n (*valve*) valvola a farfalla f.

**through** [θru:] adj diretto, di transito; finito. adv da una parte all'altra; (*to the end*) fino alla fine. prep da, per; (*place*) attraverso; (*time*) durante; (*by means of*) tramite, per mezzo di; (*past*) al di là di. **get through** (*phone*) ottenere la comunicazione; (*finish*) sbrigare. **throughout** adv completamente; (*time*) durante; (*always*) sempre.

*****throw** [θrou] n lancio m, tiro m. v lanciare, gettare; (*coll: confuse*) lasciare perplesso, sconcertare. **throw away** buttar via. **throwaway** adj (*casual*) spigliato; (*remark*) lasciato cadere; (*to be discarded*) da buttar via. **throw in** buttar dentro; (*sport*) rimettere in gioco; (*include*) comprendere. **throw out** buttar fuori, mettere alla porta; (*put forward*) dare. **throw up** lanciare in aria; (*be sick*) rigettare.

**thrown** [θroun] V throw.

**thrush**[1] [θrʌʃ] n (*bird*) tordo m.

**thrush**[2] [θrʌʃ] n (*med*) mughetto m.

*****thrust** [θrʌst] n spinta f, botta f; (*mil*) attacco m. v spingere, ficcare, lanciarsi. **thrust oneself on** imporsi a.

**thud** [θʌd] n tonfo m.

**thug** [θʌg] n delinquente m.

**thumb** [θʌm] n pollice m. **thumbmark** n impronta digitale f. v **thumb a lift** fare l'autostop.

**thump** [θʌmp] n tonfo m. v picchiare, battere.

**thunder** ['θʌndə] n tuono m. **thunderbolt** n fulmine m. **thunderstorm** n temporale m. **thunderstruck** adj sbalordito. v tuonare. **thundering** adj (*coll*) enorme. **thundery** adj temporalesco; (*menacing*) minaccioso.

**Thursday** ['θə:zdi] n giovedì m.

**thus** [ðʌs] adv così.

**thwart** [θwɔ:t] v frustrare.

**thyme** [taim] n timo m.

**thyroid** ['θairoid] n tiroide f.

**tiara** [ti'a:rə] n diadema m.

**tick**[1] [tik] n (*sound*) tictac m invar, ticchettio m; (*mark*) contrassegno m, visto m; (*moment*) attimo m. v ticchettare, fare tic-tac; contrassegnare, vistare. **tick off** (*coll: scold*) sgridare. **ticking-off** n (*coll*) lavata di capo f. **tick over** (*engine*) girare in folle.

**tick**[2] [tik] n (*insect*) zecca f, acaro m.

**ticket** ['tikit] n biglietto m; (*label, counterfoil*) scontrino m. **ticket collector** bigliettario, -a m, f. **ticket office** biglietteria f.

**tickle** ['tikl] v solleticare; (*make itch*) fare il solletico; (*gratify*) lusingare; (*amuse*) divertire. n irritazione f; (*itch*) prurito m. **ticklish** adj (*person*) che sente il solletico; (*tricky*) delicato, scabroso.

**tide** [taid] n marea f; corrente f. **tidemark** n battigia f. v **tide over** superare.

**tidy** ['taidi] adj ordinato; (*neat*) ben curato or tenuto; (*coll: considerable*) bello. v mettere in ordine. **tidy up** far pulizia. **tidiness** n ordine m.

**tie** [tai] v legare; (*join*) attaccare; (*lace up*) allacciare; (*sport*) pareggiare. **tie down** (*property, capital etc.*) vincolare. n legame m; (*neck*) cravatta f; (*bond*) vincolo m; pareggio m; (*music*) legatura f.

**tier** [tiə] n (*row*) fila f; (*rank*) gradino m; (*layer*) strato m.

**tiger** ['taigə] n tigre f.

**tight** [tait] adj stretto; (*fitting closely*) aderente; (*taut*) teso; (*coll: drunk*) brillo; (*coll: mean*) tirchio. **in a tight corner** con le spalle al muro. adv **hold tight** stringere, tenersi fermo. **sit tight** non muoversi. **tighten** v stringere, serrare. **tights** pl n collant m invar.

**tile** [tail] n (*roof*) tegola f; (*floor, wall*) piastrella f, mattonella f. v coprire con tegole or piastrelle.

**till**[1] [til] V until.

**till**[2] [til] n cassa f.

**till**[3] [til] v coltivare; (*plough*) arare.

**tiller** ['tilə] n (*rudder*) barra del timone f.

**tilt** [tilt] v inclinare. n inclinazione f. **at full tilt** di gran carriera, a tutta velocità.

**timber** ['timbə] n legname m; (*beam*) trave f. **timbered** adj costruito in legno, coperto di legno; (*wooded*) alberato.

**time** [taim] n tempo m, periodo m; (*occasion*) volta f; (*clock*) ora f; epoca f. **for a long time** (*past*) da molto tempo; (*future*) per molto tempo. **for the time being** per ora. **from time to time** ogni tanto, di quando in quando. **have a good time** divertirsi. **in time** a tempo; (*eventually*) alla fine. **one at a time** uno alla volta. **on time** in orario. **take one's time** fare con

comodo. **time bomb** bomba a orologeria f.
**timekeeper** n (sport) cronometrista m;
(overseer) controllore m. **time share** n multiproprietà d'immobili. **timesignal** segnale
orario m.
**timetable** n orario m. v misurare il tempo;
(sport) cronometrare; (choose moment)
scegliere il momento. **timeless** adj eterno,
permanente. **timely** adj opportuno, tempestivo.
**timid** ['timid] adj timido. **timidity** n
timidezza f.
**tin** [tin] n (metal) stagno m; (can) latta f,
scatola f. **tin-opener** n apriscatole m invar.
v inscatolare; stagnare. **tinny** adj (sound)
metallico.
**tinge** [tindʒ] n sfumatura f, tocco m. v
**tinged with** misto a.
**tingle** ['tiŋgl] v formicolare. n formicolio m,
prurito m.
**tinker** ['tiŋkə] v (repair) rabberciare, rattoppare; (busy oneself) affaccendarsi.
**tinkle** ['tiŋkl] v (far) tintinnare, squillare. n
tintinnio m, squillo m.
**tinsel** ['tinsəl] n orpello m.
**tint** [tint] n tinta f, tinta f. v colorire.
**tiny** ['taini] adj piccino, minuto.
**tip**[1] [tip] n (end) punta f, estremità f; (summit) cima f. **tiptoe** v camminare in punta
di piedi. **on tiptoe** in punta di piedi.
**tip**[2] [tip] v (topple) rovesciare; (dump) scaricare. n luogo di scarico m.
**tip**[3] [tip] n (money) mancia f; (hint) consiglio m; informazione riservata f. v dare la
mancia. **tip off** avvertire, prevenire.
**tipsy** ['tipsi] adj (coll) brillo. **get tipsy** ubriacarsi leggermente.
**tire**[1] ['taiə] v stancarsi, stancare; (get fed up)
stufarsi. **tired** adj stanco; (fed up) stufo.
**tireless** adj infaticabile; (unceasing) indefesso. **tiresome** adj noioso, seccante. **tiring**
adj faticoso.
**tire**[2] (US) V **tyre**.
**tissue** ['tiʃuː] n tessuto m; (handkerchief)
fazzoletto di carta m. **tissue paper** carta
velina f.
**tit** [tit] n (bird) cincia f.
**title** ['taitl] n titolo m; (law) diritto m. **title-page** n frontespizio m. **title-role** n parte
principale f. v intitolare.
**to** [tu] prep a, in; (in order to) per; (towards)
verso; da. adv **to and fro** avanti e indietro.

**to-do** n (coll) trambusto m.
**toad** [toud] n rospo m. **toadstool** n fungo
m.
**toast** [toust] n (bread) toast m invar; (speech,
drink) brindisi m. **drink a toast to** bere
alla salute di. v tostare. **toaster** n tostapane
m invar.
**tobacco** [təˈbakou] n tobacco m. **tobacconist** n tabaccaio, -a m, f.
**toboggan** [təˈbogən] n toboga m invar. v
andare in toboga.
**today** [təˈdei] adv oggi; (nowadays) oggigiorno. **a week/fortnight today** oggi a
otto/quindici. n oggi m.
**toddler** ['todlə] n bambino, -a m, f, piccino,
-a m, f. **toddle** v sgambettare.
**toe** [tou] n dito del piede m; (shoe) punta f.
**tread on someone's toes** pestare i piedi a
qualcuno.
**toffee** ['tofi] n caramella mou f.
**together** [təˈgeðə] adv insieme, assieme.
**together with** insieme con, assieme a.
**toil** [toil] n fatica f. v faticare.
**toilet** ['toilit] n (lavatory) gabinetto m;
(dressing, etc.) toilette (pl -s) f, toletta f. **toilet paper** carta igienica f. **toilet water**
acqua di toletta f. **toiletries** npl prodotti
per toletta m pl.
**token** ['toukən] n segno m, simbolo m; (gift)
omaggio m; (coin) gettone m.
**Tokyo** ['toukiou] n Tokio f.
**told** [tould] V **tell**.
**tolerate** ['toləreit] v tollerare, sopportare.
**tolerable** adj tollerabile. **tolerance** n
tolleranza f. **tolerant** adj tollerante.
**toll**[1] [toul] n pedaggio m; (duty) dazio m.
**toll**[2] [toul] n (bell) rintocco m. v rintoccare.
**tomato** [təˈmaːtou] n pomodoro m. **tomato juice/paste** succo/estratto di pomodoro
m. **tomato sauce** salsa di pomodoro f.
**tomb** [tuːm] n tomba f. **tombstone** n
pietra tombale f.
**tomorrow** [təˈmorou] nm, adv domani.
**the day after tomorrow** dopodomani.
**tomorrow morning** domattina. **tomorrow week** domani a otto.
**ton** [tʌn] n tonnellata f. **tonnage** n tonnellaggio m.
**tone** [toun] n tono m. v armonizzare. **tone down** attenuare, smorzare. **tonality** n
tonalità f.
**tongs** [toŋz] pl n pinza f sing; (fire)

molle *f pl.*

**tongue** [tʌŋ] *n* lingua *f.* **hold one's tongue** star zitto, tacere. **tongue-tied** *adj* ammutolito; (*speech defect*) scilinguato.

**tonic** ['tonik] *n* ricostituente *m;* (*water*) acqua brillante *f;* (*music*) tonica *f. adj* tonico.

**tonight** [tə'nait] *adj* (*evening*) stasera; (*night*) stanotte.

**tonsil** ['tonsil] *n* tonsilla *f.* **tonsillitis** *n* tonsillite *f.*

**too** [tu:] *adv* (*also*) anche, pure; (*moreover*) inoltre; (*more than enough*) troppo. **too many** troppi. **too much** troppo.

**took** [tuk] *V* **take**.

**tool** [tu:l] *n* attrezzo *m,* arnese *m;* strumento *m.* **tool-shed** *n* ripostiglio per attrezzi *m.* **tools of the trade** ferri del mestiere *m pl. v* lavorare.

**tooth** [tu:θ] *n, pl* **teeth** dente *m.* **have a sweet tooth** essere ghiotto di dolci. **have a tooth out** farsi cavare un dente. **in the teeth of** (*in defiance of*) a dispetto di; (*in the presence of*) in cospetto di. **toothache** *n* mal di denti *m.* **tooth-brush** *n* spazzolino da denti *m.* **toothpaste** *n* dentifricio *m.* **toothpick** *n* stuzzicadenti *m.* **toothless** *adj* sdentato.

**top¹** [top] *n* (*highest point*) cima *f,* vertice *m;* (*leading position*) testa *f,* capo *m;* (*lid*) coperchio *m.* **at the top of one's voice** a voce altissima; (*shouting*) a squarciagola. **from top to toe** da capo a piedi. **on top of** (*upon*) sopra, su; (*at the head of*) in testa a; (*following*) dopo, in seguito a. *adj* (*uppermost*) superiore, ultimo; (*greatest*) più alto; (*foremost*) principale. **at top speed** a velocità massima. **top-heavy** *adj* sovraccarico (*m pl* -chi); (*unbalanced*) sbilanciato. **topsoil** *n* terriccio *m. v* sorpassare, superare; (*be above*) sovrastare a; (*prune*) scapezzare. **top up** *v* riempire. **topless** *adj* (*dress*) a petto scoperto. **topmost** *adj* il più alto.

**top²** [top] *n* (*toy*) trottola *f.*

**topaz** ['toupaz] *n* topazio *m.*

**topic** ['topik] *n* argomento *m.* **topical** *adj* di attualità.

**topography** [tə'pogrəfi] *n* topografia *f.*

**topple** ['topl] *v* (*far*) cadere o crollare.

**topsy-turvy** [topsi'tə:vi] *adv* sottosopra.

**torch** [to:tʃ] *n* fiaccola *f;* (*electric*) lampadina tascabile *f,* torcia elettrica *f.*

**tore** [to:] *V* **tear¹**.

**torment** ['to:ment; *v* to:'ment] *n* supplizio *m,* tortura *f. v* tormentare, angosciare.

**torn** [to:n] *V* **tear¹**.

**tornado** [to:'neidou] *n* tornado *m,* turbine *m.*

**torpedo** [to:'pi:dou] *n* siluro *m,* torpedine *f. v* silurare. **torpedo-boat** *n* torpediniera *f.*

**torrent** ['torənt] *n* torrente *m.* **torrential** *adj* torrenziale.

**torso** ['to:sou] *n* torso *m.*

**tortoise** ['to:təs] *n* tartaruga *f.* **tortoise-shell** *nf, adj* tartaruga.

**tortuous** ['to:tʃuəs] *adj* tortuoso.

**torture** ['to:tʃə] *n* tortura *f. v* torturare.

**Tory** ['to:ri] *n, adj* (*coll*) conservatore, -trice.

**toss** [tos] *v* (*throw*) lanciare; (*pitch*) sballottare; (*move restlessly*) agitarsi. **toss aside** buttar via. **toss back** rilanciare. **toss up** (*coin*) far testa o croce; tirare a sorte. **toss-up** *n* questione di fortuna *f. n* **toss of the head** scrollata del capo *f.*

**tot¹** [tot] *n* (*child*) bimbo, -a *m, f,* piccino, -a *m, f;* (*drink*) bicchierino *m.*

**tot²** [tot] *v* **tot up** sommare, fare la somma di.

**total** ['toutəl] *n* totale *m,* ammontare *m. adj* totale, globale. *v* (*add up*) fare la somma di; (*add up to*) ammontare a.

**totter** ['totə] *v* barcollare, vacillare. **tottering** *adj* barcollante; (*shaky*) malsicuro.

**touch** [tʌtʃ] *n* (*sense*) tatto *m;* contatto *m;* (*music, painting*) tocco *m;* (*hint*) accenno *m;* (*med*) attacco leggero *m.* **touchstone** *n* pietra di paragone *f,* criterio *m. v* toccare; (*lightly*) sfiorare; (*handle*) maneggiare, tastare; (*move*) commuovere. **touch-and-go** *adj* rischioso. **touch down** (*plane*) atterrare. **touch up** ritoccare, ripassare. **touch wood!** tocca ferro! **touched** *adj* commosso. **touching** *adj* commovente; adiacente. **touchy** *adj* permaloso.

**tough** [tʌf] *adj* (*hard*) duro; (*hardy*) tenace; robusto; resistente; difficile. *n* teppista *m.* **toughen** *v* indurire, rinforzare. **toughness** *n* robustezza *f;* durezza *f;* resistenza *f.*

**toupee** ['tu:pei] *n* toupet *m invar,* parrucca *f.*

**tour** [tuə] *n* giro *m,* viaggio *m;* (*theatre, sport*) tournée (*pl* -s) *f. v* viaggiare, fare un giro; fare una tournée. **tourism** *n* turismo *m.* **tourist** *n* turista *m, f.*

**tournament** ['tuənəmənt] *n* torneo *m.*

**tow¹** [tou] *n* (*hemp*) stoppa *f*.

**tow²** [tou] *v* rimorchiare. **n in tow** a rimorchio. **tow-rope** *n* rimorchio *m*. **tow-path** *n* alzaia *f*.

**towards** [tə'wo:dz] *prep* verso, incontro a.

**towel** ['tauəl] *n* asciugamano *m*. *v* asciugarsi. **towelling** *n* spugna *f*.

**tower** ['tauə] *n* torre *f*. *v* elevarsi. **tower above** dominare. **towering** *adj* dominante; (*very great*) smisurato; violento.

**town** [taun] *n* città *f*; (*smaller*) cittadina *f*. **go to town** andare in città; (*do thoroughly*) mettercela tutta. **town clerk** segretario comunale *m*. **town hall** municipio *m*. **town planner** urbanista *m*, *f*. **town planning** urbanistica *f*.

**toxic** ['toksik] *adj* tossico. **toxicity** *n* tossicità *f*.

**toy** [toi] *n* giocattolo *m*. *v* (*play*) giocherellare; (*trifle*) dilettarsi.

**trace** [treis] *n* traccia *f*. *v* (*indicate, sketch*) tracciare; (*follow, discover*) rintracciare. **traceable** *adj* rintracciabile.

**track** [trak] *n* (*footpath*) sentiero *m*; (*mark, trace*) traccia *f*, orma *f*; (*sport*) pista *f*; (*set course*) percorso *m*; (*record*) banda *f*. **keep track of** seguire. **off the beaten track** fuori mano. **on the right track** sulla strada buona. *v* inseguire. **track down** scovare.

**tract¹** [trakt] *n* (*region*) zona *f*; (*anat*) apparato *m*.

**tract²** [trakt] *n* (*treatise*) trattato *m*; (*pamphlet*) manifesto *m*.

**tractor** ['traktə] *n* trattore *m*.

**trade** [treid] *n* (*work*) mestiere *m*; commercio *m*, traffico *m*; (*business*) affari *m pl*. **trademark** *n* marchio depositato *m*. **tradesman** *n* fornitore *m*, esercente *m*, negoziante *m*. **trade union** sindacato *m*. **trade unionist** sindacalista *m*, *f*. *v* fare affari, commerciare. **trade on** approfittare di. **trader** *n* commerciante *m*, *f*.

**trading** ['treidiŋ] *n* commercio *m*. *adj* commerciale.

**tradition** [trə'diʃən] *n* tradizione *f*. **traditional** *adj* tradizionale.

**traffic** ['trafik] *n* traffico *m*. **traffic jam** intasamento *or* ingorgo (del traffico) *m*. **traffic-light** *n* semaforo *m*. *v* trafficare.

**tragedy** ['tradʒədi] *n* tragedia *f*. **tragic** *adj* tragico.

**trail** [treil] *n* traccia *f*, pista *f*. *v* (*follow*) inseguire; (*drag*) trascinare. **trailer** *n* rimorchio *m*.

**train** [trein] *n* (*rail*) treno *m*; (*dress*) strascico *m*; (*following*) seguito *m*; serie *f*. **train of events** svolgimento *m*. *v* (*teach*) istruire; (*impart skill*) addestrare, ammaestrare; (*sport*) allenare. **trainee** *n* allievo, -a *m*, *f*; (*apprentice*) apprendista *m*, *f*. **trainer** *n* allenatore, -trice *m*, *f*. **training** *n* addestramento *m*; allenamento *m*.

**trait** [treit] *n* caratteristica *f*.

**traitor** ['treitə] *n* traditore *m*. **traitress** *n* traditrice *f*. **turn traitor** passare al nemico.

**tram** [tram] *n* tram *m invar*.

**tramp** [tramp] *n* (*person*) vagabondo *m*; (*walk*) passeggiata *f*; (*sound*) calpestio *m*. *v* vagabondare, percorrere a piedi.

**trample** ['trampl] *v* calpestare. **trample on** pestare.

**trampoline** ['trampəli:n] *n* trampolino *m*.

**trance** [tra:ns] *n* trance *f invar*; (*daze*) stupore *m*.

**tranquil** ['traŋkwil] *adj* sereno, calmo. **tranquillity** *n* serenità *f*, calma *f*. **tranquillizer** *n* tranquillante *m*, sedativo *m*.

**transact** [tran'zakt] *v* **transact business** trattare, entrare in trattative. **transaction** *n* affare *m*, trattativa *f*.

**transcend** [tran'send] *v* trascendere, superare. **transcendental** *adj* trascendentale.

**transcribe** [tran'skraib] *v* trascrivere. **transcript** *or* **transcription** *n* trascrizione *f*.

**transept** ['transept] *n* transetto *m*.

**transfer** ['transfə:; *v* trans'fə:] *n* trasferimento *m*; (*design*) decalcomania *f*. *v* trasferire; (*drawing*) riportare. **transferable** *adj* trasferibile.

**transform** [trans'fo:m] *v* trasformare. **transformation** *n* trasformazione *f*, mutamento *m*; (*phys*) conversione *f*. **transformer** *n* trasformatore *m*.

**transfuse** [trans'fju:z] *v* trasfondere. **transfusion** *n* trasfusione *f*.

**transgress** [trans'gres] *v* trasgredire. **transgression** *n* trasgressione *f*, infrazione *f*.

**transient** ['tranziənt] *adj* transitorio, passeggero; (*phys*) transiente.

**transistor** [tran'zistə] *n* transistor *m invar*, transistore *m*. **transistorize** *v* transistorizzare.

**transit** ['transit] *n* passaggio *m*, transito *m*.

**in transit** durante il trasporto, in transito. *adj* di passaggio *or* transito.

**transition** [tran'ziʃən] *n* transizione *f*; (*music*) modulazione *f*.

**transitive** ['transitiv] *adj* transitivo.

**translate** [trans'leit] *v* tradurre. **translation** *n* traduzione *f*. **translator** *n* traduttore, -trice *m, f*.

**translucent** [trans'lu:snt] *adj* semitrasparente, traslucido.

**transmit** [tranz'mit] *v* trasmettere. **transmission** *n* trasmissione *f*. **transmitter** *n* (*radio set*) trasmettitore *m*; (*station*) trasmittente *f*.

**transparent** [trans'peərənt] *adj* trasparente. **transparency** *n* trasparenza *f*; (*phot*) diapositiva *f*.

**transplant** [trans'pla:nt] *n* 'transpla:nt] *v* trapiantare. *n* trapianto *m*.

**transport** ['transpo:t; *v* trans'po:t] *n* trasporto *m*. *v* trasportare. **transportation** *n* trasporto *m*.

**transpose** [trans'pouz] *v* trasporre. **transposition** *n* trasposizione *f*.

**transverse** ['tranzvə:s] *adj* traverso, trasversale.

**trap** [trap] *n* trappola *f*; (*trick*) tranello *m*; (*vehicle*) carrozzetta *f*. **trapdoor** *n* trabocchetto *m*. *v* prendere in trappola.

**trapeze** [trə'pi:z] *n* trapezio *m*.

**trash** [traʃ] *n* (*rubbish*) robaccia *f*; rifiuti *m pl*; (*nonsense*) sciocchezze *f pl*. **trashy** *adj* di nessun valore.

**trauma** ['tro:mə] *n* trauma *m*. **traumatic** *adj* traumatico.

**travel** ['travl] *v* viaggiare *m*, viaggi *m pl*. **travel agency** agenzia di viaggi *f*. *v* viaggiare. **traveller** *n* viaggiatore, -trice *m, f*. **traveller's cheque** assegno turistico *m*.

**travesty** ['travəsti] *n* travestimento *m*, parodia *f*.

**trawl** [tro:l] *n* strascico (*pl* -chi) *m*. *v* pescare con strascico. **trawler** *n* peschereccio *m*.

**tray** [trei] *n* vassoio *m*.

**treachery** ['tretʃəri] *n* tradimento *m*, perfidia *f*. **treacherous** *adj* traditore, -trice, perfido; (*unreliable*) falso; (*dangerous*) pericoloso.

**treacle** ['tri:kl] *n* melassa *f*.

**\*tread** [tred] *v* (*trample*) calcare, calpestare; (*walk*) camminare. *n* passo *m*; (*stair*) gradi-

no *m*; (*tyre*) battistrada *m invar*.

**treason** ['tri:zn] *n* tradimento *m*.

**treasure** ['treʒə] *n* tesoro *m*. *v* (*cherish*) aver caro; (*prize*) apprezzare; (*retain carefully*) tener caro. **treasurer** *n* tesoriere, -a *m, f*. **treasury** *n* tesoreria *f*. **Treasury** *n* Ministero del Tesoro *m*.

**treat** [tri:t] *v* trattare; (*med*) curare. *n* piacere *m*. **treatment** *n* trattamento *m*.

**treatise** ['tri:tiz] *n* trattato *m*, dissertazione *f*.

**treaty** ['tri:ti] *n* trattato *m*.

**treble** ['trebl] *adj* triplo, triplice; di soprano. *n* soprano. *v* triplicare. *adv* tre volte tanto.

**tree** [tri:] *n* albero *m*.

**trek** [trek] *v* viaggiare (scomodamente). *n* viaggio (scomodo) *m*, migrazione *f*.

**trellis** ['trelis] *n* pergolato *m*, graticcio *m*.

**tremble** ['trembl] *v* tremare; (*be agitated*) fremere. *n* tremito *m*; fremito *m*.

**tremendous** [trə'mendəs] *adj* enorme; (*coll*) straordinario.

**tremor** ['tremə] *n* tremore *m*.

**trench** [trentʃ] *n* (*ditch*) fosso *m*; (*mil*) trincea *f*. **trenchant** *adj* tagliente, caustico.

**trend** [trend] *n* tendenza *f*; direzione *f*; (*fashion*) moda *f*. **trendy** *adj* di moda.

**trespass** ['trespəs] *v* trasgredire; (*rel*) peccare. *n* trasgressione *f*; peccato *m*.

**trestle** ['tresl] *n* trespolo *m*.

**trial** ['traiəl] *n* (*law*) processo *m*; (*test*) esame *m*, prova *f*; esperimento *m*; (*trouble*) disperazione *f*, dolore *m*. **by trial and error** (a) tentoni.

**triangle** ['traiangl] *n* triangolo *m*. **triangular** *adj* triangolare.

**tribe** [traib] *n* tribù *f*. **tribal** *adj* tribale. **tribesman** *n* membro di tribù *m*.

**tribunal** [trai'bju:nl] *n* tribunale *m*.

**tributary** ['tribjutəri] *nm, adj* tributario.

**tribute** ['tribju:t] *n* tributo *m*, omaggio *m*. **pay tribute to** rendere omaggio a.

**trick** [trik] *n* espediente *m*; (*prank*) tiro *m*; (*artifice*) trucco *m*; (*cards*) bazza *f*. **confidence trick** truffa all'americana *f*. **do the trick** ottenere l'effetto voluto. *v* ingannare, abbindolare. **trickery** *n* inganno *m*. **tricky** *adj* (*crafty*) furbo; complicato, delicato.

**trickle** ['trikl] *v* gocciolare. *n* gocciolio *m*; flusso irregolare *m*. **trickle of water** filo d'acqua *m*.

**tricycle** ['traisikl] n triciclo m.

**trifle** ['traifl] n sciocchezza f, inezia f; (food) zuppa inglese f. **a trifle** (a little) un po', alquanto. v scherzare. **trifling** adj insignificante.

**trigger** ['trigə] n grilletto m. v **trigger off** far scattare.

**trigonometry** [trigə'nomətri] n trigonometria f.

**trill** [tril] n trillo m. v trillare; (continuous) trilleggiare.

**trilogy** ['trilədʒi] n trilogia f.

**trim** [trim] adj ordinato, ben messo or tenuto, assettato. n assetto m; (ornament) guarnizione f. v (neaten) assettare; guarnire; (hair) spuntare. **trimmings** pl n guarnizioni f pl.

**trinket** ['triŋkit] n gingillo m.

**trio** ['tri:ou] n trio m.

**trip** [trip] n (excursion) gita f; (journey) viaggio m; (stumble) passo falso m. v (step lightly) saltellare; (stumble) inciampare. **trip up** far cadere, fare lo sgambetto, inciampare. **tripper** n escursionista m, f.

**tripe** [traip] n trippa f.

**triple** ['tripl] adj triplo, triplice. v triplicare. **triplet** n trigemino, -a m, f.

**tripod** ['traipod] n cavalletto m, treppiede m.

**trite** [trait] adj banale, comune.

**triumph** ['traiʌmf] n trionfo m. v trionfare, esultare. **triumphant** adj trionfante.

**trivial** ['triviəl] adj insignificante, banale. **triviality** n affare di nessuna importanza m.

**trod** [trod] V tread.

**trodden** ['trodn] V tread.

**trolley** ['troli] n carrello m.

**trombone** [trom'boun] n trombone m.

**troop** [tru:p] n banda f, gruppo m; (mil) truppa f. v **troop along** sfilare. **troop in/out** entrare/uscire in gruppo.

**trophy** ['troufi] n trofeo m.

**tropic** ['tropik] n tropico m. **tropical** adj tropicale.

**trot** [trot] v trottare. n trotto m, trottata f. **on the trot** (coll) di seguito. **trotter** n (horse) trottatore m; (pig's foot) zampa f.

**trouble** ['trʌbl] n disturbo m; difficoltà f; (unpleasantness) dispiacere m; preoccupazione f; (annoyance) fastidio m. **make trouble** creare guai. **the trouble is** il guaio è. **troublemaker** n sobillatore, -trice m, f. v disturbare, dare fastidio. **troubled** adj turbato, preoccupato, agitato. **troublesome** adj noioso, fastidioso.

**trough** [trof] n trogolo m; (drinking) abbeveratoio m.

**trousers** ['trauzəz] pl n calzoni m pl, pantaloni m pl.

**trout** [traut] n trota f.

**trowel** ['trauəl] n (plastering) cazzuola f; (gardening) vanghetto m.

**truant** ['tru:ənt] n **play truant** marinare la scuola; (shirk duty) batter la fiacca.

**truce** [tru:s] n tregua f.

**truck** [trʌk] n carro m, vagone m.

**trudge** [trʌdʒ] v trascinarsi, camminare a stento.

**true** [tru:] adj vero; corretto; genuino; (mech) centrato. **come true** avverarsi. **hold true for** valere per.

**truffle** ['trʌfl] n tartufo m.

**trump** [trʌmp] n briscola f; (bridge) atout m invar. **trump card** (coll) forte m. v (cards) tagliare; (beat) battere. **trump up** fabbricare.

**trumpet** ['trʌmpit] n tromba f. **blow one's own trumpet** vantare i propri meriti. v (proclaim loudly) strombazzare; (elephant) barrire.

**truncheon** ['trʌntʃən] n manganello m, bastone m.

**trunk** [trʌŋk] n tronco m; (chest) baule m; torso m; (elephant) proboscide f. **trunk call** telefonata interurbana f. **trunk road** strada maestra or statale f. **trunks** pl n calzoncini m pl.

**truss** [trʌs] v legare. n (framework) travatura f; (bundle) fastello; (med) cinto erniario m.

**trust** [trʌst] n fiducia f; (hope) fede f; (law) fedecommesso m; (comm) trust m invar. v fidarsi di, aver fiducia in; (hope) augurarsi. **trustworthy** adj degno di fiducia, fidato. v **trustee** n fedecommissario m; curatore, -trice m, f **trusty** adj fedele, leale.

**truth** [tru:θ] n verità f, vero m. **truthful** adj veritiero, sincero.

**try** [trai] v tentare; (test) provare; (law) giudicare, processare; (taste) assaggiare. **try on** provare. n tentativo m; (rugby) meta f. **trying** adj difficile; (distressing) penoso; (irritating) seccante.

**tsar** [za:] n zar m invar.

**T-shirt** ['ti:ʃə:t] *n* maglietta *f*.

**tub** [tʌb] *n* tino *m*; (*bath*) vasca *f*. **tubby** *adj* grassoccio.

**tuba** ['tju:bə] *n* tuba *f*.

**tube** [tju:b] *n* tubo *m*; (*for toothpaste, etc.*) tubetto *m*; (*rail*) metropolitana *f*. **inner tube** *n* camera d'aria *f*. **tubing** *n* tubo *m*.

**tubular** *adj* tubolare.

**tuber** ['tju:bə] *n* tubero *m*.

**tuberculosis** [tjubə:kju'lousis] *n* tubercolosi *f*.

**tuck** [tʌk] *n* piega *f*, rimbocco *m*. **tuck-shop** *n* spaccio di dolciumi *m*. *v* (*thrust into*) stipare; (*needlework*) rimboccare. **tuck in** ripiegare; (*coll: eat*) pappare, farsi una mangiata. **tuck up in bed** mettere a letto, coricare.

**Tuesday** ['tju:zdi] *n* martedi *m*.

**tuft** [tʌft] *n* ciuffo *m*, fiocco *m*.

**tug** [tʌg] *v* (*pull*) tirare, dare uno strappo a; (*drag*) trascinare. *n* strappo *m*; (*boat*) rimorchiatore *m*.

**tuition** [tju'iʃən] *n* insegnamento *m*, istruzione *f*.

**tulip** ['tju:lip] *n* tulipano *m*.

**tumble** ['tʌmbl] *v* cascare, ruzzolare; (*somersault*) fare un capitombolo. **tumble down** crollare. *n* caduta *f*, capitombolo *m*. **tumbler** *n* (*glass*) bicchiere *m*.

**tummy** ['tʌmi] (*coll*) pancia *f*. **tummy-ache** *n* mal di pancia *m*.

**tumour** ['tju:mə] *n* tumore *m*.

**tumult** ['tju:mʌlt] *n* tumulto *m*. **tumultuous** *adj* tumultuoso.

**tuna** ['tju:nə] *n also* **tunny** tonno *m*.

**tune** [tju:n] *n* motivo *m*; melodia *f*, aria *f*. **call the tune** essere in comando. **in tune** in tono, intonato. **out of tune** fuori tono, stonato. **sing out of tune** stonare. **to the tune of** alla bellezza di. *v* accordare; (*radio*) sintonizzare. **tuner** *n* sintonizzatore *m*.

**tunic** ['tju:nik] *n* tunica *f*.

**tunnel** ['tʌnl] *n* tunnel *m invar*, traforo *m*. *v* traforare.

**tunny** ['tʌni] *V* **tuna**.

**turban** ['tə:bən] *n* turbante *m*.

**turbid** ['tə:bid] *adj* torbido.

**turbine** ['tə:bain] *n* turbina *f*.

**turbot** ['tə:bət] *n* rombo *m*.

**turbulent** ['tə:bjulənt] *adj* turbolento. **turbulence** *n* turbolenza *f*.

**tureen** [tə'ri:n] *n* zuppiera *f*.

**turf** [tə:f] *n* zolla erbosa *f*; (*sod*) piota *f*; (*peat*) torba *f*; (*horse-racing*) ippica *f*. *v* piotare. **turf out** (*coll*) buttar fuori.

**turkey** ['tə:ki] *n* tacchino *m*.

**Turkey** ['tə:ki] *n* Turchia *f*. **Turk** *n* turco, -a *m*, *f*. **Turkish** *nm*, *adj* turco.

**turmeric** ['tə:mərik] *n* curcuma *f*.

**turmoil** ['tə:moil] *n* scompiglio *m*, confusione *f*.

**turn** [tə:n] *v* girare, voltare; (*change*) cambiare; (*change direction*) voltare. **turn against** alienare, ribellarsi a. **turn away** voltarsi da parte, guardar via; (*refuse admission*) mandar via. **turncoat** *n* rinnegato, -a *m*, *f*. **turn down** (*fold*) risvoltare; (*lower*) abbassare; (*reject*) rifiutare. **turn into** far diventare, convertire in. **turn off** (*stop flow*) chiudere; (*switch off*) spegnere; (*change direction*) voltare. **turn on** (*start flow*) aprire; (*switch on*) accendere; (*coll*) eccitare; (*attack*) aggredire. **turn out** (*switch off*) spegnere; produrre; (*send away*) cacciar via; (*empty*) vuotare; risultare; (*clothe*) vestire. **turn over** rovesciare. **turnover** *n* (*comm*) giro d'affari *m*; (*cookery*) pasticcio *m*. **turnstile** *n* tornello *m*. **turntable** *n* (*records*) giradischi *m invar*; (*rail*) piattaforma girevole *f*. **turn up** (*arrive*) capitare; (*come to light*) ricomparire; (*increase intensity*) alzare; (*occur*) succedere. *n* giro *m*, rivoluzione *f*; (*change of direction*) svolta *f*; (*in rota, game, etc.*) turno *m*. **turning** *n* curva *f*, svolta *f*. **turning point** momento critico *or* decisivo *m*.

**turnip** ['tə:nip] *n* rapa *f*.

**turpentine** ['tə:pəntain] *n* trementina *f*; (*oil*) essenza di trementina *f*.

**turquoise** ['tə:kwoiz] *n* (*stone*) turchese *f*; (*colour*) turchese *m*. *adj* turchese.

**turret** ['tʌrit] *n* torretta *f*.

**turtle** ['tə:tl] *n* testuggine *f*, tartaruga *f*. **turn turtle** cappottare, capovolgersi. **turtle-dove** *n* tortora *f*.

**Tuscany** ['tʌskəni] *n* Toscana *f*. **Tuscan** *n*, *adj* toscano, -a.

**tusk** [tʌsk] *n* zanna *f*.

**tussle** ['tʌsl] *n* zuffa *f*. *v* venire alle mani, azzuffarsi.

**tutor** ['tju:tə] *n* insegnante (privato) *m*; (*coach*) ripetitore, -trice *m*, *f*. **tutorial** *n* periodo di istruzione (privata) *m*.

**tuxedo** [tʌk'si:dou] *n* smoking *m invar*.

**tweed** [twi:d] *n* tweed *m invar*, tessuto di lana scozzese *m*.

**tweezers** ['twi:zəz] *pl n* pinzette *f pl*.

**twelve** [twelv] *nm, adj* dodici. **twelfth** *nm, adj* dodicesimo.

**twenty** ['twenti] *nm, adj* venti. **twentieth** *nm, adj* ventesimo.

**twice** [twais] *adv* due volte; (*doubly*) il doppio.

**twiddle** ['twidl] *v* (far) girare. **twiddle one's thumbs** tener le mani in mano.

**twig** [twig] *n* ramoscello *m*.

**twilight** ['twailait] *n* crepuscolo *m*, penombra *f*.

**twin** [twin] *n, adj* gemello, -a. **twin beds** letti gemelli *m pl*.

**twine** [twain] *n* spago *m*, corda *f*. *v* attorcigliare.

**twinge** [twindʒ] *n* spasimo *m*.

**twinkle** ['twiŋkl] *v* scintillare, luccicare; (*wink*) ammiccare, strizzare l'occhio. *n* luccichio *m*; strizzata d'occhio *f*.

**twirl** [twə:l] *v* girare rapidamente, piroettare.

**twist** [twist] *v* torcere, intrecciare; (*sprain*) slogarsi; alterare. *n* movimento rotatorio *m*; (*curve*) svolta *f*; (*thread*) filo ritorto *m*. **twister** *n* (*cheat*) imbroglione, -a *m, f*.

**twit** [twit] *n* (*coll*) scemo, -a *m, f*.

**twitch** [twitʃ] *v* (*jerk*) strappare, dare uno strattone; (*body*) storcere. *n* contorsione *f*, spasimo *m*. **twitching** *adj* convulsivo.

**twitter** ['twitə] *v* cinguettare. *n* cinguettio *m*.

**two** [tu:] *nm, adj* due. **in twos** due a due. **two-faced** *adj* falso. **two-piece** *n* (*garment*) duepezzi *m invar*. **two-seater** *n* a due posti. **two-way** *adj* a doppio senso; (*elec*) bipolare.

**tycoon** [tai'ku:n] *n* magnate *m*.

**type** [taip] *n* tipo *m*, genere *m*; (*print*) carattere *m*. **typeface** *n* occhio *m*, (*polizza di*) caratteri *f*. **typescript** *n* dattiloscritto *m*. **typesetter** *n* compositore *m*. **typewriter** *n* macchina da scrivere *f*. **typewritten** *adj* scritto a macchina, dattiloscritto. *v* dattilografare. **typical** *adj* tipico, caratteristico. **typify** *v* servire da esempio, simbolizzare. **typist** *n* dattilografo, -a *m, f*.

**typhoid** ['taifoid] *n* tifo *m*.

**typhoon** [tai'fu:n] *n* tifone *m*.

**typographical** [ˌtaipə'grafikl] *adj* tipografico.

**tyrant** ['tairənt] *n* tiranno *m*. **tyrannical** *adj* tirannico. **tyranny** *n* tirannia *f*.

**tyre** *or US* **tire** ['taiə] *n* gomma *f*, copertone *m*.

## U

**ubiquitous** [ju'bikwitəs] *adj* onnipresente.

**udder** ['ʌdə] *n* mammella *f*.

**UFO** *n* UFO *m*.

**ugly** ['ʌgli] *adj* (*not pretty*) brutto; (*not agreeable*) antipatico, sgradevole; (*vicious*) vile. **ugliness** *n* bruttezza *f*.

**Ukraine** *n* Ucraìna *f. n, adj* ucraìno, -a.

**ulcer** ['ʌlsə] *n* ulcera *f*.

**ulterior** [ʌl'tiəriə] *adj* ulteriore. **ulterior motive** secondo fine *m*.

**ultimate** ['ʌltimət] *adj* finale, definitivo, assoluto. **ultimately** *adv* alla fine. **ultimatum** *n* ultimatum *m invar*.

**ultrasound** ['ʌltrəsaund] *n* ultrasuono *m*.

**ultraviolet** [ʌltrə'vaiələt] *adj* ultravioletto.

**umbilical** [ʌm'bilikəl] *adj* ombilicale.

**umbrella** [ʌm'brelə] *n* ombrello *m*.

**umpire** ['ʌmpaiə] *n* arbitro *m*. *v* arbitrare.

**umpteen** [ʌmp'ti:n] *(coll) adj* innumerevole. **umpteenth** *adj* ennesimo.

**unable** [ʌn'eibl] *adj* incapace. **be unable to** non potere.

**unacceptable** [ʌnək'septəbl] *adj* inaccettabile.

**unaccompanied** [ʌnə'kʌmpənid] *adj* solo, non accompagnato.

**unaccountable** [ʌnə'kauntəbl] *adj* inspiegabile.

**unaccustomed** [ʌnə'kʌstəmd] *adj* (*not used to*) poco abituato; (*unusual*) insolito.

**unadulterated** [ʌnə'dʌltəreitid] *adj* sincero.

**unanimous** [ju'naniməs] *adj* unanime.

**unapproachable** [ʌnə'prəutʃəbl] *adj* inaccessibile.

**unarmed** [ʌn'a:md] *adj* disarmato.

**unashamed** [ʌnə'ʃeimd] *adj* svergognato, senza vergogna.

**unattainable** [ʌnə'teinəbl] *adj* irraggiungibile.

**unattractive** [ʌnə'traktiv] *adj* poco attraente, antipatico.

**unauthorized** [ʌn'ɔːθəraizd] *adj* non autorizzato, illecito.

**unavoidable** [ʌnə'vɔidəbl] *adj* inevitabile.

**unaware** [ʌnə'weə] *adj* ignaro. **be unaware of** ignorare. **unawares** *adv* di sorpresa.

**unbalanced** [ʌn'balənst] *adj* squilibrato.

**unbearable** [ʌn'beərəbl] *adj* insopportabile.

**unbelievable** [ʌnbi'liːvəbl] *adj* incredibile.

***unbend** [ʌn'bend] *v* raddrizzare. **unbending** *adj* rigido, inflessibile.

**unbiased** [ʌn'baiəst] *adj* imparziale.

**unbreakable** [ʌn'breikəbl] *adj* infrangibile.

**unbridled** [ʌn'braidld] *adj* sfrenato.

**unbroken** [ʌn'broukn] *adj* intatto; ininterrotto; (*not beaten*) imbattuto.

**unbutton** [ʌn'bʌtn] *v* sbottonare.

**uncalled-for** [ʌn'kɔːldfɔː] *adj* immeritato, gratuito.

**uncanny** [ʌn'kani] *adj* strano, misterioso.

**uncertain** [ʌn'sɜːtn] *adj* incerto, dubbio. **uncertainty** *n* incertezza *f.*

**unchanged** [ʌn'tʃeindʒd] *adj* immutato, invariato.

**uncharitable** [ʌn'tʃaritəbl] *adj* aspro, crudele.

**uncivilized** [ʌn'sivilaizd] *adj* barbaro.

**uncle** ['ʌŋkl] *n* zio *m.*

**uncomfortable** [ʌn'kʌmfətəbl] *adj* scomodo. **feel uncomfortable** sentirsi a disagio.

**uncommon** [ʌn'komən] *adj* poco comune, insolito.

**uncompromising** [ʌn'komprəmaiziŋ] *adj* intrattabile, intransigente.

**unconditional** [ʌnkən'difənl] *adj* incondizionale, senza riserve, categorico.

**unconscious** [ʌn'konfəs] *adj* (*unaware*) inconscio, inconsapevole; (*med*) privo di coscienza. *n* inconscio *m.* **become unconscious** svenire, perdere conoscenza. **be unconscious of** essere ignaro di, non accorgersi di. **unconsciously** *adv* senza rendersene conto.

**uncontrollable** [ʌnkən'troul);əbl] *adj* incontrollabile, irreprimibile.

**unconventional** [ʌnkən'venfənl] *adj* anticonformista; non convenzionale.

**unconvincing** [ʌnkən'vinsiŋ] *adj* poco convincente. **unconvinced** *adj* non convinto, poco persuaso.

**uncooked** [ʌn'kukt] *adj* crudo, non cotto.

**uncouth** [ʌn'kuːθ] *adj* rozzo, grossolano.

**uncover** [ʌn'kʌvə] *v* scoprire, rivelare, esporre.

**uncut** [ʌn'kʌt] *adj* non tagliato, integro.

**undecided** [ʌndi'saidid] *adj* indeciso, irresoluto.

**undeniable** [ʌndi'naiəbl] *adj* innegabile, incontestabile.

**under** ['ʌndə] *adv, prep* sotto, al di sotto (di). **be under the weather** sentirsi poco bene. **under age** minorenne. **under lock and key** sottochiave. **under one's breath** sottovoce. **under the circumstances** in queste circostanze.

**undercharge** [ʌndə'tʃaːdʒ] *v* far pagare meno del dovuto, non far pagare abbastanza.

**underclothes** ['ʌndəklouðz] *pl n* biancheria intima *f sing.*

**undercoat** ['ʌndəkout] *n* (*paint*) prima mano *f.*

**undercover** [ʌndə'kʌvə] *adj* segreto.

***undercut** [ʌndə'kʌt] *v* (*comm*) offrire a un prezzo inferiore a.

**underdeveloped** [ʌndədi'veləpt] *adj* sottosviluppato.

**underdog** ['ʌndədog] *n* vittima *f,* persona che ha la peggio *f.*

**underdone** [ʌndə'dʌn] *adj* (*meat*) al sangue.

**underestimate** [ʌndə'estimeit] *v* sottovalutare.

**underexpose** [ʌndərik'spouz] *v* sottoesporre.

**underfoot** [ʌndə'fut] *adv* sotto i piedi.

***undergo** [ʌndə'gou] *v* subire, supportare.

**undergraduate** [ʌndə'gradjuət] *n* studente universitario, studentessa universitaria *m, f.*

**underground** ['ʌndəgraund]; ʌndə'graund] *adj* sotterraneo; (*secret*) segreto; clandestino. **underground passage** sottopassaggio *m. adv* sottoterra. *n* resistenza *f;* (*railway*) metropolitana *f.*

**undergrowth** ['ʌndəgrouθ] *n* boscaglia *f,* macchia *f.*

**underhand** [ʌndə'hand] *adj* clandestino; (*dubious*) losco.

**\*underlie** [ʌndə'lai] v sottostare a; essere alla base di.

**underline** [ʌndə'lain] v sottolineare.

**undermine** [ʌndə'main] v minare, insidiare.

**underneath** [ʌndə'ni:θ] adv, prep sotto, al di sotto (di).

**undernourished** [ʌndə'nʌriʃt] adj malnutrito.

**underpants** ['ʌndəpants] pl n mutande f pl.

**underpass** ['ʌndəpa:s] n sottopassaggio m.

**underprivileged** [ʌndə'prɪvɪlɪdʒd] adj non privilegiato, derelitto.

**underrate** [ʌndə'reit] v sottovalutare.

**understaffed** [ʌndə'sta:ft] adj a corto di personale or manodopera.

**\*understand** [ʌndə'stand] v capire, comprendere; (realize) rendersi conto; (believe) credere. **understandable** adj comprensibile.

**understanding** [ʌndə'standiŋ] n comprensione f; (knowledge) conoscenza f; (agreement) accordo m. **on the understanding that** a condizione or premesso che. adj comprensivo, indulgente.

**understate** [ʌndə'steit] v minimizzare, attenuare. **understatement** n atto del minimizzare m.

**understudy** ['ʌndəstʌdi] v sostituire. n sostituto, -a m, f, attore, -trice supplente m, f.

**\*undertake** [ʌndə'teik] v intraprendere; (accept obligation) impegnarsi; (warrant) garantire. **undertaker** n imprenditore di pompe funebri m, becchino m. **undertaking** n impresa f; (pledge) impegno m, promessa f.

**undertone** ['ʌndətoun] n fondo m, senso occulto m. **in an undertone** a basso voce.

**underwear** ['ʌndəweə] n biancheria or maglieria intima f.

**underwater** ['ʌndəwo:tə; adv ʌndə'wo:tə] adj subacqueo. adv sott'acqua.

**underweight** [ʌndə'weit] adj di peso insufficiente.

**underworld** ['ʌndəwə:ld] n (myth) inferno m; (crime) malavita f.

**\*underwrite** [ʌndə'rait] v sottoscrivere; (support) sostenere; (finance) garantire; (insurance) riassicurare. **underwriter** n riassicuratore m, garante di una emissione m.

**undesirable** [ʌndi'zaiərəbl] adj indesiderabile, sgradito.

**undignified** [ʌn'dignifaid] adj poco dignitoso.

**\*undo** [ʌn'du:] v disfare, sciogliere, annullare; rovinare. **leave undone** tralasciare di fare. **undoing** n rovina f.

**undoubted** [ʌn'dautid] adj indubbio, incontestato, certo.

**undress** [ʌn'dres] v svestire, spogliarsi.

**undue** [ʌn'dju:] adj indebito, eccessivo.

**undulate** ['ʌndjuleit] v ondeggiare.

**unearth** [ʌn'ə:θ] v scoprire, dissotterrare. **unearthly** adj (ghostly) spettrale; (coll) assurdo.

**uneasy** [ʌn'i:zi] adj turbato, imbarazzato, a disagio.

**uneducated** [ʌn'edjukeitid] adj ignorante, senza coltura.

**unemployed** [ʌnem'ploid] adj disoccupato. **the unemployed** i disoccupati m pl. **unemployment** n disoccupazione f.

**unending** [ʌn'endiŋ] adj interminabile, che non finisce più.

**unequal** [ʌn'i:kwəl] adj disuguale; (unevenly matched) impari. **unequal to** non all'altezza di. **unequalled** adj senza pari.

**uneven** [ʌn'i:vn] adj (not level) irregolare; ineguale; (odd) dispari.

**unexpected** [ʌneks'pektid] adj inatteso.

**unfailing** [ʌn'feiliŋ] adj infallibile, immancabile.

**unfair** [ʌn'feə] adj ingiusto; (dishonest) sleale; (sport) non sportivo. **unfairness** n ingiustizia f; slealtà f.

**unfaithful** [ʌn'feiθfəl] adj infedele, disonesto; inesatto. **unfaithfulness** n infedeltà f.

**unfamiliar** [ʌnfə'miljə] adj (not conversant) poco familiare or pratico; (not well-known) poco conosciuto or noto.

**unfasten** [ʌn'fa:sn] v slegare, sciogliere, disfare.

**unfavourable** [ʌn'feivərəbl] adj sfavorevole.

**unfit** [ʌn'fit] adj (unsuitable) inadatto, non idoneo; (unable) inabile; (unwell) indisposto.

**unfold** [ʌn'fould] v (open out) schiudere; (develop) sviluppare; (reveal) rivelare.

**unforeseen** [ʌnfo:'si:n] adj imprevisto. **unforeseeable** adj imprevedibile.

**unfortunate** [ʌn'fɔ:tʃənət] *adj* sfortunato, disgraziato; (*unsuitable, unhappy*) infelice. **unfortunately** *adv* purtroppo.

**unfriendly** [ʌn'frendli] *adj* freddo; ostile.

**unfurnished** [ʌn'fə:niʃd] *adj* non ammobiliato.

**ungrateful** [ʌn'greitfəl] *adj* ingrato.

**unguarded** [ʌn'ga:did] *adj* incustodito, indifeso; imprudente, indiscreto.

**unhappy** [ʌn'hapi] *adj* infelice, triste; inopportuno; (*infelicitous*) poco felice. **unhappily** *adv* sfortunatamente. **unhappiness** *n* infelicità *f*, tristezza *f*.

**unhealthy** [ʌn'helθi] *adj* malsano; (*morbid*) morboso.

**unhurried** [ʌn'hʌrid] *adj* calmo, senza fretta.

**unhurt** [ʌn'hə:t] *adj* incolume.

**unicorn** ['ju:nikɔ:n] *n* unicorno *m*.

**uniform** ['ju:nifɔ:m] *adj* uniforme, costante. *n* uniforme *f*, divisa *f*. **uniformity** *n* uniformità *f*.

**unify** ['ju:nifai] *v* unificare. **unification** *n* unificazione *f*.

**unilateral** [ju:ni'latərəl] *adj* unilaterale.

**unimaginable** [ʌni'madʒinəbl] *adj* inconcepibile. **unimaginative** *adj* poco immaginativo.

**unimpaired** [ʌnim'peəd] *adj* intatto, in pieno vigore.

**uninhabited** [ʌnin'habitid] *adj* disabitato, deserto. **uninhabitable** *adj* inabitabile.

**unintentional** [ʌnin'tenʃənl] *adj* involontario.

**uninterested** [ʌn'intristid] *adj* disinteressato. **uninteresting** *adj* poco interessante, noioso.

**union** ['ju:njən] *n* unione *f*, unificazione *f*; associazione *f*; (*trade*) sindacato *f*; (*tech*) collegamento *m*.

**unique** [ju:'ni:k] *adj* unico, solo.

**unison** ['ju:nisn] *n* unisono *m*. **in unison** all'unisono.

**unit** ['ju:nit] *n* unità *f*; (*whole*) insieme *m*.

**unite** [ju:'nait] *v* unire, combinare, congiungere. **united** *adj* unito. **United Kingdom** Regno Unito *m*. **United Nations** Nazioni Unite *f pl*. **United States of America** Stati Uniti d'America *m pl*.

**unity** ['ju:niti] *n* unità *f*.

**universe** ['ju:nivə:s] *n* universo *m*. **universal** *adj* universale.

**university** [ju:ni'və:səti] *n* università *f*. *adj* universitario.

**unjust** [ʌn'dʒʌst] *adj* ingiusto.

**unkempt** [ʌn'kempt] *adj* spettinato; (*untidy*) sciatto.

**unkind** [ʌn'kaind] *adj* poco gentile; crudele.

**unknown** [ʌn'noun] *adj* sconosciuto, ignoto. *n* ignoto *m*; (*math*) incognita *f*. **unknown to** all'insaputa di.

**unlawful** [ʌn'lo:fəl] *adj* illegale; illecito.

**unleaded** [ʌn'ledid] *adj* senza piombo.

**unless** [ʌn'les] *conj* a meno che non, se non.

**unlike** [ʌn'laik] *adj* dissimile *or* diverso (da). **be unlike** non rassomigliarsi. **not unlike** assai simile a. *prep* a differenza di, all'inverso di.

**unlikely** [ʌn'laikli] *adj* improbabile, inverosimile.

**unload** [ʌn'loud] *v* scaricare, liberarsi di.

**unlock** [ʌn'lok] *v* aprire.

**unlucky** [ʌn'lʌki] *adj* sfortunato, disgraziato.

**unmarried** [ʌn'marid] *adj* non sposato; (*bachelor*) celibe; (*spinster*) nubile. **unmarried mother** ragazza madre *f*.

**unmistakable** [ʌnmi'steikəbl] *adj* inequivocabile, manifesto.

**unnatural** [ʌn'natʃərəl] *adj* contro natura; (*lacking natural feelings*) snaturato, disumano; anormale; forzato.

**unnecessary** [ʌn'nesəsəri] *adj* inutile, non necessario.

**unnoticed** [ʌn'noutist] *adj* inavvertito.

**unobtainable** [ʌnəb'teinəbl] *adj* irreperibile.

**unoccupied** [ʌn'okjupaid] *adj* libero, vacante, vuoto.

**unofficial** [ʌnə'fiʃəl] *adj* ufficioso.

**unopposed** [ʌnə'pouzd] *adj* incontrastato.

**unpack** [ʌn'pak] *v* (*case*) disfare (*le valige*); (*contents*) disimballare.

**unpaid** [ʌn'peid] *adj* non retribuito *or* rimunerato; (*debt, etc.*) non saldato *or* pagato.

**unpardonable** [ʌn'pa:dnəbl] *adj* imperdonabile.

**unpleasant** [ʌn'pleznt] *adj* spiacevole, sgradevole, antipatico. **unpleasantness** *n* spiacevolezza *f*; (*disagreement*) dissenso *m*.

**unpopular** [ʌn'pɔpjulə] *adj* impopolare. **be unpopular with** esser malvisto da.

**unprecedented** [ʌn'presidentid] *adj* inaudito, senza precedenti.

**unpredictable** [ʌnprə'diktəbl] *adj* imprevedibile.

**unqualified** [ʌn'kwɔlifaid] *adj* non qualificato; senza diploma; categorico, assoluto.

**unquestionable** [ʌn'kwestʃənəbl] *adj* indiscutibile, fuori questione. **unquestioned** *adj* indiscusso, incontestato.

**unravel** [ʌn'rævəl] *v* sciogliere, sbrogliare; (*clear*) chiarire.

**unreadable** [ʌn'ri:dəbl] *adj* illeggibile; (*tedious*) noioso.

**unreal** [ʌn'riəl] *adj* irreale.

**unreasonable** [ʌn'ri:zənəbl] *adj* irragionevole.

**unrecognizable** [ʌn,rekəg'naizəbl] *adj* irriconoscibile.

**unrelenting** [ʌnri'lentiŋ] *adj* inesorabile; (*dogged*) accanito.

**unreliable** [ʌnri'laiəbl] *adj* da non fidarsene; (*news*) inattendibile.

**unrepentant** [ʌnri'pentənt] *adj* impenitente.

**unrest** [ʌn'rest] *n* agitazione *f*, fermento *m*.

**unripe** [ʌn'raip] *adj* immaturo, acerbo.

**unruly** [ʌn'ru:li] *adj* indisciplinato, turbolento.

**unsafe** [ʌn'seif] *adj* malsicuro, pericoloso.

**unsatisfactory** [ʌnsatis'faktəri] *adj* poco soddisfacente, che lascia desiderare.

**unsavoury** [ʌn'seivəri] *adj* sgradevole; (*coll*) disgustoso, poco pulito.

**unscrew** [ʌn'skru:] *v* svitare.

**unscrupulous** [ʌn'skru:pjuləs] *adj* senza scrupoli.

**unselfish** [ʌn'selfiʃ] *adj* altruistico.

**unsettle** [ʌn'setl] *v* turbare; disturbare; sconcertare. **unsettled** *adj* (*weather*) variabile; (*account*) non saldato; (*not fixed*) non sistemato; (*uncertain*) incerto.

**unsightly** [ʌn'saitli] *adj* brutto, spiacevole a vedersi.

**unskilled** [ʌn'skild] *adj* inesperto, non qualificato. **unskilled worker** *n* manovale *m*.

**unsociable** [ʌn'souʃəbl] *adj* poco socievole, scontroso.

**unsound** [ʌn'saund] *adj* imperfetto, difettoso; erroneo; (*ill-founded*) poco profondo.

**unspeakable** [ʌn'spi:kəbl] *adj* indicibile, inesprimibile; (*very bad*) inqualificabile.

**unstable** [ʌn'steibl] *adj* instabile.

**unsteady** [ʌn'stedi] *adj* malfermo, instabile; incostante; (*wavering*) traballante, barcollante.

**unsuccessful** [ʌnsək'sesfəl] *adj* non *or* mal riuscito, sfortunato, fallito.

**unsuitable** [ʌn'su:təbl] *adj* inadatto; inopportuno, disadatto, sconvenevole. **unsuited** *adj* non idoneo, disadatto, sconvenevole.

**unsure** [ʌn'ʃuə] *adj* malsicuro, incerto.

**untangle** [ʌn'taŋgl] *v* districare.

**unthinkable** [ʌn'θiŋkəbl] *adj* inconcepibile, assurdo.

**untidy** [ʌn'taidi] *adj* disordinato, trascurato. **untidiness** *n* disordine *m*. trascuratezza *f*.

**untie** [ʌn'tai] *v* sciogliere, slegare.

**until** [ən'til] *prep* fino a; (*before*) prima di. *conj* finchè, fino a quando; fino al momento in cui.

**untimely** [ʌn'taimli] *adj* inopportuno, intempestivo, prematuro.

**untoward** [ʌntə'wɔ:d] *adj* disgraziato.

**untrue** [ʌn'tru:] *adj* non vero, falso, erroneo; infedele; inesatto.

**unusual** [ʌn'ju:ʒuəl] *adj* insolito, straordinario, eccezionale.

**unwanted** [ʌn'wɔntid] *adj* indesiderato, superfluo.

**unwelcome** [ʌn'welkəm] *adj* (*person*) malaccolto; (*news, etc.*) sgradito, spiacevole.

**unwell** [ʌn'wel] *adj* indisposto, ammalato.

**unwieldy** [ʌn'wi:ldi] *adj* ingombrante.

**unwilling** [ʌn'wiliŋ] *adj* restio, riluttante; (*given reluctantly*) dato controvoglia.

*****unwind** [ʌn'waind] *v* dipanare; (*relax*) rilassarsi.

**unwise** [ʌn'waiz] *adj* imprudente, insensato.

**unwittingly** [ʌn'witiŋli] *adv* senza saperlo, per inavvertenza.

**unworthy** [ʌn'wə:ði] *adj* indegno. **unworthy of** che non merita.

**unwrap** [ʌn'rap] *v* disfare.

**up** [ʌp] *adv* su; (*erect*) in piedi; (*out of bed*) alzato. **be up against** essere alle prese con. **be up to** (*capable of*) essere all'altezza di; (*mischief*) tramare. **up here** quassù. **up**

**there** lassù. **up to** fino a. **what's up?** cosa
succede? *prep* su, su per. *n* **ups and downs**
alti e bassi *m pl*.

**upbringing** ['ʌpbriŋiŋ] *n* educazione *f*.

**update** [ʌp'deit] *v* aggiornare.

**upheaval** [ʌp'hi:vl] *n* commozione *f*, sconvolgimento *m*.

**uphill** [ʌp'hil] *adv* in salita, in su. *adj* in
salita, ascendente; difficile.

*****uphold** [ʌp'hould] *v* sostenere, appoggiare.

**upholster** [ʌp'houlstə] *v* tappezzare.
**upholsterer** *n* tappezziere *m*. **upholstery**
*n* tappezzeria *f*.

**upkeep** ['ʌpki:p] *n* mantenimento *m*,
manutenzione *f*.

**uplift** [ʌp'lift] *v* edificare, incoraggiare. *n*
edificazione *f*, incoraggiamento *m*.

**upon** [ə'pon] *prep* su, sopra.

**upper** ['ʌpə] *adj* superiore, più alto. **get
the upper hand** prevalere. *n* tomaia *f*. **be
on one's uppers** essere alle strette. **uppermost** *adj* il più alto.

**upright** ['ʌprait] *adj* verticale, in piedi;
(*righteous*) retto, onesto.

**uprising** ['ʌpraiziŋ] *n* insurrezione *f*.

**uproar** ['ʌpro:] *n* tumulto, fracasso.
**uproarious** *adj* tumultuoso, chiassoso.
**uproariously funny** da crepar dal ridere.

**uproot** [ʌp'ru:t] *v* sradicare.

*****upset** [ʌp'set; *n* 'ʌpset] *v* sconvolgere, dis-
turbare; (*knock over*) rovesciare. *adj* sconvolto, turbato; rovesciato. *n* disturbo *m*,
contrattempo *m*. **upsetting** *adj* turbante,
preoccupante.

**upshot** ['ʌpʃot] *n* conclusione *f*, effetto *m*.

**upside down** [ʌpsai'daun] *adv*, *adj* sottosopra, in disordine.

**upstairs** [ʌp'steəz] *adv* di sopra, al piano
superiore.

**upstream** [ʌp'stri:m] *adv* a monte, controcorrente.

**uptight** ['ʌptait] *adj* (*coll*) nervoso.

**up-to-date** [ʌptə'deit] *adj* aggiornato, di
moda.

**upward** ['ʌpwəd] *adj* in salita, rivolto in
alto. **upwards** *adv* in su, in alto; (*more*)
più.

**uranium** [ju'reiniəm] *n* uranio *m*.

**urban** ['ə:bən] *adj* urbano.

**urchin** ['ə:tʃin] *n* monello, -a *m*, *f*.

**urge** [ə:dʒ] *n* sprone *m*, impulso *m*. *v*

esortare, spingere; insistere.

**urgent** ['ə:dʒənt] *adj* urgente. **urgency** *n*
urgenza *f*.

**urine** ['ju:rin] *n* orina *f*. **urinal** *n* orinatoio
*m*. **urinary** *adj* urinario. **urinate** *v* orinare.

**urn** [ə:n] *n* urna *f*.

**us** [ʌs] *pron* ci, ce; (*after prep*) noi.

**usage** ['ju:zidʒ] *n* uso *m*, usanza *f*.

**use** [ju:s; *v* ju:z] *n* uso *m*, impiego (*pl* -ghi)
*m*; utilità *f*. **it's no use!** è inutile! **what's
the use?** a cosa serve? *v* usare, impiegare,
adoperare. **use up** consumare. **used** *adj*
(*car*) d'occasione. **be used to** essere abituato a. **useful** *adj* utile. **useless** *adj* inutile.

**user-friendly** *adj* facile da usare, di facile
impiego.

**usher** ['ʌʃə] *n* usciere *m*. *v* **usher in** far
entrare, introdurre. **usherette** *n* maschera
*f*.

**usual** ['ju:zuəl] *adj* solito, usuale. **as usual**
come di solito. **usually** *adv* di solito, generalmente.

**usurp** [ju'zə:p] *v* usurpare.

**utensil** [ju'tensl] *n* utensile *m*, arnese *m*.

**uterus** ['ju:tərəs] *n* utero *m*.

**utility** [ju'tiləti] *n* utilità *f*, vantaggio *m*;
servizio pubblico *m*. **utilize** *v* utilizzare.

**utmost** ['ʌtmoust] *adj* massimo, supremo.
*n* massimo *m*, possibile *m*. **do one's
utmost** fare del proprio meglio.

**utter**[1] ['ʌtə] *v* (*say*) pronunciare, emettere.

**utter**[2] ['ʌtə] *adj* (*absolute*) completo, assoluto.

**U-turn** ['ju:tə:n] *n* cambio di direzione *m*.

# V

**vacant** ['veikənt] *adj* libero, vuoto; vacuo.
**vacancy** *n* (*job*) posto libero *m*; (*room*) camera libera *f*. **vacate** *v* lasciar libero,
sgomberare.

**vaccine** ['vaksi:n] *n* vaccino *m*. **vaccinate** *v*
vaccinare. **vaccination** *n* vaccinazione *f*.

**vacillate** ['vasileit] *v* vacillare.

**vacuum** ['vakjum] *n* vuoto *m*. **vacuum
cleaner** *n* aspirapolvere *m invar*. **vacuum
flask** *n* thermos *m invar*.

**vagina** [və'dʒainə] *n* vagina *f*. **vaginal**

*adj* vaginale.

**vagrant** ['veigrənt] *n*, *adj* vagabondo, -a. **vagrancy** *n* vagabondaggio *m*.

**vague** [veig] *adj* vago.

**vain** [vein] *adj* (*worthless*) vano, inutile; (*conceited*) vanitoso. **in vain** invano.

**valiant** ['valiənt] *adj* valoroso.

**valid** ['valid] *adj* (*ticket, etc.*) valevole; (*sound*) valido. **validity** *n* validità *f*.

**valley** ['vali] *n* valle *f*.

**value** ['valju:] *n* valore *m*. *v* valutare, stimare; dare importanza a. **valuable** *adj* prezioso, di valore. **valuables** *pl n* valori *m pl*, oggetti di valore *m pl*.

**value-added-tax** *n* imposta sul valore aggiunto (IVA) *f*.

**valve** [valv] *n* valvola *f*.

**vampire** ['vampaiə] *n* vampiro *m*.

**van¹** [van] *n* (*vehicle*) furgone *m*, camion *f*.

**van²** [van] *n* (*forefront*) avanguardia *f*.

**vandal** ['vandl] *n* vandalo *m*. **vandalism** *n* vandalismo *m*.

**vanilla** [və'nilə] *n* vaniglia *f*.

**vanish** ['vaniʃ] *v* sparire.

**vanity** ['vanəti] *n* vanità *f*.

**vapour** ['veipə] *n* vapore *m*. **vaporize** *v* vaporizzare.

**variance** ['veəriəns] *n* variazione *f*. **at variance** in disaccordo.

**varicose veins** ['varikous] *pl n* vene varicose *f pl*.

**variety** [və'raiəti] *n* varietà *f*, diversità *f*.

**various** ['veəriəs] *adj* vario, diverso.

**varnish** ['va:niʃ] *n* vernice *f*, lacca *f*. *v* verniciare, laccare.

**vary** ['veəri] *v* variare; modificare; differire. **variant** *n* variante *f*. **variation** *n* variazione *f*. **varied** *adj* vario, svariato.

**vase** [va:z] *n* vaso *m*.

**vasectomy** [və'sektəmi] *n* vasectomia *f*.

**vast** [va:st] *adj* vasto, immenso.

**vat** [vat] *n* tino *m*.

**VAT** *n* IVA (imposta sul valore aggiunto) *f*.

**Vatican** ['vatikən] *n* Vaticano *m*. **Vatican City** la Città del Vaticano *f*.

**vault¹** [vo:lt] *n* volta *f*; (*cellar*) cantina *f*; (*safe*) camera di sicurezza *f*.

**vault²** [vo:lt] *v* saltare, volteggiare. *n* salto *m*.

**veal** [vi:l] *n* vitello *m*.

**veer** [viə] *v* virare, cambiar direzione.

**vegetable** ['vedʒtəbl] *n* ortaggio *m*, verdura *f*. *adj* vegetale; (*food*) di verdura. **vegetarian** *n*, *adj* vegetariano, -a. **vegetate** *v* vegetare. **vegetation** *n* vegetazione *f*.

**vehement** ['vi:əmənt] *adj* violento, impetuoso.

**vehicle** ['viəkl] *n* veicolo *m*; (*means*) mezzo *m*.

**veil** [veil] *n* velo *m*. *v* velare; (*hide*) nascondere.

**vein** [vein] *n* vena *f*; (*leaf, marking*) venatura *f*.

**velocity** [və'losəti] *n* velocità *f*.

**velvet** ['velvit] *n* velluto *m*. **velvety** *adj* vellutato.

**vending machine** ['vendiŋ] *n* distributore automatico *m*.

**veneer** [və'niə] *n* piallaccio *m*; (*superficial layer*) vernice *f*.

**venerate** ['venəreit] *v* venerare. **venerable** *adj* venerabile.

**venereal disease** [və'niəriəl] *n* malattia venerea *f*.

**Venetian blind** [və'ni:ʃən] *n* veneziana *f*.

**vengeance** ['vendʒəns] *n* vendetta *f*. **with a vengeance** (*unexpectedly*) in modo insospettato; (*with violence*) violentemente.

**Venice** ['venis] *n* Venezia *f*.

**venison** ['venisn] *n* cacciagione *f*.

**venom** ['venəm] *n* veleno *m*; (*spite*) malignità *f*, cattiveria *f*. **venomous** *adj* velenoso; maligno, cattivo.

**vent** [vent] *n* (*outlet*) apertura *f*, sbocco *m*. **give vent to** sfogare. *v* esprimere, sfogare.

**ventilate** ['ventileit] *v* ventilare. **ventilation** *n* ventilazione *f*.

**venture** ['ventʃə] *n* impresa (rischiosa) *f*, avventura *f*. *v* azzardare, arrischiare.

**venue** ['venju:] *n* sede *f*; (*place*) posto *m*.

**verb** [və:b] *n* verbo *m*. **verbal** *adj* verbale. **verbatim** *adj* parola per parola.

**verdict** ['və:dikt] *n* verdetto *m*, giudizio *m*.

**verge** [və:dʒ] *n* orlo *m*, limite *m*. **on the verge of** sul punto di. *v* **verge on** tendere a, avvicinarsi a.

**verify** ['verifai] *v* verificare, confermare. **verification** *n* verifica *f*.

**vermin** ['və:min] *pl n* animali nocivi *m pl*, parassiti *m pl*; (*scum*) feccia *f sing*.

**vermouth** ['və:məθ] *n* vermut *m invar*.

**vernacular** [və'nakjulə] *adj* indigeno,

dialettale; volgare. *n* **in the vernacular** in volgare.

**versatile** ['vəːsətail] *adj* versatile, eclettico.

**verse** [vəːs] *n* verso *m*; (*poem*) poesia *f*. **in verse** in versi.

**version** ['vəːʃən] *n* versione *f*.

**versus** ['vəːsəs] *prep* contro.

**vertebra** ['vəːtibrə] *n*, *pl* **-brae** vertebra *f*. **vertebral** *adj* vertebrale. **vertebrate** *nm*, *adj* vertebrato.

**vertical** ['vəːtikl] *nf*, *adj* verticale.

**vertigo** ['vəːtigou] *n* vertigini *f pl*.

**very** ['veri] *adv* molto, assai. **the very next day** proprio il giorno dopo. *adj* proprio; esatto; (*same*) stesso; (*mere*) solo.

**vessel** ['vesl] *n* (*container*) recipiente *m*, vaso *m*; (*ship*) nave *f*, bastimento *m*.

**vest** [vest] *n* maglia *f*, maglietta *f*. *v* conferire, assegnare.

**vestige** ['vestidʒ] *n* vestigio *m*, traccia *f*.

**vestry** ['vestri] *n* sagrestia *f*.

**vet** [vet] (*coll*) *v* controllare, esaminare. *n* veterinario, -a *m*, *f*.

**veteran** ['vetərən] *n* veterano *m*; (*mil*) reduce *m*.

**veterinary** ['vetərinəri] *adj* veterinario. **veterinary surgeon** *n* veterinario, -a *m*, *f*.

**veto** ['viːtou] *n* veto *m*.

**vex** [veks] *v* vessare, irritare. **vexed question** argomento dibattuto *m*.

**via** [vaiə] *prep* per, attraverso, tramite.

**viable** ['vaiəbl] *adj* vitale, capace a vivere; (*workable*) praticabile, possibile; (*road*) transitabile. **viability** *n* praticabilità *f*; (*biol*) vitalità *f*.

**viaduct** ['vaiədʌkt] *n* viadotto *m*.

**vibrate** [vai'breit] *v* (far) vibrare. **vibration** *n* vibrazione *f*.

**vicar** ['vikə] *n* parroco *m*, vicario *m*. **vicarage** *n* parrocchia *f*.

**vicarious** [vi'keəriəs] *adj* vicario.

**vice**[1] [vais] *n* (*evil*) vizio *m*; (*fault*) difetto *m*.

**vice**[2] [vais] *n* (*tool*) morsa *f*.

**vice-chancellor** [vais'tʃaːnsələ] *n* (*university*) rettore *m*.

**vice-president** [vais'prezidənt] *n* vice-presidente *m*.

**vice versa** [vaisi'vəːsə] *adv* viceversa.

**vicinity** [vi'siniti] *n* vicinanza *f*, prossimità *f*; (*neighbourhood*) vicinanze *f pl*, dintorni *m pl*.

**vicious** ['viʃəs] *adj* (*bad*) cattivo; (*crude*) crudele, maligno. **vicious circle** circolo vizioso *m*.

**victim** ['viktim] *n* vittima *f*. **fall victim to** essere preda a. **victimize** *v* perseguitare *or* punire ingiustamente; sacrificare.

**victory** ['viktəri] *n* vittoria *f*. **victorious** *adj* vittorioso.

**video recorder** *n* videoregistratore *m*.

**videotape** ['vidiouteip] *n* videocassetta *f*.

**vie** [vai] *v* gareggiare.

**Vienna** [vi'enə] *n* Vienna *f*.

**view** [vjuː] *n* vista *f*; (*scene, opinion*) veduta *f*. **in view of** in vista di; (*considering*) dato; (*on account of*) grazie a, a causa di. **on view** esposto. **viewfinder** *n* mirino *m*. **viewpoint** *n* punto di vista *m*. **with a view to** allo scopo di. *v* vedere; osservare; ispezionare. **viewer** *n* spettatore, -trice *m*, *f*; telespettatore, -trice *m*, *f*.

**vigil** ['vidʒil] *n* veglia *f*; vigilia *f*. **vigilant** *adj* vigile.

**vigour** ['vigə] *n* vigore *m*. **vigorous** *adj* vigoroso; robusto.

**vile** [vail] *adj* vile, spregevole.

**villa** ['vilə] *n* villa *f*.

**village** ['vilidʒ] *n* villaggio *m*, paese *m*.

**villain** ['vilən] *n* farabutto *m*, villano *m*.

**vindicate** ['vindikeit] *v* rivendicare, giustificare; (*exonerate*) discolpare. **vindication** *n* rivendicazione *f*, giustificazione *f*; discolpa *f*.

**vindictive** [vin'diktiv] *adj* vendicativo, malevolo.

**vine** [vain] *n* vite *f*. **vineyard** *n* vigna *f*.

**vinegar** ['vinigə] *n* aceto *m*.

**vintage** ['vintidʒ] *n* vendemmia *f*; (*year*) annata *f*. *adj* (*wine*) pregiato; (*car*) d'epoca.

**vinyl** ['vainil] *adj* vinilico.

**viola** [vi'oulə] *n* viola *f*.

**violate** ['vaiəleit] *v* violare, trasgredire. **violation** *n* violazione *f*, trasgressione *f*.

**violence** ['vaiələns] *n* violenza *f*. **violent** *adj* violento.

**violet** ['vaiəlit] *n* (*colour*) (color) viola *m*, violetto *m*; (*flower*) viola *f*, violetta *f*. *adj* viola *invar*, violetto.

**violin** [vaiə'lin] *n* violino *m*. **violinist** *n* violinista *m*, *f*.

**viper** ['vaipə] *n* vipera *f*.

**virgin** ['vəːdʒin] *nf*, *adj* vergine. **virginity** *n* verginità f.

**Virgo** ['vəːgou] n Vergine f.

**virile** ['virail] adj virile. **virility** n virilità f.

**virtual** ['vəːtʃuəl] adj effettivo, in pratica. **virtual reality** n realtà virtuale f.

**virtue** ['vəːtʃuː] n virtù f; (admirable quality) pregio m. **by virtue of** in virtù di, grazie a. **virtuoso** n virtuoso, -a m, f. **virtuous** adj virtuoso.

**virulent** ['virələnt] adj virulento. **virulence** n virulenza f.

**virus** ['vaiərəs] n virus m invar. **viral** adj virale.

**visa** ['viːzə] n visto m.

**viscount** ['vaikaunt] n visconte m. **viscountess** n viscontessa f.

**viscous** ['viskəs] adj viscoso. **viscosity** n viscosità f.

**visible** ['vizəbl] adj visibile; (obvious) evidente. **visibility** n visibilità f.

**vision** ['viʒən] n visione f; (wisdom) sagacia f. **visionary** n, adj visionario, -a.

**visit** ['vizit] n visita f. v visitare; (person) fare una visita a, andare a trovare; (place) andare a vedere; (doctor) consultare. **visitor** n visitatore, -trice m, f; (guest) ospite m, f.

**visor** ['vaizə] n visiera f.

**visual** ['viʒuəl] adj visivo, visuale. **visualize** v immaginare, concepire.

**vital** ['vaitl] adj vitale, essenziale; capitale. **vitality** n vitalità f.

**vitamin** ['vitəmin] n vitamina f.

**vivacious** [vi'veiʃəs] adj vivace, animato. **vivacity** n vivacità f.

**vivid** ['vivid] adj vivido, vivace.

**vixen** ['viksn] n volpe femmina f.

**vocabulary** [və'kabjuləri] n vocabolario m.

**vocal** ['voukəl] adj vocale; orale.

**vocation** [vou'keiʃən] n vocazione f; professione f; (role) funzione f. **vocational** adj vocazionale, professionale.

**vociferous** [və'sifərəs] adj rumoroso, chiassoso.

**vodka** ['vodkə] n vodka f.

**voice** [vois] n voce f. v esprimere, formulare, manifestare.

**void** [void] nm, adj vuoto. v vuotare; (law) annullare.

**volatile** ['volətail] adj (chem) volatile; capriccioso; (unpredictable) imprevedibile; esplosivo.

**volcano** [vol'keinou] n vulcano m. **volcanic** adj vulcanico.

**volley** ['voli] n raffica f, scarica f; (tennis) volata f. **volleyball** n pallavolo f.

**volt** [voult] n volt m invar. **voltage** n tensione f, voltaggio m.

**volume** ['voljum] n volume m. **voluminous** adj voluminoso.

**volunteer** [volən'tiə] n volontario, -a m, f. v offrirsi volontariamente; (mil) arruolarsi volontario; (offer) dare or offrire spontaneamente. **voluntary** adj volontario.

**voluptuous** [və'lʌptʃuəs] adj voluttuoso, sensuale.

**vomit** ['vomit] v vomitare. n vomito m.

**voodoo** ['vuːduː] n vodù m.

**voracious** [və'reiʃəs] adj vorace, insaziabile. **voracity** n voracità f.

**vote** [vout] n voto m, diritto di voto m, suffragio m. v votare, dare il proprio voto; (agree generally) convenire. **voter** n elettore, -trice m, f.

**vouch** [vautʃ] v **vouch for** garantire, attestare. **vouchsafe** v degnarsi di dare, concedere.

**voucher** ['vautʃə] n buono m, tagliando m.

**vow** [vau] n voto m, giuramento m. v giurare; fare voto di.

**vowel** ['vauəl] n vocale f.

**voyage** ['voiidʒ] n viaggio m, escursione f; (crossing) traversata f. v viaggiare; attraversare.

**vulgar** ['vʌlgə] adj volgare. **vulgarity** n volgarità f. **vulgarize** v divulgare, volgarizzare; (debase) degradare.

**vulnerable** ['vʌlnərəbl] adj vulnerabile.

**vulture** ['vʌltʃə] n avvoltoio m.

# W

**wad** [wod] n tampone m; pacchetto m; (roll) rotolo m. **wadding** n (padding) imbottitura f.

**waddle** ['wodl] v camminare dondolandosi. n andatura dondolante f.

**wade** [weid] v guadare, avanzare con fatica. **wader** n (bird) trampoliere m.

**wafer** ['weifə] n cialda f, wafer m invar;

(*church*) ostia f.

**waft** [woft] v diffondere. n zaffata f.

**wag** [wag] v agitare, scuotere; (*tail*) dimenare. **set tongues wagging** suscitare pettegolezzi.

**wage** [weidʒ] n salario m, paga f. v **wage war** muover guerra.

**wager** [weidʒə] n scommessa f. v scommettere.

**wagon** [wagən] n vagone m, carrozza f. **be on the wagon** (*coll*) essere astemio.

**waif** [weif] n senzatetto m invar; (*foundling*) trovatello, -a m, f.

**wail** [weil] n gemito m, lamento m. v gemere, emettere un lamento.

**waist** [weist] n vita f. **waistcoat** n gilè m. **waistline** n misura or circonferenza della vita f.

**wait** [weit] v aspettare, attendere; servire, sostare. n attesa f; sosta f. **lie in wait** stare in agguato. **waiter** n cameriere m. **waiting-room** n sala d'aspetto f. **waitress** n cameriera f.

**waive** [weiv] v rinunciare. **waiver** n rinuncia f; (*document*) atto di rinuncia m.

**\*wake**[1] [weik] v *also* **wake up** svegliare, svegliarsi. n veglia f.

**wake**[2] [weik] n scia f. **in the wake of** subito dopo, nella scia di.

**Wales** [weilz] n Galles m.

**walk** [wo:k] v camminare; (*go on foot*) andare a piedi. **walk in** entrare. **walk out on** piantare. **walkover** n vittoria incontestata or facile f. n cammino m, passeggiata f; (*gait*) passo m. **walker** n camminatore, -trice m, f; (*sport*) podista m, f.

**wall** [wo:l] n muro m; (*internal*) parete f. **wallpaper** n carta da parati f.

**wallet** [wolit] n portafoglio m.

**wallop** [woləp] (*coll*) v (*thrash*) battere, picchiare. n (*blow*) colpo violento m.

**wallow** [wolou] v sguazzare.

**walnut** [wo:lnʌt] n (*tree*) noce m; (*fruit*) noce f.

**walrus** [wo:lrəs] n tricheco m. **walrus moustache** baffi spioventi m pl.

**waltz** [wo:lts] n valzer m invar. v ballare il valzer. **waltz through** (*coll*) superare facilmente.

**wand** [wond] n bacchetta f.

**wander** [wondə] v vagare, girare; (*stray*) allontanarsi, delirare.

**wane** [wein] v calare, declinare. n declino m; (*moon*) calare m.

**wangle** [wangl] (*coll*) n trucco m, intrigo (*pl* -ghi) m. v procurare con astuzia.

**want** [wont] v volere, desiderare, aver voglia di; (*lack*) mancare di; (*ought*) dovere. n (*need*) bisogno m, esigenza f; (*deficiency*) mancanza f. **wanted** adj (*asked for*) richiesto; (*police*) ricercato; (*advertisement*) cercasi.

**wanton** [wontən] adj deliberato, gratuito, sfrenato. n libertino m, sgualdrina f.

**war** [wo:] n guerra f. **warfare** n guerra f. **warmonger** n guerrafondaio m. **wartime** n tempo di guerra m. v far guerra, combattere.

**warble** [wo:bl] n trillo m. v trillare. **warbler** n uccello canoro m.

**ward** [wo:d] n (*district*) distretto m; (*hospital*) corsia f, padiglione m; (*law*) pupillo, -a m, f. v **ward off** parare, scansare.

**warden** [wo:dn] n guardiano, -a m, f, custode m, f.

**warder** [wo:də] n carceriere, -a m, f.

**wardrobe** [wo:droub] n guardaroba m invar; (*cupboard*) armadio m.

**warehouse** [weəhaus] n magazzino m.

**warm** [wo:m] adj caldo; cordiale, caloroso; (*lively*) animato; (*enthusiastic*) ardente. **be warm** aver caldo. **get warm** scaldarsi. v riscaldare. **warmth** n caldo m; calore m; animazione f; ardore m.

**warn** [wo:n] v mettere in guardia, ammonire; (*notify*) avvertire, preavvisare. **warning** n ammonimento m; preavviso m; allarme m. **warning triangle** triangolo d'emergenza m.

**warp** [wo:p] v deformare. n ordito m.

**warrant** [worənt] n autorizzazione f, diritto m; (*law*) mandato m. v autorizzare; giustificare; garantire. **warranty** n (*comm*) garanzia f.

**warren** [worən] n (*rabbit*) garenna f.

**warrior** [woriə] n guerriero m. **unknown warrior** n milite ignoto m.

**Warsaw** [wo:so:] n Varsavia f.

**wart** [wo:t] n verruca f.

**wary** [weəri] adj diffidente, cauto. **be wary of** diffidare di; guardarsi dal.

**was** [woz] V **be**.

**wash** [woʃ] v lavare. **wash away** portare via; (*obliterate*) cancellare. **wash-basin** n

lavandino *m.* **wash-out** *n* (*slang*) fiasco *m.*
**wash up** lavare i piatti. *n* lavata *f.*; (*clothes, etc.*) bucato *m.*; (*painting*) acquerello *m.*, guazzo *m.* **have a wash** lavarsi. **washable** *adj* lavabile. **washing** *n* bucato *m.* **washing-machine** *n* lavatrice automatica *f.*

**washer** ['wɒʃə] *n* rondella *f.*

**wasp** [wɒsp] *n* vespa *f.*

**waste** [weist] *v* sprecare, sciupare. **waste away** deperire. *n* spreco *m.*; (*rubbish*) immondizia *f.*; (*scrap*) scarti *m pl*, cascami *m pl*; (*geog*) deserto *m.* **waste-paper basket** cestino da rifiuti *m.* **waste-pipe** *n* tubo di scarico *m.* **wasteful** *adj* dispendioso, sprecone.

**watch** [wɒtʃ] *v* guardare, osservare; (*as spectator*) assistere a; (*keep an eye on*) tener d'occhio. **watch out** stare attento. **watch over** sorvegliare. *n* (*time*) orologio *m.*; osservazione *f.*; guardia *f.*, sorveglianza *f.* **keep watch** fare la guardia. **watch-dog** *n* cane da guardia *m.* **watchful** *adj* vigile.

**water** ['wɔːtə] *n* acqua *f.* *v* annaffiare, irrigare. **water down** diluire; moderare, attenuare. **watery** *adj* acquoso; (*colour*) scialbo.

**water-closet** *n* gabinetto *m.*

**water-colour** *n* acquerello *m.*

**watercress** ['wɔːtəkres] *n* crescione *m.*

**waterfall** ['wɔːtəfɔːl] *n* cascata *f.*

**waterfront** ['wɔːtəfrʌnt] *n* lungomare *m.*; (*wharf*) zona portuale *f.*

**watering-can** *n* annaffiatoio *m.*

**water-lily** *n* ninfea *f.*

**waterlogged** ['wɔːtəlogd] *adj* saturo d'acqua; (*ground*) acquitrinoso.

**water-melon** *n* cocomero *m.*

**water-mill** *n* mulino ad acqua *m.*

**water polo** *n* pallanuoto *f.*

**waterproof** ['wɔːtəpruːf] *nm*, *adj* impermeabile. *v* impermeabilizzare.

**watershed** ['wɔːtəʃed] *n* spartiacque *m invar.*

**water-ski** *n* sci nautico *m.* *v* fare dello sci nautico. **water-skiing** *n* sci nautico *m.*

**watertight** ['wɔːtətait] *adj* stagno; (*irrefutable*) inconfutabile.

**water-way** *n* corso navigabile *m.*

**waterworks** ['wɔːtəwəːks] *n* impianto idrico *m.* **turn on the waterworks** (*coll*) mettersi a piangere.

**watt** [wɒt] *n* watt *m invar.* **wattage** *n* wattaggio *m.*

**wave** [weiv] *n* onda *f.*; (*surge*) ondata *f.*; (*sign*) cenno *m.* **waveband** *n* gamma di lunghezze d'onda *f.* *v* sventolare, far segno con; (*hair*) ondulare. **wave aside** scartare. **wavy** *adj* (*hair*) ondulato; (*line*) ondeggiante.

**waver** ['weivə] *v* (*vacillate*) titubare, esitare.

**wax¹** [waks] *n* cera *f.* *v* dar la cera a, lucidare.

**wax²** [waks] *v* (*increase*) crescere; (*become*) diventare.

**way** [wei] *n* (*manner*) modo *m.*; (*respect*) rispetto *m.*, particolare *m.*; (*street*) strada *f.*; passaggio *m.* **by the way** a proposito. **give way** cedere; (*traffic*) dare la precedenza. **in a way** in un certo modo. **make way for** fare largo a. **out of the way** (*place*) fuori strada; (*unusual*) fuori del comune. **way in** entrata *f.* **way out** uscita *f.*

*****waylay** [wei'lei] *v* abbordare; (*ambush*) tendere un agguato a.

**wayward** ['weiwəd] *adj* capriccioso, ribelle.

**we** [wiː] *pron* noi.

**weak** [wiːk] *adj* debole. **weaken** *v* indebolire. **weakling** *n* persona debole *f.* **weakness** *n* debolezza *f.*; (*inclination*) debole *m.*

**wealth** [welθ] *n* ricchezza *f.*; abbondanza *f.* **wealthy** *adj* ricco.

**wean** [wiːn] *v* svezzare.

**weapon** ['wepən] *n* arma *f.*

*****wear** [weə] *v* portare, indossare; (*deteriorate*) consumare; (*last*) durare. **wear off** passare, dissiparsi. **wear out** consumare, indebolire; (*tire*) stancare. *n* (*use*) uso *m.*; (*clothing*) abiti *m pl*, abbigliamento *m.*; (*deterioration*) usura *f.*

**weary** ['wiəri] *adj* stanco, stufo. *v* stancare, stufare.

**weasel** ['wiːzl] *n* donnola *f.*

**weather** ['weðə] *n* tempo *m.* **weather-beaten** *adj* segnato dalle intemperie. **weather forecast** bollettino meteorologico *m.* *v* (*expose*) esporre all'aria, stagionare; (*overcome*) superare.

*****weave** [wiːv] *v* tessere; (*devise*) ordire. *n* armatura *f.* **weaver** *n* tessitore *m.* **weaving** *n* tessitura *f.*

**web** [web] *n* tessuto *m.*; (*spider*) ragnatela *f.* **webbed foot** piede palmato *m.*

**website** *n* sito web *m.*

**wedding** ['wediŋ] *n* matrimonio *m.*; (*cere-*

*mony*) nozze *f pl.* **wedding-dress** *n* abito nuziale *m.* **wedding-ring** *n* fede *f.*

**wedge** [wedʒ] *n* cuneo *m.* *v* incuneare, incastrare.

**Wednesday** ['wenzdi] *n* mercoledì *m.*

**weed** [wi:d] *n* erbaccia *f*, malerba *f.* **weed-killer** *n* erbicida *m.* *v* diserbare, sarchiare. **weedy** *adj* coperto di erbacce; (*person*) sparuto.

**week** [wi:k] *n* settimana *f.* **weekday** *n* giorno feriale *or* lavorativo *m.* **weekend** *n* fine settimana *f*, week-end *m invar.*

**weekly** ['wi:kli] *nm, adj* settimanale. *adv* ogni settimana.

***weep** [wi:p] *v* piangere. **weeping** *n* pianto *m.* **weeping willow** salice piangente *m.* **weepy** *adj* (*coll*) lacrimoso, sentimentale.

**weigh** [wei] *v* pesare; (*have importance*) valere. **weigh anchor** salpare. **weigh-bridge** *n* pesa a ponte *f*, pesa pubblica *f.* **weigh up** soppesare, valutare. **weight** *n* peso *m.* **carry weight** aver peso. **lose weight** dimagrire. **put on weight** ingrassare. **weighty** *adj* pesante; importante.

**weird** [wiəd] *adj* strano, misterioso.

**welcome** ['welkəm] *interj* benvenuto! **welcome home!** ben tornato! *n* benvenuto *m*, buona *or* cordiale accoglienza *f.* *adj* benvenuto, gradito. *v* accogliere; (*greet*) dare il benvenuto a; (*accept gladly*) gradire.

**weld** [weld] *v* saldare. *n* saldatura *f.*

**welfare** ['welfeə] *n* benessere *m*; assistenza sociale *f.* **welfare worker** *n* assistente sociale *m, f.*

**well**[1] [wel] *n* pozzo *m*; (*stairs*) tromba *f.*

**well**[2] [wel] *adv* bene. *interj* beh! allora! **as well** (*also*) anche.

**well-behaved** *adj* educato, beneducato.

**well-being** *n* benessere *m*, bene *m.*

**well-bred** *adj* educato, beneducato.

**well-built** *adj* ben costruito.

**wellingtons** ['weliŋtənz] *pl n* stivali impermeabili *m pl*, stivali di gomma *m pl.*

**well-known** *adj* ben noto.

**well-meaning** *adj* ben intenzionato. **well-meant** *adj* fatto a fin di bene.

**well-off** *adj* benestante, agiato.

**well-paid** *adj* ben pagato *or* retribuito.

**well-read** *adj* colto.

**well-spoken** *adj* che parla bene.

**well-to-do** *adj* benestante, abbiente.

**well-worn** *adj* logoro; (*hackneyed*) trito.

**Welsh** [welʃ] *n(m+f )*, *adj* gallese.

**went** [went] *V* **go.**

**wept** [wept] *V* **weep.**

**were** [wəː] *V* **be.**

**west** [west] *n* ovest *m*, occidente *m.* *adv also* **westward(s)** verso ovest, in direzione ovest.

**western** ['westən] *adj* occidentale, dell'ovest. *n* (*film*) western *m.*

**wet** [wet] *adj* bagnato, umido; (*rainy*) piovoso; (*paint, ink, etc.*) fresco. **wet blanket** guastafeste *m, f invar.* **wet through** bagnato fradicio; (*person*) bagnato fino alle ossa. *v* bagnare.

**whack** [wak] (*coll*) *n* colpo *m*; (*part*) fetta *f.* *v* colpire. **be whacked** essere sfinito.

**whale** [weil] *n* balena *f.* **have a whale of a time** (*coll*) divertirsi un mondo. **whaling** *n* caccia alla balena *f.*

**wharf** [woːf] *n* banchina *f*, scalo *m.*

**what** [wot] *pron* (*che*) cosa; (*relative*) quello che. *adj* che, quale. **what a ...!** che ...! **what for?** perché? **what is the matter?** cosa c'è? cosa succede?

**whatever** [wot'evə] *pron* qualsiasi *or* qualunque cosa. *adj* qualsiasi, qualunque. **none whatever** nessuno. **nothing whatever** assolutamente nulla.

**wheat** [wi:t] *n* grano *m*, frumento *m.*

**wheel** [wi:l] *n* ruota *f*; (*pottery*) tornio *m*; (*steering*) volante *m.* **wheelbarrow** *n* carretta *f*, carriola *f.* **wheelchair** *n* sedia a rotelle *f.* *v* (*make turn*) far ruotare; (*push*) spingere.

**wheeze** [wi:z] *v* ansimare. *n* respiro affannoso *m.*

**whelk** [welk] *n* buccino *m.*

**when** [wen] *adv* quando. *conj* quando; (*after which*) appena; (*whereas*) mentre. **whenever** *adv* qualora, ogni volta che.

**where** [weə] *conj, adv* dove. **whereabouts** *adv* dove, da che parte. **whereas** *conj* mentre. **whereby** *conj, adv* onde, per cui. **whereupon** *conj* dopoché, dal momento che. **wherever** *conj* dovunque. **wherewithal** *n* necessario *m.*

**whether** ['weðə] *conj* se.

**which** [witʃ] *pron* quale; (*relative*) il quale, la quale; che. *adj* quale. **which way?** da che parte?

**whichever** [witʃ'evə] *adj* qualunque, qualsiasi. *pron* quello che; (*person*) chiunque.

**whiff** [wif] *n* buffata *f*, zaffata *f*.

**while** [wail] *conj* mentre. *n* momento *m*. **a long while ago** molto tempo fa.

**whim** [wim] *n* capriccio *m*.

**whimper** ['wimpə] *v* piagnucolare. *n* piagnucolio *m*.

**whimsical** ['wimzikl] *adj* bizzarro, eccentrico.

**whine** [wain] *v* gemere; (*complain*) uggiolare. *n* uggiolio *m*, gemito *m*.

**whip** [wip] *n* frusta *f*. **whip-round** (*coll*) colletta *f*. *v* frustare; (*cookery*) frullare. **whipped cream** panna montata *f*.

**whippet** ['wipit] *n* levriere inglese *m*.

**whirl** [wə:l] *n* turbine *m*, giro vertiginoso *m*. **whirlpool** *n* vortice *m*. **whirlwind** *n* turbine *m*, tromba d'aria *f*. *v* girare (rapidamente).

**whisk** [wisk] *v* (*dust*) spolverare; (*cookery*) frullare. *n* piumino *m*; frullino *m*.

**whisker** ['wiskə] *n* pelo *m*. **whiskers** *pl n* basette *f pl*; (*moustache, cat*) baffi *m pl*.

**whisky** ['wiski] *n* whisky *m invar* .

**whisper** ['wispə] *v* bisbigliare, mormorare. *n* bisbiglio *m*, mormorio *m*.

**whist** [wist] *n* whist *m invar*.

**whistle** ['wisl] *v* fischiare; (*tune*) fischiettare. *n* (*sound*) fischio *m*; (*instrument*) fischietto *m*.

**white** [wait] *n* bianco *m*. *adj* bianco. **whitebait** *pl n* bianchetti *m pl*. **whiten** *v* imbiancare.

**whitewash** ['waitwoʃ] *n* intonaco *m*; (*cover-up*) riabilitazione *f*. *v* imbiancare, intonacare; (*cover up*) scolpare.

**whiting** ['waitiŋ] *n* (*fish*) merlango *m*.

**Whitsun** ['witsn] *n* Pentecoste *f*.

**whizz** [wiz] *v* (*hum*) sibilare; (*move*) guizzare.

**who** [hu:] *pron* chi; (*relative*) che, il quale, la quale. **whoever** *pron* chiunque.

**whole** [houl] *n* totale *m*, insieme *m*. **as a whole** nell'insieme. **on the whole** tutto considerato, in fin dei conti. *adj* intero, tutto; intatto. **wholehearted** *adj* generoso. **wholemeal** *adj* integrale. **wholesale** *adv* all'ingrosso. **wholefood** *n* alimento biologico *m*. **wholesaler** *n* grossista *m*, *f*. **wholesome** *adj* sano.

**whom** [hu:m] *pron* che; (*relative*) il quale, la quale; (*after prep*) cui.

**whooping cough** ['hu:piŋ] *n* pertosse *f*.

**whore** [ho:] *n* (*derog*) puttana *f*.

**whose** [hu:z] *pron* di chi. *adj* di cui; (*relative*) il cui, la cui.

**why** [wai] *adv, conj* perché, per cui.

**wick** [wik] *n* stoppino *m*.

**wicked** ['wikid] *adj* cattivo, malvagio. **wickedness** *n* cattiveria *f*, malvagità *f*.

**wicker** ['wikə] *n* vimini *m pl*.

**wicket** ['wikit] *n* porta *f*, sportello *m*. **a sticky wicket** una situazione scabrosa.

**wide** [waid] *adj* largo; (*spacious*) ampio. *adv* lontano. **open wide** *v* spalancare. **wide apart** spaziati. **wide awake** completamente sveglio; (*alert*) vigilante. **wide open** spalancato. **widespread** *adj* esteso, diffuso. **widen** *v* estendere, allargare.

**widow** ['widou] *n* vedova *f*. **widower** *n* vedovo *m*.

**width** [widθ] *n* larghezza *f*; (*cloth*) altezza *f*.

**wield** [wi:ld] *v* (*weapon*) brandire; (*power*) esercitare.

**wife** [waif] *n* moglie *f*.

**wig** [wig] *n* parrucca *f*.

**wiggle** ['wigl] *v* dimenare.

**wild** [waild] *adj* selvatico; (*animal, place*) selvaggio; (*unrestrained*) feroce. **spread like wildfire** divampare. **wild with anger** fuori di sé dalla rabbia. **wild with joy** folle di gioia.

**wilderness** ['wildənəs] *n* deserto *m*, solitudine *f*.

**wildlife** *n* fauna e flora selvatica *f*.

**wilful** ['wilfəl] *adj* intenzionale; premeditato; ostinato.

**will**[1] [wil] *aux translated by future tense.*

**will**[2] [wil] *n* volontà *f*; (*law*) testamento *m*. **against one's will** malvolentieri, controvoglia. **at will** a piacere.

**willing** ['wiliŋ] *adj* (*disposed*) disposto; (*ready*) pronto, volonteroso. **willingness** *n* prontezza *f*; buona volontà *f*.

**willow** ['wilou] *n* salice *m*.

**wilt** [wilt] *v* appassire.

**\*win** [win] *v* vincere. **win back** riguadagnare. *n* vittoria *f*; (*games*) vincita *f*. **winner** *n* vincitore *m*.

**wince** [wins] *v* trasalire. *n* sussulto *m*, trasalimento *m*.

**winch** [wintʃ] *n* argano *m*. *v* **winch up** sollevare con l'argano.

**wind¹** [wind] *n* vento *m*; (*breath*) fiato *m*. **get wind of** aver sentore di, fiutare. *v* sfiatare. **windy** *adj* esposto al vento.

**\*wind²** [waind] *v* (*twist*) serpeggiare. **wind up** (*roll up*) avvolgere; concludere; (*end up*) andare a finire; (*clock*) caricare; (*business*) liquidare.

**wind-cheater** *n* giacca a vento *f*.

**windfall** [windfo:l] *n* frutto fatto cadere dal vento *m*; fortuna inaspettata *f*.

**wind farm** *n* centrale eolica *f*, *m*.

**windlass** [windləs] *n* verricello *m*.

**windmill** [windˌmil] *n* mulino a vento *m*.

**window** [windou] *n* finestra *f*; (*train*) finestrino *m*; (*car*) cristallo *m*; (*cashier's*) sportello *m*. **French window** *n* portafinestra *f*. **window-dressing** *n* mostra *f*; (*show*) bella mostra *f*, inganno *m*. **window-sill** *n* davanzale *m*.

**windpipe** [windpaip] *n* trachea *f*.

**windscreen** [windskri:n] *n* parabrezza *m invar*. **windscreen wiper** tergicristallo *m*.

**windswept** [windswept] *adj* battuto dai venti.

**wine** [wain] *n* vino *m*. **wineglass** *n* bicchiere da vino *m*. **wine list** carta dei vini *f*.

**wing** [wiŋ] *n* ala *f*; (*theatre*) tra le quinte. **wingspan** *n* apertura alare *f*.

**wink** [wiŋk] *v* strizzare l'occhio, ammiccare. *n* (*signal*) cenno *m*; (*instant*) attimo *m*. **have forty winks** schiacciare un pisolino.

**winkle** [wiŋkl] *n* chiocciola di mare *f*.

**winter** [wintə] *n* inverno *m*. **wintry** *adj* invernale.

**wipe** [waip] *v* strofinare; (*dry*) asciugare. **wipe away** *or* **off** cancellare, allontanare. **wipe out** eliminare; (*debts, etc*.) liquidare; (*annihilate*) annientare. **wiper** *n* strofinaccio *m*; (*windscreen*) tergicristallo *m*.

**wire** [waiə] *n* filo *m*; telegramma *m*. **wireless** *n* radio *f invar*. *v* (*elec*) montare; (*fasten*) legare con filo metallico; telegrafare. **wiry** *adj* secco, nerboruto.

**wisdom** [wizdəm] *n* saggezza *f*. **wisdom tooth** *n* dente del giudizio *m*.

**wise** [waiz] *adj* saggio. **wisecrack** *n* battuta *f*.

**wish** [wiʃ] *n* desiderio *m*, voglia *f*. **wishes** *pl n* auguri *m pl*. *v* desiderare, volere; (*greeting*) augurare. **wishful thinking** pio desiderio *m*.

**wisp** [wisp] *n* (*hair*) ciocca *f*; (*smoke*) filo *m*.

**wistful** [wistfəl] *adj* pensoso, malinconico.

**wit** [wit] *n* spirito *m*; arguzia *f*, intelligenza *f*; (*person*) uomo di spirito *m*. **be at one's wits' end** non saper più cosa fare. **live by one's wits** vivere di espedienti.

**witch** [witʃ] *n* strega *f*. **witchcraft** *n* stregoneria *f*. **witch-doctor** *n* stregone *m*.

**with** [wið] *prep* con; (*together with*) insieme a; (*because of*) per, a causa di.

**\*withdraw** [wið'dro:] *v* ritirare; (*cash*) prelevare. **withdrawal** *n* ritiro *m*; (*mil*) ritirata *f*; prelevamento *m*.

**wither** [wiðə] *v* (*lose freshness*) appassire; atrofizzare; (*decay*) avvizzire.

**\*withhold** [wið'hould] *v* trattenere; (*hide*) nascondere.

**within** [wi'ðin] *adv* dentro. *prep* entro, in. **within reach** a portata.

**without** [wi'ðaut] *prep* senza. *adv* fuori. **do without** fare a meno (di).

**\*withstand** [wið'stand] *v* resistere a.

**witness** [witnis] *n* (*evidence*) testimonianza *f*; (*person*) testimone *m*, *f*. *v* testimoniare, attestare. **witness box** banco dei testimoni *m*.

**witty** [witi] *adj* spiritoso, arguto.

**wizard** [wizəd] *n* mago *m*.

**wobble** [wobl] *v* vacillare, traballare.

**woke** [wouk] *V* **wake¹**.

**woken** [woukn] *V* **wake¹**.

**wolf** [wulf] *n* lupo *m*. **cry wolf** gridare al lupo. *v* divorare.

**woman** [wumən] *n*, *pl* **women** donna *f*. **old woman** *n* vecchia *f*. **young woman** giovane *f*. **womanly** *adj* femminile.

**womb** [wu:m] *n* utero *m*.

**won** [wʌn] *V* **win**.

**wonder** [wʌndə] *n* meraviglia *f*; miracolo *m*. *v* meravigliarsi; (*ask oneself*) domandarsi. **wonderful** *adj* meraviglioso.

**wood** [wud] *n* (*material*) legno *m*; (*as fuel*) legna *f*; (*forest*) bosco *m*. **wooden** *adj* di legno; rigido. **woody** *adj* (*wooded*) boscoso; (*tough*) legnoso.

**woodcock** [wudkok] *n* beccaccia *f*.

**woodcut** [wudkʌt] *n* silografia *f*, incisione su legno *f*.

**woodland** [wudlənd] *n* boscaglia *f*.

**woodpecker** [wudpekə] *n* picchio *m*.

**wood-pigeon** *n* colombaccio *m*.

**wood-wind** *n* strumenti a fiato *m pl*.

**woodwork** ['wudwə:k] *n* (*carpentry*) lavoro in legno *m*, falegnameria *f*; (*wooden parts*) parti in legno *f pl*.

**woodworm** ['wudwə:m] *n* tarlo *m*.

**wool** [wul] *n* lana *f*. **dyed in the wool** *adj* radicato, convinto. **woollen** *adj* di lana; (*industry*) laniero. **woolly** *adj* di lana, lanoso; confuso.

**word** [wə:d] *n* parola *f*. **in other words** altrimenti detto. **word for word** alla lettera. *v* esprimere, redigere. **wording** *n* espressione *f*, formulazione *f*.

**word processor** *n* elaboratore testi *m*. **word processing** elaborazione testi *f*.

**wore** [wo:] *V* **wear**.

**work** [wə:k] *n* lavoro *m*; (*toil*) fatica *f*; (*product*) opera *f*. **workman** *n* operaio *m*. **works** *n* (*factory*) fabbrica *f*, stabilimento *m*. **workshop** *n* officina *f*. **workstation** *n* postazione di lavoro *f*. *v* lavorare; (*machine, etc.*) (far) funzionare. **work out** risolvere; risultare. **worker** *n* lavoratore, -trice *m*, *f*, operaio, -a *m*, *f*. **working** *n* operazione *f*, funzionamento *m*. **working class** classe operaia *f*. **working order** buon ordine *m*.

**world** [wə:ld] *n* mondo *m*. **world war** guerra mondiale *f*. **world-wide** *adj* mondiale, universale. **worldly** *adj* temporale; mondano.

**World Wide Web** *n* il web *m*.

**worm** [wə:m] *n* verme *m*. *v* insinuarsi.

**worn** [wo:n] *V* **wear**.

**worry** ['wʌri] *n* preoccupazione *f*, ansia *f*. *v* preoccupare; molestare. **worrying** *adj* preoccupante.

**worse** [wə:s] *adj* peggio, peggiore. *nm*, *adv* peggio. **from bad to worse** di male in peggio. **get worse** peggiorare. **worsen** *v* peggiorare.

**worship** ['wə:ʃip] *n* adorazione *f*, omaggio *m*; (*rel*) culto *m*, servizio religioso *m*. *v* adorare; andare a messa, andare in chiesa.

**worst** [wə:st] *adj* peggiore, il più brutto. *nm*, *adv* peggio.

**worsted** ['wustid] *nm*, *adj* pettinato.

**worth** [wə:θ] *adj* **be worth** valere. **be worthless** non valere nulla. **be worthwhile** valere la pena. *n* merito *m*, valore *m*. **worthy** *adj* degno.

**would** [wud] *aux translated by conditional or imperfect tense*.

**wound¹** [wu:nd] *n* ferita *f*. *v* ferire; offend-

ere. **wounded** *adj* ferito.

**wound²** [waund] *V* **wind²**.

**wove** [wouv] *V* **weave**.

**woven** ['wouvn] *V* **weave**.

**wrangle** ['rangl] *v* litigare, disputare. *n* lite *f*, disputa *f*.

**wrap** [rap] *v* (*envelop*) avvolgere; (*cover*) coprire; (*parcel*) incartare. *n* (*shawl*) scialle *m*; (*dressing-gown*) vestaglia *f*. **wrapper** *n* involucro *m*; (*book*) copertina *f*.

**wreath** [ri:θ] *n* ghirlanda *f*, corona *f*. **wreathe** *v* incoronare. **wreathed in smiles** raggiante.

**wreck** [rek] *n* (*ship*) naufragio *m*; (*ruin*) relitto *m*, rovina *f*. *v* rovinare; demolire; naufragare. **wreckage** *n* rottami *m pl*.

**wren** [ren] *n* scricciolo *m*.

**wrench** [rentʃ] *v* storcere. **wrench open** forzare. *n* (*movement*) strappo *m*; (*injury*) storta *f*; (*spanner*) chiave *f*.

**wrestle** ['resl] *v* lottare. **wrestling** *n* lotta *f*.

**wretch** [retʃ] *n* (*unfortunate*) disgraziato, -a *m*, *f*; (*despicable*) incosciente *m*, *f*. **wretched** *adj* disgraziato, miserabile; (*pitiful*) pietoso.

**wriggle** ['rigl] *v* dimenarsi.

***wring** [riŋ] *v* torcere. **wring out** strizzare. **wringer** *n* strizzatoio *m*. **wringing wet** fradicio.

**wrinkle** ['riŋkl] *n* crespa *f*; (*face*) ruga *f*. *v* increspare; corrugare.

**wrist** [rist] *n* polso *m*.

**writ** [rit] *n* mandato *m*.

***write** [rait] *v* scrivere. **write down** trascrivere, registrare. **write off** (*comm*) cancellare. **writer** *n* scrittore, -trice *m*, *f*. **writing** *n* calligrafia *f*. **writings** *pl n* scritti *m pl*.

**writhe** [raið] *v* contorcersi.

**written** ['ritn] *V* **write**.

**wrong** [ron] *adv* male. *adj* (*not moral*) peccato; (*incorrect*) sbagliato. **be wrong** (*person*) aver torto, sbagliarsi. *n* torto *m*; ingiustizia *f*; (*law*) violazione *f*. *v* far torto a, maltrattare. **wrongful** *adj* ingiustificato.

**wrote** [rout] *V* **write**.

**wrought iron** [rɔːt'aiən] *n* ferro battuto *m*.

**wrung** [rʌŋ] *V* **wring**.

**wry** [rai] *adj* ironico, perverso; (*askance*) di sbieco.

# X

**xenophobia** [ˌzenəˈfoubiə] n xenofobia f. **xenophobic** adj xenofobo.

**Xmas** [ˈkrisməs] V **Christmas**.

**X-ray** [ˈeksrei] n raggio X m; (photo) radiografia f. v radiografare.

**xylophone** [ˈzailəfoun] n xilofono m.

# Y

**yacht** [jot] n panfilo m. **yachting** n velismo m.

**yank** [jaŋk] v (coll) dare uno strattone a, tirare con violenza.

**yap** [jap] v guaire. n guaito m.

**yard** [jaːd] n cortile m; (site) cantiere m; (railway) scalo merci m. **yardstick** n (measure) metro m; (standard) pietra di paragone f.

**yarn** [jaːn] n (thread) filo m, filato m; storia f.

**yawn** [joːn] v sbadigliare. n sbadiglio m.

**year** [jiə] n anno m, annata f. **year-book** n annuario m. **yearly** adj annuo, annuale.

**yearn** [jəːn] v languire. **yearn for** bramare, desiderare vivamente. **yearning** n vivo desiderio m, brama f.

**yeast** [jiːst] n lievito m.

**yell** [jel] v gridare, urlare. n grido m, urlo m.

**yellow** [ˈjelou] adj giallo; (coll: cowardly) vigliacco. n giallo m. v ingiallire. **yellowy** adj giallastro.

**yelp** [jelp] v (dog) uggiolare. **yelp with pain** gridare per il dolore. n uggiolio m; grido di dolore m.

**yes** [jes] nm, adv sì.

**yesterday** [ˈjestədi] nm, adv ieri.

**yet** [jet] adv ancora; (already) già. conj ma, tuttavia. **as yet** finora.

**yew** [juː] n tasso m.

**yield** [jiːld] v produrre; (surrender) cedere; (profit, interest, etc.) rendere, fruttare. n frutto m, prodotto m; (tech) resa f; (finance) reddito m; (harvest) raccolto m.

**yob** [job] n teppista m.

**yoga** [ˈjougə] n yoga m.

**yoghurt** [ˈyogət] m iogurt m.

**yoke** [jouk] n giogo m; (dress) carrè m.

**yolk** [jouk] n tuorlo m.

**you** [juː] pron (subject: fam) tu; (subject: pl) voi; (subject: fml) Lei; (direct object) ti, vi, la; (indirect object) ti or te, vi or ve, le; (after prep) te, voi, Lei. **if I were you** se fossi (in) te.

**young** [jʌŋ] adj giovane. **youngster** n (child) bambino, -a m, f; (youth) ragazzo, -a m, f.

**your** [joː] adj (fam) (il) tuo, (la) tua, (i) tuoi, (le) tue; (pl) (il) vostro, (la) vostra, (i) vostri, (le) vostre; (fml) (il) suo, (la) sua, (i) suoi, (le) sue.

**yours** [joːz] pron (fam) il tuo, la tua, i tuoi, le tue; (pl) il vostro, la vostra, i vostri, le vostre; (fml) il suo, la sua, i suoi, le sue.

**yourself** [jəˈself] pron (fam) tu stesso; (fml) Lei stesso; (reflexive) ti, si; (after prep) te stesso, Lei stesso.

**yourselves** [jəˈselvz] pron voi stessi; (reflexive) vi.

**youth** [juːθ] n gioventù f; (boy) giovane m.

**Yugoslavia** [juːgouˈslaːvjə] n Iugoslavia f.

**Yugoslav** n, adj iugoslavo, -a.

# Z

**zeal** [ziːl] n zelo m. **zealous** adj zelante.

**zebra** [ˈzebrə] n zebra f. **zebra crossing** passaggio zebrato m.

**zero** [ˈziərou] n zero m. v mettere a zero, azzerare.

**zest** [zest] n (enjoyment) gusto m, entusiasmo m; (piquancy) nota piccante f.

**zigzag** [ˈzigzag] nm, adj zigzag. v andare a zigzag, serpeggiare.

**zinc** [ziŋk] n zinco m.

**zip** [zip] n chiusura or cerniera lampo f. **zip up** chiudere la (cerniera) lampo.

**zodiac** [ˈzoudiak] n zodiaco m.

**zone** [zoun] n zona f.

**zoo** [zuː] n giardino zoologico m, zoo m invar. **zoologist** n zoologo, -a m, f. **zoology** n zoologia f.

**zoom** [zuːm] v (noise) ronzare; (aircraft) salire in candela; (film) zumare. n ronzio m. **zoom lens** zoom m invar, obiettivo zoom m.

# Italian – Inglese

## A

**a, ad** [a, ad] *prep* to; (*stato in luogo*) at, in; (*prezzo, ora, età*) at. **a 10 metri da** 10 metres away from. **a due a due** two by two. **alle dozzina** by the dozen. **andare a casa** go home. **100 km all'ora** 100 km an hour.

**abate** [a'bate] *sm* abbot.

**abbagliare** [abba'ʎare] *v* dazzle.

**abbaiare** [abba'jare] *v* bark. **abbaiata** *sf* bark.

**abbaino** [abba'ino] *sm* attic, garret.

**abbandonare** [abbando'nare] *v* abandon, leave. **abbandonarsi a** (*darsi senza ritegno*) indulge in; give in to. **abbandono** *sm* neglect; desertion.

**abbassare** [abbas'sare] *v* lower, reduce. **abbasso** *avv* down. **abbasso ... !** *inter* down with ... !

**abbastanza** [abbas'tantsa] *avv* enough.

**abbattere** [ab'battere] *v* knock down, fell; (*uccidere*) kill; (*deprimere*) depress. **abbattersi** *v* become disheartened.

**abbazia** [abba'tsia] *sf* abbey.

**abbellire** [abbel'lire] *v* embellish, adorn.

**abbiente** [ab'bjɛnte] *agg* prosperous, well-to-do.

**abbigliare** [abbi'ʎare] *v* dress. **abbigliamento** *sm* clothes *pl*; (*modo*) dress.

**abboccare** [abbok'kare] *v* bite. **abboccato** *agg* (*vino*) medium sweet.

**abbonarsi** [abbo'narsi] *v* subscribe; take out a season ticket (for). **abbonamento** *sm* subscription; season ticket. **abbonato, -a** *sm, sf* subscriber; ticket-holder.

**abbondare** [abbon'dare] *v* be plentiful, abound. **abbondante** *agg* plentiful, abundant. **abbondanza** *sf* abundance, plenty.

**abbordare** [abbor'dare] *v* approach; (*introdurre*) broach.

**abborracciare** [abborrat'tʃare] *v* botch.

**abbottonare** [abbotto'nare] *v* button up.

**abbozzare** [abbot'tsare] *v* sketch, outline. **abbozzare un sorriso** give a faint smile. **abbozzo** *sm* sketch.

**abbracciare** [abbrat'tʃare] *v* embrace. **abbraccio** *sm* embrace, hug.

**abbreviare** [abbre'vjare] *v* abbreviate, shorten. **abbreviazione** *sf* abbreviation.

**abbronzare** [abbron'dzare] *v* tan. **abbronzatura** *sf* (sun-)tan.

**abbrustolire** [abbrusto'lire] *v* toast.

**abbuono** [ab'bwɔno] *sm* allowance; (*sport*) handicap.

**abdicare** [abdi'kare] *v* abdicate. **abdicazione** *sf* abdication.

**aberrazione** [aberra'tsjone] *sf* aberration.

**abete** [a'bete] *sm* fir(-tree). **abete rosso** spruce.

**abietto** [a'bjɛtto] *agg* abject. **abiezione** *sf* low spirits *pl*.

**abile** ['abile] *agg* clever, good (at); (*adatto*) suitable. **abilità** *sf* cleverness, skill; (*destrezza*) dexterity.

**abilitare** [abili'tare] *v* train; (*a una professione*) qualify. **abilitazione** *sf* qualification, diploma.

**abisso** [a'bisso] *sm* abyss.

**abitare** [abi'tare] *v* live. **abitante** *s(m+f)* inhabitant. **abitazione** *sf* home, dwelling.

**abitato** [abi'tato] *agg* inhabited. *sm* built-up area; (*villaggio*) hamlet.

**abito** ['abito] *sm* suit; dress; (*rel, abitudine*) habit. **abituale** *agg* customary, usual; habitual.

**abituarsi** [abitu'arsi] *v* **abituarsi a** get used to, become accustomed to.

**abitudine** [abi'tudine] *sf* habit, custom. **avere l'abitudine di** be in the habit of. **d'abitudine** as a rule.

**abolire** [abo'lire] *v* abolish. **abolizione** *sf* abolition.

**abominevole** [abomi'nevole] *agg* abominable.

**aborigeno** [abo'ridʒeno] *sm* aborigine. *agg* aboriginal.

**aborrire** [abor'rire] *v* abhor, loathe.

**abortire** [abor'tire] *v* miscarry; fail. **aborto** *sm* miscarriage. **aborto procurato** abortion.

**abrasivo** [abra'zivo] *sm, agg* abrasive. **abrasione** *sf* abrasion.

**abside** ['abside] *sf* apse.

**abusare** [abu'zare] *v* abuse. **abusivo** *agg* unauthorized, improper. **abuso** *sm* abuse.

**accademia** [akka'dɛmja] *sf* academy. **accademico** *sm, agg* academic.

***accadere** [akka'dere] *v* happen. **accaduto** *sm* occurrence.

**accampare** [akkam'pare] *v* camp; (*avanzare*) put forward. **accampamento** *sm* camp.

**accanirsi** [akka'nirsi] *v* rage; persist. **accanito** *agg* (*ostinato*) dogged, stubborn; (*spietato*) merciless; (*violento*) fierce.

**accanto** [ak'kanto] *avv* nearby; (*casa*) next door. **accanto a** next to, near to, beside.

**accantonare** [akkanto'nare] *v* set aside.

**accaparrare** [akkapar'rare] *v* corner.

**accappatoio** [akkappa'tojo] *sm* bathrobe.

**accarezzare** [akkaret'tsare] *v* caress, stroke.

**accasciare** [akka'ʃare] *v* crush. **accasciarsi** *v* collapse.

**accattone** [akkat'tone], **-a** *sm, sf* scrounger.

**accavallare** [akkaval'lare] *v* (*sovrapporre*) overlap; (*accumulare*) pile up; (*incrociare*) cross.

**accecare** [attʃe'kare] *v* blind; block up. **accecante** *agg* blinding.

***accedere** [at'tʃedere] *v* accede.

**accelerare** [attʃele'rare] *v* accelerate, speed up. **accelerato** *sm* local train. **acceleratore** *sm* accelerator. **accelerazione** *sf* acceleration.

***accendere** [at'tʃendere] *v* light; (*luce, radio*) switch on, turn on. **accendino** *sm* (*fam*) lighter.

**accennare** [attʃen'nare] *v* make a sign, nod; refer to, hint at, touch on. **accenno** *sm* indication, mention.

**accensione** [attʃen'sjone] *sf* ignition.

**accento** [at'tʃento] *sm* accent, stress; tone. **accentare** *v* accent.

**accentrare** [attʃen'trare] *v* centralize, concentrate.

**accentuare** [attʃentu'are] *v* stress; (*aumentare*) heighten.

**accerchiare** [attʃer'kjare] *v* encircle. **accerchiamento** *sm* encirclement.

**accertare** [attʃer'tare] *v* verify, ascertain; (*dir*) establish. **accertamento** *sm* verification; establishment.

**acceso** [at'tʃezo] *agg* alight, switched on; (*colore*) vivid; (*eccitato*) burning.

**accessibile** [attʃes'sibile] *agg* (*luogo*) accessible; (*persona*) approachable.

**accesso** [at'tʃesso] *sm* access; (*med*) attack, fit.

**accessorio** [attʃes'sɔrjo] *agg* complementary, secondary. *sm* accessory, fitting.

**accetta** [at'tʃetta] *sf* hatchet.

**accettare** [attʃet'tare] *v* accept; admit. **accettabile** *agg* acceptable. **accettazione** *sf* acceptance; (*sala*) reception. **bene accetto** welcome. **male accetto** unwelcome.

**acchiappare** [akkjap'pare] *v* catch, grab (hold of), seize.

**acciaio** [at'tʃajo] *sm* steel. **acciaieria** *sf* steelworks.

**accidente** [attʃi'dɛnte] *sm* accident, mishap. **mandare un accidente a** (*fam*) curse. **non capire un accidente** not understand a thing. **accidenti!** *inter* my goodness! (*ira*) damn it! **accidenti a lui!** blast him! **accidentale** *agg* accidental.

**accigliarsi** [attʃiʎ'ʎarsi] *v* frown. **accigliato** *agg* frowning.

***accingersi** [at'tʃindʒersi] *v* **accingersi a** set about; be on the point of.

**acciuffare** [attʃuffare] v seize.

**acciuga** [at'tʃuga] sf anchovy.

**acclamare** [akkla'mare] v acclaim. **acclamazione** sf acclamation.

**acclimatare** [akklima'tare] v acclimatize.

**\*accludere** [ak'kludere] v enclose.

**accoccolarsi** [akkokko'larsi] v squat.

**\*accogliere** [ak'kɔʎʎere] v receive, accept, welcome; contain. **accoglienza** sf welcome, reception.

**accomodare** [akkomo'dare] v (riparare) mend, fix; (mettere in ordine) arrange, tidy; (sistemare) settle. **accomodarsi** v make oneself comfortable; take a seat; (mettersi d'accordo) agree. **accomodamento** sm agreement; compromise. **accomodante** agg accommodating.

**accompagnare** [akkompa'nare] v accompany. **accompagnatore, -trice** sm, sf escort; (musica) accompanist.

**acconciare** [akkon'tʃare] v prepare; arrange. **acconciarsi i capelli** do one's hair. **acconciatura** sf hair-style.

**\*accondiscendere** [akkondi'ʃɛndere] v comply (with); condescend.

**acconsentire** [akkonsen'tire] v consent; acquiesce.

**accoppare** [akkop'pare] v (fam) kill, slaughter.

**accorciare** [akkor'tʃare] v shorten.

**accordare** [akkor'dare] v (uniformare) match; harmonize; (concedere) grant; (musica) tune. **accordarsi** v agree.

**accordo** [ak'kɔrdo] sm agreement. **essere** or **andare d'accordo** agree. **d'accordo!** agreed!

**\*accorgersi** [ak'kɔrdʒersi] v notice. **accorgimento** sm expedient, stratagem.

**\*accorrere** [ak'korrere] v come running, rush.

**accorto** [ak'kɔrto] agg shrewd. **fare accorto** warn, caution. **stare accorto** be wary. **accortezza** sf shrewdness.

**accostare** [akkos'tare] v approach. **accosto** avv near.

**accovacciarsi** [akkovat'tʃarsi] v crouch, huddle.

**accreditare** [akkredi'tare] v accredit.

**\*accrescere** [ak'kreʃere] v increase.

**accumulare** [akkumu'lare] v accumulate, heap. **accumulatore** sm accumulator.

**accurato** [akku'rato] agg accurate, thor-ough. **accuratezza** sf thoroughness, care.

**accusare** [akku'zare] v accuse; (notificare) acknowledge. **accusa** sf accusation, charge.

**acerbo** [a'tʃerbo] agg (immaturo) unripe; (aspro) sour.

**acero** ['atʃero] sm maple.

**aceto** [a'tʃeto] sm vinegar.

**acido** ['atʃido] sm acid. agg acid, sour. **acidità** sf acidity.

**acne** ['akne] sf acne.

**acqua** ['akkwa] sf water. **acqua minerale** mineral water. **acqua ossigenata** hydro-gen peroxide. **acqua in bocca!** keep mum!

**acquaforte** [akkwa'fɔrte] sf, pl **acqueforti** etching.

**acquaio** [ak'kwajo] sm kitchen sink.

**acquaragia** [akkwa'radʒa] sf turpentine, turps.

**acquario** [ak'kwarjɔ] sm aquarium.

**acquatico** [ak'kwatiko] agg aquatic, water.

**acquavite** [akkwa'vite] sf rough brandy.

**acquazzone** [akkwat'tsone] sm shower.

**acquedotto** [akkwe'dotto] sm aqueduct.

**acquerello** [akkwe'rɛllo] sm water-colour.

**acquistare** [akkwis'tare] v buy; (ottenere) acquire; (guadagnare) gain. **acquistarsi fama di** gain the reputation of. **acquisto** sm purchase. **buon acquisto** bargain.

**acquoso** [ak'kwozo] agg watery; (terreno) marshy.

**acre** ['akre] agg acrid, sharp.

**acrilico** [a'kriliko] agg acrylic.

**acrobata** [a'krɔbata] s(m+f) acrobat. **acrobatico** agg acrobatic. **acrobazia** sf acrobat-ics pl.

**acronimo** [a'krɔnimo] sm acronym.

**aculeo** [a'kuleo] sm sting.

**acustica** [a'kustika] sf acoustics pl. **acustico** agg acoustic. **apparecchio acustico** sm hearing-aid.

**acuto** [a'kuto] agg acute, intense; (aguzzo) pointed; (perspicace) shrewd. sm (musica) top note.

**ad** V a.

**adagiarsi** [ada'dʒarsi] v lie down.

**adagio** [a'dadʒo] avv slowly; gently. sm (musica) slow movement, adagio.

**adattabile** [adat'tabile] agg adaptable. **adattabilità** sf adaptability.

**adattare** [adat'tare] v adapt. **adattarsi** v adapt oneself, resign oneself. **adatto** agg suitable (for); (*qualificato*) suited (to).

**addebitare** [addebi'tare] *v* charge.

**addensare** [adden'sare] *v* thicken; (*raccogliere*) gather.

**addestrare** [addes'trare] *v* train. **addestramento** *sm* training.

**addetto** [ad'detto] *agg* employed (in); destined (for), intended (for); assigned. *sm* (*pol*) attaché.

**addietro** [ad'djetro] *avv* (*fa*) ago; (*prima*) before.

**addio** [ad'dio] *inter* goodbye, farewell. *sm* parting, farewell.

**addirittura** [addirit'tura] *avv* (*persino*) even; (*direttamente*) straight away; absolutely.

**additare** [addi'tare] *v* point at; (*mostrare*) point out, show.

**additivo** [addi'tivo] *sm* additive.

**addizionare** [additsjo'nare] *v* add up. **addizionale** *agg* additional. **addizione** *sf* addition.

**addolcire** [addol'tʃire] *v* sweeten; (*mitigare*) soften.

**addolorare** [addolo'rare] *v* distress.

**addome** [ad'dɔme] *sm* abdomen. **addominale** *agg* abdominal.

**addomesticare** [addomesti'kare] *v* tame.

**addormentare** [addormen'tare] *v* put to sleep. **addormentarsi** *v* fall asleep, go to sleep. **addormentato** *agg* sleeping; (*di mente*) dull; (*intorpidito*) numb.

**addossare** [addos'sare] *v* lean; (*mettere a carico*) saddle with. **addossarsi** *v* shoulder.

**addosso** [ad'dɔsso] *avv*, *prep* on. **d'addosso** off. **essere uno addosso all'altro** be crowded together.

*****addurre** [ad'durre] *v* advance, put forward; produce.

**adeguare** [ade'gware] *v* adjust.

**adempiere** [a'dempjere] *v* also **adempire** carry out.

**adenoidi** [ade'nɔidi] *sf pl* adenoids *pl*.

**aderire** [ade'rire] *v* adhere, stick. **aderire a** comply with; accept; (*associarsi*) join. **aderente** *agg* close; (*abito*) close-fitting. **aderenza** *sf* adhesion. **aderenze** *sf pl* (*fam*) contacts *pl*.

**adescare** [ades'kare] *v* lure.

**adesione** [ade'zjone] *sf* adhesion; (*consenso*) assent; support. **adesivo** *sm*, *agg* adhesive.

**adesso** [a'dɛsso] *avv* now; nowadays; (*poco fa*) just (now); (*fra poco*) any minute (now).

**per adesso** for the time being.

**adiacente** [adja'tʃɛnte] *agg* adjacent. **adiacente a** next to.

**adibire** [adi'bire] *v* turn (into).

**adirarsi** [adi'rarsi] *v* get angry.

**adito** ['adito] *sm* entry. **dare adito a** give rise to.

**adocchiare** [adok'kjare] *v* spot.

**adolescente** [adole'ʃɛnte] *agg* adolescent. *s(m+f)* adolescent, teenager. **adolescenza** *sf* adolescence.

**adombrare** [adom'brare] *v* shade; (*celare*) hide. **adombrarsi** *v* take umbrage; (*cavalli*) shy.

**adoperare** [adope'rare] *v* use. **adoperarsi** *v* do one's best.

**adorare** [ado'rare] *v* adore, worship. **adorabile** *agg* adorable. **adoratore, -trice** *sm*, *sf* admirer. **adorazione** *sf* worship.

**adornare** [ador'nare] *v* adorn, decorate. **adorno** *agg* adorned, decked out.

**adottare** [adot'tare] *v* adopt, foster. **adottivo** *agg* adoptive. **adozione** *sf* adoption.

**adrenalina** [adrena'lina] *sf* adrenaline.

**adulazione** [adula'tsjone] *sf* flattery. **adulare** *v* flatter. **adulatore, -trice** *sm*, *sf* flatterer.

**adulterare** [adulte'rare] *v* adulterate; (*corrompere*) debase.

**adultero** [a'dultero], **-a** *sm*, *sf* adulterer, -ess. *agg* adulterous. **adulterio** *sm* adultery.

**adulto** [a'dulto], **-a** *s*, *agg* adult, grown-up.

**adunare** [adu'nare] *v* assemble. **adunanza** *sf* assembly. **adunata** *sf* meeting, gathering; (*mil*) parade.

**aerare** [ae'rare] *v* air, ventilate. **aeratore** *sm* ventilator.

**aereo** [a'ɛreo] *agg* aerial, air. *sm* aeroplane.

**aerobica** [ae'robika] *sf* aerobics.

**aerodinamica** [aerodi'namika] *sf* aerodynamics. **aerodinamico** *agg* streamlined.

**aerodromo** [ae'rɔdromo] *sm* aerodrome.

**aerolinea** [aero'linea] *sf* airline.

**aeronautica** [aero'nautika] *sf* aeronautics; aviation; (*mil*) air force. **aeronautico** *agg* aeronautical.

**aeroplano** [aero'plano] *sm* aeroplane, aircraft. **aeroplano a reazione** jet. **aeroplano di bombardamento** bomber. **aeroplano di combattimento** fighter.

**aeroporto** [aero'pɔrto] *sm* airport.

**aerosol** [aero'sɔl] *sm invar* aerosol.

**afa** ['afa] *sf* oppressive heat.

**affabile** [af'fabile] *agg* affable. **affabilità** *sf* affability.

**affaccendarsi** [affattʃen'darsi] *v* busy oneself. **affaccendato** *agg* busy.

**affacciarsi** [affat'tʃarsi] *v* show oneself, appear.

**affamato** [affa'mato] *agg* starving; (*bramoso*) eager (for). **affamare** *v* reduce to starvation.

**affannare** [affan'nare] *v* worry. **affannarsi** *v* do one's utmost. **affanno** *sm* (*difficoltà di respiro*) breathlessness; anxiety, worry. **affannoso** *agg* difficult.

**affare** [af'fare] *sm* affair, business; (*questione*) matter; (*fam*) thing; (*acquisto vantaggioso*) bargain. **affari** *sm pl* (*comm*) business *sing*. **affarista** *s(m+f)* speculator.

**affascinare** [affaʃi'nare] *v* fascinate, charm.

**affastellare** [affastel'lare] *v* tie in bundles; (*ammucchiare*) pile up; (*frasi, ecc.*) string together.

**affaticare** [affati'kare] *v* tire, strain.

**affatto** [af'fatto] *avv* quite; (*con negazione*) at all.

**affermare** [affer'mare] *v* affirm; assert. **affermarsi** *v* be successful.

**afferrare** [affer'rare] *v* seize, grab, clutch at.

**affettare**[1] [affet'tare] *v* affect, pretend. **affettato** *agg* affected; mannered.

**affettare**[2] [affet'tare] *v* slice. **affettato** *sm* sliced salami *or* ham.

**affetto**[1] [af'fetto] *sm* affection, feeling. **affettuoso** *agg* affectionate, loving.

**affetto**[2] [af'fetto] *agg* affected (by); (*med*) suffering (from).

**affezionarsi** [affettsjo'narsi] *v* become fond (of). **affezionato** *agg* fond, devoted. **affezione** *sf* fondness, affection; (*med*) disorder.

**affibbiare** [affib'bjare] *v* saddle with.

**affidare** [affi'dare] *v* entrust. **affidare alla memoria** commit to memory. **affidamento** *sm* trust. **dare affidamento** inspire confidence. **fare affidamento su** rely on.

*****affiggere** [af'fiddʒere] *v* affix; (*manifesto*) put up.

**affilare** [affi'lare] *v* sharpen.

**affiliare** [affi'ljare] *v* (*dir*) foster; (*iscrivere*) enrol.

**affinché** [affin'ke] *cong* so that, in order that.

**affinità** [affini'ta] *sf* affinity. **affine** *agg* related. **affini** *sm pl* in-laws *pl*.

**affissione** [affis'sjone] *sf* bill-posting.

**affisso** [af'fisso] *agg* exhibited. *sm* poster, bill.

**affittare** [affit'tare] *v* rent, lease; (*dare in affitto*) let. **affitto** *sm* (*prezzo*) rent; (*locazione*) lease.

*****affliggere** [af'fliddʒere] *v* afflict. **affliggersi** *v* grieve, worry. **afflizione** *sf* affliction.

*****affluire** [afflu'ire] *v* flow; (*gente*) flock. **affluente** *sm* (*geog*) tributary. **affluenza** *sf* flow; (*di gente*) influx. **afflusso** *sm* flow.

**affogare** [affo'gare] *v* drown. **uovo affogato** *sm* poached egg.

**affollare** [affol'lare] *v* crowd. **affollamento** *sm* (*atto*) crowding; (*folla*) crowd.

**affondare** [affon'dare] *v* sink.

**affrancare** [affran'kare] *v* stamp. **affrancatura** *sf* postage.

**affranto** [af'franto] *agg* distraught.

**affresco** [af'fresko] *sm* fresco.

**affrettare** [affret'tare] *v* hurry, speed up.

**affrontare** [affron'tare] *v* face. **affronto** *sm* affront.

**affumicare** [affumi'kare] *v* (*annerire*) blacken (with smoke); (*gastr*) smoke; (*snidare*) smoke out. **affumicato** *agg* smoked.

**afoso** [a'fozo] *agg* sultry.

**Africa** ['afrika] *sf* Africa. **africano, -a** *s, agg* African.

**agenda** [a'dʒɛnda] *sf* diary.

**agente** [a'dʒɛnte] *sm* agent. **agente delle tasse** tax inspector. **agente di polizia** police officer.

**agenzia** [adʒen'tsia] *sf* agency.

**agevole** [a'dʒevole] *agg* easy. **agevolare** *v* facilitate. **agevolazione** *sf* concession.

**agganciare** [aggan'tʃare] *v* fasten, hook up.

**aggettivo** [addʒet'tivo] *sm* adjective.

**agghiacciare** [aggjat'tʃare] *v* freeze. **far agghiacciare il sangue** make one's blood run cold.

**aggiornare** [addʒor'nare] *v* bring up to date; (*rinviare*) postpone. **aggiornato** *agg* up-to-date.

**aggirarsi** [addʒi'rarsi] *v* **aggirarsi su**

(*approssimarsi*) be about or around.
**aggiudicare** [addʒudi'kare] v award.
**\*aggiungere** [ad'dʒundʒere] v add.
**aggiungersi** v join. **aggiunta** sf addition.
**aggiuntivo** agg additional. **aggiunto** sm assistant.
**aggiustare** [addʒus'tare] v repair, adjust; (*ordinare*) tidy, arrange.
**aggrappare** [aggrap'pare] v clutch. **aggrapparsi a** cling to.
**aggravare** [aggra'vare] v make worse. **aggravarsi** v deteriorate.
**aggredire** [aggre'dire] v attack.
**aggregare** [aggre'gare] v aggregate. **aggregato** sm, agg aggregate.
**aggressione** [aggres'sjone] sf aggression, attack. **aggressivo** agg aggressive. **aggressore** sm aggressor, assailant.
**aggrottare** [aggrot'tare] v **aggrottare le ciglia** frown, knit one's brows.
**aggruppare** [aggrup'pare] v group.
**agguato** [ag'gwato] sm ambush, trap. **stare in agguato** lie in wait.
**agiato** [a'dʒato] agg well-off. **agiatezza** sf prosperity.
**agile** ['adʒile] agg agile, nimble. **agilità** sf agility.
**agio** ['adʒo] sm comfort, ease; (*di tempo*) leisure; (*mec*) play. **sentire a proprio agio** feel at ease.
**agire** [a'dʒire] v act; (*comportarsi*) behave; (*dir*) take legal action.
**agitare** [adʒi'tare] v wave, shake; (*incitare*) stir. **agitato** agg agitated, disturbed. **agitatore, -trice** sm, sf agitator.
**agli** ['aʎi] prep+art a gli.
**aglio** ['aʎo] sm garlic.
**agnello** [a'ɲello] sm lamb.
**agnostico** [a'ɲostiko], **-a** s, agg agnostic.
**ago** ['ago] sm needle. **ago da calza** knitting needle. **lavoro ad ago** sm needlework.
**agonia** [ago'nia] sf agony. **agonizzare** v agonize, suffer anguish.
**agonismo** [ago'nizmo] sm fighting spirit.
**agopuntura** [agopun'tura] sf acupuncture.
**agosto** [a'gosto] sm August.
**agrario** [a'grarjo] sm land-owner. agg agrarian, agricultural. **riforma agraria** sf land reform. **agraria** sf agricultural science.

**agricoltore** [agrikol'tore] sm farmer.
**agrifoglio** [agri'foʎʎo] sm holly.
**agro** ['agro] agg sour, sharp, tart.
**agrumi** [a'grumi] sm pl citrus fruit pl.
**aguzzare** [agut'tsare] v sharpen.
**ahimé** [ai'me] inter alas!
**ai** ['ai] prep+art a i.
**Aia** ['aja] sf **L'Aia** The Hague.
**airone** [ai'rone] sm heron.
**aiuola** [a'jwɔla] sf flower-bed.
**aiutare** [aju'tare] v help. **aiuto** sm help, aid; assistant.
**aizzare** [ait'tsare] v incite, provoke.
**al** [al] prep+art a il.
**ala** ['ala] sf wing; (*di cappello*) brim. **apertura alare** sf wingspan.
**alabastro** [ala'bastro] sm alabaster.
**alano** [a'lano] sm Great Dane.
**alba** ['alba] sf dawn. **albeggiare** v dawn.
**albatro** ['albatro] sm albatross.
**albergare** [alber'gare] v give hospitality to; shelter, harbour.
**albergo** [al'bɛrgo] sm hotel. **albergatore** sm innkeeper. **alberghiero** agg hotel.
**albero** ['albero] sm tree; (*mar*) mast. **albero a camme** camshaft.
**albicocca** [albi'kɔkka] sf apricot. **albicocco** sm apricot tree.
**albo** ['albo] sm roll, register; (*tavola*) notice-board.
**album** ['album] sm album.
**alcali** ['alkali] sm alkali. **alcalino** agg alkaline.
**alchimia** [alki'mia] sf alchemy. **alchimista** sm alchemist.
**alcool** ['alkool] sm alcohol.
**alco(o)lismo** [alko(o)'lizmo] sm alcoholism. **alco(o)lici** sm pl alcoholic drinks pl, spirits pl. **alco(o)lico** agg alcoholic. **alco(o)lizzato, -a** sm, sf alcoholic.
**alcunché** [alkun'ke] pron something, anything.
**alcuno** [al'kuno] agg some, any, a few. pron anyone, anybody. **alcuni** pron some, a few.
**alfabeto** [alfa'bɛto] sm alphabet.
**alfiere¹** [al'fjere] sm (*portabandiera*) standard-bearer; (*fig*) forerunner.
**alfiere²** [al'fjere] sm (*scacchi*) bishop.
**alfine** [al'fine] avv in the long run.
**alga** ['alga] sf alga.

**algebra** ['aldʒebra] *sf* algebra.

**aliante** [ali'ante] *sm* glider. **aliantista** *s(m+f)* glider-pilot.

**alibi** ['alibi] *sm* alibi.

**alice** [a'litʃe] *sf* anchovy.

**alienare** [alje'nare] *v* alienate. **alienato** *agg* alienated; (*pazzo*) insane. **alienazione** *sf* alienation; (*pazzia*) madness.

**alieno** [a'ljεno] *agg* alien, foreign.

**alimentare** [alimen'tare] *agg* alimentary. *v* feed. **alimentari** *sm pl* foodstuffs *pl.* **alimentazione** *sf* feeding; (*tec*) feed. **alimenti** *sm pl* alimony *sing.* **alimento** *sm* food.

**aliquota** [a'likwota] *sf* quota, share.

**aliscafo** [alis'kafo] *sm* hydrofoil.

**alito** ['alito] *sm* breath.

**all'** [all] *prep+art* a l'.

**alla** ['alla] *prep+art* a la.

**allacciare** [allat'tʃare] *v* tie up, fasten; (*amicizia, relazioni*) establish; (*tec*) connect.

**allagare** [alla'gare] *v* flood. **allagamento** *sm* flooding.

**allargare** [allar'gare] *v* broaden; (*sport*) open up.

**allarmare** [allar'mare] *v* alarm. **allarme** *sm* alarm. **allarmista** *s(m+f)* scaremonger, alarmist. **allarmistico** *agg* alarmist.

**alle** ['alle] *prep+art* a le.

**alleanza** [alle'antsa] *sf* alliance. **alleare** *v* ally.

**alleato** [alle'ato], **-a** *agg* allied. *sm, sf* ally.

**allegare¹** [alle'gare] *v* enclose.

**allegare²** [alle'gare] *v* advance, put forward.

**alleggerire** [alleddʒe'rire] *v* lighten; (*sofferenza*) ease.

**allegoria** [allego'ria] *sf* allegory. **allegorico** *agg* allegorical.

**allegro** [al'legro] *agg* cheerful, merry. *sm* (*musica*) fast movement, allegro. **allegria** *sf* gaiety, fun, cheerfulness.

**allenare** [alle'nare] *v* train, coach. **allenatore, -trice** *sm, sf* trainer, coach.

**allentare** [allen'tare] *v* loosen. **allentare il passo** slow down.

**allergia** [aller'dʒia] *sf* allergy. **allergico** *agg* allergic.

**allestire** [alles'tire] *v* prepare, get ready; (*teatro*) stage; (*arredare*) fit out, equip. **allestimento** *sm* preparation; staging;

fitting out.

**allettare** [allet'tare] *v* entice, tempt. **allettante** *agg* enticing, tempting.

**allevare** [alle'vare] *v* (*bambini*) bring up; (*animali*) breed, keep; (*piante*) grow. **allevamento** *sm* bringing up; (*educazione*) upbringing; (*cavalli*) stud farm; (*cani*) kennels *pl.* **allevatore, -trice** *sm, sf* breeder.

**alleviare** [alle'vjare] *v* relieve, alleviate.

**allibratore** [allibra'tore] *sm* bookmaker.

**allievo** [al'ljevo], **-a** *sm, sf* pupil, student; (*apprendista*) trainee. **allievo ufficiale** (*mil*) cadet.

**alligatore** [alliga'tore] *sm* alligator.

**allineare** [alline'are] *v* line up; (*adeguare*) adjust. **allineamento** *sm* alignment, coming into line.

**allo** ['allo] *prep+art* a lo.

**allocco** [al'lɔkko] *sm* tawny owl.

**allodola** [al'lɔdola] *sf* lark.

**alloggiare** [allod'dʒare] *v* house, put up; (*mil*) billet; (*prendere alloggio*) stay, lodge. **alloggio** *sm* accommodation; lodgings *pl.*

**allontanare** [allonta'nare] *v* move away; (*tener lontano*) keep away; (*pericolo, ecc.*) avert; (*licenziare*) dismiss. **allontanarsi** *v* go away, leave. **allontanamento** *sm* removal.

**allora** [al'lora] *avv* then; in that case. **da allora** since then, from that time on. **fino allora** until then.

**alloro** [al'lɔro] *sm* laurel; (*gastr*) bay leaf.

**alluce** [al'lutʃe] *sm* big toe.

**allucinazione** [allutʃina'tsjone] *sf* hallucination. **allucinare** *v* hallucinate; (*abbagliare*) dazzle.

**\*alludere** [al'ludere] *v* allude, hint (at).

**alluminio** [allu'minjo] *sm* aluminium.

**allungare** [allun'gare] *v* lengthen, stretch; (*diluire*) water down; pass. **allungare gli orecchi** strain one's ears. **allungare il muso** (*fam*) make a long face. **allungare la strada** go the long way round. **allungamento** *sm* extension, lengthening.

**allusione** [allu'zjone] *sf* allusion.

**almeno** [al'meno] *avv* at least; if only.

**Alpi** ['alpi] *sf pl* **le Alpi** the Alps *pl.* **alpino** *agg* alpine.

**alpinismo** [alpi'nizmo] *sm* mountaineering.

**alquanto** [al'kwanto] *pron, agg* some; a fair amount of. **alquanti** *pron, agg* several; a number of. *avv* somewhat, rather.

**alt** [alt] *sm, inter* stop.

**altalena** [alta'lena] *sf* (*sospesa*) swing; (*a bilico*) seesaw; (*fig*) ups and downs *pl*.

**altare** [al'tare] *sm* altar.

**alterare** [alte'rare] *v* alter, change; (*falsificare*) forge; (*svisare*) distort; (*turbare*) upset, make angry; (*andare a male*) go off, spoil. **alterazione** *sf* alteration; forgery; deterioration.

**alternare** [alter'nare] *v* alternate; (*agric*) rotate. **alternarsi** *v* take turns. **alternativa** *sf* alternative. **alternato** *agg* alternating. **alterno** *agg* alternating, alternate.

**altero** [al'tɛro] *agg* haughty.

**altezza** [al'tettsa] *sf* height; (*profondità*) depth; (*di tessuto*) width; (*quota*) altitude; nobility; (*titolo*) Highness. **essere all'altezza di** be equal to, be up to.

**altitudine** [alti'tudine] *sf* height, altitude.

**alto** [alto] *agg* high; (*statura*) tall; (*tessuto*) wide; (*suono forte*) loud; (*suono acuto*) shrill; (*profondo*) deep; (*geog*) northern; (*nobile*) lofty; (*di grado elevato*) high-ranking. *avv* high. *sm* top, upper part. **alti e bassi** ups and downs *pl*.

**altoforno** [alto'forno] *sm, pl* **altiforni** blast furnace.

**altoparlante** [altopar'lante] *sm* loudspeaker.

**altopiano** [alto'pjano] *sm, pl* **altipiani** plateau.

**altrettanto** [altret'tanto] *pron, agg* as much *or* many (again); (*medesimo*) the same. **altrettanto ... quanto ...** as ... as .... *avv* as, as much.

**altri** ['altri] *pron* others *pl*, another (person), someone else.

**altro** ['altro] *agg* other; another; (*in più*) more; (*ulteriore*) further; (*prossimo*) next. *pron* other (one), another (one); (*persona*) somebody else. **cos'altro?** what else? **l'un l'altro** one another, each other. **l'uno e l'altro** both. **nè l'uno nè l'altro** neither. **nessun'altro** nobody else. **nient'altro** nothing else. **non altro che** nothing but. **più che altro** more than anything. **qualcos'altro** something else. **se non altro** at least. **senz'altro** certainly. **tra l'altro** among other things. **tutt'altro!** far from it!

**altronde** [al'tronde] *avv* **d'altronde** on the other hand, however.

**altrove** [al'trove] *avv* elsewhere.

**altrui** [al'trui] *agg invar* other people's, someone else's.

**altruista** [altru'ista] *s*(*m+f*) altruist, unselfish person. **altruismo** *sm* altruism, unselfishness. **altruistico** *agg* unselfish, altruistic.

**alunno** [a'lunno], **-a** *sm, sf* pupil.

**alveare** [alve'are] *sm* beehive.

**alzaia** [al'tsaja] *sf* tow-line; (*strada*) towpath.

**alzare** [al'tsare] *v* raise, lift; (*raccogliere*) pick up; (*carte da gioco*) cut. **alzarsi** *v* get up, rise. **alzare le spalle** shrug one's shoulders.

**amaca** [a'maka] *sf* hammock.

**amalgamare** [amalga'mare] *v* amalgamate, combine. **amalgama** *sm* amalgam.

**amante** [a'mante] *s*(*m+f*) lover. *agg* fond (of), keen (on).

**amare** [a'mare] *v* love, like. **amato** *agg* beloved. **amatore** *sm* lover; (*conoscitore*) connoisseur.

**amarena** [ama'rɛna] *sf* sour cherry, black cherry.

**amaro** [a'maro] *agg* bitter; (*doloroso*) painful. *sm* bitterness; (*bibita*) bitters *pl*. **amarezza** *sf* bitterness.

**ambasciata** [amba'ʃata] *sf* embassy; message. **ambasciatore, -trice** *sm, sf* ambassador, ambassadress.

**ambedue** [ambe'due] *pron, agg* both.

**ambidestro** [ambi'dɛstro] *agg* ambidextrous.

**ambientale** [ambjen'tale] *agg* environmental.

**ambientarsi** [ambjen'tarsi] *v* accustom oneself, settle down. **ambiente** *sm* environment, milieu; atmosphere. **temperatura ambiente** *sf* room temperature.

**ambiguo** [am'biguo] *agg* ambiguous; (*equivoco*) dubious; (*fam*) shady. **ambiguità** *sf* ambiguity; duplicity.

**ambito**[1] ['ambito] *sm* limits *pl*; sphere.

**ambito**[2] [am'bito] *agg* longed-for, coveted. **ambire** *v* covet.

**ambivalente** [ambiva'lɛnte] *agg* ambivalent.

**ambizione** [ambi'tsjone] *sf* ambition. **ambizioso** *agg* ambitious.

**ambo** ['ambo] *agg* both.

**ambra** ['ambra] *sf, agg* amber. **ambra grigia** ambergris.

**ambulante** [ambu'lante] *agg* wandering. **biblioteca ambulante** *sf* mobile library. **venditore ambulante** *sm* pedlar.

**ambulanza** [ambu'lantsa] *sf* ambulance; (*infermeria mobile*) field hospital.

**ambulatorio** [ambula'tɔrjo] *sm* out-patients' department, clinic.

**ameba** [a'mɛba] *sf* amoeba.

**ameno** [a'mɛno] *agg* agreeable; (*divertente*) entertaining.

**America** [a'mɛrika] *sf* America. **americano, -a** *s, agg* American.

**ametista** [ame'tista] *sf* amethyst.

**amianto** [a'mjanto] *sm* asbestos.

**amichevole** [ami'kevole] *agg* friendly.

**amico** [a'miko], **-a** *sm, sf* friend. *agg* friendly. **amicizia** *sf* friendship.

**amido** ['amido] *sm* starch.

**ammaccare** [ammak'kare] *v* dent. **ammaccatura** *sf* dent.

**ammaestrare** [ammaes'trare] *v* teach, train. **ammaestramento** *sm* teaching, training.

**ammalarsi** [amma'larsi] *v* fall ill.

**ammansire** [amman'sire] *v* tame, subdue.

**ammassare** [ammas'sare] *v* amass.

**ammazzare** [ammat'tsare] *v* kill, murder.

**ammenda** [am'mɛnda] *sf* (*dir*) fine. **fare ammenda di** make amends for.

**\*ammettere** [am'mettere] *v* admit; permit; suppose; take for granted. **ammesso che** given that.

**ammezzato** [ammed'dzato] *agg* mezzanine. *sm* mezzanine floor.

**ammiccare** [ammik'kare] *v* wink (at).

**amministrare** [amminis'trare] *v* administer, manage, run. **amministrativo** *agg* administrative. **amministratore, -trice** *sm, sf* director. **amministratore delegato** managing director. **amministrazione** *sf* administration, management. **consiglio d'amministrazione** *sm* board of directors.

**ammiraglio** [ammi'raʎo] *sm* admiral. **ammiragliato** *sm* admiralty.

**ammirare** [ammi'rare] *v* admire. **ammiratore, -trice** *sm, sf* admirer, fan. **ammirazione** *sf* admiration. **ammirevole** *agg* admirable.

**ammissibile** [ammis'sibile] *agg* admissible, acceptable.

**ammissione** [ammis'sjone] *sf* admission, admittance. **esame d'ammissione** *sm* entrance examination. **tassa d'ammissione** *sf* entrance fee.

**ammobiliare** [ammobi'ljare] *v* furnish.

**ammollare¹** [ammol'lare] *v* soften; (*nell'acqua*) soak.

**ammollare²** [ammol'lare] *v* let go, slacken.

**ammoniaca** [ammo'niaka] *sf* ammonia.

**ammonire** [ammo'nire] *v* warn; reprimand. **ammonimento** *sm* warning; reproof.

**ammontare** [ammon'tare] *sm, v* amount.

**ammorbidire** [ammorbi'dire] *v* soften.

**ammortire** [ammor'tire] *v* deaden.

**ammucchiare** [ammuk'kjare] *v* pile up.

**ammuffire** [ammuf'fire] *v* go mouldy. **ammuffito** *agg* mouldy.

**ammutinamento** [ammutina'mento] *sm* mutiny.

**amnistia** [amnis'tia] *sf* amnesty.

**amo** ['amo] *sm* hook. **abboccare all'amo** swallow the bait.

**amorale** [amo'rale] *agg* amoral.

**amore** [a'more] *sm* love; (*persona graziosa*) darling. **amor proprio** self-respect. **per amore di** for the sake of. **amoroso** *agg* loving.

**ampère** [ãʹpɛr] *sm invar* ampere, amp.

**ampio** ['ampjo] *agg* wide, spacious; (*abbondante*) full.

**amplificare** [amplifi'kare] *v* amplify, enlarge. **amplificatore** *sm* amplifier.

**ampolloso** [ampol'loso] *agg* pompous.

**amputare** [ampu'tare] *v* amputate. **amputazione** *sf* amputation.

**anacronismo** [anakro'nizmo] *sm* anachronism.

**anagrafe** [a'nagrafe] *sf* register office.

**anagramma** [ana'gramma] *sm* anagram.

**analcolico** [anal'kɔliko] *agg* non-alcoholic. *sm* soft drink.

**anale** [a'nale] *agg* anal.

**analfabeta** [analfa'bɛta] *agg, s(m+f)* illiterate. **analfabetismo** *sm* illiteracy.

**analgesico** [anal'dʒɛziko] *agg, sm* analgesic.

**analizzare** [analid'dzare] *v* analyse. **analisi** *sf* analysis (*pl* -ses). **in ultima analisi** when all is said and done. **analista** *s(m+f)* analyst. **analitico** *agg* analytic.

**analogo** [a'nalogo] *agg, m pl* -**ghi** analogous. **analogia** *sf* analogy.

**ananas** ['ananas] *sm* pineapple.

**anarchico** [a'narkiko], **-a** *agg* anarchic(al). *sm*, *sf* anarchist. **anarchia** *sf* anarchy.

**anatema** [ana'tɛma] *sm* anathema.

**anatomia** [anato'mia] *sf* anatomy. **anatomia patologica** pathology. **anatomico** *agg* anatomical. **anatomista** *s(m+f)* anatomist.

**anatra** ['anatra] *sf* duck. **anatroccolo** *sm* duckling.

**anca** ['anka] *sf* hip.

**anche** ['anke] *cong* too, as well, also; (*inoltre*) besides; (*perfino*) even.

**ancora**[1] ['ankora] *sm* anchor. **ancoraggio** *sm* moorings *pl.* **ancorare** *v* anchor.

**ancora**[2] [an'kora] *avv* still; (*in frasi negative*) yet; (*di nuovo*) again; (*un altro*) another; (*persino*) even. **ancora un po'** a little more; (*tempo*) a little longer.

*****andare** [an'dare] *v* go; (*funzionare*) work, run; (*calzare*) fit; (*essere adatto*) suit; (*dovere*) must be, have to be. **a lungo andare** in the long run. **andare a genio** be to one's liking. **andare a piedi** walk. **andare a spasso** go for a walk. **andare avanti** proceed, progress, go on. **andar bene** go well; fit; (*salute*) be well. **andare in bicicletta** cycle. **andare incontro a** go towards, go and meet. **andare via** go away, leave.

**andata** [an'data] *sf* **biglietto d'andata** *sm* single ticket.

**andirivieni** [andiri'vjeni] *sm* coming and going; (*risposta evasiva*) prevarication.

**andito** ['andito] *sm* passage.

**aneddoto** [a'nɛddoto] *sm* anecdote.

**anelare** [ane'lare] *v* pant; (*aspirare*) yearn (for). **anelante** *agg* panting, out of breath.

**anello** [a'nɛllo] *sm* ring. **anello matrimoniale/di fidanzamento** wedding/engagement ring.

**anemia** [ane'mia] *sf* anaemia. **anemico** *agg* anaemic.

**anemone** [a'nɛmone] *sm* anemone.

**anestetico** [anes'tɛtiko] *agg*, *sm* anaesthetic. **anestesia** *sf* anaesthesia. **anestetista** *s(m+f)* anaesthetist.

**anfetamina** [anfeta'mina] *sf* amphetamine.

**anfibio** [an'fibjo] *sm*, *agg* amphibian.

**angariare** [anga'rjare] *v* harass.

**angelica** [an'dʒɛlika] *sf* angelica.

**angelo** ['andʒelo] *sm* angel; (*pesce*) angelfish. **angelo custode** guardian angel.

**angelico** *agg* angelic.

**anglicano** [angli'kano], **-a** *s*, *agg* Anglican. **anglicanesimo** *sm* Anglicanism.

**angolo** ['angolo] *sm* corner; (*geom, ecc.*) angle. **angolare** *agg* angular. **pietra angolare** *sf* cornerstone.

**angoscia** [an'gɔʃa] *sf* anxiety, anguish. **angosciare** *v* distress. **angoscioso** *agg* distressed; distressing.

**anguilla** [an'gwilla] *sf* eel.

**anguria** [an'gurja] *sf* water-melon.

**anice** [a'nitʃe] *sf* aniseed.

**anima** ['anima] *sf* soul; (*parte centrale*) core; (*fervore*) heart; (*di arma da fuoco*) bore. **rodersi l'anima** torment oneself.

**animale** [ani'male] *sm* animal; (*persona*) brute. *agg* animal.

**animare** [ani'mare] *v* animate; stimulate. **animato** *agg* animate; (*vivace*) spirited. **disegno** or **cartone animato** *sm* cartoon. **essere animato da** be inspired by.

**animo** ['animo] *sm* mind; (*cuore, coraggio*) heart; (*carattere*) nature. **farsi animo** pluck up courage. **in fondo all'animo** at the back of one's mind. **mettersi l'animo in pace** resign oneself. **stato d'animo** *sm* mood.

**animosità** [animozi'ta] *sf* animosity, spite.

**annacquare** [annak'kware] *v* water down.

**annaffiare** [annaf'fjare] *v* water.

**annali** [an'nali] *sm pl* annals *pl.*

**annata** [an'nata] *sf* year; (*raccolto*) crop; (*di vino*) vintage; (*importo*) income.

**annebbiare** [anneb'bjare] *v* become foggy; (*fig*) dim, cloud.

**annegare** [anne'gare] *v* drown. **annegamento** *sm* drowning.

*****annettere** [an'nɛttere] *v* (*pol*) annex; attach. **annesso** *sm* annexe, appendage.

**annichilare** [anniki'lare] *v* annihilate, destroy.

**annientare** [annjen'tare] *v* annihilate, destroy. **annientamento** *sm* (total) destruction.

**anniversario** [anniver'sarjo] *sm*, *agg* anniversary.

**anno** ['anno] *sm* year. **anno bisestile** leap year. **anno luce** light-year.

**annodare** [anno'dare] *v* knot *or* tie (together).

**annoiare** [anno'jare] *v* bore.

**annotare** [anno'tare] *v* note, jot down;

(*postillare*) annotate.

**annoverare** [annove'rare] *v* number; enumerate.

**annuale** [annu'ale] *agg* annual, yearly.

**annuario** [annu'arjo] *sm* yearbook.

**annuire** [annu'ire] *v* nod in agreement; (*acconsentire*) agree.

**annullare** [annul'lare] *v* cancel; (*matrimonio*) annul; (*legge*) repeal. **annullamento** *sm* cancellation; annulment; repeal.

**annunciare** [annun'tʃare] *v* announce; (*precorrere*) herald. **annunciatore, -trice** *sm*, *sf* announcer. **annuncio** *sm* announcement, notice; (*pubblicità*) advertisement.

**Annunciazione** [annuntʃa'tsjone] *sf* Annunciation.

**annuo** ['annuo] *agg* yearly, annual.

**annusare** [annu'zare] *v* sniff; (*intuire*) smell.

**annuvolare** [annuvo'lare] *v* cloud (over).

**ano** ['ano] *sm* anus.

**anodo** ['anodo] *sm* anode.

**anomalia** [anoma'lia] *sf* anomaly. **anomalo** *agg* anomalous.

**anonimo** [a'nɔnimo] *agg* anonymous. **società anonima** *sf* limited company.

**anoressia nervosa** [anorɛssja ner'vɔza] *sf* anorexia nervosa.

**anormale** [anor'male] *agg* abnormal. **anormalità** *sf* abnormality.

**ansare** [an'sare] *v* puff, pant.

**ansia** ['ansja] *sf* anxiety; (*angoscia*) dread; (*desiderio*) longing. **ansioso** *agg* anxious; longing; (*impaziente*) restless.

**antagonismo** [antago'nizmo] *sm* antagonism. **antagonista** *s(m+f)* adversary.

**antartico** [an'tartiko] *agg* antarctic.

**antenato** [ante'nato] *sm* forefather, ancestor.

**antenna** [an'tenna] *sf* (*zool*) antenna; (*radio, TV*) aerial.

**anteprima** [ante'prima] *sf* preview.

**anteriore** [ante'rjore] *agg* (*nel tempo*) preceding, previous; (*nello spazio*) front, fore.

**antiabbagliante** [antiabba'ʎante] *agg* anti-dazzle. **fari antiabbaglianti** *sm pl* dipped headlights *pl*.

**antiaereo** [antia'ɛreo] *agg* anti-aircraft.

**antibiotico** [antibi'ɔtiko] *agg*, *sm* antibiotic.

**anticamera** [anti'kamera] *sf* lobby, waiting-room. **fare anticamera** be kept waiting.

**far fare anticamera** keep waiting.

**antichità** [antiki'ta] *sf* antiquity; (*oggetto*) antique.

**anticiclone** [antitʃi'klone] *sm* anticyclone.

**anticipare** [antitʃi'pare] *v* anticipate; advance; pay in advance. **anticipato** *agg* advanced; (*prima del tempo*) in advance. **anticipazione** *sf* anticipation; (*soldi*) advance.

**anticipo** [an'titʃipo] *sm* advance, deposit. **in anticipo** early; (*orologio*) fast.

**antico** [an'tiko] *agg* old; ancient; antique. **all'antica** *agg* old-fashioned.

**anticoncezionale** [antikontʃetsjo'nale] *agg*, *sm* contraceptive.

**anticonformista** [antikonfor'mista] *agg*, *s(m+f)* non-conformist.

**anticongelante** [antikondʒe'lante] *sm* antifreeze.

**anticorpo** [anti'kɔrpo] *sm* antibody.

**antidepressivo** [antidepres'sivo] *agg* antidepressant.

**antidoto** [an'tidoto] *sm* antidote.

**antifecondativo** [antifekonda'tivo] *sm*, *agg* contraceptive.

**antifurto** [anti'furto] *sm* burglar alarm.

**antilope** [an'tilope] *sf* antelope.

**antincendio** [antin'tʃendjo] *agg* **equipaggiamento antincendio** fire-fighting equipment.

**antiorario** [antio'rarjo] *agg* anti-clockwise.

**antipasto** [anti'pasto] *sm* hors d'oeuvre, starter.

**antipatia** [antipa'tia] *sf* dislike, antipathy. **prendere in antipatia** take a dislike to. **antipatico** *agg* disagreeable, unpleasant.

**antiquario** [anti'kwarjo] *sm* antique dealer. **antiquariato** *sm* antique trade; (*negozio*) antique shop.

**antiquato** [anti'kwato] *agg* (*fuori moda*) old-fashioned; (*disusato*) obsolete.

**antisemita** [antise'mita] *s(m+f)* anti-Semite. *agg* anti-Semitic. **antisemitismo** *sm* anti-Semitism.

**antisettico** [anti'sɛttiko] *sm*, *agg* antiseptic.

**antisociale** [antiso'tʃale] *agg* antisocial.

**antistaminico** [antista'miniko] *sm* antihistamine.

**antitesi** [an'titezi] *sf* antithesis (*pl* -ses).

**antologia** [antolo'dʒia] *sf* anthology.

**antro** ['antro] *sm* cave.

**antropologia** [antropolo'dʒia] *sf* anthropology. **antropologico** *agg* anthropological. **antropologo, -a** *sm, sf* anthropologist.

**anulare** [anu'lare] *agg* annular, ring-shaped. *sm* ring-finger.

**anzi** ['antsi] *cong* on the contrary; (*invece*) as a matter of fact; (*o meglio*) or better, better still; (*di più*) indeed.

**anziano** [an'tsjano], **-a** *agg* elderly; aged; senior. *sm, sf* elderly person, senior citizen.

**anziché** [antsi'ke] *cong* (*piuttosto*) rather than; (*invece*) instead of.

**anzitutto** [antsi'tutto] *avv* above all, first of all.

**apatia** [apa'tia] *sf* apathy.

**ape** ['ape] *sf* bee.

**aperitivo** [aperi'tivo] *sm* aperitif.

**aperto** [a'pɛrto] *agg* open; (*pronto*) quick. **all'aperto** in the open, outdoors.

**apice** ['apitʃe] *sm* apex, top.

**apocrifo** [a'pɔkrifo] *agg* apocryphal.

**apolide** [a'pɔlide] *agg* stateless.

**apostolo** [a'pɔstolo] *sm* apostle. **apostolico** *agg* apostolic.

**apostrofo** [a'pɔstrofo] *sm* apostrophe.

**appagare** [appa'gare] *v* satisfy.

**appalto** [ap'palto] *sm* contract.

**appannare** [appan'nare] *v* (*vista*) dim, blur; (*vetri*) mist up.

**apparato** [appa'rato] *sm* show, display; (*tec*) machinery; (*biol*) system, apparatus. **apparato scenico** set.

**apparecchiare** [apparek'kjare] *v* prepare. **apparecchiare la tavola** lay the table. **apparecchio** *sm* set; device, instrument, appliance; (*fam*) (aero)plane; (*fam*) (tele)phone.

**apparenza** [appa'rɛntsa] *sf* appearance. **apparente** *agg* apparent. **apparentemente** *avv* apparently; (*a prima vista*) to all appearances.

**\*apparire** [appa'rire] *v* appear; (*sembrare*) look, seem. **appariscente** *agg* striking.

**appartamento** [apparta'mento] *sm* flat, apartment.

**appartare** [appar'tare] *v* put aside. **appartarsi** *v* withdraw. **appartato** *agg* secluded.

**\*appartenere** [apparte'nere] *v* belong.

**appassionare** [appassjo'nare] *v* move, arouse passion; arouse interest. **appassionarsi per** be very fond of.

**appena** [ap'pena] *avv* barely, hardly; (*soltanto*) only; (*solo un po'*) only just; (*da poco*) just (recently). *cong* **appena ... che ...** no sooner ... than ....

**\*appendere** [ap'pɛndere] *v* hang.

**appendice** [appen'ditʃe] *sm* appendix. **appendicite** *sf* appendicitis.

**appetito** [appe'tito] *sm* appetite. **aver appetito** have an appetite, be hungry. **appetitoso** *agg* appetizing; tempting.

**appianare** [appja'nare] *v* level; (*dissidio, ecc.*) smooth (over), settle.

**appiccare** [appik'kare] *v* (*appendere*) hang; (*cominciare*) set off. **appiccar fuoco a** set fire to.

**appiccicare** [appittʃi'kare] *v* stick. **appiccicaticcio** *agg* sticky.

**appigionare** [appidʒo'nare] *v* let.

**appioppare** [appjop'pare] *v* give; (*affibbiare*) saddle with.

**appisolarsi** [appizo'larsi] *v* doze.

**applaudire** [applau'dire] *v* applaud. **applauso** *sm* applause.

**applicare** [appli'kare] *v* apply. **applicazione** *sf* application; concentration; (*dir*) enforcement. **applique** *sf, pl* **-s** wall-bracket.

**appoggiare** [appod'dʒare] *v* lean; (*posare*) lay; (*fondare*) base; (*favorire*) support. **appoggio** *sm* support.

**\*apporre** [ap'porre] *v* affix, append.

**apportare** [appor'tare] *v* bring about, produce. **apporto** *sm* contribution.

**apposito** [ap'pɔzito] *agg* special; (*adatto*) suitable. **appositamente** *avv* suitably; (*apposta*) deliberately; (*espressamente*) specially.

**apposta** [ap'pɔsta] *avv* deliberately, on purpose, specially. *agg invar* special.

**\*apprendere** [ap'prɛndere] *v* learn. **apprendista** *s(m+f)* apprentice, learner. **apprendistato** *sm* apprenticeship.

**apprensione** [appren'sjone] *sm* apprehension, concern. **apprensivo** *agg* apprehensive, uneasy.

**appresso** [ap'prɛsso] *avv* close by, at hand; (*con sè*) with one; (*in sequito*) later. *prep* close to; (*dietro*) close behind. *agg invar* following.

**apprestare** [appres'tare] *v* prepare; (*porgere*) bring.

**apprezzare** [appret'tsare] *v* appreciate.

**apprezzamento** *sm* appreciation; *(giudizio)* opinion; *(osservazione)* remark.

**approfittare** [approfit'tare] *v* profit (by), take advantage (of).

**approfondire** [approfon'dire] *v* deepen; *(studiare)* probe, go into.

**approntare** [appron'tare] *v* get ready.

**approssimativo** [approssima'tivo] *agg* approximate, rough. **approssimare** *v* approximate. **approssimarsi (a)** approach. **approssimazione** *sf* approximation.

**approvare** [appro'vare] *v* approve (of). **approvazione** *sf* approval.

**appuntamento** [appunta'mento] *sm* appointment; *(fam)* date.

**appunto¹** [ap'punto] *sm* note; *(osservazione)* remark. **muovere** *or* **fare un appunto** a blame, find fault with.

**appunto²** [ap'punto] *avv* precisely, just.

**appurare** [appu'rare] *v* verify.

**aprile** [a'prile] *sm* April.

**\*aprire** [a'prire] *v* open; *(luce, radio, ecc.)* switch on. **apribottiglie** *sm invar* bottle-opener. **apriscatole** *sm invar* tin-opener.

**aquila** ['akwila] *sf* eagle. **aquilone** *sm* kite.

**Arabia** [a'rabja] *sf* Arabia. **arabo, -a** *s, agg* Arab; *sm (lingua)* Arabic.

**arachide** [a'rakide] *sf* ground-nut, peanut.

**aragosta** [ara'gosta] *sf* lobster.

**araldo** [a'raldo] *sm* herald. **araldica** *sf* heraldry. **araldico** *agg* heraldic.

**arancio** [a'rantʃo] *sm* orange tree. *agg invar (colore)* orange. **arancia** *sf* orange. **arancione** *sm, agg invar* orange.

**arare** [a'rare] *v* plough. **aratro** *sm* plough.

**arazzo** [a'rattso] *sm* tapestry.

**arbitrare** [arbi'trare] *v* arbitrate; *(sport)* referee. **arbitro** *sm* referee, umpire.

**arbitrio** [ar'bitrjo] *sm* will. **arbitrario** *agg* arbitrary.

**arbusto** [ar'busto] *sm* bush.

**arca** ['arka] *sf* ark.

**arcaico** [ar'kaiko] *agg* archaic.

**arcata** [ar'kata] *sf* arcade; *(di ponte)* span; *(anat)* arch.

**archeologia** [arkeolo'dʒia] *sf* archaeology. **archeologico** *agg* archaeological. **archeologo, -a** *sm, sf* archaeologist.

**archetipo** [ar'kɛtipo] *sm* archetype. *agg* archetypal.

**archetto** [ar'ketto] *sm* bow.

**architetto** [arki'tetto] *sm* architect. **architettonico** *agg* architectural. **architettura** *sf* architecture.

**archivio** [ar'kivjo] *sm* archives *pl*; *(comm)* file. **archiviare** *v* (place on) file; *(questione, ecc.)* pigeon-hole. **archivista** *s(m+f)* archivist; *(comm)* filing clerk.

**arciduca** [artʃi'duka] *sm* archduke.

**arciere** [ar'tʃɛre] *sm* archer.

**arcigno** [ar'tʃiɲo] *agg* sullen.

**arcipelago** [artʃi'pɛlago] *sm, pl* **-ghi** archipelago.

**arcivescovo** [artʃi'veskovo] *sm* archbishop. **arcivescovado** *sm* archbishop's palace; *(dignità)* archbishopric.

**arco** ['arko] *sm* bow; *(anat, arch)* arch; *(geom)* arc. **quartetto d'archi** *sm* string quartet. **strumenti ad arco** *sm pl* strings *pl*. **tiro all'arco** *sm* archery.

**arcobaleno** ['arkobaleno] *sm* rainbow.

**arcuato** [arku'ato] *agg* arched. **dalle gambe arcuate** bow-legged.

**\*ardere** ['ardere] *v* burn. **ardente** *agg* burning; *(colore)* fiery; *(appassionato)* ardent.

**ardesia** [ar'dɛzja] *sf* slate.

**ardire** [ar'dire] *v* dare. **ardito** *agg* bold, daring; risky. **ardore** *sm (calore)* heat; passion.

**arduo** ['arduo] *agg* arduous, laborious; *(ripido)* steep.

**area** ['area] *sf* area; *(terreno)* land, ground.

**arena¹** [a'rɛna] *sf* arena.

**arena²** [a'rena] *sf (sabbia)* sand. **arenaria** [are'narja] *sf* sandstone. **arenarsi** [are'narsi] *v* run aground; *(fermarsi)* come to a standstill.

**argano** ['argano] *sm* winch; *(mar)* capstan.

**argentina** [ardʒen'tina] *sf* polo-neck sweater.

**argento** [ar'dʒento] *sm* silver. **argento vivo** quicksilver. **argentare** *v* silver(-plate). **argentato** *agg* silver-plated; *(colore)* silver. **argenteria** *sf* silver, silverware.

**argilla** [ar'dʒilla] *sf* clay.

**argine** ['ardʒine] *sm* embankment; barrier. **arginare** *v* stem, check.

**argomento** [argo'mento] *sm* argument, reason; *(materia)* subject, topic. **argomentare** *v* discuss, argue.

**arguto** [ar'guto] *agg (spiritoso)* witty;

shrewd. **arguzia** *sf* wit, humour; shrewdness.

**aria** ['arja] *sf* air; (*aspetto*) look; (*musica*) tune; (*opera*) aria. **all'aria aperta** in the open, out-of-doors. **corrente d'aria** *sf* draught. **darsi delle arie** put on airs.

**arido** ['arido] *agg* dry, arid.

**arieggiare** [arjed'dʒare] *v* air.

**ariete** [a'rjɛte] *sm* ram. **Ariete** *sm* Aries.

**aringa** [a'ringa] *sf* herring.

**arioso** [a'rjozo] *agg* airy.

**aristocratico** [aristo'kratiko], **-a** *sm*, *sf* aristocrat. *agg* aristocratic. **aristocrazia** *sf* aristocracy.

**aritmetica** [arit'mɛtika] *sf* arithmetic. **aritmetico** *agg* arithmetic(al).

**armadio** [ar'madjo] *sm* cupboard; (*per abiti*) wardrobe.

**armare** [ar'mare] *v* arm; (*mar*) rig up; reinforce. **armarsi** *v* take up arms; (*provvedersi*) arm oneself. **arma** *sf*, *pl* **-i** weapon, arms *pl*; (*mil*) force. **armamento** *sm* armament; (*tec*) equipment.

**armata** [ar'mata] *sf* army; (*flotta*) fleet.

**armato** [ar'mato] *agg* armed; equipped.

**armatura** [arma'tura] *sf* scaffolding; (*elett*) armature.

**armonia** [armo'nia] *sf* harmony. **in armonia con** in keeping with. **armonica** *sf* harmonics. **armonica a bocca** mouth-organ. **armonico** *agg* harmonic. **armonioso** *agg* melodious. **armonizzare** *v* harmonize; (*colori, ecc.*) match.

**arnese** [ar'neze] *sm* tool; gadget. **arnese da cucina** kitchen utensil. **bene/male in arnese** in good/poor shape.

**arnia** ['arnja] *sf* beehive.

**aroma** [a'rɔma] *sm* aroma; aromatic herb, spice. **aromatico** *agg* aromatic.

**arpa** ['arpa] *sf* harp. **arpeggio** *sm* arpeggio. **arpista** *s(m+f)* harpist.

**arpione** [ar'pjone] *sm* hook; (*arma*) harpoon; (*cardine*) hinge.

**arrabbiarsi** [arrab'bjarsi] *v* become angry *or* annoyed. **far arrabbiare** annoy, anger. **arrabbiato** *agg* angry; (*cane*) rabid; (*furioso*) enraged.

**arraffare** [arraf'fare] *v* snatch.

**arrampicarsi** [arrampi'karsi] *v* climb (up). **arrampicata** *sf* climbing, climb.

**arrangiare** [arran'dʒare] *v* (*aggiustare*) mend; improvise; (*fam*) fix; (*musica*)

arrange. **arrangiarsi** *v* manage; come to an agreement.

**arrecare** [arre'kare] *v* cause, bring about.

**arredare** [arre'dare] *v* furnish. **arredamento** *sm* furnishing; (*mobilio*) furniture. **arredatore, -trice** *sm*, *sf* interior decorator; (*cinema*) set decorator.

*****arrendersi** [ar'rɛndersi] *v* surrender, give oneself up. **arrendevole** *agg* yielding.

**arrestare** [arres'tare] *v* stop; (*dir*) arrest. **arresto** *sm* stop, stoppage; arrest. **arresto cardiaco** heart failure.

**arretrato** [arre'trato] *agg* behind; (*non fatto*) outstanding, overdue; (*non sviluppato*) backward; (*numero di rivista, ecc.*) back. **arretrati** *sm pl* arrears *pl*; (*di paga*) back-pay *sing*.

**arricchire** [arrik'kire] *v* enrich. **arricchirsi** become rich.

**arricciare** [arrit'tʃare] *v* curl. **arricciare il naso** pull a face. **arricciare il pelo** bristle.

**arringa** [ar'ringa] *sf* address.

**arrischiare** [arris'kjare] *v* risk, venture. **arrischiato** *agg* risky; (*imprudente*) rash.

**arrivare** [arri'vare] *v* arrive; succeed; (*capitare*) happen. **arrivare a** (*riuscire*) manage to; (*giungere*) reach, get to; (*essere ridotto a*) be reduced to. **arrivare fino a** reach, get as far as. **ben arrivato!** welcome! **arrivo** *sm* arrival.

**arrivederci** [arrive'dertʃi] *inter* goodbye! (*fam*) see you!

**arrogante** [arro'gante] *agg* arrogant. **arroganza** *sf* arrogance.

**arrossire** [arros'sire] *v* blush.

**arrostire** [arros'tire] *v* roast. **arrosto** *sm*, *agg invar* roast.

**arrotare** [arro'tare] *v* sharpen. **arrotino** *sm* knife-grinder.

**arrotolare** [arroto'lare] *v* roll up.

**arrotondare** [arroton'dare] *v* round off.

**arroventato** [arroven'tato] *agg* red-hot.

**arruffare** [arruf'fare] *v* ruffle; (*confondere*) muddle.

**arrugginirsi** [arruddʒi'nirsi] *v* rust. **arrugginito** *agg* rusty.

**arruolare** [arrwo'lare] *v* enlist.

**arsenale** [arse'nale] *sm* arsenal; (*mar*) (naval) dockyard.

**arsenico** [ar'sɛniko] *sm* arsenic.

**arso** ['arso] *agg* burnt, parched.

**arte** ['arte] *sf* art; (*attività*) craft; (*abilità*)

skill; (*astuzia*) cunning. **ad arte** on purpose; (*con artifizio*) cunningly. **artefice** *sm* craftsman.

**arteria** [ar'tɛria] *sf* artery. **arteria di traffico** main road, thoroughfare.

**artico** ['artiko] *agg* arctic.

**articolare** [artiko'lare] *v* articulate; (*suddividere*) split up.

**articolo** [ar'tikolo] *sm* article. **articoli** *sm pl* goods *pl*. **articolo di cronaca** news item. **articolo di fondo** leading article, leader.

**artificiale** [artifi'tʃale] *agg* artificial.

**artificio** [arti'fitʃo] *sm* stratagem, device. **fuochi d'artificio** *sm pl* fireworks *pl*.

**artigiano** [arti'dʒano] *sm* craftsman. **artigianato** *sm* craftsmanship; (*prodotti*) handicraft; (*classe*) craftsmen *pl*.

**artiglieria** [artiʎe'ria] *sf* artillery.

**artiglio** [ar'tiʎo] *sm* claw, talon. **cadere negli artigli di** fall into the clutches of.

**artista** [ar'tista] *s*(*m+f*) artist. **artistico** *agg* artistic.

**arto** ['arto] *sm* limb.

**artrite** [ar'trite] *sf* arthritis.

**asbesto** [az'bɛsto] *sm* asbestos.

**ascella** [a'ʃella] *sf* armpit.

**\*ascendere** [a'ʃendere] *v* rise.

**ascensore** [aʃen'sore] *sm* lift.

**ascesa** [a'ʃeza] *sf also* **ascensione** ascent, climb.

**ascesso** [a'ʃɛsso] *sm* abscess.

**asceta** [a'ʃeta] *s*(*m+f*) ascetic. **ascetico** *agg* ascetic. **ascetismo** *sm* asceticism.

**ascia** ['aʃa] *sf* axe.

**asciugare** [aʃu'gare] *v* dry. **asciugamano** *sm* towel. **asciugatoio** *sm* bath towel. **carta asciugante** *sf* blotting-paper.

**asciutto** [a'ʃutto] *agg* dry. **essere all'asciutto** (*salvo*) be safe; (*al verde*) be broke. **pasta asciutta** *sf* pasta.

**ascoltare** [askol'tare] *v* listen (to); heed, pay attention (to); (*lezioni, messa, ecc.*) attend. **ascoltatore, -trice** *sm, sf* listener. **dare ascolto a** pay attention to.

**asfalto** [as'falto] *sm* asphalt. **asfaltare** *v* asphalt.

**Asia** ['azja] *sf* Asia. **asiatico** *sm, agg* Asian, Asiatic.

**asilo** [a'zilo] *sm* refuge, shelter; (*pol*) asylum. **asilo infantile** kindergarten, nursery school. **dare asilo a** shelter.

**asino** ['azino] *sm* ass, donkey. **asineria** *sf* stupidity. **asinino** *agg* asinine. **tosse asinina** *sf* whooping cough.

**asma** ['azma] *sm* asthma. **asmatico** *agg* asthmatic.

**asola** ['azola] *sf* buttonhole.

**asparago** [as'parago] *sm* asparagus.

**aspettare** [aspet'tare] *v* await, wait (for). **aspettare con desiderio** look forward to. **aspettare un bambino** be expecting a baby. **aspettativa** *sf* expectation; (*licenza*) leave of absence.

**aspetto**[1] [as'pɛtto] *sm* appearance, look. **sotto questo aspetto** from this point of view.

**aspetto**[2] [as'pɛtto] *sm* waiting. **sala d'aspetto** *sf* waiting-room.

**aspirare** [aspi'rare] *v* inhale, breathe in; (*desiderare*) aspire. **aspirapolvere** *sm invar* vacuum cleaner.

**aspirina** [aspi'rina] *sf* aspirin.

**asportare** [aspor'tare] *v* remove, take away.

**aspro** ['aspro] *agg* sour, tart; (*vino*) rough; (*suono*) harsh; (*clima*) raw; (*fig*) hard. **asprezza** *sf* sourness; harshness.

**assaggiare** [assad'dʒare] *v* taste, try. **assaggio** *sm* taste; (*campione*) sample.

**assai** [as'sai] *avv* very; (very) much; (*abbastanza*) enough.

**assalire** [assa'lire] *v* assail, attack.

**assalto** [as'salto] *sm* attack.

**assassinare** [assassi'nare] *v* murder. **assassinio** *sm* murder. **assassino, -a** *sm, sf* murderer, murderess.

**asse**[1] ['asse] *sm* axis; (*mec*) axle.

**asse**[2] ['asse] *sf* (*tavola*) board, plank. **asse da stiro** ironing-board.

**assediare** [asse'djare] *v* besiege. **assedio** *sm* siege. **stato d'assedio** *sm* state of emergency.

**assegnare** [asseɲ'nare] *v* assign, allot. **assegnazione** *sf* allocation.

**assegno** [as'seɲo] *sm* cheque. **assegno circolare** banker's draft. **assegno in bianco** blank cheque. **assegno sbarrato** crossed cheque. **assegno turistico** traveller's cheque.

**assemblea** [assem'blɛa] *sf* assembly, meeting.

**assenso** [as'sɛnso] *sm* assent, agreement.

**assente** [as'sɛnte] *agg* absent. **assentarsi** *v* absent oneself, stay away. **assenteismo** *sm* absenteeism. **assenza** *sf* absence; *(mancanza)* lack.

**assentire** [assen'tire] *v* assent, approve.

**asserire** [asse'rire] *v* assert, affirm. **asserzione** *sf* assertion, statement.

**assessore** [asses'sore] *sm (dir)* assessor; *(comunale)* councillor.

**assestare** [asses'tare] *v* arrange, settle.

**assetato** [asse'tato] *agg* thirsty.

**assettare** [asset'tare] *v* tidy, put in order.

**assicurare** [assiku'rare] *v* assure; *(dir)* insure; *(rendere certo)* ensure; *(procurare)* secure; *(lettera)* register. **assicurarsi** *v* take out insurance. **assicuratore** *sm* underwriter. **assicurazione** *sf* insurance.

**assiduo** [as'siduo] *agg* assiduous.

**assieme** [as'sjɛme] *avv* together.

**assieparsi** [assje'parsi] *v* crowd (round).

**assillare** [assil'lare] *v* pester.

**assimilare** [assimi'lare] *v* assimilate. **assimilazione** *sf* assimilation.

**Assise** [as'size] *sf* **corte d'Assise** *sf* Assizes *pl*.

**assistente** [assis'tɛnte] *s(m+f)* assistant; *(universitario)* lecturer; *(di volo)* steward, stewardess. **assistente sociale** social worker. **assistenza** *sf* assistance; *(sociale)* welfare.

**\*assistere** [as'sistere] *v (aiutare)* assist, help; be present at; *(sport)* watch; *(lezione)* attend.

**asso** ['asso] *sm* ace; champion. **piantare in asso** leave in the lurch.

**associare** [asso'tʃare] *v* associate, join. **associarsi** *v* join; become a partner *or* member. **associazione** *sf* association, society; *(comm)* partnership.

**assoggettare** [assoddʒet'tare] *v* subject.

**assoluto** [asso'luto] *agg* absolute, complete.

**\*assolvere** [as'sɔlvere] *v (rel)* absolve; *(dir)* discharge, acquit. **assoluzione** *sf* absolution; discharge, acquittal. **assolvimento** *sm* fulfilment.

**assomigliare** [assomi'ʎare] *v* resemble.

**assonnato** [asson'nato] *agg* sleepy; *(torpido)* sluggish.

**assopirsi** [asso'pirsi] *v* nod off; calm *or* cool down.

**assorbire** [assor'bire] *v* absorb. **assorbente** *agg* absorbent. **assorbente (igienico)** *sm* sanitary towel. **carta assorbente** *sf* blotting-paper.

**assordare** [assor'dare] *v* deafen; *(attutire un suono)* deaden.

**assortire** [assor'tire] *v* sort out. **assortimento** *sm* assortment.

**\*assuefare** [assue'fare] *v* accustom.

**\*assumere** [as'sumere] *v* assume; *(personale)* take on, engage; *(procurarsi)* obtain.

**assunzione** [assun'tsjone] *sf* engagement; *(di un obbligo)* undertaking; *(elevazione)* ascent; *(filos)* assumption. **Assunzione** *sf (rel)* Assumption.

**assurdo** [as'surdo] *agg* absurd, preposterous. *sm* absurdity.

**asta** ['asta] *sf* pole; *(mec)* rod; *(scrittura)* stroke. **a mezz'asta** at half-mast. **vendita all'asta** *sf* auction.

**astante** [as'tante] *s(m+f)* bystander.

**astemio** [as'tɛmjo], **-a** *sm*, *sf* teetotaller. *agg* teetotal.

**\*astenersi** [aste'nersi] *v* abstain, refrain.

**asterisco** [aste'risko] *sm* asterisk.

**astinenza** [asti'nɛntsa] *sf* abstinence.

**astio** ['astjo] *sm* rancour, resentment. **portar astio** bear a grudge.

**\*astrarre** [as'trarre] *v* abstract. **astratto** *sm*, *agg* abstract. **astrazione** *sf* abstraction.

**astro** ['astro] *sm* star.

**astrologia** [astrolo'dʒia] *sf* astrology. **astrologico** *agg* astrological. **astrologo**, **-a** *sm*, *sf* astrologer.

**astronauta** [astro'nauta] *s(m+f)* astronaut.

**astronave** [astro'nave] *sf* spacecraft.

**astronomia** [astrono'mia] *sf* astronomy. **astronomico** *agg* astronomic(al). **astronomo**, **-a** *sm*, *sf* astronomer.

**astuccio** [as'tuttʃo] *sm* case.

**astuto** [as'tuto] *agg* astute, shrewd. **astuzia** *sf* shrewdness, cunning; *(azione)* trick.

**Atene** [a'tɛne] *sf* Athens. **ateniese** *s(m+f)*, *agg* Athenian.

**ateo** ['ateo], **-a** *sm*, *sf* atheist. *agg* atheistic.

**atlante** [at'lante] *sm* atlas.

**atlantico** [at'lantiko] *agg* Atlantic.

**atleta** [at'lɛta] *s(m+f)* athlete. **atletica** *sf* athletics. **atletico** *agg* athletic.

**atmosfera** [atmos'fɛra] *sf* atmosphere. **atmosferico** *agg* atmospheric.

**atomo** ['atomo] *sm* atom. **atomico**

*agg* atomic.

**atrio** [ˈatrjo] *sm* (entrance) hall, lobby.

**atroce** [aˈtrotʃe] *agg* dreadful, terrible; (*feroce*) cruel. **atrocità** *sf* atrocity.

**attaccare** [attakˈkare] *v* attach, fasten; (*appendere*) hang (up); (*incollare*) stick (on); apply; pass on; (*assalire, corrodere*) attack; (*iniziare*) begin. **attaccabottoni** *s(m+f)* *invar* (*fam*) bore. **attaccabrighe** *s(m+f)* *invar* (*fam*) troublemaker. **attaccapanni** *sm* (*gruccia*) coat-hanger; (*mobilia*) coat-rack. **attaccar briga** *or* **lite** pick a quarrel. **attaccaticcio** *agg* sticky. **attacco** *sm* attack; (*inizio*) opening; (*giuntura*) joint, fastening; (*elett*) plug.

**attecchire** [attekˈkire] *v* (*radicarsi*) take root; (*diffondersi*) catch on.

**atteggiare** [attedˈdʒare] *v* assume. **atteggiarsi** *v* pose. **atteggiamento** *sm* attitude, expression.

**\*attendere** [atˈtɛndere] *v* await, wait (for); (*dedicarsi*) devote oneself to, look after. **attendibile** *agg* reliable, trustworthy.

**\*attenersi** [atteˈnersi] *v* **attenersi a** keep to.

**attentato** [attenˈtato] *sm* attack; attempted murder *or* assassination.

**attento** [atˈtɛnto] *agg* attentive, alert; careful. **stare attento** pay attention, mind. *inter* careful! mind! look out!

**attenzione** [attenˈtsjone] *sf* attention, care. **fare attenzione a** pay attention to.

**atterrare** [atterˈrare] *v* (*di aereo*) land; (*gettare a terra*) knock down. **atterraggio** *sm* landing.

**attesa** [atˈteza] *sf* wait; (*aspettativa*) expectation.

**attestare** [attesˈtare] *v* certify, attest. **attestato** *sm* certificate, testimonial.

**attiguo** [atˈtiɡuo] *agg* adjoining.

**attimo** [ˈattimo] *sm* instant, moment.

**attirare** [attiˈrare] *v* attract, draw.

**attitudine¹** [attiˈtudine] *sf* (*disposizione*) aptitude, bent.

**attitudine²** [attiˈtudine] *sf* attitude.

**attivare** [attiˈvare] *v* activate, bring into action.

**attivista** [attiˈvista] *agg* activist.

**attivo** [atˈtivo] *agg* active; (*diligente*) busy. **bilancio attivo** *sm* credit balance. *sm* asset.

**attizzare** [attitˈtsare] *v* poke; (*fig*) stir up.

**atto¹** [ˈatto] *agg* suitable, fit.

**atto²** [ˈatto] *sm* action, act; gesture; (*dir*) deed. **atto di accusa** indictment. **atto di citazione** summons. **atto di nascita/ morte** birth/death certificate. **atto matrimoniale** marriage certificate. **dare atto** give notice. **in atto** in progress.

**attonito** [atˈtɔnito] *agg* astonished.

**attorcigliare** [attortʃiˈʎare] *v* twist.

**attore** [atˈtore] *sm* actor; (*dir*) plaintiff.

**attorniare** [attorˈnjare] *v* surround.

**attorno** [atˈtorno] *avv* round, around, about. **guardarsi attorno** look round; (*fig*) be wary. **qui attorno** hereabouts.

**\*attrarre** [atˈtrarre] *v* attract. **attrattiva** *sf* attraction, fascination. **attrazione** *sf* attraction.

**attraversare** [attraverˈsare] *v* cross; go through. **attraversamento** *sm* crossing.

**attrezzo** [atˈtrettso] *sm* tool, appliance. **attrezzi** *sm pl* equipment sing; kitchen utensils *pl*; (*teatro*) props *pl*. **attrezzare** *v* equip; furnish. **attrezzatura** *sf* equipment.

**attribuire** [attribuˈire] *v* ascribe, attribute; (*assegnare*) award. **attributo** *sm* attribute.

**attrice** [atˈtritʃe] *sf* actress.

**attrito** [atˈtrito] *sm* friction.

**attuale** [attuˈale] *agg* present, current; (*valido*) topical; (*filos*) actual. **attualmente** *avv* at present.

**attualità** [attualiˈta] *sf* topicality. *sf pl* news *sing*, current events *pl*. **di attualità** topical; (*di moda*) fashionable. **tornare di attualità** come back into fashion.

**attuare** [attuˈare] *v* carry out, put into effect. **attuarsi** *v* come true, be fulfilled.

**attutire** [attuˈtire] *v* mitigate; (*suono*) muffle.

**audace** [auˈdatʃe] *agg* daring, bold; risky, rash. **audacia** *sf* boldness, daring.

**audiovisivo** [audjoviˈzivo] *agg* audio-visual.

**auditorio** [audiˈtɔrjo] *sm* auditorium, studio.

**audizione** [audiˈtsjone] *sf* audition; (*dir*) hearing.

**augurare** [auɡuˈrare] *v* wish. **augurarsi** *v* hope. **augurio** *sm* wish; (*presagio*) omen.

**aula** [ˈaula] *sf* classroom; (*università*) lecture theatre; courtroom.

**aumentare** [aumenˈtare] *v* increase. **aumentare di peso** put on weight. **aumento** *sm* increase.

**aureo** ['aureo] *agg* golden.

**aureola** [au'rɛola] *sf* halo.

**aurora** [au'rora] *sf* dawn.

**ausiliare** [auzi'ljare] *sm, agg also* **ausiliario** auxiliary.

**austero** [aus'tɛro] *agg* austere.

**Australia** [aus'tralja] *sf* Australia. **australiano, -a** *s, agg* Australian.

**Austria** ['austrja] *sf* Austria. **austriaco, -a** *s, agg* Austrian.

**autarchia** [autar'kia] *sf* self-sufficiency. **autarchico** *agg* self-sufficient.

**autentico** [au'tɛntiko] *agg* authentic, genuine. **autenticare** *v* authenticate.

**autismo** [au'tismo] *sm* autism. **autistico** *agg* autistic.

**autista¹** [au'tista] *s(m+f)* driver. **autista di piazza** taxi-driver.

**autista²** [au'tista] *agg* autistic.

**auto** ['auto] *sf (fam)* car.

**autobiografia** [autobiogra'fia] *sf* autobiography. **autobiografico** *agg* autobiographical.

**autoblinda** [auto'blinda] *sf* armoured car.

**autobus** ['autobus] *sm* bus.

**autocarro** [auto'karro] *sm* lorry.

**autocollante** [autokol'lante] *sm* sticker.

**autocolonna** [autoko'lonna] *sf* convoy.

**autocontrollo** [autokon'trɔllo] *sm* self-control.

**autocratico** [auto'kratiko] *agg* autocratic.

**autodidatta** [autodi'datta] *s(m+f)* self-taught person.

**autofurgone** [autofur'gone] *sm* van.

**autolettiga** [autolet'tiga] *sf* ambulance.

**autolinea** [auto'linea] *sf* bus route.

**automa** [au'tɔma] *sm* automaton, robot.

**automatico** [auto'matiko] *agg* automatic. **distributore automatico** slot-machine. **automatizzare** *v* automate.

**automezzo** [auto'mɛddzo] *sm* motor vehicle.

**automobile** [auto'mobile] *sf* car. **automobilismo** *sm* motoring. **automobilista** *s(m+f)* motorist. **automobilistico** *agg* motor.

**autonomo** [au'tɔnomo] *agg* autonomous. **autonomia** *sf* autonomy.

**autopsia** [autop'sia] *sf* post-mortem, autopsy.

**autore** [au'tore], **-trice** *sm, sf* author; artist.

**autorevole** [auto'revole] *agg* authoritative.

**autorimessa** [autori'messa] *sf* garage.

**autorità** [autori'ta] *sf* authority. **autoritario** *agg* authoritarian.

**autoritratto** [autori'tratto] *sm* self-portrait.

**autorizzare** [autorid'dzare] *v* authorize. **autorizzazione** *sf* authorization; permit.

**autostop** [autos'tɔp] *sm invar* hitch-hiking. **fare l'autostop** hitch-hike.

**autostrada** [autos'trada] *sf* motorway.

**autosufficiente** [autosuffi'tʃente] *agg* self-sufficient.

**autotreno** [auto'trɛno] *sm* articulated lorry.

**autoveicolo** [autove'ikolo] *sm* motor vehicle.

**autunno** [au'tunno] *sm* autumn. **autunnale** *agg* autumnal.

**avambraccio** [avam'brattʃo] *sm* forearm.

**avanguardia** [avan'gwardja] *sf* forefront; (*mil*) vanguard; (*arte*) avant-garde.

**avanti** [a'vanti] *avv* forward, ahead; (*prima*) before. **andare avanti** go forward, proceed. **avanti a** before, in front of. **avanti e indietro** backwards and forwards, to and fro. **d'ora in avanti** from now on. **tirare avanti** (*fam*) scrape along, get by. *inter* come in! (*andiamo*) come now!

**avantieri** [avan'tjɛri] *avv* the day before yesterday.

**avanzare¹** [avan'tsare] *v* advance; (*presentare*) put forward. **avanzata** *sf* advance.

**avanzare²** [avan'tsare] *v* be owed; remain, be left over. **avanzo** *sm* remainder; (*cibo*) left-overs *pl*.

**avaro** [a'varo], **-a** *agg* mean. *sm, sf* miser. **avarizia** *sf* meanness, stinginess.

**avena** [a'vena] *sf* oats *pl*. **farina d'avena** *sf* oatmeal.

**\*avere** [a'vere] *v* have; get. **aver caldo/freddo** be hot/cold. **aver fame/sete** be hungry/thirsty. **aver fretta** be in a hurry. **aver paura/sonno** be afraid/sleepy. *sm* (*comm*) credit; belongings *pl*; property.

**aviazione** [avja'tsjone] *sf* aviation, flying; (*arma*) air force. **aviatore, -trice** *sm, sf* aviator, pilot.

**avido** ['avido] *agg* avid, eager.

**aviolinea** [avjo'linea] *sf* airline.

**avo** ['avo] *sm* (*nonno*) grandfather; (*antenato*) forefather, ancestor. **avito** *agg* ancestral.

**avocado** [avo'kado] *sm* avocado.

**avorio** [a'vɔrjo] *sm* ivory.

**avvampare** [avvam'pare] *v* blaze, flare up.

**avvantaggiare** [avvantad'dʒare] *v* profit, benefit.

**\*avvedersi** [avve'dersi] *v* become aware.

**avvelenare** [avvele'nare] *v* poison. **avvelenamento** *sm* poisoning. **avvelenatore**, **-trice** *sm*, *sf* poisoner.

**\*avvenire** [avve'nire] *v* happen. *sm* future. **avvenimento** *sm* event, occurrence.

**avventato** [avven'tato] *agg* rash, reckless. **avventare** *v* hurl; (*azzardare*) venture.

**avventore** [avven'tore], **-a** *sm*, *sf* patron, regular customer.

**avventurare** [avventu'rare] *v* venture, risk. **avventura** *sf* adventure; (*amorosa*) love affair. **avventuriere** *sm* adventurer.

**avverbio** [av'vɛrbjo] *sm* adverb.

**avversario** [avver'sario], **-a** *sm*, *sf* adversary, opponent. *agg* opposing.

**avversione** [avver'sjone] *sf* dislike, aversion.

**avversità** [avversi'ta] *sf* adversity.

**avverso** [av'vɛrso] *agg* adverse; opposing.

**avvertire** [avver'tire] *v* (*osservare*) notice; (*percepire*) feel; (*ammonire*) warn; (*avvisare*) inform. **avvertenza** *sf* warning, notice; (*attenzione*) care; (*istruzioni*) directions *pl*.

**avvezzare** [avvet'tsare] *v* (*educare*) train; (*abituare*) accustom.

**avviare** [avvi'are] *v* start (up), set going; (*comm*) set up; direct. **scuola d'avviamento** *sf* training college, technical college. **avviato** *agg* under way; (*prospero*) thriving.

**avvicinare** [avvitʃi'nare] *v* approach; (*portar vicino*) bring near.

**avvilire** [avvi'lire] *v* disgrace; (*scoraggiare*) dishearten; humiliate. **avvilito** *agg* downhearted; demoralized.

**avviluppare** [avvilup'pare] *v* entangle; (*avvolgere*) wrap up.

**avvincente** [avvin'tʃɛnte] *agg* fascinating.

**avvisare** [avvi'zare] *v* let know, advise; (*ammonire*) warn. **avviso** *sm* notice, note; announcement; (*pubblicità*) advertisement; opinion. **avviso circolare** circular. **come d'avviso** as advised.

**avvizzire** [avvit'tsire] *v* wither.

**avvocato** [avvo'kato] *sm* lawyer, barrister, solicitor; advocate; champion. **avvocatura** *sf* legal profession.

**\*avvolgere** [av'vɔldʒere] *v* envelop, wrap up; (*arrotolare*) roll up, wind.

**avvoltoio** [avvol'tojo] *sm* vulture.

**azalea** [adza'lɛa] *sf* azalea.

**azienda** [a'dziɛnda] *sf* firm, business, company; (*impresa*) undertaking. **azienda agricola** farm. **aziendale** *agg* business.

**azione** [a'tsjone] *sf* action; (*atto*) deed; (*mec*) movement, motion; (*dir*) lawsuit; (*comm*) share. **azionista** *s(m+f)* shareholder.

**azoto** [a'dzɔto] *sm* nitrogen.

**azzardare** [addzar'dare] *v* risk, venture. **azzardarsi** *v* dare. **azzardato** *agg* risky, rash. **azzardo** *sm* risk.

**azzuffarsi** [addzuf'farsi] *v* brawl, come to blows.

**azzurro** [ad'dzurro] *agg*, *sm* (sky) blue.

# B

**babbo** ['babbo] *sm* (*fam*) dad, daddy.

**babbuino** [babbu'ino] *sm* baboon.

**babordo** [ba'bordo] *sm* port.

**bacca** ['bakka] *sf* berry.

**baccalà** [bakka'la] *sm* dried salt cod.

**baccano** [bak'kano] *sm* row, din, uproar.

**baccello** [bat'tʃɛllo] *sm* pod.

**bacchetta** [bak'kɛtta] *sf* rod, stick; (*musica*) baton.

**baciare** [ba'tʃare] *v* kiss. **bacio** *sm* kiss.

**bacino** [ba'tʃino] *sm* basin; (*anat*) pelvis.

**baco** ['bako] *sm* larva; (*da seta*) silkworm.

**bada** ['bada] *sf* **tenere a bada** hold at bay.

**badare** [ba'dare] *v* **badare a** pay attention to, take care to. **badare di** be careful to. **senza badare a** regardless of.

**badessa** [ba'dessa] *sf* abbess.

**badia** [ba'dia] *sf* abbey.

**badile** [ba'dile] *sm* spade.

**baffo** ['baffo] *sm* **farsene un baffo** (*fam*) not care a damn. **baffi** *sm pl* moustache *sing*. **leccarsi i baffi** lick one's lips. **ridere sotto i baffi** laugh up one's sleeve.

**bagaglio** [ba'gaʎo] *sm* baggage. **bagagliaio** *sm* (*ferr*) luggage van; (*auto*) boot. **deposito bagagli** *sm* left luggage.

**bagattella** [bagat'tɛlla] *sf* (*gioco*) bagatelle;

(*inezia*) trifle.

**bagliore** [ba'ʎore] *sm* flash.

**bagnare** [ba'ɲare] *v* wet. **bagnato** *agg* wet.

**bagnino** [ba'ɲino] *sm* beach attendant, life-guard.

**bagno** [baɲo] *sm* bath; (*locale*) bathroom. **fare il bagno** take a bath. **bagnante** *s(m+f)* bather. **bagnomaria** *sm* bain-marie.

**baia** ['baja] *sf* (*geog*) bay.

**baionetta** [bajo'netta] *sf* bayonet.

**balbettare** [balbet'tare] *v* stammer.

**balbuziente** [balbut'tsjɛnte] *s(m+f)* stammerer.

**balcone** [bal'kone] *sm* balcony. **balconata** *sf* (*teatro, ecc.*) gallery.

**baldacchino** [baldak'kino] *sm* canopy; (*rel*) baldachin.

**baldanza** [bal'dantsa] *sf* self-confidence; audacity. **baldanzoso** *agg* self-confident; audacious.

**baldoria** [bal'dɔrja] *sf* merrymaking. **far baldoria** make merry.

**balena** [ba'lena] *sf* whale.

**balenare** [bale'nare] *v* flash (with lightning); (*apparire subitamente*) come in a flash. **baleno** *sm* flash.

**balia¹** ['balja] *sf* nurse.

**balia²** [ba'lia] *sf* **in balia di** in the power of, at the mercy of.

**balistica** [ba'listika] *sf* ballistics. **balistico** *agg* ballistic.

**balla** ['balla] *sf* (*involto*) bale; (*frottola*) fib, lie.

**ballare** [bal'lare] *v* dance.

**ballata** [bal'lata] *sf* ballad.

**ballerino** [balle'rino], -a *sm, sf* ballet-dancer.

**balletto** [bal'letto] *sm* ballet.

**ballo** ['ballo] *sm* ball; dance. **essere in ballo** be at stake.

**ballottaggio** [ballottad'dʒo] *sm* ballot. **ballottare** *v* ballot.

**balneare** [balne'are] *agg* bathing.

**balocco** [ba'lɔkko] *sm* toy, plaything.

**balordo** [ba'lordo] *agg* senseless, absurd; (*tonto*) dull.

**balsamo** ['balsamo] *sm* balsam; (*lenimento*) balm.

**balza** ['baltsa] *sf* (*rupe*) cliff; (*frangia*) fringe.

**balzare** [bal'tsare] *v* bounce, leap.

**bambagia** [bam'badʒa] *sf* cotton wool.

**tenere nella bambagia** pamper, spoil.

**bambinaia** [bambi'naja] *sf* (children's) nurse, nanny.

**bambino** [bam'bino], -a *sm, sf* child (*pl* -ren). **bambinata** *sf* childishness. **bambinesco** *adj* puerile.

**bamboccio** [bam'bɔttʃo] *sm* (*scioccone*) simpleton; (*fantoccio*) rag-doll; (*bambino*) bonny child.

**bambola** ['bambola] *sf* doll.

**bambù** [bam'bu] *sm* bamboo.

**banale** [ba'nale] *adj* banal.

**banana** [ba'nana] *sf* banana. **banano** *sm* banana tree.

**banca** ['banka] *sf* bank. **banca dati** database. **bancario** *agg* bank, banking. **banchiere** *sm* banker.

**bancarella** [banka'rɛlla] *sf* barrow, stall.

**bancarotta** [banka'rotta] *sf* bankruptcy.

**banchetto** [ban'ketto] *sm* banquet. **banchettare** *v* banquet, feast.

**banchina** [ban'kina] *sf* (*porto*) wharf, quay; (*stazione*) platform.

**banco** ['banko] *sm* bench; (*di vendita*) counter; (*banca*) bank. **bancogiro** *sm* giro. **banconota** *sf* banknote.

**banda¹** ['banda] *sf* (*lato*) side.

**banda²** ['banda] *sf* (*striscia*) stripe; (*radio*) band. **banda sonora** sound-track.

**banda³** ['banda] *sf* group, band; (*delinquenti*) gang.

**bandiera** [ban'djɛra] *sf* flag, banner. **bandiera di comodo** flag of convenience. **banderuola** *sf* pennant; (*ventaruola*) weather-vane; (*girella*) fickle person.

**bandire** [ban'dire] *v* proclaim; (*esiliare*) banish. **bandito** *sm* bandit. **banditore** *sm* town-crier. **bando** *sm* proclamation; banishment.

**bangio** ['bandʒo] *sm invar* banjo.

**bar** [bar] *sm invar* bar, café.

**bara** ['bara] *sf* bier, coffin. **aver un piede nella bara** have one foot in the grave.

**baracca** [ba'rakka] *sf* hut. **mandare avanti la baracca** carry on. **piantare baracca e burattini** abandon everything. **baraccone** *sm* stall, stand.

**baraonda** [bara'onda] *sf* hubbub, confusion.

**barare** [ba'rare] *v* cheat. **baro** *sm* cheat.

**barattare** [barat'tare] *v* barter. **baratto** *sm* barter, exchange.

**barattolo** [ba'rattolo] *sm* jar, tin.

**barba** ['barba] *sf* beard. **che barba!** what a bore! **barbuto** *adj* bearded.

**barbabietola** [barba'bjɛtola] *sf* beetroot.

**barbaro** ['barbaro] *sm* barbarian. *adj* barbarous.

**barbiere** [bar'bjɛre] *sm* barber.

**barbiturato** [barbitu'rato] *sm* barbiturate.

**barca** ['barka] *sf* boat. **barca a remi** rowing-boat. **barca a vela** sailing-boat. **barca a motore** motor boat. **barcamenarsi** *v* manage.

**barcollare** [barkol'lare] *v* totter, stagger.

**bardare** [bar'dare] *v* harness.

**barella** [ba'rella] *sf* stretcher. **barelliere** *sm* stretcher-bearer.

**barile** [ba'rile] *sm* barrel, cask.

**barista** [ba'rista] *sm* barman. *sf* barmaid.

**baritono** [ba'ritono] *sm* baritone.

**barlume** [bar'lume] *sm* glimmer.

**barocco** [ba'rokko] *sm, agg* baroque.

**barometro** [ba'rɔmetro] *sm* barometer.

**barone** [ba'rone] *sm* baron; (*dell'industria*) tycoon. **baronessa** *sf* baroness.

**barra** ['barra] *sf* bar, rod.

**barricare** [barri'kare] *v* barricade. **barricata** *sf* barricade.

**barriera** [bar'rjɛra] *sf* barrier.

**baruffa** [ba'ruffa] *sf* brawl.

**barzelletta** [bardzel'letta] *sf* joke, funny story.

**bascula** ['baskula] *sf* weighing machine.

**base** ['baze] *sf* basis (*pl* -ses); (*tec*) base. **a base di** made up of. **in base a** on the basis of. **basamento** *sm* pedestal; foundation. **basare** *v* base, found.

**basetta** [ba'zetta] *sf* sideburn.

**basilica** [ba'zilika] *sf* basilica.

**basilico** [ba'ziliko] *sm* basil.

**basso** ['basso] *agg* low, low-lying; (*poco profondo*) shallow. *avv* low, low down. *sm* (*musica*) bass. **a basso ... !** down with ... !

**bassofondo** [basso'fondo] *sm* shallows *pl*. **bassifondi** *sm pl* (*quartieri*) slums *pl*; (*strati sociali*) underworld *sing*.

**bassotto** [bas'sɔtto] *sm* dachshund.

**bastardo** [bas'tardo], -a *s, agg* bastard; (*non di razza*) mongrel.

**bastare** [bas'tare] *v* suffice, be enough. **basta!** *inter* enough! (*silenzio*) quiet! **basta che** provided that.

**bastimento** [basti'mento] *sm* ship.

**bastonare** [basto'nare] *v* beat, cane. **bastonata** *sf* caning, beating.

**bastone** [bas'tone] *sm* stick, cane; golf club. **bastone da passeggio** walking stick.

**battaglia** [bat'taʎa] *sf* battle; campaign. **cavallo di battaglia** hobby-horse.

**battaglio** [bat'taʎʎo] *sm* (*campana*) clapper; (*porta*) door-knocker.

**battaglione** [batta'ʎone] *sm* battalion.

**battello** [bat'tɛllo] *sm* boat.

**battere** ['battere] *v* beat. **battere a macchina** type. **battere le mani** clap (one's hands). **in un batter d'occhio** in a flash. **senza batter ciglio** without batting an eyelid.

**batteria** [batte'ria] *sf* battery; (*sport*) heat; (*insieme*) set.

**batterio** [bat'tɛrjo] *sm* bacterium (*pl* -a). **batteriologia** *sf* bacteriology. **batteriologo, -a** *sm, sf* bacteriologist.

**battesimo** [bat'tezimo] *sm* baptism, christening. **battesimale** *adj* baptismal. **battezzare** *v* baptize, christen.

**battibecco** [batti'bekko] *sm* quarrel.

**batticuore** [batti'kwɔre] *sm* **avere il batticuore** have palpitations. **far venire il batticuore** make anxious.

**battimani** [batti'mani] *sm* applause.

**battistero** [battis'tɛro] *sm* baptistry.

**battito** ['battito] *sm* beat, pulsation.

**battitore** [batti'tore] *sm* (*sport*) server, striker; (*caccia*) beater.

**battuta** [bat'tuta] *sf* (*colpo*) blow; (*spiritosaggine*) witty remark; (*musica*) beat; (*sport*) service.

**batuffolo** [ba'tuffolo] *sm* wad.

**baule** [ba'ule] *sm* trunk. **fare i bauli** (*fam*) go away.

**bava** ['bava] *sf* dribble.

**bavaglino** [bava'ʎino] *sm* bib.

**bavaglio** [bava'ʎo] *sm* gag. **mettere il bavaglio a** gag.

**bavero** ['bavero] *sm* collar.

**bazzicare** [battsi'kare] *v* associate with; frequent.

**beatitudine** [beati'tudine] *sf* beatitude.

**beato** [be'ato] *agg* blessed. **beato te!** lucky you!

**bebè** [be'bɛ] *sm* baby.

**beccaccia** [bek'kattʃa] *sf* woodcock. **beccac-**

**cino** *sm* snipe.

**beccare** [bek'kare] *v* peck; (*fam*) catch, collar.

**becchino** [bek'kino] *sm* undertaker; gravedigger.

**becco¹** ['bekko] *sm* beak; (*bruciatore*) burner.

**becco²** ['bekko] *sm* (*caprone*) goat; (*cornuto*) cuckold.

**Befana** [be'fana] *sf* Epiphany.

**beffare** [bef'fare] *v* mock. **beffarsi di** make fun of. **beffa** *sf* jest, practical joke.

**bel** ['bel] *V* bello.

**belare** [be'lare] *v* bleat.

**Belgio** ['bɛldʒo] *sm* Belgium. **belga** *s*(*m+f*), *agg*, *m* pl **-gi** Belgian.

**belletto** [bel'letto] *sm* make-up, rouge.

**bellezza** [bel'lettsa] *sf* beauty. **che bellezza!** how lovely!

**bello** ['bɛllo] *agg* beautiful; fine; fair. **il bello è che** the odd thing is (that). **nel bel mezzo** right in the middle. **oh bella!** you don't say! **questa à bella!** (*ironico*) that's a good one! **sul più bello** at the crucial moment.

**belva** ['belva] *sf* wild animal.

**bemolle** [be'mɔlle] *sm* (*musica*) flat.

**benché** [ben'ke] *cong* although.

**bendare** [ben'dare] *v* (*fasciare*) bandage; (*coprire gli occhi*) blindfold. **benda** *sf* bandage; blindfold.

**bene** ['bɛne] *avv* well. **star bene** feel well; (*abito*) suit. **va bene** all right. *sm* good; (*amore*) love; wealth, property. **beni di consumo** consumer goods *pl*. **voler bene a** be fond of. **benino** *avv* fairly well, reasonably.

**\*benedire** [bene'dire] *v* bless, consecrate. **benedetto** *agg* blessed. **benedetti voi!** lucky you!

**beneducato** [benedu'kato] *agg* well-mannered.

**beneficenza** [benefi'tʃentsa] *sf* charity.

**beneficio** [bene'fitʃo] *sm* profit; advantage. **benefico** *agg* beneficial.

**benessere** [be'nɛssere] *sm* well-being, welfare.

**benestante** [benes'tante] *agg* comfortably off, well-to-do. **benestare** *sm* well-being; (*autorizzazione*) consent.

**benevolo** [be'nɛvolo] *agg* kindly, well-disposed.

**beninteso** [benin'tezo] *avv* naturally, of course.

**benvenuto** [benve'nuto] *sm*, *agg* welcome. **dare il benvenuto a** welcome.

**benzina** [ben'dzina] *sf* petrol. **far benzina** fill up. **distributore di benzina** *sm* petrol station *or* pump.

**\*bere** ['bere] *v* drink.

**bernoccolo** [ber'nokkolo] *sm* bump; (*disposizione*) flair.

**berretto** [ber'retto] *sm* cap, hat.

**bersaglio** [ber'saʎo] *sm* target.

**bestemmia** [bes'temmja] *sf* swear-word, curse. **bestemmiare** *v* swear, curse.

**bestia** ['bɛstja] *sf* animal, beast; ignoramus. **bestiale** *agg* bestial, brutal; (*fam: intenso*) beastly.

**bestiame** [bes'tjame] *sm* livestock.

**betoniera** [beto'njera] *sf* cement-mixer.

**bettola** ['bettola] *sf* low dive.

**betulla** [be'tulla] *sf* birch.

**bevanda** [be'vanda] *sf* drink, beverage. **bevibile** *agg* drinkable.

**biada** ['bjada] *sf* fodder, forage.

**biancheria** [bjanke'ria] *sf* (*indumenti intimi*) underwear; (*da casa*) linen.

**bianchetti** [bjan'ketti] *sm pl* whitebait *pl*.

**bianchetto** [bjan'ketto] *sm* whitewash.

**bianco** ['bjanko] *agg* white; (*non scritto*) blank. *sm* white.

**biancospino** [bjanko'spino] *sm* hawthorn.

**biascicare** [bjaʃʃi'kare] *v* (*cibo*) munch; (*parole*) mumble.

**biasimare** [bjazi'mare] *v* blame. **biasimo** *sm* blame.

**Bibbia** ['bibbja] *sf* Bible. **biblico** *agg* biblical.

**bibita** ['bibita] *sf* (soft) drink, beverage.

**bibliografia** [bibljogra'fia] *sf* bibliography. **bibliografico** *agg* bibliographical. **bibliografo, -a** *sm*, *sf* bibliographer.

**biblioteca** [bibljo'tɛka] *sf* library. **bibliotecario, -a** *sm*, *sf* librarian.

**bicchiere** [bik'kjere] *sm* glass, tumbler.

**bicicletta** [bitʃi'kletta] *sf* bicycle. **andare in bicicletta** cycle.

**bicipite** [bi'tʃipite] *sm* biceps.

**bidè** [bi'dɛ] *sm* bidet.

**bidone** [bi'done] *sm* drum, can.

**bieco** ['bjɛko] *agg* **guardare con occhio bieco** look askance at.

**Bielorussia** [bjelo'russja] *sf* Belarus.

**biennale** [bien'nale] *agg* biennial. *sf* biennial event.

**bietta** ['bjetta] *sf* wedge.

**biforcarsi** [bifor'karsi] *v* branch off, fork. **biforcazione** *sf* fork, junction.

**bigamia** [biga'mia] *sf* bigamy. **bigamo** *sm* bigamist.

**bighellonare** [bigello'nare] *v* idle; (*girellare*) saunter.

**bigio** ['bidʒo] *agg* grey; (*tempo*) dull.

**bigliardo** [bi'ʎardo] *sm* billiards.

**biglietto** [bi'ʎetto] *sm* ticket; note; card. **bigliettaio, -a** *sm, sf* conductor. **biglietteria** *sf* booking-office.

**bigodino** [bigo'dino] *sm* curler, roller.

**bigotto** [bi'gɔtto], **-a** *sm, sf* bigot. *agg* bigoted.

**bilancia** [bi'lantʃa] *sf* scales *pl*; (*comm*) balance. **Bilancia** *sf* Libra. **bilanciare** *v* balance; (*pesare*) weigh.

**bilancio** [bi'lantʃo] *sm* balance sheet; budget.

**bile** ['bile] *sf* bile.

**bilico** ['biliko] *sm* **in bilico** in the balance.

**bilingue** [bi'lingwe] *agg* bilingual.

**bilione** [bi'ljone] *sm* a thousand million.

**bimbo** ['bimbo], **-a** *sm, sf* child (*pl* -ren).

**bimensile** [bimen'sile] *agg* fortnightly.

**binario** [bi'narjo] *agg* binary. *sm* rails *pl*, railway line.

**binocolo** [bi'nɔkolo] *sm* binoculars *pl*.

**biochimico** [bio'kimiko], **-a** *agg* biochemical. *sm, sf* biochemist. *sf* (*scienza*) biochemistry.

**biodegradabile** [bjodegra'dabile] *agg* biodegradable.

**biografia** [biogra'fia] *sf* biography.

**biografico** [bio'grafiko] *agg* biographical. **biografo, -a** *sm, sf* biographer.

**biologia** [biolo'dʒia] *sf* biology. **biologico** *agg* biological. **biologo, -a** *sm, sf* biologist.

**biondo** ['bjondo] *agg* blond, fair-haired.

**birbante** [bir'bante] *sm* rascal, knave.

**birbone** [bir'bone] *sm* rogue, scamp.

**birichino** [biri'kino], **-a** *sm, sf* imp, mischievous child. *agg* impish, cheeky. **birichinata** *sf* childish prank.

**birillo** [bi'rillo] *sm* skittle.

**biro** ['biro] *sf* Biro.

**birra** ['birra] *sf* beer. **birreria** *sf* public house.

**bis** [bis] *inter* encore! **dare il bis** give an encore.

**bisaccia** [bi'zattʃa] *sf* knapsack, saddlebag.

**bisbetico** [biz'betiko] *agg* cantankerous, peevish.

**bisbigliare** [bizbi'ʎare] *v* whisper. **bisbiglio** *sm* whisper.

**biscia** ['biʃa] *sf* snake.

**biscotto** [bis'kɔtto] *sm* biscuit.

**bisestile** [bizes'tile] *agg* **anno bisestile** *sm* leap year.

**bisognare** [bizo'ɲare] *v* be necessary. **bisogno** *sm* need, requirement. **aver bisogno di** need. **non c'è bisogno** there is no need. **bisognoso** *agg* needy.

**bistecca** [bis'tekka] *sf* steak.

**bisticciare** [bistit'tʃare] *v* quarrel. **bisticcio** *sm* quarrel.

**bistrattare** [bistrat'tare] *v* ill-treat.

**bitorzolo** [bi'tortsolo] *sf* pimple.

**bivio** ['bivjo] *sm* junction, fork.

**bizzarro** [bid'dzarro] *agg* strange, odd.

**bizzeffe** [bid'dzeffe] *avv* **a bizzeffe** galore.

**blandire** [blan'dire] *v* caress, entice. **blandizie** *sf pl* flattery *sing*.

**blando** ['blando] *agg* bland, mellow.

**blasfemo** [blas'femo] *agg* blasphemous.

**blatta** ['blatta] *sf* cockroach.

**blesità** [blezi'ta] *sf* lisp. **parlar bleso** lisp.

**bloccare** [blok'kare] *v* block, blockade. **blocco** *sm* block; (*massa*) lump; blockade; (*ostruzione*) blockage. **in blocco** in bulk.

**blu** [blu] *agg* blue. **bluastro** *agg* bluish.

**blusa** ['bluza] *sf* blouse.

**boa**[1] ['bɔa] *sm invar* (*zool*) boa.

**boa**[2] *sf* (*mar*) buoy.

**boato** [bo'ato] *sm* roar, rumble. **boato sonico** sonic bang.

**bobina** [bo'bina] *sf* bobbin, reel.

**bocca** ['bokka] *sf* mouth; (*apertura*) opening. **in bocca al lupo!** good luck!

**boccale** [bok'kale] *sm* tankard.

**boccata** [bok'kata] *sf* mouthful.

**bocchino** [bok'kino] *sm* mouthpiece; cigarette-holder.

**boccia** ['bɔttʃa] *sf* (*sport*) bowl; (*vaso*) decanter; (*bot*) bud.

**bocciare** [bot'tʃare] *v* (*dir*) repeal; (*esami*) fail.

**boccio** ['bɔttʃo] *sm also* **bocciolo** bud.

**boccone** [bok'kone] *sm* mouthful.

**bocconi** [bok'koni] *avv* prone, flat on one's face.

**bofonchiare** [bofon'kjare] *v* snort.

**boia** ['bɔja] *sm invar* executioner. **boiata** *sf* (*fam*) rubbish.

**boicottare** [boikot'tare] *v* boycott. **boicottaggio** *sm* boycott.

**bolide** ['bɔlide] *sm* fireball. **andare come un bolide** go like a bomb. **passare come un bolide** flash past.

**bolla¹** ['bolla] *sf* bubble; (*med*) blister.

**bolla²** ['bolla] *sf* (*sigillo*) seal; (*papale*) bull; (*comm*) bill.

**bollare** [bol'lare] *v* seal, stamp.

**bolletta** [bol'letta] *sf* (*comm*) bill, receipt. **essere in bolletta** (*fam*) be broke. **bollettino** *sm* bulletin, list.

**bollire** [bol'lire] *v* boil. **bollente** *agg* boiling. **bollito** *sm* boiled meat. **bollitore** *sm* kettle.

**bollo** ['bollo] *sm* stamp, seal. **bollo di circolazione** tax disc.

**bomba** ['bomba] *sf* bomb.

**bombardare** [bombar'dare] *v* bomb, shell. **bombardamento** *sm* bombardment, shelling.

**bombetta** [bom'betta] *sf* bowler hat.

**bombola** ['bombola] *sf* gas cylinder.

**bonario** [bo'narjo] *agg* good-natured.

**bontà** [bon'ta] *sf* goodness.

**borbottare** [borbot'tare] *v* mutter; rumble.

**bordello** [bor'dɛllo] *sm* brothel; (*confusione*) uproar.

**bordo** ['bordo] *sm* (*mar*) side; (*orlo*) border, edge. **a bordo** on board. **giornale di bordo** *sm* (ship's) log. **virare di bordo** (*mar*) tack.

**borghese** [bor'geze] *agg* bourgeois, middle-class; civilian. *s*(*m+f*) middle-class person; civilian. **in borghese** in civilian or plain clothes. **borghesia** *sf* middle class, bourgeoisie.

**borgo** ['borgo] *sm* (*paesello*) hamlet; (*sobborgo*) suburb.

**boria** ['bɔrja] *sf* conceit, arrogance. **metter su boria** put on airs. **borioso** arrogant, conceited.

**borotalco** [boro'talko] *sm invar* talcum powder.

**borsa¹** ['borsa] *sf* bag; (*della spesa*) shopping bag; (*per documenti*) brief-case; (*diplomatica*) attaché case; (*dell'acqua*) hot-water bottle. **borsa di studio** scholarship, grant. **borsaiolo** *sm* pickpocket. **borsetta** *sf* handbag. **borsista** *s*(*m+f*) scholarship-holder.

**borsa²** ['borsa] *sf* (*comm*) stock exchange. **borsa nera** black market. **borsista** *sm* stockbroker.

**bosco** ['bɔsko] *sm* wood, forest. **boscaglia** *sf* thicket. **boschereccio** *agg* woody. **boschetto** *sm* grove. **boscoso** *agg* wooded.

**Bosnia** ['bosnja] *sf* Bosnia. **bosniaco** *agg* Bosnian.

**botanico** [bo'taniko], **-a** *agg* botanical. *sm*, *sf* botanist. *sf* botany.

**botta** ['bɔtta] *sf* blow. **fare a botte** come to blows. **dare le botte a** spank, slap.

**botte** ['botte] *sf* cask, barrel.

**bottega** [bot'tega] *sf* shop; (*laboratorio*) workshop. **bottegaio, -a** *sm*, *sf* shopkeeper. **botteghino** *sm* small shop; (*teatro*) box-office.

**bottiglia** [bot'tiʎa] *sf* bottle.

**bottone** [bot'tone] *sm* button. **attaccare un bottone a** (*fam*) buttonhole. **bottoni gemelli** cuff-links *pl*.

**bozza** ['bɔttsa] *sf* draft, sketch; (*stampa*) galley proof. **bozzetto** *sm* sketch.

**bozzolo** ['bɔttsolo] *sm* cocoon.

**braccetto** [brat'tʃetto] *sm* **a braccetto** arm in arm.

**braccialetto** [brattʃa'letto] *sm* bracelet.

**bracciante** [brat'tʃante] *sm* labourer.

**bracciata** [brat'tʃata] *sf* armful.

**braccio** ['brattʃo] *sm, pl* **-a** *f* in anat sense arm. **prendere in braccio** take into one's arms. **bracciolo** *sm* (*sedia*) arm.

**braciola** [bra'tʃɔla] *sf* chop.

**bramare** [bra'mare] *v* yearn *or* long for. **brama** *sf* longing, strong desire.

**branchia** ['brankja] *sf* gill.

**branco** ['branko] *sm* flock, drove, herd.

**brancolare** [branko'lare] *v* grope.

**branda** ['branda] *sf* camp-bed.

**brandello** [bran'dello] *sm* shred, tatter.

**brandire** [bran'dire] *v* brandish.

**brano** ['brano] *sm* (*pezzo*) shred, piece; (*frammento di opera*) passage, extract.

**branzino** [bran'dzino] *sm* sea bass.

**brasare** [bra'zare] *v* braise. **brasato** *sm*

braised beef.

**bravo** ['bravo] *agg* good; capable; (*dabbene*) decent. *inter* well done! **bravura** *sf* skill.

**breccia** ['brettʃa] *sf* breach.

**bretelle** [bre'tɛlle] *sf pl* braces *pl*.

**breve** ['brɛve] *agg* brief, short. *sf* breve. **per farla breve** to cut a long story short. **tra breve** shortly. **brevità** *sf* brevity.

**brevetto** [bre'vetto] *sm* patent. **brevettare** *v* patent.

**brezza** ['brettsa] *sf* breeze.

**bricco** ['brikko] *sm* jug, pot.

**briccone** [brik'kone] *sm* knave, rascal. *agg* knavish, mischievous.

**briciola** ['britʃola] *sf* crumb. **briciolo** *sm* tiny piece, morsel.

**bridge** ['bridʒ] *sm invar* (*carte*) bridge.

**briga** ['briga] *sf* trouble. **attaccar briga** pick a quarrel. **darsi** *or* **prendersi la briga di** go to the trouble of.

**brigadiere** [briga'djɛre] *sm* sergeant-major; (*generale*) brigadier.

**brigante** [bri'gante] *sm* brigand, bandit.

**brigata** [bri'gata] *sf* company, group; (*mil*) brigade; (*uccelli*) flock.

**briglia** ['briʎa] *sf* bridle. **tenere in briglia** rein in, restrain.

**brillare** [bril'lare] *v* shine, sparkle, glitter. **brillante** *agg* sparkling, brilliant. **brillo** *agg* tipsy.

**brina** ['brina] *sf* rime, hoar-frost.

**brindare** [brin'dare] *v* **brindare a** drink to, toast.

**brindello** [brin'dɛllo] *sm* shred, tatter.

**brindisi** ['brindizi] *sm* toast. **fare un brindisi a** drink to, toast.

**brio** ['brio] *sm* liveliness, vivacity.

**britannico** [bri'tanniko], **-a** *agg* British. *sm*, *sf* Briton, British person.

**brivido** ['brivido] *sm* shudder, shiver. **aver dei brividi** shudder, shiver.

**brocca** ['brɔkka] *sf* jug, pitcher.

**broccolo** ['brɔkkolo] *sm* broccoli.

**brodo** ['brɔdo] *sm* broth, soup. **tutto fa brodo** it is all grist to the mill.

**broglio** ['brɔʎo] *sm* malpractice, racket.

**bronchite** [bron'kite] *sf* bronchitis.

**broncio** ['brontʃo] *sm* **tenere** *or* **portare il broncio** sulk.

**brontolare** [bronto'lare] *v* mutter, grumble. **brontolone**, **-a** *sm*, *sf* grumbler.

**bronzo** ['brondzo] *sm* bronze.

**bruciapelo** [brutʃa'pelo] *sm* **a bruciapelo** point-blank.

**bruciare** [bru'tʃare] *v* burn, scorch. **bruciare le tappe** hurry. **bruciatura** *sf* burn, scald. **bruciore** *sm* burning sensation, intense desire.

**bruco** ['bruko] *sm* larva, caterpillar.

**brufolo** ['brufolo] *sm* pimple.

**brughiera** [bru'gjɛra] *sf* heath, moor.

**brulicare** [bruli'kare] *v* swarm, crawl, teem. **brulichio** *sm* swarming, teeming.

**brullo** ['brullo] *agg* bleak; barren.

**bruno** ['bruno] *agg* brown; dark.

**brusco** ['brusko] *agg* sharp; brusque, harsh; (*improvviso*) sudden.

**brusio** [bru'zio] *sm* bustle, hum.

**bruto** ['bruto] *sm*, *agg* brute. **brutale** *agg* brutal.

**brutto** ['brutto] *agg* ugly, plain; (*non buono*) bad. **avere brutta cera** look poorly. **far brutta figura** cut a sorry figure, disgrace oneself. **il brutto è che** the worst is (that), the difficulty is (that).

**buca** ['buka] *sf* hole, pit. **buca delle lettere** *sf* letter-box. **bucare** *v* make a hole in; (*biglietto*) punch; (*gomma*) puncture. **bucatura** *sf* puncture.

**bucaneve** [buka'neve] *sm invar* snowdrop.

**bucato** [bu'kato] *sm* washing. **fare il bucato** do the washing.

**buccia** ['buttʃa] *sf* peel, skin, rind.

**buco** ['buko] *sm* hole. **buco nell'acqua** failure.

**buddismo** [bud'dizmo] *sm* Buddhism. **buddista** *s*(*m+f*), *agg* Buddhist.

**budello** [bu'dɛllo] *sm* gut.

**budino** [bu'dino] *sm* pudding.

**bue** ['bue] *sm*, *pl* **buoi** ox (*pl* -en); (*carne*) beef.

**bufalo** ['bufalo], **-a** *sm*, *sf* buffalo.

**bufera** [bu'fera] *sf* gale, blizzard.

**buffè** [buf'fɛ] *sm invar* (*credenza*) sideboard; (*gastr*) buffet.

**buffo** ['buffo] *agg* comic(al), amusing. *sm* (*teatro*) comic. **il buffo è che** the odd thing is (that).

**bugia¹** [bu'dʒia] *sf* lie. **dire bugie** tell lies. **bugiardo**, **-a** *sm*, *sf* liar.

**bugia²** [bu'dʒia] *sf* candlestick.

**buio** ['bujo] *sm*, *agg* dark. **al buio** in the

dark. **buio pesto** pitch-dark.

**bulbo** ['bulbo] *sm* bulb. **bulbo oculare** eyeball.

**Bulgaria** [bulga'ria] *sf* Bulgaria. **bulgaro, -a s, agg** Bulgarian.

**bullone** [bul'lone] *sm* bolt.

**buono¹** ['bwɔno], **-a** *agg* good; kind; (*giusto*) right. **a buon conto** apropos. **a buon mercato** cheap(ly). **alla buona** simply. **buoncostume** *sm* good conduct. **buongustaio, -a** *sm, sf* gourmet. **buongusto** *sm* good taste. **buono a nulla** *sm, agg* good-for-nothing. **buonsenso** *sm* good sense. **con le buone o con le cattive** by hook or by crook. *sm, sf* good person.

**buono²** ['bwɔno] *sm* (*documento*) bond, coupon, voucher.

**buonora** [bwo'nora] *sf* **alla buonora!** at last! **di buonora** early.

**burattino** [burat'tino] *sm* puppet.

**burbero** ['burbero], **-a** *agg* grumpy, gruff. *sm, sf* grumpy person.

**burlare** [bur'lare] *v* make a fool of; (*scherzare*) joke. **burlarsi di** make fun of. **burla** *sf* joke, jest.

**burocrate** [bu'rɔkrate] *sm* bureaucrat. **burocratico** *agg* bureaucratic. **burocrazia** *sf* bureaucracy; (*fam*) red tape.

**burrasca** [bur'raska] *sf* blizzard, storm. **burrascoso** *agg* stormy.

**burro** ['burro] *sm* butter.

**burrone** [bur'rone] *sm* ravine.

**bussare** [bus'sare] *v* knock.

**bussola** ['bussola] *sf* compass.

**busta** ['busta] *sf* envelope.

**bustarella** [busta'rella] *sf* bribe.

**busto** ['busto] *sm* bust; (*indumento*) corset.

**buttare** [but'tare] throw. **buttar giù** (*cibo*) gulp down; (*scritto*) jot down; (*gastr*) put in boiling water.

# C

**cabina** [ka'bina] *sf* (*aero, mar*) cabin; (*telefono, ecc.*) booth; (*ascensore*) cage.

**cablogramma** [kablo'gramma] *sm* cable.

**cacao** [ka'kao] *sm* cocoa.

**cacare** [ka'kare] *v* (*volg*) shit.

**caccia¹** ['kattʃa] *sf* hunt, chase; (*ricerca*) pursuit, search. **a caccia di** in search of. **caccia grossa** big game. **dar la caccia** pursue.

**caccia²** ['kattʃa] *sm invar* (*aero*) fighter; (*mar*) destroyer.

**cacciagione** [kattʃa'dʒone] *sf* game.

**cacciare** [kat'tʃare] *v* hunt; (*espellere*) throw or drive out; (*introdurre*) thrust; (*mettere*) stick, put.

**cacciavite** [kattʃa'vite] *sm* screwdriver.

**cachi** ['kaki] *agg, sm* khaki.

**cacio** ['katʃo] *sm* cheese.

**cactus** ['kaktus] *sm* cactus.

**cadauno** [kada'uno] *agg, pron* each.

**cadavere** [ka'davere] *sm* corpse.

**\*cadere** [ka'dere] *v* fall; (*aero*) crash. **cader dalle nuvole** be dumbfounded. **lasciar cadere** drop. **caduta** *sf* fall; (*aero*) crash.

**cadetto** [ka'detto] *sm* younger son; (*mil*) cadet.

**caffè** [kaf'fɛ] *sm* coffee; (*locale*) café. **caffettiera** *sf* coffee-pot; (*macchina*) coffee-maker.

**caffeina** [kaffe'ina] *sf* caffeine.

**cafone** [ka'fone] *sm* (*fam*) lout.

**cagionare** [kadʒo'nare] *v* cause. **cagione** *sf* cause, reason. **a cagion di** on account of, owing to.

**cagna** ['kaɲa] *sf* bitch.

**cagnara** [ka'ɲara] *sf* (*fam*) row, uproar.

**calabrone** [kala'brone] *sm* hornet.

**calamaio** [kala'majo] *sm* inkstand, ink-well.

**calamaro** [kala'maro] *sm* squid.

**calamita** [kala'mita] *sf* magnet.

**calamità** [kalami'ta] *sf* calamity.

**calare** [ka'lare] *v* lower, let down; (*maglia*) decrease, cast off; (*scendere*) go down; (*abbassarsi*) drop. **calata** *sf* descent; (*banchina*) quay.

**calcagno** [kal'kaɲo] *sm* heel. **stare alle calcagna di** follow closely.

**calcare¹** [kal'kare] *v* press (hard); (*disegno*) trace. **calco** *sm* (*impronta di rilievo*) cast; (*disegno*) tracing.

**calcare²** [kal'kare] *sm* limestone.

**calce** ['kaltʃe] *sf* lime.

**calcestruzzo** [kaltʃes'truttso] *sm* concrete.

**calcio¹** ['kaltʃo] *sm* (*chim*) calcium.

**calcio²** ['kaltʃo] *sm* (*fucile*) rifle butt.

**calcio³** ['kaltʃo] *sm* kick; (*sport*) football. **calcio di rigore** penalty (kick). **dare un**

**calcio** kick.

**calcolare** [kalko'lare] v calculate; consider. **calcolatore, -trice** sm, sf calculator, computer.

**calcolo**[1] ['kalkolo] sm calculation; (*congettura*) reckoning; (*mat*) calculus. **a calcoli fatti** all things considered.

**calcolo**[2] ['kalkolo] sm (*med*) calculus, stone.

**caldaia** [kal'daja] sf boiler.

**caldo** ['kaldo] agg warm; (*molto*) hot. sm warmth; heat. **aver** or **far caldo** be hot.

**caleidoscopio** [kaleido'skɔpjo] sm kaleidoscope.

**calendario** [kalen'darjo] sm calendar.

**calibro** ['kalibro] sm calibre; (*mec*) gauge; (*strumento*) callipers pl.

**calice** ['kalitʃe] sm goblet; (*rel*) chalice; (*bot*) calyx.

**caligine** [ka'lidʒine] sf fog.

**calligrafia** [kalligra'fia] sf handwriting.

**callo** ['kallo] sm corn. **callifugo** sm, pl **-ghi** corn-plaster.

**calmare** [kal'mare] v calm; ease. **calmarsi** v calm down. **calma** sf calm, tranquillity. **perdere la calma** lose one's temper. **prendersela con calma** take it easy. **calmante** sm sedative. **calmo** agg calm.

**calore** [ka'lore] sm heat; (*cordialità*) warmth.

**caloria** [kalo'ria] sf calorie.

**calorifero** [kalo'rifero] sm radiator.

**caloroso** [kalo'rozo] agg warm.

**calpestare** [kalpes'tare] v trample on.

**calunnia** [ka'lunnja] sf calumny; (*diffamazione orale*) slander; (*scritta*) libel. **calunniare** v slander; libel.

**calvo** ['kalvo] agg bald. **calvizie** sf baldness.

**calza** ['kaltsa] sf (*corta*) sock; (*lunga*) stocking. **fare la calza** knit. **ferro da calza** knitting needle.

**calzare** [kal'tsare] v put on; (*portare*) wear; (*convenire*) fit. **calzatura** sf footwear.

**calzolaio** [kaltso'lajo] sm shoemaker. **calzoleria** sf shoe shop.

**calzoni** [kal'tsoni] sm pl trousers pl.

**camaleonte** [kamale'onte] sm chameleon.

**cambiale** [kam'bjale] sf bill of exchange.

**cambiare** [kam'bjare] v change. **cambiar casa** move. **tanto per cambiare** just for a change. **cambiamento** sm change.

**cambio** ['kambjo] sm change; (*econ*) exchange; (*auto*) transmission, gearbox.

**camera** ['kamera] sf room; (*da letto*) bedroom; (*assemblea, tec*) chamber. **camera d'aria** (*pneumatico*) inner tube. **musica da camera** sf chamber music.

**camerata**[1] [kame'rata] sf dormitory.

**camerata**[2] [kame'rata] s(m+f) comrade; (*fam*) mate.

**cameriera** [kame'rjɛra] sf (*albergo*) chamber-maid; (*ristorante*) waitress; (*domestica*) maid.

**cameriere** [kame'rjɛre] sm (*ristorante*) waiter; servant.

**camicia** [ka'mitʃa] sf shirt; (*da donna*) blouse; (*tec*) jacket. **camicia da notte** nightgown. **camicia di forza** straitjacket. **camiciola** sf (*maglia*) vest; T-shirt.

**camino** [ka'mino] sm fireplace; chimney.

**camion** ['kamjon] sm invar lorry. **camioncino** sm van.

**cammello** [kam'mɛllo] sm camel.

**camminare** [kammi'nare] v walk; (*procedere*) go. **camminata** sf walk.

**cammino** [kam'mino] sm way; (*percorso*) journey; (*sentiero*) path. **mettersi in cammino** set out.

**camorra** [ka'mɔrra] sf racket. **camorrista** s(m+f) racketeer.

**camoscio** [ka'mɔʃo] sm chamois; (*pelle*) chamois leather.

**campagna** [kam'paɲa] sf country; (*paesaggio*) countryside; (*terreno*) land; (*villeggiatura*) holidays pl; (*mil, propaganda, ecc.*) campaign. **campagnolo** agg rural, country.

**campana** [kam'pana] sf bell; (*di lampada*) lampshade. **campanello** sm bell. **campanile** sm bell tower.

**campare** [kam'pare] v live.

**campeggiare** [kamped'dʒare] v camp. **campeggio** sm camping; (*terreno*) campsite.

**campestre** [kam'pɛstre] agg rural, country.

**campione** [kam'pjone] sm (*sport, difensore*) champion; (*piccola quantità*) sample; (*di tessuto*) pattern. **campionario** sm sample collection; pattern book. **campionessa** sf champion.

**campo** ['kampo] sm field. **campo di golf** golf course. **campo di tennis** tennis court.

**camposanto** [kampo'santo] sm cemetery.

**camuffamento** [kamuffa'mento] sm disguise; (*mil*) camouflage. **camuffare** v disguise; camouflage..

**camuso** [ka'muzo] *agg* snub-nosed.

**Canada** ['kanada] *sm* Canada. **Canadese** *s(m+f)*, *agg* Canadian.

**canaglia** [ka'naʎa] *sf* scoundrel; (*marmaglia*) rabble.

**canale** [ka'nale] *sm* canal; (*radio, TV*) channel. **Canale della Manica** (English) Channel. **canale di scarico** drain. **canale di scolo** gutter.

**canapa** ['kanapa] *sf* hemp.

**canapè** [kana'pɛ] *sm* (*mobile*) settee; (*tartina*) canapé.

**canarino** [kana'rino] *sm* canary. *agg* canary yellow.

**cancellare** [kantʃel'lare] *v* cancel, wipe out; (*con gomma*) rub out; (*con penna*) cross out.

**cancelliere** [kantʃel'ljɛre] *sm* chancellor. **cancelleria** *sf* chancellery, chancery; (*cartoleria*) stationery.

**cancello** [kan'tʃɛllo] *sm* gate. **cancellata** *sf* railings *pl*.

**cancro** [kan'kro] *sm* cancer. **Cancro** *sm* Cancer.

**cancrena** [kan'krɛna] *sf* gangrene.

**candeggiare** [kanded'dʒare] *v* bleach. **candeggina** *sf* bleach.

**candela** [kan'dela] *sf* candle; (*auto*) sparking-plug. **precipitare in candela** do a nose-dive. **candelabro** *sm* candlestick; (*a bracci*) candelabra.

**candidato** [kandi'dato], **-a** *sm*, *sf* candidate. **candidatura** *sf* candidature.

**candido** ['kandido] *agg* spotless, snow-white; (*sincero*) candid.

**candito** [kan'dito] *agg* candied, crystallized.

**cane** ['kane] *sm* dog. **cane bastardo** mongrel. **cane da guardia** watch-dog. **cane da salotto** lap-dog.

**canestro** [ka'nɛstro] *sm* basket.

**canguro** [kan'guro] *sm* kangaroo.

**canicola** [ka'nikola] *sf* heat-wave.

**canile** [ka'nile] *sm* kennel.

**canino** [ka'nino] *agg* canine.

**canna** ['kanna] *sf* cane; (*pianta*) reed; (*fucile*) barrel; (*bicicletta*) cross-bar; (*pesca*) rod; (*tubo, organo*) pipe. **cannello** *sm* tube; (*per saldare*) blowpipe.

**cannella** [kan'nɛlla] *sf* cinnamon.

**cannibale** [kan'nibale] *sm* cannibal.

**cannocchiale** [kannok'kjale] *sm* telescope.

**cannone** [kan'none] *sm* cannon. **cannonata** *sf* cannon shot. **è una cannonata!** (*fam*) it's terrific!

**cannuccia** [kan'nuttʃa] *sf* (*per bibite*) (drinking) straw; (*di pipa*) stem.

**canoa** [ka'nɔa] *sf* canoe.

**canone** ['kanone] *sm* canon; (*soldi dovuti*) fee; (*per affitto*) rent.

**canonico** [ka'nɔniko] *agg* canonical. **diritto canonico** *sm* canon law. **canonica** *sf* rectory.

**canonizzare** [kanonid'dzare] *v* canonize.

**canottaggio** [kanot'taddʒo] *sm* rowing. **canottiere** *sm* oarsman.

**canottiera** [kanot'tjɛra] *sf* T-shirt.

**canotto** [ka'nɔtto] *sm* rowing-boat; (*di salvataggio*) lifeboat.

**canovaccio** [kano'vattʃo] *sm* (*per stoviglie*) dishcloth; (*teatro*) plot.

**cantare** [kan'tare] *v* sing; (*del gallo*) crow; (*cinguettare*) chirp; (*fam: fare la spia*) squeal. **cantata** *sf* singsong; (*musica*) cantata. **canterellare** *or* **canticchiare** *v* hum.

**cantiere** [kan'tjɛre] *sm* yard; (*mar*) shipyard, dockyard.

**cantilena** [kanti'lɛna] *sf* singsong.

**cantina** [kan'tina] *sf* cellar.

**canto¹** ['kanto] *sm* song; (*poesia*) lyric; (*liturgia*) chant. **canto popolare** folk song.

**canto²** ['kanto] *sm* (*angolo*) corner; (*parte*) side. **da canto** aside. **d'altro canto** on the other hand. **da un canto** in a way.

**cantone¹** [kan'tone] *sm* corner. **cantonata** *sf* (street-)corner; (*errore*) blunder. **prendere una cantonata** blunder.

**cantone²** [kan'tone] *sm* (*geog*) canton.

**cantoniere** [kanto'njɛre] *sm* (*ferr*) signalman.

**canuto** [ka'nuto] *agg* white-haired.

**canzonare** [kantso'nare] *v* make fun of, tease, mock. **canzonatore, -trice** *sm*, *sf* mocker. **canzonatura** *sf* mockery.

**canzone** [kan'tsone] *sf* song; (*discorso noioso*) old story. **canzonetta** *sf* pop song.

**caos** ['kaos] *sm* chaos. **caotico** *agg* chaotic.

**capace** [ka'patʃe] *agg* (*abile*) capable; (*in grado di*) able. **capacità** *sf* capacity; ability.

**capanna** [ka'panna] *sf* hut. **capannone** *sm* shed; (*aero*) hangar.

**caparbio** [ka'parbjo] *agg* stubborn.

**caparra** [ka'parra] *sf* deposit.

**capello** [ka'pello] *sm* hair. **capelli** *sm pl* hair *sing.* **averne fin sopra i capelli (di)** be heartily sick (of). **capelluto** *agg* hairy. **cuoio capelluto** *sm* scalp.

**capezzale** [kapet'tsale] *sm* **al capezzale** at the bedside.

**capezzolo** [ka'pettsolo] *sm* nipple.

**capire** [ka'pire] *v* understand; (*rendersi conto*) realize. **farsi capire** make oneself understood. **si capisce** naturally.

**capitale** [kapi'tale] *sm* (*econ*) capital. *sf* capital (city). *agg* capital; fundamental; (*principale*) main. **capitalismo** *sm* capitalism. **capitalista** *s(m+f)*, *agg* capitalist.

**capitano** [kapi'tano] *sm* captain.

**capitare** [kapi'tare] *v* (*giungere*) turn up; (*presentarsi*) arise, come up; (*accadere*) happen. **capitar bene** strike lucky. **dove capita** anywhere.

**capitello** [kapi'tɛllo] *sm* capital.

**capitolo** [ka'pitolo] *sm* chapter. **aver voce in capitolo** have a say in the matter.

**capo** ['kapo] *sm* head; (*pezzo*) item; (*geog*) cape. **da capo** again, from the beginning. **da capo a fondo** from top to bottom. **da un capo all'altro** from one end to the other. **in capo a** within. **per sommi capi** briefly, in short. **venire a capo di** get to the bottom of.

**capobanda** [kapo'banda] *sm invar* ringleader; (*musica*) bandmaster.

**capodanno** [kapo'danno] *sm* New Year's Day.

**capofitto** [kapo'fitto] *agg* **a capofitto** headlong; (*con massimo impegno*) wholeheartedly.

**capogiro** [kapo'dʒiro] *sm* giddiness, dizzy spell. **fare venire il capogiro a** make dizzy.

**capolavoro** [kapola'voro] *sm* masterpiece.

**capolinea** [kapo'linea] *sm*, *pl* **capilinea** terminus.

**capoluogo** [kapo'lwɔgo] *sm*, *pl* -**ghi** main town, capital.

**capomastro** [kapo'mastro] *sm* foreman.

**capoofficina** [kapoofi'tʃina] *sm*, *pl* **capiofficina** foreman.

**caporale** [kapo'rale] *sm* corporal.

**caposala** [kapo'sala] *s(m+f)*, *pl* **capisala**, **caposala** (*fabbrica*) foreman; (*albergo*) head-waiter; (*ospedale*) ward sister.

**capostazione** [kaposta'tsjone] *sm*, *pl* **capistazione** station-master.

**capotare** [kapo'tare] *v* (*auto*) overturn; (*mar*) capsize.

**capote** [ka'pɔt] *sf*, *pl* -**s** (*auto*) hood.

**capotreno** [kapo'trɛno] *sm* guard.

*capovolgere [kapo'vɔldʒere] v overturn; (fig) turn upside down, reverse; (mar) capsize. **capovolgimento** *sm* reversal.

**cappa** ['kappa] *sf* cloak; (*di camino*) hood.

**cappella¹** [kap'pɛlla] *sf* chapel. **cappellano** *sm* chaplain.

**cappella²** [kap'pɛlla] *sf* (*di fungo*) cap.

**cappello** [kap'pɛllo] *sm* hat. **cappellaio** *sm* hatter.

**cappero** ['kappero] *sm* caper. **capperi!** *inter* gosh! good heavens!

**cappotta** [kap'pɔtta] *sf* (*auto*) hood.

**cappotto** [kap'pɔtto] *sm* coat; (*bridge*) slam.

**cappuccino** [kapput'tʃino] *sm* coffee with milk, cappuccino; (*rel*) Capuchin friar.

**cappuccio** [kap'puttʃo] *sm* hood; (*tec*) cap; (*rel*) cowl.

**capra** ['kapra] *sf* goat. **capretto** *sm* kid. **capro** *sm* he-goat. **capro espiatorio** scapegoat.

**capriccio** [ka'prittʃo] *sm* whim, fancy. **fare i capricci** have tantrums.

**Capricorno** [kapri'kɔrno] *sm* Capricorn.

**caprifoglio** [kapri'fɔʎʎo] *sm* honeysuckle.

**capriola¹** [kapri'ɔla] *sf* somersault, jump.

**capriola²** [kapri'ɔla] *sf* (*zool*) roe deer. **capriolo** *sm* roebuck.

**capsico** [kap'siko] *sm* capsicum.

**capsula** ['kapsula] *sf* capsule; (*di dente*) crown.

**carabiniere** [karabi'njɛre] *sm* policeman, soldier in police corps.

**caraffa** [ka'raffa] *sf* carafe, jug.

**caraibico** [kara'ibiko] *agg* Caribbean.

**caramella** [kara'mɛlla] *sf* sweet. **caramellato** *agg* candied; (*zucchero*) caramelized.

**carato** [ka'rato] *sm* carat.

**carattere** [ka'rattere] *sm* (*indole*) nature; (*forza, lettera*) character; characteristic; (*teatro*) role; type. **caratteristica** *sf* characteristic, (*distinctive*) feature; (*tec*) specification. **caratteristico** *agg* typical, distinctive.

**carboidrato** [karboi'drato] *sm* carbohydrate.

**carbonchio** [kar'bonkjo] *sm* carbuncle; (*vet*) anthrax; (*agric*) blight.

**carbone** [kar'bone] *sm* coal. **carbone coke** coke. **carbone di legna** charcoal. **carboncino** *sm* (*disegno*) charcoal.

**carbonio** [kar'bɔnjo] *sm* carbon.

**carburante** [karbu'rante] *sm* fuel.

**carburatore** [karbura'tore] *sm* carburettor.

**carcassa** [kar'kassa] *sf* carcass; (*fam*) wreck.

**carcere** ['kartʃere] *sm* prison, jail. **carcerato, -a** *sm, sf* prisoner. **carceriere, -a** *sm, sf* jailer.

**carciofo** [kar'tʃɔfo] *sm* artichoke.

**cardiaco** [kar'diako] *agg* cardiac. **attacco cardiaco** *sm* heart attack. **cardiologo, -a** *sm, sf* heart specialist, cardiologist.

**cardinale** [kardi'nale] *sm, agg* cardinal.

**cardine** ['kardine] *sm* hinge; (*fig*) cornerstone.

**cardo** ['kardo] *sm* (*bot*) thistle.

**carena** [ka'rena] *sf* hull. (**bacino di**) **carenaggio** *sm* dry dock.

**carestia** [kares'tia] *sf* famine.

**carezzare** [karet'tsare] *v* stroke, caress. **carezza** *sf* caress. **fare le carezze a** pat, stroke.

**cariarsi** [ka'rjarsi] *v* decay.

**carica** ['karika] *sf* (*impiego*) position; (*ufficio pubblico*) office; (*mil, elett*) charge; (*sport*) tackle.

**caricare** [kari'kare] *v* load; (*riempire*) fill; (*mil, elett*) charge; (*sport*) tackle; (*orologio, molla*) wind up.

**caricatura** [karika'tura] *sf* caricature.

**carico** ['kariko] *sm, pl* **-chi** (*di nave*) cargo; (*peso*) burden; (*tec*) load. **a carico di** (*contro*) against; (*a spese di*) at the expense of, chargeable to. **testimone a carico** witness for the prosecution. *agg* loaded, filled (with), full (of).

**carie** ['karje] *sf* (*dentaria*) tooth decay; (*di legno, cereali, ecc.*) rot.

**carino** [ka'rino] *agg* lovely, charming.

**carisma** [ka'risma] *sm* charisma. **carismatico** *agg* charismatic.

**carità** [kari'ta] *sf* charity; (*misericordia*) compassion. **aver carità di** take pity on. **fare la carità** give alms. **per carità!** God forbid!

**carlinga** [kar'linga] *sf* fuselage.

**carnagione** [karna'dʒone] *sf* complexion, skin.

**carne** ['karne] *sf* flesh; (*alimento*) meat. **carne di manzo/maiale/vitello** beef/pork/veal. **carnale** *agg* carnal. **carnoso** *agg* fleshy.

**carneficina** [karnefi'tʃina] *sf* slaughter. **carnefice** *sm* executioner.

**carnevale** [karne'vale] *sm* carnival.

**carnivoro** [kar'nivoro], **-a** *sm, sf* carnivore. *agg* carnivorous.

**caro** ['karo] *agg* dear. **aver caro** hold dear. **pagar caro** pay a lot for; (*fig*) pay dearly for. **cari** *sm pl* loved ones *pl*.

**carogna** [ka'roɲa] *sf* carrion; (*fam*) bastard, sod.

**carosello** [karo'zɛllo] *sm* merry-go-round.

**carota** [ka'rɔta] *sf* carrot.

**carovana** [karo'vana] *sf* caravan; procession.

**carpione** [kar'pjone] *sm* **in carpione** soused.

**carponi** [kar'poni] *avv* on all fours.

**carrabile** [kar'rabile] *agg* **passo carrabile** *sm* passageway.

**carreggiata** [karred'dʒata] *sf* carriageway, track. **rimettersi in carreggiata** catch up. **uscire di carreggiata** go off the road; (*fig*) go astray.

**carrello** [kar'rɛllo] *sm* (*vagoncino*) trolley; (*mec*) (under-)carriage.

**carretta** [kar'retta] *sf* cart.

**carriera** [kar'rjɛra] *sf* career; (*velocità*) full speed. **fare carriera** get on, make good.

**carriola** [kar'rjɔla] *sf* wheelbarrow.

**carro** ['karro] *sm* (*a quattro ruote*) wagon; (*a due ruote*) cart. **carro armato** armoured vehicle, tank. **carro attrezzi** breakdown van. **carro funebre** hearse. **carro merci** goods wagon.

**carrozza** [kar'rɔttsa] *sf* coach. **carrozza letto** sleeping-car, sleeper. **in carrozza!** all aboard!

**carrucola** [kar'rukola] *sf* pulley.

**carta** ['karta] *sf* paper; (*geog*) map; (*da gioco, documento*) card; (*statuto*) charter. **carta asciugante** *or* **assorbente** blotting paper. **carta carbone** carbon paper. **carta da parati** wallpaper. **carta di credito** charge card. **cartapecora** *sf* parchment. **cartapesta** *sf* papier mâché. **cartastraccia** *sf* waste paper.

**cartella** [kar'tɛlla] *sf* (*custodia per fogli*) folder; (*busta di pelle*) brief-case; (*per scolari*) satchel; (*scheda*) card, file.

**cartellino** [kartel'lino] *sm* tag.

**cartello** [kar'tɛllo] *sm* (*insegna*) sign; (*indicatore*) signpost, road sign; (*avviso*) notice, poster. **cartellone** *sm* poster.

**cartilagine** [karti'ladʒine] *sf* cartilage.

**cartolaio** [karto'lajo], **-a** *sm, sf* stationer. **cartoleria** *sf* stationer's (shop).

**cartolina** [karto'lina] *sf* postcard.

**cartone** [kar'tone] *sm* cardboard; (*disegno*) cartoon. **cartoni animati** (*cinema*) cartoons *pl*. **cartoncino** *sm* card.

**cartuccia** [kar'tuffa] *sf* cartridge.

**casa** ['kaza] *sf* home; (*edificio, dinastia*) house; (*comm*) firm. **a casa** (*stato in luogo*) at home; (*moto a luogo*) home. **a casa del diavolo** off the beaten track. **cambiar casa** move house. **casa di cura** nursing home. **casa popolare** council house.

**casalinga** [kaza'linga] *sf* housewife. **casalinghi** *sm pl* household goods *pl*. **casalingo** *agg* domestic; (*semplice*) homely, plain.

**cascame** [kas'kame] *sm* waste.

**cascare** [kas'kare] *v* fall; (*capelli, denti*) fall out; (*muri, ecc.*) fall down. **cascata** *sf* fall; (*d'acqua*) waterfall; (*perle, ecc.*) cascade.

**cascina** [ka'ʃina] *sf* dairy farm; (*casa colonica*) farmhouse.

**casco** ['kasko] *sm* helmet; (*parrucchieri*) hairdryer.

**caseggiato** [kazed'dʒato] *sm* block of buildings.

**casella** [ka'zɛlla] *sf* (*riquadro*) square; (*scompartimento*) compartment. **casella postale** post-office box. **casellario** *sm* (*mobile*) filing cabinet; (*ufficio*) registry.

**casello** [ka'zɛllo] *sm* (*fer*) signal-box; (*autostrada*) toll-booth.

**caserma** [ka'zɛrma] *sf* barracks *pl*.

**casino** [ka'zino] *sm* (*fam: confusione*) row, racket; (*postribolo*) brothel; (*casa signorile*) lodge.

**casinò** [kazi'nɔ] *sm* casino.

**caso** ['kazo] *sm* case; (*affare*) matter; (*combinazione, destino*) chance; possibility. **a caso** at random. **fare caso a** heed, attach importance to. **in caso** in case. **in caso diverso** or **contrario** otherwise. **in ogni caso** in any case, at any rate. **per caso** by chance. **poniamo il caso** let us suppose.

**cassa** ['kassa] *sf* case, box; (*istituzione*) fund; (*dove si paga*) cash desk. **cassa da morto** coffin. **cassa pronta** ready cash. **libro di cassa** cash-book.

**casseruola** [kasse'rwɔla] *sf* casserole, saucepan.

**cassetta** [kas'setta] *sf* box; (*teatro*) takings *pl*. **cassetto** *sm* drawer. **cassettone** *sm* chest of drawers.

**cassiere** [kas'sjɛre], **-a** *sm, sf* cashier.

**casta** ['kasta] *sf* caste.

**castagno** [kas'taɲo] *sm* chestnut tree; (*colore*) chestnut. **agg** chestnut. **castagna** *sf* chestnut. **castagnola** (*petardo*) cracker.

**castello** [kas'tɛllo] *sm* castle; (*impalcatura*) scaffolding. **castello di poppa** quarterdeck. **castello di prua** forecastle.

**castigare** [kasti'gare] *v* punish. **castigo** *sm, pl* **-ghi** punishment.

**casto** ['kasto] *agg* chaste. **castità** *sf* chastity.

**castoro** [kas'tɔro] *sm* beaver.

**castrare** [kas'trare] *v* castrate, geld. **castrato** *sm* (*carne*) lamb.

**casuale** [kazu'ale] *agg* fortuitous, accidental; (*dir*) contingent. **casualmente** *avv* by chance.

**catacomba** [kata'komba] *sf* catacomb.

**catafascio** [kata'faʃo] *sm* **andare a catafascio** go to rack and ruin.

**catalizzatore** [kataliddza'tore] *sm* catalyst. *agg* catalytic.

**catalogo** [ka'talogo] *sm, pl* **-ghi** catalogue, list. **catalogare** *v* catalogue, list.

**catapulta** [kata'pulta] *sf* catapult; (*missili*) launcher. **catapultare** *v* launch.

**catarifrangente** [katarifran'dʒɛnte] *sm* reflector.

**catarro** [ka'tarro] *sm* catarrh.

**catasta** [ka'tasta] *sf* pile.

**catastrofe** [ka'tastrofe] *sf* catastrophe. **catastrofico** *agg* catastrophic.

**catechismo** [kate'kizmo] *sm* catechism.

**categoria** [katego'ria] *sf* category, class. **categorico** *agg* categorical, absolute, explicit.

**catena** [ka'tena] *sf* chain. **catena di montaggio** assembly line. **catenaccio** *sm* bolt; (*fam: macchina vecchia*) old crock; (*sport*) defensive tactics *pl*.

**cateratta** [kate'ratta] *sf* cataract; (*chiusa*) floodgate.

**catetere** [kate'tɛre] *sm* catheter.

**catino** [ka'tino] *sm* basin. **piovere a catinelle** rain cats and dogs.

**catodo** ['katodo] *sm* cathode.

**catrame** [ka'trame] *sm* tar.

**cattedra** ['kattedra] *sf* (*tavola*) desk; (*ufficio di insegnante*) teaching post; (*carica universitaria*) chair.

**cattedrale** [katte'drale] *sf* cathedral.

**cattivarsi** [katti'varsi] *v* win, gain.

**cattivo** [kat'tivo] *agg* bad; (*in senso morale*) wicked; (*scortese*) nasty; (*capriccioso*) naughty. **cattiveria** *sf* wickedness, naughtiness; (*parole cattive*) spiteful remark.

**cattolico** [kat'tɔliko], **-a** s, *agg* Catholic. **Cattolicesimo** *sm* Catholicism.

**catturare** [kattu'rare] *v* capture, arrest. **cattura** *sf* capture, arrest.

**caucciù** [kaut'tʃu] *sm* rubber.

**causa** ['kauza] *sf* cause; (*dir*) lawsuit, action. **a causa di** because of, on account of. **fare causa a** sue. **causale** *agg* causal.

**causare** [kau'zare] *v* cause, give rise to, bring about.

**caustico** ['kaustiko] *agg* caustic.

**cauto** ['kauto] *agg* cautious, careful. **cautela** *sf* caution; (*precauzione*) care.

**cauzione** [kau'tsjone] *sf* (*caparra*) security, bail. **rilasciare su cauzione** release on bail. **cauzionare** *v* pay a deposit.

**cava** ['kava] *sf* quarry.

**cavalcare** [kaval'kare] *v* ride; (*ponte*) span. **cavalcata** *sf* ride. **cavalcavia** *sm invar* fly-over. **a cavalcioni** astride.

**cavaliere** [kava'ljɛre] *sm* knight; (*chi cavalca*) rider.

**cavalleria** [kavalle'ria] *sf* (*mil*) cavalry; (*medievale, cortesia*) chivalry. **cavalleresco** *agg* chivalrous. **cavallerizza** *sf* horsewoman; (*maneggio*) riding school. **cavallerizzo** *sm* horseman; (*chi insegna*) riding master.

**cavalletta** [kaval'letta] *sf* grasshopper.

**cavalletto** [kaval'letto] *sm* (*sostegno*) trestle, stand; (*da pittore*) easel.

**cavallo** [ka'vallo] *sm* horse; (*scacchi*) knight. **a cavallo** on horseback. **a cavallo di** astride, straddling. **andare a cavallo** ride. **cavallo dei pantaloni** crotch. **cavalla** *sf* mare. **cavallina** *sf* filly. **correre la cavallina** sow one's wild oats.

**cavare** [ka'vare] *v* draw *or* pull out. **cavarsela** *v* get by, manage. **cavarsi** *v* (*togliersi*)

take off. **cavatappi** *sm invar* corkscrew.

**caverna** [ka'vɛrna] *sf* cave. **cavernoso** *agg* cavernous, hollow.

**cavia** ['kavia] *sf* guinea pig.

**caviale** [ka'vjale] *sm* caviar.

**caviglia** [ka'viʎa] *sf* ankle.

**cavillare** [kavil'lare] *v* quibble.

**cavo¹** ['kavo] *sm*, *agg* (*vuoto*) hollow.

**cavo²** ['kavo] *sm* cable.

**cavolo** ['kavolo] *sm* cabbage. **cavoli di Bruxelles** Brussels sprouts *pl*. **cavolfiore** *sm* cauliflower. **testa di cavolo** (*fam*) clot.

**cazzo** ['kattso] *sm* (*volg*) prick.

**cazzotto** [kat'tsɔtto] *sm* (*fam*) punch. **fare a cazzotti** fight.

**ce** [tʃe] *V* **ci**.

**cece** ['tʃetʃe] *sm* chick-pea.

**cecità** [tʃetʃi'ta] *sf* blindness.

**ceco** ['tʃeko], **-a** s, *agg* Czech.

**cedere** ['tʃedere] *v* yield; (*trasferire*) hand over; (*piegarsi*) give way. **cedere il passo** make way. **cedere il posto** give up one's seat.

**cedola** ['tʃedola] *sf* (*scontrino*) coupon; (*di titolo*) dividend voucher.

**cedro¹** ['tʃedro] *sm* (*agrume*) citron.

**cedro²** ['tʃedro] *sm* (*conifera*) cedar.

**ceffone** [tʃef'fone] *sm* slap (in the face).

**celare** [tʃe'lare] *v* conceal, hide.

**celebrare** [tʃele'brare] *v* celebrate.

**celebre** ['tʃɛlebre] *agg* famous. **celebrità** *pf* fame; (*persona*) celebrity.

**celere** ['tʃelere] *agg* rapid. *sf* flying squad.

**celeste** [tʃe'lɛste] *agg*, *sm* sky-blue.

**celibe** ['tʃelibe] *agg* single. *sm* bachelor.

**cella** ['tʃella] *sf* cell. **cella frigorifera** cold storage.

**cellula** ['tʃellula] *sf* cell.

**cellulosa** [tʃellu'loza] *sf* cellulose.

**cemento** [tʃe'mento] *sm* cement. **cemento armato** reinforced concrete. **cementare** *v* cement.

**cena** ['tʃena] *sf* supper, dinner. **cenare** *v* have supper *or* dinner.

**cencio** ['tʃentʃo] *sm* rag; (*per stoviglie*) dishcloth; (*per spolverare*) duster. **cencioso** *agg* ragged, tattered.

**cenere** ['tʃenere] *sf* ash. **Ceneri** *sf pl* Ash Wednesday *sing*.

**cenno** ['tʃenno] *sm* sign, gesture; (*col capo*)

nod; (*con gli occhi*) wink; (*con la mano*) wave; (*allusione*) mention.

**censimento** [tʃensi'mento] *sm* census.

**censurare** [tʃensu'rare] *v* (*biasimare*) censure; (*sottoporre a censura*) censor. **censura** *sf* censorship; (*riprovazione*) censure.

**centenario** [tʃente'narjo], **-a** *sm, sf* centenarian. *sm* (*ricorrenza*) centenary. *agg* hundred-year-old.

**centesimo** [tʃen'tɛzimo] *sm* hundredth; (*soldo*) cent. *agg* hundredth.

**centigrado** [tʃen'tigrado] *agg* centigrade.

**centimetro** [tʃen'timetro] *sm* centimetre; (*nastro per misurare*) tape-measure.

**cento** ['tʃɛnto] *agg, sm* hundred. **per cento** per cent. **centinaio** *sm, pl* **-a** *f* hundred; (*circa cento*) about a hundred. **a centinaia** by the hundred, in hundreds.

**centrale** [tʃen'trale] *agg* central, principal. *sf* (*deposito*) main depot; (*del telefono*) exchange; (*di energia*) power station; (*di amministrazione*) head office. **centralino** *sm* switchboard. **centralinista** *s(m+f)* switchboard operator.

**centro** ['tʃɛntro] *sm* centre; (*mezzo*) middle; (*luogo di soggiorno*) resort; (*fam: colpo centrato*) bull's eye.

**ceppo** ['tʃeppo] *sm* (*razza*) stock; (*base di albero*) stump; (*pezzo di legno*) block; (*auto*) brake-block. **ceppi** *sm pl* fetters *pl*.

**cera**[1] ['tʃera] *sf* wax; (*per lucidare*) polish. **dare la cera** wax. **ceralacca** *sf* sealing-wax.

**cera**[2] ['tʃera] *sf* (*aspetto*) air, expression. **aver buona/brutta cera** look well/ill. **far buona cera a** welcome heartily.

**ceramica** [tʃe'ramika] *sf* (*oggetto*) piece of pottery; (*materiale*) earthenware; (*arte*) pottery. **ceramiche** *sf pl* pottery *sing*. **ceramista** *s(m+f)* potter.

**cercare** [tʃer'kare] *v* look for, search for; (*nei libri*) look up; (*tentare*) try; (*volere*) want. **cerca** *sf* search; (*questua*) begging.

**cerchia** ['tʃerkja] *sf* circle.

**cerchio** ['tʃerkjo] *sm* circle; (*giocattolo, di botte*) hoop. **fare cerchio intorno a** circle round.

**cereale** [tʃere'ale] *sm, agg* cereal.

**cerebrale** [tʃere'brale] *agg* cerebral.

**cerimonia** [tʃeri'mɔnja] *sf* ceremony. **far cerimonie** stand on ceremony. **senza ceri-**

**monie** without fuss. **cerimoniale** *sm, agg* ceremonial.

**cerino** [tʃe'rino] *sm* (*candela*) taper; (*fiammifero*) wax match.

**cerniera** [tʃer'njera] *sf* hinge; (*di borsetta*) clasp. **cerniera lampo** zip fastener.

**cernita** ['tʃernita] *sf* choice.

**cero** ['tʃero] *sm* (church) candle.

**cerotto** [tʃe'rɔtto] *sm* plaster.

**certezza** [tʃer'tettsa] *sf* certainty.

**certificare** [tʃertifi'kare] *v* certify. **certificato** *sm* certificate.

**certo** ['tʃerto] *agg* certain. *avv* certainly. **dare** *or* **sapere per certo** know for a fact. **tenere per certo** have no doubts about.

**certuni** [tʃer'tuni] *pron* some (people).

**cervello** [tʃer'vello] *sm* brain; (*intelligenza, cibo*) brains *pl*. **dare al cervello** go to one's head.

**cervo** ['tʃervo] *sm* deer, stag. **cervo volante** (*insetto*) stag beetle; (*aquilone*) kite. **cerva** *sf* deer, doe, hind.

**cesello** [tʃe'zello] *sm* (*strumento*) engraving tool, small chisel. **cesellare** *v* engrave, chisel; (*fare con cura*) polish.

**cesoie** [tʃe'zɔje] *sf pl* shears *pl*.

**cespo** ['tʃespo] *sm* (*di erbe*) tuft; (*di fiori*) cluster. **cespo di lattuga** head of lettuce.

**cespuglio** [tʃes'puʎo] *sm* shrub, bush.

**cessare** [tʃes'sare] *v* cease, stop. **cessate il fuoco** *sm* cease-fire. **cessazione** *sf* cessation; (*comm*) termination, stoppage.

**cessione** [tʃes'sjone] *sf* relinquishment; (*dir*) transfer, assignment.

**cesso** ['tʃesso] *sm* (*fam*) loo, lavatory.

**cesta** ['tʃesta] *sf* basket.

**cestino** [tʃes'tino] *sm* waste-paper basket; (*da lavoro*) work-basket. **cestino da viaggio** packed lunch. **cestinare** *v* throw away; (*scritti*) reject.

**cesto** ['tʃesto] *sm* basket.

**ceto** ['tʃɛto] *sm* class.

**cetriolo** [tʃetri'ɔlo] *sm* cucumber. **cetriolino** *sm* gherkin.

**che**[1] [ke] *pron* (*persone: soggetto*) who; (*persone: oggetto*) whom, that; (*cose*) which, that; (*quando*) when; (*dove*) where; (*interrogativo*) what; (*indefinito*) something. *inter* what! (*come*) how! *agg* (*quale*) what; (*numero limitato*) which. **non è un gran che** it's nothing much.

**che**[2] [ke] *cong* that; (*comparativa*) than;

(*quando*) when; (*dopo*) after; (*eccettuativa*) but.

**checché** [ke'ke] *pron* whatever.

**chi** [ki] *pron* (*soggetto*) who; (*oggetto*) whom; (*colui che*) he who; (*colei che*) she who; (*coloro che*) those who; (*chiunque*) whoever. **chi ... chi ...** some ... others .... **di chi** whose.

**chiacchierare** [kjakkje'rare] *v* chat. **chiacchiera** *sf* chat; (*discorso inutile*) idle talk. **far due** *or* **quattro chiacchiere** chat. **chiacchierata** *sf* chat.

**chiacchierone** [kjakkje'rone], **-a** *agg* talkative; (*pettegolo*) gossipy. *sm, sf* chatterbox, gossip.

**chiamare** [kja'mare] *v* call; (*far venire*) send for; (*al telefono*) ring (up). **chiamare in giudizio** sue. **chiamare sotto le armi** call up. **chiamata** *sf* call. **chiamata in giudizio** summons. **chiamata urbana/interurbana** local/trunk call.

**chiarire** [kja'rire] *v* clarify; (*spiegare*) explain.

**chiaro** ['kjaro] *agg* clear; (*luminoso*) bright; (*non scuro*) light. *sm* light. *avv* clearly, distinctly. **chiaro e tondo** blunt. **mettere in chiaro** clear up.

**chiasso** ['kjasso] *sm* noise, racket, row. **far chiasso** kick up a row. **chiassoso** *agg* rowdy, noisy; (*colore*) loud.

**chiavare** [kja'vare] *v* (*volg*) screw, fuck.

**chiave** ['kjave] *sf* key; (*tec*) spanner; (*segno musicale*) clef. **chiave apritutto** master key. **chiave inglese** adjustable spanner.

**chiavistello** [kjavis'tello] *sm* bolt, latch.

**chiazzare** [kjat'tsare] *v* spot; (*con colori diversi*) mottle. **chiazza** *sf* spot; (*sulla pelle*) patch, blotch. **chiazzato** *agg* spotty; blotchy; mottled.

**chicco** ['kikko] *sm* grain; (*di caffè*) bean; (*d'uva*) grape; (*di grandine*) hailstone; (*del rosario*) bead.

**\*chiedere** ['kjɛdere] *v* ask; (*per avere*) ask for; (*di diritto*) demand; (*vivamente*) beg; (*richiedere*) require; (*prezzo*) charge. **chiedersi** *v* wonder.

**chiesa** ['kjeza] *sf* church.

**chiglia** ['kiʎa] *sf* keel.

**chilo** ['kilo] *sm* kilo.

**chilometro** [ki'lɔmetro] *sm* kilometre.

**chimera** [ki'mɛra] *sf* chimera.

**chimico** ['kimiko] *agg* chemical. *sm* chemist. **chimica** *sf* (*scienza*) chemistry; (*persona*) chemist.

**china¹** ['kina] *sf* slope; decline.

**china²** ['kina] *sf* **inchiostro di china** *sm* Indian ink.

**chinare** [ki'nare] *v* bend; (*occhi*) lower. **chinarsi** *v* stoop.

**chincaglieria** [kinkaʎe'ria] *sf* fancy goods *pl*.

**chiocciare** [kjot'tʃare] *v* cluck; (*covare*) brood. **chioccia** *sf* broody hen.

**chiocciola** ['kjɔttʃola] *sf* snail; (*anat*) cochlea. **scala a chiocciola** *sf* spiral staircase.

**chiodo** ['kjɔdo] *sm* nail; fixed idea; (*fam*) debt. **chiodato** *agg* nailed; (*scarpe*) hobnailed.

**chioma** ['kjɔma] *sf* hair.

**chiosco** ['kjɔsko] *sm* kiosk, stall.

**chiostro** ['kjɔstro] *sm* cloister.

**chiromante** [kiro'mante] *s(m+f)* fortune-teller. **chiromanzia** *sf* fortune-telling.

**chirurgia** [kirur'dʒia] *sf* surgery. **chirurgico** *agg* surgical. **chirurgo** *sm* surgeon.

**chissà** [kis'sa] *avv* who knows, goodness knows; (*forse*) perhaps.

**chitarra** [ki'tarra] *sf* guitar.

**\*chiudere** ['kjudere] *v* close, shut; (*a chiave*) lock (up); (*sbattendo*) slam; (*spegnere*) turn or switch off; (*tappare*) stop up; (*recingere*) enclose. **chiudere bottega** shut up shop. **chiuder dentro** shut in. **chiudere in attivo/perdita** show a profit/loss.

**chiunque** [ki'unkwe] *pron* whoever; (*qualunque persona*) anyone.

**chiusa** ['kjuza] *sf* (*parte finale*) close; (*recinto*) enclosure; (*sbarramento artificiale*) lock; (*diga*) dam.

**chiuso** ['kjuzo] *agg* closed, shut.

**chiusura** [kju'zura] *sf* (*termine*) end; (*serratura*) fastener; (*il chiudere*) closing, shut-down.

**ci** [tʃi], **ce** *pron* (to) us; (*riflessivo*) ourselves; (*reciproco*) each other; (*impersonale*) one; (*di ciò*) about it or that. **ci conto su** I'm counting on it. **ci penso io** I'll think about it. *avv* (*lì*) there; (*qui*) here.

**ciabatta** [tʃa'batta] *sf* slipper.

**cialda** ['tʃalda] *sf* waffle; (*cialdino*) wafer.

**ciambella** [tʃam'bella] *sf* (*pasta*) doughnut; (*cuscino*) rubber ring; (*di salvataggio*) lifebuoy.

**ciambellano** [tʃambel'lano] *sm* chamberlain.

**cianciare** [tʃan'tʃare] v prattle away, talk idly.

**cianfrusaglia** [tʃanfru'zaʎa] sf knick-knack, junk.

**cianuro** [tʃa'nuro] sm cyanide.

**ciao** ['tʃao] inter (incontrandosi) hello! (congedandosi) cheerio! goodbye!

**ciarlare** [tʃar'lare] v chatter, chat. **ciarla** sf (chiacchiera) chat; (pettegolezzo) gossip.

**ciarlatano** [tʃarla'tano] sm charlatan.

**ciascuno** [tʃas'kuno] agg each; (ogni) every. pron each one; (ognuno) everyone.

**cibare** [tʃi'bare] v feed. **cibo** sm food.

**cicala** [tʃi'kala] sf cicada.

**cicalino** [tʃika'lino] sm buzzer.

**cicatrice** [tʃika'tritʃe] sf scar.

**cicca** ['tʃikka] sf (mozzicone) fag end. **non valere una cicca** be not worth a thing.

**cicchetto** [tʃik'ketto] sm (bicchierino) nip; (rimprovero) dressing-down.

**cicerone** [tʃitʃe'rone] sm (tourist) guide.

**ciclamino** [tʃikla'mino] sm cyclamen.

**ciclismo** [tʃi'klizmo] sm cycling. **ciclista** s(m+f) cyclist.

**ciclo** ['tʃiklo] sm cycle. **ciclico** agg cyclical.

**ciclomotore** [tʃiklomo'tore] sm moped.

**ciclone** [tʃi'klone] sm cyclone.

**cicogna** [tʃi'kɔɲa] sf stork.

**cicoria** [tʃi'kɔrja] sf chicory. **cicoria belga** endive.

**cicuta** [tʃi'kuta] sf hemlock.

**cieco** ['tʃɛko] -a agg blind. sm, sf blind person.

**cielo** ['tʃɛlo] sm sky; (sede divina) heaven. **a cielo aperto** in the open. **per amor del cielo!** for heaven's sake!

**cifra** ['tʃifra] sf figure, number; (somma) amount; (codice segreto) cipher.

**ciglio** ['tʃiʎo] sm, pl -a f in anat sense eyelash; (bordo) edge. **non batter ciglio** not bat an eyelid.

**cigno** ['tʃiɲo] sm swan.

**cigolare** [tʃigo'lare] v creak, squeak. **cigolio** sm creaking, squeaking.

**cilecca** [tʃi'lekka] sf **far cilecca** misfire.

**ciliegia** [tʃi'ljedʒa] sf cherry. **ciliegio** sm cherry tree.

**cilindro** [tʃi'lindro] sm cylinder; (rullo) roller; (cappello) top hat.

**cima** ['tʃima] sf top, summit. **da cima a fondo** from top to bottom. **cimare** v

(piante) trim, clip; (tessuti) shear.

**cimelio** [tʃi'mɛljo] sm (oggetto prezioso) treasure; (ricordo) relic, memento.

**cimice** ['tʃimitʃe] sf bedbug.

**ciminiera** [tʃimi'njɛra] sf chimney.

**cimitero** [tʃimi'tɛro] sm cemetery.

**cimurro** [tʃi'murro] sm distemper.

**Cina** ['tʃina] sf China. **cinese** agg, s(m+f) Chinese.

**cincia** ['tʃintʃa] sf tit(mouse). **cinciallegra** sf (great) tit.

**cincin** [tʃin'tʃin] inter cheers!

**cinema** ['tʃinema] sm invar cinema. **cinematografico** agg film. **cinematografo** sm cinema.

**cinetico** [tʃi'nɛtiko] agg kinetic. **cinetica** sf kinetics.

**\*cingere** ['tʃindʒere] v surround, encircle. **cingere d'assedio** besiege.

**cinghia** ['tʃiŋgja] sf belt.

**cinghiale** [tʃin'gjale] sm (wild) boar; (pelle) pigskin.

**cinguettare** [tʃingwet'tare] v twitter. **cinguettio** sm twittering.

**cinico** ['tʃiniko] -a agg cynical. sm, sf cynic. **cinismo** sm cynicism.

**cinquanta** [tʃin'kwanta] sm, agg fifty. **cinquantesimo** sm, agg fiftieth.

**cinque** ['tʃinkwe] sm, agg five.

**cintura** [tʃin'tura] sf belt; (giro della vita) waist. **cintura di sicurezza** safety-belt. **cinturino** sm strap.

**ciò** [tʃɔ] pron this, that. **ciò che** what. **ciò detto** having said this. **ciònondimeno** or **ciònonostante** nevertheless, just the same. **con ciò** therefore. **e con ciò?** so what?

**cioccolata** [tʃokko'lata] sf chocolate; (bevanda) (drinking) chocolate. **cioccolatino** sm (piece of) chocolate. **cioccolato** sm chocolate.

**cioè** [tʃo'ɛ] avv that is; (o piuttosto) or better.

**ciondolo** ['tʃondolo] sm pendant. **ciondolare** v dangle; (bighellonare) hang about.

**ciotola** ['tʃɔtola] sf bowl.

**ciottolo** ['tʃɔttolo] sm pebble.

**cipiglio** [tʃi'piʎo] sm frown.

**cipolla** [tʃi'pɔlla] sf onion.

**cipresso** [tʃi'prɛsso] sm cypress.

**cipria** ['tʃiprja] sf powder.

**Cipro** ['tʃipro] sm Cyprus. **cipriota** agg,

*s(m+f)* Cypriot.

**circa** ['tʃirka] *prep* (*riguardo a*) about, concerning. *avv* (*pressappoco*) about, approximately.

**circo** ['tʃirko] *sm* circus.

**circolare¹** [tʃirko'lare] *sf, agg* circular. **assegno circolare** *sm* banker's draft.

**circolare²** [tʃirko'lare] *v* circulate. **circolatorio** *agg* circulatory. **circolazione** *sf* circulation.

**circolo** ['tʃirkolo] *sm* circle.

**\*circoncidere** [tʃirkon'tʃidere] *v* circumcise. **circoncisione** *sf* circumcision.

**circondare** [tʃirkon'dare] *v* surround.

**circonferenza** [tʃirkonfe'rɛntsa] *sf* circumference.

**circonvallazione** [tʃirkonvalla'tsjone] *sf* ring road.

**\*circoscrivere** [tʃirkos'krivere] *v* circumscribe.

**circostante** [tʃirkos'tante] *agg* surrounding.

**circostanza** [tʃirkos'tantsa] *sf* circumstances *pl*; (*condizione particolare*) occurrence. **di circostanza** fitting.

**circuito** [tʃir'kuito] *sm* circuit; (*sport*) (race-)track.

**cisterna** [tʃis'tɛrna] *sf* cistern; (*serbatoio*) tank. **nave cisterna** *sf* tanker.

**citare** [tʃi'tare] *v* (*riportare parole*) quote; (*nominare*) cite; (*dir: convocare*) summon(s). **citazione** *sf* quotation; summons.

**citofono** [tʃi'tɔfono] *sm* (*fam*) intercom.

**città** [tʃit'ta] *sf* town, city. **cittadina** *sf* small town; (*persona*) citizen. **cittadinanza** *sf* citizenship, nationality; (*popolazione*) people. **cittadino** *sm* citizen.

**ciuco** ['tʃuko] *sm* donkey.

**ciuffo** ['tʃuffo] *sm* tuft.

**ciurma** ['tʃurma] *sf* crew; (*ciurmaglia*) riffraff.

**civetta** [tʃi'vetta] *sf* (*uccello*) owl; (*donna*) flirt. **civettare** *v* flirt.

**civico** ['tʃiviko] *agg* civic.

**civile** [tʃi'vile] *agg* civil; (*non militare*) civilian; (*incivilito*) civilized. **civilizzare** *v* civilize. **civismo** *sm* public spirit.

**civiltà** [tʃivil'ta] *sf* civilization; (*cortesia*) good breeding.

**clacson** ['klakson] *sm invar* horn, hooter.

**clamore** [kla'more] *sm* clamour; (*fig*) outcry, sensation. **clamoroso** *agg* noisy, sensational.

**clandestino** [klandes'tino] *agg* clandestine.

**clarinetto** [klari'netto] *sm* clarinet.

**classe** ['klasse] *sf* class; (*scuola*) form.

**classico** ['klassiko] *agg* classic, classical; typical. *sm* classic.

**classificare** [klassifi'kare] *v* classify. **classificatore** *sm* file. **classificazione** *sf* classification.

**classismo** [klas'sizmo] *sm* class-consciousness. **classista** *agg* class-conscious.

**clausola** ['klauzola] *sf* clause.

**claustrofobia** [klaustrofo'bia] *sf* claustrophobia.

**clavicembalo** [klavi'tʃembalo] *sm* harpsichord.

**clavicola** [kla'vikola] *sf* collar-bone.

**clemenza** [kle'mɛntsa] *sf* clemency; (*tempo*) mildness. **clemente** *agg* mild, clement.

**cleptomane** [klep'tɔmane] *s(m+f), agg* kleptomaniac. **cleptomania** *sf* kleptomania.

**clero** ['klɛro] *sm* clergy. **clericale** *agg* clerical.

**cliché** [kli'ʃe] *sm* (*stampa*) block; (*luogo comune*) cliché.

**cliente** [kli'ɛnte] *s(m+f)* (*di negozio*) customer; (*di professionista*) client; (*di albergo*) guest. **cliente abituale** patron. **clientela** *sf* customers *pl*, clientele; (*di professionista*) practice.

**clima** ['klima] *sm* climate. **climatico** *agg* climatic.

**clinica** ['klinika] *sf* clinic. **clinico** *agg* clinical.

**cloro** ['klɔro] *sm* chlorine.

**clorofilla** [kloro'filla] *sf* chlorophyll.

**cloroformio** [kloro'fɔrmjo] *sm* chloroform.

**cloruro** [klo'ruro] *sm* chloride.

**coabitare** [koabi'tare] *v* cohabit.

**coagulare** [koagu'lare] *v* coagulate; (*latte*) curdle; (*sangue*) clot. **coagulazione** *sf* coagulation; curdling; clotting.

**coalizione** [koali'tsjone] *sf* coalition. **coalizzarsi** *v* unite.

**coatto** [ko'atto] *agg* compulsory.

**cobalto** [ko'balto] *sm* cobalt.

**cobra** ['kɔbra] *sm invar* cobra.

**cocaina** [koka'ina] *sf* cocaine. **cocainomane** *s(m+f)* cocaine addict.

**coccarda** [kok'karda] *sf* rosette.

**cocchio** ['kɔkkjo] *sm* carriage, coach. **cocchiere** *sm* coachman.

**coccinella** [kottʃi'nella] *sf* ladybird.

**coccio** ['kɔttʃo] *sm* (*terracotta*) earthenware; (*rottame*) piece, crock.

**cocciuto** [kot'tʃuto] *agg* stubborn, pig-headed. **cocciutaggine** *sf* stubbornness, pig-headedness.

**cocco¹** ['kɔkko], **-a** *sm, sf* (*fam: amore*) pet, darling.

**cocco²** ['kɔkko] *sm* coconut tree *or* palm. **noce di cocco** *sf* coconut.

**coccodrillo** [kokko'drillo] *sm* crocodile.

**cocente** [ko'tʃɛnte] *agg* burning, scorching.

**cocomero** [ko'kɔmero] *sm* water-melon.

**cocuzzolo** [ko'kuttsolo] *sm* tip.

**coda** ['koda] *sf* tail; (*fila*) queue; (*musica*) coda. **con la coda dell'occhio** out of the corner of one's eye. **fare la coda** queue (up).

**codardo** [ko'dardo] *agg* cowardly.

**codeina** [kode'ina] *sf* codeine.

**codesto** [ko'desto] *agg* that. *pron* that (one).

**codice** ['kɔditʃe] *sm* code. **codice a barre** bar code. **codice della strada** highway code.

**coefficiente** [koeffi'tʃɛnte] *sm* coefficient; (*causa*) contributory factor.

**coerente** [koe'rɛnte] *agg* coherent; (*fig*) consistent.

**coesistere** [koe'zistere] *v* coexist. **coesistenza** *sf* coexistence.

**coetaneo** [koe'taneo], **-a** *s, agg* contemporary.

**cofano** ['kɔfano] *sm* (*auto*) bonnet; (*forziere*) chest.

***cogliere** ['kɔʎere] *v* (*staccare*) pick; (*sorprendere, capire*) catch; (*colpire*) hit. **cogliere la palla al balzo** seize the opportunity.

**coglione** [koʎʎone] (*volg*) *sm* testicle; (*sciocco*) fool. **coglioneria** *sf* foolishness.

**cognato** [ko'ɲato] *sm* brother-in-law. **cognata** *sf* sister-in-law.

**cognizione** [koɲi'tsjone] *sf* knowledge; (*dir*) cognizance.

**cognome** [ko'ɲome] *sm* surname.

**coi** ['koi] *prep+art* con i.

***coincidere** [koin'tʃidere] *v* coincide. **coincidenza** *sf* coincidence; (*treno, ecc.*) connection.

***coinvolgere** [koin'vɔldʒere] *v* involve.

**coito** ['kɔito] *sm* coitus, sexual intercourse.

**col** [kol] *prep+art* con il.

**colare** [ko'lare] *v* (*filtrare*) sieve, strain; (*gocciolare*) drip, trickle; (*fondere*) melt, cast; (*a picco*) sink. **colabrodo** *or* **colapasta** *sm invar* strainer, colander. **colatoio** *sm* strainer. **colino** *sm* sieve.

**colazione** [kola'tsjone] *sf* (*del mattino*) breakfast; (*di mezzogiorno*) lunch. **far colazione** (have) breakfast; (have) lunch.

**colei** [ko'lɛi] *pron* (*soggetto*) she; (*oggetto*) her. **colei che** (she) who.

**colera** [ko'lɛra] *sm invar* cholera.

**colesterolo** [koleste'rɔlo] *sm* cholesterol.

**coll'** [koll] *prep+art* con l'.

**colla** ['kɔlla] *sf* glue, paste.

**collaborare** [kollabo'rare] *v* collaborate; (*giornale*) contribute. **collaboratore, -trice** *sm, sf* collaborator; contributor. **collaborazione** *sf* collaboration; contribution.

**collana** [kol'lana] *sf* necklace; (*raccolta*) collection.

**collants** [kol'lã] *sm pl* tights *pl*.

**collare** [kol'lare] *sm* collar.

**collasso** [kol'lasso] *sm* collapse. **collasso cardiaco** heart failure.

**collaterale** [kollate'rale] *agg* collateral.

**collaudare** [kollau'dare] *v* test. **collaudo** *sm* test.

**colle¹** ['kɔlle] *sm* (*altura*) hill.

**colle²** ['kɔlle] *sm* (*valico*) pass.

**collega** [kol'lɛga] *s(m+f)*, *m pl* **-ghi** colleague.

**collegare** [kolle'gare] *v* connect, link (up). **collegarsi** *v* (*telefono*) get through. **collegamento** *sm* connection; link; (*mil*) liaison.

**collegio** [kol'lɛdʒo] *sm* college; (*convitto*) boarding school; (*consiglio*) board. **collegio di difesa** counsel for the defence. **collegio elettorale** constituency.

**collegiale** [kolle'dʒale] *s(m+f)* boarder. *agg* (*collettivo*) corporate, collective; (*di collegio*) college, boarding-school.

**collera** ['kɔllera] *sf* anger, rage.

**colletta** [kol'lɛtta] *sf* collection.

**collettivo** [kollet'tivo] *agg* collective.

**colletto** [kol'lɛtto] *sm* collar.

**collettore** [kollet'tore] *sm* collector; (*tec*) manifold.

**collezionare** [kolletsjo'nare] *v* collect. **collezione** *sf* collection.

**collina** [kol'lina] *sf* hill.

**collisione** [kolli'zjone] *sf* collision.

**collo¹** ['kɔllo] *sm* neck. **collo del piede** instep.

**collo²** ['kɔllo] *sm* (*pacco*) parcel, package; (*bagaglio*) item of luggage.

**collocare** [kollo'kare] *v* place. **collocare a riposo** retire, pension off. **collocamento** *sm* (*occupazione*) employment, job; (*il collocare*) placing, setting; (*vendita*) sale. **collocamento a riposo** retirement. **ufficio di collocamento** *sm* employment exchange.

**colloide** [kol'lɔide] *sm* colloid. *agg* colloidal.

**colloquio** [kol'lɔkwjo] *sm* conversation, talk; (*intervista*) interview; (*esame*) oral (examination).

**colmare** [kol'mare] *v* fill; (*fino all'orlo*) fill to the brim; (*coprire di*) shower. **colmo** *sm* top, summit; (*culmine*) height; (*situazione paradossale*) last straw, limit.

**colombo** [ko'lombo], **-a** *sm*, *sf* dove, pigeon. **colombaia** *sf* dovecote.

**colonia** [ko'lɔnja] *sf* colony; (*per bambini*) holiday camp; (*per lavoro*) settlement. **coloniale** *agg* colonial.

**colonna** [ko'lonna] *sf* column; (*sostegno*) pillar; (*fila*) line, queue. **colonna vertebrale** spinal column, backbone.

**colonnello** [kolon'nɛllo] *sm* colonel.

**colore** [ko'lore] *sm* colour; (*sostanza colorante*) paint, dye, tint; (*carte da gioco*) suit. **farne di tutti i colori** get up to all sorts of mischief. **colorante** *sm* dye. **colorare** *v* colour.

**colorire** [kolo'rire] *v* colour; (*arrossire*) blush.

**colorito** [kolo'rito] *sm* (*carnagione*) complexion; (*tinta*) colour(ing). *agg* colourful.

**coloro** [ko'loro] *pron* (*soggetto*) they; (*oggetto*) them. **coloro che** (those) who.

**colossale** [kolos'sale] *agg* colossal, tremendous. **colosso** *sm* (*statua*) colossus; (*uomo*) giant.

**colpa** ['kolpa] *sf* fault; (*colpevolezza*) guilt; (*peccato*) sin. **dare la colpa a** blame. **per colpa di** through, because of. **prendersi la colpa** take the blame.

**colpevole** [kol'pevole] *agg* (*persona*) guilty; (*azione*) culpable. *s(m+f)* culprit.

**dichiararsi colpevole** plead guilty.

**colpire** [kol'pire] *v* hit, strike.

**colpo** ['kolpo] *sm* stroke, blow; (*arma da fuoco*) shot; (*impresa*) move, raid. **colpo d'aria** draught. **far colpo** impress, cause a stir, make a hit.

**coltello** [kol'tɛllo] *sm* knife. **coltellata** *sf* stab.

**coltivare** [kolti'vare] *v* cultivate; (*far crescere*) grow. **coltivatore** *sm* grower. **coltivazione** *sf* cultivation; growing.

**colto** ['kolto] *agg* cultivated, cultured.

**coltura** [kol'tura] *sf* cultivation; (*allevamento*) breeding; (*med*) culture.

**colui** [ko'lui] *pron* (*soggetto*) he; (*oggetto*) him. **colui che** (he) who.

**coma** ['kɔma] *sm invar* coma. **comatoso** *agg* comatose.

**comandare** [koman'dare] *v* (*reggere comando*) be in command, command; (*chiedere*) order; (*mec*) control. **comandamento** *sm* commandment. **comandante** *sm* commander. **comando** *sm* command; (*sede*) headquarters; (*mec*) control, drive. **comando a distanza** remote control.

**combaciare** [komba'tʃare] *v* coincide.

**combattere** [kom'battere] *v* fight. **combattente** *sm* serviceman. **combattimento** *sm* fight. **combattivo** *agg* pugnacious. **combattuto** *agg* undecided, torn.

**combinare** [kombi'nare] *v* combine; (*mettere d'accordo*) agree; (*concludere*) arrange, bring off, achieve. **combinazione** *sf* combination; (*caso*) chance.

**combustibile** [kombus'tibile] *sm* fuel. *agg* combustible.

**combustione** [kombus'tjone] *sf* combustion.

**come** ['kome] *avv* as; (*somiglianza*) like; (*in qual modo*) how.

**comedone** [kome'done] *sm* blackhead.

**cometa** [ko'meta] *sf* comet.

**comico** ['kɔmiko], **-a** *sm*, *sf* comic, comedian. *agg* comic(al), funny; (*commedia*) dramatic.

**comignolo** [ko'miɲolo] *sm* chimney-pot.

**cominciare** [komin'tʃare] *v* begin, start. **a cominciare da** from.

**comitato** [komi'tato] *sm* committee.

**comitiva** [komi'tiva] *sf* party.

**comizio** [ko'mitsjo] *sm* meeting.

**commedia** [kom'mɛdja] *sf* play, comedy;

*(finzione)* play-acting, sham; *(scena comica)* farce. **commediante** s(*m+f*) *(fam)* ham; *(ipocrita)* humbug. **commediografo** *sm* playwright.

**commemorare** [kommemo'rare] *v* commemorate. **commemorativo** *agg* memorial.

**commentare** [kommen'tare] *v* comment (on). **commentario** *sm* commentary. **commentatore, -trice** *sm, sf* commentator. **commento** *sm* comment; *(radio)* commentary.

**commercio** [kom'mɛrtʃo] *sm* trade, commerce. **commercio all'ingrosso/al minuto** wholesale/retail trade. **mettere in commercio** put on sale.

**commesso** [kom'messo], **-a** *sm, sf* *(di negozio)* (shop) assistant; *(d'ufficio)* clerk. **commesso viaggiatore** travelling salesman.

**commestibile** [kommes'tibile] *agg* edible. **commestibili** *sm pl* foodstuffs *pl*, provisions *pl*.

**\*commettere** [kom'mettere] *v* *(fare)* commit; *(mettere insieme)* fit together, join; *(ordinare)* commission.

**commissariato** [kommissa'rjato] *sm* *(polizia)* police station. **commissario** *sm* *(polizia)* police inspector; *(sovietico)* commissar; *(amministratore)* commissioner.

**commissione** [kommis'sjone] *sf* commission; *(incombenza)* errand; *(ordinazione)* order; *(comitato)* board. **fare delle commissioni** go shopping.

**commosso** [kom'mɔsso] *agg* moved, touched.

**commozione** [kommo'tsjone] *sf* deep feelings *pl*; *(med)* concussion.

**\*commuovere** [kom'mwɔvere] *v* move, touch. **commovente** *agg* moving, touching.

**commutare** [kommu'tare] *v* commute.

**comò** [ko'mɔ] *sm* chest of drawers.

**comodamente** [komoda'mɛnte] *avv* leisurely.

**comodino** [komo'dino] *sm* bedside table.

**comodo** ['kɔmodo] *sm* convenience. *agg* comfortable; *(opportuno)* convenient; *(utile)* useful, handy. **far comodo** be useful *or* handy; *(garbare)* please, suit. **fare con comodo** take one's time. **comodare** *v* suit. **comodità** *sf* comfort.

**compagnia** [kompa'ɲia] *sf* company.

**compagno** [kom'paɲo], **-a** *sm, sf* companion, mate, friend. **compagno d'armi** fellow-soldier. **compagno di prigionia/viaggio** fellow-prisoner/traveller. **compagno di scuola** classmate.

**\*comparire** [kompa'rire] *v* appear. **comparsa** *sf* appearance; *(film)* extra.

**compartimento** [komparti'mento] *sm* compartment.

**compassione** [kompas'sjone] *sf* pity. **far compassione** arouse pity. **per compassione** out of pity. **compassionevole** *agg* *(che fa compassione)* pitiful; *(che ha compassione)* compassionate.

**compasso** [kom'passo] *sm* compasses *pl*.

**compatire** [kompa'tire] *v* be sorry for. **compatibile** *agg* compatible; *(perdonabile)* excusable.

**compatriota** [kompatri'ɔta] s(*m+f*) compatriot.

**compatto** [kom'patto] *agg* compact, dense; *(fig)* united. **compattezza** *sf* compactness; unity.

**compendio** [kom'pɛndjo] *sm* *(riassunto)* summary; *(trattato)* outline. **compendioso** *agg* brief.

**compensare** [kompen'sare] *v* compensate; *(ricompensare)* reward. **(legno) compensato** *sm* plywood. **compensazione** *sf* compensation; *(econ)* clearing. **compenso** *sm* compensation; reward. **in compenso** in return, in exchange.

**competente** [kompe'tɛnte] *agg* competent, qualified; *(adeguato)* fair. **competenza** *sf* experience, authority; *(dir)* competence.

**competere** [kom'pɛtere] *v* *(spettare)* be due; *(gareggiare)* compete, rival. **competitivo** *agg* competitive.

**\*compiacere** [kompja'tʃere] *v* please. **compiacersi** *v* be pleased, rejoice; congratulate; *(degnarsi)* be good enough. **compiaciuto** *agg* pleased, satisfied.

**\*compiangere** [kom'pjandʒere] *v* pity; *(rimpiangere)* mourn. **compianto** *sm* grief.

**compiere** ['kompjere] *v* *(finire)* complete; *(adempiere)* carry out, fulfil. **compiere ... anni** be ... years old. **compimento** *sm* fulfilment.

**compilare** [kompi'lare] *v* compile, draw up.

**compito** ['kompito] *sm* task; *(dovere)* duty; *(scuola)* homework.

**compleanno** [komple'anno] *sm* birthday.

**complementare** [komplemen'tare] *agg* complementary; (*secondario*) subsidiary. **complemento** *sm* complement; (*gramm*) object.

**complesso** [kom'plesso] *agg* complex; complicated. *sm* (*insieme*) whole; (*industria*) combine, group; (*psic*) complex; (*musica*) ensemble, band. **in complesso** (*tutto sommato*) on the whole; (*in tutto*) in all, altogether. **nel complesso** as a whole.

**completo** [kom'plɛto] *agg* complete; (*pieno*) full (up); (*assoluto*) total. *sm* (*abito*) suit; (*di maglia*) twin set; (*in generale*) outfit. **al completo** (*pieno*) full up; (*esaurito*) sold out; (*tutti presenti*) in full force. **completare** *v* complete, finish.

**complicare** [kompli'kare] *v* complicate; (*aggravare*) worsen. **complicato** *agg* complicated, complex; (*intricato*) involved. **complicazione** *sf* complication.

**complice** ['komplitʃe] *s(m+f)* accomplice; (*dir*) accessory. **complice in adulterio** co-respondent. **essere complice in** be a party to. **complicità** *sf* complicity.

**complimento** [kompli'mento] *sm* compliment. **complimenti** *sm pl* (*cerimonie*) ceremony *sing*; (*ossequi*) regards *pl*; (*auguri*) congratulations *pl*. **far complimenti** stand on ceremony. **complimentare** *v* compliment.

**complotto** [kom'plɔtto] *sm* plot. **complottare** *v* plot.

**componente** [kompo'nɛnte] *agg* component. *s(m+f)* component, member.

**\*comporre** [kom'porre] *v* (*costituire*) make up; (*assestare*) tidy; (*mettere assieme*) assemble, put together; (*musica*) compose; (*atteggiare*) put on. **comporre una lite** settle a quarrel.

**comportare** [kompor'tare] *v* (*richiedere*) involve; (*portare con sè*) imply; (*consentire*) permit. **comportarsi** *v* behave. **comportamento** *sm* behaviour.

**compositore** [kompozi'tore], **-trice** *sm, sf* (*musica*) composer; typesetter.

**composizione** [kompozi'tsjone] *sf* composition.

**composto** [kom'posto] *sm* compound, mixture. *agg* (*decoroso*) dignified; (*assestato*) neat; (*costituito*) made up (of), consisting (of); (*mat*) compound. **compostezza** *sf* self-possession; decorum; neatness.

**comprare** [kom'prare] *v* buy; (*corrompere*) bribe. **comprare all'ingrosso** buy wholesale. **compratore, -trice** *sm, sf* buyer.

**\*comprendere** [kom'prɛndere] *v* include; (*capire*) understand. **comprensibile** *agg* understandable, intelligible. **comprensione** *sf* understanding. **comprensivo** *agg* (*che include*) inclusive, comprehensive; (*tollerante*) understanding. **compreso** *agg* inclusive; (*capito*) understood.

**compressa** [kom'prɛssa] *sf* tablet, pill; (*garza*) compress.

**compressore** [kompres'sore] *sm* compressor.

**\*comprimere** [kom'primere] *v* compress; (*reprimere*) suppress.

**\*compromettere** [kompro'mettere] *v* compromise. **compromesso** *sm* compromise. **compromettente** *agg* compromising.

**comprovare** [kompro'vare] *v* confirm.

**compunto** [kom'punto] *agg* contrite.

**comune** [ko'mune] *agg* common. *sm* commune, municipality; (*autorità*) town council. **avere in comune** share. **fuori del comune** uncommon, unusual.

**comunicare** [komuni'kare] *v* communicate, announce; (*malattia*) pass on; (*rel*) administer Communion. **comunicarsi** *v* spread; receive Communion. **comunicato** *sm* communiqué, bulletin. **comunicato stampa** press release.

**comunione** [komu'njone] *sf* community; (*rel*) (Holy) Communion.

**comunismo** [komu'nizmo] *sm* communism. **comunista** *s(m+f)*, *agg* communist.

**comunità** [komuni'ta] *sf* community.

**comunque** [ko'munkwe] *avv* (*in ogni modo*) anyhow, at any rate. *cong* however, no matter how.

**con** [kon] *prep* with; (*mezzo*) with, by.

**conca** ['konka] *sf* basin; (*valle*) depression.

**concavo** [kon'kavo] *agg* concave.

**\*concedere** [kon'tʃedere] *v* grant, award; (*permettere*) allow.

**concentrare** [kontʃen'trare] *v* concentrate. **concentramento** *sm* concentration. **concentrato** *sm* concentrate.

**concentrico** [kon'tʃɛntriko] *agg* concentric.

**concepire** [kontʃe'pire] *v* conceive; (*capire*) understand; (*nutrire*) entertain, cherish. **concepibile** *agg* conceivable.

**conceria** [kontʃe'ria] *sf* tannery.

**concernere** [kon'tʃɛrnere] v concern, regard. **per quanto mi concerne** as far as I am concerned.

**concerto** [kon'tʃɛrto] sm concert.

**concessione** [kontʃes'sjone] sf concession.

**concetto** [kon'tʃɛtto] sm concept, notion, idea.

**concezione** [kontʃe'tsjone] sf conception; (pensiero) concept.

**conchiglia** [kon'kiʎa] sf shell.

**conciare** [kon'tʃare] v (pelli) tan; (tabacco) cure; (ridurre male) get into a mess; spoil. **conciare per le feste** (fam) give a thrashing.

**conciliare** [kontʃi'ljare] v reconcile.

**concilio** [kon'tʃiljo] sm council.

**concime** [kon'tʃime] sm manure; (artificiale) fertilizer.

**conciso** [kon'tʃizo] agg concise, to the point.

**concittadino** [kontʃitta'dino], **-a** sm, sf fellow-citizen.

**conclave** [kon'klave] sm conclave.

*\*concludere** [kon'kludere] v conclude; (operare con profitto) achieve. **conclusione** sf conclusion, result. **in conclusione** to sum up, in short. **conclusivo** agg final, conclusive; (determinante) decisive.

**concordare** [konkor'dare] v agree, fix. **concordato** sm agreement.

**concorrente** [konkor'rɛnte] agg concurrent; (rivale) competing. s(m+f) competitor; (a un concorso) candidate, applicant. **concorrenza** sf competition. **far concorrenza** compete (with).

*\*concorrere** [kon'korrere] v contribute; (gareggiare) compete (for); (convergere) come together.

**concorso** [kon'korso] sm (affluire) concourse, gathering; contribution; contest, competition; (esame) competitive examination.

**concreto** [kon'krɛto] sm, agg concrete. **concretare** v get done.

**condannare** [kondan'nare] v condemn; (dichiarare colpevole) sentence. **condanna** sf conviction, sentence. **condannato, -a** sm, sf condemned person.

**condensazione** [kondensa'tsjone] sf condensation. **condensare** v condense.

**condire** [kon'dire] v season; (insalata) dress. **condimento** sm seasoning, dressing.

*\*condividere** [kondi'videre] v share.

**condizione** [kondi'tsjone] sf condition. **condizioni** sf pl state sing; (comm) terms pl. **condizioni di vita** standard of living sing. **essere in condizione di** be able to. **mettere in condizione di** enable to. **condizionale** sm, agg conditional.

**condoglianza** [kondoʎ'ʎantsa] sf condolence. **fare le condoglianze** express one's sympathy.

**condonare** [kondo'nare] v remit, condone. **condono** sm remission.

**condotta** [kon'dotta] sm (comportamento) conduct, behaviour; (di un'azione, ecc.) handling; (tubazione) piping.

*\*condurre** [kon'durre] v (portare) lead; (accompagnare) take; (auto) drive; (dirigere) manage, run; (eseguire, fis) conduct; (ridurre) reduce. **condursi** v behave.

**conduttore** [kondut'tore] agg conducting. sm (fis) conductor; (conducente) driver. **conduttura** sf (tubazione) piping; (condotto) pipe.

**confederazione** [konfedera'tsjone] sf federation.

**conferenza** [konfe'rentsa] sf (congresso) conference; (discorso) lecture. **conferenza stampa** press conference. **conferenziere, -a** sm, sf lecturer, speaker.

**conferire** [konfe'rire] v award, confer; (dare) give.

**confermare** [konfer'mare] v confirm. **conferma** sf confirmation.

**confessare** [konfes'sare] v confess. **confessione** sf confession. **confessore** sm confessor.

**confetto** [kon'fɛtto] sm sugared almond.

**confettura** [konfet'tura] sf preserve.

**confezionare** [konfetsjo'nare] v make up. **confezione** sf (involucro) wrapping; (lavorazione) manufacture. **confezioni** sf pl (abiti pronti) ready-made clothes pl.

**confidare** [konfi'dare] v trust, confide. **confidenza** sf confidence. **dar confidenza a** be familiar with. **prendersi la confidenza** take the liberty. **confidenziale** agg confidential.

**confinare** [konfi'nare] v border (on); (relegare) confine; (pol) intern, banish. **confine** sm border.

**confiscare** [konfis'kare] v seize, confiscate. **confisca** sf seizure, confiscation.

**conflitto** [kon'flitto] *sm* conflict.

**\*confondere** [kon'fondere] *v* confuse; (*scambiare*) mistake for; (*mettere in imbarrazzo*) embarrass. **confondersi** *v* become mixed up.

**conformare** [konfor'mare] *v* conform, adapt. **conforme a** *agg* in conformity with, true to. **conformista** *s(m+f)* conformist.

**confortare** [konfor'tare] *v* comfort, console. **confortevole** *agg* comforting; (*comodo*) comfortable. **conforto** *sm* comfort.

**confrontare** [konfron'tare] *v* compare; (*dir*) confront. **confronto** *sm* comparison; (*dir*) confrontation. **a confronto di** compared with. **senza confronto** far and away.

**confusione** [konfu'zjone] *sf* confusion; (*ressa*) bustle; (*chiasso*) din, turmoil. **confusione mentale** mental aberration. **confuso** *agg* confused, muddled; vague; (*turbato*) bewildered.

**congedare** [kondʒe'dare] *v* dismiss; (*mil*) discharge. **congedarsi** *v* say goodbye (to); take leave (of). **congedo** *sm* (*commiato*) leave; discharge.

**congegno** [kon'dʒeɲo] *sm* device, gadget. **congegnare** *v* plan, devise.

**congelare** [kondʒe'lare] *v* freeze. **congelatore** *sm* freezer.

**congenito** [kon'dʒenito] *agg* congenital.

**congestionato** [kondʒestjo'nato] *agg* congested; (*traffico*) blocked; (*viso*) flushed. **congestione** *sf* congestion; (*traffico*) jam.

**\*congiungere** [kon'dʒundʒere] *v* (*unire*) join; (*collegare*) connect, link (up). **congiuntivite** *sf* conjunctivitis. **congiuntivo** *sm* subjunctive. **congiuntura** *sf* (*punto di unione*) joint; (*circostanza*) juncture; economic situation. **congiunzione** *sf* conjunction.

**congiura** [kon'dʒura] *sf* plot, conspiracy. **congiurato, -a** *sm, sf* plotter, conspirator.

**congratularsi** [kongratu'larsi] *v* congratulate.

**congregare** [kongre'gare] *v* congregate, gather. **congrega** *sf* band. **congregazione** *sf* congregation.

**congresso** [kon'gresso] *sm* congress.

**congruo** ['kongruo] *agg* adequate, fair.

**coniare** [ko'njare] *v* coin. **conio** *sm* coining; (*impronta, qualità*) stamp; (*matrice*) minting die.

**conico** ['kɔniko] *agg* conical.

**conifero** [ko'nifero] *agg* coniferous. **conifera** *sf* conifer.

**coniglio** [ko'niʎo] *sm* rabbit.

**coniugare** [konju'gare] *v* conjugate.

**coniuge** ['kɔnjudʒe] *s(m+f)* spouse. **coniugale** *agg* conjugal.

**\*connettere** [kon'nɛttere] *v* connect, link; associate; (*ragionare*) think straight. **connessione** *sf* connection.

**connettersi** [ko'nnɛttersi] *v* log on.

**connotati** [konno'tati] *sm pl* description *sing*, distinguishing features *pl*.

**cono** ['kɔno] *sm* cone.

**\*conoscere** [ko'noʃere] *v* know; (*fare la conoscenza*) meet. **conoscere di fama/vista** know by reputation/sight. **conoscente** *s(m+f)* acquaintance. **conoscenza** *sf* knowledge; (*conoscente*) acquaintance; (*coscienza*) consciousness, senses *pl*. **conoscitore, -trice** *sm, sf* expert, connoisseur. **conosciuto** *agg* (well) known, renowned.

**conquistare** [konkwis'tare] *v* conquer; (*fig*) gain. **conquista** *sf* conquest. **conquistatore, -trice** *sm, sf* conqueror.

**consacrare** [konsa'krare] *v* consecrate, dedicate.

**consanguineo** [konsan'gwineo], **-a** *agg* related (by blood). *sm, sf* blood relation.

**consapevole** [konsa'pevole] *agg* aware, conscious. **consapevolezza** *sf* awareness, consciousness.

**consecutivo** [konseku'tivo] *agg* consecutive; (*seguente*) following.

**consegnare** [konse'ɲare] *v* deliver, hand over; (*mil*) confine to barracks. **consegna** *sf* delivery; (*merce ordinata*) consignment; (*custodia*) care; (*deposito*) (safe) custody; (*mil: ordine*) order; (*mil: punizione*) confinement.

**conseguire** [konse'gwire] *v*. (*ottenere*) obtain, get; (*raggiungere*) achieve; (*risultare*) follow, ensue. **conseguenza** *sf* consequence, result; (*malattia*) after-effect. **di conseguenza** consequently, as a result.

**consenso** [kon'sɛnso] *sm* approval; (*accordo*) agreement; (*permesso*) consent.

**consentire** [konsen'tire] *v* (*essere d'accordo*) agree; (*accondiscendere*) consent; (*permettere*) allow. **consenziente** *agg* consenting.

**conservare** [konser'vare] *v* keep, preserve.

**conserva** *sf* preserve. **mettere in conserva** preserve; (*in scatola*) tin; (*in bottiglia*) bottle. **conservatore, -trice** *s, agg* conservative. **conservazione** *sf* preservation.

**considerare** [konside'rare] *v* consider; (*guardare*) examine; (*stimare*) esteem, think highly of; (*tener conto*) bear in mind. **consideratezza** *sf* caution. **considerato** *agg* careful, wary. **considerazione** *sf* (*prudenza*) caution; (*risguardo*) consideration; (*stima*) esteem, regard. **considerevole** *agg* considerable.

**consigliare** [konsi'ʎare] *v* advise, recommend. **consigliere** *sm* counsellor. **consigliere comunale** town councillor. **consigliere delegato** managing director. **consiglio** *sm* advice; (*organo amministrativo*) board; (*ente pubblico*) council; (*colloquio*) meeting. **consiglio d'amministrazione** board of directors.

*****consistere** [kon'sistere] *v* consist. **consistente** *agg* substantial; (*convincente*) sound. **consistenza** *sf* consistency; (*fondamento*) basis. **consistenza di cassa/magazzino** cash/stock in hand.

**consolare** [konso'lare] *v* console, comfort; (*rallegrare*) cheer (up). **consolazione** *sf* consolation, comfort; (*piacere*) delight.

**console** ['kɔnsole] *sm* consul. **consolare** *agg* consular. **consolato** *sm* consulate.

**consolidare** [konsoli'dare] *v* consolidate; (*rinforzare*) reinforce.

**consonante** [konso'nante] *sf* consonant.

**consono** ['kɔnsono] *agg* **consono a** in keeping with; in accordance with.

**consorte** [kon'sɔrte] *s(m+f), agg* consort.

**consorzio** [kon'sɔrtsjo] *sm* partnership; (*impresa commerciale, banca*) consortium, trust; (*imprese riunite*) syndicate, cooperative.

**constare** [kon'stare] *v* consist. **a quanto mi consta** to my knowledge, as far as I know.

**constatare** [konsta'tare] *v* (*notare*) see; (*accertare*) ascertain, verify; (*riconoscere*) recognize. **constatazione** *sf* verification; recognition.

**consueto** [konsu'ɛto] *agg* (*solito*) usual; (*abituato*) used. **come di consueto** as usual. **di consueto** usually. **consuetudine** *sf* habit, custom.

**consulente** [konsu'lɛnte] *s(m+f), agg* consultant. **consulenza** *sf* advice. **consultare**

*v* consult. **consultazione** *sf* consultation; (*biblioteca*) reference. **consultivo** *agg* consultative, advisory.

**consumare¹** [konsu'mare] *v* consume, use up; (*logorare*) wear out; (*dissipare*) squander; (*mangiare*) eat. **consumazione** *sf* (*bibita*) drink; (*spuntino*) snack. **consumismo** *sm* consumer society. **consumo** *sm* consumption; (*spreco*) waste. **articoli di consumo** *sm pl* consumer goods *pl*.

**consumare²** [konsu'mare] *v* (*portare a compimento*) consummate. **consumazione** *sf* consummation.

**consuntivo** [konsun'tivo] *sm* balance sheet.

**contabile** [kon'tabile] *s(m+f)* bookkeeper; (*ragioniere*) accountant. **valore contabile** *sm* book value. **contabilità** *sf* bookkeeping; accountancy. **tenere la contabilità** keep the books.

**contachilometri** [kontaki'lɔmetri] *sm invar* mileometer; (*tachimetro*) speedometer.

**contadino** [konta'dino], **-a** *agg* (*della campagna*) rustic; (*dei contadini*) peasant. *sm, sf* peasant; (*agricoltore*) farmer.

**contagioso** [konta'dʒozo] *agg* contagious, catching. **contagiare** *v* infect, contaminate.

**contagiri** [konta'dʒiri] *sm invar* rev(olution) counter.

**contaminare** [kontami'nare] *v* contaminate.

**contanti** [kon'tanti] *sm pl* cash *sing*, ready money *sing*.

**contare** [kon'tare] *v* count; (*proporsi*) think. **contato** *agg* limited. **ho i giorni contati** my days are numbered. **ho i minuti contati** I have no time to waste. **contatore** *sm* meter.

**contatto** [kon'tatto] *sm* contact. **essere/ mantenersi/mettersi in contatto** be/keep/get in touch.

**conte** ['konte] *sm* count. **contea** *sf* (*suddivisione amministrativa*) county; (*titolo, dominio di conti*) earldom. **contessa** *sf* countess.

**conteggio** [kon'teddʒo] *sm* count, counting. **conteggiare** *v* (*calcolare*) count; (*far pagare*) charge.

**contegno** [kon'teɲo] *sm* bearing, behaviour. **darsi** *or* **assumere un contegno** strike an attitude. **contegnoso** *agg* dignified, reserved.

**contemplare** [kontem'plare] *v* contemplate; consider, provide for. **contemplazione** *sf* contemplation.

**contempo** [kon'tɛmpo] *sm* **nel contempo** in the meantime, meanwhile.

**contemporaneo** [kontempo'raneo], **-a** *sm*, *sf* contemporary. *agg* contemporary; simultaneous.

***contendere** [kon'tɛndere] *v* dispute; (*litigarsi*) quarrel (over); oppose. **contendente** *s(m+f)* competitor.

***contenere** [konte'nere] *v* contain, hold; (*trattenere*) hold back. **contenersi** *v* (*dominarsi*) restrain oneself; (*comportarsi*) act. **contenitore** *sm* container.

**contentare** [konten'tare] *v* (*appagare*) satisfy; (*far contento*) please. **contentarsi** *v* be satisfied. **contentezza** *sf* satisfaction, contentment; (*gioia*) joy. **contento** *agg* (*soddisfatto*) pleased, satisfied; (*felice*) happy; (*allegro*) cheerful.

**contenuto** [konte'nuto] *sm* (*recipiente*) contents *pl*; (*argomento*) content. *agg* reserved, restrained.

**contestare** [kontes'tare] *v* contest; (*dir*) charge (with); (*impugnare*) challenge. **contestazione** *sf* dispute; notification.

**contiguo** [kon'tiguo] *agg* neighbouring, adjoining.

**continente** [konti'nɛnte] *sm*, *agg* continent. **continentale** *agg* continental. **continenza** *sf* continence.

**contingente** [kontin'dʒɛnte] *sm* quota; (*mil*) contingent. **contingenza** *sf* circumstance; contingency. **indennità di contingenza** *sf* cost of living allowance.

**continuare** [kontinu'are] *v* continue, carry on; (*riprendere*) resume; (*insistere*) keep on. **continuazione** *sf* continuation. **continuità** *sf* continuity. **continuo** *agg* endless; (*costante*) continual; (*ininterrotto*) continuous.

**conto** ['kɔnto] *sm* account; (*somma da pagare*) bill; calculation. **a conti fatti** all things considered. **a (ogni) buon conto** in any case. **far conto che** *or* **di** suppose, imagine; (*proporsi*) intend. **fare conto su** rely on. **per conto di** on behalf of. **per conto mio** as far as I'm concerned; (*da solo*) on my own. **tener conto di** make a note of; consider, take into account.

***contorcere** [kon'tɔrtʃere] *v* twist. **contorcersi** *v* writhe. **contorsione** *sf* contortion. **contorsionista** *s(m+f)* contortionist.

**contorno** [kon'torno] *sm* (*linea*) outline; (*gastr*) vegetables *pl*, side-dish; (*ornamento*) surround, border.

**contrabbandare** [kontrabban'dare] *v* smuggle. **contrabbando** *sm* contraband, smuggling. **merce di contrabbando** *sf* smuggled goods *pl*.

**contrabbasso** [kontrab'basso] *sm* double bass.

**contraccambiare** [kontrakkam'bjare] *v* reciprocate. **in contraccambio di** in return for.

**contraccolpo** [kontrak'kolpo] *sm* counter-blow; (*fig*) repercussion.

***contraddire** [kontrad'dire] *v* contradict. **contraddizione** *sf* contradiction. **spirito di contraddizione** *sm* contrariness.

**contraddittorio** [kontraddit'tɔrjo] *agg* contradictory. *sm* (*dir*) cross-examination.

**contraente** [kontra'ɛnte] *agg* contracting.

**contraereo** [kontra'ereo] *agg* anti-aircraft.

***contraffare** [kontraf'fare] *v* imitate; (*falsificare*) forge, counterfeit. **contraffattore, -trice** *sm*, *sf* counterfeiter, forger; imitator. **contraffazione** *sf* forgery.

**contralto** [kon'tralto] *sm* contralto. *agg* alto.

***contrapporre** [kontrap'porre] *v* oppose, contrast. **contrapposizione** *sf* opposition, contrast.

**contrariare** [kontra'rjare] *v* irritate, oppose.

**contrario** [kon'trarjo] *agg* opposite, contrary; (*avverso*) unfavourable. *sm* contrary, opposite. **al contrario** on the contrary. **al contrario di** unlike. **essere contrario a** be opposed to.

***contrarre** [kon'trarre] *v* contract.

**contrassegnare** [kontrasse'ɲare] *v* mark. **contrassegno** *sm* mark.

**contrastare** [kontras'tare] *v* (*ostacolare*) bar, oppose; (*essere in conflitto*) clash; dispute. **contrasto** *sm* contrast; conflict.

**contrattaccare** [kontrattak'kare] *v* counter-attack. **contrattacco** *sm* counter-attack.

**contrattempo** [kontrat'tɛmpo] *sm* hitch.

**contratto** [kon'tratto] *sm* contract. **contrattare** *v* negotiate; (*mercanteggiare*) haggle.

**contravvenzione** [kontravven'tsjone] *sf* (*violazione*) infringement; (*multa*) fine. **contravventore, -trice** *sm*, *sf* offender.

**contrazione** [kontra'tsjone] *sf* contraction.

**contribuire** [kontribu'ire] *v* contribute. **contribuente** *sm, sf* taxpayer. **contributo** *sm* contribution; (*dir*) tax.

**contristare** [kontris'tare] *v* sadden.

**contrito** [kon'trito] *agg* contrite.

**contro** ['kontro] *prep, avv* against.

**controbattere** [kontro'battere] *v* rebut.

**controbilanciare** [kontrobilan'tʃare] *v* counterbalance.

**controfirmare** [kontrofir'mare] *v* countersign. **controfirma** *sf* countersignature.

**controllare** [kontrol'lare] *v* control; (*esaminare*) check. **controllo** *sm* control; (*verifica*) check; inspection. **controllo delle nascite** birth control. **controllore** *sm* inspector.

**contromano** [kontro'mano] *avv* in the opposite direction.

**contromarcia** [kontro'martʃa] *sf* reverse (gear).

**contropelo** [kontro'pelo] *avv* against the grain.

**controproducente** [kontroprodu'tʃente] *agg* self-defeating, counter-productive.

**contrordine** [kon'trordine] *sm* countermand. **dare un contrordine** countermand.

**controsenso** [kontro'senso] *sm* nonsense, contradiction in terms.

**controversia** [kontro'vɛrsja] *sf* controversy. **controverso** *agg* controversial.

**controvoglia** [kontro'vɔʎa] *avv* unwillingly.

**conturbare** [kontur'bare] *v* perturb.

**contusione** [kontu'zjone] *sf* bruise. **contuso** *agg* bruised.

**convalescenza** [konvale'ʃɛntsa] *sf* convalescence. **convalescente** *s(m+f), agg* convalescent. **convalescenziario** *sm* convalescent home.

**convalidare** [konvali'dare] *v* confirm. **convalida** *or* **convalidazione** *sf* confirmation.

**convegno** [kon'veɲo] *sm* meeting, rendezvous. **darsi convegno** make a date; meet.

*****convenire** [konve'nire] *v* (*venire insieme*) come together, meet; (*essere d'accordo*) agree; (*ammettere*) admit; (*essere vantaggioso*) suit, pay, be worth it. **conveniente** *agg* (*vantaggioso*) favourable, reasonable; (*adatto, adeguato*) suitable. **con-**

**venienza** *sf* (*utilità*) convenience; (*decoro*) propriety; (*l'essere adatto*) suitability.

**convento** [kon'vɛnto] *sm* convent.

**convenzione** [konven'tsjone] *sf* (*patto*) agreement; (*uso*) custom, convention.

*****convergere** [kon'vɛrdʒere] *v* converge. **convergente** *agg* converging.

**conversare** [konver'sare] *v* converse. **conversazione** *sf* conversation, talk.

**conversione** [konver'sjone] *sf* conversion; (*trasformazione*) change, turn(ing).

**convertire** [konver'tire] *v* convert, turn. **convertibile** *agg* convertible. **convertito, -a** *sm, sf* convert.

**convesso** [kon'vɛsso] *agg* convex.

*****convincere** [kon'vintʃere] *v* convince. **convincente** *agg* convincing. **convinto** *agg* (*persuaso*) convinced; (*dimostrato colpevole*) convicted; (*fedele*) staunch. **convinzione** *sf* conviction.

**convitato** [konvi'tato] *sm* guest.

**convito** [kon'vito] *sm* banquet.

**convitto** [kon'vitto] *sm* boarding-school.

**convocare** [konvo'kare] *v* convoke, convene; (*radunare*) call together, rally.

**convoglio** [kon'vɔʎo] *sm* convoy. **convoglio funebre** funeral procession. **convogliare** *v* (*scortare*) convoy; (*condurre, trasportare*) convey.

**convulsione** [konvul'sjone] *sf* convulsion. **convulsivo** *agg* convulsive. **convulso** *agg* convulsed.

**cooperare** [koope'rare] *v* cooperate, collaborate; contribute. **cooperativa** *sf* cooperative. **cooperazione** *sf* cooperation, collaboration.

**coordinare** [koordi'nare] *v* coordinate. **coordinata** *sf* coordinate.

**coperchio** [ko'perkjo] *sm* lid, cover.

**coperta** [ko'pɛrta] *sf* (*drappo*) blanket; (*riparo*) cover. **copertina** *sf* (*quaderno*) cover; (*libro*) dust-jacket.

**coperto**[1] [ko'pɛrto] *agg* covered; (*riparato*) sheltered; (*chiuso*) closed; (*nuvoloso*) overcast; (*nascosto*) concealed. **al coperto** under cover. **mettersi al coperto** shelter.

**coperto**[2] [ko'pɛrto] *sm* (*a tavola*) place (setting); (*prezzo*) cover charge.

**copertone** [koper'tone] *sm* (*pneumatico*) tyre; (*telone*) tarpaulin.

**copia** ['kɔpja] *sf* copy; (*fig*) image. **bella/ brutta copia** fair/rough copy. **copiare** *v* copy. **carta copiativa** sf carbon paper. **matita copiativa** sf indelible pencil. **copiatura** sf copy; (*trascrizione*) copying.

**copioso** [ko'pjozo] agg copious.

**coppa** ['kɔppa] sf cup; (*auto*) sump.

**coppia** ['kɔppja] sf couple. **a coppie** in pairs, in twos.

\***coprire** [ko'prire] v cover; (*nascondere*) hide. **coprire un rumore** drown a noise.

**coraggio** [ko'raddʒo] sm courage, bravery; (*sfacciataggine*) nerve; (*cuore*) heart. **farsi coraggio** pluck up courage. **perdere coraggio** lose heart. **coraggioso** agg courageous, brave; (*ardito*) bold.

**corallo** [ko'rallo] sm coral.

**corazzare** [korat'tsare] v armour. **corazza** sf armour. **corazzata** sf battleship.

**corbelleria** [korbelle'ria] sf (*detto*) nonsense; (*atto*) foolery.

**corda** ['kɔrda] sf cord; (*cordicella, musica*) string; (*fune*) rope; (*geom*) chord. **avere la corda al collo** have one's back to the wall. **essere giù di corda** feel low. **tagliar la corda** (*andarsene di soppiatto*) sneak off; (*fuggire*) cut and run.

**cordiale** [kor'djale] agg cordial, warm. **cordiali saluti** kind regards pl. **cordialità** sf friendliness.

**cordoglio** [kor'dɔʎo] sm grief. **esprimere il proprio cordoglio** offer one's condolences.

**cordone** [kor'done] sm cord; (*schieramento*) cordon.

**coreografo** [kore'ɔgrafo] sm choreographer. **coreografia** sf choreography.

**coriandoli** [ko'rjandoli] sm pl confetti sing.

**coricare** [kori'kare] v lay down; (*mettere a letto*) put to bed. **coricarsi** v lie down; go to bed.

**cornacchia** [kor'nakkja] sf crow.

**cornamusa** [korna'muza] sf bagpipes pl.

**cornetto** [kor'netto] sm (*musica*) cornet; (*telefono*) receiver.

**cornice** [kor'nitʃe] sf frame; (*ambiente*) setting; (*arch*) cornice.

**corno** ['kɔrno] sm, pl **-a** f in zool sense horn; (*ramificato*) antler; (*musica*) French horn. **corno da caccia** bugle. **corno inglese** cor anglais. **dire corna di** run down. **fare le corna** (*non essere fedele*) be unfaithful; (*gesto*) make a V-sign. **non capire un corno** not understand a thing. **non valere un corno** not be worth a brass farthing.

**cornuto** agg horned.

**coro** ['kɔro] sm choir; (*canto*) chorus. **in coro** in chorus, all together.

**corpo** ['kɔrpo] sm body; (*mil, ecc.*) corps. **a corpo morto** headlong, whole-heartedly. **corpo a corpo** hand to hand. **corporatura** sf build. **corporeo** agg bodily.

**corporazione** [korpora'tsjone] sf guild, association. **corporativo** agg corporate.

**corpulento** [korpu'lɛnto] agg stout.

**corpuscolo** [kor'puskolo] sm corpuscle.

**corredo** [kor'rɛdo] sm outfit; (*mil*) equipment. **corredare** v fit out, equip; (*fig*) furnish (with).

\***correggere** [kor'reddʒere] v correct; (*bevanda*) lace.

**corrente** [kor'rɛnte] agg current; (*che scorre*) running; (*andante*) common or garden. **essere/tenere al corrente** be/keep informed or up-to-date. **mettere al corrente** acquaint, inform. sf current, stream; (*tendenza, moda*) trend. **corrente d'aria** draught.

\***correre** ['korrere] v run; (*veicoli*) go; (*circolare*) circulate. **correre dietro a** run after.

**corretto** [kor'retto] agg correct, right, exact. **correttezza** sf fairness; (*educazione*) propriety.

**correzione** [korre'tsjone] sf correction. **correzione di bozze** proof-reading.

**corridoio** [korri'dojo] sm passage, corridor.

**corridore** [korri'dore] sm runner; (*automobilista*) racing-driver; (*ciclista*) racing-cyclist. **cavallo corridore** sm racehorse.

**corriera** [kor'rjɛra] sf coach.

**corriere** [kor'rjɛre] sm messenger, courier; (*merci*) carrier; (*posta*) mail.

**corrimano** [korri'mano] sm handrail.

\***corrispondere** [korris'pondere] v correspond; (*accordarsi*) agree; (*pagare*) pay; (*ricambiare*) reciprocate. **corrispondente** s(m+f) correspondent. **corrispondenza** sf correspondence; (*posta*) mail; (*conformità*) relation; (*somiglianza*) likeness.

**corroborare** [korrobo'rare] v corroborate; (*rinforzare*) strengthen.

\***corrodere** [kor'rodere] v corrode. **corrosione** sf corrosion.

\***corrompere** [kor'rompere] v corrupt; (*con denaro*) bribe; (*guastare*) spoil. **corrotto** agg corrupt.

**corrucciarsi** [korrut'tʃarsi] v be angered and upset (by).

**corrugare** [korru'gare] v crease, wrinkle. **corrugare la fronte** knit one's brow.

**corruzione** [korru'tsjone] sf corruption; (con denaro) bribery.

**corsa** ['korsa] sf (gara) race; (azione) racing; (atletica) running; (percorso) run. **andare di corsa** (be in a) hurry. **di gran corsa** in a great hurry, in great haste. **fare una corsa (da)** (fam) pop over or round (to).

**corsia** [kor'sia] sf (teatro, ecc.) gangway; (ospedale) ward; (autostrada) lane; (tappeto) runner.

**corsivo** [kor'sivo] agg italic. sm italics pl.

**corso**[1] ['korso] sm course; (econ) circulation; (quotazione) rate; (strada principale) high street. **in corso** in progress; (in sospeso) pending; (corrente) present.

**corso**[2] ['korso], -a s, agg Corsican.

**corte** ['korte] sf court; (cortile) courtyard. **corte marziale** court-martial. **fare la corte (a)** (ragazza) court; (lusingare) play up (to). **corteggiare** v court. **corteggio** sm retinue.

**corteccia** [kor'tettʃa] sf (albero) bark; (frutto) rind; (anat) cortex.

**corteo** [kor'tɛo] sm procession.

**cortese** [kor'teze] agg polite, courteous; (gentile) kind. **cortesia** sf politeness, courtesy; kindness. **avere la cortesia di** be so kind as to. **per cortesia** (per favore) please, kindly; (per ragioni di cortesia) out of politeness.

**cortile** [kor'tile] sm courtyard; (casa colonica) farmyard. **animali da cortile** sm pl farmyard animals pl.

**cortina** [kor'tina] sf curtain. **cortina di ferro** iron curtain. **cortina di fumo** smoke-screen.

**corto** ['korto] agg short. **a farla corta** to come to the point. **essere a corto di** be short of.

**corvo** ['kɔrvo] sm (imperiale) raven; (comune) rook.

**cosa** ['kɔza] pron what. **a cosa serve?** what is it for? sf thing; (qualcosa) something; (faccenda) matter. **a cose fatte** after the event. **cosa da nulla** nothing. **cosa da poco** trifle. **gran cosa** much. **qualsiasi** or **qualunque cosa** anything. **tante cose** (augurio) best wishes pl.

**coscia** ['kɔʃa] sf thigh; (gastr) leg.

**cosciente** [koʃˈʃɛnte] agg aware. **coscienza** sf conscience; (conoscenza) consciousness; (impegno) conscientiousness. **avere la coscienza pulita/sporca** have a clear/guilty conscience. **in coscienza** morally, honestly. **coscienzioso** agg conscientious.

**coscrizione** [koskri'tsjone] sf draft, conscription. **coscritto** sm conscript, recruit.

**così** [ko'zi] avv (in questo modo) like this or that; (tanto) so; (con agg qualificante un sostantivo) such. cong so. **così ... come ...** as ... as ... **così così** so-so. **cosiddetto** agg so-called.

**cosmetico** [koz'metiko] sm, agg cosmetic. **cosmesi** or **cosmetica** sf beauty culture.

**cosmo** ['kɔzmo] sm cosmos. **cosmonauta** s(m+f) astronaut. **cosmonautica** sf astronautics.

**cosmopolita** [kozmo'pɔlita] s(m+f), agg cosmopolitan.

**coso** ['kozo] sm (fam) thingummy.

***cospargere** [kos'pardʒere] v strew.

**cospicuo** [kos'pikuo] agg conspicuous; (grande) considerable.

**cospirare** [kospi'rare] v plot.

**costa** ['kɔsta] sf coast, coastline; (litorale) shore; (coltello, libro) back; (costola) rib.

**costà** [kos'ta] avv (over) there.

**costante** [kos'tante] agg constant, firm; (saldo) steady. sf constant. **costanza** sf steadfastness, firmness.

**costare** [kos'tare] v cost. **costar caro** be expensive. **mi è costato caro** I have paid dearly for it.

**costeggiare** [kosted'dʒare] v skirt; (costa) follow the coast.

**costei** [kos'tɛi] pron this woman.

**costellare** [kostel'lare] v stud.

**costellazione** [kostella'tsjone] sf constellation.

**costernare** [koster'nare] v dismay.

**costiero** [kos'tjera] agg coastal.

**costipato** [kosti'pato] agg (stitico) constipated; (fam: raffreddato) having a bad cold.

**costituire** [kostitu'ire] v (formare) set up, form; (dar luogo) constitute; (dichiarare) appoint. **costituirsi** v (presentarsi spontaneamente) give oneself up. **costituirsi parte civile** take legal proceedings. **costituzione** sf constitution.

**costo** ['kɔsto] sm cost, price. **costoso** agg

costly, dear.

**costola** [kos'tɔla] *sf* rib.

**costoro** [kos'toro] *pron* these people.

*** costringere** [kos'trindʒere] *v* force, compel.

*** costruire** [kostru'ire] *v* build, construct. **costruzione** *sf* construction; (*edificio*) building.

**costui** [kos'tui] *pron* this man.

**costume** [kos'tume] *sm* (*usanza*) custom, use; (*condotta*) behaviour; (*indumento*) costume; (*abitudine personale*) habit. **il buon costume** morality.

**costura** [kos'tura] *sf* seam.

**cotogna** [ko'toɲa] *sf* quince.

**cotoletta** [koto'letta] *sf* cutlet.

**cotone** [ko'tone] *sm* cotton. **cotone idrofilo** cotton-wool. **cotoniero** *agg* cotton. **cotonificio** *sm* cotton mill.

**cotta** ['kɔtta] *sf* **prendere una cotta** (*fam*) fall in love.

**cottimo** ['kɔttimo] *sm* piece-work.

**cotto** ['kɔtto] *agg* cooked; (*carne*) done; (*in forno*) baked. **farne di cotte e di crude** be up to all sorts of tricks. **nè cotto nè crudo** neither one thing nor the other.

**cottura** [kot'tura] *sf* cooking; (*in forno*) baking.

**covare** [ko'vare] *v* hatch; (*fig*) brood over; (*sotto la cenere*) smoulder. **covata** *sf* brood.

**covo** ['kɔvo] *sm* lair, den.

**cozza** ['kɔttsa] *sf* mussel.

**cozzare** [kot'tsare] *v* collide *or* clash (with); (*con le corna*) butt. **cozzo** *sm* collision, clash; butt.

**crampo** ['krampo] *sm* cramp.

**cranio** ['kranjo] *sm* skull.

**cratere** [kra'tɛre] *sm* crater.

**cravatta** [kra'vatta] *sf* tie.

**creanza** [kre'antsa] *sf* (good) manners *pl*, breeding.

**creare** [kre'are] *v* create, give rise to; (*eleggere*) appoint. **creatore** *sm* maker, creator. **creatura** *sf* creature. **creazione** *sf* creation.

**credenza**¹ [kre'dɛntsa] *sf* belief (*pl* -s), opinion; (*fede*) faith; (*comm*) credit.

**credenza**² [kre'dɛntsa] *sf* (*mobile*) sideboard.

**credere** ['krɛdere] *v* believe; (*pensare*) think; (*aver fiducia*) trust. **credibile** *agg* credible, believable. **credibilità** *sf* credibility.

**credito** ['kredito] *sm* credit; (*stima*) esteem. **creditore** *sm* creditor.

**credulo** ['krɛdulo] *agg* credulous. **credulone, -a** *sm, sf* gullible person.

**crema** ['krɛma] *sf* cream. **cremoso** *agg* creamy.

**cremare** [kre'mare] *v* cremate. **crematorio** *sm* crematorium. **cremazione** *sf* cremation.

**cremisi** ['krɛmizi] *agg, sm* crimson.

**cren** [krɛn] *sm* horseradish.

**crepare** [kre'pare] *v* burst, crack; (*fam: morire*) die, kick the bucket. **crepacuore** *sm* heartbreak.

**crepitare** [krepi'tare] *v* crackle. **crepitio** *sm* crackle, crackling.

**crepuscolo** [kre'puskolo] *sm* twilight, dusk; decline.

*** crescere** ['kreʃere] *v* grow; (*maturarsi*) grow up; (*aumentare*) rise; (*sovrabbondare*) be left over. **crescita** *sf* growth.

**crescione** [kre'ʃone] *sm* (*d'acqua*) watercress; (*inglese*) mustard and cress.

**cresima** ['krɛzima] *sf* confirmation. **cresimare** *v* confirm.

**crespa** ['krespa] *sf* (*ruga*) wrinkle; (*stoffa*) crease; (*piccola ondulazione*) ripple.

**crespo** ['krespo] *agg* frizzy. *sm* crepe.

**cresta** ['kresta] *sf* crest.

**creta** ['krɛta] *sf* clay.

**cretino** [kre'tino], **-a** *sm, sf* idiot, fool. *agg* idiotic, foolish. **cretineria** *sf* stupidity; (*discorso, azione*) foolish thing.

**cricca** ['krikka] *sf* clique, gang.

**cricco** ['krikko] *sm* jack.

**criceto** [kri'tʃeto] *sm* hamster.

**criminale** [krimi'nale] *agg, s(m+f)* criminal. **crimine** *sm* crime. **criminoso** *agg* criminal.

**criniera** [kri'njɛra] *sf* mane.

**cripta** ['kripta] *sf* crypt.

**crisalide** [kri'zalide] *sf* chrysalis.

**crisantemo** [krizan'tɛmo] *sm* chrysanthemum.

**crisi** ['krizi] *sf* crisis (*pl* -ses); (*med*) fit, attack.

**cristallizzare** [kristallid'dzare] *v* crystallize.

**cristallo** [kris'tallo] *sm* crystal; (*vetro*) plate-glass, (window) pane. **cristallino** *agg* crystalline; pure, limpid.

**cristiano** [kris'tjano], **-a** *agg* Christian. *sm, sf* Christian; (*essere umano*) soul.

**Cristo** ['kristo] *sm* Christ. **non c'è cristo**

(*possibilità*) there isn't a chance. **povero cristo** poor devil.

**criterio** [kri'tɛrjo] *sm* criterion (*pl* -a), norm; sense.

**critico** ['kritiko] *agg* critical. *sm* critic. **critica** *sf* criticism; (*scritto*) review; (*persona*) critic. **criticare** *v* criticize; review; (*biasimare*) blame.

**crivellare** [krivel'lare] *v* riddle. **crivello** *sm* sieve.

**Croazia** [krɔ'attʃja] *sf* Croatia. **croato** *agg* Croatian.

**croccante** [krok'kante] *agg* crisp. *sm* (*dolce*) praline.

**crocchia** ['krɔkkja] *sf* bun, chignon.

**crocchio** ['krɔkkjo] *sm* cluster.

**croce** ['krotʃe] *sf* cross. **a occhio e croce** roughly. **croce uncinata** swastika. **crocevia** *sm invar* crossroads. **fare a testa e croce** toss a coin. **punto a croce** *sm* cross-stitch.

**crociare** [kro'tʃare] *v* cross.

**crociata** [kro'tʃata] *sf* crusade. **crociato** *sm* crusader.

**crocicchio** [kro'tʃikkjo] *sm* crossroads.

**crociera** [kro'tʃɛra] *sf* cruise.

**\*crocifiggere** [krotʃifid'dʒere] *v* crucify.

**crocifisso** [krotʃi'fisso] *sm* crucifix. *agg* crucified.

**croco** ['krɔko] *sm* crocus.

**crogiolarsi** [krodʒo'larsi] *v* bask. **crogiolo** *sm* crucible; (*fig*) melting-pot.

**crollare** [krol'lare] *v* (*cadere*) collapse, slump; (*spalle*) shrug. **crollo** *sm* collapse, slump.

**croma** ['krɔma] *sf* quaver.

**cromo** ['krɔmo] *sm* (*metallo*) chromium. **giallo cromo** chrome yellow. **cromatura** *sf* chromium-plating.

**cromosoma** [kromo'sɔma] *sm* chromosome.

**cronaca** ['krɔnaka] *sf* (*narrazione*) chronicle; (*radio, TV, stampa*) news, review.

**cronico** ['krɔniko] *agg* chronic. *sm* chronic invalid.

**cronista** [kro'nista] *s(m+f)* reporter.

**cronologico** [krono'lɔdʒiko] *agg* chronological.

**cronometro** [kro'nɔmetro] *sm* chronometer, stop-watch. **cronometrare** *v* time.

**crosta** ['krɔsta] *sf* crust; (*ferita*) scab. **crosta-ta** *sf* tart.

**crostacei** [kros'tatʃei] *sm pl* crustaceans *pl*, shellfish *pl*.

**crucciare** [krut'tʃare] *v* distress, worry.

**cruciale** [kru'tʃale] *agg* crucial.

**cruciverba** [krutʃi'vɛrba] *sm invar* crossword.

**crudele** [kru'dɛle] *agg* cruel; (*duro, aspro*) harsh; (*doloroso*) bitter. **crudeltà** *sf* cruelty; (*asprezza*) harshness.

**crudo** ['krudo] *agg* raw; (*rigido*) harsh; (*brusco*) crude; (*volgare*) coarse.

**crumiro** [kru'miro], **-a** *sm, sf* blackleg.

**cruna** ['kruna] *sf* eye (of a needle).

**crusca** ['kruska] *sf* bran.

**cruscotto** [krus'kɔtto] *sm* instrument panel; (*auto*) dashboard.

**cubo** ['kubo] *sm* cube. **cubico** *agg* cubic. **cubismo** *sm* cubism.

**cuccagna** [kuk'kaɲa] *sf* (*abbondanza*) plenty; (*allegria*) fun.

**cuccetta** [kut'tʃetta] *sf* couchette.

**cucchiaio** [kuk'kjajo] *sm* spoon; (*contenuto*) spoonful; (*da tavola*) tablespoon. **cucchiaino** *sm* teaspoon.

**cucciolo** ['kuttʃolo] *sm* puppy.

**cucina** [ku'tʃina] *sf* (*luogo*) kitchen; (*atto del cucinare*) cooking; (*cibo*) food; (*apparecchio*) cooker. **cucina casalinga** home cooking. **cucinare** *v* cook.

**cucire** [ku'tʃire] *v* sew, stitch; (*con cucitrice*) staple. **cucirino** *sm* sewing thread. **cucito** *sm* sewing, needlework. **cucitrice** *sf* (*persona*) seamstress; (*apparecchio*) stapler. **cucitura** *sf* seam.

**cuculo** ['kukulo] *sm* cuckoo.

**cuffia** ['kuffja] *sf* cap; bonnet; (*telefono, radio*) earphones *pl*, headphones *pl*.

**cugino** [ku'dʒino], **-a** *sm, sf* cousin.

**cui** ['kui] *pron* (*persone*) whom; (*cose*) which. **il cui, la cui, ecc.** whose. **in cui** (*quando*) when; (*dove*) where.

**culla** ['kulla] *sf* cradle. **cullare** *v* rock, lull. **cullarsi** *v* (*illudersi*) delude oneself.

**culmine** ['kulmine] *sm* summit, height. **culminare** *v* culminate.

**culo** ['kulo] *sm* (*fam*) bottom; (*volg*) arse.

**culto** ['kulto] *sm* worship; (*religione*) cult.

**cultura** [kul'tura] *sf* culture, learning; cultivation. **culturale** *agg* cultural.

**cumulo** ['kumulo] *sm* pile, heap.

**cuneo** ['kuneo] *sm* wedge.

**cunetta** [ku'netta] *sf* gutter.

**\*cuocere** ['kwɔtʃere] *v* (*cucinare*) cook; (*al forno*) bake; (*a lesso*) boil; (*alla griglia*) grill; (*arrosto*) roast; (*in umido*) stew; (*ceramica, ecc.*) fire. **cuocere a fuoco lento** simmer. **cuoco, -a** *sm, sf* cook.

**cuoio** ['kwɔjo] *sm* leather; (*pelle*) hide. **cuoio capelluto** scalp. **cuoio scamosciato** chamois leather, suede.

**cuore** ['kwɔre] *sm* heart. **di cuore** heartily. **di tutto cuore** with all one's heart. **mettersi il cuore in pace** set one's mind at rest. **nel cuore di** at the height of; (*notte*) at dead of. **senza cuore** heartless.

**cupido** ['kupido] *agg* greedy. **cupidigia** *sf* greed.

**cupo** ['kupo] *agg* (*profondo, suono*) deep; (*privo di luce, colore*) dark.

**cupola** ['kupola] *sf* dome.

**cura** ['kura] *sf* care; (*med*) cure, treatment. **curare** *v* look after, take care of; cure, treat. **curarsi** *v* mind *or* care about. **curativo** *agg* curative.

**curatore** [kura'tore], **-trice** *sm, sf* guardian. **curatela** *sf* guardianship.

**curioso** [ku'rjozo] *agg* curious; (*strano*) odd. **curiosità** *sf* curiosity. **curiosare** *v* pry.

**cursore** [kur'sore] *sm* cursor.

**curvare** [kur'vare] *v* bend. **curvare il capo** bow one's head. **curva** *sf* bend, curve. **curvatura** *sf* curvature, sweep. **curvo** *agg* curved, bent.

**cuscino** [ku'ʃino] *sm* cushion; (*guanciale*) pillow. **cuscinetto** *sm* (*a sfere*) ball-bearing; (*a rulli*) roller-bearing. **stato cuscinetto** *sm* buffer state.

**custode** [kus'tɔde] *s(m+f)* keeper, caretaker. **custodia** *sf* custody, care, safe keeping; (*astuccio*) case. **custodire** *v* keep; look after; (*sorvegliare*) guard.

**cutaneo** [ku'taneo] *agg* cutaneous, skin.

**cyber-spazio** [saibers'patʃjo] *sm* cyber-space.

# D

**da** [da] *prep* from; (*moto a luogo*) to; (*stato in luogo*) at; (*durata*) for; (*fin da*) since; (*causa*) of, from; (*segno distintivo*) with; (*come*) as, like. **da allora** since then. **da allora in poi** ever since. **da lontano** from afar. **da molto** for a long time. **da noi** at home; (*al mio paese*) in my country.

**dabbasso** [dab'basso] *avv* downstairs.

**dabbene** [dab'bene] *agg* decent, honest.

**daccapo** [dak'kapo] *avv* (*di nuovo*) again, once more; (*da principio*) from the beginning, all over again.

**dacché** [dak'ke] *cong* since.

**dado** ['dado] *sm* dice *pl*; (*gastr*) cube; (*mec*) nut.

**daffare** [daf'fare] *sm invar* work, business.

**dagli¹** ['daʎi] *prep+art* da gli.

**dagli²** ['daʎi] *inter* (*forza*) go on! come on! (*noioso*) not again! pack it in!

**dai** ['dai] *prep+art* da i.

**daino** ['daino] *sm* (*fallow*) deer. **daina** *sf* doe. **pelle di daino** *sf* buckskin.

**dal** [dal] *prep+art* da il.

**dalia** ['dalja] *sf* dahlia.

**dall'** [dall] *prep+art* da l'.

**dalla** ['dalla] *prep+art* da la.

**dalle** ['dalle] *prep+art* da le.

**dallo** ['dallo] *prep+art* da lo.

**daltonismo** [dalto'nizmo] *sm* colour blindness. **daltonico** *agg* colour-blind.

**dama** ['dama] *sf* lady, noblewoman; (*gioco*) draughts; (*carta*) queen.

**damasco** [da'masko] *sm* damask.

**dancing** ['daːnsin] *sm invar* dance-hall.

**Danimarca** [dani'marka] *sf* Denmark. **danese** *sm, agg* Danish; *s(m+f)* Dane.

**dannare** [dan'nare] *v* damn. **dannato, -a** *s, agg* damned. **dannazione** *sf* damnation; (*tormento*) trial.

**danneggiare** [danned'dʒare] *v* (*guastare*) damage; (*nuocere*) injure, harm. **danno** *sm* damage; injury, harm; (*pregiudizio*) detriment. **danno doloso** wilful damage. **dannoso** *agg* harmful.

**danzare** [dan'tsare] *v* dance. **danza** *sf* dancing; (*ballo*) dance. **danzatore, -trice** *sm, sf* dancer.

**dappertutto** [dapper'tutto] *avv* everywhere, all over the place.

**dappoco** [dap'pɔko] *agg invar* worthless; (*inetto*) good-for-nothing.

**dappresso** [dap'presso] *avv* close to, close up.

**dapprima** [dap'prima] *avv* at first.

**dardeggiare** [darded'dʒare] *v* dart. **dardo** *sm* dart.

**\*dare** ['dare] *v* give; (*avere come risultato*) make, come to; (*esame*) take; apply; (*colpire*) hit; (*fruttare*) yield. **dare ai** *or* **sui nervi a qualcuno** get on someone's nerves. **dare alla luce** give birth to. **dar da fare a** keep busy. **dar fine a** put an end to. **dare nell'occhio** catch the eye. **dare per scontato** take for granted. **dar retta a** listen to. **dare su** look out on to; (*affacciare*) face. **darsi a** (*dedicarsi*) devote oneself to; (*applicarsi*) go in for.

**darsena** ['darsena] *sf* dock.

**data** ['data] *sf* date. **di fresca data** recent. **di vecchia data** of long standing. **in che data?** when? **datare** *v* date; (*risalire*) go back (to).

**dato** ['dato] *agg* given; (*in vista*) considering, in view of. **dato che** supposing that, as, since. *sm* data. **dato di fatto** fact. **datore di lavoro** *sm* employer.

**dattero** ['dattero] *sm* (*frutto*) date; (*albero*) date-palm.

**dattilografo** [datti'lɔgrafo], **-a** *sm*, *sf* typist. **dattilografare** *v* type.

**davanti** [da'vanti] *avv* in front. *sm*, *agg* front. **davanti a** in front of; (*dirimpetto*) facing; (*in presenza di*) before.

**davanzale** [davan'tsale] *sm* window-sill.

**davvero** [dav'vero] *avv* really. **dici davvero?** do you (really) mean it?

**dazio** ['datsjo] *sm* (*imposta*) duty; (*ufficio*) customs (office).

**dea** ['dεa] *sf* goddess.

**debito¹** ['debito] *agg* due.

**debito²** ['debito] *sm* debt; (*comm*) debit; (*dovere*) duty. **estinguere/fare un debito** settle/incur a debt. **sentirsi in debito** be indebted. **debitore** *sm* debtor.

**debole** ['debole] *agg* weak, feeble; (*luce, suono, speranza*) faint. *sm* (*persona*) weakling; (*punto*) weak point; (*inclinazione*) weakness, foible. **debolezza** *sf* weakness; (*difetto*) failing.

**debuttare** [debut'tare] *v* make one's debut. **debutto** *sm* debut.

**decade** ['dεkade] *sf* ten days *pl*.

**\*decadere** [deka'dere] *v* decline. **decadere da** (*dir*) forfeit. **decadente** *agg* decadent. **decadenza** *sf* decline; (*dir*) forfeiture, lapse.

**decaduto** *agg* impoverished; (*scaduto*) fallen into disuse.

**decaffeinato** [dekaffei'nato] *agg* decaffeinated.

**decalcomania** [dekalkoma'nia] *sf* transfer.

**decano** [de'kano] *sm* dean; (*diplomatico*) doyen.

**decantare¹** [dekan'tare] *v* (*lodare*) sing the praises of.

**decantare²** [dekan'tare] *v* (*liquido*) decant.

**decapitare** [dekapi'tare] *v* behead.

**deceduto** [detʃe'duto] *agg* deceased.

**decennio** [de'tʃεnnjo] *sm* decade.

**decente** [de'tʃεnte] *agg* decent. **decenza** *sf* decency, propriety.

**decentrare** [detʃen'trare] *v* decentralize. **decentramento** *sm* decentralization.

**decesso** [de'tʃesso] *sm* death.

**decibel** [detʃi'bεl] *sm invar* decibel.

**\*decidere** [de'tʃidere] *v* decide (on); (*risolvere, determinare*) settle. **decidersi** make up one's mind; (*indursi*) bring oneself to.

**deciduo** [de'tʃiduo] *agg* deciduous.

**decifrare** [detʃi'frare] *v* decipher; (*fam*) make out.

**decimale** [detʃi'male] *agg*, *sm* decimal.

**decimo** ['dεtʃimo] *sm*, *agg* tenth.

**decina** [de'tʃina] *sf* ten; (*circa dieci*) ten or so. **a decine** (*fig*) by the dozen.

**decisione** [detʃi'zjone] *sf* decision, resolution; (*dir*) ruling. **decisivo** *agg* decisive; (*prova*) conclusive; (*voto*) casting.

**deciso** [de'tʃizo] *agg* (*fermo*) decided, firm, resolute; (*definito, risolto*) settled, resolved; (*spiccato*) decided, marked. **decisamente** *avv* decidedly; definitely.

**declamare** [dekla'mare] *v* declaim; (*protestare*) rail.

**declinare** [dekli'nare] *v* decline. **declinazione** *sf* (*fis*) declination; (*gramm*) declension. **declino** *sm* decline.

**declivio** [de'klivjo] *sm* slope.

**decollare** [dekol'lare] *v* take off. **decollo** *sm* take-off.

**\*decomporsi** [dekom'porsi] *v* disintegrate, decompose. **decomposizione** *sf* disintegration, decomposition.

**decorare** [deko'rare] *v* decorate. **decorazione** *sf* decoration.

**decoro** [de'kɔro] *sm* dignity; (*orgoglio*) pride. **decoroso** *agg* proper.

**decorrere** [dekor'rere] v elapse. **con decorrenza da ...** with effect from. **decorso** sm (*svolgimento*) course; (*periodo*) lapse.

**decrepito** [de'krɛpito] agg decrepit.

**decrescente** [dekre'ʃɛnte] agg decreasing, diminishing; (*luna*) on the wane.

**decreto** [de'kreto] sm decree, order. **decreto di citazione** writ; (*testimone*) subpoena. **decretare** v decree, order; (*concedere*) award.

**dedalo** ['dɛdalo] sm maze.

**dedicare** [dedi'kare] v dedicate, devote; consecrate; (*intitolare*) name after. **dedicarsi a** (*occuparsi di*) take up, go in for. **dedica** sf dedication.

**dedito** ['dɛdito] agg devoted; (*assorbito*) engrossed (in); (*vizio*) addicted.

*****dedurre** [de'durre] v deduce; (*desumere*) infer; (*prendere, derivare*) take, draw; (*sottrarre*) deduct. **deduzione** sf deduction.

**defalcare** [defal'kare] v deduct.

**deferire** [defe'rire] v defer, refer. **deferire al tribunale** sue. **deferente** agg deferential.

**deficiente** [defi'tʃɛnte] agg deficient; insufficient; (*inferiore alla media*) backward; (*fam*) moronic. s(m+f) moron, half-wit. **deficienza** sf deficiency, lack; (*scarsità*) shortage; (*idiozia*) mental deficiency.

**deficit** ['dɛfitʃit] sm invar deficit. **bilancio deficitario** sm debit balance.

**definire** [defi'nire] v define; (*risolvere*) settle. **definitivo** agg definitive. **in definitiva** (*dopo tutto*) after all; to sum up; (*in fin dei conti*) all things considered. **definizione** sf definition; settlement.

**deflazione** [defla'tsjone] sf deflation. **deflazionare** v deflate. **deflazionistico** agg deflationary.

*****deflettere** [de'flettere] v deviate. **deflessione** sf deflection; deviation.

**deformare** [defor'mare] v deform, distort; (*mec*) warp; (*senso*) twist. **deformazione** sf deformation, distortion; warping. **deforme** agg deformed, misshapen; (*viso*) disfigured.

**defunto** [de'funto], **-a** s, agg deceased.

**degenerare** [dedʒene'rare] v degenerate. **degenerato, -a** s, agg degenerate.

**degente** [de'dʒɛnte] agg bedridden. **degenza** sf (*a letto*) stay in bed; (*in ospedale*) stay in hospital.

**degli** ['deʎi] prep+art **di gli**.

**degnare** [de'ɲare] v deign; deem or consider worthy. **degnarsi di** condescend to. **degno** agg worthy, deserving. **degno di fiducia** trustworthy. **degno di lode** praiseworthy. **degno di nota** noteworthy.

**degradare** [degra'dare] v degrade. **degradazione** sf degradation.

**degustare** [degus'tare] v taste, sample.

**dei¹** ['dei] prep+art **di i**.

**dei²** ['dei] V **dio**.

**deificare** [deifi'kare] v deify.

**del** [del] prep+art **di il**.

**delatore** [dela'tore], **-trice** sm, sf informer. **delazione** sf denouncement; (*fam*) tip-off.

**delegare** [dele'gare] v delegate. **delega** sf (*procura*) proxy; (*dir*) power of attorney. **delegato, -a** sm, sf delegate. **delegazione** sf delegation.

**deleterio** [dele'tɛrjo] agg harmful.

**delfino** [del'fino] sm dolphin.

**deliberare** [delibe'rare] v deliberate; (*decidere*) resolve. **deliberato** agg determined, resolved. **deliberazione** sf deliberation, decision.

**delicato** [deli'kato] agg delicate; (*gusto*) refined. **delicatezza** sf delicacy; (*tatto*) tact; refinement.

**delimitare** [delimi'tare] v define, circumscribe. **delimitazione** sf demarcation.

**delineare** [deline'are] v sketch, outline. **delinearsi** v (*presentarsi*) appear, emerge; (*apparire*) loom up, take shape.

**delinquente** [delin'kwɛnte] s(m+f) delinquent, criminal; (*mascalzone*) rascal. **delinquenza** sf criminality.

**deliquio** [de'likwjo] sm **cadere in deliquio** faint. **essere in deliquio** be in a faint.

**delirare** [deli'rare] v be delirious; (*farneticare*) rave. **delirio** sm delirium; (*follia*) frenzy.

**delitto** [de'litto] sm crime; (*reato*) offence; (*grave*) felony; (*lieve*) misdemeanour. **delittuoso** agg criminal.

**delizia** [de'litsja] sf delight. **delizioso** agg delightful; (*sapore*) delicious.

**dell'** [dell] prep+art **di l'**.

**della** ['della] prep+art **di la**.

**delle** ['delle] prep+art **di le**.

**dello** ['dello] prep+art **di lo**.

**delta** ['dɛlta] sm invar delta.

*****deludere** [de'ludere] v disappoint; (*render*

*vano*) frustrate.

**delusione** [delu'zjone] *sf* disappointment. **deluso** *agg* disappointed.

**demente** [de'mente] *agg* insane. *s(m+f)* lunatic. **demenza** *sf* madness, insanity; (*med*) dementia.

**democratico** [demo'kratiko], **-a** *sm, sf* democrat. *agg* democratic. **democrazia** *sf* democracy.

**democristiano** [demokris'tjano], **-a** *sm, sf* Christian Democrat. *agg* Christian Democratic.

**demografia** [demogra'fia] *sf* demography. **demografico** *agg* demographic.

**demolire** [demo'lire] *v* demolish. **demolizione** *sf* demolition.

**demone** ['dɛmone] *sm* demon; (*potenza ispiratrice*) genius; passion. **demonico** *agg* demonic.

**demonio** [de'mɔnjo] *sm* devil. **brutto come il demonio** as ugly as sin. **demoniaco** *agg* demoniacal, devilish.

**demoralizzare** [demoralid'dzare] *v* demoralize. **demoralizzarsi** *v* lose heart.

**denaro** [de'naro] *sm* money; (*grossezza di filo*) denier. **denaro spicciolo** small change.

**denigrare** [deni'grare] *v* denigrate; (*fam*) run down. **denigratorio** *agg* disparaging. **denigrazione** *sf* denigration, disparagement.

**denominatore** [denomina'tore] *sm* denominator. **denominare** *v* name. **denominazione** *sf* naming; (*nome*) name.

**denotare** [deno'tare] *v* denote, show.

**denso** ['dɛnso] *agg* dense, thick. **densità** *sf* density; (*spessore*) thickness.

**dente** ['dɛnte] *sm* tooth (*pl* teeth); (*ruota*) cog; (*forchetta*) prong. **a denti stretti** tight-lipped. **avere il dente avvelenato contro** have it in for. **dente del giudizio** wisdom tooth. **dente di latte** milk-tooth. **dente finto** false tooth. **dente sporgente** buck-tooth. **mettere i denti** teethe, cut one's teeth. **restare a denti asciutti** go hungry; (*fig*) go away empty-handed. **dentario** *agg* dental. **dentato** *agg* toothed.

**dentellare** [dentel'lare] *v* indent, notch. **dentellatura** *sf* indentation.

**dentice** ['dɛntitʃe] *sm* sea bream.

**dentiera** [den'tjɛra] *sf* denture.

**dentifricio** [denti'fritʃo] *sm* toothpaste.

**dentista** [den'tista] *s(m+f)* dentist.

**dentro** ['dentro] *avv* in; (*all'interno*) inside. *prep* in, inside; (*in casa*) indoors. **andar dentro** (*fam*) go to jail.

**denunziare** [denun'tsjare] *v also* **denunciare** denounce; (*riferire*) report; (*dichiarare*) declare; (*disdire*) terminate; (*rendere palese*) show. **denunzia** or **denuncia** *sf* report; (*accusa*) charge; declaration; notice of termination.

**deodorante** [deodo'rante] *agg, sm* deodorant.

**deperire** [depe'rire] *v* (*piante*) wither; (*animali*) waste away; (*persone*) get run down; (*cibi*) perish. **deperibile** *agg* perishable.

**depilatorio** [depila'torjo] *agg* depilatory. *sm* hair-remover.

**depliant** [depli'ã] *sm, pl* **-s** leaflet.

**deplorare** [deplo'rare] *v* (*compiangere*) lament, regret; (*biasimare*) deplore, regret. **deplorevole** *agg* deplorable.

*****deporre** [de'porre] *v* put or set down, deposit, lay; (*testimoniare*) (bear) witness. **deporre in giudizio** give evidence. **deposizione** *sf* deposition, testimony.

**deportare** [depor'tare] *v* deport. **deportato, -a** *sm, sf* deportee. **deportazione** *sf* deportation.

**deposito** [de'pɔzito] *sm* deposit; (*magazzino*) warehouse, store. **deposito bagagli** left-luggage office. **depositare** *v* deposit. **depositario** *sm* trustee.

**depravare** [depra'vare] *v* deprave.

**depredare** [depre'dare] *v* plunder.

**depresso** [de'prɛsso] *agg* depressed. **depressione** *sf* depression. **depressivo** *agg* depressive, depressant.

**deprezzare** [depret'tsare] *v* depreciate. **deprezzamento** *sm* depreciation.

*****deprimere** [de'primere] *v* depress. **deprimente** *agg* depressing.

**depurare** [depu'rare] *v* purify. **depuratore** *sm* purifier. **depurazione** *sf* purification.

**deputato** [depu'tare] *v* delegate. **deputato, -a** *sm, sf* deputy; delegate; Member of Parliament.

**deragliare** [dera'ʎare] *v* be derailed, go off the rails. **deragliamento** *sm* derailment.

**derapare** [dera'pare] *v* skid.

**derelitto** [dere'litto], **-a** *agg* forsaken. *sm, sf* down-and-out; (*trovatello*) foundling.

**deretano** [dere'tano] *sm* behind.

**\*deridere** [de'ridere] *v* laugh at, mock, deride. **derisione** *sf* derision, ridicule. **derisorio** *agg* derisory, laughable.

**deriva** [de'riva] *sf* **alla deriva** adrift. **andare alla deriva** drift.

**derivare** [deri'vare] *v* derive; (*conseguire*) follow, result; (*sviare*) divert. **derivata** *sf* (*mat*) derivative. **derivato** *sm* (*chim*) derivative; (*sottoprodotto*) by-product. **derivazione** *sf* derivation, origin. **collegare in derivazione** (*elett, radio*) shunt.

**dermatite** [derma'tite] *sf* dermatitis. **dermatologo, -a** *sm, sf* dermatologist.

**derogare** [dero'gare] *v* deviate (from), depart (from); (*non osservare*) not comply (with); (*dir*) waive. **deroga** *sf* departure. **in deroga a** notwithstanding; (*dir*) waiving. **derogabile** *agg* not binding.

**derrate** [der'rate] *sf pl* provisions *pl*; (*alimentari*) foodstuffs *pl*.

**derubare** [deru'bare] *v* rob.

**\*descrivere** [des'krivere] *v* describe. **descrittivo** *agg* descriptive. **non descrivibile** indescribable. **descrizione** *sf* description, account.

**deserto** [de'zɛrto] *sm* desert, wilderness. *agg* (*vuoto*) deserted; (*disabitato*) uninhabited.

**desiderare** [dezide'rare] *v* wish; (*volere*) want; (*bramare*) long for, desire. **lasciare a desiderare** leave to be desired. **desiderabile** *agg* desirable.

**desiderio** [dezi'dɛrjo] *sm* wish; (*brama*, *rimpianto*) longing, desire. **aver desiderio di** wish *or* want to. **pio desiderio** wishful thinking.

**designare** [dezi'ɲare] *v* designate; (*denominare*) call; (*nominare, stabilire*) appoint.

**desinare** [dezi'nare] *sm* lunch, dinner. *v* lunch, dine.

**desinenza** [dezi'nɛntsa] *sf* ending.

**\*desistere** [de'zistere] *v* desist. **desistere da** give up.

**desolato** [dezo'lato] *agg* (*afflitto*) distressed; (*deserto*) desolate; (*devastato*) desolated. **desolante** *agg* distressing. **desolazione** *sf* desolation; distress.

**despota** ['dɛspota] *sm* despot.

**destare** [des'tare] *v* awake, rouse; (*suscitare*) arouse, awaken. **destar meraviglia** cause wonder.

**destinare** [desti'nare] *v* destine; (*assegnare*) intend, assign; (*dedicare*) devote; (*riservare*) set aside; (*indirizzare*) address; decide. **destinatario, -a** *sm, sf* (*lettera*) addressee; (*merci*) consignee. **esser destinato a** (*decretato dalla sorte*) be bound *or* destined to; (*condannato*) be doomed to. **destinazione** *sf* destination. **destino** *sm* destiny, fate.

**destituire** [destitu'ire] *v* dismiss. **destituito** *agg* dismissed; (*privo*) devoid. **destituzione** *sf* dismissal.

**desto** ['desto] *agg* (*sveglio*) (wide-)awake; (*vivace*) lively.

**destra** ['dɛstra] *sf* (*lato*) right, right-hand side; (*mano*) right hand; (*pol*) right (wing). **a destra** on *or* to the right. **tenere la destra** keep (to the) right.

**destro** ['dɛstro] *agg* (*lato*) right(-hand); (*abile*) skilful, dextrous; (*accorto*) clever. **destrezza** *sf* ability, skill, dexterity. **destrorso** *agg* from left to right; (*in senso orario*) clockwise.

**detenere** [dete'nere] *v* hold; (*trattenere in prigione*) detain. **detenuto, -a** *sm, sf* detainee. **detenzione** *sf* detention. **detenzione abusiva** unlawful possession.

**detergente** [deter'dʒɛnte] *sm, agg* detergent.

**deteriorare** [deterjo'rare] *v* deteriorate. **deterioramento** *sm* deterioration.

**determinare** [determi'nare] *v* determine; (*causare*) bring about. **determinante** *agg* determining, decisive. **determinato** *agg* (*preciso*) definite, distinct; (*stabilito*) appointed; (*noto*) given; (*particolare*) special; (*deciso*) determined. **determinazione** *sf* determination.

**deterrente** [deter'rɛnte] *sm, agg* deterrent.

**detersivo** [deter'sivo] *sm, agg* detergent.

**detestare** [detes'tare] *v* detest, loathe. **detestabile** *agg* hateful, odious.

**detonatore** [detona'tore] *sm* detonator. **detonante** *sm, agg* explosive. **capsula detonante** *sf* percussion cap.

**\*detrarre** [det'rarre] *v* deduct, take away; (*nuocere a*) detract (from).

**detrimento** [detri'mento] *sm* detriment, prejudice.

**detrito** [de'trito] *sm* debris; (*geol*) detritus.

**dettagliare** [detta'ʎare] *v* (*particolareggiare*) detail; (*vendere al minuto*) retail. **dettagliante** *s(m+f)* retailer. **dettaglio** *sm* detail; retail.

**dettare** [det'tare] *v* dictate. **dettar legge**

lay down the law. **dettato** *sm* dictation.

**detto** ['detto] *agg* (*già citato*) above-mentioned, aforesaid; (*chiamato*) known as, alias. **detto fatto** no sooner said than done. **detto fra noi** between you and me. *sm* saying.

**deturpare** [detur'pare] *v* disfigure, deface.

**devastare** [devas'tare] *v* ravage, devastate. **devastazione** *sf* devastation, destruction.

**devastatore** [devasta'tore] *agg* devastating, destructive. *sm* devastator, destroyer.

**deviare** [devi'are] *v* deviate; (*spostare in altra direzione*) divert. **deviazione** *sf* deviation; (*fis*) deflection; (*traffico*) diversion, detour.

**devolvere** [de'volvere] *v* devolve, assign.

**devoto** [de'voto] *agg* (*rel*) devout; (*dedicato, affezionato*) devoted. **devozione** *sf* devotion; devoutness.

**di** [di] *prep* of; (*partitivo*) some, any; (*moto da luogo*) from; (*paragone*) than.

**diabete** [dia'bɛte] *sm* diabetes. **diabetico, -a s, agg** diabetic.

**diacono** [di'akono] *sm* deacon.

**diadema** [dia'dɛma] *sm* diadem, tiara.

**diaframma** [dia'framma] *sm* diaphragm; (*divisione*) partition.

**diagnosi** ['djanozi] *sf* diagnosis (*pl* -ses). **fare la diagnosi di** diagnose.

**diagonale** [djago'nale] *sf, agg* diagonal.

**diagramma** [dia'gramma] *sm* diagram; (*grafico*) chart, curve.

**dialetto** [dia'lɛtto] *sm* dialect. **dialettale** *agg* dialect.

**dialogo** [di'alogo] *sm, pl* -ghi dialogue; (*trattative*) negotiations *pl*; (*colloquio*) conversation, talk.

**diamante** [dia'mante] *sm* diamond.

**diametro** [di'ametro] *sm* diameter. **diametrale** *agg* diametrical.

**diamine** ['djamine] *inter* heavens! **che diamine ... !** what on earth ... !

**diapason** [di'apazon] *sm* tuning fork; (*tono*) pitch; (*estensione di voce*) range.

**diapositiva** [diapozi'tiva] *sf* transparency, slide.

**diario** [di'arjo] *sm* diary, journal. **diario di bordo** log-book.

**diarrea** [diar'rɛa] *sf* diarrhoea.

**diavolo** [d'javolo] *sm* devil. **che diavolo ... !** what the devil ... ! **un buon diavolo** a good chap. **diavoleria** *sf* mischief. **diav-**

**oletto** *sm* imp; (*bigodino*) roller, curler.

**dibattere** [di'battere] *v* debate. **dibattersi** *v* struggle. **dibattimento** *sm* hearing. **dibattito** *sm* debate. **dibattuto** *agg* (*discusso*) controversial, vexed; (*tormentato*) troubled.

**dicastero** [dikas'tɛro] *sm* ministry.

**dicembre** [di'tʃɛmbre] *sm* December.

**diceria** [ditʃe'ria] *sf* rumour, gossip.

**dichiarare** [dikja'rare] *v* declare; (*gioco di carte*) bid. **dichiarazione** *sf* declaration; bid; (*attestazione*) statement; (*amore*) proposal. **dichiarazione dei redditi** tax return.

**diciannove** [ditʃan'nɔve] *agg, sm* nineteen. **diciannovesimo** *sm, agg* nineteenth.

**diciassette** [ditʃas'sɛtte] *agg, sm* seventeen. **diciassettesimo** *sm, agg* seventeenth.

**diciotto** [di'tʃɔtto] *agg, sm* eighteen. **diciottesimo** *sm, agg* eighteenth.

**dicitura** [ditʃi'tura] *sf* caption.

**didascalia** [didaska'lia] *sf* caption; (*cinema*) subtitle; (*teatro*) stage directions *pl*.

**didattico** [di'dattiko] *agg* didactic.

**didentro** [di'dɛntro] **al/dal didentro** on/from the inside.

**didietro** [di'djɛtro] *sm* behind.

**dieci** ['djɛtʃi] *sm, agg* ten.

**diesis** [di'ɛzis] *sm* (*musica*) sharp.

**dieta** ['djɛta] *sf* diet. **essere a dieta** be on a diet.

**dietro** ['djɛtro] *avv* behind. *prep* (*luogo*) behind; (*tempo*) after; (*su, in seguito a*) on. **dietro front** about turn.

**difatti** [di'fatti] *cong* in fact.

**\*difendere** [di'fɛndere] *v* defend.

**difensiva** [difen'siva] *sf* defensive. **difensivo** *agg* defensive.

**difensore** [difen'sore] *sm* defender. **avvocato difensore** counsel for the defence.

**difesa** [di'feza] *sf* defence. **difesa legittima** self-defence. **senza difesa** defenceless. **stare sulla difesa** be on the defensive.

**difeso** [di'fezo] *agg* (*riparato*) sheltered; (*fortificato*) defended, protected.

**difetto** [di'fetto] *sm* (*mancanza*) lack; (*imperfezione*) defect, fault. **difettare** *v also* **far difetto** lack; (*venir meno*) fail; (*essere difettoso*) be defective or faulty. **difettoso** *agg* defective, faulty.

**diffamare** [diffa'mare] *v* denigrate; (*a voce*) slander; (*per iscritto*) libel. **diffamatorio**

*agg* defamatory; slanderous; libellous.
**diffamatore, -trice** *sm, sf* libeller; slanderer.

**differente** [diffe'rente] *agg* different, unlike.

**differenza** [diffe'rentsa] *sf* difference. **a differenza di** unlike. **differenziale** *sm, agg* differential. **differenziare** *v* differentiate.

**differire** [diffe'rire] *v* (*rimandare*) defer; (*esser diverso*) differ, be different.

**difficile** [dif'fitʃile] *agg* difficult; (*improbabile*) unlikely; (*duro*) hard. *sm* difficulty. *s(m+f)* difficult person.

**difficoltà** [diffikol'ta] *sf* difficulty; (*ostacolo*) trouble. **difficoltoso** *agg* difficult.

**diffidare** [diffi'dare] *v* (*non fidarsi*) mistrust, be suspicious of; (*avvisare*) warn, caution. **diffida** *sf* warning, notice. **diffidente** *agg* suspicious. **diffidenza** *sf* suspicion.

**\*diffondere** [dif'fondere] *v* spread; (*luce, calore, ecc.*) diffuse; (*dilungarsi*) dwell; (*comm*) promote.

**diffusione** [diffu'zjone] *sf* spreading, diffusion; (*giornali*) circulation. **diffuso** *agg* widespread; diffused; widely circulated; (*prolisso*) long-winded.

**diga** ['diga] *sf* dam, barrier.

**digerire** [didʒe'rire] *v* digest; (*assimilare*) take in; (*tollerare*) stand, bear; (*credere*) swallow. **digeribile** *agg* digestible. **digestione** *sf* digestion. **digestivo** *sm, agg* digestive.

**digitale** [didʒi'tale] *agg* digital. **impronta digitale** *sf* fingerprint.

**digiunare** [didʒu'nare] *v also* **stare a digiuno** fast. **digiuno** *sm* fast. **a digiuno** on an empty stomach. **essere a digiuno di** (*fig*) be without.

**dignità** [diɲi'ta] *sf* dignity; (*ufficio*) (high) rank. *sf pl* dignitaries *pl*. **dignitoso** *agg* dignified.

**digredire** [digre'dire] *v* digress.

**digressione** [digres'sjone] *sf* digression.

**digrignare** [digri'ɲare] *v* **digrignare i denti** gnash one's teeth; (*animali*) bare the teeth.

**dilagare** [dila'gare] *v* flood, spread. **dilagamento** *sm* flooding.

**dilaniare** [dila'njare] *v* rend.

**dilapidare** [dilapi'dare] *v* squander.

**dilatare** [dila'tare] *v* dilate, open (wide). **dilatazione** *sf* dilation.

**dilatorio** [dila'tɔrjo] *agg* dilatory.

**dilazione** *sf* delay, deferment.

**dileguare** [dile'gware] *v* dispel. **dileguarsi** *v* disappear, fade.

**dilemma** [di'lemma] *sm* dilemma.

**dilettante** [dilet'tante] *agg, s(m+f)* amateur. **dilettantesco** *agg* amateurish.

**dilettare** [dilet'tare] *v* delight; (*far divertire*) amuse. **dilettarsi** *v* delight in, enjoy.

**diletto¹** [di'letto] *sm* (*piacere*) delight, pleasure; (*godimento*) enjoyment.

**diletto²** [di'lɛtto] *agg* beloved; (*preferito*) favourite.

**diligente** [dili'dʒente] *agg* (*che lavora*) industrious; (*accurato*) conscientious; painstaking.

**diligenza¹** [dili'dʒentsa] *sf* industry, conscientiousness. **con diligenza** conscientiously.

**diligenza²** [dili'dʒentsa] *sf* (*carrozza*) stagecoach.

**diluire** [dilu'ire] *v* dilute; (*allungare con acqua*) water down; (*vernice, ecc.*) thin (down).

**dilungarsi** [dilun'garsi] *v* (*andar per le lunghe*) talk at length, dwell.

**diluvio** [di'luvjo] *sm* flood, deluge.

**dimagrire** [dima'grire] *v also* **dimagrare** lose weight; (*di proposito*) slim; (*far sembrare snello*) make look slimmer.

**dimenare** [dime'nare] *v* wave (about); (*coda*) wag. **dimenarsi** *v* fidget, toss about.

**dimensione** [dimen'sjone] *sf* dimension. **a due/tre dimensioni** two-/three-dimensional.

**dimenticare** [dimenti'kare] *v* forget; (*perdonare*) forget about; (*trascurare*) neglect. **dimenticarsi (di)** forget (about). **dimentico** *agg, m pl* **-chi** forgetful; (*noncurante*) oblivious.

**dimestichezza** [dimesti'kettsa] *sf* familiarity. **aver dimestichezza con** be familiar with.

**dimettere** [di'mettere] *v* discharge; (*licenziare*) dismiss. **dimettersi** *v* resign.

**dimezzare** [dimed'dzare] *v* halve.

**diminuire** [diminu'ire] *v* diminish, reduce; (*calare*) drop; (*lavoro a maglia*) cast off, decrease. **diminuire di peso** lose weight. **diminuire di prezzo** cost less. **diminuire di valore** fall in value, be worth less. **diminutivo** *agg* diminutive. **diminuzione** *sf* decrease; drop, cut, fall.

**dimissione** [dimis'sjone] *sf* resignation. **dare** *or* **rassegnare le dimissioni** resign. **dimissionario** *agg* outgoing.

**dimorare** [dimo'rare] *v* stay, live. **dimora** *sf* (*abitazione*) home, abode; (*soggiorno*) stay, residence.

**dimostrare** [dimos'trare] *v* demonstrate; (*manifestare*) show, display; prove. **dimostrabile** *agg* demonstrable. **dimostrante** *s(m+f)* demonstrator. **dimostrativo** *agg* demonstrative. **dimostratore, -trice** *sm, sf* demonstrator. **dimostrazione** *sf* demonstration; (*prova*) proof.

**dinamica** [di'namika] *sf* dynamics. **dinamico** *agg* dynamic, forceful.

**dinamite** [dina'mite] *sf* dynamite.

**dinamo** ['dinamo] *sf invar* dynamo.

**dinanzi** [di'nantsi] *avv* ahead, forward. *agg invar* (*davanti a*) in front of; (*dirimpetto*) opposite; in the presence of, before.

**dinastia** [dinas'tia] *sf* dynasty. **dinastico** *agg* dynastic.

**dinoccolato** [dinokko'lato] *agg* shambling. **camminare dinoccolato** *v* slouch.

**dinosauro** [dino'sauro] *sm* dinosaur.

**dintorno** [din'torno] *avv* around, about. **dintorni** *sm pl* outskirts *pl*, surroundings *pl*.

**dio** ['dio] *sm, pl* **dei** god. **come un dio** wonderfully, beautifully.

**diocesi** ['diɔtʃezi] *sf* diocese.

**diodo** ['diodo] *sm* diode.

**dipanare** [dipa'nare] *v* unravel.

**dipartimento** [diparti'mento] *sm* department, district.

**dipendente** [dipen'dɛnte] *s(m+f)* (*impiegato*) employee. *agg* dependent, subordinate. **dipendenza** *sf* dependence; (*edificio*) annexe; (*filiale*) branch. **essere alle dipendenze di** be in the employ of.

**\*dipendere** [di'pɛndere] *v* depend (on); (*derivare*) be due (to), be caused (by). **dipende!** that depends! **dipende da te!** it is up to you!

**\*dipingere** [di'pindʒere] *v* paint; (*rappresentare*) depict. **dipingersi** *v* (*truccarsi*) make up. **dipinto** *sm* painting.

**diploma** [di'plɔma] *sm* diploma, certificate, qualification. **diplomarsi** *v* obtain a certificate, qualify.

**diplomatico** [diplo'matiko], **-a** *agg* diplomatic. *sm, sf* diplomat. **diplomazia** *sf* diplomacy.

**diporto** [di'pɔrto] *sm* pleasure, pastime.

**diradare** [dira'dare] *v* thin; (*nebbia*) clear.

**diramare** [dira'mare] *v* issue, broadcast. **diramarsi** *v* branch out *or* off. **diramazione** *sf* branch; (*comunicato, ecc.*) broadcasting, circulation.

**\*dire** ['dire] *v* say; (*raccontare, ordinare*) tell; (*significare*) mean. **a chi lo dici!** don't I know! **aver da dire su** find fault with. **è tutto dire** which is saying a lot. **inutile dire** it goes without saying. *sm* speech, words *pl*. **a dire di tutti** by all accounts. **oltre ogni dire** beyond all description.

**diretto** [di'rɛtto] *agg* direct; (*inteso*) meant, destined; (*guidato*) conducted. *sm* (*ferr*) through train. **direttissimo** *sm* (*ferr*) express train. **direttiva** *sf* directive; (*condotta*) policy. **direttivo** *agg* (*che dirige*) guiding; (*proprio di una direzione*) managerial. **direttore** *sm* manager; (*scuola*) headmaster; (*giornale*) editor; (*orchestra*) conductor. **direttrice** *sf* manageress; headmistress.

**direzione** [dire'tsjone] *sf* direction; (*il dirigere*) management, administration; (*sede*) head office. **assumere la direzione** take charge. **in che direzione?** which way?

**\*dirigere** [di'ridʒere] *v* direct; (*rivolgere*) address; (*guidare*) lead; (*amministrare*) manage; (*giornale*) edit; (*orchestra*) conduct. **dirigersi verso** go towards, head for. **dirigibile** *sm* airship.

**dirimpetto** [dirim'pɛtto] *agg invar, avv* opposite.

**diritto¹** [di'ritto] *agg* (*non curvo*) straight; (*eretto, onesto*) upright; (*fam: astuto*) crafty; (*fam: accorto*) shrewd; (*destro*) right(-hand). *avv* straight. **andar diritto** go straight ahead *or* on. *sm* (*moneta*) obverse; (*lato buono*) good side; (*tennis*) forehand.

**diritto²** [di'ritto] *sm* (*legge*) law; (*pretesa*) right; (*tassa*) due, duty. **a buon diritto** with good cause. **diritti d'autore** copyright *sing*; (*compenso*) royalties *pl*. **diritto acquisito** vested interest.

**diroccato** [dirok'kato] *agg* dilapidated.

**dirottare** [dirot'tare] *v* divert; change course.

**dirotto** [di'rotto] *agg* (*pianto*) copious; (*pioggia*) pouring.

**disabitato** [dizabi'tato] *agg* uninhabited.

**disabituare** [dizabitu'are] *v* wean.

**disaccordo** [dizak'kordo] *sm* disagreement; variance. **essere** *or* **trovarsi in disaccordo su** disagree on, be at variance over.

**disadatto** [diza'datto] *agg* ill-suited.

**disadorno** [diza'dorno] *agg* bare.

**disagevole** [diza'dʒevole] *agg* uncomfortable.

**disagio** [di'zadʒo] *sm* (*imbarazzo*) uneasiness; (*mancanza di comodità*) discomfort. **essere a disagio** be ill at ease. **sentirsi a disagio** feel uneasy. **disagiato** *agg* uncomfortable; (*duro*) hard.

**disamorarsi** [dizamo'rarsi] *v* become estranged (from), cease to care (for).

**disapprovare** [dizappro'vare] *v* disapprove. **disapprovazione** *sf* disapproval.

**disappunto** [dizap'punto] *sm* disappointment.

**disarmare** [dizar'mare] *v* disarm; (*smantellare*) dismantle; (*edificio*) remove the scaffolding from. **disarmo** *sm* disarmament.

**disarmonia** [dizarmo'nia] *sf* discord.

**disastro** [di'zastro] *sm* disaster; (*incidente*) crash; (*fam: insuccesso*) utter failure. **combinare un disastro** (*fam*) make a mess. **disastroso** *agg* disastrous.

**disattento** [dizat'tento] *agg* inattentive; (*sbadato*) careless. **disattenzione** *sf* carelessness; (*errore*) slip. **per disattenzione** through an oversight.

**disavanzo** [diza'vantso] *sm* deficit.

**disavventura** [dizavven'tura] *sf* misfortune.

**disbrigo** [diz'brigo] *sm*, *pl* **-ghi** settlement, dispatch.

**discapito** [dis'kapito] *sm* **a discapito di** at the cost of, to the prejudice of.

**\*discendere** [di'ʃendere] *v* descend; (*andar giù*) go down; (*venir giù*) come down. **discendente** *s(m+f)* descendant. **discendenza** *sf* descent; (*collettivo*) offspring. **discensore** *sm* lift.

**discepolo** [di'ʃepolo] *sm* disciple.

**discernere** [di'ʃernere] *v* discern; distinguish.

**discesa** [di'ʃesa] *sf* descent; (*declivio*) slope. **discesa in picchiata** nose-dive. **in discesa** downhill.

**\*dischiudere** [dis'kjudere] *v* open; (*svelare*) disclose.

**\*disciogliere** [di'ʃɔʎere] *v* dissolve; (*lique-*

*fare*) melt.

**disciplinare** [diʃipli'nare] *v* discipline, control. *agg* disciplinary. **disciplina** *sf* discipline. **disciplinato** *agg* (well-)disciplined, orderly.

**disco** ['disko] *sm* disc; (*grammofono*) record; (*sport*) discus; (*hockey*) puck; (*telefono*) dial. **disco rosso/verde** red/green light.

**discolo** ['diskolo] *agg* mischievous.

**discolpare** [diskol'pare] *v* clear. **discolpa** *sf* justification, defence.

**\*disconoscere** [disko'noʃere] *v* refuse to acknowledge.

**disconnettersi** [diskon'nettersi] *v* log off.

**discontinuo** [diskon'tinuo] *agg* discontinuous; (*non regolare*) erratic.

**discorde** [dis'kɔrde] *agg* *also* **discordante** discordant; (*contrastante*) conflicting; (*stonante*) clashing. **discordare** *v* disagree; conflict; clash. **discordia** *sf* disagreement.

**\*discorrere** [dis'korrere] *v* talk. **discorrere del più e del meno** talk about this and that. **e via discorrendo** and so on.

**discorso** [dis'korso] *sm* conversation, talk; (*in pubblico, gramm*) speech. **cambiare discorso** change the subject. **senza tanti discorsi** quite frankly. **tenere un discorso** make a speech, give an address.

**discoteca** [disko'tɛka] *sf* (*locale*) disco, discotheque; record collection.

**discreto** [dis'kreto] *agg* fair, reasonable; (*non importuno*) tactful, discreet; (*separato*) discrete. **discretamente** *avv* moderately well. **discrezionale** *agg* discretionary. **discrezione** *sf* discretion, moderation, tact.

**discriminazione** [diskrimina'tsjone] *sf* discrimination. **discriminare** *v* discriminate; (*dir*) extenuate.

**discussione** [diskus'sjone] *sf* discussion, debate; (*litigio*) argument. **mettere in discussione** discuss, debate; (*in dubbio*) question.

**discusso** [dis'kusso] *agg* discussed, controversial.

**\*discutere** [dis'kutere] *v* discuss, debate; (*litigare*) argue. **discutibile** *agg* debatable, questionable.

**disdegnare** [dizde'ɲare] *v* disdain, scorn. **disdegno** *sm* disdain, scorn.

**\*disdire** [diz'dire] *v* (*annullare*) cancel; (*negare*) deny; (*ritrattare*) withdraw, take back; (*mentire*) refute. **disdetta** *sf* notice; (*sfortuna*) bad luck; cancellation.

**disegnare** [dize'nare] v draw; (*progettare*) design, sketch; (*delineare*) outline. **disegnatore** sm draughtsman. **disegno** sm drawing; (*schizzo*) sketch; (*progetto*) design, plan; (*abbozzo*) outline. **a disegni** patterned. **disegno animato** (*cinema*) cartoon. **disegno di legge** bill.

**diseredare** [dizere'dare] v disinherit. **diseredato, -a** s, agg destitute.

**disertare** [dizer'tare] v desert. **disertore** sm deserter. **diserzione** sf desertion.

***disfare** [dis'fare] v undo; (*smontare*) take to pieces; (*valigia*) unpack; (*sciogliere*) melt. **disfatta** sf defeat. **disfattismo** sm defeatism. **disfattista** s(m+f), agg defeatist.

**disgelare** [dizdʒe'lare] v thaw (out); (*frigorifero*) defrost. **disgelo** sm thaw.

***disgiungere** [diz'dʒundʒere] v detach, separate.

**disgraziato** [dizgra'tsjato], **-a** agg unfortunate, unlucky; (*infelice*) wretched. sm, sf (*sventurato*) wretch; (*sciagurato*) scoundrel. **disgrazia** sf misfortune; (*incidente*) accident, mishap; (*sfavore*) disgrace; (*sfortuna*) bad luck.

**disgregare** [dizgre'gare] v break up. **disgregazione** sf break-up.

**disguido** [diz'gwido] sm (*equivoco*) misunderstanding; (*errore nel recapito*) mistake in delivery.

**disgustare** [dizgus'tare] v disgust. **disgusto** sm disgust, revulsion, loathing. **disgustoso** agg disgusting, loathsome, revolting.

**disidratare** [dizidra'tare] v dehydrate.

***disilludere** [dizil'ludere] v disillusion, disenchant. **disillusione** sf disenchantment, disillusion.

**disimpegnare** [dizimpe'nare] v free, release; (*oggetto dato in pegno*) redeem; (*mil*) relieve. **disimpegnarsi** (*cavarsela*) acquit oneself, manage. **disimpegno** sm (*adempimento*) fulfilment; (*politica*) disengagement.

**disinfettare** [dizinfet'tare] v disinfect. **disinfettante** sm disinfectant. **disinfezione** sf disinfection.

**disintegrare** [dizinte'grare] v disintegrate; (*fis*) split, decay.

**disinteressarsi** [dizinteres'sarsi] v take no interest (in). **disinteressato** agg disinterested; (*altruistico*) unselfish.

**disinvolto** [dizin'vɔlto] agg unconstrained, self-possessed; (*spigliato*) free and easy,

casual; (*senza ritegno*) uninhibited. **disinvoltura** sf ease, casualness; self-possession.

**disistima** [dizis'tima] sf lack of esteem; (*disprezzo*) contempt.

**dislivello** [dizli'vɛllo] sm difference (in level); (*fig*) inequality.

**dislocare** [dizlo'kare] v displace; (*mil*) detach.

**dismisura** [dizmi'zura] sf **a dismisura** excessively.

**disoccupato** [dizokku'pato], **-a** s, agg unemployed. **disoccupazione** sf unemployment. **sussidio di disoccupazione** sm unemployment benefit; (*fam*) dole.

**disonesto** [dizo'nɛsto] agg dishonest; (*immorale*) dishonourable; (*impudico*) shameless. **disonestà** sf dishonesty; dishonourable behaviour; shamelessness.

**disonorare** [dizono'rare] v dishonour, disgrace. **disonore** sm dishonour, disgrace. **disonorevole** agg dishonourable, disgraceful, shameful.

**disopra** [di'sopra] avv above; (*al piano superiore*) upstairs. agg invar (*superiore*) upper; (*posto più in alto*) higher up; upstairs. sm invar top, upper part. **al disopra di** (*più di*) more than; (*superiore a*) above all; (*più alto di*) above. **dal disopra** from above.

**disordinare** [dizordi'nare] v upset, turn upside down. **disordinato** agg untidy; confuso; (*sregolato*) disorderly. **disordine** sm disorder; (*confusione*) muddle.

**disorientare** [dizorjen'tare] v (*confondere*) confuse, bewilder. **disorientarsi** v lose one's bearings, become confused.

**disossare** [dizos'sare] v bone.

**disotto** [di'sotto] avv below, underneath; (*al piano inferiore*) downstairs. agg invar below; (*tra due*) lower; (*in fondo*) bottom; downstairs.

**dispaccio** [dis'pattʃo] sm dispatch.

**disparato** [dispa'rato] agg dissimilar, different.

**dispari** ['dispari] agg odd.

**disparte** [dis'parte] avv **in disparte** aside, to one side. **tenersi in disparte** keep at a distance.

**dispensa** [dis'pɛnsa] sf distribution; (*mobile*) cupboard; (*locale*) pantry, larder; (*fascicolo*) number, issue; (*esonero*) exemption. **a dispense** in instalments. **dispensa ecclesiastica** dispensation. **dispensa universitaria** lecture notes pl. **dispensare** v dispense. **dispensario** *sm* clinic.

**disperare** [dispe'rare] *v* despair. **disperato** *agg* desperate. **disperazione** *sf* despair.

***disperdere** [dis'perdere] *v* disperse, scatter; dissipate; (*sprecare*) waste. **dispersione** *sf* dispersion; waste.

**dispetto** [dis'petto] *sm* spite; (*irritazione*) annoyance. **a dispetto di** despite. **fare un dispetto** annoy. **per dispetto** out of spite. **dispettoso** *agg* spiteful, annoying.

***dispiacere** [dispja'tʃere] *v* displease. **mi dispiace** ... (*non mi piace*) I don't like ... ; (*sono spiacente*) I'm sorry .... **ti dispiace** ... ? do you mind ... ? *sm* (*rammarico*) regret; (*noia*) displeasure; (*fastidio*) trouble, worry.

**disponibile** [dispo'nibile] *agg* available; (*libero*) vacant. **posto disponibile** *sm* vacancy.

**disponibilità** [disponibili'ta] *sf* availability. *sf pl* assets *pl*.

***disporre** [dis'porre] *v* dispose; (*collocare in ordine, stabilire*) arrange; prepare; induce; order. **disporre di** have available, have at one's disposal; (*avere*) own. **disporsi** *v* prepare, get ready; (*in fila*) line up.

**dispositivo** [dispozi'tivo] *sm* device.

**disposizione** [dispozi'tsjone] *sf* arrangement, layout; (*stato d'animo*) disposition; (*inclinazione*) bent; (*norma*) provision; (*comando*) order. **a disposizione** available.

**disposto** [dis'posto] *agg* arranged, laid out; (*pronto*) ready, willing; (*stabilito*) laid down.

**disprezzare** [dispret'tsare] *v* despise, scorn. **disprezzo** *sm* scorn, contempt.

**disputare** [dispu'tare] *v* dispute; (*litigare*) argue; (*contendere*) fight (over), strive (for); (*incontro*) play; (*corsa*) run. **disputa** *sf* dispute; (*lite*) argument.

**dissanguare** [dissan'gware] *v* bleed.

**dissecare** [disse'kare] *v* dissect.

**disseccare** [dissek'kare] *v* dry up.

**disseminare** [dissemi'nare] *v* scatter; (*diffondere*) spread.

**dissenteria** [dissente'ria] *sf* dysentery.

**dissentire** [dissen'tire] *v* dissent, disagree.

**disseppellire** [disseppel'lire] *v* unearth; (*esumare*) exhume.

**dissertazione** [disserta'tsjone] *sf* dissertation.

**dissestare** [disses'tare] *v* upset, unbalance. **dissestato** *agg* ruined; (*strada*) in poor condition; (*bilancio*) adverse.

**dissetarsi** [disse'tarsi] *v* quench one's thirst. **dissetante** *agg* thirst-quenching.

**dissidente** [dissi'dɛnte] *s(m+f)*, *agg* dissident; (*rel*) non-conformist.

**dissidio** [dis'sidjo] *sm* disagreement; (*lite*) quarrel.

**dissimile** [dis'simile] *agg* different, unlike.

**dissimulare** [dissimu'lare] *v* dissimulate; (*fingere*) pretend; (*nascondere*) hide.

**dissipare** [dissi'pare] *v* dissipate; (*sospetti, dubbi, ecc.*) dispel; (*sprecare*) squander.

**dissociare** [disso'tʃare] *v* dissociate. **dissociazione** *sf* dissociation.

**dissoluto** [disso'luto] *agg* dissolute.

**dissoluzione** [dissolu'tsjone] *sf* dissolution, break-up.

***dissolvere** [dis'sɔlvere] *v* dispel; (*sciogliere*) dissolve.

**dissotterrare** [dissotter'rare] *v* unearth; (*esumare*) exhume.

***dissuadere** [dissua'dere] *v* dissuade, deter.

**distaccare** [distak'kare] *v* detach; (*sport: lasciar dietro*) leave behind. **distaccarsi** *v* (*spiccare*) stand out; (*allontanarsi*) withdraw. **distaccamento** *sm* (*mil*) detachment. **distacco** *sm* detachment; (*separazione*) parting, separation; (*sport: vantaggio*) lead.

**distante** [dis'tante] *agg* distant, remote, far. *avv* far, far off. **distanza** *sf* distance; (*tempo*) interval.

***distare** [dis'tare] *v* be far (from).

***distendere** [dis'tɛndere] *v* spread; (*allungare*) stretch; (*appendere*) hang (up); (*mettere giù*) lay; (*rilassare*) relax. **distendersi** *v* lie down, relax.

**distensione** [disten'sjone] *sf* stretching; relaxation; (*pol*) détente. **distensivo** *agg* relaxing.

**distesa** [dis'teza] *sf* expanse; (*fila*) row.

**disteso** [dis'tezo] *agg* (*teso*) stretched; (*coricato*) lying down; (*braccio*) outstretched; (*spiegato*) spread out; relaxed.

**distillare** [distil'lare] *v* distil. **distilleria** *sf* distillery.

***distinguere** [dis'tingwere] *v* distinguish, tell; (*contrassegnare*) mark; draw a distinction; (*riconoscere*) recognize. **distinguibile** *agg* distinguishable; recognizable.

**distinta** [dis'tinta] *sf* list. **distinta delle spese** statement of expenses.

**distintivo** [distin'tivo] *agg* distinctive; (*atto*

*a distinguere*) distinguishing. *sm* badge.

**distinto** [dis'tinto] *agg* distinct, different, separate; (*scelto, raffinato*) distinguished. **ben distinto** precise. **distinti saluti** yours faithfully.

**distinzione** [distin'tsjone] *sf* distinction. **fare una distinzione** make a distinction, discriminate. **senza distinzione** (*senza merito*) undistinguished; (*senza criterio*) indiscriminately; (*in modo equo*) impartially.

**\*distogliere** [dis'tɔʎere] *v* divert, turn away.

**distorsione** [distor'sjone] *sf* distortion; (*med*) sprain.

**\*distrarre** [dis'trarre] *v* distract; (*divertire*) amuse. **distrarsi** *v* amuse oneself; (*essere disattento*) be inattentive. **distratto** *agg* inattentive; (*assente*) absent-minded; (*sbadato*) careless. **distrazione** *sf* (*svago*) distraction, relaxation; (*sbadataggine*) carelessness; absent-mindedness; lack of attention.

**distretto** [dis'tretto] *sm* district.

**distribuire** [distribu'ire] *v* distribute; (*disporre*) arrange; (*assegnare*) hand out; (*le carte*) deal; (*posta*) deliver. **distributore** *sm* (*di accensione*) distributor; (*di benzina*) petrol pump, service station. **distribuzione** *sf* distribution; (*fornitura*) supply; arrangement; delivery. **distribuzione dei premi** prize-giving. **distribuzione dei ruoli** (*cinema*) casting.

**districare** [distri'kare] *v* disentangle; (*fig*) sort out. **districarsi** *v* extricate oneself.

**\*distruggere** [dis'truddʒere] *v* destroy, ruin. **distruttivo** *agg* destructive. **distrutto** *agg* destroyed, ruined; (*fig*) broken. **distruzione** *sf* destruction, ruin.

**disturbare** [distur'bare] *v* disturb; (*molestare, seccare*) trouble, bother; (*recar fastidio*) inconvenience; (*radio*) jam. **disturbo** *sm* trouble; (*incomodo*) nuisance, inconvenience; (*indisposizione*) upset, disorder; (*radio*) jamming; atmospherics *pl*, interference. **recar disturbo** trouble, inconvenience.

**disubbidire** [dizubbi'dire] *v* disobey.

**disuguale** [dizu'gwale] *agg* unequal; (*non regolare*) irregular. **disuguaglianza** *sf* difference, disparity.

**disunire** [dizu'nire] *v* separate, divide.

**disuso** [di'zuzo] *sm* disuse. **andare** or **cadere in disuso** fall into disuse, become obsolete. **disusato** *agg* obsolete, out-of-date; (*fuori moda*) old-fashioned.

**dito** ['dito] *sm, pl* **-a** *f* finger. **dito anulare/indice/medio/mignolo** ring/index/middle/little finger. **dito del piede** toe. **ditale** *sm* (*cucire*) thimble; (*guanto*) finger-stall.

**ditta** ['ditta] *sf* firm, company.

**dittatore** [ditta'tore] *sm* dictator. **dittatorio** *agg* dictatorial. **dittatura** *sf* dictatorship.

**dittico** ['dittiko] *sm* diptych.

**dittongo** [dit'tɔngo] *sm* diphthong.

**diurno** [di'urno] *agg* day(-time). **spettacolo diurno** *sm* matinee.

**diva** ['diva] *sf* (film-)star.

**divagare** [diva'gare] *v* digress, wander; (*distrarre*) distract.

**divampare** [divam'pare] *v* flare up, blaze.

**divano** [di'vano] *sm* divan, settee, couch.

**diventare** [diven'tare] *v also* **divenire** become, turn *or* grow (into). **diventar matto** go mad. **diventar pallido/rosso** go *or* turn pale/red.

**divergere** [di'vɛrdʒere] *v* diverge; (*essere diverso*) differ. **divergenza** *sf* divergence; difference.

**diversi** [di'vɛrsi] *agg* several. **pron** (*parecchi*) several (people); (*alcuni*) some (people).

**diversivo** [diver'sivo] *agg* diverting; distracting. *sm* diversion; distraction.

**diverso** [di'vɛrso] *agg* different; distinct, separate; (*di genere diverso*) various; (*comm*) sundry. **in caso diverso** otherwise. **diversamente** *avv* differently; (*se no*) otherwise. **diversità** *sf* difference, diversity.

**divertente** [diver'tɛnte] *agg* amusing, enjoyable. **divertimento** *sm* entertainment, amusement. **buon divertimento!** enjoy yourself! have a good time!

**divertire** [diver'tire] *v* amuse; (*ricreare*) entertain. **divertirsi** *v* enjoy oneself.

**dividendo** [divi'dɛndo] *sm* dividend.

**\*dividere** [di'videre] *v* divide; (*condividere*) share. **dividersi** *v* separate, part, split (up).

**divieto** [di'vjɛto] *sm* prohibition. **divieto di sorpasso/sosta/transito** no overtaking/stopping/thoroughfare.

**divinare** [divi'nare] *v* divine; (*prevedere*) foretell.

**divincolarsi** [divinko'larsi] *v* wriggle.

**divino** [di'vino] *agg* sacred, holy; (*sublime*) divine, heavenly. **divinità** *sf* divinity.

**divisa** [di'viza] *sf* uniform; motto. **divisa estera** foreign currency.

**divisibile** [divi'zibile] *agg* divisible. **divisibilità** *sf* divisibility.

**divisione** [divi'zjone] *sf* division; (*reparto*) department.

**diviso** [di'vizo] *agg* divided, separated; (*condiviso*) shared. **divisore** *sm* divisor.

**divisorio** [divi'zɔrjo] *sm* partition. *agg* dividing.

**divo** [di'vo] *sm* (film-)star.

**divorare** [divo'rare] *v* devour, eat up.

**divorzio** [di'vɔrtsjo] *sm* divorce. **divorziare** *v* divorce.

**divulgare** [divul'gare] *v* spread; (*rivelare*) divulge; (*rendere accessibile*) popularize. **divulgazione** *sf* spreading; (*notizie*) broadcasting; popularization.

**dizionario** [ditsjo'narjo] *sm* dictionary.

**dizione** [di'tsjone] *sf* diction.

**doccia** ['dottʃa] *sf* shower; (*grondaia*) gutter.

**docente** [do'tʃɛnte] *s(m+f)* lecturer, teacher.

**docile** ['dɔtʃile] *agg* docile, mild; (*materiale*) easily worked. **docilità** *sf* mildness, submissiveness; workability.

**documento** [doku'mento] *sm* document, paper. **documentare** *v* document. **documentario** *agg, sm* documentary. **documentazione** *sf* documentation; (*dir*) evidence.

**dodici** ['doditʃi] *agg, sm* twelve. **dodicesimo** *sm, agg* twelfth.

**dogana** [do'gana] *sf* customs. **doganale** *agg* customs. **doganiere** *sm* customs officer.

**doge** ['dɔdʒe] *sm* doge.

**doglie** ['dɔʎʎe] *sf pl* **doglie del parto** labour pains *pl*.

**dogma** ['dɔgma] *sm* dogma. **dogmatico** *agg* dogmatic.

**dolce** ['doltʃe] *agg* sweet; (*mite*) mild; (*morbido*) soft. *sm* sweet. **dolcezza** *sf* sweetness; mildness; softness.

**\*dolere** [do'lere] *v* (*far male*) ache, hurt. **mi duole di** *or* **che ...** I regret that ..., I'm sorry that ....

**dollaro** ['dɔllaro] *sm* dollar.

**dolo** ['dɔlo] *sm* (*dir*) malice; (*inganno*) fraud.

**dolore** [do'lore] *sm* pain; (*male fisico*) ache; (*sofferenza morale*) sorrow; (*rincrescimento*) regret. **doloroso** *agg* painful; sorrowful.

**domanda** [do'manda] *sf* question; (*richiesta*) request; (*scritta*) application; (*econ*) demand; (*dir*) petition. **domandare** *v* (*per sapere*) ask; (*per avere*) ask for; (*esigere*) demand. **domandarsi** *v* wonder.

**domani** [do'mani] *avv* tomorrow. **a domani!** see you tomorrow! **domani a otto** tomorrow week. **domani l'altro** the day after tomorrow. *sm* tomorrow; future. **un domani** one day.

**domare** [do'mare] *v* tame; (*sedare*) put down; (*spegnere*) put out; (*frenare*) curb. **domatore** *sm* tamer.

**domattina** [domat'tina] *avv* tomorrow morning.

**domenica** [do'menika] *sf* Sunday.

**domestico** [do'mɛstiko] *agg* domestic; (*della casa*) household, home. **apparecchio domestico** household appliance. *sm* servant. **domestica** *sf* maid. **domestichezza** *sf* familiarity.

**domiciliarsi** [domitʃi'ljarsi] *v* settle.

**domicilio** [domi'tʃiljo] *sm* domicile, home.

**dominare** [domi'nare] *v* dominate; (*predominare*) prevail; (*frenare*) control; (*aver potestà*) rule. **dominio** *sm* domination; rule; (*territorio*) domain; (*proprietà*) possession. **pubblico dominio** (*proprietà*) common property; (*noto a tutti*) common knowledge.

**domino** ['dɔmino] *sm* (*gioco*) dominoes.

**donare** [do'nare] *v* give, present; (*star bene*) suit, become. **donatore, -trice** *sm, sf* donor. **donazione** *sf* donation, gift.

**donde** ['donde] *avv* (*da dove*) whence, from where; (*di che*) with which.

**dondolare** [dondo'lare] *v* swing, rock. **cavallo a dondolo** *sm* rocking-horse. **sedia a dondolo** *sf* rocking-chair.

**donna** ['dɔnna] *sf* woman (*pl* women); (*domestica*) maid, servant; (*giochi*) queen. **donnaiolo** *sm* philanderer. **donnesco** *agg* feminine.

**donnola** ['dɔnnola] *sf* weasel.

**dono** ['dono] *sm* gift.

**dopo** ['dopo] *avv* after; (*poi*) then, afterwards; (*più tardi*) later (on); (*prossimo*) next. **a dopo!** see you later! **dopobarba** *agg, sm invar* aftershave. **dopo che** since. **dopo di che** whereupon. **dopodomani** *sm, avv* the day after tomorrow. **dopotutto** *avv* after all. **molto tempo dopo** long after.

**dopopranzo** [dopo'prantso] *avv* after lunch. *sm* afternoon.

**doppiare¹** [dop'pjare] *v* (*cinema*) dub. **doppiaggio** *sm* dubbing.

**doppiare²** [dop'pjare] *v* double; (*sport*) lap.

**doppio** ['doppjo] *agg* double; (*insincero*) two-faced; (*duplice*) dual, twofold. **a doppio petto** double-breasted. **fare il doppio gioco** double-cross. *sm* double, twice as much *or* many. **doppione** *sm* duplicate.

**dorare** [do'rare] *v* gild; (*gastr*) coat with egg. **doratura** *sf* gilding, gold-plating.

**dormicchiare** [dormik'kjare] *v* doze, snooze.

**dormire** [dor'mire] *v* sleep; (*esser fermo*) lie dormant. **dormita** *sf* good sleep.

**dormitorio** [dormi'tɔrjo] *sm* dormitory.

**dormiveglia** [dormi'veʎa] *sm* **essere nel dormiveglia** be half-asleep.

**dorso** ['dorso] *sm* back; (*nuoto*) backstroke.

**dose** ['dɔze] *sf* dose; quantity. **dose eccessiva** overdose. **rincarare la dose** (*fam*) pile it on. **dosaggio** *sm* dosage.

**dosso** ['dɔsso] *sm* back. **togliersi un peso di dosso** take a weight off one's mind.

**dotare** [do'tare] *v* endow, provide. **dotato** *agg* gifted; endowed *or* provided (with); (*munito*) equipped (with). **dotazione** *sf* equipment; (*rendita*) endowment. **dote** *sf* (*matrimonio*) dowry; (*donazione*) endowment; (*qualità*) quality.

**dotto¹** ['dɔtto] *agg* scholarly, learned. *sm* scholar.

**dotto²** ['dotto] *sm* (*condotto*) duct.

**dottore** [dot'tore], **-essa** *sm*, *sf* doctor.

**dottrina** [dot'trina] *sf* (*cultura*) learning; (*teoria, insieme di principi*) doctrine.

**dove** ['dove] *avv* where. *cong* (*se*) if; (*mentre*) whereas. **fin dove** as far as.

**\*dovere** [do'vere] *v* must, have to; (*esser lecito*) may; (*essere inevitabile*) be bound to; (*esser causato da*) be due to; (*al condizionale*) should, ought to. **come si deve** properly; (*persona*) proper, decent. *sm* duty. **doveroso** *agg* right and proper; (*obbligato*) (duty-) bound. **dovuto** *agg*, *sm* due.

**dovunque** [do'vunkwe] *avv* (*dappertutto*) everywhere; (*in qualsiasi luogo*) anywhere. *cong* wherever.

**dozzina** [dod'dzina] *sf* dozen. **a dozzine** by the dozen. **da dozzina** cheap, poor.

**dragare** [dra'gare] *v* dredge; (*mine*) sweep. **draga** *sf* dredge, dredger. **dragamine** *sm invar* minesweeper.

**drago** ['drago] *sm* dragon; (*aquilone*) kite. **dragone** *sm* dragon; (*mil*) dragoon.

**dramma** ['dramma] *sm* play; tragedy. **drammatico** *agg* dramatic; (*esagerato*) theatrical. **drammatizzare** *v* dramatize. **drammaturgo** *sm* playwright, dramatist.

**drappello** [drap'pɛllo] *sm* squad, band.

**drappo** ['drappo] *sm* cloth; (*funebre*) pall. **drappeggiare** *v* drape.

**drastico** ['drastiko] *agg* drastic.

**drenare** [dre'nare] *v* drain. **drenaggio** *sm* drainage.

**dritta** ['dritta] *sf* (*mano*) right (hand); (*parte*) right(-hand side); (*mar*) starboard.

**dritto** ['dritto] *agg* (*fam*) astute. *sm* (*non rovescio*) right side; (*fam*) crafty person, fast worker.

**drizzare** [drit'tsare] *v* (*raddrizzare*) straighten; (*erigere*) erect. **drizzare le orecchie** prick up one's ears.

**droga** ['drɔga] *sf* drug; (*sostanza aromatica*) spice. **drogare** *v* drug, dope; spice. **drogarsi** *v* take drugs.

**droghiere** [dro'gjɛre], **-a** *sm*, *sf* grocer. **drogheria** *sf* grocer's shop. **articoli di drogheria** groceries *pl*.

**dromedario** [drome'darjo] *sm* dromedary.

**dualismo** [dua'lizmo] *sm* dualism.

**dubbio** ['dubbjo] *sm* doubt. **essere in dubbio** be in doubt, be uncertain. **mettere in dubbio** doubt, call in question. **senza dubbio** no doubt, doubtless. *agg* also **dubbioso** doubtful, uncertain; (*ambiguo*) dubious.

**dubitare** [dubi'tare] *v* doubt; (*essere in dubbio*) be in doubt; (*diffidare*) distrust. **non dubitare!** don't worry!

**duca** ['duka] *sm* duke.

**duce** ['dutʃe] *sm* leader.

**duchessa** [du'kessa] *sf* duchess.

**due** ['due] *sm*, *agg* two. **a due a due** two by two, in twos. **duepezzi** *sm invar* two-piece. **due punti** colon. **due volte** twice. **due volte tanto** twice as much *or* many. **nessuno dei due** neither of them. **tutti e due** both of them.

**duello** [du'ɛllo] *sm* duel. **duellare** *v* duel.

**duellista** or **duellante** sm duellist.

**duetto** [du'etto] sm duet.

**duna** ['duna] sf dune.

**dunque** ['dunkwe] cong (nel discorso) well, now then; (perciò) so, therefore, hence; (rafforzativo) then. sm **trovarsi al dunque** come to the crunch. **venire al dunque** come to the point.

**duo** ['duo] sm invar duo.

**duodeno** [duo'dɛno] sm duodenum. **duodenale** agg duodenal.

**duomo** ['dwɔmo] sm cathedral.

**duplex** ['dupleks] sm invar (telefono) partyline.

**duplicare** [dupli'kare] v duplicate. **duplicato** agg, sm duplicate. **duplicatore** sm duplicator, copier. **duplice** agg double.

**durare** [du'rare] v last; (cibo) keep; (abiti) wear; (sopportare) endure.

**durata** [du'rata] sf length (of time), duration. **di breve durata** short(-lived), not lasting. **di lunga durata** lasting. **durata di una carica** term of office. **durevole** agg lasting.

**duro** ['duro] agg hard, tough. **aver la pelle dura** be thick-skinned. **aver la testa dura** be stubborn. **tener duro** hold out. **durezza** sf hardness. **durone** sm callus.

**duttile** ['duttile] agg ductile.

# E

**e** [e], **ed** cong and; (invece) and then. **e ... e** both ... and .... **tutti e due** both (of them). **tutti e tre** all three (of them).

**ebano** ['ɛbano] sm ebony. **d'ebano** (colore) jet-black. **ebanista** sm cabinet-maker.

**ebbene** [eb'bɛne] cong well (then).

**ebbro** ['ebbro] agg intoxicated, drunk. **ebbrezza** sf intoxication; (fig) rapture, elation.

**ebdomadario** [ebdoma'darjo] agg, sm weekly.

**ebete** ['ɛbete] agg dull-witted.

**ebollizione** [ebolli'tsjone] sf boiling. **punto di ebollizione** sm boiling point.

**ebraico** [e'braiko] agg Jewish, Hebrew. sm (lingua) Hebrew.

**ebreo** [e'brɛo], **-a** sm, sf Jew. agg Jewish.

**eccedere** [et'tʃedere] v exceed; surpass. **eccedere i limiti** go too far.

*****eccellere** [et'tʃɛllere] v excel, be outstanding. **eccellente** agg excellent. **eccellenza** sf excellence; (titolo) Excellency. **per eccellenza** par excellence.

**eccentrico** [et'tʃentriko] agg, sm eccentric. **eccentricità** sf eccentricity.

**eccepibile** [ettʃe'pibile] agg objectionable. **eccepire** v take exception (to), object (to).

**eccesso** [et'tʃɛsso] sm excess. **all'eccesso** excessively, to a fault. **eccesso di velocità** speeding. **eccessivo** agg excessive, exaggerated.

**eccetera** [et'tʃetera] etcetera, and so forth or on.

**eccetto** [et'tʃɛtto] prep except. **eccetto che** (tranne che) except for, but for; (a meno che) unless.

**eccettuare** [ettʃettu'are] v except, leave out.

**eccezione** [ettʃe'tsjone] sf exception. **ad eccezione di** except for. **eccezionale** agg exceptional.

**eccidio** [et'tʃidjo] sm slaughter.

**eccitare** [ettʃi'tare] v excite, stimulate; (provocare) stir up, rouse. **eccitamento** sm excitement; (stimolo) incitement. **eccitante** sm stimulant. **eccitazione** sf excitement.

**ecclesiastico** [ekkle'zjastiko] agg clerical, ecclesiastic(al). sm clergyman.

**ecco** ['ɛkko] avv this or that is; (qui) here is; (lì) there is. **ecco fatto** that is that. **ecco tutto** that is all.

**eccome** [ek'kome] avv, inter and how, certainly.

**echeggiare** [eked'dʒare] v echo; (risonare) resound.

**eclettico** [e'klettiko] agg eclectic.

**eclissare** [eklis'sare] v eclipse. **eclisse** or **eclissi** sf eclipse.

**eco** ['ɛko] s(m+f), pl **-i** m echo. **echi di cronaca** gossip (column) sing. **far eco a** echo.

**ecologia** [ekolo'dʒia] sf ecology. **ecologico** agg ecological. **ecologo**, **-a** sm, sf ecologist.

**economia** [ekono'mia] sf economy; (risparmio) thrift, saving; (scienza) economics. **fare economie** economize, save. **economico** agg economic; (a bassa spesa) economical, cheap.

**economizzare** [ekonomid'dzare] v economize, save.

**economo** [e'kɔnomo] sm steward, supply officer.

**ed** [ed] V **e**.

**edera** ['edera] sf ivy.

**edibile** [e'dibile] agg edible.

**edicola** [e'dikola] sf bookstall.

**edificare** [edifi'kare] v (erigere) construct; (stimolare al bene) edify. **edificante** agg edifying. **edificio** sm building; (fig) structure.

**edile** [e'dile] agg building. sm builder. **edilizia** sf building trade. **edilizio** agg building.

**Edimburgo** [edim'burgo] sf Edinburgh.

**editore** [edi'tore], **-trice** sm, sf publisher. agg publishing. **edito** agg published.

**editto** [e'ditto] sm edict.

**edizione** [edi'tsjone] sf edition; (tiratura) issue.

**educare** [edu'kare] v educate; (ammaestrare) train. **educativo** agg educational. **educato** agg (cortese) polite. **bene/male educato** well-/ill-mannered. **educazione** sf education, upbringing; training; (comportamento) manners pl, breeding.

**effeminato** [effemi'nato] agg effeminate. **effeminatezza** sf effeminacy.

**effervescente** [efferve'ʃɛnte] agg effervescent, sparkling.

**effetto** [ef'fɛtto] sm effect; (conseguenza) result; impression; (comm) bill. **effetto serra** greenhouse effect. **aver effetto** take effect. **dare effetto a** carry out. **fare effetto** work. **fare l'effetto di** give the impression of.

**effettuare** [effettu'are] v effect, bring about; (realizzare) carry out; (fare) make. **effettuabile** agg feasible. **effettuazione** sf execution.

**efficace** [effi'katʃe] agg effective, efficient. **efficacia** sf efficacy, effectiveness; force.

**efficiente** [effi'tʃɛnte] agg efficient. **efficienza** sf efficiency, effectiveness; (mec) working order.

**effigie** [ef'fidʒe] sf effigy; image.

**effimero** [ef'fimero] agg ephemeral.

**effluente** [efflu'ɛnte] sm effluent, sewage. **efflusso** sm outflow.

**egida** ['ɛdʒida] sf aegis.

**Egitto** [e'dʒitto] sm Egypt. **egiziano, -a** s, agg Egyptian. **egizio, -a** s, agg (ancient) Egyptian.

**egli** ['eʎi] pron he.

**egocentrico** [ego'tʃɛntriko] agg egocentric, self-centred.

**egoista** [ego'ista] s(m+f) egoist, selfish person. **egoistico** agg egoistic(al), selfish.

**egotista** [ego'tista] s(m+f) egotist, boaster. **egotistico** agg egotistic(al).

**egregio** [e'grɛdʒo] agg distinguished; (in lettere) dear.

**eguale** [e'gwale] V **uguale**.

**egualitario** [egwali'tarjo], **-a** s, agg egalitarian.

**eiettore** [ejet'tore] sm ejector. **sedile eiettore** sm ejector seat.

**elaborare** [elabo'rare] v elaborate, devise; (dati) process. **elaborato** agg elaborate. **elaboratore** sm (elettronico) computer; (dati) processor. **elaborazione** sf preparation, formulation; (dati) processing.

**elargire** [elar'dʒire] v lavish.

**elastico** [e'lastiko] agg elastic; (molleggiante) springy; (fig) flexible; (agile) nimble. sm elastic; (anello) elastic band; (materasso) spring.

**elefante** [ele'fante] sm elephant. **elefantesco** agg elephantine.

**elegante** [ele'gante] agg elegant; (vestito) smart; (fine) graceful; (ingegnoso) neat. **eleganza** sf elegance; smartness, stylishness.

**\*eleggere** [e'lɛddʒere] v elect, nominate. **eleggibile** agg eligible. **eleggibilità** sf eligibility.

**elegia** [ele'dʒia] sf elegy. **elegiaco** agg elegiac.

**elemento** [ele'mento] sm element; (individuo) fellow, individual. **elementare** agg elementary; (naturale) elemental.

**elemosina** [ele'mɔzina] sf alms, charity. **chiedere l'elemosina** beg. **fare l'elemosina** give alms.

**elenco** [e'lɛnko] sm list; (telefonico) directory; (iscritti) register. **elencare** v list; enumerate.

**eletto** [e'lɛtto] agg chosen; (scelto) select; (nominato) elected.

**elettorale** [eletto'rale] agg electoral, election. **collegio elettorale** sm constituency. **propaganda elettorale** sf electioneering. **scheda/urna elettorale** sf ballot-paper/box. **elettorato** sm electorate; (diritto di *eleggere*) franchise.

**elettore** [elet'tore], **-trice** *sm*, *sf* elector, voter; (*di collegio elettorale*) constituent.

**elettrico** [e'lɛttriko] *agg* electric(al). **elettricista** *sm* electrician. **elettricità** *sf* electricity.

**elettrificare** [elettrifi'kare] *v* electrify. **elettrificazione** *sf* electrification.

**elettrizzare** [elettrid'dzare] *v* electrify; (*fig*) thrill.

**elettrodo** [e'lɛttrodo] *sm* electrode.

**elettrodomestico** [elettrodo'mɛstiko] *sm* electric appliance.

**elettrodotto** [elettro'dotto] *sm* power line, mains.

**elettrolisi** [elet'trɔlizi] *sf* electrolysis. **elettrolitico** *agg* electrolytic.

**elettrone** [elet'trone] *sm* electron. **elettronica** *sf* electronics. **elettronico** *agg* electronic.

**elettrotecnico** [elettro'tɛkniko] *sm* electrical engineer.

**elevare** [ele'vare] *v* raise. **elevato** *agg* high; (*fig*) lofty. **elevazione** *sf* elevation; (*atto di alzare*) raising.

**elezione** [ele'tsjone] *sf* election. **elezioni politiche** general election *sing*.

**elica** ['ɛlika] *sf* propeller. **elicottero** *sm* helicopter.

**eliminare** [elimi'nare] *v* eliminate; (*escludere*) rule out. **eliminatoria** *sf* (*sport*) qualifying round. **eliminazione** *sf* elimination; exclusion.

**elio** ['ɛljo] *sm* helium.

**ella** ['ella] *pron* she; (*formula di cortesia*) you.

**ellisse** [el'lisse] *sf* ellipse. **ellittico** *agg* elliptical.

**elmetto** [el'metto] *sm also* **elmo** helmet.

**elogio** [e'lɔdʒo] *sm* praise. **elogiare** *v* praise.

**eloquente** [elo'kwɛnte] *agg* eloquent; (*significativo*) meaningful. **eloquenza** *sf* eloquence.

**elsa** ['elsa] *sf* hilt.

**\*eludere** [e'ludere] *v* elude, dodge, evade.

**emaciato** [ema'tʃato] *agg* emaciated.

**emanare** [ema'nare] *v* emanate; (*diffondere*) give off, send out; (*promulgare*) issue. **emanazione** *sf* emanation; promulgation.

**emancipare** [emantʃi'pare] *v* emancipate. **emancipazione** *sf* emancipation.

**embargo** [em'bargo] *sm* embargo.

**emblema** [em'blɛma] *sm* emblem; symbol, model. **emblematico** *agg* emblematic, symbolic.

**embolia** [embo'lia] *sf* embolism. **embolo** *sm* embolus.

**embrione** [embri'one] *sm* embryo. **embrionale** *agg* embryonic.

**emendare** [emen'dare] *v* amend. **emendamento** *sm* amendment.

**emergenza** [emer'dʒɛntsa] *sf* emergency.

**\*emergere** [e'mɛrdʒere] *v* emerge; (*distinguersi*) stand out; (*apparire*) appear.

**\*emettere** [e'mettere] *v* emit, give out; (*ordine, azioni*) issue; (*giudizio*) deliver; (*grido*) utter.

**emicrania** [emi'krania] *sf* migraine.

**emigrare** [emi'grare] *v* emigrate; (*animali*) migrate. **emigrante** *s(m+f)* emigrant. **emigrato, -a** *sm*, *sf* emigrant; (*pol*) exile. **emigrazione** *sf* emigration, migration; (*econ*) flight.

**eminente** [emi'nɛnte] *agg* eminent, distinguished; (*elevato*) high. **eminenza** *sf* eminence.

**emisfero** [emis'fɛro] *sm* hemisphere. **emisferico** *agg* hemispheric(al).

**emissario¹** [emis'sarjo] *sm* (*mandatario*) emissary.

**emissario²** [emis'sarjo] *sm* (*canale, ecc.*) outlet.

**emissione** [emis'sjone] *sf* emission; (*econ*) issue. **emittente** *agg* issuing; (*radio*) transmitting.

**emolliente** [emol'ljɛnte] *sm*, *agg* emollient.

**emorragia** [emorra'dʒia] *sf* haemorrhage, bleeding.

**emorroidi** [emor'rɔidi] *sf pl* piles *pl*.

**emotivo** [emo'tivo] *agg* emotional; (*impressionabile*) excitable; (*che provoca emozione*) emotive, thrilling.

**emozione** [emo'tsjone] *sf* emotion; excitement. **emozionale** *agg* emotive. **emozionante** *agg* exciting. **emozionare** *v* excite; (*commuovere*) move.

**empio** ['empjo] *agg* impious; (*crudele*) cruel.

**empire** [em'pire] *v* fill.

**empirico** [em'piriko] *agg* empirical.

**emporio** [em'pɔrjo] *sm* store.

**emù** [e'mu] *sm* emu.

**emulare** [emu'lare] *v* emulate. **emulazione** *sf* rivalry; *(dir)* nuisance.

**emulsione** [emul'sjone] *sf* emulsion.

**enciclopedia** [entʃiklope'dia] *sf* encyclopedia. **enciclopedico** *agg* encyclopedic.

**encomio** [en'kɔmjo] *sm* praise. **encomiabile** *agg* praiseworthy.

**endemico** [en'dɛmiko] *agg* endemic.

**energia** [ener'dʒia] *sf* energy. **energetico** *sm, agg* tonic. **energico** *agg* energetic; *(forte)* forceful, strong.

**enfasi** ['ɛnfazi] *sf* emphasis *(pl* -ses). **enfatico** *agg* emphatic.

**enfiare** [en'fjare] *v* swell, inflate.

**enigma** [e'nigma] *sm* puzzle, riddle; *(mistero, persona misteriosa)* enigma, mystery. **enigmatico** *agg* puzzling; mysterious.

**ennesimo** [en'nɛzimo] *agg* nth; *(fam)* umpteenth.

**enorme** [e'norme] *agg* enormous, huge. **enormità** *sf (causa di indignazione)* enormity; *(errore)* blunder.

**ente** ['ɛnte] *sm (filos)* being; *(azienda)* undertaking, concern; authority; *(istituzione)* body.

**enteroclisi** [entero'klizi] *sm* enema.

**entità** [enti'ta] *sf* entity; importance; *(consistenza)* extent.

**entrambi** [en'trambi] *agg, pron* both.

**entrare** [en'trare] *v* enter; *(andar dentro)* go in(to); *(con difficoltà)* get in(to); *(venir dentro)* come in(to); *(associarsi)* join. **entrare in ballo** come into play. **entrare in vigore** come into effect.

**entrata** [en'trata] *sf* entrance, entry; *(accesso)* admission. **entrate** *sf pl (redditi)* income *sing*, earnings *pl*; *(incassi)* receipts *pl*; *(di enti pubblici)* revenue *sing*.

**entro** ['entro] *prep* within; *(ora/data precisata)* by. **entro oggi** before the day is out.

**entusiasmo** [entu'zjazmo] *sm* enthusiasm. **entusiasmare** *v* thrill, excite. **entusiasta** *s(m+f)* enthusiast. **entusiastico** *agg* enthusiastic.

**enumerare** [enume'rare] *v* list. **enumerazione** *sf* listing; list.

**enunciare** [enun'tʃare] *v* enunciate; *(esprimere)* express; formulate.

**enzima** [en'dzima] *sm* enzyme.

**epatite** [epa'tite] *sf* hepatitis.

**epico** ['ɛpiko] *agg* epic, heroic. **epica** *sf* epic poetry.

**epidemia** [epide'mia] *sf* epidemic. **epidemico** *agg* epidemic.

**Epifania** [epifa'nia] *sf* Epiphany; *(festa)* Twelfth Night.

**epigramma** [epi'gramma] *sm* epigram. **epigrammatico** *agg* epigrammatic.

**epilessia** [epiles'sia] *sf* epilepsy. **epilettico, -a** *s, agg* epileptic.

**epilogo** [e'pilogo] *sm, pl* -ghi epilogue; *(fig)* end, conclusion.

**episodio** [epi'zɔdjo] *sm* episode. **episodico** *agg* episodic; *(frammentario)* bitty; *(accidentale)* incidental; isolated.

**epistola** [e'pistola] *sf* epistle. **epistolare** *agg* epistolary.

**epitaffio** [epi'taffjo] *sm* epitaph.

**epiteto** [e'piteto] *sm* epithet.

**epoca** ['ɛpoka] *sf* period; *(tempo)* time. **a quell'epoca** at that time. **che fa epoca** epoch-making. **da quell'epoca** from that time on, since then.

**eppure** [ep'pure] *cong* and yet.

**epurare** [epu'rare] *v* purge. **epurazione** *sf* purging; purge.

**equanime** [e'kwanime] *agg (imparziale)* fair; *(sereno)* even-tempered. **equanimità** *sf* fairness, equanimity.

**equatore** [ekwa'tore] *sm* equator. **equatoriale** *agg* equatorial.

**equazione** [ekwa'tsjone] *sf* equation.

**equestre** [e'kwɛstre] *agg* equestrian.

**equilibrare** [ekwili'brare] *v* balance. **equilibrio** *sm* balance, equilibrium; moderation, common sense; *(padronanza di sé)* poise. **perdere l'equilibrio** lose one's balance. **tenere in equilibrio** balance. **tenersi in equilibrio** keep one's balance. **equilibrista** *s(m+f)* acrobat.

**equinozio** [ekwi'nɔtsjo] *sm* equinox.

**equipaggiare** [ekwipad'dʒare] *v (fornire)* equip; *(nave)* man. **equipaggiamento** *sm* kit. **equipaggio** *sm* crew.

**equiparare** [ekwipa'rare] *v* level.

**equitazione** [ekwita'tsjone] *sf* (horse-)riding.

**\*equivalere** [ekwiva'lere] *v* be equivalent, correspond. **equivalente** *sm, agg* equivalent.

**equivoco** [e'kwivoko] *sm (errore)* mistake; *(malinteso)* misunderstanding. **a scanso di equivoci** to avoid misunderstandings. *agg* ambiguous; *(di dubbia moralità)* questionable, shady. **non equivoco** unambiguous, straightforward.

**equo** ['ɛkwo] *agg* fair.

**era** ['ɛra] *sf* era, age.

**erario** [e'rarjo] *sm* Treasury. **erariale** *agg* fiscal.

**erba** ['ɛrba] *sf* grass; (*gastr*) herb. **in erba** green; (*fig*) budding. **erbaceo** *agg* herbaceous.

**erbaccia** [er'battʃa] *sf* weed.

**erbicida** [erbi'tʃida] *sm* herbicide, weedkiller.

**erbivendolo** [erbi'vendolo], **-a** *sm, sf* greengrocer.

**erbivoro** [er'bivoro] *sm* herbivore. *agg* herbivorous.

**erede** [e'rɛde] *s(m+f)* heir, heiress. **erede apparente** heir presumptive. **erede universale** sole heir.

**eredità** [eredi'ta] *sf* inheritance, heritage. **ereditare** *v* inherit. **ereditario** *agg* inherited, hereditary. **principe ereditario** *sm* crown prince. **ereditiera** *sf* heiress.

**eremita** [ere'mita] *sm* hermit. **eremitaggio** *sm* hermitage.

**eretico** [e'rɛtiko], **-a** *sm, sf* heretic. *agg* heretical. **eresia** *sf* heresy; (*fam: sproposito*) rubbish.

**eretto** [e'rɛtto] *agg* erect, upright. **erettile** *agg* erectile.

**erezione** [ere'tsjone] *sf* erection.

**ergastolo** [er'gastolo] *sm* life imprisonment *or* sentence.

**erica** ['ɛrika] *sf* heather.

\***erigere** [e'ridʒere] *v* raise, erect; (*fondare, considerare*) set up.

**ermellino** [ermel'lino] *sm* ermine; (*bruno*) stoat.

**ermetico** [er'mɛtiko] *agg* (*aria*) airtight; (*acqua*) watertight; obscure.

**ernia** ['ɛrnja] *sf* hernia, rupture.

\***erodere** [e'rodere] *v* erode.

**eroe** [e'rɔe] *sm* hero. **eroico** *agg* heroic. **eroina** *sf* heroine. **eroismo** *sm* heroism; (*atto*) heroic deed.

**erogare** [ero'gare] *v* distribute, deliver; (*in donazione*) donate. **erogazione** *sf* distribution, delivery; donation.

**eroina** [ero'ina] *sf* (*stupefacente*) heroin.

**erosione** [ero'zjone] *sf* erosion.

**erotico** [e'rɔtiko] *agg* erotic. **erotismo**

*sm* eroticism.

**erpete** ['ɛrpete] *sm* herpes.

**erpice** ['erpitʃe] *sm* harrow.

**errare** [er'rare] *v* (*andare senza meta*) roam, wander; (*sbagliare*) err, be mistaken. **erratico** *agg* erratic. **errato** *agg* incorrect. **se non vado errato** if I am not mistaken.

**erroneo** [er'rɔneo] *agg* erroneous, wrong.

**errore** [er'rore] *sm* mistake, error. **errore giudiziario** miscarriage of justice. **per errore** by mistake, in error.

**erudito** [eru'dito] *agg* erudite, learned. **erudizione** *sf* learning.

**eruttare** [erut'tare] *v* (*ruttare*) belch; (*vulcano*) erupt; (*fig*) spew out. **eruzione** *sf* eruption.

**esacerbare** [ezatʃer'bare] *v* exacerbate.

**esagerare** [ezadʒe'rare] *v* exaggerate; (*caricare*) overdo. **esagerazione** *sf* exaggeration.

**esagono** [e'zagono] *sm* hexagon. **esagonale** *agg* hexagonal.

**esalare** [eza'lare] *v* exhale, give off. **esalazione** *sf* exhalation.

**esaltare** [ezal'tare] *v* exalt; (*lodare*) extol; (*entusiasmare*) thrill, stir. **esaltato, -a** *sm, sf* fanatic, hot-head.

**esame** [e'zame] *sm* examination, test; (*controllo*) inspection, check. **dare un esame** take an examination. **prendere in esame** consider, take into consideration.

**esaminare** [ezami'nare] *v* examine, test, check.

**esanime** [e'zanime] *agg* lifeless.

**esasperare** [ezaspe'rare] *v* (*irritare*) exasperate; (*inasprire*) sharpen, increase. **esasperazione** *sf* exasperation; sharpening, increase.

**esatto** [e'zatto] *agg* exact; correct; accurate; punctual. *avv* (*in punto*) exactly. **esattezza** *sf* exactness; accuracy, precision.

**esattore** [ezat'tore] *sm* (*tassa*) collector. **esattoria** *sf* tax office.

**esaudire** [ezau'dire] *v* grant.

**esaurire** [ezau'rire] *v* exhaust, use up; (*vendere completamente*) sell out; (*condurre a termine*) complete. **esaurirsi** *v* (*debilitarsi*) wear oneself out.

**esca** ['eska] *sf* bait; (*fig*) lure; (*per accendere*) tinder. **dar esca a** a fan, stir up.

**escandescenza** [eskande'ʃɛntsa] *sf* **dare in escandescenze** flare up; (*fam*) fly off the handle.

**escapismo** [eska'pismo] *sm* escapism.

**eschimese** [eski'meze] *s(m+f)*, *agg* Eskimo.

**esclamare** [eskla'mare] *v* exclaim, cry out. **punto esclamativo** *sm* exclamation mark. **esclamazione** *sf* exclamation.

**\*escludere** [es'kludere] *v* exclude. **esclusione** *sf* exclusion. **ad esclusione di** except.

**esclusivo** [esklu'zivo] *agg* exclusive. **esclusiva** *(comm)* exclusive or sole right; *(rappresentenza)* sole agency. **escluso** *agg* excluded, impossible; *(eccettuato)* except; *(non compreso)* exclusive of, not including.

**escogitare** [eskodʒi'tare] *v* devise, think up.

**escursione** [eskur'sjone] *v* excursion, trip; *(a macchina)* drive; *(a piedi)* hike. **escursionista** *s(m+f)* tripper; hiker.

**esecutivo** [ezeku'tivo] *sm*, *agg* executive.

**esecutore** [ezeku'tore], **-trice** *sm*, *sf* *(dir)* executor; *(musica)* performer; *(carnefice)* executioner.

**esecuzione** [ezeku'tsjone] *sf* execution, performance.

**eseguire** [eze'gwire] *v* carry out; *(musica, teatro)* perform; *(dir)* execute.

**esempio** [e'zɛmpjo] *sm* example; model. **ad** or **per esempio** for instance. **dare l'esempio** set an example.

**esemplare** [ezem'plare] *agg* exemplary. *sm* example, model; *(tipico)* specimen. **esemplificare** *v* exemplify, illustrate.

**esentare** [ezen'tare] *v* exempt. **esentarsi da** get out of. **esente** *agg* exempt, free. **esenzione** *sf* exemption.

**esequie** [e'zɛkwje] *sf pl* *(cerimonie)* funeral rites *pl*; funeral *sing*.

**esercente** [ezer'tʃɛnte] *s(m+f)* retailer; *(negoziante)* shopkeeper. **esercire** *v* manage, run.

**esercitare** [ezertʃi'tare] *v* practise; *(usare)* exercise. **esercitazione** *sf* practice; exercise; *(mil)* drill. **esercizio** *sm* exercise; *(attività)* practice; *(azienda)* concern.

**esibire** [ezi'bire] *v* exhibit. **esibirsi** *v* *(dar spettacolo)* perform; *(mettersi in mostra)* show off. **esibizione** *sf* exhibition, show, display. **esibizionismo** *sm* exhibitionism. **esibizionista** *s(m+f)* exhibitionist.

**\*esigere** [e'zidʒere] *v* require, need, demand. **esigente** *agg* exacting. **esigenza** *sf* requirement; *(necessità)* need; *(pretesa)* demand. **esiguo** *agg* meagre.

**esilarante** [ezila'rante] *agg* exhilarating.

**esile** ['ɛzile] *agg* slender; *(debole)* feeble.

**esiliare** [ezi'ljare] *v* exile. **esiliarsi** *v* go into exile. **esiliato**, **-a** *sm*, *sf* exile. **esilio** *sm* exile.

**\*esimere** [e'zimere] *v* exempt, free.

**esimio** [e'zimjo] *agg* distinguished, outstanding.

**esistenzialismo** [ezistentsja'lizmo] *sm* existentialism. **esistenzialista** *s(m+f)*, *agg* existentialist.

**esistere** [e'zistere] *v* exist, be. **esistente** *agg* existing. **esistenza** *sf* existence. **esistenza di cassa/magazzino** *(comm)* cash/stock in hand.

**esitare** [ezi'tare] *v* hesitate. **esitazione** *sf* hesitation.

**esito** ['ɛzito] *sm* outcome; *(dramma)* denouement. **buon esito** success.

**esodo** ['ɛzɔdo] *sm* exodus.

**esofago** [e'zɔfago] *sm* oesophagus; gullet.

**esonerare** [ezone'rare] *v* exempt. **esonero** *sm* exemption.

**esorbitante** [ezorbi'tante] *agg* exorbitant.

**esorcizzare** [ezortʃid'dzare] *v* exorcise. **esorcismo** *sm* exorcism.

**esordire** [ezor'dire] *v* start out; *(artista)* make one's debut. **esordio** *sm* start, debut.

**esortare** [ezor'tare] *v* urge. **esortazione** *sf* exhortation, encouragement.

**esoso** [e'zɔzo] *agg* *(avido)* greedy; exorbitant; odious.

**esoterico** [ezo'tɛriko] *agg* esoteric.

**esotico** [e'zɔtiko] *agg* exotic.

**\*espandere** [es'pandere] *v* expand, extend. **espandersi** *v* spread. **espansione** *sf* expansion; *(effusione d'affetto)* effusiveness. **espansivo** *agg* effusive; *(forza)* expansive.

**espatriare** [espa'trjare] *v* emigrate. **espatrio** *sm* expatriation.

**espediente** [espe'djɛnte] *sm* expedient, device; *(soluzione)* way out. **vivere di espedienti** live on one's wits.

**\*espellere** [es'pɛllere] *v* expel.

**esperienza** [espe'rjɛntsa] *sf* experience; experiment; *(conoscenza)* familiarity. **fare esperienza di** experience. **senza esperienza** inexperienced.

**esperimento** [esperi'mento] *sm* experiment; *(tentativo)* trial, test.

**esperto** [es'pɛrto], **-a** *sm*, *sf* expert, authori-

**ty.** *agg* expert (in); (*abile*) skilful (at); experienced (in).

**espiare** [espi'are] *v* expiate, atone. **capro espiatorio** *sm* scapegoat.

**espletare** [esple'tare] *v* accomplish.

**esplicito** [es'plitʃito] *agg* explicit. **esplicativo** *agg* explanatory.

**\*esplodere** [es'plɔdere] *v* explode. **far esplodere** explode, blow up.

**esplorare** [esplo'rare] *v* explore; (*investigare*) probe. **esploratore, -trice** *sm, sf* explorer; (*mil*) scout. **giovani esploratori** Boy Scouts *pl.* **esplorazione** *sf* exploration; (*mil*) reconnaissance.

**esplosione** [esplo'zjone] *sf* explosion.

**esplosivo** [esplo'zivo] *sm, agg* explosive.

**esponente** [espo'nɛnte] *sm* exponent; representative. **esponenziale** *agg* exponential.

**\*esporre** [es'porre] *v* expose; (*arrischiare*) risk; (*spiegare*) expound; (*mostrare*) exhibit, display.

**esportare** [espor'tare] *v* export. **esportatore, -trice** *sm, sf* exporter. **esportazione** *sf* export.

**esposizione** [espozi'tsjone] *sf* exhibition, show; (*spiegazione*) explanation; (*posizione, foto*) exposure.

**esposto** [es'posto] *agg* exhibited, displayed; exposed. *sm* statement.

**espressione** [espres'sjone] *sf* expression. **espressivo** *agg* expressive, eloquent.

**espresso** [es'prɛsso] *agg* express; (*manifestato*) expressed; (*dichiarato*) avowed, declared. **piatto espresso** *sm* specially prepared dish. *sm* (*lettera*) express letter; (*caffè*) espresso; (*ferr*) express train.

**\*esprimere** [es'primere] *v* express.

**espulsione** [espul'sjone] *sf* expulsion.

**essa** ['essa] *pron* (*persona: soggetto*) she; (*persona: oggetto*) her; (*cosa, animale*) it.

**esse** ['esse] *pron* (*soggetto*) they; (*oggetto*) them.

**essenza** [es'sɛntsa] *sf* essence. **essenziale** *agg* essential.

**\*essere** ['essere] *v* be; (*ausiliare con forma attiva*) have. *sm* being; (*fam*) person, creature; (*condizione*) existence.

**essi** ['essi] *pron* (*soggetto*) they; (*oggetto*) them.

**essiccare** [essik'kare] *v* dry. **essiccatoio** *sm* dryer.

**esso** ['esso] *pron* (*persona: soggetto*) he; (*persona: oggetto*) him; (*cosa, animale*) it.

**est** [est] *sm* east. **dell'est** east, eastern.

**estasi** ['ɛstazi] *sf* ecstasy. **estatico** *agg* ecstatic.

**estate** [es'tate] *sf* summer. **estate di San Martino** Indian summer.

**\*estendere** [es'tɛndere] *v* extend, stretch; (*ampliare*) broaden. **estendersi** *v* (*stendersi*) stretch; (*diffondersi*) spread.

**estensione** [esten'sjone] *sf* extension; (*dimensione*) extent; (*distesa*) expanse; (*fig, musica*) range; (*significato*) wider sense.

**estenuare** [estenu'are] *v* exhaust. **estenuante** *agg* exhausting, wearing.

**esteriore** [este'rjore] *agg* outer, exterior, external. *sm* (*parte esterna*) outside; (*apparenze*) appearances *pl.*

**esterno** [es'tɛrno] *agg* external, outer, exterior. *sm* outside; (*scolaro*) day-boy; (*film*) exterior.

**estero** ['ɛstero] *agg* foreign. *sm* foreign countries *pl.* **all'estero** abroad.

**esterrefatto** [esterre'fatto] *agg* (*atterrito*) aghast, horrified; (*sbigottito*) amazed.

**esteso** [es'tezo] *agg* large, wide-ranging; (*fig*) thorough. **per esteso** in full.

**estetica** [es'tɛtika] *sf* aesthetics. **estetico** *agg* aesthetic.

**estetista** [este'tista] *s(m+f)* beauty specialist, beautician.

**\*estinguere** [es'tingwere] *v* put out; (*far svanire*) extinguish; (*econ*) wipe out; (*debito*) pay off; (*sete*) quench. **estinguersi** *v* die out. **estinto** *agg* extinguished; (*scomparso*) extinct. **estinzione** *sf.* extinction; (*sete*) quenching; (*econ*) discharge.

**estirpare** [estir'pare] *v* eradicate.

**estivo** [es'tivo] *agg* summer.

**\*estorcere** [es'tɔrtʃere] *v* extort. **estorsione** *sf* extortion.

**Estonia** [es'tɔnja] *sf* Estonia. **estone** *agg* Estonian.

**estradare** [estra'dare] *v* extradite. **estradizione** *sf* extradition.

**estraneo** [es'traneo] *agg* extraneous, unrelated (to), unconnected (with); (*alieno*) foreign. **essere estraneo a** have no part in. **mantenersi estraneo a** have nothing to do with, keep clear of. *sm* stranger; unauthorized person. **estraniare** *v* estrange.

**\*estrarre** [es'trarre] *v* extract, draw (out);

(*miniera*) mine; (*cava*) quarry. **estratto** *sm* extract; (*compendio*) abstract; (*stralcio*) excerpt. **estrazione** *sf* extraction.

**estremo** [es'trɛmo] *agg* extreme; (*ultimo*) final; (*grandissimo*) utmost. *sm* extreme; (*colmo*) height; (*estremità*) end, tip. **estremi** *sm pl* particulars *pl*; (*dir*) essential elements *pl*. **estremismo** *sm* extremism. **estremista** *s(m+f)* extremist.

**estro** ['ɛstro] *sm* (*ghiribizzo*) whim, fancy; (*impulso*) inspiration; (*venereo*) heat. **estroso** *agg* whimsical, capricious; inspired.

**estrogeno** [es'trɔdʒeno] *sm* oestrogen.

**estroverso** [estro'vɛrso], **-a** *sm, sf* extrovert. *agg* extroverted.

**estuario** [estu'arjo] *sm* estuary.

**esuberante** [ezube'rante] *agg* exuberant. **esuberanza** *sf* exuberance.

**esule** ['ɛzule] *s(m+f)* exile. **esulare** *v* lie outside, be beyond.

**esultare** [ezul'tare] *v* rejoice. **esultante** *agg* exultant.

**esumare** [ezu'mare] *v* exhume; (*fig*) unearth.

**età** [e'ta] *v* age. **all'età di dieci anni** at (the age of) ten. **età della ragione** age of discretion.

**etere** ['ɛtere] *sm* ether.

**eterno** [e'tɛrno] *agg* eternal, everlasting; (*lunghissimo*) interminable. **eternità** *sm* eternity; (*molto tempo*) ages *pl*.

**eterodosso** [etero'dɔsso] *agg* heterodox.

**eterogeneo** [etero'dʒɛneo] *agg* heterogeneous.

**etica** ['ɛtika] *sf* ethics. **etico** *agg* ethical.

**etichetta**[1] [eti'ketta] *sf* (*cartellino*) label.

**etichetta**[2] [eti'ketta] *sf* (*regole*) etiquette.

**etimologia** [etimolo'dʒia] *sf* etymology. **etimologico** *agg* etymological.

**etnico** ['ɛtniko] *agg* ethnic.

**ettaro** ['ɛttaro] *sm* hectare.

**etto** ['ɛtto] *sm* hundred grams.

**eucalipto** [euka'lipto] *sm* eucalyptus.

**eufemismo** [eufe'mizmo] *sm* euphemism. **eufemistico** *agg* euphemistic.

**eunuco** [eu'nuko] *sm*, *pl* **-chi** eunuch.

**Europa** [eu'rɔpa] *sf* Europe. **europeo, -a** *s, agg* European.

**eutanasia** [eutana'zia] *sf* euthanasia.

**evacuare** [evaku'are] *v* evacuate.

**\*evadere** [e'vadere] *v* escape (from); (*sbrigare*) dispatch; (*fattura*) settle; (*ordini*) execute; (*fisco*) avoid.

**evanescente** [evane'ʃɛnte] *agg* (*suono*) fading; (*fugace*) fleeting; (*crema*) vanishing.

**evangelista** [evandʒe'lista] *sm* evangelist. **evangelico** *agg* evangelical.

**evaporare** [evapo'rare] *v* evaporate. **evaporatore** *sm* humidifier. **evaporazione** *sf* evaporation.

**evasione** [eva'zjone] *sf* escape; (*fisco*) evasion; (*comm*) execution.

**evasivo** [eva'zivo] *agg* evasive.

**evaso** [e'vazo], **-a** *agg* escaped; (*comm*) dispatched, dealt with. *sm, sf* fugitive, escaped convict.

**evento** [e'vɛnto] *sm* event; (*eventualità*) eventuality. **in ogni evento** in any case, at all events.

**eventuale** [eventu'ale] *agg* possible, any. **eventualità** *sf* eventuality. **nell'eventualità di** *or* **che** in the event of. **eventualmente** *cong* if, in case.

**evidente** [evi'dente] *agg* obvious, manifest, clear; (*irrefutabile*) unmistakable. **evidenza** *sf* (*chiarezza*) clarity, obviousness. **mettere in evidenza** stress, emphasize. **mettersi in evidenza** make oneself conspicuous, draw attention to oneself. **tenere un'evidenza** (*comm*) keep pending.

**evitare** [evi'tare] *v* avoid; (*non arrecare*) spare, save.

**evo** ['evo] *sm* **Medio Evo** Middle Ages *pl*.

**evocare** [evo'kare] *v* evoke.

**evoluzione** [evolu'tsjone] *sf* evolution. **evoluto** *agg* evolved, fully developed; advanced, progressive.

**evviva** [ev'viva] *inter* hurrah! **evviva ... !** long live ... !

**extra** ['ɛkstra] *agg invar* (*qualità*) first-rate; (*fuori del previsto*) additional. *sm invar* extra.

# F

**fa** [fa] *avv* ago.

**fabbisogno** [fabbi'zoɲo] *sm* requirements *pl*.

**fabbrica** ['fabbrika] *sf* factory; (*officina*)

works; (*edificio*) building. **fabbricante** *sm* manufacturer. **fabbricare** *v* manufacture, produce; (*costruire*) build; (*inventare*) make up. **fabbricato** *sm* building. **fabbricazione** *sf* manufacture, production.

**fabbro** ['fabbro] *sm* (*ferraio*) (black)smith.

**faccenda** [fat'tʃɛnda] *sf* matter; (*caso, circostanza*) business. **faccende domestiche** housework *sing*.

**facchino** [fak'kino] *sm* porter. **facchinaggio** *sm* porterage. **facchinata** *sf* (*lavoro*) drudgery.

**faccia** ['fattʃa] *sf* face; (*lato*) side. **avere una bella/brutta faccia** look well/unwell. **di faccia** opposite. **faccia tosta** (*fam*) cheek, nerve. **in faccia a** opposite. **facciata** *sf* front; (*pagina*) side.

**facezia** [fa'tʃɛtsja] *sf* pleasantry; (*detto spiritoso*) witticism. **faceto** *agg* facetious, witty.

**facile** ['fatʃile] *agg* easy; (*incline*) easily moved, prone. **facilità** *sf* ease, facility; (*l'esser facile*) easiness; (*capacità*) aptitude. **con facilità** with ease, readily; (*lingua*) fluently.

**facilitare** [fatʃili'tare] *v* facilitate; (*aiutare*) help. **facilitazione** *sf* facilitation, making easy. **facilitazioni di pagamento** easy terms *pl*.

**facoltà** [fakol'ta] *sf* faculty; (*potere*) power. **facoltativo** *agg* optional. **facoltoso** *agg* wealthy.

**faggio** ['faddʒo] *sm* beech.

**fagiano** [fa'dʒano] *sm* pheasant.

**fagiolo** [fa'dʒɔlo] *sm* bean. **andare a fagiolo** (*fam*) suit. **fagiolino** *sm* French bean.

**fagotto** [fa'gɔtto] *sm* bundle; (*musica*) bassoon. **far fagotto** pack up.

**falcata** [fal'kata] *sf* step.

**falce** ['faltʃe] *sf* sickle; (*manico lungo*) scythe. **falciare** [fal'tʃare] *v* mow; (*fig*) mow down. **falciatrice** *sf* mower.

**falco** ['falko] *sm* hawk. **falcone** *sm* falcon; (*tec*) derrick.

**falda** ['falda] *sf* (*strato*) layer, sheet; (*di pendio*) foot; (*di cappello*) brim; (*di vestito*) skirt; (*di marsina*) tail.

**falegname** [fale'name] *sm* joiner, carpenter. **falegnameria** *sf* (*arte*) joinery, carpentry; (*bottega*) joiner's shop.

**falena** [fal'lɛna] *sf* moth; (*cenere*) ash; (*persona fatua*) flighty person.

**falla** ['falla] *sf* leak. **aprire/chiudere una falla** spring/stop a leak.

**fallace** [fal'latʃe] *agg* fallacious.

**fallire** [fal'lire] *v* fail; (*non colpire*) miss; (*dir, comm*) go bankrupt. **fallimento** *sm* failure; bankruptcy.

**fallito** [fal'lito], **-a** *agg* unsuccessful. *sm, sf* bankrupt; (*fig*) failure.

**fallo**[1] ['fallo] *sm* (*errore*) fault; (*sport*) foul. **cogliere in fallo** find out. **essere in fallo** be at fault. **senza fallo** without fail, certainly.

**fallo**[2] ['fallo] *sm* (*membro virile*) phallus.

**falò** [fa'lo] *sm* bonfire.

**falsare** [fal'sare] *v* falsify; (*alterare*) distort. **falsario** *sm* (*documenti*) forger; (*monete*) counterfeiter.

**falsariga** [falsa'riga] *sf* (*modello*) pattern; (*norma*) lines *pl*.

**falsificare** [falsifi'kare] *v* falsify; (*arte*) fake. **falsificazione** *sf* falsification, faking; forgery, fake.

**falso** ['falso] *agg* false; (*falsificato*) counterfeit, faked, forged; (*fam*) bogus. *sm* (*non vero*) falsehood; (*reato*) forgery. **giurare il falso** commit perjury.

**fama** ['fama] *sf* fame, reputation.

**fame** ['fame] *sf* hunger; (*carestia*) famine. **aver fame** be hungry. **aver fame di** (*fig*) hunger for. **aver una fame da lupo** be ravenous. **fare la fame** go hungry. **morir di fame** starve to death; (*fig*) be starving.

**famelico** [fa'mɛliko] *agg* ravenous.

**famigerato** [famidʒe'rato] *agg* notorious.

**famiglia** [fa'miʎa] *sf* family. **in famiglia** at home.

**familiare** [famil'jare] *agg* domestic; (*consueto, intimo*) familiar; (*semplice*) informal. *s(m+f)* (*parente*) relative. **familiarità** *sf* familiarity. **familiarizzarsi** *v* familiarize oneself.

**famoso** [fa'moso] *agg* famous, well-known; memorable.

**fanale** [fa'nale] *sm* lamp; (*auto*) light. **fanale anteriore** headlight. **fanale di coda** tail-light.

**fanatico** [fa'natiko], **-a** *agg* fanatical; (*fam: entusiasta*) wild (about). *sm, sf* fanatic; (*tifoso*) fan. **fanatismo** *sm* fanaticism.

**fanciullo** [fan'tʃullo], **-a** *sm, sf* child (*pl* -ren). **fanciullaggine** *sf* childish behaviour. **fanciullesco** *agg* childish, puerile;

(*innocente*) child-like. **fanciullezza** *sf* childhood.

**fandonia** [fan'dɔnja] *sf* nonsense.

**fanfara** [fan'fara] *sf* (brass-)band; (*composizione*) fanfare. **fanfaronata** *sf* boasting. **fanfarone, -a** *sm, sf* boaster.

**fango** ['fango] *sm* mud. **fare i fanghi** take mud-baths. **fangoso** *agg* muddy.

**fannullone** [fannul'lone], **-a** *sm, sf* idler, loafer.

**fantascienza** [fanta'ʃɛntsa] *sf* science fiction.

**fantasia** [fanta'zia] *sf* fantasy; (*capriccio*) fancy; imagination. *agg* (*moda*) fancy, patterned.

**fantasma** [fan'tazma] *sm* ghost, phantom.

**fantasticare** [fantasti'kare] *v* daydream, dream up. **fantastico** *agg* fantastic; (*non reale*) fanciful, strange.

**fante** ['fante] *sm* (*mil*) infantryman; (*carte*) knave, jack. **fanteria** *sf* infantry. **fantino** *sm* jockey.

**fantoccio** [fan'tɔttʃo] *sm* puppet.

**farabutto** [fara'butto] *sm* rascal, rogue.

**faraona** [fara'ona] *sf* guinea-fowl.

**farcire** [far'tʃire] *v* stuff.

**fardello** [far'dello] *sm* burden.

**\*fare** ['fare] *v* (*agire*) do; (*produrre*) make; (*essere*) be; (*avere*) have; (*un mestiere, ecc.*) go in for, practise; (*comportarsi*) play; (*orologio*) say. **farcela** *v* (*riuscire*) manage; (*resistere*) be able to go on. **far attenzione** pay attention. **far bene** do good. **far bene a** be good for. **far chiamare** send for. **far entrare** let in. **fare il pieno** (*auto*) fill up. **far male** (*dolere*) hurt, ache; (*nuocere*) be bad for; (*agire male*) do the wrong thing. **far notare** point out. **fare per** be about to. **far vedere** show. **farsi** *v* (*diventare*) become, grow into; (*convertirsi*) turn into; (*tempo*) get.

**farfalla** [far'falla] *sf* butterfly; (*falena*) moth. **nuoto a farfalla** *sm* butterfly stroke.

**farina** [fa'rina] *sf* flour. **farina gialla** maize meal. **farina integrale** wholemeal. **farinaceo** *agg* floury, starchy. **farinoso** *agg* floury, mealy; (*neve*) powdery.

**faringe** [fa'rindʒe] *sf* pharynx. **faringite** *sf* pharyngitis.

**farmacia** [farma'tʃia] *sf* (*negozio*) chemist's (shop); (*scienza*) pharmacy. **farmacista** *s(m+f)* chemist. **farmaco** *sm* medicine.

**farneticare** [farneti'kare] *v* rave.

**faro** ['faro] *sm* lighthouse; (*lume, fig*) beacon; (*auto*) headlight.

**farragine** [far'radʒine] *sf* muddle, jumble.

**farsa** ['farsa] *sf* farce.

**fascia** ['faʃa] *sf* band; (*benda*) bandage; (*uniforme*) sash; (*postale*) wrapper; (*zona*) strip.

**fasciare** [fa'ʃare] *v* wrap; (*bambini*) swaddle; (*ferita*) dress, bandage.

**fascicolo** [fa'ʃikolo] *sm* (*opuscolo*) pamphlet, booklet; (*numero*) issue.

**fascino** ['faʃino] *sm* charm, fascination.

**fascio** ['faʃo] *sm* bundle, bunch.

**fascismo** [fa'ʃizmo] *sm* fascism. **fascista** *s(m+f)*, *agg* fascist.

**fase** ['faze] *sf* phase; (*auto*) stroke.

**fastidio** [fas'tidjo] *sm* trouble; (*avversione*) dislike; (*cosa fastidiosa*) bother, inconvenience. **dar fastidio** trouble; (*molestare*) annoy, bother. **darsi fastidio** put oneself out. **fastidioso** *agg* troublesome, annoying.

**fasto** ['fasto] *sm* pomp.

**fasullo** [fa'zullo] *agg* (*fam*) bogus, phoney.

**fata** ['fata] *sf* fairy.

**fatale** [fa'tale] *agg* inevitable; (*funesto*) fatal; (*decisivo*) fateful; irresistible.

**fatica** [fa'tika] *sf* (*sforzo*) effort, labour; (*stanchezza, tec*) fatigue. **a fatica** with difficulty. **costar fatica** require an effort. **durare fatica** find it difficult. **reggere alla fatica** stand the strain. **faticare** *v* labour; (*stentare*) have difficulty. **faticoso** *agg* tiring.

**fatta** ['fatta] *sf* kind.

**fattezze** [fat'tettse] *sf pl* features *pl*.

**fattibile** [fat'tibile] *agg* feasible.

**fatto¹** ['fatto] *agg* made, done. **a conti fatti** all things considered. **detto fatto** no sooner said than done. **fatto a macchina/mano** machine-/hand-made. **fatto su misura** tailor-made.

**fatto²** ['fatto] *sm* fact; (*avvenimento*) event; (*azione*) deed; (*affare*) business. **cogliere sul fatto** catch in the act. **dire il fatto suo** have one's say. **fatto compiuto** fait accompli. **fatto sta** the fact remains. **in fatto di** regarding.

**fattore** [fat'tore] *sm* factor; (*capo di fattoria*) steward.

**fattoria** [fatto'ria] *sf* farm, estate.

**fattorino** [fatto'rino] *sm* messenger; (*di*

*negozio*) errand-boy; (*di autobus*) conductor.

**fattura** [fat'tura] *sf* (*confezione*) making; (*lavorazione*) construction, workmanship; (*conto*) bill; (*comm*) invoice. **fatturare** *v* (*comm*) invoice; (*manipolare*) doctor. **fatturato** *sm* turnover.

**fatuo** [fatuo] *agg* foolish, fatuous.

**fauci** ['fautʃi] *sf pl* jaws *pl*; (*fig*) clutches *pl*.

**fauna** ['fauna] *sf* fauna.

**fausto** ['fausto] *agg* propitious.

**fautore** [fau'tore], **-trice** *sm, sf* supporter.

**fava** ['fava] *sf* broad bean.

**favilla** [fa'villa] *sf* spark. **far faville** sparkle, shine.

**favo** ['favo] *sm* honeycomb.

**favola** ['favola] *sf* fable, story. **favoloso** *agg* fabulous.

**favore** [fa'vore] *sm* favour; (*appoggio*) support. **di favore** (*biglietto*) complimentary; (*prezzo*) special. **per favore** please.

**favoreggiare** [favored'dʒare] *v* favour; (*dir*) aid and abet.

**favorevole** [favo'revole] *agg* favourable, in favour.

**favorire** [favo'rire] *v* favour; (*sostenere*) support; (*promuovere*) promote, foster. **favorito, -a** *s, agg* favourite. **favoritismo** *sm* favouritism.

**fax** [faks] *sm* fax.

**fazione** [fa'tsjone] *sf* faction, party. **fazioso** *agg* subversive.

**fazzoletto** [fatso'letto] *sm* handkerchief; (*da testa*) headsquare.

**febbraio** [feb'brajo] *sm* February.

**febbre** ['fɛbbre] *sf* temperature, fever; (*fam: sulle labbra*) cold sore; (*brama*) lust, passion. **febbre da fieno** hay fever. **febbricitante** *agg* feverish.

**feccia** ['fɛttʃa] *sf* dregs *pl*.

**feci** ['fɛtʃi] *sf pl* faeces *pl*.

**fecola** ['fɛkola] *sf* starch.

**fecondare** [fekon'dare] *v* fertilize. **fecondazione** *sf* fertilization. **fecondazione artificiale** artificial insemination. **fecondità** *sf* fertility. **fecondo** *agg* fertile; prolific, fruitful.

**fede** ['fede] *sf* faith; (*fiducia*) confidence, trust; (*anello*) wedding ring; (*attestazione*) proof.

**fedele** [fe'dele] *agg* faithful, true. *s(m+f)* believer; (*seguace*) follower. **fedeltà** *sf* faithfulness, fidelity.

**federa** ['fɛdera] *sf* pillow-case.

**federale** [fede'rale] *agg* federal.

**federazione** [federa'tsjone] *sf* federation, association.

**fedina** [fe'dina] *sf* police *or* criminal record.

**fedine** [fe'dine] *sf pl* side-whiskers *pl*.

**fegato** ['fegato] *sm* liver; (*coraggio*) guts *pl*. **mangiarsi il fegato** eat one's heart out.

**felce** ['feltʃe] *sf* fern; (*comune*) bracken.

**felice** [fe'litʃe] *agg* happy; (*fortunato*) lucky. **felicità** *sf* happiness, bliss. **felicitarsi con** congratulate. **felicitazioni** *sf pl* congratulations *pl*.

**felino** [fe'lino] *agg* feline.

**felpa** ['felpa] *sf* plush; fleece (jacket).

**feltro** ['feltro] *sm* felt.

**femmina** ['femmina] *sf* female; (*figlia*) daughter. *agg* female. **femminismo** *sm* feminism, women's movement. **femminista** *s(m+f)*, *agg* feminist.

**femminile** [femmi'nile] *agg* female; (*da donna*) feminine, womanly; (*gramm*) feminine. **scuola femminile** *sf* girls' school. *sm* feminine (gender). **femminilità** *sf* femininity.

**femore** ['femore] *sm* femur.

**\*fendere** ['fɛndere] *v* split, pierce; (*solcare*) plough (through). **fenditura** *sf* cleft; (*fessura*) crack.

**fenicottero** [feni'kɔttero] *sm* flamingo.

**fenomeno** [fe'nɔmeno] *sm* phenomenon (*pl* -a); (*prodigio*) marvel. **fenomenale** *agg* phenomenal; (*eccezionale*) extraordinary, remarkable.

**feretro** ['fɛretro] *sm* coffin.

**ferie** ['fɛrje] *sf pl* holidays *pl*. **giorno feriale** *sm* weekday.

**ferire** [fe'rire] *v* wound, injure, hurt. **ferita** *sf* wound, injury; (*persona*) casualty. **ferito** *sm* casualty.

**fermacarte** [ferma'karte] *sm invar* (*a molla*) paper-clip; (*pesante*) paperweight.

**fermaglio** [fer'maʎo] *sm* clasp, clip.

**fermare** [fer'mare] *v* stop; (*arrestare*) check; (*fissare*) secure, fasten; (*prenotare*) book. **fermarsi** stop; (*rimanere*) stay. **fermata** *sf* stop; (*tappa*) stay; (*veicoli*) halt. **fermata facoltativa** request stop.

**fermentare** [fermen'tare] *v* ferment. **fermentazione** *sf* fermentation. **fermento** *sm* ferment; (*fig*) unrest.

**fermo** ['fermo] *agg* still; (*non in moto*) stationary; (*saldo*) firm, steady. **restar fermo** stand still; (*fig*) hold good. *sm* (*mec*) catch, fastener, lock; (*dir*) detention; (*sospensione*) stop.

**feroce** [fe'rotʃe] *agg* wild; (*crudele*) savage, ferocious; (*fig*) fierce. **ferocia** *sf* cruelty, ferocity.

**ferragosto** [ferra'gosto] *sm* mid-August holiday.

**ferramenta** [ferra'menta] *sf pl* ironmongery *sing*.

**ferreo** [ˈfɛrreo] *agg* iron.

**ferro** [ˈfɛrro] *sf* iron. **essere ai ferri corti** be at loggerheads. **ferro battuto** wrought iron. **ferro da calza** knitting needle. **ferro di cavallo** horseshoe. **tocca ferro!** touch wood!

**ferrovia** [ferro'via] *sf* railway. **ferroviario** *agg* rail(way), train. **ferroviere** *sm* railwayman.

**fertile** [ˈfɛrtile] *agg* fertile, fruitful. **fertilità** *sf* fertility, fruitfulness. **fertilizzante** *sm* fertilizer. **fertilizzare** *v* fertilize.

**fervore** [fer'vore] *sm* fervour. **fervente** *agg* fervent. **fervido** *agg* ardent; (*caloroso*) heartfelt; (*vivace*) lively.

**fesso** [ˈfesso] (*volg*) *agg*, *sm* idiot, fool. **fesseria** *sf* (*azione*) foolishness; (*parole*) nonsense; (*inezia*) trifle.

**fessura** [fes'sura] *sf* crack, slit; (*gettone, moneta*) slot.

**festa** [ˈfesta] *sf* holiday; (*compleanno*) birthday; (*onomastico*) saint's day; (*festeggiamento*) celebration; (*ricevimento*) party. **far festa** (*non lavorare*) take a holiday, take time off; (*smettere il lavoro*) stop work; (*divertirsi*) make merry. **far festa a** give a warm welcome (to).

**festeggiare** [fested'dʒare] *v* celebrate; (*far festa*) give a hearty welcome (to). **festeggiamenti** *sm pl* festivities *pl*. **festeggiamento** *sm* celebration.

**festività** [festivi'ta] *sf* festivity, holiday. **festivo** *agg* festive; (*della domenica*) Sunday; (*non-feriale*) holiday.

**festone** [fes'tone] *sm* festoon; (*ricamo*) scallop.

**fetente** [fe'tɛnte] *sm* (*volg*) stinker, scoundrel. *agg also* **fetido** stinking, foul. **fetore** *sm* stench.

**feticcio** [fe'tittʃo] *sm* fetish.

**feto** [ˈfɛto] *sm* foetus.

**fetta** [ˈfetta] *sf* slice. **tagliare a fette** slice, cut into slices. **fettuccia** *sf* (*nastro*) tape, ribbon. **fettuccine** *sf pl* noodles *pl*.

**feudale** [feu'dale] *agg* feudal. **feudalesimo** *sm* feudalism. **feudo** *sm* feud; (*proprietà terriera*) lands *pl*; (*fig*) domain.

**fiaba** [ˈfjaba] *sf* story, (fairy) tale.

**fiacca** [ˈfjakka] *sf* (*stanchezza*) weariness; (*pigrizia*) laziness; (*svogliatezza*) listlessness. **battere la fiacca** (*fam: stare in ozio*) kick one's heels; (*agire svogliatamente*) be sluggish. **fiaccare** *v* (*indebolire*) weaken; (*spossare*) wear out; (*spezzare*) break. **fiacco** *agg* (*debole*) weak; (*stanco*) exhausted, weary.

**fiaccola** [ˈfjakkola] *sf* torch. **alla luce di fiaccole** by torchlight.

**fiala** [ˈfjala] *sf* phial, medicine bottle.

**fiamma** [ˈfjamma] *sf* flame; (*improvvisa, irregolare*) flare; (*molto viva*) blaze. **in fiamme** on fire. **nuovo fiammante** brand-new. **fiammata** *sf* blaze, flare.

**fiammeggiare** [fjammed'dʒare] *v* blaze, flame.

**fiammifero** [fjam'mifero] *sm* match.

**fiammingo** [fjam'mingo] *agg* Flemish.

**fiancheggiare** [fjanked'dʒare] *v* flank; (*sostenere*) help.

**fianco** [ˈfjanko] *sm* side; (*mil*) flank. **di fianco a** (*vicino*) next to, by; (*lungo*) alongside.

**fiasco** [ˈfjasko] *sm* flask, (straw-covered) bottle; (*insuccesso*) flop. **far fiasco** flop.

**fiatare** [fja'tare] *v* breathe. **fiato** *sm* breath. **fiati** *sm pl* woodwind *pl*. **senza fiato** out of breath. **strumenti a fiato** *sm pl* wind instruments *pl*. **tutto d'un fiato** in one go.

**fibbia** [ˈfibbja] *sf* buckle.

**fibra** [ˈfibra] *sf* fibre; (*fig*) constitution.

**ficcare** [fik'kare] *v* poke, stick; (*fam: mettere*) put. **ficcanaso** *sm* busybody.

**fico** [ˈfiko] *sm* fig. **fico d'India** prickly pear. **non m'importa un fico (secco)** (*fam*) I couldn't care less. **non valere un fico** be worthless.

**fidanzarsi** [fidan'tsarsi] *v* get engaged. **fidanzamento** *sm* engagement. **fidanzato, -a** *sm*, *sf* fiancé, -e.

**fidarsi** [fi'darsi] *v* (*aver fiducia*) rely (on), trust; (*osare*) trust oneself, dare.

**fido** [ˈfido] *sm* (*econ*) credit.

**fiducia** [fi'dutʃa] *sf* trust, confidence. **aver**

**fiducia in** trust. **di fiducia** (*fidato*) reliable, trustworthy; responsible. **fiduciario** *sm* (official) representative; (*dir*) trustee. **fiducioso** *agg* trusting.

**fiele** ['fjɛle] *sm* bile; (*fig*) ill-will.

**fieno** ['fjɛno] *sm* hay.

**fiera** ['fjɛra] *sf* fair; (*mostra*) exhibition; (*di beneficenza*) bazaar.

**fiero** ['fjɛro] *agg* (*orgoglioso*) proud; (*audace*) bold, spirited; (*feroce, violento*) fierce; (*austero*) severe. **fierezza** *sf* pride; boldness.

**fifa** ['fifa] (*fam*) *sf* fear. **aver fifa** be afraid. **fifone, -a** *sm, sf* coward.

**figliastro** [fiʎ'ʎastro] *sm* stepson. **figliastra** *sf* stepdaughter.

**figlio** ['fiʎo] *sm* son; (*fig: frutto*) result, product. **figli** *sm pl* children *pl*. **figlia** (*di madre*) daughter; (*comm*) counterfoil. **figliare** *v* give birth. **figliata** *sf* litter.

**figlioccio** [fiʎ'ʎottʃo] *sm* godson. **figlioccia** *sf* goddaughter.

**figliolo** [fiʎ'ɔlo] *sm* (*figlio*) son; (*ragazzo*) boy, young man; (*fam*) chap. **figliola** (*figlia*) daughter; (*ragazza*) girl. **figliolanza** *sf* offspring.

**figura** [fi'gura] *sf* figure; (*aspetto*) shape; (*illustrazione*) picture; (*tavola*) plate. **far bella figura** show up to advantage; make a good impression; (*riuscir bene*) do well. **far brutta figura** cut a sorry figure, disgrace oneself.

**figurare** [figu'rare] *v* represent, portray; (*simboleggiare*) stand for; (*mostrare*) pretend; (*risultare*) appear; (*far figura*) look smart. **figurarsi** *v* imagine. **figurati!** *inter* (*altro che*) of course! you bet! **figurina** *sf* figurine; (*cartoncino*) card. **figurino** *sm* fashion-plate; (*giornale*) fashion magazine. **figuro** *sm* shady character.

**fila** ['fila] *sf* row, line; (*coda*) queue; (*serie*) string. **di fila** (*di seguito*) in succession, in a row; (*senza interruzione*) on end, non-stop. **in fila indiana** in single file. **mettere in fila** line up. **mettersi in fila** queue up.

**filantropo** [fi'lantropo], **-a** *sm, sf* philanthropist. **filantropico** *agg* philanthropic.

**filare** [fi'lare] *v* spin; (*cavo, catena*) pay out; (*correre*) run, speed along.

**filarmonico** [filar'mɔniko] *agg* philharmonic.

**filastrocca** [filas'trɔkka] *sf* (*per bambini*) nursery rhyme; (*storia lunga*) tedious list, rigmarole.

**filatelia** [filate'lia] *sf* stamp-collecting, philately. **filatelico** *agg* stamp. **filatelista** *s(m+f)* stamp collector.

**filatura** [fila'tura] *sf* (*industria*) spinning; (*filanda*) spinning mill.

**filetto** [fi'letto] *sm* (*gastr*) fillet; border; (*filo sottile, mec*) thread; (*tipografia*) rule. **filettare** *v* (*ornare*) decorate; (*bordare*) edge; (*mec*) thread. **filettatura** *sf* edging, braid; threading.

**filiale** [fi'ljale] *sf* branch. *agg* filial.

**filibustiere** [filibus'tjɛre] *sm* pirate; (*imbroglione*) rogue.

**filigrana** [fili'grana] *sf* filigree; (*carta*) watermark.

**film** [film] *sm invar* film. **filmare** *v* film.

**filo** ['filo] *sm* thread; (*filato*) yarn; (*metallico*) wire; (*coltello*) edge; (*elettrico*) flex. **filo d'erba** blade of grass. **filo spinato** barbed wire. **lana a due/tre fili** *sf* two/three-ply wool. **perdere il filo** (*discorso*) lose track; (*taglio*) become blunt. **per filo e per segno** in detail.

**filodrammatico** [filodram'matiko], **-a** *sm, sf* amateur actor, amateur actress. *agg* amateur theatrical.

**filologo** [fi'lologo], **-a** *sm, sf* philologist. **filologia** *sf* philology. **filologico** *agg* philological.

**filone** [fi'lone] *sm* seam, vein; (*pane*) French loaf; (*fig*) current, line.

**filosofia** [filozo'fia] *sf* philosophy. **filosofico** *agg* philosophical. **filosofo, -a** *sm, sf* philosopher.

**filtrare** [fil'trare] *v* filter. **filtro** *sm* filter; (*colino*) strainer.

**filza** ['filtsa] *sf* string.

**finale** [fi'nale] *agg* final; (*ultimo*) last. *sf* (*sport*) final; (*gramm*) ending. *sm* (*musica*) finale. **finalista** *s(m+f)* finalist. **finalità** *sf* (*scopo*) purpose, aim; (*filosofia*) finality.

**finanza** [fi'nantsa] *sf* finance; (*fam: risorse economiche*) finances *pl*. **finanze** *sf pl* (*entrate dello Stato*) public revenue *sing*. **guardia di finanza** *sf* customs officer.

**finanziare** [finan'tsjare] *v* finance. **finanziamento** *sm* financing; (*fondi*) funds *pl*. **finanziario** *agg* financial. **finanziatore, -trice** *sm, agg* backer. **finanziera** *sf* frockcoat.

**finché** [fin'ke] *cong* (*per tutto il tempo che*) as long as; (*fino a quando*) until, till.

**fine¹** ['fine] *sf* end; (*libro, film, ecc.*) ending. *sm* end; (*scopo*) aim; (*esito*) conclusion. **alla fine** (*luogo*) at the end; (*tempo*) in the end; (*finalmente*) at last. **in fin dei conti** when all is said and done, in the end. **secondo fine** ulterior motive, hidden purpose. **senza fine** endless.

**fine²** ['fine] *agg* fine; (*signorile*) refined; (*acuto*) sharp; (*penetrante*) subtle. **finezza** *sf* fineness; (*raffinatezza*) finesse, polish; (*minuzie*) nicety.

**fine-settimana** [finesetti'mana] *s(m+f) invar* weekend.

**finestra** [fi'nɛstra] *sf* window.

**\*fingere** ['findʒere] *v* pretend. **fingersi** *v* pretend to be.

**finire** [fi'nire] *v* finish; (*smettere*) stop; (*terminare, sboccare*) end; (*capitare*) end up. **andare a finire** (*capitare*) get to; (*concludersi*) turn out, end up. **finimondo** *sm* pandemonium. **finissaggio** *sm* finish. **finitura** *sf* finishing off; finishing touches *pl.*

**Finlandia** [fin'landja] *sf* Finland. **finlandese** *sm, agg* Finnish; *s(m+f)* (*abitante*) Finn.

**fino¹** ['fino] *agg* fine, delicate; (*acuto*) subtle.

**fino²** ['fino] *avv* (*persino*) even. **fino a** (*tempo*) until, up to; (*luogo*) as far as. **fino a che punto?** how far? **fin da** (*passato*) since, as far back as; (*presente, futuro*) (as) from. **fin dove?** how far? **fino in fondo** right down, to the (very) end.

**finocchio** [fi'nɔkkjo] *sm* (*bot*) fennel; (*volg*) queer, gay.

**finora** [fi'nora] *avv* up to now, so far.

**finta** ['finta] *sf* pretence, sham; (*sport*) feint. **far finta di** pretend.

**finto** ['finto] *agg* false; (*simulato*) bogus; (*non reale*) mock; artificial. **fintapelle** *sf* imitation leather.

**finzione** [fin'tsjone] *sf* pretence; (*falsità*) falsehood; (*illusione*) fiction.

**fio** ['fio] *sm* **pagare il fio** pay the price.

**fioccare** [fjok'kare] *v* (*neve*) fall; (*fig*) come down thick and fast.

**fiocco** ['fjɔkko] *sm* flake; (*batuffolo*) flock; (*fibra tessile*) staple; (*nastro*) bow. **coi fiocchi** first-class, magnificent. **fiocchi d'avena** oatflakes *pl*. **fiocco di neve** snowflake.

**fioco** ['fjɔko] *agg* faint; (*luce*) dim.

**fionda** ['fjonda] *sf* catapult, sling.

**fiordo** ['fjɔrdo] *sm* fjord.

**fiore** ['fjore] *sm* flower; (*di albero*) blossom; (*meglio*) cream; (*carte da gioco*) club. **a fiori** floral. **fior di quattrini** pots of money *pl*. **in fiore** in bloom, in blossom. **fiorente** *agg* (*di fiore*) flowering; (*fig*) thriving, flourishing.

**fiorentino** [fjoren'tino], **-a** *s, agg* Florentine.

**fioretto** [fjo'retto] *sm* (*sport*) foil; (*musica, discorso*) embellishment.

**fiorire** [fjo'rire] *v* flower, bloom, blossom. **fioritura** *sf* flowering, blossoming; (*fiori*) bloom, blossom.

**Firenze** [fi'rɛntse] *sf* Florence.

**firma** ['firma] *sf* signature. **firmare** *v* sign. **firmatario** *sm* signatory.

**fisarmonica** [fizar'mɔnika] *sf* accordion.

**fiscale** [fis'kale] *agg* fiscal, tax. **fisco** *sm* treasury, tax authorities *pl*.

**fischiare** [fis'kjare] *v* whistle; (*disapprovare*) boo, hiss. **fischiata** *sf* booing, hissing. **fischiettare** *v* whistle (softly). **fischietto** *sm* whistle. **fischio** *sm* whistle, boo, hiss.

**fisica** ['fizika] *sf* physics; (*scienziata*) physicist.

**fisico** ['fiziko] *agg* physical. *sm* (*corpo*) body; (*costituzione*) make-up; (*scienziato*) physicist.

**fisima** ['fizima] *sf* whim, fancy.

**fisiologia** [fizjolo'dʒia] *sf* physiology. **fisiologico** *agg* physiological. **fisiologo, -a** *sm, sf* physiologist.

**fisionomia** [fizjono'mia] *sf* expression.

**fisioterapia** [fizjotera'pia] *sf* physiotherapy. **fisioterapista** *s(m+f)* physiotherapist.

**fissare** [fis'sare] *v* fix; (*attaccare*) fasten; (*guardare fissamente*) stare (at), gaze (at); (*prenotare*) book. **fissarsi di** be set on. **fissazione** *sf* fixation.

**fissato** [fis'sato] *agg* obsessed. *sm* (*fam*) fanatic, maniac. **essere fissato** have a bee in one's bonnet.

**fissione** [fis'sjone] *sf* fission.

**fitta** ['fitta] *sf* (*dolore*) twinge, sharp pain.

**fittizio** [fit'titsjo] *agg* fictitious.

**fitto¹** ['fitto] *agg* thick, dense; (*conficcato*) stuck, driven in; (*tessuto, ecc.*) close. *sm* thick, middle. **a capo fitto** headlong. **buio fitto** pitch dark.

**fitto²** ['fitto] *sm* (*affitto*) rent.

**fiume** ['fjume] *sm* river; (*fig*) flood, stream. **fiumana** *sf* torrent.

**fiutare** [fju'tare] *v* smell; (*annusare rumorosamente*) sniff; (*intuire*) scent. **fiutare un inganno** (*fam*) smell a rat. **fiuto** *sm* scent, nose. **al fiuto** straight off, instinctively. **aver fiuto di** get wind of.

**flaccido** ['flattʃido] *agg* flabby, limp.

**flacone** [fla'kone] *sm* small bottle.

**flagellare** [fladʒel'lare] *v* flagellate, whip. **flagello** *sm* scourge, whip.

**flagrante** [fla'grante] *agg* flagrant. **cogliere in flagrante** catch in the act, catch red-handed.

**flanella** [fla'nɛlla] *sf* flannel.

**flauto** ['flauto] *sm* flute. **flauto dolce** recorder. **flautista** *s(m+f)* flautist.

**flebile** ['flɛbile] *agg* (*debole*) faint, feeble; (*lamentevole*) mournful, melancholy.

**flemma** ['flɛmma] *sf* coolness, imperturbability. **flemmatico** *agg* cool, self-possessed, phlegmatic.

**flessibile** [fles'sibile] *agg* flexible, pliable; versatile. **flessibilità** *sf* flexibility, pliability; versatility. **flessione** *sf* bending; (*diminuzione graduale*) drop, fall; (*ginnastica*) bend.

**flessuoso** [flessu'ozo] *agg* supple, lithe. **flessuosità** *sf* suppleness.

**\*flettere** ['flɛttere] *v* bend, bow; (*membra*) flex.

**flipper** ['flipper] *sm invar* pin-table.

**flirt** [flə:t] *sm invar* (*amore superficiale*) flirtation; (*persona*) boy-friend, girl-friend. **flirtare** *v* flirt.

**flora** ['flɔra] *sf* flora.

**florido** ['flɔrido] *agg* (*prospero*) flourishing, thriving; (*colorito*) ruddy, glowing with health.

**floscio** ['flɔʃo] *agg* floppy, limp.

**flotta** ['flɔtta] *sf* fleet. **flottiglia** *sf* flotilla.

**fluido** ['fluido] *sm, agg* fluid. **fluidità** *sf* fluidity; (*scorrevolezza*) fluency; instability.

**fluire** [flu'ire] *v* flow.

**fluorescente** [fluore'ʃɛnte] *agg* fluorescent. **fluorescenza** *sf* fluorescence.

**fluoro** ['fluɔro] *sm* fluorine.

**flusso** ['flusso] *sm* flow, stream. **flusso e riflusso** ebb and flow. **flusso di sangue dal naso** nosebleed.

**fluttuare** [fluttu'are] *v* fluctuate.

**fobia** [fo'bia] *sf* phobia; (*fam*) (pet) aversion.

**foca** ['fɔka] *sf* seal.

**focaccia** [fo'kattʃa] *sf* bun. **rendere pan per focaccia** give as good as one gets.

**focale** [fo'kale] *agg* focal.

**foce** ['fotʃe] *sf* mouth, outlet.

**focena** [fo'tʃɛna] *sf* porpoise.

**focolaio** [foko'lajo] *sm* (*med*) focus; (*centro di diffusione*) hotbed, breeding ground.

**focolare** [foko'lare] *sm* hearth; (*fig*) fireside, home.

**focoso** [fo'kozo] *agg* fiery; (*ardente*) burning.

**fodera** ['fɔdera] *sf* lining; (*rivestimento*) cover. **foderare** *v* line; cover. **fodero** *sm* sheath.

**foga** ['foga] *sf* rush; (*ardore*) heat.

**foggia** ['fɔddʒa] *sf* fashion; (*forma*) shape. **foggiare** *v* shape, form, fashion.

**foglia** ['fɔʎʎa] *sf* leaf. **mettere le foglie** come into leaf. **fogliame** *sm* foliage.

**foglio** ['fɔʎʎo] *sm* sheet; (*giornale*) paper; (*banconota*) note. **foglio di via** travel-warrant. **foglio volante** leaflet.

**fogna** ['foɲa] *sf* sewer. **fognatura** *sf* sewerage.

**foia** ['fɔja] *sf* heat. **essere in foia** be on heat.

**folata** [fo'lata] *sf* gust.

**folclore** [fol'klɔre] *sm* folklore. **folcloristico** *agg* folk.

**folgorare** [folgo'rare] *v* flash; (*inveire*) rail; (*colpire con fulmine*) strike with lightning. **folgorare con lo sguardo** wither with a glance.

**folla** ['fɔlla] *sf* crowd; (*gran quantità*) host.

**folle** ['fɔlle] *agg* crazy; (*pazzo*) mad; (*sciocco*) foolish; (*auto*) neutral. **andare in folle** coast. **folletto** *sm* imp. **follia** *sf* madness, folly.

**follicolo** [fol'likolo] *sm* follicle.

**folto** ['folto] *sm, agg* thick.

**fomentare** [fomen'tare] *v* encourage; (*eccitare*) rouse. **fomento** *sm* (*impacco caldo*) poultice; (*sprone*) spur.

**fonda** ['fonda] *sf* anchorage.

**fondamento** [fonda'mento] *sm, pl* -**a** *f* in literal sense foundation. **fondamentale** *agg* fundamental, basic.

**fondare** [fon'dare] *v* found; (*istituire*) establish; base. **fondarsi su** be based on; *(fare assegnamento)* rely on. **fondatore, -trice** *sm, sf* founder. **fondazione** *sf* foundation, establishment.

\***fondere** ['fondere] *v* melt, fuse; *(in una forma)* cast, mould; *(unire)* blend, merge.

**fonderia** [fonde'ria] *sf* foundry.

**fondiario** [fon'djarjo] *agg* land. **proprietà fondiaria** *sf* real estate.

**fondina¹** [fon'dina] *sf (di pistola)* holster.

**fondina²** [fon'dina] *sf (piatto)* soup plate.

**fondista** [fon'dista] *s(m+f) (sport)* long distance runner; *(giornalista)* leader writer.

**fondo** ['fondo] *agg* deep. *sm* bottom; *(feccia)* dregs *pl; (caffè)* grounds *pl; (estremità)* end; *(sfondo)* background; *(pittura)* primer; *(denaro)* fund; *(terreno)* estate. **a fondo** *(profondamente)* thoroughly; *(con tutte le forze)* wholeheartedly. **andare a fondo** sink. **andare a fondo di** get to the bottom of. **articolo di fondo** *sm* leading article. **dar fondo a** *(consumare)* use up. **fino in fondo** to the end. **fondo (di) cassa/magazzino** cash/stock in hand. **fondo stradale** road surface. **in fondo** *(sotto)* at *or* to the bottom; *(dietro)* at *or* to the back; *(in conclusione)* after all. **mandare a fondo** sink.

**fonetica** [fo'netika] *sf* phonetics. **fonetico** *agg* phonetic.

**fontana** [fon'tana] *sf* fountain.

**fonte** ['fonte] *sf* spring; *(fig)* source. *sm (battesimale)* font.

**foraggiare** [forad'dʒare] *v* forage. **foraggio** *sm* forage.

**forare** [fo'rare] *v* perforate; *(gomma)* puncture; *(al trapano)* bore. **foratura** *sf* perforation; puncture.

**forbici** ['fɔrbitʃi] *sf pl* scissors *pl; (da siepe, cesoie)* shears *pl; (da potatura)* secateurs *pl.* **forbicina** *sf* earwig.

**forbire** [for'bire] *v* clean; *(fig)* polish.

**forca** ['forka] *sf* pitchfork; *(patibolo)* gallows. **va alla** *or* **sulla forca!** *(fam)* get stuffed! **forcella** *sf* fork; *(volatili)* wishbone.

**forchetta** [for'ketta] *sf* fork. **una buona forchetta** a hearty eater. **forchettata** *sf* forkful.

**forcina** [for'tʃina] *sf* hairpin.

**forcipe** ['fɔrtʃipe] *sm* forceps *pl.*

**forense** [fo'rɛnse] *agg* forensic.

**foresta** [fo'rɛsta] *sf* forest. **foresta plu-**

**viale** rainforest.

**forestiero** [fores'tjɛro], **-a** *agg* foreign. *sm, sf* foreigner.

**forfait¹** [for'fɛ] *sm invar (contratto)* flat rate. **a forfait** all-in.

**forfait²** [for'fɛ] *sm invar (sport)* withdrawal. **dichiarare forfait** scratch.

**forfora** ['forfora] *sf* dandruff.

**forma** ['forma] *sf* form, shape; *(stampo)* mould; *(del calzolaio)* last. **a forma di X** X-shaped.

**formaggio** [for'maddʒo] *sm* cheese.

**formale** [for'male] *agg* formal. **formalità** *sf* formality.

**formare** [for'mare] *v* form; *(modellare)* shape; *(costituire)* make up; *(numero telefonico)* dial. **formarsi un'idea** get an idea. **formato** *sm* format, size. **formazione** *sf* formation; *(addestramento)* training.

**formica** [for'mika] *sf* ant. **formicaio** *sm* ant-hill; *(fig)* teeming crowd.

**formicolare** [formiko'lare] *v* swarm; *(provare sensazione)* tingle. **formicolio** *sm* swarming; *(sensazione)* pins and needles.

**formidabile** [formi'dabile] *agg* remarkable; *(molto forte)* powerful, formidable.

**formula** ['fɔrmula] *sf* formula *(pl* -ae).

**formulare** [formu'lare] *v* formulate; *(avanzare)* put forward; *(esprimere)* express. **formulario** *sm (modulo)* form.

**fornace** [for'natʃe] *sf* kiln, furnace.

**fornaio** [for'najo], **-a** *sm, sf* baker.

**fornire** [for'nire] *v* supply, furnish. **ben fornito** well-stocked. **fornitore** *sm* supplier. **fornitura** *sf* supply.

**forno** ['forno] *sm* oven. **fornello** *sm* cooker.

**foro¹** ['foro] *sm (buco)* hole.

**foro²** ['fɔro] *sm (tribunale)* (law-)court; *(gli avvocati)* the bar; *(Roma)* forum.

**forse** ['forse] *avv* perhaps, maybe; *(circa)* about. **in forse** in doubt.

**forsennato** [forsen'nato] *agg* crazy, mad.

**forte** ['fɔrte] *agg* strong; *(grande)* large; *(bravo)* good; *(suono)* loud; *(intenso)* heavy. *avv (con forza)* hard; *(assai)* very much; *(velocemente)* fast; *(a voce alta)* loud. *sm (specialità)* strong point; *(persona)* powerful person; *(mil)* fort.

**fortezza** [for'tettsa] *sf (mil)* fortress; *(forza morale)* strength.

**fortificare** [fortifi'kare] *v* strengthen, fortify. **fortificazione** *sf* fortification.

**fortuito** [for'tuito] *agg* fortuitous, chance.

**fortuna** [for'tuna] *sf* fortune; *(buona sorte)* luck; success. **di fortuna** *(improvvisato)* makeshift; emergency. **fortuna che** fortunately. **fortunato** *agg* fortunate, lucky.

**foruncolo** [fo'runkolo] *sm* boil.

**forza** ['fɔrtsa] *sf* strength; *(potere, potenza)* power; *(fis, mil)* force. **a forza di** through, by dint of. **a tutta forza** with all one's strength. **bella forza!** there's nothing to it! **farsi forza** *(coraggio)* pluck up courage. **forza maggiore** force majeure, circumstances beyond one's control. **per forza** necessarily; *(controvoglia)* unwillingly. **per forza di cose** of necessity.

**forzare** [for'tsare] *v* force. **forzato** *sm* convict.

**foschia** [fos'kia] *sf* haze, mist.

**fosco** ['fosko] *agg* *(scuro)* dark; *(tetro)* gloomy.

**fosfato** [fos'fato] *sm* phosphate.

**fosforescente** [fosfore'ʃɛnte] *agg* phosphorescent. **fosforo** *sm* phosphorus.

**fossa** ['fɔssa] *sf* pit, hole; *(cimitero)* grave. **fossato** *sm* ditch; *(mil)* moat. **fossetta** *sf* dimple.

**fossile** ['fɔssile] *sm, agg* fossil.

**fosso** ['fɔsso] *sm* ditch. **saltare il fosso** *(fig)* take the plunge.

**foto** ['fɔto] *sf invar (fam)* snap, photo.

**fotocopia** [foto'kɔpja] *sf* photocopy.

**fotogenico** [foto'dʒɛniko] *agg* photogenic.

**fotografare** [fotogra'fare] *v* photograph. **fotografia** *sf (tecnica)* photography; *(copia)* photograph. **fotografico** *agg* photographic. **apparecchio fotografico** *sm* camera. **fotografo, -a** *sm, sf* photographer.

**fottere** ['fottere] *(volg) v* fuck. **fottuto** *agg* *(spacciato)* ruined, buggered.

**fra** [fra] *prep (fra due)* between; *(fra più di due)* among(st); *(entro)* in, within; *(partitivo)* of. **detto fra (di) noi** between ourselves. **fra l'altro** among other things; *(inoltre)* besides. **fra tutti** *(tutti insieme)* altogether, in all.

**frac** [frak] *sm invar (fam)* tails *pl*.

**fracassare** [frakas'sare] *v* smash. **fracassarsi** *v* break. **fracasso** *sm (chiasso)* racket, din, row; *(scalpore)* uproar.

**fradicio** [fraditʃo] *agg* *(inzuppato)* sopping (wet), wet through; *(guasto)* rotten. **ubriaco fradicio** dead drunk.

**fragile** ['fradʒile] *agg* fragile; *(delicato)* frail.

**fragola** ['fragola] *sf* strawberry.

**fragore** [fra'gore] *sm* din. **fragoroso** *agg* roaring, resounding.

**fragrante** [fra'grante] *agg* fragrant.

**\*fraintendere** [frain'tɛndere] *v* misunderstand, misconstrue.

**frammassone** [frammas'sone] *sm* freemason. **frammassoneria** *sf* freemasonry.

**frammento** [fram'mento] *sm* fragment; *(scheggia)* splinter. **frammentario** *agg* fragmentary.

**\*frammettersi** [fram'mettersi] *v (interporsi)* come between; *(immischiarsi)* meddle.

**frammezzo** [fram'mɛddzo] *avv* **frammezzo a** in the midst of.

**frana** ['frana] *sf* landslide. **franare** *v* slide down; *(collare)* cave in.

**francamente** [franka'mente] *avv* frankly.

**franchezza** [fran'kettsa] *sf* frankness.

**franchigia** [fran'kidʒa] *sf* exemption. **in franchigia** *(posta)* post-free; *(tassa)* tax-free.

**Francia** ['frantʃa] *sf* France. **francese** *sm, agg* French; *s(m+f)* French person.

**franco¹** ['franko] *agg (schietto)* frank, open; *(disinvolto)* (self-)confident; *(libero)* free (of), exempt (from). **in porto franco** *(comm)* carriage paid.

**franco²** ['franko] *sm (moneta)* franc.

**francobollo** [franko'bollo] *sm* (postage) stamp.

**\*frangersi** ['frandʒersi] *v* break. **frangente** *sm (ondata)* breaker; *(crisi)* spot, predicament.

**frangia** ['frandʒa] *sf* fringe.

**frantumare** [frantu'mare] *v* crush. **in frantumi** in *or* to pieces.

**\*frapporre** [frap'porre] *v* interpose.

**frase** ['fraze] *sf* phrase; *(periodo)* sentence. **frase fatta** stock phrase.

**frassino** ['frassino] *sm* ash.

**frastagliare** [frasta'ʎare] *v* indent.

**frastornato** [frastor'nato] *agg* dizzy.

**frastuono** [fras'twono] *sm* din, uproar.

**frate** ['frate] *sm* friar.

**fratello** [fra'tɛllo] *sm* brother. **fratellanza** *sf* brotherhood. **fratellastro** *sm* stepbrother.

**fraterno** [fra'tɛrno] *agg* brotherly, fraternal. **fraternizzare** *v* fraternize.

**frattaglie** [frat'taʎe] *sf pl* offal *sing*; *(di pol-*

*lame*) giblets *pl.*

**frattanto** [frat'tanto] *avv also* **nel frattempo** meanwhile, in the meantime.

**frattura** [frat'tura] *sf* fracture; (*fig*) break. **fratturare** *v* fracture, break.

**frazione** [fra'tsjone] *sf* fraction; (*borgata*) hamlet. **frazionare** *v* split up.

**freccia** ['frettʃa] *sf* arrow; (*auto*) indicator. **frecciata** *sf* shaft.

**freddo** ['freddo] *agg* cold; (*fig*) cool, chilly. *sm* cold. **aver freddo** be cold, feel cold. **fa freddo** it is cold. **fa un freddo cane** it is bitterly cold. **morir di freddo** be dying of cold. **soffrire il freddo** feel the cold.

**freddura** [fred'dura] *sf* pun.

**fregare** [fre'gare] *v* rub; (*per lucidare*) polish; (*per lavare*) scrub; (*fam: rubare*) pinch, swipe; (*volg: imbrogliare*) cheat. **fregata** *sf* rub(bing). **fregatura** *sf* (*volg: imbroglio*) swindle; (*fam: contrattempo*) wash-out, flop.

**fregio** ['fredʒo] *sm* ornament; (*arch*) frieze. **fregiare** *v* decorate.

**fremere** ['frɛmere] *v* quiver.

**fremito** ['frɛmito] *sm* quiver; (*di emozione*) thrill; (*brivido*) shudder.

**frenare** [fre'nare] *v* brake; (*fig*) restrain, control, check.

**frenesia** [frene'zia] *sf* frenzy. **frenetico** *agg* frenzied, raving.

**freno** ['freno] *sm* brake; (*fig*) check, restraint; (*cavallo*) bit. **allentare il freno** (*fig*) slacken the reins. **mordere il freno** champ at the bit. **stringere i freni** (*fig*) clamp down.

**frequentare** [frekwen'tare] *v* frequent, go to often; (*scuola, ecc.*) attend; (*persone*) mix with. **frequentatore, -trice** *sm, sf* regular. **frequente** *agg* frequent. **frequenza** *sf* frequency. **con frequenza** frequently.

**fresa** ['frɛza] *sf also* **fresatrice** cutter, milling machine.

**fresco** ['fresko] *agg* fresh; (*leggermente freddo*) cool. *sm* cool(ness); freshness; (*pittura*) fresco. **al fresco** in the cool; (*prigione*) in the cooler. **star fresco** (*nei guai*) be in a mess; (*sbagliarsi*) kid oneself.

**fretta** ['fretta] *sf* hurry. **aver fretta** be in a hurry. **far fretta** a hurry. **fatto in fretta** rushed, hurried. **frettoloso** *agg* rushed, hasty.

**\*friggere** ['friddʒere] *v* fry; (*scoppiettare bollendo*) sizzle.

**frigido** ['fridʒido] *agg* cold, frigid. **frigidità** *sf* coldness, frigidity.

**frigorifero** [frigo'rifero] *sm* refrigerator. **frigo** *sm invar* (*fam*) fridge.

**fringuello** [frin'gwɛllo] *sm* chaffinch.

**frittata** [frit'tata] *sf* omelette. **frittella** *sf* pancake.

**fritto** ['fritto] *agg* fried. *sm* fried food. **star fritto** (*fam*) be in trouble, be in for it. **frittura** *sf* (*vivanda*) fried food; (*atto del friggere*) frying.

**frivolo** ['frivolo] *agg* frivolous. **frivolezze** *sf* frivolity, trifles.

**frizione** [fri'tsjone] *sf* (*massaggio*) rub-down; (*auto*) clutch; (*attrito*) friction.

**frizzare** [frit'tsare] *v* tingle; (*bevande*) sparkle; (*metallo rovente*) hiss.

**frodare** [fro'dare] *v* defraud. **frode** *sf* fraud. **frodo** *sm* smuggling. **cacciare** *or* **pescare di frodo** poach. **cacciatore** *or* **pescatore di frodo** *sm* poacher.

**frollare** [frol'lare] *v* ripen. **frollo** *agg* ripe; (*carne*) tender; (*selvaggina*) high; (*pasta*) short.

**fronda** ['fronda] *sf* (leafy) branch; (*fig*) embellishment.

**fronte** ['fronte] *sf* (*testa*) forehead; (*faccia*) face; (*parte anteriore*) front; (*arch*) façade. *sm* (*mil*) front. **a fronte** (*in faccia*) facing. **di fronte** (*dirimpetto*) opposite; (*da davanti*) from the front. **far fronte a** face.

**fronteggiare** [fronted'dʒare] *v* face, stand up to.

**frontespizio** [frontes'pitsjo] *sm* title-page.

**frontiera** [fron'tjera] *sf* frontier, border.

**fronzoli** ['frondzoli] *sm pl* frills *pl.*

**frotta** ['frɔtta] *sf* flock, swarm.

**frottola** ['frɔttola] *sf* fib.

**frugale** [fru'gale] *agg* frugal.

**frugare** [fru'gare] *v* rummage, go through; (*perquisire*) search.

**frullare** [frul'lare] *v* whisk; (*fig*) whirl. **frullino** *sm* whisk.

**frumento** [fru'mento] *sm* wheat.

**frusciare** [fru'ʃare] *v* rustle.

**frustare** [frus'tare] *v* whip. **frusta** *sf* whip. **frustata** *sf* lash.

**frustrazione** [frustra'tsjone] *sf* frustration. **frustrare** *v* frustrate, thwart.

**frutta** ['frutta] *sf* fruit. **frutta cotta** stewed fruit. **fruttare** *v* bear fruit; yield; (*rendere*) bring in; (*procurare*) earn.

**frutteto** [frut'teto] *sm* orchard.

**fruttifero** [frut'tifero] *agg* fruitful; (*redditizio*) profitable.

**fruttivendolo** [frutti'vendolo], **-a** *sm, sf* fruiterer, greengrocer.

**frutto** ['frutto] *sm* fruit; (*interesse*) yield; (*rendita*) income; profit. **frutti di mare** seafood *sing*.

**fu** [fu] *agg invar* late, deceased.

**fucilare** [futʃi'lare] *v* shoot. **fucilata** *sf* shot. **fucilazione** *sf* execution. **fucile** *sm* rifle; (*da caccia*) shotgun.

**fucina** [fu'tʃina] *sf* forge.

**fuco¹** [fu'ko] *sm* (*ape*) drone.

**fuco²** [fu'ko] *sm* (*alga*) fucus.

**fucsia** ['fuksja] *sf* fuchsia.

**fuga** ['fuga] *sf* escape; (*musica*) fugue; (*serie*) suite. **mettere in fuga** put to flight. **prendere la fuga** take flight, flee, escape. **fugace** *agg* transient.

**fuggiasco** *sm, agg* fugitive; (*profugo*) refugee.

**fuggire** [fud'dʒire] *v* flee, escape, run away.

**fulcro** ['fulkro] *sm* fulcrum; (*fig*) heart.

**fuliggine** [fu'liddʒine] *sf* soot. **fuligginoso** *agg* sooty.

**fulminare** [fulmi'nare] *v* (*dal fulmine*) strike (by lightning); (*dalla corrente*) electrocute; (*con uno sguardo*) wither; (*allibire*) dumbfound. **fulmine** *sm* lightning, thunderbolt. **un fulmine a ciel sereno** a bolt from the blue.

**fumaiolo** [fuma'jɔlo] *sm* (*casa*) chimneypot; (*nave*) funnel, smoke-stack.

**fumare** [fu'mare] *v* smoke; (*emettere vapore*) steam. **fumata** *sf* smoke. **fumatore, -trice** *sm, sf* smoker.

**fumetto** [fu'metto] *sm* comic-strip. **fumettista** *s(m+f)* comic-strip writer.

**fumo** ['fumo] *sm* smoke. **andare in fumo** go up in smoke.

**funambolo** [fu'nambolo], **-a** *sm, sf* tightrope walker.

**fune** ['fune] *sf* rope, cable; (*per bucato*) washing line.

**funebre** ['funebre] *agg* funeral; (*lugubre*) funereal.

**funerale** [fune'rale] *sm* funeral. **funereo** *agg* funereal.

**funesto** [fu'nɛsto] *agg* fatal; (*doloroso*) distressing.

**fungo** ['fungo] *sm* mushroom; (*non mangereccio*) toadstool; (*bot*) fungus (*pl* -gi).

**funicolare** [funiko'lare] *sf* funicular railway.

**funivia** [funi'via] *sf* cable-car.

**funzionare** [funtsjo'nare] *v* function, work. **funzionale** *agg* functional, practical. **funzionamento** *sm* operation, working.

**funzionario** [funtsjo'narjo] *sm* official; (*impiegato statale*) civil servant.

**funzione** [fun'tsjone] *sf* function; (*carica*) office; (*compito*) duty. **entrare in funzione** come into operation. **essere in funzione di …** act as …

**fuochista** [fwo'kista] *sm* stoker.

**fuoco** ['fwɔko] *sm* fire; (*fis, mat, foto*) focus. **appiccare** *o* **dare fuoco a** set fire to. **a prova di fuoco** fireproof. **fuoco di Sant'Antonio** (*med*) shingles. **mettere a fuoco** (*foto*) focus. **prendere fuoco** catch fire.

**fuorché** [fwor'ke] *prep, cong* except.

**fuori** ['fwɔri] *avv* out; (*all'esterno*) outside. *prep also* **fuori di** *or* **da** out of. **esser fuori di sè** be beside oneself. **fuoribordo** *sm* (*motore*) outboard motor; (*barca*) motor boat. **fuori strada** (*veicoli*) off-road; (*fig*) on the wrong track. **mettere fuori combattimento** (*sport*) knock up; (*fig*) put out of the running.

**furbo** ['furbo] *agg* cunning, crafty. **furbacchione** *sm* cunning fellow. **furberia** *sf* cunning.

**furetto** [fu'retto] *sm* ferret.

**furfante** [fur'fante] *sm* rascal.

**furgone** [fur'gone] *sm* (delivery) van. **furgoncino** *sm* small (delivery) van.

**furia** ['furja] *sf* (*collera*) rage, fury; (*fretta*) rush, haste. **a furia di …** by dint of ….

**furibondo** [furi'bondo] *agg* furious.

**furioso** [fu'rjozo] *agg* violent, furious.

**furore** [fu'rore] *sm* fury, rage.

**furtivo** [fur'tivo] *agg* furtive, stealthy.

**furto** ['furto] *sm* theft. **furto con scasso** burglary. **piccolo furto** petty theft, petty larceny.

**fusa** ['fuza] *sf pl* **fare le fusa** purr.

**fuscello** [fu'ʃello] *sm* twig.

**fusibile** [fu'zibile] *agg* fusible. *sm* (*elett*) fuse.

**fusione** [fu'zjone] *sf* fusion; (*colata*) casting; (*scioglimento*) melting; (*fig*) merging; (*comm*) merger.

**fuso¹** ['fuzo] *agg (liquefatto)* melted, molten; *(colato)* cast.

**fuso²** ['fuzo] *sm* spindle; *(ancora)* shank. **diritto come un fuso** *(eretto)* straight as a ramrod; *(difilato)* like a shot. **fuso orario** time zone.

**fusoliera** [fuzo'ljɛra] *sf* fuselage.

**fustagno** [fus'taɲo] *sm* fustian; *(a coste)* corduroy.

**fustella** [fus'tɛlla] *sf (tec)* die.

**fustigare** [fusti'gare] *v* flog; *(fig)* lash out at.

**fusto** ['fusto] *sm* trunk; *(ossatura)* frame; *(barile)* barrel, cask; *(recipiente di metallo)* drum.

**futile** ['futile] *agg* futile; *(meschino)* petty.

**futuro** [fu'turo] *agg, sm* future.

# G

**gabbare** [gab'bare] *v* cheat.

**gabbia** ['gabbja] *sf* cage. **gabbia degli imputati** dock.

**gabbiano** [gab'bjano] *sm* seagull.

**gabinetto** [gabi'netto] *sm* study, office; *(di medico)* surgery; *(WC)* toilet, lavatory; *(pol)* cabinet; *(di scienze)* laboratory.

**gaffe** ['gaf] *sf, pl* **-s** blunder. **fare una gaffe** *(fam)* put one's foot in it.

**gagà** [ga'ga] *sm (fam)* dandy.

**gagliardo** [ga'ʎardo] *agg* vigorous; *(robusto)* strapping; *(coraggioso)* brave. **gagliardetto** *sm* pennant, flag.

**gaio** ['gajo] *agg* cheerful.

**gala** ['gala] *sf (ricevimento)* feast. *sm (mar)* flags *pl. sf (stoffa)* frill; *(cravatta)* bow-tie.

**galantuomo** [galan'twɔmo] *sm (true)* gentleman, man of honour. **galante** *agg* gallant, courteous.

**galassia** [ga'lassja] *sf* galaxy.

**galateo** [gala'tɛo] *sm* etiquette, good manners *pl.*

**galea** [ga'lɛa] *sf* galley.

**galeotto** [gale'ɔtto] *sm (carcerato)* convict; *(furfante)* scoundrel; *(vogatore forzato)* galley slave.

**galera** [ga'lɛra] *sf* prison.

**galla** ['galla] *sf* **stare** *or* **rimanere a galla** float, keep afloat. **tenersi a galla** keep afloat; *(fig)* keep one's head above water. **venire a galla** come to the surface; *(fig)* come to light, emerge.

**galleggiare** [galled'dʒare] *v* float. **galleggiante** *agg* floating. *sm* float; *(tec)* ballcock.

**galleria** [galle'ria] *sf* gallery; *(traforo)* tunnel; *(passaggio sotterraneo)* subway; *(cinema, ecc.)* circle, balcony.

**Galles** ['galles] *sm* Wales. **gallese** *sm, agg* Welsh; *s(m+f)* Welsh person.

**gallo** ['gallo] *sm* cock. **galletto** *sm* cockerel; *(tec)* wing-nut. **gallina** *sf* hen.

**gallone¹** [gal'lone] *sm (misura)* gallon.

**gallone²** [gal'lone] *sm* braid; *(mil)* stripe.

**galoppare** [galop'pare] *v* gallop. **galoppata** *sf* gallop; *(lavoro faticoso)* hard work. **galoppo** *sm* gallop.

**galvanizzare** [galvanid'dzare] *v* galvanize.

**gamba** ['gamba] *sf* leg. **andare a gambe all'aria** fall flat on one's back; *(fallire)* fail. **a tre gambe** three-legged. **darsela a gambe** take to one's heels. **gambe storte** bandy *or* bow legs *pl.* **in gamba** *(valente)* smart. *inter* take care!

**gambero** ['gambero] *sm (di acqua dolce)* crayfish; *(gamberetto)* shrimp; *(gamberone)* prawn. **rosso come un gambero** as red as a lobster.

**gambo** ['gambo] *sm (pianta)* stem, stalk; *(tec)* shank.

**gamma** ['gamma] *sf* range; *(lunghezza d'onda)* waveband.

**ganascia** [ga'naʃa] *sf* jaw; *(freno)* brake-shoe.

**gancio** ['gantʃo] *sm* hook.

**ganghero** ['gangero] *sm* hinge. **essere fuori dai gangheri** be beside oneself. **uscire dai gangheri** lose one's head.

**gara** ['gara] *sf* competition; *(corsa)* race; *(comm)* tender.

**garage** [ga'raʒ] *sm, pl* **-s** garage.

**garantire** [garan'tire] *v* guarantee; *(rendersi garante)* vouch for; *(assicurare)* assure. **essere garante per** *or* **di** vouch for. **rendersi garante per** *(dir)* stand bail for.

**garanzia** [garan'tsia] *sf* guarantee.

**garbare** [gar'bare] *v* please, suit. **garbato** *agg* polite, well-mannered. **garbo** *sm (maniera)* good manners *pl,* politeness; *(gentilezza)* charm.

**garbuglio** [gar'buʎo] *sm* muddle.

**gareggiare** [gared'dʒare] *v* compete.

**gargarismo** [garga'rizmo] *sm* gargle. **fare i gargarismi** gargle.

**garitta** [ga'ritta] *sf* cabin; (*mil*) sentry-box.

**garofano** [ga'rɔfano] *sm* carnation. **chiodo di garofano** *sm* clove.

**garrire** [gar'rire] *v* twitter. **garrito** *sm* twitter.

**garrulo** ['garrulo] *agg* (*uccello*) twittering; (*persona loquace*) garrulous.

**garza** ['gardza] *sf* gauze.

**garzone** [gar'dzone] *sm* boy, mate.

**gas** ['gas] *sm* gas. **a gas** gas. **gas asfissiante/esilarante** poison/laughing gas. **gassoso** *agg* gaseous.

**gasolio** [ga'zɔljo] *sm* fuel oil, diesel fuel.

**gassosa** [gas'soza] *sf* fizzy drink, lemonade.

**gastrico** ['gastriko] *agg* gastric.

**gastronomia** [gastrono'mia] *sf* gastronomy, cooking. **gastronomico** *agg* gastronomic(al). **gastronomo** *sm* (*buongustaio*) gourmet.

**gattabuia** [gatta'buja] *sf* (*fam*) clink.

**gatto** ['gatto] *sm* cat. **gatta** *sf* she-cat. **compare una gatta nel sacco** buy a pig in a poke. **gatta ci cova!** I smell a rat! **una gatta da pelare** a tricky job to do. **gattino** *sm* kitten; (*bot*) catkin.

**gazza** ['gaddza] *sf* magpie.

**gazzarra** [gad'dzarra] *sf* uproar, row.

**gazzella** [gad'dzɛlla] *sf* gazelle.

**gazzetta** [gad'dzetta] *sf* gazette.

**gelare** [dʒe'lare] *v* freeze. **gelata** *sf* (hard) frost.

**gelatina** [dʒela'tina] *sf* gelatine.

**gelato** [dʒe'lato] *agg* frozen. *sm* ice-cream. **gelataio** *sm* ice-cream vendor. **gelateria** *sf* ice-cream shop *or* parlour.

**gelido** ['dʒɛlido] *agg* icy.

**gelo** ['dʒɛlo] *sm* frost; intense cold; (*sensazione*) chill.

**gelone** [dʒe'lone] *sm* chilblain.

**gelosia¹** [dʒelo'zia] *sf* jealousy; (*cura attenta*) great care.

**gelosia²** [dʒelo'zia] *sf* (*finestra*) blind.

**geloso** [dʒe'lozo] *agg* jealous.

**gelso** ['dʒɛlso] *sm* (*mora*) mulberry; (*albero*) mulberry-tree.

**gelsomino** [dʒelso'mino] *sm* jasmine.

**gemello** [dʒe'mɛllo] *sm*, *agg* twin. **gemelli**

*sm pl* (*di polsino*) cuff-links *pl*. **Gemelli** *sm pl* Gemini *sing*.

**gemere** ['dʒemere] *v* groan; (*colare*) drip, ooze; (*tubare*) coo. **gemito** *sm* groan.

**gemma** ['dʒemma] *sf* gem; (*bot*) bud.

**gene** ['dʒɛne] *sm* gene.

**genealogia** [dʒenealo'dʒia] *sf* (*scienza*) genealogy; (*stirpe*) pedigree. **albero genealogico** *sm* family tree.

**generale** [dʒene'rale] *sm*, *agg* general. **in generale** in general; (*di solito*) as a rule.

**generalizzare** [dʒeneralid'dzare] *v* generalize. **generalizzazione** *sf* generalization.

**generare** [dʒene'rare] *v* generate, produce. **generazione** *sf* generation.

**genere** ['dʒenere] *sm* kind, type; (*tipo di merce*) product, article; (*stile*) genre; (*gramm*) gender. **d'ogni genere** of all kinds. **il genere umano** mankind. **nel suo genere** in his way.

**generico** [dʒe'nɛriko] *agg* generic; general.

**genero** ['dʒɛnero] *sm* son-in-law.

**generoso** [dʒene'rozo] *agg* generous; (*vino*) full-bodied; (*cavallo*) thoroughbred.

**genetica** [dʒe'nɛtika] *sf* genetics. **genetico** *agg* genetic. **genetista** *s(m+f)* geneticist.

**gengiva** [dʒen'dʒiva] *sf* gum. **gengivite** *sf* gingivitis.

**geniale** [dʒe'njale] *agg* ingenious, clever. **genialità** *sf* brilliance.

**genio¹** ['dʒɛnjo] *sm* genius; (*disposizione*) talent, gift; (*inclinazione*) taste. **andare a genio** be to one's liking, suit.

**genio²** ['dʒɛnjo] *sm* (*mil*) engineers *pl*.

**genitali** [dʒeni'tali] *sm pl* genitals *pl*.

**genitore** [dʒeni'tore] *sm* parent.

**gennaio** [dʒen'najo] *sm* January.

**Genova** ['dʒɛnova] *sf* Genoa. **genovese** *agg*, *s(m+f)* Genoese.

**gente** ['dʒɛnte] *sf* people *pl*.

**gentile** [dʒen'tile] *agg* kind; (*cortese*) polite; delicate. **gentilezza** *sf* kindness; politeness; (*atto gentile*) favour. **gentiluomo** *sm* (*nobile*) nobleman; (*persona retta*) gentleman.

**genuino** [dʒenu'ino] *agg* genuine, natural; authentic. **genuinità** *sf* authenticity, naturalness, spontaneity.

**genziana** [dʒen'tsjana] *sf* gentian.

**geografia** [dʒeogra'fia] *sf* geography. **geografico** *agg* geographical. **atlante geografico** *sm* atlas. **carta geografica** *sf* map. **geografo, -a** *sm, sf* geographer.

**geologia** [dʒeolo'dʒia] *sf* geology. **geologico** *agg* geological. **geologo, -a** *sm, sf* geologist.

**geometra** [dʒe'ɔmetra] *s(m+f)* surveyor.

**geometria** [dʒeome'tria] *sf* geometry. **geometrico** *agg* geometrical.

**geranio** [dʒe'ranjo] *sm* geranium.

**gerarchia** [dʒerar'kia] *sf* hierarchy. **gerarca** *sm* (*rel*) hierarch; (*capo*) leader. **gerarchico** *agg* hierarchical. **per via gerarchica** through official channels.

**gerente** [dʒe'rɛnte] *sm* manager.

**gergo** ['dʒɛrgo] *sm* slang, jargon.

**geriatria** [dʒerja'tria] *sf* geriatrics. **geriatrico** *agg* geriatric.

**Germania** [dʒer'manja] *sf* Germany. **germanico** *agg* German.

**germe** ['dʒɛrme] *sm* germ. **germinare** *v* germinate.

**germogliare** [dʒermoʎ'ʎare] *v* bud, sprout; (*fig*) germinate. **germoglio** *sm* shoot; (*origine*) germ.

**gesso** ['dʒɛsso] *sm* (*minerale*) gypsum; (*da disegno*) chalk; (*a pronta presa*) plaster (of Paris); (*opera*) plaster cast.

**gesta** ['dʒɛsta] *sf pl* (noble) deeds *pl*, feats *pl*.

**gesticolare** [dʒestiko'lare] *v* gesticulate.

**gestire** [dʒes'tire] *v* manage, run. **gestione** *sf* management.

**gesto** ['dʒɛsto] *sm* gesture; (*azione*) deed; (*del capo*) nod; (*della mano*) wave.

**Gesù** [dʒe'zu] *sm* Jesus.

**gesuita** [dʒezu'ita] *sm* Jesuit. **gesuitico** *agg* Jesuitical.

**gettare** [dʒet'tare] *v* throw; (*emettere*) let out; (*tec*) cast. **gettare i soldi dalla finestra** throw money down the drain. **gettare le fondamenta** lay the foundations. **gettar luce su ...** cast light on .... **gettata** *sf* cast; (*di reti*) casting.

**getto** ['dʒɛtto] *sm* (*lancio*) throw; (*di liquido o gas*) jet; (*metallo, ecc.*) casting.

**gettone** [dʒet'tone] *sm* counter, token.

**ghermire** [ger'mire] *v* clutch, grab.

**ghetto** ['getto] *sm* ghetto.

**ghiacciaia** [gjat'tʃaja] *sf* ice-box.

**ghiacciaio** [gjat'tʃajo] *sm* glacier.

**ghiacciare** [gjat'tʃare] *v* freeze. **ghiacciata** *sf* drink with crushed ice.

**ghiaccio** ['gjattʃo] *sm* ice. **di ghiaccio** (*freddissimo*) ice-cold, frozen; (*fig*) icy. **ghiacciolo** *sm* icicle; (*gelato*) ice lolly.

**ghiaia** ['gjaja] *sf* gravel.

**ghianda** ['gjanda] *sf* acorn.

**ghiandaia** [gjan'daja] *sf* jay.

**ghiandola** ['gjandola] *sf* gland. **ghiandolare** *agg* glandular.

**ghigliottina** [giʎʎot'tina] *sf* guillotine. **ghigliottinare** *v* guillotine.

**ghignare** [giɲ'ɲare] *v* sneer. **ghigno** *sm* sneer, smirk.

**ghiotto** ['gjotto] *agg* greedy; (*appetitoso*) inviting. **ghiottone, -a** *sm, sf* glutton, greedy person. **ghiottoneria** *sf* (*golosità*) gluttony; (*cibo ghiotto*) titbit. **ghiottonerie** *sm; f pl* delicatessen.

**ghiribizzo** [giri'bittso] *sm* fancy, whim.

**ghirigoro** [giri'gɔro] *sm* flourish.

**ghirlanda** [gir'landa] *sf* garland, wreath.

**ghiro** ['giro] *sm* dormouse. **dormire come un ghiro** sleep like a log.

**ghisa** ['giza] *sf* cast iron.

**già** ['dʒa] *avv* already; (*un tempo*) once; (*ex*) formerly.

**giacca** ['dʒakka] *sf* coat; (*giacchetta*) jacket.

**giacché** [dʒak'ke] *cong* as, since.

**giacchetta** [dʒak'ketta] *sf* jacket.

*****giacere** [dʒa'tʃere] *v* lie; (*in sospeso*) be in abeyance. **mettersi a giacere** lie down. **giacenza** *sf* abeyance; (*merce*) (unsold) stock; (*econ*) deposit. **giacimento** *sm* deposit.

**giacinto** [dʒa'tʃinto] *sm* hyacinth.

**giada** ['dʒada] *sf* jade.

**giaggiolo** [dʒad'dʒɔlo] *sm* iris.

**giaguaro** [dʒa'gwaro] *sm* jaguar.

**giallo** ['dʒallo] *agg* yellow. *sm* (*colore*) yellow; (*libro, film*) thriller. **giallo d'uovo** (egg) yolk. **giallastro** *agg* yellowish, sallow. **giallognolo** *agg* pale yellow, yellowish.

**giammai** [dʒam'mai] *avv* never. **se giammai** if ever.

**Giappone** [dʒap'pone] *sm* Japan. **giapponese** *s(m+f)*, *agg* Japanese.

**giardinetta** [dʒardi'netta] *sf* estate car.

**giardino** [dʒar'dino] *sm* garden. **giardino d'infanzia** kindergarten, nursery school. **giardino zoologico** zoo. **giardinaggio** *sm* gardening. **giardiniere, -a** *sm, sf* gardener.

**giarrettiera** [dʒarret'tjɛra] *sf* suspender, garter.

**giavellotto** [dʒavel'lɔtto] *sm* javelin.

**Gibilterra** [dʒibil'tɛrra] *sf* Gibraltar.

**gigante** [dʒi'gante] *sm, agg* giant. **gigantesco** *agg* gigantic, huge.

**gigione** [dʒi'dʒone] *sm* ham (actor). **fare il gigione** ham.

**giglio** ['dʒiʎo] *sm* lily.

**gilè** [dʒi'lɛ] *sm* waistcoat.

**ginecologo** [dʒine'kɔlogo], **-a** *sm, sf* gynaecologist. **ginecologia** *sm* gynaecology. **ginecologico** *agg* gynaecological.

**ginepro** [dʒi'nepro] *sm* juniper.

**ginestra** [dʒi'nɛstra] *sf* broom. **ginestrone** *sm* furze, gorse.

**Ginevra** [dʒi'nevra] *sf* Geneva.

**gingillarsi** [dʒindʒil'larsi] *v* (*divertirsi*) amuse oneself; (*perder tempo*) hang about.

**ginnasio** [dʒin'nazjo] *sm* secondary school.

**ginnastica** [dʒin'nastika] *sf* (*sport*) gymnastics; (*esercizi*) physical exercises *pl*.

**ginocchio** [dʒi'nokkjo] *sm pl* **-a** *f* knee. **ginocchioni** *avv* also **in ginocchio** on one's knees.

**giocare** [dʒo'kare] *v* play; (*in borsa*) gamble (on the Stock Exchange); (*scommettere*) bet. **giocata** *sf* (*partita*) game; (*puntata*) stake, bet. **giocatore, -trice** *sf* player; (*d'azzardo*) gambler.

**giocattolo** [dʒo'kattolo] *sm* toy.

**giocherellare** [dʒokerel'lare] *v* toy.

**giochetto** [dʒo'ketto] *sm* (*passatempo*) pastime; (*tranello*) trick; (*lavoro facile*) child's play.

**gioco** ['dʒɔko] *sm* (*divertimento, tec*) play; (*con regole, partita*) game; (*vizio*) gambling; (*combinazione di carte*) hand; (*posta*) stake; (*beffa*) trick. **entrare in gioco** come into play. **fare il doppio gioco** double-cross. **mettere in gioco** (*far agire*) bring into action; (*rischiare*) stake.

**giocoliere** [dʒoko'ljere] *sm* juggler.

**giocondo** [dʒo'kondo] *agg* cheerful, merry.

**giogo** ['dʒogo] *sm* yoke; (*valico*) pass; (*cima allungata*) ridge.

**gioia**[1] ['dʒɔja] *sf* joy, delight.

**gioia**[2] ['dʒɔja] *sf* (*gemma*) jewel.

**gioire** [dʒo'ire] *v* rejoice. **gioioso** *agg* joyful.

**giornalaio** [dʒorna'lajo], **-a** *sm, sf* news-agent.

**giornale** [dʒor'nale] *sm* (*quotidiano*) news-paper; (*registro*) journal; diary. **giornale di bordo** log(-book). **giornale radio** news (bulletin).

**giornaliero** [dʒorna'ljero] *agg* daily.

**giornalismo** [dʒorna'lizmo] *sm* journalism. **giornalista** *s*(*m+f*) journalist.

**giornata** [dʒor'nata] *sf* day. **a giornata** by the day. **di giornata** (*fresco*) fresh; (*di turno*) on duty. **donna a giornata** daily (woman). **vivere alla giornata** live from day to day.

**giorno** ['dʒorno] *sm* day. **a giorni** (*tra breve*) soon; (*a intervalli*) sometimes. **al giorno** a day. **al giorno d'oggi** nowadays. **che giorno è?** (*data*) what is the date? (*della settimana*) what day (of the week) is it? **da un giorno all'altro** (*improvvisamente*) suddenly; (*tra poco*) any day now. **di giorno** by day. **giorno festivo** holiday. **giorno libero** day off. **punto a giorno** *sm* hem-stitch. **un giorno o l'altro** one of these days.

**giostra** ['dʒɔstra] *sf* (*fiera*) merry-go-round; (*torneo*) tournament.

**giovane** ['dʒovane] *agg* young; (*giovanile*) youthful; (*non stagionato*) new. *sm* (*giovanotto*) young man, youth. *sf* young woman, girl. **giovanile** *agg* youthful, juvenile.

**giovare** [dʒo'vare] *v* help, do good.

**giovedì** [dʒove'di] *sm* Thursday.

**giovenca** [dʒo'vɛnka] *sf* heifer.

**gioventù** [dʒoven'tu] *sf* youth; (*i giovani*) young people *pl*.

**giovevole** [dʒo'vevole] *agg* useful.

**gioviale** [dʒo'vjale] *agg* genial, jolly.

**giovinezza** [dʒovi'nettsa] *sf* (*gioventù*) youth; (*qualità*) youthfulness. **seconda giovinezza** second childhood.

**giradischi** [dʒira'diski] *sm invar* record player.

**giradito** [dʒira'dito] *sm* whitlow.

**giraffa** [dʒi'raffa] *sf* giraffe.

**giramento** [dʒira'mento] *sm* **giramento di capo** dizzy spell; (fit of) dizziness.

**girandola** [dʒi'randola] *sf* (*fuochi d'artificio*) Catherine wheel; (*giocattolo*) toy windmill; (*fig*) fickle person.

**girare** [dʒi'rare] *v* turn; (*scansare*) get round, avoid; (*percorrere viaggiando*) travel, tour; (*andare da un posto all'altro*) go around; (*comm*) endorse; (*cinema*) shoot, take; (*camminare senza meta*) wander about; circulate. **girare a vuoto** (*mec*) idle. **mi gira la testa** I feel dizzy *or* giddy.

**girarrosto** [dʒirar'rɔsto] *sm* spit.

**girasole** [dʒira'sole] *sm* sunflower.

**girino** [dʒi'rino] *sm* tadpole.

**giro** ['dʒiro] *sm* turn; (*pista*) lap; (*percorso*) round; (*viaggio*) tour; (*passeggiata a piedi*) stroll, walk; (*in macchina*) drive; (*in bicicletta, a cavallo*) ride; (*periodo*) course, space; circulation; (*mec*) revolution. **andare in giro** go round. **essere in giro** (*fuori*) be out; (*in qualche posto*) be somewhere. **giro collo** neck. **giro d'affari** turnover. **giro d'orizzonte** survey. **giro manica** armhole. **guardarsi in giro** look around. **prendere in giro** make fun of.

**gironzolare** [dʒirondzo'lare] *v* stroll, wander (about).

**girovago** [dʒi'rɔvago] *sm, pl* **-ghi** vagabond, tramp. *agg* wandering. **girovagare** *v* stroll, wander (about).

**gita** ['dʒita] *sf* excursion, trip. **fare una gita** make an excursion, go on a trip.

**giù** [dʒu] *avv* down; (*dabbasso*) downstairs. **andare su e giù** (*salire e scendere*) go up and down; (*avanti e indietro*) go to and fro. **giù di lì** thereabouts. **in giù** (*moto*) down; (*stato*) low; (*in meno*) and under. **su per giù** thereabouts.

**giubba** ['dʒubba] *sf* jacket; (*mil*) tunic. **giubbotto di salvataggio** *sm* life-jacket.

**giubilare** [dʒubi'lare] *v* rejoice.

**giubileo** [dʒubi'lɛo] *sm* jubilee.

**giudaismo** [dʒuda'izmo] *sm* Judaism.

**giudicare** [dʒudi'kare] *v* judge; (*ritenere*) consider. **a giudicare da** judging by. **passare in giudicato** be beyond recall, be final.

**giudice** ['dʒuditʃe] *sm* judge. **giudice istruttore** examining magistrate.

**giudiziario** [dʒudi'tsjarjo] *agg* judicial.

**giudizio** [dʒu'ditsjo] *sm* judgment; (*parere*) opinion; (*dir*) sentence, verdict; (*buon senso*) common sense. **aver giudizio** be sensible. **citare in giudizio** summon. **comparire in giudizio** appear before a court. **dente del giudizio** *sm* wisdom tooth. **far giudizio** behave oneself. **rinviare a giudizio** commit for trial. **giudizioso** *agg* sensible.

**giugno** ['dʒuɲo] *sm* June.

**giulivo** [dʒu'livo] *agg* merry.

**giullare** [dʒul'lare] *sm* (*cantastorie*) minstrel; (*buffone*) clown.

**giunco** ['dʒunko] *sm* rush.

**\*giungere** ['dʒundʒere] *v* arrive (at), reach; (*riuscire*) manage; (*arrivare a punto di*) go so far as. **mi è giunto** I have received. **mi giunge nuovo** it is news to me.

**giungla** ['dʒungla] *sf* jungle.

**giunta¹** ['dʒunta] *sf* addition; (*peso*) make-weight; (*sartoria*) insert. **giuntare** *v* (*unire*) join; (*cucire*) sew together; (*cinema, nastro*) splice.

**giunta²** ['dʒunta] *sf* (*comitato*) council; (*mil*) junta.

**giunto** ['dʒunto] *sm* joint.

**giuntura** [dʒun'tura] *sf* joint; (*accoppiamento*) coupling.

**giunzione** [dʒun'tsjone] *sf* junction; (*giunto*) joint.

**giurare** [dʒu'rare] *v* swear. **giuramento** *sm* oath. **giuramento falso** (*spergiuro*) perjury. **mancare al giuramento** break an oath. **prestar giuramento** swear, take an oath.

**giurato** [dʒu'rato], **-a** *sm, sf* juror. *agg* sworn.

**giuria** [dʒu'ria] *sf* jury.

**giuridico** [dʒu'ridiko] *agg* legal.

**giurisdizione** [dʒurizdi'tsjone] *sf* jurisdiction.

**\*giustapporre** [dʒustap'porre] *v* juxtapose. **giustapposizione** *sf* juxtaposition.

**giustezza** [dʒus'tettsa] *sf* correctness; (*esattezza*) precision.

**giustificare** [dʒustifi'kare] *v* justify. **giustificazione** *sf* justification; (*scusa*) excuse.

**giustizia** [dʒus'titsja] *sf* justice; (*equità*) fairness. **assicurare alla giustizia** bring to justice. **fare** *or* **rendere giustizia** do justice.

**giusto** ['dʒusto] *agg* just; (*equo*) fair; (*legittimo*) rightful; (*corretto*) right. *avv* (*proprio, appena*) just; (*esattamente*) correctly. *sm* (*persona*) righteous man.

**glaciale** [gla'tʃale] *agg* glacial; (*fig*) icy.

**gladiolo** [gla'diolo] *sm* gladiolus.

**glassa** ['glassa] *sf* icing. **glassare** *v* ice.

**gli¹** [ʎi] *art* the.

**gli²** [ʎi] *pron* (*persona*) (to) him; (*cosa, animale*) (to) it.

**glicerina** [glitʃe'rina] *sf* glycerine.

**glicine** ['glitʃine] *sm* wisteria.

**globo** ['glɔbo] *sm* globe. **globo oculare** eyeball.

**globulo** ['glɔbulo] *sm* globule; (*med*) corpuscle. **globulare** *agg* globular.

**gloria** ['glɔrja] *sf* glory; (*vanto*) pride. **gloriarsi** *v* glory (in); (*vantarsi*) boast (of).

**glorificare** [glorifi'kare] *v* glorify.

**glucosio** [glu'kɔzjo] *sm* glucose.

**gnomo** ['nɔmo] *sm* gnome.

**gnomone** [no'mone] *sm* sundial.

**gobba** ['gɔbba] *sf* hump.

**gobbo** ['gɔbbo], **-a** *sm*, *sf* hunchback. *agg* hunchbacked.

**goccia** ['gottʃa] *sf* drop. **goccia a goccia** drop by drop; (*fig*) little by little. **una goccia nel mare** a drop in the ocean. **gocciolare** *v* drip.

**\*godere** [go'dere] *v* enjoy; (*rallegrarsi*) rejoice. **godimento** *sm* enjoyment; (*piacere*) pleasure.

**goffo** ['gɔffo] *agg* awkward, clumsy. **goffaggine** *sf* awkwardness, clumsiness; (*atto*) clumsy action; (*parola*) blunder.

**gol** [gɔl] *sm invar* goal.

**gola** ['gola] *sf* throat; (*golosità*) greed, gluttony. **aver l'acqua alla gola** be in deep water. **far gola** tempt.

**golf¹** [gɔlf] *sm invar* (*sport*) golf.

**golf²** [gɔlf] *sm invar* (*maglione*) sweater, jumper; (*con bottoni*) cardigan.

**golfo** ['golfo] *sm* gulf.

**goliardo** [go'ljardo] *sm* (*university*) student. **goliardico** *agg* university.

**goloso** [go'lozo] *agg* greedy. **golosità** *sf* greediness, gluttony.

**golpe¹** ['golpe] *sm* smut, blight.

**golpe²** ['golpe] *sm* coup (d'état).

**gomito** ['gomito] *sm* elbow. **gomitata** *sf* dig with the elbow. **farsi avanti a (forza di) gomitate** elbow one's way forward.

**gomitolo** [go'mitolo] *sm* ball.

**gomma** ['gomma] *sf* rubber; (*colla*) gum; (*pneumatico*) tyre. **gommapiuma** *sf* foam rubber. **gommato** *agg* rubberized; gummed. **gommoso** *agg* rubbery.

**gondola** ['gondola] *sf* gondola. **gondoliere** *sm* gondolier.

**gonfalone** [gonfa'lone] *sm* banner, standard.

**gonfiare** [gon'fjare] *v* swell (up); (*riempire di gas, ecc.*) inflate, blow up; (*montare*) puff up; exaggerate. **gonfiatura** *sf* blowing up, swelling up; (*gonfiore*) swelling; exaggeration. **gonfio** *agg* swollen, inflated. **gonfiore** *sm* swelling.

**gong** ['gɔng] *sm invar* gong.

**gonna** ['gonna] *sf also* **gonnella** skirt.

**gonorrea** [gonor'rɛa] *sf* gonorrhea.

**gonzo** ['gondzo] *sm* simpleton.

**gorgheggiare** [gorged'dʒare] *v* trill, warble. **gorgheggio** *sm* trill, warble; (*di uccello*) warbling.

**gorgo** ['gorgo] *sm* whirlpool.

**gorgogliare** [gorgo'ʎare] *v* gurgle; (*intestino*) rumble. **gorgoglio** *sm* rumble; gurgle.

**gorilla** [go'rilla] *sm invar* gorilla.

**gotico** ['gɔtiko] *agg* Gothic.

**gotta** ['gotta] *sf* gout.

**governante** [gover'nante] *sf* (*incaricata della casa*) housekeeper; (*istitutrice*) governess.

**governare** [gover'nare] *v* govern; (*dirigere*) run; (*dominare*) rule; (*pilotare*) steer. **governativo** *agg* government, governmental. **governatore** *sm* governor. **governo** *sm* government; (*dominio*) rule; (*amministrazione*) management. **governo della casa** housekeeping.

**gozzo** ['goddzo] *sm* crop; (*med*) goitre. **averla nel** *or* **sul gozzo** be unable to swallow.

**gozzovigliare** [goddzovi'ʎare] *v* revel, go on a spree.

**gracchiare** [grak'kjare] *v* croak.

**gracidare** [gratʃi'dare] *v* croak.

**gracile** ['gratʃile] *agg* frail. **gracilità** *sf* frailty.

**gradasso** [gra'dasso] *sm* boaster, braggart. **fare il gradasso** boast, brag.

**gradazione** [grada'tsjone] *sf* gradation; (*sfumatura*) shade. **gradazione alcolica** alcoholic strength.

**gradevole** [gra'devole] *agg* agreeable.

**gradiente** [gra'djɛnte] *sm* gradient.

**gradimento** [gradi'mento] *sm* (*approvazione*) liking; (*piacere*) pleasure.

**gradino** [gra'dino] *sm* step. **gradinata** *sf* flight of steps.

**gradire** [gra'dire] *v* (*trovar piacevole*) find agreeable; (*accogliere con gioia*) welcome; (*accettare*) accept; (*nelle richieste*) like.

**grado¹** ['grado] *sm* degree; (*mil, rango*) rank. **a gradi** step by step. **avanzare di**

**grado** be promoted. **essere in grado di** be able to.

**grado²** ['grado] *sm* **di buon grado** willingly.

**graduale** [gradu'ale] *agg* gradual.

**graduare** [gradu'are] *v* graduate. **graduatoria** *sf* (*elenco*) list; (*ordine*) classification.

**graffa** ['graffa] *sf* bracket; (*fermaglio*) (paper-)clip.

**graffiare** [graf'fjare] *v* scratch. **graffiatura** *sf* scratch. **graffio** *sm* scratch.

**grafico** [gra'fiko] *agg* graphic. *sm* (*diagramma*) chart, graph; (*persona*) graphic artist.

**grafologo** [gra'fɔlogo], **-a** *sm*, *sf* graphologist.

**gramigna** [gra'miɲa] *sf* couch-grass; (*malerba*) weed. **attaccarsi come la gramigna** cling like a leech.

**grammatico** [gram'matiko] *agg* grammatical. *sm* grammarian. **grammatica** *sm* grammar; (*persona*) grammarian.

**grammo** ['grammo] *sm* gram.

**grammofono** [gram'mɔfono] *sm* gramophone.

**grana¹** ['grana] *sf* (*struttura*) grain. *sm* (*formaggio*) Parmesan (cheese).

**grana²** ['grana] *sf* (*seccatura*) nuisance. **piantare una grana** make trouble.

**granaglie** [gra'naʎe] *sf pl* cereals *pl*.

**granaio** [gra'najo] *sm* barn; (*zona produttrice di grano*) granary; (*locale sottotetto*) loft.

**granata¹** [gra'nata] *sf* (*scopa*) broom.

**granata²** [gra'nata] *sf* (*mil*) grenade.

**granata³** [gra'nata] *sf* (*frutto*) pomegranate; (*pietra*) garnet.

**Gran Bretagna** [gran bre'taɲa] *sf* Great Britain.

**grancassa** [gran'kassa] *sf* (*musica*) bass drum. **batter la grancassa** blow one's own trumpet.

**granchio** [ˈgrankjo] *sm* crab. **prendere un granchio** make a blunder.

**grande** ['grande] *agg* big; (*ampio, numeroso*) large; (*largo*) wide; (*fig*) great; (*adulto*) grown-up. **in grande** on a large scale. **in gran parte** largely. **non ... un gran che** not ... much.

**grandeggiare** [granded'dʒare] *v* (*emergere*) tower, stand out; (*darsi arie*) show off.

**grandezza** [gran'dettsa] *sf* (*dimensione, taglia*) size; (*altezza*) height; (*larghezza*) width; (*ampiezza*) breadth; (*fig*) greatness; (*mat, fis*) magnitude.

**grandinare** [grandi'nare] *v* hail. **grandine** *sf* hail. **chicco di grandine** *sm* hailstone.

**grandioso** [gran'djozo] *agg* grand.

**granduca** [gran'duka] *sm*, *pl* **-chi** grand duke. **granducato** *sm* grand duchy. **granduchessa** *sf* grand duchess.

**granello** [gra'nɛllo] *sm* grain; (*di frutta*) pip. **granello di pepe** peppercorn.

**granita** [gra'nita] *sf* crushed-ice drink.

**granito** [gra'nito] *sm* granite.

**grano** ['grano] *sm* (*granello*) grain; (*frumento*) wheat; (*cereale in genere*) corn, cereal.

**granturco** [gran'turko] *sm* maize.

**granulo** ['granulo] *sm* granule. **granulare** *agg* granular.

**grappolo** ['grappolo] *sm* bunch.

**grasso** ['grasso] *agg* fat; (*unto*) greasy, oily; (*che contiene grasso*) fatty. *sm* fat; (*sostanza untuosa*) grease. **grassoccio** *agg* plump.

**grata** ['grata] *sf* grating, grille. **gratella** *sf* grill.

**graticcio** [gra'tittʃo] *sm* trellis.

**graticola** [gra'tikola] *sf* grill.

**gratifica** [gra'tifika] *sf* bonus.

**gratis** ['gratis] *agg* free. *avv* for nothing, for love.

**gratitudine** [grati'tudine] *sf* gratitude.

**grato** ['grato] *agg* grateful, obliged; (*gradevole*) pleasant; (*gradito*) welcome.

**grattacapo** [gratta'kapo] *sm* worry, headache.

**grattacielo** [gratta'tʃɛlo] *sm* skyscraper.

**grattare** [grat'tare] *v* scratch; (*grattugiare*) grate; (*raschiare*) scrape; (*fam: rubare*) pinch.

**grattugiare** [grattu'dʒare] *v* grate. **grattugia** *sf* grater.

**gratuito** [gra'tuito] *agg* free; (*non retribuito*) unpaid; (*ingiustificato*) gratuitous; (*infondato*) unfounded.

**gravare** [gra'vare] *v* burden.

**grave** ['grave] *agg* (*serio*) grave; (*pesante*) heavy; (*malattia*) serious; (*perdita*) grievous. **gravità** *sf* gravity. **gravoso** *agg* hard, onerous.

**gravido** ['gravido] *agg* pregnant. **gravidanza** *sf* pregnancy.

**grazia** ['gratsja] *sf* grace; (*fascino*) charm; (*clemenza*) pardon; favour. **grazie** *sf pl*, *inter* thanks. **grazie a** thanks to.

**Grecia** ['grɛtʃa] *sf* Greece. **greco, -a** *s, agg, m pl -ci* Greek. **naso greco** *sm* Grecian nose.

**gregge** ['greddʒe] *sm* flock, herd.

**greggio** ['greddʒo] *agg* raw, crude.

**grembiule** [grem'bjule] *sm* apron; *(con petto)* pinafore; *(con maniche)* overall.

**grembo** ['grembo] *sm* lap.

**gremire** [gre'mire] *v* fill (up). **gremirsi** *v* get crowded.

**gres** ['grɛs] *sm* stoneware.

**gretto** ['gretto] *agg* mean; *(idea, animo)* narrow-minded. **grettezza** *sf* meanness; narrow-mindedness.

**gridare** [gri'dare] *v* shout; *(strillare)* yell, scream. **gridare aiuto** call for help. **grido** *sm, pl -a f* shout; cry; scream, yell. **di grido** *(noto)* famous; *(di moda)* fashionable. **l'ultimo grido** the latest fashion, the last word.

**griffa** ['griffa] *sf* claw.

**grigio** ['gridʒo] *agg* grey; *(fig)* drab. *sm* grey. **grigiastro** *agg* greyish. **grigiore** *sm* greyness; *(fig)* drabness. **grigioverde** *sm, agg* grey-green, khaki.

**griglia** ['griʎa] *sf* grill; *(saracinesca)* shutter; *(schermo)* grille; *(radio)* grid; *(focolare)* grate.

**grilletto** [gril'letto] *sm* trigger.

**grillo** ['grillo] *sm* cricket; *(capriccio)* whim. **gli è saltato il grillo di** he got it into his head to.

**grimaldello** [grimal'dello] *sm* jemmy.

**grinza** ['grintsa] *sf* crease; *(ruga)* wrinkle. **non fare una grinza** *(calzare bene)* fit perfectly; *(filare bene)* be flawless.

**gripparsi** [grip'parsi] *v (auto)* seize up.

**grondaia** [gron'daja] *sf* gutter.

**grondare** [gron'dare] *v* drip; *(abbondantemente)* pour.

**groppa** ['grɔppa] *sf* back.

**grossa** ['grɔssa] *sf (comm)* gross. **dormire della grossa** sleep like a log.

**grossezza** [gros'settsa] *sf (volume)* bulk, size; *(spessore)* thickness.

**grossista** [gros'sista] *sm(+f)* wholesaler.

**grosso** ['grɔsso] *agg* large, big; *(spesso)* thick; *(non raffinato)* coarse; serious. **dirle grosse** tell fibs. **farne di grosse** cause all sorts of trouble. **grossolano** *agg* coarse, rough.

**grotta** ['grɔtta] *sf* cave; grotto.

**grottesco** [grot'tesko] *agg* grotesque.

**groviera** [gro'vjɛra] *s(m+f) also* **gruviera** *(formaggio)* gruyère.

**groviglio** [gro'viʎo] *sm* tangle; *(confusione)* mess.

**gru** [gru] *sf* crane.

**gruccia** ['gruttʃa] *sf* crutch; *(attaccapanni)* coat-hanger.

**grugnire** [gru'ɲire] *v* grunt. **grugnito** *sm* grunt.

**grugno** ['gruɲo] *sm (maiale)* snout; *(fam: muso)* mug.

**grullo** ['grullo] *agg* foolish.

**grumo** ['grumo] *sm* clot.

**gruppo** ['gruppo] *sm* group; *(mec)* unit.

**gruviera** [gru'vjɛra] *V* **groviera**.

**gruzzolo** ['gruttsolo] *sm* pile; *(risparmi)* nest-egg.

**guadagnare** [gwada'ɲare] *v* earn; *(ottenere)* gain; *(vincere)* win; *(raggiungere)* reach; *(risparmiare)* save.

**guadagno** [gwa'daɲo] *sm (retribuzione)* earnings *pl*; profit; advantage.

**guado** ['gwado] *sm* ford. **guadare** *v* wade.

**guaina** [gwa'ina] *sf* sheath.

**guaio** ['gwajo] *sm* trouble. **guai** *inter* woe betide you, us, etc.

**guaire** [gwa'ire] *v* whine, yelp. **guaito** *sm* whine, yelp.

**guancia** ['gwantʃa] *sf* cheek. **guanciale** *sm* pillow.

**guanto** ['gwanto] *sm* glove. **calzare come un guanto** fit like a glove. **gettare il guanto** throw down the gauntlet. **trattare coi guanti** treat with kid gloves.

**guardaboschi** [gwarda'bɔski] *sm* forester.

**guardacaccia** [gwarda'kattʃa] *sm invar* gamekeeper.

**guardacoste** [gwarda'kɔste] *sm invar* coast-guard.

**guardalinee** [gwarda'linee] *sm invar (sport)* linesman.

**guardamano** [gwarda'mano] *sm invar (sciabola)* hilt; *(fucile)* guard; *(guanto)* protective glove.

**guardare** [gwar'dare] *v* look (at); *(affacciarsi)* look out; face; *(dare un'occhiata)* have a look; *(custodire)* look after, mind; *(stare a vedere)* watch; *(considerare)* view; *(cercare)* try to, be careful to. **andare a guardare** have a look. **Dio ne guardi!** God forbid! **guarda che roba!** just look at that! **guardar di sbieco** *or* **traverso** look askance (at). **guardare fisso** stare, gaze (at). **guarda un po'!** well, well!

**guardaroba** [gwarda'rɔba] *sm invar* (*luogo*) cloakroom; (*armadio*) wardrobe. **guardarobiera** *sf* cloakroom attendant.

**guardarsi** [gwar'darsi] *v* look at oneself. **guardarsi intorno** look around. **guardarsi da** (*fare attenzione a*) beware of; (*astenersi da*) refrain from. **me ne guardo bene!** heaven forbid!

**guardata** [gwar'data] *sf* look, glance.

**guardavia** [gwarda'via] *sm invar* guardrail.

**guardia** ['gwardja] *sf* (*custodia*) watch, guard; (*turno*) duty; (*custode*) keeper, watchman; (*sentinella*) sentry; (*sport*) guard. **essere di guardia** be on duty; (*mil*) be on guard duty. **fare la guardia** (*sorvegliare*) guard, watch; (*badare*) watch over. **guardia di finanza** (*corpo*) Customs *pl*; (*singolo*) Customs officer. **mettere in guardia** warn. **guardiano** *sm* keeper, guardian.

**guardingo** [gwar'dingo] *agg* cautious, wary.

**guarire** [gwa'rire] *v* cure; (*rimettersi in salute*) recover; (*ferita*) heal. **guarigione** *sf* recovery; healing.

**guarnigione** [gwarni'dʒone] *sf* garrison.

**guarnire** [gwar'nire] *v* decorate; (*vestiario*) trim; (*gastr*) garnish; (*corredare*) equip; (*mil*) garrison. **guarnizione** *sf* decoration, trimming, garnish; (*tec*) packing; (*auto*) gasket.

**guastafeste** [gwasta'feste] *s(m+ f )* *invar* spoilsport.

**guastamestieri** [gwastames'tieri] *s(m+f )* *invar* bungler; (*fam*) menace.

**guastare** [gwas'tare] *v* spoil; (*rovinare*) ruin, damage. **guastarsi** *v* (*cibi*) go bad; (*mec*) break down; (*tempo*) change for the worse. **guasto** *agg* (*cibo*) bad, rotten; (*mec*) broken; (*salute, ecc.*) bad.

**guazzabuglio** [gwattsa'buʎo] *sm* hotchpotch, jumble.

**guazzare** [gwat'tsare] *v* splash about; (*fig*) wallow. **guazzo** *sm* pool; (*pittura*) gouache.

**guercio** ['gwertʃo] *agg* cross-eyed.

**guerra** ['gwɛrra] *sf* war; (*il guerreggiare*) warfare. **far guerra** wage war. **guerra mondiale** world war. **guerrafondaio** *sm, sf* warmonger.

**guerreggiare** [gwerred'dʒare] *v* fight.

**guerresco** [gwer'resko] *agg* (*bellicoso*) warlike; (*di guerra*) war.

**guerriero** [gwer'rjɛro] *agg* (*bellicoso*) warlike; (*combattivo*) aggressive. *sm* warrior.

**guerriglia** [gwer'riʎa] *sf* guerrilla warfare. **guerrigliero** *sm* guerrilla.

**gufo** ['gufo] *sm* owl.

**guglia** ['guʎa] *sf* (*arch*) spire; (*geog*) pinnacle.

**guida** ['gwida] *sf* guide; (*direzione, comando*) guidance, leadership; (*tappeto*) runner; (*elenco*) directory; (*auto*) drive, driving; (*comandi*) controls *pl*. **esame (di) guida** *sm* driving test. **guida a destra/sinistra** right-/left-hand drive. **scuola (di) guida** *sf* driving school.

**guidare** [gwi'dare] *v* guide; (*dirigere, comandare*) lead; (*auto*) drive; (*aero*) fly; (*nave*) steer; (*moto*) ride. **guidatore, -trice** *sm, sf* driver.

**guinzaglio** [gwin'tsaʎo] *sm* leash, lead. **mettere il guinzaglio** (*fig*) keep a tight rein (on). **tenere al guinzaglio** keep on a leash.

**guisa** ['gwiza] *sf* **a** *or* **in guisa di** in the manner of, like.

**guizzare** [gwit'tsare] *v* (*lampo*) flash; (*pesci*) dart; (*sfuggire*) wriggle; (*fiamma*) flicker. **guizzo** *sm* flash; dart; flicker.

**guscio** ['guʃo] *sm* shell; (*legumi*) pod.

**gustare** [gus'tare] *v* taste; (*trovar buono*) enjoy. **gusto** *sm* taste; (*piacere*) enjoyment. **con gusto** tastefully. **di gusto** heartily. **non aver gusto** be tasteless. **prenderci gusto** take a liking (to). **senza gusto** tasteless.

**gutturale** [guttu'rale] *agg* guttural.

# H

**hamburgher** [am'burger] *sm* beefburger.

**hascisc** [a'ʃiʃ] *sm* hashish.

**hockey** ['hɔki] *sm* hockey.

# I

**i** [i] *art* the.

**iattanza** [jat'tantsa] *sf* arrogance.

**ibernazione** [iberna'tsjone] *sf* hibernation. **ibernare** *v* hibernate.

**ibrido** ['ibrido] *sm, agg* hybrid.

**Iddio** [id'dio] *sm* God.

**idea** [i'dɛa] *sf* idea; opinion; (*proposito*) intention. **cambiare idea** change one's mind. **dare l'idea** give the impression.

**ideale** [ide'ale] *sm, agg* ideal. **idealismo** *sm* idealism. **idealista** *s(m+f)* idealist. **idealistico** *agg* idealistic.

**identico** [i'dɛntiko] *agg* identical.

**identificare** [identifi'kare] *v* identify. **identificazione** *sf* identification.

**identità** [identi'ta] *sf* identity.

**ideologia** [ideolo'dʒia] *sf* ideology. **ideologico** *agg* ideological.

**idillio** [i'dilljo] *sm* idyll. **idillico** *agg* idyllic.

**idioma** [i'djɔma] *sm* language. **frase idiomatica** *sf* idiom.

**idiota** [i'kjɔta] *s(m+f)* idiot, fool. *agg* idiotic, stupid.

**idiotismo** [idjo'tizmo] *sm* (*lingua*) idiom; (*med*) idiocy.

**idiozia** [idjo'tsia] *sf* idiocy; stupidity.

**idolo** ['idolo] *sm* idol. **idoleggiare** *v* idolize.

**idoneo** [i'dɔneo] *agg* fit, suitable; (*capace*) able. **non idoneo** unfit, unsuitable. **idoneità** *sf* ability, suitability.

**idrante** [i'drante] *sm* hydrant. **idratante** *agg* (*crema*) moisturizing.

**idraulico** [i'drauliko] *agg* hydraulic. *sm* plumber. **idraulica** *sf* hydraulics.

**idroelettrico** [idroe'lettriko] *agg* hydro-electric.

**idroestrattore** [idroestrat'tore] *sm* spin-dryer.

**idrofilo** [i'drɔfilo] *agg* **cotone idrofilo** *sm* cotton-wool.

**idrofobia** [i'drɔfobia] *sf* rabies, hydrophobia. **idrofobo** *agg* rabid, hydrophobic.

**idrogeno** [i'drɔdʒeno] *sm* hydrogen.

**idrosci** [idro'ʃi] *sm* water-skiing.

**idrovolante** [idrovo'lante] *sm* seaplane.

**iena** ['jɛna] *sf* hyena.

**ieri** ['jɛri] *avv, sm* yesterday. **ieri l'altro** the day before yesterday. **tutto ieri** all day yesterday.

**iettatore** [jetta'tore] *sm* jinx. **iettatura** *sf* bad luck; (*malocchio*) evil eye.

**igiene** [i'dʒɛne] *sf* hygiene. **igienico** *agg* hygienic; (*sano*) healthy. **assorbente igienico** *sm* sanitary towel. **carta igienica** *sf* toilet paper.

**iglù** [i'glu] *sm* igloo.

**ignaro** [i'ɲaro] *agg* unaware, ignorant.

**ignobile** [i'ɲɔbile] *agg* mean, base.

**ignominia** [iɲo'minja] *sf* disgrace.

**ignorante** [iɲo'rante] *agg* ignorant; (*non colto*) uneducated. *s(m+f)* ignoramus. **ignoranza** *sf* ignorance.

**ignorare** [iɲo'rare] *v* (*non sapere*) not know; (*trascurare, fingere di non conoscere*) ignore.

**ignoto** [i'ɲɔto] *agg* unknown. *sm* (*concetto*) unknown; (*persona*) unknown person.

**ignudo** [i'ɲudo] *agg* naked.

**il** [il] *art* the.

**ilare** ['ilare] *agg* cheerful. **ilarità** *sf* (*allegria*) cheerfulness; (*riso*) hilarity.

**illecito** [il'letʃito] *agg* illicit, unlawful.

**illegale** [ille'gale] *agg* illegal, unlawful. **illegalità** *sf* illegality.

**illeggibile** [illed'dʒibile] *agg* illegible; (*fig*) unreadable.

**illegittimo** [ille'dʒittimo] *agg* illegitimate. **illegittimità** *sf* illegitimacy.

**illeso** [il'lezo] *agg* unhurt.

**illibato** [illi'bato] *agg* pure, chaste.

**illimitato** [illimi'tato] *agg* unlimited, boundless.

**illogico** [il'lɔdʒiko] *agg* illogical, unsound. **illogicità** *sf* illogicality.

**\*illudere** [il'ludere] *v* deceive, fool. **illudersi** *v* delude oneself.

**illuminare** [illumi'nare] *v* light, illuminate; (*rischiarare*) light up; (*mostrare la verità*) enlighten; (*a giorno*) floodlight. **illuminazione** *sf* illumination, lighting. **illuminismo** *sm* Enlightenment.

**illusione** [illu'zjone] *sf* illusion; impression. **farsi (delle) illusioni** delude oneself; (*fam*) kid oneself. **non farsi (delle) illusioni** have no illusions. **illusionista** *s(m+f)* conjurer.

**illusorio** [illu'zɔrjo] *agg* illusory, vain.

**illustrare** [illus'trare] *v* illustrate; (*spiegare*) explain. **illustrativo** *agg* explanatory. **illustrato** *agg* illustrated. **illustratore, -trice** *sm, sf* illustrator. **illustrazione** *sf* illustration, explanation.

**illustre** [il'lustre] *agg* famous, illustrious. **illustre ignoto** *sm* nobody.

**imbacuccare** [imbakuk'kare] *v* wrap up.

**imballare¹** [imbal'lare] *v* pack; (*involucro*) wrap; (*in scatole*) box; (*in casse*) crate.
**imballaggio** *sm* packing; wrapping; boxing; crating.

**imballare²** [imbal'lare] *v* (*auto*) race.

**imbalsamare** [imbalsa'mare] *v* embalm.
**imbalsamatore, -trice** *sm, sf* embalmer; (*di animali*) taxidermist.

**imbambolato** [imbambo'lato] *agg* bewildered.

**imbandierare** [imbandje'rare] *v* deck with flags.

**imbandire** [imban'dire] *v* prepare.

**imbarazzare** [imbarat'tsare] *v* embarrass; (*impedire*) hamper; (*ostacolare*) block, hinder. **imbarazzo** *sm* embarrassment; (*impaccio*) hindrance, trouble. **essere in imbarazzo** be in a difficult situation, be in a fix; (*scelta difficile*) be in a quandary. **mettere in imbarazzo** (*in situazione difficile*) put in a spot; (*a disagio*) make ill at ease.

**imbarcare** [imbar'kare] *v* take aboard.
**imbarcarsi** *v* embark. **imbarcazione** *sf* craft, boat. **imbarco** *sm* embarkation; (*merci*) shipment.

**imbastire** [imbas'tire] *v* (*cucire*) tack; (*tracciare sommariamente*) draw up, outline.

**imbattersi** [im'battersi] *v* come across; (*fam*) bump into.

**imbattibile** [imbat'tibile] *agg* invincible, unbeatable.

**imbavagliare** [imbava'ʎare] *v* gag.

**imbecille** [imbe'tʃille] *agg* stupid, idiotic. *s(m+f)* fool, idiot; (*med*) imbecile.

**imbellettare** [imbellet'tare] *v* make up; (*fig*) embellish.

**imbellire** [imbel'lire] *v* beautify.

**imbevuto** [imbe'vuto] *agg* steeped (in), imbued (with).

**imbiancare** [imbjan'kare] *v* whiten; (*muri*) whitewash; (*candeggiare*) bleach. **imbianchino** *sm* house-painter.

**imbizzarrirsi** [imbiddzar'rirsi] *v* get excited.

**imboccare** [imbok'kare] *v* (*cibo*) feed; (*suggerire*) prompt; enter; (*portare alla bocca*) put to one's mouth. **imboccatura** *sf* mouth; entrance; (*bocchino*) mouthpiece.

**imbonire** [imbo'nire] *v* entice, talk into buying. **imbonimento** *sm* (*discorso*) sales talk; (*elogio immeritato*) build-up.

**imboscata** [imbos'kata] *sf* ambush. **imboscato** *sm* shirker, (draft-)dodger.

**imbottigliare** [imbotti'ʎare] *v* bottle; (*mil*) blockade; (*traffico*) jam.

**imbottire** [imbot'tire] *v* stuff; (*sarto*) pad, wad. **coperta imbottita** *sf* quilt. **panino imbottito** *sm* sandwich. **imbottitura** *sf* stuffing; padding; wadding.

**imbrattare** [imbrat'tare] *v* soil, dirty.

**imbrigliare** [imbri'ʎare] *v* bridle.

**imbroccare** [imbrok'kare] *v* (*azzeccare*) get right.

**imbrogliare** [imbro'ʎare] *v* (*gabbare*) cheat; (*mettere in disordine*) mix up, muddle up; (*ingarbugliare*) tangle (up). **imbroglio** *sm* (*faccenda confusa*) muddle, mess; (*groviglio*) tangle; (*raggiro*) trick, swindle. **imbroglione, -a** *sm, sf* cheat, trickster, swindler.

**imbronciarsi** [imbron'tʃarsi] *v* sulk; (*cielo*) cloud over.

**imbrunire** [imbru'nire] *v* darken, get dark. *sm* nightfall.

**imbruttire** [imbrut'tire] *v* spoil.

**imbucare** [imbu'kare] *v* post.

**imburrare** [imbur'rare] *v* butter.

**imbuto** [im'buto] *sm* funnel.

**imitare** [imi'tare] *v* imitate. **imitazione** *sf* imitation.

**immagazzinare** [immagaddzi'nare] *v* store.

**immaginare** [immadʒi'nare] *v* imagine. **s'immagini!** (*tutt'altro*) not in the least! (*certamente*) by all means! **immaginario** *agg* imaginary. **immaginazione** *sf* imagination.

**immagine** [im'madʒine] *sf* image; (*figura, ritratto*) picture. **immagine riflessa** reflection.

**immancabile** [imman'kabile] *agg* unfailing, certain.

**immangiabile** [imman'dʒabile] *agg* inedible, uneatable.

**immatricolarsi** [immatriko'larsi] *v* register, enrol.

**immaturo** [imma'turo] *agg* unripe; (*fig*) immature; (*prematuro*) untimely.

**immedesimarsi** [immedezi'marsi] *v* identify oneself (with).

**immediato** [imme'djato] *agg* immediate. **immediatamente** *avv* immediately; directly; (*subito*) at once.

**immemorabile** [immemo'rabile] *agg* immemorial.

**immemore** [im'mɛmore] *agg* heedless, forgetful.

**immenso** [im'menso] *agg* huge, vast; enormous. **immensità** *sf* hugeness, immensity; (*gran numero*) mass, enormous number.

**\*immergere** [im'mɛrdʒere] *v* immerse; (*intingere*) dip; (*con forza, tuffare*) plunge; (*sottomarino*) submerge. **immersione** *sf* immersion; (*tuffo*) dive.

**immeritato** [immeri'tato] *agg* undeserved. **immeritevole** *agg* undeserving.

**\*immettere** [im'mettere] *v* admit, introduce.

**immigrare** [immi'grare] *v* immigrate. **immigrante** *s(m+f)*, *agg* immigrant. **immigrato, -a** *s*, *agg* immigrant. **immigrazione** *sf* immigration.

**imminente** [immi'nɛnte] *agg* imminent. **imminenza** *sf* imminence.

**immischiare** [immis'kjare] *v* involve, mix up. **immischiarsi** *v* get involved, interfere.

**immobile** [im'mɔbile] *agg* (*che non si muove*) motionless, still; (*che non si può muovere*) immovable. **società immobiliare** *sf* building society. **immobilità** *sf* immobility, stillness. **beni immobili** *sm pl* real estate *sing*.

**immobilizzare** [immobilid'dzare] *v* immobilize; (*econ*) tie up.

**immoderato** [immode'rato] *agg* excessive. **immoderatezza** *sf* excessiveness; (*smoderatezza*) lack of moderation.

**immodesto** [immo'desto] *agg* conceited, immodest.

**immolare** [immo'lare] *v* sacrifice.

**immondo** [im'mondo] *agg* filthy. **immondezzaio** *sm* rubbish dump. **immondizia** *sf* (*sporcizia*) filth; (*spazzatura*) rubbish, garbage.

**immorale** [immo'rale] *agg* immoral.

**immortale** [immor'tale] *agg* immortal. **immortalare** *v* immortalize. **immortalità** *sf* immortality.

**immune** [im'mune] *agg* immune, free. **immunità** *sf* immunity. **immunizzare** *v* immunize.

**immutabile** [immu'tabile] *agg* immutable, unchangeable; (*costante*) unswerving. **immutabilità** *sf* immutability; firmness. **immutato** *agg* unchanged, unfailing.

**impacchettare** [impakket'tare] *v* parcel up, package.

**impacciare** [impat'tʃare] *v* hamper, hinder. **impaccio** *sm* obstacle, hindrance; (*situazione imbarazzante*) fix, predicament. **impacciato** *agg* awkward; (*imbarazzato*) ill at ease; (*goffo*) clumsy.

**impadronirsi** [impadro'nirsi] *v* **impadronirsi di** seize, take possession of; (*imparare a fondo*) master.

**impagabile** [impa'gabile] *agg* invaluable, priceless.

**impalcatura** [impalka'tura] *sf* (*struttura provvisoria*) scaffolding; (*struttura di sostegno*) framework; (*cervo*) antlers *pl*.

**impallidire** [impalli'dire] *v* turn pale; (*fig*) fade; (*offuscarsi*) grow dim.

**impanare¹** [impa'nare] *v* (*mec*) thread.

**impanare²** [impa'nare] *v* (*gastr*) dip in breadcrumbs.

**impannata** [impan'nata] *sf* window-frame.

**impantanarsi** [impanta'narsi] *v* get bogged down.

**imparare** [impa'rare] *v* learn. **imparare a memoria** learn by heart.

**impareggiabile** [impared'dʒabile] *agg* incomparable.

**impari** ['impari] *agg invar* unequal.

**impartire** [impar'tire] *v* give, impart.

**imparziale** [impar'tsjale] *agg* impartial, unbiased; (*giusto*) fair.

**impassibile** [impas'sibile] *agg* impassive, unmoved.

**impastare** [impas'tare] *v* (*pane*) knead; (*lavorare*) mix; (*incollare*) paste. **impastatrice** *sf* mixer. **impasto** *sm* mixture.

**impatto** [im'patto] *sm* impact.

**impaurire** [impau'rire] *v* frighten.

**impazietne** [impa'tsjɛnte] *agg* impatient; (*desideroso*) anxious. **impazientirsi** *v* lose one's patience.

**impazzare** [impat'tsare] *v* be in full swing; (*gastr*) curdle. **all'impazzata** wildly.

**impazzire** [impat'tsire] *v* go mad. **far impazzire** drive mad.

**impeccabile** [impek'kabile] *agg* impeccable.

**impedire** [impe'dire] *v* prevent; (*sbarrare*) block; (*impacciare*) hinder. **impedimento** *sm* impediment; obstacle; (*l'impedire*) prevention.

**impegnare** [impe'ɲare] *v* (*dare in pegno*) pledge; (*tenere impegnato*) engage; (*obbligare*) bind; (*tenere occupato*) take up;

(*prenotare*) book. **impegnarsi** *v* undertake, strive. **impegnativo** *agg* (*lavoro*) exacting, demanding; (*promessa*) binding. **impegnato** *agg* engaged; (*vincolato*) pledged; (*pol*) committed. **impegno** *sm* engagement; obligation; commitment; (*zelo*) eagerness, enthusiasm.

**impenetrabile** [impene'trabile] *agg* impenetrable, impervious.

**impenitente** [impeni'tɛnte] *agg* unrepentant. **scapolo impenitente** *sm* confirmed bachelor.

**impennarsi** [impen'narsi] *v* flare up; (*cavallo*) rear (up); (*aereo*) go into a climb.

**impensabile** [impen'sabile] *agg* unthinkable.

**impensato** [impen'sato] *agg* unforeseen.

**impensierirsi** [impensje'rirsi] *v* worry.

**imperativo** [impera'tivo] *sm, agg* imperative. **imperare** *v* rule.

**imperatore** [impera'tore] *sm* emperor. **imperatrice** *sf* empress.

**impercettibile** [impertʃet'tibile] *agg* imperceptible.

**imperdonabile** [imperdo'nabile] *agg* unforgivable.

**imperfetto** [imper'fetto] *agg* faulty, defective. *sm* imperfect (tense). **imperfezione** *sf* defect.

**imperioso** [imper'rjozo] *agg* imperious; (*ineluttabile*) pressing, impelling.

**impermalirsi** [imperma'lirsi] *v* take umbrage, take offence.

**impermeabile** [imperme'abile] *sm* raincoat. *agg* impervious; (*all'acqua*) waterproof; (*all'aria*) airtight. **impermeabilizzare** *v* waterproof.

**imperniare** [imper'njare] *v* hinge; (*fondare*) base.

**impero** [im'pɛro] *sm* (*territorio*) empire; (*autorità*) rule.

**imperscrutabile** [imperskru'tabile] *agg* inscrutable.

**impersonale** [imperso'nale] *agg* impersonal.

**impersonare** [imperso'nare] *v* (*simboleggiare*) personify; (*attore*) impersonate. **impersonarsi** *v* be the personification (of).

**imperterrito** [imper'tɛrrito] *agg* undaunted; unperturbed.

**impertinente** [imperti'nɛnte] *agg* impertinent, cheeky.

**imperturbabile** [impertur'babile] *agg* unruffled, imperturbable, calm. **imperturbato** *agg* unperturbed, unruffled.

**impeto** ['impeto] *sm* impetus, force; (*accesso*) outburst. **agire d'impeto** act on impulse.

**impettito** [impet'tito] *agg* stiff, erect. **camminare impettito** strut.

**impetuoso** [impe'twozo] *agg* impetuous.

**impiallacciato** [impjallat'tʃato] *agg* veneered. **impiallacciatura** *sf* veneer.

**impiantare** [impjan'tare] *v* set up; (*fondare*) establish; (*tec*) install. **impianto** *sm* plant, installation; (*fondazione*) establishment.

**impiantito** [impjan'tito] *sm* flooring.

**impiastrare** [impjas'trare] *v* smear. **impiastro** *sm* (*cataplasma*) poultice; (*persona uggiosa*) bore.

**impiccare** [impik'kare] *v* hang. **impiccato** *sm* hanged man.

**impicciare** [impit'tʃare] *v* be in the way, hamper. **impicciarsi** *v* meddle, interfere.

**impiccio** [im'pittʃo] *sm* (*ostacolo*) hindrance; (*guaio*) mess, trouble. **essere d'impiccio** *v* be in the way.

**impiegare** [impje'gare] *v* employ; spend. **impiegatizio** *agg* clerical. **impiegato, -a** *sm, sf* employee; (*funzionario*) official. **impiegati** *pl* (*collettivo*) staff *sing*, personnel *sing*.

**impiego** [im'pjɛgo] *sm, pl* -**ghi** use; (*denaro*) investment; (*posto, occupazione*) employment, job.

**impietrito** [impje'trito] *agg* petrified.

**impigliarsi** [impi'ʎarsi] *v* get entangled, get mixed up.

**impiparsi** [impi'parsi] *v* (*fam*) not care a damn.

**implacabile** [impla'kabile] *agg* implacable.

**implicare** [impli'kare] *v* (*coinvolgere*) involve; (*comportare*) imply, entail.

**implicito** [im'plitʃito] *agg* implicit.

**implorare** [implo'rare] *v* implore, entreat.

**impolverare** [impolve'rare] *v* cover with dust.

**imponderabile** [imponde'rabile] *agg* imponderable.

**imponente** [impo'nɛnte] *agg* imposing, impressive.

**imponibile** [impo'nibile] *agg* taxable. *sm* taxable income.

**impopolare** [impopo'lare] *agg* unpopular.

**impopolarità** *sf* unpopularity.

**\*imporre** [im'porre] *v* impose; (*costringere*) oblige; (*ordinare*) order; (*comportare*) involve. **imporsi** *v* (*farsi valere*) assert oneself; (*incontrar favore*) go down well; (*rendersi necessario*) become necessary.

**importante** [impor'tante] *agg* important. *sm* important thing, main point. **importanza** *sf* importance. **di nessuna importanza** unimportant.

**importare** [impor'tare] *v* (*aver peso*) matter; (*comportare*) involve; (*introdurre dall'estero*) import. **non importa!** it doesn't matter! never mind! **non me ne importa niente!** (*fam*) I couldn't care less!

**importazione** [importa'tsjone] *sf* import; (*atto*) importation.

**importo** [im'porto] *sm* amount.

**importunare** [importu'nare] *v* trouble, bother. **importuno** *agg* troublesome, tiresome, boring.

**imposizione** [impozi'tsjone] *sf* imposition.

**impossessarsi** [imposses'sarsi] *v* get hold of, seize.

**impossibile** [impos'sibile] *agg* impossible. **fare l'impossibile** do all one can. **impossibilità** *sf* impossibility.

**imposta**[1] [im'posta] *sf* (*finestra*) shutter.

**imposta**[2] [im'posta] *sf* (*econ*) tax, duty.

**impostare**[1] [impos'tare] *v* (*spedire*) post.

**impostare**[2] [impos'tare] *v* (*avviare*) get under way; (*questione, ecc.*) set out, state; (*nave*) lay down; (*voce*) pitch. **impostazione** *sf* approach.

**impostore** [impos'tore] *sm* imposter.

**impotente** [impo'tɛnte] *agg* powerless; (*med*) impotent. **impotenza** *sf* powerlessness; impotence.

**impoverire** [impove'rire] *v* impoverish. **impoverimento** *sm* impoverishment.

**impraticabile** [imprati'kabile] *agg* (*strada*) impassable; (*campo sportivo*) unfit for play.

**impratichirsi** [imprati'kirsi] *v* practise.

**imprecare** [impre'kare] *v* curse. **imprecazione** *sf* curse.

**impreciso** [impre'tʃizo] *agg* (*inesatto*) inaccurate; (*indeterminato*) imprecise, vague. **imprecisabile** *agg* indefinable. **imprecisione** *sf* inaccuracy; vagueness.

**impregnare** [impre'ɲare] *v* impregnate; (*fig*) imbue; (*inzuppare*) soak.

**imprenditore** [imprendi'tore] *sm* contrac-

tor; entrepreneur. **imprenditore di pompe funebri** undertaker. **imprenditore edile** building contractor. **piccolo imprenditore** tradesman.

**impreparato** [imprepa'rato] *agg* unprepared; (*lavoro*) untrained. **impreparazione** *sf* unpreparedness; lack of training.

**impresa** [im'preza] *sf* undertaking, enterprise; (*azienda*) concern, firm; (*azione*) deed; (*azione pericolosa*) exploit. **impresario** *sm* entrepreneur; (*theatre*) manager, impresario.

**imprescindibile** [impreʃin'dibile] *agg* that cannot be disregarded.

**impressionare** [impressjo'nare] *v* make an impression; (*spaventare*) frighten; (*turbare*) shock, upset; (*foto*) expose. **impressionarsi** *v* be upset, be shocked; be affected. **impressionabile** *agg* impressionable, easily affected; easily frightened. **impressionante** *agg* striking, impressive; frightening; upsetting.

**impressione** [impres'sjone] *sf* impression; sensation.

**imprestare** [impres'tare] *v* lend.

**imprevidenza** [imprevi'dentsa] *sf* lack of foresight. **imprevedibile** *agg* unforeseeable. **imprevidente** *agg* heedless.

**imprevisto** [impre'visto] *agg* unforeseen. **salvo imprevisti** if all goes well.

**imprigionare** [impridʒo'nare] *v* imprison.

**\*imprimere** [im'primere] *v* imprint, impress; (*dare*) impart; (*pittura*) prime.

**improbabile** [impro'babile] *agg* unlikely, improbable. **improbabilità** *sf* unlikelihood.

**improduttivo** [improdut'tivo] *agg* unproductive.

**impronta** [im'pronta] *sf* impression, mark, stamp. **impronta del piede** footprint. **impronta digitale** fingerprint. **improntare** *v* stamp. **all'impronto** at sight.

**improprio** [im'prɔprjo] *agg* (*inadatto*) inappropriate; (*inopportuno*) out of place; (*mat*) improper.

**improrogabile** [improro'gabile] *agg* **termine improrogabile** *sm* deadline.

**improvvisare** [improvvi'zare] *v* improvise. **improvvisamente** *avv* suddenly, all of a sudden. **improvvisata** *sf* surprise. **improvvisazione** *sf* improvisation.

**imprudente** [impru'dɛnte] *agg* rash, imprudent. **imprudenza** *sf* imprudence.

**commettere un'imprudenza** do something rash.

**impudente** [impu'dɛnte] *agg* impudent.

**impudico** [impu'diko] *agg, m pl* **-chi** immodest.

**impugnare¹** [impu'ɲare] *v* (*contestare*) challenge; (*dir*) contest.

**impugnare²** [impu'ɲare] *v* (*afferrare*) grasp. **impugnare le armi** take up arms. **impugnatura** *sf* handle; (*spada*) hilt; (*racchetta*) grip.

**impulso** [im'pulso] *sm* impulse. **dare impulso** boost. **impulsivo** *agg* impulsive.

**impunemente** [impune'mente] *avv* with impunity.

**impunito** [impu'nito] *agg* (*delitto*) unpunished.

**impuntarsi** [impun'tarsi] *v* refuse to budge, dig one's heels in.

**impuro** [im'puro] *agg* impure. **impurità** *sf* impurity.

**imputare** [impu'tare] *v* impute, attribute, ascribe; (*dir*) charge. **imputabile** *agg* attributable. **imputato, -a** *sm, sf* defendant, accused. **imputazione** *sf* charge.

**imputridire** [imputri'dire] *v* rot.

**in** [in] *prep* in; (*su, sopra*) on; (*moto a luogo*) to; (*dentro*) into; (*moto per luogo*) round, through; (*entro*) within; (*durante*) during.

**inabile** [in'abile] *agg* (*non capace*) unable, incapable; (*non idoneo*) unfit; (*per infortunio*) disabled; (*dir*) ineligible.

**inabitabile** [inabi'tabile] *agg* uninhabitable. **inabitato** *agg* uninhabited.

**inaccessibile** [inattʃes'sibile] *agg* inaccessible.

**inaccettabile** [inattʃet'tabile] *agg* unacceptable.

**inadatto** [ina'datto] *agg* unsuitable (for); (*incapace*) unfit (for).

**inadeguato** [inade'gwato] *agg* insufficient, inadequate.

**inalare** [ina'lare] *v* inhale. **inalatore** *sm* inhaler.

**inalienabile** [inalje'nabile] *agg* inalienable.

**inalterabile** [inalte'rabile] *agg* unchangeable. **inalterato** *agg* unchanged.

**inamidare** [inami'dare] *v* starch.

**inammissibile** [innammis'sibile] *agg* inadmissible.

**inanimato** [inani'mato] *agg* inanimate, lifeless.

**inappagabile** [innappa'gabile] *agg* insatiable. **inappagato** *agg* unsatisfied.

**inapplicabile** [inappli'kabile] *agg* inapplicable.

**inarcare** [inar'kare] *v* arch, bend. **inarcare le sopracciglia** raise one's eyebrows.

**inargentare** [inardʒen'tare] *v* silver.

**inaridire** [inari'dire] *v* dry up.

**inaspettato** [inaspet'tato] *agg* unexpected.

**inasprire** [inas'prire] *v* exacerbate, make worse.

**inattendibile** [inatten'dibile] *agg* unreliable.

**inatteso** [inat'tezo] *agg* unexpected.

**inattivo** [inat'tivo] *agg* idle.

**inattuabile** [inat'twabile] *agg* impracticable.

**inaudito** [inau'dito] *agg* (*non udito prima*) unheard of; incredible, extraordinary.

**inaugurare** [inaugu'rare] *v* inaugurate, open. **inaugurazione** *sf* inauguration, opening.

**inavveduto** [inavve'duto] *agg* thoughtless, careless.

**inavvertenza** [inavver'tɛntsa] *sf* carelessness, oversight.

**incagliarsi** [inka'ʎarsi] *v* (*mar*) run aground; (*fig*) get stuck.

**incalcolabile** [inkalko'labile] *agg* incalculable.

**incalzare** [inkal'tsare] *v* follow closely; (*fig*) press.

**incamminare** [inkammi'nare] *v* start (off). **incamminarsi** *v* set off; (*avviarsi*) be on the way (to).

**incanalare** [inkana'lare] *v* channel.

**incantare** [inkan'tare] *v* enchant, charm. **incantarsi** *v* (*rimanere intontito*) be in a daze; (*mec*) jam, break down. **incantato** *agg* enchanted; (*intontito*) dazed, spellbound. **incantatore, -trice** *sm, sf* charmer. **incantesimo** *sm* charm, spell. **incantevole** *agg* charming, enchanting.

**incanto¹** [in'kanto] *sm* spell, magic. **stare d'incanto** suit perfectly.

**incanto²** [in'kanto] *sm* (*vendita*) auction.

**incapace** [inka'patʃe] *agg* incapable. **incapacità** *sf* inability; (*fisica*) disability; (*dir*) incapacity.

**incappare** [inkap'pare] *v* run into, come up against.

**incarcerare** [inkartʃe'rare] v imprison, jail.

**incaricare** [inkari'kare] v charge, entrust; order. **incaricarsi** v take charge. **incaricato, -a** sm, sf person in charge; (università) lecturer; (funzionario) official.

**incarico** [in'kariko] sm, pl -chi task, assignment, charge.

**incarnare** [inkar'nare] v embody; (personaggio) impersonate.

**incartare** [inkar'tare] v wrap (up).

**incasellare** [inkazel'lare] v pigeon-hole.

**incassare** [inkas'sare] v (riscuotere) collect, cash; (sport) take; (inserire) embed. **incasso** sm collection; (entrata) takings pl.

**incastellatura** [inkastella'tura] sf (impalcatura) scaffolding; (mec) casing.

**incastonare** [inkasto'nare] v set, mount. **incastonatura** sf setting, mounting.

**incastrare** [inkas'trare] v wedge, drive; (imprigionare) jam, sandwich; (falegnameria) mortise. **incastro** sm joint; (cavità) hollow, recess; mortise.

**incatenare** [inkate'nare] v chain; (fig) tie.

**incatramare** [inkatra'mare] v tar.

**incauto** [in'kauto] agg incautious.

**incavare** [inka'vare] v hollow out. **incavo** sm hollow; (scanalatura) groove.

**incendiare** [intʃen'djare] v set on fire; (fig) fire.

**incendiario** [intʃen'djarjo] agg incendiary. sm arsonist, fire-raiser.

**incendio** [in'tʃendjo] sm fire. **bocca d'incendio** sf (fire) hydrant. **incendio doloso** arson.

**incenerire** [intʃene'rire] v burn down; (fig) wither.

**incenso** [in'tʃenso] sm incense.

**incensurabile** [intʃensu'rabile] agg beyond reproach. **essere incensurato** have a clean record.

**inceppare** [intʃep'pare] v obstruct, hamper.

**incertezza** [intʃer'tettsa] sf uncertainty; (dubbio) doubt; (indecisione) hesitation.

**incerto** [in'tʃerto] agg uncertain; dubious; (indeciso) hesitant; (malsicuro) unsure. sm uncertainty.

**incespicare** [intʃespi'kare] v stumble, trip up.

**incessante** [intʃes'sante] agg ceaseless, constant.

**incesto** [in'tʃesto] sm incest. **incestuoso** agg incestuous.

**incettare** [intʃet'tare] v also **fare incetto di** corner, buy up. **incetta** sf cornering.

**inchiesta** [in'kjesta] sf inquiry, investigation; (giornalismo) report; (scandalo) probe.

**inchinare** [inki'nare] v bow, bend; (abbassare) lower. **inchinarsi** v bend down, bow; (donna) curtsey. **inchino** sm bow, curtsey.

**inchiodare** [inkjo'dare] v nail.

**inchiostro** [in'kjostro] sm ink. **inchiostro di china** Indian ink.

**inciampare** [intʃam'pare] v stumble (over), trip up. **inciampo** sm obstacle, stumbling block.

**incidente** [intʃi'dɛnte] sm (episodio) incident; (infortunio) accident; (disputa) argument.

**incidenza** [intʃi'dɛntsa] sf incidence.

***incidere¹** [in'tʃidere] v cut (into); carve; (intagliare) engrave; (ad acquaforte) etch; (registrare) record; (med) incise, lance. **incisione** sf incision; cut; engraving; etching; recording. **incisivo** agg incisive. **per inciso** by the way, incidentally. **incisore** sm engraver.

***incidere²** [in'tʃidere] v **incidere su** affect.

**incinta** [in'tʃinta] agg pregnant.

**incipriare** [intʃi'prjare] v powder.

**incitare** [intʃi'tare] v incite. **incitamento** sm incitement, spur.

**incivile** [intʃi'vile] agg uncivilized; (villano) boorish, uncivil.

**incivilire** [intʃivi'lire] v civilize.

**inclemente** [inkle'mɛnte] agg harsh.

**inclinare** [inkli'nare] v incline; (propendere) tend, be inclined. **inclinazione** sf inclination; (pendenza) slope; (disposizione d'animo) leaning; (simpatia) liking; (strada) gradient. **incline** agg prone.

***includere** [in'kludere] v (comprendere) include; (accludere) enclose; (implicare) imply. **inclusione** sf inclusion. **incluso** agg included; (comm) inclusive.

**incoerente** [inkoe'rɛnte] agg incoherent; (fig) inconsistent.

**incognita** [in'kɔnita] sf (matematica) unknown; (fatto imprevedibile) unknown factor, uncertainty; (persona) mystery, dark horse.

**incognito** [in'kɔnito] agg unknown. sm incognito; (ignoto) unknown.

**incollare** [inkol'lare] v (attaccare) glue; (spal-

*mare*) paste.
**incolore** [inko'lore] *agg* colourless.
**incolpare** [inkol'pare] *v* blame.
**incolto** [in'kolto] *agg* (*non coltivato*) uncultivated; (*trascurato*) untidy; (*privo di coltura*) uncultured.
**incolume** [in'kɔlume] *agg* unharmed.
**incombente** [inkom'bɛnte] *agg* (*imminente*) impending; (*spettante*) incumbent.
**incominciare** [inkomin'tʃare] *v* begin, start. (**tanto**) **per cominciare** to begin with.
**incomodo** [in'kɔmodo] *agg* (*disagevole*) uncomfortable; (*inopportuno*) inconvenient. *sm* trouble, inconvenience. **il terzo incomodo** the odd man out. **incomodare** *v* inconvenience, trouble.
**incomparabile** [inkompa'rabile] *agg* incomparable.
**incompatibile** [inkompa'tibile] *agg* incompatible. **incompatibilità** *sf* incompatibility.
**incompetente** [inkompe'tɛnte] *agg* incompetent. *s(m+f)* incompetent person.
**incompiuto** [inkom'pjuto] *agg* unfinished.
**incompleto** [inkom'plɛto] *agg* incomplete.
**incomprensibile** [inkompren'sibile] *agg* incomprehensible. **incomprensibilità** *sf* incomprehensibility.
**incompreso** [inkom'prezo] *agg* misunderstood.
**inconcepibile** [inkontʃe'pibile] *agg* inconceivable.
**inconciliabile** [inkontʃi'ljabile] *agg* irreconcilable.
**inconcludente** [inkonklu'dɛnte] *agg* inconclusive.
**incondizionato** [inkonditsjo'nato] *agg* unconditional; (*pieno*) complete.
**inconsapevole** [inkonsa'pevole] *agg* unaware, unconscious.
**inconscio** [in'kɔnʃo] *agg* unconscious; (*persona*) unaware. *sm invar* unconscious.
**inconsiderabile** [inkonside'rabile] *agg* negligible. **inconsiderato** *agg* thoughtless. **inconsideratezza** *sf* thoughtlessness.
**inconsistente** [inkonsis'tɛnte] *agg* flimsy; (*infondato*) groundless.
**inconsolabile** [inkonso'labile] *agg* inconsolable.
**inconsueto** [inkonsu'ɛto] *agg* unusual.
**incontenibile** [inkonte'nibile] *agg* uncontrollable.

**incontentabile** [inkonten'tabile] *agg* hard to please, exacting.
**incontrare** [inkon'trare] *v* meet; (*esser popolare*) be a success. **incontrar favore** find favour. **incontrarsi per caso** run into.
**incontrario** [inkon'trarjo] *sm* **all'incontrario** (*a rovescio*) the wrong way round.
**incontrastato** [inkontras'tato] *agg* unopposed.
**incontro¹** [in'kontro] *sm* meeting; (*partita*) match; (*gioco*) game; (*favore*) reception, success. **incontro alla pari** (*sport*) tie, draw.
**incontro²** [in'kontro] *avv* towards. **all'incontro** on the contrary. **andare incontro a** go towards, approach; (*fig*) meet halfway.
**incontrollabile** [inkontrol'labile] *agg* uncontrollable.
**inconveniente** [inkonve'njɛnte] *sm* drawback, snag.
**incoraggiare** [inkorad'dʒare] *v* encourage.
**incorniciare** [inkorni'tʃare] *v* frame.
**incoronare** [inkoro'nare] *v* crown. **incoronazione** *sf* coronation.
**incorporare** [inkorpo'rare] *v* incorporate; annex.
**incorreggibile** [inkorred'dʒibile] *agg* incorrigible.
**\*incorrere** [in'korrere] *v* incur.
**incorruttibile** [inkorrut'tibile] *agg* incorruptible.
**incosciente** [inko'ʃɛnte] *agg* unconscious; (*sconsiderato*) irresponsible.
**incredibile** [inkre'dibile] *agg* incredible, unbelievable.
**incredulo** [in'krɛdulo] *agg* incredulous, disbelieving.
**incremento** [inkre'mento] *sm* (*aumento*) increase; (*sviluppo*) growth, expansion; (*mat*) increment. **incrementare** *v* increase; (*far prosperare*) promote.
**increspare** [inkres'pare] *v* (*acqua*) ripple; (*capelli*) curl. **increspare la fronte** frown.
**incrinare** [inkri'nare] *v* crack.
**incrociare** [inkro'tʃare] *v* cross. **incrociatore** *sm* cruiser. **incrocio** *sm* crossing; (*accoppiamento*) cross-breeding; (*frutto*) cross, hybrid.
**incrostato** [inkros'tato] *agg* encrusted.
**incubatrice** [inkuba'tritʃe] *sf* incubator. **incubazione** *sf* incubation.
**incubo** ['inkubo] *sm* nightmare.

**incudine** [in'kudine] *sf* anvil.

**inculcare** [inkul'kare] *v* inculcate.

**incuneare** [inkune'are] *v* wedge.

**incurabile** [inku'rabile] *agg* incurable.

**incurante** [inku'rante] *agg* heedless, unconcerned.

**incuriosire** [inkurjo'zire] *v* arouse curiosity.

**incursione** [inkur'sjone] *sf* incursion, raid. **incursione aerea** air-raid.

**incustodito** [inkusto'dito] *agg* unattended.

**indagare** [inda'gare] *v* investigate, inquire into. **indagine** *sf* inquiry, investigation; (*scientifica*) research; (*studio*) survey.

**indebitamente** [indebita'mente] *avv* unduly; (*ingiustamente*) unlawfully.

**indebitarsi** [indebi'tarsi] *v* run into debt. **indebitato** *agg* indebted.

**indebolire** [indebo'lire] *v* weaken. **indebolimento** *sm* weakening; (*debolezza*) weakness.

**indecente** [inde'tʃɛnte] *agg* indecent. **indecenza** *sf* indecency; (*vergogna*) disgrace.

**indecifrabile** [indetʃi'frabile] *agg* illegible.

**indecisione** [indetʃi'zjone] *sf* indecision.

**indeciso** [inde'tʃizo] *agg* undecided; (*non risolto, instabile*) unsettled.

**indefesso** [inde'fɛsso] *agg* tireless.

**indefinibile** [indefi'nibile] *agg* indefinable.

**indefinito** [indefi'nito] *agg* indefinite; (*non risolto*) unsettled.

**indegno** [in'deɲo] *agg* unworthy. **indegnità** *sf* base action.

**indelicato** [indeli'kato] *agg* tactless; indiscreet.

**indemagliabile** [indema'ʎabile] *agg* nonrun, ladder-proof.

**indenne** [in'dɛnne] *agg* unharmed, unscathed.

**indennità** [indenni'ta] *sf* (*risarcimento*) allowance; (*dir*) indemnity. **indennizzare** *v* compensate. **indennizzo** *sm* compensation.

**inderogabile** [indero'gabile] *agg* binding, irrevocable.

**indescrivibile** [indeskri'vibile] *agg* indescribable.

**indesiderabile** [indezide'rabile] *agg* undesirable.

**indeterminabile** [indetermi'nabile] *agg* indeterminate, imprecise..

**indi** ['indi] *avv* (*dopo*) then; (*da quel luogo*)

from there. **indi a poco** soon after.

**India** ['indja] *sf* India. **indiano, -a** *s, agg* Indian.

**indiavolato** [indjavo'lato] *agg* (*molto agitato*) wild; (*eccessivo*) awful; (*indemoniato*) frenzied.

**indicare** [indi'kare] *v* indicate, show; (*significare*) mean. **indicativo** *agg* indicative. **indicato** *agg* indicated; (*adatto*) suitable. **indicatore** [indika'tore] *sm* indicator; (*tec*) gauge; (*stradale*) signpost.

**indicazione** [indika'tsjone] *sf* indication; (*dato, notizia*) information; (*istruzione per l'uso*) direction.

**indice** ['inditʃe] *sm* index; (*dito*) index finger; (*tec*) pointer.

**indietreggiare** [indjetred'dʒare] *v* draw back, withdraw.

**indietro** [in'djetro] *avv* (*in arretrato*) in arrears; (*debole*) weak; (*moto*) back(wards).

**indifeso** [indi'fezo] *agg* undefended; (*fig*) defenceless.

**indifferente** [indiffe'rɛnte] *agg* indifferent; (*lo stesso*) all the same; (*che non interessa*) unimportant. **indifferenza** *sf* indifference, lack of interest.

**indigeno** [in'didʒeno] *sm, agg* native.

**indigesto** [indi'dʒesto] *agg* indigestible; (*non digerito*) undigested.

**indignare** [indi'ɲare] *v* fill with indignation.

**indimenticabile** [indimenti'kabile] *agg* unforgettable.

**indipendente** [indipen'dɛnte] *agg* independent. **indipendenza** *sf* independence.

**\*indire** [in'dire] *v* announce; (*radunare*) call.

**indiretto** [indi'rɛtto] *agg* indirect.

**indirizzare** [indirit'tsare] *v* address; (*rivolgere*) direct. **indirizzo** *sm* address; (*tendenza*) trend; direction.

**indisciplinato** [indiʃipli'nato] *agg* undisciplined.

**indiscreto** [indis'krɛto] *agg* indiscreet.

**indiscusso** [indis'kusso] *agg* beyond dispute, incontrovertible.

**indispensabile** [indispen'sabile] *agg* indispensable, essential.

**indispettire** [indispet'tire] *v* irritate.

**indisposizione** [indispozi'tsjone] *sf* indisposition, slight illness. **indisposto** *agg* indisposed, unwell.

**indistinto** [indis'tinto] *agg* indistinct.

**indistinguibile** *agg* indistinguishable.

**indivia** [in'divja] *sf* endive.

**individuale** [individu'ale] *agg* individual.

**individuare** [individu'are] *v* (*determinare*) locate; (*riconoscere*) single out; (*scoprire*) discover, recognize.

**individuo** [indi'viduo] *sm* person; (*spreg*) fellow, character.

**indivisibile** [indivi'zibile] *agg* indivisible. **indiviso** *agg* undivided.

**indizio** [in'ditsjo] *sm* sign, indication; (*dir*) (*circumstantial*) evidence.

**indole** ['indole] *sf* nature, character.

**indolenzire** [indolen'tsire] *v* make sore, make ache. **indolenzito** *agg* sore, aching.

**indomani** [indo'mani] *sm* **l'indomani** the following day.

**indossare** [indos'sare] *v* (*mettersi indosso*) put on; (*portare*) wear. **indossatrice** *sf* model. **indosso** *avv* on.

**indotto** [in'dotto] *agg* induced.

**indovinare** [indovi'nare] *v* guess. **indovinato** *agg* (*riuscito*) successful; (*che sta bene*) becoming. **indovinello** *sm* puzzle, riddle. **indovino, -a** *sm, sf* fortune-teller.

**indù** [in'du] *s(m+f)*, *agg* Hindu.

**indubbio** [in'dubbjo] *agg* certain, unmistakable.

**indubitabile** [indubi'tabile] *agg* unquestionable. **indubitato** *agg* certain, unquestioned.

**indugiare** [indu'dʒare] *v* delay; (*soffermarsi*) linger (over). **indugio** *sm* delay.

**indulgente** [indul'dʒɛnte] *agg* lenient. **indulgenza** *sf* indulgence.

**indumento** [indu'mento] *sm* garment.

**indurire** [indu'rire] *v* harden. **indurimento** *sm* hardening.

**\*indurre** [in'durre] *v* induce. **indurre in errore** mislead; (*fig*) lead astray. **indurre in tentazione** lead into temptation.

**industria** [in'dustrja] *sf* industry; (*attività industriale*) business.

**industriale** [indus'trjale] *agg* industrial. *sm* industrialist, manufacturer. **industrializzare** *v* industrialize. **industrializzazione** *sf* industrialization.

**inebriare** [inebri'are] *v* intoxicate.

**inedito** [in'edito] *agg* unpublished.

**ineducato** [inedu'kato] *agg* ill-mannered.

**ineguale** [ine'gwale] *agg* unequal; (*non uniforme*) uneven.

**ineluttabile** [inelut'tabile] *agg* relentless; (*inevitabile*) unavoidable.

**inerente** [ine'rɛnte] *agg* (*riferentesi*) concerning; (*implicito*) inherent.

**inerme** [i'nɛrme] *agg* unarmed; (*senza difesa*) defenceless.

**inerpicarsi** [inerpi'karsi] *v* scramble up.

**inerte** [i'nɛrte] *agg* inert. **inerzia** *sf* sluggishness; (*fis*) inertia.

**inesatto** [ine'zatto] *agg* (*sbagliato*) wrong, incorrect; imprecise, inaccurate.

**inesistente** [inezis'tɛnte] *agg* non-existent.

**inesorabile** [inezo'rabile] *agg* inexorable.

**inesperienza** [inesper'jɛntsa] *sf* inexperience.

**inesperto** [ines'pɛrto] *agg* inexperienced.

**inesplicabile** [inespli'kabile] *agg* inexplicable.

**inespressivo** [inespres'sivo] *agg* expressionless.

**inesprimibile** [inespri'mibile] *agg* indescribable.

**inetto** [i'nɛtto] *agg* inept, inadequate; (*incapace*) unsuited (to), incapable (of).

**inevaso** [ine'vazo] *agg* outstanding.

**inevitabile** [inevi'tabile] *agg* unavoidable.

**inezia** [i'nɛtsja] *sf* trifle.

**infagottare** [infagot'tare] *v* bundle up, wrap up.

**infallibile** [infal'libile] *agg* infallible. **infallibilità** *sf* infallibility.

**infame** [in'fame] *agg* infamous, vile. **infamia** *sf* infamy, disgrace.

**infangare** [infan'gare] *v* muddy.

**infante** [in'fante] *s(m+f)* infant, newborn baby. **infantile** *agg* childlike; (*puerile*) childish, infantile. **asilo infantile** *sm* nursery school. **infanzia** *sf* infancy, childhood.

**infarcire** [infar'tʃire] *v* stuff.

**infarinare** [infari'nare] *v* (dip in) flour. **infarinatura** *sf* coating of flour; (*fig*) smattering.

**infastidire** [infasti'dire] *v* bother, trouble.

**infaticabile** [infati'kabile] *agg* tireless.

**infatti** [in'fatti] *cong* in fact, as a matter of fact, indeed.

**infatuarsi** [infatu'arsi] *v* become infatuated (with); fall (for).

**infausto** [in'fausto] *agg* inauspicious, unlucky.

**infedele** [infe'dele] *agg* unfaithful.

**infelice** [infe'litʃe] *agg* unhappy; (*inopportuno*) unfortunate; (*disgraziato*) wretched, unlucky; (*cattivo*) bad. *s(m+f)* unhappy person, wretch.

**inferiore** [infe'rjore] *agg* lower; (*di grado più basso*) inferior; (*numeri*) below, less than. **inferiorità** *sf* inferiority.

**inferire** [infe'rire] *v* (*arrecare*) inflict, cause; (*dedurre*) infer.

**infermeria** [inferme'ria] *sf* infirmary. **infermiere, -a** *sm, sf* nurse. **infermità** *sf* illness. **infermo** *sm, agg* invalid.

**inferno** [in'fɛrno] *sm* hell. **infernale** *agg* infernal, hellish.

**inferriata** [infer'rjata] *sf* grille.

**infestare** [infes'tare] *v* infest.

**infettare** [infet'tare] *v* infect; (*fig*) taint. **infettivo** *agg* infectious, catching. **infezione** *sf* infection.

**infiacchire** [infjak'kire] *v* weaken.

**infiammare** [infjam'mare] *v* set on fire; (*eccitare, med*) inflame. **infiammabile** *agg* inflammable. **infiammazione** *sf* inflammation.

**infido** [in'fido] *agg* untrustworthy.

**infierire** [infje'rire] *v* rage.

**infilare** [infi'lare] *v* thread, string; (*introdurre*) insert; (*imboccare*) turn into, take. **infilata** *sf* row, string.

**infiltrarsi** [infilt'rarsi] *v* infiltrate.

**infimo** ['infimo] *agg* (the) lowest.

**infine** [in'fine] *avv* in the end, finally.

**infinito** [infi'nito] *agg* infinite; (*interminabile*) endless; (*innumerevole*) countless. *sm* infinity; (*gramm*) infinitive. **infinità** *sf* infinity; (*gran numero*) large number, crowd.

**infischiarsi** [infis'kjarsi] *v* not give a damn.

**infisso** [in'fisso] *sm* frame.

**inflazione** [infla'tsjone] *sf* inflation.

**inflessibile** [infles'sibile] *agg* inflexible. **inflessione** *sf* inflection.

***infliggere** [in'fliddʒere] *v* inflict.

**influenza** [influ'entsa] *sf* influence; (*med*) influenza, flu. **influenzare** *v* influence.

**influire** [influ'ire] *v* have an influence. **influire su** affect, influence. **influsso** *sm* influence.

**infondato** [infon'dato] *agg* groundless, unfounded.

***infondere** [in'fondere] *v* instil, inspire.

**informare** [infor'mare] *v* inform, tell; (*plasmare*) form, shape. **informarsi** *v* inquire, find out. **informazione** *sf* information.

**informe** [in'forme] *agg* shapeless.

**informicolirsi** [informiko'lirsi] *v* have pins and needles.

**infortunio** [infor'tunjo] *sm* accident.

**infossato** [infos'sato] *agg* hollow.

***inframmettersi** [infram'mettersi] *v* interfere.

***infrangere** [in'frandʒere] *v* break. **infrangibile** *agg* unbreakable.

**infrazione** [infra'tsjone] *sf* infringement, breach.

**infreddarsi** [infred'darsi] *v* catch a cold. **infreddatura** *sf* cold.

**infrequente** [infre'qwente] *agg* infrequent.

**infuori** [in'fwori] *avv* **all'infuori di** apart from, except.

**infuriare** [infu'rjare] *v* rage. **infuriarsi** *v* fly into a temper.

**ingannare** [ingan'nare] *v* deceive; (*truffare*) cheat; (*essere infedele*) be unfaithful. **inganno** *sm* deceit, deception, trick.

**ingarbugliarsi** [ingarbuˈʎarsi] *v* get entangled.

**ingegnarsi** [indʒe'narsi] *v* get by, manage.

**ingegnere** [indʒe'nere] *sm* engineer. **ingegneria** *sf* engineering.

**ingegno** [in'dʒeɲo] *sm* genius, talent. **ingegnoso** *agg* ingenious, clever.

**ingenuo** [in'dʒɛnwo] *agg* ingenuous, naive. *sm* naive person. **fare l'ingenuo** feign innocence; pretend not to understand.

**ingerirsi** [indʒe'rirsi] *v* meddle, interfere.

**ingessare** [indʒes'sare] *v* put in plaster.

**Inghilterra** [ingil'terra] *sf* England.

**inghiottire** [ingjot'tire] *v* swallow.

**inginocchiarsi** [indʒinok'kjarsi] *v* kneel (down).

**ingiuria** [in'dʒurja] *sf* offence; insult; (*fig*) damage. **ingiuriare** *v* insult; (*oltraggiare*) offend. **ingiurioso** *agg* insulting, offensive.

**ingiusto** [in'dʒusto] *agg* unjust; unfair.

**inglese** [in'gleze] *sm* (*persona*) Englishman; (*lingua*) English. *sf* Englishwoman. *agg* English. **filare all'inglese** take French leave. **zuppa inglese** *sf* trifle.

**ingoiare** [ingo'jare] *v* gulp (down),

swallow (down).

**ingolfarsi** [ingol'farsi] *v* (*auto*) flood; (*debiti*) be swamped.

**ingombrare** [ingomb'rare] *v* obstruct, get in the way.

**ingombro** [in'gombro] *agg* cluttered (with). *sm* obstruction; (*spazio*) space.

**ingommare** [ingom'mare] *v* stick.

**ingordo** [in'gordo] *agg* greedy. **ingordigia** *sf* greed.

**ingorgarsi** [ingor'garsi] *v* be blocked up. **ingorgo** *sm* obstruction; (*traffic*) jam.

**ingranare** [ingra'nare] *v* engage; (*fam*) get on. **ingranaggio** *sm* (*mec*) gear; (*fig*) works *pl*, mechanism.

**ingrandire** [ingran'dire] *v* enlarge, magnify. **ingrandimento** *sm* enlargement.

**ingrassare** [ingras'sare] *v* fatten, make fat; (*ungere*) grease. **ingrassarsi** *v* put on weight, get fat; (*arricchirsi*) profit.

**ingrato** [in'grato] *agg* ungrateful; (*sgradevole*) thankless. **ingratitudine** *sf* ingratitude.

**ingrediente** [ingre'djɛnte] *sm* ingredient.

**ingresso** [in'grɛsso] *sm* entrance; admission.

**ingrossare** [ingros'sare] *v* swell.

**ingrosso** [in'grɔsso] *avv* **all'ingrosso** wholesale.

**ingualcibile** [ingwal'tʃibile] *agg* crease-resistant.

**inguaribile** [ingwa'ribile] *agg* incurable.

**inguine** ['ingwine] *sm* groin.

**inibire** [ini'bire] *v* inhibit, forbid. **inibizione** *sf* inhibition.

**iniettare** [injet'tare] *v* inject. **iniezione** *sf* injection.

**inimicizia** [inimi'tʃitsja] *sf* enmity, hostility.

**inimitabile** [inimi'tabile] *agg* inimitable.

**inimmaginabile** [inimmadʒi'nabile] *agg* unimaginable.

**inintelligibile** [inintelli'dʒibile] *agg* unintelligible.

**ininterrotto** [ininter'rotto] *agg* uninterrupted, continuous.

**iniziale** [ini'tsjale] *agg* initial. *sf* initial (letter).

**iniziare** [ini'tsjare] *v* start, begin; (*avviare*) initiate. **iniziativa** *sf* initiative, enterprise. **inizio** *sm* beginning.

**innaffiare** [innaf'fjare] *v* water.

**innalzare** [innal'tsare] *v* raise.

**innamorarsi** [innamo'rarsi] *v* fall in love (with).

**innanzi** [in'nantsi] *prep* before. **innanzi tutto** first of all; (*sopratutto*) above all. *avv* (*prima*) before; (*avanti*) on, ahead. **d'ora innanzi** from now on, henceforth.

**innato** [in'nato] *agg* innate.

**innegabile** [inne'gabile] *agg* undeniable.

**innestare** [innes'tare] *v* (*piante*) graft; insert; (*med*) inoculate. **innestare una marcia** (*auto*) put into gear. **innesto** *sm* graft; (*auto*) clutch; (*med*) inoculation.

**inno** ['inno] *sm* hymn. **inno nazionale** national anthem.

**innocente** [inno'tʃɛnte] *agg* innocent. **dichiararsi innocente** (*dir*) plead not guilty. **innocenza** *sf* innocence.

**innocuo** [in'nɔkuo] *agg* innocuous, harmless.

**innominabile** [innomi'nabile] *agg* unmentionable.

**innovare** [inno'vare] *v* innovate. **innovatore, -trice** *sm*, *sf* innovator. **innovazione** *sf* innovation.

**innumerevole** [innume'revole] *agg* innumerable.

**inoculare** [inoku'lare] *v* inoculate.

**inoffensivo** [inoffen'sivo] *agg* inoffensive, harmless.

**inoltrare** [inol'trare] *v* send on, forward. **inoltrarsi** *v* advance.

**inoltre** [i'noltre] *avv* besides, furthermore.

**inondare** [inon'dare] *v* flood. **inondazione** *sf* flood.

**inoperoso** [inope'rozo] *agg* idle; (*econ*) unemployed.

**inopportuno** [inoppor'tuno] *agg* untimely; inopportune. **inopportunità** *sf* unsuitability; inappropriateness.

**inorridire** [inorri'dire] *v* horrify; be horrified.

**inospitale** [inospi'tale] *agg* inhospitable.

**inosservato** [inosser'vato] *agg* unobserved.

**inossidabile** [inossi'dabile] *agg* stainless.

**inquadrare** [inkwa'drare] *v* (*mettre in cornice*) frame; (*fig*) set; (*mil*) organize. **inquadratura** *sf* (*cine*, *TV*) shot.

**inquietare** [inkwje'tare] *v* worry. **inquietante** *agg* worrying. **inquieto** *agg* restless; (*preoccupato*) uneasy. **inquietudine** *sf* restlessness, worry.

**inquilino** [inkwi'lino], **-a** *sm, sf* tenant.

**inquinare** [inkwi'nare] *v* pollute. **inquinamento** *sm* pollution.

**insabbiare** [insab'biare] *v* (*pratica*) shelve.

**insalata** [insa'lata] *sf* salad; (*confusione*) muddle. **insalatiera** *sf* salad-bowl.

**insalubre** [insa'lubre] *agg* unhealthy.

**insanabile** [insa'nabile] *agg* incurable.

**insanguinare** [insangwi'nare] *v* stain with blood.

**insaputa** [insa'puta] *sf* **all'insaputa di** without the knowledge of.

**insaziabile** [insa'tsjabile] *agg* insatiable.

**inscatolare** [inskato'lare] *v* tin, can.

**inscenare** [inʃe'nare] *v* stage.

**insegna** [in'seɲa] *sf* (*emblema*) insignia *pl*; (*stemma*) coat of arms; motto; (*cartello*) sign.

**insegnare** [inse'ɲare] *v* teach. **insegnamento** *sm* teaching, education. **insegnante** *s(m+f)* teacher.

**inseguire** [inse'gwire] *v* pursue, chase. **inseguimento** *sm* pursuit, chase.

**insensato** [insen'sato] *agg* senseless, foolish.

**insensibile** [insen'sibile] *agg* (*leggerissimo*) imperceptible, very slight; (*indifferente*) insensitive, unfeeling.

**inseparabile** [insepa'rabile] *agg* inseparable.

**inserire** [inse'rire] *v* insert. **inserirsi** *v* introduce oneself, appear. **inserto** *sm* supplement. **inserzione** *sf* insertion; (*pubblicitaria*) advertisement.

**inservibile** [inser'vibile] *agg* useless.

**inserviente** [inser'vjɛnte] *s(m+f)* attendant.

**insetto** [in'sɛtto] *sm* insect. **insetticida** *sm* insecticide.

**insicuro** [insi'kuro] *agg* insecure.

**insidia** [in'sidja] *sf* snare, trap; (*pericolo*) danger. **insidioso** *agg* insidious.

**insieme** [in'sjɛme] *avv* together; (*allo stesso tempo*) at the same time. *sm* whole; (*abbigliamento*) outfit.

**insigne** [in'siɲe] *agg* notable, illustrious.

**insignificante** [insiɲifi'kante] *agg* insignificant, trivial.

**insignire** [insi'ɲire] *v* decorate, honour.

**insincero** [insin'tʃero] *agg* insincere.

**insinuare** [insinu'are] *v* insinuate, creep. **insinuazione** *sf* insinuation.

**insipido** [in'sipido] *agg* insipid, tasteless.

*__insistere__ [in'sistere] *v* insist (on). **insistente** *agg* insistent; (*incessante*) persistent, ceaseless. **insistenza** *sf* insistence.

**insocievole** [inso'tʃevole] *agg* unsociable.

**insoddisfatto** [insoddis'fatto] *agg* dissatisfied.

**insofferente** [insoffe'rɛnte] *agg* intolerant, impatient.

**insoffribile** [insof'fribile] *agg* unbearable.

**insolazione** [insola'tsjone] *sf* sunstroke.

**insolente** [inso'lɛnte] *agg* insolent. **insolenza** *sf* insolence.

**insolito** [in'sɔlito] *agg* unusual, strange.

**insolubile** [inso'lubile] *agg* insoluble. **insoluto** *agg* unsolved; (*non pagato*) outstanding.

**insomma** [in'somma] *inter* well! now then! *avv* (*in conclusione*) in short, in other words.

**insonnia** [in'sonnja] *sf* insomnia, sleeplessness. **insonne** *agg* sleepless; (*fig*) indefatigable.

**insopportabile** [insoppor'tabile] *agg* unbearable, intolerable.

*__insorgere__ [in'sordʒere] *v* rebel, rise (up against); protest.

**insormontabile** [insormon'tabile] *agg* insurmountable.

**insospettato** [insospet'tato] *agg* unexpected, unsuspected.

**insostenibile** [insoste'nibile] *agg* (*non difensibile*) untenable; (*non sopportabile*) unbearable.

**insostituibile** [insostitu'ibile] *agg* irreplaceable.

**insperato** [inspe'rato] *agg* undreamt of, unexpected.

**inspiegabile** [inspje'gabile] *agg* inexplicable.

**installare** [instal'lare] *v* install, establish. **installarsi** *v* settle (down). **installazione** *sf* installation.

**insù** [in'su] *avv* up.

**insubordinato** [insubordi'nato] *agg* insubordinate.

**insuccesso** [insut'tʃɛsso] *sm* failure.

**insudiciare** [insudi'tʃare] *v* soil, dirty.

**insufficiente** [insuffi'tʃɛnte] *agg* insufficient, inadequate. **insufficienza** *sf* insufficiency; (*mancanza*) shortage.

**insulina** [insu'lina] *sf* insulin.

**insultare** [insul'tare] *v* insult. **insulto** *sm* insult, abuse; (*accesso*) fit.

**insuperabile** [insupe'rabile] *agg* insuperable, insurmountable; (*imbattibile*) unbeatable.

**insurrezione** [insurre'tsjone] *sf* insurrection.

**insussistente** [insussis'tɛnte] *agg* nonexistent, baseless.

**intaccare** [intak'kare] *v* attack; (*far tacche*) notch, nick; (*consumare*) eat into.

**intagliare** [inta'ʎare] *v* carve, cut.

**intangibile** [intan'dʒibile] *agg* intangible.

**intanto** [in'tanto] *avv* meanwhile, in the meantime; (*fam: invece*) but, whereas, while.

**intasare** [inta'zare] *v* clog, block. **intasamento** *sm* obstruction, blockage.

**intascare** [intas'kare] *v* pocket.

**intatto** [in'tatto] *agg* intact.

**intavolare** [intavo'lare] *v* (*iniziare*) begin.

**integrale** [inte'grale] *agg* complete, total. **calcolo integrale** *sm* integral calculus. **pane integrale** *sm* wholemeal bread.

**integrare** [inte'grare] *v* integrate.

**integro** ['integro] *agg* complete; (*onesto*) upright. **integrità** *sf* integrity.

**intelletto** [intel'lɛtto] *sm* intellect. **intellettuale** *s(m+f)*, *agg* intellectual.

**intelligente** [intelli'dʒɛnte] *agg* intelligent. **intelligenza** *sf* intelligence. **intelligibile** *agg* intelligible.

**intemperie** [intem'pɛrje] *sf pl* bad weather *sing*.

**intempestivo** [intempes'tivo] *agg* untimely. **intempestività** *sf* untimeliness.

**intendente** [inten'dɛnte] *sm* superintendent, administrator. **intendenza** *sf* administration.

**\*intendere** [in'tɛndere] *v* (*udire*) hear; (*comprendere*) understand; (*aver intenzione, volere*) intend; (*significare*) mean. **intendersi** *v* (*andar d'accordo*) agree, get on; (*essere competente*) be knowledgeable (about). **s'intende** of course, it goes without saying.

**intenditore** [intendi'tore], **-trice** *sm*, *sf* connoisseur, good judge.

**intenso** [in'tɛnso] *agg* intense. **intensificare** *v* intensify. **intensità** *sf* intensity.

**intento** [in'tɛnto] *agg* busy. *sm* object, end.

**intenzione** [inten'tsjone] *sf* intention. **aver l'intenzione di** intend to. **bene/male**

**intenzionato** *agg* well-/ill-disposed.

**interattivo** [interat'tivo] *agg* interactive.

**intercettare** [intertʃet'tare] *v* intercept.

**\*interdire** [inter'dire] *v* (*proibire*) forbid; (*dir*) disqualify. **interdizione** *sf* ban, disqualification.

**interessare** [interes'sare] *v* interest; (*riguardare*) concern; (*stare a cuore*) matter. **interessarsi** *v* take an interest (in); (*prendersi cura*) look after, take care (of). **interessante** *agg* interesting. **interessato** *agg* interested, concerned; (*opportunistico*) self-interested. **interesse** *sm* interest; (*tornaconto*) profit.

**interferire** [interfe'rire] *v* interfere. **interferenza** *sf* interference.

**interiore** [inte'rjore] *agg* inner, interior.

**intermedio** [inter'mɛdjo] *agg* intermediate. **intermediario, -a** *s*, *agg* intermediary.

**interminabile** [intermi'nabile] *agg* endless, never-ending.

**internare** [inter'nare] *v* intern; (*med*) commit. **internamento** *sm* internment; commitment. **internato** *sm* (*convitto*) boarding school; (*scolaro*) boarder.

**internazionale** [internatsjo'nale] *agg* international.

**interno** [in'tɛrno] *agg* inner, internal. *sm* inside, interior; (*telefono*) extension.

**intero** [in'tero] *sm*, *agg* whole. **per intero** in full.

**interpellare** [interpel'lare] *v* ask, consult.

**interpretare** [interpre'tare] *v* interpret, explain; (*teatro, ecc.*) play. **interpretazione** *sf* interpretation. **interprete** *s(m+f)* interpreter; (*teatro, ecc.*) actor, performer; (*cantante*) singer.

**interrare** [inter'rare] *v* inter, bury.

**interrogare** [interro'gare] *v* interrogate, question; examine, test; consult. **interrogatorio** *sm* examination; questioning. **interrogazione** *sf* interrogation; (*domanda*) question; (*dir*) questioning, examination.

**\*interrompere** [inter'rompere] *v* interrupt, break (off).

**interruttore** [interrut'tore] *sm* switch.

**interruzione** [interru'tsjone] *sf* interruption, break.

**interurbano** [interur'bano] *agg* **chiamata** or **telefonata interurbana** *sf* trunk-call.

**intervallo** [inter'vallo] *sm* interval, break.

**\*intervenire** [interve'nire] v intervene; (*assistere*) take part, attend; (*med*) operate. **intervento** *sm* intervention; operation.

**intervista** [inter'vista] *sf* interview. **intervistare** v interview. **intervistatore, -trice** *sm, sf* interviewer.

**intesa** [in'teza] *sf* agreement, understanding; (*pol*) entente. **inteso** *agg* (*volto a un fine*) intended, meant; (*compreso*) understood; (*convenuto*) agreed. **ben inteso** understood.

**intestare** [intes'tare] v head; (*mettere a nome di*) make out to. **intestatario, -a** *sm, sf* holder.

**intestino** [intes'tino] *sm* intestine.

**intimare** [inti'mare] v order; (*dichiarare*) declare.

**intimidire** [intimi'dire] v intimidate.

**intimità** [intimi'ta] *sf* intimacy; (*ambiente intimo, fig*) privacy.

**intimo** ['intimo] *agg* intimate; (*interno*) innermost. *sm* (*amico*) close friend; (*anima*) heart of hearts. **biancheria intima** *sf* underwear.

**intimorire** [intimo'rire] v intimidate, frighten.

**\*intingere** [in'tindʒere] v dip.

**intingolo** [in'tingolo] *sm* (*piatto*) stew; (*salsa*) sauce, gravy.

**intirizzire** [intirit'tsire] v grow numb. **intirizzito** *agg* numb.

**intitolare** [intito'lare] v entitle; dedicate.

**intollerabile** [intolle'rabile] *agg* intolerable, unbearable.

**intollerante** [intolle'rante] *agg* intolerant.

**intonaco** [in'tɔnako] *sm* plaster. **intonacare** v plaster, whitewash.

**intonare** [into'nare] v (*accordare*) tune, (*cominciare a cantare*) intone, strike up; (*armonizzare*) match.

**intontire** [inton'tire] v daze.

**intorno** [in'torno] *avv* around; (*circa*) about; (*argomento*) on, about.

**intorpidire** [intorpi'dire] v grow numb.

**intossicante** [intossi'kante] *agg* poisoning. **intossicazione** *sf* poisoning.

**intraducibile** [intradu'tʃibile] *agg* untranslatable.

**intralciare** [intral'tʃare] v hold up, hinder. **intralcio** *sm* hindrance, obstacle.

**intransigente** [intransi'dʒɛnte] *agg* intransigent.

**intransitivo** [intransi'tivo] *agg* intransitive.

**\*intraprendere** [intra'prɛndere] v undertake, take on, begin. **intraprendente** *agg* enterprising. **intraprendenza** *sf* enterprise, initiative.

**intrattabile** [intrat'tabile] *agg* intractable; (*fam*) impossible, difficult.

**\*intrattenere** [intratte'nere] v entertain. **intrattenersi** v linger; (*indugiare su*) dwell (on).

**\*intravedere** [intrave'dere] v catch a glimpse (of); (*intuire*) sense.

**intreccio** [in'trettʃo] *sm* plaiting; (*trama*) plot. **intrecciare** v intertwine; (*capelli*) braid.

**intrepido** [in'trɛpido] *agg* intrepid, brave.

**intrigo** [in'trigo] *sm, pl* **-ghi** plot, intrigue. **intrigare** v plot, intrigue.

**intrinseco** [in'trinseko] *agg* intrinsic.

**intriso** [in'trizo] *agg* soaked.

**\*introdurre** [intro'durre] v introduce; (*inserire*) insert; (*far entrare*) show in. **introdotto** *agg* (*conosciuto*) well-known, well-established; (*esperto*) well up in. **introduzione** *sf* introduction.

**introito** [in'trɔito] *sm* income; (*incasso*) takings *pl*.

**\*intromettersi** [intro'mettersi] v meddle, intervene.

**intronare** [intro'nare] v deafen.

**introspettivo** [introspet'tivo] *agg* introspective.

**introvabile** [intro'vabile] *agg* unobtainable, not to be found.

**introverso** [intro'vɛrso], **-a** *s, agg* introvert.

**intrusione** [intru'zjone] *sf* intrusion. **intruso, -a** *sm, sf* intruder.

**intuitivo** [intui'tivo] *agg* intuitive. **intuire** v sense. **intuito** *sm* intuition, instinct, insight.

**inumano** [inu'mano] *agg* inhuman.

**inumidire** [inumi'dire] v moisten.

**inusitato** [inuzi'tato] *agg* uncommon.

**inutile** [i'nutile] *agg* useless; (*non necessario*) unnecessary.

**invadente** [inva'dɛnte] *agg* intrusive. *s(m+f)* busybody.

**\*invadere** [in'vadere] v invade, flood.

**invalido** [in'valido], **-a** *agg* invalid; (*privo di valore*) null and void; (*mutilato*) disabled. *sm, sf* invalid; disabled person. **invalidare**

*v* (*dir*) invalidate.

**invano** [in'vano] *avv* in vain. *agg* vain, useless.

**invariabile** [inva'rjabile] *agg* invariable, even. **invariato** *agg* unchanged.

**invasione** [inva'zjone] *sf* invasion.

**invecchiare** [invek'kjare] *v* age. **invecchiamento** *sm* ageing.

**invece** [in'vetʃe] *avv* instead (of); (*mentre*) whereas, while.

**invendibile** [inven'dibile] *agg* unsaleable. **invenduto** *agg* unsold.

**inventare** [inven'tare] *v* invent. **inventore** *sm* inventor. **invenzione** *sf* invention.

**inventario** [inven'tarjo] *sm* inventory.

**inverno** [in'vɛrno] *sm* winter. **invernale** *agg* winter, wintry.

**inverosimile** [invero'simile] *agg* unlikely.

**inverso** [in'vɛrso] *agg* contrary, opposite; (*mat*) inverse. *agg* contrary, opposite. **inversione** *sf* inversion; (*tec*) reversal.

**invertebrato** [inverte'brato] *sm, agg* invertebrate.

**investigare** [investi'gare] *v* investigate.

**investire** [inves'tire] *v* (*comm*) invest; (*scontrare*) collide, hit; (*scontrare persone*) hit, run down. **investimento** *sm* investment; collision, crash.

**invetriata** [invetri'ata] *sf* (*porta*) glass door; (*finestra*) window.

**invettiva** [invet'tiva] *sf* invective.

**inviare** [invi'are] *v* dispatch, send (off). **inviato, -a** *sm, sf* (*diplomatico*) envoy; (*giornale*) correspondent. **invio** *sm* dispatch.

**invidiare** [invi'djare] *v* envy. **invidia** *sf* envy. **invidioso** *agg* envious.

**invigorire** [invigo'rire] *v* invigorate, strengthen.

**invincibile** [invin'tʃibile] *agg* invincible.

**invisibile** [invi'zibile] *agg* invisible.

**invitare** [invi'tare] *v* invite. **invitato, -a** *sm, sf* guest. **invito** *sm* invitation.

**invocare** [invo'kare] *v* invoke, call for.

**invogliare** [invo'ʎare] *v* tempt.

***involgere** [in'vɔldʒere] *v* wrap (up).

**involontario** [involon'tarjo] *agg* involuntary.

**involtino** [invol'tino] *sm* (*gastr*) roulade, olive.

**involto** [in'vɔlto] *sm* bundle, package.

**involucro** [in'vɔlukro] *sm* covering, wrapper.

**invulnerabile** [invulne'rabile] *agg* invulnerable.

**inzaccherare** [indzakke'rare] *v* spatter with mud.

**inzuppare** [indzup'pare] *v* soak.

**io** ['io] *pron* I. *sm* self.

**iodio** ['jɔdjo] *sm* iodine.

**ione** ['jone] *sm* ion.

**iperattivo** [iperat'tivo] *agg* hyperactive.

**iperbole** [i'pɛrbole] *sf* hyperbole. **iperbolico** *agg* exaggerated; (*mat*) hyperbolic.

**ipermercato** [ipermer'kato] *sm* hypermarket.

**ipertensione** [iperten'sjone] *sf* hypertension. **iperteso** *agg* hypertensive.

**ipnosi** [ip'nɔzi] *sf* hypnosis. **ipnotico** *agg* hypnotic. **ipnotismo** *sm* hypnotism.

**ipnotizzare** [ipnotid'dzare] *v* hypnotize. **ipnotizzatore, -trice** *sm, sf* hypnotist.

**ipocondriaco** [ipokon'driako], **-a** *s, agg* hypochondriac. **ipocondria** *sf* hypochondria.

**ipocrita** [i'pɔkrita] *s(m+f)* hypocrite. *agg* hypocritical. **ipocrisia** *sf* hypocrisy.

**ipoteca** [ipo'tɛka] *sf* mortgage. **ipotecare** *v* mortgage.

**ipotenusa** [ipote'nuza] *sf* hypotenuse.

**ipotesi** [i'pɔtezi] *sf* hypothesis (*pl* -ses). **nella migliore delle ipotesi** at best. **nella peggiore delle ipotesi** if the worst comes to the worst. **ipotetico** *agg* hypothetical.

**ippica** ['ippika] *sf* horse-racing. **ippico** *agg* horse.

**ippocampo** [ippo'kampo] *sm* sea-horse.

**ippocastano** [ippokas'tano] *sm* horse-chestnut.

**ippodromo** [ip'pɔdromo] *sm* racecourse.

**ippopotamo** [ippo'pɔtamo] *sm* hippopotamus.

**ira** ['ira] *sf* rage, anger. **irascibile** *agg* irascible.

**iride** ['iride] *sf* iris; (*arcobaleno*) rainbow.

**Irlanda** [ir'landa] *sf* Ireland. **Irlanda del Nord** Northern Ireland. **irlandese** *sm, agg* Irish. **gli irlandesi** the Irish.

**ironia** [iro'nia] *sf* irony. **ironico** *agg* ironic(al).

**irradiare** [irra'djare] *v* radiate; (*fig*) irradiate.

**irraggiungibile** [irraddʒun'dʒibile] *agg*

unattainable.

**irragionevole** [irrad3o'nɛvole] *agg* unreasonable.

**irrazionale** [irratsjo'nale] *agg* irrational.

**irreale** [irre'ale] *agg* unreal.

**irregolare** [irrego'lare] *agg* irregular. **irregolarità** *sf* irregularity.

**irreperibile** [irrepe'ribile] *agg* that cannot be found.

**irreguieto** [irre'kwjɛto] *agg* restless.

**irresistibile** [irrezis'tibile] *agg* irresistible.

**irresoluto** [irrezo'luto] *agg* wavering, undecided. **irresolutezza** *sf* indecision, wavering.

**irresponsabile** [irrespon'sabile] *agg* irresponsible. **irresponsabilità** *sf* irresponsibility.

**irrigare** [irri'gare] *v* irrigate. **irrigazione** *sf* irrigation.

**irrigidire** [irrid3i'dire] *v* stiffen. **irrigidimento** *sm* stiffening; (*fig*) obstinacy.

**irrimediabile** [irrime'djabile] *agg* irreparable.

**irrisorio** [irri'zɔrjo] *agg* derisory, ridiculous.

**irritare** [irri'tare] *v* irritate; (*dar fastidio*) annoy. **irritabile** *agg* irritable. **irritante** *agg* irritating; (*med*) irritant. **irritazione** *sf* irritation.

**irriverenza** [irrive'rɛntsa] *sf* disrespect.

***irrompere** [ir'rompere] *v* burst into; (*riversarsi*) pour into.

**irsuto** [ir'suto] *agg* shaggy, hairy.

**irto** ['irto] *agg* bristling (with).

***iscrivere** [is'krivere] *v* enrol, register; (*diventar socio*) join. **iscritto** *sm* member. **iscrizione** *sf* registration, enrolment; (*scritta*) inscription.

**Islanda** [is'landa] *sf* Iceland. **islandese** *sm*, *agg* Icelandic; *s*(*m+f*) Icelander.

**isola** ['izola] *sf* island.

**isolare** [izo'lare] *v* isolate; (*fis*) insulate. **isolamento** *sm* isolation; insulation.

**ispettore** [ispet'tore], **-trice** *sm*, *sf* inspector.

**ispezionare** [ispetsjo'nare] *v* inspect. **ispezione** *sf* inspection.

**ispirare** [ispi'rare] *v* inspire.

**issare** [is'sare] *v* hoist.

**istamina** [ista'mina] *sf* histamine.

**istante** [is'tante] *sm* instant, moment. **istantanea** *sf* snapshot. **istantaneo** *agg*

instantaneous.

**istanza** [is'tantsa] *sf* (*domanda*) application, petition.

**isterico** [is'tɛriko] *agg* hysterical. **attacco isterico** *sm* hysterics *pl*. **isteria** *sf* hysteria.

**istigare** [isti'gare] *v* instigate.

**istillare** [istil'lare] *v* instil.

**istinto** [is'tinto] *sm* instinct.

**istituire** [istitu'ire] *v* institute, establish.

**istituto** [isti'tuto] *sm* institute; (*ente*) institution, organization. **istituzione** *sf* institution.

**istrice** ['istritʃe] *sm* porcupine; (*persona scontrosa*) touchy person.

***istruire** [istru'ire] *v* instruct, educate. **istruire un processo** (*dir*) prepare a case. **istruttore, -trice** *sm*, *sf* instructor, -tress, teacher. **giudice istruttore** *sm* examining magistrate. **istruttoria** *sf* (*dir*) examination. **istruttorio** *agg* preliminary. **istruzione** *sf* instruction, education, tuition.

**Italia** [i'talja] *sf* Italy. **italiano, -a** *s*, *agg* Italian.

**itinerario** [itine'rarjo] *sm* itinerary, route.

**itterizia** [itte'ritsja] *sf* jaundice.

**Iugoslavia** [jugo'slavja] *sf* Yugoslavia. **iugoslavo, -a** *s*, *agg* Yugoslav.

**iuta** ['juta] *sf* jute.

# L

**la¹** [la] *art* the.

**la²** [la] *pron* (*cosa, animale*) it; (*persona*) her; (*formula di cortesia*) you.

**là** [la] *avv* there. **di là** (*nell'altra stanza*) in the other room; (*da quella parte*) that way. **in là** (*oltre*) further. **va là!** come off it!

**labbro** ['labbro] *sm*, *pl* **-a** *f* in anat sense lip; (*orlo*) brim.

**labirinto** [labi'rinto] *sm* labyrinth, maze.

**laboratorio** [labora'tɔrjo] *sm* laboratory; (*industria*) workshop.

**laborioso** [labo'rjozo] *agg* laborious.

**laburista** [labu'rista] *agg* Labour.

**lacca** ['lakka] *sf* lacquer.

**laccio** ['lattʃo] *sm* noose; (*trappola*) snare, trap; (*legame*) tie. **laccio da scarpe** shoelace.

**lacerare** [latʃe'rare] v lacerate, tear.

**lacrima** ['lakrima] sf tear.

**lacrimogeno** [lakri'mɔdʒeno] agg **gas lacrimogeno** sm tear-gas.

**lacuna** [la'kuna] sf gap.

**ladro** ['ladro] sm thief. **al ladro!** stop thief! **vestito come un ladro** dressed like a tramp.

**laggiù** [lad'dʒu] avv down there.

**lagnarsi** [la'ɲarsi] v complain. **lagna** sf bore.

**lago** ['lago] sm lake.

**laico** ['laiko] agg lay. sm layman.

**lama¹** ['lama] sf blade. **lametta** sf razorblade.

**lama²** ['lama] sm invar (zool) llama.

**lambiccarsi** [lambik'karsi] v **lambiccarsi il cervello** rack one's brains.

**lambire** [lam'bire] v lick, lap.

**lamentare** [lamen'tare] v lament. **lamentarsi (di)** complain (about). **lamentela** sf complaint. **lamentevole** agg pitiful. **lamento** sm lament. **lamentoso** agg plaintive.

**lamiera** [la'mjɛra] sf sheet.

**lamina** ['lamina] sf thin layer; (metallo) foil. **laminare** v (ridurre in lamine) roll; (coprire con lamine) laminate. **laminato** sm laminate. **laminatoio** sm rolling-mill.

**lampada** ['lampada] sf lamp. **lampadario** sm chandelier. **lampadina** sf (light) bulb. **lampadina tascabile** torch.

**lampeggiare** [lamped'dʒare] v flash.

**lampione** [lam'pjone] sm lamp-post.

**lampo** ['lampo] sm flash; (temporale) lightning. **cerniera lampo** sf zip.

**lampone** [lam'pone] sm raspberry.

**lampreda** [lam'prɛda] sf lamprey.

**lana** ['lana] sf wool. **di lana** woollen. **industria laniera** sf wool industry. **lanificio** sm woollen mill.

**lancetta** [lan'tʃetta] sf hand.

**lancia¹** ['lantʃa] sf (arma) lance.

**lancia²** ['lantʃa] sf (barca) launch. **lancia di salvataggio** lifeboat.

**lanciare** [lan'tʃare] v throw, fling; (diffondere) launch; (bombe) drop. **lanciafiamme** sm invar flame-thrower. **lanciamissili** sm invar rocket-launcher. **lanciare un grido** utter a cry. **lancio** sm throw, fling; launching.

**languire** [lan'gwire] v languish; (diminuire di forza) flag. **languido** agg languid.

**lanterna** [lan'tɛrna] sf lantern.

**lanugine** [la'nudʒine] sf down.

**lapide** ['lapide] sf (sepolcrale) tombstone; (commemorativa) memorial tablet.

**lapis** ['lapis] sm pencil.

**lardo** ['lardo] sm lard, dripping.

**largo** ['largo] agg wide, broad. **al largo di** away from, off. **far largo di** make room for. **larghezza** sf width, breadth; (fig) generosity.

**larice** ['laritʃe] sm larch.

**laringe** [la'rindʒe] sf larynx. **laringite** sf laryngitis.

**larva** ['larva] sf larva; (spettro) shadow.

**lasciare** [la'ʃare] v leave; (permettere) let. **lascito** sm legacy.

**lascivo** [la'ʃivo] agg lascivious.

**laser** ['lazer] sm invar laser.

**lassativo** [lassa'tivo] sm, agg laxative.

**lasso** ['lasso] sm (periodo) lapse. agg (rilassato) loose.

**lassù** [las'su] avv up there.

**lastra** ['lastra] sf plate; sheet.

**lastricare** [lastri'kare] v pave. **lastrico** sm pavement; (miseria) poverty.

**latente** [la'tɛnte] agg latent.

**laterale** [late'rale] agg lateral, side.

**laterizi** [late'ritsi] sm pl bricks pl, tiles pl.

**latice** [la'titʃe] sm latex.

**latino** [la'tino] sm, agg Latin.

**latitante** [lati'tante] agg fugitive. **rendersi latitante** abscond.

**latitudine** [lati'tudine] sf latitude.

**lato¹** ['lato] sm side. **da un lato ... dall'altro ...** on the one hand ... on the other .... **d'altro lato** on the other hand.

**lato²** ['lato] agg **in senso lato** in a broad sense.

**latrare** [la'trare] v bark.

**latrina** [la'trina] sf latrine.

**latta** ['latta] sf (lamiera) tin, tinplate; (recipiente) tin, can.

**lattaio** [lat'tajo] sm milkman.

**latte** ['latte] sm milk. **latte magro** skimmed milk. **latteo** agg milky. **latteria** sf dairy. **lattiera** sf milk jug.

**lattuga** [lat'tuga] sf lettuce.

**laurea** ['laurea] sf degree; sf, sm graduation.

**laurearsi** v graduate. **laureato, -a** sm, sf graduate. **essere laureato in ...** have a degree in ....

**lauro** ['lauro] sm laurel.

**lauto** ['lauto] agg generous, sumptuous.

**lava** ['lava] sf lava.

**lavabo** [la'vabo] sm wash-basin.

**lavaggio** [la'vaddʒo] sm washing. **lavaggio a secco** dry-cleaning. **lavaggio del cervello** brainwashing.

**lavagna** [la'vaɲa] sf slate; (scolastica) blackboard.

**lavanda**¹ [la'vanda] sf (bot) lavender.

**lavanda**² [la'vanda] sf wash(ing).

**lavandaia** [lavan'daja] sf laundress, washerwoman.

**lavanderia** [lavande'ria] sf laundry; (a gettoni) launderette.

**lavandino** [lavan'dino] sm sink.

**lavapiatti** [lava'pjatti] sm also **lavastoviglie** invar dishwasher.

**lavatrice** [lava'tritʃe] sf washing machine.

**lavare** [la'vare] v wash. **lavare a secco** dry-clean. **lavare il capo a** tell off. **lavarsi** v (have a) wash. **lavata di capo** sf telling-off. **lavatura** sf washing; (acqua sporca) dishwater.

**lavativo** [lava'tivo] sm (fam) bore, pain in the neck.

**lavorare** [lavo'rare] v work; (con fatica) labour; (aziende, negozi, ecc.) do business; (il terreno) till; (teatro, ecc.) act, play. **lavorativo** agg working. **lavorato** agg finished; (metallo) wrought; (a macchina) machined.

**lavoratore** [lavora'tore], **-trice** sm, sf worker. **lavoratore a cottimo** piece-worker.

**lavorazione** [lavora'tsjone] sf manufacture; (fattura) workmanship; work. **lavorazione in serie** mass-production.

**lavoro** [la'voro] sm work; (occupazione) job; (teatro, ecc.) play. **lavori di casa** sm pl housework sing. **lavoro a cottimo** sm piece-work. **lavoro straordinario** sm overtime.

**lazzarone** [laddza'rone] sm scoundrel.

**le**¹ [le] art the.

**le**² [le] pron (persona) (to) her; (cosa, animale) (to) it; (formula di cortesia) (to) you; (pl) them.

**leale** [le'ale] agg sincere; (onesto) fair. **lealtà** sf loyalty, fairness.

**lebbroso** [leb'brozo], **-a** agg leprous. sm, sf leper. **lebbra** sf leprosy.

**leccare** [lek'kare] v lick. **leccalecca** sm invar (fam) lollipop. **leccapiedi** sm invar (fam) bootlicker. **leccare i piedi a** lick the boots of. **leccornia** sf titbit, tasty morsel.

**lecito** ['letʃito] agg (dir) lawful; (permesso) allowed.

**lega** ['lega] sf league, alliance; (metalli) alloy.

**legale** [le'gale] agg legal; (legittimo) lawful. **medicina legale** sf forensic medicine. **numero legale** sm quorum. **ora legale** sf summer-time. **legalizzare** v legalize, certify.

**legame** [le'game] sm tie, bond; (fig) link; (amoroso) liaison.

**legare** [le'gare] v tie (up), bind; (assicurare) fasten. **matto da legare** crazy, mad as a hatter.

**legato** [le'gato] agg tied (up); (libro) bound; (impacciato) stiff. sm (papale) legate; (testamento) legacy.

**legatura** [lega'tura] sf binding.

**legge** ['leddʒe] sf law; (votata dal parlamento) act (of parliament); (norma di condotta) rule. **progetto di legge** sm bill. **proposta di legge** sf draft bill.

**leggenda** [led'dʒɛnda] sf legend; (didascalia) caption. **leggendario** agg legendary.

**\*leggere** ['leddʒere] v read.

**leggero** [led'dʒɛro] agg light; (lieve) slight. **leggerezza** sf lightness; (frivolezza) levity; (sconsideratezza) thoughtlessness.

**leggiadro** [led'dʒadro] agg graceful, lovely.

**leggibile** [led'dʒibile] agg readable, legible.

**leggio** [led'dʒio] sm music stand; (chiesa) lectern.

**legione** [le'dʒone] sf legion.

**legislazione** [ledʒizla'tsjone] sf legislation. **legislatore** sm legislator.

**legittimo** [le'dʒittimo] agg lawful; (tale per legge) legitimate; proper; justifiable.

**legna** ['leɲa] sf invar firewood. **mettere legna al fuoco** add fuel to the fire.

**legname** [le'ɲame] sm timber; (in tronchi) logs pl.

**legnata** [le'ɲata] sf blow. **un sacco di legnate** sm (fam) a good hiding.

**legno** ['leɲo] sm wood. **di legno** wooden, wood. **lavoro in legno** sm woodwork; (edilizia) timberwork. **legno compensato**

plywood. **legno impiallacciato** veneer.

**lei** ['lɛi] *pron (soggetto)* she; *(oggetto)* her; *(formula di cortesia)* you.

**lembo** ['lembo] *sm (orlo)* edge, border; *(striscia)* strip.

**lemme lemme** ['lɛmme 'lɛmme] *avv (fam)* very leisurely.

**lena** ['lena] *sf* vigour. **lavorare di buona lena** *(fam)* put one's back into it.

**lente** ['lɛnte] *sf* lens. **lente a contatto** contact lens. **lente d'ingrandimento** magnifying glass. **lenti** *sf pl* glasses *pl*.

**lenticchia** [len'tikkja] *sf* lentil.

**lentiggine** [len'tiddʒine] *sf* freckle. **lentigginoso** *agg* freckled.

**lento** ['lɛnto] *agg* slow; *(allentato)* loose. **lento a capire** slow in the uptake.

**lenza** ['lɛntsa] *sf* (fishing-)line.

**lenzuolo** [len'tswɔlo] *sm, pl* **-a** *f when referring to a pair* sheet.

**leone** [le'one] *sm* lion. **leonessa** *sf* lioness.

**leopardo** [leo'pardo] *sm* leopard.

**lepido** ['lɛpido] *agg* witty.

**lepre** ['lɛpre] *sf* hare. **lepre in salmi** jugged hare. **labbro leporino** *sm* hare-lip.

**lesbico** ['lɛzbiko] *agg* lesbian. **lesbica** *sf* lesbian.

**lesina** ['lezina] *sf* awl; *(fam: taccagneria)* meanness. **lesinare** *v* skimp.

**lesione** [le'zjone] *sf* injury; *(med)* lesion; *(danno)* damage. **parte lesa** *sf* injured party.

**lessare** [les'sare] *v* boil. **lesso** *sm* boiled meat.

**lessico** ['lɛssiko] *sm* lexicon; vocabulary.

**lesto** ['lɛsto] *agg* swift, quick. **lesto di lingua** glib. **lesto di mano** light-fingered. **lestofante** *sm* swindler.

**letale** [le'tale] *agg* lethal, deadly.

**letame** [le'tame] *sm* manure, dung; *(fig)* filth. **letamaio** *sm* dung-heap; *(luogo sudicio)* pigsty.

**letargico** [le'tardʒiko] *agg* lethargic. **letargo** *sm (zool)* hibernation; *(med, torpore)* lethargy.

**letizia** [le'titsja] *sf* joy, gladness.

**lettera** ['lettera] *sf* letter. **alla lettera** literally; verbatim. **lettera d'accompagnamento** covering letter. **lettera di sollecitazione** reminder. **lettera maiuscola/minuscola** capital/small letter.

**letterario** [lette'rarjo] *agg* literary.

**letteratura** [lettera'tura] *sf* literature.

**lettiga** [let'tiga] *sf* litter; *(barella)* stretcher.

**letto** ['lɛtto] *sm* bed.

**Lettonia** [let'tɔnja] *sf* Latvia. **lettone** *s(m+f)*, *agg* Latvian.

**lettore** [let'tore], **-trice** *sm, sf* reader; *(universitario)* modern language lecturer.

**lettura** [let'tura] *sf* reading.

**leucemia** [leutʃe'mia] *sf* leukaemia.

**leva**[1] ['lɛva] *sf (mec)* lever; *(fig)* incentive. **far leva** lever. **far leva su** exploit, play on.

**leva**[2] ['lɛva] *sf* call-up; conscripts *pl*.

**levante** [le'vante] *sm* east.

**levare** [le'vare] *v (alzare)* raise, lift; *(togliere)* take away *or* off; *(estrarre)* pull out. **levare di mezzo** get rid of, remove. **levarsi** *v (alzarsi)* rise; *(dal letto)* get up. **levarsi la fame** satisfy one's hunger. **levarsi la sete** quench one's thirst. **levata della posta** *sf* mail collection. **levata del sole** *sf* sunrise.

**levatoio** [leva'tojo] *agg* **ponte levatoio** *sm* drawbridge.

**levatrice** [leva'tritʃe] *sf* midwife.

**levigare** [levi'gare] *v* smooth; polish; *(pomiciare)* rub down; *(con carta vetrata)* sand down.

**levriere** [le'vrjɛre] *sm* greyhound.

**lezione** [le'tsjone] *sf* lesson; class; *(durata)* period; *(universitaria)* lecture.

**lezioso** [le'tsjozo] *agg* affected, mannered.

**lezzo** ['lɛttso] *sm* stench; *(sudiciume)* filth.

**li** [li] *pron* them.

**lì** [li] *avv* there. **giù di lì** thereabouts. **lì per lì** *(sul momento)* there and then; *(dapprima)* at first.

**libbra** ['libbra] *sf* pound.

**libellula** [li'bellula] *sf* dragonfly.

**liberale** [libe'rale] *s(m+f)*, *agg* liberal.

**liberare** [libe'rare] *v* free, liberate; *(salvare)* save, rescue. **liberazione** *sf* liberation; release.

**libero** ['libero] *agg* free; *(sgombro)* clear; exempt. **aria libera** *sf* open air. **libero pensatore** *sm* freethinker. **tempo libero** *sm* time off.

**libertà** [liber'ta] *sf* freedom, liberty. **giorno di libertà** *sm* day off. **libertà condizionata** probation. **libertà provvisoria** bail. **mettere in libertà** set free.

**Libra** ['libra] *sf* Libra.

**libraio** [li'brajo] *sm* bookseller. **libreria** *sf* (*negozio*) bookshop; (*raccolta di libri*) library; (*casa editrice*) publishers *pl*.

**libro** ['libro] *sm* book. **a libro** hinged. **libro di cassa** cash register. **libro giallo** thriller. **libro mastro** ledger. **libro nero** blacklist.

**licenza** [li'tʃɛntsa] *sf* licence, permission; (*scuola*) leaving certificate.

**licenziare** [litʃen'tsjare] *v* dismiss. **licenziamento** *sm* dismissal.

**liceo** [li'tʃɛo] *sm* secondary school, high school.

**lichene** [li'kɛne] *sm* lichen.

**lido** ['lido] *sm* shore.

**lieto** ['ljɛto] *agg* glad, happy.

**lieve** ['ljɛve] *agg* slight, light.

**lievito** ['ljɛvito] *sm* yeast; (*fig*) ferment.

**lignaggio** [li'naddʒo] *sm* lineage, pedigree.

**ligustro** [li'gustro] *sm* privet.

**lilla** ['lilla] *agg, sm invar* lilac.

**lima** ['lima] *sf* file. **limare** *v* file. **limatura** *sf* filing; (*polvere*) filings *pl*.

**limitare** [limi'tare] *v* limit, restrict. **limitazione** *sf* limitation, restraint.

**limite** ['limite] *sm* limit; (*confine*) boundary. **caso limite** *sm* borderline case. **limitrofo** *agg* bordering.

**limo** ['limo] *sm* mud, slime.

**limone** [li'mone] *sm* (*albero*) lemon-tree; (*frutto*) lemon. **limonata** *sf* lemonade.

**limpido** ['limpido] *agg* clear.

**lince** ['lintʃe] *sf* lynx.

**linciare** [lin'tʃare] *v* lynch. **linciaggio** *sm* lynching.

**lindo** ['lindo] *agg* clean, tidy.

**linea** ['linea] *sf* line; (*corpo umano*) figure. **linea ferroviaria** railway line. **lineetta** *sf* dash.

**lineamenti** [linea'menti] *sm pl* features *pl*; (*elementi essenziali*) outlines *pl*.

**lineare** [line'are] *agg* linear; coherent; (*di indirizzo stabile*) unswerving.

**linfa** ['linfa] *sf* lymph; (*bot*) sap.

**lingua** ['lingwa] *sf* tongue; (*linguaggio*) language. **linguaggio** *sm* language. **linguista** *s*(*m+f*) linguist. **linguistico** *agg* linguistic.

**lino** ['lino] *sm* (*pianta*) flax; (*tessuto*) linen. **olio di lino** *sm* linseed oil.

**liocorno** [lio'kɔrno] *sm* unicorn.

**liquefare** [likwe'fare] *v* liquefy, melt. **liquefazione** *sf* liquefaction.

**liquidare** [likwi'dare] *v* liquidate; (*conti*) settle; (*merci*) sell off; (*sciogliere*) wind up. **liquidazione** *sf* liquidation, settlement; (*svendita*) clearance sale; winding-up; (*indennità*) leaving bonus. **liquidatore** *sm* receiver.

**liquido** ['likwido] *sm, agg* liquid, fluid.

**liquirizia** [likwi'ritsja] *sf* liquorice.

**liquore** [li'kwore] *sm* liqueur.

**lira¹** ['lira] *sf* (*moneta*) lira. **lira sterlina** pound sterling.

**lira²** ['lira] *sf* (*musica*) lyre.

**lirico** ['liriko] *agg* lyrical; opera. **cantante lirico** *s*(*m+f*) opera singer. **dramma lirico** *sm* opera. **teatro lirico** *sm* opera house. **lirica** *sf* lyric poetry.

**lisca** ['liska] *sf* fishbone.

**lisciare** [li'ʃare] *v* smooth. **liscio** *agg* smooth; (*bevanda*) neat. **andar liscio** go smoothly. **passarla liscia** get off scot-free.

**liseuse** [li'zøz] *sf, pl* -s bed-jacket.

**liso** ['lizo] *agg* worn.

**lista** ['lista] *sf* (*striscia*) strip; (*elenco*) list. **lista elettorale** electoral register. **listare** *v* border. **listino** *sm* list.

**litania** [lita'nia] *sf* litany.

**lite** ['lite] *sf* quarrel; (*dir*) (law)suit.

**litigare** [liti'gare] *v* quarrel. **litigio** *sm* quarrel, row. **litigioso** *agg* quarrelsome; (*dir*) contentious.

**litorale** [lito'rale] *agg* coastal. *sm* shore.

**litro** ['litro] *sm* litre.

**Lituania** [li'twanja] *sf* Lithuania. **lituano** *s*(*m+f*), *agg* Lithuanian.

**liturgia** [litur'dʒia] *sf* liturgy. **liturgico** *agg* liturgical.

**liuto** [li'uto] *sm* lute.

**livellare** [livel'lare] *v* level. **livella** *sf* level. **livellatore, -trice** *sm, sf* leveller.

**livello** [li'vello] *sm* level. **livello del mare** sea-level. **passaggio a livello** *sm* level crossing.

**livido** ['livido] *agg* livid. *sm* bruise.

**Livorno** [li'vorno] *sf* Leghorn.

**livrea** [li'vrea] *sf* livery.

**lizza** ['littsa] *sf* **entrare in lizza** compete.

**lo¹** [lo] *art* the.

**lo²** [lo] *pron* (*persona*) him; (*cosa, animale*) it.

**lobo** ['lɔbo] *sm* lobe.

**locale¹** [lo'kale] *agg* local.

**locale²** [lo'kale] *sm* room, spot. **locale notturno** night-club. **località** *sf* locality.

**localizzare** [lokalid'dzare] *v* (*individuare*) locate; (*circoscrivere*) localize.

**locanda** [lo'kanda] *sf* inn. **locandiere, -a** *sm, sf* innkeeper.

**locatario** [loka'tarjo] *sm* tenant.

**locatore** [loka'tore] *sm* landlord.

**locazione** [loka'tsjone] *sf* lease, tenancy.

**locomotiva** [lokomo'tiva] *sf* locomotive, engine.

**lodare** [lo'dare] *v* praise. **lode** *sf* praise. **lodevole** *agg* praiseworthy.

**logaritmo** [loga'ritmo] *sm* logarithm.

**loggia** [lɔdd'ʒa] *sf* loggia; (*massone*) lodge. **loggione** *sm* gallery.

**logica** [lɔ'dʒika] *sf* logic. **logico** *agg* logical.

**logistica** [lo'dʒistika] *sf* logistics. **logistico** *agg* logistic(al).

**logorare** [logo'rare] *v* wear out. **logoramento** *sm* wear; (*mentale*) strain. **logorio** *sm* wear and tear. **logoro** *agg* worn out.

**Londra** [lɔndra] *sf* London. **londinese** *s*(*m+f*) Londoner.

**longevo** [lon'dʒɛvo] *agg* long-lived. **longevità** *sf* longevity.

**longitudine** [londʒi'tudine] *sf* longitude. **longitudinale** *agg* longitudinal.

**lontano** [lon'tano] *agg* far, far away; (*assente*) absent; distant; vague. *avv* far. **lontananza** *sf* distance.

**lontra** [lɔntra] *sf* otter.

**loquace** [lo'kwatʃe] *agg* loquacious.

**lordo** [lɔrdo] *agg* (*peso*) gross; (*sporco*) filthy.

**loro** [loro] *pron* (*soggetto*) they; (*oggetto*) them; (*formula di cortesia*) you; (*di essi*) theirs. *agg* their.

**losco** [losko] *agg* sinister.

**loto** [lɔto] *sm* lotus.

**lotta** [lɔtta] *sf* struggle, fight; (*sport*) wrestling. **lottare** *v* struggle, fight; wrestle.

**lotteria** [lotte'ria] *sf* lottery.

**lotto** [lɔtto] *sm* portion; (*comm*) lot; lottery.

**lozione** [lo'tsjone] *sf* lotion.

**lubrificante** [lubrifi'kante] *agg* lubricating. *sm* lubricant. **lubrificare** *v* lubricate. **lubrificazione** *sf* lubrication.

**lucchetto** [luk'ketto] *sm* padlock.

**luccicare** [luttʃi'kare] *v* shine, sparkle.

**luccio** [luttʃo] *sm* pike.

**lucciola** [luttʃola] *sf* firefly.

**luce** [lutʃe] *sf* light.

**lucernario** [lutʃer'narjo] *sm* skylight.

**lucertola** [lu'tʃertola] *sf* lizard.

**lucidare** [lutʃi'dare] *v* polish.

**lucido** [lutʃido] *agg* shiny, glossy; (*fig*) lucid. *sm* polish.

**luglio** [luʎo] *sm* July.

**lugubre** [lugubre] *agg* lugubrious.

**lui** [lui] *pron* (*soggetto*) he; (*oggetto*) him.

**lumaca** [lu'maka] *sf* snail; (*persona*) slow-coach.

**lume** [lume] *sm* light; lamp. **far lume su** throw light on.

**luminoso** [lumi'nozo] *agg* bright, shining.

**luna** [luna] *sf* moon. **avere la luna** be in a bad mood. **luna di miele** honeymoon. **luna-park** *sm invar* funfair. **lunare** *agg* lunar. **sbarcare il lunario** make ends meet.

**lunedì** [lune'di] *sm* Monday.

**lungo¹** [lungo] *agg* long; (*alto*) tall; (*lento*) slow; (*diluito*) weak. **alla lunga** in the long run. **a lungo** (for) long. **di gran lunga** by far. **lunghezza** *sf* length.

**lungo²** [lungo] *prep* along. **lungomare** *sm* seashore.

**luogo** [lwɔgo] *sm* place. **aver luogo** take place. **fuori luogo** out of place. **in luogo di** instead of. **luogotenente** *sm* lieutenant.

**lupo** [lupo] *sm* wolf. **lupa** *sf* she-wolf.

**luppolo** [luppolo] *sm* hop.

**lurido** [lurido] *agg* filthy.

**lusingare** [luzin'gare] *v* flatter; (*illudere*) delude. **lusinga** *sf* flattery; delusion. **lusinghiero** *agg* flattering, alluring.

**Lussemburgo** [lussem'burgo] *sm* Luxembourg.

**lusso** [lusso] *sm* luxury. **di lusso** luxury, de luxe. **lussuoso** *agg* luxurious.

**lustrare** [lus'trare] *v* polish. **lustrino** *sm* sequin. **lustro** *sm* polish, sheen; lustre.

**lutto** [lutto] *sm* mourning; (*dolore*) grief.


# M

**ma** [ma] *cong* but. **macché!** *inter* (*neanche*

*per sogno)* of course not! not on your life! **ma davvero?** really? **ma no!** of course not! **ma sì!** of course!

**macabro** ['makabro] *agg* macabre.

**maccheroni** [makke'roni] *sm pl* macaroni *sing.*

**macchia**¹ ['makkja] *sf* spot; stain.

**macchia**² ['makkja] *sf (arbusti)* bush.

**macchiare** [mak'kjare] *v* stain. **caffè macchiato** *sm* coffee with a dash of milk.

**macchietta** [mak'kjetta] *sf (persona)* character.

**macchina** ['makkina] *sf* machine; *(automobile)* car. **macchina da scrivere** typewriter. **macchina fotografica** camera.

**macchinare** [makki'nare] *v* plot.

**macchinario** [makki'narjo] *sm* machinery.

**macchinista** [makki'nista] *s(m+f)* machinist; *(ferr)* engine driver.

**macedonia** [matʃe'dɔnja] *sf* fruit salad.

**macellare** [matʃel'lare] *v* slaughter. **macelleria** *sf* butcher's shop. **macellaio** *sm* butcher. **macello** *sm* slaughterhouse; *(fig)* shambles.

**macerare** [matʃe'rare] *v* soak; macerate.

**macerie** [ma'tʃɛrje] *sf pl* ruins *pl.*

**macina** ['matʃina] *sf* millstone, grindstone. **macinare** *v* grind. **macinino** *sm (da caffè)* coffee-mill; *(da pepe)* pepper-mill.

**madido** ['madido] *agg* soaking wet.

**Madonna** [ma'donna] *sf* **la Madonna** the Virgin Mary.

**madornale** [mador'nale] *agg* gross.

**madre** ['madre] *sf* mother; *(comm)* counterfoil. **madreperla** *sf* mother-of-pearl.

**madrigale** [madri'gale] *sm* madrigal.

**maestà** [mae'sta] *sf* majesty. **maestoso** *agg* majestic; imposing.

**maestro** [ma'estro] *sm* master; teacher. *agg* principal, main. **colpo maestro** *sm* masterstroke. **maestra** *sf* mistress; teacher. **maestranze** *sf pl* work force *sing.*

**mafia** ['mafja] *sf* mafia. **mafioso, -a** *sm, sf* member of the Mafia.

**magagna** [ma'gaɲa] *sf* flaw, fault.

**magari** [ma'gari] *inter* most certainly! *(oh se ...)* if only ... . *avv (forse)* perhaps; *(perfino)* even.

**magazzino** [magad'dzino] *sm* store, warehouse. **magazzinaggio** *sm* warehousing. **magazziniere** *sm* warehouseman.

**maggio** ['maddʒo] *sm* May.

**maggiorana** [maddʒo'rana] *sf* marjoram.

**maggioranza** [maddʒo'rantsa] *sf* majority.

**maggiore** [mad'dʒore] *s(m+f)*, *agg* major; *(più grande)* greater, larger; *(più vecchio)* older; *(di due fratelli)* elder; *(superlativo)* greatest, oldest, eldest. *sm* major. **andare per la maggiore** be a hit.

**maggiorenne** [maddʒor'mɛnne] *agg* of age. *s(m+f)* major.

**maggiormente** [maddʒor'mɛnte] *avv* (all the) more; *(di più)* most.

**magia** [ma'dʒia] *sf* magic. **magico** *agg* magic(al).

**magistero** [madʒis'tɛro] *sm* teaching (profession). **scuola di magistero** *sf* college of education. **magistrale** *agg (di maestro)* magisterial; *(da maestro)* masterly.

**magistrato** [madʒis'trato] *sm* magistrate.

**maglia** ['maʎa] *sf* stitch; *(rete)* mesh; *(indumento intimo)* vest; T-shirt; *(maglione)* jersey. **fare la maglia** knit. **lavoro a maglia** *sm* knitting. **maglieria** *sf* knitwear. **maglione** *sm* jersey, pullover.

**magnanimo** [ma'ɲanimo] *agg* magnanimous.

**magnete** [ma'ɲɛte] *sm (auto)* magneto; *(calamita)* magnet. **magnetismo** *sm* magnetism.

**magnetofono** [maɲe'tɔfono] *sm* tape recorder.

**magnifico** [ma'ɲifiko] *agg* magnificent, splendid. **magnificenza** *sf* magnificence.

**magnolia** [ma'nɔlja] *sf* magnolia.

**mago** ['mago] *sm (stregone)* sorcerer; *(illusionista)* magician.

**magro** ['magro] *agg* thin; *(fig)* meagre; *(povero di grasso)* lean. **magra** *sf (fiume)* low level; *(fig)* shortage.

**mai** ['mai] *avv* never, ever. **caso** *or* **se mai** in case, if ever. **come mai** how (on earth).

**maiale** [ma'jale] *sm* pig; *(carne)* pork.

**maionese** [majo'neze] *sf* mayonnaise.

**mais** ['mais] *sm* maize.

**maiuscolo** [ma'juskolo] *agg* capital. **maiuscola** *sf* capital (letter).

**malaccorto** [malak'kɔrto] *agg* ill-advised.

**malafede** [mala'fede] *sf* bad faith.

**malandato** [malan'dato] *agg* in bad condition.

**malanno** [ma'lanno] *sm* misfortune, trouble.

**malapena** [mala'pena] *sf* **a malapena** scarcely.

**malaria** [ma'larja] *sf* malaria.

**malato** [ma'lato], **-a** *agg* sick, ill. *sm, sf* sick person, patient. **malattia** *sf* illness, disease.

**malavita** [mala'vita] *sf* underworld.

**malavoglia** [mala'voʎa] *sf* reluctance.

**malavveduto** [malavve'duto] *agg* unwise.

**malconcio** [mal'kontʃo] *agg* shabby.

**malcontento** [malkon'tɛnto] *agg* dissatisfied. *sm* dissatisfaction.

**maldestro** [mal'dɛstro] *agg* awkward.

**maldicente** [maldi'tʃɛnte] *agg* slanderous.

**male** ['male] *avv* (*non bene*) badly; (*in modo non buono*) ill; (*in modo imperfetto*) not well; (*indisposto*) unwell. **sentirsi male** feel unwell *or* ill. *sm* evil; (*dolore*) pain. **andare a male** go bad. **di male in peggio** from bad to worse. **far male** hurt. **mal di denti** toothache. **mal di gola** sore throat. **mal di mare** sea-sickness. **mal di testa** headache.

*****maledire** [male'dire] *v* curse, damn. **maledizione** *sf* curse.

**maleducato** [maledu'kato] *agg* ill-mannered, rude.

**malefico** [ma'lɛfiko] *agg* harmful.

**malerba** [ma'lɛrba] *sf* weed.

**malessere** [ma'lɛssere] *sm* malaise.

**malevolo** [ma'lɛvolo] *agg* hostile.

**malfamato** [malfa'mato] *agg* ill-famed.

**malfatto** [mal'fatto] *agg* badly made.

**malfattore** [malfat'tore] *sm* evil-doer.

**malfermo** [mal'fermo] *agg* unsteady.

**malfido** [mal'fido] *agg* unreliable.

**malgrado** [mal'grado] *prep* notwithstanding, in spite of.

**malia** [ma'lia] *sf* charm. **maliardo** *agg* bewitching.

**maligno** [ma'liɲo] *agg* spiteful; (*med*) malignant.

**malinconia** [malinko'nia] *sf* melancholy, gloom. **malinconico** *agg* gloomy, dismal.

**malincuore** [malin'kwɔre] *avv* **a malincuore** reluctantly, half-heartedly.

**malinteso** [malin'tezo] *agg* misunderstood, mistaken. *sm* misunderstanding.

**malizia** [ma'litsja] *sf* cunning, malice. **malizioso** *agg* malicious, cunning.

**mallevadore** [malleva'dore] *sm* guarantor, surety.

**malmenare** [malme'nare] *v* manhandle.

**malnutrito** [malnu'trito] *agg* undernourished.

**malora** [ma'lora] *sf* ruin. **andare in malora** (*fam*) go to the dogs. **va in malora!** (*al diavolo*) go to hell!

**malsano** [mal'sano] *agg* unhealthy.

**malsicuro** [malsi'kuro] *agg* unsafe.

**malta** ['malta] *sf* mortar.

**maltempo** [mal'tempo] *sm* bad weather.

**malto** [mal'to] *sm* malt.

**maltrattare** [maltrat'tare] *v* ill-treat. **maltrattamento** *sm* ill-treatment.

**malumore** [malu'more] *sm* bad temper.

**malva** ['malva] *sm invar* (*colore*) mauve. *sf* (*bot*) mallow.

**malvagio** [mal'vadʒo] *agg* wicked.

**malversare** [malver'sare] *v* embezzle. **malversatore**, **-trice** *sm, sf* embezzler. **malversazione** *sf* embezzlement.

**malvisto** [mal'visto] *agg* unpopular.

**malvivente** [malvi'vɛnte] *sm* crook.

**malvolentieri** [malvolen'tjɛri] *avv* reluctantly.

**mamma** ['mamma] *sf* mother, mum(my). **mamma mia!** good gracious!

**mammella** [mam'mɛlla] *sf* breast.

**mammifero** [mam'mifero] *sm* mammal.

**mammola** ['mammola] *sf* violet.

**manata** [ma'nata] *sf* handful.

**mancare** [man'kare] *v* (*aver difetto*) lack; (*essere assente*) be missing; (*fallire, sentire la mancanza*) miss. **ci mancherebbe altro!** that would be the limit! **mancare alla parola** not keep one's word. **sentirsi mancare** feel faint.

**mancia** ['mantʃa] *sf* tip. **dar la mancia** tip.

**mancino** [man'tʃino], **-a** *sm, sf* left-hander. *agg* left-handed, left. **colpo mancino** *sm* underhand trick.

**mandare** [man'dare] *v* send. **mandare a fondo** sink. **mandare avanti** run. **mandar giù** (*cibo*) swallow. **mandar via** dismiss.

**mandarino**[1] [manda'rino] *sm* (*cinese*) mandarin.

**mandarino**[2] [manda'rino] *sm* (*albero*) mandarin tree; (*frutto*) mandarin, tangerine.

**mandato** [man'dato] *sm* commission; (*pol*) mandate; (*dir*) warrant.

**mandibola** [man'dibola] *sf* jaw.

**mandolino** [mando'lino] *sm* mandolin.

**mandorla** ['mandorla] *sf* almond. **mandorlo** *sm* almond-tree.

**mandria** ['mandrja] *sf* herd, flock.

**mandrino** [man'drino] *sm* (*tec*) spindle, mandrel.

**maneggiare** [maned'dʒare] *v* handle. **maneggio** *sm* handling; (*addestramento cavalli*) riding-school; (*intrigo*) plot.

**manette** [ma'nette] *sf pl* handcuffs *pl*.

**mangano** ['mangano] *sm* mangle.

**mangereccio** [mandʒe'rettʃo] *agg* edible.

**mangiare** [man'dʒare] *v* eat; (*corrodere*) eat into; (*dissipare*) squander; (*carte, scacchi, ecc.*) take. **dar da mangiare a** feed. **far da mangiare** prepare a meal. **mangiare la foglia** smell a rat. **mangiarsi il fegato** fret. **mangime** *sm* food.

**mangiatoia** [mandʒa'toja] *sf* manger.

**mangime** [man'dʒime] *sm* fodder.

**maniaco** [ma'niako], **-a** *agg* maniacal. *sm*, *sf* maniac. **mania** *sf* mania.

**manica** ['manika] *sf* sleeve. **senza maniche** sleeveless.

**manichino** [mani'kino] *sm* mannequin, (tailor's) dummy.

**manico** ['maniko] *sm* handle; (*violino, ecc.*) neck.

**manicomio** [mani'kɔmjo] *sm* lunatic asylum.

**maniera** [ma'njɛra] *sf* manner.

**manifattura** [manifat'tura] *sf* manufacture.

**manifestare** [manifes'tare] *v* show; express; (*pol*) demonstrate. **manifestazione** *sf* display, show; expression; demonstration.

**manifesto**[1] [mani'fɛsto] *sm* poster, bill; (*pol*) manifesto. **manifestino** *sm* leaflet.

**manifesto**[2] [mani'fɛsto] *agg* clear, manifest.

**maniglia** [ma'niʎa] *sf* handle.

**manipolare** [manipo'lare] *v* manipulate.

**mano** ['mano] *sf*, *pl* **-i** hand; (*strato*) coat. **alla mano** ready, to hand. **a portata di mano** within reach. **dar** *or* **stringere la mano a** shake hands with. **di prima/seconda mano** first/second-hand. **far man bassa** make a clean sweep. **fuori mano** outlying, off the beaten track. **man mano che** as. **mettere le mani avanti** take precautions. **sotto mano** handy.

**manodopera** [mano'dɔpera] *sf invar* labour, workforce.

**\*manomettere** [mano'mettere] *v* tamper with, violate.

**manopola** [ma'nɔpola] *sf* (*manubrio*) handgrip; (*guanto*) mitten; (*radio, ecc.*) knob.

**manoscritto** [mano'skritto] *sm* manuscript. *agg* handwritten.

**manovale** [mano'vale] *sm* labourer.

**manovella** [mano'vɛlla] *sf* handle, crank.

**manovrare** [manov'rare] *v* handle, manoeuvre. **manovra** *sf* manoeuvre.

**mansione** [man'sjone] *sf* function, duty.

**mansueto** [mansu'ɛto] *agg* gentle, meek.

**mantello** [man'tɛllo] *sm* coat, cloak.

**\*mantenere** [mante'nere] *v* maintain, keep. **mantenimento** *sm* maintenance.

**mantice** ['mantitʃe] *sm* bellows *pl*.

**manto** ['manto] *sm* cloak, mantle.

**manuale** [manu'ale] *agg*, *sm* manual.

**manubrio** [ma'nubrjo] *sm* handlebar.

**manutenzione** [manuten'tsjone] *sf* maintenance, upkeep; (*auto*) servicing.

**manzo** ['mandzo] *sm* (*animale*) steer; (*carne*) beef.

**mappa** ['mappa] *sf* map. **mappamondo** *sm* globe.

**maratona** [mara'tona] *sf* marathon.

**marca** ['marka] *sf* brand.

**marcare** [mar'kare] *v* mark; (*sport*) score; accentuate.

**marchese** [mar'keze] *sm* marquis. **marchesa** *sf* marchioness.

**marchio** ['markjo] *sm* mark; (*comm*) trademark. **marchio depositato** registered trade-mark.

**marcia**[1] ['martʃa] *sf* march; (*auto*) gear; (*sport*) walking. **fare marcia indietro** reverse; (*fig*) back out. **mettere in marcia** get going, set off.

**marcia**[2] ['martʃa] *sf* (*materia*) pus.

**marciapiede** [martʃa'pjɛde] *sm* pavement.

**marciare** [mar'tʃare] *v* march; (*sport*) walk; (*fam: funzionare*) work.

**marcio** ['martʃo] *agg* rotten; (*fig*) corrupt. *sm* rottenness; rotten part.

**marcire** [mar'tʃire] *v* rot, go bad. **marciume** *sm* rot.

**marco** ['marko] *sm* mark.

**mare** ['mare] *sm* sea; (*grande quantità*) host. **alto mare** high sea. **essere in alto mare** (*fig*) be floundering, be at sea. **mare agitato** *or* **mosso** rough sea. **maretta** *sf* choppy sea.

**marea** [ma'rɛa] *sf* tide.

**maresciallo** [mare'ʃallo] *sm* (*sottufficiale*) sergeant major; (*ufficiale*) field-marshal.

**margarina** [marga'rina] *sf* margarine.

**margherita** [marge'rita] *sf* daisy.

**margine** ['mardʒine] *sm* edge, border; (*fig*) margin.

**marina** [ma'rina] *sf* navy. **marinaio** *sm* sailor.

**marinare** [mari'nare] *v* marinate. **marinare la scuola** play truant.

**marionetta** [marjo'netta] *sf* puppet.

**maritare** [mari'tare] *v* marry; (*mescolare*) mix. **maritarsi** *v* get married.

**marito** [ma'rito] *sm* husband.

**marittimo** [ma'rittimo] *agg* sea; maritime.

**marmaglia** [mar'maʎa] *sf* rabble.

**marmellata** [marmel'lata] *sf* jam; (*di agrumi*) marmalade.

**marmo** ['marmo] *sm* marble.

**marra** ['marra] *sf* hoe.

**marrone** [mar'rone] *sm* chestnut. *agg* brown.

**marsupiale** [marsu'pjale] *sm, agg* marsupial.

**martedì** [marte'di] *sm* Tuesday.

**martellare** [martel'lare] *v* hammer; (*fig*) pound. **martellata** *sf* hammer-blow; (*fig*) heavy blow. **martello** *sm* hammer; (*porta*) knocker; (*orologio*) striker.

**martinetto** [marti'netto] *sm* jack.

**martin pescatore** [mar'tin peska'tore] *sm* kingfisher.

**martire** ['martire] *s(m+f)* martyr. **martirio** *sm* martyrdom. **martoriare** *v* torture.

**marxismo** [mar'ksizmo] *sm* Marxism. **marxista** *s(m+f)*, *agg* Marxist.

**marzapane** [martsa'pane] *sm* marzipan.

**marziale** [mar'tsjale] *agg* martial.

**marzo** ['martso] *sm* march.

**mascalzone** [maskal'tsone] *sm* rascal, scoundrel. **mascalzonata** *sf* nasty trick.

**mascara** [mas'kara] *sm* mascara.

**mascella** [ma'ʃella] *sf* jaw.

**maschera** ['maskera] *sf* mask; (*travestimento*) disguise; (*cinema, teatro*) usherette. **mascherare** *v* mask; (*con costumi*) dress up; (*celare*) disguise; (*schermare*) screen; (*mimetizzare*) camouflage.

**maschile** [mas'kile] *agg* male; (*gramm*) masculine; (*per ragazzi*) boys'; (*per uomini*) men's.

**maschio** ['maskjo] *sm* male; (*ragazzo*) boy.

**masochismo** [mazo'kizmo] *sm* masochism. **masochista** *s(m+f)* masochist.

**massa** ['massa] *sf* mass; (*gran numero*) heap, lot; (*elett*) earth.

**massacrare** [massa'krare] *v* massacre. **massacro** *sm* massacre.

**massaggiare** [massad'dʒare] *v* massage. **massaggio** *sm* massage.

**massaia** [mas'saja] *sf* housewife.

**masserizie** [masse'ritsje] *sf pl* fixtures and fittings *pl*.

**massiccio** [mas'sittʃo] *agg* solid.

**massima** ['massima] *sf* maxim; (*norma*) rule. **di massima** general, informal. **in linea di massima** as a general rule, on the whole.

**massimo** ['massimo] *agg* greatest; (*estremo*) utmost; (*il più alto*) highest; (*il migliore*) best; (*fis*) maximum. *sm* maximum; (*tutto ciò che*) most; (*meglio*) best.

**massone** [mas'sone] *sm* freemason. **massoneria** *sf* freemasonry.

**masticare** [masti'kare] *v* chew; (*borbottare*) ɪгutter. **gomma da masticare** *sf* chewing gum.

**mastice** ['mastitʃe] *sm* mastic; (*per vetri*) putty.

**mastino** [mas'tino] *sm* mastiff.

**mastro** ['mastro] *sm* ledger.

**matassa** [ma'tassa] *sf* skein, hank.

**matematico** [mate'matiko], **-a** *agg* mathematical. *sm, sf* mathematician. *sf* mathematics.

**materasso** [mate'rasso] *sm* mattress. **materassino (pneumatico)** *sm* air-bed.

**materia** [ma'tɛrja] *sf* matter; substance; (*argomento, disciplina*) subject; (*fam: marcia*) pus. **entrare in materia** broach a subject. **materia prima** raw material.

**materiale** [mate'rjale] *sm, agg* material. **materialismo** *sm* materialism. **materialista** *s(m+f)* materialist.

**materno** [ma'tɛrno] *agg* maternal, motherly. **scuola materna** *sf* nursery school. **maternità** *sf* motherhood; (*ospedale*) maternity hospital.

**matita** [ma'tita] *sf* pencil.

**matriarcale** [matriar'kale] *agg* matriarchal.

**matrice** [ma'tritʃe] *sf* matrix; (*modulo*)

counterfoil.

**matricola** [ma'trikola] *sf* register; (*numero*) serial number; (*studente*) freshman. **matricolare** *v* register.

**matrigna** [ma'triɲa] *sf* stepmother.

**matrimonio** [matri'mɔnjo] *sm* marriage, matrimony; (*festa nuziale*) wedding. **matrimoniale** *agg* matrimonial. **letto matrimoniale** *sm* double bed.

**matta** ['matta] *sf* (*carte*) joker.

**mattatoio** [matta'tɔjo] *sm* slaughterhouse.

**matterello** [matte'rɛllo] *sm* rolling-pin.

**mattina** [mat'tina] *sf* morning. **mattinata** *sf* morning; (*teatro*) matinée. **mattiniero** *agg* early rising.

**matto** ['matto] *agg* mad. **andar matto per** be crazy about. **matto da legare** mad as a hatter. **scacco matto** checkmate.

**mattone** [mat'tone] *sm* brick; (*fam: noioso*) bore. **mattonella** *sf* tile; (*biliardo*) cushion.

**mattutino** [mattu'tino] *agg* morning.

**maturare** [matu'rare] *v* mature, ripen; (*med*) come to a head. **maturazione** *sf* ripening. **maturità** *sf* maturity. **esame di maturità** *sm* school-leaving examination, A level(s). **maturo** *agg* ripe; mature.

**mausoleo** [mauzo'lɛo] *sm* mausoleum.

**mazza** ['mattsa] *sf* club; (*martello*) sledge-hammer. **mazzata** *sf* heavy blow.

**mazzo** ['mattso] *sm* bunch; (*carte*) pack. **fare il mazzo** shuffle the cards *or* pack.

**me** [me] *pron* me. *V* **mi**.

**meccanico** [mek'kaniko] *agg* mechanical. *sm* mechanic. **meccanica** *sf* mechanics. **meccanismo** *sm* mechanism, works. **meccanizzare** *v* mechanize. **meccanizzazione** *sf* mechanization.

**meccanografico** [mekkano'grafiko] *agg* data processing.

**medaglia** [me'daʎa] *sf* medal. **medaglione** *sm* medallion; (*gioiello*) locket.

**medesimo** [me'dezimo] *agg* same.

**media** ['mɛdja] *sf* mean, average; (*scuola*) secondary school. **fare la media di** average.

**mediana** [me'djana] *sf* median. **mediano** *agg* median, medial.

**mediante** [me'djante] *prep* through, by (means of).

**mediatore** [medja'tore], **-trice** *sm, sf* intermediary; (*comm*) broker. **mediazione** *sf* mediation; brokerage.

**medicare** [medi'kare] *v* treat; (*ferita*) dress. **medicina** *sf* medicine.

**medicinale** [meditʃi'nale] *agg* medicinal. *sm* medicine.

**medico** ['mɛdiko] *sm* doctor, physician. *agg* medical. **medico chirurgo** surgeon. **medico condotto** medical officer. **medico generico** general practitioner.

**medievale** [medje'vale] *agg* medieval.

**medio** ['mɛdjo] *agg* middle; average; (*scuola*) secondary. *sm* middle finger.

**mediocre** [me'djɔkre] *agg* mediocre, poor.

**meditare** [medi'tare] *v* meditate, ponder. **meditazione** *sf* meditation.

**mediterraneo** [mediter'raneo] *sm, agg* Mediterranean.

**medium** ['mɛdjum] *s(m+f) invar* medium.

**medusa** [me'duza] *sf* jelly-fish.

**megafono** [me'gafono] *sm* loudspeaker.

**megera** [me'dʒera] *sf* harridan.

**meglio** ['mɛʎo] *agg, avv* (*comparativo*) better; (*superlativo*) best. *sm* best. **alla meglio** as well as possible. **tanto meglio!** so much the better!

**mela** ['mela] *sf* apple. **mela cotogna** quince. **melo** *sm* apple-tree.

**melagrana** [mela'grana] *sf* pomegranate. **melograno** *sm* pomegranate tree.

**melanzana** [melan'dzana] *sf* aubergine, egg-plant.

**melassa** [me'lassa] *sf* treacle, molasses.

**melma** ['melma] *sf* slime.

**melodia** [melo'dia] *sf* melody. **melodico** *agg* melodious. **melodioso** *agg* melodious, sweet-sounding.

**melodramma** [melo'dramma] *sm* melodrama.

**melone** [me'lone] *sm* melon.

**membrana** [mem'brana] *sf* membrane; (*acustica*) diaphragm.

**membro** ['mɛmbro] *sm, pl* **-a** *f in collective sense* member; (*anat*) limb.

**memoria** [me'mɔrja] *sf* memory; (*oggetto ricordo*) souvenir; (*scritto*) memoir. **a memoria** by heart. **prendere memoria di** make a note of. **memoriale** *sm* memorial; petition; (*raccolta di documenti*) record. **memorizzare** *v* memorize.

**menare** [me'nare] *v* lead; (*portare*) take, bring; (*assestare*) strike. **a menadito** at one's fingertips.

**mendicare** [mendi'kare] *v* beg. **mendicante** *s(m+f)* beggar.

**meno** ['meno] *avv* (*comparativo*) less; (*superlativo*) least; (*mat*) minus. *agg invar* (*minore*) less; (*in minor numero*) fewer. *prep* (*eccetto*) but (for), except (for). **a meno che** unless. **fare a meno di** do without. **meno male!** thank goodness! **o meno** (*o no*) or not. **tanto meno** let alone. **venir meno** (*svenire*) faint; (*mancare*) fail, **venir meno alla parola** break one's word. *sm invar* (the) least. **i meno** *sm pl* (the) minority *sing*.

**menomare** [meno'mare] *v* diminish; (*danneggiare*) injure, disable. **menomato, -a** *s*, *agg* disabled.

**menopausa** [meno'pauza] *sf* menopause.

**mensa** ['mɛnsa] *sf* table; refectory; (*mil*) mess.

**mensile** [men'sile] *agg* monthly. *sm* (*giornale*) monthly; (*paga*) monthly pay.

**mensola** ['mɛnsola] *sf* bracket, shelf; (*caminetto*) mantelpiece.

**menta** ['menta] *sf* mint; (*peperina*) peppermint; (*romana*) spearmint.

**mente** ['mente] *sf* mind; intellect. **venire in mente** occur; come to mind. **mentale** *agg* mental. **mentalità** *sf* mentality.

**mentire** [men'tire] *v* lie. **mentito** *agg* false.

**mento** ['mento] *sm* chin.

**mentre** ['mentre] *cong* while, as; (*laddove*) whereas.

**menu** [mə'ny] *sm* menu.

**menzionare** [mentsjo'nare] *v* mention. **menzione** *sf* mention.

**menzogna** [men'dzoɲa] *sf* lie. **menzognero** *agg* lying, false.

**meraviglia** [mera'viʎa] *sf* wonder, marvel; (*stupore*) surprise. **a meraviglia** wonderfully. **meravigliare** *v* surprise, amaze. **meraviglioso** *agg* marvellous, wonderful.

**mercante** [mer'kante] *sm* merchant, trader. **mercanteggiare** *v* trade, deal; (*contrattare*) haggle, bargain. **mercantile** *agg* mercantile. **nave mercantile** *sf* merchant ship.

**mercanzia** [merkan'tsia] *sf* merchandise, goods *pl*.

**mercato** [mer'kato] *sm* market. **a buon mercato** cheap, inexpensive.

**merce** ['mɛrtʃe] *sf* merchandise, goods *pl*; (*in magazzino*) stock.

**mercenario** [mertʃe'narjo] *agg*, *sm* mercenary.

**merciaio** [mer'tʃajo], **-a** *sm*, *sf* haberdasher. **merceria** *sf* haberdashery.

**mercoledì** [mercole'di] *sm* Wednesday.

**mercurio** [mer'kurjo] *sm* mercury.

**merda** ['mɛrda] *sf* (*volg*) shit.

**merenda** [me'rɛnda] *sf* (afternoon) snack, tea.

**meridiano** [meri'djano] *sm* (*geog*) meridian. *agg* (*di mezzogiorno*) midday. **meridiana** *sf* (*geog*) meridian line; (*orologio solare*) sundial.

**meridionale** [meridjo'nale] *agg* southern, south. *s(m+f)* southerner. **meridione** *sm* south.

**meringa** [me'ringa] *sf* meringue.

**meritare** [meri'tare] *v* deserve, merit. **meritevole** *agg* deserving, worthy.

**merito** ['mɛrito] *sm* merit. **a pari merito** equal. **in merito a** regarding, as to, about. **per merito di** thanks to.

**merletto** [mer'letto] *sm* lace.

**merlo** ['merlo] *sm* blackbird; (*sempliciotto*) fool.

**merluzzo** [mer'luttso] *sm* cod; (*nasello*) hake.

**mero** ['mɛro] *agg* mere.

**meschino** [mes'kino] *agg* wretched, mean.

**mescolare** [mesko'lare] *v* mix; (*unire*) blend. **mescolatore, -trice** *sm*, *sf* mixer.

**mese** ['meze] *sm* month.

**messa**[1] ['messa] *sf* (*rel*) Mass. **messale** *sm* missal.

**messa**[2] ['messa] *sf* (*il mettere*) placing, putting.

**messaggio** [mes'saddʒo] *sm* message. **messaggero** *sm* messenger; (*fig*) herald.

**Messico** ['messiko] *sm* Mexico. **messicano, -a** *s*, *agg* Mexican.

**messo** ['messo] *sm* usher.

**mestiere** [mes'tjɛre] *sm* job, trade; (*manuale*) craft; profession. **di mestiere** by profession. **essere del mestiere** be an expert. **ferri del mestiere** *sm pl* tools of the trade *pl*.

**mesto** ['mesto] *agg* sad, mournful. **mestizia** *sf* sadness.

**mestolo** ['mestolo], **-a** *sm*, *sf* ladle, kitchen spoon.

**mestruazione** [mestrua'tsjone] *sf* menstruation; (*fam*) period. **mestruale** *agg* menstrual.

**meta** ['mɛta] *sf* goal, aim; destination; (*rugby*) try.

**metà** [me'ta] *sf* half; (*centro*) middle. **a metà strada** half-way. **fare a metà** halve; (*fam*) go halves.

**metabolismo** [metabo'lizmo] *sm* metabolism. **metabolico** *agg* metabolic.

**metafisico** [meta'fiziko], **-a** *agg* metaphysical. *sm*, *sf* metaphysician. *sf* metaphysics.

**metafora** [me'tafora] *sf* metaphor, figure of speech. **metaforico** *agg* metaphorical.

**metallo** [me'tallo] *sm* metal. **metallico** *agg* metallic. **metallurgia** *sf* metallurgy.

**metamorfosi** [meta'mɔrfozi] *sf* metamorphosis, transformation.

**metano** [me'tano] *sm* methane.

**meteora** [me'tɛɔra] *sf* meteor. **meteorico** *agg* meteoric.

**meteorologia** [meteorolo'dʒia] *sf* meteorology. **meteorologico** *agg* meteorological, weather. **bollettino meteorologico** *sm* weather report. **previsioni meteorologiche** *sf pl* weather forecast *sing*.

**meticcio** [me'tittʃo], **-a** *s*, *agg* half-caste.

**meticoloso** [metiko'lozo] *agg* meticulous.

**metodista** [meto'dista] *s(m+f)*, *agg* methodist.

**metodo** [me'tɔdo] *sm* method. **metodico** *agg* methodical.

**metro** ['mɛtro] *sm* metre; (*per misurare*) rule; (*a nastro*) tape-measure. **metrico** *agg* (*misura*) metric; (*poesia*) metrical.

**metropoli** [me'trɔpoli] *sf* metropolis. **metropolitana** *sf* underground (railway).

**\*mettere** ['mettere] *v* put; place; lay (down); (*indossare*) put on, wear; (*supporre*) suppose. **mettersi sotto** get down to it.

**mezzo** [meddzo] *agg* half; (*medio*) middle. **mezzogiorno** *sm* noon, midday; (*geog*) south. *sm* half; (*centro*) middle; (*strumento*) means. **a** *or* **per mezzo di** by, through. **mezzi** *pl* means *pl*. *avv* half; (*quasi*) nearly. **andarci di mezzo** (*avere la peggio*) suffer for it; (*essere in gioco*) be at stake. **togliere di mezzo** get rid of.

**mi** [mi], **me** *pron* (to) me; (*riflessivo*) myself.

**miagolare** [mjago'lare] *v* mew, miaow. **miagolio** *sm* mewing.

**mica¹** ['mika] *avv* (*fam*) at all.

**mica²** ['mika] *sf* mica.

**miccia** ['mittʃa] *sf* fuse.

**microbo** ['mikrobo] *sm* microbe.

**microcosmo** [mikro'kɔzmo] *sm* microcosm.

**microfilm** ['mikrofilm] *sm invar* microfilm.

**microfono** [mi'krɔfono] *sm* microphone; (*telefono*) mouthpiece.

**microscopio** [mikro'skɔpjo] *sm* microscope. **microscopico** *agg* microscopic.

**midollo** [mi'dollo] *sm* marrow; (*bot*) pith. **bagnato fino al midollo** soaked to the skin. **fino al midollo** to the core. **midollo spinale** spinal cord.

**miele** ['mjɛle] *sm* honey.

**mietere** ['mjɛtere] *v* reap, harvest; (*uccidere*) mow down. **mietitore, -trice** *sm*, *sf* reaper, harvester. **mietitrebbiatrice** *sf* combine harvester. **mietitura** *sf* reaping, harvesting; (*periodo, messe*) harvest.

**migliaio** [mi'ʎajo] *sm*, *pl f* thousand; (*circa mille*) about a thousand.

**miglio¹** ['miʎo] *sm*, *pl* **-a** *f* mile.

**miglio²** ['miʎo] *sm* (*bot*) millet.

**migliore** [mi'ʎore] *agg* (*comparativo*) better; (*superlativo*) best. *sm* best.

**mignolo** ['miɲolo] *sm* (*della mano*) little finger; (*del piede*) little toe.

**migrare** [mi'grare] *v* migrate. **migratorio** *agg* migratory. **migrazione** *sf* migration.

**milione** [mi'ljone] *sm* million. **milionesimo** *sm*, *agg* millionth.

**militare** [mili'tare] *agg* military. *sm* soldier. *v* militate. **militarismo** *sm* militarism. **militarista** *s(m+f)*, *agg* militarist.

**milite** ['milite] *sm* soldier, warrior. **milizia** *sf* (*corpo armato*) militia.

**millantare** [millan'tare] *v* boast. **millantato credito** false pretences *pl*. **millantatore, -trice** *sm*, *sf* braggart, show-off. **millanteria** *sf* boasting.

**mille** ['mille] *agg*, *sm* thousand. **millennio** *sm* millennium. **millesimo** *agg*, *sm* thousandth.

**milligrammo** [milli'grammo] *sm* milligram.

**millimetro** [mil'limetro] *sm* millimetre.

**mimetizzare** [mimetid'dzare] *v* camouflage. **mimetizzazione** *sf* camouflage.

**mimica** ['mimika] *sf* mime. **mimico** *agg* mimic. **mimo** *sm* mime; (*uccello*) mockingbird.

**mina** ['mina] *sf* mine; (*di matita*) lead. **minare** *v* mine; (*insidiare*) undermine. **minatore** *sm* miner.

**minaccia** [mi'nattʃa] *sf* threat. **minacciare**

*v* threaten. **minaccioso** *agg* threatening.
**minareto** [mina'reto] *sm* minaret.
**minerale** [mine'rale] *agg*, *sm* mineral.
**minerario** [mine'rarjo] *agg* mining.
**minestra** [mi'nɛstra] *sf* soup.
**mingherlino** [minger'lino] *agg* skinny.
**miniatura** [minja'tura] *sf* miniature.
**miniera** [mi'njɛra] *sf* mine.
**minimo** ['minimo] *agg* (*il più piccolo*) least, smallest, slightest; (*più basso*) minimum; (*piccolissimo*) very small, very slight; (*molto basso*) very low. *sm* minimum; (*la minima cosa*) least.
**ministero** [mini'stɛro] *sm* (*pol*) ministry. **pubblico ministero** public prosecutor.
**ministro** [mi'nistro] *sm* minister.
**minore** [mi'nore] *s(m+f)*, *agg* (*più piccolo*) less, smaller; (*più basso*) lower; (*più giovane*) younger; (*superlativo*) least, lowest, youngest; (*mat, musica*) minor. **minorità** *sf* minority.
**minorenne** [mino'rɛnne] *s(m+f)* minor. *agg* under age.
**minuetto** [minu'etto] *sm* minuet.
**minuscolo** [mi'nuskolo] *agg* small, diminutive. **minuscola** *sf* small letter.
**minuta** [mi'nuta] *sf* draft.
**minuto¹** [mi'nuto] *agg* small, minute; detailed. **al minuto** retail. **vendere al minuto** retail.
**minuto²** [mi'nuto] *sm* (*primo*) minute. **minuto secondo** second. **spaccare il minuto** be dead on time.
**mio** ['mio], *m pl* **miei** *agg* my. *pron* mine.
**miope** [miope] *agg* short-sighted. **miopia** *sf* short-sightedness.
**mira** ['mira] *sf* aim.
**miracolo** [mi'rakolo] *sm* miracle. **miracoloso** *agg* miraculous.
**miraggio** [mi'raddʒo] *sm* mirage.
**mirare** [mi'rare] *v* aim; (*prendere la mira*) take aim. **mirino** *sm* sight; (*foto*) viewfinder.
**mirtillo** [mir'tillo] *sm* bilberry. **mirtillo rosso** cranberry.
**miscela** [miʃela] *sf* mixture; (*caffè, tè, tabacco*) blend. **miscelare** *v* mix, blend.
**mischia** ['miskja] *sf* fray.
**mischiare** [mis'kjare] *v* mix; (*carte*) shuffle.
**miscuglio** [mis'kuʎo] *sm* mixture.
**miseria** [mi'zɛrja] *sf* poverty; (*inezia*) pit-

tance; squalor. **miserabile** *agg* miserable, wretched.
**misericordia** [mizeri'kɔrdja] *sf* mercy. **senza misericordia** merciless; (*spietato*) ruthless.
**misero** ['mizero] *agg* poor, wretched.
**missile** ['missile] *sm* missile.
**missione** [mis'sjone] *sf* mission. **missionario, -a** *s*, *agg* missionary.
**mistero** [mis'tɛro] *sm* mystery. **misterioso** *agg* mysterious.
**mistico** ['mistiko], **-a** *agg* mystical. *sm*, *sf* mystic. *sf* mysticism. **misticismo** *sm* mysticism.
**misto** ['misto] *agg* mixed.
**misura** [mi'zura] *sf* measure; (*taglia, dimensione*) size; (*atto e modo del misurare*) measurement; moderation. **fatto su misura** made to measure. **prendere delle misure** take steps.
**misurare** [mizu'rare] *v* measure; limit; (*indumenti*) try on. **misurato** *agg* measured, moderate.
**mite** ['mite] *agg* mild, moderate.
**mito** ['mito] *sm* myth. **mitico** *agg* mythical. **mitologia** *sf* mythology. **mitologico** *agg* mythological.
**mitra¹** ['mitra] *sf* (*rel*) mitre.
**mitra²** ['mitra] *sm invar* tommy-gun.
**mitragliatrice** [mitraʎa'tritʃe] *sf* machine-gun. **mitragliamento** *sm* machine-gun fire; (*fig*) bombarding. **mitragliare** *v* machine-gun; (*fig*) bombard.
**mittente** [mit'tɛnte] *s(m+f)* sender.
**mobile** ['mɔbile] *agg* mobile, moving; movable. **squadra mobile** *sf* flying squad. *sm* piece of furniture. **mobili** *sm pl* furniture *sing*.
**mobilia** [mo'bilja] *sf* furnishings *pl*; (*mobili*) furniture.
**mobiliare** [mobi'ljare] *agg* movable. *v* furnish.
**mobilitare** [mobili'tare] *v* mobilize. **mobilitazione** *sf* mobilization.
**mocassino** [mokas'sino] *sm* moccasin.
**moccolo** ['mɔkkolo] *sm* candle-end. **reggere il moccolo** play gooseberry. **tirare dei moccoli** (*fam*) swear.
**moda** ['mɔda] *sf* fashion. **di** *or* **alla moda** in fashion, fashionable. **fuori moda** out of fashion. **passare di moda** go out of fashion.

**modalità** [modali'ta] *sf* procedure, formality.

**modellare** [model'lare] *v* model. **modella** *sf* model. **modello** *sm* model; (*disegno*) pattern.

**moderare** [mode'rare] *v* moderate, lower; control. **moderatore** *sm* moderator; (*TV, radio*) chairman. **moderazione** *sf* moderation, restraint.

**moderno** [mo'dɛrno] *agg* modern; (*al passo coi tempi*) up-to-date. **modernizzare** *v* modernize, bring up-to-date.

**modestia** [mo'dɛstja] *sf* modesty. **modesto** *agg* modest, unassuming; (*umile*) humble.

**modificare** [modifi'kare] *v* modify, alter. **modifica** *sf* alteration, modification.

**modista** [mo'dista] *sf* milliner.

**modo** ['mɔdo] *sm* manner, way; opportunity; (*gramm*) mood. **ad ogni modo** anyhow, in any case. **di modo che** (*affinchè*) so that; (*e così*) and so. **in modo da** so that. **in qualche modo** somehow. **modo di dire** expression, idiom. **modo di fare** manner. **per modo di dire** so to speak.

**modulare** [modu'lare] *v* modulate.

**modulo** ['mɔdulo] *sm* form; (*mat, tec*) modulus.

**mogano** ['mɔgano] *sm* mahogany.

**mogio** ['mɔdʒo] *agg* downhearted.

**moglie** ['moʎe] *sf* wife.

**moina** [mo'ina] *sf* **fare moine** coax.

**molare** [mo'lare] *v* grind. *agg* molar. **pietra molare** *sf* millstone. **mola** *sf* grinding wheel.

**Moldavia** [mol'davja] *sf* Moldova.

**mole** ['mɔle] *sf* pile, mass; (*grandezza*) size.

**molecola** [mo'lɛkola] *sf* molecule.

**molesto** [mo'lɛsto] *agg* troublesome, annoying. **molestare** *v* trouble, annoy. **molestia** *sf* annoyance, nuisance.

**molla** ['mɔlla] *sf* spring; (*stimolo*) mainspring. **molle** *sf pl* tongs *pl*. **mollare** *v* (*lasciar andare*) let go; (*allentare*) loosen, slacken. **molleggiato** *agg* sprung. **molletta** *sf* (*biancheria*) (clothes-)peg; (*capelli*) hair-pin.

**molle** ['mɔlle] *agg* soft; (*bagnato*) wet; (*debole*) weak. **mettere in molle** steep.

**mollusco** [mol'lusko] *sm* mollusc.

**molo** ['mɔlo] *sm* jetty; (*banchina*) wharf.

**molteplice** [mol'teplitʃe] *agg* manifold; varied.

**moltiplicare** [moltipli'kare] *v* multiply.

**moltitudine** [molti'tudine] *sm* multitude, host.

**molto** ['molto] *agg* a lot of, lots of, much; (*pl*) many; (*tempo*) long. *avv* much, a lot; (*con agg e avv positivi*) very. *pron*. a lot, much; (*pl*) many.

**momento** [mo'mento] *sm* moment. **a momenti** (*tra poco*) shortly; (*quasi*) almost. **al momento d'oggi** nowadays. **dal momento che** since.

**monaca** ['mɔnaka] *sf* nun. **monaco** *sm* monk.

**Monaco** ['mɔnako] *sf* (*principato*) Monaco; (*di Baviera*) Munich.

**monarca** [mo'narka] *sm* monarch, king. **monarchia** *sf* monarchy. **monarchico, -a** *sm, sf* monarchist.

**monastero** [monas'tɛro] *sm* monastery. **monastico** *agg* monastic.

**monco** ['monko] *agg* maimed. **essere monco di ...** have ... missing. **moncherino** *sm* stump.

**mondezzaio** [mondet'tsajo] *sm* rubbish heap; (*ambiente sudicio*) pigsty. **mondare** *v* (*sbucciare*) peel; (*togliere erbacce*) weed.

**mondo** ['mondo] *sm* world. **mandare all'altro mondo** (*fam*) send to hell. **mettere al mondo** give birth to. **vivere nel mondo della luna** have one's head in the clouds. **mondiale** *agg* world; (*diffuso*) world-wide.

**monello** [mo'nɛllo] *sm* urchin. **monelleria** *sf* prank.

**moneta** [mo'neta] *sf* coin; (*denaro*) money; (*spicciola*) (small) change. **monetario** *agg* monetary.

**monito** ['mɔnito] *sm* warning.

**monocolore** [monoko'lore] *agg* plain; (*pol*) one-party.

**monocromo** [mo'nɔkromo] *agg, sm* monochrome.

**monogamo** [mo'nɔgamo], **-a** *agg* monogamous. *sm, sf* monogamist. **monogamia** *sf* monogamy.

**monolitico** [mono'litiko] *agg* monolithic.

**monologo** [mo'nɔlogo] *sm, pl* **-ghi** monologue.

**monopolio** [mono'pɔljo] *sm* monopoly. **monopolizzare** *v* monopolize.

**monossido di carbonio** [mo'nɔssido di kar'bonjo] *sm* carbon monoxide.

**monoteismo** [monote'izmo] *sm* monotheism.

**monotono** [mo'nɔtono] *agg* monotonous. **monotonia** *sf* monotony.

**monovolume** [monovo'lume] *sm* people carrier.

**monsone** [mon'sone] *sm* monsoon.

**monta** ['monta] *sf* (*accoppiamento*) mounting; (*luogo*) stud-farm; (*modo di cavalcare*) riding.

**montacarichi** [monta'kariki] *sm* goods lift.

**montaggio** [mon'taddʒo] *sm* assembly; (*cinema*) editing.

**montagna** [mon'taɲa] *sf* mountain. **montagne russe** switchback *sing*.

**montare** [mon'tare] *v* (*salire*) climb; (*tec*) assemble; (*incorniciare*) mount; (*film*) edit; (*macchina*) get in(to). **montare a cavallo** get on a horse; (*cavalcare*) ride. **montatura** *sf* assembly; (*occhiali*) frame; (*pubblicitaria*) stunt.

**monte** ['monte] *sm* mountain; (*davanti a nome*) Mount. **a monte** above, upstream. **andare a monte** fall through. **mandare a monte** upset; (*disdire*) cancel. **monte di pietà** pawnshop. **monte premi** jackpot. **montuoso** *agg* mountainous.

**montone** [mon'tone] *sm* ram; (*carne*) mutton.

**monumento** [monu'mento] *sm* monument. **monumentale** *agg* monumental.

**moquette** [mɔ'kɛtt] *sf* fitted carpet.

**mora** ['mɔra] *sf* (*gelso*) mulberry; (*rovo*) blackberry.

**morale** [mo'rale] *agg* moral. *sf* (*dottrina*) ethics *pl*; morality, morals *pl*; (*insegnamento*) moral. *sm* morale. **essere su/giù di morale** be cheerful/depressed. **moralizzare** *v* moralize.

**morbido** ['mɔrbido] *agg* soft.

**morbillo** [mor'billo] *sm* measles.

**morbo** ['mɔrbo] *sm* disease. **morboso** *agg* morbid; pathological.

*****mordere** ['mɔrdere] *v* bite; (*afferrare*) grip. **mordere il freno** strain at the leash. **mordace** *agg* biting, caustic.

**morfina** [mor'fina] *sf* morphine.

**morigerato** [moridʒe'rato] *agg* sober, clean-living.

*****morire** [mo'rire] *v* die. **avere una fame/sete da morire** be terribly hungry/thirsty.

**mormorare** [mormo'rare] *v* murmur. **mormorio** *sm* murmur.

**moro**[1] ['mɔro] *agg* dark; (*nero*) black; (*carnagione*) swarthy; (*capelli*) brown.

**moro**[2] ['mɔro] *sm* (*gelso*) mulberry.

**morsa** ['mɔrsa] *sf* vice. **morsetto** *sm* clamp; (*elett*) terminal.

**morsicare** [morsi'kare] *v* gnaw, bite. **morso** *sm* bite; (*fig*) sting; (*cavallo*) bit.

**mortaio** [mor'tajo] *sm* mortar.

**mortale** [mor'tale] *agg* mortal; (*implacabile*) deadly. **mortalità** *sf* mortality.

**morte** ['mɔrte] *sf* death.

**morto** ['mɔrto] *agg* dead. *sm* dead person; (*carte*) dummy. **fare il morto** float (on one's back).

**mosaico** [mo'zaiko] *sm* mosaic.

**mosca** ['moska] *sf* fly; (*barbetta*) goatee. **mosca cieca** blindman's buff. **moscerino** *sm* small fly.

**Mosca** ['moska] *sf* Moscow.

**moscato**[1] [mos'kato] *agg* muscat(el). **noce moscata** *sf* nutmeg.

**moscato**[2] [mos'kato] *agg* (*cavallo*) dappled.

**moschea** [mos'kɛa] *sf* mosque.

**moschetto** [mos'ketto] *sm* musket. **moschettiere** *sm* musketeer.

**mossa** ['mɔssa] *sf* movement; (*fig*) move.

**mosso** ['mɔsso] *agg* (*mare*) rough; (*capelli*) wavy.

**mostarda** [mos'tarda] *sf* mustard.

**mostrare** [mos'trare] *v* show. **mostra** *sf* show, exhibition; ostentation; (*campione*) sample. **mettere in mostra** display.

**mostro** ['mɔstro] *sm* monster. **mostruosità** *sf* monstrosity. **mostruoso** *agg* monstrous.

**motivo** [mo'tivo] *sm* ground, reason; (*diseno, musica*) motif. **motivare** *v* motivate. **motivazione** *sf* motivation.

**moto**[1] ['mɔto] *sm* motion; (*sommossa*) rebellion. **mettere in moto** set in motion, start (up).

**moto**[2] ['mɔto] *sf* (*fam*) motor-bike.

**motocicletta** [mototʃik'letta] *sf* motorcycle. **motociclista** *s(m+f)* motor-cyclist.

**motore** [mo'tore] *sm* engine. *agg* motor. **albero motore** *sm* crankshaft. **motorino d'avviamento** *sm* starter (motor). **motore di ricerca** *sm* search engine.

**motoscafo** [moto'skafo] *sm* motor-boat.

**motto** ['mɔtto] *sm* motto; (*detto*) saying.

**movimento** [movi'mento] *sm* movement; activity. **movimentato** *agg* lively, busy.

**mozione** [mo'tsjone] *sf* motion.

**mozzare** [mot'tsare] *v* cut off; (*coda*) dock. **mozzare il fiato** take one's breath away.

**mozzicone** [mottsi'kone] *sm* butt.

**mucca** ['mukka] *sf* cow.

**mucchio** ['mukkjo] *sm* heap.

**muco** ['muko] *sm* mucus. **mucosa** *sf* mucous membrane.

**muda** ['muda] *sf* moulting.

**muffa** ['muffa] *sf* mould. **muffoso** *agg* mouldy.

**muggire** [mud'dʒire] *v* also **mugghiare** bellow; (*mare*) roar; (*vento*) howl.

**mughetto** [mu'getto] *sm* lily of the valley.

**mugnaio** [mu'najo] *sm* miller.

**mugolare** [mugo'lare] *v* howl, whine.

**mulattiera** [mulat'tjɛra] *sf* (mule-)track.

**mulino** [mu'lino] *sm* mill; (*a vento*) windmill. **mulinello** *sm* whirlpool; (*pesca*) reel.

**mulo** ['mulo] *sm* mule.

**multa** ['multa] *sf* fine.

**multicolore** [multiko'lore] *agg* multicoloured.

**multiplo** ['multiplo] *agg*, *sm* multiple.

**mummia** ['mummja] *sf* mummy. **mummificare** *v* mummify.

**\*mungere** ['mundʒere] *v* milk.

**municipio** [muni'tʃipjo] *sm* (*comune*) municipality; (*sede*) town hall. **municipale** *agg* municipal.

**munire** [mu'nire] *v* supply; fortify.

**munizione** [muni'tsjone] *sf* munitions *pl*; (military) stores *pl*. **munizioni** *sf pl* ammunition *sing*.

**\*muovere** ['mwɔvere] *v* move.

**muraglia** [mu'raʎa] *sf* wall.

**muratore** [mura'tore] *sm* bricklayer.

**muro** ['muro] *sm* wall. **mura** *sf pl* city walls *pl*. **parlare al muro** talk to a brick wall.

**musa** ['muza] *sf* muse.

**muschio**¹ ['muskjo] *sm* (*bot*) moss. **muscoso** *agg* mossy.

**muschio**² ['muskjo] *sm* (*odore*) musk.

**muscolo** ['muskolo] *sm* muscle.

**museo** [mu'zɛo] *sm* museum.

**museruola** [muze'rwɔla] *sf* muzzle.

**musica** ['muzika] *sf* music. **musicale** *agg* musical, music. **musicista** *s(m+f)* musician.

**muso** ['muzo] *sm* snout; (*spreg*) mug. **mettere il muso lungo** pull a long face.

**mussolina** [musso'lina] *sf* muslin.

**mutande** [mu'tande] *sf pl* also **mutandine** (*da donna*) panties *pl*; (*da uomo*) underpants *pl*; (*da bagno*) swimming trunks *pl*.

**mutare** [mu'tare] *v* change; (*fare la muta*) shed. **mutabile** or **mutevole** *agg* changeable; (*fig*) fickle. **mutamento** *sm* change. **mutazione** *sf* mutation.

**mutilare** [muti'lare] *v* maim, mutilate. **mutilato, -a** *sm*, *sf* disabled person.

**muto, -a** *agg* silent; (*affetto da mutismo*) dumb. *sm*, *sf* mute. **linguaggio dei muti** *sm* deaf-and-dumb language.

**mutuo** ['mutuo] *agg* mutual. *sm* loan. **mutuo ipotecario** mortgage. **mutua** *sf* insurance.

# N

**nafta** ['nafta] *sf* fuel oil.

**nailon** ['nailon] *sm invar* nylon.

**nanna** ['nanna] *sf* **fare la nanna** (*fam*) sleep.

**nano** ['nano], **-a** *s*, *agg* dwarf.

**Napoli** ['napoli] *sf* Naples. **napoletano, -a** *s*, *agg* Neapolitan.

**nappa** ['nappa] *sf* tassel; (*fam: naso*) conk; (*pelle*) nappa.

**narciso** [nar'tʃizo] *sm* narcissus; (*giunchiglia*) daffodil.

**narcotico** [nar'kɔtiko] *agg*, *sm* narcotic. **narcosi** *sf* narcosis.

**narice** [na'ritʃe] *sf* nostril.

**narrare** [nar'rare] *v* tell. **narrativa** *sf* fiction. **narrazione** *sf* tale.

**\*nascere** ['naʃere] *v* be born; (*fig*) (a) rise, start (up). **far nascere** give rise to. **nascita** *sf* birth. **atto di nascita** *sm* birth certificate.

**\*nascondere** [nas'kondere] *v* hide. **nascondiglio** *sm* hide-out. **nascondino** *sm* hide-and-seek.

**nascosto** [nas'kosto] *agg* hidden.

**nasello** [na'zɛllo] *sm* hake.

**naso** ['nazo] *sm* nose. **cacciare** *or* **ficcare il naso (in)** poke one's nose (into).

**nastro** ['nastro] *sm* ribbon; *(tec)* tape. **nastro sonoro** sound-track. **nastro trasportatore** conveyor belt.

**nasturzio** [nas'turtsjo] *sm* nasturtium.

**natale** [na'tale] *agg* native. **Natale** *sm* Christmas. **natalizio** *agg* Christmas. **giorno natalizio** *sm* birthday.

**natatoia** [nata'toja] *sf* flipper, fin.

**natica** ['natika] *sf* buttock.

**nativo** [na'tivo] *agg* native.

**nato** ['nato] *agg* born. **appena nato** newborn. **... nato e sputato** the (spitting) image of ... . **nato morto** stillborn.

**natura** [na'tura] *sf* nature. **naturale** *agg* natural. **naturalezza** *sf* spontaneity; simplicity. **naturalistico** *agg* naturalistic.

**naturalizzare** [naturalid'dzare] *v* naturalize. **naturalizzazione** *sf* naturalization.

**naufragio** [nau'fradʒo] *sm* shipwreck; *(fig)* wreck. **naufragare** *v* be shipwrecked; *(fig)* come to grief. **naufrago, -a** *sm, sf* survivor.

**nausea** ['nauzea] *sf* nausea. **dare la nausea a** make sick. **provar nausea** feel sick. **nauseante** *agg* nauseating, sickening. **nauseato** *agg* nauseated, sickened.

**nautico** ['nautiko] *agg* nautical. **sport nautici** *sm pl* water sports *pl*.

**navata** [na'vata] *sf (centrale)* nave; *(laterale)* aisle.

**nave** ['nave] *sf* ship. **nave cisterna** tanker. **nave di salvataggio** lifeboat. **nave traghetto** ferry. **navale** *agg* naval. **navalmeccanica** *sf* shipbuilding. **navalmeccanico** *sm* shipyard worker.

**navetta** [na'vetta] *sf* shuttle.

**navigare** [navi'gare] *v* sail, navigate; *(Internet)* browse. **navigatore** *sm* navigator. **navigazione** *sf* navigation.

**nazionalizzare** [natsjonalid'dzare] *v* nationalize. **nazionalizzazione** *sf* nationalization.

**nazione** [na'tsjone] *sf* nation. **nazionale** *agg* national; *(econ)* domestic. **nazionalismo** *sm* nationalism. **nazionalista** *s(m+f)*, *agg* nationalist. **nazionalità** *sf* nationality.

**nazismo** [na'dzizmo] *sm* Nazism, National Socialism. **nazista** *s(m+f)*, *agg* Nazi.

**ne** [ne] *pron* of it *or* them, about it *or* them; *(partitivo)* some, any. *avv* from there.

**nè** [ne] *cong* neither, nor; *(con altra negazione)* either. **nè ... nè ...** neither ... nor ... .

**neanche** [ne'anke] *avv, cong, also* **nemmeno, neppure** neither; either; *(rafforzativo)* not even.

**nebbia** ['nebbja] *sf* fog; *(foschia)* haze, mist. **nebbioso** *agg* foggy.

**necessario** [netʃes'sarjo] *agg* necessary, needed (for). *sm* necessary. **lo stretto necessario** the bare necessities *pl*.

**necessità** [netʃessi'ta] *sf* necessity, need. **di prima necessità** essential. **in caso di necessità** if necessary. **trovarsi nella necessità di** be obliged to.

**negare** [ne'gare] *v* deny. **negato** *agg* denied; *(senza disposizione)* hopeless (at). **negazione** *sf* denial, negation.

**negativa** [nega'tiva] *sf* negative. **negativo** *agg* negative.

**negli** ['neʎi] *prep+art* in gli.

**negligente** [negli'dʒɛnte] *agg* negligent. **negligenza** *sf* negligence.

**negoziare** [nego'tsjare] *v* negotiate.

**negozio** [ne'gɔtsjo] *sm* shop; *(affare)* deal. **negoziante** *s(m+f)* shopkeeper; dealer; *(all'ingrosso)* wholesaler; *(al minuto)* retailer.

**negro** ['negro], **-a** *agg* black. *sm, sf* black person. **negriere** *sm* slaver; *(fig)* slave-driver.

**nei** ['nei] *prep+art* in i.

**nel** [nel] *prep+art* in il.

**nell'** [nell] *prep+art* in l'.

**nella** ['nella] *prep+art* in la.

**nelle** ['nelle] *prep+art* in le.

**nello** ['nello] *prep+art* in lo.

**nemico** [ne'miko], **-a** *agg* enemy, hostile; *(dannoso)* bad. *sm, sf* enemy.

**nemmeno** [nem'meno] *V* **neanche**.

**neo** ['nɛo] *sm* mole; *(posticcio)* beauty-spot.

**neon** ['nɛon] *sm* neon.

**neonato** [neo'nato], **-a** *agg* new-born. *sm, sf* new-born baby.

**neozelandese** [neodzelan'deze] *agg* New Zealand. *sm, sf* New Zealander.

**nepotismo** [nepo'tizmo] *sm* nepotism.

**neppure** [nep'pure] *V* **neanche**.

**nerbo** ['nɛrbo] *sm* whip; *(fig)* force.

**nero** ['nero] *agg, sm* black. **bestia nera** *sf* bugbear. **borsa nera** *sf* black market. **nerastro** *agg* blackish.

**nervo** ['nɛrvo] *sm* nerve; (*bot*) rib, vein; (*corda*) string. **avere i nervi** be on edge, be irritable. **dare ai** *or* **sui nervi a qualcuno** get on somebody's nerves. **nervoso** *agg* nervous; irritable; (*eccitabile*) highly strung. **esaurimento nervoso** *sm* nervous breakdown.

**nesso** ['nɛsso] *sm* connection.

**nessuno** [nes'suno] *agg* no. *pron* (*persone*) nobody, no-one; (*cose*) none; (*qualcuno*) anybody.

**nettare** [net'tare] *sm* nectar.

**netto** ['netto] *agg* clean; (*fig*) clear, sharp; (*peso, comm*) net. **nettezza** *sf* cleanliness; (*precisione*) clarity. **nettezza urbana** *sf* street-cleaning; refuse collection.

**neutrale** [neu'trale] *s*(*m+f*), *agg* neutral. **neutralità** *sf* neutrality. **neutralizzare** *v* neutralize; (*fig*) counteract.

**neutro** ['nɛutro] *sm*, *agg* neutral; (*gramm, sesso*) neuter. **neutrone** *sm* neutron.

**neve** ['neve] *sf* snow. **cumulo di neve** *sm* snowdrift. **pupazzo di neve** *sm* snowman. **nevato** *or* **nevoso** *agg* snowy.

**nevicare** [nevi'kare] *v* snow. **nevicata** *sf* snowfall.

**nevischio** [ne'viskjo] *sm* sleet.

**nevralgia** [nevral'dʒia] *sf* neuralgia.

**nevrosi** [ne'vrɔzi] *sf* neurosis. **nevrotico, -a** *s*, *agg* neurotic.

**nibbio** ['nibbjo] *sm* kite.

**nicchia** ['nikkja] *sf* niche, recess.

**nichel** ['nikel] *sm* nickel. **nichelare** *v* nickel-plate. **nichelatura** *sf* nickel-plating.

**nichilismo** [niki'lizmo] *sm* nihilism. **nichilista** *s*(*m+f*) nihilist.

**nicotina** [niko'tina] *sf* nicotine.

**nido** ['nido] *sm* nest. **nido d'ape** honeycomb. **nido d'infanzia** crèche, day nursery. **nidiata** *sf* brood.

**niente** ['njɛnte] *pron* nothing; (*con altra negazione*) anything. *sm* nothing; (*cosa da poco*) slightest thing. **da niente** unimportant. **niente paura!** don't be afraid! **non fa niente** (*non importa*) it doesn't matter.

**ninfa** ['ninfa] *sf* nymph. **ninfomane** *sf*, *agg* nymphomaniac.

**ninfea** [nin'fɛa] *sf* water lily.

**ninna-nanna** [ninna'nanna] *sm* lullaby.

**ninnolo** ['ninnolo] *sm* (*balocco*) toy; (*gingillo*) knick-knack.

**nipote** [ni'pote] *sm* (*di nonni*) grandson; (*di zii*) nephew. *sf* (*di nonni*) grand-daughter; (*di zii*) niece.

**nitido** ['nitido] *agg* neat; (*fig*) clear.

**nitrire** [ni'trire] *v* neigh. **nitrito** *sm* neigh.

**no** [nɔ] *avv* no. no; (*rifiuto*) refusal. **come no!** of course! and how! **se no** otherwise, or else. **uno sì e uno no** every other one.

**nobile** ['nɔbile] *agg* noble. *sm* nobleman. *sf* noblewoman. **nobiltà** *sf* nobility.

**nocca** ['nɔkka] *sf* knuckle; (*del cavallo*) fetlock.

**nocciola** [not'tʃɔla] *sf* hazel-nut. *agg*, *sm invar* (*colore*) hazel. **nocciolina** (**americana**) *sf* peanut. **nocciolo** *sm* (*pianta*) hazel.

**nocciolo** [not'tʃɔlo] *sm* (*bot*) stone, kernel; (*fig*) heart, point; (*tec*) core.

**noce** ['notʃe] *sm* (*albero*) walnut(-tree); (*legno*) walnut. *sf* (*frutto*) walnut. **noce di burro** pat of butter. **noce di cocco** coconut. **noce moscata** nutmeg. **nocepesca** *sf* nectarine.

**nocivo** [no'tʃivo] *agg* harmful.

**nodo** ['nɔdo] *sm* knot; (*incrocio*) junction; (*trama*) plot. **avere un nodo alla gola** have a lump in one's throat. **nodo scorsoio** slip-knot. **nodoso** *agg* knotty.

**noi** ['noi] *pron* (*soggetto*) we; (*oggetto*) us.

**noia** ['nɔja] *sf* (*tedio*) boredom; (*fastidio*) nuisance; (*fam*) bore. **avere delle noie con** have trouble with. **dare noia (a)** trouble, bother. **noioso** *agg* boring; (*fastidioso*) troublesome.

**noleggiare** [noled'dʒare] *v* hire, rent. **noleggio** *sm* hire; (*prezzo*) rental. **nolo** *sm* freight. **dare a nolo** hire (out). **prendere a nolo** hire, rent.

**nomade** ['nɔmade] *agg* nomadic. *s*(*m+f*) nomad.

**nome** ['nome] *sm* name; (*gramm*) noun. **a nome di** on behalf of. **conoscere di nome** know by name. **fare il nome di** mention; (*proporre*) propose. **nome di battaglia** pseudonym. **nomignolo** *sm* nickname.

**nomina** ['nɔmina] *sf* appointment. **nominare** *v* mention; name; (*eleggere*) appoint.

**non** [non] *avv* not. **non ... affatto** not at all. **non ... mai** never. **non ... nessuno** nobody. **non ... niente** *or* **nulla** nothing. **nonché** *cong* as well as.

**noncurante** [nonku'rante] *agg* heedless.

**nondimeno** [nondi'meno] *cong* nevertheless.

**nonno** ['nɔnno] *sm* grandfather; (*fam*) grand-dad. **nonna** *sf* grandmother; (*fam*) grandma, granny. **nonni** *sm pl* grandparents *pl*.

**nono** ['nɔno] *sm, agg* ninth.

**nonostante** [nonos'tante] *prep* notwithstanding, in spite of. *cong* (al)though.

**nontiscordardimè** [nontiskordardi'mɛ] *sm* forget-me-not.

**nord** [nɔrd] *sm* north. **a nord** north. **del nord** north, northern. **nord-est** *sm* northeast. **nord-ovest** *sm* north-west.

**norma** ['nɔrma] *sf* rule, standard; (*istruzione*) direction; regulation. **a norma di legge** according to (the) law.

**normale** [nor'male] *agg* normal, regular; standard. *sf* perpendicular. **normalmente** *avv* as a rule.

**Norvegia** [nor'vedʒa] *sf* Norway. **norvegese** *s(m+f)*, *agg* Norwegian.

**nostalgia** [nostal'dʒia] *sf* nostalgia; (*della casa*) homesickness. **aver nostalgia di** miss. **nostalgico** *agg* nostalgic, homesick.

**nostro** ['nɔstro] *agg* our. *pron* ours. **nostrano** *agg* local, home-grown.

**nota** ['nɔta] *sf* note; list.

**notaio** [no'tajo] *sm* notary.

**notare** [no'tare] *v* note; (*osservare*) notice. **far notare** point out.

**notificare** [notifi'kare] *v* notify; inform. **notificazione** *sf* notification; (*avviso*) notice.

**notizia** [no'titsja] *sf* news (item), information. **notiziario** *sm* news (bulletin).

**noto** ['nɔto] *agg* well-known, renowned. **render noto** make known.

**notorio** [no'tɔrjo] *agg* renowned; (*spreg*) notorious. **notorietà** *sf* renown.

**notte** ['nɔtte] *sf* night. **buona notte!** goodnight! **dare la buona notte** bid goodnight. **nottata** *sf* night.

**notturno** [not'turno] *agg* night, nocturnal. *sm* (*musica*) nocturne.

**novanta** [no'vanta] *sm, agg* ninety. **novantesimo** *sm, agg* ninetieth.

**nove** ['nɔve] *sm, agg* nine.

**novella** [no'vella] *sf* short story. **novellista** *s(m+f)* short-story writer.

**novello** [no'vello] *agg* new.

**novembre** [no'vɛmbre] *sm* November.

**novità** [novi'ta] *sf* novelty; (*notizie*) news.

**novizio** [no'vitsjo] *sm* beginner, novice.

**nozione** [no'tsjone] *sf* notion, idea.

**nozze** ['nɔttse] *sf pl* wedding *sing*. **viaggio di nozze** *sm* honeymoon.

**nube** ['nube] *sf* cloud. **nubifragio** *sm* cloudburst.

**nubile** ['nubile] *agg* unmarried, single.

**nuca** ['nuka] *sf* nape of the neck.

**nucleo** ['nukleo] *sm* nucleus. **nucleo familiare** family. **nucleare** *agg* nuclear.

**nudo** ['nudo] *agg* bare, naked. *sm* nude. **a piedi nudi** barefoot. **nudismo** *sm* nudism. **nudista** *s(m+f)* nudist. **nudità** *sf* nudity, nakedness.

**nulla** ['nulla] *pron* nothing; (*con altra negazione*) anything. *sm* nothing; (*cosa da poco*) slightest thing. **da nulla** unimportant. **non fa nulla!** (*non importa*) it doesn't matter!

**nullo** ['nullo] *agg* null. **dichiarar nullo** annul. **nullaosta** *sm invar* clearance. **nullità** *sf* cipher.

**numero** ['numero] *sm* number; (*segno*) numeral. **numero chiuso** quota. **numero legale** quorum.

**numismatica** [numiz'matika] *sf* numismatics. **numismatico, -a** *sm, sf* numismatist.

**\*nuocere** ['nwɔtʃere] *v* harm.

**nuora** ['nwɔra] *sf* daughter-in-law.

**nuotare** [nwo'tare] *v* swim. **nuotatore, -trice** *sm, sf* swimmer. **nuoto** *sm* swimming.

**nuovo** ['nwɔvo] *agg* new. **Nuova York** *sf* New York. **Nuova Zelanda** *sf* New Zealand.

**nutrire** [nu'trire] *v* feed, nourish. **nutrire affetto per** feel affection for. **nutriente** *agg* nourishing. **nutrimento** *sm* nourishment.

**nuvola** ['nuvola] *sf* cloud. **senza nuvole** cloudless. **nuvoloso** *agg* cloudy; (*cielo*) overcast.

**nuziale** [nu'tsjale] *agg* wedding.

# O

**o** [o] *cong* or. **o ... o ...** either … or …. **o l'uno o l'altro** either.

**oasi** ['ɔazi] *sf* oasis (*pl* -ses).

**\*obbedire** [obbe'dire] *v* obey. **obbedienza** *sf* obedience.

**obbligare** *v* bind, force. **obbligarsi** *v* undertake. **obbligato** *agg* fixed, set; (*riconoscente*) obliged. **obbligatorio** *agg* compulsory. **obbligazione** *sf* (*dir*) obligation; (*comm*) bond, debenture. **obbligo** *sm*, *pl* -ghi duty, obligation. **essere d'obbligo** be compulsory *or* obligatory.

**obbrobrio** [ob'brɔbrjo] *sm* disgrace.

**obeso** [o'bɛzo] *agg* obese. **obesità** *sf* obesity.

**obiettare** [objet'tare] *v* object. **obiezione** *sf* objection.

**obiettivo** [objet'tivo] *sm* objective; (*scope*) aim; (*foto, ecc.*) lens. *agg* objective.

**obitorio** [obi'tɔrjo] *sm* morgue.

**oblazione** [obla'tsjone] *sf* offering.

**oblio** [o'blio] *sm* oblivion.

**obliquo** [o'blikwo] *agg* oblique.

**oblò** [o'blɔ] *sm* porthole.

**oblungo** [o'blungo] *agg* oblong.

**oboe** ['ɔboe] *sm* oboe.

**oca** ['ɔka] *sf* goose (*pl* geese); (*maschio*) gander.

**occasionale** [okkazjo'nale] *agg* (*fortuito*) chance; immediate; (*saltuario*) occasional.

**occasione** [okka'zjone] *sf* chance, opportunity; (*buon affare*) bargain; (*circostanza*) occasion.

**occhiali** [ok'kjali] *sm pl* glasses *pl*, spectacles *pl*. **occhiali da sole** sun-glasses *pl*. **occhialuto** *agg* bespectacled.

**occhio** ['ɔkkjo] *sm* eye; (*bot*) bud. **a occhi chiusi** blindly. **a occhio** by sight. **a occhio nudo** with the naked eye. **a quattr'occhi** in private. **costare un occhio della testa** cost the earth. **dare nell'occhio** catch the eye. **tenere d'occhio** keep an eye on.

**occidente** [ottʃi'dɛnte] *sm* west. **occidentale** *agg* west, western.

**\*occorrere** [ok'korrere] *v* be necessary. **all'occorrenza** in case of need.

**occulto** [ok'kulto] *agg* occult; (*nascosto*) hidden.

**occupare** [okku'pare] *v* occupy; (*far lavorare*) employ; (*tempo*) spend; (*carica*) hold; (*tener occupato*) keep busy. **occuparsi di** concern oneself with. **occupato** *agg* engaged; (*indaffarato*) busy. **occupazione** *sf* occupation.

**oceano** [o'tʃeano] *sm* ocean.

**ocra** ['ɔkra] *sf* ochre.

**oculare** [oku'lare] *agg* **testimone oculare** *sm* eye-witness.

**oculista** [oku'lista] *s(m+f)* oculist.

**ode** ['ɔde] *sf* ode.

**odiare** [o'djare] *v* hate, loathe. **odio** *sm* hatred, hate, loathing. **avere in odio** hate, detest. **odioso** *agg* hateful.

**odierno** [o'djɛrno] *agg* of today; modern.

**odissea** [odis'sɛa] *sf* odyssey.

**odontoiatria** [odontoja'tria] *sf* dentistry.

**odorare** [odo'rare] *v* smell. **odorato** *sm* sense of smell. **odore** *sm* smell, odour. **sentir un odore di** smell. **odoroso** *agg* sweet-smelling.

**\*offendere** [of'fɛndere] *v* offend; (*ledere*) injure, hurt. **offendere la legge** break the law. **offendersi** *v* take offence. **offensiva** *sf* offensive. **offensivo** *agg* offensive. **offensore** *sm* attacker; (*dir*) offender.

**offerta** [of'fɛrta] *sf* offer; (*comm*) bid; (*econ*) supply. **offerente** *s(m+f)* bidder.

**offesa** [of'feza] *sf* offence; insult; (*danno*) harm.

**officina** [offi'tʃina] *sf* works, workshop. **capo officina** *sm* (works) foreman.

**\*offrire** [of'frire] *v* offer; (*comm*) bid. **offrirsi** *v* offer; present oneself.

**offuscare** [offus'kare] *v* dim; (*foto, ecc.*) blur; (*fig*) obscure.

**oggetto** [od'dʒetto] *sm* object; (*argomento*) subject; (*cosa*) thing. **oggettività** *sf* objectivity. **oggettivo** *agg* objective.

**oggi** ['oddʒi] *avv*, *sm* today. **al giorno d'oggi** nowadays. **oggi a otto** a week today.

**ogni** ['oɲi] *agg* every, each. **ad** *or* **in ogni modo** in any case. **ogni tanto** every so often, now and then.

**Ognissanti** [oɲis'santi] *sm* All Saints' Day.

**ognuno** [o'ɲuno] *pron* everybody, everyone; (*ciascuno*) each.

**ohimè** [oi'mɛ] *inter* alas!

**Olanda** [o'landa] *sf* Holland. **olandese** *agg* Dutch. **gli olandesi** the Dutch.

**oleodotto** [oleo'dotto] *sm* (*oil*) pipeline.

**oleoso** [ole'ozo] *agg* oily.

**olfatto** [ol'fatto] *sm* sense of smell.

**olimpiade** [olim'piade] *sf* Olympic games *pl*. **olimpico** *agg* Olympian. **olimpionico** *agg* Olympic.

**olio** ['ɔljo] *sm* oil. **olio combustibile** (*gasolio*) fuel oil.

**oliva** [o'liva] *sf* olive. **oliveto** *sm* olive grove. **olivo** *sm* olive-tree.

**olmo** ['olmo] *sm* elm-tree.

**olocausto** [olo'kausto] *sm* holocaust, sacrifice.

**oltraggiare** [oltrad'dʒare] *v* outrage. **oltraggio** *sm* outrage. **oltraggio al pudore** indecent behaviour. **oltraggioso** *agg* outrageous.

**oltranza** [ol'trantsa] *sf* **ad oltranza** to the (bitter) end.

**oltre** ['oltre] *avv* (*luogo*) further, farther; (*tempo*) beyond. *prep* beyond; (*più di*) more than, over. **oltre a** besides, apart from.

**oltremare** [oltre'mare] *avv* overseas.

**oltremodo** [oltre'mɔdo] *avv* exceedingly.

**oltrepassare** [oltrepas'sare] *v* exceed; surpass.

**omaggio** [o'maddʒo] *sm* (*dono*) (complimentary) gift. **porgere omaggi a** pay respects to. **rendere omaggio a** pay homage to.

**ombelico** [ombe'liko] *sm*, *pl* **-chi** navel. **ombelicale** *agg* umbilical.

**ombra** ['ombra] *sf* shadow; (*opposto di luce*) shade. **ombretto** *sm* eye-shadow.

**ombrello** [om'brɛllo] *sm* umbrella.

**omeopatico** [omeo'patiko] *agg* homeopathic.

**omero** ['ɔmero] *sm* humerus.

**\*omettere** [o'mettere] *v* omit, leave out.

**omicida** [omi'tʃida] *agg* murderous. *s(m+f)* murderer, murderess. **omicidio** *sm* homicide, murder. **omicidio colposo** manslaughter.

**omissione** [omis'sjone] *sf* omission.

**omogeneo** [omo'dʒɛneo] *agg* homogeneous. **omogeneità** *sf* homogeneity.

**omologare** [omolo'gare] *v* ratify.

**omonimo** [o'mɔnimo] *agg* homonymous. *nm* namesake; (*parola*) homonym.

**omosessuale** [omosessu'ale] *s(m+f)*, *agg* homosexual. **omosessualità** *sf* homosexuality.

**oncia** ['ontʃa] *sf* ounce.

**onda** ['onda] *sf* wave. **a onde** wavy. **ondata** *sf* wave, surge.

**onde** ['onde] *avv* whence. *cong* so that.

**ondeggiare** [onded'dʒare] *v* wave, sway, roll; (*fig*) waver.

**ondulare** [ondu'lare] *v* (*capelli*) wave. **ondulato** *agg* wavy; (*lastra, cartone*) corrugated.

**onere** ['ɔnere] *sm* burden. **oneroso** *agg* burdensome.

**onesto** [o'nɛsto] *agg* honest; (*prezzo*) fair. **onestà** *sf* honesty, integrity.

**onice** ['ɔnitʃe] *sf* onyx.

**onnipotente** [onnipo'tɛnte] *agg* omnipotent.

**onnivoro** [on'nivoro] *agg* omnivorous.

**onomastico** [ono'mastiko] *sm* saint's day.

**onorare** [ono'rare] *v* honour.

**onorario** [ono'rarjo] *agg* honorary. *sm* fee.

**onore** [o'nore] *sm* honour. **a onor del vero** to tell the truth. **far onore a** honour; do credit *or* justice to. **farsi onore** distinguish oneself. **onorevole** *agg* honourable.

**onorificenza** [onorifi'tʃɛntsa] *sf* honour. **onorifico** *agg* honorary.

**onta** ['onta] *sf* shame.

**ontano** [on'tano] *sm* alder.

**opaco** [o'pako] *agg*, *m pl* **-chi** opaque, dull.

**opale** [o'pale] *sm* opal.

**opera** ['ɔpera] *sf* work; (*teatro*) opera; (*azione*) deed; institution. **mettere in opera** put into practice; instal. **per opera di** thanks to. **operetta** *sf* operetta, light opera. **operoso** *agg* active.

**operaio** [ope'rajo], **-a** *sm*, *sf* worker. *agg* working.

**operare** [ope'rare] *v* function, work; (*med*) operate. **farsi operare** have an operation. **operatore** *sm* (*cinema*) cameraman; (*di borsa*) stockbroker. **operatorio** *agg* operating. **operazione** *sf* operation.

**opinione** [opi'njone] *sf* opinion.

**oppio** ['ɔppjo] *sm* opium.

**opponente** [oppo'nɛnte] *agg* opposing. *s(m+f)* adversary.

**\*opporre** [op'porre] *v* oppose. **opporre resistenza** offer resistance. **opporsi a** set oneself against; object to.

**opportuno** [oppor'tuno] *agg* opportune. **opportunismo** *sm* opportunism. **opportunista** *s(m+f)* opportunist. **opportunità** *sf* opportunity.

**opposizione** [oppozi'tsjone] *sf* opposition.

**opposto** [op'posto] *agg*, *sm* opposite. **all'opposto** on the contrary.

**oppressione** [oppres'sjone] *sf* oppression. **oppresso** *agg* oppressed. **oppressore** *sm* oppressor.

**\*opprimere** [op'primere] *v* oppress, burden.

**oppure** [op'pure] *cong* or, or else.

**opulento** [opu'lɛnto] *agg* opulent.

**opuscolo** [o'puskolo] *sm* pamphlet, booklet.

**ora¹** ['ora] *sf* hour; (*tempo*) time. **alla buon'ora!** at last! **all'ora** (*velocità*) per hour. **di buon'ora** early. **ora di punta** rush-hour. **ora legale** summer-time. **ora straordinaria** overtime.

**ora²** ['ora] *avv* (*adesso*) now; (*appena*) just. **d'ora in poi** from now on, henceforth. **or ora** just (now).

**orale** [o'rale] *agg* oral. *sm* (*esame*) viva.

**orario** [o'rarjo] *agg* (*all'ora*) per hour; time. **in senso orario** clockwise. **segnale orario** time-signal. *sm* (*ore*) hours *pl*; (*tabella*) timetable. **in orario** on time.

**orazione** [ora'tsjone] *sf* speech. **oratore** *sm* orator. **oratorio** *sm* (*chiesa*) oratory; (*musica*) oratorio.

**orbene** [or'bɛne] *avv* well (now).

**orbita** [or'bita] *sf* orbit. **orbitare** *v* orbit.

**orchestra** [or'kɛstra] *sf* orchestra. **orchestrare** *v* orchestrate. **orchestrazione** *sf* orchestration.

**orchidea** [orki'dɛa] *sf* orchid.

**orco** ['ɔrko] *sm* ogre.

**orda** ['ɔrda] *sf* horde.

**ordigno** [or'diɲo] *sm* device.

**ordinare** [ordi'nare] *v* order; (*mettere in ordine*) tidy up; (*sistemare*) arrange; (*rel*) ordain. **ordinamento** *sm* order; arrangement; system. **ordinazione** *sf* order; (*rel*) ordination.

**ordinario** [ordi'narjo] *agg, sm* ordinary.

**ordine** ['ordine] *sm* order. **ordine del giorno** agenda.

**ordire** [or'dire] *v* (*tessile*) warp; (*fig*) hatch. **ordito** *sm* warp; (*fig*) plot.

**orecchio** [o'rekkjo] *sm* ear. **a orecchio** by ear. **a portato d'orecchio** within earshot. **orecchino** *sm* ear-ring. **orecchioni** *sm pl* mumps *sing*.

**orefice** [o'refitʃe] *sm* goldsmith, jeweller, **oreficeria** *sf* jewellery; (*negozio*) jeweller's (shop).

**orfano** ['ɔrfano], **-a** *s*, *agg* orphan. **orfano-**

**trofio** *sm* orphanage.

**organico** [or'ganiko] *agg* organic. *sm* personnel. **organismo** *sm* organism; (*fig*) body.

**organizzare** [organid'dzare] *v* organize, arrange. **organizzazione** *sf* organization, body. **organizzatore, -trice** *sm, sf* organizer.

**organo** ['ɔrgano] *sm* organ. **organetto** *sm* barrel-organ.

**orgasmo** [or'gazmo] *sm* orgasm.

**orgia** ['ɔrdʒa] *sf* orgy.

**orgoglio** [or'goʎo] *sm* pride. **orgoglioso** *agg* proud.

**orientare** [orjen'tare] *v* orient(ate); direct. **orientarsi** *v* find one's bearings; tend. **orientamento** *sm* orientation; (*direzione*) trend. **senso d'orientamento** *sm* sense of direction.

**oriente** [o'rjɛnte] *sm* East. **orientale** *agg* oriental, eastern, east.

**orifizio** [ori'fitsjo] *sm* orifice, opening.

**origano** [o'rigano] *sm* oregano.

**originare** [oridʒi'nare] *v* (*avere origini*) originate; (*dare origini*) give rise to.

**origine** [o'ridʒine] *sf* origin; (*inizio*) beginning. **originale** *sm, agg* original; eccentric. **originalità** *sf* originality; eccentricity. **originario** *agg* native.

**origliare** [ori'ʎare] *v* eavesdrop.

**orina** [o'rina] *sf* urine. **orinare** *v* urinate. **orinatorio** *agg* urinary.

**oriundo** [o'rjundo] *agg* native.

**orizzonte** [orid'dzonte] *sm* horizon. **giro d'orizzonte** *sm* general survey. **orizzontale** *agg* horizontal. **orizzontarsi** *v* find one's bearings.

**orlo** ['orlo] *sm* edge; (*abisso*) brink; (*bicchiere*) rim; (*tessuto*) hem. **orlare** *v* hem; (*bordare*) trim.

**orma** ['orma] *sf* footprint; track.

**ormai** [or'mai] *avv* by now; (*passato*) by then.

**ormeggiare** [ormed'dʒare] *v* moor. **ormeggio** *sm* mooring.

**ormone** [or'mone] *sm* hormone.

**ornare** [or'nare] *v* adorn, decorate. **ornamentale** *agg* ornamental. **ornamento** *sm* ornament, decoration.

**ornitologia** [ornitolo'dʒia] *sf* ornithology. **ornitologo, -a** *sm, sf* ornithologist.

**oro** ['ɔro] *sm* gold. **d'oro** gold, golden.

**orologio** [oro'lɔdʒo] sm clock; (*da polso o tasca*) watch. **orologeria** sf clockwork; (*negozio*) watchmaker's (shop). **bomba ad orologeria** sf time-bomb. **orologiaio** sm watchmaker.

**oroscopo** [o'rɔskopo] sm horoscope.

**orpello** [or'pɛllo] sm tinsel.

**orrendo** [or'rɛndo] agg hideous, horrifying.

**orribile** [or'ribile] agg horrible, dreadful.

**orrore** [or'rore] sm horror, dread, loathing. **avere orrore di** loathe.

**orso** ['orso], **-a** sm, sf bear. **orsacchiotto** sm bear-cub; (*giocattolo*) teddy-bear.

**ortica** [or'tika] sf nettle. **orticaria** sf nettlerash.

**orto** ['ɔrto] sm kitchen garden. **ortaggi** sm pl vegetables pl. **orticoltore** sm horticulturist. **orticoltura** sf horticulture. **ortolano** sm greengrocer.

**ortodosso** [orto'dɔsso] agg orthodox. **ortodossia** sf orthodoxy.

**ortografia** [ortogra'fia] sf spelling. **errore ortografico** sm spelling mistake.

**ortopedia** [ortope'dia] sf orthopaedics. **ortopedico** agg orthopaedic.

**orzaiolo** [ordza'jɔlo] sm stye.

**orzo** ['ɔrdzo] sm barley.

**osare** [o'zare] v dare; risk.

**osceno** [o'ʃɛno] agg obscene. **oscenità** sf obscenity.

**oscillare** [oʃil'lare] v swing, oscillate.

**oscurare** [osku'rare] v darken; (*fig*) obscure. **oscuramento** sm darkening; (*guerra*) blackout. **oscurità** sf dark; (*fig*) obscurity.

**ospedale** [ospe'dale] sm hospital. **ospedaliero** agg hospital.

**ospitare** [ospi'tare] v offer hospitality (to); (*albergare*) put up. **ospitale** agg hospitable.

**ospite** ['ɔspite] s(m+f) (*persona ospitata*) guest; (*oste*) host, hostess.

**ospizio** [os'pitsjo] sm hostel.

**ossatura** [ossa'tura] sf (*arch*) framework; (*anat*) bone structure.

**ossequio** [os'sɛkwjo] sm homage. **ossequi** sm pl (*saluti*) regards pl. **ossequioso** agg respectful.

**osservare** [osser'vare] v obscure; (*notare*) notice. **osservanza** sf observance. **osservatore, -trice** sm, sf observer. **osservatorio** sm observatory. **osservazione** sf observation; (*nota*) remark. **fare un'osservazione** comment; criticize.

**ossessionare** [ossessjo'nare] v haunt. **ossessionante** agg haunting. **ossessione** sf obsession. **ossesso** agg possessed.

**ossessivo** [osses'sivo] agg obsessive.

**ossia** [os'sia] cong or rather, in other words.

**ossigeno** [os'sidʒeno] sm oxygen. **ossidare** v oxidize. **ossido** sm oxide.

**osso** ['ɔsso] sm, pl **-a** f in collective sense bone. **ossuto** agg bony.

**ostacolare** [ostako'lare] v hinder, obstruct. **ostacolo** sm obstacle, hindrance; (*atletica*) hurdle. **corsa a ostacoli** sf obstacle race; hurdling.

**ostaggio** [os'taddʒo] sm hostage.

**oste** ['ɔste] sm host, innkeeper.

**ostello** [os'tɛllo] sm refuge; (*per la gioventù*) (youth-)hostel.

**ostentare** [osten'tare] v show off. **ostentato** agg ostentatious.

**osteria** [oste'ria] sf inn.

**ostetrico** [os'tɛtriko] sm obstetrician. **ostetrica** sf obstetrician; (*levatrice*) midwife. **ostetricia** sf obstetrics; midwifery.

**ostia** ['ɔstja] sf (*rel*) host; (*cialda*) wafer.

**ostile** [os'tile] agg hostile. **ostilità** sf hostility.

**ostinarsi** [osti'narsi] v persist. **ostinatezza** sf obstinacy, stubbornness. **ostinato** agg obstinate, stubborn.

**ostrica** ['ɔstrika] sf oyster.

**ostruire** [ostru'ire] v obstruct, block. **ostruzione** sf obstruction.

**otite** [o'tite] sf otitis.

**otorinolaringoiatra** [otorinolaringo'jatra] s(m+f) ear, nose, and throat specialist.

**ottagono** [ot'tagono] sm octagon.

**ottano** [ot'tano] sm octane.

**ottanta** [ot'tanta] agg eighty. **ottantesimo** agg sm eightieth.

**ottava** [ot'tava] sf octave. **ottavo** sm, agg eighth.

**\*ottenere** [otte'nere] v obtain, get. **ottenibile** agg obtainable.

**ottico** ['ɔttiko] agg optic. sm optician. **ottica** sf (*persona*) optician; (*scienza*) optics.

**ottimismo** [otti'mizmo] agg optimistic.

**ottimo** ['ɔttimo] agg excellent, very good.

**otto** ['ɔtto] agg, sm eight.

**ottobre** [ot'tobre] sm October.

**ottone** [ot'tone] sm brass. **ottoni** sm pl

(*musica*) brass *pl*.

**otturare** [ottu'rare] *v* plug; (*dente*) fill. **otturatore** *sm* (*foto*) shutter.

**ottuso** [ot'tuzo] *agg* dull; (*non tagliente*) blunt; (*angolo*) obtuse.

**ovaia** [o'vaja] *sf* ovary.

**ovale** [o'vale] *agg, sm* oval.

**ovatta** [o'vatta] *sf* wadding; (*cotone idrofilo*) cotton wool.

**ovazione** [ova'tsjone] *sf* ovation.

**ovest** ['ɔvest] *sm* west. **a ovest di** (to the) west of. **dell'ovest** west, western.

**ovile** [o'vile] *sm* sheepfold.

**ovulo** ['ɔvulo] *sm* ovum; (*bot*) ovule. **ovulazione** *sf* ovulation.

**ovunque** [o'vunkwe] *avv* everywhere. *cong* wherever.

**ovvero** [ov'vero] *cong* or (rather).

**ovvio** ['ɔvvjo] *agg* obvious. **ovviamente** *avv* obviously.

**oziare** [o'tsjare] *v* loaf. **ozio** *sm* (*pigrizia*) idleness; (*tempo libero*) leisure, spare time. **ozioso** *agg* idle.

**ozono** [ot'tʃono] *sm* ozone.

# P

**pacato** [pa'kato] *agg* calm.

**pacchia** ['pakkja] *sf* godsend.

**pacco** ['pakko] *sm* parcel. **pacchetto** *sm* packet, small parcel.

**pace** ['patʃe] *sf* peace.

**Pachistan** [pakistan] *sm* Pakistan. **pachistano**, **-a** *s*, *agg* Pakistani.

**pacificare** [patʃifi'kare] *v* pacify, appease; reconcile. **pacifico** *agg* peaceful; (*ovvio*) self-evident.

**pacifismo** [patʃi'fizmo] *sm* pacifism. **pacifista** *s*(*m+f*) pacifist.

**padella** [pa'dɛlla] *sf* frying pan.

**padiglione** [padi'ʎone] *sm* pavilion.

**Padova** ['padova] *sf* Padua.

**padre** ['padre] *sm* father. **padre adottivo** foster-father. **padrino** *sm* godfather.

**padrone** [pa'drone], **-a** *sm, sf* master, mistress; owner; (*fam*) boss. **padronale** *agg* private; (*non di servizio*) owner's. **padro-**

**nanza** *sf* mastery. **padroneggiarsi** *v* control oneself.

**paesaggio** [pae'zaddʒo] *sm* landscape.

**paese** [pa'eze] *sm* country; village; (*città*) town. **paesano** *agg* rural, country.

**paffuto** [paf'futo] *agg* plump.

**paga** ['paga] *sf* pay, wages *pl*.

**pagaia** [pa'gaja] *sf* paddle.

**pagano** [pa'gano], **-a** *s*, *agg* pagan, heathen.

**pagare** [pa'gare] *v* pay. **pagamento** *sm* payment.

**pagella** [pa'dʒella] *sf* school report.

**paggio** ['paddʒo] *sm* page(-boy).

**pagina** ['padʒina] *sf* page.

**paglia** ['paʎa] *sf* straw. **pagliericcio** *sm* palliasse. **paglietta** *sf* steel wool; (*cappello*) straw hat.

**pagliaccio** [pa'ʎattʃo] *sm* clown. **pagliacciata** *sf* buffoonery.

**pagnotta** [pa'ɲɔtta] *sf* loaf (of bread).

**pago** ['pago] *agg* contented (with).

**pagoda** [pa'gɔda] *sf* pagoda.

**paio** ['pajo] *sm*, *pl* **-a** *f* pair; (*due o circa due*) couple.

**pala** ['pala] *sf* shovel; (*di remo*) blade. **palata** *sf* shovel(ful). **soldi a palate** *sm pl* pots or bags of money *pl*.

**palato** [pa'lato] *sm* palate.

**palazzo** [pa'lattso] *sm* (*edificio*) building; (*appartamenti*) block of flats; (*casa di principe, ecc.*) palace. **palazzina** *sf* villa.

**palco** ['palko] *sm* platform, stand; (*teatro*) box. **palcoscenico** *sm* stage.

**palese** [pa'leze] *agg* obvious, clear. **palesare** *v* reveal.

**palestra** [pa'lestra] *sf* gymnasium.

**paletto** [pa'letto] *sm* bolt.

**palio** ['paljo] *sm* **mettere in palio** offer as a prize.

**palla** ['palla] *sf* ball. **pallacanestro** *sf* basketball. **pallanuoto** *s f* water polo.

**palleggiare** [palled'dʒare] *v* (*tennis*) knock up; (*calcio*) dribble. **palleggio** *sm* knockup, dribbling.

**pallido** ['pallido] *agg* pale; (*fig*) faint.

**pallino** [pal'lino] *sm* (*bocce*) jack; (*fig*) craze. **a pallini** with polka dots.

**pallone** [pal'lone] *sm* ball; (*calcio*) football; (*aerostato*) balloon.

**pallottola** [pal'lɔttola] *sf* pellet; (*rivoltella*) bullet.

**palma¹** ['palma] *sf* (*albero*) palm(-tree).

**palma²** ['palma] *sf* (*anat*) palm. **piede palmato** *sm* webbed foot.

**palmo** ['palmo] *sm* palm.

**palo** ['palo] *sm* pole; (*di porta*) post.

**palombaro** [palom'baro] *sm* diver.

**palpare** [pal'pare] *v* feel; *pat.* **palpabile** *agg* palpable.

**palpebra** ['palpebra] *sf* eyelid. **battere le palpebre** blink.

**palpitare** [palpi'tare] *v* throb.

**paltò** [pal'tɔ] *sm invar* overcoat.

**palude** [pa'lude] *sf* marsh, swamp. **terreno paludoso** *sm* marshland.

**panca** ['panka] *sf* bench. **panchetto** *sm* (foot)stool. **panchina** *sf* bench, garden seat. **pancone** *sm* work-bench.

**pancetta** [pan'tʃetta] *sf* bacon.

**pancia** ['pantʃa] *sf* belly; (*fam*) tummy. **mal di pancia** *sm* (*fam*) tummy-ache. **panciotto** *sm* waistcoat. **panciuto** *agg* (*persona*) pot-bellied; (*cosa*) bulging.

**pancreas** ['pankreas] *sm invar* pancreas.

**panda** ['panda] *sm invar* panda.

**pandemonio** [pande'mɔnjo] *sm* uproar.

**pane** ['pane] *sm* bread; (*forma*) loaf. **buono come il pane** as good as gold. **guadagnarsi il pane** earn one's living. **pan grattato** breadcrumbs *pl.* **pan tostato** toast. **panettiere** *sm* baker. **panificio** *sm* bakery.

**panfilo** ['panfilo] *sm* yacht.

**panico** ['paniko] *sm* panic.

**paniere** [pa'njɛre] *sm* basket.

**panino** [pa'nino] *sm* roll. **panino imbottito** sandwich.

**panna¹** ['panna] *sf* cream. **panna montata** whipped cream.

**panna²** ['panna] *sf* (*mec*) breakdown.

**pannello** [pan'nɛllo] *sm* panel.

**panno** ['panno] *sm* cloth. **panni** *sm pl* (*vestiti*) clothes *pl.* **pannolino** *sm* nappy.

**panorama** [pano'rama] *sm* panorama, view.

**pantaloni** [panta'loni] *sm pl* trousers *pl*; (*corti*) shorts *pl.*

**pantano** [pan'tano] *sm* bog.

**pantera** [pan'tɛra] *sf* panther.

**pantofola** [pan'tɔfola] *sf* slipper.

**pantomima** [panto'mima] *sf* play-acting.

**paonazzo** [pao'nattso] *agg* purple.

**papa** ['papa] *sm* pope. **ogni morte di papa** once in a blue moon. **vivere come un papa** live like a lord. **papale** *agg* papal.

**papà** [pa'pa] *sm* (*fam*) dad(dy).

**papavero** [pa'pavero] *sm* poppy.

**papera** ['papera] *sf* slip, blunder. **prendere una papera** slip up.

**papero** ['papero], **-a** *sm*, *sf* gosling.

**papiro** [pa'piro] *sm* papyrus; (*fam*) paper.

**pappa** ['pappa] *sm* mush. **pappare** *v* gobble up.

**pappagallo** [pappa'gallo] *sm* parrot.

**paprica** ['paprika] *sf* paprika.

**parabola** [pa'rabola] *sf* (*storia*) parable; (*mat*) parabola. **parabola satellitare** satellite dish.

**parabrezza** [para'brettsa] *sm invar* windscreen.

**paracadute** [paraka'dute] *sm invar* parachute. **paracadutista** *s*(*m+f*) parachutist; (*mil*) paratrooper.

**paradiso** [para'dizo] *sm* paradise, heaven.

**paradosso** [para'dɔsso] *sm* paradox. **paradossale** *agg* paradoxical.

**parafango** [para'fango] *sm* mudguard.

**paraffina** [paraf'fina] *sf* paraffin.

**parafrasi** [pa'rafrazi] *sf* paraphrase.

**parafulmine** [para'fulmine] *sm* lightning conductor.

**parafuoco** [para'fwɔko] *sm*, *pl* **-chi** fireguard, firescreen.

**paragonare** [parago'nare] *v* compare. **paragonabile** *agg* comparable. **paragone** *sm* comparison. **senza paragone** without equal.

**paragrafo** [pa'ragrafo] *sm* paragraph.

**paralisi** [pa'ralizi] *sf* paralysis (*pl* -ses). **paralitico, -a** *sm*, *sf* cripple. **paralizzare** *v* paralyse.

**parallelo** [paral'lɛlo] *agg*, *sm* parallel. **parallela** *sf* parallel (line). **parallelogrammo** *sm* parallelogram.

**paralume** [para'lume] *sm* lampshade.

**paramedico** [para'mediko] *sm* paramedic.

**paranoia** [para'nɔja] *sf* paranoia. **paranoico** *agg* paranoid.

**parapetto** [para'pɛtto] *sm* parapet.

**parare** [pa'rare] *v* adorn; (*evitare*) ward off; (*sport*) save.

**parasole** [para'sole] *sm* sunshade.

**parassita** [paras'sita] *agg* parasitic. *s(m+f)* parasite.

**parata**[1] [pa'rata] *sf* (*sfilata*) parade.

**parata**[2] [pa'rata] *sf* (*scherma*) parry; (*calcio, ecc.*) save.

**parato** [pa'rato] *sm* **carta da parati** *sf* wallpaper.

**paraurti** [para'urti] *sm invar* bumper.

**paravento** [para'vɛnto] *sm* screen.

**parcheggiare** [parked'dʒare] *v* park. **parcheggio** *sm* parking; (*luogo*) car park.

**parchimetro** [par'kimetro] *sm* parking meter.

**parco**[1] ['parko] *sm* park; (*industriale*) depot; (*auto*) fleet.

**parco**[2] ['parko] *agg* frugal, moderate.

**parecchio** [pa'rekkjo] *agg* quite a lot of, several. **parecchio tempo** quite a long time. *pron* quite a lot, several. *avv* quite a lot.

**pareggiare** [pared'dʒare] *v* equal; (*sport*) draw; (*comm*) balance. **pareggio** *sm* balance; draw.

**parente** [pa'rɛnte] *s(m+f)* relative, relation. **parentela** *sf* relationship; (*parenti*) relations *pl*.

**parentesi** [pa'rɛntezi] *sf* bracket, parenthesis (*pl* -ses). **fra parentesi** incidentally.

**\*parere** [pa'rere] *v* seem, appear; (*suono*) sound; (*tatto*) feel. **faccio come mi pare** I do as I like. *sm* opinion.

**parete** [pa'rete] *sf* wall; (*monte*) face.

**pari** ['pari] *agg* equal, same; (*non dispari*) even; equivalent. **alla pari** (*in famiglia*) au pair. **essere pari** be quits; (*forze*) be equal *or* level. *s(m+f)* equal, peer.

**Parigi** [pa'ridʒi] *sf* Paris. **parigino, -a** *s, agg* Parisian.

**parità** [pari'ta] *sf* parity. **a parità di condizioni** all things being equal.

**parlamento** [parla'mento] *sm* parliament. **parlamentare** *agg* parliamentary.

**parlare** [par'lare] *v* speak, talk. **parlar chiaro** speak clearly; (*fig*) speak one's mind. *sm* talk; (*parlata*) way of speaking, dialect.

**parmigiano** [parmi'dʒano] *agg* Parmesan. *sm* Parmesan cheese.

**parodia** [paro'dia] *sf* parody.

**parola** [pa'rɔla] *sf* word. **parola d'ordine** password. **parole crociate** *sf pl* crossword *sing*.

**parolacce** [paro'lattʃe] *sf pl* bad language *sing*.

**parrochia** [par'rɔkkja] *sf* parish. **parroco** *sm*, *pl* **-chi** parish priest.

**parrucca** [par'rukka] *sf* wig.

**parrucchiere** [parruk'kjɛre] *sm* hairdresser.

**parte** ['parte] *sf* part; (*porzione*) share; (*lato*) side; (*dir*) party. **a parte** apart; extra. **dall' altra parte** on the other hand. **da parte** aside. **da parte mia** from me. **da queste parti** round here. **per parte mia** as far as I am concerned.

**partecipare** [partetʃi'pare] *v* participate, take part in; (*condividere*) share; announce. **partecipazione** *sf* sharing; announcement; presence.

**partenza** [par'tɛntsa] *sf* departure; (*sport*) start.

**participio** [parti'tʃipjo] *sm* participle.

**particolare** [partiko'lare] *agg* particular, special. *sm* detail.

**partigiano** [parti'dʒano], **-a** *s, agg* partisan.

**partire** [par'tire] *v* leave; go away; start.

**partita** [par'tita] *sf* game; (*incontro*) match; (*contabilità*) entry; (*merci*) lot.

**partito** [par'tito] *sm* party; condition; decision. **mal partito** predicament. **per partito preso** having made up one's mind.

**partitura** [parti'tura] *sf* score.

**parto** ['parto] *sm* birth; (*umano*) childbirth; (*atto*) delivery. **partorire** *v* give birth (to).

**parziale** [par'tsjale] *agg* partial; (*predisposto*) biased.

**pascere** [pa'ʃere] *v* feed (on). **ben pasciuto** well-fed, plump.

**pascolare** [pasko'lare] *v* graze. **pascolo** *sm* pasture.

**Pasqua** ['paskwa] *sf* Easter. **Pasqua degli ebrei** Passover.

**passabile** [pas'sabile] *agg* fair.

**passaggio** [pas'saddʒo] *sm* passage; (*traversata*) crossing. **dare un passaggio** give a lift. **diritto di passaggio** *sm* right of way. **essere di passaggio** be on the way through. **vietato il passaggio** no thoroughfare.

**passaporto** [passa'pɔrto] *sm* passport.

**passare** [pas'sare] *v* pass; go past; (*gastr*) strain.

**passatempo** [passa'tɛmpo] *sm* pastime.

**passato** [pas'sato] *agg* past; (*scorso*) last. *sm* past.

**passatoia** [passa'toja] *sf* runner.

**passeggero** [passed'dʒero], **-a** *agg* passing, transient. *sm*, *sf* passenger.

**passeggiare** [passed'dʒare] *v* go for a walk *or* stroll. **passeggiata** *sf* walk, stroll; (*non a piedi*) ride.

**passeggino** [passed'ʒino] *sm* buggy.

**passerella** [passe'rɛlla] *sf* footbridge.

**passero** ['passero] *sm* sparrow.

**passibile** [pas'sibile] *agg* liable (to).

**passione** [pas'sjone] *sf* passion.

**passivo** [pas'sivo] *agg* passive; (*comm*) debit. *sm* (*gramm*) passive; (*comm*) liability.

**passo** ['passo] *sm* step; (*andatura*) pace; (*velocità*) rate; (*geog*) pass; (*di vite*) thread. **cedere il passo** give way. **fare due passi** go for a stroll. **sbarrare il passo** block the way. **segnare il passo** mark time.

**pasta** ['pasta] *sf* dough; (*minestra*) pasta; (*impasto*) paste; (*dolce*) pastry. **pasta frolla** shortcrust pastry. **pasta sfoglia** puff pastry.

**pastello** [pas'tɛllo] *sm* pastel.

**pasticca** [pas'tikka] *sf* lozenge.

**pasticceria** [pastittʃe'ria] *sf* (*negozio*) confectioner's (shop); (*pasticcini*) pastries *pl*. **pasticciere** *sm* confectioner.

**pasticciare** [pastit'tʃare] *v* bungle, mess up. **pasticcio** *sm* mess; (*gastr*) pie.

**pastiglia** [pas'tiʎa] *sf* tablet.

**pasto** ['pasto] *sm* meal. **vino da pasto** *sm* table wine.

**pastore** [pas'tore] *sm* shepherd; (*prete*) minister. **cane pastore** *sm* sheepdog. **pastorale** *agg* pastoral.

**pastorizzare** [pastorid'dzare] *v* pasteurize. **pastorizzazione** *sf* pasteurization.

**pastoso** [pas'tozo] *agg* mellow.

**pastrano** [pas'trano] *sm* overcoat.

**pastura** [pas'tura] *sf* pasture.

**patata** [pa'tata] *sf* potato. **patatine fritte** *sf pl* French fries.

**patella** [pa'tɛlla] *sf* (*anat*) knee-cap; (*zool*) limpet.

**patente¹** [pa'tɛnte] *agg* patent.

**patente²** [pa'tɛnte] *sf* licence.

**paterno** [pa'tɛrno] *agg* paternal. **paternale** *sf* lecture. **paternità** *sf* paternity.

**patetico** [pa'tɛtiko] *agg* pathetic, moving.

**patibolo** [pa'tibolo] *sm* gallows.

**patina** ['patina] *sf* coat.

**patire** [pa'tire] *v* suffer. **patimento** *sm* suffering, pain. **patito** *sm* (*fam*) fan.

**patologico** [pato'lɔdʒiko] *agg* pathological.

**patria** ['patrja] *sf* country; home.

**patrigno** [pa'triɲo] *sm* stepfather.

**patrimonio** [patri'mɔnjo] *sm* estate; fortune. **patrimonio pubblico** public heritage.

**patriota** [patri'ɔta] *s(m+f)* patriot. **patriottico** *agg* patriotic. **patriottismo** *sm* patriotism.

**patrocinio** [patro'tʃinjo] *sm* defence. **patrocinare** *v* defend.

**patrono** [pa'trono] *sm* patron. **patronato** *sm* patronage; institution.

**pattinare** [patti'nare] *v* skate. **pattinaggio** *sm* skating. **pattino** *sm* skate; (*mec*) slide.

**patto** ['patto] *sm* pact, agreement; condition, term. **pattuire** *v* agree.

**pattuglia** [pat'tuʎa] *sf* patrol.

**pattumiera** [pattu'mjɛra] *sf* dustbin.

**paura** [pa'ura] *sf* fear; (*spavento*) fright. **aver paura di** be afraid of, fear. **far paura** scare. **pauroso** *agg* (*che fa paura*) frightening; (*che ha paura*) timid, afraid.

**pausa** ['pauza] *sf* pause, interval.

**pavimento** [pavi'mento] *sm* floor.

**pavone** [pa'vone] *sm* peacock. **pavonessa** *sf* peahen.

**pavoneggiarsi** [pavoned'dʒarsi] *v* show off.

**paziente** [pa'tsjɛnte] *s(m+f)*, *agg* patient. **pazientare** *v* wait patiently. **pazienza** *sf* patience.

**pazzo** ['pattso], **-a** *agg* crazy, insane. *sm*, *sf* lunatic. **pazzesco** *agg* mad; incredible. **pazzia** *sf* madness, folly.

**peccare** [pek'kare] *v* sin. **pecca** *sf* fault. **peccato** *sm* sin. **che peccato!** what a pity! **peccatore, -trice** *sm*, *sf* sinner.

**pece** ['petʃe] *sf* pitch.

**pecora** ['pɛkora] *sf* sheep; (*femmina*) ewe.

**peculiare** [peku'ljare] *agg* peculiar.

**pedaggio** [pe'daddʒo] *sm* toll.

**pedale** [pe'dale] *sm* pedal. **pedalare** *v* pedal.

**pedana** [pe'dana] *sf* platform; (*sport*) springboard.

**pedante** [pe'dante] *agg* pedantic. *s(m+f)* pedant.

**pedata** [pe'data] *sf* kick; (*orma*) footprint.

**pedestre** [pe'dɛstre] *agg* pedestrian.

**pediatria** [pedja'tria] *sf* paediatrics. **pediatra** *s(m+f)* paediatrician. **pediatrico** *agg* paediatric.

**pedicure** [pedi'kure] *s(m+f)* *invar* chiropodist.

**pedina** [pe'dina] *sf* piece; (*scacchi*) pawn. **muovere una pedina** make a move; (*fig*) pull strings.

**pedinare** [pedi'nare] *v* shadow.

**pedone** [pe'done] *s(m+f)* pedestrian. **pedonale** *agg* pedestrian.

**peggio** ['pɛddʒo] *agg* (*comparativo*) worse; (*superlativo*) the worst. *sm* the worst. **alla peggio** if the worst comes to the worst.

**peggiorare** [pɛddʒo'rare] *v* (*stare*) get worse; (*rendere*) make worse. **peggioramento** *sm* worsening.

**peggiore** [pɛd'dʒore] *agg* (*comparativo*) worse; (*superlativo*) the worst. *s(m+f)* the worst.

**pegno** ['peɲo] *sm* pledge, pawn.

**pelare** [pe'lare] *v* peel, skin; (*fig*) fleece. **pelarsi** *v* (*fam*) go bald.

**pelle** ['pɛlle] *sf* skin; (*cuoio*) hide; (*frutta*) peel; (*carnagione*) complexion. **rimetterci la pelle** lose one's life.

**pellegrino** [pelle'grino] *sm* pilgrim. **pellegrinaggio** *sm* pilgrimage.

**pellicano** [pelli'kano] *sm* pelican.

**pelliccia** [pel'littʃa] *sf* fur; (*mantello*) fur coat. **pellicciaio** *sm* furrier.

**pellicola** [pel'likola] *sf* film; membrane.

**pelo** ['pelo] *sm* hair; (*pelame*) coat. **cercare il pelo nell'uovo** split hairs. **contro pelo** against the grain. **per un pelo** by a whisker.

**peltro** ['peltro] *sm* pewter.

**peluria** [pe'lurja] *sf* down.

**pelvi** ['pɛlvi] *sf* pelvis.

**pena** ['pena] *sf* (*dolore*) pain; (*disturbo*) trouble; punishment. **valere la pena** be worth it, be worthwhile.

**penale** [pe'nale] *agg* criminal, penal. *sf* fine.

**penare** [pe'nare] *v* find difficult, be hardly able to.

**pendente** [pen'dɛnte] *agg* hanging; (*dir, comm*) pending; (*torre*) leaning. *sm* pendant. **pendenza** *sf* slope, incline.

**pendere** ['pɛndere] *v* hang (down); incline, slope; (*dir*) be pending.

**pendio** [pen'dio] *sm* slope.

**pendolare** [pendo'lare] *v* swing. *s(m+f)* commuter. **pendolo** *sm* pendulum.

**pene** ['pɛne] *sm* penis.

**penetrare** [pene'trare] *v* penetrate, pierce. **penetrante** *agg* penetrating, piercing; acute. **penetrazione** *sf* penetration.

**penicillina** [penitʃil'lina] *sf* penicillin.

**penisola** [pe'nizola] *sf* peninsula.

**penitente** [peni'tɛnte] *s(m+f)*, *agg* penitent. **penitenza** *sf* penance; (*gioco*) forfeit. **penitenziario** *sm* jail.

**penna** ['penna] *sf* feather; (*da scrivere*) pen. **penna a sfera** ball-point pen. **penna stilografica** fountain pen. **pennuto** *agg* feathered.

**pennello** [pen'nɛllo] *sm* brush.

**penombra** [pe'nombra] *sf* twilight.

**penoso** [pe'nozo] *agg* painful.

**pensare** [pen'sare] *v* think; intend. **pensarci** *v* think about it. **pensarci sopra** think it over. **pensatore, -trice** *sm*, *sf* thinker.

**pensiero** [pen'sjɛro] *sm* thought; (*mente, parere*) mind. **essere in pensiero** worry. **pensieroso** *agg* thoughtful; pensive.

**pensile** ['pɛnsile] *agg* hanging.

**pensionare** [pensjo'nare] *v* pension off. **pensionato** *sm* pensioner; (*collegio*) boarding-school. **pensione** *sf* pension. **essere in pensione** be retired. **mezza pensione** half board. **pensione completa** full board.

**pentagono** [pen'tagono] *sm* pentagon. **pentagonale** *agg* pentagonal.

**Pentecoste** [pente'kɔste] *sf* Whitsun.

**pentirsi** [pen'tirsi] *v* regret, be sorry for; (*rel*) repent. **pentimento** *sm* regret; repentance.

**pentola** ['pentola] *sf* pot.

**penultimo** [pe'nultimo] *agg* penultimate.

**penzolare** [pendzo'lare] *v* dangle. **penzoloni** *avv* dangling.

**pepe** ['pepe] *sm* pepper. **pepare** *v* pepper. **pepato** *agg* peppery, hot. **peperone** *sm* capsicum; (*frutto*) pepper; (*peperoncino*) chili.

**pepita** [pe'pita] *sf* nugget.

**per** ['per] *prep* for; (*attraverso*) through; (*mat, entro, tramite*) by. **per caso** by chance. **per cento** per cent. **per di più** in addition. **per lo meno** at least. **per ora** for the present. **per terra** on the floor. **per volta** at a time. **stare per** be about to, be on the point of.

**pera** ['pera] *sf* pear. **pero** *sm* pear tree.
**perbacco** [per'bakko] *inter* by Jove!
**perbene** [per'bɛne] *agg invar* respectable,
nice. *avv* well, nicely.
**percentuale** [pertʃentu'ale] *agg* per cent. *sf*
percentage.
**percepire** [pertʃe'pire] *v* notice, be aware
(of); (*riscuotere*) receive. **percepibile** *agg*
noticeable; (*comm*) due. **percettibile** *agg*
perceptible. **percezione** *sf* perception.
**perché** [per'ke] *avv* why. *cong* because, as;
(*affinché*) so that. *sm* reason.
**perciò** [per'tʃo] *cong* so, therefore.
*****percorrere** [per'korrere] *v* cover.
**percorso** [per'korso] *sm* trip, run.
**percossa** [per'kɔssa] *sf* blow, impact.
*****percuotere** [per'kwɔtere] *v* strike, hit.
**percussione** [perkus'sjone] *sf* percussion.
*****perdere** ['pɛrdere] *v* lose; (*colare*) leak;
(*sprecare*) waste. **lascia perdere!** skip it!
**perdere di vista** lose sight of. **perdersi** *v*
get lost. **perdita** *sf* loss; leak; waste.
**perdonare** [perdo'nare] *v* forgive. **perdono**
*sm* forgiveness, pardon.
**perenne** [pe'rɛnne] *agg* perpetual.
**perfetto** [per'fetto] *agg* perfect.
**perfezionare** [perfetsjo'nare] *v* (*migliorare*)
improve; make perfect. **perfezionarsi** *v*
specialize. **perfezionamento** *sm* specialization. **perfezione** *sf* perfection. **perfezion-
ista** *s(m+f)* perfectionist.
**perfidia** [per'fidja] *sf* treachery, wickedness.
**perfido** *agg* treacherous, wicked.
**perfino** [per'fino] *avv* even.
**perforare** [perfo'rare] *v* pierce, perforate.
**pergamena** [perga'mɛna] *sf* parchment.
**pericolo** [pe'rikolo] *sm* danger; risk. **peri-
colante** *agg* unsafe. **pericoloso** *agg* dangerous; risky.
**periferia** [perife'ria] *sf* periphery; (*città*)
suburbs *pl*. **periferico** *agg* suburban;
peripheral.
**perimetro** [pe'rimetro] *sm* perimeter.
**periodico** [peri'ɔdiko] *agg* periodic. *sm*
periodical.
**periodo** [pe'riodo] *sm* period.
**peripezia** [peripe'tsia] *sf* vicissitude.
**perire** [pe'rire] *v* perish, die.
**periscopio** [peri'skɔpjo] *sm* periscope.
**perito** [pe'rito], **-a** *s*, *agg* expert. **perizia** *sf*

(*bravura*) skill, expertise; (*pratica*) experience; (*valutazione*) examination, expert
opinion.
**perizoma** [perit'tʃoma] *sm* (*indumento*)
thong.
**perla** ['pɛrla] *sf* pearl.
**perlomeno** [perlo'meno] *avv* at least.
**perlustrare** [perlus'trare] *v* patrol; (*mil*)
reconnoitre. **perlustrazione** *sf* patrol;
reconnaissance.
**permaloso** [perma'lozo] *agg* touchy.
**permanente** [perma'nɛnte] *agg* permanent, lasting. *sf* (*fam*) perm. **permanenza**
*sf* (*soggiorno*) stay. **in permanenza** perma-
nently. **permanere** *v* remain.
**permeare** [perme'are] *v* permeate. **perme-
abile** *agg* permeable.
**permesso** [per'messo] *sm* permission;
licence; (*congedo*) leave, pass. **(con) permesso?** may I? (*inter*) allow me!
*****permettere** [per'mettere] *v* allow, permit.
**pernice** [per'nitʃe] *sf* partridge.
**perno** ['pɛrno] *sm* pivot, pin. **far perno su**
hinge on.
**pernottare** [pernot'tare] *v* spend the night.
**però** [pe'ro] *cong* but; (*tuttavia*) still, yet,
however.
**perossido** [pe'rɔssido] *sm* peroxide.
**perpendicolare** [perpendiko'lare] *agg, sf*
perpendicular.
**perpetuo** [per'pɛtuo] *agg* perpetual.
**perplesso** [per'plɛsso] *agg* puzzled; (*incerto*)
undecided. **perplessità** *sf* perplexity; indecision.
**perquisire** [perkwi'zire] *v* search. **perquisizione** *sf* search.
**perseguire** [perse'gwire] *v* pursue.
**perseguimento** *sm* pursuit.
**perseguitare** [persegwi'tare] *v* persecute.
**persecuzione** *sf* persecution.
**perseverare** [perseve'rare] *v* persevere.
**perseveranza** *sf* perseverance.
**persiana** [per'sjana] *sf* shutter, blind.
**persiano** [per'sjano] *agg* Persian.
**persico** ['pɛrsiko] *agg* Persian. **(pesce) persico** *sm* perch.
**persino** [per'sino] *avv* even.
*****persistere** [per'sistere] *v* persist. **persis-
tenza** *sf* persistence.
**perso** ['pɛrso] *agg* lost. **a tempo perso** in
one's spare time.

**persona** [per'sona] *sf* person; (*qualcuno*) somebody. **di** *or* **in persona** in person, personally; (*personificato*) personified. **persona di servizio** domestic (help).

**personaggio** [perso'naddʒo] *sm* (*teatro, ecc.*) character; celebrity.

**personale** [perso'nale] *agg* personal. *sm* (*aspetto*) figure; (*dipendenti*) staff. *sf* (*mostra*) one-man show. **personale di direzione** management. **personale qualificato** skilled workers *pl*.

**personalità** [personali'ta] *sf* personality.

**personificare** [personifi'kare] *v* personify. **personificazione** *sf* personification.

**perspicace** [perspi'katʃe] *agg* keen, shrewd.

***persuadere** [persua'dere] *v* persuade; convince. **persuasione** *sf* persuasion; conviction. **persuasivo** *agg* convincing. **persuaso** *agg* convinced.

**pertanto** [per'tanto] *cong* thus, therefore, so.

**pertica** ['pɛrtika] *sf* pole.

**pertinace** [perti'natʃe] *agg* stubborn; (*deciso*) determined.

**pertinente** [perti'nɛnte] *agg* pertaining (to); (*domanda*) relevant.

**pertosse** [per'tosse] *sf* whooping cough.

***pervadere** [per'vadere] *v* pervade.

***pervenire** [perve'nire] *v* arrive (at).

**pervertire** [perver'tire] *v* corrupt, pervert. **perverso** *agg* perverse. **pervertito, -a** *sm, sf* pervert.

**pesare** [pe'zare] *v* weigh. **pesa** *sf* (*pesatura*) weighing; (*basculla*) weigh-bridge. **pesante** *agg* heavy; (*aria*) stuffy; (*duro*) rough. **peso** *sm* weight; (*onere*) burden.

**pesca¹** ['pɛska] *sf* (*bot*) peach. **pesco** *sm* peach-tree.

**pesca²** ['peska] *sf* fishing; (*industria*) fishery; (*quantità*) catch. **pescare** *v* fish; (*trovare*) pick up, get hold of; (*acciuffare*) catch. **pescatore** *sm* fisherman; (*con lenza*) angler.

**pesce** ['peʃe] *sm* fish. **buttarsi a pesce su** make a dive for. **pesce d'aprile** April fool. **sano come un pesce** fit as a fiddle. **pescivendolo, -a** *sm, sf* fishmonger.

**pessimismo** [pessi'mizmo] *sm* pessimism.

**pessimista** *s(m+f)* pessimist. **pessimistico** *agg* pessimistic.

**pessimo** ['pɛssimo] *agg* very bad; (*scadente, incapace*) very poor.

**pestare** [pes'tare] *v* crush; (*fam: picchiare*) give a (good) hiding. **pestare i piedi a qualcuno** tread on someone's toes. **pestello** *sm* pestle.

**peste** ['pɛste] *sf* plague; (*fig*) pest, curse.

**pesto** ['pesto] *agg* crushed. **essere buio pesto** be pitch dark.

**petalo** ['pɛtalo] *sm* petal.

**petizione** [peti'tsjone] *sf* petition.

**petrolifero** [petro'lifero] *agg* oil.

**petrolio** [pe'trɔljo] *sm* oil. **lampada a petrolio** *sf* paraffin lamp. **petroliera** *sf* (oil-)tanker.

**pettegolo** [pet'tegolo], **-a** *sm, sf* gossip. *agg* gossipy. **pettegolezzo** *sm* gossip.

**pettinare** [petti'nare] *v* comb. **pettinarsi** *v* comb one's hair. **pettinato** *sm* (*tessuto*) worsted. **pettinatura** *sf* combing; (*acconciatura*) hair-style. **pettine** *sm* comb.

**petto** ['pɛtto] *sm* breast; (*torace*) chest. **a doppio/un petto** double-/single-breasted.

**petulante** [petu'lante] *agg* pert.

**pezza** ['pɛttsa] *sf* rag; (*toppa*) patch; (*pannolino*) napkin. **pezza da piedi** doormat. **pezza di tessuto** roll of cloth. **pezzato** *agg* spotted. **pezzente** *s(m+f)* beggar.

**pezzo** ['pɛttso] *sm* piece; (*tempo*) period; (*giornale*) article. **pezzo di ricambio** spare part. **pezzo di terreno** plot of land. **pezzo grosso** (*fam*) VIP, big shot.

***piacere** [pja'tʃere] *v* please. **mi piace ...** I like .... *sm* pleasure; favour. **a piacere** ad lib, freely. **far piacere a** please. **per piacere** please, if you please. **piacevole** *agg* pleasant.

**piaga** ['pjaga] *sf* sore; (*fig*) wound.

**piagnucolare** [pjanuko'lare] *v* whine, whimper. **piagnucolio** *sm* whining, whimpering. **piagnucolone, -a** *sm, sf* (*fam*) cry-baby.

**pialla** ['pjalla] *sf* plane. **piallare** *v* plane.

**pianella** [pja'nɛlla] *sf* (*mattonella*) tile; (*pantofola*) mule, slipper.

**pianerottolo** [pjane'rɔttolo] *sm* landing.

**pianeta** [pja'neta] *sm* planet.

***piangere** ['pjandʒere] *v* weep, cry. **far piangere** *v* move to tears; (*ironico*) be pathetic.

**pianificare** [pjanifi'kare] *v* plan. **pianificatore, -trice** *sm, sf* planner. **pianificazione** *sf* planning.

**pianista** [pja'nista] *s(m+f)* pianist.

**piano¹** ['pjano] *agg* flat, level; (*chiaro*) clear.

*avv* (*adagio*) slow, slowly; (*con cautela*) carefully; (*a voce bassa*) softly. **pian piano** very slowly, very softly; (*poco alla volta*) little by little.

**piano²** ['pjano] *sm* plane, level; (*casa*) floor, storey; (*autobus*) deck. **primo piano** foreground. **secondo piano** background.

**piano³** ['pjano] *sm* (*progetto*) plan. **piano di studi** syllabus. **piano regolatore** town plan.

**pianoforte** [pjano'fɔrte] *sm* pianoforte; (*fam*) piano. **pianoforte a coda** grand piano.

**pianta** ['pjanta] *sf* (*bot*) plant; (*disegno*) plan; (*carta di città*) map. **di sana pianta** from scratch. **in pianta stabile** on the permanent staff. **pianta del piede** sole.

**piantagione** [pjanta'dʒone] *sf* plantation.

**piantare** [pjan'tare] *v* plant; (*conficcare*) drive; (*tenda*) pitch; (*abbandonare*) quit. **piantare grane** (*fam*) make trouble. **piantare in asso** leave in the lurch.

**pianterreno** [pjanter'reno] *sm* ground floor.

**pianto** ['pjanto] *sm* crying; tears *pl*.

**pianura** [pja'nura] *sf* plain.

**piastra** ['pjastra] *sf* plate. **piastrella** *sf* tile. **piastrellare** *v* tile.

**piattaforma** [pjatta'forma] *sf* platform. **piattaforma di lancio** launching pad. **piattaforma girevole** turntable.

**piatto** ['pjatto] *agg* flat. *sm* plate; (*portata*) dish, course; (*bilancia*) pan. **lavare i piatti** wash up.

**piazza** ['pjattsa] *sf* square; (*comm*) market; (*posto*) place; (*fam: calvizie*) bald patch. **a due piazze** (*letto, ecc.*) double. **a una piazza** single. **far piazza pulita** make a clean sweep. **scendere in piazza** demonstrate. **piazzaforte** *sf* stronghold. **piazzale** *sm* square. **piazzare** *v* place. **piazzista** *sm* salesman, commercial traveller.

**picca** ['pikka] *sf* pike. **picche** *sf pl* (*carte*) spades *pl*. **rispondere picche** turn down flat.

**piccante** [pik'kante] *agg* sharp, spicy; (*arguto*) spirited; (*licenzioso*) racy.

**picchiare** [pik'kjare] *v* hit, strike; (*colpire*) beat; (*bussare*) knock. **picchiata** *sf* (*aereo*) (nose-)dive.

**picchio** ['pikkjo] *sm* woodpecker.

**piccino** [pit'tʃino] *agg* tiny. *sm* child (*pl* -ren).

**piccione** [pit'tʃone] *sm* pigeon, dove. **piccionaia** *sf* dovecot; (*fam: teatro*) (the) gods.

**picco** ['pikko] *sm* peak. **a picco** sheer. **colare** *or* **mandare a picco** sink.

**piccolo** ['pikkolo], **-a** *agg* small, little. *sm, sf* little one, child (*pl* -ren). **da piccolo** as a child. **fin da piccolo** since childhood. **in piccolo** on a small scale. **piccolezza** *sf* (*inezia*) trifle.

**piccone** [pik'kone] *sm* pick-axe.

**pidocchio** [pi'dokkjo] *sm* louse (*pl* lice). **pidocchioso** *agg* lousy; (*fig*) mean.

**piede** ['pjɛde] *sm* foot (*pl* feet). **a piedi** on foot. **a piedi nudi** barefoot. **essere tra i piedi** be in the way. **fatto con i piedi** (*fam*) slipshod. **in piedi** standing. **togliersi dai piedi** get out of the way. **piedistallo** *sm* pedestal.

**piega** ['pjɛga] *sf* fold; crease; (*ornamento*) pleat. **messa in piega** *sf* set. **mettere in piega** *v* set. **prendere una brutta piega** take a turn for the worse.

**piegare** [pje'gare] *v* bend; (*foglio, tessuto*) fold.

**pieghettare** [pjeget'tare] *v* pleat.

**pieghevole** [pje'gevole] *agg* folding; flexible.

**piena** ['pjɛna] *sf* flood, spate; (*folla*) crowd.

**pieno** ['pjɛno] *agg* full. **in pieno** completely; exactly. (*nel mezzo*) in the middle of. **pieno zeppo** full up, chock full. **fare il pieno** (*auto*) fill up.

**pietà** [pje'ta] *sf* pity, compassion; (*devozione*) piety. **fare pietà** arouse pity. **pietoso** *agg* pitiful.

**pietanza** [pje'tantsa] *sf* dish, course.

**pietra** ['pjɛtra] *sf* stone. **pietra dura** semi-precious stone. **pietra di paragone** touchstone. **pietrina** *sf* flint.

**piffero** ['piffero] *sm* pipe; (*sonatore*) piper.

**pigiama** [pi'dʒama] *sm* pyjamas *pl*.

**pigiare** [pi'dʒare] *v* press, squeeze. **pigiatura** *sf* pressing.

**pigione** [pi'dʒone] *sf* rent.

**pigliare** [pi'ʎare] (*fam*) *V* **prendere**.

**pigmento** [pig'mento] *sm* pigment. **pigmentazione** *sf* pigmentation.

**pigmeo** [pig'mɛo] *sm* pygmy.

**pigna** ['piɲa] *sf* pine-cone.

**pignatta** [pi'ɲatta] *sf* pot.

**pignolo** [pi'ɲɔlo], **-a** *agg* fussy, pedantic. *sm, sf* pedant.

**pigolare** [pigo'lare] v peep, chirp. **pigolio** sm peeping, chirping.

**pigro** ['pigro], -**a** agg idle, lazy. sm, sf lazy person, loafer. **pigrizia** sf laziness, idleness.

**pila** ['pila] sf pile; (elett) battery.

**pilastro** [pi'lastro] sm pillar, column.

**pillola** ['pillola] sf pill.

**pilone** [pi'lone] sm pillar; (ponte) pier; (elett) pylon.

**pilotare** [pilo'tare] v pilot; (auto) drive. **pilota** sm pilot.

**pinacoteca** [pinako'tɛka] sf picture gallery.

**pineta** [pi'neta] sf pine forest.

**pingue** ['pingwe] agg fat.

**pinguino** [pin'gwino] sm penguin.

**pinna** ['pinna] sf fin.

**pinnacolo** [pin'nakolo] sm pinnacle.

**pino** ['pino] sm pine (tree). **pinolo** sm pine-seed.

**pinza** ['pintsa] sf pliers pl; (zool) pincer. **pinzetta** sf tweezers pl.

**pio** ['pio] agg pious.

**pioggia** ['pjoddʒa] sf rain. **pioggerella** sf also **pioggia fine** drizzle. **pioggia acida** sm acid rain.

**piolo** [pi'ɔlo] sm peg; (scala) rung.

**piombare**[1] [pjom'bare] v hurtle, plunge; (avventarsi) pounce.

**piombare**[2] [pjom'bare] v (otturare) fill; (sigillare) seal (with lead). **piombo** sm lead; (piombino) plummet.

**pioniere** [pjo'njɛre], -**a** sm, sf pioneer.

**pioppo** ['pjoppo] sm poplar.

*****piovere** ['pjɔvere] v rain; (fig) pour (in). **piovere a catinelle** rain cats and dogs. **piovigginare** v drizzle. **piovoso** agg rainy.

**piovra** ['pjɔvra] sf (giant) squid; (persona) blood-sucker.

**pipa** ['pipa] sf pipe.

**pipistrello** [pipi'strɛllo] sf bat.

**pira** ['pira] sf pyre.

**piramide** [pi'ramide] sf pyramid.

**pirata** [pi'rata] sm pirate. **pirata della strada** hit-and-run driver. **pirateria** sf piracy.

**piroscafo** [pi'rɔskafo] sm steamer; (da carico) freighter; (di linea) liner.

**piscia** ['piʃa] (volg) sf piss. **pisciare** v piss.

**piscina** [pi'ʃina] sf swimming pool.

**pisello** [pi'zɛllo] sm pea. **pisello odoroso** sweet pea.

**pisolino** [pizo'lino] sm **fare** or **schiacciare un pisolino** take a nap.

**pista** ['pista] sf track; (aero) runway.

**pistola** [pis'tɔla] sf pistol. **pistola a spruzzo** spray-gun. **pistolettata** sf pistol-shot.

**pistone** [pis'tone] sm piston.

**pitocco** [pi'tɔkko], -**a** sm, sf beggar; (avaro) miser.

**pitone** [pi'tone] sm python.

**pittore** [pit'tore] sm painter.

**pittoresco** [pitto'resko] agg picturesque.

**pittura** [pit'tura] sf painting; (descrizione) picture; (vernice) paint. **pitturare** v paint.

**più** [pju] avv (comparativo) more; (superlativo) most. **al più presto** as soon as possible. **il più** the majority. **il più possibile** as much as possible. **più volte** several times. **sempre più** ... more and more .... **tanto più** especially. **tutt'al più** at most.

**piuma** ['pjuma] sf feather. **piumino** sm down; (per cipria) powder-puff; (letto) eider-down, duvet.

**piuttosto** [pjut'tɔsto] avv rather.

**piviere** [pi'vjɛre] sm plover.

**pizzicare** [pittsi'kare] v pinch; (pungere) sting; (musica) pluck. **pizzico** sm, pl -**chi** pinch, dash. **pizzicore** sm itch. **pizzicotto** sm pinch.

**pizzo** ['pittso] sm (merletto) lace; (barba) goatee.

**placare** [pla'kare] v calm down, placate.

**placca** ['plakka] sf plate; (ornamento) plaque; (med) patch.

**placenta** [pla'tʃɛnta] sf placenta.

**placido** ['platʃido] agg placid.

**plagiare** [pla'dʒare] v plagiarize. **plagiario**, -**a** sm, sf plagiarist.

**planare** [pla'nare] v glide. **planata** sf glide.

**plasmare** [plaz'mare] v mould. **plasma** sm plasma.

**plastica** ['plastika] sf (arte) modelling; (med) plastic surgery; (materia) plastic. **plasticare** v model. **plastico** agg plastic.

**platano** ['platano] sm plane-tree.

**platea** [pla'tɛa] sf stalls pl.

**platino** ['platino] sm platinum.

**platonico** [pla'tɔniko] agg platonic.

**plausibile** [plau'zibile] agg plausible.

**plebe** ['plɛbe] sf plebs pl; (plebaglia) mob, riff-raff. **plebeo** agg plebeian; common.

**plebiscito** [plebi'ʃito] *sm* plebiscite.

**pleurite** [pleu'rite] *sf* pleurisy.

**plico** ['pliko] *sm* parcel.

**plotone** [plo'tone] *sm* platoon.

**plumbeo** ['plumbeo] *agg* leaden.

**plurale** [plu'rale] *agg, sm* plural.

**plutocratico** [pluto'kratiko] *agg* plutocratic. **plutocrate** *sm* plutocrat. **plutocrazia** *sf* plutocracy.

**pneumatico** [pneu'matiko] *sm* tyre. *agg* (*mec*) pneumatic; (*gonfiabile*) inflatable.

**po'** [po] *V* poco.

**pochino** [po'kino] *agg* not much or many. *avv, pron* very little or few. *sm* bit.

**poco** ['pɔko] *agg* little; (*tempo*) short. *avv* little, not very. *pron* little, not much. **a poco a poco** little by little. **da poco** unimportant. **fra poco** soon. **pochi** *pron, agg* few *pl*. **poco dopo** not long after. **poco fa** a short while ago. **poco male!** never mind! **un poco** or **po'** a little.

**podere** ['podere] *sm* estate.

**podestà** [podes'ta] *sm* mayor.

**podio** ['pɔdjo] *sm* platform.

**podismo** [po'dizmo] *sm* track events *pl*; (*corsa*) running. **podista** *s*(*m+f*) track athlete; runner.

**poema** [po'ɛma] *sm* poem.

**poi** ['pɔi] *avv* then; (*più tardi*) later. *sm* future. **da ... in poi** from ... onwards. **il senno di poi** hindsight.

**poiché** [pɔi'ke] *cong* as, since.

**polacco** [po'lakko], **-a** *agg* Polish. *sm, sf* Pole. *sm* (*lingua*) Polish.

**polarizzare** [polarid'dzare] *v* polarize. **polare** *agg* polar. **stella polare** *sf* pole star.

**polca** ['pɔlka] *sf* polka.

**polemica** [po'lɛmika] *sf* polemic; controversy. **polemico** *agg* contentious, polemical.

**polenta** [po'lɛnta] *sf* (*gastr*) maize porridge; (*fam: persona lenta*) slow-coach.

**policlinico** [poli'kliniko] *sm* hospital.

**poligamo** [po'ligamo], **-a** *agg* polygamous. *sm, sf* polygamist. **poligamia** *sf* polygamy.

**poligono** [po'ligono] *sm* polygon.

**polimero** [po'limero] *sm* polymer.

**polistirolo** [polisti'rɔlo] *sm* polystyrene.

**politecnico** [poli'tekniko] *sm* polytechnic.

**politene** [poli'tene] *sm* polythene.

**politico** [po'litiko] *agg* political. *sm* politician. **politica** *sf* politics; (*linea di con-*

*dotta*) policy.

**polizia** [poli'tsia] *sf* police. **poliziesco** *agg* police. **romanzo** or **film poliziesco** *sm* thriller. **poliziotto** *sm* policeman.

**polizza** ['pɔlittsa] *sf* policy; (*ricevuta*) voucher.

**pollame** [pol'lame] *sm* poultry. **pollaio** *sm* chicken coop. **pollastra** *sf* pullet; (*fam*) lass, chick. **pollastro** *sm* cockerel; (*fam*) gullible person, mug.

**pollice** ['pɔllitʃe] *sm* thumb; (*del piede*) big toe.

**polline** ['pɔlline] *sm* pollen.

**pollo** ['pollo] *sm* chicken. **far ridere i polli** be ridiculous.

**polmone** [pol'mone] *sm* lung. **polmonare** *agg* pulmonary. **polmonite** *sf* pneumonia.

**polo** ['pɔlo] *sm* pole. **essere ai poli opposti** be poles apart.

**Polonia** [po'lɔnja] *sf* Poland.

**polpa** ['polpa] *sf* flesh; (*carne*) meat; (*fig*) substance. **polpetta** *sf* meatball. **polposo** *agg* fleshy.

**polpaccio** [pol'pattʃo] *sm* (*anat*) calf.

**polso** ['polso] *sm* wrist; (*med*) pulse; (*polsino*) cuff.

**poltiglia** [pol'tiʎa] *sf* mush; mixture.

**poltrona** [pol'trona] *sf* easy chair, armchair; (*teatro*) stall.

**poltrone** [pol'trone], **-a** *sm, sf* idler, loafer.

**polvere** ['pɔlvere] *sf* dust; powder. **polveriera** *sf* powder-keg. **polverizzare** *v* pulverize. **polveroso** *agg* dusty.

**pomata** [po'mata] *sf* ointment.

**pomeriggio** [pome'riddʒo] *sm* afternoon. **pomeridiano** *agg* afternoon.

**pomice** ['pɔmitʃe] *sf* pumice-stone.

**pomo** ['pomo] *sm* (*frutto*) apple; (*albero*) apple-tree.

**pomodoro** [pomo'dɔro] *sm* tomato.

**pompa¹** ['pompa] *sf* pump. **pompa antincendio** fire-engine. **pompare** *v* pump (up).

**pompa²** ['pompa] *sf* pomp. **far pompa di** show off. **impresario di pompe funebri** *sm* undertaker. **pomposo** *agg* pompous.

**pompelmo** [pom'pɛlmo] *sm* grapefruit.

**pompiere** [pom'pjɛre] *sm* fireman.

**ponderare** [ponde'rare] *v* consider. **ponderato** *agg* careful. **ponderoso** *agg* ponderous.

**ponente** [po'nɛnte] *sm* west.

**ponte** ['ponte] *sm* bridge; (*impalcatura*) scaffolding. **ponte aereo** air-lift. **ponte radio** radio link. **ponte sospeso** suspension bridge.

**pontefice** [pon'tefitʃe] *sm* pontiff. **pontificare** *v* pontificate. **pontificio** *agg* papal.

**pontile** [pon'tile] *sm* pier; (*da sbarco*) landing stage.

**popolare** [popo'lare] *agg* popular; working-class; (*tradizionale*) folk. **casa popolare** *sf* council house. **v** populate. **popolarità** *sf* popularity. **popolarizzare** *v* popularize.

**popolo** ['pɔpolo] *sm* people; common people. **popolazione** *sf* population.

**popone** [po'pone] *sm* melon.

**poppa**[1] ['poppa] *sf* (*mar*) stern. **avere il vento in poppa** sail before the wind.

**poppa**[2] ['poppa] *sf* (*anat*) breast. **poppare** *v* suck.

**porcellana** [portʃel'lana] *sf* porcelain, china.

**porco** ['pɔrko] *sm, pl* **-ci** pig. *agg* (*volg*) bloody. **porcaio** *sm* pig-sty. **porcellino d'India** *sm* guinea-pig. **porcheria** *sf* muck, filth; (*cibo*) disgusting stuff; (*cosa malfatta*) rubbish. **porcospino** *sm* porcupine.

*****porgere** ['pɔrdʒere] *v* give, hand. **porgere aiuto** offer help.

**pornografia** [pornogra'fia] *sf* pornography. **pornografico** *agg* pornographic.

**poro** ['pɔro] *sm* pore. **poroso** *agg* porous.

**porpora** ['porpora] *agg invar, sf* purple.

*****porre** ['porre] *v* put; set, place. **porre in dubbio** question. **porre in evidenza** stress. **porre rimedio** set right.

**porro** ['pɔrro] *sm* leek.

**porta** ['pɔrta] *sf* door. **a porte chiuse** behind closed doors; (*dir*) in camera. **mettere alla porta** (*fig*) throw out. **porta di sicurezza** emergency exit.

**portabagagli** [portaba'ɡaʎi] *sm invar* luggage-rack; (*facchino*) porter.

**portabile** [por'tabile] *agg* portable.

**portacenere** [porta'tʃenere] *sm invar* ashtray.

**portachiavi** [porta'kjavi] *sm invar* keyring.

**portaerei** [porta'ɛrei] *sf* aircraft-carrier.

**portafinestra** [portafi'nɛstra] *sf, pl* **portefinestre** French window.

**portafoglio** [porta'fɔʎʎo] *sm* wallet; (*borsa*) briefcase; (*pol*) portfolio.

**portalettere** [porta'lettere] *sm invar* postman.

**portamonete** [portamo'nete] *sm invar* purse.

**portare** [por'tare] *v* bring; (*prendere*) take; (*trasportare*) carry; (*indossare*) wear; (*addurre*) put forward. **essere portato** have a gift (for). **portatore** *sm* carrier; (*comm*) bearer.

**portasapone** [portasa'pone] *sm invar* soap-dish.

**portasigarette** [portasiga'rette] *sm invar* cigarette-case.

**portaspilli** [porta'spilli] *sm invar* pincushion.

**portauovo** [portauovo] *sm invar* egg-cup.

**portavoce** [porta'votʃe] *sm invar* spokesman, mouthpiece.

**portento** [por'tɛnto] *sm* portent; (*persona*) prodigy.

**portico** ['pɔrtiko] *sm* arcade; (*di casa*) porch.

**portinaio** [porti'najo] **-a** *sm, sf* doorkeeper; caretaker. **portineria** *sf* caretaker's lodge.

**porto**[1] ['pɔrto] *sm* port, harbour.

**porto**[2] ['pɔrto] *sm* (*comm*) carriage. **porto d'armi** gun licence.

**porto**[3] ['pɔrto] *sm* (*vino*) port.

**Portogallo** [porto'gallo] *sm* Portugal. **portoghese** *agg*, *s(m+f)* Portuguese; *sm* (*lingua*) Portuguese. **fare il portoghese** gate-crash.

**portone** [por'tone] *sm* front door.

**porzione** [por'tsjone] *sf* portion, share.

**posa** ['poza] *sf* (*atteggiamento*) pose; (*foto*) exposure.

**posare** [po'zare] *v* put *or* lay down; rest; (*ritratto*) pose.

**poscritto** [pos'kritto] *sm* postscript.

**positivo** [pozi'tivo] *agg* positive; affirmative; practical. **positiva** *sf* (*foto*) positive.

**posizione** [pozi'tsjone] *sf* position.

*****posporre** [pos'porre] *v* postpone; (*mettere dopo*) place after. **posposizione** *sf* postponement.

*****possedere** [posse'dere] *v* possess, own. **possedimento** *sm* also **possesso** possession. **possessore** *sm* owner.

**possibile** [pos'sibile] *agg* possible. **fare il possibile** do one's best. **possibilità** *sf* possibility; (*capacità*) means. **possibilmente** *avv* if possible.

**posta¹** ['pɔsta] *sf* post, mail; (*ufficio*) post office. **a giro di posta** by return of post. **mettersi alla posta (di)** be on the lookout (for). **posta aerea** air mail. **postale** *agg* postal.

**posta²** ['pɔsta] *sf* (*gioco*) bet, stake.

**post-bellico** [post'bɛlliko] *agg* post-war.

**posteggiare** [posted'dʒare] *v* park. **posteggio** *sm* parking; (*spazio*) parking space.

**posteriore** [poste'rjore] *agg* back, rear; (*tempo*) later.

**posterità** [posteri'ta] *sf* posterity.

**posticcio** [pos'tittʃo] *agg* artificial. *sm* hairpiece.

**posticipare** [postitʃi'pare] *v* defer.

**postino** [pos'tino] *sm* postman.

**posto** ['pɔsto] *sm* (*luogo*) place; (*spazio*) room; (*impiego*) position; (*sedere*) seat. **essere a posto** be in order; (*star bene*) be well, be content. **mettere a posto** tidy up; repair. **sul posto** on the spot.

**postumo** ['pɔstumo] *agg* posthumous.

**potabile** [po'tabile] *agg* (*spreg*) drinkable. **acqua potabile** *sf* drinking water.

**potare** [po'tare] *v* prune.

**potassio** [po'tassjo] *sm* potassium. **potassa** *sf* potash.

**potente** [po'tɛnte] *agg* powerful; (*efficace*) potent; (*valido*) forceful. **potenza** *sf* power; (*forza*) strength; (*efficacia*) potency.

**potenziale** [poten'tsjale] *agg*, *sm* potential. **potenzialità** *sf* capacity.

**potenziare** [poten'tsjare] *v* strengthen, expand. **potenziamento** *sm* strengthening, expansion.

**\*potere¹** [po'tere] *v* can, be able; (*possibilità, permesso*) may. **non poterne più** (*essere sfinito*) be exhausted; (*essere al limite della sopportazione*) be unable to stand it any longer. **può darsi** maybe.

**potere²** [po'tere] *sm* power.

**povero** ['pɔvero], **-a** *agg* poor. *sm*, *sf* poor person. **povero di** lacking in. **povertà** *sf* poverty; (*scarsità*) want, lack.

**pozza** ['pɔtsa] *sf* pool. **pozzanghera** *sf* puddle.

**pozzo** ['pɔtso] *sm* well; (*cavità*) shaft. **pozzo nero** cesspool.

**pranzare** [pran'tsare] *v* have dinner; (*a mezzogiorno*) have lunch. **pranzo** *sm* dinner; lunch. **dopo pranzo** (*nel pomeriggio*) in the afternoon. **sala da pranzo** *sf* dining room.

**pratica** ['pratika] *sf* practice; experience; (*incartamento*) file. **praticante** *s(m+f)* apprentice; (*rel*) churchgoer. **praticare** *v* practise; (*fare*) make; frequent; associate (with).

**pratico** ['pratiko] *agg* practical; (*esperto*) skilled; (*funzionale*) useful, handy. **all'atto pratico** in practice. **essere pratico di** be familiar with.

**prato** ['prato] *sm* meadow; (*giardino*) lawn. **pratolina** *sf* daisy.

**preavvisare** [preavvi'zare] *v also* **preavvertire** inform in advance; (*ammonire*) warn. **preavviso** *sm* (advance) notice; warning.

**pre-bellico** [pre'bɛlliko] *agg* pre-war.

**precario** [pre'karjo] *agg* precarious.

**precauzione** [prekau'tsjone] *sf* (*cautela*) caution, care; (*provvedimento*) precaution. **precauzionale** *agg* precautionary.

**precedente** [pretʃe'dɛnte] *agg* previous, preceding, former. *sm* (*dir*) precedent. **precedenti (penali)** *sm pl* (criminal) record *sing*. **precedentemente** *avv* before. **precedenza** *sf* priority. **in precedenza** previously.

**precedere** [pre'tʃedere] *v* precede.

**precipitare** [pretʃipi'tare] *v* hurl (down); (*affrettare*) hasten; (*chim*) precipitate; (*cadere*) crash; (*piombare*) plunge. **precipitoso** *agg* hurried; (*fig*) rash.

**precipizio** [pretʃi'pitsjo] *sm* precipice.

**precisare** [pretʃi'zare] *v* specify; (*fam*) spell out. **precisazione** *sf* clarification. **precisione** *sf* precision. **preciso** *agg* precise, exact; identical.

**precoce** [pre'kɔtʃe] *agg* precocious; premature, untimely.

**preconcetto** [prekon'tʃetto] *sm* preconceived idea, prejudice.

**precursore** [prekur'sore] *sm* forerunner.

**preda** ['preda] *sf* prey; (*bottino*) booty. **essere in preda a** be struck by. **in preda alle fiamme** in flames. **predare** *v* plunder.

**predecessore** [predetʃes'sore] *sm* predecessor.

**predestinare** [predesti'nare] *v* preordain.

**predetto** [pre'detto] *agg* aforesaid.

**predica** ['prɛdika] *sf* sermon; (*ramanzina*) telling-off. **predicare** *v* preach.

**prediletto** [predi'lɛtto], **-a** *s*, *agg* favourite.

**\*predire** [pre'dire] *v* predict, foretell.

**\*predisporre** [predis'porre] v arrange (in advance); predispose.

**predominare** [predomi'nare] v prevail. **predominio** sm sway.

**prefabbricato** [prefabbri'kato] agg prefabricated.

**prefazione** [prefa'tsjone] sf preface, foreword.

**preferire** [prefe'rire] v prefer. **preferenza** sf preference. **preferibile** agg preferable.

**prefetto** [pre'fetto] sm prefect. **prefettura** sf prefecture.

**\*prefiggere** [pre'fiddʒere] v fix (in advance); (gramm) prefix. **prefiggersi** v resolve.

**prefisso** [pre'fisso] sm (gramm) prefix; (telefono) (area) code.

**pregare** [pre'gare] v pray. **prego** inter (per favore) please! (risposta) don't mention it!

**pregevole** [pre'dʒevole] agg valuable.

**preghiera** [pre'gjɛra] sf prayer; (domanda) request.

**pregiato** [pre'dʒato] agg valued. **pregio** sm regard; merit. **di nessun pregio** worthless.

**pregiudicare** [predʒudi'kare] v prejudice; (danneggiare) harm. **pregiudicato** sm exconvict.

**pregiudizio** [predʒu'ditsjo] sm prejudice, bias.

**pregustare** [pregus'tare] v look forward to.

**preistorico** [preis'tɔriko] agg prehistoric.

**prelato** [pre'lato] sm prelate.

**prelevare** [prele'vare] v withdraw.

**prelibato** [preli'bato] agg exquisite.

**preliminare** [prelimi'nare] agg preliminary. sm element.

**preludio** [pre'ludjo] sm prelude.

**prematuro** [prema'turo] agg premature.

**premeditato** [premedi'tato] agg premeditated.

**premere** ['prɛmere] v press. **mi preme (di) sapere** I am anxious to know.

**premiare** [pre'mjare] v award a prize to; (ricompensare) reward. **premio** sm prize; reward; (comm) premium.

**preminente** [premi'nente] agg pre-eminent.

**premura** [pre'mura] sf (fretta) haste; (riguardo) solicitude, attention. **fare premura a** hurry up. **farsi premura** take care. **pre-**

**muroso** agg thoughtful, solicitous.

**\*prendere** ['prɛndere] v take; (cogliere, subire, catturare) catch; (ricevere) receive; (ritirare) pick up; (occupare) take up; (assumere) take on; (ottenere) get. **andare a prendere** fetch. **prendere alla lettera** take literally. **prendere per il naso** mock. **prendere qualcuno per il bavero** pull someone's leg. **prendere un granchio** (fig) make a blunder. **prendersela** v take it amiss; (con qualcuno) get angry with; (a cuore) take it to heart.

**prenatale** [prena'tale] agg antenatal.

**prenotare** [preno'tare] v book, reserve. **prenotazione** sf booking, reservation.

**preoccupare** [preokku'pare] v worry. **preoccupazione** sf worry.

**preparare** [prepa'rare] v prepare; (tavola) lay; (letto) make. **preparare la strada** pave the way. **preparativo** sm arrangement. **preparazione** sf preparation.

**preposizione** [preposi'tsjone] sf preposition.

**prepotente** [prepo'tɛnte] agg overbearing. s(m+f) (fam) bully.

**prerequisito** [prerekwi'zito] sm prerequisite.

**prerogativa** [preroga'tiva] sf privilege.

**presa** ['preza] sf hold; (stretta) grasp; (elett) socket; (carte) trick; (cattura) capture. **cane da presa** sm retriever. **essere alle prese con** wrestle with. **far presa** set. **macchina da presa** sf cine-camera. **presa di posizione** taking sides. **presa in giro** leg-pull. **venire alle prese** come to grips.

**presbite** ['prɛzbite] agg long-sighted.

**prescindere** [pre'ʃindere] v **a prescindere da** apart from.

**\*prescrivere** [pre'skrivere] v prescribe. **prescrizione** sf ordinance. **prescrizione medica** doctor's orders pl; (ricetta) prescription.

**presentare** [prezen'tare] v present; (far conoscere) introduce; (mostrare) show; offer. **presentatore, -trice** sm, sf compere, question-master.

**presente** [pre'zɛnte] agg present; in the presence of; (questo) this. sm present. **i presenti** those present pl. **tener presente** keep in mind.

**presentimento** [presenti'mento] sm presentiment, foreboding.

**presenza** [pre'zɛntza] sf presence; appearance. **di presenza** personally. **fare atto di**

**presenza** put in an appearance. **presenziare (a)** v attend.

**preservare** [prezer'vare] v preserve; protect. **preservativo** sm preservative; (*guaina profilattica*) condom. **preservazione** sf preservation.

**preside** ['prɛzide] sm headmaster; (*di facoltà*) dean. sf headmistress.

**presidente** [prezi'dɛnte] sm president; (*di assemblea*) chairman. **presidente della camera** (pol) speaker. **presidente del Consiglio** (pol) Prime Minister. **presidenza** sf (pol) presidency; chairmanship. **assumere la presidenza** take the chair.

**presidio** [pre'zidjo] sm garrison; (*fig*) protection. **presidiare** v garrison; protect.

**\*presiedere** [pre'sjɛdere] v be in charge (of).

**pressa** ['prɛssa] sf press. **pressare** v press.

**pressappoco** [pressap'pɔko] avv about, roughly.

**pressione** [pres'sjone] sf pressure.

**presso** ['prɛsso] prep near; (*insieme a, fra*) with; (*accanto a*) by; (*indirizzo*) care of, c/o. avv nearby. **pressoché** avv almost.

**prestabilire** [prestabi'lire] v prearrange.

**prestare** [pres'tare] v lend. **prestare aiuto** help. **prestar fede** believe. **prestar giuramento** take an oath. **prestazione** sf (*rendimento*) performance. **prestazioni** sf pl services pl.

**prestigio** [pres'tidʒo] sm prestige. **gioco di prestigio** sm conjuring trick. **prestigiatore, -trice** sm, sf conjurer. **prestigioso** agg prestigious.

**prestito** ['prɛstito] sm loan. **dare in prestito** lend. **prendere in prestito** borrow.

**presto** ['prɛsto] avv (*tra poco*) soon; (*in fretta*) quickly; (*di buon'ora*) early. **si fa presto** (*facilmente*) it's easy.

**\*presumere** [pre'zumere] v imagine. **presunto** agg presumed; (*erede*) presumptive. **presuntuoso** agg presumptuous. **presunzione** sf presumption.

**presumibilmente** [prezumibil'mɛnte] avv presumably.

**\*presupporre** [presup'porre] v presuppose, assume; (*richiedere*) require. **presupposizione** sf assumption.

**prete** ['prɛte] sm priest.

**\*pretendere** [pre'tendere] v (*esigere, presumere*) expect; (*sostenere*) claim. **preten-**

**sioso** agg pretentious.

**pretesa** [pre'teza] sf claim; (*presunzione*) pretention. **aver poche/molte pretese** be easy/difficult to please.

**pretesto** [pre'testo] sm pretext; (*occasione*) opportunity.

**prettamente** [pretta'mente] avv typically.

**\*prevalere** [preva'lere] v prevail.

**\*prevedere** [preve'dere] v foresee; (*considerare*) provide for. **prevedibile** agg foreseeable.

**\*prevenire** [preve'nire] v (*precedere*) arrive before; (*fig*) anticipate; (*evitare*) avert; (*avvertire*) warn. **prevenuto** agg (*maldisposto*) biased.

**preventivo** [preven'tivo] agg precautionary; (*dir*) preventive. sm estimate. **preventivare** v estimate. **prevenzione** sf (*preconcetto*) bias; (*provvedimento*) prevention.

**previdente** [previ'dɛnte] agg far-sighted, provident. **previdenza** sf foresight. **previdenza sociale** social security.

**previo** ['prɛvjo] agg prior.

**previsione** [previ'zjone] sf forecast; (*aspettativa*) anticipation; (*comm*) estimate. **previsto** agg foreseen; (*dir*) provided for. **meno/più del previsto** less/more than anticipated.

**prezioso** [pre'tsjozo] agg precious, valuable.

**prezzemolo** [pret'tsemolo] sm parsley.

**prezzo** ['prettso] sm price; (*tariffa*) rate; (*trasporto pubblico*) fare. **a buon prezzo** cheaply.

**prigione** [pri'dʒone] sf prison, jail. **prigionia** sf captivity. **prigioniero, -a** sm, sf prisoner.

**prima** ['prima] avv (*in anticipo*) first, in advance; (*precedentemente*) before; (*più presto*) earlier; (*una volta*) once; (*in primo luogo*) first. sf (*teatro*) première; (*auto*) first gear; (*treno*) first class.

**primario** [pri'marjo] agg primary. sm (*med*) consultant.

**primato** [pri'mato] sm supremacy; record.

**primavera** [prima'vera] sf spring. **primaverile** agg spring.

**primitivo** [primi'tivo] agg primitive; original.

**primizia** [pri'mitsja] sf early produce; (*notizia*) latest news.

**primo** ['primo] *agg* first; (*precedente*) former; (*principale*) main. **per primo** first.

**primula** ['primula] *sf* primrose.

**principale** [printʃi'pale] *agg* principal, main. *sm* principal; (*fam*) boss.

**principe** ['printʃipe] *sm* prince. **principato** *sm* principality. **principesco** *agg* princely. **principessa** *sf* princess.

**principio** [prin'tʃipjo] *sm* beginning; (*fondamento*) principle; origin. **da** *or* **in principio** at first. **per principio** on principle.

**priorità** [priori'ta] *sf* priority.

**prisma** ['prizma] *sm* prism.

**privare** [pri'vare] *v* deprive.

**privato** [pri'vato], **-a** *agg* private; personal. *sm*, *sf* private citizen. **privatista** *s(m+f)* (*scolaro*) private school pupil; (*candidato*) external student. **privativa** *sf* monopoly. **privazione** *sf* privation, loss.

**privilegio** [privi'ledʒo] *sm* privilege. **privilegiato** *agg* privileged.

**privo** ['privo] *agg* devoid (of), without. **privo di denaro** penniless. **privo di sensi** (*svenuto*) unconscious.

**probabile** [pro'babile] *agg* probable, likely. **poco probabile** unlikely. **probabilità** *sf* probability, likelihood; (*possibilità*) chance.

**problema** [pro'blɛma] *sm* problem. **problematico** *agg* problematic; doubtful.

**proboscide** [pro'boʃide] *sf* trunk.

**procedere** [pro'tʃɛdere] *v* proceed; (*comportarsi*) behave. **procedimento** *sm* (*svolgimento*) course; (*tec*) process; (*dir*) proceedings *pl*.

**processione** [protʃes'sjone] *sf* procession.

**processo** [pro'tʃesso] *sm* process; (*dir*) trial, lawsuit. **essere sotto processo** be on trial. **processo verbale** minutes *pl*.

**procinto** [pro'tʃinto] *sm* **essere in procinto di** be on the point of, be about to.

**proclamare** [prokla'mare] *v* proclaim. **proclamazione** *sf* proclamation.

**proclive** [pro'klive] *agg* prone (to).

**procreare** [prokre'are] *v* procreate. **procreazione** *sf* procreation.

**procurare** [proku'rare] *v* get; (*dare, causare*) give. **procura** *sf* power of attorney. **per procura** by proxy. **procuratore** *sm* proxy; (*magistrato*) attorney; (*comm*) agent.

**proda** ['prɔda] *sf* bank.

**prode** ['prɔde] *agg* valiant.

**prodigare** [prodi'gare] *v* lavish. **prodigo**

*agg, m pl* **-ghi** prodigal, lavish.

**prodigio** [pro'didʒo] *sm* prodigy. **prodigioso** *agg* wonderful, marvellous.

**prodotto** [pro'dotto] *sm* product; (*alimentare*) foodstuff; (*chimico*) chemical.

**\*produrre** [pro'durre] *v* produce; cause; (*mostrare*) show; (*fare*) make. **produrre un testimone** call a witness. **produttivo** *agg* productive. **produttività** *sf* productivity. **produttore** *sm* producer. **produzione** *sf* production; (*fabbricazione*) manufacture; (*quantità*) output.

**profanare** [profa'nare] *v* desecrate; (*contaminare*) debase. **profano** *agg* profane; (*empio*) sacrilegious; (*inesperto*) ignorant.

**\*proferire** [profe'rire] *v* utter, pronounce.

**professare** [profes'sare] *v* profess. **professionale** *agg* professional; vocational; (*connesso alla professione*) occupational. **professione** *sf* profession; (*mestiere*) trade. **di professione** by profession. **professionista** *s(m+f)* professional (person).

**professore** [profes'sore], **-essa** *sm*, *sf* teacher. **professore titolare/incaricato** university professor/lecturer.

**profeta** [pro'fɛta] *sm* prophet. **profetico** *agg* prophetic. **profezia** *sf* prophecy.

**proficuo** [pro'fikuo] *agg* useful.

**profilo** [pro'filo] *sm* profile; (*contorno*) outline. **profilare** *v* outline; (*mec*) profile. **profilato** *sm* (*mec*) section.

**profittare** [profit'tare] *v* profit; (*approfittare*) take advantage; (*progredire*) make progress. **profittatore** *sm* profiteer. **profitto** *sm* profit; advantage. **trarre profitto** benefit.

**profondo** [pro'fondo] *agg* deep; (*radicato*) deep-rooted. *sm* depth. **profondare** *v* sink. **profondità** *sf* depth.

**profugo** ['prɔfugo], **-a** *sm, pl* **-ghi**, *sf* refugee.

**profumare** [profu'mare] *v* perfume. **profumato** *agg* perfumed; fragrant. **profumeria** *sf* perfumery. **profumo** *sm* fragrance, scent.

**profusione** [profu'zjone] *sf* profusion.

**progettare** [prodʒet'tare] *v* plan; (*tec*) design. **progettazione** *sf* planning. **progetto** *sm* project, plan. **progetto di legge** bill. **progetto di massima** preliminary plan.

**prognosi** ['prɔɲozi] *sf* prognosis.

**programma** [pro'gramma] *sm* programme; prospectus; (*scuola*) syllabus. **program-**

**mare** v programme. **programmatore, -trice** sm, sf programmer. **programmazione** sf programming.

**progredire** [progre'dire] v make progress, get on. **progressione** sf progression. **progressivo** agg progressive. **progresso** sm progress. **fare progressi** improve, make progress.

**proibire** [proi'bire] v forbid, prohibit. **proibito** agg forbidden. **proibizionismo** sm prohibition.

**proiettare** [projet'tare] v project; (gettar fuori) eject; (cine) screen. **proiettile** sm projectile; (mil) shell. **a prova di proiettile** bullet-proof. **proiettore** sm projector.

**prole** ['prɔle] sf offspring.

**proletario** [prole'tarjo], **-a** s, agg proletarian. **proletariato** sm proletariat.

**prolifico** [pro'lifiko] agg prolific.

**prolisso** [pro'lisso] agg long-winded.

**prologo** ['prɔlogo] sm, pl **-ghi** prologue.

**prolungare** [prolun'gare] v extend; (tempo) prolong; (spazio) lengthen. **prolungarsi** v (dilungarsi) dwell (on). **prolunga** sf extension. **prolungamento** sm extension.

**promemoria** [prome'mɔrja] sm invar memorandum.

***promettere** [pro'mettere] v promise. **promessa** sf promise. **promesso** agg promised. **promettente** agg promising.

**prominente** [promi'nente] agg prominent, jutting (out). **prominenza** sf prominence, projection.

**promiscuo** [pro'miskuo] agg mixed; (scuola) co-educational; (relazioni) promiscuous.

**promontorio** [promon'tɔrjo] sm headland.

**promozione** [promo'tsjone] sf promotion.

***promuovere** [pro'mwɔvere] v promote; provoke.

**pronome** [pro'nome] sm pronoun.

**pronosticare** [pronosti'kare] v forecast. **pronostico** sm forecast.

**pronto** ['pronto] agg ready; (rapido) prompt; (vivace) lively. **inter** (telefono) hello!

**prontuario** [prontu'arjo] sm handbook.

**pronunciare** [pronun'tʃare] v pronounce. **pronunciarsi a favore di** declare oneself in favour of. **pronuncia** sf pronunciation.

**propaganda** [propa'ganda] sf propaganda. **propagandista** s(m+f) propagandist.

**propagare** [propa'gare] v propagate.

**propenso** [pro'penso] agg inclined; favourable.

**propizio** [pro'pitsjo] agg propitious; favourable.

**proponimento** [proponi'mento] sm resolution.

***proporre** [pro'porre] v propose; intend; suggest.

**proporzione** [propor'tsjone] sf proportion; (mat) ratio. **in proporzione a** compared with. **proporzionale** agg proportional.

**proposito** [pro'pɔzito] sm purpose; intention; (scopo) aim; (progetto) plan. **a proposito** (opportunamente) at the right time; (inter) by the way; (opportuno) to the point. **a proposito di** with regard to. **cambiare proposito** change one's mind.

**proposizione** [propozi'tsjone] sf proposition; clause.

**proposta** [pro'posta] sf proposal.

**proprietà** [proprje'ta] sf property; (precisione, decoro) propriety; (possesso) ownership. **essere di proprietà di** belong to. **proprietà letteraria** copyright.

**proprio** ['prɔprjo] agg one's (own); (mat, gramm) proper, characteristic. **avv** exactly, just; (veramente) really.

**propulsione** [propul'sjone] sf propulsion.

**prora** ['prɔra] sf prow.

**prorogare** [proro'gare] v (rinviare) put off, adjourn; (prolungare) extend. **proroga** sf adjournment; extension.

***prorompere** [pro'rompere] v burst out.

**prosa** ['prɔza] sf prose; theatre. **prosaico** agg prosaic.

**prosciugare** [proʃu'gare] v drain.

**prosciutto** [pro'ʃutto] sm ham.

***proscrivere** [pro'skrivere] v proscribe.

**proseguire** [prose'gwire] v continue, go on. **proseguimento** sm continuation.

**prosperare** [prospe'rare] v prosper, thrive. **prosperità** sf prosperity. **prospero** agg prosperous, thriving.

**prospettiva** [prospet'tiva] sf (tec) perspective; (previsione) prospect, outlook. **prospettare** v (esporre) show; (guardare) look out (on). **prospettarsi** v (essere in vista) be in sight.

**prospetto** [pros'petto] sm (tabella) list; (pubblicità) prospectus.

**prossimo** ['prɔssimo] agg near; (seguente) next; (vicino nel futuro, stretto) close. **pas-**

**sato/trapassato prossimo** *sm* (*gramm*) present/past perfect. **prossimità** *sf* proximity.

**prostituire** [prostitu'ire] *v* prostitute. **prostituta** *sf* prostitute. **prostituzione** *sf* prostitution.

**protagonista** [protago'nista] *s(m+f)* protagonist, chief character.

***proteggere** [pro'teddʒere] *v* protect, shelter; favour.

**proteina** [prote'ina] *sf* protein.

**protesi** ['prɔtezi] *sf* prosthesis.

**protesta** [pro'tɛsta] *sf* protest. **protestare** *v* protest; (*dichiarare*) declare. **protesto** *sm* protest.

**protestante** [protes'tante] *s(m+f)*, *agg* Protestant.

**protetto** [pro'tɛtto], **-a** *agg* protected; favourite. *sm*, *sf* protégé; favourite. **protettorato** *sm* protectorate. **protettore** *sm* protector, defender. **santo protettore** patron saint.

**protezione** [prote'tsjone] *sf* protection; (*mecenatismo*) patronage. **protezione antincendio** fireproofing.

**protocollo** [proto'kɔllo] *sm* protocol; register. **carta protocollo** *sf* foolscap (paper).

**protone** [pro'tone] *sm* proton.

**prototipo** [pro'tɔtipo] *sm* prototype.

***protrarre** [pro'trarre] *v* protract; (*prorogare*) put off.

**prova** ['prɔva] *sf* proof; evidence; (*esame, testimonianza*) test; (*cimento*) trial; (*tentativo*) try; (*sarto*) fitting; (*teatro*) rehearsal. **a prova di acqua** waterproof. **a prova di fuoco** fireproof. **dar buona prova di sè** give a good account of oneself. **reggere alla prova** stand the test.

**provare** [pro'vare] *v* try (out); (*collaudare*) test; (*spettacolo*) rehearse; (*assaggiare*) taste; (*dimostrare*) prove; (*mettere alla prova*) put to the test; (*abito, ecc.*) try on.

***provenire** [prove'nire] *v* come (from); (*fig*) spring (from), be caused (by). **provenienza** *sf* origin, source.

**proverbio** [pro'vɛrbjo] *sm* proverb, saying. **proverbiale** *agg* proverbial.

**provetta** [pro'vetta] *sf* test-tube.

**provincia** [pro'vintʃa] *sf* province. **di provincia** provincial.

**provocare** [provo'kare] *v* provoke, cause. **provocatorio** *agg* provocative. **provo-** cazione *sf* provocation.

***provvedere** [provve'dere] *v* make provision for, provide for; (*prendere provvedimenti*) take steps; (*badare a*) see to; (*procurare*) provide. **provvedimento** *sm* step, measure. **provveditore** *sm* administrator; (*agli studi*) education officer.

**provvidenza** [provvi'dentsa] *sf* providence; (*fam*) godsend. **provvidenziale** *agg* providential.

**provvigione** [provvi'dʒone] *sf* commission.

**provvisorio** [provvi'zɔrjo] *agg* provisional.

**provvista** [provv'vista] *sf* provisions *pl*, stock. **provvisto** *agg* supplied, provided.

**prua** ['prua] *sf* prow.

**prudente** [pru'dɛnte] *agg* prudent, careful, cautious. **prudenza** *sf* care, caution.

***prudere** ['prudere] *v* itch. **prurito** *sm* itch.

**prugna** ['pruɲa] *sf* plum; (*secca*) prune. **prugno** *sm* plum-tree.

**pseudonimo** [pseu'dɔnimo] *sm* pseudonym.

**psicanalisi** [psica'nalizi] *sf* psycho-analysis. **psicanalista** *s(m+f)* psycho-analyst. **psicanalitico** *agg* psycho-analytical.

**psichiatra** [psi'kjatra] *s(m+f)* psychiatrist. **psichiatria** *sf* psychiatry.

**psichico** ['psikiko] *agg* psychic.

**psicologo** [psi'kɔlogo], **-a** *sm* psychologist. **psicologia** *sf* psychology. **psicologico** *agg* psychological.

**psicopatico** [psiko'patiko], **-a** *agg* psychopathic. *sm*, *sf* psychopath.

**psicosi** [psi'kɔzi] *sf* psychosis. **psicotico, -a** *s*, *agg* psychotic.

**psicosomatico** [psikoso'matiko] *agg* psychosomatic.

**psicoterapia** [psikotera'pia] *sf* psychotherapy. **psicoterapista** *s(m+f)* psychotherapist.

**pubblicare** [pubbli'kare] *v* publish. **pubblicazione** *sf* publication, issue. **pubblicista** *s(m+f)* (freelance) journalist.

**pubblicità** [pubblitʃi'ta] *sf* publicity; advertising. **fare pubblicità** advertise. **piccola pubblicità** classified advertisements *pl*. **pubblicitario** *agg* advertising, publicity.

**pubblico** ['pubbliko] *agg* public. *sm* public; (*teatro*) audience.

**pubertà** [puber'ta] *sf* puberty.

**pudico** [pu'diko] *agg*, *m pl* **-chi** modest; (*vergognoso*) bashful.

**pudore** [pu'dore] *sm* modesty; *(vergogna)* shame. **oltraggio al pudore** *sm* indecent behaviour. **senza pudore** shameless.

**puerile** [pue'rile] *agg* puerile.

**pugilato** [pudʒi'lato] *sm* boxing. **fare del pugilato** box. **pugile** *sm* boxer. **pugilistico** *agg* boxing.

**pugnalare** [puɲa'lare] *v* stab. **pugnalata** *sf* stab. **pugnale** *sm* dagger.

**pugno** ['puɲo] *sm* fist; *(colpo)* punch; *(piccola quantità)* fistful. **essere un pugno in un occhio** be an eyesore. **fare a pugni** fight; *(fig)* clash. **prendere a pugni** punch, **tenere in pugno** clutch; *(fig)* control.

**pulce** ['pultʃe] *sf* flea. **gioco della pulce** *sm* tiddly-winks.

**pulcino** [pul'tʃino] *sm* chick. **bagnato come un pulcino** wet through.

**puledro** [pu'ledro] *sm* colt. **puledra** *sf* filly.

**puleggia** [pu'leddʒa] *sf* pulley.

**pulire** [pu'lire] *v* clean; *(lavando)* wash; *(con strofinaccio, ecc.)* wipe (clean); *(con spazzola)* brush; *(sfregando)* scour; *(lucidare)* polish. **pulirsi il naso** blow one's nose. **pulito** *agg* clean.

**pulizia** [puli'tsia] *sf (il pulire)* cleaning; *(l'essere pulito)* cleanliness. **far le pulizie** do the cleaning. **far pulizia** clean; *(sgombrare)* clear out.

**pullman** ['pullman] *sm invar* coach.

**pullover** [pul'lɔver] *sm invar* pullover.

**pullulare** [pullu'lare] *v* swarm.

**pulpito** ['pulpito] *sm* pulpit. **montare in pulpito** preach.

**pulsare** [pul'sare] *v* throb, beat. **pulsante** *sm* button; *(campanello)* buzzer.

**\*pungere** ['pundʒere] *v* sting; *(morsicare)* bite; *(con spillo)* prick. **pungente** *agg* pungent; *(fig)* sharp; *(ispido)* prickly.

**pungiglione** *sm* sting. **pungolo** *sm* goad.

**punire** [pu'nire] *v* punish. **punibile** *agg* punishable. **punitivo** *agg* punitive. **punizione** *sf* punishment; *(sport)* penalty.

**punta** ['punta] *sf* point; *(estremità)* tip. **ora di punta** *sf* rush hour. **prendere di punta** clash (with).

**puntare** [pun'tare] *v* point, direct; *(scommettere)* bet.

**puntata** [pun'tata] *sf (scritto)* instalment, part.

**punteggiare** [punted'dʒare] *v* punctuate. **punteggiatura** *sf* punctuation.

**punteggio** [pun'teddʒo] *sm* score.

**puntellare** [puntel'lare] *v* prop up. **puntello** *sm* prop; *(fig)* support.

**puntiglioso** [puntiʎozo] *agg* stubborn. **puntiglio** *sm* stubbornness.

**puntina** [pun'tina] *sf (da disegno)* drawing pin; *(grammofono)* stylus.

**punto** ['punto] *sm* point; *(segno)* dot; *(med, ricamo, maglia)* stitch. *avv (affatto)* at all. **di punto in bianco** point-blank. **due punti** colon. **in punto** *(tempo)* on the dot, sharp. **mettere a punto** put right; *(auto)* tune; *(fig)* clarify. **punto esclamativo/interrogativo** exclamation/question mark. **punto e virgola** semicolon. **punto fermo** full stop.

**puntuale** [puntu'ale] *agg* punctual, on time.

**puntualizzare** [puntualid'dzare] *v* define, precisely.

**puntura** [pun'tura] *sf* sting, bite; *(di spillo, ecc.)* prick; *(med)* injection, puncture; *(dolore)* stitch.

**punzecchiare** [pundzek'kjare] *v* sting, bite, prick; *(stuzzicare)* tease.

**punzonare** [puntso'nare] *v* punch. **punzonatrice** *sf* punch. **punzone** *sm* punch, die.

**pupa** ['pupa] *sf (fam)* baby; *(bambola)* doll. **pupattola** *sf* doll. **pupazzo** *sm* puppet. **pupo** *sm (fam)* baby, little boy.

**pupilla** [pu'pilla] *sf* pupil.

**purché** [pur'ke] *cong* provided that, as long as.

**pure** ['pure] *avv* also, too. *cong* even (though); *(tuttavia)* yet.

**purè** [pu're] *sm invar* purée. **purè di patate** mashed potatoes *pl.*

**purgare** [pur'gare] *v* purge; purify. **purga** *sf* purge; *(il purgare)* purging, cleansing; *(purgante)* laxative; *(gastr)* soaking.

**purgatorio** [purga'tɔrjo] *sm* purgatory.

**purificare** [purifi'kare] *v* purify.

**puritano** [puri'tano], **-a** *s, agg* puritan.

**puro** ['puro] *agg* pure. **purezza** *sf* purity. **purosangue** *sm, agg invar* throughbred.

**purpureo** [pur'pureo] *agg* purple.

**purtroppo** [pur'trɔppo] *avv* unfortunately.

**pus** [pus] *sm invar* pus.

**\*putrefare** [putre'fare] *v* putrefy, rot. **putrefatto** *or* **putrido** *agg* putrid, rotten.

**puttana** [put'tana] *sf* whore; *(fam)* tart.

**puzzare** [put'tsare] *v* stink, smell. **puzzo** *sm* stench, smell. **puzzolente** *agg* stinking.

# Q

**qua** [kwa] *avv* here. **(al) di qua di** on this side of. **di qua** (*stato in luogo*) here; (*moto a luogo*) over here; (*da qui*) from here. **fin qua** (*spazio*) up to here; (*tempo*) so far. **per di qua** this way. **qua sopra/sotto/vicino** up/down/near here.

**quacchero** ['kwakkero], -a *sm, sf* Quaker.

**quaderno** [kwa'dɛrno] *sm* exercise-book.

**quadrante** [kwa'drante] *sm* (*mat, astron*) quadrant; (*orologio*) dial; (*solare*) sundial.

**quadrato** [kwa'drato] *agg* square; (*assenato*) level-headed. *sm* square. **quadrare** *v* square; (*star bene*) fit, suit; (*garbare*) please.

**quadretto** [kwa'dretto] *sm* small square; (*fig*) scene. **a quadretti** check(ed), chequered.

**quadrifoglio** [kwadri'fɔʎʎo] *sm* four-leafed clover; (*autostrada*) clover-leaf.

**quadro¹** ['kwadro] *agg* square.

**quadro²** ['kwadro] *sm* (*dipinto*) picture; (*ambito*) scope; (*tabella*) table. **quadri** *sm pl* (*carte*) diamonds *pl*. **a quadri** check(ed), chequered.

**quadrupede** [kwa'drupede] *agg, sm* quadruped.

**quaggiù** [kwad'dʒu] *avv* down here.

**quaglia** ['kwaʎa] *sf* quail.

**qualche** ['kwalke] *agg* some, any; (*alcuni*) a few. **in qualche luogo** somewhere. **in qualche modo** somehow. **qualcosa** *pron also* **qualche cosa** something, anything. **qualcuno** *pron* somebody, anybody.

**quale** ['kwale] *agg, pron* what; (*fra numero limitato*) which; (*come*) as. **tale e quale** just like. *inter* what! *avv* as.

**qualificare** [kwalifi'kare] *v* qualify. **qualifica** *sf* title; position; (*doti professionali*) qualification; (*giudizio*) report. **qualificativo** *agg* qualifying. **qualificato** *agg* skilled.

**qualità** [kwali'ta] *sf* quality; (*specie*) sort, kind. **qualitativo** *agg* qualitative.

**qualora** [kwa'lora] *cong* in case.

**qualunque** [kwa'lunkwe] *agg invar also* **qualsiasi** any; (*ogni*) every; (*non importa quale*) whatever, whichever. **l'uomo qualunque** the man in the street.

**quando** ['kwando] *avv* when. *cong* when; (*ogniqualvolta*) whenever; (*mentre*) whereas; (*giacché*) since. **da quando** (*dacché*) (*ever*) since; (*da quanto tempo*) since when. **di quando in quando** from time to time. **fino a quando** until; (*interrogativo*) until when; (*per quanto tempo*) how long.

**quantità** [kwanti'ta] *sf* quantity. **quantitativo** *sm* amount.

**quanto** ['kwanto] *agg* how much *or* many; (*esclamativo*) what (a lot of); (*relativo*) as much *or* many … as. *pron* how much *or* many; as much *or* many; (*quello che*) what. *avv* how (much *or* many); (*tempo*) how long; (*distanza*) how far; (*come*) as; (*nella misura che*) as much as. **da quanto** (*tempo*) how long; (*per ciò che*) as far as. **per quanto** however; (*per ciò che*) as far as. **quanto a** as for. **quanto fa?** how much is it? **quanto mai** very much indeed. **quanto prima** soon. **quanto tempo** how long.

**quaranta** [kwa'ranta] *agg, sm* forty. **quarantena** *sf* quarantine. **quarantesimo** *sm, agg* fortieth.

**quaresima** [kwa'rezima] *sf* Lent.

**quarta** ['kwarta] *sf* (*auto*) fourth *or* top gear; (*musica*) fourth. **partire in quarta** (*fam*) be off like a shot.

**quartetto** [kwar'tetto] *sm* quartet.

**quartiere** [kwar'tjɛre] *sm* district, quarter. **quartieri bassi** slums *pl*.

**quarto** ['kwarto] *agg* fourth. *sm* quarter. **sono le due e/meno un quarto** it is a quarter past/to two.

**quarzo** ['kwartso] *sm* quartz.

**quasi** ['kwazi] *avv* nearly, almost; (*con valore negativo*) hardly. *cong* (*come se*) as if.

**quassù** [kwas'su] *avv* up here.

**quatto quatto** ['kwatto 'kwatto] *avv* very quickly.

**quattordici** [kwat'tɔrditʃi] *agg, sm* fourteen. **quattordicesimo** *agg, sm* fourteenth.

**quattrini** [kwat'trini] *sm pl* money *sing*; (*fam*) cash *sing*. **quattrini a palate** loads of money *sing*. **senza quattrini** penniless.

**quattro** ['kwattro] *sm, agg* four. **dirne quattro a qualcuno** give someone a piece of one's mind. **far quattro passi** go for a stroll. **farsi in quattro** go out of one's way.

**quegli** ['kweʎi] *V* **quello**.

**quei** ['kwei] *V* **quello**.

**quel** [kwel] *V* **quello**.

**quello** ['kwello] *agg* that (*pl* those). *pron* that (one) (*pl* those); (*lo stesso*) the same. **di quello che** than. **quello che** the one who (*pl* those who); (*ciò che*) what.

**quercia** ['kwertʃa] *sf* oak.

**querela** [kwe'rela] *sf* lawsuit, action. **presentare** *or* **sporgere querela** bring an action. **querelante** *s(m+f)* plaintiff.

**questionario** [kwestjo'narjo] *sm* questionnaire.

**questione** [kwes'tjone] *sf* question; (*affare*) matter; problem; (*disputa*) argument. **fare una questione** make an issue. **mettere in questione** question.

**questo** ['kwesto] *agg* this (*pl* these). *pron* this (one) (*pl* these). **con questo** (*con queste parole*) with these words; (*ciononostante*) in spite of this.

**questura** [kwes'tura] *sf* police station. **questore** *sm* police inspector.

**qui** ['kwi] *avv* here. **di qui** from here; (*moto a luogo*) here; (*tempo*) from now (on). **fin qui** up to here; (*tempo*) up to now.

**quietanza** [kwje'tantsa] *sf* receipt.

**quietare** [kwje'tare] *v* calm. **quiete** *sf* calm; (*assenza di moto*) rest.

**quindi** ['kwindi] *cong* so. *avv* afterwards.

**quindici** ['kwinditʃi] *agg, sm* fifteen. **quindici giorni** a fortnight. **quindicesimo** *agg, sm* fifteenth. **quindicinale** *sm* fortnightly.

**quinta** ['kwinta] *sf* (*teatro*) wing. **dietro le quinte** behind the scenes.

**quintessenza** [kwintes'sɛntsa] *sf* quintessence.

**quintetto** [kwin'tetto] *sm* quintet.

**quinto** ['kwinto] *sm, agg* fifth.

**quota** ['kwɔta] *sf* (*porzione*) share; (*altitudine*) height; (*livello*) level; (*econ*) quota. **quota zero** square one. **quotare** *v* appreciate; (*borsa*) quote. **quotazione** *sf* quotation.

**quotidiano** [kwoti'djano] *agg, sm* daily.

**quoziente** [kwo'tsjɛnte] *sm* quotient.

# R

**rabarbaro** [ra'barbaro] *sm* rhubarb.

**rabberciare** [rabber'tʃare] *v* patch, mend; (*scritto*) re-hash.

**rabbia** ['rabbja] *sf* fury, rage; (*idrofobia*) rabies. **che rabbia!** how infuriating! **fare rabbia a** make angry. **rabbioso** *agg* furious; (*idrofobo*) rabid.

**rabbino** [rab'bino] *sm* rabbi. **rabbinico** *agg* rabbinical.

**rabbonire** [rabbo'nire] *v* calm down, soothe.

**rabbrividire** [rabbrivi'dire] *v* shiver; (*fig*) shudder.

**rabbuffare** [rabbuf'fare] *v* (*scompigliare*) ruffle; (*sgridare*) scold. **rabbuffo** *sm* telling-off, scolding.

**rabbuiarsi** [rabbu'jarsi] *v* darken.

**raccapezzare** [rakkapet'tsare] *v* scrape together. **raccapezzarsi** *v* make out.

**raccapricciare** [rakkaprit'tʃare] *v* be horrified. **raccapricciante** *agg* horrifying.

**raccattare** [rakkat'tare] *v* pick up, collect.

**racchetta** [rak'ketta] *sf* racket; (*ping-pong*) bat.

**\*raccogliere** [rak'kɔʎere] *v* pick; (*riprendere da terra*) pick up; (*riunire*) collect; (*fare il raccolto*) gather, harvest. **raccoglimento** *sm* attention. **raccoglitore** *sm* (*cartella*) binder.

**raccolta** [rak'kɔlta] *sf* collecting; collection; (*agric*) harvesting. **fare la raccolta (di)** collect.

**raccolto** [rak'kɔlto] *agg* (*concentrato nei pensieri*) deep in thought; (*rannicchiato*) crouching. *sm* harvest, crop.

**raccomandare** [rakkoman'dare] *v* recommend; (*esortare*) urge. **mi raccomando!** please do! **raccomandarsi** a rely on. **(lettera) raccomandata** *sf* registered letter. **raccomandato, -a** *sm, sf* protégé. **raccomandazione** *sf* recommendation.

**raccomodare** [rakkomo'dare] *v* also **racconciare** repair, mend.

**raccontare** [rakkon'tare] *v* tell. **racconto** *sm* story, tale; (*resoconto*) account.

**raccorciare** [rakkor'tʃare] *v* shorten.

**raccordare** [rakkor'dare] *v* connect. **raccordo** *sm* connection; (*strada, ecc.*) junction.

**racimolare** [ratʃimo'lare] v scrape together.

**radar** ['radar] sm invar radar.

**raddolcire** [raddol'tʃire] v sweeten; (acqua) soften.

**raddoppiare** [raddop'pjare] v double; (fig) redouble.

**raddrizzare** [raddrit'tsare] v straighten; (elett) rectify. **raddrizzatore** sm rectifier.

**\*radere** ['radere] v (sbarbare) shave; (sfiorare) graze. **radere al suolo** raze to the ground.

**radiale** [ra'djale] agg radial.

**radiare** [ra'djare] v expel; (mil) cashier; cancel. **radiare dall'albo** strike off the register.

**radiatore** [radja'tore] sm radiator.

**radiazione[1]** [radja'tsjone] sf (fis) radiation.

**radiazione[2]** [radja'tsjone] sf expulsion; cancellation.

**radica** ['radika] sf briar.

**radicale** [radi'kale] agg radical. sm (chim) radical; (mat) root.

**radicare** [radi'kare] v (take) root. **radicato** agg deep-rooted.

**radicchio** [ra'dikkjo] sm chicory.

**radice** [ra'ditʃe] sf root. **mettere radici** take root. **radice quadrata/cubica** square/cube root.

**radio[1]** ['radjo] sm invar radium.

**radio[2]** ['radjo] sf invar radio. **giornale radio** sm news (broadcast). **segnale radio** sm time signal.

**radioattivo** [radjoat'tivo] agg radioactive. **radioattività** sf radioactivity.

**radiocontrollato** [radjokontrol'lato] agg radio-controlled.

**radiodiffusione** [radjodiffu'zjone] sf also **radiotrasmissione** broadcast. **radiodiffuso** agg broadcast.

**radiografare** [radjogra'fare] v X-ray. **radiografia** sf (immagine) X-ray; (procedimento) radiography.

**radiologo** [ra'djɔlogo], -a sm, pl -ghi, sf radiologist.

**rado** ['rado] agg sparse. **di rado** rarely. **radura** sf clearing.

**radunare** [radu'nare] v gather. **radunarsi** v assemble. **radunata** sf assembly, meeting. **raduno** sm meeting.

**rafano** ['rafano] sm radish.

**raffica** ['raffika] sf (vento) gust; (colpi) volley.

**raffigurare** [raffigu'rare] v represent.

**raffinare** [raffi'nare] v refine. **raffinatezza** sf refinement. **raffinazione** sf refining. **raffineria** sf refinery.

**rafforzare** [raffor'tsare] v reinforce.

**raffreddare** [raffred'dare] v cool. **raffreddarsi** v (diventar freddo) cool down; (fam: prendersi un raffreddore) catch a cold. **raffreddamento** sm cooling (down or off). **raffreddore** sm cold.

**raffrenare** [raffre'nare] v restrain.

**raffrontare** [raffron'tare] v compare. **raffronto** sm comparison.

**rafia** ['rafia] sf raffia.

**raganella** [raga'nɛlla] sf rattle.

**ragazza** [ra'gattsa] sf girl; (innamorata) girlfriend. **da ragazza** as a girl. **nome da ragazza** sm maiden name. **ragazza madre** unmarried mother.

**ragazzo** [ra'gattso] sm boy, lad; (fam) fellow, chap; (innamorato) boy-friend. **da ragazzo** as a boy. **fin da ragazzo** since childhood.

**raggiare** [rad'dʒare] v radiate.

**raggio** ['raddʒo] sm ray; (geom) radius; (ambito) range; (ruota) spoke. **raggio d'azione** range; (fig) scope. **fare i raggi** X-ray.

**raggirare** [raddʒi'rare] v trick. **raggiro** sm trick.

**\*raggiungere** [rad'dʒundʒere] v reach; (riunirsi) join; (allinearsi) catch up (with); (conseguire) attain. **raggiungibile** agg within reach; attainable.

**raggiustare** [raddʒus'tare] v mend; (fig) set right.

**raggomitolare** [raggomito'lare] v roll up. **raggomitolarsi** v curl up.

**raggrinzare** [raggrin'tsare] v also **raggrinzire** wrinkle, crease.

**raggrumare** [raggru'mare] v clot.

**raggruppare** [raggrup'pare] v group (together). **raggrupparsi** v assemble. **raggruppamento** sm grouping; (gruppo) group; (mil) unit.

**ragguagliare** [raggwa'ʎare] v level; (paragonare) compare; inform; (mat) convert. **ragguaglio** sm comparison; information; (resoconto) report; conversion.

**ragia** ['radʒa] sf **acqua ragia** sf turpentine.

**ragionare** [radʒo'nare] v reason; discuss. **ragionamento** sm reasoning; discussion.

**ragione** [ra'dʒone] *sf* reason; (*diritto*) right; (*rapporto*) rate; (*spiegazione*) account; (*mat*) ratio. **a ragione** rightly. **a ragion veduta** after due consideration. **aver ragione** be right. **dar ragione a qualcuno** admit that someone is right. **rendersi ragione (di)** account (for).

**ragioneria** [radʒone'ria] *sf* accountancy. **ragioniere, -a** *sm, sf* accountant.

**ragionevole** [radʒo'nevole] *agg* reasonable.

**ragliare** [ra'ʎare] *v* bray. **raglio** *sm* bray.

**ragno** ['raɲo] *sm* spider. **ragnatela** *sf* cobweb.

**ragù** [ra'gu] *sm* meat sauce.

**raid** ['reid] *sm invar* (*mil*) raid; (*sport*) rally.

**raion** ['rajon] *sm invar* rayon.

**rallegrare** [ralleg'rare] *v* cheer up. **rallegrarsi** *v* be delighted; congratulate. **rallegramenti** *sm pl* congratulations *pl*.

**rallentare** [rallen'tare] *v* slacken, slow down. **rallentamento** *sm* slackening, slowing down.

**rame** ['rame] *sm* copper. **ramaiolo** *sm* ladle.

**ramengo** [ra'mengo] *sm* **andare a ramengo** (*fam*) go to the dogs.

**ramificare** [ramifi'kare] *v* ramify. **ramificazione** *sf* ramification.

**ramino** [ra'mino] *sm* rummy.

**rammaricarsi** [rammari'karsi] *v* regret; (*lamentarsi*) complain. **rammarico** *sm, pl* **-chi** regret.

**rammendare** [rammen'dare] *v* darn. **rammendo** *sm* (*atto*) darning; (*parte rammendata*) darn.

**rammentare** [rammen'tare] *v* (*ricordare*) recall; (*richiamare alla memoria*) call to mind.

**rammollire** [rammol'lire] *v* soften. **rammollito** *agg* soft; (*rimbambito*) doddering.

**ramo** ['ramo] *sm* branch. **ramoscello** *sm* twig.

**rampa** ['rampa] *sf* ramp; (*scala*) flight. **rampante** *agg* rampant.

**rampicante** [rampi'kante] *agg* climbing. *sm* (*pianta*) creeper.

**rampino** [ram'pino] *sm* hook.

**rampollo** [ram'pɔllo] *sm* offspring; (*pianta*) shoot; (*acqua*) spring.

**rampone** [ram'pone] *sm* (*pesca*) harpoon; (*alpinismo*) crampon.

**rana** ['rana] *sf* frog; (*nuoto a rana*) breaststroke. **uomo rana** *sm* frogman.

**rancido** ['rantʃido] *agg* rancid.

**rancio** ['rantʃo] *sm* meal.

**rancore** [ran'kore] *sm* grudge.

**randagio** [ran'dadʒo] *agg* stray.

**randello** [ran'dɛllo] *sm* club.

**rango** ['rango] *sm* rank; (*posizione sociale*) standing.

**rannicchiarsi** [rannik'kjarsi] *v* crouch, huddle.

**rannuvolarsi** [rannuvo'larsi] *v* cloud over; (*fig*) darken.

**ranocchio** [ra'nokkjo] *sm* frog.

**rantolare** [ranto'lare] *v* wheeze.

**ranuncolo** [ra'nunkolo] *sm* buttercup.

**rapa** ['rapa] *sf* turnip.

**rapace** [ra'patʃe] *agg* rapacious. **uccello rapace** *sm* bird of prey.

**rapare** [ra'pare] *v* crop.

**rapido** ['rapido] *agg* quick, rapid. *sm* express (train).

**rapina** [ra'pina] *sf* robbery. **rapinare** *v* rob.

**rapire** [ra'pire] *v* (*rapinare*) rob; (*persone*) kidnap, abduct; (*estasiare*) enrapture. **rapimento** *sm* kidnapping; (*estasi*) rapture.

**rappezzare** [rappet'tsare] *v* patch.

**rapporto** [rap'porto] *sm* (*legame*) connection; relationship; (*resoconto*) report; (*mec, mat*) ratio.

***rapprendersi** [rap'prendersi] *v* coagulate; (*latte*) curdle.

**rappresaglia** [rappre'zaʎa] *sf* reprisal.

**rappresentare** [rappresen'tare] *v* represent; (*significare*) mean; (*teatro*) show. **rappresentante** *s(m+f)* representative, agent. **rappresentanza** *sf* agency. **rappresentativo** *agg* representative. **rappresentazione** *sf* representation; description; (*teatro, cine*) performance.

**raro** ['raro] *agg* rare; exceptional. **rarità** *sf* rarity.

**rasare** [ra'zare] *v* shave; (*erba, ecc.*) cut. **rasoio** *sm* razor.

**raschiare** [ras'kjare] *v* scrape; (*cancellare*) scratch out. **raschiatura** *sf* scratching; scratch. **raschietto** *sm* scraper.

**rasentare** [razen'tare] *v* go close (to); (*fig*) come close (to).

**raso** ['razo] *agg* (*liscio*) smooth; (*sbarbato*) shaved. *sm* (*tessuto*) satin.

**raspa** ['raspa] *sf* rasp. **raspare** *v* rasp.

**rassegnare** [rasse'ɲare] *v* **rassegnare le dimissioni** resign. **rassegnarsi** *v* resign oneself. **rassegna** *sf* review; inspection; (*resoconto*) survey.

**rasserenarsi** [rassere'narsi] *v* clear up; (*fig*) cheer up.

**rassettare** [rasset'tare] *v* tidy up; (*accomodare*) repair.

**rassicurare** [rassiku'rare] *v* reassure.

**rassomigliare** [rassomiʎ'ʎare] *v* resemble. **rassomigliarsi** *v* look alike.

**rastrello** [ras'trɛllo] *sm* rake. **rastrellamento** *sm* (*polizia*) round-up. **rastrellare** *v* rake; (*fig*) comb. **rastrelliera** *sf* rack.

**rata** ['rata] *sf* instalment.

**ratificare** [ratifi'kare] *v* ratify. **ratifica** *sf* ratification.

**ratto¹** ['ratto] *sm* (*zool*) rat.

**ratto²** ['ratto] *sm* (*rapimento*) rape.

**rattoppare** [rattop'pare] *v* patch. **rattoppo** *sm* (*toppa*) patch.

**rattrappire** [rattrap'pire] *v* make numb.

**rattristare** [rattris'tare] *v* sadden. **rattristarsi** *v* become sad, grieve.

**rauco** ['rauko] *agg* hoarse.

**ravanello** [rava'nɛllo] *sm* radish.

***ravvedersi** [ravve'dersi] *v* mend one's ways.

**ravviare** [ravvi'are] *v* tidy (up).

**ravvicinare** [ravvitʃi'nare] *v* bring near; reconcile. **ravvicinamento** *sm* (*pol*) rapprochement.

**ravvisare** [ravvi'zare] *v* recognize.

**ravvivare** [ravvi'vare] *v* revive.

***ravvolgere** [rav'vɔldʒere] *v* wrap (up).

**raziocinio** [ratsjo'tʃinjo] *sm* reason; common sense.

**razionale** [ratsjo'nale] *agg* rational. **razionalizzare** *v* rationalize. **razionalizzazione** *sf* rationalization.

**razionare** [ratsjo'nare] *v* ration. **razionamento** *sm* rationing. **razione** *sf* ration.

**razza¹** ['rattsa] *sf* race; (*specie*) kind; (*stirpe*) descent; (*animali*) breed. **di ogni razza** of all sorts. **di razza incrociata** crossbred. **di razza (pura)** (*animali*) pedigree, thoroughbred. **razziale** *agg* racial. **razzismo** *sm* racialism, racism. **razzista** *agg, s(m+f)* racist, racialist.

**razza²** ['rattsa] *sf* (*pesce*) ray, skate.

**razzia** [rat'tsia] *sf* raid.

**razzo** ['rattso] *sm* rocket.

**re** [re] *sm* king.

**reagire** [rea'dʒire] *v* react. **reagente** *sm* reagent.

**reale¹** [re'ale] *agg* real. **realismo** *sm* realism. **realista** *s(m+f)* realist. **realistico** *agg* realistic. **realtà** *sf* reality. **in realtà** in (actual) fact.

**reale²** [re'ale] *agg* (*regale*) royal. **realista** *agg, s(m+f)* royalist.

**realizzare** [realid'dzare] *v* realize; (*effettuare*) put into effect; (*sport*) score. **realizzabile** *agg* feasible. **realizzazione** *sf* realization; (*teatro, ecc.*) production. **prezzo di realizzo** cost price.

**reato** [re'ato] *sm* offence; (*grave*) crime.

**reattivo** [reat'tivo] *agg* reactive. *sm* (*chim*) reagent; (*psic*) test.

**reattore** [reat'tore] *sm* reactor; (*aereo*) jet.

**reazione** [reat'tsjone] *sf* reaction. **motore a reazione** jet engine. **reazionario, -a** *s, agg* reactionary.

**rebbio** ['rebbjo] *sm* prong.

**recapito** [re'kapito] *sm* (*indirizzo*) address; (*consegna*) delivery. **recapitare** *v* deliver.

**recare** [re'kare] *v* (*portare*) bear; (*arrecare*) cause.

**recensire** [retʃen'sire] *v* review. **recensione** *sf* review. **recensore, -a** *sm, sf* reviewer.

**recente** [re'tʃɛnte] *agg* recent. **recentissime** *sf pl* latest news *sing*.

**recessione** [retʃes'sjone] *sf* recession.

**recinto** [re'tʃinto] *sm* enclosure; (*per animali*) pen. **recintare** *v* enclose.

**recipiente** [retʃi'pjɛnte] *sm* container.

**reciproco** [re'tʃiproko] *agg* reciprocal, mutual. **reciprocare** *v* reciprocate. **reciprocità** *sf* reciprocity.

**recitare** [retʃi'tare] *v* (*versi, ecc.*) recite; (*una parte*) play; (*sostenere un ruolo*) act; (*fingere*) put on an act. **recita** *sf* performance. **recital** *sm invar* recital. **recitazione** *sf* recitation.

**reclamare** [rekla'mare] *v* complain; (*richiedere*) demand; protest. **reclamo** *sm* complaint.

**reclame** [re'klam] *sf invar* advertisement. **fare (della) reclame** advertise.

**reclusione** [reklu'zjone] *sf* confinement; imprisonment.

**reclutare** [reklu'tare] *v* recruit. **recluta**

*sf* recruit.

**record** ['rekord] *sm invar* record.

**recriminare** [rekrimi'nare] *v* recriminate.

**redarguire** [redargu'ire] *v* rebuke.

**redattore** [redat'tore], **-trice** *sm, sf* editor. **redazione** *sf* editorial staff; (*ufficio*) editor's office; (*atto del redigere*) editing, compiling.

**reddito** ['reddito] *sm* income; (*statale*) revenue; (*utile*) return. **imposta sul reddito** *sf* income tax. **reddito imponibile** taxable income.

**redentore** [reden'tore] *agg* redeeming. *sm* redeemer.

*****redigere** [re'didʒere] *v* (*compilare*) draw up; (*scrivere*) write; (*giornale*) edit.

*****redimere** [re'dimere] *v* redeem. **redimibile** *agg* redeemable.

**redini** ['redini] *sf pl* reins *pl*.

**redivivo** [redi'vivo] *agg* (*fig*) another.

**reduce** ['redutʃe] *agg* returning. *sm* (*mil*) veteran; (*superstite*) survivor.

**refe** ['refe] *sm* thread.

**referendum** [refe'rɛndum] *sm invar* referendum.

**referenza** [refe'rɛntsa] *sf* reference.

**refettorio** [refet'tɔrjo] *sm* refectory.

**refrattario** [refrat'tarjo] *agg* refractory; (*fig*) unmoved (*by*).

**refrigerare** [refridʒe'rare] *v* refresh, cool.

**regalare** [rega'lare] *v* give (away). **regalo** *sm* gift, present.

**regale** [re'gale] *agg* regal.

**regata** [re'gata] *sf* regatta.

**reggente** [red'dʒɛnte] *sm* ruler. *agg* ruling.

*****reggere** ['rɛddʒere] *v* (*sostenere*) hold; support; (*resistere*) stand; (*dirigere*) run; (*gramm*) govern; (*durare*) last. **reggere al confronto con** bear comparison with. **reggere alla prova** stand the test. **reggersi** *v* stand.

**reggia** ['rɛddʒa] *sf* royal palace.

**reggimento** [reddʒi'mento] *sm* regiment.

**reggipetto** [reddʒi'pɛtto] *sm* bra.

**regia** [re'dʒia] *sf* (*cinema*) direction; (*teatro*) production.

**regime** [re'dʒime] *sm* regime. **essere a regime** be on a diet. **regime di vita** way of life.

**regina** [re'dʒina] *sf* queen.

**regio** ['rɛdʒo] *agg* royal.

**regione** [re'dʒone] *sf* region. **regionale** *agg* regional.

**regista** [re'dʒista] *sf* (*cine*) director; (*teatro, TV*) producer.

**registrare** [redʒis'trare] *v* record; (*in registro*) register; (*mettere a punto*) adjust. **registratore** *sm* recorder; register. **registrazione** *sf* record; registration; adjustment; (*radio, TV*) recording. **registro** *sm* register. **cambiar registro** (*fam*) change one's tune.

**regnare** [re'ɲare] *v* rule, reign. **regno** *sm* (*territorio*) kingdom, realm; (*periodo, potere*) reign.

**regola** ['rɛgola] *sf* rule; norm. **di regola** normally. **in regola** in order. **per vostra regola** for your information. **regolamentare** *agg* prescribed. **regolamento** *sm* (*il regolare*) regulation; (*norme*) rules *pl*; (*comm*) settlement.

**regolare** [rego'lare] *v* regulate; (*mettere a punto*) adjust; (*comm*) settle. **regolarsi** *v* act; control oneself. *agg* regular. **regolarità** *sf* regularity. **regolarizzare** *v* regularize.

**regolo** ['rɛgolo] *sm* ruler; (*calcolatore*) slide-rule.

**reincarnazione** [reinkarna'tsjone] *sf* reincarnation.

**reintegrare** [reinte'grare] *v* reinstate. **reintegrazione** *sf* reinstatement.

**relativo** [rela'tivo] *agg* relative; concerning; (*corrispondente*) relevant. **relativamente a** regarding. **relatività** *sf* relativity.

**relazione** [rela'tsjone] *sf* relation(ship), connection; (*resoconto*) report. **essere in buone relazioni** be on good terms. **in relazione a** as regards. **mettere in relazione** relate.

**relegare** [rele'gare] *v* relegate.

**religione** [reli'dʒone] *sf* religion. **religiosa** *sf* nun. **religioso** *agg* religious.

**reliquia** [re'likwja] *sf* relic. **reliquiario** *sf* reliquary.

**relitto** [re'litto] *sm* wreck; (*rottame*) wreckage.

**remare** [re'mare] *v* row. **remata** *sf* stroke. **fare una remata** go for a row.

**reminiscenza** [remini'ʃɛntsa] *sf* recollection.

**remissivo** [remis'sivo] *agg* meek.

**remoto** [re'mɔto] *agg* remote.

*****rendere** ['rɛndere] *v* return; (*fruttare*) bring in; (*far diventare*) make; be efficient. **render conto di** account for. **render l'idea** make oneself clear. **rendere omaggio** pay homage. **rendersi conto** (*spiegare*) explain; (*capire*) realize. **rendere un servizio** do a favour.

**rendimento** [rendi'mento] *sm* (*utile*) yield; (*resa*) output; (*fis*, *mec*) efficiency.

**rendita** ['rendita] *sf* income; (*econ*) revenue; (*reddito*) yield.

**rene** ['rɛne] *sm* kidney. **reni** *sf pl* (*fam*) back *sing*.

**renna** ['rɛnna] *sf* reindeer.

**reparto** [re'parto] *sm* department; (*mil*) unit. **capo reparto** departmental head; (*maestranza*) foreman; (*negozio*) supervisor.

**repellente** [repel'lɛnte] *agg* repellent; (*ripugnante*) repulsive.

**repentaglio** [repen'taʎo] *sm* **mettere a repentaglio** jeopardize.

**reperibile** [repe'ribile] *agg* to be found; (*disponibile*) available.

**repertorio** [reper'tɔrjo] *sm* repertoire; (*elenco*) list.

**replica** ['rɛplika] *sf* repetition; (*risposta*) reply; (*teatro*) performance; objection; copy. **replicare** *v* repeat; reply; perform again; object.

**repressione** [repres'sjone] *sf* repression. **represso** *agg* repressed.

**\*reprimere** [re'primere] *v* repress, control.

**repubblica** [re'pubblika] *sf* republic. **repubblicano** *agg* republican.

**Repubblica Ceca** [re'pubblika 'ʃɛka] *sf* Czech Republic.

**reputare** [repu'tare] *v* consider. **reputazione** *sf* reputation.

**requisire** [rekwi'zire] *v* requisition. **requisito** *sm* requirement. **requisitoria** *sf* (*dir*) indictment; (*rimprovero*) reproof.

**resa** ['reza] *sf* (*l'arrendersi*) surrender; (*restituzione*) return; (*rendimento*) yield. **resa dei conti** statement (of accounts); (*fig*) reckoning.

**\*rescindere** [re'ʃindere] *v* rescind.

**residente** [rezi'dɛnte] *s*(*m+f*), *agg* resident. **residenza** *sf* residence; (*permanenza*) stay.

**residuo** [re'ziduo] *agg* residual. *sm* residue; (*fig*) trace. **residuato** *sm* surplus.

**resina** ['rezina] *sf* resin.

**resistere** [re'zistere] *v* resist; (*sopportare*) bear; (*non essere danneggiato*) be resistant (to). **resistente** *agg* resistant, proof (against). **resistenza** *sf* resistance; (*capacità* di resistere*) endurance.

**resoconto** [rezo'konto] *sm* report.

**\*respingere** [res'pindʒere] *v* push back, repel; (*rifiutare*) reject; (*bocciare*) fail. **respingente** *sm* buffer.

**respirare** [respi'rare] *v* breathe. **respiratore** *sm* respirator. **respiratorio** *agg* respiratory. **respirazione** *sf* respiration. **respiro** *sm* breath; (*fig*) breathing space. **sentirsi mancare il respiro** feel breathless.

**responsabile** [respon'sabile] *agg* responsible. *s*(*m+f*) person responsible. **responsabilità** *sf* responsibility. **prendersi la responsabilità** take the responsibility.

**ressa** ['rɛssa] *sf* crowd.

**restare** [res'tare] *v* remain; (*avanzare*) be left (over). **restarci male** (*delusi*) be disappointed; (*offesi*) be offended. **restare d'accordo** agree. **restante** *sm* remainder.

**restaurare** [restau'rare] *v* restore. **restauro** *sm* restoration; (*riparazione*) repair.

**restio** [res'tio] *agg* restive; (*bambini*) fractious.

**restituire** [restitu'ire] *v* return; (*fig*) restore. **restituzione** *sf* return.

**resto** ['rɛsto] *sm* remainder; (*di denaro*) change. **del resto** (*d'altronde*) on the other hand; (*inoltre*) besides.

**\*restringere** [res'trindʒere] *v* (*limitare*) restrict; (*ridurre di larghezza*) narrow; (*vestiario*) take in; (*tessuto*) shrink. **restringimento** *sm* shrinkage, narrowing. **restrizione** *sf* restriction.

**rete** ['rete] *sf* net; (*sistema*, *tec*) network; (*calcio*) goal; (*inganno*) trap. **rete metallica** wire netting.

**reticente** [reti'tʃente] *agg* reticent.

**reticolato** [retiko'lato] *sm* (*disegno*) grid; (*graticcio*) grating. **reticolo** *sm* lattice, grating.

**retina** ['rɛtina] *sf* retina.

**retorica** [re'tɔrika] *sf* rhetoric. **retorico** *agg* rhetorical.

**retribuire** [retribu'ire] *v* reward. **retribuzione** *sf* reward; (*paga*) payment.

**retro** ['rɛtro] *sm* back.

**retroattivo** [retroat'tivo] *agg* retrospective.

**\*retrocedere** [retro'tʃedere] *v* recede; (*ritirarsi*) retreat; (*mil*) demote; (*sport*) move down.

**retrodatare** [retroda'tare] *v* back-date.

**retrogrado** [re'trɔgrado] *agg* retrograde;

(*fig*) backward, reactionary.

**retroguardia** [retro'gwardja] *sf* rearguard.

**retromarcia** [retro'martʃa] *sf* reverse.

**retroscena** [retro'ʃɛna] *sm invar* backstage; (*fig*) background.

**retrospettivo** [retrospet'tivo] *agg* retrospective.

**retrovisore** [retrovi'zore] *sm* rear-view mirror.

**retta¹** ['rɛtta] *sf* (*geom*) straight line.

**retta²** ['rɛtta] *sf* **dar retta a** listen to, pay attention to.

**retta³** [rɛtta] *sf* fee for board and lodging.

**rettangolo** [ret'tangolo] *sm* rectangle. **rettangolare** *agg* right-angled, rectangular.

**rettificare** [rettifi'kare] *v* rectify, correct; (*mec*) grind. **rettifica** *sf* rectification, correction; grinding.

**rettile** ['rɛttile] *sm* reptile.

**rettilineo** [retti'lineo] *agg* straight.

**retto** ['rɛtto] *agg* straight; (*leale*) upright, straightforward; correct; (*geom*) right.

**rettore** [ret'tore] *sm* rector.

**reumatismo** [reuma'tizmo] *sm* rheumatism. **reumatico** *agg* rheumatic.

**reverendo** [reve'rɛndo] *agg* reverend. *sm* (*fam*) priest.

**reversibile** [rever'sibile] *agg* reversible.

**revisione** [revi'zjone] *sf* revision; (*tec*) overhaul; (*dei conti*) audit; (*dir*) review. **revisore** *sm* auditor; (*di bozze*) proof-reader.

**revocare** [revo'kare] *v* revoke.

**riabbassare** [riabbas'sare] *v* lower again.

**riabbottonare** [riabbotto'nare] *v* button up.

**riabbracciare** [riabbrat'tʃare] *v* embrace again.

**riabilitare** [riabili'tare] *v* rehabilitate. **riabilitazione** *sf* rehabilitation.

**riaccompagnare** [riakkompa'ɲare] *v* take back.

**riacquistare** [riakkwis'tare] *v* (*ricomprare*) buy back; (*ricuperare*) recover.

**riaddormentarsi** [riaddormen'tarsi] *v* fall asleep again.

**riaffermare** [riaffer'mare] *v* reaffirm.

**riallacciare** [riallat'tʃare] *v* re-tie; (*fig*) renew.

**rialto** [ri'alto] *sm* rise.

**rialzare** [rial'tsare] *v* raise (again). **rialzo** *sm* rise.

**\*riammettere** [riam'mettere] *v* re-admit. **riammissione** *sf* re-admission.

**riammogliarsi** [riammoʎ'ʎarsi] *v* remarry.

**rianimare** [riani'mare] *v* revive; (*fig*) cheer (up).

**\*riapparire** [riappa'rire] *v* reappear.

**\*riaprire** [riap'rire] *v* reopen; (*riprendere*) resume. **riapertura** *sf* reopening; resumption.

**riarmare** [riar'mare] *v* rearm; (*nave*) refit; (*edificio*) reinforce. **riarmamento** *sm* rearmament.

**riassestare** [riasses'tare] *v* rearrange.

**riassettare** [riasset'tare] *v* tidy up.

**riassicurare** [riassiku'rare] *v* reassure; (*dir*) reinsure. **riassicurazione** *sf* reassurance; reinsurance.

**\*riassumere** [rias'sumere] *v* take on again; (*compendiare*) sum up; (*condensare*) summarize. **riassunto** *sm* summary. **riassunzione** *sf* re-employment; (*dir*) resumption.

**riattaccare** [riattak'kare] *v* (*con filo*) sew on again; (*con colla*) stick on again; (*riprendere*) resume.

**riattivare** [riatti'vare] *v* reactivate; put back into service; (*strada*) reopen.

**\*riavere** [ria'vere] *v* have again; (*ricuperare*) recover.

**riavvicinare** [riavvitʃi'nare] *v* approach again; (*fig*) reconcile. **riavvicinamento** *sm* (*pol*) rapprochement.

**ribadire** [riba'dire] *v* rivet; (*fig*) confirm.

**ribaldo** [ri'baldo] *sm* rogue.

**ribaltare** [ribal'tare] *v* turn over; (*mandar sottosopra*) overturn. **ribalta** *sf* (*asse*) flap; (*teatro*) proscenium; (*fig*) limelight. **tornare alla ribalta** (*questione*) come up again. **venire alla ribalta** come on to the scene. **ribaltabile** *agg* folding; (*tavolo*) drop-leaf; (*camion*) tip-up.

**ribassare** [ribas'sare] *v* reduce. **ribasso** *sm* reduction. **essere in ribasso** drop.

**ribattere** [ri'battere] *v* hit back; (*chiodo*) rivet; (*sport*) return; (*confutare*) refute; (*replicare*) answer back.

**ribelle** [ri'bɛlle] *agg* rebellious. *s* (*m+f*) rebel. **ribellarsi** *v* revolt. **ribellione** *sf* rebellion.

**ribes** ['ribes] *sm* (red)currant. **ribes nero** blackcurrant.

**riboccare** [ribok'kare] *v* overflow.

**ribollire** [ribol'lire] *v* boil (again); ferment; (*fig*) seethe.

**ribrezzo** [ri'brettso] *sm* disgust. **far ribrezzo** disgust. **provar ribrezzo** be disgusted (by).

**ributtare** [ribut'tare] *v* throw again; (*buttar fuori*) throw out; vomit; (*rifiutare*) reject.

**ricacciare** [rikat'tʃare] *v* turn out (again); (*rimettere*) push back.

***ricadere** [rika'dere] *v* fall (back); (*pendere*) hang (down). **ricaduta** *sf* relapse.

**ricalcare** [rikal'kare] *v* (*disegno*) trace; (*fig*) follow faithfully. **ricalco** *sm* tracing.

**ricamare** [rika'mare] *v* embroider. **ricamo** *sm* embroidery.

**ricambiare** [rikam'bjare] *v* (*sostituire*) change; (*scambiare*) exchange; (*di nuovo*) change again. **di ricambio** spare.

**ricapitolare** [rikapito'lare] *v* sum up.

**ricaricare** [rikari'kare] *v* recharge; (*armi*) reload; (*orologio*) wind up again; (*pipa*) refill.

**ricattare** [rikat'tare] *v* blackmail. **ricattatore, -trice** *sm*, *sf* blackmailer. **ricatto** *sm* blackmail.

**ricavare** [rika'vare] *v* obtain, get; (*dedurre*) deduce. **ricavato** *or* **ricavo** *sm* proceeds *pl*.

**ricchezza** [rik'kettsa] *sf* wealth.

**riccio**[1] ['rittʃo] *agg* curly. *sm* curl; (*voluta*) scroll. **riccioluto** *or* **ricciuto** *agg* curly.

**riccio**[2] ['rittʃo] *sm* (*zool*) hedgehog; (*castagna*) (chestnut) husk. **riccio di mare** sea-urchin.

**ricco** ['rikko], **-a** *agg* rich. *sm*, *sf* rich person.

**ricerca** [ri'tʃerka] *sf* search; (*scientifica*) research; (*indagine*) investigation. **ricercare** *v* search (for); investigate. **ricercato** *agg* (much-)wanted; in (great) demand; (*affettato*) precious; (*raffinato*) refined. **ricercatezza** *sf* affectation; refinement. **ricercatore, -trice** *sm*, *sf* (*persona*) research worker; (*apparecchio*) detector.

**ricetta** [ri'tʃetta] *sf* recipe.

**ricettare** [ritʃet'tare] *v* receive. **ricettatore** *sm* receiver (of stolen goods).

**ricettivo** [ritʃet'tivo] *agg* receptive. **ricettività** *sf* receptivity.

***ricevere** [ri'tʃevere] *v* receive; (*accogliere*) welcome. **ricevimento** *sm* reception; (*ricevuta*) receipt. **ricevitore** *sm* receiver; (*impiegato*) collector. **ricevuta** *sf* receipt. **ricezione** *sf* reception.

**richiamare** [rikja'mare] *v* call back; (*far tornare*, *ricordare*) recall; (*rimproverare*) rebuke. **richiamare in vita** revive. **richiamo** *sm* call; recall; rebuke. **far da richiamo** act as a decoy.

***richiedere** [ri'kjedere] *v* (*aver bisogno*) require; (*per sapere*) ask; (*per ottenere*) ask for. **richiesta** *sf* request; (*econ*) demand; (*burocratica*) application. **richiesto** *agg* in (great) demand; necessary.

**riciclare** [ritʃi'klare] *v* recycle. **riciclaggio** *sm* recycling.

**ricino** ['ritʃino] *sm* **olio di ricino** *sm* castoroil.

**ricominciare** [rikomin'tʃare] *v* start again.

**ricompensa** [rikom'pɛnsa] *sf* reward. **ricompensare** *v* (*contraccambiare*) repay; (*premiare*) reward.

**riconciliare** [rikontʃi'ljare] *v* reconcile; (*procurare di nuovo*) win back. **riconciliarsi** *v* make it up.

**ricondurre** [rikon'durre] *v* take back; (*di nuovo*) take again.

***riconoscere** [riko'noʃere] *v* recognize; (*ammettere*) admit. **riconoscente** *agg* grateful. **riconoscenza** *sf* gratitude. **riconoscibile** *agg* recognizable. **riconoscimento** *sm* recognition; admission; identification.

**riconquistare** [rikonkwis'tare] *v* win back.

**ricopiare** [riko'pjare] *v* copy.

***ricoprire** [riko'prire] *v* cover (again); (*occupare*) hold; (*rivestire*) coat; (*colmare*) smother.

**ricordare** [rikor'dare] *v* remember; (*richiamare alla memoria*) recall; (*far ricordare*) remind. **ricordo** *sm* recollection; (*oggetto*) souvenir. **ricordo di famiglia** heirloom. **ricordo d'infanzia** childhood memory. **ricordi** *sm pl* (*libro*) memoirs *pl*.

***ricorrere** [ri'korrere] *v* resort; (*dir*) appeal; (*ripetersi*) recur. **ricorso** *sm* resort, recourse; (*dir*) appeal.

**ricostituente** [rikostitu'ente] *sm* tonic. **ricostituire** *v* reconstitute.

***ricostruire** [rikostru'ire] *v* rebuild; (*fig*) reconstruct. **ricostruzione** *sf* reconstruction.

**ricotta** [ri'kɔtta] *sf* cottage cheese.

**ricoverare** [rikove'rare] *v* take in; (*all'ospedale*) send to hospital. **ricoverato, -a** *sm*, *sf* (*ospedale*) patient; (*ospizio*) inmate. **ricovero** *sm* shelter; (*ospizio*) home; (*in ospedale*) admission to hospital.

**ricrearsi** [rikre'arsi] *v* amuse oneself. **ricreazione** *sf* recreation; (*scuola*) playtime; (*pausa*) break.

**ricredersi** [ri'kredersi] *v* change one's mind.

**ricuperare** [rikupe'rare] *v* recover; (*mar*) salvage. **ricupero** *sm* recovery; salvage.

**ricurvo** [ri'kurvo] *agg* bent.

**ricusare** [riku'zare] *v* decline.

*ridare** [ri'dare] *v* (*dare nuovamente*) give again; (*restituire*) give back.

*ridere** ['ridere] *v* laugh. **(cosa) da ridere** (*divertene*) funny; (*inezia*) of no importance. **far ridere** be funny; be ridiculous. *sm* laughter.

**ridicolo** [ri'dikolo] *agg* ridiculous. *sm* absurdity; (*derisione*) ridicule.

**ridimensionare** [ridimensjo'nare] *v* reorganize; (*ridurre*) cut down; (*fig*) reappraise.

*ridire** [ri'dire] *v* (*riferire*) tell; (*criticare*) find fault with; (*dire di nuovo*) repeat.

**ridosso** [ri'dɔsso] *sm* **a ridosso di** close to; (*dietro*) behind.

*ridurre** [ri'durre] *v* reduce; (*trasformare*) turn. **riduzione** *sf* reduction; cut; adaptation.

**rielaborare** [rielabo'rare] *v* work out again; modify.

*riempire** [riem'pire] *v* fill; (*compilare*) fill in; (*gastr*) stuff. **riempitivo** *sm* filler; (*fig*) stopgap.

**rientrare** [rien'trare] *v* (*tornare*) return; (*rincasare*) come or go home; (*far parte*) come within, form part of; (*entrare nuovamente*) re-enter. **rientro** *sm* return; re-entry; (*rientranza*) recess.

**riepilogare** [riepilo'gare] *v* summarize. **riepilogo** *sm*, *pl* **-ghi** recapitulation.

**riesumare** [riezu'mare] *v* exhume; (*fig*) unearth.

**rievocare** [rievo'kare] *v* recall; commemorate.

*rifare** [ri'fare] *v* make or do again; (*ricostruire*) rebuild; imitate.

**riferire** [rife'rire] *v* relate; report. **riferimento** *sm* reference. **punto di riferimento** *sm* landmark.

**rifilare** [rifi'lare] (*fam*) *v* palm off; (*dire d'un fiato*) reel off.

**rifinire** [rifi'nire] *v* (*dare l'ultima mano*) give the finishing touch; (*ritoccare*) touch up. **rifinitura** *sf* finishing touches *pl*; (*guarnizione*) fittings *pl*.

**rifiutare** [rifju'tare] *v* refuse; decline. **rifiuto** *sm* refusal; (*scarto*) refuse, rubbish.

**riflessione** [rifles'sjone] *sf* reflection; (*osservazione*) remark.

**riflessivo** [rifles'sivo] *agg* thoughtful; (*gramm*) relexive.

**riflesso** [ri'flɛsso] *sm* reflection; (*med*) reflex. **di riflesso** indirectly.

*riflettere** [ri'flɛttere] *v* reflect; (*pensarci su*) think (over or about). **riflettersi su** (*ripercuotersi*) affect. **riflettore** *sm* reflector; (*cinema, ecc.*) floodlight.

*rifondere** [ri'fondere] *v* recast; (*ricomporre*) recompose; (*risarcire*) refund.

**riformare** [rifor'mare] *v* reform; (*formare di nuovo*) re-form. **riforma** *sf* reform.

**rifornire** [rifor'nire] *v* supply (with). **rifornirsi di benzina** (*auto*) fill up. **rifornimento** *sm* supply.

**rifuggire** [rifud'dʒire] *v* escape (again); (*fig*) shrink (from).

**rifugiarsi** [rifu'dʒarsi] *v* (take) shelter. **rifugiato, -a** *sm*, *sf* refugee.

**rifugio** [ri'fudʒo] *sm* shelter. **rifugio antiaereo** air-raid shelter. **rifugio fiscale** tax-haven.

*rifulgere** [ri'fuldʒere] *v* glow.

**riga** ['riga] *sf* line; (*fila*) row; (*righello*) ruler. **a righe** striped. **riga a T** T-square. **rigare** *v* rule; (*tracciar strisce*) stripe; (*scalfire*) score.

**rigaglie** [ri'gaʎe] *sf pl* giblets *pl*.

**rigettare** [ridʒet'tare] *v* (*buttar fuori*) throw out; (*fig*) reject; vomit; (*gettare indietro*) throw back.

**rigido** ['ridʒido] *agg* rigid, stiff; (*freddo*) severe. **rigidezza** or **rigidità** *sf* rigidity; (*fig*) rigour, severity.

**rigirare** [ridʒi'rare] *v* turn round; (*fig*) twist round. **rigiro** *sm* twist. **giri e rigiri** *sm pl* twists and turns *pl*.

**rigo** ['rigo] *sm* line; (*musica*) stave.

**rigoglioso** [rigo'ʎozo] *agg* blooming.

**rigonfio** [ri'gonfjo] *agg* swollen.

**rigore** [ri'gore] *sm* rigour; (*calcio*) penalty (kick). **a rigor di logica** strictly speaking. **a rigore** in point of fact. **di rigore** compulsory. **rigoroso** *agg* rigorous.

**rigovernare** [rigover'nare] *v* (*i piatti*) wash up; (*animali*) tend.

**riguardare** [rigwar'dare] *v* regard. **riguardo** *sm* regard; (*cautela*) care; consideration. **di riguardo** of consequence. **riguardo a** regarding. **riguardo a me** as for me. **senza riguardo** inconsiderate. **riguardoso** *agg* thoughtful, respectful.

**rilanciare** [rilan'tʃare] v launch; (*asta, carte*) raise.

**rilasciare** [rila'ʃare] v (*liberare*) release; (*con-segnare*) issue.

**rilassare** [rilas'sare] v relax; (*allentare*) slacken. **rilassamento** sm relaxation.

**rilegare** [rile'gare] v bind; (*incastonare*) set. **rilegatura** sf binding.

***rileggere** [ri'leddʒere] v re-read.

**rilevare** [rile'vare] v (*notare*) notice; (*comm*) take over; (*topografia*) survey.

**rilievo** [ri'ljevo] sm relief; importance; (*asservazione*) remark; survey. **mettere in rilievo** stress, emphasize.

**riluttante** [rilut'tante] agg reluctant.

**rima** ['rima] sf rhyme.

**rimandare** [riman'dare] v send back; (*posporre*) defer.

***rimanere** [rima'nere] v remain; (*essere*) be. **rimanere d'accordo** agree. **rimanere in dubbio** be left in doubt. **rimaner male** be put out; (*deluso*) be disappointed; (*offeso*) be hurt.

**rimasugli** [rima'zuʎi] sm pl left-overs pl.

**rimbalzare** [rimbal'tsare] v bounce; (*proiettile*) ricochet.

**rimbambire** [rimbam'bire] v become childish. **rimbambito** agg (*fam*) gaga.

**rimbeccare** [rimbek'kare] v retort. **di rimbecco** sharply.

**rimboccare** [rimbok'kare] v turn down. **rimboccarsi le maniche** roll up one's sleeves.

**rimbombare** [rimbom'bare] v resound.

**rimborsare** [rimbor'sare] v reimburse. **rimborso** sm refund.

**rimediare** [rime'djare] v remedy; (*fam: racimolare*) scrape together; (*accomodare*) patch; (*provvedere*) take care. **rimedio** sm remedy.

**rimescolare** [rimesko'lare] v stir; (*carte*) shuffle.

**rimessa** [ri'messa] sf (*deposito*) depot; garage; (*trasferimento*) remittance; (*perdita*) loss. **rimessa in gioco** (*calcio*) throw-in.

***rimettere** [ri'mettere] v put back; (*indossare*) put back on; (*spedire*) send; (*denaro*) remit. **rimetterci** v lose. **rimettersi** v (*riaversi*) recover; (*affidarsi*) trust.

**rimodernare** [rimoder'nare] v modernize.

**rimontare** [rimon'tare] v (*mettere insieme*) reassemble; (*sport*) catch up; (*risalire*) go up;

(*a cavallo*) remount; (*auto*) get back in.

**rimorchiare** [rimor'kjare] v (have in) tow. **rimorchio** sm trailer. **cavo da rimorchio** sm tow-rope.

**rimorso** [ri'morso] sm remorse. **rimorso di coscienza** pangs of conscience pl.

**rimostrare** [rimos'trare] v remonstrate.

**rimpasto** [rim'pasto] sm (*fig*) reshuffle.

**rimpatriare** [rimpa'trjare] v repatriate. **rimpatrio** sm repatriation.

***rimpiangere** [rim'pjandʒere] v regret. **rimpianto** sm regret.

**rimpiattino** [rimpjat'tino] sm hide-and-seek.

**rimpiazzare** [rimpjat'tsare] v replace.

**rimpiccolire** [rimpikko'lire] v make smaller.

**rimpinzarsi** [rimpin'tsarsi] v stuff oneself, gorge.

**rimproverare** [rimprove'rare] v reproach; (*sgridare*) scold; (*fam*) tell off; (*biasimare*) blame. **rimprovero** sm reproach; blame.

***rimuovere** [ri'mwovere] v remove; (*distogliere*) dissuade.

**Rinascimento** [rinaʃi'mento] sm Renaissance.

**rinascita** [ri'naʃita] sf rebirth; (*fig*) revival.

**rincagnato** [rinka'ɲato] agg **naso rincagnato** sm pug nose, snub nose.

**rincalzare** [rinkal'tsare] v (*sorreggere*) prop up; (*lenzuola*) tuck in.

**rincarare** [rinka'rare] v (*rendere più caro*) raise (the price of); (*essere più caro*) rise, become more expensive.

**rincasare** [rinka'zare] v return home.

***rinchiudere** [rin'kjudere] v shut in.

**rinchiuso** [rin'kjuzo] agg shut in; (*aria*) stale, fusty. sm enclosure. **saper di rinchiuso** smell fusty or musty.

***rincorrere** [rin'korrere] v run after, chase. **rincorsa** sf run-up.

***rincrescere** [rin'kreʃere] v cause regret or sorrow. **mi rincresce di ...** I'm sorry to ... . **ti rincresce ... ?** do you mind ... ? **rincrescimento** sm regret.

**rinculare** [rinku'lare] v recoil.

**rinforzare** [rinfor'tsare] v reinforce, strengthen. **rinforzo** sm reinforcement.

**rinfrescare** [rinfres'kare] v cool; (*pulire*) freshen up; (*memoria*) refresh; (*ravvivare*) brush up. **rinfrescata** sf cooling. **darsi una rinfrescata** freshen up. **rinfreschi** sm pl refreshments pl. **rinfresco** sm (*ricevi-*

*mento*) party.

**rinfusa** [rin'fuza] *sf* **alla rinfusa** higgledy-piggledy.

**ringhiare** [rin'gjare] *v* growl, snarl.

**ringhiera** [rin'gjɛra] *sf* railing; (*delle scale*) banister.

**ringiovanire** [rindʒova'nire] *v* rejuvenate; (*nell'aspetto*) make look younger.

**ringraziare** [ringra'tsjare] *v* thank. **ringraziamento** *sm* thanks *pl.* **lettera di ringraziamento** *sf* thank-you letter.

**rinnegare** [rinne'gare] *v* deny. **rinnegato, -a** *s, agg* renegade.

**rinnovare** [rinno'vare] *v* renew. **rinnovabile** *agg* renewable. **rinnovamento** *sm* renewal; (*rimodernamento*) renovation. **rinnovazione** *sf* renewal; renovation.

**rinoceronte** [rinotʃe'ronte] *sm* rhinoceros.

**rinomato** [rino'mato] *agg* renowned. **rinomanza** *sf* renown.

**rinsaldare** [rinsal'dare] *v* consolidate; (*inamidare*) starch.

**rintoccare** [rintok'kare] *v* (*campana*) toll; (*orologio*) strike. **rintocco** *sm* toll; stroke.

**rintracciare** [rintrat'tʃare] *v* trace; track down.

**rintronare** [rintro'nare] *v* thunder; (*assordare*) deafen.

**rintuzzare** [rintut'tsare] *v* (*rendere ottuso*) blunt; (*respingere*) repel; (*ribattere*) refute; (*frenare*) check.

**rinunciare** [rinun'tʃare] *v* give up; (*fare a meno*) forgo; (*dir*) renounce; (*non voler fare*) refrain (from). **rinunce** *sf pl* (*privazioni*) hardship *sing*. **rinuncia** *sf* abandonment; renunciation.

**\*rinvenire[1]** [rinve'nire] *v* (*ritrovare*) recover.

**\*rinvenire[2]** [rinve'nire] *v* (*ritornare in sè*) come to; (*riprendere freschezza*) revive.

**rinviare** [rinvi'are] *v* (*mandare indietro*) send back; (*posporre*) put off; (*dir*) adjourn; (*indirizzare*) refer. **rinvio** *sm* postponement; adjournment; (*testo*) (cross-)reference.

**rinvigorire** [rinvigo'rire] *v* invigorate; (*ritornar vigoroso*) regain strength.

**rione** [ri'one] *sm* district. **rionale** *agg* local.

**riordinare** [riordi'nare] *v* rearrange; (*comm*) reorder.

**riorganizzare** [riorganid'dzare] *v* reorganize. **riorganizzazione** *sf* reorganization.

**ripagare** [ripa'gare] *v* pay back.

**riparare** [ripa'rare] *v* (*aggiustare*) repair; (*porre rimedio*) make up (for), redress; protect; (*esame*) repeat. **ripararsi** *v* take shelter. **riparazione** *sf* repair; redress.

**riparo** [ri'paro] *sm* shelter; (*protezione*) cover; (*mec*) guard. **mettersi al riparo** (**da**) shelter (from).

**ripartire[1]** [ripar'tire] *v* (*partire di nuovo*) leave *or* start (up) again.

**ripartire[2]** [ripar'tire] *v* (*dividere*) split up; distribute.

**ripassare** [ripas'sare] *v* (*tornare*) pass again; (*visitare*) call back; (*attraversare*) cross again; (*rivedere*) review; (*mec*) overhaul. **ripassata** *sf* (*pittura*) fresh coat of paint; revision, overhaul; (*stirata*) press.

**ripensare** [ripen'sare] *v* think (over); (*mutare pensiero*) reconsider. **ripensare a** (*tornare col pensiero*) recall.

**ripentirsi** [ripen'tirsi] *v* repent; (*cambiar pensiero*) have second thoughts.

**\*ripercuotersi** [riper'kwɔtersi] *v* (*suono*) reverberate; (*fig*) have an effect.

**ripercussione** [riperkus'sjone] *sf* repercussion.

**ripetere** [ri'petere] *v* repeat. **ripetizione** *sf* repetition; (*studio*) coaching.

**ripiano** [ri'pjano] *sm* terrace; (*scomparto*) shelf.

**ripido** ['ripido] *agg* steep.

**ripiegare** [ripje'gare] *v* fold again; (*fig*) make do. **di ripiego** makeshift.

**ripieno** [ri'pjɛno] *agg* filled, stuffed. *sm* filling, stuffing.

**\*riporre** [ri'porre] *v* put (back).

**riportare** [ripor'tare] *v* (*portare indietro*) bring back; (*ricondurre*) take again; (*riferire*) report; (*ricevere*) get; (*mat*) carry. **riporto** *sm* carrying forward; amount carried forward.

**riposare** [ripo'zare] *v* rest. **riposarsi** *v* take a rest. **riposo** *sm* rest. **andare a riposo** retire. **mettere a riposo** pension off. **senza riposo** without interruption.

**ripostiglio** [ripos'tiʎo] *sm* cubby-hole.

**\*riprendere** [ri'prɛndere] *v* take again; (*recuperare*) recover; (*ricominciare*) resume. **riprendersi** (**da**) get over.

**ripresa** [ri'preza] *sf* resumption; (*innovamento*) renewal; (*calcio*) second half; (*boxe*) round; (*auto*) acceleration; (*cine*) shot.

**ripristinare** [ripristi'nare] *v* restore. **ripristino** *sm* restoration.

**\*riprodurre** [ripro'durre] v reproduce. **riproduzione** sf reproduction.

**riprova** [ri'prɔva] sf fresh proof; confirmation. **riprovare** v blame; (esame) fail.

**ripudiare** [ripu'djare] v repudiate.

**ripugnante** [ripu'ɲante] agg repugnant. **ripugnare** v disgust.

**ripulsione** [ripul'sjone] sf repulsion.

**risaia** [ri'zaja] sf rice-field.

**risalire** [risa'lire] v (andar su) go up (again); (nel tempo) go back.

**risaltare** [risal'tare] v (distinguersi) stand out; (sporgere) project. **far risaltare** bring out. **risalto** sm emphasis; projection.

**risanare** [risa'nare] v heal; (fig) improve; (bonificare) reclaim.

**risaputo** [risa'puto] agg well-known.

**risarcire** [rizart'fire] v compensate. **risarcimento** sm compensation.

**risata** [ri'zata] sf laugh. **fare** or **farsi una bella risata** have a good laugh. **scoppiare in una risata** burst out laughing.

**riscaldare** [riskal'dare] v heat, warm up. **riscaldamento** sm heating; (impianto) heating system. **riscaldamento globale** global warming.

**riscatto** [ris'katto] sm ransom; (econ) redemption. **riscattare** v ransom; redeem.

**rischiarare** [riskja'rare] v illuminate.

**rischiare** [ris'kjare] v risk. **rischiare di** run the risk of. **rischio** sm risk. **rischioso** agg risky.

**risciacquare** [riʃa'kware] v rinse. **risciacquatura** sf (atto) rinsing; (acqua) dishwater. **risciacquo** sm mouthwash.

**riscontrare** [riskon'trare] v (rilevare) find; (confrontare) compare; (controllare) check. **riscontro** sm finding; comparison; check; (lettera) reply.

**riscossa** [ris'kɔssa] sf (riconquista) recovery; (insurrezione) revolt.

**\*riscuotere** [ris'kwɔtere] v (ritirare denaro) draw; (riportare) win, earn; (scuotere) shake.

**risentire** [risen'tire] v (provare) feel; (mostrare) show; (udire di nuovo) hear again; (soffrire) feel the effects of. **risentirsi** v resent. **risentimento** sm resentment; consequence.

**riserbo** [ri'serbo] sm reserve.

**riserva** [ri'sɛrva] sf (provvista) supply; (scorta, sport) reserve; (dubbio) reservation. **riservare** v reserve, keep; (prenotare) book;

(dimostrare) show. **riservatezza** sf discretion; (segretezza) confidential nature; (carattere) reserve. **riservato** agg reserved; confidential.

**risibile** [ri'zibile] agg laughable.

**risiedere** [ri'sjɛdere] v reside.

**risma** ['rizma] sf (carta) ream; (spreg) kind.

**riso¹** ['rizo] sm (bot) rice.

**riso²** ['rizo] sm, pl -a f laughter; (risata) laugh; ridicule.

**risoluto** [riso'luto] agg resolute. **risolutezza** sf decisiveness.

**risoluzione** [risolu'tsjone] sf resolution; (mat) solution; (dir) cancellation.

**\*risolvere** [ri'sɔlvere] v resolve; (mat, indovinello) solve; (dir) cancel; (scomporre) break down. **risolversi** v (fig) turn out; decide.

**risonare** [riso'nare] v also **risuonare** ring; (echeggiare) resound.

**\*risorgere** [ri'sɔrdʒere] v rise again. **far risorgere** revive. **risorgimento** sm revival.

**risorsa** [ri'sorsa] sf resource.

**risparmiare** [rispar'mjare] v spare; (economizzare, mettere da parte) save. **risparmiatore, -trice** sm, sf saver. **risparmio** sm saving; (denaro) savings pl. **fare risparmio (di)** save.

**rispecchiare** [rispek'kjare] v reflect.

**rispettare** [rispet'tare] v respect; (mantenere) keep.

**rispettivo** [rispet'tivo] agg respective.

**rispetto** [ris'pɛtto] sm respect. **rispetto a** (in relazione a) with respect to, as to; (in confronto) compared to. **rispettoso** agg respectful.

**risplendere** [ris'plɛndere] v shine.

**\*rispondere** [ris'pondere] v answer; (rimbeccare) answer back; (obbedire) respond; (carte) follow suit. **rispondere di no/si** say no/yes. **rispondere male** give a wrong answer; (sgarbatamente) answer back. **rispondere picche** give a flat refusal.

**risposta** [ris'posta] sf answer, reply. **botta e risposta** tit for tat. **per tutta risposta** merely. **senza risposta** unanswered.

**rissa** ['rissa] sf brawl.

**ristabilire** [ristabi'lire] v restore.

**ristagnare** [rista'ɲare] v stagnate; (fig) come to a standstill; (comm) be slack. **ristagno** sm stagnation; (econ) slump.

**ristampare** [ristam'pare] v reprint. **ristam-**

**pa** sf reprint.

**ristorante** [risto'rante] sm restaurant. **vagone ristorante** sm dining car.

**ristorare** [risto'rare] v restore. **ristorarsi** v refresh oneself. **ristoro** sm refreshment.

**ristretto** [ris'tretto] agg (limitato) restricted; (angusto) narrow; (caffè) very strong. **brodo ristretto** sm consommé.

**risultare** [rizul'tare] v appear; gather; (conseguire) ensue. **mi risulta che ...** I gather that ... .

**risultato** [rizul'tato] sm result.

**risuonare** [riswo'nare] V **risonare**.

**risurrezione** [rizurre'tsjone] sf resurrection.

**risuscitare** [risuʃi'tare] v revive; (rel) resurrect.

**risvegliare** [rizve'ʎare] v wake (up); (fig) awaken, revive.

**ritaglio** [ri'taʎo] sm cutting.

**ritardare** [ritar'dare] v be late; (orologio) be slow; (differire) delay. **ritardatario, -a** sm, sf latecomer. **ritardo** sm delay. **in ritardo** late.

**ritegno** [ri'teɲo] sm reserve; (freno) restraint.

**\*ritenere** [rite'nere] v think; consider; (trattenere) hold.

**ritirare** [riti'rare] v withdraw; (ottenere in consegna) collect. **ritirarsi** v withdraw; (interrompere un'attività) retire. **ritirata** sf retreat. **ritiro** sm withdrawal; (il prendere) collection; (luogo appartato) retreat.

**ritmo** [ˈritmo] sm rhythm. **ritmico** agg rhythmic(al).

**rito** [ˈrito] sm rite; (usanza) custom. **di rito** customary.

**ritoccare** [ritok'kare] v touch up.

**ritornare** [ritor'nare] v return; (andare indietro) go back. **biglietto di andata e ritorno** return ticket. **di ritorno** back. **viaggio di andata e ritorno** round trip. **ritornello** sm refrain.

**\*ritrarre** [ri'trarre] v (tirare indietro) draw back; (rappresentare) portray.

**ritratto** [ri'tratto] sm portrait. **ritrattista** s(m+f) portrait painter.

**ritroso** [ri'trozo] agg (scontroso) contrary; (restio) unwilling. **a ritroso** (indietro) backwards; (controcorrente) against the stream.

**ritrovare** [ritro'vare] v find (again); (recuperare) recover; (incontrare) meet again. **ritrovarsi** v meet (again); (orientarsi) get

one's bearings; (essere a proprio agio) feel at ease. **ritrovato** sm invention; expedient. **ritrovo** sm meeting-place; club.

**ritto** [ˈritto] agg upright.

**rituale** [ritu'ale] agg, sm ritual.

**riunire** [riu'nire] v gather; (ricongiungere) reunite; (convocare) call. **riunione** sf meeting.

**\*riuscire** [riu'ʃire] v succeed; (andare a finire) turn out; (aver capacità) be good (at). **mi riesce antipatico/simpatico I** dislike/like him. **riuscita** sf result; success.

**riva** [ˈriva] sf shore; (fiume) bank.

**rivale** [ri'vale] s(m+f), agg rival. **rivalità** sf rivalry.

**rivalutare** [rivalu'tare] v (econ) revalue; (fig) reappraise. **rivalutazione** sf revaluation; reappraisal.

**\*rivedere** [rive'dere] v see again; (incontrare) meet again; (ripassare) go over. **rivedere i conti** audit (the accounts).

**rivelare** [rive'lare] v reveal. **rivelatore** sm (tec) detector. **rivelazione** sf revelation.

**rivendere** [ri'vendere] v resell; (al dettaglio) retail. **rivendita** sf resale; (negozio) shop.

**rivendicare** [rivendi'kare] v claim.

**riverberare** [riverbe'rare] v reverberate.

**riverire** [rive'rire] v revere; respect; (salutare) pay one's respects (to). **riverenza** sf reverence; respect; (inchino) bow; (di donne) curtsy.

**rivestire** [rives'tire] v cover; (vernice) coat; (fodera) line. **rivestire una carica** hold an office; (conferirla) confer an office. **rivestirsi** v dress again, change (clothes). **rivestimento** sm covering; coating; lining.

**rivetto** [ri'vetto] sm rivet.

**riviera** [ri'vjera] sf coastal region. **Riviera** sf Riviera.

**rivincita** [ri'vintʃita] sf return match. **prendersi la rivincita** take one's revenge.

**rivista** [ri'vista] sf review; (periodico) magazine; (teatro) revue.

**\*rivolgere** [ri'vɔldʒere] v turn. **rivolgersi** v (indirizzare) address; (ricorrere) turn to; (per domandare, ecc.) apply.

**rivolta** [ri'vɔlta] sf revolt; (mar, mil) mutiny.

**rivoltare** [rivol'tare] v turn; (ripugnare) revolt; (insalata) toss. **rivoltarsi** v (ribellarsi) revolt.

**rivoltella** [rivol'tella] sf revolver. **rivoltellata** sf shot.

**rivoluzione** [rivolu'tsjone] *sf* revolution. **rivoluzionario, -a** *s, agg* revolutionary.

**rivulsione** [rivul'sjone] *sf* revulsion.

**rizzare** [rit'tsare] *v* raise; erect. **far rizzare i capelli** make one's hair stand on end. **rizzare le orecchie** prick up one's ears.

**roba** ['rɔba] *sf* stuff, things *pl.* **bella roba!** that's a fine thing! **robaccia** *sf* rubbish.

**robusto** [ro'busto] *agg* sturdy; solid. **robustezza** *sf* sturdiness; (*fig*) vigour.

**rocca**[1] ['rɔkka] *sf* fortress. **cristallo di rocca** sm rock-crystal.

**rocca**[2] ['rɔkka] *sf* (*conocchia*) distaff; (*bobina*) reel. **rocchetto** *sm* reel; (*elett*) coil.

**roccia** ['rɔttʃa] *sf* rock; (*sport*) rock-climbing. **roccioso** *agg* rocky.

**rodaggio** [ro'daddʒo] *sm* running-in.

**\*rodere** ['rɔdere] *v* gnaw. **rodersi il fegato** (*fig*) be eaten up. **roditore** *sm* rodent.

**rododendro** [rodo'dɛndro] *sm* rhododendron.

**rogna** ['rɔɲa] *sf* (*animali*) mange; (*agric*) scab; (*fam*) pain in the neck. **rognoso** *agg* mangy; (*noioso*) boring.

**rognone** [ro'ɲone] *sm* kidney.

**rogo** ['rɔgo] *sm* stake; (*incendio*) fire.

**Roma** ['roma] *sf* Rome. **romano, -a** *s, agg* Roman. **fare alla romana** go Dutch.

**Romania** [roma'nia] *sf* Romania. **romeno, -a** *s, agg* Romanian.

**romanico** [ro'maniko] *agg* Romanesque.

**romantico** [ro'mantiko] *agg* romantic. **romanticismo** *sm* romanticism; sentimentalism.

**romanza** [ro'mandza] *sf* romance.

**romanzo**[1] [ro'mandzo] *sm* novel; (*storia inventata*) fiction. **romanzo a fumetti** comic strip. **romanzo d'appendice** serial story. **romanzo fiume** saga. **romanzesco** *agg* romantic; fantastic.

**romanzo**[2] [ro'mandzo] *agg* (*lingua*) Romance.

**rombo**[1] ['rɔmbo] *sm* (*geom*) rhombus; (*pesce*) turbot.

**rombo**[2] ['rombo] *sm* roar. **rombare** *v* roar.

**\*rompere** ['rompere] *v* break; (*spezzare*) break off. **rompere l'anima** (*volg*) pester. **rompicapo** *sm* (*fam*) headache; (*indovinello*) puzzle. **a rompicollo** at breakneck speed. **rompiscatole** *s(m+f)* (*fam*) pain in the neck.

**ronda** ['ronda] *sf* **fare la ronda** (*mil*) be on watch; (*polizia*) be on the beat.

**rondella** [ron'dɛlla] *sf* washer.

**rondine** ['rondine] *sf* swallow.

**rondò**[1] [ron'do] *sm* (*musica*) rondo.

**rondò**[2] [ron'do] *sm* (*incrocio*) roundabout.

**rondone** [ron'done] *sm* swift.

**ronfare** [ron'fare] *v* (*fam*) snore.

**ronzare** [ron'dzare] *v* buzz. **ronzio** *sm* buzz(ing).

**ronzino** [ron'dzino] *sm* nag.

**rosa** ['rɔza] *sf* rose. **all'acqua di rose** (*fam*) watered-down. *agg invar* pink. **veder tutto rosa** see everything through rose-coloured spectacles. **rosato** *agg* (*vino*) rosé. **roseo** *agg* rosy. **rosetta** *sf* (*coccarda*) rosette; (*mec*) washer.

**rosario** [ro'zarjo] *sm* rosary.

**rosbif** [rɔz'bif] *sm invar* roast beef.

**rosicare** [rozi'kare] *v also* **rosicchiare** nibble; (*rodere*) gnaw.

**rosmarino** [rozma'rino] *sm* rosemary.

**rosolare** [rozo'lare] *v* brown.

**rosolia** [rozo'lia] *sf* German measles.

**rospo** ['rɔspo] *sm* toad.

**rossetto** [ros'setto] *sm* lipstick; (*belletto*) rouge.

**rosso** ['rosso] *agg* red. *sm* red; (*l'essere rosso*) redness. **rosso d'uovo** egg-yolk. **rossastro** *or* **rossiccio** *agg* reddish. **rossore** *sm* blush.

**rosticceria** [rostittʃe'ria] *sf* rotisserie.

**rostro** ['rɔstro] *sm* rostrum.

**rotaia** [ro'taja] *sf* rail.

**rotare** [ro'tare] *v* rotate. **rotatorio** *agg* rotatory. **rotazione** *sf* rotation.

**roteare** [rote'are] *v* wheel; (*occhi*) roll.

**rotella** [ro'tɛlla] *sf* small wheel; (*mobili*) castor; (*ginocchio*) knee-cap. **gli manca una rotella** (*fam*) he has a screw loose. **pattino a rotelle** *sm* roller-skate.

**rotolare** [roto'lare] *v* roll. **rotolo** *sm* roll. **andare a rotoli** *or* **rotoloni** go to rack and ruin. **rotoloni** *avv* rolling (over and over).

**rotondo** [ro'tondo] *agg* round.

**rotta**[1] ['rotta] *sf* route. **cambiar rotta** change course.

**rotta**[2] ['rotta] *sf* (*disfatta*) rout; (*breccia*) breach. **a rotta di collo** at breakneck speed. **mettere in rotta** (put to) rout.

**rotto** ['rotto] *agg* broken. **per il rotto della cuffia** by the skin of one's teeth. **rottame** *sm* fragment. **rottami** *sm pl* scrap *sing.* **rottura** *sf* break; (*violazione*) breach; (*interruzione*) breakdown.

**rovente** [ro'vɛnte] *agg* red-hot.

**rovere** ['rɔvere] *sm* oak.

**rovesciare** [rove'ʃare] *v* upset; (*abbattere*) overthrow; (*gettare*) throw (back). **rovesciarsi** *v* overturn; (*barca, ecc.*) capsize; (*affluire*) pour. **rovescio** *sm* shower; (*retro*) back; (*danno*) setback; (*sport*) backhand. **andare a rovescio** go wrong. **a rovescio** the wrong way round; (*capovolto*) upside-down; (*col dentro fuori*) inside out.

**rovinare** [rovi'nare] *v* ruin. **rovina** *sf* ruin. **andare in rovina** collapse. **mandare in rovina** ruin. **rovinoso** *agg* ruinous.

**rovistare** [rovis'tare] *v* ransack.

**rovo** ['rɔvo] *sm* bramble.

**rozzo** ['roddzo] *agg* rough; (*fig*) coarse.

**ruba** ['ruba] *sf* **andare a ruba** sell like hot cakes.

**rubacchiare** [rubak'kjare] *v* pilfer.

**rubare** [ru'bare] *v* steal. **rubacuori** *s(m+f)* charmer. **rubare il tempo a qualcuno** take up someone's time. **ruberia** *sf* theft.

**rubinetto** [rubi'netto] *sm* tap. **rubinetto di chiusura** stopcock.

**rubino** [ru'bino] *sm* ruby.

**rubrica** [ru'brika] *sf* (*indirizzi*) address-book; (*telefonica*) directory; (*quaderno*) index-book; (*giornale*) feature.

**rude** ['rude] *agg* rough.

**rudere** ['rudere] *sm* ruin; (*persona*) wreck.

**ruffiano** [ruf'fjano] *sm* pimp; (*adulatore*) bootlicker.

**ruga** ['ruga] *sf* wrinkle. **rugoso** *agg* wrinkled.

**ruggine** ['ruddʒine] *sf* rust; (*astio*) ill feeling. **rugginoso** *agg* rusty.

**ruggire** [rud'dʒire] *v* roar. **ruggito** *sm* roar.

**rugiada** [ru'dʒada] *sf* dew. **goccia di rugiada** *sf* dewdrop.

**rullare** [rul'lare] *v* roll; (*aereo*) taxi. **rullio** *sm* rolling. **rullo** *sm* roll; (*tec*) roller.

**rum** [rum] *sm* rum.

**ruminare** [rumi'nare] *v* ruminate.

**rumore** [ru'more] *sm* noise; (*diceria*) rumour; sensation. **rumoreggiare** *v* make a noise; rumble. **rumoroso** *agg* noisy.

**ruolo** ['rwɔlo] *sm* roll; (*teatro, funzione*) role. **insegnante non di ruolo** supply teacher. **personale di ruolo** permanent staff.

**ruota** ['rwɔta] *sf* wheel. **andare a ruota libera** free-wheel. **a ruota** circular. **far la ruota** (*pavoneggiarsi*) show off. **seguire a ruota** follow close behind.

**rupe** ['rupe] *sf* cliff.

**rupia** [ru'pia] *sf* rupee.

**rurale** [ru'rale] *agg* rural.

**ruscello** [ru'ʃɛllo] *sm* stream.

**ruspa** ['ruspa] *sf* bulldozer. (**pollo**) **ruspante** *sm* free-range chicken.

**russare** [rus'sare] *v* snore.

**Russia** ['russja] *sf* Russia. **russo, -a** *s*, *agg* Russian.

**rustico** ['rustiko] *agg* rustic; (*contadino*) rural; (*rozzo*) rough.

**ruttare** [rut'tare] *v* belch. **rutto** *sm* belch.

**ruvido** ['ruvido] *agg* rough. **ruvidezza** *sf* roughness.

**ruzzare** [rut'tsare] *v* romp.

**ruzzolare** [ruttso'lare] *v* tumble; (*rotolare*) roll (down). **ruzzolone** *sm* tumble. **fare un ruzzolone** (*fam*) come a cropper.

# S

**sabato** ['sabato] *sm* Saturday. **il** *or* **di sabato** on Saturdays.

**sabbia** ['sabbja] *sf* sand. **sabbie mobili** quicksand *sing.* **sabbiare** *v* sand-blast. **sabbioso** *agg* sandy.

**sabotaggio** [sabo'taddʒo] *sm* sabotage. **sabotare** *v* sabotage. **sabotatore, -trice** *sm, sf* saboteur.

**sacca** ['sakka] *sf* bag; (*fig*) pocket.

**saccarina** [sakka'rina] *sf* saccharine.

**saccente** [sat'tʃɛnte] *s(m+f)*, *agg* know-all.

**saccheggiare** [sakked'dʒare] *v* sack, loot. **saccheggiatore** *sm* plunderer, looter. **saccheggio** *sm* sacking, looting.

**sacco** ['sakko] *sm* sack. **cogliere con le mani nel sacco** catch red-handed. **sacco a pelo** sleeping-bag. **sacco da montagna** rucksack. **sacco postale** mail-bag. **un sacco di** lots of.

**sacerdote** [satʃer'dɔte] *sm* priest. **sacerdozio** *sm* priesthood.

**sacramento** [sakra'mento] *sm* sacrament.

**sacrificare** [sakrifi'kare] *v* sacrifice; (*rinun-*

*ciare*) give up; (*non valorizzare*) waste. **sacrificio** *sm* sacrifice; (*di sè*) self-sacrifice.

**sacrilegio** [sakri'ledʒo] *sm* sacrilege; (*fig*) crime. **sacrilego** *agg, m pl* **-ghi** sacrilegious; criminal.

**sacro** ['sakro] *agg* sacred. *sm* (*osso*) sacrum. **sacrosanto** *agg* sacrosanct.

**sadico** ['sadiko], **-a** *agg* sadistic. *sm, sf* sadist. **sadismo** *sm* sadism.

**saetta** [sa'etta] *sf* flash (of lightning); (*mec*) bit; (*freccia*) arrow.

**sagace** [sa'gatʃe] *agg* sagacious. **sagacia** *sf* sagacity.

**saggio**[1] ['saddʒo], **-a** *agg* wise; (*sapiente*) sage. *sm, sf* sage. **saggezza** *sf* wisdom.

**saggio**[2] ['saddʒo] *sm* trial; (*metalli preziosi*) assay; (*prova*) proof; (*dimostrazione pubblica*) display; (*scritto critico*) essay. **saggiare** *v* test; assay. **saggiatura** *sf* assay; (*segno*) hallmark. **saggista** *s(m+f)* essayist.

**Sagittario** [sadʒit'tarjo] *sm* Sagittarius.

**sagoma** ['sagoma] *sf* outline; (*forma, modello*) pattern. **sagomare** *v* shape.

**sagra** ['sagra] *sf* feast.

**sagrestano** [sagres'tano] *sm* sacristan. **sagrestia** *sf* vestry.

**sala** ['sala] *sf* room, hall. **sala da pranzo** dining-room. **sala d'aspetto** waiting-room. **sala di lettura/macchine** reading/engine-room. **sala giochi** amusement arcade. **sala operatoria** operating theatre.

**salace** [sa'latʃe] *agg* salacious.

**salamandra** [sala'mandra] *sf* salamander.

**salame** [sa'lame] *sm* salami; (*fig*) fool.

**salamoia** [sala'mɔja] *sf* brine. **mettere in salamoia** pickle.

**salare** [sa'lare] *v* salt. **salato** *agg* salty; (*conservato*) salted. (*caro*) dear.

**salario** [sa'larjo] *sm* pay; (*settimanale*) wages *pl*; (*mensile*) salary. **salariale** *agg* pay.

**salassare** [salas'sare] *v* bleed.

**salda** ['salda] *sf* size, sizing. **dare la salda a** size; (*inamidare*) starch.

**saldare** [sal'dare] *v* (*tec*) solder; (*autogeno*) weld; (*econ*) settle, pay. **saldatore** *sm* (*operaio*) solderer, welder; (*utensile*) soldering iron. **saldatrice** *sf* welder. **saldatura** *sf* welding; soldering.

**saldo**[1] ['saldo] *agg* solid; firm. **saldezza** *sf* solidity; firmness.

**saldo**[2] ['saldo] *sm* settlement; (*somma da pagare*) balance. **saldi** *sm pl* (*merce*)

remnants *pl*.

**sale** ['sale] *sm* salt. **non aver sale in zucca** be stupid. **restar di sale** be dumbfounded. **salgemma** *sm* rock-salt. **salino** *agg* saline.

**salice** ['salitʃe] *sm* willow(-tree). **salice piangente** weeping willow.

**saliente** [sa'ljɛnte] *agg, sm* salient.

**\*salire** [sa'lire] *v* climb, go up; (*autobus, treno*) board, get on; (*auto*) get in; (*alzarsi, crescere*) rise. **far salire** send up. **saliscendi** *sm invar* (*chiusura*) latch; (*fig*) ups and downs *pl*. **salita** *sf* climb; entrance; (*tratto che sale*) slope. **in salita** uphill; (*che aumenta*) rising.

**saliva** [sa'liva] *sf* saliva. **salivale** *agg* salivary. **salivare** *v* salivate.

**salma** ['salma] *sf* corpse.

**salmo** ['salmo] *sm* psalm.

**salmone** [sal'mone] *sm* salmon.

**salone** [sa'lone] *sm* living room; (*esposizione*) show; (*parrucchiere*) salon.

**salotto** [sa'lɔtto] *sm* drawing room, lounge.

**salpare** [sal'pare] *v* weigh anchor.

**salsa** ['salsa] *sf* sauce; (*a base di carne*) gravy. **in tutte le salse** in all kinds of ways. **salsiera** *sf* sauce-boat; gravy-boat.

**salsiccia** [sal'sittʃa] *sf* sausage.

**salso** ['salso] *agg* salt(y). **salsedine** *sf* saltiness.

**saltare** [sal'tare] *v* jump; (*balzare*) leap; (*tralasciare*) skip; (*bottone, etc.*) come off; (*gastr*) sauté. **far saltare** destroy, blow up; (*serratura*) force; (*governo*) bring down. **saltare di palo in frasca** switch from one subject to another. **saltare (in aria)** (*esplodere*) blow up. **saltare in bestia** fly into a rage. **saltare in mente** cross one's mind, get into one's head.

**saltellare** [saltel'lare] *v also* **salterellare** skip *or* hop about.

**saltimbanco** [saltim'banko] *sm* acrobat; (*spreg*) charlatan.

**salto** ['salto] *sm* jump, leap; (*omissione*) gap. **in un salto** in a jiffy. **salto con l'asta** pole-vault. **salto in alto/lungo** high/long-jump. **saltuario** *agg* intermittent, occasional.

**salubre** [sa'lubre] *agg* healthy.

**salumeria** [salume'ria] *sf* delicatessen. **salumi** *sm pl* cold meats *pl*. **salumiere, -a** *sm, sf* pork-butcher; grocer.

**salutare** [salu'tare] v greet; (mil) salute. **salutami tuo fratello** remember me to your brother. **saluto** sm greeting; salute. **cordiali/distinti saluti** yours sincerely/faithfully.

**salute** [sa'lute] sf health; (benessere) welfare. inter (a chi starnutisce) bless you! (nei brindisi) cheers!

**salvare** [sal'vare] v save; (trarre in salvo) rescue; protect. **salvacondotto** sm pass. **salvadanaio** sm money-box. **salvagente** sm (ciambella) lifebelt; (giacca) life-jacket; (strada) traffic island. **salvaguardare** v safeguard. **salvaguardia** sf safeguard. **salvaschermo** [salvas'kɛrmo] sm screensaver. **salvataggio** sm rescue.

**salve** [ˈsalve] inter hello! (salute) bless you!

**salvia** [ˈsalvja] sf sage.

**salvietta** [sal'vjetta] sf (tovagliolo) napkin; (asciugamano) towel.

**salvo** [ˈsalvo] agg safe. **mettere in salvo** save, put aside. prep except (for), bar(ring). **salvo che** except that; (a meno che) unless. **salvezza** sf salvation; (sicurezza) safety.

**sambuco** [sam'buko] sm, pl -chi elder.

**sanare** [sa'nare] v heal; (porre rimedio) rectify; (bonificare) reclaim. **sanatorio** sm sanatorium.

**sancire** [san'tʃire] v sanction; ratify.

**sandalo**[1] [ˈsandalo] sm sandal.

**sandalo**[2] [ˈsandalo] sm (legno) sandal-wood.

**sangue** [ˈsangwe] sm blood. **al sangue** (gastr) rare. **a sangue caldo/freddo** warm-/cold-blooded. **farsi cattivo sangue** get worked up. **puro sangue** thoroughbred. **sangue freddo** sang-froid, composure. **sanguemisto** sm half-breed.

**sanguigno** [san'gwiɲo] agg blood; (colore) blood-red; (costituzione) sanguine.

**sanguinare** [sangwi'nare] v bleed. **sanguinario** agg bloodthirsty. **sanguinolento** agg bleeding; (insanguinato) bloody. **sanguinoso** agg bloody.

**sanguisuga** [sangwi'suga] sf leech.

**sanità** [sani'ta] sf health; (salubrità) wholesomeness. **sanità mentale** sanity. **sanitario** agg sanitary; (di medicina) medical.

**sano** [ˈsano] agg healthy; (integro) sound; (salubre) wholesome; (di mente) sane; intact. **sano come un pesce** sound as a bell. **sano e salvo** safe and sound.

**santo** [ˈsanto], **-a** agg holy; (seguito da nome) Saint; pious; sacred; (rafforzativo) blessed. sm, sf saint. **santerello, -a** sm, sf (fam) goody-goody. **santificare** v sanctify; (venerare) hallow; canonize. **santità** sf holiness; (fig) sanctity. **santuario** sm sanctuary.

**sanzione** [san'tsjone] sf sanction. **sanzionare** v sanction.

*__sapere__ [sa'pere] v know; (essere capace, aver imparato) can, know how (to); (aver odore) smell (of); (aver sapore) taste (of). **buono a sapersi** worth knowing. **far sapere a** let know, inform. **non ne voglio sapere I** don't want to have anything to do with it. **non si sa mai** you never can tell. **per quanto ne sappia** as far as I know. **saperla lunga** know a thing or two. **venire a sapere** learn, gather. sm knowledge, learning.

**sapienza** [sa'pjɛntsa] sf wisdom; learning. **sapiente** agg wise; learned. **sapientone, -a** sm, sf (fam) know-all.

**sapone** [sa'pone] sm soap. **sapone in polvere** soap-powder. **saponetta** sf bar of soap. **saponiera** sf soap-dish. **saponoso** agg soapy.

**sapore** [sa'pore] sm taste, flavour. **saporito** agg tasty; (salato) rather salty; (arguto) witty.

**saracinesca** [saratʃi'nɛska] sf roller-blind; (di chiusa) floodgate.

**sarcasmo** [sar'kazmo] sm sarcasm. **sarcastico** agg sarcastic.

**sarchio** [ˈsarkjɔ] sm hoe. **sarchiare** v hoe.

**sarda** [ˈsarda] sf also **sardina** pilchard, sardine.

**Sardegna** [sar'deɲa] sf Sardinia. **sardo, -a** s, agg Sardinian.

**sardonico** [sar'dɔniko] agg sardonic.

**sarta** [ˈsarta] sf dressmaker. **sarto** sm tailor. **sartoria** sf (laboratorio) dressmaker's or tailor's workshop; (tecnica) dressmaking, tailoring.

**sasso** [ˈsasso] sm stone; (ciottolo) pebble; (roccia) rock. **prendere a sassate** pelt with stones, stone. **sassoso** agg stony.

**sassofono** [sas'sɔfono] sm saxophone. **sassofonista** s(m+f) saxophonist.

**Satana** [ˈsatana] sm Satan. **satanico** agg satanic.

**satellite** [sa'tɛllite] agg, sm satellite.

**satirico** [sa'tiriko] agg satirical. **satira** sf satire. **satireggiare** v also **mettere in satira** satirize.

**satiro** ['satiro] *sm* satyr.

**satollo** [sa'tollo] *agg* full up.

**saturare** [satu'rare] *v* saturate; *(fig)* cram. **saturazione** *sf* saturation. **saturo** *agg* saturated; crammed, full.

**savio** ['savjo] *agg* wise; prudent.

**saziare** [sa'tsjare] *v* satisfy; *(riempire presto)* be filling. **saziarsi** *v* have one's fill; *(stancarsi)* tire. **sazietà** *sf* surfeit. **a sazietà** more than enough. **mangiare a sazietà** eat *or* have one's fill. **sazio** *agg* satisfied; *(fam)* full up; *(stanco)* tired.

**sbadato** [zba'dato] *agg* careless, thoughtless. **sbadataggine** *sf* carelessness, thoughtlessness.

**sbadigliare** [zbadi'ʎare] *v* yawn. **sbadiglio** *sm* yawn.

**sbafare** [zba'fare] *v* *(scroccare)* scrounge; *(mangiare avidamente)* gobble up. **mangiare/vivere a sbafo** scrounge a meal/living.

**sbagliare** [zba'ʎare] *v* make a mistake; *(scambiare)* mistake. **sbagliare i calcoli** miscalculate; *(fig)* make a (big) mistake. **sbagliar il passo** stumble; *(mil)* be out of step. **sbagliar numero** get the wrong number. **sbagliare ortografia** spell incorrectly. **sbagliarsi sul conto di** be wrong about. **sbagliato** *agg* wrong, mistaken. **calcolo sbagliato** *sm* miscalculation. **pronuncia sbagliata** *sf* mispronunciation. **sbaglio** *sm* mistake.

**sbalestrato** [zbales'trato] *agg* unsettled; *(smarrito)* lost.

**sballare** [zbal'lare] *v* *(merce)* unpack. **sballato** *agg* wild.

**sballottare** [zballot'tare] *v* toss about. **sballottamento** *sm* tossing.

**sbalordire** [zbalor'dire] *v* astonish; *(turbare)* bewilder, shock. **sbalordimento** *sm* astonishment; shock, bewilderment. **sbalorditivo** *agg* amazing; *(incredibile)* staggering.

**sbalzare**[1] [zbal'tsare] *v* throw, fling. **sbalzo** *sm* jerk, jolt; *(fig)* jump. **a sbalzi** jerkily; *(fig)* by fits and starts.

**sbalzare**[2] [zbal'tsare] *v* *(metallo)* emboss. **lavoro a sbalzo** *sm* embossing.

**sbandare** [zban'dare] *v* *(auto)* skid; *(mar)* list; *(aero)* bank; *(disperdere)* break *or* split up. **sbandata** *sf* skid. **prendere una sbandata per** have a crush on. **sbandato** *agg* scattered; *(fig)* bewildered.

**sbaragliare** [zbara'ʎare] *v* (put to) rout. **andare** *or* **buttarsi allo sbaraglio** risk

everything. **mettere allo sbaraglio** jeopardize.

**sbarazzarsi** [zbarat'tsarsi] *v* get rid of.

**sbarbare** [zbar'bare] *v* shave. **sbarbatello** *sm* novice.

**sbarcare** [zbar'kare] *v* land; *(merce)* unload. **sbarco** *sm* landing; unloading.

**sbarra** ['zbarra] *sf* bar, barrier; *(segno grafico)* stroke. **sbarramento** *sm* barrage; block(age). **sbarrare** *v* bar, block; *(porta)* bolt; *(assegno)* cross; *(occhi)* open wide.

**sbatacchiare** [zbatak'kjare] *v* slam; *(ali)* flap.

**sbattere** ['zbattere] *v* *(scaraventare)* fling; *(chiudere violentemente)* slam; *(urtare)* bash; *(ali)* flap; *(gastr)* whip, beat. **non saper dove sbattere la testa** not know which way to turn. **sbatter fuori** *(fam)* chuck out.

**sbavare** [zba'vare] *v* *(emettere bava)* dribble; *(colore, ecc.)* smudge. **sbavatura** *sf* dribble; smudge.

**sberla** ['zberla] *sf* slap.

**sbiadire** [zbja'dire] *v* fade. **sbiadito** *agg* faded; *(fig)* dull.

**sbiancare** [zbjan'kare] *v* whiten.

**sbianchire** [zbjan'kire] *v* whiten; *(gastr)* blanch.

**sbieco** ['zbjɛko] *agg* crooked. **guardar di sbieco** look askance at. **tagliar di sbieco** cut on the bias.

**sbigottire** [zbigot'tire] *v* astonish; *(turbare)* dismay. **sbigottimento** *sm* astonishment; dismay.

**sbilancio** [zbi'lantʃo] *sm* *(squilibrio)* lack of equilibrium; *(econ)* deficit. **sbilanciare** *v* unbalance.

**sbilenco** [zbi'lɛnko] *agg* crooked.

**sbloccare** [zblok'kare] *v* free, release; *(prezzi)* unfreeze.

**sboccare** [zbok'kare] *v* come out; *(condurre)* lead; *(fiume)* flow (into). **sbocco** *sm* outlet.

**sbocciare** [zbot'tʃare] *v* bloom, blossom.

**sbollentare** [zbollen'tare] *v* blanch.

**sbornia** [zbɔrnja] *sf* postumi di una sbornia *sm pl* hangover *sing*. **prendere una sbornia** get drunk.

**sborsare** [zbor'sare] *v* pay out, disburse. **sborso** *sm* disbursement.

**sbottare** [zbot'tare] *v* burst out.

**sbottonare** [zbotto'nare] *v* unbutton.

**sbozzare** [zbot'tsare] *v* sketch; *(fig)* outline.

**sbracciarsi** [zbrat'tʃarsi] v gesticulate; (*rimboccarsi le maniche*) roll up one's sleeves; (*fig*) do one's utmost. **sbracciato** *agg* (*abito*) sleeveless.

**sbraitare** [zbrai'tare] v yell; protest.

**sbranare** [zbra'nare] v tear to pieces.

**sbrattare** [zbrat'tare] v tidy up. **stanza di sbratto** *sf* lumber-room.

**sbriciolare** [zbritʃo'lare] v crumble.

**sbrigare** [zbri'gare] v get done, finish (off); (*risolvere*) settle. **sbrigarsi** v (*far presto*) hurry up; (*liberarsi*) get rid (of). **sbrigativo** *agg* quick; (*superficiale*) hasty.

**sbrigliare** [zbri'ʎare] v unbridle, give free rein (to). **sbrigliatezza** *sf* unruliness. **sbrigliato** *agg* unruly, wild.

**sbrindellare** [zbrindel'lare] v tear to shreds. **sbrindellato** *agg* in rags *or* tatters.

**sbrodolare** [zbrodo'lare] v (*insudiciare*) soil; (*fig*) spin out; (*fam*) waffle.

**sbrogliare** [sbro'ʎare] v disentangle. **sbrogliarsi** v extricate oneself.

**sbronzo** ['zbrondzo] *agg* drunk. **prendersi una sbronza** get drunk.

**sbruffare** [zbruf'fare] v spurt; (*fig*) brag.

**sbucare** [zbu'kare] v come out, emerge; (*fig*) spring up.

**sbucciare** [zbut'tʃare] v peel; (*escoriare*) scrape. **sbucciapatate** *sm invar* potato peeler. **sbucciatura** *sf* scrape, graze.

**sbudellare** [zbudel'lare] v disembowel; (*gastr*) gut. **sbudellarsi dal ridere** split one's sides laughing.

**sbuffare** [zbuf'fare] v puff, pant; (*rabbia*) snort.

**scabbia** ['skabbia] *sf* scabies. **scabbiosa** *sf* (*bot*) scabious.

**scabroso** [ska'brozo] *agg also* **scabro** rough; (*problema*) thorny, knotty.

**scacciare** [skat'tʃare] v drive out *or* away; (*fig*) expel.

**scacco** ['skakko] *sm* (*quadretto*) check; (*figurina del gioco*) chessman. **scacchi** *sm pl* (*gioco*) chess *sing*. **scacco matto** check-mate. **subire uno scacco** suffer a setback. **scacchiera** *sf* chess-board; (*per dama*) draught-board.

***scadere** [ska'dere] v expire; (*perdere valore*) decline; (*econ*) fall due. **scadente** *agg* poor. **scadenza** *sf* expiry; (*effetti*) maturity. **a breve/lunga scadenza** short/long-term. **scadimento** *sm* decline.

**scafandro** [ska'fandro] *sm* diving-suit; (*astronauta*) space-suit.

**scaffale** [skaf'fale] *sm* shelf. **scaffalatura** *sf* shelving.

**scafo** ['skafo] *sm* hull.

**scagionare** [skadʒo'nare] v exonerate.

**scaglia** ['skaʎa] *sf* scale; (*sapone*) flake. **scagliare** v flake.

**scagliare** [ska'ʎare] v (*lanciare*) fling, hurl.

**scaglione** [ska'ʎone] *sm* group; (*mil*) echelon. **scaglionare** v stagger; (*mil*) range. **scaglionamento** *sm* staggering.

**scala** ['skala] *sf* stairs *pl*, staircase; (*piano*) level; (*misura, rapporto*) scale; (*apparecchio*) ladder. **far le scale** climb the stairs; (*musica*) practise scales. **scala a chiocciola** spiral staircase. **scala di corda** rope-ladder. **scala portatile** steps *pl*, step-ladder. **scalinata** *sf* flight of stairs.

**scalare** [ska'lare] v scale. *agg* graduated; (*fis*) scalar. **scalata** *sf* climb. **scalatore, -trice** *sm, sf* climber.

**scalcagnato** [skalka'ɲato] *agg* shabby.

**scaldare** [skal'dare] v warm (up); (*a temperatura più elevata*) heat (up). **scaldabagno** *sm* water-heater.

**scalfire** [skal'fire] v scratch.

**scalmanato** [skalma'nato] *agg* flustered. *sm, sf* hothead. **scalmana** *sf* chill; (*fig*) craze.

**scalo** ['skalo] *sm* (*banchina*) pier; (*porto d'approdo*) port of call; (*aero*) stopover. **far scalo** (*mar*) land, stop. **scalo merci** (*mar*) wharf; (*ferr*) goods yard. **senza scalo** non-stop.

**scalogna** [ska'loɲa] *sf* bad luck. **scalognato** *agg* unlucky.

**scaloppa** [ska'lɔppa] *sf* cutlet. **scaloppina** *sf* escalope.

**scalpello** [skal'pɛllo] *sm* chisel; (*chirurgia*) scalpel. **scalpellare** v chisel; cut away.

**scalpore** [skal'pore] *sm* sensation.

**scaltro** ['skaltro] *agg* shrewd.

**scalzo** ['skaltso] *agg* barefoot.

**scambiare** [skam'bjare] v (*dare in cambio*) exchange; (*confondere*) mistake, mix up. **scambievole** *agg* mutual. **scambio** *sm* exchange; (*ferr*) points *pl*. **libero scambio** free trade.

**scamosciato** [skamo'ʃato] *agg* suede.

**scampagnata** [skampa'ɲata] *sf* outing.

**scampanato** [skampa'nato] *agg* flared.

**scampare** [skam'pare] v escape; (evitare) avoid. **Dio ce ne scampi!** God forbid! **scamparla bella** have a narrow escape. **scampato, -a** sm, sf (superstite) survivor. **scampo** sm way out.

**scampo** ['skampo] sm prawn.

**scampolo** ['skampolo] sm remnant.

**scanalare** [skana'lare] v groove; (colonna) flute. **scanalatura** sf groove; flute.

**scandagliare** [skanda'ʎare] v sound (out). **scandaglio** sm sounding.

**scandalizzare** [skandalid'dzare] v shock; (dar scandalo) scandalize. **scandalo** sm scandal. **scandaloso** agg scandalous.

**scandire** [skan'dire] v (pronunciare) articulate; (versi) scan.

**scanno** ['skanno] sm stall.

**scansare** [skan'sare] v dodge, shirk; (spostare) shift. **scansarsi** v get out of the way. **scansafatiche** s(m+f) invar loafer.

**scapaccione** [skapat'tʃone] sm slap.

**scapestrato** [skapes'trato], -a agg wild, unruly. sm, sf madcap, daredevil.

**scapigliato** [skapi'ʎato] agg dishevelled; (fig) reckless.

**scapitare** [skapi'tare] sm loss; (danno) injury. **a scapito di** to the detriment of.

**scapola** ['skapola] sf shoulder-blade.

**scapolo** ['skapolo] agg single. sm bachelor.

**scappamento** [skappa'mento] sm (auto) exhaust.

**scappare** [skap'pare] v run away; escape, flee. **devo scappare** (ho fretta) I must rush. **lasciarsi scappar di bocca** blurt out. **scappare di mente** slip one's mind. **scappatella** sf escapade. **scappatoia** sf way out; (fig) loophole.

**scappellotto** [skapel'lɔtto] sm smack. **passare a scappellotti** (fam) scrape through.

**scarabocchio** [skara'bɔkkjo] sm (macchia) blot; (sgorbio) scrawl; (disegno) doodle. **scarabocchiare** v scrawl; doodle.

**scarafaggio** [skara'faddʒo] sm cockroach.

**scaramanzia** [skaraman'tsia] sf spell. **per scaramanzia** for luck.

**scaramuccia** [skara'muttʃa] sf skirmish.

**scaraventare** [skaraven'tare] v hurl, fling.

**scarcerare** [skartʃe'rare] v release (from prison). **scarceramento** sm release.

**scardinare** [skardi'nare] v unhinge.

**scaricare** [skari'kare] v discharge; (deporre)

un carico) unload; (sfogare) vent; (liquido) empty; (gas) let out; (Internet) download. **scaricare la colpa** shift the blame. **scarica** sf discharge; (raffica) volley. **scaricalasino** sm invar piggy-back.

**scarico** ['skariko] sm, pl -chi discharge; unloading; (di rifiuti) dumping; (i rifiuti stessi) rubbish; (deposito di rifiuti) dump; (auto) exhaust. **a mio scarico** in my defence. **a scarico di coscienza** to clear one's conscience. agg (vuoto) empty; (batteria) flat.

**scarlattina** [skarlat'tina] sf scarlet fever.

**scarlatto** [skar'latto] agg, sm scarlet.

**scarno** ['skarno] agg skinny; (spoglio) bare; (povero) scanty.

**scarpa** ['skarpa] sf shoe. **scarpe da ginnastica** or **tennis** plimsolls pl. **scarpone** sm boot. **scarponi da calciatore/sci** football/ski-boots pl.

**scarso** ['skarso] agg poor; (manchevole) lacking (in); (insufficiente) short. **un chilo scarso** just under a kilo. **scarseggiare** v be scarce; be short (of); (fig) lack (in). **scarsezza** or **scarsità** sf shortage; lack.

**scartabellare** [skartabel'lare] v skim or flip through.

**scartare¹** [skar'tare] v (togliere dalla carta) unwrap; (respingere) discard, reject. **scarto** sm (cosa scartata) reject; (alle carte) discard. **merci di scarto** sf pl inferior goods pl, rejects pl.

**scartare²** [skar'tare] v (spostarsi lateralmente) swerve. **scarto** sm swerve, skid; difference.

**scassare** [skas'sare] v (fam: guastare) smash, bust; (il terreno) break up. **furto con scasso** sm burglary.

**scassinare** [skassi'nare] v force (open). **scassinatore, -trice** sm, sf burglar; (di banche) bank-robber.

**scatenare** [skate'nare] v unleash; cause. **scatenarsi** v break out.

**scatola** ['skatola] sf box; carton; (di latta) tin. **averne piene le scatole** (fam) be fed up to the back teeth (with). **cibo in scatola** sm tinned food. **rompere le scatole** (fam) be a nuisance. **scatolame** sm tinned goods pl.

**scattare** [skat'tare] v spring; (rilasciarsi) spring up; (armi) go off; (aprirsi) spring open; (chiudersi) snap shut. **far scattare** release. **scattare a vuoto** misfire. **scatto**

*sm* release; (*rumore*) click; (*sport*) spurt; (*accesso*) outburst. **a scatti** jerkily. **di scatto** suddenly.

**scaturire** [skatu'rire] *v* gush; (*fig*) arise.

**scavalcare** [skaval'kare] *v* step *or* climb over; (*saltando*) jump over; (*sbalzare di sella*) throw; (*superare*) overtake.

**scavare** [ska'vare] *v* dig; (*miniera*) sink; (*trovare*) dig up; (*sartoria*) widen. **scavatore** *sm* digger. **scavatura** *sf* excavation. **scavo** *sm* excavation.

*****scegliere** ['ʃeʎere] *v* choose. **c'è (molto) da scegliere** there is plenty to choose from. **c'è poco da scegliere** there is little choice.

**scellerato** [ʃelle'rato], **-a** *agg* wicked. *sm, sf* wicked person. **scelleratezza** *sf* wickedness; (*atto*) misdeed.

**scelta** ['ʃelta] *sf* choice, selection; quality. **a scelta** according to preference. **non aver possibilità di scelta** have no choice. **scelto** *agg* chosen, picked; (*eccellente*) choice.

**scemare** [ʃe'mare] *v* diminish.

**scemo** ['ʃemo], **-a** *agg* stupid, idiotic; (*sciocco*) foolish. *sm, sf* fool, idiot. **scemenza** *sf* (*azione*) idiocy, foolishness; (*parole*) nonsense.

**scena** ['ʃena] *sf* scene; (*palcoscenico*) stage. **mettere in scena** stage, produce. **scenario** *sm* (*teatro*) set; (*cinema*) scenario, script; (*fig*) setting. **scenata** *sf* scene, row. **sceneggiare** *v* adapt, dramatize. **sceneggiatura** *sf* script. **scenico** *agg* scenic.

*****scendere** ['ʃendere] *v* (*andar giù*) go down; (*venir giù*) come down; (*autobus, treno*) get off; (*auto*) get out; (*calare*) drop; (*sostare*) stop. **scendere a un accordo** reach an agreement. **scendere dal letto** get up. **scendiletto** *sm invar* (*tappetino*) bedside rug; (*vestaglia*) dressing-gown.

**sceriffo** [ʃe'riffo] *sm* sheriff.

**scervellarsi** [ʃervel'larsi] *v* rack one's brains. **scervellato** *agg* hare-brained.

**scettico** ['ʃettiko], **-a** *agg* sceptical. *sm, sf* sceptic. **scetticismo** *sm* scepticism.

**scettro** ['ʃettro] *sm* sceptre.

**scheda** ['skeda] *sf* card; (*di schedario*) index-card; (*elettorale*) ballot(-paper). **scheda gratta e vinci** scratch card. **schedare** *v* catalogue; (*archiviare*) file. **schedario** *sm* file; (*mobile*) filing cabinet; (*elenco*) list. **schedina** *sf* coupon.

**scheggia** ['skeddʒa] *sf* splinter. **scheggiare** *v* splinter, chip.

**scheletro** ['skɛletro] *sm* skeleton; (*tec*) framework. **scheletrico** *agg* skeletal; (*fig*) bare.

**schema** ['skɛma] *sm* scheme; (*abbozzo*) outline; (*modello*) pattern. **schema di legge** bill. **schematico** *agg* schematic.

**scherma** ['skerma] *sf* fencing. **tirare di scherma** fence. **schermaglia** *sf* skirmish. **schermitore, -trice** *sm, sf* fencer.

**schermo** ['skermo] *sm* screen; (*difesa*) shield. **schermare** *v* screen, shield. **schermire** *v* protect.

**schernire** [sker'nire] *v* scorn, mock. **schernitore, -trice** *agg* scornful, mocking. **scherno** *sm* mockery, derision; (*oggetto di scherno*) laughing-stock.

**scherzare** [sker'tsare] *v* joke; (*prendere alla leggera*) trifle (with); (*giocare*) play. **c'è poco da scherzare** it is not a laughing matter. **scherzi!** *inter* you must be joking! **scherzo** *sm* joke; (*tiro*) trick; (*musica*) scherzo. **per scherzo** for fun, as a joke. **scherzoso** *agg* playful; (*giocoso*) jocular.

**schettinare** [sketti'nare] *v* roller-skate. **schettinaggio** *sm* roller-skating. **schettino** *sm* roller-skate.

**schiacciare** [skjat'tʃare] *v* (*spiaccicare*) squash; (*frantumare*) crush; (*noci*) crack. **schiacciare un pisolino** have a nap. **schiacciante** *agg* crushing. **schiaccianoci** *sm* nutcrackers *pl*. **schiacciasassi** *sm* steamroller.

**schiaffare** [skjaf'fare] *v* (*fam*) chuck.

**schiaffo** ['skjaffo] *sm* slap. **schiaffeggiare** *v* slap.

**schiamazzare** [skjamat'tsare] *v* cackle; (*far baccano*) make a row. **schiamazzo** *sm* cackle; row.

**schiantare** [skjan'tare] *v* shatter, burst. **schianto** *sm* crash.

**schiappa** ['skjappa] *sf* (*fam*) washout.

**schiarire** [skja'rire] *v* clear (up). **schiarimento** *sm* clearing up; (*spiegazione*) explanation; information.

**schiavo** ['skjavo], **-a** *s, agg* slave. **schiavitù** *sf* slavery.

**schiena** ['skjɛna] *sf* back. **colpire alla schiena** stab in the back. **mal di schiena** *sm* backache. **schienale** *sm* back.

**schiera** ['skjɛra] *sf* band; (*moltitudine*) mass, crowd. **schieramento** *sm* formation; line-up. **schierare** *v* line up; (*mil*) deploy.

**schierarsi contro** take sides against.
**schierarsi dalla parte di** side with.
**schietto** ['skjetto] *agg* sincere; genuine;
frank. **a dirla schietta** (to speak) frankly.
**schiettezza** *sf* genuineness; frankness.

**schifo** ['skifo] *sm* disgust. **avere a schifo**
loathe. **far schifo** *v* (*essere disgustoso*) be
disgusting; (*disgustare*) (fill with) disgust.
**schifare** *v* disgust. **schifezza** *sf* rubbish,
muck. **schifiltoso** *agg* fussy; (*esigente*) fastidious. **schifoso** *agg* disgusting.

**schioccare** [skjok'kare] *v* crack; (*dita*) snap.

**schioppo** ['skjɔppo] *sm* gun; (*da caccia*)
shotgun. **schioppettata** *sf* (gun)shot.

**\*schiudersi** ['skjudersi] *v* open (up).

**schiuma** ['skjuma] *sf* foam; (*birra*) froth;
(*sapone*) lather; (*feccia*) scum. **aver la
schiuma alla bocca** foam at the mouth.
**schiumare** *v* skim. **schiumoso** *agg* foamy;
frothy; lathery.

**schivare** [ski'vare] *v* avoid; (*fam*) dodge;
(*boxe*) duck.

**schizofrenia** [skitsofre'nia] *sf* schizophrenia. **schizofrenico, -a** *s*, *agg* schizophrenic.

**schizzare** [skit'tsare] *v* (*zampillare*) spurt;
(*spruzzare*) squirt; (*sporcare*) splash; (*disegnare*) sketch. **schizzar via** dash off.
**schizzetto** *sm* spray; syringe; (*giocattolo*)
water-pistol. **schizzo** *sm* spurt; squirt;
splash; sketch.

**schizzinoso** [skittsi'nozo] *agg* fastidious;
squeamish.

**sci** [ʃi] *sm* (*attrezzo*) ski; (*attività*) skiing. **fare
dello sci** ski, go skiing. **sci nautico** water-
ski; water-skiing. **sciare** *v* ski. **sciatore,
-trice** *sm, sf* skier.

**scia** ['ʃia] *sf* wake; (*traccia*) trail. **seguire la
scia di** follow in the footsteps of.

**sciabola** ['ʃabola] *sf* sabre.

**sciacallo** [ʃa'kallo] *sm* jackal.

**sciacquare** [ʃak'kware] *v* rinse (out). **sciac-
quata** *sf* rinse. **sciacquatura** *sf* (*azione*)
rinsing; (*acqua*) dishwater. **sciacquo** *sm*
rinsing; (*liquido*) mouthwash.

**sciagura** [ʃa'gura] *sf* disaster; (*incidente*)
accident, crash. **sciagurato** *agg*
(*sfortunato*) unlucky, wretched; (*malvagio*)
wicked.

**scialacquare** [ʃalak'kware] *v* squander.
**scialacquatore, -trice** *sm, sf* spendthrift.

**scialbo** ['ʃalbo] *agg* pale; faint; (*fig*) dull.

**scialle** ['ʃalle] *sm* shawl.

**scialo** ['ʃalo] *sm* waste.

**sciame** ['ʃame] *sm* swarm. **sciamare** *v*
swarm.

**sciancato** [ʃan'kato] *agg* lame; (*sedia, ecc.*)
shaky, rickety.

**sciarada** [ʃa'rada] *sf* charade.

**sciarpa** ['ʃarpa] *sf* scarf.

**sciatica** ['ʃatika] *sf* sciatica. **sciatico** *agg* sciatic.

**sciatto** ['ʃatto] *agg* slovenly; (*fam*) sloppy.

**scientifico** [ʃen'tifiko] *agg* scientific.

**scienza** ['ʃɛntsa] *sf* science. **scienziato, -a**
*sm, sf* scientist; (*studioso*) scholar.

**scimmia** ['ʃimmja] *sf* monkey; (*senza coda*)
ape. **brutto come una scimmia** as ugly as
sin. **scimmiottare** *v* also **fare la scimmia
a** ape.

**scimpanzè** [ʃimpan'tse] *sm* chimpanzee.

**scimunito** [ʃimu'nito] **, -a** *agg* foolish. *sm, sf*
fool.

**\*scindere** ['ʃindere] *v* separate; divide.

**scintilla** [ʃin'tilla] *sf* spark. **dare** *or* **emettere scintille** spark. **scintillare** *v* sparkle;
(*lampeggiare*) flash.

**sciocco** ['ʃɔkko] **, -a** *agg* foolish. *sm, sf* fool.
**sciocchezza** *sf* foolish thing; (*cosa da
niente*) trifle; (*l'essere sciocco*) foolishness.
**dire sciocchezze** talk nonsense.

**\*sciogliere** ['ʃɔʎere] *v* (*fondere*) melt; dissolve; (*porre fine*) break up; (*disfare*) undo;
(*allentare*) loosen; (*slegare*) untie; (*società*)
wind up. **scioglimento** *sm* dissolution;
breaking up; melting.

**sciolto** ['ʃɔlto] *agg* loose; (*agile*) nimble.
**aver la lingua sciolta** have the gift of the
gab. **versi sciolti** *sm pl* blank verse *sing*.
**scioltezza** *sf* nimbleness; (*fig*) fluency.

**scioperare** [ʃope'rare] *v* (go on) strike. **sci-
operante** *s(m+f)* striker. **scioperato** *agg*
lazy. **sciopero** *sm* strike. **entrare in
sciopero** go on strike. **far sciopero** strike.
**sciopero bianco/selvaggio** sit-
down/wildcat strike.

**sciorinare** [ʃori'nare] *v* (*bucato*) hang out;
(*fig*) show off; (*spreg*) dash off. **sciorinare
bugie** tell a string of lies.

**sciovinismo** [ʃovi'nizmo] *sm* chauvinism.
**sciovinista** *s(m+f)* chauvinist.

**scipito** ['ʃipito] *agg* insipid.

**scippare** [ʃip'pare] *v* snatch. **scippatore,
-trice** *sm, sf* bag-snatcher.

**scirocco** [ʃi'rɔkko] *sm* sirocco.

**sciroppo** [ʃi'rɔppo] *sm* syrup. **sciroppato** *agg* in syrup. **sciropposo** *agg* syrupy.

**scisma** ['ʃizma] *sm* schism. **scismatico** *agg* schismatic.

**scissione** [ʃis'sjone] *sf* split. **scisso** *agg* split.

**sciupare** [ʃu'pare] *v* (*rovinare*) ruin, spoil; (*perdere*) waste. **sciuparsi** *v* (*salute*) ruin one's health; (*sgualcirsi*) get creased. **sciupato** *agg* ruined; wasted; (*di aspetto*) haggard. **sciupio** *sm* waste. **sciupone, -a** *sm*, *sf* wastrel.

**scivolare** [ʃivo'lare] *v* slide; (*sfuggire, sdrucciolare*) slip; (*aero*) glide. **scivolata** *sf* slide; glide. **scivolo** *sm* chute; (*mar*) slipway. **scivolone** *sm* slip; (*caduta*) tumble. **scivoloso** *agg* slippery.

**sclerosi** [skle'rɔzi] *sf* sclerosis. **sclerotico** *agg* sclerotic.

**scoccare** [skok'kare] *v* (*orologio*) strike; (*scagliare*) fling.

**scocciare** [skot'tʃare] *v* bother. **scocciarsi** *v* get bored. **scocciatore, -trice** *sm*, *sf* bore; (*fam*) pest. **scocciatura** *sf* bore.

**scodella** [sko'dɛlla] *sf* bowl. **scodellare** *v* serve; (*minestra*) ladle out; (*fig*) come out with.

**scoglio** ['skɔʎo] *sm* rock; (*fig*) stumbling block. **scogliera** *sf* cliff; (*a fior d'acqua*) reef. **scoglioso** *agg* rocky.

**scoiattolo** [sko'jattolo] *sm* squirrel.

**scolare** [sko'lare] *v* drain; (*gastr*) strain. **scolapiatti** *sm invar* draining-board. **scolo** *sm* drainage; (*condotto*) drain.

**scolaro** [sko'laro] **-a** *sm*, *sf* pupil; disciple. **scolastico** *agg* (*della scuola*) school; (*spreg*) bookish; (*filosofio*) scholastic.

**scollato** [skol'lato] *agg* low-necked.

**scolorire** [skolo'rire] *v also* **scolorare** discolour, fade. **scolorito** *agg* faded.

**scolpire** [skol'pire] *v* sculpt; (*incidere*) carve; (*fig*) impress.

**scombinare** [skombi'nare] *v* upset. **scombinato** *agg* (*mal combinato*) badly arranged; confused.

**scombro** ['skombro] *sm also* **sgombro** mackerel.

**scombussolare** [skombusso'lare] *v* upset; (*stordire*) stun.

**\*scommettere** [skom'mettere] *v* bet. **scommessa** *sf* bet. **scommettitore, -trice** *sm*, *sf* punter.

**scomodare** [skomo'dare] *v* trouble, inconvenience. **scomodità** *sf* discomfort; (*disagio*) inconvenience. **scomodo** *agg* (*non comodo*) uncomfortable; inconvenient.

**scompaginare** [skompadʒi'nare] *v* throw into disarray; (*fig*) upset.

**\*scomparire** [skompa'rire] *v* disappear; (*fig*) look insignificant.

**scomparso** [skom'parso], **-a** *agg* vanished. *sm*, *sf* deceased. *sf* disappearance.

**scompartimento** [skomparti'mento] *sm* compartment. **scomparto** *sm* compartment; (*parete*) partition.

**scompigliare** [skompi'ʎare] *v* upset; confuse; (*capelli*) ruffle. **scompiglio** *sm* confusion.

**\*scomporre** [skom'porre] *v* take apart; resolve; decompose; (*turbare*) perturb. **senza scomporsi** unperturbed. **scomposto** *agg* broken down; (*in disordine*) untidy; (*indecoroso*) unseemly.

**scomunicare** [skomuni'kare] *v* excommunicate. **scomunica** *sf* excommunication.

**sconcertare** [skontʃer'tare] *v* baffle. **sconcertato** *agg* bewildered.

**sconcio** ['skontʃo] *agg* indecent; obscene. *sm* disgrace. **sconcezza** *sf* obscenity. **dire sconcezze** use foul language. **sconciare** *v* spoil.

**sconfessare** [skonfes'sare] *v* repudiate.

**\*sconfiggere** [skon'fiddʒere] *v* defeat. **sconfitta** *sf* defeat. **sconfitto** *agg* defeated, beaten. **dichiararsi sconfitto** acknowledge defeat.

**sconfortante** [skonfor'tante] *agg* disheartening. **sconforto** *sm* discouragement; depression.

**scongelare** [skondʒe'lare] *v* defrost.

**scongiurare** [skondʒu'rare] *v* beseech; (*evitare*) avoid; (*rel*) exorcise. **scongiuro** *sm* exorcism.

**\*sconnettere** [skon'nettere] *v* disconnect. **sconnesso** *agg* (*fig*) disjointed.

**sconosciuto** [skono'ʃuto], **-a** *agg* unknown. *sm*, *sf* stranger.

**sconquassare** [skonkwas'sare] *v* smash; shake (up). **sconquassato** *agg* shattered.

**sconsiderato** [skonside'rato] *agg* thoughtless. **sconsideratezza** *sf* thoughtlessness.

**sconsigliare** [skonsi'ʎare] *v* advise against; dissuade.

**sconsolato** [skonso'lato] *agg* disconsolate.

**scontare** [skon'tare] v (*detrarre*) deduct; (*econ*) discount; (*debito*) pay off. **sconto** sm discount.

**scontentare** [skonten'tare] v dissatisfy; (*lasciare scontento*) disappoint. **scontentezza** sf dissatisfaction; disappointment. **scontento** agg displeased; disappointed.

**scontrarsi** [skon'trarsi] v meet; (*veicoli*) crash. **scontro** sm encounter; (*discussione*) argument; (*violento*) clash; crash.

**scontrino** [skon'trino] sm check.

**scontroso** [skon'trozo] agg surly. **scontrosità** sf surliness.

*****sconvenire** [skonve'nire] v be unsuitable; (*non essere decoroso*) be unbecoming. **sconveniente** agg unfavourable; unbecoming.

*****sconvolgere** [skon'voldʒere] v upset. **sconvolgimento** sm upset; confusion. **sconvolto** agg upset.

**scopa** ['skopa] sf broom. **scopare** v sweep; (*volg*) screw.

**scoperchiare** [skoper'kjare] v take the lid off.

**scoperto** [sko'pɛrto] agg uncovered; (*aperto*) open; (*nudo*) bare. sm open; (*conto*) overdraft. **allo scoperto** outdoors, in the open (air). **scoperta** sf discovery.

**scopo** ['skɔpo] sm purpose. **a** or **allo scopo di** in order to. **senza scopo** pointless.

**scoppiare** [skop'pjare] v burst; explode; (*manifestarsi*) break out. **scoppiettare** v crackle. **scoppio** sm explosion; outbreak; (*rumore*) bang.

*****scoprire** [sko'prire] v (*fatti, cose nuove*) discover; (*togliere copertura*) uncover, bare; (*esporre*) expose; (*manifestare*) show. **scoprire le (proprie) carte** lay one's cards on the table.

**scoraggiare** [skorad'dʒare] v discourage, dishearten.

**scorbuto** [skor'buto] sm scurvy. **scorbutico** agg (*fig*) cantankerous.

**scorciare** [skor'tʃare] v shorten. **scorciatoia** sf short cut.

**scordare** [skor'dare] v also **scordarsi** forget.

**scordato** [skor'dato] agg (*musica*) out of tune.

**scoreggia** [sko'reddʒa] (*volg*) sf fart. **scoreggiare** v fart.

*****scorgere** [skɔrdʒere] v notice.

**scoria** ['skɔrja] sf slag; (*fig*) dross.

**scorno** ['skɔrno] sm humiliation.

**scorpione** [skor'pjone] sm scorpion. **Scorpione** sm Scorpio.

**scorrazzare** [skorrat'tsare] v run about. **scorrazzata** sf trip.

*****scorrere** ['skorrere] v (*liquido*) run, flow; (*tempo*) pass (by); (*scivolare*) glide; (*leggere in fretta*) run through. **scorrevole** agg flowing. **scorrevolezza** sf fluidity; (*fig*) fluency.

**scorretto** [skor'rɛtto] agg incorrect; (*sgarbato*) impolite; (*non leale*) unfair. **scorrettezza** sf incorrectness, lack of manners; unfairness.

**scorsa** ['skɔrsa] sf glance.

**scorso** ['skɔrso] agg last. **l'anno scorso** last year.

**scorsoio** [skor'sɔjo] agg **nodo scorsoio** sm slip-knot.

**scorta** ['skɔrta] sf escort; (*provvista*) stock, supply; reserve. **di scorta** spare. **fare la scorta a** escort. **fare una scorta (di)** stock up (on). **sotto la scorta di** under the guidance of. **sulla scorta di** on the basis of. **scortare** v escort.

**scortese** [skor'teze] agg rude. **scortesia** sf rudeness.

**scorticare** [skorti'kare] v skin; (*escoriare*) graze.

**scorza** ['skɔrtsa] sf skin; (*corteccia*) bark.

**scosceso** [sko'ʃezo] agg steep.

**scossa** ['skɔssa] sf shock; (*scatto, sbalzo*) jerk; (*tremore*) shake. **a scosse** jerkily. **scosso** agg shaken.

**scostare** [skos'tare] v shift. **scostarsi** v move aside; (*deviare*) stray. **scostamento** sm shifting; (*mat*) deviation. **scostante** agg unpleasant.

**scostumato** [skostu'mato] agg dissolute, licentious. **scostumatezza** sf licentiousness.

**scotennare** [skoten'nare] v skin; (*di cuoio capelluto*) scalp.

**scottare** [skot'tare] v burn; (*con liquido bollente*) scald; (*causare bruciatura*) scorch; (*essere caldo*) be hot. **scottatura** sf burning; scalding; (*ustione*) burn, scald.

**scovare** [sko'vare] v (*stanare*) flush out; (*rintracciare*) track down; (*trovare*) find.

**Scozia** ['skɔtsja] sf Scotland. **scozzese** agg Scottish, Scotch; s(m+f) Scot.

**screanzato** [skrean'tsato] agg rude.

**screditare** [skredi'tare] v discredit.

**scremare** [skre'mare] *v* skim.

**screpolare** [skrepo'lare] *v* crack. **screpolatura** *sf* crack.

**screziato** [skre'tsjato] *agg* variegated.

**scribacchiare** [skribak'kjare] *v* scribble.

**scricchiolare** [skrikkjo'lare] *v* creak. **scricchiolio** *sm* creaking noise.

**scricciolo** ['skrittʃolo] *sm* wren.

**scrigno** ['skriŋo] *sm* casket.

**scriminatura** [skrimina'tura] *sf* parting.

**scritta** ['skritta] *sf* inscription; (*dir*) document.

**scritto** ['skritto] *agg* written. *sm* writing; letter; document. **scrittoio** *sm* (writing-)desk. **scrittore, -trice** *sm, sf* writer.

**scrittura** [skrit'tura] *sf* writing; (*contratto*) engagement; (*calligrafia*) handwriting. (*Sacra*) Scrittura (Holy) Scripture. **scritturare** *v* engage.

**scrivania** [skriva'nia] *sf* (writing-)desk.

**\*scrivere** ['skrivere] *v* write; (*compitando*) spell. **scrivere bene/male** (*calligrafia*) have good/bad handwriting; (*stile*) write well/badly; (*compitare*) spell correctly/incorrectly.

**scroccare** [skrok'kare] *v* scrounge. **vivere a scrocco** scrounge a living. **scroccone, -a** *sm, sf* scrounger.

**scrocco** ['skrɔkko] *sm* **coltello a scrocco** *sm* clasp-knife. **serratura a scrocco** *sf* springlock, latch.

**scrofa** ['skrɔfa] *sf* sow.

**scrollare** [skrol'lare] *v* shake; (*spalle*) shrug.

**scrosciare** [skro'ʃare] *v* thunder; (*pioggia*) pelt down. **scroscio** *sm* (*pioggia*) downpour. **scroscio di applausi** thunderous applause. **scroscio di risa** roar of laughter.

**scrostare** [skros'tare] *v* scrape (off).

**scroto** ['skrɔto] *sm* scrotum.

**scrupolo** ['skrupolo] *sm* scruple, qualm. **avere** *or* **farsi scrupoli (di)** have qualms (about). **essere onesto fino allo scrupolo** be scrupulously honest. **senza scrupoli** unscrupulous. **scrupoloso** *agg* scrupulous, meticulous.

**scrutare** [skru'tare] *v* scan; (*indagare*) delve into. **scrutatore, -trice** *sm, sf* scrutineer. **scrutinare** *v* scrutinize. **scrutinio** *sm* scrutiny; (*elezioni*) poll.

**scucire** [sku'tʃire] *v* unstitch. **scucitura** *sf* rip.

**scudo** ['skudo] *sm* shield. **farsi scudo** shield oneself. **scuderia** *sf* (*ricovero*) stable; (*allevamento*) stud; (*auto*) racing team. **scudetto** *sm* (*calcio*) league championship.

**scugnizzo** [sku'ɲittso] *sm* urchin.

**sculacciare** [skulat'tʃare] *v* spank. **sculacciata** *sf* spanking.

**scultore** [skul'tore] *sm* sculptor. **scultrice** *sf* sculptress. **scultura** *sf* sculpture.

**scuola** ['skwɔla] *sf* school. **scuola dell'obbligo** compulsory schooling. **scuola guida** driving school. **scuola materna** nursery school. **scuola pubblica** state school.

**\*scuotere** ['skwɔtere] *v* shake; (*le spalle*) shrug. **scuotersi di dosso** shrug off.

**scure** ['skure] *sf* axe.

**scuro** ['skuro] *agg* dark. *sm* dark, darkness. **scuretto** *sm* (window-)shutter. **scurire** *v* darken.

**scusa** ['skuza] *sf* excuse; apology. **chiedere scusa a qualcuno** beg someone's pardon. **scusabile** *agg* excusable; justifiable. **scusante** *sf* excuse; justification. **scusare** *v* excuse; pardon. **scusarsi** *v* apologize; justify oneself. **mi scusi!** (I'm) sorry! I beg your pardon!

**sdegnare** [zde'ɲare] *v* (*disprezzare*) scorn; irritate. **sdegnato** *agg* indignant; irritated. **sdegno** *sm* indignation. **sdegnoso** *agg* disdainful.

**sdoppiare** [zdop'pjare] *v* split (in two). **sdoppiamento** *sm* split. **sdoppiamento della personalità** split personality.

**sdraiarsi** [zdra'jarsi] *v* (*stendersi*) stretch out; (*mettersi a giacere*) lie down. **sdraia** *sf* also **sedia a sdraio** deck-chair.

**sdrucciolare** [zdruttʃo'lare] *v* slip. **sdrucciolevole** *agg* slippery. **sdrucciolone** *sm* slip.

**sdrucire** [zdru'tʃire] *v* rip.

**se¹** [se] *cong* if; whether; (*se solo*) if only. **come se** as though. **se non altro** if nothing else, at least.

**se²** [se] *V* **si**.

**sé** [se] *pron* one(self); (*lui*) him(self); (*lei*) her(self); (*cosa, animale*) it(self); (*loro*) them(selves). **da sé** on one's own. **di per sé** in itself. **fra sé e sé** to oneself. **va da sé** it goes without saying.

**sebbene** [seb'bɛne] *cong* (al)though.

**seccare** [sek'kare] *v* dry (up); (*importunare*) bother. **seccarsi** *v* (*diventar secco*) dry up; (*annoiarsi*) get bored; (*infastidirsi*) get annoyed. **secca** *sf* shallow; (*fig*) fix. **seccante** *agg* boring; annoying. **seccato** *agg*

annoyed; (*fam*) fed up. **seccatore, -trice** *sm, sf* nuisance. **seccatura** *sf* nuisance.
**secco** *agg* dry; (*essiccato*) dried; (*fig*) sharp. **lavare a secco** dry-clean. **rimanere in secco** be left high and dry.

**secchia** ['sekkja] *sf* bucket. **secchio** *sm* pail; (*per carbone*) coal-scuttle. **secchione** *sm* (*fam: sgobbone*) swot.

**\*secernere** [se'tʃɛrnere] *v* secrete.

**secessione** [setʃes'sjone] *sf* secession.

**secolo** ['sɛkolo] *sm* century; (*periodo*) age. **al secolo** alias. **secolare** *agg* centuries old; (*laico*) secular.

**secondino** [sekon'dino] *sm* warder.

**secondo¹** [se'kondo] *sm, agg* second. **in un secondo tempo** on a later occasion. **secondo fine** *sm* ulterior motive.

**secondo²** [se'kondo] *prep* according to; depending on. *inter* it depends!

**secrezione** [sekre'tsjone] *sf* secretion.

**sedano** ['sɛdano] *sm* celery. **sedano rapa** celeriac.

**sedare** [se'dare] *v* calm; (*reprimere*) quell. **sedativo** *agg, sm* sedative.

**sede** ['sɛde] *sf* seat; (*comm*) office; residence; (*seduta*) sitting. **in altra sede** (*luogo*) elsewhere; (*tempo*) some other time. **Santa Sede** Holy See. **sede centrale** headquarters. **sede legale** registered office.

**\*sedere** [se'dere] *v* sit (down). **dar da sedere** offer a seat. **sedersi** *v* sit down, take a seat. **tirarsi su a sedere** sit up. *sm* (*deretano*) bottom. **sedentario** *agg* sedentary.

**sedia** ['sɛdja] *sf* chair.

**sedicente** [sedi'tʃɛnte] *agg* so-called, would-be.

**sedici** ['seditʃi] *agg, sm* sixteen. **sedicesimo** *sm, agg* sixteenth.

**sedile** [se'dile] *sm* seat.

**sedimento** [sedi'mento] *sm* sediment. **sedimentazione** *sf* sedimentation.

**sedizione** [sedi'tsjone] *sf* sedition; rebellion. **sedizioso** *agg* seditious.

**\*sedurre** [se'durre] *v* seduce; (*attrarre*) entice. **seducente** *agg* alluring, tempting. **seduttore, -trice** *agg* seductive. **seduzione** *sf* seduction; temptation.

**seduta** [se'duta] *sf* session; (*pasto, posa*) sitting; (*riunione*) meeting. **seduta spiritica** seance. **seduta stante** forthwith.

**sega** ['sega] *sf* saw. **a sega** saw-toothed. **sega a catena** chain-saw. **sega da traforo** fretsaw. **segare** *v* saw. **segatrice** *sf* saw. **segatura** *sf* (*azione*) sawing; (*frammenti*) sawdust.

**segale** ['segale] *sf* rye.

**seggio** ['sɛddʒo] *sm* seat; (*carica*) chair. **seggiola** *sf* chair. **seggiolino** *sm* seat. **seggiolone** *sm* armchair; (*per bambini*) high chair.

**seggiovia** [sedd ʒo'via] *sf* chair-lift.

**seghettare** [seget'tare] *v* serrate.

**segmento** [seg'mento] *sm* segment. **segmentare** *v* divide up. **segmentazione** *sf* segmentation; (*fig*) breaking up.

**segnalare** [seɲa'lare] *v* signal; (*indicare*) point out; (*render noto*) report. **segnalato** *agg* announced, reported; (*straordinario*) outstanding. **segnalatore** *sm* (*persona*) signaller; indicator; alarm. **segnalazione** *sf* signalling; report; notification; (*nota informativa*) notice. **segnalazione stradale** road sign. **segnale** *sm* signal; (*cartello*) sign; (*telefono*) tone. **segnaletica** *sf* road signs *pl*.

**segnalibro** [seɲa'libro] *sm* bookmark.

**segnapunti** [seɲa'punti] *sm invar* (*tabellone*) score-board; (*libretto*) score-book.

**segnare** [se'ɲare] *v* mark; (*marchiare*) brand. **segnare i punti** keep the score. **segnare le ore** tell the time.

**segno** ['seɲo] *sm* sign; (*traccia*) mark. **come** or **in segno di** as a sign of, in token of. **essere segno che** mean. **tiro a segno** *sm* target practice.

**sego** ['sego] *sm* tallow.

**segregare** [segre'gare] *v* segregate, set apart. **segregazione** *sf* segregation; isolation. **segregazione cellulare** solitary confinement.

**segretario** [segre'tarjo], **-a** *sm, sf* secretary; (*chi redige verbali, ecc.*) clerk. **segretariato** *sm* secretariat. **segreteria** *sf* secretary's office; (*enti pubblici*) secretariat.

**segreto** [se'greto] *agg* secret. *sm* secret; (*intimità*) depth; (*segretezza*) secrecy. **in segreto** in secret; (*riservatamente*) confidentially. **nel segreto più assoluto** in utmost secrecy. **segreti del mestiere** tricks of the trade *pl*. **segreto di Pulcinella** open secret. **segreta** *sf* dungeon. **segretezza** *sf* secrecy.

**seguace** [se'gwatʃe] *s(m+f)* follower; disciple.

**seguente** [se'gwɛnte] *agg* following; (*futuro*) next.

**segugio** [se'gudʒo] *sm* bloodhound; (*fig*) sleuth.

**seguire** [se'gwire] *v* follow; (*frequentare*) attend. **segue a tergo** continued overleaf, PTO. **seguitare** *v* continue. **seguito** *sm* following; succession; favour; continuation; consequence. **di seguito** on end, non-stop. **in seguito** later (on). **in seguito a** as a result of, because of.

**sei** ['sɛi] *agg, sm* six.

**selce** ['sɛltʃe] *sf* flint; (*strada*) paving-stone. **selciato** *sm* paving.

**selettivo** [selet'tivo] *agg* selective. **selettività** *sf* selectivity. **selettore, -trice** *sm, sf* selector.

**selezionare** [seletsjo'nare] *v* select; grade. **selezionamento** *sm* selection. **selezione** *sf* selection; (*scelta*) choice. **selezione automatica** (*telefono*) automatic dialling, STD.

**sella** ['sɛlla] *sf* saddle. **sellare** *v* saddle.

**seltz** ['sɛlts] *sm invar* soda-water.

**selva** ['selva] *sf* forest. **selvoso** *agg* wooded.

**selvaggio** [sel'vaddʒo], **-a** *agg* wild; (*incivile*) savage. *sm, sf* savage. **selvaggina** *sf* game. **selvatico** *agg* wild; (*scontroso*) uncouth.

**semaforo** [se'maforo] *sm* traffic lights *pl*.

**semantica** [se'mantika] *sf* semantics. **semantico** *agg* semantic.

**sembrare** [sem'brare] *v* seem. **cosa te ne sembra?** what do you think of it?

**seme** ['seme] *sm* seed; (*di mele, pere, ecc.*) pip; (*carte da gioco*) suit. **sementa** *sf* (*operazione*) sowing; (*semente*) seed. **semente** *sf* seed. **semenza** *sf* seed; (*perle*) seed-pearls *pl*.

**semestre** [se'mɛstre] *sm* half-year. **semestrale** *agg* half-yearly.

**semibreve** [semi'brɛve] *sf* semibreve.

**semicerchio** [semi'tʃerkjo] *sm* semicircle.

**semicircolare** [semitʃirko'lare] *agg* semicircular.

**semicroma** [semi'krɔma] *sf* semiquaver.

**semidio** [semi'dio] *sm* demi-god.

**semifinale** [semifi'nale] *sf* semifinal. **semifinalista** *s(m+f)* semifinalist.

**semiminima** [semi'minima] *sf* crotchet.

**seminare** [semi'nare] *v* sow; (*fig*) scatter, strew. **semina** *sf* sowing. **seminale** *agg* seminal. **uscire dal seminato** digress.

**seminario** [semi'narjo] *sm* (*rel*) seminary; (*università*) seminar. **seminarista** *sm* seminarist.

**seminterrato** [seminter'rato] *sm* basement.

**seminudo** [semi'nudo] *agg* half-naked.

**semita** [se'mita] *s(m+f)* Semite. *agg also* **semitico** Semitic.

**semitono** [semi'tɔno] *sm* semitone.

**semivivo** [semi'vivo] *agg* half-dead.

**semola** ['semola] *sf* (*crusca*) bran. **semolino** *sm* semolina.

**semovente** [semo'vɛnte] *agg* self-propelled.

**semplice** ['semplitʃe] *agg* simple; (*di un solo elemento*) single; (*senza affettazione*) plain. **semplicemente** *avv* simply; (*soltanto*) only. **semplicione** *sm* simpleton. **semplicità** *sf* simplicity. **semplificare** *v* simplify; facilitate. **semplificazione** *sf* simplification.

**sempre** ['sempre] *avv* always; (*ancora*) still. **da sempre** from the beginning. **per sempre** for ever. **sempre che** (*purché*) as long as, provided that; (*ammesso che*) supposing that. **sempre più** more and more. **sempreverde** *s(m+f)*, *agg* evergreen. **una volta per sempre** once and for all.

**senape** ['senape] *sf* mustard.

**senato** [se'nato] *sm* senate. **senatore** *sm* senator.

**senile** [se'nile] *agg* senile. **senilità** *sf* senility.

**senno** ['senno] *sm* wits *pl*; (*sensatezza*) (common) sense. **con senno** sensibly. **senno di poi** hindsight. **uscir di senno** go out of one's mind.

**seno** ['seno] *sm* bosom, breast; (*grembo*) womb; (*anat*) sinus; (*mat*) sine; (*geog*) inlet. **allattare al seno** breast-feed. **in seno a** (*nel mezzo di*) within; (*tra le braccia*) in the arms of.

**sensale** [sen'sale] *sm* broker.

**sensato** [sen'sato] *agg* sensible. **sensatezza** *sf* good sense.

**sensazione** [sensa'tsjone] *sf* feeling, sensation. **sensazionale** *agg* sensational.

**sensibile** [sen'sibile] *agg* (*che sente*) sensitive; (*notevole*) appreciable; perceptible; susceptible. **sensibilità** *sf* sensitivity. **sensibilizzare** *v* sensitize.

**sensitivo** [sensi'tivo] *agg* (*funzione*) sensory; (*sensibile*) sensitive. **sensitività** *sf* sensitivity.

**senso** ['senso] *sm* sense; (*significato*) meaning; (*direzione, modo*) way. **a senso** in one's own words; (*tradurre*) freely. **far senso**

(*ripugnare*) disgust. **in senso antiorario** anticlockwise. **in senso orario** clockwise. **non aver senso** not make sense; be pointless. **senso proibito** no entry. **senso unico** one-way. **sensorio** *agg* sensory. **sensuale** *agg* sensual; sensuous. **sensualità** *sf* sensuality; sensuousness.

**sentenza** [sen'tɛntsa] *sf* sentence, judgment; (*massima*) saying. **sputare sentenze** be sententious. **sentenziare** *v* pass judgment *or* sentence; rule; decree. **sentenzioso** *agg* sententious.

**sentiero** [sen'tjɛro] *sm* path.

**sentimento** [senti'mento] *sm* feeling; (*concetto*) sense. **sentimenti** *sm pl* (*modo di sentire*) sentiments *pl*.

**sentinella** [senti'nɛlla] *sf* sentry.

**sentire** [sen'tire] *v* feel; (*col gusto*) taste; (*con l'udito*) hear; (*con l'olfatto*) smell; (*dare ascolto*) listen to; (*aver notizia*) gather. **al mio modo di sentire** to my way of thinking. **sentirsela** *v* feel like. **sentirsi** *v* feel.

**sentito** [sen'tito] *agg* (*udito*) heard; sincere. **per sentito dire** by hearsay.

**sentore** [sen'tore] *sm* inkling.

**senza** ['sentsa] *prep* without. **rimanere senza** run out of. **senza contare** apart from; over and above. **senza dire** not to mention. **senza fallo** certainly. **senz'altro** definitely. **senza soldi** penniless. **senzatetto** *s(m+f)* (*invar*) homeless person.

**separare** [sepa'rare] *v* separate, divide. **separarsi** *v* part; (*coniugi*) separate. **separazione** *sf* separation, division; parting.

**sepolcro** [se'polkro] *sm* tomb. **sepolcrale** *agg* sepulchral.

**sepolto** [se'polto] *agg* buried. **sepoltura** *sf* burial.

**\*seppellire** [seppel'lire] *v* bury.

**seppia** ['seppja] *sf* (*zool*) cuttlefish. *agg*, *sm invar* (*colore*) sepia.

**seppure** [sep'pure] *cong* even though, even if.

**sequela** [se'kwɛla] *sf* succession.

**sequestrare** [sekwes'trare] *v* seize, confiscate; (*persona*) imprison unlawfully; (*rapire*) kidnap. **sequestro** *sm* seizure, confiscation; kidnapping; illegal confinement.

**sera** ['sera] *sf* evening, night. **buona sera!** (*di pomeriggio*) good afternoon! (*di sera*) good evening! **si fa sera** it is getting dark. **serale** *agg* evening, night. **serata** *sf* evening, night; (*ricevimento*) party;

(*teatro*) performance.

**serbare** [ser'bare] *v* (*mantenere*) keep; (*metter da parte*) put aside. **serbare gratitudine verso** be grateful to. **serbatoio** *sm* tank; (*penna*) barrel; (*fucile, ecc.*) magazine.

**Serbia** ['zɛrbja] *sf* Serbia. **serbo, -a** *s*, *agg* Serbian.

**serbo** ['sɛrbo] *sm* **dare in serbo** put into custody. **mettere in serbo** put by *or* aside. **tenere in serbo** keep in store.

**serenata** [sere'nata] *sf* serenade.

**serenella** [sere'nɛlla] *sf* lilac.

**sereno** [se'reno] *agg* calm, serene; (*cielo*) clear; (*senza preoccupazioni*) carefree; objective. *sm* clear sky; (*aperto*) open air. **serenità** *sf* serenity; objectivity.

**sergente** [ser'dʒɛnte] *sm* sergeant.

**serico** ['sɛriko] *agg* silk.

**serie** ['sɛrje] *sf invar* (*assortimento*) set; (*sport*) division. **fuori serie** (*auto*) custom-built. **modello di serie** *sm* production model. **prodotto in serie** mass-produced. **produzione in serie** *sf* mass-production.

**serio** ['sɛrjo] *agg* serious; (*degno di fiducia*) trustworthy; (*comm*) reputable. *sm* seriousness. **sul serio** (*seriamente*) seriously; (*davvero*) really. **serietà** *sf* seriousness; (*fidatezza*) reliability.

**sermone** [ser'mone] *sm* sermon; (*rimprovero*) lecture.

**serpeggiare** [serped'dʒare] *v* wind.

**serpente** [ser'pɛnte] *sm* snake, serpent. **serpente a sonagli** rattlesnake. **serpentino** *agg* snake-like.

**serra** ['sɛrra] *sf* greenhouse, hothouse.

**serraglio** [ser'raʎo] *sm* menagerie.

**serrare** [ser'rare] *v* close; (*a chiave*) lock; (*stringere*) tighten; (*denti, pugni*) clench. **serrare al cuore** embrace. **serramento** *sm* (*di finestra*) window-frame; (*di porta*) doorframe. **serrata** *sf* lock-out. **serrato** *agg* closed; (*fila*) serried; (*fig*) to the point.

**serratura** [serra'tura] *sf* lock. **buco della serratura** *sm* keyhole. **serratura a cilindro** Yale lock ®. **serratura a lucchetto** padlock. **serratura a scatto** latch.

**servire** [ser'vire] *v* serve; (*fam: occorrere*) be useful; (*carte da gioco*) deal. **a cosa serve?** what is the use? **cosa ti serve?** what do you need? **posso servirti?** can I help you? **servirsi** *v* use; make use; (*di cibo*) help oneself. **servile** *agg* servile; (*fig*) slavish. **servitore** *sm* servant. **servitù** *sf* (*schiavitù*)

slavery; (*personale di servizio*) servants *pl*.
**ridurre in servitù** enslave.

**servizio** [ser'vitsjo] *sm* service; (*lavoro*)
work; favour; (*giornale*) report; (*turno*) duty.
**a mezzo servizio** part-time. **donna di
servizio** *sf* maid. **fare servizio** (*transporto*)
run; (*negozio*) be open. **fuori servizio** off
duty; (*che non funziona*) out of order. **in
servizio** on duty. **servizievole** *agg* obliging.

**servo** ['sɛrvo], **-a** *sm*, *sf* servant.

**sesamo** ['sɛzamo] *sm* sesame.

**sessanta** [ses'santa] *agg*, *sm* sixty. **sessantesimo** *agg*, *sm* sixtieth.

**sessione** [ses'sjone] *sf* session.

**sesso** ['sɛsso] *sm* sex. **sessista** *agg* sexist.
**sessuale** *agg* sexual. **sessualità** *sf* sexuality.

**sestetto** [ses'tetto] *sm* sextet.

**sesto¹** ['sɛsto] *sm*, *agg* sixth.

**sesto²** ['sɛsto] *sm* order; (*di arco*) curve.
**mettere in sesto** tidy up. **rimettersi in
sesto** get back on one's feet again.

**seta** ['seta] *sf* silk.

**setaccio** [se'tattʃo] *sm* sieve. **setacciare** *v
also* **passare al setaccio** sift, sieve.

**sete** ['sete] *sf* thirst. **aver sete** be thirsty.
**mettere seta a** make thirsty.

**setola** ['setola] *sf* bristle.

**setta** ['sɛtta] *sf* sect. **agg**, *sm* sectarian.

**settanta** [set'tanta] *agg*, *sm* seventy. **settantesimo** *agg*, *sm* seventieth.

**sette** ['sɛtte] *agg*, *sm* seven. **settimo** *agg*,
*sm* seventh.

**settembre** [set'tembre] *sm* September.

**settentrione** [setten'trjone] *sm* north. **settentrionale** *agg* northern, north.

**settico** ['sɛttiko] *agg* septic. **setticemia** *sf*
blood-poisoning.

**settimana** [setti'mana] *sf* week; (*paga*)
week's wages. **a metà settimana** mid-
week. **a settimane** by the week; (*una si e
una no*) every other week. **fine settimana**
*sm* week-end. **settimanale** *agg*, *sm* weekly.

**settore** [set'tore] *sm* sector; (*campo*) field.

**severo** [se'vɛro] *agg* severe, strict; (*grave*)
serious. **severità** *sf* severity.

**seviziare** [sevi'tsjare] *v* torture; (*violentare*)
rape. **sevizie** *sf pl* torture *sing*.

**sezione** [se'tsjone] *sf* section; (*tribunale*)
division; (*sezionamento*) dissection.
**sezionare** *v* dissect; (*dividere in sezioni*) section.

**sfaccendato** [sfattʃen'dato], **-a** *agg* idle. *sm*,
*sf* loafer.

**sfaccettare** [sfattʃet'tare] *v* cut.

**sfacchinare** [sfakki'nare] *v* slave. **sfacchinata** *sf* heavy work.

**sfacciato** [sfat'tʃato], **-a** *agg* impudent;
(*svergognato*) shameless; (*vistoso*) gaudy.
*sm*, *sf* impudent *or* shameless person.
**sfacciataggine** *sf* impudence; shamelessness.

**sfacelo** [sfa'tʃɛlo] *sm* ruin; (*disfacimento*)
decay. **andare in sfacelo** break up; (*fam*)
go to rack and ruin.

**sfaldarsi** [sfal'darsi] *v* flake; (*sbriciolarsi*)
crumble. **sfaldatura** *sf* flaking; crumbling.

**sfalsare** [sfal'sare] *v* stagger.

**sfamare** [sfa'mare] *v* feed. **sfamarsi** *v* satisfy one's hunger.

**sfarfallare** [sfarfal'lare] *v* (*svolazzare*) flutter; (*esser volubile*) flit; (*auto*) wobble.

**sfarzo** ['sfartso] *sm* magnificence, pomp.
**senza sfarzo** simply. **sfarzosità** *sf* sumptuousness; ostentation. **sfarzoso** *agg* sumptuous; ostentatious.

**sfasciare** [sfa'ʃare] *v* (*rompere*) smash.

**sfatare** [sfa'tare] *v* refute.

**sfavillante** [sfavil'lante] *agg* glittering,
sparkling.

**sfavore** [sfa'vore] *sm* disfavour, discredit.
**andare a sfavore di** go against. **sfavorevole** *agg* unfavourable; (*contrario*) adverse.

**sfegatato** [sfega'tato] *agg* passionate.

**sfera** ['sfɛra] *sf* sphere; (*ambiente*) circle;
(*campo*) field. **cuscinetto a sfere** *sm* ball-
bearing. **penna a sfera** *sf* ball-point pen.
**sferico** *agg* spherical.

**sferrare** [sfer'rare] *v* (*attacco*) launch;
(*pugno*) deal. **sferrare un calcio** kick.

**sferza** ['sfɛrtsa] *sf* whip. **sferzare** *v* whip;
lash.

**sfiatato** [sfja'tato] *agg* breathless; (*strumento musicale*) cracked; (*fam*) hoarse.

**sfibrare** [sfi'brare] *v* (*indebolire*) weaken.
**sfibrante** *agg* enervating. **sfibrato** *agg*
exhausted.

**sfida** ['sfida] *sf* challenge. **sfidare** *v* challenge; (*invitare*) defy; (*fig*) brave.

**sfiducia** [sfi'dutʃa] *sf* distrust. **avere sfiducia in** distrust; lack confidence in. **sfidu-
ciarsi** *v* lose confidence. **sfiduciato** *agg*
distrustful; (*di sé stesso*) diffident; (*scoraggiato*) disheartened.

**sfigurare** [sfigu'rare] v disfigure; make a bad impression.

**sfilacciare** [sfilat't∫are] v fray.

**sfilare**[1] [sfi'lare] v (togliere di dosso) take off; (ago) unthread.

**sfilare**[2] [sfi'lare] v parade. **sfilata** sf parade; (lunga fila) long row.

**sfilza** ['sfiltsa] sf string.

**sfinge** ['sfindʒe] sf sphinx.

**sfinire** [sfi'nire] v wear out. **sfinimento** sm exhaustion.

**sfiorare** [sfjo'rare] v skim (over); (toccando) graze, barely touch; (successo, ecc.) be on the verge of.

**sfiorito** [sfjo'rito] agg withered.

**sfitto** ['sfitto] agg vacant.

**sfocato** [sfo'kato] agg (foto) out of focus; (fig) hazy.

**sfociare** [sfo't∫are] v flow (into); (fig) result. **sfocio** sm outlet.

**sfogare** [sfo'gare] v let out; (fig) give vent to. **sfogarsi** v (sfogar l'ira) give vent to one's anger; (confidarsi) pour out one's heart; (bambino) run wild. **sfogo** sm outlet; (sollievo) relief.

**sfoggiare** [sfod'dʒare] v show off. **sfoggio** sm display; ostentation.

**sfogliare**[1] [sfo'ʎare] v also **dare una sfogliata a** (pagine) leaf or skim through.

**sfogliare**[2] [sfo'ʎare] v (levar le foglie) strip (of leaves). **sfoglia** sf leaf; (gastr) puff pastry.

**sfolgorare** [sfolgo'rare] v blaze; (occhi) shine.

**sfollare** [sfol'lare] v disperse; evacuate. **sfollamento** sm evacuation. **sfollato, -a** sm, sf evacuee.

**sfondare** [sfon'dare] v break through; (schiantare) smash; (logorare) wear out. **sfondato** agg (senza fondo) bottomless; (logoro) worn out. **ricco sfondato** rolling in money. **sfondo** sm background, setting.

**sformare** [sfor'mare] v pull out of shape; (estrarre dalla forma) turn out. **sformato** sm (gastr) pie.

**sfornito** [sfor'nito] agg **sfornito di** lacking in, without.

**sfortuna** [sfor'tuna] sf bad luck; (contrattempo) misfortune. **sfortunato** agg unlucky; (senza successo) unfortunate.

**sforzare** [sfor'tsare] v force, strain. **sforzarsi di** try hard to. **sforzo** sm effort.

**sfottere** ['sfottere] v (fam) take the mickey (out of). **sfottimento** sm teasing, ridicule.

**sfracellare** [sfrat∫el'lare] v shatter.

**sfrangiato** [sfran'dʒato] agg fringed.

**sfrattare** [sfrat'tare] v turn out, evict. **sfratto** sm eviction.

**sfregare** [sfre'gare] v rub; (lucidando) polish; (lavando) scrub. **sfregamento** sm rubbing; polishing; scrubbing.

**sfrenare** [sfre'nare] v let loose. **sfrenatezza** sf lack of restraint; wild behaviour. **sfrenato** agg unbridled; (senza ritegno) immoderate.

**\*sfriggere** ['sfriddʒere] v also **sfrigolare** sizzle.

**sfrondare** [sfron'dare] v prune.

**sfrontato** [sfron'tato] agg impudent, brazen; (fam) cheeky. **sfrontatezza** sf effrontery; (fam) cheek.

**sfruttare** [sfrut'tare] v exploit. **sfruttamento** sm exploitation; utilization. **sfruttatore, -trice** sm, sf exploiter.

**sfuggire** [sfud'dʒire] v shun; (scappare) escape from. **lasciarsi sfuggire** let slip; (occasione) let go by. **sfuggire di mano** slip out of one's hand. **sfuggire di mente** slip one's mind. **sfuggente** agg (mento, fronte) receding. **di sfuggita** fleetingly.

**sfumare** [sfu'mare] v (svanire) disappear; (colori, suoni) fade away, tone down. **sfumato** agg (pittura) shaded; (fig) vague. **sfumatura** sf nuance.

**sfuriata** [sfu'rjata] sf outburst; (tempesta) storm; (rabbuffo) telling-off.

**sfuso** ['sfuzo] agg (sciolto) loose; (liquefatto) melted.

**sgabello** [zga'bɛllo] sm stool.

**sgabuzzino** [zgabut'tsino] sm cubby-hole.

**sgambettare** [zgambet'tare] v (camminare a piccoli passi) toddle (along); (fare lo sgambetto) trip up.

**sganciare** [zgan't∫are] v unhook; (bombe) release; (fam: sborsare) fork out.

**sgangherato** [zgange'rato] agg (sfasciato) rickety; (sconnesso) incoherent; (esagerato) boisterous.

**sgarbato** [zgar'bato] agg rude, discourteous. **sgarbatezza** sf rudeness, discourtesy.

**sgarbugliare** [zgarbu'ʎare] v disentangle.

**sgargiante** [zgar'dʒante] agg showy.

**sgarrare** [zgar'rare] v be or go wrong.

**sgelare** [zdʒe'lare] v thaw out; (surgelati) defrost.

**sghembo** ['zgembo] *agg* crooked. **di sghembo** askew.

**sgherro** ['zgɛrro] *sm* thug.

**sghignazzare** [zgiɲaʦare] *v* laugh sarcastically, sneer; (*sguaiatamente*) guffaw. **sghignazzata** *sf* sarcastic laughter; guffaw.

**sghiribizzo** [zgiriˈbiʦo] *sm* whim.

**sgobbare** [zgobˈbare] (*fam*) *v* slave. **sgobbata** *sf* grind. **sgobbone, -a** *sm, sf* slogger; (*studente*) swot.

**sgocciolare** [zgotʧoˈlare] *v* drip; (*vuotare*) drain. **sgocciolatura** *sf* dripping; (*macchie*) drips *pl*. **essere agli sgoccioli** be *or* have nearly finished.

**sgolarsi** [zgoˈlarsi] *v* shout oneself hoarse.

**sgombrare** [zgomˈbrare] *v also* **sgomberare** clear; (*vuotare*) empty; (*portar via*) clear away; evacuate; (*lasciar libero*) vacate.

**sgombro¹** ['zgombro] *sm also* **sgombero** (*trasloco*) move; clearing (away); evacuation. *agg* clear; empty.

**sgombro²** ['zgombro] *V* **scombro**.

**sgomentare** [zgomenˈtare] *v* dismay. **sgomento** *sm* dismay.

**sgonfiare** [zgonˈfjare] *v* deflate; (*fam*) annoy. **sgonfiarsi** *v* go down; (*pneumatico*) go flat; (*fig*) be deflated. **sgonfio** *agg* deflated, flat.

**sgorbia** ['zgɔrbja] *sf* gouge.

**sgorbio** ['zgɔrbjo] *sm* (*macchia*) blot; (*scarabocchio*) scrawl.

**sgorgare** [zgorˈgare] *v* gush (out); (*uscire*) spring.

**sgradevole** [zgraˈdevole] *agg* disagreeable, unpleasant. **sgradito** *agg* disagreeable; (*non gradito*) unwelcome.

**sgrammaticato** [zgrammatiˈkato] *agg* ungrammatical.

**sgranare** [zgraˈnare] *v* shell; (*occhi*) open wide.

**sgranchire** [zgranˈkire] *v* stretch.

**sgravare** [zgraˈvare] *v* relieve; (*partorire*) give birth.

**sgraziato** [zgraˈtsjato] *agg* ungainly, awkward.

**sgretolare** [zgretoˈlare] *v* break up. **sgretolarsi** *v* crumble. **sgretolato** *agg* crumbling.

**sgridare** [zgriˈdare] *v* scold; (*fam*) tell off. **sgridata** *sf* scolding; (*fam*) telling-off.

**sguaiato** [zgwaˈjato] *agg* unseemly; vulgar; (*grossolano*) coarse. **sguaiataggine** *sf* vulgarity; coarseness.

**sgualcire** [zgwalˈtʃire] *v* crease, crumple.

**sgualdrina** [zgwalˈdrina] *sf* (*spreg*) tart.

**sguardo** ['zgwardo] *sm* look; (*occhiata*) glance; (*fisso*) stare; (*prolungato*) gaze. **al primo sguardo** at first sight. **fissare lo sguardo su** stare at. **gettare uno sguardo su** glance at.

**sguarnire** [zgwarˈnire] *v* strip.

**sguattero** ['zgwattero], **-a** *sm, sf* skivvy.

**squazzare** [zgwatˈtsare] *v* splash about; (*fig*) wallow.

**sguinzagliare** [zgwintsaˈʎare] *v* let loose.

**sgusciare¹** [zguˈʃare] *v* (*scivolare*) slip.

**sgusciare²** [zguˈʃare] *v* shell; (*uova, noci*) crack.

**shampoo** [ʃamˈpu] *sm invar* shampoo.

**si** [si] *pron* (*lui*) himself; (*lei*) herself; (*cosa, animale*) itself; (*loro*) themselves; (*reciproco*) each other; (*riflessivo*) oneself; (*indefinito*) one.

**sì** [si] *avv* yes. **credo di sì** I think so. **dire di sì** say yes. **far cenno di sì** nod. **spero di sì** I hope so. **un giorno sì e uno no** every other day.

**sia** ['sia] *cong* **sia ... sia ...** whether ... or ... ; (*entrambi*) both.

**siamese** [siaˈmeze] *agg*, *s(m+f)* Siamese.

**sibilare** [sibiˈlare] *v* hiss. **sibilo** *sm* hiss.

**sicario** [siˈkarjo] *sm* hired assassin.

**sicché** [sikˈke] *cong* (*di modo che*) and so; (*e perciò*) so that.

**siccità** [sittʃiˈta] *sf* drought.

**siccome** [sikˈkome] *cong* as, since.

**Sicilia** [siˈtʃilja] *sf* Sicily. **siciliano, -a** *agg s*, *agg* Sicilian.

**sicomoro** [sikoˈmɔro] *sm* sycamore.

**sicura** [siˈkura] *sf* safety catch.

**sicurezza** [sikuˈrettsa] *sf* safety; certainty; (*garanzia*) security; (*confidenza*) self-assurance. **di sicurezza** safety. **per maggior sicurezza** to be on the safe side. **publica sicurezza** police. **sicurezza sociale** social security; welfare.

**sicuro** [siˈkuro] *agg* safe; (*tranquillo*) secure; certain, sure; (*fidato*) reliable; (*saldo*) steady. *sm* safety; safe place. **andar sul sicuro** take no chances. **dare per sicuro** be certain about. **di sicuro** certainly. **star sicuro** not worry.

**sidro** ['sidro] *sm* cider.

**siepe** ['sjɛpe] *sf* hedge.

**siero** ['sjɛro] *sm* serum.

**siesta** ['sjɛsta] *sf* siesta; (*fam*) nap. **fare la siesta** take a nap.

**sifilide** [si'filide] *sf* syphilis.

**sifone** [si'fone] *sm* siphon.

**sigaretta** [siga'retta] *sf* cigarette. **sigaro** *sm* cigar.

**sigillare** [sidʒil'lare] *v* seal. **sigillatura** *sf* sealing, seal. **sigillo** *sm* seal. **anello con sigillo** *sm* signet-ring.

**sigla** ['sigla] *sf* initials *pl*; (*auto*) registration number. **sigla musicale** signature tune. **siglare** *v* initial.

**significare** [siɲifi'kare] *v* mean; (*simboleggiare*) stand for. **significativo** *agg* meaningful, significant; important. **significato** *sm* meaning; importance.

**signora** [si'ɲora] *sf* lady; (*donna*) woman (*pl* women); (*cortesia*) madam; (*seguito dal cognome*) Mrs; (*padrona*) mistress; (*moglie*) wife. **fare la signora** live like a lady.

**signore** [si'ɲore] *sm* gentleman; (*uomo*) man (*pl* men); (*cortesia*) sir; (*seguito dal cognome*) Mr; (*padrone*) master.

**signoreggiare** [siɲored'dʒare] *v* rule.

**signoria** [siɲo'ria] *sf* domination.

**signorile** [siɲo'rile] *agg* elegant, high-class; (*uomo*) gentlemanly; (*donna*) lady-like. **signorilità** *sf* elegance; refinement.

**signorina** [siɲo'rina] *sf* young lady *or* woman; (*cortesia*) madam; (*seguito dal cognome*) Miss; (*non sposata*) unmarried woman. **nome da signorina** *sm* maiden name.

**silenzio** [si'lɛntsjo] *sm* silence. **far silenzio** be quiet. **silenziare** *v* muffle. **silenziatore** *sm* silencer. **silenzioso** *agg* silent, quiet.

**silicio** [si'litʃo] *sm* silicon. **silice** *sf* silica. **silicone** *sm* silicone. **silicosi** *sf* silicosis.

**sillaba** ['sillaba] *sf* syllable. **sillabare** *v* (*gramm*) syllabify; (*fig*) spell out. **sillabario** *sm* spelling book.

**silo** ['silo] *sm* silo.

**silofono** [si'lɔfono] *sm* xylophone.

**silurare** [silu'rare] *v* torpedo; (*far fallire*) wreck; (*destituire*) dismiss. **siluramento** *sm* torpedoing; wrecking; dismissal. **siluro** *sm* torpedo.

**silvestre** [sil'vɛstre] *agg* woody; (*selvaggio*) wild.

**silvia** ['silvja] *sf* (*bot*) wood anemone; (*zool*) warbler.

**simbolo** ['simbolo] *sm* symbol; (*rel*) creed. **simboleggiare** *v* symbolize. **simbolico** *agg* symbolic.

**simile** ['simile] *agg* like, similar; (*predicato*) alike; (*tale*) such. **similitudine** *sf* simile.

**simmetria** [simme'tria] *sf* symmetry. **simmetrico** *agg* symmetrical.

**simpatia** [simpa'tia] *sf* (*sentimento di attrazione*) liking; (*qualità*) likeableness; (*affinità*) sympathy. **avere** *or* **provare simpatia per** like, take to. **simpatico** *agg* nice, likeable; (*piacevole*) agreeable; (*anat*) sympathetic. **simpatizzare** *v* sympathize.

**simposio** [sim'pɔzjo] *sm* symposium.

**simulare** [simu'lare] *v* feign; (*imitare*) simulate. **simulacro** *sm* image; (*fig*) semblance. **simulazione** *sf* simulation.

**simultaneo** [simul'taneo] *agg* simultaneous. **simultaneità** *sf* simultaneity.

**sinagoga** [sina'gɔga] *sf* synagogue.

**sincero** [sin'tʃero] *agg* sincere, true; (*non artefatto*) genuine. **sincerità** *sf* sincerity.

**sincopare** [sinko'pare] *v* syncopate. **sincope** *sf* syncope; (*musica*) syncopation.

**sincronizzare** [sinkronid'dzare] *v* synchronize. **sincronizzatore** *sm* synchronizer. **sincronizzazione** *sf* synchronization.

**sindacale** [sinda'kale] *agg* (*di sindacato*) (trade) union. **sindacalismo** *sm* trade unionism. **sindacalista** *s(m+f)* trade unionist.

**sindacare** [sinda'kare] *v* check; (*contabilità*) audit; (*fig*) criticize.

**sindacato** [sinda'kato] *sm* (*operaio*) trade union; (*padronale, d'impresa*) consortium; (*finanziario*) syndicate.

**sindaco** ['sindako] *sm* mayor; (*comm*) auditor.

**sindrome** ['sindrome] *sf* syndrome.

**sinfonia** [sinfo'nia] *sf* symphony. **sinfonico** *agg* symphonic. **orchestra sinfonica** *sf* symphony orchestra.

**singhiozzare** [singjot'tsare] *v* (*avere il singhiozzo*) hiccup; (*piangere*) sob. **singhiozzo** *sm* sob; hiccup. **a singhiozzi** by fits and starts.

**singolare** [singo'lare] *agg* singular; (*strano*) strange. *sm* singular. **singolarità** *sf* singularity; strangeness.

**singolo** ['singolo] *agg* single, individual. *sm* (*persona*) individual; (*telefono*) private line; (*tennis*) singles; (*canottaggio*) skiff.

**sinistra** [si'nistra] *sf* left(-hand side); *(mano)* left hand. **a sinistra** on *or* to the left. **tenere la sinistra** keep to the left. **uomo di sinistra** *sm* left-winger.

**sinistrare** [sinis'trare] *v* damage. **sinistrato, -a** *sm, sf* victim. **zona sinistrata** *sf* disaster area.

**sinistro** [si'nistro] *agg* left; *(lato)* lefthand; *(fig)* sinister. *sm* accident; *(pugilato)* left.

**sino** ['sino] *cong* **sino a** *(tempo)* until; *(luogo)* as far as. *avv (persino)* even. **sinora** *avv (per ora)* so far; *(fino ad ora)* up to now.

**sinossi** [si'nɔssi] *sf* synopsis *(pl* -ses). **sinottico** *agg* synoptic.

**sintassi** [sin'tassi] *sf* syntax. **sintattico** *agg* syntactic(al).

**sintesi** ['sintezi] *sf* synthesis *(pl* -ses). **in sintesi** *(in poche parole)* in short; *(sommariamente)* summing up. **sintetico** *agg* synthetic; *(fig)* concise. **sintetizzare** *v* synthesize; *(riassumere)* summarize.

**sintomo** ['sintomo] *sm* symptom. **sintomatico** *agg* symptomatic.

**sintonizzare** [sintoniď'dzare] *v* tune in.

**sinuoso** [sinu'ozo] *agg* sinuous, winding.

**sinusite** [sinu'zite] *sf* sinusitis.

**sipario** [si'parjo] *sm* curtain.

**sirena** [si'rɛna] *sf* siren; *(creatura)* mermaid.

**siringa** [si'ringa] *sf* syringe; *(bot)* lilac; catheter. **siringare** *v* syringe; catheterize.

**sismico** ['sizmiko] *agg* seismic. **sismografo** *sm* seismograph.

**sistema** [sis'tɛma] *sm* system; *(modo di fare)* way; method. **sistemare** *v (mettere a posto)* arrange; *(put in)* order; *(risolvere)* settle; organize; *(collocare)* place; install. **sistemarsi** *v* settle (down); *(lavoro)* get a job. **sistematico** *agg* systematic; methodical. **sistemazione** *sf* arrangement; *(composizione)* settlement; *(alloggio)* accommodation; *(lavoro)* job.

**sito web** *sm* website.

**situare** [situ'are] *v* place; *(collocare)* locate. **situazione** *sf* situation. **situazione di fatto** state of affairs.

**slabbrare** [zlab'brare] *v (vasellame)* chip; *(tessuto)* tear.

**slacciare** [zlat'tʃare] *v* undo, untie.

**slanciare** [zlan'tʃare] *v* hurl. **slanciato** *agg* slender, slim. **slancio** *sm* swing; *(di passione, ecc.)* burst. **di slancio** in a rush; *(fig)* on impulse.

**slattare** [zlat'tare] *v* wean.

**slavato** [zla'vato] *agg* washed out; *(fig)* dull.

**sleale** [zle'ale] *agg* disloyal; *(fatto senza lealtà)* unfair. **gioco sleale** *sm* foul play. **slealtà** *sf* disloyalty; unfairness.

**slegare** [zle'gare] *v* untie. **slegato** *agg* untied; *(non rilegato)* unbound; *(fig)* disjointed.

**slip** [zlip] *sm invar (mutande)* briefs *pl*; *(da bagno)* swimming trunks *pl*.

**slitta** ['zlitta] *sf* sleigh, sledge; *(tec)* slide. **slittare** *v* slip; *(ruote)* skid; *(scivolare)* slide.

**slogan** ['zlɔgan] *sm invar* slogan.

**slogare** [zlo'gare] *v* dislocate. **slogatura** *sf* dislocation.

**sloggiare** [zlod'dʒare] *v* dislodge.

**Slovacchia** [zlo'vakkja] *sf* Slovakia. **slovacco, -a** *s, agg* Slovakian.

**Slovenia** [zlo'vɛnja] *sf* Slovenia. **sloveno, -a** *s, agg* Slovenian.

**smacchiare** [zmak'kjare] *v* clean. **smacchiatore** *sm* stain-remover. **smacchiatura** *sf* cleaning.

**smacco** ['zmakko] *sm* defeat.

**smagliante** [zma'ʎante] *agg* dazzling.

**smagliarsi** [zma'ʎarsi] *v (calze)* ladder; *(pelle)* stretch.

**smagrire** [zma'grire] *v* slim.

**smaltare** [zmal'tare] *v* enamel; *(unghie)* paint; *(ceramica)* glaze. **smalto** *sm* enamel; glaze; *(per le unghie)* nail-varnish.

**smaltire** [zmal'tire] *v* digest; *(fig)* swallow; *(comm)* dispose of.

**smanceroso** [zmantʃe'rozo] *agg* affected; *(smorfioso)* mawkish. **smanceria** *sf* affectation.

**smania** ['zmanja] *sf* craving; *(agitazione)* frenzy. **aver la smania addosso** fidget. **smaniare** *v (essere agitato)* fret; *(essere furioso)* rave; *(desiderare)* crave (for).

**smantellare** [zmantel'lare] *v* dismantle; *(fig)* pull to pieces.

**smargiassata** [zmardʒas'sata] *sf* brag; bravado. **smargiasso, -a** *sm, sf* braggart. **fare lo smargiasso** brag.

**smarrire** [zmar'rire] *v* lose; *(non riuscire a trovare)* mislay. **smarrirsi** *v (persone)* lose one's way; *(cose)* be mislaid, go astray. **smarrimento** *sm* loss; *(svenimento)* fainting-fit; *(turbamento)* bewilderment.

**smascherare** [zmaske'rare] *v* unmask,

reveal. **smascheramento** *sm* unmasking.

**smembrare** [zmem'brare] *v* dismember.

**smemorato** [zmemo'rato], **-a** *agg* forgetful; (*distratto*) absent-minded, *sm*, *sf* forgetful or absent-minded person. **smemorataggine** *sf* forgetfulness; (*dimenticanza*) lapse of memory. **smemoratezza** *sf* forgetfulness; absent-mindedness.

**smentire** [zmen'tire] *v* deny; (*ritrattare*) retract; (*dimostrare la falsità*) belie. **smentita** *sf* denial.

**smeraldo** [zme'raldo] *sm* emerald. *agg invar* (*colore*) emerald-green.

**smerciare** [zmer'tʃare] *v* sell. **smercio** *sm* sale.

**smerigliare** [zmeri'ʎare] *v* (*mec*) grind; (*vetro*) frost. **carta smerigliata** *sf* (*grossa*) emery paper; (*fine*) sandpaper. **vetro smerigliato** *sm* frosted glass. **smeriglio** *sm* emery.

**smerlare** [zmer'lare] *v* scallop. **smerlo** *sm* scallop.

**\*smettere** ['zmettere] *v* stop.

**smidollato** [zmidol'lato] *agg* spineless.

**smilitarizzare** [zmilitarid'dzare] *v* demilitarize. **smilitarizzazione** *sf* demilitarization.

**smilzo** [zmiltso] *agg* lean.

**sminuire** [zminu'ire] *v* diminish; (*fig*) belittle.

**sminuzzare** [zminut'tsare] *v* break into small pieces; (*sbriciolare*) crumble.

**smistare** [zmis'tare] *v* sort (out); (*ferr*) shunt.

**smisurato** [zmizu'rato] *agg* boundless; enormous.

**smobilitare** [zmobili'tare] *v* demobilize. **smobilitazione** *sf* demobilization.

**smoderato** [zmode'rato] *agg also* **smodato** immoderate. **smoderatezza** *sf* lack of moderation; excess.

**smoking** ['zmɔkiŋ] *sm invar* dinner-jacket.

**smontare** [zmon'tare] *v* (*scomporre*) dismantle, take apart; (*totalmente*) strip; (*da veicoli*) get out or off. **smontaggio** *sm* dismantling; stripping.

**smorfia** ['zmɔrfja] *sf* wry face. **fare una smorfia** pull a face; (*di dolore*) wince with pain. **smorfioso** *agg* simpering.

**smorto** ['zmɔrto] *agg* pale, wan; (*fig*) colourless.

**smorzare** [zmor'tsare] *v* (*colori*) tone down; (*suoni*) muffle; (*luce*) dim; (*fig*) dampen.

**smorzata** *sf* (*tennis*) drop-shot.

**smunto** ['zmunto] *agg* emaciated.

**\*smuovere** ['zmwɔvere] *v* shift; (*commuovere*) touch; dissuade.

**smussare** [zmus'sare] *v* smooth; (*angolo*) round off; (*fig*) soften. **smussarsi** *v* become blunt.

**snaturare** [znatu'rare] *v* distort. **snaturato** *agg* unnatural; degenerate.

**snazionalizzare** [znatsjonalid'dzare] *v* denationalize. **snazionalizzazione** *sf* denationalization.

**snellire** [znel'lire] *v* slim (down); simplify; speed up. **snellezza** *sf* slimness. **snello** *agg* slim; (*agile*) nimble; simple, easy.

**snervare** [zner'vare] *v* exhaust.

**snidare** [zni'dare] *v* drive out.

**snob** ['znɔb] *agg*, *s(m+f)* *invar* snob. **snobbare** *v* snub. **snobismo** *sm* snobbery.

**snocciolare** [znottʃo'lare] *v* stone; (*fam: spendere*) shell out; (*fam: spiattellare*) rattle off.

**snodare** [zno'dare] *v* unknot; (*articolare meglio*) loosen (up); (*piegare*) bend. **snodabile** *agg* (*tec*) articulated. **snodato** *agg* flexible, loose.

**soave** [so'ave] *agg* delicate, sweet. **soavità** *sf* sweetness, delicacy.

**sobbalzare** [sobbal'tsare] *v* jolt; (*trasalire*) jump. **di sobbalzo** with a start.

**sobbarcarsi** [sobbar'karsi] *v* undertake.

**sobbollire** [sobbol'lire] *v* simmer.

**sobborgo** [sob'borgo] *sm* suburb.

**sobillare** [sobil'lare] *v* incite, stir up. **sobillatore**, **-trice** *sm*, *sf* trouble-maker.

**sobrio** ['sɔbrjo] *agg* sober. **sobrietà** *sf* sobriety.

**\*socchiudere** [sok'kjudere] *v* half-close. **socchiuso** *agg* half-closed; (*porta*) ajar.

**soccombere** [sok'kombere] *v* succumb.

**\*soccorrere** [sok'korrere] *v* assist; come to the aid of; (*salvare*) rescue.

**soccorritore** [sokkorri'tore], **-trice** *agg* helping. *sm*, *sf* helper.

**soccorso** [sok'korso] *sm* help, assistance; rescue. **pronto soccorso** first aid; (*all'ospedale*) casualty ward. **soccorsi** *sm pl* (*rinforzi*) reinforcements *pl*; (*rifornimenti*) supplies *pl*.

**socialdemocratico** [sotʃaldemo'kratiko], **-a** *sm*, *sf* social democrat. **socialdemocrazia** *sf* social democracy.

**sociale** [so'tʃale] *agg* social; (*benessere*) welfare; (*comm*) relating to a firm, company. **assistente sociale** *s(m+f)* welfare officer, social worker. **assistenza sociale** *sf* welfare. **tessera sociale** *sf* membership card.

**socialismo** [sotʃa'lizmo] *sm* socialism. **socialista** *agg*, *s(m+f)* socialist.

**società** [sotʃe'ta] *sf* society; (*comm*) company, partnership; association. **gioco di società** *sm* parlour game. **mettersi in società** go into partnership. **società anonima** limited company. **società dei consumi** consumer society. **società per azioni** limited company.

**socievole** [so'tʃevole] *agg* social; (*persona*) sociable. **socievolezza** *sf* sociability.

**socio** ['sɔtʃo], **-a** *sm*, *sf* partner; member.

**sociologia** [sotʃolo'dʒia] *sf* sociology. **sociologico** *agg* sociological. **sociologo, -a** *sm*, *sf* sociologist.

**soda** ['sɔda] *sf* soda.

**sodalizio** [soda'litsjo] *sm* brotherhood; (*amicizia*) fellowship.

**\*soddisfare** [soddis'fare] *v* satisfy; (*appagare*) gratify; (*riparare*) make amends for. **soddisfacente** *agg* satisfactory; satisfying. **soddisfatto** *agg* satisfied; (*contento*) pleased. **soddisfazione** *sf* satisfaction. **bella satisfazione!** big deal!

**sodio** ['sɔdjo] *sm* sodium.

**sodo** ['sɔdo] *agg* firm; (*fig*) sound. **uovo sodo** *sm* hard-boiled egg. *avv* hard; (*profondamente*) soundly.

**sofà** [so'fa] *sm* sofa, settee.

**sofferente** [soffe'rɛnte] *agg* suffering. **sofferenza** *sf* suffering.

**soffermarsi** [soffer'marsi] *v* linger (over).

**soffiare** [sof'fjare] *v* blow; (*sbuffare*) puff; (*dama, scacchi*) huff. **soffiare di rabbia** fume (with rage). **soffio** *sm* puff; (*med*) murmur. **in un soffio** in a flash. **per un soffio** by a whisker.

**soffice** ['sɔffitʃe] *agg* soft.

**soffietto** [sof'fjetto] *sm* bellows *pl*; (*fam: articoletto*) plug. **a soffietto** folding. **lavorar di soffietto** (*fam*) tell tales.

**soffitta** [sof'fitta] *sf* attic.

**soffitto** [sof'fitto] *sm* ceiling.

**soffocare** [soffo'kare] *v* suffocate, choke; (*reprimere*) suppress, stifle. **soffocamento** *sm* suffocation.

**\*soffriggere** [soffrid'dʒere] *v* brown.

**\*soffrire** [sof'frire] *v* suffer (from); (*sopportare*) bear, stand; (*consentire*) allow. **soffrire la fame** go hungry. **soffrir di (mal di) cuore** have heart trouble.

**sofisma** [so'fizma] *sm* sophistry. **sofisticare** *v* (*sottilizzare*) quibble; (*fam*) split hairs; (*adulterare*) doctor.

**soggetto** [sod'dʒetto] *sm* subject; (*argomento*) topic; person. **recitare a soggetto** improvise. *agg* subject, liable; (*sottomesso*) subjected; (*predisposto*) prone. **soggettivo** *agg* subjective. **soggezione** *sf* subjection; embarrassment; (*timore*) awe. **aver soggezione di** (*sentirsi imbarazzato*) feel uneasy in the presence of; (*averne timore*) be overawed by. **ispirare soggezione a** make uneasy; overawe.

**sogghignare** [soggi'ɲare] *v* sneer.

**\*soggiacere** [soddʒa'tʃere] *v* be subjected to; succumb.

**soggiorno** [sod'dʒorno] *sm* stay; (*luogo*) resort; (*stanza*) living room. **permesso di soggiorno** *sm* residence permit. **soggiornare** *v* stay.

**\*soggiungere** [sod'dʒundʒere] *v* add.

**soglia** ['sɔʎa] *sf* threshold.

**sogliola** ['sɔʎola] *sf* sole.

**sognare** [so'ɲare] *v* dream; (*ad occhi aperti*) daydream. **sognatore, -trice** *sm*, *sf* dreamer. **sogno** *sm* dream. **fare un sogno** have a dream. **neanche per sogno!** not likely!

**soia** ['sɔja] *sf* soya (bean).

**solaio** [so'lajo] *sm* (*soffitta*) loft; (*piano di edificio*) floor.

**solare** [so'lare] *agg* solar. **luce solare** *sf* sunlight.

**solco** ['solko] *sm* (*agric*) furrow; (*traccia*) track; (*lampo*) streak; (*disco*) groove.

**soldato** [sol'dato] *sm* soldier. **andare soldato** join up. **fare il soldato** be in the army.

**soldo** ['sɔldo] *sm* penny. **soldi** *sm pl* (*denaro*) money *sing*. **essere al soldo di** be in the pay of. **essere senza soldi** be penniless.

**sole** ['sole] *sm* sun. **al sole** in the sun. **chiaro come il sole** clear as daylight. **fare un bagno di sole** sunbathe. **occhiali da sole** *sm pl* sun-glasses *pl*. **soleggiato** *agg* sunny.

**solenne** [so'lɛnne] *agg* solemn; (*fig*) tremendous. **solennità** *sf* solemnity; (*festa*) holiday. **solennizzare** *v* solemnize.

**\*solere** [so'lere] v be in the habit of.

**soletta** [so'letta] sf sole; (*suola interna*) insole.

**solfato** [sol'fato] sm sulphate. **solforico** agg sulphuric. **solfuro** sm sulphide.

**solidale** [soli'dale] agg (*tec*) integral; (*d'accordo*) in agreement (with); (*dir*) joint. **solidarietà** sf solidarity.

**solidificare** [solidifi'kare] v harden. **solidificarsi** v set. **solidificazione** sf hardening; setting.

**solido** ['sɔlido] agg solid; stable; (*robusto, valido*) sound; (*colori*) fast. sm solid. **solidità** sf solidity; stability; soundness; fastness.

**soliloquio** [soli'lɔkwjo] sm soliloquy.

**solista** [so'lista] s(m+f) soloist.

**solitario** [soli'tarjo], **-a** agg solitary. sm, sf loner. sm (*brillante, gioco*) solitaire.

**solito** ['sɔlito], **-a** agg usual. pron same. sm (*abitudine*) habit; (*cosa*) usual. **come al solito** as usual. **di solito** usually, as a rule. **essere solito a fare** be used to doing.

**solitudine** [soli'tudine] sf solitude.

**sollazzare** [sollat'tsare] v amuse.

**sollecitare** [solletʃi'tare] v press for; (*affrettare*) speed up; (*mec*) stress; (*chiedere con insistenza*) solicit. **sollecitazione** sf solicitation, entreaty; (*mec*) stress. **lettera di sollecitazione** sf reminder.

**sollecito** [sol'letʃito] agg (*fatto con premura*) prompt; (*premuroso*) solicitous. **sollecitudine** sm (*prontezza*) dispatch; (*preoccupazione*) solicitude.

**solleticare** [solleti'kare] v tickle; (*fig*) arouse. **solletico** sm tickle. **fare il solletico** tickle. **sentire** or **soffrire il solletico** be ticklish.

**sollevare** [solle'vare] v raise; (*tirar su*) lift (up). **sollevarsi** v rise; (*riprendersi*) recover.

**sollievo** [sol'ljevo] sm relief.

**solo** ['solo] agg alone; by oneself; (*unico*) only, sole; (*semplice*) mere; (*musica*) unaccompanied. avv (*soltanto*) only; (*ma*) but. **da solo** alone, by oneself. **solo che** only. **solo soletto** quite alone. **una sola volta** once only. **un solo** just one, only one.

**solstizio** [sol'stitsjo] sm solstice.

**soltanto** [sol'tanto] avv only.

**solubile** [so'lubile] agg soluble. **solubilità** sf solubility. **soluzione** sf solution.

**solvente** [sol'vɛnte] agg, sm solvent. **solvibile** agg (*comm*) solvent. **solvibilità** sf (*comm*) solvency.

**soma** ['sɔma] sf burden.

**somaro** [so'maro] sm donkey.

**somigliare** [somiʎ'ʎare] v resemble, be like. **somigliante** agg similar. **somiglianza** sf resemblance.

**somma** ['somma] sf sum. **fare la somma** add up. **tirare le somme** sum up. **sommare** v add or sum up. **tutto sommato** all things considered.

**sommario** [som'marjo] agg brief; (*dir*) summary. sm summary, outline.

**\*sommergere** [som'merdʒere] v submerge. **sommergibile** sm submarine.

**sommesso** [som'messo] agg meek.

**somministrare** [somminis'trare] v administer.

**sommità** [sommi'ta] sf peak, summit.

**sommo** ['sommo] agg highest; (*fig*) supreme. sm peak.

**sommossa** [som'mɔssa] sf riot.

**sommozzatore** [sommottsa'tore] sm skindiver; (*mil*) frogman.

**sonaglio** [so'naʎo] sm bell. **serpente a sonagli** sm rattlesnake.

**sonare** [so'nare] v also **suonare** sound; (*campanello*) ring; (*musica*) play; (*orologio*) strike; (*fam: imbrogliare*) cheat. **sonata** sf (*musica*) sonata; (*fam: bastonatura*) caning; (*fam: fregatura*) swindle. **prendersi una sonata** be taken in. **sonato** agg (*compiuto*) past; (*rimbambito*) gaga.

**sonda** ['sonda] sf probe. **sondaggio** sm probing, sounding; (*indagine*) poll. **sondare** v sound, probe.

**sonnambulo** [son'nambulo], **-a** sm, sf sleep-walker.

**sonnecchiare** [sonnek'kjare] v doze.

**sonnifero** [son'nifero] agg soporific. sm sleeping pill.

**sonno** ['sonno] sm sleep; (*senso di torpore*) drowsiness. **aver sonno** be sleepy. **fare un bel sonno** have a good sleep. **sonnolento** agg sleepy, drowsy. **sonnolenza** sf drowsiness.

**sonoro** [so'nɔro] agg sound; (*che risona*) resonant; (*consonanti*) voiced. **sonorità** sf resonance; (*fis*) acoustics pl.

**sontuoso** [sontu'ozo] agg sumptuous. **sontuosità** sf sumptuousness.

**soporifero** [sopo'rifero] agg, sm soporific.

**sopperire** [soppe'rire] *v* provide for.

**soppesare** [soppe'zare] *v* weigh up.

**soppiantare** [soppjan'tare] *v* supplant.

**soppiatto** [sop'pjatto] *agg* **di soppiatto** stealthily. **entrare/uscire di soppiatto** steal in/away.

**sopportare** [soppor'tare] *v* (*reggere*) support; (*fig*) bear, stand. **sopportabile** *agg* bearable. **sopportazione** *sf* endurance.

*****sopprimere** [sop'primere] *v* suppress; abolish. **soppressione** *sf* suppression; abolition.

**sopra** ['sopra] *prep* on, upon; (*senza contatto diretto*) over, above. **al di sopra di** above; (*oltre*) beyond. *avv* on; (*più in su*) above; (*al piano superiore*) upstairs. **come/vedi sopra** (*nei rinvii*) as/see above.

**soprabito** [so'prabito] *sm* overcoat.

**sopracciglio** [soprat'tʃiʎo] *sm* eyebrow.

**sopraccitato** [soprattʃi'tato] *agg* abovementioned.

**sopraccoperta** [soprakko'pɛrta] *sf* (*letto*) counterpane; (*libro*) dust-jacket.

*****sopraffare** [sopraf'fare] *v* overcome; dominate.

**sopraffino** [sopraf'fino] *agg* excellent; highly refined.

**sopraggiungere** [soprad'dʒundʒere] *v* turn up; (*accadere improvvisamente*) happen, arise.

**sopralluogo** [sopral'lwɔgo] *sm, pl* **-ghi** (*on the spot*) inspection; (*statistica*) poll.

**sopralzo** [so'praltso] *sm* extension.

**soprammobile** [sopram'mɔbile] *sm* knickknack.

**soprannaturale** [soprannatu'rale] *agg, sm* supernatural.

**soprannome** [sopran'nome] *sm* nickname. **soprannominare** *v* call.

**soprannumero** [sopran'numero] *sm* excess.

**soprano** [so'prano], **-a** *sm, sf* soprano.

**soprappensiero** [soprappen'sjero] *avv* lost in thought.

**soprappiù** [soprap'pju] *sm* surplus; (*aggiunta*) addition. **di** *or* **per soprappiù** in addition, besides.

**soprapprezzo** [soprap'prɛttso] *sm* (*econ*) premium; (*maggiorazione*) increase in price.

**soprassalto** [sopras'salto] *sm* sudden start. **di soprassalto** suddenly.

**soprassedere** [soprasse'dere] *v* put off.

**soprattassa** [soprat'tassa] *sf* additional charge.

**soprattutto** [soprat'tutto] *avv* above all; (*per la maggior parte*) mainly.

**sopravanzare** [sopravan'tsare] *v* be left over.

**sopravvalutare** [sopravvalu'tare] *v* overrate. **sopravvalutazione** *sf* overestimate.

*****sopravvenire** [sopravve'nire] *v* turn up; (*accadere d'improvviso*) happen, arise.

**sopravvento** [soprav'vɛnto] *agg, avv* windward. *sm* (*fig*) upper hand.

*****sopravvivere** [soprav'vivere] *v* survive. **sopravvissuto, -a** *sm, sf* survivor. **sopravvivenza** *sf* survival.

**soprelevare** [soprele'vare] *v* raise.

*****soprintendere** [soprin'tɛndere] *v* supervise; be in charge of. **soprintendente** *s*(*m+f*) superintendent. **soprintendenza** *sf* (*atto*) supervision; (*ufficio*) superintendence.

**sopruso** [so'pruzo] *sm* outrage.

**soqquadro** [sok'kwadro] *sm* **mettere a soqquadro** turn upside down.

**sorbetto** [sor'betto] *sm* sorbet, water ice.

**sorbire** [sor'bire] *v* sip. **sorbirsi** *v* (*sopportare*) put up with.

**sorcio** ['sortʃo] *sm* mouse (*pl* mice).

**sordido** ['sordido] *agg* sordid. **sordidezza** *sf* sordidness.

**sordina** [sor'dina] *sf* (*musica*) mute. **in sordina** (*fig*) on the quiet.

**sordo** ['sordo], **-a** *agg* deaf; (*smorzato*) dull; (*fig*) hidden. **sordo come una campana** deaf as a post. *sm, sf* deaf person. **fare il sordo** feign deafness. **sordità** *sf* deafness.

**sordomuto** [sordo'muto], **-a** *agg* deaf and dumb. *sm, sf* deaf-mute.

**sorella** [so'rella] *sf* sister. **sorellastra** *sf* step-sister, half-sister.

*****sorgere** ['sordʒere] *v* rise; (*aver origine*) arise. **sorgente** *sf* source. **acqua sorgiva** *sf* spring water.

**soriano** [so'rjano] *sm, agg* tabby.

**sormontare** [sormon'tare] *v* surmount; (*stoffa*) overlap.

**sornione** [sor'njone] *agg* sly.

**sorpassare** [sorpas'sare] *v* (*oltrepassare*) overtake; (*eccedere*) exceed. **sorpassare in altezza/lunghezza** be higher/longer. **sorpassato** *agg* (*non più attuale*) out of date.

**sorpasso** *sm* overtaking. **divieto di sorpasso** *sm* no overtaking.

**\*sorprendere** [sor'prɛndere] *v* surprise; (*cogliere all'improvviso*) catch. **sorprendente** *agg* surprising. **sorpresa** *sf* surprise.

**\*sorreggere** [sor'rɛddʒere] *v* hold up; sustain. **sorreggersi** *v* stand upright.

**\*sorridere** [sor'ridere] *v* smile; (*destar piacere*) appeal. **sorridente** *agg* smiling. **sorriso** *sm* smile.

**sorso** ['sorso] *sm* (*sorsata*) sip; (*d'un fiato*) gulp; (*piccola quantità*) drop. **sorseggiare** *v* also **bere a piccoli sorsi** sip.

**sorta** ['sorta] *sf* kind, sort. **di sorta** (*di nessun tipo*) whatever.

**sorte** ['sorte] *sf* fate; fortune; (*condizione propria*) lot. **sorteggiare** *v* also **tirare a sorte** draw lots. **sorteggio** *sm* draw.

**sortilegio** [sorti'lɛdʒo] *sm* spell.

**sorvegliare** [sorve'ʎare] *v* watch; (*sovrintendere*) oversee; (*vigilare*) keep an eye on. **sorvegliante** *s*(*m+f*) overseer; (*custode*) caretaker; (*guardiano*) watchman. **sorveglianza** *sf* surveillance, watch.

**sorvolare** [sorvo'lare] *v* fly over; (*fig*) skip.

**sosia** ['sɔzja] *sm invar* double.

**\*sospendere** [sos'pɛndere] *v* suspend; (*attaccare in alto*) hang; interrupt; (*seduta*) adjourn; defer. **sospendere il lavoro** stop work. **sospensione** *sf* suspension; interruption; (*cessazione*) stoppage. **sospeso** *agg* hanging; (*non definito*) outstanding. **col fiato sospeso** with bated breath. **in sospeso** in suspense; (*non risolto*) pending.

**sospettare** [sospet'tare] *v* suspect; (*diffidare*) distrust, be suspicious (of).

**sospetto** [sos'petto] *agg* suspect, suspicious. **persona sospetta** *sf* suspect. *sm* suspicion. **sospettoso** *agg* distrustful.

**\*sospingere** [sos'pindʒere] *v* push; (*fig*) drive. **a ogni piè sospinto** at every step.

**sospirare** [sospi'rare] *v* sigh; (*aspettare con ansia*) long *or* yearn for. **sospiro** *sm* sigh.

**sosta** ['sɔsta] *sf* stop; pause; (*riposo*) rest; (*aspettare*) wait. **divieto di sosta** no waiting. **senza sosta** ceaselessly; without stopping. **sostare** *v* stop; pause; wait; rest.

**sostantivo** [sostan'tivo] *agg* substantive. *sm* noun.

**sostanza** [sos'tantsa] *sf* matter; (*parte utile*) substance; (*parte nutritiva*) nourishment; (*patrimonio*) property. **cibo di sostanza** nourishing food. **in sostanza** essentially.

**sostanza alimentare** food-stuff.
**sostanziale** *agg* substantial; essential.
**sostanzioso** *agg* nourishing.

**sostegno** [sos'teɲo] *sm* support.

**\*sostenere** [soste'nere] *v* support; (*asserire*) maintain; (*tenere alto*) keep up; (*tollerare*) stand. **sostenere una carica** hold an office. **sostenere una parte** act a part. **sostenersi** *v* (*star su*) hold oneself up, stand up; (*fig*) hold water. **sostenibile** *agg* tenable.

**sostenitore** [sosteni'tore], **-trice** *agg* supporting. *sm*, *sf* supporter.

**\*sostentare** [sosten'tare] *v* support; maintain. **sostentamento** *sm* support; maintenance.

**sostenuto** [soste'nuto] *agg* (*contegnoso*) reserved; (*musica*) sostenuto. **sostenutezza** *sf* reserve.

**sostituire** [sostitu'ire] *v* substitute; (*rimpiazzare*) replace. **sostituto, -a** *sm*, *sf* deputy, substitute. **sostituzione** *sf* substitution; replacement.

**sottaceto** [sotta'tʃeto] *avv* **mettere sottaceto** pickle. **sottaceti** *sm pl* pickles *pl*.

**sottalimentazione** [sottalimenta'tsjone] *sf* undernourishment.

**sottana** [sot'tana] *sf* skirt; (*sottoveste*) slip, underskirt; (*rel*) cassock.

**sottecchi** [sot'tekki] *avv* **di sottecchi** stealthily.

**sottentrare** [sotten'trare] *v* replace.

**sotterfugio** [sotter'fudʒo] *sm* subterfuge.

**sotterraneo** [sotter'raneo] *agg* underground. *sm* basement. **sotterranea** *sf* underground (railway); (*fam*) tube.

**sotterrare** [sotter'rare] *v* bury. **sotterra** *avv* underground.

**sottile** [sot'tile] *agg* thin; fine; (*acuto*) sharp. **sottigliezza** *sf* thinness; sharpness; (*sofisticheria*) nicety.

**sottinsù** [sottin'su] *avv* **di sottinsù** from below.

**\*sottintendere** [sottin'tɛndere] *v* imply; infer; (*non esprimere*) leave out. **sottinteso** *agg* implied; (*chiaro da sé*) understood. *sm* allusion. **senza sottintesi** plainly.

**sotto** ['sotto] *prep* under; (*al di sotto di*) below, beneath; (*in cambio di*) on. *avv* underneath; below; (*al piano di sotto*) downstairs. **andar sotto le armi** join up. **metter sotto** (*investire*) run down. **mettersi sotto** get down to. **sotto la pioggia** in the rain. **sotto questo punto di vista** from this point of view. **sotto questo riguardo** in this respect. **sotto sotto** deep down.

**sottobanco** [sotto'banko] *avv* under the counter.

**sottobicchiere** [sottobik'kjɛre] *sm* mat, coaster.

**sottobraccio** [sotto'brattʃo] *avv* arm-in-arm. **prendere sottobraccio qualcuno** take someone's arm.

**sottocchio** [sot'ɔkkjo] *avv* **tenere sottocchio** keep an eye on.

**sottocommissione** [sottokommis'sjone] *sf* subcommittee; subcommission.

**sottocoppa** [sotto'kɔppa] *sm invar* mat; (*piattino*) saucer.

**\*sottoesporre** [sottoes'porre] *v* underexpose.

**sottofondo** [sotto'fondo] *sm* foundation; (*suono*) background noise. **musica in sottofondo** *sf* background music.

**sottolineare** [sottoline'are] *v* underline; (*fig*) stress.

**sottomano** [sotto'mano] *avv* (*a portata di mano*) within (easy) reach, on hand; (*di nascosto*) on the quiet; (*sport*) underhand.

**\*sottomettere** [sotto'mettere] *v* (*assoggettare*) subject; (*costringere a sottostare*) subdue; subordinate. **sottomettersi** *v* submit. **sottomesso** *agg* subdued; (*obbediente*) submissive.

**sottopassaggio** [sottopas'saddʒo] *sm* underpass.

**\*sottoporre** [sotto'porre] *v* (*presentare*) submit; (*costringere*) subject, expose. **sottoporsi a un'operazione** undergo an operation. **sottoposto, -a** *sm, sf* subordinate.

**sottoprodotto** [sottopro'dotto] *sm* by-product.

**sottordine** [sot'tordine] *sm* suborder. **in sottordine** of minor importance.

**\*sottoscrivere** [sotto'skrivere] *v* sign; (*fig*) support; (*econ*) underwrite, subscribe. **sottoscritto, -a** *sm, sf* undersigned; (*fam*) yours truly. **sottoscrizione** *sf* subscription.

**sottosopra** [sotto'sopra] *avv* upside down.

**\*sottostare** [sotto'stare] *v* be under; (*sottomettersi*) give in. **sottostante** *agg* (down) below.

**sottosuolo** [sotto'swɔlo] *sm* subsoil.

**sottoterra** [sotto'tɛrra] *avv* underground.

**sottotitolo** [sotto'titolo] *sm* subtitle.

**sottovalutare** [sottovalu'tare] *v* underestimate.

**sottoveste** [sotto'vɛste] *sf* slip.

**sottovoce** [sotto'votʃe] *avv* in a low voice, softly.

**\*sottrarre** [sot'trarre] *v* remove; (*mat*) subtract; (*salvare*) save (from). **sottrarsi a** escape; (*evitare*) avoid. **sottrazione** *sf* subtraction; removal.

**sottufficiale** [sottuffi'tʃale] *sm* non-commissioned officer; (*mar*) petty officer.

**sovente** [so'vɛnte] *avv* also **di sovente** frequently.

**soverchio** [so'verkjo] *agg* excessive. **soverchieria** *sf* bullying; (*sopruso*) outrage.

**sovietico** [so'vjɛtiko], **-a** *s, agg* Soviet.

**sovrabbondante** [sovrabbon'dante] *agg* plentiful; excessive. **sovrabbondanza** *sf* plenty; excess.

**sovraccaricare** [sovrakkari'kare] *v* overburden; (*tec*) overload. **sovraccarica** *sf* overcharge. **sovraccarico** *agg, m pl* **-chi** overloaded.

**\*sovr(a)esporre** [sovr(a)es'porre] *v* overexpose. **sovresposizione** *sf* over-exposure.

**sovraffollato** [sovraffol'lato] *agg* overcrowded.

**sovrano** [so'vrano], **-a** *agg* sovereign, supreme. *sm, sf* sovereign. **sovranità** *sf* sovereignty; (*fig*) supremacy.

**sovrappopolato** [sovrappopo'lato] *agg* overpopulated.

**\*sovrapporre** [sovrap'porre] *v* superimpose; (*fig*) set over; (*accavallare*) overlap.

**sovrastante** [sovra'stante] *agg* towering; (*imminente*) impending.

**sovreccitare** [sovrettʃi'tare] *v* over-excite. **sovreccitarsi** *v* become over-excited. **sovreccitazione** *sf* over-excitement.

**sovrumano** [sovru'mano] *agg* superhuman.

**sovvenzione** [sovven'tsjone] *sf* subsidy. **sovvenzionare** *v* subsidize.

**sovversione** [sovver'sjone] *sf* subversion. **sovversivo, -a** *s, agg* subversive. **sovvertire** *v* subvert.

**sozzo** ['sottso] *agg* filthy; (*fig*) loathsome. **sozzura** *sf* filth; loathsomeness.

**spaccare** ['spakkare] *v* (*fendere*) split; (*rompere*) break; (*legna*) chop. **spaccarsi** *v* split (open); break (up). **spaccare il minu-**

**to** be dead on time. **fare la spaccata** do the splits. **spacco** *sm* split; (*strappo*) tear; (*giacca*) vent.

**spacciare** ['spattʃare] *v* (*vendere*) sell off; (*mettere in circolazione*) peddle; (*dichiarar inguaribile*) give up. **spacciato** *agg* (*fam: rovinato*) done for. **spacciatore, -trice** *sm, sf* pedlar; (*di droghe*) pusher; (*di notizie false*) rumour-monger. **spaccio** *sm* sale; (*negozio*) shop; (*mil, fabbrica*) canteen.

**spaccone** [spak'kone] *sm* braggart. **fare lo spaccone** brag.

**spada** ['spada] *sf* sword; (*sport*) épée. **a spada tratta** vigorously. **pesce spada** *sm* sword-fish. **tirar di spada** fence. **spadaccino** *sm* swordsman. **spadista** *s*(*m+f*) fencer.

**spadroneggiare** [spadroned'dʒare] *v* be bossy.

**spaesato** [spae'zato] *agg* lost.

**Spagna** ['spaɲa] *sf* Spain. **spagnolo, -a** *agg, sm* Spanish; *sf* (*abitante*) Spaniard.

**spago** ['spago] *sm* string, twine.

**spalancare** [spalan'kare] *v* open wide. **spalancare gli orecchi** prick up one's ears. **spalancato** *agg* wide open.

**spalare** [spa'lare] *v* shovel.

**spalla** ['spalla] *sf* shoulder; (*dorso*) back. **alle spalle di** (*stato*) behind; (*moto*) from behind. **aver le spalle grosse** be broad-shouldered. **aver sulle spalle** (*fig*) be responsible for. **alzar le spalle** shrug one's shoulders. **ridere alle spalle di qualcuno** laugh behind someone's back. **vivere alle spalle di** live off. **spallata** *sf* (*spinta*) push with the shoulder; (*alzata di spalle*) shrug. **spalletta** *sf* parapet.

**spalmare** [spal'mare] *v* spread.

**spanare** [spa'nare] *v* strip.

**spanciare** [span'tʃare] *v* bulge. **spanciarsi dalle risa** split one's sides laughing.

**\*spandere** ['spandere] *v* (*versare*) shed; (*involontariamente*) spill; (*stendere, divulgare*) spread.

**spanna** ['spanna] *sf* span.

**spappolare** [spappo'lare] *v* crush.

**sparare** [spa'rare] *v* fire; (*tirare*) shoot. **spararle grosse** (*fam*) shoot a line; tell tall stories. **sparata** *sf* volley. **sparo** *sm* shot.

**sparecchiare** [sparek'kjare] *v* clear (away).

**spareggio** [spa'reddʒo] *sm* (*sport*) decider.

**\*spargere** ['spardʒere] *v* scatter; (*versare*)

shed; (*involontariamente*) spill; (*sale, pepe, ecc.*) sprinkle; (*diffondere*) spread.

**\*sparire** [spa'rire] *v* disappear. **far sparire** (*nascondere*) hide; (*fam: rubare*) pinch.

**sparlare** [spar'lare] *v* speak ill (of).

**sparo** ['sparo] *sm* shot.

**sparpagliare** [sparpa'ʎare] *v* scatter.

**spartire** [spar'tire] *v* divide; (*in parti*) share out; (*musica*) score. **spartiacque** *sm invar* watershed. **spartineve** *sm invar* snow-plough. **spartitraffico** *sm* traffic island. **spartito** *sm* score.

**sparuto** [spa'ruto] *agg* gaunt; (*esiguo*) scanty.

**sparviere** [spar'vjɛre] *sm* sparrow-hawk.

**spasimare** [spazi'mare] *v* suffer agonies; (*fig*) crave, long (for). **spasimo** *sm* pang; (*med*) spasm. **spasmodico** *agg* spasmodic.

**spassarsela** [spas'sarsela] *v* enjoy oneself.

**spassionato** [spassjo'nato] *agg* dispassionate.

**spasso** ['spasso] *sm* fun. **andare a spasso** go for a walk. **mandare a spasso** (*fam: licenziare*) sack; (*fam: liberarsene*) get rid of. **portare a spasso** take for a walk. **quel ragazzo è uno spasso!** that boy is a scream! **spassoso** *agg* amusing.

**spastico** ['spastiko], **-a** *s, agg* spastic. **spasticità** *sf* spasticity.

**spatola** ['spatola] *sf* spatula; (*di pittore*) palette-knife; (*zool*) spoonbill.

**spatriare** [spatri'are] *v* expatriate.

**spaurire** [spau'rire] *v* scare. **spauracchio** *sm* scarecrow.

**spavaldo** [spa'valdo] *agg* defiant; (*baldanzoso*) bold; (*arrogante*) cocky. **spavalderia** *sf* defiance; boldness; cockiness.

**spaventare** [spaven'tare] *v* frighten, scare. **spaventarsi** *v* get frightened, get scared. **spaventapasseri** *sm* scarecrow. **spaventevole** *agg* terrifying. **spavento** *sm* fright. **fare spavento** frighten, scare. **prendersi uno spavento** have a fright. **spaventoso** *agg* frightful; (*terribile*) dreadful; (*enorme*) tremendous.

**spazientirsi** [spatsjen'tirsi] *v* lose one's patience.

**spazio** ['spatsjo] *sm* space; (*estensione limitata*) room; distance. **spaziale** *agg* space, spatial. **spaziare** *v* space; (*fig*) range. **spazioso** *agg* roomy.

**spazzare** [spat'tsare] *v* sweep; (*spazzarvia*)

sweep away. **spazzacamino** *sm* chimney-sweep. **spazzaneve** *sm invar* snowplough. **spazzatura** *sf* cleaning; sweeping; (*rifiuti*) rubbish. **spazzaturaio** *sm* dustman. **spazzino** *sm* road sweeper.

**spazzola** ['spattsola] *sf* brush. **capelli a spazzola** crew-cut. **spazzola per capelli** hairbrush. **spazzolare** *v* brush. **spazzolino da denti/unghie** *sm* tooth-/nail-brush. **spazzolone** (*per lavare*) scrubbing brush.

**specchio** ['spɛkkjo] *sm* mirror; model; (*prospetto*) table; summary. **specchio d'acqua** sheet of water. **specchio retrovisore** driving mirror. **specchiarsi** *v* (*guardarsi*) look at oneself in the mirror; (*riflettersi*) be reflected. **specchiato** *agg* (*fig*) exemplary. **specchiera** *sf* large mirror; (*toletta*) dressing-table. **specchietto** *sm* small mirror; (*tavola*) table, summary.

**speciale** [spe'tʃale] *agg* special; particular; (*fuori del solito*) peculiar. **specialista** *s*(*m+f*) specialist. **specialità** *sf* speciality; (*prodotto speciale*) specialty; (*farmaceutica*) proprietary medicine. **specializzarsi** *v* specialize. **specializzato** *agg* specialized; (*operaio*) skilled; (*medico*) specialist. **specializzazione** *sf* specialization.

**specie** ['spɛtʃe] *sf invar* kind, sort; (*bot, zool*) species; surprise. **mi fa specie** it surprises me. **sotto specie di** in the form of.

**specificare** [spetʃifi'kare] *v* specify. **specifica** *sf* detailed list. **specificazione** *sf* specification. **specifico** *agg* specific.

**speculare** [speku'lare] *v* speculate. **speculativo** *agg* speculative. **speculatore, -trice** *sm, sf* speculator; (*di borsa*) stockbroker. **speculazione** *sf* speculation.

**spedalità** [spedali'ta] *sf* hospitalization.

**spedire** [spe'dire] *v* send; post; (*inoltrare*) forward. **spedire all'altro mondo** (*fam*) bump off. **spedito** *agg* (*veloce*) quick; (*corrente*) fluent. **speditore, -trice** *sm, sf* sender; (*comm*) shipper. **spedizione** *sf* dispatch; (*trasporto*) shipment; (*cosa spedita*) consignment. **casa di spedizione** forwarding *or* shipping agents *pl.* **fare una spedizione** send a consignment. **spedizioniere** *sm* shipping *or* forwarding agent.

*\****spegnere** ['spenere] *v* extinguish, put out; (*con interruttore*) switch *or* turn off; (*sete*) quench. **spegnersi** *v* go out; (*motore*) stall.

**spelacchiato** [spelak'kjato] *agg* (*con pochi peli*) mangy; (*logoro*) threadbare.

**spellare** [spel'lare] *v* skin; (*escoriare*) graze.

**spellarsi** *v* peel. **spellatura** *sf* skinning; grazing; peeling.

**spelonca** [spe'lonka] *sf* hovel.

*\****spendere** ['spendere] *v* spend. **senza spender fatica** effortlessly. **spendere bene/male** use one's money wisely/unwisely. **spendereccio** *agg* extravagant.

**spennacchiare** [spennak'kjare] *v also* **spennare** pluck; (*fig*) fleece.

**spensierato** [spensje'rato] *agg* carefree. **spensierataggine** *sf* thoughtlessness; irresponsibility. **spensieratezza** *sf* light-heartedness.

**spento** ['spento] *agg* out, off; (*fig*) dull.

**spenzolare** [spendzo'lare] *v* dangle.

**speranza** [spe'rantsa] *sf* hope. **avere buone speranze** have high hopes. **avere una speranza** have a chance. **filo di speranza** *sm* glimmer of hope. **senza speranza** hopeless.

**sperare** [spe'rare] *v* hope; (*aspettarsi*) expect. **sperare (in)** have hope for the best. **sperare in Dio** trust in God. **spero di no/si** I hope not/so.

*\****sperdersi** ['spɛrdersi] *v* get lost. **sperduto** *agg* lost; (*fuori mano*) out-of-the-way; (*solo*) lonely.

**spergiurare** [sperdʒu'rare] *v* commit perjury, perjure oneself. **spergiuro** *sm* perjury; (*persona*) perjurer.

**spericolato** [speriko'lato] *agg* reckless.

**sperimentare** [sperimen'tare] *v* experiment (with); (*mettere alla prova*) try out, test; (*farne esperienza*) experience. **sperimentale** *agg* experimental.

**sperma** ['sperma] *sm* sperm.

**sperone** [spe'rone] *sm* spur; (*mar*) ram. **sperone di cavaliere** larkspur. **speronare** *v* ram.

**sperperare** [sperpe'rare] *v* squander. **sperpero** *sm* waste.

**sperticato** [sperti'kato] *agg* (*fig*) excessive.

**spesa** ['speza] *sf* expenditure; (*costo*) expense; (*acquisto*) purchase; (*compra*) shopping. **a spese di** at the expense of. **con poca spesa** cheaply; (*fig*) easily. **conto spese** *sm* expense account. **far la spesa** go shopping. **non badare a spese** spare no expense. **senza spesa** free. **spese** *sf pl* cost *sing*, charges *pl.* **spese generali** overheads *pl.* **essere spesato** have one's expenses paid.

**spesso** ['spesso] *agg* thick. *avv* often, frequently. **spesse volte** very often, frequently. **spessore** sm thickness.

**spettacolo** [spet'takolo] sm show; (*rappresentazione*) performance; (*vista*) sight. **dare spettacolo di sé** make an exhibition of oneself. **spettacolo pomeridiano** matinée. **spettacoloso** agg spectacular.

**spettare** [spet'tare] v (*competere per dovere*) be up (to); (*appartenere per diritto*) be due (to); (*essere di pertinenza*) be the concern (of).

**spettatore** [spetta'tore], **-trice** sm, sf spectator; (*testimone*) witness. **spettatori** sm pl audience *sing*.

**spettinare** [spetti'nare] v ruffle the hair of. **spettinato** agg unkempt, dishevelled.

**spettro** ['spettro] sm ghost; (*fig*) spectrum.

**spezie** ['spetsje] sf pl spices pl.

**spezzare** [spet'tsare] v break; (*staccando*) break off; (*fare a pezzi*) break up; (*gastr*) cut up. **spezzatino** sm stew. **spezzettare** v chop (up). **spezzone incendiario** sm incendiary bomb.

**spia** ['spia] sf spy, informer; (*indizio*) sign; (*apertura*) spy-hole; (*tec*) warning light. **fare la spia** be a spy; (*polizia*) inform; (*riportare*) tell tales.

**spiaccicare** [spjattʃi'kare] v squash.

***spiacere** [spja'tʃere] v displease. **mi spiace ... I** dislike ... **mi spiace di ...** (*rammarico*) I'm sorry ... **se non ti spiace** if you don't mind. **spiacevole** agg unpleasant, disagreeable; (*increscioso*) regrettable.

**spiaggia** ['spjaddʒa] sf (sea-)shore, beach.

**spianare** [spja'nare] v level; (*render liscio*) smooth; (*radere al suolo*) flatten, raze (to the ground); (*fig*) iron out. **spianato** agg smooth. **spianatoia** sf pastry board. **spianatoio** sm rolling-pin. **a tutto spiano** flat out.

**spiantare** [spjan'tare] v uproot; (*rovinare*) ruin.

**spiare** [spi'are] v spy (on); (*aspettare*) look out for; explore.

**spiazzo** ['spjattso] sm open space; (*radura*) clearing.

**spiccare** [spik'kare] v pick; (*pronunciare distintamente*) spell out; (*dir*) issue; (*comm*) draw; (*risaltare*) stand out. **spiccare il volo** take off. **spiccato** agg distinct, marked; (*notevole*) striking. **spicco** sm prominence. **far spicco** catch the eye.

**spicchio** ['spikkjo] sm segment; (*aglio*) clove.

**spicciare** [spit'tʃare] v dispatch. **spicciarsi** v hurry up. **spicciativo** agg quick; (*brusco*) abrupt. **spiccio** agg swift. **alla spicciolata** in dribs and drabs. **spiccioli** sm pl (small) change *sing*. **spicciolo** agg small.

**spiedo** ['spjɛdo] sm spit. **spiedino** sm skewer.

**spiegare** [spje'gare] v (*distendere*) unfold; (*ali*) spread; (*vele*) unfurl; (*render chiaro*) explain. **spiegarsi** v (*capire*) understand; (*diventar comprensibile*) explain oneself, make oneself understood. **spieghiamoci!** let's get it straight! **spiegabile** agg explicable.

**spiegazione** [spjega'tsjone] sf explanation; (*ragione*) reason.

**spiegazzare** [spjegat'tsare] v crumple (up), crease.

**spietato** [spje'tato] agg (*senza pietà*) pitiless; (*accanito*) relentless.

**spifferare** [spiffe'rare] v blab, blurt out. **spiffero** sm (*fam*) draught.

**spiga** ['spiga] sf ear. **disegno a spiga** sm herringbone pattern.

**spigliato** [spi'ʎato] agg (free and) easy; (*padrone di sè*) self-possessed. **spigliatezza** sf ease.

**spigola** ['spigola] sf bass.

**spigolare** [spigo'lare] v glean. **spigolature** sf pl tit-bits pl.

**spigolo** ['spigolo] sm corner; edge.

**spilla** ['spilla] sf brooch. **spilla da cravatta** tie-pin.

**spillare** [spil'lare] v tap; (*attingere*) draw.

**spillo** ['spillo] sm pin. **spillo di sicurezza** safety-pin.

**spilluzzicare** [spilluttsi'kare] v nibble.

**spilorcio** [spi'lortʃo], **-a** agg stingy. sm, sf miser. **spilorceria** sf meanness.

**spina** ['spina] sf (*bot*) thorn; (*aculeo*) sting; (*riccio*) quill; (*elett*) plug. **birra alla spina** sf draught beer. **spina di pesce** fish-bone. **spina dorsale** backbone. **star sulle spine** be on tenterhooks. **spinare** v bone. **spinato** agg (*pesce*) filleted; (*filo*) barbed.

**spinacio** [spi'natʃo] sm (*bot*) spinach. **spinaci** sm pl (*gastr*) spinach *sing*.

***spingere** ['spindʒere] v push, drive; (*stimolare*) urge; (*premere*) press.

**spino** ['spino] sm (*bot*) blackthorn, bramble. **spineto** sm bramble bush. **spinoso** agg prickly, thorny.

**spinta** ['spinta] *sf* push; pressure; (*aiuto*) (helping) hand; (*stimolo*) boost; (*fis*) thrust. **spinto** *agg* pushed; disposed; (*fam*) extremist. **spintone** *sm* hard push, shove; (*raccomandazione*) good word.

**spionaggio** [spio'naddʒo] *sm* espionage. **spione** *sm* (*fam*) tell-tale.

**spiovente** [spjo'vɛnte] *agg* (*baffi*) drooping; (*spalle*) stooping; (*tetto*) sloping.

**spira** ['spira] *sf* coil. **spirale** *agg*, *sf* spiral.

**spiraglio** [spi'raʎo] *sm* chink; (*di luce, speranza*) glimmer; (*aria*) breath of air.

**spirare¹** [spi'rare] *v* (*soffiare*) blow; (*emettere*) give off or out; (*emanare*) be given off or out.

**spirare²** [spi'rare] *v* (*morire*) expire.

**spirito** ['spirito] *sm* spirit; (*animo*) mind; sense of humour. **bello spirito** wit. **condizioni di spirito** *sm pl* mood *sing*. **con spirito** wittily. **pieno di spirito** (*vivace*) lively; (*arguto*) witty.

**spiritosaggine** [spirito'zaddʒine] *sf* witticism.

**spiritoso** [spiri'tozo], **-a** *agg* witty. *sm, sf* funny person.

**spirituale** [spiritu'ale] *agg* spiritual. **spiritualismo** *sm* spiritualism. **spiritualista** *s(m+f)* spiritualist.

**spiumare** [spju'mare] *v* pluck.

**spizzicare** [spittsi'kare] *v* nibble. **a spizzico** *or* **spizzichi** in dribs and drabs.

***splendere** ['splɛndere] *v* shine. **splendido** *agg* brilliant; (*meraviglioso*) splendid. **splendore** *sm* brilliance; splendour.

**spodestare** [spodes'tare] *v* (*cacciare*) oust; (*privare di beni*) dispossess.

**spogliare** [spoʎ'ʎare] *v* strip; (*svestire*) undress; (*esaminare*) go through; sort out. **spogliarsi** *v* undress. **spogliarello** *sm* strip-tease. **spogliatoio** *sm* changing-room. **spoglie** *sf pl* (*bottino*) spoils *pl*; (*mortali*) (mortal) remains *pl*. **spoglio** *agg* (*nudo*) bare; (*privo*) devoid (of); (*libero*) free (from). **fare lo spoglio** (*corrispondenza*) sort out; (*dati*) extract; (*voti*) scrutinize.

**spola** ['spɔla] *sf* shuttle; (*macchina da cucire*) spool, bobbin. **far la spola** shuttle, ply. **spoletta** *sf* bobbin; (*tec, mil*) fuse.

**spolmonarsi** [spolmo'narsi] *v* shout oneself hoarse.

**spolverare** [spolve'rare] *v* dust. **spolverat(ur)a** *sf* dusting.

**sponda** ['sponda] *sf* (*mare, lago*) shore; (*fiume*) bank; (*bordo*) edge; (*biliardo*) cushion.

**spontaneo** [spon'taneo] *agg* spontaneous. **di mia spontanea volontà** of my own free will. **spontaneità** *sf* spontaneity.

**spopolare** [spopo'lare] *v* depopulate; (*vuotare*) empty; (*aver successo*) be a hit.

**spora** ['spɔra] *sf* spore.

**sporadico** [spo'radiko] *agg* sporadic.

**sporco** ['spɔrko] *agg* dirty; dishonest. **aver la coscienza sporca** have a guilty conscience. **sporcizia** *sf* dirt, filth; (*fam*) muck.

***sporgere** ['spɔrdʒere] *v* stick out, project, protrude. **sporgersi** *v* lean out. **sporgere querela contro** sue. **sporgente** *agg* jutting out; (*dente*) protruding; (*occhio*) bulging. **sporgenza** *sf* projection.

**sport** [spɔrt] *sm invar* sport. **fare per sport** do for fun.

**sporta** ['spɔrta] *sf* (*sacca*) shopping-bag; (*quantità*) bagful. **una sporta di legnate** a good hiding. **un sacco e una sporta** a lot.

**sportello** [spor'tɛllo] *sm* counter; (*per biglietti*) ticket office; (*porta*) door. **sportello automatico** *sm* cash dispenser.

**sportivo** [spor'tivo] *agg* sports; (*interessato*) sporty, sporting; (*leale*) sportsmanlike, sporting. *sm* sportsman. **sportiva** *sf* sportswoman.

**sposa** ['spɔza] *sf* bride. **sposalizio** *sm* wedding. **sposare** *v* marry; (*fig*) wed. **sposarsi** *v* get married. **sposata** *sf* married woman. **sposato** *sm* married man. **sposino, -a** *sm, sf* newly-wed. **sposo** *sm* bridegroom.

**spossare** [spos'sare] *v* exhaust. **spossatezza** *sf* exhaustion; (*stanchezza*) weariness. **spossato** *agg* worn out, weary.

**spossessare** [sposses'sare] *v* dispossess.

**spostare** [spos'tare] *v* shift; (*rimuovere*) displace; (*turbare*) upset; transfer. **spostamento** *sm* shift; displacement; transfer. **spostato, -a** *agg* (*fuori posto*) out of place; (*fig*) unsettled. *sm, sf* misfit.

**spranga** ['spranga] *sf* crossbar; (*chiavistello*) bolt. **sprangare** *v* bolt.

**sprazzo** ['sprattso] *sm* flash.

**sprecare** [spre'kare] *v* waste. **è tempo/fiato sprecato** it is a waste of breath/time. **spreco** *sm* waste. **sprecone, -a** *sm, sf* spendthrift.

**spregevole** [spre'dʒevole] *agg* despicable.

**spregiare** v despise, spurn. **spregiativo** agg disparaging; (gramm) pejorative.

**spregiudicato** [spredʒudiˈkato], -a agg (senza pregiudizi) open-minded; (senza scrupoli) unscrupulous. sm unscrupulous person. **spregiudicatezza** sf open-mindedness; unscrupulousness.

**spremere** [ˈsprɛmere] v squeeze. **spremersi il cervello** rack one's brains. **spremilimoni** sm lemon squeezer. **spremuta** sf (bevanda) juice.

**sprezzare** [spretˈtsare] v despise. **sprezzante** agg contemptuous. **sprezzo** sm scorn.

**sprigionare** [spridʒoˈnare] v give off.

**sprint** [sprint] sm invar (sport) sprint; (auto) pick-up. sf sports car.

**sprizzare** [spritˈtsare] v (acqua) squirt; (sangue) spurt; (fig) burst with.

**sprofondare** [sprofonˈdare] v collapse; (affondare) sink; (lasciarsi sopraffare) be overwhelmed (by). **sprofondarsi** v sink; (fig) immerse oneself. **sprofondamento** sm collapse. **sprofondato** agg (fig) immersed, engrossed.

**spronare** [sproˈnare] v spur (on). **spronata** sf spur. **sprone** sm spur.

**sproporzionato** [sproporttsjoˈnato] agg out of proportion; disproportionate. **sproporzione** sf lack of proportion.

**sproposito** [sproˈpɔzito] sm blunder; (strafalcione) howler. **a sproposito** (inopportunamente) at the wrong time; (fuori luogo) in the wrong place. **commettere uno sproposito** do something silly. **costare uno sproposito** cost the earth. **spropositato** agg excessive.

**sprovvisto** [sprovˈvisto] agg also **sprovveduto** short (of); (privo) lacking (in). **alla sprovvista** unawares.

**spruzzare** [sprutˈtsare] v spray; (senza intenzione) splash. **spruzzata** sf sprinkling. **spruzzatore** sm sprinkler; (profumi) atomizer. **spruzzo** sm spray; (schizzo) spurt; splash.

**spudorato** [spudoˈrato] agg shameless. **spudoratezza** sf shamelessness.

**spugna** [ˈspuɲa] sf sponge; (tessuto) towelling; (fam) boozer. **bere come una spugna** drink like a fish. **spugnatura** sf sponging down. **spugnoso** agg spongy.

**spuma** [ˈspuma] sf froth. **spumante** sm sparkling wine. **spumare** v (bevande gassate) fizz; (vino) sparkle. **spumare dalla rabbia** (fam) foam at the mouth. **spumeggiare** v froth. **spumoso** agg frothy.

**spuntare** [spunˈtare] v (germogliare) sprout; (apparire improvvisamente) emerge; (sorgere) rise; (fig) overcome; (capelli, ecc.) trim. **spuntato** agg (matita) blunt; (vino) sour.

**spuntino** [spunˈtino] sm snack.

**spunto** [ˈspunto] sm cue; idea; (sport) spurt. **prendere lo spunto da** start (off) from.

**spuntone** [spunˈtone] sm spike.

**spurgare** [spurˈgare] v clear out. **spurgarsi** v clear one's throat.

**spurio** [ˈspurjo] agg spurious.

**sputacchiare** [sputakˈkjare] v splutter. **sputacchiera** sf spitoon.

**sputare** [spuˈtare] v spit. **sputa fuori!** spit it out! **sputar sentenze** talk sententiously. **sputar veleno** speak spitefully. **sputo** sm spit(tle), saliva; (espettorato) sputum.

**squadernare** [skwaderˈnare] v leaf through.

**squadra**[1] [ˈskwadra] sf (strumento) square. **a squadra** at right angles. **fuori squadra** crooked; (fuori posto) out of place; (disordinato) disorderly. **squadrare** v square; (fig) eye.

**squadra**[2] [ˈskwadra] sf (mil) section, squad; (aero) squadron; (gruppo) gang; (sport) team. **squadra mobile** flying squad.

**squadriglia** sf band; (mar, aero) squadron.

**squadro** [ˈskwadro] sm angel-fish.

**squagliarsi** [skwaˈʎarsi] v melt. **squagliarsela** v sneak off.

**squalificare** [skwalifiˈkare] v disqualify. **squalifica** sf disqualification.

**squallido** [ˈskwallido] agg dismal; (fig) squalid. **squallore** sm dreariness, squalor.

**squalo** [ˈskwalo] sm dog-fish; (pescecane) shark.

**squama** [ˈskwama] sf scale. **squamare** v scale. **squamoso** agg scaly.

**squarciare** [skwarˈtʃare] v tear (to pieces), rend. **a squarciagola** at the top of one's voice. **squarcio** sm (stoffa) tear; (ferita) gash; (fig) passage.

**squartare** [skwarˈtare] v quarter. **squartatoio** sm cleaver.

**squassare** [skwasˈsare] v shake violently.

**squattrinato** [skwattriˈnato] agg penniless.

**squilibrare** [skwiliˈbrare] v unbalance. **squilibrarsi** v lose one's balance. **squili-**

**brato** *agg* (mentally) unbalanced. **squilibrio** *sm* lack of equilibrium; (*econ*) imbalance; disproportion; (*mentale*) derangement.

**squillare** [skwil'lare] *v* ring; (*tromba*) sound; (*voce*) be shrill. **squillo** *sm* ring; (*suono*) squeal; (*tromba*) sound. **ragazza squillo** *sf* call-girl.

**squinternare** [skwinter'nare] *v* take to pieces; (*fig*) upset.

**squisito** [skwi'zito] *agg* excellent; delicious; (*raffinato*) exquisite. **squisitezza** *sf* deliciousness; delicacy.

**squittire** [skwit'tire] *v* (*uccelli*) chirp; (*topi*) squeak.

**sradicare** [sradi'kare] *v* (*divellere*) uproot; (*fig*) root out, eradicate.

**sregolato** [srego'lato] *agg* (*smodato*) immoderate; (*scapestrato*) wild.

**stabbio** ['stabbjo] *sm* pen; (*porcile*) pigsty; (*letame*) dung.

**stabile** ['stabile] *agg* stable; (*che non oscilla*) steady; permanent; (*durevole*) lasting.

**stabilimento** [stabili'mento] *sm* establishment; (*fabbrica*) factory, works; (*edificio*) building.

**stabilire** [stabi'lire] *v* establish; decide. **stabilirsi** *v* settle. **stabilità** *sf* stability. **stabilito** *agg* (*istituito*) established; (*fissato*) fixed; (*convenuto*) agreed. **stabilizzare** *v* stabilize. **stabilizzarsi** *v* settle. **stabilizzazione** *sf* stabilization.

**staccare** [stak'kare] *v* (*togliere*) take off; (*separare*) detach; (*tagliando*) cut off; (*strappando*) pluck; (*sganciare*) unhook; (*risaltare*) stand out. **staccare il lavoro** (*fam*) knock off work. **staccarsi** *v* move away; (*venir via*) come off; separate. **staccato** *agg* detached; separate; (*musica*) staccato.

**stadio** ['stadjo] *sm* (*sport*) stadium; (*tec, fase*) stage.

**staffa** ['staffa] *sf* stirrup; (*mec*) bracket; (*calza*) heel. **perdere le staffe** (*fig*) lose one's temper. **staffetta** *sf* courier; (*sport*) relay(-race).

**staffilare** [staffi'lare] *v* lash; (*fig*) lash out (at). **staffilata** *sf* lash; (*fig*) lashing criticism. **staffile** *sm* stirrup-strap; (*sferza*) lash.

**stagione** [sta'dʒone] *sf* season; (*condizioni atmosferiche*) weather. **fuori stagione** out of season; (*fig*) untimely. **stagionale** *agg* seasonal. **stagionare** *v* season; (*invecchiare*) age; mature. **stagionatura** *sf* ageing; maturing; seasoning.

**stagno¹** ['staɲo] *sm* (*metallo*) tin. **stagnare** *v* tin; (*saldare*) solder; (*chiudere*) seal. **stagnola** *sf* tin foil.

**stagno²** ['staɲo] *sm* (*bacino d'acqua*) pool. *agg* (*a tenuta d'acqua*) watertight. **stagnare** *v* stagnate; (*sangue*) stanch; (*fermare*) stop.

**stalagmite** [stalag'mite] *sf* stalagmite.

**stalattite** [stalat'tite] *sf* stalactite.

**stalla** ['stalla] *sf* stable; (*bovini*) cow-shed; (*fig*) pigsty. **stallaggio** *sm* stabling. **stallone** *sm* stallion.

**stallo** ['stallo] *sm* seat; (*scacchi*) stalemate. **andare in stallo** (*aero*) stall.

**stamattina** [stamat'tina] *avv also* **stamani** this morning.

**stamberga** [stam'bɛrga] *sf* hovel.

**stambugio** [stam'budʒo] *sm* cubby-hole.

**stame** ['stame] *sm* (*bot*) stamen; (*tessile*) fine yarn.

**stamigna** [sta'miɲa] *sf* bunting.

**stampa** ['stampa] *sf* printing; (*giornali*) press; (*immagine, foto*) print. **errore di stampa** *sm* misprint. **stampe** *sf pl* (*posta*) printed matter *sing*. **stampaggio** (*foto*) printing; (*metallo*) forging; (*plastici*) moulding. **stampare** *v* print; publish; (*con pressa*) press; forge; mould. **stampatello** *sm* block letters *pl*. **stampato** *sm* printed matter; (*modulo*) form; (*disegno*) print. **stampatore, -trice** *sm, sf* printer.

**stampella** [stam'pɛlla] *sf* crutch.

**stampiglia** [stam'piʎa] *sf* stamp. **stampigliare** *v* stamp.

**stampino** [stam'pino] *sm* stencil; (*punzone*) punch.

**stampo** ['stampo] *sm* mould; (*matrice*) die; (*fig*) kind, sort.

**stanare** [sta'nare] *v* drive out.

**stancare** [stan'kare] *v* tire; (*annoiare*) bore. **stancarsi** *v* get tired, tire. **stanchezza** *sf* tiredness; (*fiacchezza*) fatigue. **stanco** *agg* tired; bored.

**standard** ['standard] *sm invar* standard. **standardizzare** *v* standardize. **standardizzazione** *sf* standardization.

**stanga** ['stanga] *sf* bar. **stangare** *v* (*colpire*) thrash; (*bocciare*) fail; (*scuola*) give a bad mark; (*far pagare troppo*) rob. **stangata** *sf* blow.

**stanotte** [sta'nɔtte] *avv* tonight.

**stante** ['stante] *agg* **a sè stante** apart.

**seduta stante** straight away. *prep* (*a causa di*) on account of.

**stantio** [stan'tio] *agg* stale.

**stantuffo** [stan'tuffo] *sm* piston; (*di pressa idraulica*) plunger.

**stanza** ['stantsa] *sf* room; (*poesia*) stanza. **stanza da bagno** bathroom. **stanza da pranzo** dining-room.

**stanziare** [stan'tsjare] *v* allocate; deliberate.

**stappare** [stap'pare] *v* uncork.

***stare** ['stare] *v* stay, remain; (*abitare*) live; (*essere*) be; (*vestiario*) suit; (*spettare*) be up to. **come stai?** how are you? **lasciar stare** leave alone. **non poter stare senza** be unable to do without. **stare a dieta** be on a diet. **stare in guardia** be on one's guard. **stare per** be about to. **sto bene** I am well. **sto male** I am not well.

**starna** ['starna] *sf* partridge.

**starnutire** [starnu'tire] *v* sneeze. **starnuto** *sm* sneeze.

**stasera** [sa'sera] *avv* this evening.

**stasi** ['stazi] *sf* standstill.

**statale** [sta'tale] *agg* state. **strada statale** *sf* trunk road. *s(m+f)* civil servant.

**statica** ['statika] *sf* statics. **statico** *agg* static; (*senza movimento*) motionless.

**statista** [sta'tista] *sm* statesman.

**statistica** [sta'tistika] *sf* statistics. **statistico** *agg* statistical.

**stato** ['stato] *sm* state; condition; (*posizione sociale*) status. **colpo di stato** *sm* coup d'état. **Stati Uniti** *sm pl* United States *pl*. **stato d'animo** mood. **ufficio di stato civile** *sm* register office. **statunitense** *s(m+f)*, *agg* American.

**statua** ['statua] *sf* statue. **statuario** *agg* statuary.

**statura** [sta'tura] *sf* (*altezza*) height; (*fig*) stature.

**statuto** [sta'tuto] *sm* statute; constitution. **statutario** statutory.

**stavolta** [sta'vɔlta] *avv* this time.

**stazione** [sta'tsjone] *sf* station; (*località di soggiorno*) resort. **stazionamento** *sm* parking. **stazionare** *v* stop; park. **stazionario** *agg* stationary.

**stecca** ['stekka] *sf* small stick; (*biliardo*) cue; (*persiane*) slat; (*sigarette*) carton; (*hockey*) stick. **steccare** *v* fence (in); (*sonare*) play a wrong note. **steccato** *sm* fence. **a stecchetto** (*senza soldi*) hard up; (*senza cibo*) on short rations. **stecchito** *agg* (*rinsecchito*) dried up; (*magrissimo*) skinny. **morto stecchito** stone dead. **stecco** *sm* dry twig. **steccone** *sm* post.

**stella** ['stella] *sf* star. **alle stelle** (*prezzi*) sky-high. **stella alpina** edelweiss. **stella cadente** *or* **filante** shooting star; (*di carta*) streamer. **stella di mare** starfish. **stellare** *agg* (*astron*) stellar; (*forma*) starshaped; (*bot*) stellate. **stellato** *agg* starry; (*fig*) studded. **stelletta** (*mil*) star; (*fam*) pip.

**stelo** ['stelo] *sm* stem; (*fiore*) stalk; (*gambo di utensile*) shank.

**stemma** ['stemma] *sm* coat of arms.

**stemp(e)rare** [stempe(e)'rare] *v* dissolve.

**stendardo** [sten'dardo] *sm* standard.

***stendere** ['stendere] *v* (*allungare*) stretch (out); (*distendere*) spread (out); (*bucato*) hang out; (*contratto*) draw up. **stendersi** *v* stretch out.

**stenodattilografia** [stenodattilogra'fia] *sf* shorthand typing. **stenodattilografo, -a** *sm, sf* shorthand typist. **stenografare** *v* take down in shorthand. **stenografia** *sf* shorthand. **stenografo, -a** *sm, sf* stenographer.

**stentare** [sten'tare] *v* find it hard, have difficulty. **stentatezza** *sf* difficulty. **stentato** *agg* laboured; (*di crescita arrestata*) stunted; (*pieno di stenti*) hard. **stento** *sm* hardship; difficulty. **a stento** barely.

**steppa** ['steppa] *sf* steppe.

**sterco** ['sterko] *sm* excrement; (*letame*) dung.

**stereo** ['stereo] *agg*, *sm* stereo.

**stereofonico** [stereo'fɔniko] *agg* stereophonic; (*fam*) stereo.

**stereotipato** [stereoti'pato] *agg* stereotyped; (*fisso*) frozen. **concezione stereotipata** *sf* stereotype.

**sterile** ['sterile] *agg* sterile; (*fig*) vain. **sterilire** *v* sterilize. **sterilità** *sf* sterility; (*fig*) uselessness. **sterilizzare** *v* sterilize. **sterilizzatore** *sm* sterilizer. **sterilizzazione** *sf* sterilization.

**sterlina** [ster'lina] *sf* pound (sterling).

**sterminare** [stermi'nare] *v* exterminate. **sterminato** *agg* boundless. **sterminio** *sm* extermination.

**sterna** ['sterna] *sf* tern.

**sterno** ['sterno] *sm* breastbone.

**sterzo** ['stertso] *sm* (*auto*) steering;

(*bicicletta*) handlebars *pl.* **sterzare** *v* (*auto*) steer; (*fig*) swerve. **sterzata** *sf* steering; swerve. **fare una sterzata** make a sharp turn.

**stesso** ['stesso] *agg* same; (*proprio*) very; (*personificato*) itself; (*in persona*) personally; (*rafforzativo, riflessivo*) myself, yourself, etc.

**stesura** [ste'zura] *sf* drafting; draft.

**stetoscopio** [stetos'kɔpjo] *sm* stethoscope.

**stia** ['stia] *sf* chicken coop. **essere (pigiati) come in una stia** be cooped up.

**stigma** ['stigma] *sm* stigma. **stigmatizzare** *v* stigmatize.

**stilare** [sti'lare] *v* draw up.

**stile** ['stile] *sm* style; (*eleganza*) stylishness. **di stile** stylish. **in grande stile** in style. **stilista** *s*(*m+f*) stylist. **stilistico** *agg* stylistic. **stilizzare** *v* stylize.

**stilla** ['stilla] *sf* drop. **a stilla a stilla** drop by drop. **stillare** *v* (*trasudare*) ooze, exude; (*gocciolare*) drip. **stillarsi il cervello** rack one's brains. **stillicidio** *sm* constant trickle.

**stilo** ['stilo] *sm* (*per scrivere*) stylus; (*stadera*) beam. **stilografica** *sf* fountainpen.

**stima** ['stima] *sf* (*buona opinione*) esteem, regard; (*giudizio*) estimation; (*valutazione*) estimate. **a mia stima** in my estimation. **aver stima di** hold in high esteem. **con (la massima) stima** (*in lettere*) yours faithfully.

**stimare** [sti'mare] *v* estimate; (*apprezzare*) value, esteem; consider. **stimatore, -trice** *sm, sf* (*perito*) valuer; (*ammiratore*) admirer.

**stimolare** [stimo'lare] *v* stimulate; (*fig*) arouse; (*appetito*) whet. **stimolante** *sm* stimulant. **stimolatore cardiaco** *sm* pacemaker. **stimolazione** *sf* (*med*) stimulation; (*fig*) arousal. **stimolo** *sm* stimulus (*pl* -li).

**stinco** ['stinko] *sm* shin. **stincata** *sf* blow on the shin.

***stingere** ['stindʒere] *v* (*macchiare*) run; (*sbiadire*) fade.

**stipare** [sti'pare] *v* pack, cram.

**stipendio** [sti'pɛndjo] *sm* salary. **stipendio arretrato** back pay.

**stipite** ['stipite] *sm* doorpost.

**stipulare** [stipu'lare] *v* stipulate. **stipulazione** *sf* stipulation.

**stiracchiare** [stirak'kjare] *v* stretch; (*lesinare*) skimp. **stiracchiare sul prezzo** haggle. **stiracchiamento** *sm* stretching;

haggling. **stiracchiatura** *sf* distortion.

**stirare** [sti'rare] *v* (*col ferro*) iron, press. **stirarsi** *v* stretch. **stiro** *sm* ironing; pressing. **ferro da stiro** *sm* iron. **tavolo da stiro** *sm* ironing board.

**stirpe** ['stirpe] *sf* (*origine*) descent, extraction; (*razza*) race; family; (*discendenti*) offspring.

**stitico** ['stitiko] *agg* constipated; (*fig*) stingy. **stitichezza** *sf* constipation.

**stiva** ['stiva] *sf* hold. **stivaggio** *sm* stowage.

**stivale** [sti'vale] *sm* boot. **lustrar gli stivali a** (*fig*) lick the boots of. **rompere gli stivali a** (*fig*) pester.

**stivaletto** [stiva'letto] *sm* bootee.

**stizza** ['stittsa] *sf* anger. **avere** *or* **provare stizza per** be angry about. **stizzire** *v* anger. **stizzirsi** *v* get angry. **stizzito** *agg* angry. **stizzoso** *agg* irritable.

**stoccafisso** [stokka'fisso] *sm* dried cod.

**stoccata** [stok'kata] *sf* stab; (*scherma*) thrust; (*battuta*) gibe. **stocco** *sm* rapier.

**Stoccolma** [stok'kolma] *sf* Stockholm.

**stoffa** ['stɔffa] *sf* fabric, material; (*dote*) makings *pl.* **ha della stoffa** he has what it takes.

**stoico** ['stɔiko], **-a** *agg* stoical. *sm, sf* stoic.

**stoino** [sto'ino] *sm* doormat.

**stola** ['stɔla] *sf* stole.

**stolto** ['stolto], **-a** *agg* foolish. *sm, sf* fool. **stoltezza** *sf* foolishness; (*azione*) foolish action; (*parole*) nonsense.

**stomaco** ['stɔmako] *sm* stomach; (*fam*) tummy; (*fam: coraggio*) guts. **mal di stomaco** *sm* stomach-ache. ... **mi sta** *or* **rimane sullo stomaco** I cannot stomach ... . **stomacare** *v* nauseate. **stomachevole** *agg* revolting.

**stonare** [sto'nare] *v* (*cantare*) sing out of tune; (*sonare*) play out of tune; (*contrastare*) clash. **stonata** *sf* wrong note. **stonato** *agg* out of tune; clashing; (*turbato*) upset.

**stoppa** ['stoppa] *sf* tow. **stoppare** *v* (*otturare*) block; (*sport*) stop. **stoppaccio** *sm* wad. **stoppie** *sf pl* stubble *sing.* **stoppino** *sm* wick.

***storcere** ['stortʃere] *v* twist; (*piegare*) bend. **storcere il naso** turn up one's nose. **storcere la bocca** make a wry face. **storcersi per il dolore** writhe in pain. **storcimento** *sm* twisting; wrench.

**stordire** [stor'dire] *v* stun; (*rumore*) deafen.

**stordimento** *sm* (*stato d'animo*) bewilderment. **stordito** *agg* stunned; bewildered; (*distratto*) scatter-brained.

**storia** ['stɔrja] *sf* history; (*racconto*) story, tale; (*frottola*) fib, lie; (*faccenda*) business. **la solita storia** the same old story. **libro di storia** history book. **storie** *sf pl* (*trambusto*) fuss *sing*. **storiella** *sf* little story; (*barzelletta*) joke; (*fandonia*) fib.

**storico** ['stɔriko], -a *agg* (*della storia*) historical; (*famoso*) historic. *sm, sf* historian.

**storione** [sto'rjone] *sm* sturgeon.

**stormo** ['stormo] *sm* (*uccelli*) flock; (*cani*) pack; (*persone*) crowd; (*fig*) mess. **sonare a stormo** sound the alarm.

**stornare** [stor'nare] *v* (*allontanare*) avert; dissuade; transfer; annul. **storno** *sm* transfer.

**stornello** [stor'nɛllo] *sm also* **storno** (*uccello*) starling.

**storno** ['storno] *agg* dapple-grey.

**storpio** ['stɔrpjo], -a *agg* crippled. *sm, sf* cripple. **storpiare** *v* cripple; mispronounce.

**storto** ['stɔrto] *agg* crooked; (*sbagliato*) wrong. **aver gli occhi storti** squint. **aver le gambe storte** be bandy-legged. **storta** *sf* twist, sprain; (*recipiente*) retort. **prendersi una storta alla caviglia** twist one's ankle.

**stoviglie** [sto'viʎe] *sf pl* crockery *sing*. **lavar le stoviglie** wash the dishes, wash up.

**strabico** ['strabiko] *agg* cross-eyed. **strabismo** *sm* squint. **essere affetto da strabismo** have a squint.

**strabiliante** [strabi'ʎante] *agg* amazing.

**straboccare** [strabok'kare] *v* overflow. **strabocchevole** *agg* excessive.

**stracarico** [stra'kariko] *agg*, *m pl* -chi overloaded; (*fig*) overburdened.

**stracciare** [strat'tʃare] *v* tear; (*facendo a pezzi*) tear up.

**straccio** ['strattʃo] *sm* rag. *agg* waste. **straccione, -a** *sm, sf* ragamuffin; beggar.

**stracco** ['strakko] (*fam*) *agg* worn out, done in. **stracco morto** dead beat.

**stracotto** [stra'kɔtto] *agg* overcooked. **cotto e stracotto** overdone. *sm* (*gastr*) stew, casserole.

**strada** ['strada] *sf* road, street; (*percorso*) way; (*itinerario*) route; (*cammino*) journey; (*varco*) path. **a mezza strada** halfway. **che strada fai?** which way are you going? **far**

**strada a qualcuno** show someone the way. **farsi strada** (*aprirsi un passaggio*) clear a way for oneself; (*ottener successo*) do well for oneself. **fuori strada** off the road; (*fig*) on the wrong track. **lungo** *or* **per la strada** on the way. **strada facendo** on the way. **stradale** *agg* road. **codice stradale** *sm* highway code. **lavori stradali** *sm pl* roadworks *pl*.

**strafalcione** [strafal'tʃone] *sm* blunder.

**\*strafare** [stra'fare] *v* overdo it.

**straforo** [stra'fɔro] *sm* **di straforo** indirectly; (*di nascosto*) on the quiet; (*di sfuggita*) in passing.

**strage** ['stradʒe] *sf* slaughter; (*distruzione*) havoc; (*fam*) mass.

**stragrande** [stra'grande] *agg* huge. **stragrande maggioranza** *sf* great majority.

**stralciare** [stral'tʃare] *v* take out; (*dedurre*) deduct; (*mettere in liquidazione*) wind up. **stralcio** *sm* removal; extract; liquidation. **vendere a stralcio** sell off.

**stralunare** [stralu'nare] *v* roll one's eyes. **stralunato** *agg* (*fig*) distraught.

**stramazzare** [stramat'tsare] *v* fall to the ground.

**strambo** ['strambo] *agg* odd; eccentric. **stramberia** *sf* oddity; eccentricity.

**strampalato** [strampa'lato] *agg* weird.

**strangolare** [strango'lare] *v* strangle. **strangolarsi** *v* choke. **strangolamento** *sm* strangulation.

**straniero** [stra'njɛro], -a *agg* foreign. *sm, sf* foreigner; (*termine burocratico*) alien.

**strano** ['strano] *agg* strange, odd. *sm* strange *or* odd thing. **strano a dirsi** oddly enough. **stranezza** *sf* peculiarity; (*atteggiamento*) odd behaviour.

**straordinario** [straordi'narjo] *agg* extraordinary; (*insolito*) unusual; special. **lavoro straordinario** *sm* overtime. *sm* unusual thing; overtime.

**strapagare** [strapa'gare] *v* (*fam*) pay through the nose.

**strapazzare** [strapat'tsare] *v* wear out; (*trattar male*) ill-treat. **uova strapazzate** *sf pl* scrambled eggs *pl*. **strapazzata** *sf* (*sgridata*) dressing-down; (*faticata*) strain. **strapazzo** *sm* strain; ill-treatment. **vestiti da strapazzo** *sm pl* working clothes *pl*.

**strapieno** [stra'pjɛno] *agg* full up.

**strapiombare** [strapjom'bare] *v* overhang, jut out. **a strapiombo** sheer, overhanging.

**strappare** [strap'pare] *v* snatch; (*portar via*) pull off *or* out; (*rompendo*) tear (off *or* out); (*in più pezzi*) tear up. **strappata** *sf* tug. **strappo** *sm* pull, tug; (*strattone*) jerk; tear. **strappo muscolare** pulled *or* torn muscle.

**straripare** [strari'pare] *v* overflow. **straripamento** *sm* overflowing.

**strascicare** [straʃi'kare] *v* trail; (*con fatica*) drag; (*fig*) drag out; (*pronuncia*) drawl. **strascico** *sm*, *pl* -**chi** (*fig*) after-effect; (*vestito*) train.

**strascinare** [straʃi'nare] *v* drag along.

**stratagemma** [strata'dʒɛmma] *sm* stragem; (*fig*) trick.

**strategia** [strate'dʒia] *sf* strategy. **strategico** *agg* strategic. **stratego, -a** *sm*, *sf* strategist.

**strato** ['strato] *sm* layer; (*vernice*) coat; (*geol*, *classe*) stratum (*pl* -a). **stratificato** *agg* stratified.

**strattone** [strat'tone] *sm* pull, jerk. **a strattoni** jerkily.

**stravagante** [strava'gante] *agg* extravagant. **stravaganza** *sf* extravagance.

**stravecchio** [stra'vɛkkjo] *agg* very old.

*****stravincere** [stra'vintʃere] *v* win hands down; (*battere*) beat hollow.

**straviziare** [stravi'tsjare] *v* over-indulge. **stravizio** *sm* over-indulgence.

*****stravolgere** [stra'vɔldʒere] *v* twist; (*fig*) affect deeply. **stravolgere gli occhi** roll one's eyes. **stravolgimento** *sm* twisting; contortion. **stravolto** *agg* twisted; (*fig*) deeply upset.

**straziare** [stra'tsjare] *v* torture, torment. **straziare il cuore a qualcuno** break someone's heart. **cuore straziato** *sm* broken heart. **strazio** *sm* torment, agony. **far strazio di** (*fig*) play havoc with.

**strega** ['strega] *sf* witch. **stregare** *v* bewitch. **stregone** *sm* wizard; (*mago*) sorcerer; (*popoli primitivi*) witch-doctor. **stregoneria** *sf* witchcraft; sorcery. **fare stregonerie** cast spells.

**stregua** ['stregwa] *sf* **alla stregua di** in the same way as. **a questa stregua** at this rate.

**stremato** [stre'mato] *agg* exhausted.

**stremo** ['strɛmo] *sm* limit.

**strenna** ['strɛnna] *sf* gift.

**strenuo** ['strɛnuo] *agg* valiant; (*fig*) untiring.

**strepitare** [strepi'tare] *v* make a din; (*gridando*) shout. **strepito** *sm* clamour, uproar. **fare strepito** cause a stir. **strepitoso** *agg* noisy; (*fragoroso*) resounding; (*fig*) tremendous.

**streptococco** [strepto'kɔkko] *sm* streptococcus. **streptomicina** *sf* streptomycin.

**stretta** ['stretta] *sf* hold; (*abbraccio*) embrace; (*presa*) grip; critical point; (*situazione difficile*) predicament. **essere** *or* **trovarsi alle strette** be in a tight corner. **stretta alla gola** lump in the throat. **stretta di mano** handshake.

**stretto** ['stretto] *agg* narrow; (*vestiario*) tight; (*rigoroso*) strict; (*denti, pugni*) clenched. *sm* strait. **strettoia** *sf* (*strada*) narrowing of the road; (*fig*) tight spot.

**striato** [stri'ato] *agg* striped.

**stricnina** [strik'nina] *sf* strychnine.

**stridere** ['stridere] *v* (*strillare*) shriek, screech; (*insetti*) chirp; (*cigolare*) squeak; (*fig*) clash. **stridente** *agg* strident; clashing. **strido** *sm*, *pl* -**a** *f* shriek, screech; squeak; chirp.

**strigliata** [stri'ʎata] *sf* dressing-down.

**strillare** [stril'lare] *v* scream; (*parlare ad alta voce*) shout. **strillo** *sm* scream. **strillone** *sm* news-vendor.

**striminzito** [strimin'tsito] *agg* skimpy; (*magro*) skinny.

**strimpellare** [strimpel'lare] *v* strum.

**strinare** [stri'nare] *v* scorch.

**stringa** ['stringa] *sf* lace. **stringare** *v* lace (up); (*fig*) condense.

*****stringere** [strin'dʒere] *v* (*avvicinare*) squeeze *or* press (together); (*serrare*) clasp, clutch; (*vestiario*) pinch; (*concludere*) make; (*denti, pugni*) clench. **il tempo stringe** time is getting short. **stringere i tempi** speed things up; (*musica*) quicken the tempo. **stringere la cinghia** (*fig*) tighten one's belt. **stringere la mano a** shake hands with. **stringere un'amicizia** strike up a friendship. **stringi stringi** when all is said and done.

**striscia** ['striʃa] *sf* strip; (*riga larga*) stripe; (*traccia*) streak. **a strisce** striped. **strisce pedonali** *sf pl* zebra crossing *sing*. **strisciare** *v* creep, crawl; (*sfiorando*) slide; (*sfiorare*) graze. **strisciare i piedi** drag one's feet. **colpire di striscio** graze. **striscione** *sm* banner.

**stritolare** [strito'lare] *v* crush.

**strizzare** [strit'tsare] *v* wring out; (*spremere*)

**strofinare** [strofi'nare] *v* rub. **strofinaccio** *sm* rag. **strofinata** *sf* quick rub. **strofinio** *sm* prolonged rubbing.

**strombazzare** [strombat'tsare] *v* shout from the roof-tops. **strombazzare i propri meriti** blow one's own trumpet.

**strombettare** [strombet'tare] *v* blare; (*auto*) blow the horn.

**stroncare** [stron'kare] *v* break off; (*tagliando*) cut off; (*fig*) cut short; (*criticare*) slate. **stroncatura** *sf* slating.

**stronzo** ['strontso] *sm* (*volg*) turd; (*fig*) idiot.

**stropicciare** [stropit'tʃare] *v* rub. **stropicciarsene** *v* (*fam*) not care a damn.

**strozzare** [strot'tsare] *v* strangle, choke; (*med*) strangulate. **strozzatura** *sf* narrowing; (*occlusione*) bottle-neck; strangling. **strozzino, -a** *sm, sf* usurer.

**\*struggere** ['struddʒere] *v* melt; (*fig*) eat up. **struggersi** *v* be consumed.

**strumento** [stru'mento] *sm* instrument; (*arnese*) tool. **strumento ad arco** stringed instrument. **strumento a fiato** woodwind instrument. **strumentale** *agg* instrumental. **strumentare** *v* orchestrate.

**strusciare** [stru'ʃare] *v* scrape.

**strutto** ['strutto] *sm* lard.

**struttura** [strut'tura] *sf* structure. **strutturale** *agg* structural. **strutturare** *v* structure. **strutturazione** *sf* organization.

**struzzo** ['struttso] *sm* ostrich. **fare lo struzzo** bury one's head in the sand.

**stuccare¹** [stuk'kare] *v* plaster; (*decorare*) stucco. **stuccatore** *sm* plasterer; stucco-worker. **stucco** *sm* plaster; (*per finestre*) putty; (*arte*) stucco. **rimaner di stucco** be dumbfounded.

**stuccare²** [stuk'kare] *v* (*nauseare*) make sick; (*annoiare*) bore. **stucchevole** *agg* sickly; boring. **stucco** *agg* sick (of).

**studente** [stu'dɛnte], **-essa** *sm, sf* student. **studentesco** *agg* (*di scuola*) school; university.

**studiare** [stu'djare] *v* study; (*cercar di trovare*) try and find. **studiare a memoria** learn by heart. **studiato** *agg* studied; affected.

**studio** ['studjo] *sm* study; (*progetto*) plan; (*di avvocato*) office; (*di medico*) surgery; (*di artista, fotografo, ecc.*) studio. **allo studio** under consideration. **fare gli studi** study.

**studioso** [stu'djozo], **-a** *agg* studious. *sm, sf* scholar.

**stufa** ['stufa] *sf* stove, heater. **stufare** *v* (*gastr*) stew; (*fam: annoiare*) bore. **stufarsi di** get sick and tired of. **stufato** *sm* stew. **stufo** *agg* fed up (with).

**stuoia** ['stwɔja] *sf* mat. **stuoino** *sm* doormat.

**stuolo** ['stwɔlo] *sm* crowd.

**\*stupefare** [stupe'fare] *v* astound. **stupefacente** *sm* drug, narcotic. **stupefatto** *agg* astonished, amazed.

**stupendo** [stu'pɛndo] *agg* stupendous.

**stupido** ['stupido] *agg* stupid; (*sciocco*) foolish. **stupidaggine** *sf* stupidity; (*atto*) foolish thing; (*parole*) nonsense; (*inezia*) trifle. **dir stupidaggini** talk nonsense. **stupidità** *sf* stupidity.

**stupire** [stu'pire] *v* amaze, astonish. **stupirsi** *v* be amazed *or* astonished (at). **stupore** *sm* astonishment, amazement; (*med*) stupor.

**stuprare** [stu'prare] *v* rape. **stupro** *sm* rape.

**sturare** [stu'rare] *v* uncork. **sturabottiglie** *sm invar* corkscrew. **sturalavandini** *sm invar* plunger.

**stuzzicare** [stuttsi'kare] *v* prod; (*molestare*) annoy; (*punzecchiare*) tease; (*stimolare*) excite. **stuzzicadenti** *sm invar* tooth-pick. **stuzzicar l'appetito** whet the appetite. **stuzzicante** *agg* exciting; appetizing.

**su** [su] *prep* on; (*senza contatto*) over; (*più in alto di*) above; (*vicino*) by; (*verso*) towards; (*intorno a, circa*) about; (*oltre*) after. **dare su** look out over. **novanta volte su cento** (*fig*) nine times out of ten. *avv* (*in alto*) up; (*indosso*) on; (*al piano superiore*) upstairs. **avercela su con** (*fam*) be cross with. **in su** up; (*età, numero*) upwards. **su per giù** roughly. *inter* come on!

**subacqueo** [su'bakkweo] *agg* underwater.

**subaffittare** [subaffit'tare] *v* sublet. **dare in subaffitto** sublet.

**subalterno** [subal'tɛrno], **-a** *s, agg* subordinate.

**subappaltare** [subappal'tare] *v* subcontract. **subappalto** *sm* subcontract.

**subbia** ['subbja] *sf* chisel.

**subbio** ['subbjo] *sm* beam.

**subbuglio** [sub'buʎo] *sm* turmoil; confusion.

**subconscio** [sub'kɔnʃo] *sm, agg* subconscious.

**subdolo** ['subdolo] *agg* underhand.

**subentrare** [suben'trare] *v* take the place of; succeed.

**subire** [su'bire] *v* suffer; (*sottoporsi a*) undergo.

**subissare** [subis'sare] *v* (*fig*) overwhelm. **subisso** *sm* (*fam*) load; (*rovina*) ruin.

**subito** ['subito] *avv* at once, immediately. **subito prima** just before. **subitaneità** *sf* suddenness. **subitaneo** *agg* sudden.

**sublimare** [subli'mare] *v* sublimate. **sublimato** *sm* sublimate. **sublimazione** *sf* sublimation.

**sublime** [sub'lime] *agg*, *sm* sublime.

**subnormale** [subnor'male] *agg*, *sm* subnormal.

**subodorare** [subodo'rare] *v* **subodorare un inganno** smell a rat.

**subordinare** [subordi'nare] *v* subordinate. **subordinato, -a** *agg*, *s* subordinate. **subordinazione** *sf* subordination.

**subornare** [subor'nare] *v* suborn. **subornazione** *sf* subornation.

**suburbano** [subur'bano] *agg* suburban.

**\*succedere** [sut'tʃedere] *v* follow; succeed; (*capitare*) happen. **cosa sta succedendo?** what is happening? **cosa ti succede?** what is the matter with you? **sono cose che succedono** these things will happen.

**successione** [suttʃes'sjone] *sf* succession. **successione delle colture** crop rotation. **tasse di successione** *sf pl* death duties *pl*. **successivamente** *avv* subsequently. **successivo** *agg* (*seguente*) following; (*uno dopo l'altro*) consecutive. **successore** *sm* successor.

**successo** [sut'tʃɛsso] *sm* success. **aver cattivo successo** be unsuccessful. **aver successo** be successful.

**succhiare** [suk'kjare] *v* suck. **succhietto** *or* **succhiotto** *sm* dummy. **succhione** *sm* sucker.

**succhiello** [suk'kjɛllo] *sm* gimlet.

**succinto** [sut'tʃinto] *agg* scanty; (*fig*) succinct.

**succitato** [suttʃi'tato] *agg* above-mentioned.

**succo** ['sukko] *sm* juice; (*fig*) essence, gist. **succoso** *agg* juicy; (*fig*) meaty. **succulento** *agg* succulent, juicy; (*pasto*) tasty.

**succube** ['sukkube] *s(m+f)* slave.

**succursale** [sukkur'sale] *sf* branch.

**sud** [sud] *sm* south. **abitante del sud** *s(m+f)* southerner. **al sud** (*stato*) in the south; (*moto*) to the south. **del sud** south, southern.

**Sud Africa** [zud 'afrika] *sm* South Africa. **sudafricano, -a** *s, agg* South African.

**Sud America** [zud a'merika] *sm* South America. **sudamericano, -a** *s, agg* South American.

**sudare** [su'dare] *v* sweat, perspire; (*lavorar molto*) toil. **sudar freddo** be in a cold sweat. **sudata** *sf* sweat. **sudaticcio** *agg* sweaty.

**suddetto** [sud'detto] *agg* above-mentioned.

**suddito** ['suddito], **-a** *sm*, *sf* subject.

**\*suddividere** [suddi'videre] *v* subdivide, divide. **suddivisione** *sf* division, subdivision.

**sud-est** [sud'ɛst] *sm* south-east. **del sudest** south-east(ern).

**sudicio** ['suditʃo] *agg* dirty; (*molto sporco*) filthy. *sm invar* filth. **sudiciume** *sm* filth.

**sudore** [su'dore] *sm* sweat, perspiration.

**sud-ovest** [sud'ɔvest] *sm* south-west. **del sud-ovest** south-west(ern).

**sufficiente** [suffi'tʃɛnte] *agg* enough; (*adeguato*) sufficient; presumptuous. **sufficiente a se stesso** self-sufficient. *sm* enough. **avere il sufficiente per vivere** have enough to live on. **sufficienza** *sf* sufficiency. **a sufficienza** more than enough.

**suffisso** [suf'fisso] *sm* suffix.

**suffragio** [suf'fradʒo] *sm* suffrage. **suffragetta** *sf* suffragette.

**suffumicare** [suffumi'kare] *v* fumigate. **suffumicazione** *sf* fumigation.

**suga** ['suga] *agg* **carta suga** *or* **sugante** *sf* blotting paper.

**suggello** [sud'dʒɛllo] *sm* seal. **suggellare** *v* seal.

**suggerire** [suddʒe'rire] *v* suggest; (*consigliare*) advise; (*richiamare*) bring to mind; (*teatro*) prompt. **suggerimento** *sm* suggestion; piece of advice. **suggeritore, -trice** *sm, sf* prompter.

**suggestione** [suddʒes'tjone] *sf* suggestion; impression; (*fascino*) charm. **suggestionabile** *agg* easily influenced, impressionable. **suggestionabilità** *sf* suggestibility. **suggestionare** *v* influence; (*persuadere*) induce. **suggestivo** *agg* suggestive; evocative. **domanda suggestiva** *sf* leading question.

**sughero** ['sugero] *sm* cork.

**sugli** ['suʎi] *prep+art* su gli.

**sugna** ['suɲa] *sf* pork fat.

**sugo** ['sugo] *sm* (*succo*) juice; (*salsa*) sauce; (*fig*) (main) point. **senza sugo** (*fig*) pointless. **sugoso** *agg* juicy; (*fig*) meaty.

**sui** ['sui] *prep+art* su i.

**suicida** [sui'tʃida] *agg* suicidal. *s(m+f)* suicide. **suicidarsi** *v* commit suicide. **suicidio** *sm* suicide.

**suino** [su'ino] *sm* pig, swine. *agg* pig. **carne suina** *sf* pork.

**sul** [sul] *prep+art* su il.

**sulfureo** [sul'fureo] *agg* sulphurous.

**sull'** [sull] *prep+art* su l'.

**sulla** ['sulla] *prep+art* su la.

**sulle** ['sulle] *prep+art* su le.

**sullo** ['sullo] *prep+art* su lo.

**sultano** [sul'tano] *sm* sultan. **(uva) sultanina** *sf* sultana.

**sunto** ['sunto] *sm* summary. **sunteggiare** *v also* **fare il sunto** sum up, summarize.

**suo** ['suo], *m pl* **suoi** *agg* (*uomo*) his; (*donna*) her; (*cosa, animale*) its; (*riflessivo*) one's. *pron* his; hers. **a ciascuno il suo** to each his own.

**suocera** ['swɔtʃera] *sf* mother-in-law; (*spreg*) battle-axe. **suocero** *sm* father-in-law.

**suola** ['swɔla] *sf* sole. **suolare** *v* (*mettere la suola*) sole.

**suolo** ['swɔlo] *sm* ground; (*terreno*) soil.

**suonare** [swo'nare] *V* **sonare**.

**suono** ['swɔno] *sm* sound; tone. **suono falso** discord; (*fig*) false ring.

**suora** ['swɔra] *sf* nun, sister.

**super** ['super] *agg* (*benzina*) four-star.

**superare** [supe'rare] *v* (*dimensione, quantità*) exceed; (*oltrepassare*) go beyond, surpass; (*di passaggio*) pass, overtake; (*sostenere*) get over *or* through. **superato** *agg* (*antiquato*) old-fashioned; (*non più valido*) obsolete.

**superbo** [su'perbo] *agg* haughty; (*fiero*) proud; (*fig*) magnificent, superb. **superbia** *sf* haughtiness. **senza superbia** modestly.

**supercongelato** [superkondʒe'lato] *agg* deep-frozen.

**superficie** [super'fitʃe] *sf* surface; area. **alla superficie** on the surface. **superficiale**

*agg* superficial; (*geom*) plane. **tensione superficiale** *sf* surface tension.

**superfluo** [su'perfluo] *agg* (*eccessivo*) superfluous; (*inutile*) unnecessary. *sm* surplus.

**superiore** [supe'rjore] *agg* (*più in alto*) upper; (*maggiore*) higher; (*fig*) superior; (*di grado*) senior; advanced. **superiore alla media** above average. **superiorità** *sf* superiority.

**superlativo** [superla'tivo] *sm, agg* superlative.

**supermercato** [supermer'kato] *sm* supermarket.

**supero** ['supero] *sm* surplus.

**supersonico** [super'sɔniko] *agg* supersonic.

**superstite** [su'perstite] *agg* surviving. *s(m+f)* survivor.

**superstizione** [supersti'tsjone] *sf* superstition. **superstizioso** *agg* superstitious.

**superuomo** [supe'rwɔmo] *sm* superman.

**supervisione** [supervi'zjone] *sf* supervision. **supervisore** *sm* supervisor.

**supino** [su'pino] *agg* supine. **giacere supino** lie on one's back.

**suppellettili** [suppel'lettili] *sf pl* furnishings *pl*; (*di casa*) household goods *pl*.

**suppergiù** [supper'dʒu] *avv* roughly, more or less.

**supplemento** [supple'mento] *sm* supplement; (*prezzo*) additional charge; (*biglietto*) excess fare. **supplementare** *agg* additional, extra; (*econ, mat*) supplementary.

**supplicare** [suppli'kare] *v* implore. **supplica** *sf* plea. **in atto di supplica** imploringly. **supplicante** *s(m+f)* supplicant. **supplichevole** *agg* imploring.

**supplire** [sup'plire] *v* make up for; (*fare le veci*) stand in for. **supplente** *s(m+f)* supply teacher.

**supplizio** [sup'plitsjo] *sm* torture; (*pena di morte*) capital punishment. **suppliziare** *v* torture.

**\*supporre** [sup'porre] *v* suppose; imagine. **supposizione** *sf* supposition. **supposto che** assuming that, supposing.

**supporto** [sup'pɔrto] *sm* support; (*mec*) bearing; (*sostegno*) stand.

**supposta** [sup'posta] *sf* suppository.

**suppurare** [suppu'rare] *v* fester. **suppurazione** *sf* festering.

**supremo** [su'prɛmo] *agg* supreme; (*massimo*) highest. **supremazia** *sf* supremacy.

**surgelare** [surdʒe'lare] v freeze. **surgelato** sm frozen food.

**surreale** [surre'ale] agg unreal. **surrealismo** sm surrealism. **surrealista** s(m+f), agg surrealist.

**surriscaldare** [surriskal'dare] v overheat. **surriscaldamento** sm overheating.

**surrogare** [surro'gare] v substitute. **surrogato** sm, agg substitute. **surrogazione** sf surrogation.

**suscettibile** [suʃet'tibile] agg capable (of), susceptible; (facile a risentirsi) touchy. **suscettibilità** sf susceptibility. **offendere la suscettibilità di qualcuno** hurt someone's feelings.

**suscitare** [suʃi'tare] v provoke, give rise to.

**susina** [su'zina] sf plum, damson. **susino** sm plum-tree, damson-tree.

**susseguirsi** [susse'gwirsi] v follow (each other). **susseguente** agg following, subsequent.

**sussidiare** [sussi'djare] v subsidize. **sussidiario** agg subsidiary. **sussidio** sm aid; (di denaro) subsidy.

**sussistere** [sus'sistere] v exist; (esser fondato) subsist. **sussistenza** sf subsistence; (mil) catering.

**sussultare** [sussul'tare] v (give a) start. **far sussultare** startle. **sussulto** sm start.

**sussurrare** [sussur'rare] v murmur; (dire a bassa voce) whisper. **sussurro** sm murmur; whisper.

**sutura** [su'tura] sf suture. **suturare** v suture.

**suvvia** [suv'via] inter come on!

**svago** ['zvago] sm diversion; (divertimento) amusement. **svagare** v distract. **svagarsi** v amuse oneself. **svagatezza** sf absent-mindedness. **svagato** agg absent-minded.

**svaligiare** [zvali'dʒare] v ransack. **svaligiatore, -trice** sm, sf burglar.

**svalutare** [zvalu'tare] v devalue. **svalutazione** sf devaluation.

**svanire** [zva'nire] v vanish; (fig) fade away; (esaurirsi) lose strength. **svanito** agg (odore) evaporated; (mente) feeble-minded.

**svantaggio** [zvan'taddʒo] sm disadvantage; (pregiudizio) drawback; (danno) detriment. **svantaggiato** agg handicapped. **svantaggioso** agg disadvantageous; detrimental.

**svariare** [zva'rjare] v vary; diversify. **svariato** agg various.

**svasato** [zva'zato] v flared. **svasatura** sf flare.

**svastica** ['zvastika] sf swastika.

**svecchiare** [zvek'kjare] v renew.

**svedese** [zve'deze] agg Swedish. sm (lingua) Swedish; (fiammifero) safety match. s(m+f) (persona) Swede.

**svegliare** [zve'ʎare] v wake up; (fig) arouse. **svegliarsi** v wake up. **sveglia** sf call; (mil) reveille; (orologio) alarm-clock. **sveglio** agg awake; (fig) quick (-witted).

**svelare** [zve'lare] v reveal.

**svelto** ['zvelto] agg quick; intelligent; (slanciato) slim. **svelto di mano** light-fingered. **sveltezza** sf quickness; (rapidità) speed; slimness. **sveltire** v quicken; (render disinvolto) smarten or liven up; make (more) slender.

**svendere** ['zvendere] v sell off. **svendita** sf sale.

**\*svenire** [zve'nire] v faint. **svenevole** agg mawkish. **svenimento** sm fainting fit.

**sventare** [zven'tare] v foil. **sventatezza** sf thoughtlessness. **sventato** agg thoughtless.

**sventola** ['zventola] sf fan; (pugilato) hook; (schiaffo) slap. **sventolare** v flutter; (arieggiare) air.

**sventrare** [zven'trare] v rip open; (animale) disembowel; (fig) demolish. **sventramento** sm demolition.

**sventura** [zven'tura] sf misfortune; (mala sorte) bad luck. **per colmo di sventura** to crown it all. **per mia sventura** unluckily for me. **sventurato** agg unlucky.

**svergognare** [zvergo'nare] v (put to) shame. **svergognatezza** sf impudence. **svergognato, -a** sm, sf shameless or impudent person.

**svernare** [zver'nare] v winter.

**sverza** ['zvertsa] sf splinter. **sverzare** v splinter.

**svestire** [zves'tire] v undress.

**Svezia** ['zvetsja] sf Sweden.

**svezzare** [zvet'tsare] v wean. **svezzamento** sm weaning.

**sviare** [zvi'are] v divert; (fig) lead astray. **sviare il discorso** change the subject. **sviamento** sm diversion. **sviato** agg misguided.

**svignarsela** [zvi'narsela] v sneak away.

**svigorire** [zvigo'rire] v weaken.

**sviluppo** [zvi'luppo] *sm* development; (*crescita*) growth. **età dello sviluppo** *sf* puberty. **sviluppare** *v* develop; (*produrre*) generate; (*estendersi*) grow.

**svincolare** [zvinko'lare] *v* release; (*riscattare*) redeem. **svincolarsi** *v* free oneself (from). **svincolo** *sm* release; (*comm*) clearance; (*autostrada*) exit.

**svisare** [zvi'zare] *v* twist.

**sviscerare** [zviʃe'rare] *v* disembowel; (*fig*) exhaust. **sviscerarsi per** dote on. **sviscerato** *agg* passionate; (*spreg*) obsequious.

**svista** ['zvista] *sf* oversight.

**svitare** [zvi'tare] *v* unscrew. **svitato, -a** *sm*, *sf* (*fam*) nut.

**Svizzera** ['zvittsera] *sf* Switzerland. **svizzero, -a** *s*, *agg* Swiss.

**svogliato** [zvoˈʎato] *agg* listless; unenthusiastic; (*indolente*) slack. **svogliatezza** *sf* listlessness.

**svolazzare** [zvolat'tsare] *v* flutter. **svolazzo** *sm* flourish.

***svolgere** ['zvɔldʒere] *v* develop. **svolgersi** *v* proceed, go; (*distendersi*) unfold; (*voltarsi*) turn. **svolgimento** *sm* development. **svolta** *sf* turning; (*fig*) turning point; curve.

**svuotare** [zvwo'tare] *v* empty.

# T

**tabacco** [taˈbakko] *sm* tobacco. **tabaccaio, -a** *sm*, *sf* tobacconist. **tabaccheria** *sf* tobacconist's (shop).

**tabella** [taˈbella] *sf* table; list. **tabellone** *sm* notice-board; (*per affissioni murali*) hoarding; (*sport*) score-board.

**tabù** [taˈbu] *agg*, *sm* taboo.

**tabulatore** [tabulaˈtore], **-trice** *sm*, *sf* tabulator.

**tacca** ['takka] *sf* nick; (*macchia*) blotch; (*qualità*) kind; (*difetto*) fault.

**taccagno** [takˈkaɲo] *agg* stingy. **taccagneria** *sf* stinginess.

**taccheggiatore** [takkeddʒaˈtore], **-trice** *sm*, *sf* shop-lifter. **taccheggio** *sm* shoplifting.

**tacchino** [takˈkino] *sm* turkey.

**taccia** ['tattʃa] *sf* (bad) reputation. **tacciare**

*v* accuse.

**tacco** ['takko] *sm* heel. **battere i tacchi** click one's heels.

**taccuino** [takkuˈino] *sm* note-book.

***tacere** [taˈtʃere] *v* be *or* keep quiet; (*fam*) shut up; (*non dir nulla*) say nothing. **far tacere** hush.

**tachimetro** [taˈkimetro] *sm* speedometer.

**tacito** [ˈtatʃito] *agg* tacit; (*silenzioso*) silent. **taciturno** *agg* taciturn.

**tafano** [ˈtafano] *sm* horsefly.

**tafferuglio** [taffeˈruʎo] *sm* brawl.

**taglia** [ˈtaʎa] *sf* (*premio*) reward; (*statura*) size.

**tagliando** [taˈʎando] *sm* coupon; (*scontrino*) voucher.

**tagliare** [taˈʎare] *v* cut; (*staccare, interrompere*) cut off; (*trinciare*) carve; (*in più parti*) cut up; (*vino*) blend. **tagliaboschi** *sm invar* woodcutter. **tagliacarte** *sm invar* paper-knife. **tagliapietre** *sm invar* stonemason. **tagliare la testa al toro** settle a matter once and for all.

**tagliente** [taˈʎente] *agg* cutting.

**tagliere** [taˈʎere] *sm* chopping board.

**taglio** [ˈtaʎo] *sm* cut; (*parte staccata*) piece; (*parte tagliente*) (cutting) edge; (*importo*) denomination.

**tagliola** [taˈʎɔla] *sf* trap.

**tagliuzzare** [taʎutˈtsare] *v* chop up; (*a strisce*) cut to shreds.

**tailleur** [taˈjœr] *sm* suit.

**talco** [ˈtalko] *sm* talc.

**tale** [ˈtale] *agg* such; certain. **tal dei tali** so-and-so. **tale quale** exactly like. **tale ... tale ...** like ... like .... **un (certo) tale** a certain person.

**talento** [taˈlento] *sm* talent.

**talismano** [talizˈmano] *sm* talisman, charm.

**talloncino** [tallonˈtʃino] *sm* counterfoil.

**tallone** [talˈlone] *sm* heel. **tallonare** *v* shadow; (*sport*) mark.

**talora** [taˈlora] *avv* at times.

**talpa** [ˈtalpa] *sf* mole.

**taluni** [taˈluni] *pron*, *agg* some.

**talvolta** [talˈvɔlta] *avv* sometimes.

**tamburo** [tamˈburo] *sm* drum; (*sonatore*) drummer; (*mec*) barrel, drum. **tamburellare** *v* drum. **tamburello** *sm* tambourine.

**Tamigi** [taˈmidʒi] *sm* Thames.

**tamponare** [tampo'nare] *v* plug; (*auto*) bump into. **tamponare una falla** stop a leak. **tampone** *sm* plug; tampon.

**tana** ['tana] *sf* den.

**tanfo** ['tanfo] *sm* musty smell.

**tangente** [tan'dʒɛnte] *sf* tangent. **tangenziale** *sf* (*strada*) ring road.

**tangibile** [tan'dʒibile] *agg* tangible.

**tango** ['tango] *sm* tango.

**tanto** ['tanto] *agg* (so) much *or* many; (*altrettanto*) as much *or* many; (*molto*) a lot (of). **tanto ... quanto ...** as much ... as ... *pron* a lot; much *or* many. **tanti** *pron* (*persone*) so many (people). **tanto per** so much for. *avv* so (much); (*soltanto*) just. **da tanto** (*tempo*) for such a long time. **di tanto in tanto** from time to time. **ogni tanto** from time to time. **tanti auguri!** best wishes! congratulations! **tanto meglio** so much the better. **tanto più che** especially as.

**tappa** ['tappa] *sf* stage; (*sosta*) stop.

**tappare** [tap'pare] *v* shut; (*con tappo*) bung (up). **tapparsi il naso** hold one's nose. **tapparsi le orecchie** close one's ears.

**tapparella** [tappa'rɛlla] *sf* blind.

**tappeto** [tap'peto] *sm* carpet; (*piccolo*) rug; (*sport, tec*) mat. **mettere al tappeto** knock down.

**tappezzare** [tappet'tsare] *v* (*di carta*) paper; (*di legno*) panel; (*di stoffa*) cover, upholster. **tappezzeria** *sf* (*carta*) wallpaper; (*stoffa*) tapestry; (*legno*) panelling; (*mobili*) upholstery. **tappezziere** *sm* decorator; upholsterer.

**tappo** ['tappo] *sm* stopper, plug; (*sughero*) cork; (*a vite*) screw-cap.

**tara** ['tara] *sf* tare; defect. **tarato** *agg* (*tec*) calibrated; (*difettoso*) tainted.

**tarantola** [ta'rantola] *sf* tarantula.

**tarchiato** [tar'kjato] *agg* sturdy.

**tardare** [tar'dare] *v* be late. **tardi** *avv* late. **tardivo** *agg* late; retarded. **tardo** *agg* (*lento*) slow; (*tempo*) late; (*età*) ripe old.

**targa** ['targa] *sf* plate; (*auto*) numberplate. **targare** *v* (*auto*) register.

**tariffa** [ta'riffa] *sf* rate; (*trasporto pubblico*) fare; (*dogana*) tariff.

**tarlo** ['tarlo] *sm* woodworm. **tarlo del dubbio** gnawing doubt. **tarlato** *agg* worm eaten.

**tarma** ['tarma] *sf* moth.

**tarpare** [tar'pare] *v* **tarpare le ali a** clip the wings of.

**tartagliare** [tarta'ʎare] *v* stammer.

**tartaro** ['tartaro] *sm* tartar.

**tartaruga** [tarta'ruga] *sf* tortoise.

**tartassare** [tartas'sare] *v* ill-treat.

**tartina** [tar'tina] *sf* canapé.

**tartufo** [tar'tufo] *sm* truffle.

**tasca** ['taska] *sf* pocket. **avere le tasche piene (di)** (*fam*) be sick and tired (of). **conoscere come le proprie tasche** know like the back of one's hand. **tascabile** *agg* pocket.

**tassa** ['tassa] *sf* tax; (*imposta*) duty; (*giudiziaria, scolastica*) fee. **tassametro** *sm* meter.

**tassare** [tas'sare] *v* tax. **tassare troppo** (*fig*) overtax. **tassabile** *agg* taxable; subject to duty. **tassativo** *agg* express; definite.

**tassello** [tas'sɛllo] *sm* dowel; (*prelievo*) wedge; (*indumento*) gusset.

**tassi** [tas'si] *sm* taxi. **tassista** *sm* taxi-driver.

**tasso**¹ ['tasso] *sm* (*zool*) badger.

**tasso**² ['tasso] *sm* (*bot*) yew(-tree).

**tasso**³ ['tasso] *sm* (*rapporto*) rate.

**tasso d'interessi** *sm* interest rate.

**tastare** [tas'tare] *v* feel. **tastare il terreno** (*fig*) see how the land lies. **tastiera** *sf* keyboard. **tasto** *sm* key; (*argomento*) subject; (*tatto*) touch. **a tastoni** feeling one's way.

**tattica** ['tattika] *sf* tactics *pl*. **tattico** *agg* tactical.

**tatto** ['tatto] *sm* touch; (*fig*) tact. **con tatto** tactfully. **mancare di tatto** be tactless. **senza tatto** tactlessly.

**tatuaggio** [tatu'addʒo] *sm* tattoo. **tatuare** *v* tattoo.

**tautologia** [tautolo'dʒia] *sf* tautology. **tautologico** *agg* tautological.

**taverna** [ta'vɛrna] *sf* inn, pub.

**tavola** ['tavola] *sf* table; (*asse*) board. **tavola calda** snack-bar. **tavola da disegno/stiro** drawing/ironing board. **tavola di comando** console. **tavola nera** blackboard. **tavola reale** (*gioco*) backgammon.

**tavolato** [tavo'lato] *sm* (*pavimento*) flooring; (*assito*) partition; (*geog*) plateau.

**tavolo** ['tavolo] *sm* table; (*ufficio, studio*) desk.

**tavolozza** [tavo'lɔttsa] *sf* palette.

**tazza** ['tattsa] *sf* cup; (*gabinetto*) lavatory pan; (*fontana*) basin.

**te** [te] *pron* you. *V* **ti.**

**tè** [tɛ] *sm* tea.

**teatro** [te'atro] *sm* theatre; *(attività professionale)* stage; *(complesso di opere)* plays *pl*. **teatro lirico** *(edificio)* opera house; *(genere)* opera. **teatrale** *agg* theatrical.

**tecnica** ['tɛknika] *sf* technique; technology.

**tecnico** ['tɛkniko], **-a** *agg* technical. *sm*, *sf* technician, engineer; expert. **tecnicismo** *sm* technicality.

**tecnologia** [teknolo'dʒia] *sf* technology. **tecnologico** *agg* technological. **tecnologia dell'informazione** *sf* information technology.

**tedesco** [te'desko], **-a** *s*, *agg* German.

**tedio** ['tɛdjo] *sm* tediousness. **tedioso** *agg* tedious.

**tegame** [te'game] *sm* (frying-)pan. **uova al tegame** *sf pl* fried eggs *pl*.

**teglia** ['teʎa] *sf* baking tin.

**tegola** ['tegola] *sf* (roofing-)tile. **coprire di tegole** tile. **tetto di tegole** *sm* tiled roof.

**tela** ['tela] *sf* cloth; *(pittura)* canvas; *(teatro)* curtain. **tela cerata** oilcloth. **tela da lenzuola** sheeting. **tela di lino** linen.

**telaio** [te'lajo] *sm* loom; *(auto)* chassis; *(tec)* frame.

**telecabina** [teleka'bina] *sf* cable-car.

**telecomando** [teleko'mando] *sm* remote control. **telecomandare** *v* operate by remote control.

**telecronaca** [tele'krɔnaka] *sf* news bulletin. **telecronista** *s(m+f)* television commentator.

**telefonare** [telefo'nare] *v* telephone; *(fam)* phone. **telefonata** *sf* telephone call. **telefonata urbana/interurbana/con preavviso** local/trunk/personal call. **telefonico** *agg* telephone. **telefonista** *s(m+f)* telephonist. **telefono** *sm* telephone.

**telegiornale** [teledʒor'nale] *sm* television news.

**telegrafare** [telegra'fare] *v* telegraph. **telegrafico** *agg* telegraph; *(conciso)* telegraphic. **telegrafista** *s(m+f)* telegraph operator.

**telegramma** [tele'gramma] *sm* telegram.

**telepatia** [telepa'tia] *sf* telepathy. **telepatico** *agg* telepathic.

**teleschermo** [tele'skɛrmo] *sm* television screen.

**telescopio** [tele'skɔpjo] *sm* telescope.

**telespettatore** [telespetta'tore], **-trice** *sm*, *sf* viewer.

**teletrasmissione** [teletrazmis'sjone] *sf* television programme.

**televendita** [tele'vendita] *sf* telesales.

**televisione** [televi'zjone] *sf* television; *(fam)* TV. **televisore** *sm* television set.

**telone** [te'lone] *sm* tarpaulin.

**tema** ['tɛma] *sm* theme, subject; *(scolastico)* essay. **fuori tema** off the point.

**temerario** [teme'rarjo] *agg* reckless; *(avventato)* rash. **temerità** *sf* temerity.

**temere** [te'mere] *v* fear, be afraid. **non temere!** don't worry!

**temperamento** [tempera'mento] *sm* temperament.

**temperare** [tempe'rare] *v* temper; *(matita)* sharpen. **temperato** *agg* temperate. **temperino** *sm* pen-knife.

**temperatura** [tempera'tura] *sf* temperature.

**tempesta** [tem'pɛsta] *sf* storm. **tempestare** *v* storm; *(ornare)* stud; *(importunare)* bombard. **tempestoso** *agg* stormy.

**tempestivo** [tempes'tivo] *agg* timely. **tempestività** *sf* timeliness.

**tempia** ['tɛmpja] *sf* temple.

**tempio** ['tɛmpjo] *sm* temple.

**tempista** [tem'pista] *s(m+f)* opportunist.

**tempo** ['tɛmpo] *sm* time; *(atmosferico)* weather; *(gramm)* tense; *(musica)* tempo, movement. **a suo tempo** *(passato)* originally; *(futuro)* in due course; *(al momento giusto)* at the right time. **a tempo debito** in due course. **a tempo perso** in one's spare time. **da tempo** for some time. **in un primo tempo** at first. **tempo da cani** foul weather.

**temporale¹** [tempo'rale] *agg* temporal.

**temporale²** [tempo'rale] *sm* (thunder)storm. **temporalesco** *agg* stormy.

**temporaneo** [tempo'raneo] *agg* temporary.

**temporeggiare** [tempored'dʒare] *v* mark time, temporize.

**temprare** [tem'prare] *v* temper. **tempra** *sf* *(tec)* tempering; temper; *(fig)* fibre; *(voce)* timbre.

**tenace** [te'natʃe] *agg* firm; *(fig)* tenacious. **tenacia** *sf* tenacity. **tenacità** *sf* tenacity, firmness.

**tenaglie** [te'naʎe] *sf pl* pincers *pl*; (*pinze*) pliers *pl*; (*molle*) tongs *pl*.

**tenda** ['tɛnda] *sf* (*drappo*) curtain; (*da campo*) tent; (*tendone da sole*) awning. **tenda alla veneziana** Venetian blind. **tendina** *sf* net curtain.

**tendenza** [ten'dɛntsa] *sf* tendency; (*attitudine*) bent; (*orientamento, econ*) trend. **tendenziale** *agg* potential. **tendenzioso** *agg* tendentious.

**\*tendere** ['tɛndere] *v* (*mettere in tensione*) stretch; (*porgere*) hold out; (*reti*) cast. **tendere a** (*mirare*) aim at; be inclined to; (*volgersi verso*) tend towards. **tendere un tranello** set a trap.

**tendine** ['tɛndine] *sm* tendon.

**tenebre** ['tɛnebre] *sf pl* darkness *sing*. **tenebroso** *agg* dark; (*fig*) mysterious.

**tenente** [te'nɛnte] *sm* lieutenant.

**\*tenere** [te'nere] *v* hold; (*mantenere, trattenere*) keep; (*seguire una direzione*) keep to. **tenerci a** attach great importance to. **tenere a** (*volere*) want. **tener d'occhio** keep an eye on. **tener presente** bear in mind.

**tenero** ['tɛnero] *agg* tender. **tenerezza** *sf* tenderness.

**tenia** ['tɛnja] *sf* tapeworm.

**tennis** ['tɛnnis] *sm* tennis. **tennista** *s(m+f)* tennis player.

**tenore** [te'nore] *sm* tenor; content. **a tenore di** in accordance with. **tenore di vita** living standard.

**tensione** [ten'sjone] *sf* tension.

**tentacolo** [ten'takolo] *sm* tentacle.

**tentare** [ten'tare] *v* (*cercare*) try; (*sperimentare*) try out; (*cercare di fare*) attempt; (*invogliare*) tempt. **tentativo** *sm* attempt. **tentatore** *sm* tempter. **tentatrice** *sf* temptress. **tentazione** *sf* temptation. **aver la tentazione (di)** be tempted (to).

**tentennare** [tenten'nare] *v* wobble; hesitate.

**tentoni** [ten'toni] *avv* **a tentoni** groping one's way.

**tenue** ['tɛnue] *agg* slender; (*debole*) faint; (*fig*) slight.

**tenuta** [te'nuta] *sf* (*divisa*) uniform; (*possedimento fondiario*) estate; capacity; (*auto*) road-holding; (*tec*) seal. **a tenuta d'acqua** water-tight. **a tenuta d'aria** airtight.

**teologia** [teolo'dʒia] *sf* theology. **teologico**
*agg* theological. **teologo, -a** *sm, sf* theologian.

**teorema** [teo'rɛma] *sm* theorem.

**teoria** [teo'ria] *sf* theory. **in teoria** theoretically.

**teorico** [te'ɔriko], **-a** *agg* theoretical. *sm, sf* theorist.

**tepore** [te'pore] *sm* warmth.

**teppa** ['teppa] *sf also* **teppaglia** rabble. **teppismo** *sm* hooliganism. **teppista** *s(m+f)* hooligan.

**terapia** [tera'pia] *sf* therapy. **terapeutico** *agg* therapeutic. **terapista** *s(m+f)* therapist.

**tergicristallo** [terdʒikris'tallo] *sm* windscreen-wiper.

**tergiversare** [terdʒiver'sare] *v* prevaricate.

**tergo** ['tɛrgo] *sm* **a tergo** (*di dietro*) behind. **vedi a tergo** (*nei rinvii*) please turn over, PTO.

**terme** ['tɛrme] *sf pl* (thermal) baths *pl*. **termale** *or* **termico** *agg* thermal.

**terminare** [termi'nare] *v* end. **terminazione** *sf* ending. **termine** *sm* term; limit; (*punto estremo*) end; (*comm*) expiry (date). **a breve/lungo termine** short-/long-term. **ai termini di legge** by law. **a rigor di termini** strictly speaking. **terminologia** *sf* terminology.

**termodinamica** [termodi'namika] *sf* thermodynamics.

**termometro** [ter'mɔmetro] *sm* thermometer.

**termonucleare** [termonukle'are] *agg* thermonuclear.

**termos** *V* thermos.

**termosifone** [termosi'fone] *sm* radiator.

**termostato** [ter'mɔstato] *sm* thermostat. **termostatico** *agg* thermostatic.

**terra** ['tɛrra] *sf* earth; (*estensione di terreno, paese*) land; (*suolo*) soil. **a terra** (*senza soldi*) broke; (*depresso*) in low spirits; (*gomma*) flat. **collegare** *or* **mettere a terra** (*elett*) earth. **raso terra** close to the ground.

**terraglia** [ter'raʎa] *sf* earthenware. **terraglie** *sf pl* (*vasellame*) crockery *sing*.

**terrapieno** [terra'pjɛno] *sm* embankment.

**terrazza** [ter'rattsa] *sf* terrace. **terrazzo** *sm* terrace; (*alpinismo*) ledge.

**terremoto** [terre'mɔto] *sm* earthquake. **terremotato, -a** *sm, sf* earthquake victim.

**terreno¹** [ter'reno] *agg* earthly, worldly.

**piano terreno** ground floor.

**terreno**[2] [ter'reno] *sm* land; (*suolo*) ground; (*podere*) plot (of land); (*fig*) field.

**terreo** ['tɛrreo] *agg* earthy; (*colorito*) deathly pale.

**terrestre** [ter'rɛstre] *agg* terrestrial.

**terribile** [ter'ribile] *agg* terrible.

**territorio** [terri'tɔrjo] *sm* territory. **territoriale** *agg* territorial.

**terrore** [ter'rore] *sm* terror. **aver terrore (di)** be terrified (of). **terrorismo** *sm* terrorism. **terrorista** *s(m+f)* terrorist. **terroristico** *agg* terrorist. **terrorizzare** *v* terrorize.

**terzo** ['tɛrtso] *agg*, *sm* third. **terzi** *sm pl* (*comm, dir*) third party *sing*. **terzina** *sf* triplet.

**tesa** ['teza] *sf* (*cappello*) brim; (*reti*) spreading.

**teschio** ['tɛskjo] *sm* skull.

**tesi** ['tɛzi] *sf* thesis (*pl* -es).

**teso** ['tezo] *agg* taut; (*nervoso*) tense. **stare con le orecchie tese** prick up one's ears.

**tesoro** [te'zɔro] *sm* treasure; (*tesoreria, pol*) treasury. **far tesoro (di)** treasure. **tesoriere** *sm* treasurer.

**tessera** ['tɛssera] *sf* card; (*lasciapassare*) pass; (*ferr*) season-ticket. **tesseramento** *sm* rationing. **tesserare** *v* give a membership card; ration.

**tessere** ['tɛssere] *v* weave. **tessitura** *sf* weaving; (*stabilimento*) (weaving) mill; (*trama*) plot. **tessuto** *sm* fabric; (*bot, zool, fig*) tissue.

**tessile** ['tɛssile] *agg* textile. *sm* textile; (*operaio*) textile worker.

**testa** ['tɛsta] *sf* head. **a testa** (*ciascuno*) each, per head. **colpo di testa** *sm* (*sport*) header; (*fig*) whim. **essere in testa** be in the lead. **fare a testa e croce** toss up. **passare in testa** take the lead. **rompersi la testa** rack one's brains.

**testamento** [testa'mento] *sm* will; (*bibbia*) testament.

**testardo** [tes'tardo] *agg* stubborn. **testardaggine** *sf* stubbornness.

**testata** [tes'tata] *sf* (*intestazione*) heading; (*colpo di testa*) butt; (*auto*) cylinder head; (*parte anteriore*) head.

**testicolo** [tes'tikolo] *sm* testicle.

**testimone** [testi'mɔne] *s(m+f)* witness. **testimoniale** *sm* evidence. **testimonianza** *sf* testimony; (*prova*) evidence. **testimoniare**

*v* testify; (*deporre in giudizio*) (bear) witness.

**testo** ['tɛsto] *sm* text; (*libro*) text-book. **far testo** be an authority. **testuale** *agg* exact.

**testone** [tes'tone] *sm* (*stupido*) blockhead; (*testardo*) pig-headed person.

**testuggine** [tes'tuddʒine] *sf* tortoise; (*di mare*) turtle.

**tetano** ['tɛtano] *sm* tetanus.

**tetro** ['tɛtro] *agg* gloomy.

**tetta** ['tetta] *sf* (*fam*) breast. **tettarella** *sf* dummy.

**tetto** ['tetto] *sm* roof (*pl* -s). **essere senza tetto** be homeless. **tettoia** *sf* roofing, canopy.

**Tevere** ['tevere] *sm* Tiber.

**thermos** ® *or* **termos** ['tɛrmos] *sm invar* thermos (flask) ®.

**ti** [ti], **te** *pron* (to) you; (*riflessivo*) yourself.

**tiara** ['tjara] *sf* tiara.

**tic** [tik] *sm invar* tic.

**ticchettare** [tikket'tare] *v* click; (*pioggia*) patter; (*orologio*) tick.

**ticchio** ['tikkjo] *sm* whim.

**tictac** [tik'tak] *sm* tick.

**tiepido** ['tjɛpido] *agg* lukewarm.

**tifo** ['tifo] *sm* (*med*) typhus; (*fam: sport*) fanaticism. **fare il tifo per** be a fan of. **(febbre) tifoide** *sf* typhoid (fever).

**tifone** [ti'fone] *sm* typhoon.

**tifoso** [ti'fozo], **-a** *sm*, *sf* fan.

**tiglio** ['tiʎo] *sm* lime(-tree); (*fibra*) bast.

**tigna** ['tiɲa] *sf* ringworm.

**tignola** [ti'ɲɔla] *sf* moth.

**tigre** ['tigre] *sf* tiger.

**timbrare** [tim'brare] *v* stamp; (*posta*) postmark. **timbro** *sm* stamp; postmark; (*suono*) timbre.

**timido** ['timido] *agg* shy; (*timoroso*) timid.

**timo** ['timo] *sm* (*bot*) thyme.

**timone** [ti'mone] *sm* rudder; (*fig*) helm. **timoniere** *sm* helmsman; (*canottaggio*) cox.

**timore** [ti'more] *sm* fear. **senza timore** fearless. **timoroso** *agg* fearful; (*preoccupato*) anxious.

**timpano** ['timpano] *sm* (*anat*) ear-drum; (*musica*) kettle-drum. **timpani** *sm pl* timpani *pl*.

**tinca** ['tinka] *sf* tench.

**\*tingere** ['tindʒere] *v* dye; (*macchiare*) spot.

**tino** ['tino] *sm* tub, vat.

**tinta** ['tinta] *sf* colour; (*sfumatura*) shade. **tintarella** *sf* tan. **tinto** *agg* dyed; (*macchiato*) tinged. **tintore** *sm* dyer. **tintoria** *sf* cleaners. **tintura** *sf* dyeing; (*med*) tincture.

**tipo** ['tipo] *sm* type; (*genere*) sort, kind. **tipico** *agg* typical.

**tipografia** [tipogra'fia] *sf* typography; (*stamperia*) press. **tipografico** *agg* typographical. **tipografo, -a** *sm, sf* printer.

**tiranneggiare** [tiranned'dʒare] *v* tyrannize. **tirannia** *sf* tyranny. **tirannico** *agg* tyrannical. **tiranno** *sm* tyrant.

**tirante** [ti'rante] *sm* (connecting) rod; brace.

**tirapiedi** [tira'pjɛdi] *sm invar* hanger-on.

**tirare** [ti'rare] *v* pull, draw; (*lanciare*) throw; (*sparare*) shoot. **tirare avanti** keep going. **tirar fuori** pull out; (*estrarre*) take out. **tirare in lungo** draw out. **tirarsi indietro** draw back. **tirarsi su** draw oneself up; (*fam*) get back on one's feet. **tirata** *sf* pull; (*discorso*) tirade. **tiratura** *sf* printing; (*numero*) run.

**tirchio** ['tirkjo] *agg* stingy.

**tiritera** [tiri'tɛra] *sf* rigmarole.

**tiro** ['tiro] *sm* (*lancio*) throw; (*arma*) shot. **fuori tiro** out of range.

**tirocinio** [tiro'tʃinjo] *sm* apprenticeship.

**tiroide** [ti'rɔide] *sf* thyroid.

**titolare** [tito'lare] *agg* titular, regular. *s(m+f)* proprietor.

**titolo** ['titolo] *sm* title; (*comm*) share; (*obbligazione*) bond; (*filato*) count. **a titolo di** out of.

**titubare** [titu'bare] *v* hesitate.

**tizio** ['titsjo] *sm* fellow. **Tizio, Caio, e Sempronio** Tom, Dick, and Harry.

**tizzo** ['tittso] *sm* ember.

**toboga** [to'bɔga] *sm invar* toboggan.

**toccare** [tok'kare] *v* touch; (*riguardare*) concern. **tocca a me** it is my turn; (*spettare di diritto*) I am entitled; (*spettare di dovere*) it is up to me. **toccasana** *sm invar* panacea.

**tocco¹** ['tokko] *sm* touch; (*campana*) stroke; (*l'una*) one o'clock.

**tocco²** ['tɔkko] *sm* (*pezzo*) hunk.

**toga** ['tɔga] *sf* toga.

***togliere** ['tɔʎere] *v* take away; (*indumenti*) take off. **ciò non toglie che** it does not alter the fact that. **togliere di mezzo** get out of the way. **togliersi** *v* (*levarsi*) take off; (*soddisfare*) satisfy.

**toletta** [to'letta] *sf also* **toilette** toilet; (*mobile*) dressing table; (*acconciatura*) toilette; (*abito*) outfit.

**tollerare** [tolle'rare] *v* tolerate, stand; (*permettere*) allow. **tollerabile** *agg* bearable. **tollerante** *agg* tolerant. **tolleranza** *sf* tolerance.

**tomaia** [to'maja] *sf* upper.

**tomba** ['tomba] *sf* tomb.

**tombola¹** ['tombola] *sf* (*gioco*) tombola; bingo.

**tombola²** ['tombola] *sf* (*caduta*) fall.

**tomo** ['tɔmo] *sm* tome; (*tipo strano*) odd type.

**tonaca** ['tɔnaka] *sf* (*frati, monache*) habit; (*preti*) cassock.

**tonalità** [tonali'ta] *sf* tonality; (*colore*) shade.

**tonare** [to'nare] *v* thunder.

**tonchio** ['tonkjo] *sm* weevil.

**tondo** ['tondo] *agg* round. *sm* round plate; (*forma*) circle. **parlar chiaro e tondo** speak bluntly.

**tonfo** ['tonfo] *sm* thud; (*nell'acqua*) splash.

**tonico** ['tɔniko] *agg* tonic. **tonica** *sf* (*musica*) tonic.

**tonnellata** [tonnel'lata] *sf* ton. **tonnellaggio** *sm* tonnage.

**tonno** ['tonno] *sm* tuna, tunny.

**tono** ['tɔno] *sm* tone. **cambiar tono** change (one's) tune. **fuori tono** out of tune. **giù di tono** out of sorts. **in tono** in tune; (*fisicamente*) fit.

**tonsilla** [ton'silla] *sf* tonsil. **tonsillite** *sf* tonsillitis.

**tonto** ['tonto], **-a** *agg* silly. *sm, sf* fool.

**topazio** [to'patsjo] *sm* topaz.

**topico** ['tɔpiko] *agg* local; (*fig*) topical.

**topo** ['tɔpo] *sm* mouse (*pl* mice); (*campagnolo*) fieldmouse. **topo di biblioteca** bookworm.

**topografia** [topogra'fia] *sf* topography. **topografico** *agg* topographical.

**toporagno** [topo'raɲo] *sm* shrew.

**toppa** ['tɔppa] *sf* patch; (*serratura*) keyhole.

**torace** [to'ratʃe] *sm* chest.

**torba** ['tɔrba] *sf* peat.

**torbido** ['tɔrbido] *agg* turbid, muddy. **c'è del torbido** there's something fishy going on.

***torcere** ['tɔrtʃere] *v* twist; (*strizzare*) wring

out. **torcere il collo a qualcuno** wring someone's neck. **torcere il naso** turn up one's nose. **torcersi il collo** crane one's neck. **torcicollo** sm crick in the neck.

**torchio** ['tɔrkjo] sm press. **torchiare** v press.

**torcia** ['tɔrtʃa] sf torch.

**tordo** ['tordo] sm thrush.

**Torino** [to'rino] sf Turin.

**torma** ['torma] sf herd; (persone) throng.

**tormentare** [tormen'tare] v torment. **tormento** sm torment; (infastidire) plague.

**tornaconto** [torna'konto] sm advantage.

**tornante** [tor'nante] sm hairpin bend.

**tornare** [tor'nare] v return; (andare di nuovo) go back; (venire di nuovo) come back; (ricominciare) start again. **ben tornato!** welcome back! **qualcosa non torna** something is not quite right.

**torneo** [tor'nɛo] sm tournament.

**tornio** ['tɔrnjo] sm lathe. **tornire** v turn. **tornitore** sm (tec) lathe operator; (di legno) wood turner.

**toro** ['tɔro] sm bull. **Toro** sm Taurus.

**torpedine** [tor'pedine] sf torpedo.

**torpedone** [torpe'done] sm coach.

**torpido** ['tɔrpido] agg sluggish. **torpore** sm sluggishness.

**torre** ['torre] sf tower; (scacchi) rook, castle. **torretta** sf turret.

**torrefare** [torre'fare] v roast. **torrefazione** sf roasting.

**torrente** [tor'rɛnte] sm torrent. **torrenziale** agg torrential.

**torrido** ['tɔrrido] agg torrid.

**torrone** [tor'rone] sm nougat.

**torso** ['torso] sm stalk; (frutta) core; (anat) torso. **a torso nudo** bare-chested.

**torsolo** ['torsolo] sm stalk; (frutta) core.

**torta** ['torta] sf cake; (di frutta) tart; (pasticcio) pie.

**tortiglione** [torti'ʎone] sm spiral. **a tortiglione** spiral.

**torto**[1] ['tɔrto] sm wrong; (colpa) fault. **a torta** wrongfully. **aver torto** be wrong. **dar torto a** prove wrong.

**torto**[2] ['tɔrto] agg twisted.

**tortora** ['tortora] sf turtle-dove.

**tortuoso** [tortu'ozo] agg tortuous.

**torturare** [tortu'rare] v torture. **tortura** sf torture.

**torvo** ['torvo] agg surly.

**tosare** [to'zare] v shear; (cani) clip; (fig) fleece. **tosatrice** sf (capelli) hair-clippers pl; (erba) lawn-mower. **tosatura** sf shearing; clipping.

**Toscana** [tos'kana] sf Tuscany. **toscano, -a s, agg** Tuscan.

**tosse** ['tosse] sf cough. **tossire** v cough.

**tossico** ['tɔssiko] agg poisonous. sm poison. **tossicità** sf toxicity. **tossicomane** s(m+f) drug addict. **tossicomania** sf drug addiction. **tossina** sf toxin.

**tostare** [tos'tare] v roast; (pane) toast. **tostapane** sm invar toaster.

**tosto** ['tɔsto] agg **faccia tosta** sf (fam) cheek.

**totale** [to'tale] agg, sm total. **totalità** sf entirety.

**totalitario** [totali'tarjo] agg (pol) totalitarian.

**totano** ['tɔtano] sm squid.

**totocalcio** [toto'kalfʃo] sm football pools pl.

**tovaglia** [to'vaʎa] sf table-cloth. **tovagliolo** sm napkin, serviette.

**tozzo**[1] ['tottso] agg squat; (persone) stocky.

**tozzo**[2] ['tottso] sm piece.

**tra** [tra] prep among(st); (tra due) between; (nel mezzo) in the midst of; (tempo) in. **tra breve** or **poco** soon. **tra l'altro** among other things; (inoltre) besides.

**traballare** [trabal'lare] v wobble; (persone, fig) totter.

**traboccare** [trabok'kare] v overflow. **trabocchetto** sm trap.

**tracannare** [trakan'nare] v gulp down.

**traccia** ['trattʃa] sf track, trail; (orma) footprint; (indizio) trace. **tracciare** v trace; (abbozzare) sketch (out); (a grandi linee) outline. **tracciato** sm layout.

**trachea** [tra'kɛa] sf windpipe.

**tracolla** [tra'kɔlla] sf shoulder-strap. **a tracolla** over one's shoulder. **borsetta a tracolla** sf shoulder-bag.

**tradire** [tra'dire] v betray; (coniugi) be unfaithful (to). **tradimento** sm treachery; (dir) treason. **a tradimento** by surprise. **traditore** sm traitor. **traditrice** sf traitress.

**tradizione** [tradi'tsjone] sf tradition. **tradizionale** agg traditional.

*****tradurre** [tra'durre] v translate; (condurre) convey. **traduttore, -trice** sm, sf translator. **traduzione** sf translation.

**trafelato** [trafe'lato] *agg* out of breath.

**trafficare** [traffi'kare] *v* (*commerciare*) trade, deal; (*spreg*) traffic; (*darsi da fare*) busy oneself. **traffico** *sm* traffic.

***trafiggere** [tra'fiddʒere] *v* pierce.

**trafila** [tra'fila] *sf* (*operazione*) (lengthy) procedure. **trafilare** *v* draw. **trafiletto** *sm* paragraph.

**traforare** [trafo'rare] *v* bore, drill; (*legno*) cut with a fretsaw. **traforatrice** *sf* drill; (*sega*) fretsaw. **traforo** *sm* tunnel; fretsaw.

**tragedia** [tra'dʒɛdja] *sf* tragedy.

**traghetto** [tra'getto] *sm* ferry. **traghettare** *v* ferry (across).

**tragico** ['tradʒiko] *agg* tragic. *sm* tragedy; (*autore*) tragedian; (*attore*) tragic actor. **prendere sul tragico** dramatize.

**tragitto** [tra'dʒitto] *sm* journey; (*traversata*) crossing.

**traguardo** [tra'gwardo] *sm* finish; (*sport*) winning-post; (*fig*) goal.

**traiettoria** [trajet'tɔrja] *sf* trajectory; (*di volo*) flight-path.

**trainare** [trai'nare] *v* pull *or* haul along; (*rimorchiare*) tow. **traino** *sm* haulage; (*rimorchio*) trailer; (*con pattini*) sledge.

**tralasciare** [trala'ʃare] *v* leave out; interrupt; (*trascurare*) neglect.

**tralcio** ['traltʃo] *sm* shoot.

**traliccio** [tra'littʃo] *sm* (*tessuto*) ticking; (*struttura*) truss; (*graticcio*) trellis.

**tram** [tram] *sm invar* tram.

**trama** ['trama] *sf* (*tessile*) weft; (*fig*) plot. **tramare** *v* plot.

**tramandare** [traman'dare] *v* hand down.

**trambusto** [tram'busto] *sm* turmoil.

**tramezzare** [tramed'dzare] *v* interpose; (*dividere un locale*) partition (off). **tramezzo** *sm* partition.

**tramite** ['tramite] *sm* means *pl*; intermediary. *prep* (*per mezzo di*) through.

**tramontana** [tramon'tana] *sf* (*nord*) north; (*vento*) north wind.

**tramontare** [tramon'tare] *v* set; (*aver fine*) come to an end; (*dileguarsi*) wane. **tramonto** *sm* sunset; (*fig*) decline.

**tramortire** [tramor'tire] *v* stun.

**trampolino** [trampo'lino] *sm* springboard; (*piscina*) diving-board; (*palestra*) trampoline; (*sci*) ski-jump.

**trampolo** ['trampolo] *sm* stilt.

**tramutare** [tramu'tare] *v* transform.

**trancia** ['trantʃa] *sf* (*taglierina*) cutter; (*gastr*) slice.

**tranello** [tra'nɛllo] *sm* trap; (*fig*) catch.

**trangugiare** [trangu'dʒare] *v* gulp down; (*fig*) swallow.

**tranne** ['tranne] *prep* except *or* but (for).

**tranquillo** [tran'kwillo] *agg* quiet, calm. **stare tranquillo** keep quiet or calm; (*non turbarsi*) not worry. **tranquillità** *sf* calm. **tranquillante** *sm* tranquillizer.

**transatlantico** [transat'lantiko] *agg* transatlantic. *sm* ocean liner.

**transazione** [transa'tsjone] *sf* (*comm*) transaction; (*dir*) settlement.

**transistor** [tran'sistor] *sm invar* transistor.

**transitivo** [transi'tivo] *agg* transitive.

**transito** ['transito] *sm* transit. **transito interrotto** road closed. **transitabile** *agg* practicable. **transitorio** *agg* transitory; (*fis*) transient.

**transizione** [transi'tsjone] *sf* transition.

**tranvai** [tran'vaj] *sm* tram. **tranvia** *sf* tramway.

**trapanare** [trapa'nare] *v* drill. **trapanatrice** *sf* drill. **trapanatura** *sf* drilling. **trapano** *sm* drill.

**trapassare** [trapas'sare] *v* run through; pass. **trapassato** *sm* past perfect. **trapasso** *sm* passing; transition; (*dir*) transfer.

**trapelare** [trape'lare] *v* leak out.

**trapezio** [tra'pɛtsjo] *sm* (*geom*) trapezium; (*sport*) trapeze. **trapezista** *s(m+f)* trapeze artist.

**trapiantare** [trapjan'tare] *v* transplant. **trapianto** *sm* transplant; (*agric*) transplantation.

**trappola** ['trappola] *sf* trap, snare.

**trapuntare** [trapun'tare] *v* quilt; (*ricamare*) embroider. **trapunta** *sf* quilt.

***trarre** ['trarre] *v* draw. **trarre in inganno** deceive. **trarre in tentazione** lead into temptation.

**trasalire** [trasa'lire] *v* jump.

**trasandato** [trazan'dato] *agg* untidy.

***trascendere** [tra'ʃɛndere] *v* transcend.

**trascinare** [traʃi'nare] *v* drag; (*fig*) carry away.

***trascorrere** [tras'korrere] *v* spend; (*tempo*) pass.

***trascrivere** [tras'krivere] *v* transcribe.

**trascrizione** sf transcription.

**trascurare** [trasku'rare] v neglect; (omettere) fail. **trascurato** agg neglected; (noncurante) careless; (sciatto) slovenly.

**trasferire** [trasfe'rire] v transfer. **trasferirsi** v (traslocare) move. **trasferibile** agg transferable. **trasferimento** sm transfer.

**trasferta** sf (sport) away match; (viaggio) business trip; (indennità) travelling expenses pl.

**trasformare** [trasfor'mare] v transform; (cambiare) change. **trasformare in** turn into. **trasformatore** sm transformer. **trasformazione** sf transformation.

**trasfusione** [trasfu'zjone] sf (med) transfusion.

**trasgredire** [trazgre'dire] v disobey; (legge) infringe. **trasgressione** sf infringement.

**traslocare** [trazlo'kare] v move; (impiegato) transfer. **trasloco** sm, pl -chi move; transfer.

**\*trasmettere** [traz'mettere] v transmit; (communicare, dir) convey; (radio) broadcast. **trasmettitore** sm transmitter; (malattia) carrier. **trasmissione** sf transmission; broadcast. **trasmittente** sf transmitter.

**trasmodato** [trazmo'dato] agg excessive.

**trasognato** [traso'ɲato] agg dreamy.

**trasparente** [traspa'rɛnte] agg transparent. sm transparency. **trasparenza** sf transparency.

**trasparire** [traspa'rire] v show through; (alla luce) shine through; (palesarsi) appear.

**traspirare** [traspi'rare] v transpire.

**trasportare** [traspor'tare] v carry; (trascinare) transport, carry away. **trasportatore** sm carrier; (tec) conveyor. **trasporto** sm transport; (comm) carriage; (inoltro) forwarding; (per nave) shipping.

**trastullare** [trastul'lare] v amuse. **trastullo** sm amusement; (fig) plaything.

**trasudare** [trasu'dare] v ooze.

**trasversale** [trazver'sale] agg transverse.

**trasvolare** [trazvo'lare] v fly across; (fig) barely touch.

**tratta** ['tratta] sf (comm) draft; (traffico illecito) trade.

**trattare** [trat'tare] v treat, deal with, handle. **si tratta di ...** it is about ..., it is a question of ... . **trattabile** agg negotiable; (persona) tractable. **trattamento** sm treatment. **trattativa** sf negotiation. **trattato**

sm (opera) treatise; (dir) treaty.

**tratteggiare** [tratted'dʒare] v hatch; (abbozzare) outline.

**\*trattenere** [tratte'nere] v (far rimanere) keep (back); (frenare) restrain, hold back; (detrarre) withhold. **trattenersi** v (restare) stay; restrain oneself. **trattenimento** sm reception; (spettacolo) show.

**tratto** ['tratto] agg drawn. sm stroke; (elemento caratteristico) feature; (frazione) stretch; (brano) passage. **a tratti** at times. **di tratto in tratto** every now and then. **d'un tratto** all of a sudden.

**trattore** [trat'tore] sm tractor.

**trattoria** [tratto'ria] sf restaurant.

**traudire** [trau'dire] v mishear.

**trauma** ['trauma] sm trauma. **traumatico** agg traumatic.

**travagliare** [trava'ʎare] v torment. **travaglio** sm torment; (angoscia) distress. **travaglio di parto** labour.

**travasare** [trava'zare] v decant.

**trave** ['trave] sf beam; (di tetto) rafter; (di soffitto) joist. **fare una trave di ogni fuscello** make a mountain out of a molehill.

**traversare** [traver'sare] v cross; (da parte a parte) go through. **traversata** sf crossing. **traversina** sf sleeper.

**traverso** [tra'vɛrso] agg cross, transverse. sm breadth, width. **andare di traverso** (cibo) go down the wrong way. **a traverso** sideways on. **guardare di traverso** look askance at. **prendere di traverso** take the wrong way.

**travestire** [traves'tire] v disguise. **travestito, -a** sm, sf (psic) transvestite.

**traviare** [travi'are] v lead astray. **traviamento** sm straying; corruption.

**travisare** [travi'zare] v distort. **travisamento** sm distortion.

**\*travolgere** [tra'voldʒere] v sweep away; (investire) knock down; (fig) overwhelm. **travolgente** agg sweeping; overwhelming.

**trazione** [tra'tsjone] sf traction; (auto) drive.

**tre** [tre] agg, sm three.

**trebbiare** [treb'bjare] v thresh. **trebbia** or **trebbiatrice** sf threshing machine. **trebbiatura** sf threshing.

**treccia** ['trettʃa] sf braid, plait. **farsi le trecce** plait one's hair.

**tredici** ['treditʃi] agg, sm thirteen. **tredice-**

**simo** *sm, agg* thirteenth.

**tregua** ['trɛgwa] *sf* truce; (*riposo*) rest. **senza tregua** unremitting; without respite; (*senza sosta*) non-stop.

**tremare** [tre'mare] *v* tremble; (*di freddo*) shiver; (*per emozioni*) shudder. **la tremarella** *sf* (*fam*) the shivers *pl*.

**tremendo** [tre'mɛndo] *agg* terrible, dreadful.

**trementina** [tremen'tina] *sf* turpentine.

**tremito** ['trɛmito] *sm* shaking, shudder(ing).

**tremolare** [tremo'lare] *v* quiver; (*stelle*) twinkle; (*luce*) flicker.

**tremore** [tre'more] *sm* tremor; (*agitazione*) trembling.

**treno** ['trɛno] *sm* train. **treno accelerato/diretto/direttissimo/rapido** slow/fast/through/express train. **treno di gomme/ruote** set of tyres/wheels.

**trenta** ['trenta] *sm, agg* thirty. **trentesimo** *sm, agg* thirtieth.

**trepidare** [trepi'dare] *v* be anxious.

**trespolo** ['trespolo] *sm* trestle; (*sgabello*) stool.

**triangolo** [tri'angolo] *sm* triangle. **triangolare** *agg* triangular.

**tribolare** [tribo'lare] *v* suffer; (*far soffrire*) torment. **vita tribolata** *sf* hard life.

**tribordo** [tri'bordo] *sm* starboard.

**tribù** [tri'bu] *sf* tribe. **membro di tribù** *sm* tribesman.

**tribuna** [tri'buna] *sf* platform; (*palco riservato*) gallery; (*campo sportivo*) stand; (*coperta*) grandstand.

**tribunale** [tribu'nale] *sm* court.

**tributo** [tri'buto] *sm* tribute. **tributare** *v* render. **tributario** *agg* (*tributi*) tax; (*fiume*) tributary.

**tricheco** [tri'keko] *sm* walrus.

**triciclo** [tri'tʃiklo] *sm* tricycle.

**tricolore** [triko'lore] *sm, agg* tricolour.

**tric-trac** ['tric'trac] *sm invar* backgammon.

**tridimensionale** [tridimensjo'nale] *agg* three-dimensional.

**trifoglio** [tri'fɔʎʎo] *sm* clover.

**triglia** ['triʎa] *sf* red mullet. **far l'occhio di triglia** (*fam*) make sheep's eyes.

**trigonometria** [trigonome'tria] *sf* trigonometry.

**trillare** [tril'lare] *v* trill. **trillo** *sm* trill.

**trilogia** [trilo'dʒia] *sf* trilogy.

**trimestre** [tri'mɛstre] *sm* quarter; (*scolastico*) term. **trimestrale** *agg* quarterly.

**trina** ['trina] *sf* lace.

**trincare** [trin'kare] *v* drink.

**trincea** [trin'tʃɛa] *sf* (*mil*) trench; (*ferr*) cutting. **trincerare** *v* entrench. **trinceramento** *sm* entrenchment.

**trinciare** [trin'tʃare] *v* cut up; (*pollo, ecc.*) carve; (*in strisce sottili*) shred. **trinciato** *sm* (*tabacco*) shag.

**trinità** [trini'ta] *sf* trinity.

**trio** ['trio] *sm* trio.

**trionfare** [trion'fare] *v* triumph. **trionfale** *agg* triumphal. **trionfante** *agg* triumphant. **trionfo** *sm* triumph; success.

**triplice** ['triplitʃe] *agg* threefold. **in triplice copia** in triplicate. **triplo** *agg* treble, triple; (*di tre parti*) threefold. **il triplo** *sm* three times as much.

**tripode** ['tripode] *sm* tripod.

**trippa** ['trippa] *sf* tripe.

**tripudiare** [tripu'djare] *v* rejoice. **tripudio** *sm* jubilation.

**triste** ['triste] *agg* sad. **tristezza** *sf* sadness.

**tristo** ['tristo] *agg* (*malvagio*) wicked; (*meschino*) mean.

**tritare** [tri'tare] *v* grind; (*carne*) mince. **carne tritata** *sf* mince. **tritacarne** *sm invar* mincer. **trito** *agg* chopped, ground, minced; (*fig*) trite.

**tritatutto** [trita'tutto] *sm; f* food processor.

**trittico** ['trittiko] *sm* triptych.

**trivellare** [trivel'lare] *v* drill, bore. **trivella** *sf* auger; (*succhiello*) gimlet; (*miniera*) drill. **trivellazione** *sf* drilling, boring.

**triviale** [tri'vjale] *agg* vulgar; (*banale*) trivial. **trivialità** *sf* vulgarity; triviality.

**trofeo** [tro'fɛo] *sm* trophy.

**trogolo** ['trɔgolo] *sm* trough.

**troia** ['trɔja] *sf* (*volg*) (*scrofa*) sow; (*prostituta*) whore. **troiaio** *sm* pigsty. **troiata** *sf* (*lavoro mal fatto*) awful mess; (*azione sudicia*) dirty trick.

**tromba** ['tromba] *sf* trumpet; (*mil*) bugle; (*auto*) horn; (*ascensore, scale*) well; (*anat*) tube. **tromba d'aria** tornado. **trombetta** *sm* trumpeter; (*trombettiere*) bugler. **trombone** *sm* trombone. **trombonista** *s(m+f)* trombonist.

**trombosi** [trom'bɔzi] *sf* thrombosis.

**troncare** [tron'kare] **v** cut off; (*spezzare*, *fig*) break off.

**tronco¹** ['tronko] **agg** cut off, broken off; (*mat*, *parole*) truncated.

**tronco²** ['tronko] **sm** trunk; (*tratto*) section; (*arch*) shaft.

**tronfio** ['tronfjo] **agg** puffed up, pompous.

**trono** ['trono] **sm** throne.

**tropico** ['tropiko] **sm** tropic. **tropicale** **agg** tropical.

**troppo** ['troppo] **agg** too much; (*pl*) too many. **avv** too much; (*con agg e avv*) too.

**trota** ['trota] **sf** trout.

**trottare** [trot'tare] **v** trot. **trotto** **sm** trot; (*andatura svelta*) brisk pace. **andare al piccolo trotto** jog-trot. **rompere il trotto** break into a gallop. **trotterellare** **v** jog (along); (*bambini*) toddle (along).

**trottola** ['trottola] **sf** (spinning) top.

**trovare** [tro'vare] **v** find. **andare a trovare** go to see, call on. **trovare in fallo** catch red-handed. **trovarsi** **v** (*essere*) be; (*per caso*) happen to be; (*sentirsi*) get on; (*incontrarsi*) meet; (*pensare*) think. **trovata** **sf** good idea; expedient. **trovata pubblicitaria** publicity stunt. **trovatello, -a** **sm**, **sf** foundling.

**truccare** [truk'kare] **v** make up; (*falsificare*) doctor; (*auto*) soup up; (*sport*) fix. **truccarsi** **v** disguise oneself; (*imbellettarsi*) put make-up on. **truccatore, -trice** **sm**, **sf** make-up artist. **truccatura** **sf** (*teatro*) making-up; (*belletto*, *ecc.*) make-up. **trucco** **sm** make-up; (*inganno*) trick.

**truce** [trutʃe] **agg** grim.

**truciolo** ['trutʃolo] **sm** (wood) chip, shaving.

**truffare** [truf'fare] **v** cheat, swindle; (*dir*) defraud. **truffa** **sf** swindle; (*dir*) fraud. **truffatore, -trice** **sm**, **sf** swindler, cheat.

**truppa** ['truppa] **sf** troop; (*fig*) horde.

**tu** [tu] **pron** you. **a tu per tu** face to face.

**tuba** ['tuba] **sf** (*musica*) tuba; (*cappello*) top-hat; (*anat*) tube.

**tubare** [tu'bare] **v** coo.

**tubercolosi** [tuberko'lɔzi] **sf** tuberculosis.

**tubo** ['tubo] **sm** pipe, tube; (*flessibile*) hose(-pipe); (*anat*) canal. **tubazione** **sf** piping. **tubetto** **sm** tube. **tubolare** **agg** tubular.

**tuffare** [tuf'fare] **v** plunge, dip. **tuffarsi** **v** plunge; (*fare un tuffo*) dive. **tuffo** **sm** dive.

**tulipano** [tuli'pano] **sm** tulip.

**tumefatto** [tume'fatto] **agg** swollen.

**tumore** [tu'more] **sm** tumour.

**tumulto** [tu'multo] **sm** uproar; (*sommossa*) riot. **tumultuoso** **agg** tumultuous; (*chiassoso*) rowdy.

**tunica** ['tunika] **sf** tunic.

**tuo** ['tuo], **m pl tuoi** **agg** your. **pron** yours.

**tuono** ['twɔno] **sm** thunder. **tuonare** **v** thunder.

**tuorlo** ['twɔrlo] **sm** yolk.

**turare** [tu'rare] **v** plug; (*con sughero*) cork. **turarsi il naso** hold one's nose. **turacciolo** **sm** stopper; (*di sughero*) cork; (*botte*) bung.

**turba** ['turba] **sf** mob.

**turbante** [tur'bante] **sm** turban.

**turbare** [tur'bare] **v** trouble; disturb; (*sconvolgere*) upset. **turbarsi** **v** get upset. **turbamento** **sm** disturbance, anxiety.

**turbina** [tur'bina] **sf** turbine.

**turbine** ['turbine] **sm** whirl; (*neve*, *sabbia*) storm; (*fig*) (seething) horde. **turbine di vento** whirlwind. **turbolento** **agg** turbulent; (*inquieto*) unruly.

**turchese** [tur'keze] **s**(*m+f*), **agg** turquoise.

**Turchia** [tur'kia] **sf** Turkey. **turco, -a** **sm**, **agg** Turkish; **sm**, **sf** (*persona*) Turk. **bestemmiare come un turco** swear like a trooper. **fumare come un turco** smoke like a chimney. **parlare (in) turco** (*fam*) talk double Dutch.

**turchino** [tur'kino] **agg**, **sm** deep blue.

**turismo** [tu'rizmo] **sm** tourism; (*culturale*) sight-seeing. **fare del turismo** tour, travel. **turista** **s**(*m+f*) tourist; sightseer.

**turlupinare** [turlupi'nare] **v** swindle; (*fam*) take in.

**turno** ['turno] **sm** (*volta*) turn; (*lavoro*) shift; (*mil*) guard. **essere di turno** be on duty. **fare a turno** take turns. **lavoro a turni** **sm** shift-work.

**turpe** ['turpe] **agg** foul. **turpiloquio** **sm** foul language.

**tuta** ['tuta] **sf** overalls **pl**; (*sport*) tracksuit.

**tutela** [tu'tɛla] **sf** defence; (*dir*) guardianship, protection. **tutelare** **v** protect; (*salvaguardare*) safeguard.

**tuttavia** [tutta'via] **cong** nevertheless.

**tutto** ['tutto] **agg** all; (*intero*) the whole (of); (*pl*) every. **pron** everything; (*pl*) everybody **sing**. **avv** completely. **a tutta velocità** at full speed. **il tutto** the whole (thing), everything. **innanzi tutto** first of all. **in tutti i modi** anyhow. **noi tutti** all of us. **tutt'ad un tratto** all of a sudden. **tutt'altro** anything but. **tutti e due** both (of them). **tutti i giorni** every day. **una volta per tutte** once and for all.

**tuttora** [tut'tora] *avv* still.

# U

**ubbia** [ub'bia] *sf* silly idea; prejudice.

**ubbidire** [ubbi'dire] *v* obey; (*essere ubbidiente*) be obedient; (*dar retta*) listen (to). **ubbidiente** *agg* obedient. **ubbidienza** *sf* obedience.

**ubriacare** [ubria'kare] *v* make drunk, intoxicate. **ubriacarsi** *v* get drunk. **ubriachezza** *sf* drunkenness. **ubriaco, -a** *s, agg, m pl* -**chi** drunk. **ubriaco fradicio** dead drunk.

**uccello** [ut'tʃɛllo] *sm* bird.

**\*uccidere** [ut'tʃidere] *v* kill; (*assassinare*) murder. **uccisione** *sf* killing; murder. **ucciso** *agg* killed; murdered. **uccisore** *sm* killer; murderer.

**\*udire** [u'dire] *v* hear. **udibile** *agg* audible. **udienza** *sf* hearing; (*formale*) audience. **uditivo** *agg* (*fis*) audible; (*med*) auditory. **udito** *sm* hearing. **uditore, -trice** *sm, sf* listener. **uditorio** *sm* audience.

**Ucraina** [ukra'ina] *sf* Ukraine. **ucraino, -a** *s, agg* Ukrainian.

**uffa** ['uffa] *inter* **uffa, che noia!** what a bore!

**ufficiale** [uffi'tʃale] *agg* official. *sm* officer. **ufficiale di stato civile** registrar.

**ufficio** [uffi'tʃo] *sm* office; (*dovere, compito*) duty. **d'ufficio** official; (*ufficialmente*) officially; (*in veste ufficiale*) ex officio. **ufficio di collocamento** employment exchange. **ufficioso** *agg* unofficial.

**ufo** ['ufo] *avv* **a ufo** for nothing. **mangiare a ufo** scrounge a meal.

**uggia** ['uddʒa] *sf* boredom. **avere in uggia** dislike. **prendere in uggia** take a dislike to. **uggioso** *agg* boring.

**uggiolare** [uddʒo'lare] *v* whine.

**ugola** ['ugola] *sf* (*anat*) uvula; (*fig*) voice.

**uguagliare** [ugwa'ʎare] *v* (*essere uguale*) equal; (*rendere uguale*) equalize, even out; (*livellare*) level. **uguaglianza** *sf* equality.

**uguale** [u'gwale] *agg also* **eguale** the same; uniform; (*mat*) equal. *sm* equal. **ugualmente** *avv* equally; uniformly; (*tuttavia*) just *or* all the same.

**ulcera** ['ultʃera] *sf* ulcer.

**uliva** [u'liva] *V* **oliva**.

**ulteriore** [ulte'rjore] *agg* further. **ulteriormente** *avv* further; (*più avanti*) farther on; (*in seguito*) subsequently.

**ultimo** ['ultimo], **-a** *agg* last; (*più recente*) latest; (*fondamentale*) ultimate. *sm, sf* last. **all'ultimo** at the end; (*in fine*) finally. **fino all'ultimo** to the very end. **ultimamente** *avv also* **negli ultimi tempi** lately. **ultimare** *v* finish. **ultimatum** *sm invar* ultimatum. **ultimazione** *sf* completion.

**ultrasensibile** [ultrasen'sibile] *agg* hypersensitive.

**ultrasonico** [ultra'sɔniko] *agg* supersonic.

**ultrasuono** [ultra'zwɔno] *sm* ultrasound.

**ultravioletto** [ultravio'letto] *agg* ultraviolet.

**ululare** [ulu'lare] *v* howl. **ululato** *sm* howling; (*urlo*) howl.

**umanesimo** [uma'nɛzimo] *sm* humanism. **umanista** *s(m+f)* humanist. **umanistico** *agg* humanist.

**umano** [u'mano] *agg* human; (*compassionevole*) humane; (*comprensivo*) understanding. **umanità** *sf* humanity. **umanitario** *agg* humanitarian.

**umettare** [umet'tare] *v* moisten.

**umido** ['umido] *agg* damp; (*clima*) humid. *sm* dampness; humidity; (*gastr*) stew. **cuocere in umido** stew. **umidità** *sf* dampness; humidity.

**umile** ['umile] *agg* humble. **umiltà** *sf* (*virtù, sentimento*) humility; (*qualità*) humbleness.

**umiliare** [umi'ljare] *v* humiliate, humble. **umiliazione** *sf* humiliation.

**umore** [u'more] *sm* (*disposizione*) mood; (*indole*) temperament; (*liquido*) humour. **essere di buon/cattivo umore** be in a good/bad mood; (*abitualmente*) be good-/bad-tempered. **umorismo** *sm* humour. **umorista** *s(m+f)* humorist. **umoristico** *agg* humorous; (*spiritoso*) witty.

**un** [un] *V* **uno**.

**unanime** [u'nanime] *agg* unanimous. **unanimità** *sf* unanimity. **all'unanimità** unanimously.

**uncino** [un'tʃino] *sm* hook. **uncinare** *v*

hook. **croce uncinata** *sf* swastika.
**uncinetto** *sm* crochet-hook. **lavorare
all'uncinetto** crochet.

**undici** ['unditʃi] *agg, sm* eleven. **undicesimo** *sm, agg* eleventh.

*****ungere** ['undʒere] *v* grease; (*rel*) anoint.

**Ungheria** [unge'ria] *sf* Hungary. **ungherese**
*s(m+f)*, *agg* Hungarian.

**unghia** ['ungja] *sf* nail; (*artiglio*) claw; (*minima distanza*) hair's breadth. **unghie** *sf pl*
(*fig*) clutches *pl*. **unghiata** *sf* scratch; (*temperino*) indentation.

**unguento** [un'gwento] *sm* ointment.

**unico** ['uniko] *agg* only; (*esclusivo*) sole;
(*senza pari*) unique; (*enfatico*) one and only.
**unicamente** *avv* only.

**unicorno** [uni'kɔrno] *sm* unicorn.

**unificare** [unifi'kare] *v* unify; (*fondere*)
merge; standardize. **unificazione** *sf* union;
merger; standardization.

**uniforme** [uni'fɔrme] *sf, agg* uniform. **uniformare** *v* (*adattare*) bring into line (with);
(*render piano*) level out; standardize. **uni-
formarsi** *v* comply (with); adapt (to). **uniformità** *sf* uniformity; (*di superficie*)
evenness; (*accordo*) agreement.

**unione** [un'njone] *sf* union; (*concordia*) unity.

**Unione Europea** [un'njone euro'pea] *sf*
European Union.

**unire** [u'nire] *v* join; (*fig*) unite. **unirsi** *v*
join; (*insieme con altri*) join up with.

**unità** [uni'ta] *sf* unity; (*misura, mil*) unit.
**unità di misura** measure.

**unito** [u'nito] *agg* united; (*tinta*) plain. **uni-
tamente a** together with.

**università** [universi'ta] *sf* university. **universitario, -a** *sm, sf* university student.

**universo** [uni'verso] *sm* universe. **universale** *agg* universal.

**uno** ['uno] *agg* one, a. *art* a, an. *pron* one;
(*qualcuno*) someone. **fare un po' per uno**
share equally. **nè l'uno nè l'altro** neither.
**non me ne va bene una!** I can't get one
thing right! **tutt'uno** the same thing. **uno
a uno** one by one.

**unto** ['unto] *agg* (*cosparso di grasso*) greasy,
oily; (*spalmato*) greased, oiled; (*sporco*)
dirty. *sm* grease; (*gastr*) fat. **untuoso** *agg*
greasy; (*fig*) unctuous.

**uomo** ['wɔmo] *sm, pl* **uomini** man (*pl*
men). **l'uomo qualunque** the man in the
street. **uomo d'affari** businessman. **uomo**

**di fiducia** right-hand man. **uomo di spirito** wit.

**uopo** ['wɔpo] *sm* **all'uopo** (*a tale scopo*) for
this purpose; (*al momento opportuno*) at the
right moment. **essere d'uopo** be necessary.

**uovo** ['wɔvo] *sm, pl* **-a f** egg. **uovo al burro**
or **tegame** fried egg. **uovo alla coque**
boiled egg. **uovo in camicia** poached egg.
**uovo sodo/strapazzato**
hardboiled/scrambled egg.

**uragano** [ura'gano] *sm* hurricane;
(*tempesta*) storm.

**uranio** [u'ranjo] *sm* uranium.

**urbano** [ur'bano] *agg* (*di città*) town,
urban; (*cortese*) urbane. **nettezza urbana**
refuse collection. **urbanistica** *sf* town-
planning. **urbanista** *s(m+f)* town-planner.

**urgente** [ur'dʒente] *agg* urgent. **urgenza** *sf*
urgency. **aver urgenza di** need urgently.
**chiamata d'urgenza** *sf* emergency call.

**urgere** ['urdʒere] *v* (*sollecitare*) urge;
(*abbisognare*) be required urgently.

**urina** [u'rina] *sf* urine. **urinare** *v* urinate.
**urinario** *agg* urinary.

**urlare** [ur'lare] *v* scream; (*animali*) howl;
(*dire ad alta voce*) shout. **urlo** *sm, pl* **-a f**
shout; howl; scream.

**urna** ['urna] *sf* urn. **andare alle urne** go to
the polls.

**urrà** [ur'ra] *inter* hurrah!

**urtare** [ur'tare] *v* knock *or* bump (into);
(*dare uno spintone*) jostle; (*fig*) annoy.
**urtarsi** *v* (*scontrarsi*) clash; (*auto*) collide;
(*fig*) get irritated. **urto** *sm* (*spinta*) push;
(*scontro*) clash, collision.

**usare** [u'zare] *v* use; (*essere solito a*) be
accustomed to; (*essere di moda*) be fashionable; (*servirsi di*) make use of; (*fig*) exercise.
**usanza** *sf* custom; habit.

**uscio** ['uʃo] *sm* door. **mettere fuori
dell'uscio** turn out (of the house). **uscio
di casa** front door.

*****uscire** [u'ʃire] *v* leave; (*andar fuori*) go out;
(*venir fuori*) come out; (*scendere*) get off;
(*sboccare*) lead. **uscir di mente** slip one's
mind. **uscir di strada** go off the road.
**uscire in macchina** go for a drive. **uscita**
*sf* (*passaggio*) exit, way out; (*sbocco*) outlet;
(*motto di spirito*) witty remark; (*spesa*) outlay; (*a carte*) lead. **essere in libera uscita**
be off duty. **giorno di libera uscita** *sm*
day off. **uscita di sicurezza** emergency
exit.

**usignolo** [uzi'ɲɔlo] *sm* nightingale.

**uso** ['uzo] *sm* use; (*usanza*) custom; (*voga*) fashion. **c'è l'uso** it is customary. **uso e consumo** wear and tear. **usuale** *agg* usual; customary; common.

**ustionare** [ustjo'nare] *v* scald. **ustione** *sf* scald.

**usufruire** [uzufru'ire] *v* benefit (from).

**usura¹** [u'zura] *sf* usury. **a usura** with interest. **usuraio, -a** *sm, sf* usurer.

**usura²** [u'zura] *sf* (*tec*) wear. **resistente all'usura** hard-wearing.

**usurpare** [uzur'pare] *v* usurp. **usurpatore, -trice** *sm, sf* usurper.

**utensile** [u'tɛnsile] *sm* tool, utensil. **macchina utensile** *sf* machine tool.

**utente** [u'tɛnte] *s(m+f)* user.

**utero** ['utero] *sm* womb.

**utile** ['utile] *agg* useful; (*persona di aiuto*) helpful. **in tempo utile** in good time. **tornar utile** come in handy. *sm* profit. **utili** *sm pl* (*reddito*) income *sing*. **utilità** *sf* usefulness, use; profit. **utilizzare** *v* utilize. **utilizzazione** *sf* utilization.

**utopia** [uto'pia] *sf* utopia.

**uva** ['uva] *sf* grapes *pl*. **acino d'uva** *sm* grape. **uva secca** *or* **passa** raisins *pl*. **uva spina** gooseberry.

# V

**vacanza** [va'kantsa] *sf* holiday; (*l'essere vacante*) vacancy. **vacante** *agg* vacant.

**vacca** ['vakka] *sf* cow. **vaccata** *sf* (*volg*) rubbish. **vacchetta** *sf* (*cuoio*) cowhide.

**vaccinare** [vattʃi'nare] *v* vaccinate. **vaccinazione** *sf* vaccination. **vaccino** *sm* vaccine.

**vacillare** [vatʃil'lare] *v* totter; (*essere incerto*) waver.

**vagabondo** [vaga'bondo] **-a** *agg* roving. *sm, sf* vagrant; (*spreg*) loafer. **vagabondare** *v* wander (about).

**vagare** [va'gare] *v* stray.

**vagina** [va'dʒina] *sf* vagina.

**vagire** [va'dʒire] *v* wail. **vagito** *sm* wail(ing).

**vaglia¹** ['vaʎa] *sm invar* money order.

**vaglia postale** postal order.

**vaglia²** ['vaʎa] *sf* **di vaglia** of note.

**vagliare** [va'ʎare] *v* sift; (*argomenti, ecc.*) weigh (up). **vagliatura** *sf* sifting; (*esame attento*) careful consideration. **vaglio** *sm* sieve; close examination.

**vago** ['vago] *agg* vague. **vaghezza** *sf* vagueness.

**vagone** [va'gone] *sm* (*per passeggeri*) carriage; (*per merci*) wagon. **vagone letto/ristorante** sleeping-/dining-car.

**vaiolo** [va'jɔlo] *sm* smallpox.

**valanga** [va'langa] *sf* avalanche; (*fig*) shower.

**valente** [va'lɛnte] *agg* skilled, clever.

**\*valere** [va'lere] *v* (*aver valore*) be worth; (*aver merito*) be good; (*aver forza legale*) apply; (*esser regolare*) be valid; (*contare*) count; (*essere utile*) be of use; (*importare*) matter. **far valere** assert. **farsi valere** demand respect; (*imporsi*) assert oneself. **vale a dire** that is to say. **tanto vale** one might as well. **valere la pena** be worth it. **valere un occhio della testa** be worth a fortune.

**valevole** [va'levole] *agg* valid.

**valicare** [vali'kare] *v* cross. **valico** *sm, pl* **-chi** pass; crossing.

**valido** ['valido] *agg* valid; (*efficace*) effective; (*forte*) strong. **validità** *sf* validity.

**valigia** [va'lidʒa] *sf* suitcase. **far le valigie** pack. **valigeria** *sf* (*merce*) travel goods *pl*.

**valle** ['valle] *sf also* **vallata** valley. **a valle di** below. **scendere a valle** go downhill. **vallone** *sm* deep valley; (*depressione*) gorge.

**valletto** [val'letto] *sm* page; assistant.

**valore** [va'lore] *sm* value; (*pregio*) worth; validity; (*significato*) meaning; (*coraggio*) valour. **aver valore di** amount to. **carte valori** *sf pl* securities *pl*. **di valore** of value, valuable; (*professionista*) leading. **imposta di valore aggiunto (IVA)** valued added tax (VAT). **privo di valore** worthless; of no value. **valori** *sm pl* valuables *pl*.

**valorizzare** [valorid'dzare] *v* exploit; (*mettere in evidenza*) make the most of. **valorizzazione** *sf* exploitation.

**valuta** [va'luta] *sf* currency.

**valutare** [valu'tare] *v* value; (*calcolare*) estimate; (*tenere in considerazione*) rate; (*vagliare*) weigh. **valutazione** *sf* evaluation; estimation; (*calcolo approssimativo*) estimate.

**valvola** ['valvola] *sf* valve; (*elett*) fuse. **valvola di sicurezza** safety-valve.

**valzer** ['valtser] *sm invar* waltz.

**vampa** ['vampa] *sf* blaze; (*arrossamento*) flush. **vampata** *sf* blaze; (*fig*) burst; flush; (*al viso*) blush.

**vampiro** [vam'piro] *sm* vampire.

**vandalo** ['vandalo] *sm* vandal. **vandalismo** *sm* vandalism.

**vaneggiare** [vaned'dʒare] *v* rave.

**vanesio** [va'nɛzjo] *agg* fatuous, vain.

**vangare** [van'gare] *v* dig (over). **vanga** *sf* spade.

**vangelo** [van'dʒɛlo] *sm* gospel.

**vaniglia** [va'niʎa] *sf* vanilla.

**vanità** [vani'ta] *sf* vanity. **vanitoso** *agg* vain.

**vano** ['vano] *agg* vain. *sm* (*locale*) room; (*spazio*) space. **rendere vano** make useless. **riuscir vano** be unsuccessful.

**vantaggio** [van'taddʒo] *sm* advantage; (*sport*) lead, handicap; profit. **vantaggiare** *v* favour. **vantaggioso** *agg* advantageous.

**vantare** [van'tare] *v* boast (of). **vantarsi** *v* boast, brag. **vantatore, -trice** *sm, sf* boaster, braggart. **vanteria** *sf* boasting, bragging. **vanto** *sm* (*vanteria*) boasting, bragging; (*atto*) boast.

**vanvera** ['vanvera] *sf* **a vanvera** (*senza riflettere*) without thinking; (*a casaccio*) at random.

**vapore** [va'pore] *sm* steam; (*nave*) steamer. **a tutto vapore** full steam ahead. **vaporizzare** *v* vaporize. **vaporizzatore** *sm* vaporizer; (*profumi*) atomizer.

**varare** [va'rare] *v* launch. **varo** *sm* launch(ing).

**varcare** [var'kare] *v* cross; (*eccedere*) go beyond. **varco** *sm* opening. **aspettare al varco** lie in wait (for).

**variare** [va'rjare] *v* change; (*esser diverso*) vary. (**tanto**) **per variare** (just) for a change. **variare d'aspetto** look different. **variabile** *sf, agg* variable. **variabilità** *sf* variability. **variante** *sf* variant. **variato** *agg* varied. **variazione** *sf* variation.

**varicella** [vari'tʃella] *sf* chicken-pox.

**varicoso** [vari'kozo] *agg* varicose.

**varietà** [varje'ta] *sf* variety. *sm* (*teatro*) variety.

**vario** ['varjo] *agg* (*variato*) varied; (*diverso*) various, different; (*non regolare*) variable.

**variopinto** *agg* multicoloured. **vari** *pron pl* various people *pl*, several people *pl*.

**vasca** ['vaska] *sf* basin; (*da bagno*) bathtub; (*tino*) vat; (*piscina*) (swimming-) pool. **fare una vasca** (*sport*) swim a length.

**vascello** [va'ʃello] *sm* vessel, warship. **ufficiale di vascello** *sm* naval officer.

**vasellame** [vazel'lame] *sm* crockery; (*di metallo prezioso*) plate; (*di porcellana*) china; (*di vetro*) glassware.

**vaso** ['vazo] *sm* pot; (*per fiori recisi*) vase; (*anat*) vessel. **vaso da fiori** flower-pot. **vaso da notte** chamber-pot. **vasaio, -a** *sm*, *sf* potter.

**vassoio** [vas'sojo] *sm* tray; (*del muratore*) mortar-board.

**vasto** ['vasto] *agg* wide, vast. **vastità** *sf* vastness.

**Vaticano** [vati'kano] *sm* Vatican. **città del Vaticano** *sf* Vatican City.

**vaticinio** [vati'tʃinjo] *sm* prediction. **vaticinare** *v* predict.

**ve** [ve] *V* **vi**.

**vecchio** ['vekkjo] *agg* old. *sm* old man. **vecchia** *sf* old woman. **vecchiaia** *sf* old age. **vecchiotto** *agg* oldish, fairly old; (*fuori moda*) out-of-date.

**vece** ['vetʃe] *sf* **fare le veci di** take the place of. **in mia vece** in my place.

*****vedere** [ve'dere] *v* see. **avere a che vedere con** have to do with. **dare a vedere** let it be understood. **far vedere** show. **non vederci più** (*fam*) be furious. **non veder l'ora di** look forward to. **stare a vedere** (*attendere*) see; (*guardare*) watch; (*scommettere*) bet. **vedere di buon occhio** approve (of). **vediamo un po'** let's see *sm*. **a mio vedere** in my opinion.

**vedetta** [ve'detta] *sf* look-out.

**vedova** ['vedova] *sf* widow. **vedovo** *sm* widower. **rimaner vedova** or **vedovo** be widowed. **vedovanza** *sf* widowhood.

**veemente** [vee'mɛnte] *agg* vehement.

**vegetale** [vedʒe'tale] *agg, sm* vegetable. **vegetariano, -a** *agg* vegetarian. **vegetativo** *agg* vegetative. **vegetazione** *sf* vegetation.

**vegetare** [vedʒe'tare] *v* vegetate. **vegeto** *agg* flourishing. **vivo e vegeto** alive and kicking.

**vegliare** [ve'ʎare] *v* (*vigilare*) watch; (*fare la veglia*) keep watch; (*star sveglio*) stay up. **veglia** *sf* watch, vigil; (*lo star desto*) wakefulness; (*festa*) party; (*funebre*) wake. **veglione** *sm* ball, party.

**veicolo** [ve'ikolo] *sm* vehicle; (*malattia*) carrier.

**vela** ['vela] *sf* sail; (*sport*) sailing. **a gonfie vele** booming. **barca a vela** *sf* sailing-boat. **volo a vela** *sm* gliding. **veleggiare** *v* sail; (*velivolo*) glide. **veliero** *sm* sailingship.

**velare** [ve'lare] *v* veil; cover; (*offuscare*) cloud, dim; (*suono*) muffle.

**veleno** [ve'leno] *sm* poison. **avere il veleno in corpo** (*fam*) have a chip on one's shoulder. **sputare veleno** (*fig*) vent one's spleen. **velenoso** *agg* poisonous; (*fig*) venomous.

**velino** [ve'lino] *agg* **carta velina** *sf* flimsy (paper). **velina** *sf* (*copia*) carbon copy.

**velivolo** [ve'livolo] *sm* aircraft; (*aliante*) glider.

**velleità** [vellei'ta] *sf* vain ambition.

**vellicare** [velli'kare] *v* titillate.

**vello** ['vello] *sm* fleece.

**velluto** [vel'luto] *sm* velvet. **di velluto** velvet. **vellutato** *agg* velvety.

**veloce** [ve'lotʃe] *agg* quick, fast. **velocista** *s(m+f)* sprinter. **velocità** *sf* speed; (*fis*) velocity. **eccedere la velocità** (*auto*) speed.

**velodromo** [ve'ɔdromo] *sm* cycle-track.

**veltro** ['veltro] *sm* greyhound.

**vena** ['vena] *sf* vein; (*fig*) talent; inspiration. **essere in vena** be in the mood.

**venale** [ve'nale] *agg* saleable; (*spreg*) mercenary.

**vendemmiare** [vendem'mjare] *v* harvest (grapes). **vendemmia** *sf* grape harvest.

**vendere** ['vendere] *v* sell. **aver ... da vendere** have ... to spare; have plenty of .... **vendere a contanti** sell for cash. **vendere al dettaglio** *or* **minuto** retail. **vendere all'asta** auction. **vendere all'ingrosso** sell wholesale. **vendere fumo** bluff. **vendibile** *agg* saleable; (*messo in vendita*) for sale.

**vendetta** [ven'detta] *sf* revenge; (*castigo meritato*) vengeance.

**vendicare** [vendi'kare] *v* avenge. **vendicarsi** take revenge. **vendicativo** *agg* vindictive.

**vendita** ['vendita] *sf* sale. **vendita a rate** hire-purchase. **venditore, -trice** *sm*, *sf* vendor; (*negoziante*) shopkeeper.

**venerare** [vene'rare] *v* revere; (*rel*) worship.

**venerabile** *agg* venerable. **venerazione** *sf* veneration.

**venerdì** [vener'di] *sm* Friday. **Venerdì Santo** Good Friday.

**venereo** [ve'nɛreo] *agg* venereal.

**Venezia** [ve'netsja] *sf* Venice. **veneziana** *sf* Venetian blind. **veneziano, -a** *s*, *agg* Venetian.

**veniale** [ve'njale] *agg* venial.

**\*venire** [ve'nire] *v* come; (*riuscire*) come out; (*essere*) be. **far venire** (*mandare a chiamare*) call, send for. **mi viene da ...** I feel like ... . **venire alle mani** come to blows. **venire incontro** come towards; (*incontrare*) meet; (*fig*) meet halfway. **venir meno** (*mancare*) be lacking; (*svenire*) pass out.

**ventaglio** [ven'taʎo] *sm* fan.

**venti** ['venti] *agg*, *sm* twenty. **ventesimo** *agg*, *sm* twentieth.

**ventilare** [venti'lare] *v* air; (*agric*) winnow. **ventilato** *agg* airy, ventilated. **ventilazione** *sf* ventilation.

**vento** ['vɛnto] *sm* wind.

**ventosa** [ven'toza] *sf* sucker.

**ventre** ['vɛntre] *sm* stomach; abdomen; (*forma*) belly; (*grembo materno*) womb. **ventrale** *agg* ventral.

**ventricolo** [ven'trikolo] *sm* ventricle.

**ventriloquo** [ven'trilokwo], **-a** *sm*, *sf* ventriloquist.

**ventura** [ven'tura] *sf* fortune. **alla ventura** at random. **andare** *or* **mettersi alla ventura** trust to luck; take a chance. **soldato di ventura** *sm* mercenary.

**venturo** [ven'turo] *agg* next.

**vera** ['vera] *sf* wedding ring.

**verace** [ve'ratʃe] *agg* (*veritiero*) truthful; (*vero*) true, real. **veracità** *sf* truthfulness.

**veranda** [ve'randa] *sf* veranda.

**verbale** [ver'bale] *sm* record, minutes *pl*. **mettere a verbale** put on record. *agg* verbal.

**verbo** ['vɛrbo] *sm* verb; (*parola*) word. **verboso** *agg* verbose, long-winded.

**verde** ['verde] *agg* green. *sm* green; (*natura*) greenery; (*zona*) green belt. **essere** *or* **trovarsi al verde** be broke. **verdastro** *agg* greenish. **verdeggiare** *v* be verdant; (*diventar verde*) turn green.

**verdetto** [ver'detto] *sm* verdict.

**verdura** [ver'dura] *sf* greens *pl*, vegetables *pl*.

**verga** ['verga] *sf* rod. **verga magica** magic wand. **vergare** *v* line; (*scrivere*) write.

**vergine** ['verdʒine] *sf, agg* virgin. **Vergine** *sf* Virgo. **verginale** *agg* virginal. **verginità** *sf* virginity.

**vergogna** [ver'goɲa] *sf* shame; (*disonore*) disgrace. **fare vergogna** shame. *inter* shame on you! **vergognarsi** *v* be *or* feel ashamed (of); (*non osare*) be too shy (to). **vergognoso** *agg* shameful; shy.

**verificare** [verifi'kare] *v* check. **verificarsi** *v* (*avvenire*) occur; (*avverarsi*) come true. **verifica** *sf* control; verification; (*dei conti*) audit. **verificabile** *agg* verifiable. **verificazione** *sf* verification, check; audit.

**verità** [veri'ta] *sf* truth; (*giustezza*) truthfulness. **veritiero** *agg* truthful.

**verme** ['verme] *sm* worm; (*larva di insetto*) maggot.

**vermiglio** [ver'miλo] *agg, sm* vermilion.

**vermut** ['vermut] *sm invar* vermouth.

**verniciare** [verni'tʃare] *v* paint; (*con vernice trasparente*) varnish; (*a smalto*) enamel. **vernice** *sf* varnish, lacquer; (*apparenza*) veneer; (*strato sottile*) film. **verniciata** *sf* coat of paint. **verniciatura** *sf* painting; varnishing.

**vero** ['vero] *agg* true; real. *sm* truth. **a onor del vero** to tell the truth. **di vero cuore** from the bottom of one's heart. **vero e proprio** out and out.

**verosimile** [vero'simile] *agg* likely. **aver del verosimile** be likely.

**verricello** [verri'tʃello] *sm* winch.

**verro** ['verro] *sm* boar.

**verruca** [ver'ruka] *sf* wart.

**versare** [ver'sare] *v* pour (out); (*rovesciare*) spill; (*spargere*) shed; (*pagare*) pay; (*trovarsi*) find oneself. **versamento** *sm* payment, deposit. **versante** *sm* side. **versato** *agg* paid (up); (*pratico*) skilled.

**versatile** [ver'satile] *agg* versatile. **versatilità** *sf* versatility.

**versione** [ver'sjone] *sf* version; (*traduzione*) translation.

**verso**[1] ['verso] *prep* towards; (*circa*) about. **verso il basso** down(wards). **verso l'alto** up(wards).

**verso**[2] ['verso] *sm* (*metrica*) verse; (*suono particolare*) sound; gesture; direction; (*modo*) means. **in verso antiorario** anticlockwise. **in verso orario** clockwise. **per**

**un verso o per un altro** in one way or another.

**vertebra** ['vertebra] *sf* vertebra (*pl* -brae). **vertebrato** *agg, sm* vertebrate.

**vertenza** [ver'tentsa] *sf* dispute; (*dir*) lawsuit.

**verticale** [verti'kale] *agg, sf* vertical.

**vertice** ['vertitʃe] *sm* summit; (*mat*) vertex.

**vertigini** [ver'tidʒini] *sf pl* dizziness *sing*; (*attacco*) dizzy spell *sing*; (*med*) vertigo *sing*. **aver le vertigini** feel dizzy *or* giddy. **vertiginoso** *agg* dizzy.

**vescica** [ve'ʃika] *sf* bladder; (*bolla cutanea*) blister.

**vescovo** ['veskovo] *sm* bishop. **vescovado** *sm* (*dignità*) bishopric; (*territorio*) diocese; (*palazzo*) bishop's palace. **vescovile** *agg* episcopal.

**vespa** ['vespa] *sf* wasp. **vespaio** *sm* wasps' nest.

**vestaglia** [ves'taλa] *sf* dressing-gown; (*vestaglietta*) housecoat.

**veste** ['veste] *sf* dress; (*rel*) vestment; (*fig*) capacity. **in veste di amico** as a friend. **in veste ufficiale** in an official capacity. **vestiario** *sm* wardrobe; (*indumenti*) clothes *pl*. **capo di vestiario** *sm* item of clothing.

**vestibolo** [ves'tibolo] *sm* vestibule, lobby.

**vestigio** [ves'tidʒo] *sm* trace.

**vestire** [ves'tire] *v* dress; (*indossare*) wear; (*detto di abiti*) fit. **vestirsi** *v* dress. **vestito** *sm* dress.

**veterano** [vete'rano], **-a** *s, agg* veteran.

**veterinario** [veteri'narjo] *agg* veterinary. *sm* veterinary surgeon, vet. **veterinaria** *sf* veterinary science.

**veto** ['veto] *sm invar* veto.

**vetro** ['vetro] *sm* glass; (*di finestra*) pane. **vetro smerigliato** frosted glass. **vetraio** *sm* glazier. **vetrata** *sf* (*porta*) glass door; (*finestra*) stained-glass window.

**vetta** ['vetta] *sf* top.

**vettore** [vet'tore] *sm* vector; (*comm*) carrier.

**vettovaglie** [vetto'vaλe] *sf pl* provisions *pl*.

**vettura** [vet'tura] *sf* carriage; (*auto*) car. **biglietto di vettura** *sm* (*comm*) bill of lading.

**vezzeggiare** [veddzed'dʒare] *v* fondle.

**vi** [vi], **ve** *pron* (to) you; (*riflessivo*) yourselves; (*reciproco*) each other. *avv* (*qui*) here; (*lì*) there.

**via**[1] ['via] *sf* way; (*strada*) street; (*sentiero*)

path. **in via di costruzione** under construction. **in via eccezionale** exceptionally. **per via aerea** by air. **per via di** (a causa di) because of. **via mare/terra** by sea/land.

**via²** ['via] avv away; (suvvia) come on. sm invar starting signal. **e così via** and so on. **va via!** go on! **via le mani!** hands off! **via** gradually; (a mano a mano) as.

**viabilità** [viabili'ta] sf road conditions pl.

**viadotto** [via'dotto] sm viaduct.

**viaggiare** [viad'dʒare] v travel; (veicoli) run; (essere trasportato) be carried. **viaggiatore, -trice** sm, sf traveller; passenger. **piccione viaggiatore** sm carrier pigeon.

**viaggio** [vi'addʒo] sm journey, trip. **mettersi in viaggio** set out or off. **viaggio d'andata/di ritorno** outward/return journey. **viaggio d'andata e ritorno** round trip. **viaggio di nozze** honeymoon.

**viale** [vi'ale] sm avenue.

**viandante** [vian'dante] s(m+f) wayfarer.

**viavai** [via'vaj] sm coming and going.

**vibrare** [vib'rare] v vibrate; (fig) quiver; (assestare) hurl. **vibrare un colpo** deal a blow. **vibrazione** sf vibration; (fremito) quiver.

**vicario** [vi'karjo] sm vicar.

**viceconsole** [vitʃe'kɔnsole] s(m+f) vice-consul.

**vicedirettore** [vitʃediret'tore], **-trice** sm, sf assistant manager; (scuola) deputy head.

**vicenda** [vi'tʃɛnda] sf event; succession. **vicendevolmente** avv also **a vicenda** (a turno) in turns; (scambievolmente) each other, one another.

**vicepresidente** [vitʃeprezi'dɛnte], **-essa** sm, sf vice-president, vice-chairman.

**viceversa** [vitʃe'vɛrsa] avv vice versa; (invece) but.

**vicinanza** [vitʃi'nantsa] sf vicinity.

**vicinato** [vitʃi'nato] sm neighbourhood.

**vicino** [vi'tʃino], **-a** agg near; (accanto) next; (confinante) neighbouring; (fig) close. avv close (by); near (by); (accanto a) beside, by. **da vicino** at close quarters. sm, sf neighbour. **vicino di casa** next-door neighbour.

**vicolo** ['vikolo] sm alley.

**video** ['video] sm invar (television) screen.

**videocamera** [video'kamra] sf camcorder.

**videocassetta** ['video kas'sɛtta] sf video cassette.

**videoregistratore** [videoreʒistra'tɔre] sm video recorder.

**vidimare** [vidi'mare] v certify. **vidimazione** sf certification.

**vietare** [vje'tare] v prohibit; (impedire) prevent. **vietato** agg forbidden. **ingresso vietato** no admission. **sosta vietata** no parking.

**vigente** [vi'dʒɛnte] agg current; (dir) in force.

**vigilare** [vidʒi'lare] v watch (over); keep a watch (on). **vigilante** agg watchful. **vigilanza** sf vigilance; (controllo) supervision; (urbana) police.

**vigile** ['vidʒile] agg watchful. sm policeman. **vigile del fuoco** fireman.

**vigilia** [vi'dʒilja] sf eve; (rel) vigil. **vigilia di Natale/Capodanno** Christmas/New Year's Eve.

**vigliacco** [vi'ʎakko] agg cowardly. sm, sf coward. **vigliaccheria** sf cowardice; cowardly action.

**vigna** ['viɲa] sf vineyard.

**vignetta** [vi'ɲetta] sf sketch; (umoristica) cartoon.

**vigore** [vi'gore] sm force; (forza vitale) vigour. **entrare in vigore** (dir) come into force. **vigoria** sf energy.

**vile** ['vile] agg (vigliacco) cowardly; (basso) base, low. s(m+f) coward. **vilipendio** sm contempt.

**villa** ['villa] sf villa. **villa di campagna** country house.

**villaggio** [vil'laddʒo] sm village.

**villano** [vil'lano], **-a** agg rude; (rozzo) uncouth; offensive. sm, sf lout, boor. **villania** sf rudeness.

**villeggiare** [villed'dʒare] v spend a holiday. **villeggiatura** sf holidays pl.

**viltà** [vil'ta] sf cowardice; cowardly action.

**viluppo** [vi'luppo] sm tangle.

**vimini** ['vimini] sm pl wicker sing. **di vimini** wicker. **lavoro in vimini** sm wickerwork.

**\*vincere** ['vintʃere] v win; (battere) beat; (sopraffare) overcome; (sconfiggere) defeat. **lasciarsi vincere (da)** yield (to). **vincita** sf win.

**vincitore** [vintʃi'tore], **-trice** sm, sf winner; (di battaglia) victor. agg winning, victorious.

**vincolare** [vinko'lare] v bind; (comm) tie up.

(*scherma*) mask.

**vino** ['vino] *sm* wine. **vino di mele** cider.
**vinicolo** *agg* wine.

**viola¹** [vi'ɔla] *sf* (*bot*) violet. *agg*, *sm invar* (*colore*) violet. **viola del pensiero** pansy.
**violacciocca** *sf* stock; (*gialla*) wallflower.
**violaceo** *agg* violet.

**viola²** [vi'ɔla] *sf* (*musica*) viola.

**violare** [vio'lare] *v* violate; (*una donna*) rape; (*domicilio*) break into. **violare l'ordine pubblico** cause a breach of the peace. **violazione** *sf* violation. **violazione carnale** rape. **violazione della pace** breach of the peace. **violazione di domicilio** house-breaking.

**violentare** [violen'tare] *v* force; (*una donna*) rape. **violentatore** *sm* rapist. **violento** *agg* violent. **violenza** *sf* violence.

**violetta** [vio'letta] *sf* violet. **violetto** *agg*, *sm invar* violet.

**violino** [vio'lino] *sm* violin. **violinista** *s(m+f)* violinist.

**violoncello** [violon'tʃɛllo] *sm* (violon)cello. **violoncellista** *s(m+f)* (violon)cellist.

**viottolo** [vi'ɔttolo] *sm* path.

**vipera** [vipera] *sf* viper.

**virale** [vi'rale] *agg* viral.

**virare** [vi'rare] *v* (*alare*) haul (in); (*mutar direzione*) veer, change course; (*aero*) turn.

**virgola** [virgola] *sf* comma; (*mat*) point. **tra virgolette** in inverted commas.

**virile** [vi'rile] *agg* virile; masculine; (*fig*) manly. **virilità** *sf* virility.

**virtù** [vir'tu] *sf* virtue; faculty. **in virtù di** by virtue of, in accordance with. **virtuale** *agg* virtual.

**virtuoso** [virtu'ozo], **-a** *agg* virtuous. *sm*, *sf* virtuoso.

**virulento** [viru'lɛnto] *agg* virulent.

**virus** ['virus] *sm invar* virus.

**viscere** [viʃere] *sm* internal organ. *sf pl* intestines *pl*; (*di animali*) entrails *pl*. **le viscere della terra** the bowels of the earth *pl*.

**vischio** [viskjo] *sm* mistletoe; (*estratto*) bird-lime; (*fig*) snare. **viscido** *agg* slimy.

**visconte** [vis'konte] *sm* viscount.

**viscoso** [vis'kozo] *agg* viscous. **viscosa** *sf* viscose. **viscosità** *sf* viscosity.

**visibile** [vi'zibile] *agg* visible. **andare/mandare in visibilio** go/send into raptures. **visibilità** *sf* visibility.

**visiera** [vi'zjera] *sf* visor; (*berretto*) peak;

**visione** [vi'zjone] *sf* sight; (*apparizione*) vision; idea; (*cinema*) showing. **prendere in visione** inspect. **ricevere in visione** receive on approval. **visionario, -a** *sm*, *sf* visionary.

**visita** ['vizita] *sf* visit; (*persona*) visitor; (*esame*) examination. **visita domiciliare** domiciliary visit; (*perquisizione*) house search. **visitare** *v* visit; (*andare a trovare*) call on; (*med*) examine. **visitatore, -trice** *sm*, *sf* visitor.

**visivo** [vi'zivo] *agg* visual. **campo visivo** *sm* field of vision.

**viso** ['vizo] *sm* face. **a viso aperto** openly. **far buon viso a cattiva sorte** make the best of it. **fare il viso lungo** sulk.

**visone** [vi'zone] *sm* mink.

**vispo** ['vispo] *agg* lively; (*svelto*) brisk.

**vista** ['vista] *sf* sight; (*spettacolo*) view. **avere in vista** have in mind. **a vista** on sight. **a vista d'occhio** before one's very eyes. **conoscere di vista** know by sight. **perdere di vista** lose sight (of).

**visto** ['visto] *sm* visa. **visto di soggiorno** tourist visa.

**vistoso** [vis'tozo] *agg* showy; (*notevole*) considerable.

**visuale** [vizu'ale] *agg* visual. *sf* view; line of vision. **visualizzare** *v* visualize.

**vita¹** ['vita] *sf* life. (*durata*) lifetime. **a vita** for life. **condanna a vita** life sentence. **essere in fin di vita** be at death's door. **guadagnarsi la vita** earn one's living.

**vita²** ['vita] *sf* (*corpo*) waist.

**vitale** [vi'tale] *agg* vital. **vitalità** *sf* vitality.

**vitalizio** [vita'litsjo] *agg* life(long). *sm* (*rendita*) annuity.

**vitamina** [vita'mina] *sf* vitamin.

**vite¹** ['vite] *sf* (*bot*) vine. **viticcio** *sm* tendril. **viticoltura** *sf* viticulture.

**vite²** ['vite] *sf* (*mec*) screw. **cadere in vite** (*aero*) go into a spin.

**vitello** [vi'tɛllo] *sm* calf; (*gastr*) veal. **vitellone** *sm* bullock; (*fig*) loafer.

**vitreo** ['vitreo] *agg* glassy, vitreous.

**vittima** ['vittima] *sf* victim; (*chi subisce danni*) casualty. **essere vittima di un incidente** be involved in an accident. **fare la vittima** (*fig*) be a martyr.

**vitto** ['vitto] *sm* food; (*nutrimento giornaliero*) board. **vitto e alloggio** board and lodging.

**vittoria** [vit'ɔrja] sf victory; (sport) win. **vittorioso** agg victorious.

**vituperare** [vitupe'rare] v berate. **vituperio** sm insult; (causa) disgrace.

**viva** ['viva] inter hurrah! **viva ...!** long live ...!

**vivacchiare** [vivak'kjare] v manage.

**vivace** [vi'vatʒe] agg lively; (intenso) bright. **vivacità** sf liveliness; brightness.

**vivaio** [vi'vajo] sm nursery; (pesci) fishpond.

**vivanda** [vi'vanda] sf food; (piatto) dish.

**\*vivere** ['vivere] v live; (trascorrere) spend. **avere di che vivere** have enough to live on. **lasciar vivere** leave in peace. **vivere alla giornata** live from hand to mouth. sm life; (modo di vivere) living.

**viveri** ['viveri] sm pl provisions pl.

**vivido** ['vivido] agg vivid.

**vivisezione** [vivise'tsjone] sf vivisection.

**vivo** ['vivo] agg living; (vivace) lively; (intenso) bright. **a viva forza** by force. **farsi vivo** show up; (mettersi in contatto) get in touch. sm living person; (fig) heart. **ferire nel vivo** wound to the quick.

**viziare** [vi'tsjare] v spoil; (dir) vitiate.

**vizio** [vitsjo] sm vice; bad habit; defect; (peccato) sin. **vizio parziale (di mente)** diminished responsibility. **vizioso** agg depraved.

**vizzo** ['vittso] agg withered.

**vocabolo** [vo'kabolo] sm word. **vocabolario** sm vocabulary; dictionary.

**vocale** [vo'kale] agg vocal. sf vowel.

**vocazione** [voka'tsjone] sf vocation; (inclinazione naturale) leaning. **vocazionale** agg vocational.

**voce** ['votʃe] sf voice; expression; (elemento di elenco) heading; opinion. **a bassa voce** softly. **ad alta voce** out loud. **aver voce in capitolo** have a say in the matter. **corre voce** rumour has it. **dire a (viva) voce** tell personally. **sotto voce** in an undertone.

**vociare** [vo'tʃare] v bawl.

**vociferare** [votʃife'rare] v talk at the top of one's voice; (fig) rumour.

**vodka** ['vɔdka] sf vodka.

**vogare** [vo'gare] v row. **vogatore** sm oarsman.

**voglia** ['voʎa] sf wish; (disposizione) will; (capriccio) fancy; (med) birthmark. **avere una gran voglia di** be dying to. **aver**

**voglia di (fare)** feel like (doing), want to (do). **di buona voglia** willingly. **di cattiva** or **mala voglia** unwillingly.

**voi** ['voi] pron you.

**volano** [vo'lano] sm (mec) flywheel; (sport) shuttlecock.

**volare** [vo'lare] v fly. **volar giù** hurtle down. **volata** sf (sport) sprint; (corsa rapida) dash. **di volata** in a rush. **fare una volata** make a dash.

**volatile** [vo'latile] agg volatile.

**volentieri** [volen'tjeri] avv willingly; with pleasure. **fare volentieri** like doing.

**\*volere** [vo'lere] v want; (desiderare) wish; (comando) will; (intendere) mean; (cortesia) like. **l'hai voluto tu!** you've asked for it! **neanche a volere** not even if you try. **non vuol dire** (non ha importanza) it doesn't matter. **se Dio vuole** God willing. **senza volere** without meaning to. **volerci** v take. **voler bene a** (aver affetto) be fond of; (amare) love. **voler dire** mean.

**volgare** [vol'gare] agg vulgar; common. sm (lingua) vernacular. **volgarità** sf vulgarity. **volgarizzare** v popularize.

**\*volgere** ['vɔldʒere] v turn. **col volgere degli anni** with the passing of time. **volgere alla fina** near the end. **volgere la parola a** address.

**volgo** ['volgo] sm common people pl.

**volo** ['volo] sm flight. **cogliere al volo** seize. **volo a vela** gliding. **volo in picchiata** nose-dive.

**volontà** [volon'ta] sf will. **di mia spontanea** or **propria volontà** of my own free will.

**volontario** [volon'tarjo], -**a** voluntary. sm, sf volunteer. **volontario del sangue** blood donor. **volontariato** sm voluntary service.

**volonteroso** [volonte'rozo] agg willing.

**volpe** ['volpe] sf fox; (femmina) vixen.

**volta¹** ['vɔlta] sf time; turn. **alla volta** at a time. **alla volta di** towards. **a volte** sometimes. **spesse volte** often. **una buona volta** once and for all. **una volta** once; (nelle fiabe) once upon a time.

**volta²** ['vɔlta] sf (arch) vault.

**voltare** [vol'tare] v turn. **voltagabbana** s(m+f) invar fickle person.

**volto** ['volto] sm face.

**volubile** [vo'lubile] agg fickle.

**volume** [vo'lume] sm volume; (mole) size.

**voluminoso** *agg* voluminous; (*ingombrante*) bulky.

**voluta** [vo'luta] *sf* scroll.

**voluttuoso** [volutu'ozo] *agg* voluptuous. **voluttà** *sf* voluptuousness.

**vomitare** [vomi'tare] *v* vomit, be sick. **aver voglia di vomitare** feel sick. **vomito** *sm* (*atto*) vomiting; (*materia*) vomit. **mi viene il vomito** I feel sick.

**vongola** ['vongola] *sf* clam.

**vorace** [vo'ratʃe] *agg* greedy.

**voragine** [vo'radʒine] *sf* chasm, gulf.

**vortice** ['vɔrtitʃe] *sm* vortex; (*gorgo*) whirlpool; (*fig*) whirl.

**vostro** ['vɔstro] *agg* your. *pron* yours.

**votare** [vo'tare] *v* vote; (*approvare*) pass; put to the vote; (*dedicare*) devote. **votazione** *sf* voting; (*scrutinio*) ballot; (*scuola*) marks *pl*. **voto** *sm* vote; (*promessa*) vow; (*scuola*) mark. **a pieni voti** with full marks. **pronunciare i voti** take one's vows.

**vulcano** [vul'kano] *sm* volcano. **vulcanico** *agg* volcanic; (*fig*) brilliant.

**vulnerabile** [vulne'rabile] *agg* vulnerable. **vulnerabilità** *sf* vulnerability.

**vuotare** [vwo'tare] *v* empty. **vuotare il sacco** (*fig*) spill the beans.

**vuoto** ['vwɔto] *agg* empty. *sm* void; (*fis*) vacuum; (*fig*) emptiness, gap. **andare a vuoto** fail. **a vuoto** in vain. **girare a vuoto** (*mec*) idle.

# X

**xenofobo** [kse'nɔfobo], **-a** *agg* xenophobic. *sm, sf* xenophobe. **xenofobia** *sf* xenophobia.

**xerocopiare** [kseroko'pjare] *v* Xerox®.

**xilofono** [ksi'lɔfono] *sm* xylophone.

# Y

**yoga** ['jɔga] *sm invar* yoga.

**yoghurt** ['jɔgurt] *sm invar* yoghurt.

# Z

**zacchera** ['dzakkera] *sf* splash (of mud).

**zaffata** [dzaf'fata] *sf* whiff; (*getto di liquido*) splash.

**zafferano** [dzaffe'rano] *sm* saffron.

**zaffiro** [dzaf'firo] *sm* sapphire.

**zaino** ['dzajno] *sm* kit-bag; (*alpinisti*) rucksack.

**zampa** ['dzampa] *sf* leg; (*con unghie*) paw; (*maiale*) trotter. **a quattro zampe** on all fours. **zampe di gallina** *sf pl* (*rughe*) crow's-feet *pl*; (*scrittura*) scrawl *sing*. **zampare** *v* paw (the ground). **aver lo zampino in** have a hand in. **mettere lo zampino** interfere.

**zampillare** [dzampil'lare] *v* spurt, gush. **zampillo** *sm* spurt.

**zampogna** [dzam'poɲa] *sf* bagpipes *pl*.

**zangola** ['dzangola] *sf* churn. **zangolare** *v* churn.

**zanna** ['dzanna] *sf* fang; (*di elefante, cinghiale*) tusk.

**zanzara** [dzan'dzara] *sf* mosquito. **zanzariera** *sf* mosquito-net.

**zappare** [dzap'pare] *v* hoe. **zappa** *sf* hoe.

**zattera** ['dzattera] *sf* raft.

**zazzera** ['dzaddzera] *sf* mop of hair.

**zebra** ['dzebra] *sf* zebra. **zebre** *sf pl* (*passaggio*) zebra crossing *sing*. **zebrato** *agg* striped.

**zecca¹** ['dzekka] *sf* mint. **nuovo di zecca** brand-new. **zecchino** *sm* gold coin.

**zecca²** ['dzekka] *sf* (*zool*) tick.

**zelo** ['dzelo] *sm* zeal. **zelante** *agg* keen, zealous.

**zenzero** ['dzendzero] *sm* ginger.

**zeppa** ['dzeppa] *sf* wedge. **zeppare** *v* wedge.

**zeppo** ['dzeppo] *agg* **(pieno) zeppo** packed, cram-full.

**zerbino** [dzer'bino] *sm* (door-)mat.

**zero** ['dzero] *sm* nought; (*fig, mat*) zero; (*sport*) nil; (*tennis*) love.

**zia** ['dzia] *sf* aunt.

**zibellino** [dzibel'lino] *sm* sable.

**zibetto** [dzi'betto] *sm* civet.

**zigzag** [dzig'dzag] *sm* zigzag. **andare a zigzag** zigzag.

**zimbello** [dzim'bɛllo] *sm* decoy; (*oggetto di scherno*) laughing-stock. **zimbellare** *v* lure.

**zinco** ['dzinko] *sm* zinc.

**zingaro** ['dzingaro], **-a** *s*, *agg* gipsy.

**zio** ['dzio] *sm* uncle.

**zirlare** [dzir'lare] *v* chirp.

**zitella** [dzi'tɛlla] *sf* spinster. **vecchia zitella** (*spreg*) old maid.

**zittire** [dzit'tire] *v* (*far tacere*) hush; (*disapprovazione*) hiss.

**zitto** ['dzitto] *agg* quiet. **star zitto** keep quiet; (*fam*) shut up.

**zoccolo** ['dzɔkkolo] *sm* clog; (*zool*) hoof; base; (*parete*) skirting-board.

**zodiaco** [dzo'diako] *sm* zodiac.

**zolfo** ['dzolfo] *sm* sulphur.

**zolla** ['dzolla] *sf* clod.

**zona** ['dzɔna] *sf* zone; area. **zona pedonale** pedestrian precinct. **zona verde** (*periferica*) green belt.

**zonzo** ['dzondzo] *avv* **andare a zonzo** wander about.

**zoo** [dzo] *sm invar* zoo.

**zoologia** [dzoolo'dʒia] *sf* zoology. **zoologico** *agg* zoological. **zoologo**, **-a** *sm*, *sf* zoologist.

**zoppicare** [dzoppi'kare] *v* limp; (*tavolo, ecc.*) be rickety; (*fig*) be shaky. **zoppo** *agg* lame; rickety; shaky.

**zotico** ['dzɔtiko], **-a** *agg* boorish. *sm*, *sf* boor.

**zucca** ['dzukka] *sf* pumpkin; (*fam*: *testa*) nut. **zuccone** *sm* (*fam*) blockhead.

**zucchero** ['dzukkero] *sm* sugar. **zucchero a velo** icing sugar. **zucchero semolato** castor sugar. **zuccherare** *v* sweeten.

**zucchino** [dzuk'kino], **-a** *sm*, *sf* courgette.

**zuffa** ['dzuffa] *sf* scuffle, brawl.

**zuppa** ['dzuppa] *sf* soup. **zuppa inglese** trifle. **zuppiera** *sf* tureen. **zuppo** *agg* drenched.